FAMILY LAW

CASES, COMMENTS, AND QUESTIONS

Eighth Edition

■ ■ ■

Harry D. Krause
Max L. Rowe Professor of Law Emeritus
University of Illinois

Linda D. Elrod
Richard S. Righter Distinguished Professor of Law
Washburn University School of Law

J. Thomas Oldham
John H. Freeman Professor of Law
University of Houston Law Center

AMERICAN CASEBOOK SERIES®

WEST
ACADEMIC
PUBLISHING

American Casebook Series is a trademark registered in the U.S. Patent and Trademark Office.

© 1976, 1983, 1989, 1998 West Publishing Company
© West, a Thomson business, 2003
© 2007 Thomson/West
© 2013 Thomson Reuters
© 2018 LEG, Inc. d/b/a West Academic
      444 Cedar Street, Suite 700
      St. Paul, MN 55101
      1-877-888-1330

West, West Academic Publishing, and West Academic are trademarks of West Publishing Corporation, used under license.

Printed in the United States of America

ISBN: 978-1-68328-451-2

This eighth edition is dedicated to:

Dr. Marion Llewellynn Drake, who believed in his grandson.

J.T.O.

To my children—Carson and Bree who
have made parenting a delight!

L.D.E.

A NOTE OF THANKS

Tom Oldham would like to thank Kristan Withers, Christina Gonzalez, and Paola Gonzalez for help preparing this manuscript.

Linda Elrod would like to thank Shirley Jacobson and Russell Budden for their work on the eighth edition.

Both would like to thank Harry Krause, the father of the original text.

SUMMARY OF CONTENTS

TABLE OF CONTENTS

TABLE OF CASES

The principal cases are in bold type.

———————

FAMILY LAW

CASES, COMMENTS, AND QUESTIONS

Eighth Edition

CHAPTER 1

AMERICAN FAMILY LAW: DEFINITIONS, POLICY AND TRENDS

■ ■ ■

> *The family is the natural and fundamental group unit of society and is entitled to protection by society and the State.*
>
> UNIVERSAL DECLARATION OF HUMAN RIGHTS, Art. 16(3)
>
> *Unfortunately, the American family is confronted with the problem whether it shall continue to exist, and the American people, whether they like it or not, should look the problems of their family life squarely in the face as the greatest of all their social problems.*
>
> Charles Ellwood, 1909
>
> *No matter how many communes anybody invents, the family always creeps back.*
>
> Margaret Mead

1. THE NEW FAMILY AND THE NEW FAMILY LAW

A. THE NEW FAMILY

MARY ANN GLENDON, THE NEW FAMILY AND THE NEW PROPERTY
3–7, 11, 13–20, 28–38, 41–45, 245 (1981).

* * *

The "new family" is a convenient way of referring to that group of changes that characterizes 20th century Western marriage and family behavior, such as increasing fluidity, detachability and interchangeability of family relationships; the increasing appearance, or at least visibility, of family behavior outside formal legal categories, and to changing attitudes and behavior patterns in authority structure and economic relations within

1

the family. It follows from these changes that the new family is *no* family in the sense of a single model that can be called typical for modern industrialized societies. The new family is a concept that represents a variety of co-existing family types.

As an example of the kinds of developments that can be illuminated by the analysis that will be set forth here, consider two pairs of interesting but at first sight unrelated legal events of the 1970s—one in family law, the other in the law of employment contracts. In 1973, Sweden and the American state of Washington changed their laws to permit one spouse unilaterally to terminate a marriage for any reason, or no reason. In 1974, Sweden extended protection against dismissal without cause to all employees in the labor force, and the Supreme Court of New Hampshire became the first in the nation to repudiate the time-honored common-law rule that an employer may terminate an at-will employment contract for any reason, or no reason. When viewed from a civilian, comparative, and historical perspective, and placed in the context of other private law developments, the American and Swedish innovations, while strikingly coincidental are seen to be neither isolated phenomena nor mere curiosities.

* * *

When comparative analysis is brought to bear on the two pairs of developments, it becomes clear that Sweden and the United States are not special or extreme cases. Comparison of the marriage and employment law of England, France, Sweden, West Germany and the United States * * * shows that the once fundamental legal concepts that one spouse cannot repudiate the other at will and that an employer can fire an employee for any reason that suits him are legally moribund in fact in all those legal systems. Finally, from a historical perspective, the two legal trends are— to use characterizations employed by the French historian Braudel in another context—simultaneously "motors," "indicators," and "multipliers" of a vast reorganization of social relationships.

* * *

A.   CIRCUMSCRIBING THE FAMILY UNIT: THE LAW OF COMPANIONATE MARRIAGE

The husband-wife relationship has become the "central zone" of the modern family. This came about only gradually. The pre-modern family included a wide circle of people from different households related by blood ties and by a feeling that they belonged together in a different way from the way in which they belonged to a neighborhood, community or larger political entity. Lawrence Stone calls the pre-modern family the "open lineage" family to emphasize that its outer boundaries were relatively weak and permeable in contrast to what he perceives as the close-knit, inward-turning modern family. The strong sense of kinship did not exclude a wide range of connections with others through marriage or spiritual affinity (e.g., godparents and children) and with non-relatives. Over time, however, the feeling of being united by a common tie within the kinship group weakened, and the term "family" slowly came to be identified primarily with the household, conceived of as containing a husband, wife and minor children. * * *

The French Civil Code of 1804 appeared at just the right time to preserve the image of the older order, especially in the *conseil de famille,* to ensconce the conjugal household as the "family of the Civil Code," and to foreshadow the future in its short-lived introduction of divorce.

* * *

Comparing th[is] * * * Code * * * with the German Civil Code of 1896, one can observe the progress of the trends we have been following. In the "modern" German Civil Code, which went into effect in 1900, the family law sections were more decisively organized around the conjugal family of husband-wife and children. The kinship group had receded further into the background. Collaterals were dropped from the list of relatives entitled to a forced share in a decedent's estate, and the surviving spouse was added. English and American statutory and case law developments were following a similar general pattern. * * * By the turn of the 20th century, Western legal systems had come to share, generally speaking, a common set of assumptions. Marriage was an important support institution and a decisive determinant of the status of spouses and children. Marriage was in principle to last until the death of a spouse and should be terminable during the lives of the spouses, if at all, only for serious cause. The community aspect of marriage and the family was emphasized over the individual personalities of each member. Within the family, the standard pattern of authority and role allocation was that the husband-father was predominant in decision-making and was to provide for the material needs of the family, while the wife-mother fulfilled her role primarily by caring for the household and children. Procreation and child-rearing were assumed to be major purposes of marriage, and sexual relations within marriage were supposed to be exclusive, at least for the wife. Marriage and divorce were supposed to take place within legal categories. Underlying all these particular assumptions were general assumptions that "the" family was "a basic social institution" and that state regulation of its formation, organization and dissolution and even the conduct of its everyday affairs was proper.

* * *

B.   THE BONDING OF THE NEW FAMILY

In the 20th century, as marriage and family both declined as focal points of security and standing, a family type has emerged that is characterized by, among other things, relatively loose bonding. In contrast to pre-modern, early modern and 19th century families, both kinship ties and marital ties are attenuated in the new family.

* * *

Outside the nuclear core the loosening of family ties is especially pronounced. While research in many countries has demonstrated that extensive kinship networks still exist and can be quite important even in modernized, urbanized industrial societies—more especially in some sectors than in others—it nevertheless seems generally true, as Konig says, that "one does not any more simply 'have' relatives; rather one decides with whom one will have contact, so that kin relationships can be compared to those among friends." It is common to hear people describe certain relatives approvingly as "not only my (mother, son, wife, brother, etc.) but also my friend." Konig's observation is neatly illustrated in the 1964 amendments to the French Civil Code provisions on the appointment of a family council when this becomes necessary to supervise the personal care of a child. Since 1964, little is presumed from the mere existence of a family tie, and the possibly greater significance of non-familial ties in individual cases is recognized. Article 408 of the Civil Code now requires the judge, in choosing the members of the council, to consider "before all else, the habitual relationships that the mother and father had with their various blood relatives and in-laws." Article 409, as amended, then goes on to introduce the possibility for the judge to appoint to the council "friends, neighbors, or any other persons who seem to him to have concern for the child."

* * *

2.a. Fluidity, Detachability and Interchangeability

1.   Marriage

In historical perspective, two facts stand out that distinguish the modern couple relationship. They at first appear contradictory. One is that modern marriage, while it lasts, is companionate, its bonding seemingly close and intense; the other is that it is fragile, its close bonding seemingly unstable. This version of reality is faithfully reflected in modern marriage law which simultaneously expresses the closeness and intensity, yet the instability of the modern couple bonded more by emotional than economic ties.

This can best be observed by comparing the legal rights a spouse has in inheritance with those he or she has in divorce. The common thread running through the changes in the spouses' position in succession law stands out in contrast to the diversity of the responses of various legal systems to the problem of the increase in marriage termination by divorce. It is obvious why legal treatment of these two situations has become sharply differentiated in recent years. The surviving spouse has steadily gained against blood relations in inheritance, a natural consequence of the decline of kinship and the companionate nature of those marriages (still a majority) that last until death. The divorced spouse, on the other hand, is either increasingly required in principle to be self-sufficient, or the spousal support obligation is continued, but shifted over to a new utilitarian basis— the protection of the public purse. Both approaches are natural consequences of the perishability of the modern couple unit and the rise in successive marriages while the prior spouse is still alive. In the United States and England it has been estimated that 30 to 40 percent of marriages formed in the 1970s will end in divorce. Since most divorced persons remarry, the New Marriage is often a subsequent marriage, and the New Family a reconstituted family.

But what is modern about the New Marriage is not that it is perishable or that it is often a remarriage. * * * The information being assembled about marriage in the early modern period from 1500 to 1800 indicates that marriages then were dissolved by death almost as often as they are dissolved by divorce. * * * What is modern is that the doors do not revolve merely to the pearly gates. In close personal relationships today, impermanence, fluidity and interchangeability are mainly the result not of death, but of the exercise of choice, a choice made possible only by the opportunities which individuals have for finding economic subsistence outside the family.

The marriage bond seems to have been relatively durable when the conjugal family functioned as a productive unit. So long as this pattern prevailed, the husband was predominant in the legal authority structure of the family. But his superior legal authority was held in check in practice

> * * * by a dependence on the productive labor force of his wife and her ability to bear children. Children are in this phase—in their quality as labour force—a considerable asset. Although the relationship between the partners was asymmetrical it was however at the same time characterized by an economic interdependence. * * *

When the productive work which formed the basis of the maintenance of the family was removed from the home through industrialization, women and children were vulnerable because the breadwinner upon whom they now depended entirely was released from his dependence on them. From being economic assets, women and children became a strain on resources in the marriage type where the husband worked outside the home and the wife was exclusively occupied with the household. This was the beginning of the end of marriage as a reliable support institution.

As women, too, entered the labor force, their economic vulnerability lessened somewhat, but at the same time it seems that the actual or potential participation of married women in the labor force makes it easier for men as well as women to leave marriages. * * *

Meanwhile, as marriage declined as a support institution, women decreasingly defined their social position with reference to their husbands or lack thereof. The notion, long taken for granted, that the "husband's occupation alone supposedly defines class and status for the family," and the assumption, attributed to Talcott Parsons, that "the family as a whole shares a status and that the man is the link with the economic system," have been undermined by the course of events in the 20th century. * * *

The fact that marriage in itself is no longer so important as a determinant of wealth, rank, and status has made it easy for "freedom to marry" to be established as a fundamental legal principle, coincidentally at about the same time, in France, West Germany and the United States. Ironically, marriage has become a basic human right just when it is losing much of its former economic importance. This is also why marriage is becoming freely terminable on the request of one party in countries where a century ago divorce was available, if at all, only for grave and serious cause, and why "legitimacy" is decreasingly tied to formal, legal marriage. In its encounter with informal marriage and family behavior, the law itself has become more fluid and informal.

* * *

b.   *Parents and Children*

Like the bonds between husband and wife, those between parents and children have been reduced and relaxed in the modern family. Relationships between parent and child are said to have become looser, not only because the child upon reaching a certain age typically leaves the family, but because the child's psychological dependence on the family decreases even earlier. Surveying changes in American family life cycles over an 80-year period ending in the 1970s, Census Bureau senior demographer Paul Glick has stated that, contrary to what might be expected, the father and mother of today's smaller families are apparently not spending more time with their children than their great-grandparents did. In fact the period of child-rearing has been shortened by about three years. Those who believe that children today achieve emotional independence from their families earlier than in the recent past attribute this, variously, to the fact that children move in non-family milieus at an early age, and to the outside influences from television and the peer group that penetrate the family circle through the children.

Legally, these looser ties find expression in the decline of parental control over a child's marriage decision, the rise of "children's rights," the substitution of social for family responsibility for support of aged parents or more distant relatives and the near disappearance of patriarchal authority over wives and children. Laurence Tribe, in a perceptive analysis of recent Supreme Court cases affecting the parent-child relationship, observes that what the Court and commentators often characterize as "'family rights' emerge as rights of individuals only." He reaches this conclusion by comparing cases "pitting the child against outside institutions" with cases where "the child seeks aid from outside institutions," finding that both lines of decisions "move in the parallel direction of reduced parental control."

Fluidity and interchangeability of relationships characterize many recent developments in child law just as they do marriage law. * * * [W]ith increasing acceptance of the notion that close attention should be paid in custody matters to the "psychological parent," neither the biological nor the legal tie is necessarily decisive for purposes of custody or termination of parental rights. In the area of post-divorce custody, wider kinship ties seem to reappear in the sprinkling of American cases that have begun to accord visitation rights to grandparents. But these cases do not represent a reinforcement of legal kinship ties so much as they do legal adaptation to the fluidity and shifting composition of families, a process in which grandparents are often lumped in with "significant others" who are not kinfolk, such as foster parents, cohabitants, step-parents and even babysitters. The step-relationship has begun to draw a number of legal incidents to itself, even in cases where it has not been formalized through legal adoption. At the same time, in the United States, the very theory of adoption is changing. While the aim of adoption was once to integrate the adopted child as fully as possible into the adoptive family, severing all other ties, the idea of "open adoption" has recently emerged to permit the adopted child to retain her old family ties while entering into new ones. * * *

C.   THE EMERGENCE OF THE INDIVIDUAL

* * * It was to the declining influence of the family in determining an individual's security and standing that Sir Henry Maine was referring in his constantly quoted statement that "the movement of the progressive societies has hitherto been a movement *from Status to Contract.*"

* * *

Maine was more right than he knew and probably more right than he wanted to be. Particularly since the 1960s, the law in the countries discussed here has come increasingly to emphasize the individuality of the members of the conjugal family as well as to facilitate their independence from it and each other. For example, so far as the spouses are concerned, Rheinstein and Glendon's survey of the law of several countries on the personal and property relationships of husband and wife during marriage showed that legal and symbolic rules, which had captured and reinforced the trend toward viewing companionate marriage as a community of life between the spouses, are significantly affected by trends toward emphasizing the separateness and autonomy of the individual spouses.

* * *

The fact is that we may now carry Maine's analysis one step further: we have left a time when one's position in society was fixed by one's family, *not* for the reign of contract, but for a situation in which one's status is derived from one's occupation or fixed, in a negative way, by one's lack of occupation. Occupations are less and less governed by contract. The collective bargaining agreement is *sui generis*, with mixed elements of contract, statute and constitution, and with its terms, like other employment relationships and other aspects of work, increasingly fixed and regulated by law. The relationships which, unlike marriage and contract, are relatively hard to enter and leave today are the preferred sorts of New Property—good jobs with good fringe benefits. * * *

Current changes in family behavior, property and law, and ways of thinking about them, contain bewildering possibilities for good and ill, for renewal or deterioration. It seems likely that, in the future, what we have here called the new family and the new property will be seen as transitional phenomena and identified with a period of extreme separation of man from man, and man from nature. * * *

NOTES AND QUESTIONS

1.   Throughout the Western industrialized world, experts see a trend that started in the 1960s toward smaller families, more nonmarital cohabitation, more nonmarital births, more single-parent and single person households. The latter family form is the fastest growing household type. In the United States, the 2010 Census Data revealed that the percent increase for nonfamily households between 2000 and 2010 was double that for family households. There was a 41% increase in unmarried partner households; an increase in multigenerational households; and fewer households with children. *See* http://2010census.gov/news/releases/operations/cb12-68. Between 1970 and 2000, the proportion of family households in the United States declined from 81% to 69%. The most dramatic drop was in the number of married couples with their own minor children, which declined from 40.3% to 24.1%. During the same time period, the number of households with unmarried individuals and no children increased as did the number of households headed by single mothers. *Id.* By 2015, the share of two parent households with a breadwinner father and a stay-at-home mother was 26%. STEPHANIE COONTZ, THE WAY WE *NEVER* WERE: AMERICAN FAMILIES AND THE NOSTALGIA TRAP (REV. ED. 2016).

Households by Type: Selected Years, 1970-2010
(Percent distribution)

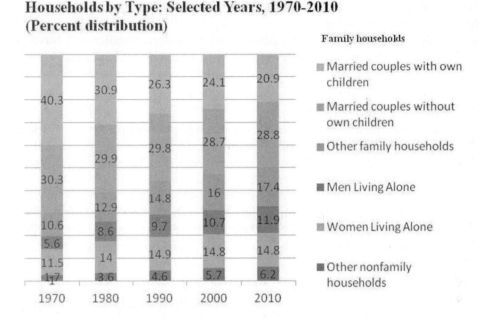

Source: U.S. Census Bureau, Current Population Survey,
Statistical Abstract of the United States, Table 59 (2012).

2.   One author noted, "This rich diversity of family forms won't come into being without pain and anguish. For any change in family structure also forces change in the roles we live. Every society, through its institutions, creates its own architecture of roles or social expectations." ALVIN TOFFLER, THE THIRD WAVE 222–23 (1981). What are the roles and expectations of the family today? Which of its functions are most important to individual family members? to the public?

B. THE NEW FAMILY LAW

Dramatic changes in family form and function have altered not only American family life, but also our family law. Family law is evolving to meet the challenges of new family forms. Today's family law must resolve disputes involving nonmarital cohabitants and participants in new forms of reproduction, such as surrogate parenting and in vitro fertilization. It must resolve challenges to traditional definitions of marriage, parenting, property, and the family itself.

Not surprisingly, the process of fashioning rules that are fair and workable for today's rapidly changing family has been far from smooth and uncontroversial. Family law is now central to many of the most difficult, and emotional, of social issues: Should couples who live together without marriage be entitled to benefits that have traditionally been available only to "family members"? Should a law degree be considered marital property to be "divided" at divorce? Who is the mother of a child born to one woman with genetic material from another? Should a lesbian "co-parent" be able to adopt her partner's child? Absent an adoption, should she have an entitlement to visitation if her relationship with the child's mother ends? These are some of the issues with which family law now contends and which you will be studying.

Family law issues arouse controversy for a variety of reasons. Family relationships are intimate, generating strong, often conflicting, emotions. Family law often draws on other disciplines, such as sociology, psychology, mediation, medicine, and law enforcement, and thus becomes embroiled in debates within these other fields. Many issues of family law are also issues of morality, religious doctrine and cultural values; they can be—and are— debated in these terms as well as in terms of law. Traditionally, much of family law has been based on widely accepted religious and cultural values. But a more diverse populace challenges our ability to achieve consensus on many family law issues.

The one issue on which there is widespread consensus is the importance of the family as a cornerstone of our society. The United Nations recognizes that the family is "the natural and fundamental group unit of society and is entitled to protection by society and the State." Universal Declaration of Human Rights § 16(3). But exactly what makes a group of individuals a "family" remains unclear.

NOTES AND QUESTIONS

1. How does "family law" differ from other types of law? How does the family law of today differ from the law of the 1950s? 1890s? *See* Janet Halley, *What is Family Law?: A Genealogy Part II*, 23 YALE L.J. & HUMANITIES 189 (2011).

2. Are there any recurrent themes in family law? Does the law influence how people choose to live? Consider the following:

> [I]n the channeling function the law creates or (more often) supports social institutions which are thought to serve desirable ends * * *. Generally, the channeling function does not specifically require people to use these social institutions, although it may offer incentives and disincentives for their use. Primarily, rather, it is their very presence, the social currency they have, and the governmental support they receive which combine to make it seem reasonable and natural for people to use them.

Carl E. Schneider, *The Channelling Function in Family Law*, 20 HOFSTRA L. REV. 495, 496 (1992) (using marriage and parenthood as examples).

> Family law may be instrumental, designed to affect people's behavior in some ways that policy makers believe is desirable. It may be retrospective, concerned less with changing what might happen in

the future, than with changing the consequences of what has already happened, to make the outcome more fair.

Ira Ellman, *Why Making Family Law is Hard*, 35 ARIZ. L. REV. 699 (2003).

3.   What is "public policy" as it relates to family law? How should courts determine what policies the law should advance? *See* HERBIE DIFONZO & RUTH STERN, INTIMATE ASSOCIATIONS: THE LAW AND CULTURE OF AMERICAN FAMILIES (2013).

2. A FAMILY BY ANY NAME?

Membership in a family may confer entitlement to benefits, such as health insurance, and determine legal obligations. Should family status be determined based on standardized criteria or on the understanding of the individuals involved? If a standardized definition is employed, on what factors should it rely? What entity—the state, the federal government, or the parties themselves—should determine what constitutes a family?

In Village of Belle Terre v. Boraas, 416 U.S. 1 (1974), the Supreme Court upheld a zoning ordinance that defined a family as "one or more persons related by blood, adoption or marriage, living and cooking together as a single housekeeping unit, exclusive of household servants. * * * " In oft-quoted statements, Justices Douglas and Marshall eloquently disagreed about the effect of the ordinance. To Justice Douglas, the Village ordinance was a benign edict:

> A quiet place where yards are wide, people few, and motor vehicles restricted are legitimate guidelines in a land-use project addressed to family needs. This goal is a permissible one. * * * The police power is not confined to elimination of filth, stench, and unhealthy places. It is ample to lay out zones where family values, youth values, and the blessings of quiet seclusion and clean air make the area a sanctuary for people. *Id.* at 9.

To Justice Marshall, on the other hand, the ordinance represented active discrimination against nonconformists:

> Belle Terre imposes upon those who deviate from the community norm in their choice of living companions significantly greater restrictions than are applied to residential groups who are related by blood or marriage, and compose the established order within the community. The village has, in effect, acted to fence out those individuals whose choice of lifestyle differs from that of its current residents. *Id.* at 16–17.

When considering the definitions of "family" contained in the following cases, try to determine both whether the definition was drawn for benign or discriminatory reasons and how much latitude government actors have to "fence out" certain lifestyles.

MOORE V. CITY OF EAST CLEVELAND, OHIO
Supreme Court of the United States, 1977.
431 U.S. 494.

JUSTICE POWELL delivered the opinion of the Court.

East Cleveland's housing ordinance, like many throughout the country, limits occupancy of a dwelling unit to members of a single family.

But the ordinance contains an unusual and complicated definitional section that recognizes as a "family" only a few categories of related individuals. Section 1341.08 provides:

"Family" means a number of individuals related to the nominal head of the household living as a single housekeeping unit in a single dwelling unit, but limited to the following:

(a) Husband or wife of the nominal head of the household.

(b) Unmarried children of the nominal head of the household or of the spouse of the nominal head of the household, provided, however, that such unmarried children have no children residing with them.

(c) Father or mother of the nominal head of the household or of the spouse of the nominal head of the household.

(d) * * * a family may include not more than one dependent married or unmarried child of the nominal head of the household or of the spouse of the nominal head of the household and the spouse and dependent children of such dependent child. For the purpose of this subsection, a dependent person is one who has more than fifty percent of his total support furnished for him by the nominal head of the household and the spouse of the nominal head of the household.

(e) A family may consist of one individual.

Because her family, living together in her home, fits none of those categories, appellant stands convicted of a criminal offense. The question in this case is whether the ordinance violates the Due Process Clause of the Fourteenth Amendment.

* * *

Appellant, Mrs. Inez Moore, lives in her East Cleveland home together with her son, Dale Moore, Sr., and her two grandsons, Dale, Jr., and John Moore, Jr. The two boys are first cousins rather than brothers; we are told that John came to live with his grandmother and with the elder and younger Dale Moores after his mother's death.

In early 1973, Mrs. Moore received a notice of violation from the city, stating that John was an "illegal occupant" and directing her to comply with the ordinance. When she failed to remove him from her home, the city filed a criminal charge. Mrs. Moore moved to dismiss, claiming that the ordinance was constitutionally invalid on its face. Her motion was overruled, and upon conviction she was sentenced to five days in jail and a $25 fine. * * *

But one overriding factor sets this case apart from *Belle Terre*. The ordinance there affected only *unrelated* individuals. It expressly allowed all who were related by "blood, adoption, or marriage" to live together, and in sustaining the ordinance we were careful to note that it promoted "family needs" and "family values." East Cleveland, in contrast, has chosen to regulate the occupancy of its housing by slicing deeply into the family itself. This is no mere incidental result of the ordinance. On its face it selects certain categories of relatives who may live together and declares that others may not. In particular, it makes a crime of a grandmother's choice to live with her grandson in circumstances like those presented here.

When a city undertakes such intrusive regulation of the family, neither Belle Terre nor Euclid governs; the usual judicial deference to the legislature is inappropriate. "This Court has long recognized that freedom of personal choice in matters of marriage and family life is one of the liberties protected by the Due Process Clause of the Fourteenth Amendment." Cleveland Board of Education v. Lafleur, 414 U.S. 632, 639–640 (1974). A host of cases * * * have consistently acknowledged a "private realm of family life which the state cannot enter." Of course, the family is not beyond regulation. But when the government intrudes on choices concerning family living arrangements, this Court must examine carefully the importance of the governmental interests advanced and the extent to which they are served by the challenged regulation.

When thus examined, this ordinance cannot survive. * * *

Appropriate limits on substantive due process come not from drawing arbitrary lines but rather from careful "respect for the teachings of history [and], solid recognition of the basic values that underlie our society". Our decisions establish that the Constitution protects the sanctity of the family precisely because the institution of the family is deeply rooted in this Nation's history and tradition. It is through the family that we inculcate and pass down many of our most cherished values, moral and cultural.

Ours is by no means a tradition limited to respect for the bonds uniting the members of the nuclear family. The tradition of uncles, aunts, cousins, and especially grandparents sharing a household along with parents and children has roots equally venerable and equally deserving of constitutional recognition. Over the years millions of our citizens have grown up in just such an environment, and most, surely, have profited from it. Even if conditions of modern society have brought about a decline in extended family households, they have not erased the accumulated wisdom of civilization, gained over the centuries and honored throughout our history, that supports a larger conception of the family. Out of choice, necessity, or a sense of family responsibility, it has been common for close relatives to draw together and participate in the duties and the satisfactions of a common home. Decisions concerning child rearing, which *Yoder, Meyer, Pierce* and other cases have recognized as entitled to constitutional protection, long have been shared with grandparents or other relatives who occupy the same household—indeed who may take on major responsibility for the rearing of the children. Especially in times of adversity, such as the death of a spouse or economic need, the broader family has tended to come together for mutual sustenance and to maintain or rebuild a secure home life. This is apparently what happened here.

Whether or not such a household is established because of personal tragedy, the choice of relatives in this degree of kinship to live together may not lightly be denied by the State. *Pierce* struck down an Oregon law requiring all children to attend the State's public schools, holding that the Constitution "excludes any general power of the State to standardize its children by forcing them to accept instruction from public teachers only." 268 U.S., at 535. By the same token the Constitution prevents East Cleveland from standardizing its children—and its adults—by forcing all to live in certain narrowly defined family patterns.

JUSTICE STEWART, with whom JUSTICE REHNQUIST joins, dissenting.

* * * [T]he appellant contends that the importance of the "extended family" in American society requires us to hold that her decision to share her residence with her grandsons may not be interfered with by the State. This decision, like the decisions involved in bearing and raising children, is said to be an aspect of "family life" also entitled to substantive protection under the Constitution. Without pausing to inquire how far under this argument an "extended family" might extend, I cannot agree. When the Court has found that the Fourteenth Amendment placed a substantive limitation on a State's power to regulate, it has been in those rare cases in which the personal interests at issue have been deemed "implicit in the concept of ordered liberty." The interest that the appellant may have in permanently sharing a single kitchen and a suite of contiguous rooms with some of her relatives simply does not rise to that level. To equate this interest with the fundamental decisions to marry and to bear and raise children is to extend the limited substantive contours of the Due Process Clause beyond recognition.

* * *

JUSTICE WHITE, dissenting.

That the Court has ample precedent for the creation of new constitutional rights should not lead it to repeat the process at will. The judiciary, including this Court, is the most vulnerable and comes nearest to illegitimacy when it deals with judge-made constitutional law having little or no cognizable roots in the language or even the design of the Constitution. Realizing that the present construction of the Due Process Clause represents a major judicial gloss on its terms, as well as on the anticipation of the Framers, and that much of the underpinning for the broad, substantive application of the Clause disappeared in the conflict between the executive and the judiciary in the 1930's and 1940's, the Court should be extremely reluctant to breathe still further substantive content into the Due Process Clause so as to strike down legislation adopted by a State or city to promote its welfare. Whenever the judiciary does so, it unavoidably pre-empts for itself another part of the governance of the country without express constitutional authority.

NOTES AND QUESTIONS

1.　What standard of review did the Court use? Why? What is the determining factor in the *Moore* decision? Is it tradition, current household residence patterns, economic and racial factors, or the Court's reluctance to see a grandmother evicted for housing two grandsons?

2.　Typical residence and family patterns vary significantly by race and ethnicity and by education.

> Over the past 50 years, a quiet revolution has taken place . . . At the center of this transformation is the shrinking institution of marriage. In 1960, 72% of American adults were married. By 2008, that share had fallen to 52%.

> Marriage rates are now more strongly linked to education than they have been in the past, with college graduates (64%) much more likely to be married than those who have never attended college (48%).

> The racial differences are even larger. Blacks (32%) are much less likely than whites (56%) to be married, and this gap has increased significantly over time. And black children (52%) are nearly three times as likely as white children (18%) and nearly twice as likely as Hispanic children (27%) to live with one parent.

> As the country shifts away from marriage, a smaller proportion of adults are experiencing the economic gains that typically accrue from marriage. In 2008, the median household income of married adults was 41% greater than that of unmarried adults, even after controlling for differences in household size. In 1960, this gap was only 12%. The widening of the gap is explained partly by the increased share of wives in the workforce (61% in 2008 versus 32% in 1960) and partly by the increased differential in the educational attainment of the married and unmarried.

The net result is that a marriage gap and a socio-economic gap have been growing side by side for the past half century, and each may be feeding off the other. Adults on the lower rungs of the socio-economic ladder (whether measured by income or education) are just as eager as other adults to marry. But they place a higher premium on economic security as a prerequisite for marriage than do those with higher levels of income and education.

PEW RESEARCH CENTER SOCIAL TRENDS STAFF, THE DECLINE OF MARRIAGE AND RISE OF NEW FAMILIES, Nov. 18, 2010, available at http://pewresearch.org/pubs/1802/decline-marriage-rise-new-families.

3. Long before the Pew Report, some opined that because family forms vary widely by race, ethnicity, and socioeconomic status, family law may not be equally responsive to the needs and interests of all Americans. See Lenore Weitzman, *Legal Regulation of Marriage: Tradition and Change*, 62 CAL. L. REV. 1169 (1974). Weitzman argued that in its provisions regarding marriage, divorce, property, support, alimony and custody, the traditional model of universal legal marriage and universal legal divorce incorporate a white, middle-class ideal. Do you agree?

4. Is a legally-recognized relationship necessary to be considered a "family"? Miguel Braschi and Leslie Blanchard, an unmarried gay couple, lived in Blanchard's rent-controlled apartment in New York City from 1975 until Blanchard's death in 1986. When the property owner tried to evict Braschi, Braschi argued that he was a member of Blanchard's "family" and thus protected from eviction under the rent control code. That code did not define family. The owner argued that "family" under the code should be defined as it is for purposes of determining intestate succession, which would require a relationship based on blood, marriage, or adoption. Braschi argued that the code's purpose, protecting family members from the sudden loss of their home, required a more expansive definition. The Court agreed with Mr. Braschi:

> * * * [W]e conclude that the term family, as used in 9 NYCRR 2204.6(d), should not be rigidly restricted to those people who have formalized their relationship by obtaining, for instance, a marriage certificate or an adoption order. The intended protection against sudden eviction should not rest on fictitious legal distinctions or genetic history, but instead should find its foundation in the reality of family life. In the context of eviction, a more realistic, and certainly equally valid, view of a family includes two adult lifetime partners whose relationship is long term and characterized by an emotional and financial commitment and interdependence. This view comports both with our society's traditional concept of "family" and with the expectations of individuals who live in such nuclear units. * * * In fact, Webster's Dictionary defines "family" first as "a group of people united by certain convictions or common affiliation" (Webster's Ninth New Collegiate Dictionary 448 (1984); see Ballantine's Law Dictionary 456 (3d ed. 1969) ("family" defined as "[p]rimarily, the

collective body of persons who live in one house and under one head or management"); Black's Law Dictionary 543 (Special Deluxe 5th ed. 1979)). Hence, it is reasonable to conclude that, in using the term "family," the Legislature intended to extend protection to those who reside in households having all of the normal familial characteristics. Appellant Braschi should therefore be afforded the opportunity to prove that he and Blanchard had such a household.

This definition of "family" is consistent with both of the competing purposes of the rent-control laws: the protection of individuals from sudden dislocation and the gradual transition to a free market system. Family members, whether or not related by blood, or law who have always treated the apartment as their family home will be protected against the hardship of eviction following the death of the named tenant, thereby furthering the Legislature's goals of preventing dislocation and preserving family units which might otherwise be broken apart upon eviction. This approach will foster the transition from rent control to rent stabilization by drawing a distinction between those individuals who are, in fact, genuine family members, and those who are mere roommates * * * or newly discovered relatives hoping to inherit the rent-controlled apartment after the existing tenant's death.

The determination as to whether an individual is entitled to noneviction protection should be based upon an objective examination of the relationship of the parties. In making this assessment, the lower courts of this State have looked to a number of factors, including the exclusivity and longevity of the relationship, the level of emotional and financial commitment, the manner in which the parties have conducted their everyday lives and held themselves out to society, and the reliance placed upon one another for daily family services. * * * These factors are most helpful, although it should be emphasized that the presence or absence of one or more of them is not dispositive since it is the totality of the relationship as evidenced by the dedication, caring and self-sacrifice of the parties which should in the final analysis, control.

Braschi v. Stahl Associates Company, 543 N.E.2d 49 (N.Y. 1989).

Under *Moore*, could the City have defined "family" in the Rent Control Code to exclude all relationships except those based on blood, marriage, or consanguinity? Since July 2011, New York has allowed gay marriage. If the couple had the option to marry and chose not to, would they still be considered a family?

5.　Can a group of college students be a "family"? After one too many loud parties hosted by college students, a Borough passed a zoning ordinance which defined a family as "[o]ne or more persons occupying a dwelling unit as a single non-profit housekeeping unit, who are living together as a stable and permanent living unit, being a traditional family unit or the functional equivalency [sic] thereof." The Borough's statement of purpose specified an intention to confine college students either to college dormitories or to other zoning districts that permitted apartments and townhouses. The defendants had purchased a house in an area zoned for families for use by a college student (who was the brother of a defendant) and his friends. After ten unrelated students moved into the house, the Borough sought an injunction against their continued occupancy, arguing that they did not constitute a family. The New Jersey court stated that:

> [t]he uncontradicted testimony reflects a plan by ten sophomore college students to live together for three years under conditions that correspond substantially to the ordinance's requirement of a "stable and permanent living unit." To facilitate the plan, the house had been purchased by relatives of one of the students. The students ate together, shared household chores, and paid expenses from a common fund. Although the students signed four-month leases, the leases were renewable if the house was "in order" at the end of the term. Moreover, the students testified to their intention to remain in the house throughout college.

> * * * It is a matter of common experience that the costs of college and the variables characteristic of college life and student relationships do not readily lead to the formation of a household as stable and potentially durable as the one described in this record. On these facts, however, we cannot quarrel with the Law Division's conclusion that the occupancy at issue here "shows stability, permanency, and can be described as the functional equivalent of a family."

Borough of Glassboro v. Vallorosi, 568 A.2d 888 (N.J. 1990). *See* Edward D. Crane, Note, *Five is a Crowd: A Constitutional Analysis of the Boston Zoning Amendment Prohibiting More than Four College Students From Living Together*, 43 SUFFOLK U. L. REV. 217 (2009). Could (and should) a group of students be defined as a "family" for any purpose other than zoning?

6.   How will family be defined in the future? Consider the statement that:

> [t]he Family that will emerge—and endure—in the 21st Century will be one defined overwhelmingly not by tradition or transitory choice, but by a consensus, yet to emerge in any detail, over what human intimacy and commitment is truly valuable.

Harry D. Krause & David D. Meyer, *What Family for the 21st Century?* 50 AM. J. COMPAR. L. 101, 120 (Supp. 2002). Do you agree with Krause and Meyer's assessment? What factors will likely affect lawmakers' decisions on defining families?

Problem 1-1:

A local housing authority has denied an application for low-income housing assistance on the sole basis that the applicants, who had three children, were unmarried. The housing authority (HACE) interpreted the term "family" to mean "two or more persons who live together in the dwelling and are related by blood, marriage or adoption." What arguments support a reversal of the housing authority's interpretation? *See* Hann v. Housing Authority of the City of Easton, 709 F. Supp. 605 (E.D. Pa. 1989).

Problem 1-2:

The City's zoning ordinance defines "family" as "a group of individuals living as a single housekeeping unit in a single dwelling unit. A group of three or more individuals will not be considered a family unless each individual is related to the nominal household head(s) by ties of consanguinity, affinity, or adoption. A family may also consist of one individual." Based on the zoning ordinance, John and Jane Jones, who have contracted with the State Department of Social Services to accept up to eight adolescent children in state foster care for a per-child monthly fee, recently received a notice of violation from the City. Mr. and Mrs. Jones have appealed the determination, arguing that the ordinance is unconstitutional under *Moore*. You are the City Attorney and have been asked to evaluate the merits of their claim.

Problem 1-3:

The Town of Surrey is a wealthy suburb of Hartford, Connecticut. The zoning ordinance defines a family as "those related by blood, marriage, civil union or legal adoption." It prohibits more than three unrelated people living together. Mary and Mike Mitchell were close friends with Sarah and Sam Smith who have three children and a childless couple Tim and Tanya Tyler. As all were struggling with housing costs, Mary and Mike proposed buying a large house in Surrey for all of them to live in. The house has 6000 square feet, nine bedrooms and two acres of land. Mary and Mike are on the title and the mortgage. All three couples move in and contribute to a household account which pays the monthly mortgage, utilities, and groceries. The couples take turns cooking dinner and have regular "family night" activities. Some of the neighbors have complained to the city council that this group violates the zoning ordinance. Mary and Mike have received a cease and desist order. What arguments can you make on behalf of Mike and Mary before the Zoning Board of Appeals? The neighbors?

3. THE FEDERAL TRADITION OF NON-INVOLVEMENT—THE TENTH AMENDMENT AND MORE

The 10th Amendment to the United States Constitution specifies that "[t]he powers not delegated to the United States by the Constitution, nor prohibited by it to the States, are reserved to the States respectively, or to the people." Unlike taxation and interstate commerce, family matters are not among the enumerated powers of the federal government. As a result, and in contrast to other federal systems (i.e., Australia, Canada, Germany, Switzerland) where family law is predominantly federal law, in the United States, state legislatures have traditionally defined the family and enacted the laws that regulate marriage, parentage, divorce, family support obligations, and family property rights.

Congress has conferred federal jurisdiction in cases or controversies between citizens of different states where the amount in controversy exceeds $75,000. 28 U.S.C. § 1332(a). Theoretically, federal courts could exercise diversity jurisdiction over family matters. However, as a result of the court-created "domestic relations exception" and various abstention doctrines, federal courts seldom entertain family law matters. Indeed, the United States Supreme Court has often repeated that "[t]he whole subject of the domestic relations of husband and wife, parent and child, belongs to the laws of the State, and not the laws of the United States." Simms v. Simms, 175 U.S. 162 (1899); accord, McCarty v. McCarty, 453 U.S. 210 (1981).

ANKENBRANDT V. RICHARDS
Supreme Court of the United States, 1992.
504 U.S. 689.

JUSTICE WHITE delivered the opinion of the Court.

This case presents the issue whether the federal courts have jurisdiction or should abstain in a case involving alleged torts committed by the former husband of petitioner and his female companion against petitioner's children, when the sole basis for federal jurisdiction is the diversity-of-citizenship provision of 28 U.S.C. § 1332.

Petitioner Carol Ankenbrandt, a citizen of Missouri, brought this lawsuit on September 26, 1989, on behalf of her daughters L.R. and S.R. against respondents Jon A. Richards and Debra Kesler, citizens of Louisiana, in the United States District Court for the Eastern District of Louisiana. * * * Ankenbrandt's complaint sought monetary damages for alleged sexual and physical abuse of the children committed by Richards and Kesler. Richards is the divorced father of the children and Kesler his female companion * * * [t]he District Court granted respondents' motion to dismiss * * *

* * *

We granted certiorari limited to the following questions: "(1) Is there a domestic relations exception to federal jurisdiction? (2) If so, does it permit a district court to abstain from exercising diversity jurisdiction over a tort action for damages? and (3) Did the District Court in this case err in abstaining from exercising jurisdiction under the doctrine of *Younger v. Harris?*" * * * We address each of these issues in turn.

The domestic relations exception upon which the courts below relied to decline jurisdiction has been invoked often by the lower federal courts. The seeming authority for doing so originally stemmed from the announcement in *Barber v. Barber*, 21 How. 582, 16 L. Ed. 226 (1859), that the federal courts have no jurisdiction over suits for divorce or the allowance of alimony. In that case, the Court heard a suit in equity brought by a wife (by her next friend) in federal district court pursuant to diversity jurisdiction against her former husband. She sought to enforce a decree from a New York state court, which had granted a divorce and awarded her alimony. The former husband thereupon moved to Wisconsin to place himself beyond the New York court's jurisdiction so that the divorce decree there could not be enforced against him; he then sued for a divorce in a Wisconsin court, representing to that court that his wife had abandoned him and failing to disclose the existence of the New York decree. In a suit brought by the former wife in Wisconsin Federal District Court, the former husband alleged that the court lacked jurisdiction. The court accepted jurisdiction and gave judgment for the divorced wife.

* * *

Counsel argued in *Barber* that the Constitution prohibited federal courts from exercising jurisdiction over domestic relations cases. An examination of Article III, *Barber* itself, and our cases since *Barber* makes clear that the Constitution does not exclude domestic relations cases from the jurisdiction otherwise granted by statute to the federal courts.

Article III, § 2, of the Constitution provides in pertinent part:

> The judicial Power shall extend to all Cases in Law and Equity, arising under this Constitution, the Laws of the United States, and Treaties made, * * * to Controversies between two or more States; between a State and Citizens of another State; between Citizens of different states * * *

This section delineates the absolute limits on the federal courts' jurisdiction. But in articulating three different terms to define jurisdiction—"Cases in Law and Equity," "Cases," and "Controversies"—this provision contains no limitation on subjects of a domestic relations nature. Nor did *Barber* purport to ground the domestic relations exception in these constitutional limits on federal jurisdiction. The Court's discussion of federal judicial power to hear suits of a domestic relations nature contains no mention of the Constitution, and it is logical to presume that the Court based its statement limiting such power on narrower statutory, rather than broader constitutional, grounds.

* * *

That Article III, § 2, does not mandate the exclusion of domestic relations cases from federal-court jurisdiction, however, does not mean that such courts necessarily must retain and exercise jurisdiction over such cases.

* * *

The Judiciary Act of 1789 provided that "the circuit courts shall have original cognizance, concurrent with the courts of the several States, of *all suits of a civil nature at common law or in equity, where the matter in dispute exceeds*, exclusive of costs, the sum or value of *five hundred dollars*, and * * * an alien is a party, or the suit is *between a citizen of the State where the suit is brought, and a citizen of another State.*" (Emphasis added.) The defining phrase, "all suits of a civil nature at common law or in equity," remained a key element of statutory provisions demarcating the terms of diversity jurisdiction until 1948, when Congress amended the diversity jurisdiction provision to eliminate this phrase and replace in its stead the term "all civil actions."

The *Barber* majority itself did not expressly refer to the diversity statute's use of the limitation on "suits of a civil nature at common law or in equity." The dissenters in *Barber*, however, implicitly made such a reference, for they suggested that the federal courts had no power over certain domestic relations actions because the court of chancery lacked authority to issue divorce and alimony decrees. Stating that "the origin and the extent of [the federal courts'] jurisdiction must be sought in the laws of the United States, and in the settled rules and principles by which those laws have bound them," the dissenters contended that "as the jurisdiction of the chancery in England does not extend to or embrace the subjects of divorce and alimony, and as the jurisdiction of the courts of the United States in chancery is bounded by that of the chancery in England, all power or cognizance with respect to those subjects by the courts of the United States in chancery is equally excluded." Hence, in the dissenters' view, a suit seeking such relief would not fall within the statutory language "all suits of a civil nature at common law or in equity." Because the *Barber* Court did not disagree with this reason for accepting the jurisdictional limitation over the issuance of divorce and alimony decrees, it may be inferred fairly that the jurisdictional limitation recognized by the Court rested on this statutory basis and that the disagreement between the Court and the dissenters thus centered only on the extent of the limitation.

We have no occasion here to join the historical debate over whether the English court of chancery had jurisdiction to handle certain domestic relations matters. * * * We thus are content to rest our conclusion that a domestic relations exception exists as a matter of statutory construction not on the accuracy of the historical justifications on which it was seemingly based, but rather on Congress' apparent acceptance of this construction of the diversity jurisdiction provisions in the years prior to 1948, when the statute limited jurisdiction to "suits of a civil nature at common law or in equity." As the court in *Phillips, Nizer, Benjamin, Krim & Ballon v. Rosenstiel*, 490 F.2d 509, 514 (2d Cir. 1973) observed, "[m]ore than a century has elapsed since the *Barber* dictum without any intimation of Congressional grant." Considerations of *stare decisis* have particular strength in this context, where "the legislative power is implicated, and Congress remains free to alter what we have done."

When Congress amended the diversity statute in 1948 to replace the law/equity distinction with the phrase "all civil actions," we presume Congress did so with full cognizance of the Court's nearly century-long interpretation of the prior statutes, which had construed the statutory diversity jurisdiction to contain an exception for certain domestic relations matters. * * *

In the more than 100 years since this Court laid the seeds for the development of the domestic relations exception, the lower federal courts have applied it in a variety of circumstances. Many of these applications go well beyond the circumscribed situations posed by *Barber* and its progeny. *Barber* itself disclaimed federal jurisdiction over a narrow range of domestic relations issues involving the granting of a divorce and a decree of alimony * * *.

* * *

The holding of the case itself sanctioned the exercise of federal jurisdiction over the enforcement of an alimony decree that had been properly obtained in a state court of competent jurisdiction. Contrary to the *Barber* dissenters' position, the enforcement of such validly obtained orders does not "regulate the domestic relations of society" and produce an "inquisitorial authority" in which federal tribunals "enter the habitations and even into the chambers and nurseries of private families, and inquire into and pronounce upon the morals and habits and affections or antipathies of the members of every household." And from the conclusion that the federal courts lacked jurisdiction to issue divorce and alimony decrees, there was no dissent.

* * *

Subsequently, this Court expanded the domestic relations exception to include decrees in child custody cases. In a child custody case brought pursuant to a writ of habeas corpus, for instance, the Court held void a writ issued by a Federal District Court to restore a child to the custody of the father. "As to the right to the control and possession of this child, as it is contested by its father and its grandfather, it is one in regard to which neither the Congress of the United States nor any authority of the United States has any special jurisdiction." *In re Burrus*, 136 U.S. 586, 594 (1890).

* * * We conclude, therefore, that the domestic relations exception, as articulated by this Court since *Barber*, divests the federal courts of power to issue divorce, alimony, and child custody decrees. Given the long passage of time without any expression of congressional dissatisfaction, we have no trouble today reaffirming the validity of the exception as it pertains to divorce and alimony decrees and child custody orders.

Not only is our conclusion rooted in respect for this long-held understanding, it is also supported by sound policy considerations. Issuance of decrees of this type not infrequently involves retention of jurisdiction by the court and deployment of social workers to monitor compliance. As a matter of judicial economy, state courts are more eminently suited to work of this type than are federal courts, which lack the close association with state and local government organizations dedicated to handling issues that arise out of conflicts over divorce, alimony, and child custody decrees. Moreover, as a matter of judicial expertise, it makes far more sense to retain the rule that federal courts lack power to issue these types of decrees because of the special proficiency developed by state tribunals over the past century and a half in handling issues that arise in the granting of such decrees.

By concluding, as we do, that the domestic relations exception encompasses only cases involving the issuance of a divorce, alimony, or child custody decree, we necessarily find that the Court of Appeals erred by affirming the District Court's invocation of this exception. This lawsuit in no way seeks such a decree; rather, it alleges that respondents Richards and Kesler committed torts against L.R. and S.R., Ankenbrandt's children by Richards. Federal subject-matter jurisdiction pursuant to § 1332 thus is proper in this case. We now address whether, even though subject-matter jurisdiction might be proper, sufficient grounds exist to warrant abstention from the exercise of that jurisdiction.

The courts below cited *Younger v. Harris*, 401 U.S. 37 (1971), to support their holdings to abstain in this case. In so doing, the courts clearly erred. *Younger* itself held that, absent unusual circumstances, a federal court could not interfere with a pending state criminal prosecution. Though we have extended *Younger* abstention to the civil context, we have never applied the notions of comity so critical to *Younger's* "Our Federalism" when no state proceeding was pending nor any assertion of important state interests made. In this case, there is no allegation by respondents of any pending state proceedings, and Ankenbrandt contends that such proceedings ended prior to her filing this lawsuit. Absent any pending proceeding in state tribunals, therefore, application by the lower courts of *Younger* abstention was clearly erroneous.

It is not inconceivable, however, that in certain circumstances, the abstention principles * * * might be relevant in a case involving elements of the domestic relationship even when the parties do not seek divorce, alimony, or child custody. This would be so when a case presents "difficult questions of state law bearing on policy problems of substantial public import whose importance transcends the result in the case then at bar." Such might well be the case if a federal suit were filed prior to effectuation of a divorce, alimony, or child custody decree, and the suit depended on a determination of the status of the parties. Where, as here, the status of the domestic relationship has been determined as a matter of state law, and in any event has no bearing on the underlying torts alleged, we have no difficulty concluding that _Burford_ abstention is inappropriate in this case.

We thus conclude that the Court of Appeals erred by affirming the District Court's rulings to decline jurisdiction based on the domestic relations exception to diversity jurisdiction and to abstain under the doctrine of *Younger v. Harris*.

* * *

JUSTICE BLACKMUN, concurring in the judgment.

I agree with the Court that the District Court had jurisdiction over petitioner's claims in tort. Moreover, I agree that the federal courts should not entertain claims for divorce, alimony, and child custody. I am unable to agree, however, that the diversity statute contains any "exception" for domestic relations matters. The Court goes to remarkable lengths to craft an exception that is simply not in the statute and is not supported by the case law. In my view, the longstanding, unbroken practice of the federal courts in refusing to hear domestic relations cases is precedent at most for continued discretionary abstention rather than mandatory limits on federal jurisdiction. For these reasons I concur only in the Court's judgment.

NOTES AND QUESTIONS

1. Congress has not amended 28 U.S.C.A. § 1332(a) since the *Ankenbrandt* case. Are there continuing justifications for the exception? What impact might congressional or judicial repeal of the domestic relations exception have on the federal court system?

2. After *Ankenbrandt*, what is the scope of the domestic relations exception? If the case involves a federal question, the exception has no application. *See* Rubin v. Smith, 817 F. Supp. 987 (D. N.H. 1993). When no federal question is involved, lower courts struggle with the line between "cases involving the issuance of a divorce, alimony, or child custody decree," and cases in which "the status of the domestic relationship has been determined as a matter of state law and has no bearing on the underlying [action]." *Compare* Johnson v. Thomas, 808 F. Supp. 1316 (W.D. Mich. 1992) (applying exception to action based on alleged domestic partnership agreement) and McLaughlin v. Cotner, 193 F.3d 410 (6th Cir. 1999) (applying exception to wife's attempt to

enforce divorce decree ordering ex-husband to sell marital home) *with* Stone v. Wall, 135 F.3d 1438 (11th Cir. 1998) (not applying exception to tort claim for custodial interference) and Lannan v. Maul, 979 F.2d 627 (8th Cir. 1992) (not applying exception to child's action based on father's breach of divorce agreement to maintain life insurance policy).

3.   The *Ankenbrandt* case mentioned the *Younger* abstention which is based on Younger v. Harris, 401 U.S. 37 (1971). In order for a federal court to abstain under *Younger,* (1) there must be ongoing state judicial proceedings; (2) the state proceedings must implicate important state interests; and (3) the state proceedings must afford an adequate opportunity to raise the federal claims.

There are several other abstention doctrines: The *Rooker-Feldman* doctrine (District of Columbia Court of Appeals v. Feldman, 460 U.S. 462 (1983); Rooker v. Fidelity Trust Co., 263 U.S. 413 (1923)) restricts lower federal court review of state-court judgments and evaluation of constitutional claims that are "inextricably intertwined" with the state court's decision in a judicial proceeding. *See* Silverman v. Silverman, 338 F.3d 886 (8th Cir. 2003); McKnight v. Middleton, 699 F. Supp. 2d 507 (E.D. N.Y. 2010). The *Burford* abstention (Burford v. Sun Oil Co., 319 U.S. 315 (1943)) allows a federal court to dismiss a case when it is asked to entertain litigation involving specialized aspects of a complicated state regulatory scheme, the enforcement of which is better left to state administrative agencies or courts. The *Colorado River* abstention (Colorado River Water Conservation District v. United States, 424 U.S. 800, 818 (1976)) permits a federal court to defer to a concurrent state court proceeding as a matter of wise judicial administration.

4.   If family issues are of national importance, then why shouldn't federal courts hear family law cases? Consider the following two excerpts:

> * * * A first possibility is that federal court involvement in family life is bad, per se, at a structural level. This claim takes seriously the arguments made in the many cases espousing (slight pun intended) state control over family life and fearing that the federal courts would become hopelessly "enmeshed" in family disputes. Under this vision, the states (and Indian tribes) as smaller units of government are closer to "the people", and thus a more appropriate level of government to determine matters affecting intimate life.
>
> Possible justifications for this view exist. Contemporary innovations of the domestic relations exception discard arguments based on ecclesiastical authority, the alleged lack of jurisdictional diversity between married couples, that the claim that divorces lack monetary value—all in favor of a "modern view that state courts have historically decided these matters and have developed both a well-known expertise in these cases and a strong interest in disposing of them." * * * Holding aside the ever-present question of boundaries, doctrine might shift in a variety of ways when ideological claims

about the relationship between federal courts and families are revised.

First, one could insist that, despite recognition of federal laws of the family, the claim of deference to state governance remains strong and, as a matter of doctrine, complete abstention (a form of reverse presumption) is desirable. To the extent recent federal law in bankruptcy, pensions, and benefits law points in the other direction, that erosion should be stopped—by legislation or judicial interpretation. But were one really to press this claim—that states are specially situated and should be controlling family life-one would not seek only to cabin the federal courts. This position would also require urging Congress and agencies to avoid defining families by rewriting statutes and regulations to incorporate state law, so as to permit state governance of interpersonal relations. An array of federal statutes would have to incorporate state definitions of families, and what would be lost in uniformity and national norms would be gained in recognition of the special relationship of states in defining family life.

Alternatively, one might instruct the federal courts to adopt a somewhat weaker form of deference, reminiscent of eleventh amendment doctrine and conscious of the many instances of congressional silence. * * * Yet a third alternative is to have selective federal court interpretation of congressional silence as a basis for federal law to override state law. * * *

Yet a problem remains. The current hierarchy stipulates the federal courts as most powerful; the supremacy clause confirms that sense of authority. Further, federal courts theorists might affirmatively argue that federal courts are needed in this area—either because of their special capacity to protect the politically disfavored or because federal sovereign and administrative interests are at stake. While neither the appeal to the community envisioned by the claim of closeness of the state to the family nor the concern about attitudes and knowledge of federal judges should be discounted, the "inevitability of federal involvement" in family life remains, as does a sense that the rejection of that role by federal courts reconfirms the marginalization of women and families from national life.

Federal involvement emerges here, as it does in torts, land use, health regulation, criminal law, and other areas, because of the wealth of interactions that make the imagined coherence of the very categories "federal" and "state" themselves problematic. Whether looking at the problem from the top down, and seeing "joint governance" or considering the issue from the perspective of individuals and speaking of "membership in multiple communities," the point is the same: an interlocking, enmeshed regulatory structure covers the host of human activity in the United States. There is not a

priori line one can invoke to separate legal regulation into two
bounded boxes "state" and "federal." Uniform state laws demonstrate
the limits of state court borders and the need for regulatory
structures that bridge them. State and federal court interpretation of
"family" are unavoidable. * * *

Judith Resnick, *"Naturally" Without Gender: Women, Jurisdiction, and the
Federal Courts*, 66 N.Y.U. L. REV. 1682, 1750–1757 (1991).

Despite the federalism rhetoric that still marks political debate and
judicial opinions, family law in the United States today is a complex
mixture of state and federal law. * * * Congress has used its spending
power to reconfigure state child support and child welfare laws on a
cooperative federalism basis and its powers under the Commerce and
Full Faith and Credit Clauses to legislate in areas that pose
horizontal federalism problems. National laws may also preempt
state family law in areas including civil rights, economic regulation,
immigration, and foreign relations. Congress has been primarily
responsible for defining the balance of national and state power over
families, with the federal courts resisting national family legislation
only if it seems likely to shift significant responsibility from the state
courts to the federal courts.

Ann Laquer Estin, *Sharing Governance: Family Law in Congress and the
States*, 18 CORNELL J.L. & PUB. POL'Y 267 (2009).

Problem 1-4:

Herbert and Wilma separated and, approximately a year ago, Herbert
obtained a divorce in Wisconsin based on a marital settlement agreement.
Herbert then remarried and moved to Texas. Based on information she has
recently acquired, Wilma has now brought an action against Herbert in
federal court alleging that, during the pendency of the divorce proceedings,
Herbert concealed assets, committed perjury, and misrepresented his
financial dealings so as to intentionally deprive Wilma of her interest in
the couple's marital property. Herbert has filed a motion to dismiss. What
arguments are available to Wilma? to Herbert? What result? *See* Strasen
v. Strasen, 897 F. Supp. 1179 (E.D. Wis. 1995).

Problem 1-5:

Tara filed for divorce from Todd in state district court. Todd then filed
an identity theft tort claim in a diversity action in the federal court against
Tara. He claims that during their marriage she had purloined his personal
information and used it to obtain several credit cards in his name upon
which she charged about $40,000 in purchases, resulting in his being sued
for non-payment. Tara moves to dismiss the claim based on the domestic
relations exception. What result? Why? *See* Wallace v. Wallace, 736 F.3d
764 (8th Cir. 2013).

4. THE FUTURE—AND INEVITABILITY—OF FEDERAL INVOLVEMENT IN FAMILY LAW

A. FEDERAL LEGISLATION

Despite the tradition of federal noninvolvement, in recent years Congress and the United States Supreme Court have become involved in many aspects of family law. Using the Commerce Clause, the Fourteenth Amendment, and conditioning state receipt of federal welfare funding on compliance with federal requirements, Congress has legislated on many family law subjects.

The lengthiest list of federal laws is in the area of child support. Federal activism here has been spurred by rising rates of single parenthood and children's poverty which resulted in an increase in welfare funding, first with Aid to Families with Dependent Children and now with Temporary Assistance to Needy Families. Since 1974 when Congress enacted Title-IVD to the Social Security Act and established the Office of Child Support Enforcement, the federal government has revolutionized the process for establishing and enforcing child support. A unanimous Congress enacted the Child Support Enforcement Amendments of 1984 which required expedited establishment and enforcement of child support orders and the creation of numerical child support guidelnes. *See* Linda D. Elrod, *The Federalization of Child Support Guidelines*, 6 J. AM. ACAD. MATRIM. LAWYERS 103 (1990). Congress then enacted the Family Support Act and the Full Faith and Credit to Child Support Orders Act. In 1996, the Personal Responsibility and Work Opportunity Reconciliation Act directed all states to adopt the Uniform Interstate Family Support Act by January 1, 1998. *See generally* Paul Legler, *The Coming Revolution in Child Support Policy: Implications of the 1996 Welfare Act*, 30 FAM. L. Q. 519 (1996). Federal appellate courts have uniformly rejected arguments that Congress has violated the Tenth Amendment or exceeded its power under the Commerce Clause in enacting the Child Support Enforcement Amendments. *See* United States v. Faasse, 265 F.3d 475 (6th Cir. 2001) (citing other cases). Congress also made it a federal crime to cross state lines to avoid paying child support if one owes more than a certain amount of child support. See Child Support Recovery Act of 1992 and Deadbeat Parents Punishment Act of 1998. See generally Chapter 17.

Although child custody has traditionally been an issue left to the states, Congress acted to settle interstate jurisdictional disputes over child custody by enacting the Parental Kidnapping Prevention Act (PKPA). When the United States ratified the Hague Convention on the Civil Aspects of International Child Abduction, Congress enacted the International Child Abduction Remedies Act (ICARA) which, among other things, granted federal and state courts concurrent jurisdiction over international child abduction cases. In addition, Congress made international parental kidnapping a federal crime (International Parental Kidnapping Act).

Congress stepped into the area of child abuse in 1974 with the Child Abuse Prevention and Treatment Act (CAPTA). The Adoption Assistance and Child Welfare Act of 1980 (AACWA), the Adoption and Safe Families Act (ASFA) (1997), the Foster Care Independence Act (1999), and Preventing Sex Trafficking and Strengthening Families Act (2014). *See* Chapter 10. To protect Indian children from being placed with non-Indian families, Congress enacted the Indian Child Welfare Act of 1978. Because of problems placing children in the welfare system for adoption, Congress enacted the Multiethnic Placement Act (1994) and Interethnic Placement Provisions. See Chapter 8.

Congress ventured into the area of family violence with the Violence Against Women Act (VAWA) of 1994 (reauthorized in 2005 and 2013). VAWA provided funds for many services, including police and prosecutor training, battered women shelters, a national domestic violence hotline. The Supreme Court struck only the section which created a new federal private right of action for damages suffered in the course of "a crime of violence motivated by gender," 42 U.S.C. § 13981(b). Noting that "[t]he Constitution requires a distinction between what is truly national and what is truly local," the Supreme Court found that Congress had exceeded its powers in creating the VAWA claim. United States v. Morrison, 529 U.S. 598, 617–18 (2000). Congress has also mandated that states must grant full faith and credit to civil protection orders issued in another state. 18 U.S.C. § 2265 (2014).

B. LACK OF FEDERAL POLICY

Despite the recent proliferation of federal laws that impact state regulation of families, family policy in the United States has lacked general goals. Legislation has been passed to meet particular perceived needs, not to further a larger policy agenda. Historian John Demos sees the United States as standing alone in its lack of a coherent family policy:

> * * * [O]ur inherited habits and values—our constricted capacity for extrafamilial caring—partly explain public indifference to the blighted conditions in which many families even now are obliged to live. The results are especially tragic as they affect children, and they leave us with a terrible paradox. In this allegedly most child-centered of nations, we find it hard to care very much or very consistently about other people's children. * * *

JOHN DEMOS, IMAGES OF THE AMERICAN FAMILY, THEN AND NOW, CHANGING IMAGES OF THE FAMILY 43–60 (1978).

In 1987, President Reagan attempted to establish a national family policy through issuance of this Executive Order:

EXECUTIVE ORDER 12,606 OF SEPTEMBER 2, 1987

52 Fed. Reg. 34188 (Sept. 9, 1987).

THE FAMILY

Section 1. *Family Policymaking Criteria.* In formulating and implementing policies and regulations that may have significant impact on family formation, maintenance, and general well-being, executive departments and agencies shall, to the extent permitted by law, assess such measures in light of the following questions:

(a)   Does this action by government strengthen or erode the stability of the family and, particularly, the marital commitment?

(b)   Does this action strengthen or erode the authority and rights of parents in the education, nurture and supervision of their children?

(c)   Does this action help the family perform its functions, or does it substitute governmental activity for the function?

(d)   Does this action by government increase or decrease family earnings? Do the proposed benefits of this action justify the impact on the family budget?

(e)   Can this activity be carried out by a lower level of government or by the family itself?

(f)   What message, intended or otherwise, does this program send to the public concerning the status of the family?

(g)   What message does it send to young people concerning the relationship between their behavior, their personal responsibility, and the norms of our society?

The Order remained in effect until April 21, 1997, when it was superseded by President Clinton's Executive Order 13045, directing federal agencies to assess environmental health risks that affect children. The new order appears to be much more limited in scope. In response, a bill was introduced in Congress in 1997 which would forbid enactment of new federal policies without study of how the policy would affect families; thus far the bill has not been enacted.

NOTES AND QUESTIONS

1.   Is the Reagan Executive Order an adequate account of national family policy goals? What, if any, issues does the Executive Order fail to address?

2.   There have been other attempts to formulate a cohesive family policy. For example, in its 1996 report to Congress, the Commission on Child and Family Welfare made recommendations for greater use of alternative dispute resolution procedures and addressing family problems more "holistically," but

failed to contain specific policy proposals. A minority report of the Commission did set out a legislative agenda. *See* Minority Report and Policy Recommendations to the President and Congress, July 1996. It urged:

(1) A national commitment to the preservation and encouragement of the institution of marriage;

(2) A national commitment to the re-inclusion and re-involvement of fathers in family life, whether married or not;

(3) A national commitment to support more and better involvement of both mothers and fathers with raising a child, regardless of marital status;

(4) A national commitment to decreasing the number of children raised solely by single-parents;

(5) A national commitment to welfare reform that reverses prior policy and places father-inclusiveness as a cornerstone of all new policy.

How does this agenda differ from the Reagan policy statement? Is it a better or worse attempt to formulate a national policy? Why?

Many of the recent federal family law enactments—and all of the child support initiatives—were spurred by rising rates of children's poverty and welfare dependence. The poverty rate for children in single-parent households is more than five times that of children living in married-couple households. U.S. Dep't of Commerce, Bureau of the Census, Statistical Abstract of the United States: 1993 tbls. 737, 740. Children in single parent households are more likely to experience poor health, behavioral problems, delinquency, and low educational attainment than are their peers in intact families; as adults they have higher rates of poverty, early childbearing, and divorce. *See* Wendy Sigle-Rushton & Sara McLanahan, *Father Absence and Child Well-Being: A Critical Review*, *in* THE FUTURE OF THE FAMILY 116, 120–22 (Daniel P. Moynihan et al., eds. 2004).

So should public policy focus on improving the living standard of children in single-parent households? Or on deterring single parenthood? Some commentators see the decline of marriage as the key problem.

* * *

Marriage is the cultural creation that restricts and channels men's sexual access to women. For several thousand years, both in the West and the East, the stable life-long monogamous marriage has been the norm. * * * Marriage is a cultural invention. It is designed to harness men's energies to support the only offspring they may legitimately have, or are likely to have, legitimately or otherwise, in a world in which marriage is the norm. We lose sight of this truth at our peril.

* * *

Western society * * * in the very recent past understood marriage as an allocation of separate spheres of power to husbands and wives based on their cultural and biological specialization and accepted hierarchy. That as a formal matter in law, and, as a practical matter, in most marriages, men have been on top of the hierarchy may be a reflection of men's greater physical strength, women's greater front-end investment in marriage, or the symbolic meaning of the sexual act itself. * * *

[I]t is not my belief that consciousness has not changed nor that the change in consciousness has not generated changes in behavior. Rather, I believe that those changes have less to do with women per se and more to do with mankind generally, and that present marriage patterns are as much, if not more, a function of men's changed consciousness as of women's. Specifically, if men no longer recognize the same duty to adhere to their commitments as their great-great-grandfathers, and neither society nor the law holds them to those commitments, the security of marriage and of women's investment in marriage dissolves. * * *

Lloyd R. Cohen, *Rhetoric, the Unnatural Family, and Women's Work,* 81 VA. L. REV. 2275, 2282, 2287, 2290–95 (1995). Responding to arguments like Cohen's—and hoping to reduce federal welfare expenditures—in 2002, Congress earmarked $300 million to encourage getting and staying married. *See* Wade F. Horn & Isabel Sawhill, *Making Room for Daddy: Fathers, Marriage, and Welfare Reform,* THE NEW WORLD OF WELFARE (Ronald Haskins et al. eds. 2001).

Other scholars believe that the real problem is not single parenthood, but money: First, the lower standard of living associated with single parenthood appears to explain half or more of the variation between single and two-parent households. Moreover, childhood poverty—whether or not coupled with single parenthood—is correlated with risks to childhood functioning and adult attainments much like those attributed to single parenthood. For example, child maltreatment is highly concentrated among disadvantaged families: a U.S. national incidence study found that children from families with annual incomes below $15,000 were 60 times more likely to die from maltreatment and 22 times more like to be seriously harmed by it than were children from families with annual incomes above $30,000. Single and adolescent parenting, substance abuse, mental health problems, adult family violence, and lack of social supports are all highly correlated with child maltreatment; these various maltreatment-risk factors are also highly correlated with each other and with low socioeconomic status. *See* Marsha Garrison, *Reforming Child Protection: A Public Health Perspective,* 12 VA. J. SOC. POL'Y & L. 590, 612–16 (2005) (reviewing research data).

Some experts believe that poverty is an important factor in explaining why U.S. children fare poorly when compared to children in other wealthy, industrialized nations. The United States has the *highest* rate of:

- child poverty (about 4 times higher than countries with the lowest rate);

- death from child maltreatment (12 times higher than countries with the lowest rates and 2 to 3 times the median rate);

- infant mortality (about 70% higher than the lowest rate and about 50% higher than the median rate);

- teenage pregnancy (12 times higher than countries with the lowest rates); and

- children living in single parent families.

The United States has the *highest* per capita income, but it also has the *lowest* level of public transfers to children.

These experts argue that U.S. family policy should focus on family support, not family form. As one commentator put it:

all that we know about families demonstrates that family form simply does not correlate with family function or developmental health * * * No single form of family is essential nor is it a guarantor of healthy, happy children * * * The empirical evidence supports correlation but not causation between father absence and children's difficulties or lack of success, and much of that * * * connects economics, not the absence of a developmentally required father.

NANCY E. DOWD, IN DEFENSE OF SINGLE PARENT FAMILIES at xv, 29 (1997).

The National Marriage Project issues regular "State of Our Unions" reports that analyze trends in marriage, divorce and cohabitation. The 2010 report indicated that "[m]arriage is an emerging dividing line between America's moderately educated middle [high school diploma] and those with college degrees." The Report noted multiple disparities that pervaded everything from the likelihood of having a child outside of marriage to the quality of the marriage. Inequality of family structure is linked to inequalities of income, health, longevity and positive indicators for children. *See* NAOMI CAHN & JUNE CARBONE, RED FAMILIES V. BLUE FAMILIES: LEGAL POLARIZATION AND THE CREATION OF CULTURE (2010).

What information do we need to fashion an optimal U.S. family policy? Is it possible to formulate a sensible policy in the absence of such information? The issues of family formation, dissolution, support, and public policy will be discussed throughout the book.

5. INTERNATIONAL AND FOREIGN LAW IN AMERICAN COURTS

A. TREATIES AND PRIVATE INTERNATIONAL LAW AGREEMENTS

International law and foreign laws are of increasing importance to family lawyers today. Increased mobility across country lines and globalization have led to the proliferation of five Hague treaties dealing with family law topics. The United States has ratified three of them—the Hague Convention on the Civil Aspects of International Child Abduction (1980), the Hague Convention on Cooperation with Respect to Intercountry Adoption (1993), and the Hague Convention on the International Enforcement of Child Support and Other Forms of Family Maintenance (2016). Before the 2016 election, the State Department was looking at the possible enactment of the Hague Convention on Jurisdiction, Applicable Law, Recognition, Enforcement and Co-operation in Respect of Parental Responsibility and Measures for the Protection of Children (1996). A fifth family convention on International Protection of Adults (2000) has not received much attention in the United States.

The United Nations Convention on the Rights of the Child (1989) has been ratified by 193 countries, including Somalia in 2015. The UNCRC is a "Bill of Rights" for children which recognizes that the child's interests may be separate from the parents in legal proceedings. It also sets the "best interests of the child" as the standard for all decisions affecting children. Although the United States has not adopted the Convention, it has adopted two of the optional protocols—Optional Protocol on the Rights of the Child on the Sale of Children, Child Prostitution and Pornography and the Optional Protocol on Child Soldiers (2002). The United States Supreme Court acknowledged the Convention in Roper v. Simmons, 543 U.S. 551, 575–76 (2005):

> As respondent and a number of *amici* emphasize, Article 37 of the United Nations Convention on the Rights of the Child, which every country in the world has ratified save for the United States and Somalia, contains an express prohibition on capital punishment for crimes committed by juveniles under 18. * * * No ratifying country has entered a reservation to the provision prohibiting the execution of juvenile offenders. Parallel

prohibitions are contained in other significant international covenants.

B. USE OF FOREIGN LAW IN AMERICAN COURTS

An increasing number of cases involve transnational families which can lead to difficult choice of law issues. Citizens of another country may marry and move to the United States. One may wish to divorce. An American citizen may marry a foreign national, have children, and seek a divorce. The custody laws of the foreign country may be vastly different than American laws.

Another instance that may arise is that one party obtains an order or judgment from a foreign country and the U.S. courts have to decide whether to enforce the foreign judgment. For example, in Aleem v. Aleem, 947 A.2d 489 (Md. 2008), the couple, foreign nationals, had lived in Maryland for twenty years and had children. The wife filed for divorce in Maryland. The husband then obtained a talaq, a nonjudicial divorce, which is authorized under the laws of Pakistan which gave the wife no property or alimony. The husband petitioned the Maryland court to dismiss the divorce because the parties were divorced pursuant to the talaq. The wife argued that the Maryland court should not give comity to the law of Pakistan. The Maryland Court cited the state's Equal Rights Amendment in finding that the enforcement of a talaq divorce "where only the male, i.e. husband, has an independent right to utilize talaq . . . is contrary to Maryland's constitutional provisions and thus is contrary to the public policy of Maryland."

Recently there have been attempts in several states to limit the use of shari'a law. These enactments raise the issue of whether the law applicable to a family dispute should depend upon what religious tradition the couple accepts.

AWAD V. ZIRIAX
Western District of Oklahoma, 2010.
754 F. Supp. 2d 1298.

This order addresses issues that go to the very foundation of our country, our Constitution, and particularly, the Bill of Rights. Throughout the course of our country's history, the will of the "majority" has on occasion conflicted with the constitutional rights of individuals, an occurrence which our founders foresaw and provided for through the Bill of Rights. * * *

Before the Court is plaintiff's Complaint Seeking a Temporary Restraining Order and Preliminary Injunction, filed November 4, 2010. * * *

State Question 755, which was on Oklahoma's November 2, 2010 ballot, provides:

This measure amends the State Constitution. It changes a section that deals with the courts of this state. It would amend Article 7, Section 1. It makes courts rely on federal and state law when deciding cases. It forbids courts from considering or using international law. It forbids courts from considering or using Sharia Law.

International law is also known as the law of nations. It deals with the conduct of international organizations and independent nations, such as countries, states and tribes. It deals with their relationship with each other. It also deals with some of their relationships with persons.

The law of nations is formed by the general assent of civilized nations. Sources of international law also include international agreements, as well as treaties.

Sharia Law is Islamic law. It is based on two principal sources, the Koran and the teaching of Mohammed.

State Question 755 was put on the ballot through the legislative adoption of Enrolled House Joint Resolution 1056. Said resolution proposes to amend Section 1 of Article VII of the Oklahoma Constitution by adding the following section:

C.   The Courts provided for in subsection A of this section when exercising their judicial authority, shall uphold and adhere to the law as provided in the United States Constitution, the Oklahoma Constitution, the United States Code, federal regulations promulgated pursuant thereto, established common law, the Oklahoma Statutes and rules promulgated pursuant thereto, and if necessary the law of another state of the United States provided the law of the other state does not include Sharia Law, in making judicial decisions. The courts shall not look to the legal precepts of other nations or cultures. Specifically, the courts shall not consider international law or Sharia Law. The provisions of this subsection shall apply to all cases before the respective courts including, but not limited to, cases of first impression.

Election results show that 70.08 per cent of the voters approved State Question 755. Once the Oklahoma State Board of Elections certifies the election results, the amendment set forth above will become a part of the Oklahoma Constitution.

On November 4, 2010, plaintiff filed the instant action, challenging the constitutionality of State Question 755's amendment to the Oklahoma Constitution. Specifically, plaintiff asserts that the ban on the state courts' use and consideration of Sharia Law violates the Establishment Clause and the Free Exercise Clause of the First Amendment to the United States Constitution. * * *

Under Article III, federal courts have jurisdiction only to decide "Cases" and "Controversies." U.S. Const. art. III, § 2. An essential part of the case-or-controversy requirement is the concept that a plaintiff must have standing. * * *

Having carefully reviewed the briefs on this issue, and having heard the evidence and arguments presented at the hearing, the Court finds that plaintiff has shown that he will suffer an injury in fact, specifically, an invasion of his First Amendment rights which is concrete, particularized and imminent. * * *

[Plaintiff] has sufficiently set forth a personal stake in this action by alleging that he lives in Oklahoma, is a Muslim, that the amendment conveys an official government message of disapproval and hostility toward his religious beliefs, that sends a clear message he is an outsider, not a full member of the political community, thereby chilling his access to the government and forcing him to curtail his political and religious activities. Further, the Court finds the consequences—the condemnation—that plaintiff believes will result from the amendment are objectively justified. Finally, the Court would note that it would be incomprehensible if, as plaintiff alleges, Oklahoma could condemn the religion of its Muslim citizens, yet one of those citizens could not defend himself in court against his government's preferment of other religious views. * * *

A movant seeking a preliminary injunction must show: (1) a substantial likelihood of success on the merits; (2) irreparable injury to the movant if the injunction is denied; (3) the threatened injury to the movant outweighs the injury to the party opposing the preliminary injunction; and (4) the injunction would not be adverse to the public interest. * * *

When a claim asserting a violation of the Establishment Clause has been made, "[t]o pass constitutional muster, the governmental action (1) must have a secular legislative purpose, (2) its principal or primary effect must be one that neither advances nor inhibits religion, and (3) it must not foster an excessive government entanglement with religion. * * *

The Court finds plaintiff has made a strong showing of a substantial likelihood of success on the merits of his claim asserting a violation of the Establishment Clause. Specifically, the Court finds that plaintiff has made a strong showing that State Question 755's amendment's primary effect inhibits religion and that the amendment fosters an excessive government entanglement with religion. While defendants contend that the amendment is merely a choice of law provision that bans state courts from applying the law of other nations and cultures, regardless of what faith they may be based on, if any, the actual language of the amendment reasonably, and perhaps more reasonably, may be viewed as specifically singling out Sharia Law, conveying a message of disapproval of plaintiff's faith. The amendment creates two independent restrictions on use/consideration of Sharia Law: (1) the amendment requires that Oklahoma courts "shall not consider ... Sharia Law", and (2) the amendment allows Oklahoma courts to use/consider the law of another state of the United States but only if "the other state does not include Sharia Law". No other "legal precepts of other nations or cultures" is similarly restricted with respect to the law of another state.

Furthermore, plaintiff has presented testimony that "Sharia Law" is not actually "law", but is religious traditions that provide guidance to plaintiff and other Muslims regarding the exercise of their faith. Plaintiff has presented testimony that the obligations that "Sharia Law" imposes are not legal obligations but are obligations of a personal and private nature dictated by faith. Plaintiff also testified that "Sharia Law" differs depending on the country in which the individual Muslim resides. For example, plaintiff stated that marrying more than one wife is permissible in Islam but in the United States, where that is illegal, Muslims do not marry more than one wife because Sharia in the United States mandates Muslims to abide by the law of the land and respect the law of their land. Based upon this testimony, the Court finds that plaintiff has shown "Sharia Law" lacks a legal character, and, thus, plaintiff's religious traditions and faith are the only non-legal content subject to the judicial exclusion set forth in the amendment. As a result, the Court finds plaintiff has made a strong showing that the amendment conveys a message of disapproval of plaintiff's faith and, consequently, has the effect of inhibiting plaintiff's religion.

Additionally, the Court finds that plaintiff has made a strong showing that the amendment will foster an excessive government entanglement with religion. Because, as set forth above, Sharia Law is not "law" but is religious traditions that differ among Muslims, the Court finds that plaintiff has shown that to comply with the amendment, Oklahoma courts will be faced with determining the content of Sharia Law, and, thus, the content of plaintiff's religious doctrines. The United States Supreme Court has held: "[i]t is well established . . . that courts should refrain from trolling through a person's or institution's religious beliefs."

Plaintiff also asserts that State Question 755's amendment to the Oklahoma Constitution violates the First Amendment's Free Exercise Clause. "At a minimum, the protections of the Free Exercise Clause pertain if the law at issue discriminates against some or all religious beliefs or regulates or prohibits conduct because it is undertaken for religious reasons. * * *Further, "[a]lthough a law targeting religious beliefs as such is never permissible, if the object of a law is to infringe upon or restrict practices because of their religious motivation, the law is not neutral, and it is invalid unless it is justified by a compelling interest and is narrowly tailored to advance that interest." However, "a law that is neutral and of general applicability need not be justified by a compelling governmental interest even if the law has the incidental effect of burdening a particular religious practice."

Having carefully reviewed the briefs on this issue, and having heard the evidence and arguments presented at the hearing, the Court finds plaintiff has made a strong showing of a substantial likelihood of success on the merits of his claim asserting a violation of the Free Exercise Clause. * * * Plaintiff has shown that the actual language of the amendment reasonably, and perhaps more reasonably, may be viewed as specifically singling out Sharia Law (plaintiff's faith) and, thus, is not facially neutral. Additionally, as set forth above, the Court finds that plaintiff has shown that there is a reasonable probability that the amendment would prevent plaintiff's will from being fully probated by a state court in Oklahoma because it incorporates by reference specific elements of the Islamic prophetic traditions. Further, plaintiff has presented evidence that there is a reasonable probability that Muslims, including plaintiff, will be unable to bring actions in Oklahoma state courts for violations of the Oklahoma Religious Freedom Act and for violations of their rights under the United States Constitution if those violations are based upon their religion. Finally, the Court finds that defendants have presented no evidence which would show that the amendment is justified by any compelling interest or is narrowly tailored. * * *

Therefore, . . . the Court GRANTS plaintiff's request for a preliminary injunction and ENJOINS defendants from certifying the election results for State Question 755 until this Court rules on the merits of plaintiff's claims.

NOTES AND QUESTIONS

1. The court's decision to grant a preliminary injunction was upheld in 2012. *See* Awad v. Ziriax, 670 F.3d 1111 (10th Cir. 2012). How might Sharia law be used in American courts? Should it be applied to all Muslim couples? Should Jewish law govern all Jewish couples? *See* Joel A. Nichols, *Religion, Marriage, and Pluralism*, 25 EMORY INTERNAT'L L. REV. 967 (2011).

2. In what type of instances might a court have to look at the law of another country?

3. The largest category of immigrants to the United States are those related by marriage or birth to a citizen. *See* Contreras-Salinas v. Holder, 585 F.3d 710 (2d Cir. 2009). The immigration system expresses a strong preference for certain types of familial relationships. There is an unlimited number of visas for immediate family members of U.S. citizens, which includes spouses, unmarried children under age 21, and parents if the sponsor is over age 21. For all other categories, there are statutory ceilings. Consider the expanding definitions of family in the first part of this chapter. Is there a reason to be

more "traditional" in immigration law? *See* Kerry Abrams, *Immigration Law and the Regulation of Marriage*, 91 MINN. L. REV. 1625 (2007).

Problem 1-6:

The State of Ames is considering enacting the following statute:

Any court, arbitration, tribunal or administrative agency ruling or decision shall violate the public policy of this state and be void and unenforceable if the court, arbitration, tribunal or administrative agency bases its rulings or decisions in the matter at issue in whole or in part on any foreign law, legal code or system that would not grant the parties affected by the ruling or decision the same fundamental liberties, rights and privileges granted under the United States and Ames constitutions, including, but not limited to, equal protection, due process, free exercise of religion, freedom of speech or press, and any right of privacy or marriage.

Is this better than the Initiative adopted in Oklahoma? Why or why not? Can you think of instances when a court should use foreign law? See Ghassemi v. Ghassemi, 998 So. 2d 731 (La. Ct. App. 2008).

CHAPTER 2

FAMILY PRIVACY: WHEN SHOULD THE STATE INTERVENE?

■ ■ ■

The makers of our Constitution undertook to secure conditions favorable to the pursuit of happiness. They recognized the significance of man's spiritual nature, of his feelings and of his intellect. They knew that only a part of the pain, pleasure and satisfactions of life are to be found in material things. They sought to protect Americans in their beliefs, their thoughts, their emotions and their sensations. They conferred, as against the Government, the right to be let alone—the most comprehensive of rights and the right most valued by civilized men.

Olmstead v. U.S., 277 U.S. 438, 478 (1928) (Brandeis, J., dissenting)

[T]he family, with its narrow privacy and tawdry secrets, is the source of all our discontents.

Sir Edmund Leach (1967)

1. CULTURES OF PRIVACY

JAMES Q. WHITMAN, THE TWO WESTERN CULTURES OF PRIVACY: DIGNITY VERSUS LIBERTY
113 YALE L.J. 1151, 1151–60 (2004).

In every corner of the Western world, writers proclaim "privacy" as a supremely important human good, as a value somehow at the core of what makes life worth living. Without our privacy, we lose "our very integrity as persons," Charles Fried declared over thirty-five years ago. Many others have since agreed that privacy is somehow fundamental to our "personhood." * * *

43

At the same time, honest advocates of privacy protections are forced to admit that the concept of privacy is embarrassingly difficult to define. "Nobody," writes Judith Jarvis Thomson dryly, "seems to have any very clear idea what [it] is." Not every author is as skeptical as Thomson, but many of them feel obliged to concede that privacy, fundamentally important though it may be, is an unusually slippery concept. In particular, the sense of what must be kept "private," of what must be hidden before the eyes of others, seems to differ strangely from society to society. This is a point that is frequently made by citing the literature of ethnography, which tells us that there are some societies in which people cheerfully defecate in full view of others, and at least a few in which the same is true of having sex. But the same point can be made by citing a large historical literature, which shows how remarkably ideas of privacy have shifted and mutated over time. Anyone who wants a vivid example can visit the ruins of Ephesus, where the modern tourist can set himself down on one of numerous ancient toilet seats in a public hall where well-to-do Ephesians gathered to commune, two thousand years ago, as they collectively emptied their bowels.

If privacy is a universal human need that gives rise to a fundamental human right, why does it take such disconcertingly diverse forms? This is a hard problem for privacy advocates who want to talk about the values of "personhood," harder than they typically acknowledge. It is a hard problem because of the way they usually try to make their case: Overwhelmingly, privacy advocates rely on what moral philosophers call "intuitionist" arguments. In their crude form, these sorts of arguments suppose that human beings have a direct, intuitive grasp of right and wrong—an intuitive grasp that can guide us in our ordinary ethical decision-making. Privacy advocates evidently suppose the same thing. Thus, the typical privacy article rests its case precisely on an appeal to its reader's intuitions and anxieties about the evils of privacy violations. Imagine invasions of your privacy, the argument runs. Do they not seem like violations of your very personhood? Since violations of privacy seem intuitively horrible to everybody, the argument continues, safeguarding privacy must be a legal imperative, just as safeguarding property or contract is a legal imperative. Indeed, privacy matters so much to us that laws protecting it must be a basic element of human rights.

* * * [Yet] all the evidence seems to suggest that human intuitions and anxieties about privacy differ. We do not need to refer to the practices of exotic ancient or modern cultures to demonstrate as much: It is true even as between the familiar societies of the modern West. In fact, we are in the midst of significant privacy conflicts between the United States and the countries of Western Europe—conflicts that reflect unmistakable differences in sensibilities about what ought to be kept "private." * * *

For sensitive Europeans, indeed, a tour through American law may be an experience something like a visit to the latrines of Ephesus. Correspondingly, it has become common for Europeans to maintain that they respect a "fundamental right to privacy" that is either weak or wholly absent in the "cultural context" of the United States. Here, Europeans point with pride to Article 8 of the European Convention on Human Rights, which protects "the right to respect for private and family life," and to the European Union's new Charter of Fundamental Rights, which demonstratively features articles on both "Respect for Private and Family Life" and "Protection of Personal Data." By the standards of those great documents, American privacy law seems, from the European point of view, simply to have "failed."

But it is not just that Europeans resent and distrust the American approach to privacy: The reverse is also true. Anyone who has lived in the United States knows that Americans can be just as obsessively attached to their "privacy" as Europeans, sometimes defending it by resort to firearms. As for American law, it too is obsessed with privacy. Indeed, some of the most violently controversial American social issues are conceived of as privacy matters. This has been true of abortion for thirty years. * * * It is simply false to say that privacy doesn't matter to Americans. * * *

* * * There are numerous aspects of European law that can seem not only ridiculous, but somewhat shocking to Americans. For example, continental governments assert the authority to decide what names parents will be permitted to give their children—a practice affirmed by the European Court of Human Rights as recently as 1996. This is an application of state power that Americans will view with complete astonishment, as a manifest violation of proper norms of the protection of privacy and personhood. How can the state tell you what you are allowed to call your baby? * * *

* * * [I]t is impossible to ignore the fact that Americans and Europeans are, as the Americans would put it, coming from different places. At least as far as the law goes, we do not seem to possess general "human" intuitions about the "horror" of privacy violations. * * * What we must acknowledge, instead, is that there are * * * different cultures of privacy, which are home to different intuitive sensibilities, and which have produced * * * significantly different laws of privacy.

In this chapter, we look at two privacy doctrines, both of which have had a major impact on the development of American family law. These two doctrines express very different privacy "cultures"; they have different historical roots and contemporary dimensions. But they are alike in treating certain kinds of decisions and actions as inappropriate subjects for state regulation because these decisions and actions take place within a "private" sphere of family life. As you read the materials that follow, try to analyze the concerns and values that underlie these different conceptions of privacy.

2. THE CULTURE OF RELATIONAL HARMONY

A. DISPUTES WITHIN THE INTACT FAMILY

McGUIRE v. McGUIRE

Supreme Court of Nebraska, 1953.
157 Neb. 226, 59 N.W.2d 336.

MESSMORE, JUSTICE.

The plaintiff, Lydia McGuire, brought this action in equity in the district court for Wayne County against Charles W. McGuire, her husband, as defendant, to recover suitable maintenance and support money, and for costs and attorney's fees. Trial was had * * * and a decree was rendered in favor of the plaintiff. * * *

The record shows that the plaintiff and defendant were married in Wayne, Nebraska, on August 11, 1919. At the time of the marriage the defendant was a bachelor 46 or 47 years of age and had a reputation for more than ordinary frugality, of which the plaintiff was aware. She had visited in his home and had known him for about 3 years prior to the marriage. After the marriage the couple went to live on a farm of 160 acres located in Leslie precinct, Wayne County, owned by the defendant and upon which he had lived and farmed since 1905. The parties have lived on this place ever since. The plaintiff had been previously married. Her first husband died in October 1914, leaving surviving him the plaintiff and two daughters. He died intestate, leaving 80 acres of land in Dixon County. The plaintiff and each of the daughters inherited a one-third interest therein. At the time of the marriage of the plaintiff and defendant the plaintiff's daughters were 9 and 11 years of age. By working and receiving financial assistance from the parties to this action, the daughters received a high school education in Pender. One daughter attended Wayne State Teachers College for 2 years and the other daughter attended a business college in Sioux City, Iowa, for 1 year. Both of these daughters are married and have families of their own.

On April 12, 1939, the plaintiff transferred her interest in the 80-acre farm to her two daughters. The defendant signed the deed.

At the time of trial plaintiff was 66 years of age and the defendant nearly 80 years of age. No children were born to these parties. The defendant had no dependents except the plaintiff.

The plaintiff testified that she was a dutiful and obedient wife, worked and saved, and cohabited with the defendant until the last 2 or 3 years. She worked in the fields, did outside chores, cooked, and attended to her household duties such as cleaning the house and doing the washing. For a number of years she raised as high as 300 chickens, sold poultry and eggs, and used the money to buy clothing, things she wanted, and for groceries. She further testified that the defendant was the boss of the house and his word was law; that he would not tolerate any charge accounts and would not inform her as to his finances or business; and that he was a poor companion. The defendant did not complain of her work, but left the impression to her that she had not done enough. On several occasions the plaintiff asked the defendant for money. He would give her very small amounts, and for the last 3 or 4 years he had not given her any money nor provided her with clothing, except a coat about 4 years previous. The defendant had purchased the groceries the last 3 or 4 years, and permitted her to buy groceries, but he paid for them by check. There is apparently no complaint about the groceries the defendant furnished. The defendant had not taken her to a motion picture show during the past 12 years. They did not belong to any organizations or charitable institutions, nor did he give her money to make contributions to any charitable institutions. The defendant belongs to the Pleasant Valley Church which occupies about 2 acres of his farm land. At the time of trial there was no minister for this church so there were no services. For the past 4 years or more, the defendant had not given the plaintiff money to purchase furniture or other household necessities. Three years ago he did purchase an electric, wood-and-cob combination stove which was installed in the kitchen, also linoleum floor covering for the kitchen. The plaintiff further testified that the house is not equipped with a bathroom, bathing facilities, or inside toilet. The kitchen is not modern. She does not have a kitchen sink. Hard and soft water is obtained from a well and cistern. She has a mechanical Servel refrigerator, and the house is equipped with electricity. There is a pipeless furnace which she testified had not been in good working order for 5 or 6 years, and she testified she was tired of scooping coal and ashes. She had requested a new furnace but the defendant believed the one they had to be satisfactory. She related that the furniture was old and she would like to replenish it, at least to be comparable with some of her neighbors; that her silverware and dishes were old and were primarily gifts, outside of what she purchased; that one of her daughters was good about furnishing her clothing, at least a dress a year, or sometimes two; that the defendant owns a 1929 Ford coupe equipped with a heater which is not efficient, and on the average of every 2 weeks he drives the plaintiff to Wayne to visit her mother; and that he also owns a 1927 Chevrolet pickup which is used for different purposes on the farm. The plaintiff has the privilege to use all of the rent money she wanted to from the 80-acre farm, and when she goes to see her daughters, which is not frequent, she uses part of the rent money for that purpose, the defendant providing no funds for such use. The defendant ordinarily raised hogs on his farm, but the last 4 or 5 years has leased the farm land to tenants, and he generally keeps up the fences and the buildings. At the present time the plaintiff is not able to raise chickens and sell eggs. She has about 25 chickens. The plaintiff has had three abdominal operations for which the defendant has paid. She selected her own doctor, and there were no restrictions placed in that respect. When she has requested various things for the home or personal effects, defendant has informed her on many occasions that he did not have the money to pay for the same. She would like to have a new car. She visited one daughter in Spokane, Washington, in March 1951 for 3 or 4 weeks, and visited the other daughter living in Fort Worth, Texas, on three occasions for 2 to 4 weeks at a time. She had visited one of her daughters when she was living in Sioux City some weekends. The plaintiff further testified that she had very little funds, possibly $1,500 in the bank which was chicken money and money which her father furnished her, he having departed this life a few years ago; and that use of the telephone was restricted, indicating that defendant did not desire that she make long distance calls, otherwise she had free access to the telephone.

It appears that the defendant owns 398 acres of land with 2 acres deeded to a church, the land being of the value of $83,960; that he has bank deposits in the sum of $12,786.81 and government bonds in the amount of $104,500; and that his income, including interest on the bonds and rental for his real estate, is $8,000 or $9,000 a year. There are apparently some Series E United States Savings Bonds listed and registered in the names of Charles W. McGuire or Lydia M. McGuire purchased in 1943, 1944, and 1945, in the amount of $2,500. Other bonds seem to be in the name of Charles W. McGuire, without a beneficiary or co-owner designated. The plaintiff has a bank account of $5,960.22. This account includes deposits of some $200 and $100 which the court required the defendant to pay his wife as temporary allowance during the pendency of these proceedings. One hundred dollars was withdrawn on the date of each deposit. * * *

* * * There are no cases cited by the plaintiff and relied upon by her from this jurisdiction or other jurisdictions that will sustain the action such as she has instituted in the instant case. * * *

There are * * * several cases, under statutes of various states, in which separate maintenance was refused the wife, where the husband and wife were living in the same house. These cases are to the effect that it is indispensable requirement of a maintenance statute that the wife should be living separate and apart from her husband without her fault, and that therefore, a wife living in the same house with her husband, occupying a different room and eating at a different time, was not entitled to separate maintenance. * * *

In the instant case the marital relation has continued for more than 33 years, and the wife has been supported in the same manner during this time without complaint on her part. The parties have not been separated or living apart from each other at any time. In the light of the cited cases it is clear, especially so in this jurisdiction, that to maintain an action such as the one at bar, the parties must be separated or living apart from each other.

The living standards of a family are a matter of concern to the household, and not for the courts to determine, even though the husband's attitude toward his wife, according to his wealth and circumstances, leaves little to be said in his behalf. As long as the home is maintained and the parties are living as husband and wife it may be said that the husband is legally supporting his wife and the purpose of the marriage relation is being carried out. Public policy requires such a holding. It appears that the plaintiff is not devoid of money in her own right. She has a fair-sized bank account and is entitled to use the rent from the 80 acres of land left by her first husband, if she so chooses. * * *

For the reasons given in this opinion, the judgment rendered by the district court is reversed and the cause remanded with directions to dismiss the cause.

YEAGER, JUSTICE (dissenting).

I respectfully dissent. In doing so I do not question the correctness of the statement of facts set forth in the majority opinion. I, however, do not think some important considerations have received appropriate emphasis. * * *

* * * [T]he district court decreed that plaintiff was legally entitled to use the credit of defendant and to obligate him to pay for a large number of items, some of which were in the nature of improvements and repairs to the house and some of which were furniture and appliances to be placed in the home. The total cost of these improvements and additions, as is apparent from the decree, would amount to several thousand dollars. As an alternative to a part of this defendant was permitted, in agreement with plaintiff, to purchase a modern house elsewhere. The defendant was ordered to purchase a new automobile with an effective heater within 30 days. He was ordered to pay traveling expenses of plaintiff for a visit to each of her daughters at least once each year. It was decreed that plaintiff was entitled in the future to pledge the credit of defendant for what may constitute necessaries of life. The plaintiff was awarded a personal allowance in the amount of $50 a month. An award of $800 was made for services for plaintiff's attorney. * * *

It is true that in all cases examined which uphold the right of a wife to maintain an action in equity for maintenance the parties were living apart, but no case has been cited or found which says that separation is a condition precedent to the right to maintain action in equity for maintenance. Likewise none has been cited or found which says that it is not.

In primary essence the rule contemplates the enforcement of an obligation within and not without the full marriage relationship. * * *

> "The question is, whether or not the plaintiff shall be compelled to resort to a proceeding for a divorce, which she does not desire to do, and which probably she is unwilling to do, from conscientious convictions, or, in failing to do so, shall be deprived of that support which her husband is bound to give her."

Earle v. Earle. This reasoning has received the approval of this court in the later * * * cases. * * *

It is thought that the following from the same opinion should be regarded as controlling here: "It seems to us that a declaration of such a doctrine as the law of the land would place it within the power of every man, who, unrestrained by conscience, seeks to be freed from his obligations to his wife and family, by withholding the necessary comforts and support due them, to compel her to do that for him which the law would not do upon his own application."

I conclude therefore that the conclusion of the decree that the district court had the power to entertain the action was not contrary to law. * * *

NOTES AND QUESTIONS

1. Although the case law is sparse, U.S. law generally supports the noninterventionist approach taken in *McGuire*. Thus, in Kilgrow v. Kilgrow, 107 So. 2d 885 (Ala. 1958), the Supreme Court of Alabama dismissed a petition in which a father and husband sought an injunction restraining his wife from interfering with their daughter's continued education at a religious school that she had attended the previous year. The Kilgrows, perhaps anticipating future disagreement, had entered into a premarital agreement specifying that their child would attend a religious school. The *Kilgrow* court nonetheless refused to entertain their dispute:

> In none of our cases has the court intervened to settle a controversy between unseparated parents as to some matter incident to the well-being of the child, where there was no question presented as to which parent should have custody. * * * The inherent jurisdiction of courts of equity over infants is a matter of necessity, coming into exercise only where there has been a failure of that natural power and obligation which is the province of parenthood. It is a jurisdiction assumed by the courts only when it is forfeited by a natural custodian incident to a broken home * * *.
>
> It would be anomalous to hold that a court of equity may sit in constant supervision over a household and see that either parent's

will and determination in the upbringing of a child is obeyed, even though the parents' dispute might involve what is best for the child. Every difference of opinion between parents concerning their child's upbringing necessarily involves the question of the child's best interest.

It may well be suggested that a court of equity ought to interfere to prevent such a direful consequence as divorce or separation, rather than await the disruption of the marital relationship. Our answer to this is that intervention, rather than preventing or healing a disruption, would quite likely serve as the spark to a smoldering fire. A mandatory court decree supporting the position of one parent against the other would hardly be a composing situation for the unsuccessful parent to be confronted with daily. One spouse could scarcely be expected to entertain a tender, affectionate regard for the other spouse who brings him or her under restraint. The judicial mind and conscience is repelled by the thought of disruption of the sacred marital relationship, and usually voices the hope that the breach may somehow be healed by mutual understanding by the parents themselves.

The prenuptial agreement as to the child's religious education has no bearing on the question of the trial court's jurisdiction in this case. * * *

Id. at 888–89.

2.   Commentators have disagreed over whether the noninterventionist approach to family disputes represents sound public policy. Professor Hafen, arguing in favor of nonintervention, contends that "constant legal intervention (or the threat of it) will destroy the continuity that is critically necessary for meaningful, ongoing relations and developmental nurturing" and that "increas[ing] state intervention in an ongoing family to protect the autonomy of some family members * * * may simply exchange one threat to autonomy for another." Bruce C. Hafen, *The Family as an Entity*, 22 U.C. DAVIS L. REV. 865, 912 (1989). Would intervention on behalf of Mrs. McGuire destroy "ongoing relations and developmental nurturing" in the *McGuire* household? Would intervention destroy relationships and nurturing in the *Kilgrow* household.

Dean Teitelbaum, arguing against nonintervention, urges that Mrs. McGuire should have been granted support; otherwise "the practical consequence of * * * the [*McGuire*] decision is to confer or ratify the power of one family member over others" and thus to "ratif[y] the naturally existing or socially created inequalities which have led to the victory of one over the other." Lee E. Teitelbaum, *Family History and Family Law*, 1985 WIS. L. REV. 1135, 1145. This claim is the flip side of Professor Hafen's argument that state intervention would protect the autonomy of some family members at the expense of others: if the state refuses to intervene, it ratifies Mr. McGuire's and Mrs. Kilgrow's power; if it does intervene, it confers power on Mrs. McGuire and Mr. Kilgrow. When should the state ratify the status quo and when should it confer the power to alter it through offering a dispute-resolution forum? Was *McGuire* an appropriate case for intervention? Was *Kilgrow*?

3.   *The Necessaries Doctrine:* The *McGuire* case also illustrates the common law duty of a husband to support his wife. The common law necessaries doctrine gave the creditor who provided a wife with "necessaries" an action against her husband for the value of the goods provided:

> This doctrine traditionally required the creditor to show that he supplied to the wife an item that was, in fact, a necessary and that the defendant had previously failed or refused to provide his wife with this item. When such a showing was made, the creditor was entitled to recovery as against the husband despite the fact that the husband had not contractually bound himself by his own act or by the act of an agent. The doctrine of necessaries is not imposed by the law of agency. This duty is placed upon a husband by virtue of the legal relationship of marriage. It arises as an obligation placed on him as a matter of public policy.

Sharpe Furniture, Inc. v. Buckstaff, 299 N.W.2d 219, 222 (Wis. 1980).

Although the necessaries doctrine dates from the common law era when a wife could neither sue nor be sued, the doctrine survives in most American jurisdictions:

> We are of the opinion that the doctrine of necessaries serves a legitimate and proper purpose in our system of common law. The heart of this common law rule is a concern for the support and the sustenance of the family and the individual members thereof. The sustenance of the family unit is accorded a high order of importance in the scheme of Wisconsin law. It has been codified as a part of our statutes, and it has been recognized as a part of our case law. The necessaries rule encourages the extension of credit to those who in an individual capacity may not have the ability to make these basic purchases. In this manner it facilitates the support of the family unit and its function is in harmony with the purposes behind the support laws of this state. The rule retains a viable role in modern society.

Id. at 119, 222. The modern trend is toward gender-neutral application of the necessaries doctrine, although some states have eliminated it.

In interpreting the meaning of "necessaries," most courts have used a "station of life" approach that takes account of the family's socioeconomic status. They have also tended to define necessaries expansively. *See, e.g.,* Gimbel Bros. v. Pinto, 145 A.2d 865 (Pa. Super. 1958) (finding a $3300 mink coat necessary); Daggett v. Neiman-Marcus Co., 348 S.W.2d 796 (Tex. Civ. App. 1961) (finding $2000 worth of clothes necessary). The necessaries doctrine typically applies to purchases made by or on behalf of a minor child, although courts "are sharply divided" on whether a child-support order sets a boundary on the liability of a nonresidential parent. Roger D. Colton, *Limiting The*

"Family Necessaries" Doctrine As A Means Of Imposing Third Party Liability For Utility Bills, 35 CLEARINGHOUSE REV. 193 (July/Aug. 2001).

4.   Why is an aggrieved spouse like Mrs. McGuire permitted to bind her husband's credit under the necessaries doctrine when she cannot sue him for increased support directly? Why do you think Mrs. McGuire did not employ the necessaries doctrine?

5.   Does the contrast between the necessaries doctrine and the rule followed in *McGuire* suggest that the real source "of the court's reluctance to grant Mrs. McGuire the remedy she wants is * * * simply the sheer number of Mrs. McGuires: those with a heated car and indoor plumbing but no refrigerator; those with a refrigerator but no car at all; and those with a refrigerator and heated car and indoor plumbing but an outmoded wardrobe. It is, in short, the specter of the floodgates opened, those same floodgates that have led courts to hold that schools have no duty to educate, the police no duty to protect the public, parents no duty to supervise their children, and bystanders no duty to rescue a fellow being in distress." Marsha Garrison, *Toward a Contractarian Account of Family Governance*, 1998 UTAH L. REV. 241. If the "floodgates specter" is an important source of nonintervention in cases like *McGuire*, what does this tell us about the doctrine of family privacy?

6.   Should the doctrine of necessaries apply to couples who are still legally married but have been separated for years or have filed for divorce at the time the expense was incurred? *See* Southern New Hampshire Medical Center v. Hayes, 992 A.2d 596 (N.H. 2010) (noting the nondebtor spouse's liability under the doctrine of necessaries depends on mutual expectation that the spouses will share assets, expenses and debts so that if marriage has broken down, it makes little sense to hold the nondebtor spouse responsible). See also St. Catherine Hospital v. Alvarez, 383 P.3d 184 (Kan. Ct. App. 2016).

7.   The problem in *McGuire* is created by the assumption that the husband should have the power to determine how to spend "his" wages. Does this seem to be a sensible rule? Or should both parties have the power to manage the income of the household? This topic is addressed in Chapter 4.

B. FAMILY VIOLENCE

1. The Language of Privacy and Love

REVA B. SIEGEL, "THE RULE OF LOVE": WIFE BEATING AS PREROGATIVE AND PRIVACY
105 YALE L.J. 2117, 2118–19 (1996).

The Anglo-American common law originally provided that a husband, as master of his household, could subject his wife to corporal punishment or "chastisement" so long as he did not inflict permanent injury upon her. During the nineteenth century, an era of feminist agitation for reform of marriage law, authorities in England and the United States declared that a husband no longer had the right to chastise his wife. Yet, for a century after courts repudiated the right of chastisement, the American legal system continued to treat wife beating differently from other cases of assault and battery. While authorities denied that a husband had the right to beat his wife, they intervened only intermittently in cases of marital violence: Men who assaulted their wives were often granted formal and informal immunities from prosecution, in order to protect the privacy of the family and to promote "domestic harmony." * * *

* * * This new body of common law differed from chastisement doctrine, both in rule structure and rhetoric. Judges no longer insisted that a husband had the legal prerogative to beat his wife; instead, they often asserted that the legal system should not interfere in cases of wife beating, in order to protect the privacy of the marriage relationship and to promote domestic harmony. Judges most often invoked considerations of marital privacy when contemplating the prosecution of middle-and upper-class men for wife beating. Thus, * * * the body of formal and informal immunity rules that sprang up in criminal and tort law during the Reconstruction Era was both gender-and class-salient: It functioned to preserve authority relations between husband and wife, and among men of different social classes as well.

These changes in the rule structure of marital status law were justified in a distinctive rhetoric * * *. Instead of reasoning about marriage in the older, hierarchy-based norms of the common law, jurists began to justify the regulation of domestic violence in the language of privacy and love associated with companionate marriage in the industrial era. Jurists reasoning in this discourse of "affective privacy" progressively abandoned tropes of hierarchy and began to employ tropes of interiority to describe the marriage relationship, justifying the new regime of common law immunity rules in languages that invoked the feelings and spaces of domesticity. Once translated from an antiquated to a more contemporary gender idiom, the state's justification for treating wife beating differently from other kinds of assault seemed reasonable in ways the law of chastisement did not.

Well into the twentieth century, the "language of privacy and love" was used to justify formal and informal noninterventionist policies toward family violence. These policies were evident both within tort and criminal law.

2.   Intrafamilial Tort Immunities

Like the marital chastisement privilege, spousal tort immunities originated in common law doctrine. The relevant concept was "marital unity," which served to justify the negation of a woman's legal identity upon her marriage. As William Blackstone put it, "The husband and wife are one, and the husband is that one." Because of the marital unity doctrine, a wife could not sue without joining her husband as a plaintiff. Spouses were also precluded from suing each other as such a suit would represent an action against one's self.

The Married Women's Property Acts, widely enacted during the nineteenth century, abolished the marital unity doctrine. But courts nonetheless continued to disallow tort actions between spouses, relying on the language of privacy and love. Courts variously claimed that

> (a) Such suits would disturb the harmony of the marital relation. (b) They would involve the courts in endless litigation over trivial disputes between the spouses. (c) They would encourage fraud and collusion between spouses where the conduct constituting the tort is covered by insurance. (d) The criminal law provides an adequate remedy. (e) Such suits would reward the defendant spouse for his own wrong, since, if the parties are living together, they both share in the benefits of the judgment.

HOMER H. CLARK, LAW OF DOMESTIC RELATIONS 253 (1st ed. 1968).

Similar claims were used to justify parent-child immunity, a nineteenth century innovation that had no roots in common law doctrine. Parent-child immunity originated in an 1891 opinion of the Mississippi Supreme Court which dismissed an emancipated daughter's claim against her mother for committing her to an insane asylum after the daughter had exhibited "immoral habits." "The peace of society and of the families composing society," the Court urged, "forbid to the minor child a right to appear in court in the assertion of a claim for civil redress for personal injuries suffered at the hands of the parent." Hewlett v. George, 9 So. 885 (Miss. 1891). Two other American high courts quickly adopted the reasoning of *Hewlett*. In McKelvey v. McKelvey, 77 S.W. 664 (Tenn. 1903), the high court of Tennessee held that a minor child could not sue her father for "cruel and inhuman treatment" allegedly inflicted by her stepmother with the consent of her father. In Roller v. Roller, 79 P. 788 (Wash. 1905), the Washington Supreme Court held that a minor child could not sue her father for rape, even if he had been criminally convicted. "This 'great trilogy' was the inauspicious beginning of the doctrine of parental immunity, which was soon embraced by almost every state." Broadbent v. Broadbent, 907 P.2d 43, 46 (Ariz. 1995).

Over the past half century, intrafamilial tort immunity has fallen into disfavor. By 1997, spousal immunity had been completely abrogated in 45 states and the District of Columbia; the remaining five states (Georgia, Massachusetts, Nevada, Rhode Island, and Vermont) had abrogated the immunity in limited circumstances. For a discussion of issues regarding liability of spouses for torts against each other, *see* Sarah M. Buel, *Access to Meaningful Remedy: Overcoming Doctrinal Obstacles in Tort Litigation Against Domestic Violence Offenders,* 83 OR. L. REV. 945 (2004). Over the same time period, most courts abandoned parent-child immunity for intentional torts, although some have retained a limited form of the immunity. *See* DAN B. DOBBS & PAUL T. HAYDEN, TORTS AND COMPENSATION 388–89 (4th ed. 2000).

Despite the demise of intrafamilial tort immunities, many courts continue to restrict tort actions for conduct that would not be tortious in the absence of a family relationship. For example, some courts have refused to countenance suits against parents for the negligent exercise of uniquely parental responsibilities. *See* Restatement (Second) of Torts § 895G ("repudiation of a general tort immunity does not establish liability for an act or omission that, because of the parent-child relationship, is otherwise privileged or is not tortious."). Many courts have also been skeptical about emotional distress actions by one spouse against another. *See* Chapter 4, Section 4.

3.   Marital Sex-Offense Immunity

Not only did the common law authorize a husband to chastise his wife, it also permitted him to rape her. One basis for rape immunity was the marital-unity doctrine. Another was the notion of marital contract. Under Lord Hale's influential version of this contract thesis, "a husband cannot be guilty of a rape committed by himself upon his lawful wife, for by their mutual matrimonial consent and contract the wife hath given up herself in this kind unto her husband which she cannot retreat."1 Hale P.C. 629, *quoted in* Warren v. State, 336 S.E.2d 221 (Ga. 1985). Other justifications for marital sex-offense immunity were privacy concerns like those used to justify tort immunities, including, "Prevention of fabricated charges; Preventing wives from using rape charges for revenge; Preventing state intervention into marriage so that possible reconciliation will not be thwarted." *Id.*

As late as 1980, the Model Penal Code recognized the marital rape exclusion and justified that recognition with the language of privacy and love:

> * * * The problem with abandoning the immunity * * * is that the law of rape, if applied to spouses, would thrust the prospect of criminal sanctions into the ongoing process of adjustment in the marital relationship. Section 213.1, for example, defines as gross sexual imposition intercourse coerced "by any threat that would prevent resistance by a woman of ordinary resolution." It may well be that a woman of ordinary resolution would be prevented from resisting by her husband's threat to expose a secret to her mother, for example. Behavior of this sort within the marital relationship is no doubt unattractive, but it is risky business for the law to

intervene by threatening criminal sanctions. Retaining the spousal exclusion avoids this unwarranted intrusion of the penal law into the life of the family.

AM. LAW INST., MODEL PENAL CODE AND COMMENTARY PART II, Vol. 1, Comment to § 213.1, p. 341, 345–46 (1980).

During the 1980s and 1990s, states began to reject the reasoning of the Model Penal Code. By 2003, 24 states had abolished marital immunity for all sex offenses. But 26 retained marital immunity in one form or another: 20 states granted marital immunity for sex with a woman who was incapacitated or unconscious and thus incapable of consent, and 15 mandated conditions, such as extra force or separation. Some states continue to punish marital rape less severely than stranger rape. *See* John F. Decker & Peter G. Baroni, *"No" Still Means "Yes," The Failure of the Nonconsent Reform Movement in American Rape and Sexual Assault Law*, 101 J. CRIM. L. & CRIMINOLOGY 1081 (2011).

4. Marital Violence: From Nonintervention to Mandatory Arrest and Prosecution

Until the last quarter of the twentieth century, law enforcement officials in many communities continued to follow the approach described by Professor Siegel: they treated all but the most serious incidents of marital violence as private matters for which arrest and prosecution were inappropriate. For example, in Balistreri v. Pacifica Police Dept., 901 F.2d 696 (9th Cir. 1988), the plaintiff alleged that, after she was severely beaten by her husband, the responding police officers removed the husband from the home but refused to place him under arrest and were "rude, insulting, and unsympathetic." After this incident, Mrs. Balistreri's complaint alleged that:

> Throughout 1982, Balistreri continually complained to the Pacifica police of instances of vandalism and of receiving hundreds of harassing phone calls. She named her husband, from whom she is now divorced, as the suspected culprit.

> In November 1982, Balistreri obtained a restraining order which enjoined her former husband from "harassing, annoying or having any contact with her." Subsequent to the service of this order, Balistreri's former husband crashed his car into her garage, and Balistreri immediately called the police, who arrived at the scene but stated that they would not arrest the husband or investigate the incident. During the remainder of 1982, Balistreri reported additional acts of phone harassment and vandalism, but the police "received her complaints with ridicule," denied that any restraining order was on file, ignored her requests for protection

and investigation, and on one occasion hung up on her when she called to report an instance of vandalism. * * *

Throughout 1983–85, Balistreri was continually subjected to telephone harassment and vandalism. Balistreri contacted Pacific Bell to "trace" the calls. Pacific Bell reported that some of these calls were traced to the former husband's family, but the police refused to act on this information.

Id. at 698. During the 1970s and 80s, the pattern of nonintervention evident in *Balistreri* was reversed. Spurred by women's advocates and heightened public awareness of domestic violence, all states established shelters for abused women and passed legislation that criminalized violence between intimate partners. Many states and localities went so far as to adopt *mandatory* arrest and prosecution policies in such cases.

Mandated arrest policies were spurred by a landmark study conducted in Minneapolis in 1984 that compared the deterrent effects of three different police responses to domestic violence: arrest plus a night in jail; mediation; and requiring the offender to leave the house for eight or more hours. The researchers concluded that arrest was the most effective response in deterring subsequent violence. The U.S. Attorney General recommended arrest as the standard police response to domestic assault. Many mandatory arrest statutes require a police officer to arrest an abuser whenever the officer has probable cause to believe that a domestic assault has occurred or a protection order violated.

The benefits remain unclear. Critics argue that mandatory-arrest policies may lead to the arrest of intimate partners who are acting in self-defense and may discourage victims who do not want their assailants arrested from calling the police. The available data suggests that this is not an insignificant number of cases. Between 1998 and 2002, about 40% of family violence victimizations were *not* reported to the police. The most common reason victims gave for failing to report was that the incident was a "private/personal matter" (34%); another 12% of non-reporting victims said that they did not report the crime to "protect the offender." *See* MATTHEW R. DUROSE ET AL., FAMILY VIOLENCE STATISTICS (U.S. Bureau Criminal Justice Statistics, 2005).

Finally, critics argue that mandatory arrest can promote as well as deter violence. Evidence to support this claim comes from studies that sought to replicate the Minneapolis findings:

Two of them confirmed the deterrent effect of arrest found in Minneapolis, but in three others, arrest correlated with an increase in subsequent violence. Although these studies were intended to be replications, generalization across and comparison between them is difficult because their experimental designs actually varied considerably. One consistent finding across all six studies that may explain the inconsistent results, however, was a robust correlation between the deterrent effect of arrest and the employment status of the batterer: arrest correlated with increased violence when the batterers were unemployed, but it correlated with decreased subsequent abuse by employed batterers. Another possible reason for the diverse findings may lie in differential prosecution or conviction rates. For example, in the Milwaukee study, only five percent of those arrested were prosecuted and only one percent were eventually convicted. The study's conclusion that arrest correlated with a subsequent increase in violence thus might suggest not that mandatory arrest is ineffective, but that the stakes need to be higher and prosecution more vigorous in order to achieve a substantial deterrent effect.

Developments in the Law—Legal Responses to Domestic Violence, 106 HARV. L. REV. 1501, 1539–40 (1993).

Mandatory prosecution policies are just as controversial as mandated arrest. "As many as 80% of domestic violence victims do not appear at trial," a pattern "related to several issues":

Some studies have noted that mandatory prosecutions may not reflect the wishes of the victims, many of whom call the police as (reasonable) strategy for ending the violence at hand without necessarily wishing to enter the criminal justice system. Women may seek to avoid the system for many reasons, including fear of retribution and a desire to remain in the relationship (particularly where financial dependence is a consideration). * * *

Fear of [prosecution] * * * may be further reinforced by evidence of adverse consequences experienced by women who have pursued criminal remedies, such as intervention by state child protective services. Women wish to avoid the anguish of disclosing personal details about their relationship at trial and the diminution of their reputation by prosecutors who may interpret victims' unwillingness to testify as weakness in character and deficiency of judgment, and who may even threaten arrest and prosecution for contempt * * *.

Deborah Weissman, Crawford v. Washington: *Implications for Public Health Policy and Practice in a Domestic Violence Context*, 121 PUB. HEALTH RPTS. 464, 466 (2006). *See also* Tom Lininger, *The Sound of Silence: Holding Batterers Accountable for Silencing Their Victims*, 87 TEX. L. REV. 857 (2009).

5. Intimate-Partner Violence: Continuing Controversy

While no expert today would argue for a return to noninterventionist policies, there is no consensus on what governmental policy is best. Mandatory arrest and prosecution create risks as well as benefits:

> * * * The gains from these categorical strategies are essentially twofold. First, we send a message to men who batter their partners that their battering has consequences. This message is intended to have a deterrent effect, and indeed, some of the arrest studies demonstrate that it probably does. Second, we gain a standard by which we can hold officers, prosecutors, and physicians accountable for not intervening in domestic violence cases. These two gains are significant and reflect important policy goals.
>
> On the other hand, we lose a great deal from mandatory arrest and prosecution policies. First, these policies may result in high rates of retaliatory violence, especially against African-American battered women and battered women involved with men who are unemployed or otherwise without community ties. Second, these policies reinforce the negative dynamics of rejection, degradation, terrorization, isolation, missocialization, exploitation, emotional unresponsiveness, and confinement intrinsic to the battering relationship. * * * [S]tudies of emotional trauma's impact on its victims suggest that this form of abuse would have long-term and devastating effects.

Linda G. Mills, *Killing Her Softly: Intimate Abuse and the Violence of State Intervention*, 113 HARV. L. REV. 550, 612–13 (1999). *See also* Laurie S. Kohn, *The Justice System and Domestic Violence: Engaging the Case but Divorcing the Victim*, 32 N.Y.U. REV. L. & SOC. CHANGE 191 (2008) (arguing that mandatory arrest and prosecutorial no-drop policies ignore the victims without necessarily making them safer).

Programs that channel violent partners into therapeutic prevention programs also fail to show a clear balance of benefit over risk, however. These programs are responsive to two facts: first, as many as half of adult, intimate-partner victims remain in the abusive relationship; second, the victim's process of leaving an abusive relationship often takes place over weeks, months, or years. *See* Linda G. Mills et al., *Enhancing Safety and Rehabilitation in Intimate Violence Treatments: New Perspectives*, 121 PUB. HEALTH RPTS. 363, 363–64 (2006). But "the results of * * * experimental investigations which incorporate the highest degree of control over confounding facts suggest that BIP [i.e., batterer intervention program] interventions produce, at best, quite modest benefits. * * * A large percentage of men (around 40%–60%) either do not attend or drop out of BIP, and there is only a negligible relationship between attending BIP and [violence] * * * cessation." Christopher I. Eckhardt et al. *Intervention Programs for Perpetrators of Intimate Partner Violence: Conclusions from a Clinical Research Perspective*, 121 PUB. HEALTH RPTS. 369, 370–72 (2006).

Civil protection orders are the most frequently used and possibly the most effective remedy against domestic violence and may be more advantageous to the victim than criminal prosecution of the abuser. Many women do not want their partners jailed, especially when there are mutual children. *See* Sally F. Goldfarb, *Reconceiving Civil Protection Orders for Domestic Violence: Can Law Help End the Abuse Without Ending the Relationship?*, 29 CARDOZO L REV. 1487, 1492 (2008). One study that evaluated the association between civil protection orders and subsequent police-reported violence found that permanent (12-month), but not temporary (2-week), protective orders were associated with a significant (80%) decrease in the reported incidence of physical violence in the year following the initial incident. *See* Victoria L. Holt et al., *Civil Protection Orders and Risk of Subsequent Police-Reported Violence*, 288 JAMA 589 (2002). An earlier federal survey, however, had found that such orders, obtained by 17% of surveyed battered women, were violated more often than not; more than two-thirds of orders involving rape or stalking and more than one-half of those involving physical assault were violated. *See* PATRICIA TJADEN & NANCY THOENNES, EXTENT, NATURE AND CONSEQUENCES OF INTIMATE PARTNER VIOLENCE: FINDINGS FROM THE NATIONAL VIOLENCE AGAINST WOMEN SURVEY (2000). Civil protection orders work only to the extent that law enforcement will enforce them. *See* Town of Castle Rock, Colorado v. Gonzales, 545 U.S. 748 (2005) (finding mother domestic violence victim had no basic constitutional right to state protection against private harm when the father violated a protection order and killed the three children).

One approach that seems to be working is the use of "lethality assessments screening tools." The District of Columbia and Maryland have experienced drops in domestic violence-related deaths which some attribute to an eleven question screening tool. Apparently fourteen states and the District of Columbia use some form of lethality assessment. *See* Editorial, *Predicting and Preventing Murder*, WASH. POST, Sept. 29, 2011, at p. A15.

6.   The Incidence, Consequences, and Cost of Intimate-Partner Violence (IPV)

Although the right response remains controversial, it is clear that violence between intimate partners is common and that its consequences are serious and costly. Twenty-four people per minute are victims of sexual assault, physical violence or stalking by an intimate partner in the United States, and women are disproportionately affected. One in four women will be a victim of domestic violence or sexual assault at some point in their lives. CENTERS FOR DISEASE CONTROL, NATIONAL INTIMATE PARTNER AND SEXUAL VIOLENCE SURVEY (2010). Women who experience intimate partner violence are not only at increased risk of injury and death but also a wide range of physical, emotional and social problems. Such violence is associated with "a 50% to 70% increase in gynecological, central nervous system, and stress-related problems" as well as significantly enhanced rates of "depression, anxiety, suicidality, post traumatic stress disorder, mood and eating disorders, substance dependence, antisocial personality disorders, and nonaffective psychosis." C. Nadine Wathen & Harriet L. MacMillan, *Interventions for Violence Against Women*, 289 JAMA 589 (2003). The U.S. Centers for Disease Control has reported that IPV is significantly associated with eight out of ten leading health indicators, including obesity, tobacco use, substance abuse, responsible sexual behavior, mental health, injury, immunization, and access to health care. The financial costs of IPV are thus estimated to exceed $5.8 billion each year.

These cost estimates do not take account of the impact of IPV on children. Most research suggests that, on average, children whose mothers are victims of IPV are about twice as likely to be abused as children whose mothers are not IPV victims. *See* LUNDY BANCROFT & JAY SILVERMAN, THE BATTERER AS PARENT 42 (2002) (noting that 40–70 percent of victims report concurrent child abuse). The risk of child abuse also increases with the frequency of adult violence. Thus, in one national family-violence survey, among parents who admitted to more than 50 acts of physical violence against a partner during the previous year, "virtually all the fathers and 30% of the mothers acknowledged physical abuse against a child." S.M. Ross, *Risk of Physical Abuse to Children of Spouse Abusing Parents*, 20 CHILD ABUSE & NEGLECT 589 (1996).

Studies now show that children are harmed by witnessing domestic violence even if they are not the target. Among the effects are post traumatic stress disorder, depression, and other emotional and behavioral problems. Amy Lewis Gilbert et al., *Child Exposure to Parental Violence and Psychological Distress Associated with Delayed Milestones*, 132 PEDIATRICS 1577 (2015). Violence is often associated with other parental characteristics such as substance abuse, mental illness, and low socio-economic status that are themselves risk factors for child development. See S.R. Dube et al., *Exposure to Abuse, Neglect and Household Dysfunction Among Adults Who Witnessed Intimate Partner Violence as Children*, 17 VIOLENCE & VICTIMS 3 (2002).

The negative impact of family violence also appears to continue into an exposed child's adulthood. Some research evidence suggests that witnessing intimate partner violence increases the risk being an adult victim or perpetrator of intimate partner violence. Moreover, the U.S.

Adverse Childhood Experiences (ACE) project has charted a startling large array of adverse health behaviors—smoking, intravenous drug use, obesity, unintentional pregnancy—that are significantly linked both to the experience of child maltreatment and exposure to intimate partner violence. The ACE study also found that these adverse childhood experiences were significantly correlated with a wide range of adult mental and physical health problems; conditions ranging from depression and suicidality to hypertension and bone fractures were all positively associated with childhood trauma. *See* Victor J. Felitti et al., *The Relationship of Adult Health Status to Childhood Abuse and Household Dysfunction*, 14 AM. J. PREVENTIVE MED. 245 (1998) http://www.acestudy. org/publications.php. *See also* Jan Jeske & Mary Louise Klas, *Adverse Childhood Experiences: Implications for Family Law Practice and the Family Court System*, 50 FAM. L. Q. 123 (2016).

NOTES AND QUESTIONS

1.   *Distribution of Family Violence:* In the United States, 11% of all reported and unreported violence between 1998 and 2002 involved intimate partners or other family members. Of the roughly 3.5 million violent crimes committed against family members between 1998 and 2002, 49% involved spouses, 11% sons or daughters victimized by a parent, and 41% other family members. About three-fourths of all family violence occurred in or near the victim's residence. Less than half of 1% of all family-violence incidents during 1998–2002 involved murder, although 40% of family violence victims were injured during the incident. Three-fourths of family-violence offenders were male, and almost three-quarters (73%) of victims were female. Women were 84% of spouse-abuse victims and 86% of boyfriend or girlfriend victims. Women were 58% of family-murder victims, and family members were responsible for 43% of all female homicides. Children under age 13 were 23% of murder victims killed by a family member, and just over 3% of nonfamily murder victims. Eight in ten murderers who killed a family member were male. *See* MATTHEW R. DUROSE ET AL., FAMILY VIOLENCE STATISTICS (U.S. Bureau of Criminal Justice Statistics, 2005).

2.   *Family Violence in International Context:* A World Health Organization report notes that, in "48 population-based surveys from around the world, 10–69% of women reported being physically assaulted by an intimate male partner at some point in their lives." The same report indicates that "[m]ost victims of physical aggression are subjected to multiple acts of violence over extended periods of time" and "tend to suffer from more than one type of abuse. For example, a study of 613 abused women in Japan found that less than 10% were victims of physical violence alone, while 57% had suffered physical, psychological and sexual abuse. A study in Mexico found that over half of the women who had been physically assaulted had also been sexually abused by their partners." WORLD HEALTH ORGANIZATION, WORLD REPORT ON VIOLENCE AND HEALTH: SUMMARY (2002).

3.   To what extent should victims' privacy concerns shape government policy toward family violence?

4.   Given the high risks inherent in family violence and the available evidence on intervention efficacy, what approach or combination of approaches should government adopt and what research should be undertaken?

5.   Why does family harmony no longer seem an adequate justification for tort immunities between family members? For non-interventionist criminal-law policies toward family violence? If family harmony is no longer an adequate basis for a noninterventionist approach to family torts and family violence, is family harmony necessarily an inadequate basis for a noninterventionist approach to nonviolent family disputes like those in *McGuire* and *Kilgrow*?

7.   The Parental Chastisement Privilege

IN THE MATTER OF PETER G. & OTHERS

Supreme Court, Appellate Division, First Department, New York, 2004.
6 A.D.3d 201, 774 N.Y.S.2d 686, app. dismissed 3 N.Y.3d 655, 816 N.E.2d 566,
782 N.Y.S.2d 693.

Orders of fact-finding and disposition, Family Court, * * * insofar as it was found that respondents had neglected the subject children, reversed, on the law and the facts * * *.

SULLIVAN, J. (concurring)

* * * [T]he parents appeal from orders * * *, which, after a * * * determination that the parents neglected their children, released one of their children, Peter, to their custody, under certain conditions, with 12 months of supervision by a child protective agency * * *.

The petition charged the parents, Steven G. and Angela G., with neglecting their children, Peter, born February 22, 1990, Venitia, born May 7, 1992 and Demitri, born January 20, 1995, alleging that the father used excessive corporal punishment in that he disciplined the children with a belt and cane and caused injuries. After a fact-finding hearing, Family Court found that the father used excessive corporal punishment against Peter and that the mother knew or should have known of the excessive corporal punishment and failed to protect the child.

The case against the father consisted of the testimony of Ronna Rosen, employed by the New York City Board of Education as a school psychologist, who was qualified as an expert in child psychology "for the limited purpose of giving opinions about this matter," and Margaret Young, a caseworker for the Administration for Children's Services (ACS). On December 1 and 9, 1999, Dr. Rosen conducted a five-hour evaluation of Peter, who, without specifying how often this occurred, told her that the father disciplined him and Venitia by striking them with a cane or belt. Dr.

Rosen was unable to see any marks when Peter rolled up his pants to show where on his legs he had been struck. Peter described an incident in which his father struck him and Venitia while they were pinned between a table and wall. These incidents were usually a response to their being disobedient, for example, watching television without permission. After discussing the matter with the school principal, Dr. Rosen notified the State Central Registry because both she and the principal "thought that Peter felt he was in danger."

On December 21, 1999, Ms. Young, after receiving a report made through the State Central Registry, visited the G. home and spoke separately to each of the children. Venitia tearfully told Ms. Young that the father had struck Peter with a cane but denied that he had ever struck her with a cane. When Ms. Young asked Peter if he had ever been hit with a cane, he said "yes, [o]nly to his leg" and pointed to his right leg, just above the ankle. Ms. Young did not see any bruises. Peter also indicated that the father sometimes struck the bed with the cane, which he also used to pull the children towards him. Peter also stated that the father had threatened him with a belt; he did not indicate that he had ever been struck with the belt. Peter was afraid of his father and concerned that he might hurt Venitia. Four-year-old Demitri told Ms. Young that he had not been hit with the cane but that he had seen Peter being hit.

Testifying for the mother, the children's maternal uncle, a New York City Police Officer, stated that over the past 10 years he had, on average, visited the G. home two evenings a week. He stated that he had a "[v]ery good, excellent" relationship with the children, none of whom ever complained to him about the parents or mentioned a cane. He stated that he "might have" seen the parents hit the children and that he had seen them discipline the children with "time outs." While the father had a tendency to yell at the children, the mother was the disciplinarian, a fact the mother confirmed. The mother also testified that the father had never struck the children except for an occasional spanking on the buttocks. The father testified that he never used a belt or cane to strike or discipline his children. * * *

Pursuant to Family Court Act § 1012 (f) (i), a finding of neglect requires proof that the child's "physical, mental or emotional condition has been impaired or is in imminent danger of becoming impaired" as a result of the parent's failure "to exercise a minimum degree of care." Parents are entitled to use reasonable corporal punishment to maintain discipline; they are guilty of neglect if they use "excessive corporal punishment" * * *. *See* Penal Law § 35.10 [1] [a parent may use "physical force . . . when and to the extent that he reasonably believes it necessary to maintain discipline or to promote the welfare of (the child)"]). The petitioner has the burden of proving the allegations of neglect by a preponderance of the evidence. "Unsworn out-of-court statements of the victim may be received and, if properly corroborated, will support a finding of abuse or neglect". Although such statements may be corroborated by "[a]ny other evidence tending to support [their] reliability", there is a "threshold of reliability that the evidence must meet."

Here, the evidence * * *, consisting mainly of Peter's out-of-court statements * * *, was lacking in context, detail and specificity. Peter did not state the number of instances in which he was struck with a cane, that is, whether a single, isolated event or a common occurrence was involved, or how many blows were struck. He did not indicate how hard he was hit or whether he felt pain. Although Peter rolled up his pants to show where he had been struck, neither the school psychologist nor the ACS caseworker was able to see any bruises or other marks on his leg. Peter also told the school psychologist that the father struck him with a belt, but indicated to the ACS caseworker that the father had threatened, not struck, him with a belt. * * *

While children's statements can corroborate each other, the statements of Venitia and Demitri failed in that regard because * * * they were too general to bear the mark of reliability. * * * Although, according to the caseworker, Venitia stated that the father struck Peter with a cane, her statement, like Peter's, lacked detail and specificity. Furthermore, it contradicted Peter's in an important detail, in that Peter said that both he and Venitia had been struck by the father while Venitia said that the father never struck her. * * * Although four-year-old Demitri stated that he saw the father hit Peter with his cane, his statement was extremely general. * * *

Even assuming that the burden of proving that the father struck Peter with a cane has been met, there has been no showing that the father used more force than was reasonable. It is important that we not lose sight of a parent's common-law privilege to use reasonable physical force to discipline his or her children, which has been codified in New York. In this case, there was no evidence of bruising or injury of any kind, and, while there was testimony that the father became angry, there was no showing that the father's actions were extreme or unnecessarily degrading or prompted by rage or administered solely for self-gratification. * * *

ELLERIN, J. (dissenting in part).

I would affirm the finding against the father on the grounds that the children's statements cross-corroborate each other and the evidence as a whole preponderates against the father.

Peter told the school psychologist that his father uses a cane and a belt to discipline him and his siblings. Pointing to his leg, he said, "I have bruises here if I do something bad." He told her that when his father threatens the children with the cane, "we have to run away, [he] has red in his eye." He said, "Sometimes I don't think we did anything—always threatens with the cane." Peter said his mother "sometimes gets very mad at him because he is threatening us with the cane. So she is trying to be on our side." He said she screams at the father not to hit them with his cane. Peter related an incident in which his father trapped him and Venitia behind a table and struck them with his cane. He said that two days before the interview with the school psychologist, his father had hit Venitia on the leg with his cane. Peter expressed anxiety over Venitia's welfare and his father's inability to control himself when disciplining her. He said, "He's so mad, he's controlling himself, when really mad hits her." He described his family as a "hitting family." In his interview with the Administration for Children's Services (ACS) caseworker, Peter said his father hits him on the leg with the cane. He said he was frightened of his father, frightened that his father would hurt Venitia. * * *

I see no error in the court's determination that Peter's statements that his father hits him with a cane were reliably corroborated by Venitia's and Demitri's independent statements that their father hits Peter with his cane. The children's statements were neither confusing nor lacking in the kind of detail that would cast doubt on their assertion that the father uses his cane on Peter. Both children described their father as having "red in his eye" when angry, both said he had difficulty controlling himself when angry, and both said he hits Peter with his cane.

The instant record also supports the court's conclusion that the credible evidence preponderated against the father. * * * Angela testified that * * * she has asked Steven many times to leave the home when they have been arguing and that the manner in which he disciplines the children is one of the issues she has raised with him on those occasions. * * *

Steven * * * testified that he and Angela learned the expression, "red in the eye," in a conflict resolution course they attended and that it referred to "when you know you have anger, and you're yelling and shouting." * * * He said that he was taking these courses because he is not "trained to handle" Peter.

* * * Recognizing a parent's common-law privilege to use reasonable physical force to discipline his children, we are concerned with "the dimensions of reasonable parental use of physical force." Punishment is not reasonable if the means by which it are administered are not moderate, if it is more severe than other equally effective available means, or if it is "unnecessarily degrading," "brutal" or "protracted beyond the child's power of endurance." * * *

In the instant case, the court apparently found both parents less than credible on the subject of Steven's caning of Peter. In matters such as this, the nisi prius court's findings must be accorded the greatest respect. I must note, however, that even without the benefit of that court's superior vantage point, I find that the cold record alone transmits the picture of an enraged father, unable to control himself, reaching for his cane and lashing out at his son, who does not always understand what has put the "red in his [father's] eye." * * * Thus, the court's finding that Steven uses excessive corporal punishment against Peter should be affirmed.

NOTES AND QUESTIONS

1.   The parental chastisement privilege survives in all American states. Thus, in Lovan C. v. Dep't of Children & Families, 860 A.2d 1283 (Conn. App. 2004), the appellate court noted that "[t]he great preponderance of authority is to the effect that a parent has a right to punish a child within the bounds of moderation and reason, so long as he does it for the welfare of the child" and accordingly held that:

> In a substantiation of abuse hearing, if it is shown that a child has sustained a nonaccidental injury as a result of parent administered corporal punishment, the hearing officer must determine whether the punishment was reasonable and whether the parent believed the punishment was necessary to maintain discipline or to promote the child's welfare. * * * The hearing officer must assess the reasonableness of the punishment in light of the child's misbehavior and the surrounding circumstances, including the parent's motive, the type of punishment administered, the amount of force used and the child's age, size and ability to understand the punishment. * * * If it is determined that the parent used reasonable physical force on the child in order to maintain discipline or to promote the child's welfare, a substantiation of physical abuse cannot stand.

Id. at 299, 1289.

Lovan C. involved an appeal from an abuse finding against a mother who found her five-year-old daughter "swinging and jumping on her canopy bed":

> Although the plaintiff rarely used physical discipline, she picked up a child's belt and spanked her daughter three times with a portion of the strap, which left a bruise approximately one inch in diameter on her thigh. The incident was investigated by a police officer, who had received a complaint from the child's father.

Id. at 292, 1285. Although the investigating police officer decided that the plaintiff's actions "did not rise to the level of child abuse," the local child protection department nonetheless substantiated the complaint based on the statutory definition of abuse (a "physical injury") and a department policy manual which gave examples of physical injury that included " * * * bruises * * *." Because the plaintiff's actions produced a bruise, the hearing examiner determined that it was a physical injury and ordered the plaintiff's name to be entered in the state child abuse and neglect registry.

Noting that the plaintiff's career as a schoolteacher would be adversely affected by the placement of her name in the abuse registry, the appellate court found that application of the "reasonableness of the punishment" approach required reversal:

> * * * The act at issue was a one time occurrence, not part of a pattern of physical punishment. The child was struck three times on the backside with the strap of a child's belt, resulting in a bruise. The plaintiff did not intend to hurt or to injure the child, but rather to discipline her for her misbehavior. There was no finding by the hearing officer of any apparent malice or ill motive behind the plaintiff's actions, and the child sustained only a minor injury. *Id.* at 301

Under the *Lovan C.* standard, was an abuse finding warranted against the father in *Peter G.*? Against the mother? Under the standards enunciated in *Peter G.*, was an abuse finding warranted in *Lovan C.*? For a survey of state laws, *see* Doriane Lambelet Coleman, et al, *Where and How to Draw the Line Between Reasonable Corporal Punishment and Abuse*, 73 LAW & CONTEMP. PROBS. 107, 114–119 (2010).

2.   Delaware defines what is "reasonable force." DEL. CODE ANN. Tit 11, § 468(c) provides:

> The force shall not be justified if it includes . . . : Throwing the child, kicking, burning, cutting, striking with a closed fist, interfering with breathing, use of or threatened use of a deadly weapon, prolonged deprivation of sustenance or medication, or doing any other act that is likely to cause or does cause physical injury, disfigurement, mental distress, unnecessary degradation or substantial risk of serious physical injury or death.

Would this standard have resulted in a different outcome in *Lovan C.* or *Peter G.*?

3.   In Western Europe, the parental chastisement privilege has been under attack in both the courts and legislatures. In A. v. United Kingdom, 27 Eur. H.R. Rep. 611 (1998), the European Court of Human Rights ruled that beatings with a garden cane suffered by a nine-year-old, which left bruises and "had been applied with considerable force on more than one occasion," represented a violation of Article 3 of the European Convention on Human Rights, which prohibits "inhuman or degrading treatment or punishment." The Court found the U.K. to be in violation of Article 3 despite the fact that the relevant authorities had prosecuted the stepparent who administered the beatings:

> [U]nder English law it is a defense to a charge of assault on a child that the treatment in question amounted to "reasonable chastisement." The burden of proof is on the prosecution to establish beyond reasonable doubt that the assault went beyond the limits of lawful punishment. In the present case, despite the fact that the applicant had been subjected to treatment of sufficient severity to fall within the scope of Article 3, the jury acquitted his stepfather, who

had administered the treatment. In the Court's view, the law did not provide adequate protection to the applicant against treatment or punishment contrary to Article 3. * * * In the circumstances of the present case, the failure to provide adequate protection constitutes a violation of Article 3 of the Convention. *Id.*

Across the world, legislatures have grown increasingly hostile to corporal punishment. By 2011, thirty-two countries, including several South American countries and some African, had total bans on corporal punishment. Another 91 ban corporal punishment by teachers or administrators.

4.   In 2004, the Canadian Supreme Court upheld section 43 of the Canadian Criminal Code, permitting "reasonable" physical punishment of children, against a challenge under the nondiscrimination guarantees of the Canadian Charter of Rights and Freedoms. The Court was:

> satisfied that a reasonable person acting on behalf of a child, apprised of the harms of criminalization that § 43 avoids, the presence of other governmental initiatives to reduce the use of corporal punishment, and the fact that abusive and harmful conduct is still prohibited by the criminal law, would not conclude that the child's dignity has been offended in the manner contemplated by § 15(1). Children often feel a sense of disempowerment and vulnerability; this reality must be considered when assessing the impact of § 43 on a child's sense of dignity. Yet, as emphasized, the force permitted is limited and must be set against the reality of a child's mother or father being charged and pulled into the criminal justice system, with its attendant rupture of the family setting, or a teacher being detained pending bail, with the inevitable harm to the child's crucial educative setting. Section 43 is not arbitrarily demeaning. It does not discriminate. Rather, it is firmly grounded in the actual needs and circumstances of children. * * *

Canadian Foundation For Children, Youth & Law v. Canada (Attorney General), [2004] 1 S.C.R. 76. However, the Court also limited the range of permissible parental punishments:

> Corporal punishment of children under two years is harmful to them, and has no corrective value given the cognitive limitations of children under two years of age. Corporal punishment of teenagers is harmful, because it can induce aggressive or antisocial behaviour. Corporal punishment using objects, such as rulers or belts, is physically and emotionally harmful. Corporal punishment which involves slaps or blows to the head is harmful. These types of punishment, we may conclude, will not be reasonable. * * * *Id.*

Under the *Canadian Foundation* opinion, would state intervention be warranted in *Peter G.*? In *Lovan C.*? In *A v. United Kingdom*?

5.   *Should the Chastisement Privilege Survive?* Consider the following facts:

> A mother and daughter enter a supermarket. An accident occurs when the daughter pulls the wrong orange from the pile and 37 oranges are given their freedom. The mother grabs the daughter, shakes her vigorously, and slaps her. What is your reaction? Do you ignore the incident? Do you consider it a family squabble and none of your business? Or do you go over and advise the mother not to hit her child? If the mother rejects your advice, do you physically restrain her? If she persists, do you call the police? * * *
>
> Now let me change one detail. *The girl was not that mother's daughter.* Do you feel different[ly]? Would you act differently? Why? Do "real" parents have the right to abuse their children because they "own" them? Now let me change another detail. Suppose the daughter was 25 years old, and yelled, "Help me! Help me!" * * * How does [calling the police] * * * sound with a mere change in the age of the victim?

Roger W. McIntire, *Parenthood Training or Mandatory Birth Control: Take Your Choice*, PSYCH. TODAY 34 (Oct. 1973).

a.   Under *Peter G.* and *Lovan C.*, would state intervention be warranted in the case described by McIntire? Would intervention be warranted under *A. v. United Kingdom*? Under the *Canadian Foundation* opinion?

b.   Why has the parental chastisement privilege survived when the marital chastisement privilege has not?

c.   On balance, should the parental chastisement privilege be abandoned? What are the pros and cons of retaining the privilege and of eliminating it? *See* DAN MARKET, JENNIFER COLLINS & ETHAN LIEB, PRIVILEGE OR PUNISH (2009) (arguing the use of parental discipline as a defense to child abuse is untenable in exposing children to a form of violence permitted by statute); *Symposium, Corporal Punishment*, 73(2) LAW & CONTEM. PROBS. (2010); Elizabeth T. Gershoff & Susan H. Bitensky, *The Case Against Corporal Punishment of Children*, 13(4) PSYCHOL., PUB. POL'Y & L. 231 (2007).

3. THE CULTURE OF DECISIONAL AUTONOMY

Many trace the origins of the right to privacy within the family to two cases in the 1920s. In Meyer v. Nebraska, 262 U.S. 390 (1923), the United States Supreme Court struck a Nebraska statute which barred the teaching of German to children who had not reached the eighth grade. The Court stated:

> While this Court has not attempted to define with exactness the liberty thus guaranteed [by the Fourteenth Amendment], * * *

> some of the included things have been definitely stated. Without
> doubt, it denotes not merely freedom from bodily restraint but also
> the right of the individual to contract, to engage in any of the
> common occupations of life, to acquire useful knowledge, to marry,
> establish a home and bring up children, to worship God according
> to the dictates of his own conscience, and generally to enjoy those
> privileges long recognized at common law as essential to the
> orderly pursuit of happiness by free men.

Id. at 399.

In the second case, Pierce v. Society of Sisters, 268 U.S. 510 (1925), the
Supreme Court found that Oregon's compulsory education statute that
required parents to enroll their children in public schools "unreasonably
interferes with the liberty of parents and guardians to direct the
upbringing and education of children under their control."

GRISWOLD V. CONNECTICUT
Supreme Court of the United States, 1965.
381 U.S. 479.

JUSTICE DOUGLAS delivered the opinion of the Court:

Appellant Griswold is Executive Director of the Planned Parenthood
League of Connecticut. Appellant Buxton is a licensed physician and a
professor at the Yale Medical School who served as Medical Director for the
league at its Center in New Haven—a center open and operating from
November 1 to November 10, 1961, when appellants were arrested. They
gave information, instruction, and medical advice to married persons as to
the means of preventing conception. They examined the wife and
prescribed the best contraceptive device or material for her use. Fees were
usually charged, although some couples were serviced free.

The statutes whose constitutionality is involved in this appeal * * *
provide:

> Any person who uses any drug, medicinal article or instrument
> for the purpose of preventing conception shall be fined not less
> than fifty dollars or imprisoned not less than sixty days nor more
> than one year or be both fined and imprisoned. * * *

> Any person who assists, abets, counsels, causes, hires or
> commands another to commit any offense may be prosecuted and
> punished as if he were the principal offender.

> The appellants were found guilty as accessories and fined $100
> each. * * *

Coming to the merits, we are met with a wide range of questions that
implicate the Due Process Clause of the Fourteenth Amendment. * * * We

do not sit as a super-legislature to determine the wisdom, need, and propriety of laws that touch economic problems, business affairs, or social conditions. This law, however, operates directly on an intimate relation of husband and wife and their physician's role is one aspect of that relation.

The association of people is not mentioned in the Constitution nor in the Bill of Rights. The right to educate a child in a school of the parent's choice—whether public or private or parochial—is also not mentioned. Nor is the right to study any particular subject or any foreign language. Yet the First Amendment has been construed to include certain of those rights.

By *Pierce v. Society Of Sisters*, 268 U.S. 510, the right to educate one's children as one chooses is made applicable to the states by the force of the First and Fourteenth Amendments. By *Meyer v. State of Nebraska*, 262 U.S. 390, the same dignity is given the right to study the German language in a private school. In other words, the State may not, consistently with the spirit of the First Amendment, contract the spectrum of available knowledge. The right of freedom of speech and press includes not only the right to utter or to print, but the right to distribute, the right to receive, the right to read and freedom on inquiry, freedom of thought, and freedom to teach—indeed the freedom of the entire university community. * * * Without these peripheral rights the specific rights would be less secure, and so we reaffirm the principle of the *Pierce* and *Meyer* cases.

In *NAACP v. State of Alabama*, 357 U.S. 449, 462, we protected the "freedom to associate and privacy in one's associations," noting that freedom of association was a peripheral First Amendment right. Disclosure of membership lists of a constitutionally valid association, we held, was invalid "as entailing the likelihood of a substantial restraint upon the exercise by petitioner's members of the right to freedom of association." Id. In other words, the First Amendment has a penumbra where privacy is protected from governmental intrusion. In like context, we have protected forms of "association" that are not political in the customary sense but pertain to the social, legal, and economic benefit of the members. *NAACP v. Button*, 371 U.S. 415, 430–431. * * *

Those cases involved more than the "right of assembly" a right that extends to all irrespective of their race or ideology. The right of "association," like the right of belief is more than the right to attend a meeting; it includes the right to express one's attitudes or philosophies by membership in a group by affiliation with it or by other lawful means. Association in that context is a form of expression of opinion; and while it is not expressly included in the First Amendment its existence is necessary in making the express guarantees fully meaningful.

The foregoing cases suggest that specific guarantees in the Bill of Rights have penumbras, formed by emanations from those guarantees that help give them life and substance. * * * Various guarantees create zones of privacy. The right of association contained in the penumbra of the First Amendment is one, as we have seen. The Third Amendment in its prohibition against the quartering of soldiers "in any house" in time of peace without the consent of the owner is another facet of that privacy. The Fourth Amendment explicitly affirms the "right of the people to be secure in their persons, houses, papers, and effects, against unreasonable searches and seizures." The Fifth Amendment in its Self-Incrimination Clause enables the citizen to create a zone of privacy which government may not force him to surrender to his detriment. The Ninth Amendment provides: "The enumeration in the Constitution, of certain rights, shall not be construed to deny or disparage others retained by the people."

* * *

The present case, then, concerns a relationship lying within the zone of privacy created by several fundamental constitutional guarantees. And it concerns a law which, in forbidding the use of contraceptives rather than regulating their manufacture or sale, seeks to achieve its goals by means of having a maximum destructive impact upon that relationship. Such a law cannot stand in light of the familiar principle, so often applied by this Court, that a "government purpose to control or prevent activities constitutionally subject to state regulation may not be achieved by means which sweep unnecessarily broadly and thereby invade the area of protected freedoms." *NAACP v. Alabama*, 377 U.S. 288, 307. Would we allow the police to search the sacred precincts of marital bedrooms for telltale signs of the use of contraceptives? The very idea is repulsive to the notions of privacy surrounding the marriage relationship.

We deal with a right of privacy older than the Bill of Rights—older than our political parties, older than our school system. Marriage is a coming together for better or worse, hopefully enduring, and intimate to the degree of being sacred. It is an association that promotes a way of life, not causes; a harmony in living, not political faiths; a bilateral loyalty, not commercial or social projects. Yet it is an association for as noble a purpose as any involved in our prior decisions.

Reversed.

JUSTICE GOLDBERG, the CHIEF JUSTICE and JUSTICE BRENNAN, concurring.

* * * The language and history of the Ninth Amendment reveal that the Framers of the Constitution believed that there are additional fundamental rights, protected from governmental rights, protected from governmental infringement, which exist alongside those fundamental rights specifically mentioned in the first eight constitutional amendments.

The Ninth Amendment reads, "The enumeration in the Constitution, of certain rights, shall not be construed to deny or disparage others retained by the people." The Amendment is almost entirely the work of James Madison. It was introduced in Congress by him and passed the House and Senate with little or no debate and virtually no change in the language. It was proffered to quiet expressed fears that a bill of specifically enumerated rights could not be sufficiently broad to cover all essential rights and that the specific mention of certain rights would be interpreted as a denial that others were protected. * * *

Although the Constitution does not speak in so many words of the right of privacy in marriage, I cannot believe that it offers these fundamental rights no protection. * * *

Finally, it should be said of the court's holding today that it in no way interferes with a state's proper regulation of sexual promiscuity or misconduct. As my brother Harlan so well states in his dissenting opinion in *Poe v. Ullman*,

> Adultery, homosexuality and the like are sexual intimacies which the State forbids * * * but the intimacy of husband and wife is necessarily an essential and accepted feature of the institution of marriage, an institution which the State not only must allow, but which always and in every age it has fostered and protected. It is one thing when the State exerts its power either to forbid extra-marital sexuality * * * or to say who may marry, but it is quite another when, having acknowledged a marriage and the intimacies inherent in it, it undertakes to regulate by means of the criminal law the details of that intimacy.

In sum, I believe that the right of privacy in the marital relation is fundamental and basic—a personal right "retained by the people" within the meaning of the Ninth Amendment. Connecticut cannot constitutionally abridge this fundamental right, which is protected by the Fourteenth Amendment from infringement by the States. I agree with the Court that petitioners' convictions must therefore be reversed.

JUSTICE BLACK, with whom JUSTICE STEWART joins, dissenting.

* * *

One of the most effective ways of diluting or expanding a [constitutional] * * * right is to substitute for the crucial word or words of a constitutional guarantee another word or words. * * * This fact is well illustrated by the use of the term "right of privacy" as a comprehensive substitute for the Fourth Amendment's guarantee against "unreasonable searches and seizures." * * *

This brings me to [the due process clause and Ninth Amendment arguments. O]n analysis they turn out to be the same thing—merely using different words to claim for this Court * * * power to invalidate any legislative act which the judges find irrational, unreasonable or offensive.

* * * The Due Process Clause * * * was liberally used by this Court to strike down economic legislation in the early decade of this century, threatening, many people thought, the tranquility and stability of the Nation. That formula, based on subjective considerations of "natural justice," is no less dangerous when used to enforce this Court's views about personal rights than those about economic rights. * * *

NOTES AND QUESTIONS

1.   Do the various *Griswold* opinions place more emphasis on family privacy or individual privacy? Is Justice Black correct that "the zone of privacy created by several fundamental constitutional guarantees" identified by the *Griswold* majority as a basis for its holding is identical to the "additional fundamental rights * * * protected from governmental infringement [under the Ninth Amendment]" identified by concurring Justice Goldberg as a basis for the Court's holding?

2.   What constitutional standards and level of scrutiny did the majority apply?

3.   In Eisenstadt v. Baird, 405 U.S. 438 (1972), the Supreme Court was faced with a Massachusetts statute criminalizing the dispensing of contraceptives to anyone other than a married person. Noting that "the question for our determination * * * is whether there is some ground of difference that rationally explains the different treatment accorded married and unmarried persons under [the statute]," the Court "conclude[d] that no such ground exists." The Court went on to say:

> If under *Griswold* the distribution of contraceptives to married persons cannot be prohibited, a ban on distribution to unmarried persons would be equally impermissible. It is true that in *Griswold* the right of privacy in question inhered in the marital relationship. Yet the marital couple is not an independent entity with a mind and heart of its own, but an association of two individuals each with a separate intellectual and emotional makeup. If the right of privacy means anything, it is the right of the individual, married or single, to be free from unwarranted governmental intrusion into matters so fundamentally affecting a person as the decision whether to bear or beget a child. *Id.* at 453.

How do the various strands of constitutional doctrine utilized by the *Griswold* majority to find a constitutional privacy right apply in *Eisenstadt*? Which strands seem less relevant? More relevant? *See* Khiara Bridges, *Privacy Rights and Public Families*, 34 HARV. J. L. & GENDER 113 (2011).

4.   *Abortion and Spousal Disagreement:* In Roe v. Wade, 410 U.S. 113 (1973), the Supreme Court extended its holdings in *Griswold* and *Eisenstadt* to abortion. Abortion, in contrast to contraception, necessarily implicates the procreational liberties of *two* individuals, who may not agree. In Planned Parenthood v. Danforth, 428 U.S. 52 (1976), the Supreme Court struck down a

Missouri statute that conditioned a married woman's abortion on the consent of her husband:

> Clearly, since the State cannot regulate or proscribe abortion during the first stage, when the physician and his patient make that decision, the State cannot delegate authority to any particular person, even the spouse, to prevent abortion during that same period.

> * * *

> It seems manifest that, ideally, the decision to terminate a pregnancy should be one concurred in by both the wife and her husband. * * * But it is difficult to believe that the goal of fostering mutuality and trust in a marriage, and of strengthening the marital relationship and the marriage institution, will be achieved by giving the husband a veto power exercisable for any reason whatsoever or for no reason at all. Even if the State had the ability to delegate to the husband a power it itself could not exercise, it is not at all likely that such action would further, as the District Court majority phrased it, the "interest of the state in protecting the mutuality of decisions vital to the marriage relationship."

> We recognize, of course, that when a woman, with the approval of her physician but without the approval of her husband, decides to terminate her pregnancy, it could be said that she is acting unilaterally. The obvious fact is that when the wife and the husband disagree on this decision, the view of only one of the two marriage partners can prevail. Since it is the woman who physically bears the child and who is the more directly and immediately affected by the pregnancy, as between the two, the balance weighs in her favor.

In Planned Parenthood v. Casey, 505 U.S. 833 (1992), the Court extended its *Danforth* ruling to a spousal notification rule:

> The District Court heard the testimony of numerous expert witnesses and made detailed findings of fact regarding the effect of [the statute's requirement that, with certain exceptions, a married woman must sign a statement indicating that she has notified her husband of her intended abortion before obtaining abortion services. It concluded that the requirement would deter women who were victims of domestic violence from obtaining abortions and that, although the statutes contained exemptions for some forms of domestic violence, these were insufficient.] "Because of the nature of the battering relationship, battered women are unlikely to avail themselves of the exceptions to * * * the Act, regardless of whether the section applies to them." * * *

> These findings are supported by studies of domestic violence. [The Court cites statistics, like those described in Section 1, on the frequency and severity of intimate-partner violence.]

This information and the District Court's findings reinforce what common sense would suggest. In well-functioning marriages, spouses discuss important intimate decisions such as whether to bear a child. But there are millions of women in this country who are the victims of regular physical and psychological abuse at the hands of their husbands. * * * The spousal notification requirement is thus likely to prevent a significant number of women from obtaining an abortion. * * *

[The Act] embodies a view of marriage consonant with the common-law status of married women but repugnant to our present understanding of marriage and of the nature of the rights secured by the Constitution. Women do not lose their constitutionally protected liberty when they marry. The constitution protects all individuals, male or female, married or unmarried, from the abuse of governmental power even where that power is employed for the supposed benefit of a member of the individual's family. These considerations confirm our conclusion that [the spousal notification rule] * * * is invalid.

Are *Danforth* and *Casey* consistent with *McGuire* and *Kilgrow*? How does the concept of privacy evident in these abortion-decision-making cases differ from that contained in the family-dispute decisions?

5. Some lower courts, interpreting *Griswold* and *Eisenstadt*, found that "[n]ecessarily implicit in the right to make decisions regarding childbearing is the right to engage in sexual intercourse." Doe v. Duling, 603 F. Supp. 960 (E.D. Va. 1985) (striking down state law criminalizing fornication). But in Bowers v. Hardwick, 478 U.S. 186 (1986), the Supreme Court (5–4) upheld a statute criminalizing consensual sodomy:

[W]e think it evident that none of the rights announced in those cases [i.e., *Griswold, Eisenstadt, Roe*] bears any resemblance to the claimed constitutional right of homosexuals to engage in acts of sodomy that is asserted in this case. No connection between family, marriage, or procreation on the one hand and homosexual activity on the other has been demonstrated, either by the Court of Appeals or by respondent. * * *

[T]he Court has sought to identify the nature of rights qualifying for heightened judicial protection. In *Palko v. Connecticut*, it was said that this category includes those fundamental liberties that are "implicit in the concept of ordered liberty" * * * A different description of fundamental liberties appeared in *Moore v. East Cleveland*, where they are characterized as those liberties that are "deeply rooted in this nation's history and tradition."

It is obvious to us that neither of these formulations would extend a fundamental right to homosexuals to engage in acts of consensual sodomy. Proscriptions against that conduct have ancient roots. * * *

Against this background, to claim that a right to engage in such conduct is "deeply rooted in this Nation's history and tradition" or "implicit in the concept of ordered liberty" is, at best, facetious. *Id.*

In 2003 the Supreme Court revisited *Bowers*.

LAWRENCE V. TEXAS
Supreme Court of the United States, 2003.
539 U.S. 558.

JUSTICE KENNEDY delivered the opinion of the Court.

* * * The question before the Court is the validity of a Texas statute making it a crime for two persons of the same sex to engage in certain intimate sexual conduct. * * *

The petitioners * * * challenged the statute as a violation of the Equal Protection Clause of the Fourteenth Amendment * * * [, but were convicted,] * * * fined $200 and assessed court costs of $141.25. * * * [The appellate court affirmed the convictions, relying in part on * * * *Bowers v. Hardwick*].

II.

We conclude the case should be resolved by determining whether the petitioners were free as adults to engage in the private conduct in the exercise of their liberty under the due process clause of the Fourteenth Amendment to the Constitution. For this inquiry we deem it necessary to reconsider the court's holding in *Bowers*. * * *

The facts in *Bowers* had some similarities to the instant case. A police officer, whose right to enter seems not to have been in question, observed Hardwick, in his own bedroom, engaging in intimate sexual conduct with another adult male. The conduct was in violation of a Georgia statute making it a criminal offense to engage in sodomy. One difference between the two cases is that the Georgia statute prohibited the conduct whether or not the participants were of the same sex, while the Texas statute, as we have seen, applies only to participants of the same sex. * * *

The Court began its substantive discussion in *Bowers* as follows: "The issue presented is whether the Federal Constitution confers a fundamental right upon homosexuals to engage in sodomy and hence invalidates the laws of the many States that still make such conduct illegal and have done so for a very long time." That statement, we now conclude, discloses the Court's own failure to appreciate the extent of the liberty at stake. To say that the issue in *Bowers* was simply the right to engage in certain sexual conduct demeans the claim the individual put forward, just as it would demean a married couple were it to be said marriage is simply about the right to have sexual intercourse. The laws involved in *Bowers* and here are, to be sure, statutes that purport to do no more than prohibit a particular sexual act. Their penalties and purposes, though, have more far-reaching consequences, touching upon the most private human conduct, sexual behavior, and in the most private of places, the home. The statutes do seek to control a personal relationship that, whether or not entitled to formal recognition in the law, is within the liberty of persons to choose without being punished as criminals.

This, as a general rule, should counsel against attempts by the State, or a court, to define the meaning of the relationship or to set its boundaries absent injury to a person or abuse of an institution the law protects. It suffices for us to acknowledge that adults may choose to enter upon this relationship in the confines of their homes and their own private lives and still retain their dignity as free persons. When sexuality finds overt expression in intimate conduct with another person, the conduct can be but one element in a personal bond that is more enduring. The liberty protected by the Constitution allows homosexual persons the right to make this choice.

Having misapprehended the claim of liberty there presented to it, and thus stating the claim to be whether there is a fundamental right to engage in consensual sodomy, the *Bowers* Court said: "Proscriptions against that conduct have ancient roots." * * *

At the outset it should be noted that there is no longstanding history in this country of laws directed at homosexual conduct as a distinct matter. * * * [The Court finds that "[l]aws prohibiting sodomy do not seem to have been enforced against consenting adults acting in private," and that "[t]he policy of punishing consenting adults for private acts was not much discussed in the early legal literature."] We can infer that one reason for this was the very private nature of the conduct. Despite the absence of prosecutions, there may have been periods in which there was public criticism of homosexuals as such and an insistence that the criminal laws be enforced to discourage their practices. But far from possessing "ancient roots," * * * [i]t was not until the 1970's that any State singled out same-sex relations for criminal prosecution, and only nine States have done so. * * *

* * * In all events we think that our laws and traditions in the past half century are of most relevance here. The[y] * * * show an emerging awareness that liberty gives substantial protection to adult persons in deciding how to conduct their private lives in matters pertaining to sex. * * *

* * * A committee advising the British Parliament recommended in 1957 repeal of laws punishing homosexual conduct. Parliament enacted the substance of those recommendations 10 years later.

Of even more importance, almost five years before *Bowers* was decided, the European Court of Human Rights considered a case with parallels to

Bowers and to today's case. * * * The court held that the laws proscribing the conduct were invalid under the European Convention on Human Rights. Dudgeon v. United Kingdom, 45 Eur. Ct. H. R. (1981). Authoritative in all countries that are members of the Council of Europe (21 nations then, 45 nations now), the decision is at odds with the premise in *Bowers* that the claim put forward was insubstantial in our Western civilization.

In our own constitutional system the deficiencies in *Bowers* became even more apparent in the years following its announcement. The 25 states with laws prohibiting the relevant conduct referenced in the *Bowers* decision are reduced now to 13, of which 4 enforce their laws only against homosexual conduct. In those states where sodomy is still proscribed, whether for same-sex or heterosexual conduct, there is a pattern of nonenforcement with respect to consenting adults acting in private. * * *

Two principal cases decided after *Bowers* cast its holding into even more doubt. * * * The *Casey* decision again confirmed that our laws and tradition afford constitutional protection to personal decisions relating to marriage, procreation, contraception, family relationships, child rearing, and education. In explaining the respect the Constitution demands for the autonomy of the person in making these choices, we stated as follows:

> "These matters, involving the most intimate and personal choices a person may make in a lifetime, choices central to personal dignity and autonomy, are central to the liberty protected by the Fourteenth Amendment. At the heart of liberty is the right to define one's own concept of existence, of meaning, of the universe, and of the mystery of human life. Beliefs about these matters could not define the attributes of personhood were they formed under compulsion of the State."

Persons in a homosexual relationship may seek autonomy for these purposes, just as heterosexual persons do. The decision in *Bowers* would deny them this right.

The second post-*Bowers* case of principal relevance is *Romer v. Evans*, 517 U.S. 620 (1996). There the Court struck down class-based legislation directed at homosexuals as a violation of the Equal Protection Clause. *Romer* invalidated an amendment to Colorado's constitution which named as a solitary class persons who were homosexuals, lesbians, or bisexual either by "orientation, conduct, practices or relationships,", and deprived them of protection under state antidiscrimination laws. We concluded that the provision was "born of animosity toward the class of persons affected" and further that it had no rational relation to a legitimate governmental purpose. * * *

The foundations of *Bowers* have sustained serious erosion from our recent decisions in *Casey* and *Romer*. When our precedent has been thus weakened, criticism from other sources is of greater significance. * * * The courts of five different States have declined to follow it in interpreting provisions in their own state constitutions parallel to the Due Process Clause of the Fourteenth Amendment. * * *

To the extent *Bowers* relied on values we share with a wider civilization, it should be noted that the reasoning and holding in *Bowers* have been rejected elsewhere. * * * The right the petitioners seek in this case has been accepted as an integral part of human freedom in many other countries. There has been no showing that in this country the governmental interest in circumscribing personal choice is somehow more legitimate or urgent. * * *

Bowers was not correct when it was decided, and it is not correct today. It ought not to remain binding precedent. *Bowers v. Hardwick* should be and now is overruled.

The present case does not involve minors. It does not involve persons who might be injured or coerced or who are situated in relationships where consent might not easily be refused. It does not involve public conduct or prostitution. It does not involve whether the government must give formal recognition to any relationship that homosexual persons seek to enter. The case does involve two adults who, with full and mutual consent from each other, engaged in sexual practices common to a homosexual lifestyle. The petitioners are entitled to respect for their private lives. The State cannot demean their existence or control their destiny by making their private sexual conduct a crime. Their right to liberty under the Due Process Clause gives them the full right to engage in their conduct without intervention of the government. "It is a promise of the Constitution that there is a realm of personal liberty which the government may not enter." The Texas statute furthers no legitimate state interest which can justify its intrusion into the personal and private life of the individual. * * *

The judgment [below] * * * is reversed. * * *

JUSTICE SCALIA, with whom the CHIEF JUSTICE and JUSTICE THOMAS join, dissenting.

"Liberty finds no refuge in a jurisprudence of doubt." *Planned Parenthood Of Southeastern Pa. v. Casey*. That was the Court's sententious response, barely more than a decade ago, to those seeking to overrule *Roe v. Wade*. The Court's response today, to those who have engaged in a 17-year crusade to overrule *Bowers v. Hardwick* is very different. The need for stability and certainty presents no barrier.

Most of the rest of today's opinion has no relevance to its actual holding—that the Texas statute "furthers no legitimate state interest which can justify" its application to petitioners under rational-basis review. * * * [N]owhere does the Court's opinion declare that homosexual sodomy is a "fundamental right" under the Due Process Clause; nor does it subject the Texas law to the standard of review that would be appropriate (strict scrutiny) if homosexual sodomy were a "fundamental right." Thus, while overruling the outcome of *Bowers*, the Court leaves strangely untouched its central legal conclusion. * * * Instead the Court simply describes petitioners' conduct as "an exercise of their liberty"—which it undoubtedly is—and proceeds to apply an unheard-of form of rational-basis review that will have far-reaching implications beyond this case. * * *

Our opinions applying the doctrine known as "substantive due process" hold that the Due Process Clause prohibits States from infringing fundamental liberty interests, unless the infringement is narrowly tailored to serve a compelling state interest. We have held repeatedly, in cases the Court today does not overrule, that only fundamental rights qualify for this so-called "heightened scrutiny" protection—that is, rights which are " 'deeply rooted in this Nation's history and tradition.' " All other liberty interests may be abridged or abrogated pursuant to a validly enacted state law if that law is rationally related to a legitimate state interest. * * *

* * * *Bowers'* conclusion that homosexual sodomy is not a fundamental right "deeply rooted in this Nation's history and tradition" is utterly unassailable.

Realizing that fact, the Court instead says: "We think that our laws and traditions in the past half century are of most relevance here. These references show an emerging awareness that liberty gives substantial protection to adult persons in deciding how to conduct their private lives in matters pertaining to sex." Apart from the fact that such an "emerging awareness" does not establish a "fundamental right," the statement is factually false. States continue to prosecute all sorts of crimes by adults "in matters pertaining to sex": prostitution, adult incest, adultery, obscenity, and child pornography. Sodomy laws, too, have been enforced "in the past half century," in which there have been 134 reported cases involving prosecutions for consensual, adult, homosexual sodomy. * * *

In any event, an "emerging awareness" is by definition not "deeply rooted in this Nation's history and traditions," as we have said "fundamental right" status requires. Constitutional entitlements do not spring into existence because some States choose to lessen or eliminate criminal sanctions on certain behavior. Much less do they spring into existence, as the Court seems to believe, because foreign nations decriminalize conduct. * * *

The Texas statute undeniably seeks to further the belief of its citizens that certain forms of sexual behavior are "immoral and unacceptable," *Bowers*,—the same interest furthered by criminal laws against fornication, bigamy, adultery, adult incest, bestiality, and obscenity. *Bowers* held that this was a legitimate state interest. The Court today reaches the opposite conclusion. The Texas statute, it says, "furthers no legitimate state interest which can justify its intrusion into the personal and private life of the individual". * * * This effectively decrees the end of all morals legislation. If, as the Court asserts, the promotion of majoritarian sexual morality is not even a legitimate state interest, none of the above-mentioned laws can survive rational-basis review.

Today's opinion is the product of a Court, which is the product of a law-profession culture, that has largely signed on to the so-called homosexual agenda, by which I mean the agenda promoted by some homosexual activists directed at eliminating the moral opprobrium that has traditionally attached to homosexual conduct. * * * So imbued is the Court with the law profession's anti-anti-homosexual culture, that it is seemingly unaware that the attitudes of that culture are not obviously "mainstream"; that in most States what the Court calls "discrimination" against those who engage in homosexual acts is perfectly legal; that proposals to ban such "discrimination" under Title VII have repeatedly been rejected by congress; that in some cases such "discrimination" is mandated by federal statute, see 10 U.S.C. § 654(b)(1) (mandating discharge from the armed forces of any service member who engages in or intends to engage in homosexual acts); and that in some cases such "discrimination" is a constitutional right, see Boy Scouts of America v. Dale, 530 U.S. 640 (2000).

Let me be clear that I have nothing against homosexuals, or any other group, promoting their agenda through normal democratic means. * * * But persuading one's fellow citizens is one thing, and imposing one's views in absence of democratic majority will is something else. I would no more require a State to criminalize homosexual acts—or, for that matter, display any moral disapprobation of them—than I would forbid it to do so. What Texas has chosen to do is well within the range of traditional democratic action, and its hand should not be stayed through the invention of a brand-new "constitutional right" by a Court that is impatient of democratic change. * * *

One of the benefits of leaving regulation of this matter to the people rather than to the courts is that the people, unlike judges, need not carry things to their logical conclusion. The people may feel that their disapprobation of homosexual conduct is strong enough to disallow homosexual marriage, but not strong enough to criminalize private homosexual acts—and may legislate accordingly. The Court today pretends that it possesses a similar freedom of action, so that we need not fear judicial imposition of homosexual marriage * * *. At the end of its opinion— after having laid waste the foundations of our rational-basis jurisprudence—the Court says that the present case "does not involve whether the government must give formal recognition to any relationship that homosexual persons seek to enter." Do not believe it. * * * Today's opinion dismantles the structure of constitutional law that has permitted a distinction between heterosexual and homosexual unions, insofar as formal recognition of marriage is concerned. If moral disapprobation of homosexual conduct is "no legitimate state interest" for purposes of proscribing that conduct; and if, as the Court coos (casting aside all pretense of neutrality), "when sexuality finds overt expression in intimate conduct with another person, the conduct can be but one element in a personal bond that is more enduring"; what justification could there possibly be for denying the benefits of marriage to homosexual couples exercising "the liberty protected by the Constitution"? Surely not the encouragement of procreation, since the sterile and the elderly are allowed to marry. This case "does not involve" the issue of homosexual marriage only if one entertains the belief that principle and logic have nothing to do with the decisions of this Court. Many will hope that, as the Court comfortingly assures us, this is so.

* * * Texas's prohibition of sodomy neither infringes a "fundamental right" (which the Court does not dispute), nor is unsupported by a rational relation to what the Constitution considers a legitimate state interest, nor denies the equal protection of the laws. I dissent.

NOTES AND QUESTIONS

1.   What is the holding of *Lawrence*? Does the court find a fundamental right to privacy or use a rational basis test to invalidate the Texas law? Does *Lawrence* recognize a fundamental right to intimate or family associations beyond the boundaries of "deeply rooted traditions"? *Compare* Laurence H. Tribe, Lawrence v. Texas: *The Fundamental Rights That Dare Not Speaks Its Name*, 117 HARV. L. REV. 1893 (2004) *with* Cass R. Sunstein, *What Did* Lawrence *Hold? Of Autonomy, Desuetude, Sexuality, and Marriage*, 55 SUP. CT. REV. 27 (2003).

2.   Is the expansion of the right to privacy in *Lawrence* based on a "broadening conception of family?" *See* David D. Meyer, *Domesticating* Lawrence, 2004 U. CHI. L. FORUM 453.

3.   In *Dudgeon v. U.K.*, cited by the *Lawrence* majority, the Court relied primarily on Article 8 of the European Convention on Human Rights, providing that:

> Everyone has the right to respect for his private and family life, his home and his correspondence. There shall be no interference by a public authority with the exercise of this right except such as is in accordance with the law and is necessary in a democratic society in the interests of national security, public safety or the economic well-being of the country, for the prevention of disorder or crime, for the protection of health or morals, or for the protection of the rights and freedoms of others.

The *Dudgeon* court noted that "the moral climate * * * in sexual matters * * * is one of the matters which the national authorities may legitimately take into account in exercising their discretion." The Court also accepted that there was "a strong body of opposition stemming from a genuine and sincere conviction shared by a large number of responsible members of the Northern Irish community that a change in the law would be seriously damaging to the moral fabric of society." But even in Northern Ireland, the Court found that "the authorities have refrained in recent years from enforcing the law in respect of private homosexual acts between consenting males over the age of 21 years capable of valid consent":

> No evidence has been adduced to show that this has been injurious to moral standards in Northern Ireland or that there has been any public demand for stricter enforcement of the law. It cannot be maintained in these circumstances that there is a "pressing social need" to make such acts criminal offenses, there being no sufficient justification provided by the risk of harm to vulnerable sections of society requiring protection or by the effects on the public. On the issue of proportionality, the Court considers that such justifications as there are for retaining the law in force unamended are outweighed by the detrimental effects which the very existence of the legislative provisions in question can have on the life of a person of homosexual orientation like the applicant. Although members of the public who regard homosexuality as immoral may be shocked, offended or disturbed by the commission by others of private homosexual acts, this cannot on its own warrant the application of penal sanctions when it is consenting adults alone who are involved.

Id. How does the text of the European Convention alter the arguments available to the plaintiff and the state? Did the text of the Convention ensure that the *Dudgeon* plaintiff would win?

4.   Professor Daniel Solove has argued that *Griswold* and its progeny provide protection against "decisional interference," i.e., "governmental interference with people's decisions regarding certain matters of their lives." He notes that:

> Many commentators have argued that the language of privacy is inappropriate for decisional interference cases, since they primarily concern a harm to autonomy and liberty, not to privacy. Thus, Laurence Tribe argues that the central issue in *Roe v. Wade* is "not privacy, but autonomy." Similarly, Louis Henkin contends that the Supreme Court's substantive due process right-to-privacy cases are about protecting a "zone of autonomy, of presumptive immunity to governmental regulation," not about protecting privacy. * * *

> [However, t]he decisional interference cases are deeply connected to information privacy. * * * [J]ust a few years after *Roe v. Wade*, the Court explained in *Whalen v. Roe* [, involving mandated reporting of names and addresses of patients receiving certain categories of drugs], that the constitutionally protected "zone of privacy" extends not only to the "interest in independence in making certain kinds of

important decisions" but also to the "individual interest in avoiding disclosure of personal matters." This gave rise to the constitutional right to information privacy, which, although not developed further by the Supreme Court, has been recognized by most federal circuit courts. * * *

* * * The decisional interference cases track traditional areas that are widely considered to be private, such as the home, family, and body. Decisional interference, therefore, does not apply to all decisions, but only to a subset of decisions; this aspect of decisional interference resembles exposure in its focus on those aspects of life which are socially considered to be the most private. * * *

Decisional interference also bears an indirect resemblance to blackmail, in that laws restricting consensual private sexual behavior often give rise to blackmail. The *Lawrence* court noted that in 1955, when crafting the Model Penal Code, the American Law Institute recommended against criminalizing "consensual sexual relations conducted in private" in part because "the statutes regulated private conduct not harmful to others," and because "the laws were arbitrarily enforced and thus invited the danger of blackmail." Indeed, * * * blackmail historically occurred in the shadow of laws that punished consensual sexual activities in private. * * *

Daniel J. Solove, *A Taxonomy of Privacy*, 154 U. PA. L. REV. 477, 562–63 (2006).

Do the cases in this section (*Griswold, Eisenstadt, Danforth, Casey, Lawrence*) support Professor Solove's claim that decisional interference claims are "deeply connected to information privacy"?

5.   Are the central issues in *Griswold* and its progeny more accurately characterized as autonomy or privacy claims? Does it matter whether we think of these claims in autonomy or privacy terms? Put differently, is the language of privacy helpful in analyzing when actors should have decisional autonomy and when they should not?

6.   *Lawrence* figured prominently in striking down Proposition 8, the California constitutional amendment limiting marriage to a man and a woman. *Consider* Perry v. Schwarzenegger, 704 F. Supp. 2d 921 (N.D. Cal. 2010):

The evidence here shows that Proposition 8 was a hard-fought campaign and that the majority of California voters supported the initiative. * * * The arguments surrounding Proposition 8 raise a question similar to that addressed in *Lawrence*, when the Court asked whether a majority of citizens could use the power of the state to enforce "profound and deep convictions accepted as ethical and moral principles" through a criminal code. 539 U.S. at 571. The question here is whether California voters can enforce those same principles through regulation of marriage licenses. They cannot.

California's obligation is to treat its citizens equally, not to "mandate [its] own moral code." *Id.* "[M]oral disapproval, without any other asserted state interest," has never been a rational basis for legislation. [*Id.* at 582 (O'Connor, J., concurring)]. Tradition alone cannot support legislation. * * *

As you move into Chapter 3 on marriage regulation, consider whether you agree that the comparison between a criminal law and issuance of a marriage license are the same.

CHAPTER 3

THE REGULATION OF MARRIAGE

■ ■ ■

* * * Marriage, as creating the most important relation in life, as having more to do with the morals and civilization of a people than any other institution, has always been subject to the control of the legislature. That body prescribes the age at which parties may contract to marry, the procedure or form essential to constitute marriage, the duties and obligations it creates, its effects upon the property rights of both, present and prospective, and the acts which may constitute grounds for its dissolution * * *

Maynard v. Hill, 125 U.S. 190 (1888)

1. A BRIEF HISTORY OF MARRIAGE REGULATION

From ancient times to modern, entry into and exit from marriage have been subject to legal regulation. The Babylonian Code of Hammurabi provided that, "[i]f a man take a wife and does not arrange with her the proper contracts, that woman is not his legal wife." Roman law, although it proscribed bigamy, also viewed marriage as essentially contractual. A valid marriage required mutual consent but no particular ceremony; spouses themselves determined marital obligations and could obtain a divorce based on consent or unilateral withdrawal from the marriage relationship. Although the law recognized both secular and religious rules governing family relationships, the religious law applied only to its adherents. *See* MARRIAGE, DIVORCE, AND CHILDREN IN ANCIENT ROME (BERYL RAWSON ED., 1991).

The advent of Christianity profoundly affected both social attitudes toward marriage and marriage law. Between the fifth and sixteenth centuries, canon law gradually merged with local marriage laws and customs. In England, marriage was recognized as a sacrament during the twelfth century. By the thirteenth century the ecclesiastical courts had gained exclusive jurisdiction over marriage and its incidents.

Under canon law, marriage represented a sexual union blessed and sanctified by God—what God has joined together, let no man put asunder. Thus sex outside of marriage was criminalized, divorce was forbidden, and husband and wife were treated as one legal person. (*See* Chapter 4). Based on Biblical prohibitions, the law forbade marriage between persons related by consanguinity or affinity. Based on the view that entry into the marriage relationship required capacity, the law also invalidated marriages in cases of insanity, impotence, or nonage. Violations of the law produced civil and/or religious penalties.

The most famous "victim" of this inflexible marriage law was Henry VIII, who broke with the Roman Catholic Church in 1534 because of its refusal to annul his marriage to Catherine of Aragon. Thereafter Anglican, rather than Catholic, law prevailed. While the Anglican ecclesiastical courts continued to have jurisdiction over marriage and divorce until passage of the Matrimonial Causes Act of 1857, which transferred disputes over marriage and divorce to the civil courts, Parliament also played a substantial role in marriage regulation. *See* FRANCIS & JOSEPH GIES, MARRIAGE AND THE FAMILY IN THE MIDDLE AGES (1987); LAWRENCE STONE, THE FAMILY, SEX AND MARRIAGE 1500–1800 (1977).

In the United States, marriage and divorce have always been subject to the civil law, although many substantive and formal marriage requirements have their roots in ecclesiastical law and practice. But the Establishment Clause of the First Amendment forbids any "official" deference to the views of a particular religion. Thus, in dissolving a marriage over a wife's religious objection, the Oklahoma court in Williams v. Williams, 543 P.2d 1401 (Okla. 1975) noted that:

> We have no jurisdiction to regulate or enforce scriptural obligations. * * * The action of the trial court only dissolved the civil contract of marriage between the parties. No attempt was made to dissolve it ecclesiastically. Therefore, there is no infringement upon her constitutional right of freedom of religion. She still has her constitutional prerogative to believe that in the eyes of God, she and her estranged husband are ecclesiastically wedded as one * * * Any transgression by her husband of their ecclesiastical vows, is, in this instance, outside the jurisdiction of the court.

See also Sharma v. Sharma, 667 P.2d 395 (Kan. App. 1983) (granting divorce over objections of Hindu wife who argued that her religion not only forbade divorce, but also would treat her as legally dead if a divorce were to be granted).

Traditionally, each state has determined its requirements for who can marry, how they marry, and how the marriage can be dissolved. For histories of marriage law in the United States, *see* NANCY F. COTT, PUBLIC

VOWS: A HISTORY OF MARRIAGE AND THE NATION (2001); HENRIK HARTOG,
MAN AND WIFE IN AMERICA (2000).

2. CONSTITUTIONAL LIMITATIONS ON STATE MARRIAGE REGULATION

ZABLOCKI V. REDHAIL
Supreme Court of the United States, 1978.
434 U.S. 374.

JUSTICE MARSHALL delivered the opinion of the Court.

At issue * * * is the constitutionality of a Wisconsin statute §§ 245.10(1), (4), (5) (1973), which provides that a certain class of Wisconsin residents may not marry within the State or elsewhere, without first obtaining a court order granting permission to marry. The class is defined by the statute to include any "Wisconsin resident having minor issue not in his custody and which he is under obligation to support by any court order or judgment." The Statute specifies that court permission cannot be granted unless the marriage applicant submits proof of compliance with the support obligation and, in addition, demonstrates that the children covered by the support order "are not then and are not likely thereafter to become public charges." No marriage license may lawfully be issued in Wisconsin to a person covered by the statute, except upon court order; any marriage entered into without compliance with § 245.10 is declared void; and persons acquiring marriage licenses in violation of the section are subject to criminal penalties. * * *

[In a 1972 paternity action, appellee had been found to be the father of a baby girl and ordered to pay child support. In 1974, after not having paid his child support for over two years, he sought a marriage license which was denied for failure to satisfy the statute. It was stipulated that the child, who was on welfare, would have been "a public charge even if appellee had been current in his support payments."]

[T]he three-judge panel analyzed the * * * statute under the Equal Protection Clause and concluded that "strict scrutiny" was required because the classification created by the statute infringed upon a fundamental right to marry. The court then proceeded to evaluate the interests advanced by the State to justify the statute, and, finding that the classification was not necessary for the achievement of those interests, the court held the statute invalid. * * *

Appellant brought this direct appeal. * * * Appellee defends the lower court's equal protection holding and, in the alternative, urges affirmance * * * on the ground that the statute does not satisfy the requirements of

8

substantive due process. We agree with the District Court that the statute violates the Equal Protection Clause.

In evaluating [the statute] under the Equal Protection Clause, "we must first determine what burden of justification the classification created thereby must meet, by looking to the nature of the classification and the individual interests affected." *Memorial Hospital v. Maricopa County*, 415 U.S. 250, 253 (1974). Since our past decisions make clear that the right to marry is of fundamental importance, and since the classification of that right, we believe that "critical examination" of the state interests advanced in support of the classification is required.

The leading decision of this Court on the right to marry is *Loving v. Virginia*, 388 U.S. 1 (1967). In that case, an interracial couple who had been convicted of violating Virginia's miscegenation laws challenged the statutory scheme on both equal protection and due process grounds. The Court's opinion could have rested solely on the ground that the statutes discriminated on the basis of race in violation of the Equal Protection Clause. But the Court went on to hold that the laws arbitrarily deprived the couple of a fundamental liberty protected by the Due Process Clause, the freedom to marry. The Court's language on the latter point bears repeating:

> The freedom to marry has long been recognized as one of the vital personal rights essential to the orderly pursuit of happiness by free men.
>
> Marriage is one of the "basic civil rights of man," fundamental to our very existence and survival.

Id., quoting *Skinner v. Oklahoma ex rel. Williamson*, 316 U.S. 535, 541 (1942).

More recent decisions have established that the right to marry is part of the fundamental "right of privacy" implicit in the Fourteenth Amendment's Due Process Clause. In *Griswold v. Connecticut*, 381 U.S. 479 (1965), the Court observed:

> We deal with a right of privacy older than the Bill of Rights—older than our political parties, older than our school system. Marriage is a coming together for better or for worse, hopefully enduring, and intimate to the degree of being sacred. It is an association that promotes a way of life, not causes; a harmony in living, not political faiths; a bilateral loyalty, not commercial or social projects. Yet it is an association for as noble a purpose as any involved in our prior decisions.

Cases subsequent to *Griswold* and *Loving* have routinely categorized the decision to marry as among the personal decisions protected by the right of privacy.

* * *

It is not surprising that the decision to marry has been placed on the same level of importance as decisions relating to procreation, childbirth, child rearing, and family relationships. As the facts of this case illustrate, it would make little sense to recognize a right of privacy with respect to other matters of family life and not with respect to the decision to enter the relationship that is the foundation of the family in our society. The woman whom appellee desired to marry had a fundamental right to seek an abortion of their expected child, or to bring the child into life to suffer the myriad social, if not economic, disabilities that the status of illegitimacy brings. Surely, a decision to marry and raise a child in a traditional family setting must receive equivalent protection. And, if appellee's right to procreate means anything at all, it must imply some right to enter the only relationship in which the State of Wisconsin allows sexual relations legally to take place.

[W]e do not mean to suggest that every state regulation which relates in any way to the incidents of or prerequisites for marriage must be subjected to rigorous scrutiny. To the contrary, reasonable regulations that do not significantly interfere with decisions to enter into the marital relationship may legitimately be imposed. The statutory classification at issue here, however, clearly does interfere directly and substantially with the right to marry.

Under the challenged statute, no Wisconsin resident in the affected class may marry in Wisconsin or elsewhere without a court order, and marriages contracted in violation of the statute are both void and punishable as criminal offenses. Some of those in the affected class, like appellee, will never be able to obtain the necessary court order, because they either lack the financial means to meet their support obligations or cannot prove that their children will not become public charges. These persons are absolutely prevented from getting married. Many others, able in theory to satisfy the statute's requirements, will be sufficiently burdened by having to do so that they will in effect be coerced into foregoing their right to marry. And even those who can be persuaded to meet the statute's requirements suffer a serious intrusion into their freedom of choice in an area in which we have held such freedom to be fundamental.

When a statutory classification significantly interferes with the exercise of a fundamental right, it cannot be upheld unless it is supported by sufficiently important state interests and is closely tailored to effectuate only those interests. Appellant asserts that two interests are served by the challenged statute: the permission-to-marry proceeding furnishes an opportunity to counsel the applicant as to the necessity of fulfilling his prior support obligations; and the welfare of the out-of-custody children is protected. We may accept for present purposes that these are legitimate and substantial interests, but, since the means selected by the State for achieving these interests unnecessarily impinges on the right to marry, the statute cannot be sustained.

There is no evidence that the challenged statute, as originally introduced in the Wisconsin Legislature, was intended merely to establish a mechanism whereby persons with support obligations to children from prior marriages could be counseled before they entered into new marital relationships and incurred further support obligations. Court permission was automatically to be granted after counseling was completed. The statute actually enacted, however, does not expressly require or provide for any counseling whatsoever, nor for any automatic granting of permission to marry by the court, and thus it can hardly be justified as a means for ensuring counseling * * * Even assuming that counseling does take place— a fact as to which there is no evidence in the record—this interest obviously cannot support the withholding of court permission to marry once counseling is completed.

With regard to safeguarding the welfare of the out-of-custody children, appellant's brief does not make clear the connection between the State's interest and the statute's requirements. At argument, appellant's counsel suggested that, since permission to marry cannot be granted unless the applicant shows that he has satisfied his court-determined support obligations to the prior children and that those children will not become public charges, the statute provides incentive for the applicant to make support payments to his children. This "collection device" rationale cannot justify the statute's broad infringement on the right to marry.

First, with respect to individuals who are unable to meet the statutory requirements, the statute merely prevents the applicant from getting married, without delivering any money at all into the hands of the applicant's prior children. More importantly, regardless of the applicant's ability or willingness to meet the statutory requirements, the State already has numerous other means for exacting compliance with support obligations, means that are at least as effective as the instant statutes and yet do not impinge upon the right to marry. Under Wisconsin law, whether the children are from a prior marriage or were born out of wedlock, court-determined support obligations may be enforced directly via wage assignments, civil contempt proceedings, and criminal penalties. And, if the State believes that parents of children out of their custody should be responsible for ensuring that those children do not become public charges, this interest can be achieved by adjusting the criteria used for determining the amounts to be paid under their support orders.

There is also some suggestion that * * * [the statute] protects the ability of marriage applicants to meet support obligations to prior children by preventing the applicants from incurring new support obligations. But the challenged provisions of [the statute] are grossly underinclusive with respect to this purpose, since they do not limit in any way new financial commitments by the applicant other than those arising out of the contemplated marriage. The statutory classification is substantially overinclusive as well: Given the possibility that the new spouse will actually better the applicant's financial situation, by contributing income from a job or otherwise, the statute in many cases may prevent affected individuals from improving their ability to satisfy their prior support obligations. And, although it is true that the applicant will incur support obligations to any children born during the contemplated marriage, preventing the marriage may only result in the children being born out of wedlock, as in fact occurred in appellee's case. Since the support obligation is the same whether the child is born in or out of wedlock, the net result of preventing the marriage is simply more illegitimate children.

The statutory classification * * * thus cannot be justified by the interests advanced in support of it. The judgment of the District Court is, accordingly, Affirmed.

JUSTICE STEWART, concurring in the judgment.

I cannot join the opinion of the Court. To hold, as the Court does, that the Wisconsin statute violates the Equal Protection Clause seems to me to misconceive the meaning of that constitutional guarantee. The Equal Protection Clause deals not with substantive rights or freedoms but with invidiously discriminatory classifications. The paradigm of its violation is, of course, classification by race.

Like almost any law, the Wisconsin statute now before us affects some people and does not affect others. But to say that it thereby creates "classifications" in the equal protection sense strikes me as little short of fantasy. The problem in this case is not one of discriminatory classifications, but of unwarranted encroachment upon a constitutionally protected freedom. I think that the Wisconsin statute is unconstitutional because it exceeds the bounds of permissible state regulation of marriage, and invades the sphere of liberty protected by the Due Process Clause of the Fourteenth Amendment.

I do not agree with the Court that there is a "right to marry" in the constitutional sense. That right, or more accurately, that privilege, is under our federal system peculiarly one to be defined and limited by state law. A State may not only "significantly interfere with the decision to enter into the marriage relationship," but may in many circumstances absolutely prohibit it. Surely, for example, a State may legitimately say that no one can marry his or her sibling, that no one can marry who is not at least 14 years old, that no one can marry without first passing an examination for venereal disease, or that no one can marry who has a living husband or wife. But, just as surely, in regulating the intimate human relationship of marriage, there is a limit beyond which a State may not constitutionally go.

* * *

The Wisconsin law makes no allowance for the truly indigent. The State flatly denies a marriage license to anyone who cannot afford to fulfill his support obligations and keep his children from becoming wards of the State. We may assume that the State has legitimate interests in collecting delinquent support payments and in reducing its welfare load. We may also assume that as applied to those who can afford to meet the statute's financial requirements but choose not to do so, the law advances the State's objectives in ways superior to other means available to the State. The fact remains that some people simply cannot afford to meet the statute's financial requirements. To deny these people permission to marry penalizes them for failing to do that which they cannot do. Insofar as it applies to indigents, the state law is an irrational means of achieving these objectives of the State.

As directed against either the indigent or the delinquent parent, the law is substantially more rational if viewed as a means of assuring the financial viability of future marriages. In this context, it reflects a plausible judgment that those who have not fulfilled their financial obligations and have not kept their children off the welfare rolls in the past are likely to encounter similar difficulties in the future. But the State's legitimate concern with the financial soundness of prospective marriages must stop short of telling people they may not marry because they are too poor or because they might persist in their financial irresponsibility. The invasion of constitutionally protected liberty and the chance of erroneous prediction are simply too great. A legislative judgment so alien to our traditions and so offensive to our shared notions of fairness offends the Due Process Clause of the Fourteenth Amendment.

JUSTICE POWELL, concurring in the judgment.

I concur in the judgment of the Court that Wisconsin's restrictions on the exclusive means of creating the marital bond * * * cannot meet applicable constitutional standards. I write separately because the majority's rationale sweeps too broadly in an area which traditionally has been subject to pervasive state regulation. The Court apparently would subject all state regulation which "directly and substantially" interferes with the decision to marry in a traditional family setting to "critical examination" or "compelling state interest" analysis. Presumably, "reasonable regulations that do not significantly interfere with decisions to enter into the marital relationship may legitimately be imposed." The Court does not present, however, any principled means for distinguishing between the two types of regulations. Since state regulation in this area typically takes the form of a prerequisite or barrier to marriage or divorce,

CONSTITUTIONAL LIMITATIONS ON

the degree of "direct" interference with the decision to marry or to divorce is unlikely to provide either guidance for state legislatures or a basis for judicial oversight.

* * *

In my view, analysis must start from the recognition of domestic relations as "an area that has long been regarded as a virtually exclusive province of the States." * * * The State, representing the collective expression of moral aspirations, has an undeniable interest in ensuring that its rules of domestic relations reflect the widely held values of its people. * * * State regulation has included bans on incest, bigamy, and homosexuality, as well as various preconditions to marriage, such as blood tests. Likewise, a showing of fault on the part of one of the partners traditionally has been a prerequisite to the dissolution of an unsuccessful union. A "compelling state purpose" inquiry would cause doubt on the network of restrictions that the States have fashioned to govern marriage and divorce.

State power over domestic relations is not without constitutional limits. The Due Process Clause requires a showing of justification "when the government intrudes on choices concerning family living arrangements" in a manner which is contrary to deeply rooted traditions. * * * Due process constraints also limit the extent to which the State may monopolize the process of ordering certain human relationships while excluding the truly indigent from that process. * * *

The Wisconsin measure in this case does not pass muster under either due process or equal protection standards. Appellant identifies three objectives which are supposedly furthered by the statute in question: (1) a counseling function; (2) an incentive to satisfy outstanding support obligations; and (3) a deterrent against incurring further obligations. The opinion of the Court amply demonstrates that the asserted counseling objective bears no relation to this statute. * * *

The so-called "collection device" rationale presents a somewhat more difficult question. I do not agree with the suggestion in the Court's opinion that a State may never condition the right to marry on satisfaction of existing support obligations simply because the State has alternative methods of compelling such payments.

* * *

[But] the marriage applicant is required by the Wisconsin statute not only to submit proof of compliance with his support obligation, but also to demonstrate * * * that his children "are not then and are not likely thereafter to become public charges." This statute does more than simply "fail to alleviate the consequences of differences in economic circumstances that exist wholly apart from any state action." It tells the truly indigent, whether they have met their support obligations or not, that they may not marry so long as their children are public charges or there is a danger that their children might go on public assistance in the future. Apparently, no other jurisdiction has embraced this approach as a method of reducing the number of children on public assistance. Because the State has not established a justification for this unprecedented foreclosures of marriage to many of its citizens solely because of their indigency, I concur in the judgment of the Court.

JUSTICE STEVENS, concurring in the judgment.

* * * When a State allocates benefits or burdens, it may have valid reasons for treating married and unmarried persons differently. Classification based on marital status has been an accepted characteristic of tax legislation, Selective Service rules, and Social Security regulations.

* * *

A classification based on marital status is fundamentally different from a classification which determines who may lawfully enter into the marriage relationship. The individual's interest in making the marriage decision independently is sufficiently important to merit special constitutional protection. It is not, however, an interest which is constitutionally immune from evenhanded regulation. Thus, laws prohibiting marriage to a child, a close relative, or a person afflicted with venereal disease, are unchallenged even though they "interfere directly and substantially with the right to marry." This Wisconsin statute has a different character.

Under this statute, a person's economic status may determine his eligibility to enter into a lawful marriage. A noncustodial parent whose children are "public charges" may not marry even if he has met his court-ordered obligations. Thus, within the class of parents who have fulfilled their court-ordered obligations, the rich may marry and the poor may not. This type of statutory discrimination is, I believe, totally unprecedented, as well as inconsistent with our tradition of administering justice equally to the rich and to the poor.

The statute appears to reflect a legislative judgment that persons who have demonstrated an inability to support their offspring should not be permitted to marry and thereafter to bring additional children into the world. Even putting to one side the growing number of childless marriages and the burgeoning number of children born out of wedlock, that sort of reasoning cannot justify this deliberate discrimination against the poor.

The statute prevents impoverished parents from marrying even though their intended spouses are economically independent. Presumably, the Wisconsin Legislature assumed (a) that only fathers would be affected by the legislation, and (b) that they would never marry employed women.

The first assumption ignores the fact that fathers are sometimes awarded custody, and the second ignores the composition of today's work force. To the extent that the statute denies a hardpressed parent any opportunity to prove that an intended marriage will ease rather than aggravate his financial straits, it not only rests on unreliable premises, but also defeats its own objectives.

These questionable assumptions also explain why this statutory blunderbuss is wide of the target in another respect. The prohibition on marriage applies to the noncustodial parent but allows the parent who has custody to marry without the State's leave. Yet the danger that new children will further strain an inadequate budget is equally great for custodial and noncustodial parents * * *.

* * * Even assuming that the right to marry may sometimes be denied on economic grounds, this clumsy and deliberate legislative discrimination between the rich and the poor is irrational in so many ways that it cannot withstand scrutiny under the Equal Protection Clause of the Fourteenth Amendment.

NOTES AND QUESTIONS

1.   The *Zablocki* majority subjects the Wisconsin statute to an equal protection analysis. Justice Stewart, by contrast, sees the case not as a problem of discriminatory classification, but of the state's invasion of "the sphere of liberty protected by the Due Process Clause of the Fourteenth Amendment." What is the difference?

2.   *Zablocki* makes a distinction between statutes that "interfere directly and substantially" with the choice to marry and "reasonable regulations that do not significantly interfere" with free choice. What are some examples of "reasonable regulations" that are not subject to heightened scrutiny?

3.   The Universal Declaration of Human Rights, article 16, provides that:

1.   Men and women of full age, without any limitation due to race, nationality or religion, have the right to marry and to found a family. They are entitled to equal rights as to marriage, during marriage and its dissolution * * *

2.   Marriage shall be entered into only with the free and full consent of the intending spouses. Adopted by the United National General Assembly on December 10, 1948, U.N. Doc. No. A/810, Gen. Ass. Off. Rec., 3d Sess. (I), Resolutions, at 71.

How does the right guaranteed by the Declaration differ from the right guaranteed by *Zablocki*?

Problem 3-1:

The State Division of Corrections recently refused several inmates permission to marry, based on a state prison regulation that permits an inmate to marry only with the permission of the superintendent of the prison. The regulation also specifies that approval should be given only "when there are compelling reasons to do so." Although the term "compelling" is not defined, prison officials have historically considered pregnancy or the birth of an illegitimate child as a compelling reason for marriage. All of the prisoners who were recently denied permission to marry met their prospective spouses through classified ads and correspondence and thus could not meet the "compelling reasons" test.

You are a lawyer at the Prisoners' Legal Assistance Project and have been consulted by one of the prisoners, who wants to know if there is any basis for challenging the regulation. You have already corresponded with prison officials, who indicate that the basis for the regulation is "security and rehabilitation concerns." Officials indicate that "some inmates will marry simply to obtain conjugal visits—and through those visits may incur support obligations they cannot possibly meet in prison. Nor can the prisoner provide either financial or meaningful emotional support to his new family. Finally, any marriage based on a classified ad and brief correspondence holds a high possibility of failure."

What arguments are available to the prisoners and State under *Zablocki*? How do you expect the Supreme Court would rule? *See* Turner v. Safley, 482 U.S. 78 (1987); Langone v. Coughlin, 712 F. Supp. 1061 (N.D. N.Y. 1989).

Problem 3-2:

Janet is a police officer in Smallville. One requirement of her job is that she live within twenty miles of Smallville. Janet married Tom, a police officer who lives in Greenville which has a similar residency restriction and is more than twenty miles from Smallville. When Janet moved in with Tom, she was terminated from her job. Under *Zablocki*, is the Smallville residency restriction constitutional? *See* Klatt v. Labor & Indus. Rev. Com'n, 669 N.W.2d 752 (Wis. App. 2003).

3. SUBSTANTIVE REQUIREMENTS FOR ENTERING MARRIAGE

All marriage restrictions have the effect of approving some marriages and disapproving others. In reading the materials that follow, ask yourself what policies underlie current restrictions and whether those policies are justifiable in the context of the modern, flexible approach to defining family.

A. VOID AND VOIDABLE MARRIAGES

An attempted marriage that does not comply with state regulations may be *void, voidable* or *partially valid*. Technically, a *void* marriage is non-existent and has never existed; no formal procedure is necessary to terminate it. (Nevertheless, an annulment or a declaratory judgment to the effect that a void marriage is really void may sometimes be useful to prevent confusion, unexpected claims or a prosecution for bigamy). A void marriage can be attacked even after death of one of the spouses. *See In re* Estate of Santolino, 895 A.2d 506 (N.J. Super. Ch. Div. 2005). A *voidable* marriage, on the other hand, is effective until it is formally voided, usually as a result of a court order in an annulment action. The invalidity of a voidable marriage can be asserted only by the spouses while both are alive. Traditionally, once a *voidable* marriage was voided, the effect was retroactive and, as in the case of a *void* marriage, the law treated the marriage as nonexistent. Given the inequities that may result from this approach, modern marriage law takes a more flexible approach. *See* Chapter 12, § 4(B).

The classification of invalid marriages into void or voidable marriages usually is (or at least should be) related to the intensity of the state's interest in the particular regulation that has been violated. For example, generally considered "void" is an attempted incestuous marriage, or one involving a party below the absolute minimum age for marriage, or one between persons one or both of whom are currently married to someone else (bigamy). *See* Seaton v. Seaton, 133 Cal. Rptr. 3d 50 (Ct. App. 2011). Generally considered "voidable" is an attempted marriage between partners above the minimum age who need, but lack, parental consent for marriage, one procured through fraud or duress, or one entered into in violation of "collateral", formal requirements, such as absence of health checks. Generally the fraud must go the essentials of the marriage. *See* Kerry Abrams, *Marriage Fraud*, 100 CAL. L. REV. 1 (2012).

To be distinguished further are situations best described as "non-marriages" involving, for instance, a failure to comply with "essential" formal requirements, such as an attempted common law marriage in a jurisdiction not recognizing common law marriage.

B. CONFLICTS OF LAW

In general, the validity of a marriage is governed by the law of the place of celebration. RUSSELL J. WEINTRAUB, COMMENTARIES ON THE CONFLICT OF LAWS § 5.1A, 333–336 (6th ed. 2010). There are two exceptions to this *lex loci* approach. One exception permits nonrecognition based on public policy. "A marriage which satisfies the requirements of the state where the marriage was contracted will everywhere be recognized as valid *unless* it violates the strong public policy of another state which had the most significant relationship to the spouses and the marriage at the time of the marriage." The RESTATEMENT (SECOND) OF CONFLICT OF LAWS § 283 (1971) (emphasis added).

The other exception applies when a domiciliary of one state goes to another state for the purpose of avoiding his own state's marriage requirements. *See* WEINTRAUB, *supra*. Thirteen states have statutes modeled on the Uniform Marriage Evasion Act, even though it was withdrawn in 1943. For example, WIS. STAT. ANN. § 765.04 provides that:

> If any person residing and intending to continue to reside in this state who is disabled or prohibited from contracting marriage under the laws of this state goes into another state or country and there contracts a marriage prohibited or declared void under the laws of this state, such marriage shall be void for all purposes in this state with the same effect as though it had been entered into in this state.

Because the evasion exception is intent-based, a state may recognize a marriage that is invalid under its own laws if the evidence shows that the parties did not intend to evade state law and the marriage does not violate a strong public policy. *See In re* Estate of Loughmiller, 629 P.2d 156 (Kan. 1981) (finding a valid marriage in Colorado even though parties were first cousins from Kansas and Oklahoma because there was no attempt to evade Kansas law, no criminal law was violated, and a large number of states recognize first-cousin marriages).

C. ONE AT A TIME

The law in the United States allows only one spouse at a time. Polygamy became a political issue in the United States when Utah, settled by the polygamous Mormons, aspired to statehood. In Reynolds v. United States, 98 U.S. (8 Otto) 145 (1878), a Mormon brought an Establishment Clause challenge to his conviction under a federal law criminalizing bigamy. In sustaining the conviction and the statute, the Supreme Court noted that:

> Polygamy has always been odious among the northern and western nations of Europe, and, until the establishment of the Mormon Church, was almost exclusively a feature of the life of Asiatic and of African people. At common law, the second marriage was always void (2 Kent, Com. 79), and from the earliest history of England polygamy has been treated as an offence against society.

> * * *

> [W]e think it may safely be said there never has been a time in any State of the union when polygamy has not been an offence

against society, cognizable by the civil courts and punishable with more or less severity. In the face of all this evidence, it is impossible to believe that the constitutional guaranty of religious freedom was intended to prohibit legislation in respect to this most important feature of social life. Marriage, while from its very nature a sacred obligation, is nevertheless, in most civilized nations, a civil contract, and usually regulated by law. Upon it society may be said to be built, and out of its fruits spring social relations and social obligations and duties, with which government is necessarily required to deal. In fact, according as monogamous or polygamous marriages are allowed, do we find the principles on which the government of the people, to a greater or less extent, rests. Professor Lieber says, polygamy leads to the patriarchal principle, and which, when applied to large communities, fetters the people in stationary despotism, while that principle cannot long exist in connection with monogamy. Chancellor Kent observes that this remark is equally striking and profound. 2 Kent, Com. 81, note (e).

An exceptional colony of polygamists under an exceptional leadership may sometimes exist for a time without appearing to disturb the social condition of the people who surround it; but there cannot be a doubt that, unless restricted by some form of constitution, it is within the legitimate scope of the power of every civil government to determine whether polygamy or monogamy shall be the law of social life under its dominion.

* * *

In our opinion, the statute immediately under consideration is within the legislative power of Congress. * * * Laws are made for the government of actions, and while they cannot interfere with mere religious belief and opinions, they may with practices. Suppose one believed that human sacrifices were a necessary part of religious worship, would it be seriously contended that the civil government under which he lived could not interfere to prevent a sacrifice? Of if a wife religiously believed it was her duty to burn herself upon the funeral pile of her dead husband, would it be beyond the power of the civil government to prevent her carrying her belief into practice?

So here, as a law of the organization of society under the exclusive dominion of the United States, it is provided that plural marriages shall not be allowed. Can a man excuse his practices to the contrary because of his religious belief? To permit this would be to make the professed doctrines of religious belief superior to the law of the land, and in effect to permit every citizen to become a law unto himself. Government could exist only in name under such circumstances.

STATE V. GREEN

Supreme Court of Utah, 2004.
99 P.3d 820.

PARRISH, J.

A jury convicted Thomas Green of criminal nonsupport and four counts of bigamy. Green appeals his bigamy convictions. * * *

An avowed polygamist, Green has participated in simultaneous conjugal-type relationships with multiple women. These women all use Green's surname and have borne children who also use the Green surname. Between 1970 and 1996, Green formed relationships with Lynda Penman, Beth Cook, Linda Kunz, Shirley Beagley, June Johnson, LeeAnn Beagley, Cari Bjorkman, Hannah Bjorkman, and Julie Dawn McKinley. Through his relationships with these women, Green has fathered approximately twenty-five children.

Some of the women entered into licensed marriages with Green. The remaining women participated in unlicensed ceremonies, after which they considered themselves married to Green. Green avoided being in more than one licensed marriage at a time by terminating each licensed marriage by divorce prior to obtaining a license for a new marriage. Green then continued his relationships with each of the women he divorced as if no divorce had occurred.

In 1995, Green and his family moved to Juab County, Utah, where they resided together in a collection of shared mobile homes that the family called "Green Haven." Green quartered in one mobile home, while the women and children quartered in others. Some of the mobile home areas were set aside as common dining and laundry areas, and the family shared the bathrooms scattered among the mobile homes. The women spent nights individually with Green in his mobile home on a rotating schedule.

Each of the women shared with Green the duties of raising the children and managing the family by dividing the tasks of cooking for the entire family, doing the family laundry, and home schooling all of the children. In addition, the women assisted with the family business, which consisted of selling magazine subscriptions. All money earned by the family business was pooled into "the Green Family Household account."

Between 1988 and 2001, Green appeared on various television shows with the women, consistently referring to the women as his wives, and the women likewise acknowledged spousal relationships. In these television appearances, Green acknowledged that his conduct was potentially punishable under Utah criminal statutes. In April 2000, the State filed an information charging Green with, among other things, four counts of bigamy. * * *

[W]e will restrict our review of this case to * * * Green's claims that (1) Utah's bigamy statute violates his federal constitutional right to free exercise of religion; [and] (2) Utah's bigamy statute is unconstitutionally vague in light of Green's conduct. * * *

Utah's bigamy statute provides, in relevant part, as follows:

> A person is guilty of bigamy when, knowing he has a husband or wife or knowing the other person has a husband or wife, the person purports to marry another person or cohabits with another person.

Utah Code Ann. § 76–7–101(1) (2003). Green argues that this statute is unconstitutional under the First Amendment to the United States Constitution because it punishes his marital practices in violation of his right to freely exercise his religion. Specifically, Green argues that a law effectively prohibiting religiously motivated bigamy (which we refer to as polygamy) cannot withstand a challenge under the standards articulated by the United States Supreme Court. * * *

First, Green is not the first polygamist to launch an attack on the constitutionality of a law burdening the practice of polygamy. In 1878, polygamist George Reynolds challenged the constitutionality of the Morrill Antibigamy Act, which prohibited bigamy in all territories of the United States. Reynolds v. United States, 98 U.S. 145 (1878). * * * The Supreme Court reviewed the practice of polygamy, found it to be socially undesirable, and upheld Reynolds' bigamy conviction.

We are cognizant of the fact that *Reynolds* was decided over a century ago and may be antiquated in its wording and analysis. We are similarly cognizant of the fact that its reasoning may not necessarily comport with today's understanding of the language and apparent purpose of the Free Exercise Clause. Nevertheless, the Supreme Court has never explicitly overruled the decision.

* * *

We follow the analysis set forth by the Supreme Court in [Employment Div., Dep't. of Human Res. v. Smith, 494 U.S. 872 (1990) (upholding state laws penalizing ceremonial ingestion of peyote as not violating the Free Exercise Clause) and Church of the Lukumi Babalu Aye, Inc. v. City of Hialeah, 508 U.S. 520 (1993) (invalidating city ordinances prohibiting ritual slaughter of animals because the regulations were not neutral, not of general applicability, and not justified by a compelling state interest)] and, accordingly, examine Utah's bigamy statute to determine whether it is neutral and of general applicability.

[I]n the case now before us, Green and amici curiae argue that Utah's bigamy statute is not facially neutral. They contend that use of the word "cohabit" in the statute's text amounts to impermissible targeting of the religiously motivated marital practices of polygamists. In furtherance of their contention, Green and amici assert that "cohabit" must be read as plainly referring to polygamists because Utah is the only state that outlaws cohabitation between parties as bigamy and because early federal laws enacted in response to polygamy also made cohabitation an element of the crime of bigamy. We disagree.

* * * Utah's bigamy statute explains what it prohibits in secular terms, without referring to religious practices. The statute does not on its face mention polygamists or their religion. In addition, the word "cohabit" does not have religious origins or connotations; rather, it is a word of secular meaning. Green and amici attempt to infuse the word "cohabit" with religious animus, but in doing so they erroneously circumvent and ignore the word's plain meaning. Utah's bigamy statute is not a statute that "refers to a religious practice without a secular meaning discernable from the language." We accordingly hold that it is facially neutral.

[W]e also must assess the statute's operational neutrality. * * * Utah's bigamy statute does not similarly operate to isolate and punish only that bigamy which results from the religious practices of polygamists. It contains no exemptions that would restrict the practical application of the statute only to polygamists. In fact, the last reported decision of a prosecution under the current bigamy statute in our state courts involved a man who committed bigamy for non-religious reasons. * * * We thus find that Utah's bigamy statute is operationally, as well as facially, neutral. * * *

[W]e move [next] to the second requirement of the Free Exercise Clause—the requirement that "laws burdening religious practice must be of general applicability." * * * As noted above, Utah's bigamy statute does not attempt to target only religiously motivated bigamy. Any individual who violates the statute, whether for religious or secular reasons, is subject to prosecution. * * *

It is true that Utah's bigamy statute has an adverse impact on those wishing to practice polygamy as a tenet of their religion. An adverse impact on religion does not by itself, however, prove impermissible targeting because "a social harm may have been a legitimate concern of government for reasons quite apart from [religious] discrimination." [citations omitted]. Indeed, "[i]n many instances, the Congress or state legislatures conclude that the general welfare of society, wholly apart from any religious considerations," demands "regulation of conduct whose reason or effect merely happens to coincide or harmonize with the tenets of some or all religions." McGowan v. Maryland, 366 U.S. 420, 442 (1961).

The Utah legislature has determined that prohibiting bigamy serves this state's best interests. Because Utah's bigamy statute is neutral and of general applicability, the State is not required to show that the interests it serves are compelling or that the statute is narrowly tailored in pursuit of those interests. Instead, the State need show only that the statute is rationally related to a legitimate government end. [W]e assess whether the State has met its burden in this regard. We conclude that Utah's bigamy statute is rationally related to several legitimate government ends.

First, this state has an interest in regulating marriage. * * * Zablocki v. Redhail, 434 U.S. 374 (1978). The State of Utah's interest in regulating marriage has resulted in a network of laws, many of which are premised upon the concept of monogamy. * * *

Beyond the State's interest in regulating marriage as an important social unit, or in maintaining its network of laws, Utah's bigamy statute serves additional legitimate government ends. Specifically, prohibiting bigamy implicates the State's interest in preventing the perpetration of marriage fraud, as well as its interest in preventing the misuse of government benefits associated with marital status.

Most importantly, Utah's bigamy statute serves the State's interest in protecting vulnerable individuals from exploitation and abuse. The practice of polygamy, in particular, often coincides with crimes targeting women and children. Crimes not unusually attendant to the practice of polygamy include incest, sexual assault, statutory rape, and failure to pay child support. Moreover, the closed nature of polygamous communities makes obtaining evidence of and prosecuting these crimes challenging.

All of the foregoing interests are legitimate, if not compelling, interests of the State, and Utah's bigamy statute is rationally related to the furthering of those interests. We therefore hold that Utah's bigamy statute does not violate the Free Exercise Clause of the First Amendment of the United States Constitution. Having so determined, we turn our attention to Green's assertion that Utah's bigamy statute is unconstitutionally vague.

Green argues that Utah's bigamy statute is unconstitutionally vague [because] the statute left him "in a quandary" over how often he could legally reside with and have sexual contact with the women. We disagree and hold that the word "cohabit" is not vague as applied to Green's conjugal-type associations.

The record is clear that Green intended to create and maintain spousal-type relationships with Shirley Beagley, LeeAnn Beagley, Cari Bjorkman, and Hannah Bjorkman. He referred to each of these women as a wife, regardless of whether a licensed marriage existed. The women likewise considered themselves Green's wives and adopted the Green surname. Green spent nights with each woman on a rotating schedule and succeeded in impregnating these four women eighteen times, collectively. * * * Together, Green and the women undertook spousal and parental obligations. * * * With these facts in mind, it is difficult to see how Green could be unsure whether he might be "cohabiting" within the meaning of Utah's bigamy statute. Indeed, Green's conduct produced precisely the situation that bigamy statutes aim to prevent. * * *

[In addition,] Green and amici argue that Utah's bigamy statute affords enforcement officials too much prosecutorial discretion because it does not specifically indicate which of the "myriad of modern living arrangements" should be prosecuted. * * * We find that law enforcement officials encountering Green's circumstances would not be left to pursue their own personal predilections in determining the applicability of Utah's bigamy statute. As we already have discussed, Green's conduct fell unmistakably within the statute's purview. * * * We therefore hold that Green's vagueness challenge fails. * * *

We affirm * * *.

NOTES AND QUESTIONS

1.   Do you agree with the *Green* court's assessment of the state interests involved? The same Thomas Green, the "husband" of five wives, was convicted of criminal nonsupport of twenty-five children and of statutory rape. The latter charge arose from the fact that wife number 5, the daughter of wife number 2 and his stepdaughter, was 13 when he impregnated her and 14 when they "married." State v. Green, 108 P.3d 710 (Utah 2005). In a subsequent case, Bronson v. Swensen, 394 F. Supp. 2d 1329 (D. Utah 2005), the federal district court upheld the constitutionality of Utah's ban on polygamous marriages, finding that *Lawrence v. Texas* did not require the State to recognize polygamous marriages.

2.   Is polygamy inherently exploitive of women? The United Nations Commission on the Status of Women has declared that marriage should offer women "freedom of choice * * *, monogamy and equal rights to dissolution." How would Green's wives likely respond to the Commission? Whose views are more persuasive? *See* Keith E. Sealing, *Polygamists Out of the Closet: Statutory and State Constitutional Prohibitions against Polygamy are Unconstitutional under the Free Exercise Clause,* 17 GA. ST. L. REV. 691 (2001).

3.   The Islamic religion permits polygamy. According to the Koran, a man may have as many as four wives at one time if they are treated equally. Even in Islamic countries, however, there appears to be a trend toward monogamy. Islamic Tunisia and Turkey have outlawed polygamy; Sierra Leone and Malaysia permit the practice only among Muslims. *See Symposium on Marriage and Divorce Recognition in Sixteen Countries,* 29 FAM. L. Q. 497, 613, 655, 701 (1995); ABA Section of Family Law, *A White Paper: An Analysis of the Law Regarding Same-Sex Marriage, Civil Unions and Domestic*

Partnerships, 38 FAM. L. Q. 339, 349–50 (2004)(discussing polygamy in Islamic cultures).

4.   Should a polygamous marriage valid where contracted be recognized in a state disallowing polygamy? Immigration law denies admission into the United States for persons intending to practice polygamy. 8 U.S.C. § 1182(a)(10)(A)(2000). In England, although a polygamous marriage cannot be celebrated, § 1 of the Matrimonial Proceedings (Polygamous Marriages) Act of 1972 allows a court to grant matrimonial relief or a declaration concerning validity of the marriage notwithstanding that it is polygamous. *See* S.M. POULTER, ENGLISH LAW AND ETHNIC MINORITY CUSTOMS 53–55 (1986).

5.   The Mormon Church has formally rejected polygamy for over a century. Still, experts estimate that there could be from 30,000–1,000,000 fundamentalist Mormons living in polygamous relationships in Utah. *See* PHILIP L. KILBRIDE AND DOUGLAS R. PAGE, PLURAL MARRIAGE FOR OUR TIMES: A REINVENTED OPTION? (2012). The Utah attorney general has generally declined to enforce the bigamy statute against consenting adults. Tom Green's prosecution was the first in almost fifty years. *See* Pamela Manson, *The Law Has Been Slow to Step In*, SALT LAKE TRIB., Mar. 14, 2004, at G1. Why do you think there are so few prosecutions? In 2008, the State of Texas removed approximately 468 children from their homes on an emergency basis without a hearing because they lived on a ranch associated with the Fundamentalist Church of Jesus Christ of Latter Day Saints. A mandamus proceeding brought by the mothers found that the state failed to prove imminent harm. *In re* Texas Dep't of Family & Protective Servs., 255 S.W.3d 613 (Tex. 2008). Some prosecutions, however, have been successful. In 2011, Warren Jeffs was convicted for the sexual assault of an underage girl he took as a bride in a "spiritual marriage." *Texas: Polygamist Leader Gets Life Sentence*, N.Y. TIMES, Aug. 10, 2011, at A15. Sister Wives star Kody Brown brought an action to find Utah's statute unconstitutional. A federal district court held that the policy of limiting prosecution rendered the lawsuit moot. *See* Brown v. Buhman, 822 F.3d 1151 (10th Cir. 2016).

6.   For a discussion of polygamy, *compare* IRWIN ALTMAN & JOSEPH GINAT, POLYGAMOUS FAMILIES IN CONTEMPORARY SOCIETY (1996) *with* JOHN KRAKAUER, UNDER THE BANNER OF HEAVEN: A STORY OF VIOLENT FAITH (2003). *See also* Adrienne D. Davis, *Regulating Polygamy: Intimacy, Default Rules, and Bargaining for Equality*, 110 COLUM. L. REV. 1955 (2010).

7.   Bigamy has both civil and criminal consequences. A marriage contracted while one party is legally married to another is void. *See In re* Estate of Vargas, 111 Cal. Rptr. 779 (App. 1974). Many states also criminalize bigamy, although these statutes are rarely enforced. *See* ALA. CRIM. CODE § 13A–13–1. A defense to a bigamy charge may be available under an "Enoch Arden" statute if the first spouse disappeared for several years (usually five to seven) before the second marriage. *See* DEL. CODE ANN. tit. 11, §§ 381, 384. Other states have statutes that allow one spouse to have an absent spouse declared legally dead. *See* N.Y. DOM. REL. L. §§ 220, 221.

D. OF DIFFERENT SEXES

Marriage has historically been defined as the voluntary union of a man and a woman. Until recently, all states had rejected legal challenges by same-sex couples to marry. See Baker v. Nelson, 191 N.W.2d 185 (Minn. 1971). States rejected privacy based challenges because same-sex marriage was not a right "deeply rooted in our nation's history and tradition." In Baehr v. Lewin, 852 P.2d 44 (Hawaii 1993), the Hawaiian Supreme Court found that sex was a suspect category for purposes of equal protection analysis under the Hawaiian Constitution. On remand, the trial court held that the state had not established a compelling state interest to prohibit same-sex marriages. Baehr v. Miike, 910 P.2d 112 (Hawaii 1996). The decision became moot when voters subsequently amended the constitution to prohibit same-sex marriages. The decision prompted several states to enact statutes or to amend the state constitution to provide that a marriage other than between a man and a woman was against the strong public policy of the state and would not be recognized.

Partly in reaction to the Hawaii decision, in 1996 Congress enacted, and President Clinton signed, the Defense of Marriage Act (DOMA), which provided:

> Sec. 2.   [N]o state, territory, or possession of the United States, or Indian tribe, shall be required to give effect to any public act, record, or judicial proceeding of any other State, territory, possession, or tribe respecting a relationship between persons of the same-sex that is treated as a marriage under the laws of such other State * * * or a right or claim arising from such relationship." 28 U.S.C.A. § 1738C (2000).

> Sec. 3.   In determining the meaning of any Act of Congress, or of any ruling, regulation, or interpretation of the various bureaus and agencies of the United States, the word "marriage" means only a legal union between one man and one woman as husband and wife and the word "spouse" refers only to a person of the opposite sex who is a husband or a wife. 1 U.S.C. § 7.

Forty-one states enacted their own Defense of Marriage Acts (called mini-DOMAs) to prevent their states from having to recognize a same-sex marriage from another state. There were, however, other states moving in the direction of recognizing same-sex unions even if not called marriage. In 1999, the Supreme Court of Vermont found that same-sex couples did not have a constitutional right to marry, but that their exclusion from "the legal benefits and protections afforded their opposite-sex counterparts" violated Vermont's "common benefits" clause. The court ordered the Vermont legislature to either allow same-sex marriage or enact rules permitting same-sex couples "to obtain the same benefits and protections afforded by Vermont law to married opposite-sex couples." Baker v. State, 744 A.2d 864, 886 (Vt. 1999).

Shortly after the United States Supreme Court decision in Lawrence v. Texas, 539 U.S. 558 (2003), the Massachusetts Supreme Court in Goodridge v. Department of Public Health, 798 N.E.2d 941 (Mass. 2003), held that the state constitution required Massachusetts to allow same-sex individuals to enter civil marriage. The court noted that the state determines the terms of civil marriage and could define who can marry as well as what obligations and benefits attach. The Court emphasized the numerous positive benefits that flow from marriage, tangible and intangible. The state's asserted legislative rationales for prohibiting same-sex marriage were: (1) providing a favorable setting for procreation; (2) ensuring the optimal setting for child rearing; and (3) preserving scarce state and private financial resources. The Massachusetts Supreme Court concluded that none satisfied a rational basis review, noting that the present marriage ban works a "deep add scarring hardship" on a very real segment of the community for no rational reason. Many nonresident same-sex couples went to marry in Massachusetts, even though the validity of the marriage was questionable in many of their home states.

Until 2008, most state courts rejected the *Goodridge* majority's reasoning. Then things changed quickly. In April 2009, Vermont became the first state to legalize same-sex marriage by legislative action. In 2012, Maine, Maryland and Washington legalized same-sex marriage by referendum. By the end of 2013, Delaware, the District of Columbia, Hawaii, Illinois, Minnesota, New Hamshire, New York, and Rhode Island had statutes allowing same sex marriages. Courts in Connecticut, Iowa, New Jersey, New Mexico, Oregon, and Pennsylvania also invalidated state bans on same-sex marriage.

California saga. California has had domestic partnership legislation since 1999. California passed a Defense of Marriage Act, which the California Supreme Court invalidated in 2008. *In re* Marriage Cases, 183 P.3d 384 (Cal. 2008) (finding "sexual orientation is a characteristic * * * that is associated with a stigma of inferiority and second-class citizenship, manifested by the group's history of legal and social disabilities."). Approximately 18,000 same-sex marriages were performed between June 16 and November 4, 2008, when voters approved Proposition 8 amending the California Constitution to restrict marriage to a woman and a man. In 2009, the California Supreme Court upheld the constitutionality of Proposition 8 but found that the marriages entered into in the interim period were valid. Strauss v. Horton, 207 P.3d 48 (Cal. 2009). The debate then shifted to federal court with the argument that the ban violated the federal constitution. The California attorney general refused to defend the statute so the court allowed proponents of Proposition 8 to defend the ban. In August 2010, a federal district court found that Proposition 8 unconstitutionally burdens the exercise of the fundamental right to marry and discriminated against gays and lesbians on the basis of their sexual orientation. Perry v. Schwarzenegger, 704 F. Supp. 2d 921 (N.D. Cal. 2010). The Ninth Circuit affirmed on narrower grounds. Perry v. Brown, 671 F.3d 1052 (9th Cir. 2012). The United States Supreme Court held that the proponents lacked standing to defend Proposition 8 and declined to address the merits. Hollingsworth v. Perry, 133 S. Ct. 2652 (2013) (vacating the 9th Circuit opinion).

DOMA Challenges in Federal Court. Married same-sex couples were not treated the same as heterosexual couples under federal law. Same-sex couples could not file taxes jointly, could not take advantage of the unlimited estate tax marital deduction, could not file jointly in bankruptcy, and could not take Social Security survivor benefits.

Federal district courts began to find Section 3 of DOMA unconstitutional on various grounds. *See* Massachusetts v. U.S. Dep't of Health and Human Services, 698 F. Supp. 2d 234 (D. Mass. 2010) (violates the spending clause and the Tenth Amendment); *In re* Levenson, 560 F.3d 1145 (9th Cir. 2009) (violates due process to not allow same-sex spouse to have health insurance); Gill v. OPM, 699 F. Supp. 2d 374 (D. Mass. 2010) (violates equal protection). The U.S. Attorney General informed Congress that the Department of Justice would not defend suits based on Section 3 of DOMA. Letter from Eric J. Holder, Jr. Attorney General of the United States to John A. Bochner, Speaker of the U.S. House of Representatives (Feb. 23, 2011). The DOMA issue reached the United States Supreme Court in United States v. Windsor, 133 S. Ct. 2675 (2013). Edith Windsor and Thea Spyer had been in a long term relationship and married in Canada. They lived in New York which recognized the marriage. When Thea died, the estate taxes exceeded $360,000. If their marriage were recognized, there would be no estate tax liability. The United States Supreme Court found that Section 3 of DOMA was unconstitutional. Justice Kennedy's majority opinion discussed the significance of marriage:

> This status is a far-reaching legal acknowledgment of a legal relationship between two people, a relationship deemed by the State worthy of dignity in the community equal with other marriages. It reflects both the community's considered perspective on the historical roots of the institution of marriage and its evolving understanding of the meaning of equality.

Windsor, 133 S. Ct. at 2692.

Justice Scalia dissented, predicting the majority opinion would be used to legalize same-sex marriage. *Id.* at 2709. Post *Windsor*, five circuit courts of appeal invalidated state same-sex marriage bans either on the basis of due process or equal protection. See Kitchen v. Swensen, 755 F.3d 1193 (10th Cir. 2014); Baskins v. Bogan, 766 F.3d 648 (7th Cir. 2014); Bostic v.

Schaefer, 760 F.3d 352 (4th Cir. 2014); Latta v. Otter, 771 F.3d 456 (9th Cir. 2014). The Supreme Court denied certiorari in those cases in the fall of 2014. A circuit split occurred when the Sixth Circuit upheld the ban on same-sex marriage. DeBoer v. Snyder, 772 F.3d 388 (6th Cir. 2014). The United States Supreme Court granted certiorari in January 2015. On June 26, 2015, the Court issued its landmark decision.

OBERGEFELL V. HODGES

Supreme Court of United States, 2015.
576 U.S. ____, 135 S. Ct. 2584.

JUSTICE KENNEDY delivered the opinion of the Court.

The Constitution promises liberty to all within its reach, a liberty that includes certain specific rights that allow persons, within a lawful realm, to define and express their identity. The petitioners in these cases seek to find that liberty by marrying someone of the same sex and having their marriages deemed lawful on the same terms and conditions as marriages between persons of the opposite sex.

These cases come from Michigan, Kentucky, Ohio, and Tennessee, States that define marriage as a union between one man and one woman. The petitioners are 14 same-sex couples and two men whose same-sex partners are deceased. The respondents are state officials responsible for enforcing the laws in question. The petitioners claim the respondents violate the Fourteenth Amendment by denying them the right to marry or to have their marriages, lawfully performed in another State, given full recognition.

* * *

II. A

From their beginning to their most recent page, the annals of human history reveal the transcendent importance of marriage. The lifelong union of a man and a woman always has promised nobility and dignity to all persons, without regard to their station in life. Marriage is sacred to those who live by their religions and offers unique fulfillment to those who find meaning in the secular realm. Its dynamic allows two people to find a life that could not be found alone, for a marriage becomes greater than just the two persons. Rising from the most basic human needs, marriage is essential to our most profound hopes and aspirations.

The centrality of marriage to the human condition makes it unsurprising that the institution has existed for millennia and across civilizations. Since the dawn of history, marriage has transformed strangers into relatives, binding families and societies together. * * * It is fair and necessary to say these references were based on the understanding that marriage is a union between two persons of the opposite sex.

That history is the beginning of these cases. The respondents say it should be the end as well. To them, it would demean a timeless institution if the concept and lawful status of marriage were extended to two persons of the same sex. Marriage, in their view, is by its nature a gender-differentiated union of man and woman. This view long has been held—and continues to be held—in good faith by reasonable and sincere people here and throughout the world.

The petitioners acknowledge this history but contend that these cases cannot end there. * * * Far from seeking to devalue marriage, the petitioners seek it for themselves because of their respect—and need—for its privileges and responsibilities. And their immutable nature dictates that same-sex marriage is their only real path to this profound commitment.

* * *

Petitioner James Obergefell, a plaintiff in the Ohio case, met John Arthur over two decades ago. They fell in love and started a life together, establishing a lasting, committed relation. In 2011, however, Arthur was diagnosed with amyotrophic lateral sclerosis, or ALS. This debilitating disease is progressive, with no known cure. Two years ago, Obergefell and Arthur decided to commit to one another, resolving to marry before Arthur died. To fulfill their mutual promise, they traveled from Ohio to Maryland, where same-sex marriage was legal. It was difficult for Arthur to move, and so the couple were wed inside a medical transport plane as it remained on the tarmac in Baltimore. Three months later, Arthur died. Ohio law does not permit Obergefell to be listed as the surviving spouse on Arthur's death certificate. By statute, they must remain strangers even in death, a state-imposed separation Obergefell deems "hurtful for the rest of time." He brought suit to be shown as the surviving spouse on Arthur's death certificate. [other petitioner's circumstances listed]

* * *

B

The ancient origins of marriage confirm its centrality, but it has not stood in isolation from developments in law and society. The history of marriage is one of both continuity and change. That institution—even as confined to opposite-sex relations—has evolved over time.

For example, marriage was once viewed as an arrangement by the couple's parents based on political, religious, and financial concerns; but by the time of the Nation's founding it was understood to be a voluntary contract between a man and a woman. As the role and status of women changed, the institution further evolved. Under the centuries-old doctrine of coverture, a married man and woman were treated by the State as a single, male-dominated legal entity. As women gained legal, political, and property rights, and as society began to understand that women have their own equal dignity, the law of coverture was abandoned. These and other developments in the institution of marriage over the past centuries were not mere superficial changes. Rather, they worked deep transformations in its structure, affecting aspects of marriage long viewed by many as essential.

These new insights have strengthened, not weakened, the institution of marriage. Indeed, changed understandings of marriage are characteristic of a Nation where new dimensions of freedom become apparent to new generations, often through perspectives that begin in pleas or protests and then are considered in the political sphere and the judicial process.

This dynamic can be seen in the Nation's experiences with the rights of gays and lesbians. Until the mid-20th century, same-sex intimacy long had been condemned as immoral by the state itself in most Western nations, a belief often embodied in the criminal law. For this reason, among others, many persons did not deem homosexuals to have dignity in their own distinct identity. A truthful declaration by same-sex couples of what was in their hearts had to remain unspoken.

* * *

In the late 20th century, following substantial cultural and political developments, same-sex couples began to lead more open and public lives and to establish families. * * *

This Court first gave detailed consideration to the legal status of homosexuals in *Bowers v. Hardwick* (1986). There it upheld the constitutionality of a Georgia law deemed to criminalize certain homosexual acts. Ten years later, in *Romer v. Evans* (1996), the Court invalidated an amendment to Colorado's Constitution that sought to foreclose any branch or political subdivision of the State from protecting persons against discrimination based on sexual orientation. Then, in 2003, the Court overruled *Bowers,* holding that laws making same-sex intimacy a crime "demea [n] the lives of homosexual persons." *Lawrence v. Texas.*

Against this background, the legal question of same-sex marriage arose. In 1993, the Hawaii Supreme Court held Hawaii's law restricting marriage to opposite-sex couples constituted a classification on the basis of sex and was therefore subject to strict scrutiny under the Hawaii Constitution. Although this decision did not mandate that same-sex marriage be allowed, some States were concerned by its implications and reaffirmed in their laws that marriage is defined as a union between opposite-sex partners. So too in 1996, Congress passed the Defense of Marriage Act (DOMA), defining marriage for all federal-law purposes as "only a legal union between one man and one woman as husband and wife." 1 U.S.C. § 7.

The new and widespread discussion of the subject led other States to a different conclusion. In 2003, the Supreme Judicial Court of Massachusetts held the State's Constitution guaranteed same-sex couples the right to marry. See *Goodridge v. Department of Public Health,* . . . . After that ruling, some additional States granted marriage rights to same-sex couples, either through judicial or legislative processes. Two Terms ago, in *United States v. Windsor* (2013), this Court invalidated DOMA to the extent it barred the Federal Government from treating same-sex marriages as valid even when they were lawful in the State where they were licensed. * * *

III

Under the Due Process Clause of the Fourteenth Amendment, no State shall "deprive any person of life, liberty, or property, without due process of law." The fundamental liberties protected * * * include most of the rights enumerated in the Bill of Rights. In addition these liberties extend to certain personal choices central to individual dignity and autonomy, including intimate choices that define personal identity and beliefs. *See, e.g., Eisenstadt v. Baird* (1972); *Griswold v. Connecticut* (1965).

The identification and protection of fundamental rights is an enduring part of the judicial duty to interpret the Constitution. That responsibility, however, "has not been reduced to any formula." *Poe v. Ullman* (1961) (Harlan, J., dissenting). Rather, it requires courts to exercise reasoned judgment in identifying interests of the person so fundamental that the State must accord them its respect. That process is guided by many of the same considerations relevant to analysis of other constitutional provisions that set forth broad principles rather than specific requirements. History and tradition guide and discipline this inquiry but do not set its outer boundaries. *Lawrence.* That method respects our history and learns from it without allowing the past alone to rule the present.

The nature of injustice is that we may not always see it in our own times. The generations that wrote and ratified the Bill of Rights and the Fourteenth Amendment did not presume to know the extent of freedom in all of its dimensions, and so they entrusted to future generations a charter protecting the right of all persons to enjoy liberty as we learn its meaning. * * *

[T]he Court has long held the right to marry is protected by the Constitution. In *Loving v. Virginia* (1967), which invalidated bans on interracial unions, a unanimous Court held marriage is "one of the vital personal rights essential to the orderly pursuit of happiness by free men." The Court reaffirmed that holding in *Zablocki v. Redhail* (1978), which held the right to marry was burdened by a law prohibiting fathers who were behind on child support from marrying. The Court again applied this principle in *Turner v. Safley* (1987), which held the right to marry was

abridged by regulations limiting the privilege of prison inmates to marry.
* * *

It cannot be denied that this Court's cases describing the right to marry presumed a relationship involving opposite-sex partners. * * * In defining the right to marry these cases have identified essential attributes of that right based in history, tradition, and other constitutional liberties inherent in this intimate bond. And in assessing whether the force and rationale of its cases apply to same-sex couples, the Court must respect the basic reasons why the right to marry has been long protected. See, *e.g., Eisenstadt*; *Poe* (Harlan, J., dissenting).

This analysis compels the conclusion that same-sex couples may exercise the right to marry. The four principles and traditions to be discussed demonstrate that the reasons marriage is fundamental under the Constitution apply with equal force to same-sex couples.

A first premise of the Court's relevant precedents is that the right to personal choice regarding marriage is inherent in the concept of individual autonomy. * * *

Choices about marriage shape an individual's destiny. As the Supreme Judicial Court of Massachusetts has explained, because "it fulfils yearnings for security, safe haven, and connection that express our common humanity, civil marriage is an esteemed institution, and the decision whether and whom to marry is among life's momentous acts of self-definition." *Goodridge.*

The nature of marriage is that, through its enduring bond, two persons together can find other freedoms, such as expression, intimacy, and spirituality. This is true for all persons, whatever their sexual orientation. *See Windsor.* There is dignity in the bond between two men or two women who seek to marry and in their autonomy to make such profound choices.

A second principle in this Court's jurisprudence is that the right to marry is fundamental because it supports a two-person union unlike any other in its importance to the committed individuals. * * *

As this Court held in *Lawrence,* same-sex couples have the same right as opposite-sex couples to enjoy intimate association. * * *

A third basis for protecting the right to marry is that it safeguards children and families and thus draws meaning from related rights of childrearing, procreation, and education. * * * By giving recognition and legal structure to their parents' relationship, marriage allows children "to understand the integrity and closeness of their own family and its concord with other families in their community and in their daily lives." *Windsor.* Marriage also affords the permanency and stability important to children's best interests.

As all parties agree, many same-sex couples provide loving and nurturing homes to their children, whether biological or adopted, and hundreds of thousands of children are presently being raised by such couples. Most States have allowed gays and lesbians to adopt, either as individuals or as couples, and many adopted and foster children have same-sex parents. This provides powerful confirmation from the law itself that gays and lesbians can create loving, supportive families.

Excluding same-sex couples from marriage thus conflicts with a central premise of the right to marry. Without the recognition, stability, and predictability marriage offers, their children suffer the stigma of knowing their families are somehow lesser. They also suffer the significant material costs of being raised by unmarried parents, relegated through no fault of their own to a more difficult and uncertain family life. The marriage laws at issue here thus harm and humiliate the children of same-sex couples.

That is not to say the right to marry is less meaningful for those who do not or cannot have children. An ability, desire, or promise to procreate is not and has not been a prerequisite for a valid marriage in any State. In light of precedent protecting the right of a married couple not to procreate, it cannot be said the Court or the States have conditioned the right to marry on the capacity or commitment to procreate. The constitutional marriage right has many aspects, of which childbearing is only one.

Fourth and finally, this Court's cases and the Nation's traditions make clear that marriage is a keystone of our social order. * * *

For that reason, just as a couple vows to support each other, so does society pledge to support the couple, offering symbolic recognition and material benefits to protect and nourish the union. Indeed, while the States are in general free to vary the benefits they confer on all married couples, they have throughout our history made marriage the basis for an expanding list of governmental rights, benefits, and responsibilities. These aspects of marital status include: taxation; inheritance and property rights; rules of intestate succession; spousal privilege in the law of evidence; hospital access; medical decisionmaking authority; adoption rights; the rights and benefits of survivors; birth and death certificates; professional ethics rules; campaign finance restrictions; workers' compensation benefits; health insurance; and child custody, support, and visitation rules. Valid marriage under state law is also a significant status for over a thousand provisions of federal law. See *Windsor*. The States have contributed to the fundamental character of the marriage right by placing that institution at the center of so many facets of the legal and social order.

There is no difference between same- and opposite-sex couples with respect to this principle. Yet by virtue of their exclusion from that institution, same-sex couples are denied the constellation of benefits that the States have linked to marriage. This harm results in more than just material burdens. Same-sex couples are consigned to an instability many opposite-sex couples would deem intolerable in their own lives. * * *

The limitation of marriage to opposite-sex couples may long have seemed natural and just, but its inconsistency with the central meaning of the fundamental right to marry is now manifest. With that knowledge must come the recognition that laws excluding same-sex couples from the marriage right impose stigma and injury of the kind prohibited by our basic charter.

Washington v. Glucksberg (1997) * * * did insist that liberty under the Due Process Clause must be defined in a most circumscribed manner, with central reference to specific historical practices. Yet while that approach may have been appropriate for the asserted right there involved (physician-assisted suicide), it is inconsistent with the approach this Court has used in discussing other fundamental rights, including marriage and intimacy. * * *

The right to marry is fundamental as a matter of history and tradition, but rights come not from ancient sources alone. They rise, too, from a better informed understanding of how constitutional imperatives define a liberty that remains urgent in our own era. Many who deem same-sex marriage to be wrong reach that conclusion based on decent and honorable religious or philosophical premises, and neither they nor their beliefs are disparaged here. But when that sincere, personal opposition becomes enacted law and public policy, the necessary consequence is to put the imprimatur of the State itself on an exclusion that soon demeans or stigmatizes those whose own liberty is then denied. Under the Constitution, same-sex couples seek in marriage the same legal treatment as opposite-sex couples, and it would disparage their choices and diminish their personhood to deny them this right.

The right of same-sex couples to marry that is part of the liberty promised by the Fourteenth Amendment is derived, too, from that Amendment's guarantee of the equal protection of the laws. The Due Process Clause and the Equal Protection Clause are connected in a profound way, though they set forth independent principles. Rights implicit in liberty and rights secured by equal protection may rest on different precepts and are not always co-extensive, yet in some instances each may be instructive as to the meaning and reach of the other. * * *

The Court's cases touching upon the right to marry reflect this dynamic. In *Loving* the Court invalidated a prohibition on interracial marriage under both the Equal Protection Clause and the Due Process Clause. * * * The reasons why marriage is a fundamental right became more clear and compelling from a full awareness and understanding of the hurt that resulted from laws barring interracial unions.

The synergy between the two protections is illustrated further in *Zablocki.* * * * Each concept—liberty and equal protection—leads to a stronger understanding of the other.

* * *

This dynamic also applies to same-sex marriage. It is now clear that the challenged laws burden the liberty of same-sex couples, and it must be further acknowledged that they abridge central precepts of equality.

* * *

 These considerations lead to the conclusion that the right to marry is a fundamental right inherent in the liberty of the person, and under the Due Process and Equal Protection Clauses of the Fourteenth Amendment couples of the same-sex may not be deprived of that right and that liberty. The Court now holds that same-sex couples may exercise the fundamental right to marry.

IV

There may be an initial inclination in these cases to proceed with caution—to await further legislation, litigation, and debate. The respondents warn there has been insufficient democratic discourse before deciding an issue so basic as the definition of marriage. * * *

The Constitution contemplates that democracy is the appropriate process for change, so long as that process does not abridge fundamental rights. * * *

The dynamic of our constitutional system is that individuals need not await legislative action before asserting a fundamental right. The Nation's courts are open to injured individuals who come to them to vindicate their own direct, personal stake in our basic charter. * * *

[I]t must be emphasized that religions, and those who adhere to religious doctrines, may continue to advocate with utmost, sincere conviction that, by divine precepts, same-sex marriage should not be condoned. * * * The Constitution, however, does not permit the State to bar same-sex couples from marriage on the same terms as accorded to couples of the opposite sex.

V

 These cases also present the question whether the Constitution requires States to recognize same-sex marriages validly performed out of State. * * *

The Court, in this decision, holds same-sex couples may exercise the fundamental right to marry in all States. It follows that the Court also must hold—and it now does hold—that there is no lawful basis for a State to refuse to recognize a lawful same-sex marriage performed in another State on the ground of its same-sex character.

* * *

No union is more profound than marriage, for it embodies the highest ideals of love, fidelity, devotion, sacrifice, and family. In forming a marital union, two people become something greater than once they were. As some of the petitioners in these cases demonstrate, marriage embodies a love that may endure even past death. It would misunderstand these men and women to say they disrespect the idea of marriage. Their plea is that they do respect it, respect it so deeply that they seek to find its fulfillment for themselves. Their hope is not to be condemned to live in loneliness, excluded from one of civilization's oldest institutions. They ask for equal dignity in the eyes of the law. The Constitution grants them that right.

The judgment of the Court of Appeals for the Sixth Circuit is reversed.

CHIEF JUSTICE ROBERTS, with whom JUSTICE SCALIA and JUSTICE THOMAS join, dissenting.

Although the policy arguments for extending marriage to same-sex couples may be compelling, the legal arguments for requiring such an extension are not. The fundamental right to marry does not include a right to make a State change its definition of marriage. And a State's decision to maintain the meaning of marriage that has persisted in every culture throughout human history can hardly be called irrational. In short, our Constitution does not enact any one theory of marriage. The people of a State are free to expand marriage to include same-sex couples, or to retain the historic definition.

Today, however, the Court takes the extraordinary step of ordering every State to license and recognize same-sex marriage. Many people will rejoice at this decision, and I begrudge none their celebration. But for those who believe in a government of laws, not of men, the majority's approach is deeply disheartening. * * *

The majority's decision is an act of will, not legal judgment. The right it announces has no basis in the Constitution or this Court's precedent.

I

* * * There is no serious dispute that, under our precedents, the Constitution protects a right to marry and requires States to apply their marriage laws equally. The real question in these cases is what constitutes "marriage," or—more precisely—*who decides* what constitutes "marriage"?

A

As the majority acknowledges, marriage "has existed for millennia and across civilizations." For all those millennia, across all those civilizations, "marriage" referred to only one relationship: the union of a man and a woman. * * *

The premises supporting this concept of marriage are so fundamental that they rarely require articulation. The human race must procreate to survive. Procreation occurs through sexual relations between a man and a woman. When sexual relations result in the conception of a child, that child's prospects are generally better if the mother and father stay together rather than going their separate ways. Therefore, for the good of children and society, sexual relations that can lead to procreation should occur only between a man and a woman committed to a lasting bond.

* * *

The majority may be right that the "history of marriage is one of both continuity and change," but the core meaning of marriage has endured.

* * *

The majority purports to identify four "principles and traditions" in this Court's due process precedents that support a fundamental right for same-sex couples to marry. In reality, however, the majority's approach has no basis in principle or tradition, except for the unprincipled tradition of judicial policymaking * * *

Allowing unelected federal judges to select which unenumerated rights rank as "fundamental"—and to strike down state laws on the basis of that determination—raises obvious concerns about the judicial role. Our precedents have accordingly insisted that judges "exercise the utmost care" in identifying implied fundamental rights, "lest the liberty protected by the Due Process Clause be subtly transformed into the policy preferences of the Members of this Court." *Washington v. Glucksberg.*

* * *

In short, the "right to marry" cases stand for the important but limited proposition that particular restrictions on access to marriage *as traditionally defined* violate due process. These precedents say nothing at all about a right to make a State change its definition of marriage, which is the right petitioners actually seek here. See *Windsor.* Neither petitioners nor the majority cites a single case or other legal source providing any basis for such a constitutional right. None exists, and that is enough to foreclose their claim.

The Court also invoked the right to privacy in *Lawrence* which * * * relied on the position that criminal sodomy laws, like bans on contraceptives, invaded privacy by inviting "unwarranted government intrusions" that "touc[h] upon the most private human conduct, sexual ehavior . . . in the most private of places, the home."

. . . the marriage laws at issue here involve no government intrusion. They create no crime and impose no punishment. Same-sex couples remain free to live together, to engage in intimate conduct, and to raise their families as they see fit. No one is "condemned to live in loneliness" by the laws challenged in these cases—no one. At the same time, the laws in no way interfere with the "right to be let alone."

* * *

One immediate question invited by the majority's position is whether States may retain the definition of marriage as a union of two people. Although the majority randomly inserts the adjective "two" in various places, it offers no reason at all why the two-person element of the core definition of marriage may be preserved while the man-woman element may not. Indeed, from the standpoint of history and tradition, a leap from opposite-sex marriage to same-sex marriage is much greater than one from a two-person union to plural unions, which have deep roots in some cultures around the world. If the majority is willing to take the big leap, it is hard to see how it can say no to the shorter one.

I do not mean to equate marriage between same-sex couples with plural marriages in all respects. There may well be relevant differences that compel different legal analysis. But if there are, petitioners have not pointed to any. When asked about a plural marital union at oral argument, petitioners asserted that a State "doesn't have such an institution." But that is exactly the point: the States at issue here do not have an institution of same-sex marriage, either.

In addition to their due process argument, petitioners contend that the Equal Protection Clause requires their States to license and recognize same-sex marriages. The majority does not seriously engage with this claim. Its discussion is, quite frankly, difficult to follow. The central point seems to be that there is a "synergy between" the Equal Protection Clause and the Due Process Clause, and that some precedents relying on one Clause have also relied on the other. . . .

* * *

The majority goes on to assert in conclusory fashion that the Equal Protection Clause provides an alternative basis for its holding. Yet the majority fails to provide even a single sentence explaining how the Equal Protection Clause supplies independent weight for its position, nor does it attempt to justify its gratuitous violation of the canon against unnecessarily resolving constitutional questions. In any event, the marriage laws at issue here do not violate the Equal Protection Clause, because distinguishing between opposite-sex and same-sex couples is rationally related to the States' "legitimate state interest" in "preserving the traditional institution of marriage." *Lawrence* (O'Connor, J., concurring in judgment).

* * *

Federal courts are blunt instruments when it comes to creating rights. They have constitutional power only to resolve concrete cases or controversies; they do not have the flexibility of legislatures to address concerns of parties not before the court or to anticipate problems that may arise from the exercise of a new right. Today's decision, for example, creates serious questions about religious liberty. Many good and decent people oppose same-sex marriage as a tenet of faith, and their freedom to exercise religion is—unlike the right imagined by the majority—actually spelled out in the Constitution. Amdt. 1.

* * * The majority offers a cursory assurance that it does not intend to disparage people who, as a matter of conscience, cannot accept same-sex marriage. That disclaimer is hard to square with the very next sentence, in which the majority explains that "the necessary consequence" of laws codifying the traditional definition of marriage is to "demea[n] or stigmatiz[e]" same-sex couples. * * *

I respectfully dissent.

JUSTICE SCALIA, with whom JUSTICE THOMAS joins, dissenting.

I join THE CHIEF JUSTICE's opinion in full. I write separately to call attention to this Court's threat to American democracy.

The substance of today's decree is not of immense personal importance to me. The law can recognize as marriage whatever sexual attachments and living arrangements it wishes, and can accord them favorable civil consequences, from tax treatment to rights of inheritance. * * * It is of overwhelming importance, however, who it is that rules me. Today's decree says that my Ruler, and the Ruler of 320 million Americans coast-to-coast, is a majority of the nine lawyers on the Supreme Court. The opinion in these cases is the furthest extension in fact—and the furthest extension one can even imagine—of the Court's claimed power to create "liberties" that the Constitution and its Amendments neglect to mention.

I

* * *

The Constitution places some constraints on self-rule—constraints adopted *by the People themselves* when they ratified the Constitution and its Amendments. * * * Aside from these limitations, those powers "reserved to the States respectively, or to the people" can be exercised as the States or the People desire. These cases ask us to decide whether the Fourteenth Amendment contains a limitation that requires the States to license and recognize marriages between two people of the same sex. Does it remove *that* issue from the political process?

Of course not. * * * When the Fourteenth Amendment was ratified in 1868, every State limited marriage to one man and one woman, and no one doubted the constitutionality of doing so. That resolves these cases. * * * [t]he public debate over same-sex marriage must be allowed to continue.

But the Court ends this debate, in an opinion lacking even a thin veneer of law. Buried beneath the mummeries and straining-to-be-memorable passages of the opinion is a candid and startling assertion: No matter *what* it was the People ratified, the Fourteenth Amendment protects those rights that the Judiciary, in its "reasoned judgment," thinks the Fourteenth Amendment ought to protect. * * *

This is a naked judicial claim to legislative—indeed, *super-*legislative—power; a claim fundamentally at odds with our system of government. Except as limited by a constitutional prohibition agreed to by the People, the States are free to adopt whatever laws they like, even those that offend the esteemed Justices' "reasoned judgment." A system of government that makes the People subordinate to a committee of nine unelected lawyers does not deserve to be called a democracy.

* * *

II

But what really astounds is the hubris reflected in today's judicial Putsch. The five Justices who compose today's majority are entirely comfortable concluding that every State violated the Constitution for all of the 135 years between the Fourteenth Amendment's ratification and Massachusetts' permitting of same-sex marriages in 2003. They have discovered in the Fourteenth Amendment a "fundamental right" overlooked by every person alive at the time of ratification, and almost everyone else in the time since. * * *

[T]he opinion's showy profundities are often profoundly incoherent. "The nature of marriage is that, through its enduring bond, two persons together can find other freedoms, such as expression, intimacy, and spirituality." (Really? Who ever thought that intimacy and spirituality [whatever that means] were freedoms? And if intimacy is, one would think Freedom of Intimacy is abridged rather than expanded by marriage. Ask the nearest hippie. Expression, sure enough, *is* a freedom, but anyone in a long-lasting marriage will attest that that happy state constricts, rather than expands, what one can prudently say.) * * * The world does not expect logic and precision in poetry or inspirational pop-philosophy; it demands them in the law. The stuff contained in today's opinion has to diminish this Court's reputation for clear thinking and sober analysis.

* * *

JUSTICE THOMAS, with whom JUSTICE SCALIA joins, dissenting.

The Court's decision today is at odds not only with the Constitution, but with the principles upon which our Nation was built. Since well before 1787, liberty has been understood as freedom from government action, not entitlement to government benefits. * * *

The majority's decision today will require States to issue marriage licenses to same-sex couples and to recognize same-sex marriages entered in other States largely based on a constitutional provision guaranteeing "due process" before a person is deprived of his "life, liberty, or property." I have elsewhere explained the dangerous fiction of treating the Due Process Clause as a font of substantive rights. It distorts the constitutional text, which guarantees only whatever "process" is "due" before a person is deprived of life, liberty, and property. Worse, it invites judges to do exactly what the majority has done here—" 'roa[m] at large in the constitutional field' guided only by their personal views" as to the " 'fundamental rights' " protected by that document. * * *

II A 1

* * *

As used in the Due Process Clauses, "liberty" most likely refers to "the power of locomotion, of changing situation, or removing one's person to whatsoever place one's own inclination may direct; without imprisonment or restraint, unless by due course of law." 1 W. Blackstone, Commentaries on the Laws of England 130 (1769) (Blackstone). That definition is drawn from the historical roots of the Clauses and is consistent with our Constitution's text and structure.

* * *

[T]his Court's earliest Fourteenth Amendment decisions appear to interpret the Clause as using "liberty" to mean freedom from physical restraint. * * * That the Court appears to have lost its way in more recent years does not justify deviating from the original meaning of the Clauses.

2

Even assuming that the "liberty" in those Clauses encompasses something more than freedom from physical restraint, it would not include the types of rights claimed by the majority. In the American legal tradition, liberty has long been understood as individual freedom from governmental action, not as a right to a particular governmental entitlement.

* * *

B

Whether we define "liberty" as locomotion or freedom from governmental action more broadly, petitioners have in no way been deprived of it.

Petitioners cannot claim, under the most plausible definition of "liberty," that they have been imprisoned or physically restrained by the States for participating in same-sex relationships. To the contrary, they have been able to cohabitate and raise their children in peace. They have been able to hold civil marriage ceremonies in States that recognize same-sex marriages and private religious ceremonies in all States. They have been able to travel freely around the country, making their homes where they please. Far from being incarcerated or physically restrained, petitioners have been left alone to order their lives as they see fit.

* * *

Nor have the States prevented petitioners from approximating a number of incidents of marriage through private legal means, such as wills, trusts, and powers of attorney.

Instead, the States have refused to grant them governmental entitlements. Petitioners claim that as a matter of "liberty," they are entitled to access privileges and benefits that exist solely because of the government. * * * But receiving governmental recognition and benefits has nothing to do with any understanding of "liberty" that the Framers would have recognized.

To the extent that the Framers would have recognized a natural right to marriage that fell within the broader definition of liberty, it would not have included a right to governmental recognition and benefits. Instead, it would have included a right to engage in the very same activities that petitioners have been left free to engage in—making vows, holding religious ceremonies celebrating those vows, raising children, and otherwise enjoying the society of one's spouse—without governmental interference. At the founding, such conduct was understood to predate government, not to flow from it. * * * Petitioners misunderstand the institution of marriage when they say that it would "mean little" absent governmental recognition.

* * * As a philosophical matter, liberty is only freedom from governmental action, not an entitlement to governmental benefits. And as a constitutional matter, it is likely even narrower than that, encompassing only freedom from physical restraint and imprisonment. * * *

III

The majority's inversion of the original meaning of liberty will likely cause collateral damage to other aspects of our constitutional order that protect liberty.

A

The majority apparently disregards the political process as a protection for liberty. * * *

B

Aside from undermining the political processes that protect our liberty, the majority's decision threatens the religious liberty our Nation has long sought to protect.

* * *

* * * In our society, marriage is not simply a governmental institution; it is a religious institution as well. Today's decision might change the former, but it cannot change the latter. It appears all but inevitable that the two will come into conflict, particularly as individuals and churches are confronted with demands to participate in and endorse civil marriages between same-sex couples.

The majority appears unmoved by that inevitability. * * *

IV

* * * Human dignity has long been understood in this country to be innate. * * * [It] cannot be taken away by the government. Slaves did not lose their dignity (any more than they lost their humanity) because the government allowed them to be enslaved. Those held in internment camps did not lose their dignity because the government confined them. * * * The government cannot bestow dignity, and it cannot take it away.

* * *

JUSTICE ALITO, with whom JUSTICE SCALIA and JUSTICE THOMAS join, dissenting.

Until the federal courts intervened, the American people were engaged in a debate about whether their States should recognize same-sex marriage. The question in these cases, however, is not what States should do about same-sex marriage but whether the Constitution answers that question for them. It does not. The Constitution leaves that question to be decided by the people of each State.

I

* * *

Although the Court expresses the point in loftier terms, its argument is that the fundamental purpose of marriage is to promote the well-being of those who choose to marry. Marriage provides emotional fulfillment and the promise of support in times of need. * * *

This understanding of marriage, which focuses almost entirely on the happiness of persons who choose to marry, is shared by many people today, but it is not the traditional one. For millennia, marriage was inextricably linked to the one thing that only an opposite-sex couple can do: procreate. / *religion*

* * *

If this traditional understanding of the purpose of marriage does not ring true to all ears today, that is probably because the tie between marriage and procreation has frayed. Today, for instance, more than 40% of all children in this country are born to unmarried women. This development undoubtedly is both a cause and a result of changes in our society's understanding of marriage.

While, for many, the attributes of marriage in 21st-century America have changed, those States that do not want to recognize same-sex marriage have not yet given up on the traditional understanding. They worry that by officially abandoning the older understanding, they may contribute to marriage's further decay. It is far beyond the outer reaches of this Court's authority to say that a State may not adhere to the understanding of marriage that has long prevailed, not just in this country and others with similar cultural roots, but also in a great variety of countries and cultures all around the globe.

* * *

III

Today's decision usurps the constitutional right of the people to decide whether to keep or alter the traditional understanding of marriage. The decision will also have other important consequences.

It will be used to vilify Americans who are unwilling to assent to the new orthodoxy. In the course of its opinion, the majority compares traditional marriage laws to laws that denied equal treatment for African-Americans and women. The implications of this analogy will be exploited by those who are determined to stamp out every vestige of dissent.

* * * I assume that those who cling to old beliefs will be able to whisper their thoughts in the recesses of their homes, but if they repeat those views *right* in public, they will risk being labeled as bigots and treated as such by governments, employers, and schools.

NOTES AND QUESTIONS

1.   What is the difference in the majority and dissenting justices views on the meaning of marriage? The relationship between equality and liberty?

2.   What is the scope of the fundamental right to marry? Are the petitioners asserting a fundamental right or a new right not recognized in the Constitution?

3.   Does *Obergefell* answer the question whether classifications based on sexual orientation warrant heightened scrutiny?

4.   Does *Obergefell* require states to treat same-sex married couples identically to opposite-sex couples for all purposes, including things like adoption, custody and assisted reproduction? See Pavan v. Smith, 137 S. Ct. 2075 (2017) (requiring Arkansas to put married same-sex spouse's name on child's birth certificate).

5.   Before same-sex marriage was allowed, transgendered individuals complicated the issue. The majority American view is that a person's gender is determined at birth. *See In re* Marriage of Simmons, 825 N.E.2d 303 (Ill. App. 2005); and Kantaras v. Kantaras, 884 So. 2d 155 (Fla. Dist. Ct. App. 2004). A New Jersey court took a functional approach to transsexuals:

> In sum, it has been established that an individual suffering from the condition of transsexualism is one with a disparity between his or her genitalia or anatomical sex and his or her gender, that is, the individual's strong and consistent emotional and psychological sense of sexual being. A transsexual in a proper case can be treated medically by certain supportive measures and through surgery to remove and replace existing genitalia with sex organs which will coincide with the person's gender. If such sex reassignment surgery is successful and the postoperative transsexual is, by virtue of medical treatment, thereby possessed of the full capacity to function sexually as a male or female, as the case may be, we perceive no legal barrier, cognizable social taboo, or reason grounded in public policy to prevent that person's identification at least for purposes of marriage of the sex finally indicated. * * *

> In this case the transsexual's gender and genitalia are no longer discordant; they have been harmonized through medical treatment. Plaintiff has become physically and psychologically unified and fully capable of sexual attributes of gender and anatomy. Consequently, plaintiff should be considered a member of the female sex for marital purposes. * * *

M.T. v. J.T., 355 A.2d 204 (N. J. Super. App. Div. 1976).

The European Court of Human Rights found a violation of Articles 8 (guaranteeing respect for private life) and 12 (securing the fundamental right of a man and woman to marry and to found a family) when the United Kingdom denied a male-to-female transsexual the right to change a number of official government records that listed her as a male. Goodwin v. United Kingdom, [2002] 35 E.H.R.R., 18 ECHR.

E. UNRELATED BY BLOOD

7 INTERNATIONAL ENCYCLOPEDIA OF
THE SOCIAL SCIENCES 120 (1968)

Incest taboos, as one aspect of the regulation of sex and marriage, are integral to all known forms of social organization. Their form and function have varied extremely from one culture to another, in small and large societies, and in simple and complex societies. There seem to be no grounds for attributing the formation of this sanctioning system, by which an equilibrium is maintained between close and wide social ties, to any single set of innate human characteristics or to any specific set of historical circumstances. The universality of the occurrence of incest regulations, whatever form they may take or particular functions they may serve in a specific culture, suggests that they are part of a very complex system with deep biological roots, a system that is both a condition and a consequence of human evolution. Variations in the form and function of incest taboos suggest also that the formation of human character and the functioning of social systems are so intricately related to specific historical forms that changes within a social system are necessarily accompanied by some breakdown in the previously recognized pattern of personal relationships. Widespread failure to observe incest regulations is an index of the disruption of a sociocultural system that may be even more significant than the more usual indexes of crime, suicide, and homicide. (Margaret Mead).

Incest prohibitions may have existed as long as written law. In the Bible, Leviticus 18:6–18 sets out incest prohibitions. Roman Catholic canon law, which regulated marriage in Europe during the medieval period, prohibited marriages within the fourth degree of consanguinity; it also prohibited marriage in some cases of relationship by affinity (i.e., through marriage), as well as between godfather and godchild or godfather's daughter and godson.

Today, incestuous marriages are prohibited in all states, although the relationships defined as incestuous vary. For example, Uniform Marriage and Divorce Act (UMDA) § 207(a) (9A U. L. A. 168 (1987)) prohibits:

* * *

(2) a marriage between an ancestor and a descendant, or between a brother and a sister, whether the relationship is by the half or the whole blood, or by adoption;

(3) a marriage between an uncle and a niece or between an aunt and a nephew, whether the relationship is by the half or the whole

blood, except as to marriages permitted by the established customs of aboriginal cultures.

All states and the District of Columbia prohibit marriages between parent and child, siblings, aunt and nephew, uncle and niece. Twenty-four states ban first-cousin marriages. Some states do not forbid marriages between relatives by adoption.

Most states have statutes criminalizing incest, sometimes drafted more broadly than the marriage prohibitions. Consider whether the following justifications of a *criminal* incest prohibition offered by the drafters of the Model Penal Code support prohibitions on marriage based on consanguinity:

(a) *Religion.* The incest law may represent simply the use of criminal sanctions to enforce a religious tenet. The Bible defines and prohibits incest, and the offense was the exclusive concern of the church courts until 1908, with one brief interruption. * * * The specification of the forbidden degrees of kinship in legislation that prevailed at the time the Model Code was drafted was also largely derived from the religious history of the offense.

(b) *Genetics.* The laws against incest may have a genetic justification in that they may serve the civil and utilitarian function of preventing such inbreeding as would result in defective offspring. Mating between consanguineous relatives is non-random in the sense that close kinsmen are more likely to be genetically similar than are persons randomly selected from the population. Inbreeding therefore yields an increased probability of homozygosity with respect to a particular trait—that is, a greater chance that the offspring will receive an identical genetic contribution from each parent. If the pedigree contains a recessive abnormality—a genetic defect that does not appear in an individual unless both parents transmit the appropriate determinant—the increased probability of homozygosity in the first generation of offspring may have tragic consequences.

There are, however, a number of problems with relying upon a genetic theory to justify a law of incest. It must be noted first that none of the incest laws in the United States, or in the English ecclesiastical history from which they are derived, is limited to childbearing. The prohibition typically relates to marriage and sexual intercourse and, particularly in a day when contraceptive techniques are widely employed, is thus overbroad. It is clear, moreover, that former laws do not reflect genetic considerations insofar as marriages are prohibited between persons not related by blood, as in the extension to persons related by affinity such as stepchildren   or   daughters-in-law.   As   one   anthropologist

[Murdock] noted, "incest taboos, in their application to persons outside of the nuclear family, fail strikingly to coincide with nearness of actual biological relationship. * * * Very commonly * * * [they] exempt certain close consanguineal kinsmen but apply to adoptive, affinal, or ceremonial relatives with whom no biological kinsmen can be traced."

Even with respect to consanguineous mating, the science of human genetics has less solid guidance to offer than might be supposed. Geneticists are not agreed in their assessments of the relative dangers posed by inbreeding, and the number of serious genetic disorders related to inbreeding is quite limited. More importantly, some have argued that any decrease in the number of first-generation defectives resulting from the prevention of consanguineous marriages will be balanced by an increase in later generations, as the dispersal of unfavorable genes among the general population through exogamous matings raises the frequency with which the marriage of unrelated persons produces the unfavorable characteristic. "Thus," as one authority [Stern] put it, "the exclusion of consanguinity in one generation transfers the load of affected individuals to later generations." There is also the point that technological advance [pre-birth diagnosis] coupled with the general availability of abortion may provide at least a partial response to the problem of producing defective offspring, whether or not they result from consanguineous relationships.

(c) *Protection of the Family Unit.* The incest taboo and its origins are frequent topics of discussion in sociological and anthropological literature. Scholars from these disciplines have suggested various social objectives that the incest prohibition might serve. Perhaps the most persuasive theory is that social strictures against incest promote the solidarity of the nuclear family. This theory explains the universality of the concept of incest by reference to the universality of the nuclear family and derives strength from the anthropological verification of the existence of both across a wide range of cultural traditions.

The essentials of a nuclear family are a man and a woman in a relation of sexual intimacy and bearing a responsibility for the upbringing of the woman's children. This institution is the principal context for socialization of the individual. A critical component of that process is the channeling of the individual's erotic impulses into socially acceptable patterns. The incest prohibition regulates erotic desire in two ways that contribute to preservation of the nuclear family. First, the prohibition controls sex rivalries and jealousies within the family unit. It inhibits competing relations of sexual intimacy that would disorganize the family structure and undermine the family's role as the unit of socialization and personality development. Second, by ensuring suitable role models, the incest restriction prepares the individual for assumption of familial responsibility as an adult. Eventually, it propels the individual toward creation of a new nuclear family by his own marriage. It is worth noting also that this theory of the relation of incest to the nuclear family is consistent with Freudian psychology, which posits intrafamily sexual attraction as one of the basic facts of mental life and attributes much psychic disturbance to failure of the personality to resolve the internal conflict between such desires and societal repression of them.

(d) *Reinforcing Community Norms.* Even if it were demonstrable that the incest laws promote no secular goal, it might nevertheless be desirable to have a penal law on the subject. Where there is a general and intense hostility to behavior, a penal law will neither be accepted nor respected if it does not seek to repress that which is universally regarded by the community as misbehavior.

(e) *Sexual Imposition.* The actual incidence of prosecution for incest suggests that such laws have operated primarily against a kind of imposition on young and dependent females. A study of 30 appellate decisions on incest in the United States from 1846 to 1954 disclosed that all prosecutions were against males and that in 28 of the 30 cases the other party was the daughter or stepdaughter of the defendant. In the 21 instances where the court noted the age of the female, 18 involved girls aged 16 or younger, and none concerned a woman older than 22. Other research suggests that incest between stepfathers and stepdaughters occurs far more frequently than does incest between the parallel natural relations. In this aspect, therefore, the crime of incest can be viewed as supplementing other offenses of sexual imposition and assault.

(f) *Conclusion.* In light of the foregoing, it would appear that a modern penal code can appropriately contain a prohibition of incest, although attention plainly should be focused upon the scope of the prohibition. * * * It would seem * * * that a modern incest statute, carrying felony penalties, should be confined to relationships that present a high likelihood of threatening the solidarity of the nuclear family, that provide the occasion for sexual imposition of the experienced upon the inexperienced, and that coincide most closely with the intensely felt mores of the community. It may be permissible for a jurisdiction to adopt broader civil restrictions upon marriages regarded as undesirable, but the violation of any such regulations should not carry the infamy or penalty commonly associated with the crime of incest.

It seems clear, therefore, that the law of incest should be separated from the civil law regulating the institution of marriage and that it should be confined more narrowly than the history of the offense might otherwise suggest.

AMERICAN LAW INSTITUTE, MODEL PENAL CODE AND COMMENTARIES § 230.2, at 403–407 (1980).

ISRAEL V. ALLEN

Supreme Court of Colorado, 1978.
195 Colo. 263, 577 P.2d 762.

PRINGLE, CHIEF JUSTICE.

Plaintiffs, Martin Richard Israel and Tammy Lee Bannon Israel, are brother and sister related by adoption and are not related by either the half or the whole blood.

Raymond Israel (the natural father of Martin Richard Israel) and Sylvia Bannon (the natural mother of Tammy Lee Bannon Israel) were married on November 3, 1972. At the time of their marriage, Martin was 18 years of age and was living in the State of Washington; Tammy was 13 years of age and was living with her mother in Denver, Colorado. Raymond Israel adopted Tammy on January 7, 1975.

Plaintiffs desired to be married in the State of Colorado. Defendant, Clerk and Recorder of Jefferson County, however, denied plaintiffs a license to marry. * * *

While the practice of adoption is an ancient one, the legal regulation of adoptive relationships in our society is strictly statutory in nature. The legislative intent in promulgating statutes concerning adoption was, in part, to make the law affecting adopted children in respect to equality of inheritance and parental duties *in pari materia* with that affecting natural children. It is clear, however, that adopted children are not engrafted upon their adoptive families for all purposes. *See e.g.*, the criminal incest statute, which does not include sexual relationships between adopted brother and sister.

Nonetheless, defendant argues that this marriage prohibition provision furthers a legitimate state interest in family harmony. *See* § 14–2–102(2)(a), C.R.S. 1973. We do not agree. As the instant case illustrates, it is just as likely that prohibiting marriage between brother and sister related by adoption will result in family discord. While we are not, strictly speaking, dealing with an affinity based relationship in this case, we find the following analysis equally applicable to the situation presently before us:

According to the English law, relationship by affinity was an impediment to marriage to the same extent and in the same degree as consanguinity. While this principle, derived from the ecclesiastically administered canon law, still strongly persists, in the United States the statutory law governing the marriage relationship nowhere so sweeping condemns the marriage of persons related only by affinity. * * * The objections that exist against consanguineous marriages are not present where the relationship is merely by affinity. The physical detriment to the offspring of persons related to blood is totally absent. The natural repugnance of people toward marriages of blood relatives, that has resulted in well-nigh universal moral condemnation of such marriages, is quite generally lacking in application to the union of those related only by affinity. It is difficult to construct any very logical case for the prohibition of marriage on grounds of affinity * * *.

1 VERNIER, AMERICAN FAMILY LAWS 183.

We hold that it is just as illogical to prohibit marriage between adopted brother and sister.

NOTES AND QUESTIONS

1.   Is it so illogical not to allow adoptive siblings to marry? Would you distinguish the "step-parent adoption" involved in *Israel* from the typical adoption situation? What if the stepfather had been the residential parent of Martin and had adopted Tammy when she was three years old? Would the state's interests in protecting the integrity of the family unit and protecting against inbreeding be sufficiently important to justify the incest prohibition?

2.   Was it crucial to the *Israel* court's decision that, in contrast to the rule in many states, Colorado's criminal incest statute does not cover brothers and sisters related by adoption? After *Lawrence*, may states use criminal law to enforce moral judgments without demonstrating concrete social injury?

3.   Is the court's near total reliance on the affinity analogy persuasive? A few states do prohibit marriages between persons related by affinity, i.e., CONN. GEN. STAT. ANN. § 46b–21, "No man may marry his * * * stepmother or stepdaughter, and no woman may marry her * * * stepfather or stepson. Any marriage within these degrees is void." In England relationships based on marriage or adoption are prohibited along with those based on consanguinity. Matrimonial Causes Act (MCA) 1973 § 11. What legitimate state interests uphold marriage impediments based on affinity, adoption, or a step-relationship? Is there a stronger case for impediments based on adoption or step-relationships than for impediments based on affinity? What type of law would have prevented Woody Allen from marrying Soon-Yi, the adopted daughter of Mia Farrow, with whom he had had an intimate relationship for thirteen years? Would such a law be a good idea? *See* Christina McNiece Metter, *Some "Incest" is Harmless Incest, Determining the Fundamental Right*

to Marry of Adults Related by Affinity, 10 KAN. J. L. & PUB. POL'Y 262 (2000) (attacking legitimacy of restrictions on affinity marriages).

4. Twenty-four states ban first cousins from marrying. *See In re* Estate of Everhart, 783 N.W.2d 1 (App. 2010) (finding first cousin marriage void so surviving cousin could not inherit as spouse). Seven states have limitations, such as counseling requirements. What is the basis for the proscription on first-cousin marriage?

Problem 3-3:

In 2008, Wilma and Fred adopted a fifteen year-old girl, Mary. Wilma and Fred divorced in November 2016. In July 2017, Mary gave birth to Fred's child. Mary thereafter petitions the court to abrogate her adoption by Fred (but not Wilma) so that she and Fred can marry. What public policies are implicated? What should the court do? *See In re* Adoption of M., 722 A.2d 615 (N.J. Super. Ch. Div. 1998).

Problem 3-4:

In 1986 Tara and Hamid, first cousins, were married in Iran which allows first cousin marriages. In 2006, Tara and Hamid moved to Louisiana. In 2017, Tara filed for divorce and a division of the parties' community assets. Hamid answered the petition by refuting the marriage because first cousins are not allowed to marry in Louisiana. The district court agreed and dismissed the divorce. Tara appeals. What result? What principles are involved? *See* Ghassemi v. Ghassemi, 998 So. 2d 731 (La. App. 2008).

F. OF SUFFICIENT AGE

Citizens of Rome contract lawful matrimony when they unite according to the precepts of the law; the males having attained the age of puberty, and the females a marriageable age. And this whether the males are fathers or sons of a family; but, if the latter, they must first have the consent of the parents under whose power they are. For both natural reason and the law convinces us that this consent of parents should precede marriage.

JUSTINIAN'S INSTITUTES, Book I, Title X (A.D. 533)

As the quote indicates, at one time parental consent was considered important for marriage. Today, the rules on the age of marriage are many. The age at which a person can marry without anyone's permission is generally the age of majority. After passage of the Twenty-Sixth Amendment to the United States Constitution, which lowered the voting age to eighteen, most states selected 18 as the minimum age at which a person can marry without parental or judicial consent.*See* CAL. FAM. CODE § 302.

Is there a "minimum" age? At common law the ages of capacity were fourteen for men and twelve for women. Below these ages, a marriage would be void.

UNIFORM MARRIAGE AND DIVORCE ACT § 205
9A U.L.A. 168 (1987).

(a) The [_____] court, after a reasonable effort has been made to notify the parents or guardian of each underaged party, may order the [marriage license] clerk to issue a marriage license and a marriage certificate form:

> [(1)] to a party aged 16 or 17 years who has no parent capable of consenting to marriage, or whose parent or guardian has not consented to his marriage; [or (2) to a party under the age of 16 years who has the consent of both parents to his marriage, if capable of giving consent, or his guardian].

(b) A marriage license and a marriage certificate form may be issued under this section only if the court finds that the underaged party is capable of assuming the responsibilities of marriage and the marriage will serve his best interest. Pregnancy alone does not establish that the best interest of the party will be served.

MOE V. DINKINS
United States District Court, S.D. New York, 1981.
533 F. Supp. 623, aff'd 669 F.2d 67 (2d Cir. 1982).

[Plaintiffs, Maria Moe, age 15, Raoul Roe, age 18, and Ricardo Roe, their one year old son born out of wedlock, seek to have New York's parental consent to marry laws declared unconstitutional as violating due process and equal protection. New York Domestic Relations Law § 15.2 provides that male applicants for a marriage license between ages 16 and 18 and females between ages 14 and 18 must obtain written consent to the marriage from both parents, if living. Section 15.3 requires that a woman between ages 14 and 16 must also obtain judicial approval. Maria's mother who was receiving welfare for Maria would not consent to the marriage.

The Court notes that marriage is a liberty interest protected by the Constitution.]

* * *

While it is true that a child, because of his minority, is not beyond the protection of the Constitution, the Court has recognized the State's power to make adjustments in the constitutional rights of minors. The power of the State to control the conduct of children reaches beyond the scope of authority over adults. This power to adjust minors' constitutional rights flows from the State's concern with the unique position of minors. In *Bellotti v. Baird*, the Court noted "three reasons justifying the conclusion that the constitutional rights of children cannot be equated with those of adults: the peculiar vulnerability of children; their inability to make critical decisions in an informed and mature manner; and the importance of the parental role in child-rearing."

Likewise, marriage occupies a unique position under the law. It has been the subject of extensive regulation and control, within constitutional limits, in its inception and termination and has "long been regarded as a virtually exclusive province of the State." *Sosna v. Iowa.*

While it is evident that the New York law before this court directly abridges the right of minors to marry, *in the absence of parental consent,* the question is whether the State interests that support the abridgement can overcome the substantive protection of the Constitution. The unique position of minors and marriage under the law leads this court to conclude that § 15 should not be subjected to strict scrutiny, the test which the Supreme Court has ruled must be applied whenever a state statute burdens the exercise of a fundamental liberty protected by the Constitution. Applying strict scrutiny would require determination of whether there was a compelling state interest and whether the statute had been closely tailored to achieve that state interest. * * * It is this court's view that § 15 should be looked at solely to determine whether there exists a rational relation between the means chosen by the New York legislature and the legitimate state interests advanced by the State. Section 15 clearly meets this test.

The State interests advanced to justify the parental consent requirement of § 15 include the protection of minors from immature decision-making and preventing unstable marriages. The State possesses paternalistic power to protect and promote the welfare of children who lack the capacity to act in their own best interest. The State interests in mature decision-making and in preventing unstable marriages are legitimate under its *parens patriae* power.

An age attainment requirement for marriage is established in every American jurisdiction. The requirement of parental consent ensures that at least one mature person will participate in the decision of a minor to marry. That the State has provided for such consent in § 15 is rationally related to the State's legitimate interest in light of the fact that minors often lack the "experience, perspective and judgment" necessary to make "important, affirmative choices with potentially serious consequences."

Yet, plaintiffs fault the parental consent requirement of § 15 as possibly arbitrary, suggesting that courts, as non-interested third parties, are in a better position to judge whether a minor is prepared for the responsibilities that attach to marriage. Although the possibility for parents to act in other than the best interest of their child exists, the law presumes that the parents "possess what the child lacks in maturity" and that "the natural bonds of affection lead parents to act in the best interest of their children." *Parham v. J.R.*, 442 U.S. 584 (1979). "That the governmental power should supersede parental authority in all cases because some parents" may act in other than the best interest of their children is "repugnant to the American tradition."

Plaintiffs also contend that § 15 denied them the opportunity to make an individualized showing of maturity and denies them the only means by which they can legitimize their children and live in the traditional family unit sanctioned by law. On the other hand, New York's § 15 merely delays plaintiffs' access to the institution of marriage. Moreover, the prohibition does not bar minors whose parents consent to their child's marriage. Assuming arguendo that the illegitimacy of plaintiff Moe's child * * * is a harm, it is not a harm inflicted by § 15. It is merely an incidental consequence of the lawful exercise of State power. The illegitimacy of plaintiffs' children, like the denial of marriage without parental consent, is a temporary situation at worst. A subsequent marriage of the parents legitimatizes the child, thereby erasing the mark of illegitimacy. The rights or benefits flowing from the marriage of minors are only temporarily suspended by § 15. Any alleged harm to these rights and benefits is not inflicted by § 15, but is simply an incidental consequence of the valid exercise of State power.

The fact that the State has elected to use a simple criterion, age, to determine probable maturity in the absence of parental consent, instead of requiring proof of maturity on a case by case basis, is reasonable, even if the rule produces seemingly arbitrary results in individual cases. * * *

Plaintiffs' reliance on the abortion and contraception cases is misplaced. * * * These cases can be distinguished from the instant case in that

> a pregnant minor's options are much different than those facing a minor in other situations, *such as deciding whether to marry*. A minor not permitted to marry before the age of maturity is required simply to postpone her decision. She and her intended spouse may preserve the opportunity for a later marriage should they continue to desire it.

Bellotti v. Baird, supra, (emphasis added). Giving birth to an unwanted child involves an irretrievable change in position for a minor as well as for an adult, whereas the temporary denial of the right to marry does not. Plaintiffs are not irretrievably foreclosed from marrying. The gravamen of the complaint, in the instant case, is not total deprivation but only delay.

This court concludes that § 15's requirement of parental consent is rationally related to the State's legitimate interests in mature decision-making with respect to marriage by minors and preventing unstable marriages. It is also rationally related to the State's legitimate interest in supporting the fundamental privacy right of a parent to act in what the parent perceives to be the best interest of the child free from state court scrutiny. Section 15, therefore, does not offend the constitutional rights of minors but represents a constitutionally valid exercise of state power.

Accordingly, plaintiffs' motion for summary judgment in their favor is denied and summary judgment is entered in favor of defendants.

NOTES AND QUESTIONS

1.   While nearly every state technically prohibits persons under age 18 from marrying, in 34 states, 16 and 17 year olds can marry with parents' permission; in 36 states minors can marry with judicial consent. Laws in 27 states do not specify an age below which a child cannot marry. State statutes typically provide that a person less than 16 years of age may marry only if he has the consent of a parent or legal guardian or can show extraordinary circumstances. Is pregnancy an extraordinary circumstance? See State Dep't of Hum. Resources v. Lott, 16 So. 3d 104 (Ala. Civ. App. 2009). Is religious belief such a circumstance? Child marriage is a reality in many parts of the world. In the United States, it is rare but most common in Texas and West Virginia. See David McClendon & Aleksandra Sandstrom, *Child Marriage is Rare in the U.S., though this varies by State,* Factank, Pew Research Center, (Nov. 16, 2016). See also Nicholas Kristof, *11 Years Old, A Mom, and Pushed to Marry Her Rapist in Florida,* N.Y. TIMES (May 26, 2017). In 2017, New York and Texas passed laws forbidding underage marriage unless a judge approves the marriage.

2.   Is a parent who consents to the marriage of an underage child committing child abuse? *See* New Jersey Div. of Youth & Fam. Services v. R.W., 641 A.2d 1124 (N. J. Super. Ch. Div. 1994). Can (or should) a parent be criminally liable for consenting to the marriage of an underage child? *See* State v. Chaney, 989 P.2d 1091 (Utah App. 1999).

3.   Is the marriage of an underage child without parental consent void or voidable? The majority view seems to disfavor permitting parents to interfere with a *fait accompli.* Should, in these circumstances, the "child" be permitted to attack his or her own marriage based on lack of parental consent? What should be the role of the public, i.e., the juvenile authorities or the state's attorney, in these cases? *See* Kirkpatrick v. Dist. Ct., 64 P.3d 1056 (Nev. 2003).

4.   Does the minimum age statute only apply to formal marriages? Could someone under the minimum age form a common law marriage? *See In re* Marriage of J.M.H., 143 P.3d 1116 (Colo. App. 2006) (using common law ages of 14 and 12).

5.   The Personal Responsibility and Work Opportunity Reconciliation Act (PRWORA) contained several economic incentives to encourage young mothers of nonmarital children to marry. H.R. 240, 109th Cong. (2005).

However, researchers have found that teen marriages are less stable than older marriages, with half of them ending within fifteen years; teens who have a nonmarital birth, marry and divorce are also worse off economically than those who did not marry; teen mothers are more likely to have a second birth quickly if they marry; teen marriage leads to decreased educational attainment for girls; teen fathers earn less in early adulthood than males who wait until age 20 to have a child; and teen marriages often involve high levels of domestic violence. *See* Naomi Seiler, *Is Teen Marriage a Solution?*, CENTER FOR L. & SOC. POL'Y REPORT 7–8 (Aug. 2002). See also Vivian Hamilton, *The Age of Marital Capacity: Reconsidering Civil Recognition of Adolescent Marriage*, 92 B.U.L. Rev. 1773 (2012).

G. IN PROPER HEALTH AND WITH GOOD GENES?

WILLIAM VUKOWICH, THE DAWNING OF THE BRAVE NEW WORLD—LEGAL, ETHICAL, AND SOCIAL ISSUES OF EUGENICS
1971 U. ILL. L. F. 189, 214 (1971).

In the early 1900s many states enacted laws that prohibited marriage by criminals, alcoholics, imbeciles, feebleminded persons, and the insane. Today most states prohibit marriage by persons with venereal disease, but only a few states have laws which are similar to those of the early 1900's.

* * *

In addition to the existing marital restrictions, Nobel Prize winner Linus Pauling has suggested that legislation prohibit marriages between heterozygotes for the same recessive gene if the recessive gene can be detected in the heterozygous state. The suggestion was made in reference to sickle-cell anemia, but is equally applicable to other serious defects which are caused by recessive genes that can or will become detectable in heterozygotes. Professor Pauling would require that heterozygotes for serious defects be conspicuously marked so that two heterozygotes for the same defect would not fall in love. In any event, their marriage would be prohibited, although there is only a 25 percent chance for two heterozygotes to have a homozygous child. Professor Pauling believes that severe marital restrictions are warranted because of the grave suffering borne by children with the diseases that the restrictions would prevent. If heterozygotes for the same deleterious gene never intermarry, however, there would be an *increase* in the incidence of the gene.

NOTES AND QUESTIONS

1. Muster arguments for and against the constitutionality of Professor Pauling's (who did not get his Nobel prize for this) proposal.

2. An example of an old-line eugenic statute is N.D. CENT. CODE § 14–03–07: "Marriage by a woman under the age of forty-five years or by a man of any age, unless he marries a woman over the age of forty-five years, is prohibited if such a man or woman is [a chronic alcoholic, an habitual criminal, a mentally deficient person, an insane person, a person who has been afflicted with hereditary insanity, or with any contagious venereal disease]". Overwhelmingly, when referring to "insanity", "imbecility", "idiocy" and the like, modern legislation deals with *capacity to consent to marriage*, not mental or emotional capability to function in a marriage or with genetic problems that may be passed on to the children.

3. If it is "genetic risk" that affords a legitimate basis for upholding incest prohibitions, can you justify a marriage law that does not apply equally strong prohibitions to marriages between nonrelatives who have known genetic defects that pose a risk to their offspring?

4. While disease-based marriage prohibitions are rare, a number of states require premarital health examinations to detect venereal and/or other diseases, including rubella, Rh incompatibility, tuberculosis, and drug addiction. Today there are tests available for a wide variety of genetically-linked disorders. Should premarital testing for these disorders be required?

Problem 3-5:

UTAH CODE ANN. tit. 30 § 1–2 prohibited marriages "with a person afflicted with acquired immune deficiency syndrome, syphilis, or gonorrhea that is communicable or that may become communicable." Is the statute constitutional under *Zablocki*? Does it conflict with other federal legislation, such as the Americans with Disabilities Act, 42 U.S.C.A. § 1201 et. seq. *See* T.E.P. v. Leavitt, 840 F. Supp. 110 (D. Utah 1993).

4. PROCEDURES RELATING TO ENTRY INTO MARRIAGE

In the last section we looked at the *substantive* requirements for marriage that are typically found in state statutes. We now turn to the *procedural* requirements for a valid marriage.

A. CONSENT TO MARRY

1. Capacity to Contract

To marry requires *the capacity to contract*. Although state statutes invariably require mental capacity, they provide no effective mechanism to ascertain a marriage applicant's mental condition. Typically, the matter lies entirely in the hands of the clerks authorized to issue marriage licenses, few of whom are qualified mental health diagnosticians. Appellate cases involving the refusal of a marriage license on grounds of mental capacity are scarce, indicating either that marriage licenses are rarely refused on that ground or that, when refused, couples go to more hospitable jurisdictions.

UNIFORM MARRIAGE AND DIVORCE ACT § 208
9A U.L.A. 170 (1987).

The [___] court shall enter its decree declaring the invalidity of a marriage entered into under the following circumstances:

(1)   a party lacked capacity to consent to the marriage at the time the marriage was solemnized, either because of mental incapacity or infirmity or because of the influence of alcohol, drugs, or other incapacitating substances, or a party was induced to enter into a marriage by force or duress, or by fraud involving the essentials of marriage;

(2)   a party lacks the physical capacity to consummate the marriage by sexual intercourse, and at the time the marriage was solemnized the other party did not know of the incapacity;

(3)   a party [was under the age of 16 years and did not have the consent of his parents or guardian and judicial approval or] was aged 16 or 17 years and did not have the consent of his parents or guardian or judicial approval; or

(4)   the marriage is prohibited. [See § 207].

LARSON V. LARSON
Illinois Court of Appeals, 1963.
42 Ill. App. 2d 467, 192 N.E.2d 594.

CROW, PRESIDING JUSTICE.

* * * When the celebration of a marriage is shown, the contract of marriage, the capacity of the parties, and, in fact, everything necessary to the validity of the marriage, in the absence of proof to the contrary, will be presumed; the burden of proof was upon the plaintiff to show the marriage was invalid; to enable a party legally to contract a marriage he or she must be capable of understanding the nature of the act. When a marriage is shown the law raises a strong presumption in favor of its validity, and the burden is upon the party objecting thereto to prove such facts and circumstances as necessarily establish its invalidity; there is no clear dividing line between competency and incompetency, and each case must be judged by its own peculiar facts; the parties must have sufficient mental

capacity to enter into the status, but proof of lack of mental capacity must be clear and definite; if the party possesses sufficient mental capacity to understand the nature, effect, duties, and obligations of the marriage contract into which he or she is entering, the marriage contract is binding, as long as they are otherwise legally competent to enter into the relation.

A marriage contract will be invalidated by the want of consent of capable persons; it requires the mutual consent of two persons of sound mind, and if at the time one is mentally incapable of giving an intelligent consent to what is done, with an understanding of the obligations assumed, the solemnization is a mere idle ceremony,—they must be capable of entering understandingly into the relation. It is impossible to prescribe a definite rule by which the mental condition as to sanity or insanity in regard to a marriage can in every case be tested; the question is not altogether of brain quantity or quality in the abstract, but whether the mind could and did act rationally regarding the precise thing in contemplation,—marriage,—and the particular marriage in dispute,—not whether his or her conduct was wise, but whether it proceeded from a mind sane as respects the particular thing done. The decree here [denying annulment] is not contrary to the manifest weight of the evidence or to the law. Prior to and at the time of the marriage the plaintiff noticed nothing abnormal about the defendant. There is no evidence that any of the unusual things she thought and did some months after the marriage had also occurred prior to and at the time of the marriage. Her first commitment to Elgin State Hospital was in 1952, more than two years after the marriage. In 1954 she was found to have recovered and was restored to all her civil rights. She got along for a while thereafter. Her second commitment was in 1956, more than four and one-half years after the marriage. The plaintiff continued to live regularly with the defendant as husband and wife except for such times as she was actually physically confined at the Hospital. The doctor who testified had never examined, or treated the defendant and his entire testimony is based, necessarily, on a hypothetical question. The ostensible diagnosis was evidently made by another or other doctors, who were not available or did not testify here. No doctor, nurse, or attendant at the Hospital who might have observed, examined, or treated her testified. In this doctor's opinion, even, a patient of that type may have lucid intervals for months or years—she may not have had any symptoms which a layman would recognize as insanity,—she might be all right for years,—and he would not say a patient of such type could never be cured. Even he said such a patient might be legally all right,—not legally insane,—though medically it may be very difficult to say. The other witness' testimony was either quite remote in point of time, or related to an incident eight years after the marriage, or had to do with matters having no great legal significance.

The plaintiff has not satisfied the burden of proving, clearly and definitely, that the defendant was an "insane person" at the particular time of this marriage, March 21, 1950,—that she was at that time incapable of understanding the nature of the act, that she had insufficient mental capacity to enter into the status and understand the nature, effect, duties, and obligations of the marriage contract, that she was mentally incapable of giving an intelligent, understanding consent, or that her mind could not and did not act rationally regarding the precise thing in contemplation, marriage, and this particular marriage in dispute. The decree is correct and it will be affirmed.

NOTES AND QUESTIONS

1.   Is the *Larson* court concerned with capacity to *make* the contract or to *perform* the contract?

2.   Less capacity is required to consent to a marriage than is required to execute a will, sign a deed, or to make a business contract. The fact that a spouse has a guardian or conservator will not, by itself, invalidate a marriage based on lack of capacity. *See* Uniform Probate Code §§ 5–401, 5–309.

3.   Incapacity may derive from disease, mental retardation, or the influence of alcohol or drugs. But the burden of proof is on the party attacking the marriage, who is often required to show lack of capacity by clear and convincing evidence. *See In re* Estate of Hendrickson, 805 P.2d 20 (Kan. 1991). Would a prior adjudication of mental incompetence be conclusive on the issue of capacity to marry? *Compare* Geitner v. Townsend, 312 S.E.2d 236 (N.C. App. 1984) (no) *with* May v. Leneair, 297 N.W.2d 882 (Mich. App. 1980) (yes).

Problem 3-6:

Greg is 86 years old and suffers from Alzheimer's disease. He can remember events from forty years ago as if they were yesterday but has severe short-term memory loss. He seldom knows what day or year it is. Betty, a 30 year-old neighbor, convinces Greg to marry her. They go through a ceremony and Betty moves into Greg's house and puts her name on the joint checking account. Greg's children would like to annul the marriage. Do they have a basis? *See* Moss v. Davis, 794 A.2d 1288 (Del. Fam. 2001); Campbell v. Thomas, 897 N.Y.S.2d 460 (App. Div. 2010).

2.   Intent to Contract

The parties must intend to marry. If consent to marry was obtained by force, duress, or fraud, the party with clean hands may be able to annul the marriage. Fraud generally must go to the essentials of the marriage. What goes to the "essentials" is determined on a case-by-case basis. *See* Chapter 11, Section 4B.

In contrast to a fraudulently obtained marriage, a "sham" marriage is a marriage for a limited purpose and with a limited intent, for example a marriage entered simply to "give the baby a name." Most courts have upheld such marriages. *See* Schibi v. Schibi, 136 Conn. 196, 69 A.2d 831 (1949) (husband was denied annulment where parties married to legitimize an unborn child but never intended to cohabit as husband and wife). *See generally* J.H. Wade, *Limited Purpose Marriages*, 45 MOD. L. REV. 159 (1982).

Until 1986, when Congress substantially tightened the immigration laws, the most typical sham marriage was one arranged for the sole purpose of obtaining a visa to enter the United States. Typically, the foreign national paid money to an American citizen whom he or she married without any intention of maintaining a marital relationship. *See* Bu Roe v. Immigration & Naturalization Service, 771 F.2d 1328 (9th Cir. 1985); Faustin v. Lewis, 427 A.2d 1105 (N.J. 1981); Eileen P. Lynsky, Note, *Immigration Marriage Fraud Amendments of 1986: Till Congress Do Us Part*, 41 U. MIAMI L. REV. 1087 (1987).

Marriage to a United States citizen exempts an alien from the quota restrictions of the Immigration and Nationality Act (INA), 8 U.S.C. § 1151(a), (b). The Immigration Marriage Fraud Amendments (IMFA), 8 U.S.C. § 1154(b) require that an alien obtaining residence through a marriage less than two years old is given a *conditional* permanent residence. The United States Citizen and Immigration Services (USCIS) tries to interpret the true intention of the couple entering into a marriage when reviewing immigration petitions. The relevant factors are: the length of time the couple has known each other; the frequency of meetings of the couple prior to the marriage; whether the couple have lived together or presently live together; whether the couple married only after one party became the subject of an investigation, removal, or deportation proceedings. The person has to come back two years later with the petitioning spouse and show they are still married or if the marriage was terminated, that the marriage was entered in good faith. Prior to the two-year anniversary of receiving permanent residence, the parties are required to file a petition to "remove the condition." The parties must submit documents showing the continuity of the bona fides of the marriage, such as cohabitation, income tax records, bank records, car and medical insurance records, rent/mortgage documents and birth certificates of children born to the union. *See* Nicole Lawrence Ezer, *The Intersection of Immigration Law and Family Law*, 40 FAM. L. Q. 339 (2006). The United States Citizenship and Immigration Services (CIS) became the successor organization to the INS after Congress moved immigration functions from the Department of Justice to the Department of Homeland Security (DHS).

An immigration petition may not be approved for the alien who was married after the commencement of removal, exclusion, or deportation proceeding until the alien has resided outside the United States for at least two years, unless the alien spouse can prove the marriage was a good faith marriage and not solely for immigration purposes. INA § 204(g), § 245 (e). Amendments allow an exemption when the alien establishes by clear and convincing evidence that the marriage was entered in good faith, was not for immigration purposes, and was not connected with the payment of anything but a lawyer's fee. 8 C.F.R. 2204.2(a)(1)(iii)(D) and (E).

The Department of Homeland Security (DHS) can revoke an alien's conditional status and begin removal procedures if it learns that the marriage is fraudulent. 8 C.F.R. 204.2(a)(1)(ii); 8 CFR 216.3(b). If DHS ever determines that an alien has entered or attempted or conspired to enter a fraudulent marriage, no residency petition for that alien may ever be approved. *See* INA § 204(c); *Family Based Avenues to Permanent Residence in* ROBERT C. DIVINE AND R. BLAKE CHISAM, IMMIGRATION LAW PRACTICE: 2005–2006 EDITION.

Problem 3-7:

Abigail and Jake entered into a marriage so that Jake could avoid deportation proceedings. Jake was killed in an automobile accident. Can Jake's heirs attack the marriage? *See* Kunz v. Kunz, 136 P.3d 1278 (Utah App. 2006).

B. SOLEMNIZATION AND LICENSING

All states regulate the process of obtaining a marriage license and solemnization of marriage. The Uniform Marriage and Divorce Act has served as the model for a number of state licensing and solemnization statutes.

UNIFORM MARRIAGE AND DIVORCE ACT
9A U.L.A. 163, 166 (1987).

Section 203.

(a) When a marriage application has been completed and signed by both parties to a prospective marriage and at least one party has appeared before the [marriage license] clerk and paid the marriage license fee of [_____], the [marriage license] clerk shall issue a license to marry and a marriage certificate form upon being furnished:

(1) satisfactory proof that each party to the marriage will have attained the age of 18 years at the time the marriage license is effective, or will have attained the age of 16 years and has either the consent to the marriage of both parents or his guardian, or judicial approval; [or if under the age of 16 years, has both the consent of both parents or his guardian and judicial approval;] and

(2) satisfactory proof that the marriage is not prohibited; [and]

[(3) a certificate of the results of any medical examination required by the laws of this State].

Section 206. [Solemnization and Registration]

(a) A marriage may be solemnized by a judge of a court of record, by a public official whose powers include solemnization of marriages, or in accordance with any mode of solemnization recognized by any religious denomination, Indian Nation or Tribe, or Native Group. Either the person solemnizing the marriage, or, if no individual acting alone solemnized the marriage, a party to the marriage, shall complete the marriage certificate form and forward it to the [marriage license] clerk.

(b) If a party to a marriage is unable to be present at the solemnization, he may authorize in writing a third person to act as his proxy. If the person solemnizing the marriage is satisfied that the absent party is unable to be present and has consented to the marriage, he may solemnize the marriage by proxy. If he is not satisfied, the parties may petition the [_____] court for an order permitting the marriage to be solemnized by proxy.

(c) Upon receipt of the marriage certificate, the [marriage license] clerk shall register the marriage.

(d) The solemnization of the marriage is not invalidated by the fact that the person solemnizing the marriage was not legally qualified to solemnize it, if either party to the marriage believed him to be so qualified.

COLO. REV. STAT. § 14–2–109

A marriage may be solemnized by a judge of a court, by a court magistrate, by a retired judge of a court, by a public official whose powers include solemnization of marriages, by the parties to the marriage, or in accordance with any mode of solemnization recognized by any religious denomination or Indian nation or tribe. * * *

CARABETTA V. CARABETTA

Supreme Court of Connecticut, 1980.
182 Conn. 344, 438 A.2d 109.

PETERS, J.

The plaintiff and the defendant exchanged marital vows before a priest in the rectory of Our Lady of Mt. Carmel Church of Meriden, on August 25, 1955, according to the rite of the Roman Catholic Church, although they had failed to obtain a marriage license. Thereafter they lived together as husband and wife, raising a family of four children, all of whose birth certificates listed the defendant as their father. Until the present action, the defendant had no memory or recollection of ever having denied that the plaintiff and the defendant were married.

The issue before us is whether, under Connecticut law, despite solemnization according to an appropriate religious ceremony, a marriage is void where there has been noncompliance with the statutory requirement of a marriage license. This is a question of first impression in this state.

* * *

The governing statutes at the time of the purported marriage between these parties contained two kinds of regulations concerning the requirements for a legally valid marriage. One kind of regulation concerned substantive requirements determining those eligible to be married. * * * The other kind of regulation concerns the formalities prescribed by the state for the effectuation of a legally valid marriage. These required formalities, in turn, are of two sorts: a marriage license and a solemnization. In *Hames v. Hames*, * * * we interpreted our statutes not to make void a marriage consummated after the issuance of a license but deficient for want of due solemnization. Today we examine the statutes in the reverse case, a marriage duly solemnized but deficient for want of a marriage license.

* * *

In the absence of express language in the governing statute declaring a marriage void for failure to observe a statutory requirement, this court has held in an unbroken line of cases that such a marriage, though imperfect, is dissoluble rather than void. We see no reason to import into the language "[n]o persons shall be joined in marriage until [they have applied for] a license," a meaning more drastic than that assigned in *Gould v. Gould*, [78 Conn. 242, 61 A. 604 (1905)] to the statute that * * * provided that "[n]o man and woman, either of whom is epileptic * * * shall intermarry." Although the state may well have a legitimate interest in the health of those who are about to marry, *Gould v. Gould* held that the legislature would not be deemed to have entirely invalidated a marriage contract in violation of such health requirements unless the statute itself expressly declared the marriage to be void. Then as now, the legislature had chosen to use the language of voidness selectively, applying it to some but not to all of the statutory requirements for the creation of a legal marriage. Now as then, the legislature has the competence to choose to sanction those who solemnize a marriage without a marriage license rather than those who marry without a marriage license. In sum, we conclude that the legislature's failure to expressly characterize as void a marriage properly celebrated without a license means that such a marriage is not invalid.

* * *

The conclusion that a ceremonial marriage contracted without a marriage license is not null and void finds support, furthermore, in the decisions in other jurisdictions. In the majority of states, unless the licensing statute plainly makes an unlicensed marriage invalid, "the cases find the policy favoring valid marriages sufficiently strong to justify upholding the unlicensed ceremony. This seems the correct result. Most such cases arise long after the parties have acted upon the assumption that they are married, and no useful purpose is served by avoiding the long-standing relationship. Compliance with the licensing laws can better be attained by safeguards operating before the license is issued, as by a more careful investigation by the issuing authority or the person marrying the parties." Clark, Domestic Relations, p. 41 (1968).

Since the marriage that the trial court was asked to dissolve was not void, the trial court erred in granting the motion to dismiss for lack of jurisdiction over the subject matter.

NOTES AND QUESTIONS

1.   The Connecticut court concludes that a marriage without a license is neither invalid nor "null and void" and finds that the trial court had jurisdiction over the subject matter. Does this fuzzy rhetoric mean that the marriage is valid? Connecticut does not recognize common law marriage. Is this case a "near-revival"? Weigh state policies favoring and disfavoring upholding the marriage in this case. A couple of other states have found that marriages performed without a license were "absolutely void." *See* Yaghoubinejad v. Haghighi, 894 A.2d 1173 (N.J. Super. Ct. App. Div. 2006); Nelson v. Marshall, 869 S.W.2d 132 (Mo. App. 1993). *But see In re* Estate of Peacock, 788 S.E.2d 191 (N.C. App. 2016).

2.   Waiting periods between the issuance of a marriage license and solemnization of the marriage are imposed by approximately three quarters of the states and range from one to ten days, with three days the most common requirement. Why have waiting periods? Under *Carabetta,* is a marriage performed before the expiration of a state-mandated waiting period invalid?

3.   With destination weddings on the rise, problems occasionally arise over who is authorized to solemnize a marriage. For example, some courts and the Attorney General of Tennessee (Opinion No. U97–041) have found that "ordained" ministers of the Universal Life Church are not "ministers" within the meaning of state laws describing who can administer the rites of marriage. *See* State v. Lynch, 272 S.E.2d 349 (N.C. 1980) (reversing a bigamy conviction where first marriage was performed by person holding $10.00 mail order certificate from Universal Life Church); Ranieri v. Ranieri, 539 N.Y.S.2d 382 (App. Div. 1989). *But see* Matter of Blackwell, 531 So. 2d 1193 (Miss. 1988) (sustaining marriage performed by minister of Universal Life Church). Would a marriage solemnized by a Universal Life Church minister be valid under *Carabetta*? Under UMDA § 206(d)? Under the Colorado statute?

4.   UMDA § 206(b) and many other state statutes permit a marriage to be solemnized by proxy. The usual reason for a proxy marriage is that the bride and groom are in different states (or countries). The parties may designate a "stand in" who appears for the absent party at the ceremony. Some states require both parties to be present at the ceremony. Would an internet connection be sufficient (with video)? *See* Farah v. Farah, 429 S.E.2d 626 (Va. App. 1993) (not recognizing proxy marriage between Algerian citizen and Pakistani citizen celebrated in England (where neither were present).

5.   *Premarital Education:* Several state legislatures have authorized money incentives for couples who take certain premarital education classes. One study indicates that premarital education classes work to promote healthy marriages and reduce divorce in three ways: (1) they foster greater deliberation in entering marriage; (2) reinforce the idea that marriage is worthy of commitment and depends primarily on knowledge and skills rather than romance and luck; and (3) couples who have had counseling are more likely to seek marital therapy for relationship problems earlier. *See* Scott Stanley, *Premarital Education, Marital Quality, and Marital Stability: Findings From a Large Random Household Survey*, 20 J. FAM. PSYCH. 117 (2006). *See also* Alan J. Hawkins, *Will Legislation to Encourage Premarital Education Strengthen Marriage and Reduce Divorce*, 9 J. L. & FAM. STUDIES 79 (2007).

5. EXCEPTIONS TO THE FORMAL REQUIREMENTS

A. COMMON LAW MARRIAGE

P. BROMLEY, FAMILY LAW
27–29 (4th ed. 1971).

In England, until the middle of the eighteenth century a marriage could be contracted in one of three ways:

(a) *In facie ecclesiae*, after the publishing of banns or upon a license, before witnesses, and with the consent of the parent or guardian of a party who was a minor. Such a marriage was obviously valid for all purposes.

(b) Clandestinely, *per verba de praesenti* before a clerk in holy orders, but not *in facie ecclesiae*. This * * * was as valid as if it had been solemnized *in facie ecclesiae*.

(c) *Per verba de praesenti* or *per verba de futuro* with subsequent sexual intercourse, but where the words were not spoken in the presence of an ordained priest or deacon. Whilst such a marriage would no longer produce all the legal effects of coverture at common law, it was nevertheless valid for many purposes. Such a union was indissoluble, so that, if either party to it subsequently married another, the later marriage could be annulled. Moreover, either party could obtain an order from an ecclesiastical court calling upon the other to solemnize the marriage *in facie ecclesiae*.

Lord Hardwicke's Act.—It needs little imagination to picture the social evils which resulted from such a state of law. A person who had believed himself to be validly married for years would suddenly find that his marriage was a nullity because of a previous clandestine or irregular union, the existence of which he had never before suspected. Children would marry without their parents' consent, and if the minor was a girl with a large fortune, the old common law rule that a wife's property vested in her husband on marriage made her a particularly attractive catch. The "Fleet" parsons thrived—profligate clergy who traded in clandestine marriages. By the middle of the eighteenth century matters had come to such a pass that there was a danger in certain sections of society that such marriages would become the rule rather than the exception.

It was to stop these abuses that Lord Hardwicke's Act was passed in 1753. The principle underlying this Act was to secure publicity by enacting that no marriage should be valid unless it was solemnized according to the rites of the Church of England in the parish church of one of the parties in the presence of a clergyman and two other witnesses. Unless a license had been obtained, banns had to be published in the parish churches of both parties for three Sundays. If either party was under the age of 21, parental consent had to be obtained as well, unless this was impossible to obtain or was unreasonably withheld, in which case the consent of the Lord Chancellor had to be obtained. If these stringent provisions were not observed, the marriage would in the vast majority of cases be void. Furthermore, the Act abolished the jurisdiction of the Ecclesiastical Courts to compel persons to celebrate the marriage *in facie ecclesiae* if they had contracted a marriage *per verba de praesenti* or *futuro* followed by consummation.

Marriage Act 1823.—Whilst Lord Hardwicke's Act effectively put a stop to clandestine marriages in England, it caused an almost greater social evil. For the new law was so stringent and the consequence of failing to observe it—the avoidance of the marriage—so harsh, that many couples deliberately evaded it by getting married in Scotland. This was particularly the case when one of the parties was a minor and parental consent was withheld; so that the 70 years following the passing of the Act saw an increasing number of "Gretna Green" marriages. It was in an attempt to prevent this that the Legislature in 1823 repealed Lord Hardwicke's Act and replaced it by a new Marriage Act. So far as the positive directions of the earlier Act were concerned, *viz.* the necessity of the solemnization of the marriage in the church of the parish in which one of the parties resided after the publication of banns or the grant of a license, they were reenacted with only a few minor alterations of detail; where the new Act differed largely was in the effect of non-compliance with these directions. A marriage was now to be void only if both parties *knowingly and wilfully* intermarried in any other place than the church wherein the banns might be published, or without the due publication of banns or the obtaining of a license, or if they *knowingly and wilfully* consented to the solemnization of the marriage by a person not in holy orders. In all other cases the marriage was to be valid notwithstanding any breach in the prescribed formalities.

———————

At one time nearly two-thirds of the states recognized common law marriages. American acceptance of common law marriage reflected the vast expanses of the American frontier, where there were few clergymen or state officials to perform marriage ceremonies. "[A] rigid execution of [the laws requiring ceremonial marriage]," courts opined, "would bastardize a vast majority of the children which have been born within the state for half a century." Rodebaugh v. Sanks, 2 Watts 9, 11 (Pa. 1833). *See also* Walter Otto Weyrauch, *Metamorphoses of Marriage*, 13 FAM. L. Q. 415 (1980); Note, *Governing Through Contract: Common Law Marriage in the Nineteenth Century*, 107 YALE L. J. 185 (1998).

In 2017, only a handful of jurisdictions—Colorado, Iowa, Kansas, Montana, New Hampshire (persons cohabitating and acknowledging each other as husband and wife), Rhode Island, South Carolina, Texas, and Utah—continue to recognize common law marriage. Several states which formerly allowed common law marriage will recognize those formed before the date of its abolition: Alabama (1/1/2017), Georgia (11/1/97), Idaho (1/1/96), Ohio (10/10/91), Oklahoma (11/1/98), Pennsylvania (1/1/05). But because a marriage valid where contracted is valid everywhere, absent a serious public policy concern, common law marriage has broader application.

When established, a common law marriage is legally no different than a formal, ceremonial marriage. But the fact of the marriage must be established by showing:

(1) intent to marry on the part of both parties;

(2) capacity to marry; and

(3) "holding out" (cohabitation) by the parties that they are husband and wife. Some states require "consummation" of the marriage.

The burden of proof is on the party asserting the existence of a marriage. As one court noted:

> [T]he courts do not look on * * * [common law] marriages with favor, and * * * where a common-law marriage is claimed, the courts will carefully scrutinize the evidence and require that the

marriage be established by clear and convincing evidence. C.J.S. Marriage § 6, p. 818. If any of the essentials of a common-law marriage are lacking, the relationship is illicit and meretricious and is not a marriage. * * * There is no presumption that persons are married. Accordingly, the burden of proving a marriage rests on the party who asserts it, particularly where a common-law marriage is asserted; and an allegation that a party was not married does not thereby require a pleader to assume the burden of proof of non-marriage. * * * A claim of common-law marriage is regarded with suspicion, and will be closely scrutinized. Thus, in order to establish a common-law marriage, all of the essential elements of such a relationship must be shown by clear, consistent and convincing evidence, especially must all of the essential elements of such a relationship be shown when one of the parties is dead; and such marriage must be proved by a preponderance.

In re Estate of Fisher, 176 N.W.2d 801, 804–805 (Iowa 1970). *See also* Staudenmayer v. Staudenmayer, 714 A.2d 1016 (Pa. 1998) (noting that common law marriages are tolerated, but not encouraged).

IN RE ESTATE OF KEIMIG
Supreme Court of Kansas, 1974.
215 Kan. 869, 528 P.2d 1228.

HARMAN, COMMISSIONER.

This is an appeal from a judgment denying the claim of an alleged common law wife to her purported husband's estate.

The plaintiff-appellant, Ruth Ann Huss, was first married in 1920 to Joseph Cavanaugh. A daughter was born as a result of this marriage. In 1922 appellant secured a divorce from Mr. Cavanaugh.

In 1925 appellant was married in Kansas City, Kansas to Walter A. Keimig, the decedent whose estate she now claims. Eventually marital difficulties developed between appellant and Walter and they started living apart. Appellant filed suit for divorce in Atchison, Kansas, and obtained it March 21, 1935. That evening Walter went to appellant to discuss their situation. They decided to forgive and forget and go back together again. The couple spent the night together at plaintiff's father's home. The next day they returned to the same home in which they had resided prior to the separation and divorce.

After the reconciliation the couple held each other out as man and wife for the next nine years. During this time they resided in Shannon in Atchison County, Kansas, where Walter farmed extensively and conducted a farm equipment business. Appellant helped in this latter business and also carried out domestic tasks including cooking for the hired help and caring for Walter's father who lived with them. She signed her name as Mrs. Keimig; Walter introduced her as Mrs. Walter Keimig or "my wife;" she was known by Walter's employees as Mrs. Keimig; when appellant's daughter married in 1938, the nuptial announcements were made by "Mr. and Mrs. Walter Keimig."

In the spring of 1944 appellant made out a check to herself for $500.00, cashed it, left decedent and went to Plainville, Kansas. There she joined Albert Huss, a former farm employee of Walter. A short while thereafter she returned to Walter at Shannon for about a week, then departed again and went to Great Bend, Kansas, where she commenced living with Albert Huss. Appellant worked for a while in Great Bend using the name Cavanaugh. She lived with Mr. Huss in several western Kansas towns and eventually began using the name Huss. As time passed she and Mr. Huss acquired real estate in the names of Albert and Ruth Huss, husband and wife; their insurance was carried in the same way; appellant was listed in the census record as Ruth Huss; she received her driver's license and was assessed for personal property under that name; Huss named her as his wife in a deed conveying to her his interest in realty; she signed mortgages under the name of Ruth Huss. In 1954 appellant filed suit in Barton County, Kansas, for divorce from Albert Huss. Later she had this action dismissed on the ground she and Albert had reconciled their marital differences. Upon reaching the requisite ages Huss and appellant applied for and received social security benefits as husband and wife. Appellant lived continuously with Mr. Huss and on January 13, 1972—which was subsequent to Walter Keimig's death—they were formally married in a ceremony at Stillwater, Oklahoma.

Meanwhile, Walter Keimig dated other women. In 1962 he and defendant-appellee Goldie Keimig, then Goldie Sherrer, started living together at the Keimig home in Doniphan County. On July 20, 1967, Walter and appellee Goldie were married in a civil ceremony at Miami, Oklahoma. Walter told appellee he was divorced, single and free to marry. Prior to his marriage to Goldie, Walter executed documents conveying interests in realty in which he was described as an unmarried man. On March 26, 1970, Walter executed his last will which provided:

"I give, devise and bequeath all of my property, real, personal and mixed, and wheresoever situated unto my beloved wife, Goldie Keimig."

In a prior will executed in 1946 in which he referred to himself as unmarried, he had directed that all his property should go to his brother Philip Keimig.

On June 21, 1971, Walter died in Ray County, Missouri, where he and appellee were then living. On June 29, 1971, upon appellee's petition the probate court of Doniphan County, Kansas, admitted Walter's last will to probate and appointed her as his executrix. On December 29, 1971, appellant, using the name of Ruth Ann Keimig, petitioned the probate court for an order extending the statutory period of time for a surviving spouse to file an election. The probate court granted a thirty day extension.

On January 25, 1972, twelve days after her ceremonial marriage to Albert Huss, appellant filed an election to take under the law, alleging she was Walter's surviving spouse and sole heir at law. An evidentiary hearing was held upon this election. The probate court ruled against appellant on the ground she was not Walter's legal wife at the time of his death. Appellant appealed to the district court of Doniphan County where the matter was heard anew. That court likewise ruled against appellant. After making certain factual findings it held:

> 17. That Claimant has failed to show the establishment of a common law marriage with Walter A. Keimig subsequent to their divorce, in that Claimant did not show a marriage agreement in addition to an agreement to cohabit.

> 18. The Claimant has failed to overcome the presumption of the validity of a subsequent marriage of Walter A. Keimig and Goldie Sherrer.

Appellant's motion for new trial was denied and the present appeal ensued * * * appellant's points on appeal as to the trial court's first finding are embraced in the assertion the trial court erred under all the evidence in failing to find appellant was the common law wife of Walter Keimig at the time of his death. She urges that Walter was rendered incapable of contracting marriage with appellee by reason of the fact appellant remained his legal spouse.

Kansas has long recognized the validity of common law marriage, the essential elements of which are: (1) A capacity of the parties to marry; (2) a present marriage agreement between the parties; and (3) a holding out of each other as husband and wife to the public. Common law marriages between persons previously divorced from each other have been considered judicially in other states. It is generally held, and we think correctly so, that the same tests and standards used in determining whether persons with no previous matrimonial history have entered into a common law marriage are to be applied in determining whether a common law remarriage exists between divorced spouses. This does not mean the fact of the previous marriage and divorce is to be removed from consideration or placed in a vacuum apart from other facts in the case.

The district court here specifically found appellant had failed to show the establishment of a common law marriage with Keimig in that she did not show a marriage agreement in addition to consent to cohabit. * * *

[I]n *In re Estate of Freeman*, 171 Kan. 211, 231 P.2d 261, we said:

In order to constitute a valid common law marriage there must also be a present marriage agreement rather than an agreement to be married in the future and a holding out of each other to the public as husband and wife. (p. 213)

However, the present marriage agreement need not be in any particular form.

We have already summarized the testimony respecting the resumption of cohabitation between appellant and Walter following their divorce and there is no question a holding out as man and wife was shown. The whole evidence concerning what occurred when Walter went to see appellant at her father's home on the evening the divorce was granted is disclosed by the testimony of appellant as follows:

Q.   All right, during the course of the evening in connection with your discussion about your marriage problems, tell us please what you said and he said as nearly as you recall about this divorce and about the marriage?

A.   Well, we decided we never had no divorce, we just went back as we always had been when we first got married.

Q.   And during the course of that evening did you have any discussion forgiving one another about what had gone on?

A.   Yes.

Q.   You say yes?

A.   Yes.

Q.   And what were those discussions, what did you say and what did he say as near as you recall about the things that had been, that bothered you before?

A.   We were going to forget them and go back and live as we should have lived.

Although the evidence revealed a considerable period of living together as man and wife, we cannot say the trial court was compelled or required by it or by all the evidence to find that appellant and Walter actually contemplated or entered into a new agreement to become husband and wife at the critical time in question. They did not say so and, aside from holding out, their subsequent conduct belied the fact. They may have considered remarriage in the future if and when that became mutually agreeable. Each definitely considered himself single for a period of time after their twice repeated separation and each became interested in new marital partners to the extent of a long time holding out by appellant as the wife of another, of whom she sought formal riddance by divorce, and of a ceremonial marriage by Walter. It appears it was only some time after Walter's death that appellant perceived herself as his widow. By coincidence she was in Atchison, Kansas, visiting her granddaughter at the time of Walter's death. She learned of his death then but did nothing about the funeral nor did she attend it. At that time she made no inquiry about Walter's estate and did nothing until after her daughter contacted her. Her testimony was she did not want Walter's not inconsiderable estate for herself—she wanted to give it to her daughter and to Walter's brother Philip, who appeared as a witness in support of her cause. Appellant's inconsistency in her marital positions was such as to render her entire testimony suspect. The most that can be said in her favor is that a factual issue was presented by reason of differing interpretations which could be placed upon all the evidence and the trial court after hearing it resolved any conflict by finding there was no present marriage agreement when appellant and Walter resumed cohabitation. We simply cannot say there was no substantial evidence in support thereof and the finding must be approved.

Having reached the foregoing conclusion it becomes unnecessary to consider whether the trial court correctly found that appellant had failed to overcome the presumption of the validity of Walter's subsequent marriage to appellee. The judgment is affirmed.

NOTES AND QUESTIONS

1. If Walter Keimig had died in 1942, would the Kansas court have found Ruth to be the common law wife for purposes of inheritance?

2. One source of hostility to common law marriage is the fact that common law marriage claims are most typically made when one "spouse" dies and the other claims a right to inherit or obtain some other form of death benefit, such as worker's compensation or Social Security survivor's benefits; the court's determination is thus retrospective rather than prospective. *See In re* Estate of Dallman, 228 N.W.2d 187 (Iowa 1975); Renshaw v. Heckler, 787 F.2d 50 (2d Cir. 1986). Of course, a "spouse" might also seek to establish a common law marriage in order to obtain divorce entitlements, such as alimony and marital property distribution, at separation. What problems does retrospective marriage determination create?

3. Courts require clear and convincing evidence of common law marriage. Reese v. Holston, 67 So. 3d 109 (Ala. Civ. App. 2011). What is the purpose of the holding out requirement? Over how long a period must the holding out occur? Is signing a hotel register enough? *See* Winfield v. Renfro, 821 S.W.2d 640 (Tex. App. 1991) (no); Boswell v. Boswell, 497 So. 2d 479 (Ala. 1986).

4. A common law marriage requires capacity to marry. If, as in *Keimig*, one spouse is married when cohabitation begins, when must the present

agreement to marry be formed? For another case involving impediments to the marriage and three states, *see* Orr v. Bowen, 648 F. Supp. 1510 (D. Nev. 1986).

5.   Where a couple has lived in several different states and one recognizes common law marriage, the issue arises whether the parties' contacts with that state were sufficient to establish a common law marriage. *See* Travers v. Reinhardt, 205 U.S. 423 (1907) (parties living in New Jersey which recognized common law marriage at time of husband's death sufficient to establish marriage); Jennings v. Hurt, 554 N.Y.S.2d 220 (App. Div. 1990) (finding that actor William Hurt and Sandra Jennings did not establish a common law marriage while in South Carolina filming "The Big Chill"); Clark Sand Co., Inc. v. Kelly, 60 So. 3d 149 (Miss. 2011) (recognizing common law marriage created in Alabama).

6.   Compare two recent "modern" common law marriage statutes:

UTAH CODE ANN. § 30–1–4.5

(1)   A marriage which is not solemnized according to this chapter shall be legal and valid if a court or administrative order establishes that it arises out of a contract between two consenting parties who:

    (a)   are capable of giving consent;

    (b)   are legally capable of entering a solemnized marriage under the provisions of this chapter;

    (c)   have cohabited;

    (d)   mutually assume marital rights, duties, and obligations; and

    (e)   hold themselves out as and have acquired a uniform and general reputation as husband and wife.

(2)   The determination or establishment of a marriage under this section must occur during the relationship described in Subsection (1), or within one year following the termination of that relationship. Evidence of a marriage recognizable under this section may be manifested in any form, and may be proved under the same general rules of evidence as facts in other cases.

TEX. FAM. CODE § 2.402

(a)   A declaration of informal marriage shall be executed on a form prescribed by the Bureau of Vital Statistics * * * and provided by the county clerk. Each party to the declaration shall provide the information required in the form.

(b)   The declaration form shall contain: * * *

(5)   a printed declaration and oath reading: "I SOLEMNLY SWEAR (OR AFFIRM) THAT WE, THE UNDERSIGNED, ARE MARRIED TO EACH OTHER BY VIRTUE OF THE FOLLOWING FACTS: ON OR ABOUT (DATE) WE AGREED TO BE MARRIED, AND AFTER THAT DATE WE LIVED TOGETHER AS HUSBAND AND WIFE AND IN THIS STATE

WE REPRESENTED TO OTHERS THAT WE WERE MARRIED. SINCE THE DATE OF MARRIAGE TO THE OTHER PARTY I HAVE NOT BEEN MARRIED TO ANY OTHER PERSON. THIS DECLARATION IS TRUE AND THE INFORMATION IN IT WHICH I HAVE GIVEN IS CORRECT" * * *

What, if any, problems with common law marriage do these statutes attempt to cure? How successful are they? *See* Kelley v. Kelley, 9 P.3d 171 (Utah App. 2000).

7.   Does acceptance of common law marriage require the creation of common law divorce? If yes, is the Utah statute a good way to deal with the problem?

Problem 3-8:

In 2012, Gail and Tom were married in Missouri, which has abolished common law marriage. In 2013, Gail moved out of the marital home but did not obtain a divorce. Thereafter, Gail met and married Jim in Kansas, which recognizes common law marriage. In 2015, Gail and Jim moved to Missouri. Jim first learned about Tom when he and Gail were notified of Tom's death in January 2016. Outraged, Jim moved back to Kansas. After a short separation, Gail moved back in with him in July 2016. In December 2016, Gail was killed in a car accident. Is Jim a lawful spouse for inheritance purposes? *See* Kelderhaus v. Kelderhaus, 467 S.E.2d 303 (Va. App. 1996).

B. THE PUTATIVE SPOUSE DOCTRINE

The putative spouse doctrine derives from the civil law and was first found in former French or Spanish colonies, including California, Louisiana, and Texas. The doctrine was recognized in the Uniform Marriage and Divorce Act, however, and has spread to a number of common law states.

UNIFORM MARRIAGE AND DIVORCE ACT § 209
9A U.L.A. 174 (1987).

Any person who has cohabited with another to whom he is not legally married in the good faith belief that he was married to that person is a putative spouse until knowledge of the fact that he is not legally married terminates his status and prevents acquisition of further rights. A putative spouse acquires the rights conferred upon a legal spouse, including the right to maintenance following termination of his status, whether or not the marriage is prohibited (§ 207) or declared invalid (§ 208). If there is a legal spouse or other putative spouses, rights acquired by a putative spouse do not supersede the rights of the legal spouse or those acquired by other putative spouses, but the court shall apportion property, maintenance, and support rights among the claimants as appropriate in the circumstances and in the interests of justice.

IN RE ESTATE OF VARGAS

California Court of Appeals, 1974.
36 Cal. App. 3d 714, 111 Cal. Rptr. 779.

FLEMING, ASSOCIATE JUSTICE.

For 24 years Juan Vargas lived a double life as husband and father to two separate families, neither of which knew of the other's existence. This terrestrial paradise came to an end in 1969 when Juan died intestate in an automobile accident. In subsequent heirship proceedings the probate court divided his estate equally between the two wives. Juan's first wife Mildred appeals, contending that the evidence did not establish Juan's second wife Josephine as a putative spouse, and that even if Josephine were considered a putative spouse an equal division of the estate was erroneous.

Mildred presented evidence that she and Juan married in 1929, raised three children, and lived together continuously in Los Angeles until Juan's death in 1969. From 1945 until his death Juan never spent more than a week or 10 days away from home. They acquired no substantial assets until after 1945.

Josephine countered with evidence that she met Juan in 1942 while employed in his exporting business. They married in Las Vegas in February 1945 and went through a second marriage ceremony in Santa Ana in May 1945. Josephine knew Juan had been previously married, but Juan assured her he had acquired a divorce. In July 1945 they moved into a home in West Los Angeles and there raised a family of four children. After 1949 Juan no longer spent his nights at home, explaining to Josephine that he spent the nights in Long Beach in order to be close to his business, but he and Josephine continued to engage in sexual relations until his death in 1969. He visited Josephine and their children every weekday for dinner, spent time with them weekends, supported the family, and exercised control over its affairs as husband and father. Throughout the years Josephine continued to perform secretarial work for Juan's business at home without pay.

The foregoing evidence amply supports the court's finding that Josephine was a putative spouse. An innocent participant who has duly solemnized a matrimonial union which is void because of some legal infirmity acquires the status of putative spouse. Although Josephine's marriage was void because Juan was still married to Mildred, Josephine, according to her testimony, married Juan in the good-faith belief he was divorced from his first wife. Her testimony was not inherently improbable; her credibility was a question for determination by the trial court; and court appearance of her testimony established her status as a putative spouse.

Query d

The more difficult question involves the equal division of Juan's estate between Mildred and Josephine.

California courts have relied on at least two legal theories to justify the award of an interest in a decedent's estate to a putative spouse. The theory of "quasi-marital property" equates property rights acquired during a putative marriage with community property rights acquired during a legal marriage. Subsequent to the time of Juan's death this theory was codified in Civil Code § 4452.

A second legal theory treats the putative marriage as a partnership: "In effect, the innocent putative spouse was in partnership or a joint enterprise with her spouse, contributing her services—and in this case, her earnings—to the common enterprise. Thus, their accumulated property was held in effect in tenancy-in-common in equal shares. Upon death of the husband, only his half interest is considered as community property, to which the rights of the lawful spouse attach."

In practice, these sometimes-conflicting theories have proved no more than convenient explanations to justify reasonable results, for when the theories do not fit the facts, courts have customarily resorted to general principles of equity to effect a just disposition of property rights. For example, in *Brown v. Brown*, 274 Cal. App. 2d 178, 82 Cal. Rptr. 238, the court found that a legal wife's acquiescence in a putative wife's 28-year marriage equitably estopped the legal wife from claiming any interest in the community property.

The present case is complicated by the fact that the laws regulating succession and the disposition of marital property are not designed to cope with the extraordinary circumstance of purposeful bigamy at the expense of two innocent parties. The laws of marital succession assume compliance with basic law and do not provide for contingencies arising during the course of felonious activity. For this reason resort to equitable principles becomes particularly appropriate here. * * * Equity acts "in order to meet the requirements of every case, and to satisfy the needs of a progressive social condition, in which the primary rights and duties are constantly arising, and new kinds of wrongs are constantly committed." Equity need not wait upon precedent "but will assert itself in those situations where right and justice would be defeated but for its intervention." * * * For example, in *Estate of Krone*, where the putative husband died intestate and there was no legal wife, the court awarded the entire quasi-marital estate to the putative wife, even though the putative wife had no legal claim to the husband's share of the quasi-marital estate.

In the present case, depending on which statute or legal theory is applied, both Mildred, as legal spouse, and Josephine, as putative spouse, have valid or plausible claims to at least half, perhaps three-quarters, possibly all, of Juan's estate. The court found that both wives contributed in indeterminable amounts and proportions to the accumulations of the community. Since statutes and judicial decisions provide no sure guidance for the resolution of the controversy, the probate court cut the Gordian knot of competing claims and divided the estate equally between the two wives, presumably on the theory that innocent wives of practicing bigamists are entitled to equal shares of property accumulated during the active phase of the bigamy. No injury has been visited upon third parties, and the wisdom of Solomon is not required to perceive the justice of the result. The judgment is affirmed.

NOTES AND QUESTIONS

1.   Would the plaintiff in *Keimig* be a putative spouse? Are common law marriage and the putative spouse doctrine mutually exclusive categories, or can the concepts operate together, i.e., might a bona fide, but false, belief in the existence of a common law marriage make the "believer" a putative spouse? *See* Garduno v. Garduno, 760 S.W.2d 735 (Tex. App. 1988). Does it matter if the state recognizes common law marriages? *See In re* Estate of Marson, 120 P.3d 382 (Mont. 2005).

2.   If Josephine had died before Juan, could he have been a putative spouse? Did he have a "reasonable" belief in the validity of the marriage? *See* Xia Guo v. Xiao Hua Sun, 112 Cal. Rptr. 3d 906 (Ct. App. 2010) (finding that a husband who had not yet divorced his first wife could not be a putative spouse of another woman because he lacked a good faith belief that they were married).

3.   The federal government applies a putative spouse test for awarding of Social Security benefits. If an applicant "in good faith went through a marriage ceremony resulting in a purported marriage between them which, but for a legal impediment not known to the applicant at the time of such ceremony, would have been a valid marriage, and such applicant and the insured individual were living in the same household at the time of the death of such insured individual such purported marriage shall be deemed a valid marriage." 42 U.S.C. § 416(h)(1)(B).

4.   In states which recognize common law marriage and same-sex marriages, such as Iowa, can there now be a same-sex common law marriage?

Problem 3-9:

State A does not recognize common law marriage but does accept the putative spouse doctrine. Jan and Tom were married for five months, divorced—and then continued to live together for 14 years. Tom listed Jan as his wife on all documents and accounts, apparently thinking that he and Jan were still married. When Jan discovered that she and Tom were legally divorced, she threatened to leave Tom. Tom begged her to stay because he feared he would lose his job if it were discovered that they were not married. Four years later, Tom left Jan. Is Jan entitled to alimony and property distribution as a putative spouse? *See* Manker v. Manker, 644 N.W.2d 522 (Neb. 2002).

CHAPTER 4

MARITAL RIGHTS AND OBLIGATIONS: GAINS AND LOSSES

■ ■ ■

> *When a marriage has equal partners, I fear not.*
>
> AESCHYLUS, PROMETHEUS BOUND

Marriage changes legal status. After the marriage ceremony, two individuals formerly classified by the state as single persons are classified as a family unit. Marriage also creates private rights and obligations: as you learned in Chapter 2, each spouse takes on legal support obligations to the other; as you will see in this chapter, marriage also creates rights to property, to compensatory damages, and to evidentiary privileges. Marriage additionally affects public obligations and entitlements: the amount of taxes one owes and the public benefits one receives are typically dependent on marital status. In this chapter, we explore these effects of the decision to marry.

1. PRIVATE RIGHTS AND OBLIGATIONS: FROM PATRIARCHY TO EQUALITY

BEATRICE GOTTLIEB, THE FAMILY IN THE WESTERN WORLD: FROM THE BLACK DEATH TO THE INDUSTRIAL AGE
90–92 (Oxford University Press, 1993).

While it is probably no surprise that [marital] inequality was rife in earlier centuries, it is important to recognize that what we see as a blemish was for a long time considered to be positive. * * * Husband and wife each had an "authentic place." * * *

The main elements of the theory appear in Paul's Epistle to the Ephesians, where they are treated as long-established ideas:

Wives, submit yourselves unto your own husbands * * * for the husband is the head of the wife, even as Christ is the head of the church* * * Let the wives be to their own husbands in everything. Husbands, love your wives, even as Christ also loved the church * * * So ought men to love their wives as their own bodies. He that loveth his wife loveth himself* * * For this cause shall a man leave his father and mother, and shall be joined unto his wife, and they two shall be one flesh* * * Let every one of you in particular so love his wife even as himself, and the wife see that she reverence her husband. (5:22–23)

This idea of a loving despotism was buttressed by the idea of the natural inferiority of women, an idea whose antiquity argued for its truth. It was stated clearly in Aristotle and obliquely but unmistakably in the Old Testament. Worshipers in Anglican churches were regularly reminded that the woman is "the weaker vessel, of a frail heart." Frailty justified control, but a control that should not be too harsh. "Although she is inferior," said a handbook for French confessors in the sixteenth century, "yet she is not a slave or a servant but the companion and flesh of the flesh of her husband." * * *

The legal systems of the Western world supported the theory. When a woman married, her identity was swallowed up in her husband's. As William Blackstone pithily put it in the eighteenth century, summing up the thrust of English common law, "The husband and wife are one, and the husband is that one." What this meant was that, with a few exceptions, a wife could not bring a legal action in a court, make a contract, or own property. If she technically had title to property, it was controlled by her husband. The commonest way of looking at the property of a married couple saw it as a community of pooled resources, to which the wife sometimes made a major contribution in the form of her dowry. As long as the marriage lasted she had next to no say in how it was managed or spent. * * *

––––––––––

In contrast to the patriarchal ideal embedded in the common law notion of marriage, modern family law is based on the ideal of marital equality. The move from patriarchy to equality as a governing marital norm has been gradual and uneven. In the United States, one of the first legal reforms marking the shift was the Married Women's Property Acts. State legislatures began enacting these laws in the 1850s and, by the end of the nineteenth century, every state had one in its statute books. The Acts restored to the married woman the rights she had when unmarried, including the right to acquire, own, or transfer property, to make a will and enter contracts, to engage in business or be employed, to keep her own earnings, to sue and be sued, and to testify in civil and criminal trials.

The Acts did not succeed in conferring full legal capacity on married women without a lengthy struggle, however:

The general and sometimes inappropriate language which they contained was often used by the courts as an excuse for restrictive interpretation. Part of this judicial conservatism reflected a desire to protect the married woman and to preserve family institutions, but it nonetheless ran counter to the clear spirit and purpose of the statutes. The legislatures were thereby led, over a long period, to pass specific provisions correcting the courts' mistakes. The outcome * * * was that most of the married women's disabilities were ultimately removed.

HOMER H. CLARK, JR., THE LAW OF DOMESTIC RELATIONS IN THE UNITED STATES 289–90 (2d ed. 1988).

The primary focus of the Acts was the married woman's legal relationships with individuals outside the family. Thus the Acts did not abolish spousal immunity, which prevented one spouse from maintaining a tort action against another. Nor did they alter other legal principles that fostered continued male dominance within the family. For example, many state family law codes continued to contain provisions like this one:

> N.D. CENT. CODE § 14–07–02: Head of Family—The husband is the head of the family. He may choose any reasonable place or mode of living and the wife must conform thereto.

> Repealed, March 3, 1979, Ch. 195, N.D. Sess. Laws, p. 426.

The second wave of reform, focusing on the marital relationship itself, did not really take off until the 1960s. Like the earlier reform movement, the progress of this one has been fitful and uneven. Writing in 1968, the author of a leading family law treatise reported that only seventeen states had abolished spousal immunity and that, while "one might suppose that other states would join the chorus and discard the immunity, this does not seem to be happening." HOMER H. CLARK, THE LAW OF DOMESTIC RELATIONS 254 (1st ed. 1968).

Although the second wave of reforms undeniably produced greater equality in the legal status of husband and wife, the new egalitarianism represents, for many couples, an aspirational ideal more than a lived reality. Researchers continue to report that the typical American husband has more power within marriage than does his wife. Husbands are more likely to dominate major spending decisions; they are less likely, even when the wife works full-time outside the home, to perform house work or child care. *See, e.g.*, PHILIP BLUMSTEIN & PEPPER SCHWARTZ, AMERICAN COUPLES 53–59, 62–64; 144–46 (1983); Carole B. Burgoyne, *Heart Strings and Purse Strings: Money in Heterosexual Marriage*, 14 FEMINISM PSYCH. 165 (2004); Catherine T. Kenney, *Allocative Systems and Inequality in Couple Households*, 20 GENDER & SOC. 354 (2006).

One reason for continued inequality in marital relationships is inequality in men's and women's earnings. Although the proportion of wives who earn as much or more than their husbands has increased considerably, seventy to eighty percent of wives in dual-earner families still earn less than their husbands, and less than ten percent earn more than their husbands over a five-year period. *See* Sarah Winslow-Bowe, *The Persistence of Wives' Income Advantage*, 68 J. MARRIAGE & FAM. 824, 832 (2006); Anne E. Winkler et al., *Wives Who Outearn Their Husbands: A Transitory or Persistent Phenomenon for Couples?*, 42 DEMOGRAPHY 523 (2005). Some evidence suggests that the relative power of husband and wife is influenced by their monetary contributions to the household. A pioneering study of American couples found that, three-quarters of the time, it was money that established the balance of power in a relationship. Among both married couples and heterosexual cohabitants, women gained power when they earned more. *See* BLUMSTEIN & SCHWARTZ, *supra*, at 53–54, 309. *See also* Makiko Fuwa, *Macro-Level Gender Inequality and the Division of Household Labor in 22 Countries*, 69 AM. SOC. REV. L651 (2004); Michael Bittman et al., *When Gender Trumps Money: Bargaining and Time in Household Work*, 109 AM. J. SOC. 186 (2003).

Spousal power is also significantly affected by the extent to which husband and wife express belief in the "male provider" philosophy and, looking across societies, by gender norms and economic development. Indeed, some research suggests that these cultural factors may "trump" money as a determinant of spousal power relationships. For example, one group of researchers found that women's earnings were associated with reductions in their housework only when they contributed less than half of family income; when a woman contributed more than half, her contribution of a greater share of family income was associated with *more* housework on her part. The researchers speculated that this phenomenon reflects "an attempt to neutralize the gender deviance of the husband earning less than his wife." Bittman et al., *supra*.

Given the impact of money and cultural norms, it is unsurprising that many marriages fail to conform to the new egalitarian ideal. Nor is it entirely clear just what the new ideal means. One vision of egalitarianism emphasizes marital community; another emphasizes the individual autonomy of husband and wife. Changes in the law over the past few decades evidence the pull of both visions and demonstrate no consistent preference or ordering principle. The slogans "partnership" and "equality" do not tell us which of these visions should be preferred or what balance between autonomy and community is best.

The choice between autonomy and community is complicated by the continuance of economic and power disparities between men and women. For example, the autonomy-focused Married Women's Property Acts did very little to improve the position of married women without property or earnings. If the husband worked outside the home and the wife did not, the husband retained control of all property (except what the wife acquired by gift or inheritance) during the marriage. But other reforms emphasizing individual autonomy—the abolition of spousal immunity, for example— have undeniably enhanced wives' power.

The choice is also complicated by the fact that the passing of the doctrine of marital unity has not substantially altered the long-standing view that the family is not just a collection of individual members but also a transcending entity. Because of its "deep root[s] in this Nation's history and tradition," because "[i]t is through the family that we inculcate and pass down many of our most cherished values, moral and cultural," the Supreme Court has held that "the Constitution protects the sanctity of the *family* * * *." Moore v. City of East Cleveland, [p. (emphasis added)]. But an emphasis on the individual rights of family members necessarily undermines the importance of the family to which they belong. Some commentators thus worry that the recent wave of reforms

> has contributed to a climate in which individuals are permitted, and even encouraged, to pursue narrow self-interest at great cost to other family members and to the family itself. * * * By maintaining a stance of moral neutrality toward the choices that people make about intimate associations, the law undermines the shared values that define the family. In this environment, family relationships are weakened, and the long-term viability of the family itself is threatened.

Elizabeth Scott, *Rehabilitating Liberalism in Modern Divorce Law*, 1994 UTAH L. REV. 687, 710 (summarizing views of various commentators).

As you read the materials in this chapter, try to chart which rules enhance marital community and which individual autonomy. Ask yourself whether, and how, we can attain an egalitarian marital ideal in the face of spousal inequality both in the marketplace and in different levels of engagement in unpaid service to the household. And ask yourself how the claims of individual husbands and wives should be balanced against "the shared values that define the family."

2. NAMES

KRUZEL V. PODELL
Supreme Court of Wisconsin, 1975.
67 Wis. 2d 138, 226 N.W.2d 458.

HEFFERNAN, JUSTICE.

This case presents the question of whether upon marriage a woman is required by law to assume the surname of her husband. We conclude that a woman upon marriage adopts the surname of her husband by thereafter customarily using that name, but no law requires that she do so. If she continues to use her anti-nuptial [sic! Freudian slip?] surname, her name is unchanged by the fact that marriage has occurred.

Kathleen Rose Harney married Joseph Michael Kruzel on July 31, 1971. She is an art teacher in the Milwaukee school system and was issued a teacher's certificate under her birth-given surname. She was employed by the Milwaukee school system under that name and exhibited works of art under the name Harney. She at all times used the name Harney and not Kruzel.

The Milwaukee School Board insisted, however, for group insurance purposes, that Kathleen either use her husband's surname or "legally" change her surname to Harney.

Kathleen accordingly petitioned the circuit court for Milwaukee county for an order "changing" her surname from Kruzel to Harney. At the hearing it was shown that at no time had the petitioner ever used the name Kruzel. The only time she had used Kruzel as her surname was in the petition for the instant proceeding, and then only for the purpose of "changing" that name to Harney.

The trial judge [denied Kathleen's petition, relying] * * * on 57 Am. Jur. 2d, Name, § 9, page 281, which states: "It is well settled by common-law principles and immemorial custom that a woman upon marriage abandons her maiden name and assumes the husband's surname." * * *

[T]he trial judge [also] stated that to permit Kathleen to bear the surname Harney and her husband the name Kruzel would be contrary to the best interests of any children that might thereafter be born to the marriage. * **

* * *

It is undoubtedly true that the tendency of a wife to take her husband's surname was spawned by the common law theory of marriage. Under that theory, upon marriage, a man and a woman became one and that one was the husband. * * * Obviously, the conditions that led to the practice of having women adopt their husbands' surnames no longer have their foundation in existing law. * * *

We conclude that the statutes of Wisconsin are consistent with the common law, which does not require a wife to assume her husband's surname and when the husband's surname was acquired, it was the result of usage and her holding out to the world that the surname is the same as the husband's.

Since we conclude in this case that Kathleen Rose Harney was never compelled to change her name, nor did she ever in fact adopt the surname Kruzel by usage, her petition, although ostensibly brought under § 296.36, Stats., amounted only to a request for judicial recognition that she had been correct in using her maiden surname in the past. The recognition of her right should have been given by the mandate of the court. Accordingly, the order is vacated and the cause remanded to the trial court for the entry of an order declaring her right to use the name of Kathleen Rose Harney.

NOTES AND QUESTIONS

1. A married woman in the United States is nowhere *required* to take her husband's name. And to avoid the kind of issue litigated in *Kruzel*, many states have enacted legislation prescribing methods by which wives—and husbands—may register their name choices. Some additionally offer prospective spouses an extensive menu of name options. For example, in New York, all marriage license applications must state that:

1) A person's last name (surname) does not automatically change upon marriage, and neither party to the marriage must change his or her last name. Parties to a marriage need not have the same last name.

2) One or both parties to a marriage may elect to change the surname by which he or she wishes to be known after the solemnization of the marriage by entering the new name in the space below. Such entry shall consist of one of the following surnames:

i) the surname of the other spouse; or

ii) any former surname of either spouse; or

iii) a name combining into a single surname all or a segment of the premarriage surname or any former surname of each spouse; or

iv) a combination name separated by a hyphen, provided that each part of such combination surname is the premarriage surname, or any former surname, of each of the spouses.

3) The use of this option will have the effect of providing a record of the change of name. The marriage certificate, containing the new name, if any, constitutes proof that the use of the new name, or the retention of the former name, is lawful.

4) Neither the use of, nor the failure to use, this option of selecting a new surname by means of this application abrogates the right of each person to adopt a different name through usage at some future date.

N.Y. DOM. REL. L. § 15.1(B). Under the New York statute, Ms. Harney and Mr. Kruzel could have become, say, Mr. Harney and Mrs. Kruzel—or Mr. and Mrs. Harzel or Kruney or Harkru or Zelney. New York is one of seven states that provide a statutory right for a man to change his name upon marriage. *See Note*, 16 DUKE J. GENDER L. & POL'Y 155 (2009).

2.   There is some evidence that the number of married women who choose to keep their maiden names has declined in recent years. A survey of married Harvard alumnae found that 44% of the class of 1980 and 32% of the class of 1990 retained their birth names after marriage. And Massachusetts marriage records reveal that 23% of female college graduates chose to keep their own names in 1990, as compared to 17% in 2000. *See* Rich Lowry, *Ms. Goes Mrs.,* NAT. REV., Aug. 6, 2004. Looking at the seeming trend in favor of name switching, one commentator urged that "it will strengthen marriage. It's a sign that * * * it is for the duration." Another pair theorize that "surname-keeping seems less salient as a way of publicly supporting equality for women than it did in the late 1970s and 1980s" and speculate that "a general drift to more conservative social values has made surname-keeping less attractive." *Id.* What do you think?

3.   Most states have established procedures enabling the woman who adopted her husband's name at marriage to resume her maiden name upon divorce. For example, UMDA § 314(d) provides that, "[u]pon request by a wife whose marriage is dissolved * * *, the court may, and if there are no children of the parties shall, order her maiden name or a former name restored."

4.   In Dunn v. Palermo, 522 S.W.2d 679 (Tenn. 1975), the Tennessee Supreme Court reached the same conclusion as the court in *Kruzel* regarding the impact of marriage upon a woman's surname. The opinion surveys some nineteenth-century cases that gave rise to the view that a woman's surname did automatically change upon marriage, and also reviews the history of surnames in England after the Norman Conquest.

3.   THE LAW OF EVIDENCE

TRAMMEL V. UNITED STATES

Supreme Court of the United States, 1980.
445 U.S. 40.

CHIEF JUSTICE BURGER delivered the opinion of the Court.

We granted certiorari to consider whether an accused may invoke the privilege against adverse spousal testimony so as to exclude the voluntary testimony of his wife.

* * *

According to the indictment, petitioner and his wife flew from the Philippines to California in August 1975, carrying with them a quantity of heroin. Freeman and Roberts assisted them in its distribution. Elizabeth Trammel then traveled to Thailand where she purchased another supply of the drug. On November 3, 1975, with four ounces of heroin on her person, she boarded a plane for the United States. During a routine customs search in Hawaii, she was searched, the heroin was discovered, and she was arrested. After discussions with Drug Enforcement Administration agents, she agreed to cooperate with the Government.

* * *

The privilege claimed by petitioner has ancient roots. Writing in 1628, Lord Coke observed that "it hath been resolved by the Justices that a wife cannot be produced either against or for her husband." This spousal disqualification sprang from two canons of medieval jurisprudence: first, the rule that an accused was not permitted to testify in his own behalf because of his interest in the proceeding; second, the concept that husband and wife were one, and that since the woman had no recognized separate legal existence, the husband was that one. From those two now long-abandoned doctrines, it followed that what was inadmissible from the lips of the defendant-husband was also inadmissible from his wife.

Despite its medieval origins, this rule of spousal disqualification remained intact in most common-law jurisdictions well into the 19th century. It was applied by this Court * * *, where it was deemed so well established a proposition as to "hardly requir[e] mention." Indeed, it was not until 1933 * * * that this Court abolished the testimonial disqualification in the federal courts, so as to permit the spouse of a defendant to testify in the defendant's behalf. * * * [H]owever, [we] left undisturbed the rule that either spouse could prevent the other from giving adverse testimony. The rule thus evolved into one of privilege rather than one of absolute disqualification.

The modern justification for this privilege against adverse spousal testimony is its perceived role in fostering the harmony and sanctity of the marriage relationship. Notwithstanding this benign purpose, the rule was sharply criticized. Professor Wigmore termed it "the merest anachronism in legal theory and an indefensible obstruction to truth in practice." The Committee on the Improvement of the Law of Evidence of the American Bar Association called for its abolition. In its place, Wigmore and others suggested a privilege protecting only private marital communications, modeled on the privilege between priest and penitent, attorney and client, and physician and patient.

These criticisms influenced the American Law Institute, which, in its 1942 Model Code of Evidence advocated a privilege for marital confidences, but expressly rejected a rule vesting in the defendant the right to exclude all adverse testimony of his spouse. In 1953 the Uniform Rules of Evidence, drafted by the National Conference of Commissioners on Uniform State Laws, followed a similar course; it limited the privilege to confidential communications and "abolishe[d] the rule, still existing in some states, and largely a sentimental relic, of not requiring one spouse to testify against the other in a criminal action." Several state legislatures enacted similarly patterned provisions into law.

In *Hawkins v. United States*, 358 U.S. 74 (1958), this Court * * * took note of the critical comments that the common-law rule had engendered, but chose not to abandon it. * * * Since 1958, when *Hawkins* was decided, support for the privilege against adverse spousal testimony has been eroded further. Thirty-one jurisdictions, including Alaska and Hawaii, then allowed an accused a privilege to prevent adverse spousal testimony. The number has now declined to 24. * * * The trend in state law toward divesting the accused of the privilege to bar adverse spousal testimony has special relevance because the law of marriage and domestic relations are concerns traditionally reserved to the states. Scholarly criticism of the *Hawkins* rule has also continued unabated.

* * *

It is essential to remember that the *Hawkins* privilege is not needed to protect information privately disclosed between husband and wife in the confidence of the marital relationship—once described by this Court as "the best solace of human existence." Those confidences are privileged under the independent rule protecting confidential marital communications. The *Hawkins* privilege is invoked, not to exclude private marital communications, but rather to exclude evidence of criminal acts and of communications made in the presence of third persons.

No other testimonial privilege sweeps so broadly. The privileges between priest and penitent, attorney and client, and physician and patient limit protection to private communications. These privileges are rooted in the imperative need for confidence and trust. The priest-penitent privilege recognizes the human need to disclose to a spiritual counselor, in total and absolute confidence, what are believed to be flawed acts or thoughts and to receive priestly consolation and guidance in return. The lawyer-client privilege rests on the need for the advocate and counsel to know all that relates to the client's reasons for seeking representation if the professional mission is to be carried out. Similarly, the physician must know all that a patient can articulate in order to identify and to treat disease; barriers to full disclosure would impair diagnosis and treatment.

The *Hawkins* rule stands in marked contrast to these three privileges. Its protection is not limited to confidential communications; rather it permits an accused to exclude all adverse spousal testimony. As Jeremy Bentham observed more than a century and a half ago, such a privilege goes far beyond making "every man's house his castle," and permits a person to convert his house into "a den of thieves." It "secures, to every man, one safe and unquestionable and ever ready accomplice for every imaginable crime."

The ancient foundations for so sweeping a privilege have long since disappeared. Nowhere in the common-law world—indeed in any modern society—is a woman regarded as chattel or demeaned by denial of a separate legal identity and the dignity associated with recognition as a whole human being. Chip by chip, over the years those archaic notions have been cast aside. * * *

The contemporary justification for affording an accused such a privilege is also unpersuasive. * * * When one spouse is willing to testify against the other in a criminal proceeding—whatever the motivation— their relationship is almost certainly in disrepair; there is probably little in the way of marital harmony for the privilege to preserve. In these circumstances, a rule of evidence that permits an accused to prevent adverse spousal testimony seems far more likely to frustrate justice than to foster family peace. Indeed, there is reason to believe that vesting the privilege in the accused could actually undermine the marital relationship. For example, in a case such as this the Government is unlikely to offer a wife immunity and lenient treatment if it knows that her husband can prevent her from giving adverse testimony. If the Government is dissuaded from making such an offer, the privilege can have the untoward effect of permitting one spouse to escape justice at the expense of the other. It hardly seems conducive to the preservation of the marital relation to place a wife in jeopardy solely by virtue of her husband's control over her testimony.

Our consideration of the foundations for the privilege and its history satisfy us that "reason and experience" no longer justify so sweeping a rule as that found acceptable by the Court in *Hawkins*. Accordingly, we conclude that the existing rule should be modified so that the witness spouse alone has a privilege to refuse to testify adversely; the witness may be neither compelled to testify nor foreclosed from testifying. This modification—vesting the privilege in the witness spouse—furthers the important public interest in marital harmony without unduly burdening legitimate law enforcement needs.

Here, petitioner's spouse chose to testify against him. That she did so after a grant of immunity and assurances of lenient treatment does not render her testimony involuntary. Accordingly, the District Court and the Court of Appeals were correct in rejecting petitioner's claim of privilege, and the judgment of the Court of Appeals is affirmed.

NOTES AND QUESTIONS

1. As the Court notes, information "privately disclosed between husband and wife in the confidence of the marital relationship" remains fully protected under *Trammel*. "[U]nlike the testimonial privilege, the confidential communication privilege survives termination of the marriage by annulment, divorce or death. The husband-wife confidential communication privilege barring disclosure by either spouse belongs to both spouses and may be asserted by either in his or her own right." MARK GRAHAM, HANDBOOK OF FEDERAL EVIDENCE 335–336 (1981).

2.   Does the *Trammel* court strike a reasonable balance in upholding the witness spouse's privilege and striking down the accused spouse's privilege? What are the pros and cons of the *Trammel* approach as compared one in which the witness spouse may testify adversely against the defendant spouse only when the defendant has committed a "personal wrong" against the witness? *See* People v. Eberhardt, 205 Mich. App. 587, 518 N.W.2d 511 (1994). Are you convinced by the court's argument that "when one spouse is willing to testify against the other in a criminal proceeding . . . there is probably little in the way of marital harmony for the privilege to preserve"? Reading between the lines, why does it seem the wife is willing to testify in *Trammel*?

3.   Although the states remain divided on adverse spousal testimony, the trend reported in *Trammel* continues. By 1995, only thirteen states permitted a spouse to veto adverse spousal testimony. *See* Milton C. Regan, Jr., *Spousal Privilege and the Meanings of Marriage*, 81 VA. L. REV. 2045, 2060–61 (1995).

4.   Many federal and state courts have considered recognizing a parent-child evidentiary privilege, and virtually all have declined to do so. *See In re* Grand Jury, 103 F.3d 1140, 1146 (3d Cir. 1997) ("The overwhelming majority of all courts—federal or state—have rejected such a privilege."). Many civil law countries, on the other hand, protect a broad range of family members from compelled testimony. *See id.* at 1162. In declining to extend the spousal privilege to the parent-child relationship, the Third Circuit Court of Appeals noted that:

> A privilege should be recognized only where such a privilege would be indispensable to the survival of the relationship that society deems should be fostered. For instance, because complete candor and full disclosure by the client is absolutely necessary in order for the attorney to function effectively, society recognizes an attorney-client privilege. Without a guarantee of secrecy, clients would be unwilling to reveal damaging information. As a corollary, clients would disclose negative information, which an attorney must know to prove effective representation, only if they were assured that such disclosures are privileged.In contrast, it is not clear whether children would be more likely to discuss private matters with their parents if a parent-child privilege were recognized than if one were not. It is not likely that children, or even their parents, would typically be aware of the existence or non-existence of a testimonial privilege covering parent-child communications.

Id. at 1153. Would the marital confidential-communications privilege pass this test? If not, should it be abandoned? Why have American courts embraced the confidential-communications privilege for spouses and rejected it for parents and children?

5.   Some states have enacted rules that compel the testimony of one spouse allegedly abused by the other. *See* Commonwealth v. Kirkner, 805 A.2d 514 (Pa. 2002). These statutes have not always worked as intended. For example, in a case involving Houston pro football player Warren Moon, Mrs.

Moon—compelled to testify against her wishes—testified that she had started the fight which led to criminal charges against her husband. Despite other evidence supporting the prosecution, the jury acquitted Mr. Moon. *See* Verhovek, *Athlete and Legal Issue on Trial*, N.Y. TIMES, Feb. 19, 1996, at A6, col. 1. Seven years later the same thing happened in a case involving a Houston professional baseball player, Julio Lugo. *See* Jeffrey Gilbert, *Jurors Acquit Ex-Astro Lugo In Assault Trial*, HOUST. CHRON., July 17, 2003, http://www.chron.com/cda/archives/archive.mpl/2003_3672546/jurors-acquit-ex-astro-lugo-in-assault-trial.html. Commentators strongly disagree about the propriety of mandated testimony in cases like *Moon*. *Compare* Cheryl Hanna, *No Right to Choose: Mandated Victim Participation in Domestic Violence Prosecutions*, 109 HARV. L. REV. 1849, 1906–08 (1996) (arguing that "if prosecutors had to choose between dismissing the case or forcing Ms. Moon to testify, then they made the right decision even though in the end the jury found Mr. Moon not guilty." * * * In the long run, such decisions to mandate participation will begin to erase the misconception that these cases are not worth pursuing criminally because domestic violence is a private family matter, not a crime) *with* Linda G. Mills, *Killing Her Softly: Intimate Abuse and the Violence of State Intervention*, 113 HARV. L. REV. 550, 613 (1999) (arguing that, because mandated prosecution reinforces powerlessness of the victim and does not demonstrate clear benefits to victims as a group, prosecution should depend on victim consent).

6.   What are the advantages of a testimonial rule under which:

a.   Neither spouse may testify;

b.   The defendant spouse may compel the witness spouse to testify;

c.   The defendant spouse may preclude the witness spouse from testifying;

d.   The witness spouse may elect whether or not to testify;

e.   The prosecution may compel the witness spouse to testify;

f.   The witness spouse may be "bribed" to testify against the defendant (*Trammel*).

On balance, which rule or rule-combination is best?'

4. THE LAW OF TORTS

A. INTERSPOUSAL TORTS AND "HEART BALM" ACTIONS

BAILEY V. FAULKNER
Supreme Court of Alabama, 2006.
940 So. 2d 247.

WOODALL, JUSTICE.

M. Floyd Bailey, Jr., appeals from a judgment entered on a jury verdict in favor of James H. Faulkner III in Faulkner's action against Bailey arising out of a consensual, sexual relationship between Bailey and Paris Faulkner, who, at the time of that relationship, was Faulkner's wife. We reverse and remand.

I. FACTUAL BACKGROUND

In December 1999, the Faulkners were attending the Dalraida Church of Christ in Montgomery ("Dalraida"). Bailey, who has a bachelor of arts degree in Bible from Faulkner University, was Dalraida's pastor. At that time, the elders of Dalraida hired Paris to serve as the church secretary. The job responsibilities of the secretary and the pastor occasioned frequent personal interaction between Paris and Bailey.

Bailey soon discovered that the Faulkners were engaged in marriage counseling with Dr. Terry Gunnels, a licensed counselor. In March 2000, Bailey began advising the Faulkners regarding their marital problems, and they discontinued their counseling sessions with Dr. Gunnels. According to James Faulkner, Bailey "assured" them that "he could spend a lot more time with [them] than [Dr.] Gunnels," and "guaranteed" them that "he could fix [their] marriage." That same month, Bailey and Paris secretly began a consensual, sexual relationship that lasted until July 2000.

In April 2000, Bailey learned that James had been offered employment in Baldwin County and that Paris did not want to move. Bailey urged James to decline the job offer, saying that the move "could break [the Faulkners'] marriage." James took Bailey's advice and declined the offer.

The relationship ended after James discovered it and confronted Paris and Bailey. After initially denying his involvement with Paris, Bailey eventually admitted it and resigned as pastor of Dalraida. Paris unsuccessfully sought reconciliation with James, who initiated divorce proceedings. The Faulkners were divorced on January 4, 2001.

On February 5, 2002, Faulkner sued Bailey. * * * During the trial, Bailey filed timely motions for a judgment as a matter of law * * * [alleging that] "this is . . . a case of alienation of affection * * * couched in terms of negligent counseling."

The trial court denied those motions. * * * The jury awarded $67,000 compensatory damages and $2,000,000 punitive damages, [and] * * * Bailey appealed. * * *

II. DISCUSSION

* * * "The so-called 'heart balm' or amatory torts," were abolished by [Ala. Code] § 6–5–331, which provides: "There shall be no civil claims for alienation of affections, criminal conversation, or seduction of any female person of the age of 19 years or over."

"The gist of an alienation of affections action is the intentional or purposeful . . . interference with the marriage relationship." "An action for alienation of affection permitted recovery for 'loss of consortium, humiliation, shame, mental anguish, loss of sexual relations, and the disgrace the tortious acts of the defendant have brought.'" Another element of damage is pecuniary loss, such as loss of income. Additionally, "punitive damages [could] be recovered for the tort of alienation of affections." (Citations omitted.)

Since the abolition in Alabama of the heart-balm torts, this Court has refused to recognize "any claim for damages against a third party, no matter how denominated, that is based on allegations of interference with the marriage relationship." *D.D.*, 600 So. 2d at 223. For example, in *D.D.*, this Court affirmed a summary judgment for the paramour and against the husband in his action against his wife's paramour for interfering with, and causing the dissolution of, his marriage.

The husband's action purported to state claims of (1) abuse of process, (2) invasion of privacy, (3) negligence, (4) wantonness, and (5) intentional infliction of emotional distress. * * * Although the complaint was conspicuously devoid of any claim denominated as an amatory claim, this Court held that each of the husband's claims was * * *, "in effect, one alleging alienation of affections"; and was, therefore, "barred by § 6–5–331."

Other courts have held that a husband's claim of negligent marital counseling or clergy malpractice, based on allegations that his wife and the minister or marriage counselor had engaged in sexual misconduct under the auspices of a counselor-counselee relationship, was merely a restyled alienation-of-affections claim, for which no relief was afforded. (Citations omitted.)

In *Strock*, for example, Richard Strock and his wife, Suzanne, sought marital counseling from "James Pressnell, minister of the Shepherd of the Ridge Lutheran Church." During the counseling period, Pressnell and Suzanne "engaged in consensual sexual relations." After Richard discovered the relationship, he divorced Suzanne and sued Pressnell asserting claims of "clergy malpractice, breach of a fiduciary duty, fraud, misrepresentation, nondisclosure, and intentional infliction of emotional distress." The trial court dismissed the action * * * [and t]he Ohio Supreme Court agreed with the trial court. * * *

Significantly, the court at first rejected the validity of the clergy-malpractice claim, on the ground that malpractice is not an "intentional tort." * * * The conclusion in *Strock* that a husband's allegations of consensual sexual misconduct between his wife and a pastor arising out of the counselor-counselee relationship do not sound in negligence is consistent with *D.D., supra.* This is so, because, of course, the "gist of a malpractice action is negligence," whereas the intentional or purposeful "interference with the marriage relationship" is the "the gist of an alienation of affections action." *D.D.*, at 222. Thus, it is immaterial whether Faulkner purports to allege negligent ministerial counseling, i.e., clergy malpractice, as Bailey insists, or negligent marital counseling, as Faulkner characterizes his claim. Neither theory is valid under the facts of this case.

This is so, because, despite the allegation in the complaint that Bailey "negligently [and/or wantonly]" counseled "[Faulkner] and his wife . . . concerning their marriage," Faulkner's actual theory of the case is that Bailey's illicit relationship with Paris destroyed his marriage. All the damages Faulkner seeks flow, not from alleged negligence or wantonness, but from Bailey's intentional conduct. * * *

Faulkner also contends that he suffered mental anguish during the counseling sessions because Bailey always sided with Paris and because he was ashamed that he was suspicious of the relationship between Bailey and Paris. However, he concedes that Bailey's support for Paris during the sessions was based on a bias resulting from their relationship. According to Faulkner, Bailey gave him advice that was calculated to make Paris angry, because, he states, "Bailey knew what buttons to push to aggravate the situation." Such allegations evidence deliberate—not negligent—conduct. * * *

In short, this case is not about negligence or wantonness—it is about intentional conduct. The only claims stated by the allegations in this case assert the amatory torts abolished by § 6–5–331. Damages sought here are the species of damages recoverable for those torts. * * *

III. CONCLUSION

The judgment is * * * reversed, and the cause is remanded for the entry of a judgment in favor of Bailey.

LYONS, JUSTICE (concurring specially).

* * * If I were a member of the Alabama Legislature, I would immediately amend § 6–5–331 so as to provide that nothing in the statute

should preclude a civil cause of action when a person who has assumed a duty toward a husband and wife with respect to the status of their marital relationship thereafter has sexual contact * * * with one of the parties to the marriage during the existence of the marital relationship. * * * But I am not a member of the legislature, and I must concur in reversing the judgment in favor of Faulkner.

PARKER, JUSTICE (concurring specially).

* * * Although I agree with the holding of the main opinion, I write separately to caution that it not be extended so far as to bar an action against a state-licensed professional such as an attorney who seduces his client or a doctor who seduces his patient. * * *

Although a church clergyman is also a professional—in fact, a member of one of the first professions historically recognized—his status derives from the church, not the state, and his professional standards are based on the Bible and church doctrine, not on civil government statutes. * * * Given the fact that the state has neither the ability nor the authority to identify or enforce the proper standard of care for religious counseling, the State of Alabama has wisely and consistently refused to recognize a tort of clergy malpractice. * * *

The case before us presents only two logical alternatives: either Bailey's conduct was alienation of affections or it was clergy malpractice. To the extent it was alienation of affections, the cause of action was abolished by § 6–5–331. To the extent it was clergy malpractice, Alabama has never before recognized that tort and should not start recognizing it today.

NOTES AND QUESTIONS

1. Is the majority correct that legislative action would be needed in order to countenance Bailey's suit? If yes, is concurring Justice Lyons right that legislative reform is desirable?

2. The common law action for "criminal conversation" permitted recovery of damages based on the defendant's adulterous sexual intercourse with the plaintiff's wife; it applied to both rape and consensual sexual relations. The related action for "alienation of affections" protected the husband's relational interest; as the name of the tort suggests, this action was based on the defendant's actions which altered the wife's attitudes and affections. See KEETON, PROSSER, & KEETON ON TORTS 918–31 (5th ed. 1984).

Today, one or another heart balm action survives in gender-neutral form in only a handful of states; in these states, wives as well as husbands can sue. See generally J.T. OLDHAM, DIVORCE, SEPARATION, AND THE DISTRIBUTION OF PROPERTY § 8.01[4] (2017). Although reported heart-balm actions are few in number, the high courts of Mississippi and South Dakota have reaffirmed the availability of the tort. See Fitch v. Valentine, 959 So. 2d 1012 (Miss. 2007);

Veeder v. Kennedy, 589 N.W.2d 610 (S.D. 1999). In 1999, a North Carolina appellate court affirmed an award of $1 million dollars in compensatory and punitive damages. *See* Hutelmyer v. Cox, 514 S.E.2d 554 (N.C. App. 1999). More recently a North Carolina trial court in 2010 awarded $9 million in damages. Shackelford v. Lundquist, 07 CVD 12047 (N.C. Guilford Cnty. Super. Ct., March 19, 2010). In 2011 a judge awarded damages of $30 million in an alienation of affections case, *See* Jean M. Cary & Sharon Scudder, *Breaking Up Is Hard to Do: North Carolina Refuses to End Its Relationship with Heartbalm Torts,* 4 ELON L. REV. 1, 3 n.8 (2012).

Note that, even if all parties involved live elsewhere, a claim for criminal conversation can be successfully asserted if parties engaged in sexual activity once in a state that still recognizes the claim. *See* Jones v. Shelley, 673 S.E.2d 385 (N.C. App. 2009).

3.   Cases similar to *Faulkner* have been litigated with some frequency, and the weight of the case law is in accord with the conclusions of the Alabama Supreme Court. But in Doe v. Zwelling, 620 S.E.2d 750 (Va. 2005), faced with facts similar to *Faulkner*, the Virginia Supreme Court reversed a judgment dismissing the husband's cause of action. The defendant in *Doe* was a clinical social worker instead of a clergyman. The Court noted that malpractice actions against social workers "are subject to the same laws as those governing such actions against physicians". It reviewed prior case law dismissing claims that sounded in alienation of affections and found that, in the earlier cases,

> all of the plaintiff's injuries were ascribed to the effect of the defendant's conduct upon the plaintiff's marriage. In the present case, that cannot be said. Here, the plaintiff has alleged facts constituting breaches of the defendant's professional standard of care that would be compensable in damages even if the plaintiff were unmarried. Such breaches might include maligning him to a third person and administering improper treatment, as well as subjecting him to the humiliation and embarrassment of having his most intimate confidences disclosed to a third party without his authorization.

Id. at 752–53. The Court thus allowed the plaintiff to proceed in his professional malpractice action and directed the trial court to "exclude from the fact-finder's consideration any effect the defendant's conduct may have had upon the plaintiff's marriage." *Id.* at 753.

How does the "actionable-if-the-plaintiff-were-unmarried" test adopted by the *Doe* court differ from the approach outlined in *Faulkner*? What are the pros and cons of the *Doe* and *Faulkner* approaches?

If a social worker can be found liable for professional misconduct on facts like those in *Faulkner*, are there convincing reasons to immunize a clergyman for liability on the same facts?

4.   In Osborne v. Payne, 31 S.W.3d 911 (Ky. 2000) the Kentucky Supreme Court reversed a summary judgment granted the defendant when a

plaintiff husband sued a priest for having an affair with his wife while she was receiving counseling from him. The court held that, despite the repeal of the Heart Balm statutes, the defendant's actions were outrageous and could constitute conduct that would allow recovery for intentional infliction of emotional distress.

5.   *Spousal Immunity:* Although most states have banned actions against third parties for criminal conversation and alienation of affection, most states have now abrogated the doctrine of interspousal tort immunity. As a result, courts have increasingly been forced to determine whether particular allegations against a spouse or former spouse state a viable tort action. Most courts that have considered the issue have held that allegations of adultery alone are not actionable. *See, e.g.,* Whittington v. Whittington, 766 S.W.2d 73, 74 (Ky. App. 1989); Ruprecht v. Ruprecht, 599 A.2d 604, 608 (N.J. Super. Ch. Div. 1991); Strauss v. Cilek, 418 N.W.2d 378 (Iowa App. 1987); McDermott v. Reynolds, 530 S.E.2d 902 (Va. 2000). Courts have divided when the allegation of adultery is enhanced with the claim that the wife has misrepresented the husband's paternity of the couple's children, although the majority have refused to countenance such claims. *Compare* Doe v. Doe, 747 A.2d 617 (Md. 2000) (dismissing husband's claim because the husband's action sought to recover damages, using a different label, for the same type of conduct which formerly gave rise to criminal conversation action) *with* Miller v. Miller, 956 P.2d 887 (Okla. 1998) (permitting intentional infliction of emotional distress action against misrepresenting wife and her parents) *and* G.A.W. v. D.M.W., 596 N.W.2d 284 (Minn. App. 1999) (permitting claim for intentional infliction of emotional distress and fraud but dismissing negligent misrepresentation claim because it did not arise out of a business or commercial relationship). *See generally* George L. Blum, *Intentional Infliction of Distress in Marital Context*, 110 A.L.R.5th 371, 398 (2003).

6.   *Intercepting Private Communications:* Email that is an "electronic storage" is protected from unauthorized access by the Stored Communications Act, 18 U.S.C. § 2701. In Miller v. Myers, 766 F. Supp. 2d 919 (W.D. Ark. 2011), a man installed keylogging software on his former wife's computer, and then used the passwords he obtained to obtain access to her email and social networking accounts. The court ruled this constituted a violation of the Act.

7.   *Obtaining Evidence—Wiretapping:* A number of federal courts have considered whether the Omnibus Crime Control and Safe Streets Act of 1968, 18 U.S.C.A. § 2510 et seq. (Title III), which proscribes wiretapping, is applicable when the wiretapping occurs in the marital home and is conducted by a spouse. For example, in Kempf v. Kempf, 677 F. Supp. 618 (E.D. Mo. 1988), Mr. Kempf became suspicious that his wife was engaging in extra-marital affairs because of frequent phone calls in which the caller hung up or claimed he had reached a wrong number. After this had gone on long enough that Mr. Kempf began to recognize some of the voices, he connected a cassette tape recorder, in full view, to one of the three telephones in the home. Mr. Kempf thereafter filed for divorce and offered into evidence tapes he had made of his wife's telephone conversations. The tapes were admitted over the objections of

Mrs. Kempf's lawyer and judgment was entered in Mr. Kempf's favor. Mrs. Kempf thereafter filed suit in federal court under Title III, seeking money damages. After noting that the federal courts were divided on the applicability of Title III to domestic wiretapping, the trial court found that:

> Congress did not intend to give a remedy for interspousal wiretapping when the parties involved were sharing a home and living together as husband and wife at the time the wiretap was utilized. Extending federal law into such a purely domestic matter runs counter to the tradition federal courts have followed in leaving family matters to the discretion of the state courts. * * * This type of spouse-snooping might be morally reprehensible in some respects. Nonetheless, it is an inappropriate subject for federal litigation, and the Court does not believe * * * that Congress meant for Title III to apply to the facts herein.

677 F. Supp. 618 (E.D. Mo. 1988). The Court of Appeals reversed, noting that the legislative history of Title III does not demonstrate any intention to treat interspousal wiretapping differently and that Title III itself contains "no express exception for instances of willful, unconsented to electronic surveillance between spouses." 868 F.2d 970, 973 (8th Cir. 1989) (quoting Pritchard v. Pritchard, 732 F.2d 372 (4th Cir. 1984)). Most federal courts have followed the Eighth Circuit approach. *But see* Simpson v. Simpson, 490 F.2d 803 (5th Cir. 1974) (establishing spousal exception).

8.   *Spousal Immunity and Divorce:* The abolition of spousal immunity has also produced litigation regarding whether a tort action should, or may, be joined with a divorce action. The issue is complicated by the fact that some states permit spousal fault to be taken into account in dividing marital property and awarding alimony. *See* Chapters 15 and 16. At this point, no consensus on the right approach has emerged. *Compare* Twyman v. Twyman, 855 S.W.2d 619 (Tex. 1993) (joinder encouraged) *and* Weil v. Lammon, 503 So. 2d 830 (Ala. 1987) (joinder required) *with* Heacock v. Heacock, 520 N.E.2d 151 (Mass. 1988) (joinder barred) *and* Stuart v. Stuart, 421 N.W.2d 505 (Wis. 1988) (joinder permitted but discouraged). *See generally* Steven J. Gaynor, *Joinder of Tort Actions Between Spouses with Proceeding for Dissolution of Marriage,* 4 A.L.R. 5th 972 (2003).

9.   *The Right Line:* Professors Ellman and Sugarman have argued that "it is probably a mistake for the courts to make tort law available for claims between divorcing spouses, apart from cases which the abusive conduct is criminal. This would bar most, if not all, claims for IIED or invasion of privacy, while allowing claims for physical violence and the like." Ira Mark Ellman & Stephen D. Sugarman, *Spousal Emotional Abuse as a Tort?,* 55 MD. L. REV. 1268, 1343 (1996). What are the pros and cons of the line proposed by Ellman and Sugarman? On balance, when should tort actions between spouses be allowed and when should they be precluded?

B. TORTS AGAINST OTHERS: SPOUSAL CONSORTIUM CLAIMS

Under the common law, a husband was entitled to maintain an action against a tortfeasor who had intentionally injured his wife so as to deprive him of her services, society, and conjugal relations. As the negligence action developed during the nineteenth century, most courts extended the husband's consortium claim to negligent tortfeasors. A wife did not have a corresponding consortium claim because she could not sue in her own name and had no legal entitlement to her husband's services.

While the Married Women's Property Acts might have been expected to result in extension of the consortium claim to wives, they did not. It was not until 1950, in Hitaffer v. Argonne Co., 183 F.2d 811 (D.C. Cir. 1950), cert. denied 340 U.S. 852 (1950), that an American court held that a wife could maintain a consortium action based on an injury to her husband. In the years since 1950, the vast majority of states have followed *Hitaffer* and extended the consortium claim to wives on the same basis as husbands; in a handful of others, the doctrine has been rejected for both spouses. *See* Boucher By Boucher v. Dixie Medical Center, 850 P.2d 1179 (Utah 1992) (rejecting action).

Under current law, both husband and wife may recover when a spouse has been injured by the negligence or intentional conduct of a third person. In order to avoid the risk of double recovery, many states require that the consortium claim be brought with the underlying tort action and permit the defendant to raise any defenses available against the victim against the victim's spouse as well.

Damage awards for loss of consortium generally reflect the value of damages awarded to the tort victim. Sometimes the awards are substantial. *See, e.g.,* Uniroyal Goodrich Tire Co. v. Martinez, 928 S.W.2d 64 (Tex. App. 1995) (affirming $500,000 award for loss of spousal consortium and $1,000,000 award for consortium losses of each of two children). Some courts have rejected enhancement of consortium damages when the victim spouse's injury allegedly caused a divorce. *See* Prill v. Hampton, 453 N.W.2d 909 (Wis. App. 1990); Chizmar v. Mackie, 896 P.2d 196 (Alaska 1995).

5. OWNERSHIP AND CONTROL OF PROPERTY DURING MARRIAGE

A. COMMON LAW STATES

Since the adoption of the Married Women's Property Acts, title determines asset ownership and management rights in "common law" states.

As a general rule, during an intact marriage in a common law state the property rights of the spouses are not impacted by the marriage. They are generally treated, for purposes of their property rights during marriage, as roommates. Property titled in the name of the husband alone is his property, and property held in the wife's name is hers. Each has sole control over his or her property. Of course, spouses in these states could choose to take title jointly when they purchase something, or have joint bank accounts, but are under no obligation to do so. Creditors of one spouse can attach property owned by that spouse, but generally not property owned by the other. In a number of states, however, one spouse is liable for "necessaries" provided by third parties to the other spouse. *See* Moses H. Cone Memorial Hospital v. Haisley, 672 S.E.2d 742 (N.C.App. 2009) *See generally* the discussion on the notes after *McGuire* in Chapter 2.

The doctrine of necessaries originally required only the *husband* to pay for necessities provided to the *wife*. *See* Note, 82 MICH. L. REV. 1767 (1984). As a result, a few states abolished the doctrine as an unconstitutional gender-based classification. *See* Wal Mart Stores v. Holmes, 7 A.3d 13 (Md. 2010). In many states, the obligation is now reciprocal. See, e.g., 750 ILL. CONS. STATS. 65/15 (a) (1). In some states, one spouse is obligated to pay for necessities provided the other spouse only if the creditor has first tried to collect from the contracting spouse. *See, e,g.,* Hickory Creek at Connersville v. Estate of Combs, 992 N.E.2d 209 (Ind. App. 2013); 23 PA. CONS. STAT. ANN. § 4102. A Kansas court has ruled that, if spouses are living in separate residences when the debt arose, the non-contracting spouse is not liable unless the creditor can show that it relied on the credit of both spouses when extending services. *See* St. Catherine's Hospital v. Alvarez, 383 P.3d 184 (Kan. App. 2016).

In Chapter 15, we will learn that spouses have shared rights in "marital property" property accumulated during marriage from the efforts of either. But these shared rights arise only after a divorce is filed. In U.S. v. Donahue, 2016 WL 3615260 (M.D. Pa. July 6, 2016) the husband was taken into custody during marriage on a criminal charge while possessing $7,876 in cash. The wife filed a petition requesting the court to release the cash because it was "marital property." The court ruled that, under Pennsylvania marital property law, the wife was given no ownership interest in property in the possession of her husband outside the context of a divorce case.

LAW COMMISSION (LONDON), WORKING PAPER NO. 42
Family Property Law (1971) p. 5 et seq.

* * * It is said that equality of power, which separation of property achieves, does not of itself lead to equal opportunity to exercise that power; it ignores the fact that a married woman, especially if she has young

children, does not in practice have the same opportunity as her husband or as an unmarried woman to acquire property; it takes no account of the fact that marriage is a form of partnership to which both spouses contribute, each in a different way, and that the contribution of each is equally important to the family welfare and to society. * * *

0.15 Criticisms of the present law are not limited to its unfairness. It is complained that the law is uncertain. This has been graphically illustrated by reference to the Jones family: Mr. and Mrs. Jones have been married for ten years and have three children. When they married they bought a house on mortgage. The deposit was paid partly from Mrs. Jones' savings and partly from a loan from Mr. Jones' employer. The mortgage installments have usually been paid by Mr. Jones. At the beginning Mrs. Jones had a job; she went back to part-time work when the children were older. From her wages she paid a large part of the household expenses and bought some of the furniture. Occasionally she paid the mortgage installments. A car and a washing machine were bought on hire-purchase in Mr. Jones' name, but the installments were sometimes paid by him and sometimes by her. * * *

0.16 If, in the above situation, Mrs. Jones asks what her property rights are * * * she will receive no clear answer. * * * It is said that this is unsatisfactory, and that the law should give "a clear and definite ruling as to what belongs to whom." * * *

Legal doctrines which complicate ownership of the Joneses' property include the presumption of gift and "resulting trust." For example,

> If a husband buys property out of his earnings and takes the title in the joint names of himself and his wife, he is presumed in law to have intended to make a gift to her of one-half of the value of the property. Similarly, if he buys property in her name, the law presumes that he has made a gift of the entire property to her. This is called the "presumption of advancement" and applies only in one direction: if a wife buys property from her earnings and takes the title in joint names or in her husband's name alone, the presumption is that she retains the full interest, and that he holds the property, or a share in it, as a trustee for her. This is the presumption of "resulting trust." Both presumptions can be rebutted by evidence showing that the intention of the purchaser was different from what is presumed, but in the absence of such evidence wives take property purchased by their husbands under these conditions as gifts, while they retain the full beneficial interest in property that they have purchased and placed in their husband's names.

LAW REFORM COMMISSION OF CANADA, WORKING PAPER NO. 8, FAMILY PROPERTY 10 (March 1975). Another doctrine that might apply to the Joneses' case is that of "constructive trust." Constructive trust is a flexible remedy imposed in a variety of situations to prevent unjust enrichment. In order to establish a constructive trust, the plaintiff typically must show: (1) a confidential relationship; (2) a promise, express or implied; (3) a transfer of property made in reliance on such promise; and (4) unjust enrichment. Sometimes courts interpret these requirements loosely, imposing a constructive trust simply to prevent unjust enrichment. *See* 5 AUSTIN W. SCOTT, TRUSTS §§ 461–552 (William F. Fratcher ed., 4th ed. 1987).

Finally, while the facts do not specify, some of the Joneses' assets may be held in a tenancy by the entireties or joint tenancy with right of survivorship. Surveys suggest that the marital home, often the couple's most valuable asset, is typically held jointly. One divorce survey, for example, found that approximately 89% of couples who owned their home held joint title. *See* Marsha Garrison, *Good Intentions Gone Awry: The Impact of New York's Equitable Distribution Law on Divorce Outcomes*, 57 BROOKLYN L. REV. 621, 655 (1991).

The tenancy by the entireties was, under the common law, the primary exception to the principle of individual spousal control. Such a tenancy was created when husband and wife took the subject property by name, by the same conveyance, to take effect at the same time. When property was so held, neither spouse could independently convey, encumber, or use the property to the exclusion of the other; the tenancy thus could not be severed as could a joint tenancy with right of survivorship. On the death of one spouse, title vested automatically in the survivor. At common law, property held in a tenancy by the entireties was subject to the husband's management. Some states have abolished this feature of the tenancy (*see, e.g.*, Robinson v. Trousdale County, 516 S.W.2d 626 (Tenn. 1974)); the majority of states have abolished the tenancy by the entireties itself. While the tenancy by the entireties is now available in only twenty or so states, joint tenancy with right of survivorship is universally recognized. Joint tenancy establishes equal rights to the subject property; when one joint tenant dies, the other automatically succeeds to his or her interest.

B. COMMUNITY PROPERTY STATES

1. In General

Nine states—Arizona, California, Idaho, Louisiana, New Mexico, Nevada, Texas, Washington, and Wisconsin—have adopted community property systems. Wisconsin's community property system is the most recent, deriving from its adoption of the Uniform Marital Property Act during the 1980s. While there are only nine community property states, about 30% of all residents of the United States live in one. About 20% of all Americans live in either California or Texas.

The community property concept is part of the civil law tradition of the European continent and was first enacted in states that were former French or Spanish colonies. Community property reverses the individual ownership principle of the common law and treats individual earnings acquired during marriage as the joint property of husband and wife, regardless of title.

Although different types of community property systems have evolved, including "universal" community property, (where all property owned by either spouse is treated as community property regardless of when or how the property was acquired), American systems all restrict application of the community property principle to a "community of acquests." Under this approach, only those accumulations viewed as acquisitions of the marital partnership are considered community property.

Community property states agree that accumulations by one spouse before marriage and a gift or inheritance received by one spouse during marriage should not be included in the community of acquests. This "separate" property is owned and managed solely by one spouse. So, under American community property systems, during an intact marriage a couple may hold three types of property: the wife's separate property (owned solely by her), the husband's separate property (owned solely by him), and community property (owned equally by each). In contrast, in a common law state (as mentioned above) there is generally only the husband's property and the wife's property.

The various community property states do not agree, however, on how broadly the community of acquests should extend:

TEX. FAM. CODE

§ 3.001. A spouse's separate property consists of:

1)   the property owned or claimed by the spouse before marriage;

2)   the property acquired by the spouse during marriage by gift, devise, or descent; and

3)   the recovery for personal injuries sustained by the spouse during the marriage, except any recovery for loss of earning capacity during marriage.

§ 3.002. Community property consists of the property, other than separate property, acquired by either spouse during marriage.

ARIZ. REV. STAT.

§ 25–211.

All property acquired by either husband or wife during the marriage is the community property of the husband and wife except for property that is:

1. Acquired by gift, devise or descent.

2. Acquired after service of a petition for dissolution of marriage, legal separation or annulment if the petition results in a decree of dissolution of marriage, legal separation or annulment.

§ 25–213.

A spouse's real and personal property that is owned by that spouse before marriage and that is acquired by that spouse during the marriage by gift, devise or descent, and the increase, rents, issues and profits of that property, is the separate property of that spouse. Property that is acquired by a spouse after service of a petition for dissolution of marriage, legal separation or annulment is also the separate property of that spouse if the petition results in a decree of dissolution of marriage, legal separation or annulment.

UNIFORM MARITAL PROPERTY ACT
9A U.L.A. 109 (1987).

§ 4. Classification of Property of Spouses

(a) All property of spouses is marital property except that which is classified otherwise by this [Act].

(b) All property of spouses is presumed to be marital property.

(c) Each spouse has a present undivided one-half interest in marital property.

(d) Income earned or accrued by a spouse or attributable to property of a spouse during marriage and after the determination date is marital property.

(e) Marital property transferred to a trust remains marital property.

(f) Property owned by a spouse at a marriage after the determination date is individual property.

(g) Property acquired by a spouse during marriage and after the determination date is individual property if acquired:

(1) by gift or a disposition at death made by a third person to the spouse and not to both spouses;

(2) in exchange for or with the proceeds of other individual property of the spouse;

(3) from appreciation of the spouse's individual property except to the extent that the appreciation is classified as marital property under § 14;

(4) by a decree, marital property agreement, written consent, or reclassification under § 7(b) designating it as the individual property of the spouse;

(5) as a recovery for damage to property under § 15, except as specifically provided otherwise in a decree, marital property agreement, or written consent; or

(6) as a recovery for personal injury except for the amount of that recovery attributable to expenses paid or otherwise satisfied from marital property.

NOTES AND QUESTIONS

1.   What important differences do you see between a typical common law state's rules and those of (a) Texas; (b) Arizona; and (c) the UMPA?

2.   About what types of property do Texas, Arizona, and the UMPA agree? Disagree? What are the sources of disagreement?

3.   The "dim" line of distinction between appreciation of and income from separate property is between gain that is "intrinsic" to the property and gain that is "detached." *See* UMPA §§ 4(d) & (4)(g)(3); Thomas Andrews, *Income from Separate Property: Toward a Theoretical Foundation*, 56 LAW & CONTEMP. PROB. 171 (1993). In an ideal marital property system, should income from and appreciation of separate property be subject to the same rules? If yes, should both be community property? Separate property? Or should we distinguish between the two?

Should the classification of appreciated separate property depend on the source of the increased value? If yes, should increased value resulting from inflation be classified as separate or marital? What about increased value resulting from the owner spouse's hard work? Her speculation in the stock market?

Problem 4-1:

In 2000, Bernie inherited a stock portfolio worth $75,000 and real estate worth $500,000. The real estate was an apartment building with sixteen rental units; the net monthly profits from the building were $6,000. In 2001, Bernie married Susan. Shortly after the marriage, Bernie began to use the rents to make improvements to the building. All work was performed by a local contractor, although Bernie decided what should be done. As a result of the improvements, the building is now worth $1,000,000 and produces net monthly profits of $12,000. Although Bernie has neither bought nor sold any of the securities in his stock portfolio, it, too, has increased in value to $250,000. What, if any, part of the value of Bernie's stock and real estate are community property in Arizona? Texas? a UMPA state?

2. Management of Community Property

Under traditional community property rules both spouses were theoretically equal owners, but the husband was legally entitled to manage community assets. The Louisiana management statute, for example, provided that "[t]he husband is the head and master of the partnership or community of gains; he administers its effects, disposes of the revenues which they produce, and may alienate them by an onerous title, without the consent and permission of his wife." LA. CIV. CODE ANN. ART. 2404 (repealed). These rules were already on the way out when, in Kirchberg v. Feenstra, 450 U.S. 455 (1981), the Supreme Court held that the Louisiana statute impermissibly discriminated on the basis of gender.

Today, all community property states have moved from male management to one or another combination of sole management, joint management, and equal management:

TEX. FAM. CODE

§ 3.101.

Each spouse has the sole management, control, and disposition of that spouse's separate property.

§ 3.102.

(a) During marriage, each spouse has the sole management, control, and disposition of the community property that he or she would have owned if single, including but not limited to:

(1) personal earnings;

(2) revenue from separate property;

(3) recoveries for personal injuries; and

(4) the increase and mutations of, and the revenue from, all property subject to his or her sole management, control, and disposition.

(b) If the community property subject to the sole management, control, and disposition of one spouse is mixed or combined with community property subject to the sole management, control, and disposition of the other spouse, then the mixed or combined community property is subject to the joint management, control, and disposition of the spouses, unless the spouses provide otherwise by power of attorney in writing or other agreement.

(c) Except as provided in Subsection (a) of this section, the community property is subject to the joint management, control, and disposition of the spouses, unless the spouses provide otherwise by power of attorney in writing or other agreement.

ARIZ. REV. STAT. § 25–214

A. Each spouse has the sole management, control and disposition rights of his or her separate property.

B. The spouses have equal management, control and disposition rights over their community property, and have equal power to bind the community.

C. Either spouse separately may acquire, manage, control or dispose of community property, or bind the community, except that joinder of both spouses is required in any of the following cases:

1. Any transaction for the acquisition, disposition or encumbrance of an interest in real property other than an unpatented mining claim or a lease of less than one year.

2. Any transaction of guaranty, indemnity or suretyship.

CAL. FAM. CODE

§ 1100.

(a) Except as provided in subdivisions (b), (c), and (d) * * * either spouse has the management and control of the community personal property * * * with like absolute power of disposition, other than testamentary, as the spouse has of the separate estate of the spouse.

(b) A spouse may not make a gift of community personal property, or dispose of community personal property for less than fair and reasonable value, without the written consent of the other spouse. This subdivision does not apply to gifts mutually given by both spouses to third parties and to gifts given by one spouse to the other spouse.

(c) A spouse may not sell, convey, or encumber community personal property used as the family dwelling, or the furniture, furnishings, or fittings of the home, or the clothing or wearing apparel of the other spouse or minor children which is community personal property, without the written consent of the other spouse.

(d) Except as provided in subdivisions (b) and (c), and in § 1102, a spouse who is operating or managing a business or an interest in a business that is all or substantially all community personal property has the primary management and control of the business or interest. Primary management and control means that the managing spouse may act alone in all transactions but shall give prior written notice to the other spouse of any sale, lease, exchange, encumbrance, or other disposition of all or substantially all of the personal property used in the operation of the business (including personal property used for agricultural purposes), whether or not title to that property is held in the name of only one spouse. Written notice is not, however, required when prohibited by the law otherwise applicable to the transaction. Remedies for the failure by a managing spouse to give prior written notice as required by this subdivision are only as specified in § 1101. A failure to give prior written notice shall not adversely affect the validity of a transaction nor of any interest transferred.

(e) Each spouse shall act with respect to the other spouse in the management and control of the community assets and liabilities in accordance with the general rules governing fiduciary relationships which control the actions of persons having relationships of personal confidence * * *, until such time as the assets and liabilities have been divided by the parties or by a court. This duty includes the obligation to make full disclosure to the other spouse of all material facts and information regarding the existence, characterization, and valuation of all assets in which the community has or may have an interest and debts for which the community is or may be liable, and to provide equal access to all information, records, and books that pertain to the value and character of those assets and debts, upon request.

§ 1102.

(a) * * * [E]ither spouse has the management and control of the community real property, * * * but both spouses * * * must join in executing any instrument by which that community real property or any interest therein is leased for a longer period than one year, or is sold, conveyed, or encumbered.

(b) Nothing in this section shall be construed to apply to a lease, mortgage, conveyance, or transfer of real property or of any interest in real property between husband and wife.

(c) Notwithstanding subdivision (b): * * *

2) The sole lease, contract, mortgage, or deed of either spouse, holding the record title to community real property to a lessee, purchaser, or encumbrancer, in good faith without knowledge of the marriage relation, shall be presumed to be valid. * * *

In a common law state, until the marriage breaks down there are no limits on what a title-holding spouse may do with her property: a unilateral gift during marriage to a third party thus will not generally be taken into account at divorce unless the court finds that the transfer was made in contemplation of divorce. *See* Panhorst v. Panhorst, 390 S.E.2d 376 (S.C.

App. 1990). By contrast, community property states impose significant limits on a spouse's unilateral management power over community property in an intact marriage.

MARTIN V. MARTIN

California Court of Appeal, First District, Division 1, 1984 (A012041), 1 Civ. No. 52320.
(Sup. Ct. No. 230798) (unpublished).

HOLMDAHL, J.

Husband Thomas J. Martin (hereafter, "Husband") and wife Jean Martin (hereafter, "Wife"), appellant here and the petitioner below, were married on June 27, 1948, and separated on February 28, 1979. There is no minor child. Wife abandoned a career as a professional dancer when she married Husband. Husband graduated from law school, but worked as a building contractor and developer during the marriage. Toward the later part of the marriage, Husband developed an intimate friendship with another woman. Over a period of about 15 years, Husband gave the woman money and other gifts and traveled with her extensively, paying all or most of her expenses.

The San Mateo County Superior Court found that, at the time of separation, there were assets of the community having a total value of $3,555,006 (not including funds already distributed to the parties). The court also found that Husband had, during marriage, misappropriated community funds in the amount of $67,604 in connection with his extra-marital relationship. * * * It awarded that sum to Husband and awarded to Wife assets of equal value as an offset. In essence, the action required Husband to pay to Wife her one-half share of the assets he had misappropriated. Thus, Wife was restored to the position she would have occupied had the assets not been misappropriated (ignoring the loss of the use of the funds).

* * *

Wife contends the court should have awarded interest (preferably compound interest) on the misappropriated assets. She argues that a fiduciary relationship exists between a husband and wife, in the nature of a trustee-beneficiary relationship, and that allowance of interest is permitted in such circumstances pursuant to Civil Code §§ 2237 and 2238. * * * A misappropriated asset is one which, by definition, does not exist at the time of trial. In other words, it is an asset which was removed from the community's control at some time in the past. Given this fact, we think it is significant that the statute dealing with misappropriation makes no provision for interest but, rather, expressly refers only to the "sum [the court] determines to have been deliberately misappropriated." Had the Legislature intended that interest be awarded, it would have expressly so provided.

Husband contends that because he received some value in connection with his expenditure of funds relative to his extramarital affair, the expenditures do not constitute misappropriations. He cites *In re Marriage of Moore,* 28 Cal.3d 366 (1980), in which the husband was found to have disposed of various items of community property, evidently to finance his acquisition of large amounts of alcoholic beverages. The California Supreme Court made the following observation: "Lydie, however, has failed to prove that David made a gift of the missing items or disposed of them without valuable consideration. The only evidence presented on the question—Lydie's belief that he disposed of the items to buy alcoholic beverages—indicates to the contrary. David could not have purchased alcoholic beverages with the items if he had not received valuable consideration for them."

To the extent, then, that valuable consideration was received, the expenditures were not misappropriations. He then goes on to argue that he derived a great deal of benefit from the expenditures, that the stipend he paid to his illicit companion was offset by the amount he saved by avoiding, with her help, undue consumption of alcohol (the parties agree Husband had an alcohol problem), and that he was entitled to have some recreation given the fact he had made for the community so much money. He gives examples of gifts which should not be considered misappropriations, including, for example, a gift to the S.P.C.A. He also suggests that the amount of the gift compared to the wealth of the community should be considered in determining whether a misappropriation occurred.

Husband's arguments do not persuade us. A spouse cannot be allowed to defeat a claim of misappropriation by claiming he derived benefit from expending the community's assets. The test should be whether the expenditure benefitted the community or occurred with its express or implied consent. As for Husband's suggestion that he was responsible for amassing the wealth of the community, we decline to establish some sort of a test relative to misappropriation which permits a spouse to spend in whatever way he chooses some of the community's assets because he was responsible for accumulating the assets. To do so would create a second category of community property and run counter to the very foundation of our community property system. Neither are we tempted to create exceptions based on the recipient of a gift. A gift to the S.P.C.A. might very well constitute misappropriation, if it is made over the other spouse's objection. Nor can the wealth of the community be the basis of any sort of workable test, even ignoring the fact that this too would tend to create two categories of community property.

This leads us to the other significant point raised by Husband relative to this issue. Husband says it was error for the court to prevent him from introducing evidence to the effect that "the reason he started spending money on [his illicit companion] in the first place was that he and his wife had not had sexual relations since 1958 and that she had denied him the affection and companionship of a normal marriage. Husband offered this evidence in order to show the circumstances surrounding his relationship with [her]. In Husband's view, this evidence would have negated any deliberate misappropriation on his part." Husband's point is not well-taken. The relevant question is not whether there was a good reason for his relationship with his companion, but whether the relationship and the related expenditures benefitted the community or occurred with its consent.

The proffered evidence was not offered for a proper purpose and, therefore, the trial court did not abuse its discretion in excluding it. * * * The judgment is affirmed in all respects.

NOTES AND QUESTIONS

1. In California, each spouse may rescind any type of unilateral gift of community property made by the other spouse. Under the UMPA and Texas law, a spouse may make a "reasonable" unilateral gift of community property. What are the pros and cons of each approach? Under the Texas/UMPA approach, how should a court determine whether a gift is "reasonable"?

2. The American Law Institute has proposed that spouses should be able to undo unilateral gifts of marital property only when the gift is "substantial relative to the total value of the marital property at the time of the gift," and the gift is made shortly before a divorce action is filed. *See* AM. LAW INSTITUTE, PRINCIPLES OF THE LAW OF FAMILY DISSOLUTION § 4.10 (2002). On what assumptions is the ALI approach based? What are the pros and cons of the ALI approach as compared to the California and Texas/UMPA approaches?

3. In some community property states, a spouse is liable to the community estate if he or she does something intentionally that dissipates the community estate. For example, in Marriage of Beltran, 227 Cal. Rptr. 924 (App. 1986) the husband had earned certain military retirement benefits, a portion of which would have been community property. He was convicted during marriage of committing a crime; as a result, he was dismissed from the Army and forfeited all retirement benefits. In the parties' divorce, he was required to pay the wife 50% of the value of the forfeited benefits. Is this fair?

4. Although the question whether a spouse has exceeded her management authority is typically litigated, as in *Martin*, in the context of a divorce proceeding, California has provided remedies for spouses who remain married. Under CAL. FAM. CODE § 1101, a court may order "an accounting of the property and obligations of the parties to a marriage"; it may also, with exceptions for certain types of property, (in order to facilitate each spouse's equal management power) order "that the name of a spouse shall be added to community property held in the name of the other spouse." Is giving one spouse a remedy of this nature a good idea?

5. A major loss through gambling is typically treated as dissipation of marital assets, but a bad investment made in good faith is not. *Compare* Reaney v. Reaney, 505 S.W.2d 338 (Tex. App. 1974) (husband liable at divorce for $53,000 in gambling losses) *with* Andrews v. Andrews, 677 S.W.2d 171 (Tex. App. 1984) (husband is not liable for bad investments.) What is the difference between gambling and a bad investment? Is this a sound distinction?

6. *Creditors' Rights in Community Property States:* Community property states accept the necessaries doctrine. *See, e.g.,* TEX. FAM. CODE § 3.201; CAL. FAM. CODE § 914. But in contrast to the common law states, creditors' rights are not limited to debts for necessaries. Some community property states provide that the creditor of a spouse may attach all property over which that spouse has management power; in Texas, for example, a contract creditor of one spouse may attach a debtor-spouse's separate property as well as all property over which the spouse has sole or joint management power. *See* TEX. FAM. CODE §§ 3.201, 3.202. Other states base the creditor's rights on whether the debt is a separate or community debt; for a community debt, a creditor may attach all community property and the debtor-spouse's separate property. *See* ARIZ. REV. STAT. § 25–215; N.M. STAT. ANN. § 40–3–11; WIS. STAT. ANN. § 766.55. For a separate debt, some of the "community vs. separate debt" states restrict the creditor's rights to the spouse's separate property; the remainder permit the creditor to attach the debtor-spouse's interest in community assets as well. *See* N.M. STAT. ANN. § 40–3–10; WIS. STAT. ANN. § 766.55.

Many community property states also distinguish tort judgments from other debts. Most permit the tort-judgment creditor to attach at least the tortfeasor's half of the community estate, but some distinguish between a "separate" and "community" tort. In California, for example, the tort-judgment creditor must first exhaust community property before attaching the tortfeasor's separate property if the tort is a community tort; for a separate tort the creditor must first exhaust separate property before the tortfeasor's share of community assets may be attached. *See* CAL. FAM. CODE § 1000.

7. Is sole, joint, or equal management the best system?

Each system has its drawbacks. Joint management ensures that both owners will have the opportunity to participate in management of the community, but this requirement could place a substantial burden upon commerce, particularly if it were applied to all transactions involving any amount of community property. Furthermore, some spouses might not want to manage; the joint management system would burden them, unless some way of opting out were created. Also, what should occur under such a system if only one spouse purports to transfer community property? * * *

The sole management system clearly specifies who will have management power over each item of community property. However, if each spouse does not accumulate (or in some states have record ownership of) the same amount of property during marriage, this system would grant one spouse power over more than half of the community estate, even though both spouses possess a present, vested fifty percent interest. If one spouse works outside the home and the other does not, in many instances the spouse working in the home would manage little or no community property.

The equal management system, like the joint management system, reflects a general norm of equality; it does present a problem, however, if the spouses disagree, and especially if they give contradictory instructions to a third party. In addition, even though either spouse in theory may exercise management power, one might argue that the system facilitates the usurpation of management of the community by the dominant spouse. Also, equal and sole management both permit one spouse to affect the property interests of the other without giving that spouse notice.

No state has accepted one of these management systems for all transactions involving community property. Each has adopted a combination of management rules, in which some transactions are governed by one set of rules, and others by another set. * * *

J. Thomas Oldham, *Management of the Community Estate During An Intact Marriage*, 56 L. & CONTEMP. PROB. 99, 106–07 (1993).

Is the best management system some combination of sole, joint, and equal management, as Professor Oldham suggests? If yes, what is the best combination? What rule should govern household property? A community property business? Real estate? Why do most community property states require both spouses to consent to the sale or encumbrance of community realty?

Problem 4-2:

Wanda would like to invest funds she has earned during her marriage to Harry in an oil well. Harry thinks this is a bad idea and would like to veto it. Is there a legal remedy available to Harry: a) in a common law state? b) in a community property state? Which state's management rules are most helpful to Harry? In which states, if any, will Wanda be liable to Harry if she makes the investment and loses the money?

Problem 4-3:

Hank works outside the home and Wilma is a homemaker. Hank deposits his paycheck in an account in his own name. Wilma wants the power to manage these funds, too. Is there a legal remedy available to Wilma: a) in a common law state? b) in a community property state? Which state's management rules are most helpful to Wilma?

Problem 4-4:

Harvey is a homemaker and Willa works outside the home, where she earns a substantial amount of money. All savings accrued during the marriage are in accounts in Willa's name alone. If Harvey buys a piece of art on credit for the living room, may the art dealer attach Willa's property? Does it matter if they live in a common law or community property state?

C. "TIL DEATH US DO PART": SPOUSAL PROPERTY RIGHTS AT DEATH

Under a community property regime, each spouse holds an equal, undivided interest in all community assets. When the first spouse dies, that spouse may dispose of her half of community property by will without restriction; the survivor spouse has no inheritance entitlement either to the decedent spouse's separate property or his half interest in community assets, but the survivor does, of course, retain his or her half interest in the community estate.

The traditional common law approach, which held that all property was owned by the husband, granted the surviving wife a right to "dower," i.e., a life estate in one-third of any land of which the husband was seized in fee at any time during the marriage. As a result of the wife's dower right, the husband could not alienate his lands during his lifetime so as to bar the wife's right of dower unless the wife consented. But the husband's personalty was his to dispose of as he wished:

> He can, even by his will, give all of it away from her except her necessary clothes, and with that exception his creditors can take all of it. A further exception, of which there is not much to be read, is made of jewels, trinkets, and ornaments of the person, under the name of *paraphernalia*. The husband may sell or give these away in his lifetime, and even after his death they may be taken for his debts; but he can not give them away by will. If the husband dies during the wife's life and dies intestate, she is entitled to a third, or if there be no living descendant of the husband, to one-half of his personalty. But this is a case of pure intestate succession; she only has a share of what is left after payment of her husband's debts.

2 F. POLLOCK & F. MAITLAND, THE HISTORY OF THE ENGLISH LAW 405 (1899).

The wife's dower right, in most common law states, has been replaced or augmented by a spousal "right of election" that applies to both husband and wife and guarantees the surviving spouse a fixed fractional share (typically the dower fraction, one-third) of the decedent spouse's probate assets. J. Thomas Oldham, *You Can't Take It With You, and Maybe You Can't Even Give It Away: The Case of Elizabeth Baldwin Rice*, 41 U. MEMPHIS L. REV. 95 (2010). Although the details of right of election schemes vary substantially from state to state, only one of the common law states (Georgia) has no elective share scheme; most statutes grant an entitlement to *ownership*, not a life estate or income, of assets equal to the spousal share. *See* Laura A. Rosenbury, *Two Ways To End a Marriage: Divorce or Death*, 2005 UTAH L. REV. 1227 (2005); J. Thomas Oldham, *Should the Surviving Spouse's Forced Share Be Retained?*, 38 CASE W. RES. L. REV. 225 (1988). Note that the survivor's claim extends to *all* of the decedent's estate, including property acquired before marriage or by gift or inheritance.

If the spouses have been living separately for a substantial period when a spouse dies, should this affect the survivor's claim? *See In re Peterson Estate*, 889 N.W.2d 753 (Mich. App. 2016). What if the claimant has been cohabiting with another?

In many common law states, the spousal right of election has been extended to assets, such as joint tenancy property, that are not part of the probate estate. This extension (under the Uniform Probate Code (UPC), the "augmented estate") is designed both to prevent the decedent spouse from rendering the right of election meaningless through illusory or fraudulent lifetime transfers and to ensure that the surviving spouse's entitlement is fairly based on all the decedent's assets and all the survivor's assets derived from the decedent. Some states have not adopted the augmented estate concept, however. And many have included in the augmented estate some types of probate assets but not others, with the result that the spouse who wants to defeat his or her spouse's right of election can, with some careful planning, still do so in most states.

A third round of reform is just now underway, this one motivated by the discrepancy between elective-share rules and the widely accepted view that marriage is an equal partnership. The elective-share fraction—typically one-third of the decedent's estate—does not comport with the partnership model, which would mandate one-half of all property accumulated during the marriage. Nor does it comport with survey evidence, which uniformly demonstrates that the typical U.S. spouse prefers to leave everything to the survivor.[1] Moreover, the elective-share fraction applies to what would be separate assets in a community property system and does so without regard to marital duration; the spouse married for one day to the multimillionaire gets exactly the same share of her estate as the spouse married for thirty years.

---

[1] The one exception is where there are children from a prior marriage. *See, e.g.,* Contemporary Studies Project, *A Comparison of Iowans' Dispositive Preferences with Selected Provisions of the Iowa and [the Pre-1990] Uniform Probate Codes*, 63 Iowa L. Rev. 1041 (1978); Mary L. Fellows et al., *Public Attitudes About Property Distribution at Death and Intestate Succession Laws in the United States*, 1978 A.B.F. RES. J. 391; Mary L. Fellows, et al., *An Empirical Study of the Illinois Statutory Estate Plan*, 1978 U. ILL. L. F. 717; John Price, *The Transmission of Wealth at Death in a Community Property Jurisdiction*, 50 WASH. L. REV. 277 (1975). Earlier studies are cited in these publications. A strong preference for the surviving spouse has also been reported in England. U.K. LAW COMM'N, FAMILY LAW: DISTRIBUTION ON INTESTACY (No. 187), at app. C, 36–37, 40–45 (1989).

The aim of the new reform movement has been to infuse elective-share law with community property concepts. But this is not so easy in states that do not recognize community property. The ingenious, if complex, system adopted by the 1990 Uniform Probate Code retains the common law approach of granting the surviving spouse a fractional share of the decedent's property without regard to whether it would be classified as separate or community property. But the revised elective share expands with the duration of the marriage; a surviving spouse married to the decedent for one year is entitled to only 3% of the augmented estate, while a survivor married for fifteen years is entitled to 50%. *See generally* Lawrence W. Waggoner, *The Multiple-Marriage Society and Spousal Rights Under the Revised Uniform Probate Code,* 76 IOWA L. REV. 223 (1991).

If the decedent and the spouse were married to each other:	The elective-share percentage is:
Less than 1 year	Supplemental Amount Only
1 year but less than 2 years	3% of the augmented estate
2 years but less than 3 years	6% of the augmented estate
3 years but less than 4 years	9% of the augmented estate
* * *	
15 or more years	50% of the augmented estate

UPC § 2–201.

These varying percentages are coupled with a newly defined augmented estate that includes the *surviving* spouse's assets as well as those of the decedent. UPC §§ 2–202, 2–203. Less than a dozen states have adopted the 1990 version of the Uniform Probate Code elective-share provisions, either as drafted or with minor variations. Two others, Alaska and North Dakota, adopted the 1990 UPC elective-share scheme without the phased-in percentage share provisions; Alaska's fixed-share entitlement is one-third (ALASKA STAT. ANN. § 13.12.202) and North Dakota's one-half (N.D. CENT. CODE § 30.1–05–01). *See* JESSE DUKEMINIER & STANLEY M. JOHANSEN, WILLS, TRUSTS, AND ESTATES 512 (6th ed. 2000).

In some respects, the accrual system is similar to the U.S. community property system. Of course, the two systems are not identical. Most significantly, in a community property system, the time and manner of acquisition determine the property's character. Absent commingling or a subsequent spousal agreement, the character, once established, never changes. Property acquired before marriage, for example, is separate and, absent action by the parties, will remain so. In contrast, under the UPC accrual system all property is treated the same, notwithstanding when or how it was acquired, and gradually becomes marital property over time without any action by the spouses.

After fifteen years, all property is considered marital. Functionally, after fifteen years of marriage, the UPC system could be characterized as a system of "universal" community property, as opposed to the "community of acquests" system that has been accepted in U.S. community property states, in the sense that all property owned by either spouse is shared.

A few examples clarify how the UPC system operates. Assume A and B have been married for 5 years when A dies and that A's net estate is $400,000 and B's is $200,000. A devised nothing to B. Under the revised UPC, the total, or "augmented," estate, or the sum of A's and B's net estate is $600,000. Further, the UPC assumes that 30% of the total assets, $180,000, are marital after five years of marriage. The elective share is 50% of the marital share, or $90,000. But that does not mean B gets $90,000 because the UPC assumes B already owns $60,000 of marital assets, or 30% of B's $200,000. B's claim from A's estate is the elective share amount, $90,000, minus the amount of marital assets owned by B, $60,000. Thus, B is entitled to $30,000. After the transfer of $30,000 from A's estate, B would then own 50% of the accrued marital estate of $180,000.

In the same example, if A dies and the marriage exceeded fifteen years in duration, rather than five, all the parties' $600,000 would be considered marital. B's aggregate forced share claim would be $300,000, or half of the amount of the total marital estate. Since the total value of B's estate is $200,000, the survivor's claim under the UPC would be $100,000 from A's estate, or $300,000 less the $200,000 already owned by B.

If instead A had died with a net probate estate of $300,000, A left nothing to B, and B's net assets were also worth $300,000 in a fifteen-year marriage, the result would be significantly different. The augmented estate is still $600,000, and all the assets would be considered marital under the UPC schedule, given the fifteen-year martial duration. The elective share again is 50% of the marital estate, or $300,000. However, unlike the previous examples, B would have no net claim against A's estate because B already owns $300,000 in marital assets.

One difference between rights of spouses at death in a common law state and a community property state can be highlighted by the story of the dispute that arose between Mr. and Mrs. William Marsh Rice at the end of the 19th century. Mr. Rice, who had extensive business interests in Texas, shortly after the end of the Civil War married a woman from Texas. Throughout their marriage, they had a house in New York and spent a great deal of time in Texas, due to Mr. Rice's business interests. After 30 years of marriage, Mrs. Rice died. Her will revealed her assumption that she could devise 50% of all property acquired by Mr. Rice during marriage; this would be true if the parties had been domiciled in Texas when she died. Mr. Rice contended that they were domiciled in New York, and that under New York law Mrs. Rice could devise only that property titled in her name when she died. Mr. Rice eventually settled with her executor by paying a relatively small amount of "his" fortune, thereby giving him the ability to endow what would become Rice University with most of the assets acquired by him during his marriage with Mrs. Rice. *See* J. Thomas Oldham, *You Can't Take It with You, and Maybe You Can't Even Give it Away: The Case of Elizabeth Baldwin Rice*, 41 U. MEMPHIS L. REV. 95 (2010). Does the law of Texas or New York seem preferable in this situation?

One unusual aspect of U.S. inheritance law is that almost all states allow a parent to leave nothing to his children when the parent dies. Only Louisiana generally requires a parent to leave a fraction of his or her estate to a surviving child, but only if the child is younger than 24.

Problem 4-5:

Consider the following fact patterns and determine each surviving spouse's entitlement in a community property state, a common law state with an elective share equal to one-third of the decedent's probate estate, and under the 1990 UPC. None of the spouses entered into a premarital agreement.

a.   John and Marla married in February 2007. At the time of the marriage, each had assets worth $20,000. In 2010, they had a child. In January 2017, John and Marla separated. One month later John died, leaving his entire estate to the National Audubon Society. John's probate estate (which represents all of his assets) is worth $400,000; $380,000 represents money inherited from his mother in 2000. Marla owns assets worth $25,000.

b.   Tom and Joanne married in 1977. At the time of the marriage, each had no debts. Tom died testate in 2017, leaving his entire estate to his disabled brother, Philip. Tom's probate estate (representing all of his assets) is worth $1 million; all assets were acquired with Tom's earnings during the marriage. Joanne owns assets worth $5,000.

c.   Harry and Sally married in June 2016. It was the third marriage for both; each had children from prior marriages. At the time of the marriage, Harry had assets worth $300,000; Sally had assets worth $1,900,000. Harry died testate in August 2017, leaving his entire estate to his children, in equal shares. Harry's estate is worth $300,000; Sally has assets worth $2,000,000.

d.   Harry and Sally married in June 2016. It was the third marriage for both; each had children from prior marriages. At the time of the marriage, Harry had assets worth $300,000. Sally had assets worth $15,000; as a result of the marriage, she also lost her claim to alimony from her former husband, worth $2000 per month. Harry died testate in August 2017, leaving his entire estate to his children, in equal shares. Harry's estate is worth $300,000; Sally has assets worth $15,000.

In what types of cases does the community property approach seem most fair? The common law right of election? The UPC approach? Is there some combination that seems preferable to any one approach alone?

D. SOME CONCLUDING THOUGHTS

So, is a community property system better than the common law approach? The common law states certainly have not leaped toward community property norms; in the decade and a half since it was promulgated, the Uniform Marital Property Act (UMPA) has been adopted in only one state.

Is there some belated wisdom in the common law approach?

There is still one small fact that gives rise to a nagging doubt about our * * * efforts [to reform the common law]. This is that in West Germany and Sweden, home of systems like those we are trying to establish, discontent is being registered with the deferred community. In Sweden, law reforms are in progress which seem likely to result in the curtailment or abolition of the deferred community and its replacement with another system, more responsible to current needs and desires. What is this ultra modern system? Separation of assets. O tempora, o mores!

Why should we be concerned with what is happening in West Germany and Sweden? Their societies and economies are not just like ours. What are the reasons for their re-examination of deferred community and why are they casting their eyes toward our old system of the Married Women's Separate Property Acts? In both West Germany and Sweden, the feeling is being expressed in some quarters that legal devices developed for the situation where one spouse works outside and the other works inside the home are increasingly inappropriate. In Sweden, the exclusively housewife marriage is said now to be becoming uncommon. In West Germany, the two-earner marriage is said to have replaced *Hausfrauenehe* as the dominant pattern. The official family policy statement of the Social Democratic Party and government sponsored legislation are designed to reflect and respond to the changing social situation. Already, many West German couples are going to the trouble to contract out of the deferred community in favor of separation of assets.

Mary Ann Glendon, *Is There a Future for Separate Property?*, 8 FAM. L.Q. 315, 322–25 (1974).

Despite the developments described by Professor Glendon, many wives continue to earn less than their husbands and play a disproportionate role in child-care activities that typically reduce long-term earning capacity. In the case of a long-term homemaker, the common law approach can produce results that seem unfair. Perhaps we need a property rule that varies based on marital roles: it is theoretically possible to impose a community property regime on traditional, homemaker/ breadwinner couples and a separate property regime on those with relatively equal earnings and careers. Or perhaps, as in many civil law countries, it would be preferable to require spouses to opt into one regime or the other at the time of their marriage. These alternatives have their own disadvantages, of course. The one thing we can say with confidence is that no marital property regime seems fair in all cases.

Problem 4-6:

You are counsel to the state legislature's Committee on Family Law. The legislature is considering marital property reform. Its goals are improvements in fairness and efficiency. Advise the Committee on how, if at all, your state's property classification and management scheme should be revised.

6. PUBLIC OBLIGATIONS AND BENEFITS

Marital status determines a wide range of benefits and obligations. We have already considered some of the private benefits associated with marriage: Spouses acquire certain rights against their marriage partner, including support, an interest in assets acquired during after marriage, and the right (except in Georgia) to take a share of the decedent spouse's estate. Spouses also acquire rights against third parties. Tort law, as you have already learned, provides spouses with the right to maintain a wrongful death action and an action for loss of spousal consortium. More meaningful to the typical spouse are employment-benefit rights, including participation as a family member in the earner-spouse's health insurance plan, the right to death benefits payable under a pension plan governed by the federal Employment and Retirement Income Security Act (ERISA), and other "family" benefits related to employment. Additionally, marital status often affects public obligations and benefits.

SCHWEIKER V. GRAY PANTHERS
Supreme Court of the United States, 1981.
453 U.S. 34.

JUSTICE POWELL delivered the opinion of the Court.

The Medicaid program provides federal funds to States that pay for medical treatment for the poor. An individual's entitlement to Medicaid benefits depends on the financial resources "available" to him. Some States determine eligibility by assuming—"deeming"—that a portion of the spouse's income is "available" to the applicant. "Deeming" thus has the effect of reducing both the number of eligible individuals and the amount of assistance paid to those who qualify. The question in this case is whether *issue* the federal regulations that permit States to "deem" income in this manner are arbitrary, capricious, or otherwise unlawful.

I.   * * *   [The Medicaid regulations at issue describe] the circumstances in which the income of one spouse may be "deemed" available to the other. In [some] states, "deeming" is conducted in the following manner: When the applicant and his spouse live in the same household, the spouse's income and resources always are considered in determining eligibility, "whether or not they are actually contributed." When the applicant and spouse cease to share the same household, the spouse's income is disregarded the next month, unless both are eligible for assistance. In the latter case, the income of both is considered for six months after their separation. [In other states, i.e., the so-called § 209 (b) states, the regulations permit deeming beyond this six-month period.] * * *

II.   Respondent, an organization dedicated to helping the nation's elderly, filed this suit * * * attacking some of the Secretary's regulations applicable in § 209 (b) States. Respondent argued that "deeming" impermissibly employs an "arbitrary formula" to impute a spouse's income to an institutionalized Medicaid applicant. According to respondent, "deeming" is inconsistent with * * * the Act, which provides that only income "available" to the applicant may be considered in establishing entitlement to and the amount of Medicaid benefits. In respondent's view, before a state may take into account the income of a spouse in calculating *respondent's argument* the benefits of any institutionalized applicant, the State must make a factual determination that the spouse's income actually is contributed to that applicant.

The District Court agreed with respondent and declared the regulations invalid. The Court of Appeals for the District of Columbia Circuit affirmed, [having found] * * * the Secretary, in authorizing *history* "deeming" of income between noncohabiting spouses, had failed to "[take] . . . into account" two "relevant factors." First, where spouses are separated they maintain two households rather than one. For those already put to this additional expense, it is unfair to continue to treat the couple as a "single economic unit" jointly responsible for the medical expenses of each. Second, the requirement of support carries with it the potential to interject "disruptive forces" into people's lives. The noninstitutionalized spouse is "faced with the 'choice' of reducing his or her standard of living to a point apparently set near the poverty line, or being responsible for the eviction of his or her spouse from the institution."

One aspect of this "disruption," according to the court, was the fact that the "deeming" requirement creates an incentive for couples to divorce. Because the court believed that the Secretary had not adequately considered these effects of "deeming," it affirmed the District Court's order invalidating the regulations and remanded to the Secretary for reconsideration. * * *

III. * * *

A. * * * [O]ur task is the limited one of ensuring that the Secretary did not "[exceed] his statutory authority" and that the regulation is not arbitrary or capricious.

B. We do not think that the regulations at issue, insofar as they authorize some "deeming" of income between spouses, exceed the authority conferred on the Secretary by Congress. Section 1902 (A)(17)(D) of the Act, * * * provides that, in calculating benefits, state medicaid plans must not

> "take into account the financial responsibility of any individual for any applicant or recipient of assistance under the plan *unless such applicant or recipient is such individual's spouse* or such individual's child who is under age 21 or [in certain circumstances] is blind or disabled. . . " (Emphasis added.)

It thus is apparent that, from the beginning of the Medicaid program, Congress authorized States to presume spousal support.

The legislative history of this provision is fully consistent with its language. The Senate and House Reports accompanying the 1965 amendments used virtually identical language in endorsing the concept of "deeming" between spouses. The Senate Report states in pertinent part:

> The committee believes it is proper to expect spouses to support each other and parents to be held accountable for the support of their minor children. . . Such requirements for support may reasonably include the payment by such relative, if able, for medical care. Beyond such degree of relationship, however, requirements imposed are often destructive and harmful to the relationships among members of the family group. Thus, States may not include in their plans provisions for requiring contributions from relatives *other than a spouse or the parent of a minor child.* . . S. Rep. No. 404, 89th Cong., 1st Sess., 78 (1965) (emphasis added).

* * *

If "deeming" were not permissible, subsection (17)(D) would be superfluous. Payments *actually received* by a Medicaid applicant—whether from a spouse or a more distant relative—are taken into account automatically. Thus, if there is to be content to subsection (17)(D)'s distinction between the responsibility of a spouse and that of a more distant relative, the subsection must envision that States can "deem" the income of the former but not the latter. * * *

C.   Respondent nevertheless insists that the Secretary's regulation is inconsistent with provisions of the statute and also contrary to statements in the legislative history. The Act requires Medicaid determinations to be made only on the basis of the income "available to the applicant." according to respondent, the use of that term demonstrates that Medicaid entitlements must be determined on the basis of income "actually in the hands . . . of the institutionalized spouse," not imputed on the basis of an "arbitrary formula." Respondent acknowledges the duty of spousal support as a general matter, but argues that the act nevertheless requires an individualized determination of availability in each case.

We take a different view. It is clear beyond doubt that Congress was wary of imputing the income of others to a Medicaid applicant. Yet, as we noted above, Congress treated spouses differently from most other relatives by explicitly authorizing state plans to "take into account the financial responsibility" of the spouse. Congress thus demonstrated that "deeming" is not antithetical to the general statutory requirement that Medicaid eligibility be based solely on resources "available" to the applicant. "Available" resources are different from those in hand. We think that the requirement of availability refers to resources left to a *couple* after the spouse has deducted a sum on which to live. It does not, as respondent argues, permit the State only to consider the resources actually paid by the spouse to the applicant. * * *

We are not without sympathy for those with minimal resources for medical care. But our "sympathy is an insufficient basis for approving a recovery" based on a theory inconsistent with law.[20]

* * * Accordingly, we reverse the decision under review and remand for proceedings consistent with this opinion.

NOTES AND QUESTIONS

1.   Was the Senate correct that deeming poses a greater threat to family harmony when applied to relatives who aren't spouses or children? How do the Senate's family-harmony concerns differ from those of the *McGuire* court? From those of the nineteenth century courts that favored parent-child and spousal immunity rules?

2.   *The Assumptions Behind Deeming:* Deeming relies on the assumption that the married couple is an economic unit in which the income of one spouse is fully available to the other. This assumption—which is reflected in U.S. tax law as well as the Social Security Act and a wide range of other benefit-conferring statutes—flows from both legal and social norms: marriage partners

---

[20] We note, in any event, that respondent's position would not eliminate difficult choices for the contributing spouse. This lawsuit seeks only to enjoin the "deeming" of income to an institutionalized spouse. Respondent thus concedes the legality of "deeming" where spouses cohabit. To adopt respondent's construction of the statute would create an incentive to shunt ailing spouses into nursing homes to circumvent the "deeming" that otherwise would occur.

have legal support obligations to each other; both the marriage ceremony and widely accepted notions of spousal unity tend to foster a marital income-pooling ethic. Thus, the evidence suggests that even those spouses who view some assets—inheritances, for example, or premarital savings—as "mine" instead of "ours," rarely divide the monthly bills and split them as roommates would. Instead, they pool earnings to provide for their combined living expenses or pay expenses based on income. *See* Marsha Garrison, *Is Consent Necessary? An Evaluation of the Emerging Law of Cohabitant Obligation*, 52 UCLA L. REV. 815, 840 n. 99, 846 n. 124 (2005) (summarizing research).

Income pooling produces significant economic benefits. Indeed, the U.S. government calculates that the income necessary to get above the poverty line is about 50% less for a two-person family than for two, single-person households. *See* U.S. BUREAU OF THE CENSUS, POVERTY THRESHOLDS 2012, http://www.census.gov/hhes/www/poverty/data/threshld/thresh11.xls.

3. *Profit or Penalty?* The marital-unit approach does not uniformly profit or penalize married couples. For purposes of federal income tax, for example, marital-unit classifications have tended to disadvantage married couples whose incomes are relatively similar and benefit those whose incomes are disparate. *See* Mapes v. United States, 576 F.2d 896, 897–98 (Ct. Cl. 1978), which upholds the "marriage penalty" and notes that "not all married couples are penalized taxwise by reason of their status. To the contrary, many, if not most, married couples achieve considerable tax savings through income splitting on a joint return. It is when both spouses generate somewhat comparable incomes that the benefits of income-splitting cease to exist." This will be discussed in more detail in Chapter 19.

4. *The Evasion Possibility:* Marital-unit classifications offer opportunities to evade taxes and other public obligations. For example in 2012, under current Earned Income Tax Credit (EITC) rules, a low-income mother can obtain almost $6000 in tax credits for herself and her children if she remains unmarried, she has 3 children, and her income is less than $17,090. *See* IRS Rev. Proc. 2011–52, 2011–45 I.R.B. 701; But if she marries, she could lose a significant portion of those credits even if she marries a man who also qualifies for the credit. Married couples begin to lose the EITC once their combined income exceeds $22,300. See *Id.;* 26 U.S.C. § 32. So, a mother whose annual adjusted gross income is $15,000 is entitled to the maximum credit. If she marries, she will lose the maximum credit if her husband's adjusted gross income exceeds $7300. In contrast, if her partner has no income, the EITC could create an incentive to marry. For example, in 2011 an unmarried woman with 2 children and an annual income of $25,000 was entitled to a tax credit of $3,367. A married couple with 2 children and $25,000 in combined annual income gets a tax credit of $4,426. See http://www.irs.gov/aub/irs-pdf/p596.pdf (page 51).

5. Many other countries, including Australia, Canada, and Sweden, have rejected the marital-unit approach to taxation. In these nations, each individual must file a separate tax return and pay taxes based on his or her

individual income. What are the pros and cons of the marital-unit and single-payer systems: Which system is more equitable? More efficient? More capable of preventing fraud? Do the advantages of the single-payer system also apply to benefit-calculation problems like those posed by *Schweiker*?

6.   *Decision-Making Rights:* A different sort of deeming underlies rules that cast spouses as default decision makers. For example, at least 37 states have enacted "family-consent" laws that authorize specified family members to make medical decisions on behalf of an incompetent patient. All of these statutes permit the patient to nominate his own decision maker; if he or she fails to exercise this right, the statutes set out a hierarchical list of relatives empowered to decide on the incompetent's behalf. Unless a separation has occurred, a patient's spouse invariably tops the list, typically followed by adult children, parents, and adult siblings. *See* Catherine A. West, Comment, *Gay and Lesbian Partners Are Family Too: Why Wisconsin Should Adopt a Family Consent Law*, 19 WIS. WOMEN'S L.J. 119, 134 (2004). What assumptions underlie these family consent laws? How do they differ from the assumptions that underlie the deeming principles described in *Schweiker* and the Internal Revenue Code?

———————————

The rights and obligations that you have learned about in this chapter have, with few exceptions, been restricted to couples who establish that they are married. They do not apply to cohabiting couples. In recent years, cohabitants have challenged this approach. Courts have typically reacted negatively. For example, in ruling against a long-term cohabitant who sought to recover for loss of consortium, the Massachusetts Supreme Judicial Court held that:

> A loss of consortium claim presupposes a legal right to consortium of the injured person. While [cohabitants] * * * well may have a "stable, significant romantic relationship," * * * they chose not to marry and, consequently, have neither the obligation nor the "benefit of the rules of law that govern property, financial, and other matters in a marital relationship." To recognize a right to recover for loss of consortium by a person who could have but has declined to accept the correlative responsibilities of marriage undermines the "deep interest" that the Commonwealth has that the integrity of marriage "is not jeopardized."

Fitzsimmons v. Mini Coach of Boston, Inc., 799 N.E.2d 1256, 1257 (Mass. 2003). Most courts have agreed with the reasoning of *Fitzsimmons*.

However, in Lozoya v. Sanchez, 66 P.3d 948 (N.M. 2003), the New Mexico Supreme Court extended the consortium claim to a cohabiting partner who shares with the plaintiff an exclusive, "intimate familial relationship." New Mexico also has an unusual family-consent statute which varies the typical family-priority list so that an individual in a long-term relationship of indefinite duration with the patient in which the individual has demonstrated an actual commitment to the patient similar to the commitment of a spouse and in which the individual and patient consider themselves to be responsible for each other's well-being takes precedence over all other family claimants except a legal spouse.

See N.M. STAT. ANN. § 24–7A–5(B). Why have most states followed the Massachusetts model? What are the pros and cons of the New Mexico and Massachusetts approaches? Should there be legal distinctions between married couples and unmarried couples who have established a long-term relationship? Keep these questions in mind as you read Chapter 6!

CHAPTER 5

MARITAL AGREEMENTS

■ ■ ■

Any intelligent woman who reads the marriage contract and then [marries] deserves all the consequences.

Isadora Duncan

[Without a premarital agreement, the football star you see] on any given Sunday wins the Superbowl and drives off in a Hyundai.

Kanye West, "Gold Digger"

1. MARRIAGE: CONTRACT OR STATUS?

UMDA § 201: "Marriage is a personal relationship between a man and a woman arising out of a civil contract to which the consent of the parties is essential * * * "

MAYNARD V. HILL
Supreme Court of the United States, 1888.
125 U.S. 190.

JUSTICE FIELD.

* * * It is also to be observed that, while marriage is often termed by text writers and in decisions of courts as a civil contract, generally to indicate that it must be founded upon the agreement of the parties, and does not require any religious ceremony for its solemnization, it is something more than a mere contract. The consent of the parties is of course essential to its existence, but when the contract to marry is executed by the marriage, a relation between the parties is created which they cannot change. Other contracts may be modified, restricted, or enlarged, or entirely released upon the consent of the parties. Not so with marriage. The relation once formed, the law steps in and holds the parties to various obligations and liabilities. It is an institution, in the maintenance of which in its purity the public is deeply interested, for it is the foundation of the family and of society, without which there would be neither civilization nor progress. This view is well expressed by the supreme court of Maine in

215

Adams v. Palmer, 51 Me. 480, 483: "It is not then a contract within the meaning of the clause of the constitution which prohibits the impairing the obligation of contracts. It is rather a social relation like that of parent and child, the obligations of which arise not from the consent of concurring minds, but are the creation of the law itself, a relation the most important, as affecting the happiness of individuals, the first step from barbarism to incipient civilization, the purest tie of social life, and the true basis of human progress."

NOTES AND QUESTIONS

1.   The Supreme Court observes that, at least in 1888, an agreement to marry is "something more than a mere contract," and that, as a result of the marriage, "a relation between the parties is created which they cannot change." In the previous chapter, we discussed the rights and responsibilities that customarily flow from marriage.

2.   To what extent, if any, should parties be able to modify these rights and responsibilities via a premarital agreement?

WALTON V. WALTON

California Court of Appeals, 1972.
28 Cal. App. 3d 108, 104 Cal. Rptr. 472.

Kaufman, Acting Presiding Justice.

Wife appeals from an interlocutory judgment granting Husband's petition for dissolution of marriage and denying Wife's request for legal separation. * * *

Wife's contention that dissolution of her marriage on the ground of irreconcilable differences as prescribed in The Family Law Act constitutes an unconstitutional impairment of her rights is untenable. In the first place, marital rights and obligations are not contractual rights and obligations within the meaning of Article I, § 10 of the United States Constitution or Article I, § 16 of the California Constitution. (*Maynard v. Hill*). Marriage is much more than a civil contract; it is a relationship that may be created and terminated only with consent of the state and in which the state has a vital interest. Secondly, even if marital obligations were treated as contractual obligations protected by the constitutional prohibitions, a statutory change in the grounds for divorce would not constitute an unconstitutional impairment thereof. * * * When persons enter into a contract or transaction creating a relationship infused with a substantial public interest, subject to plenary control by the state, such contract or transaction is deemed to incorporate and contemplate not only the existing law but the reserve power of the state to amend the law or enact additional laws for the public good and in pursuance of public policy, and such legislative amendments or enactments do not constitute an unconstitutional impairment of contractual obligations.

Similarly, Wife's contention that the dissolution of her marriage on the ground of irreconcilable differences under The Family Law Act unconstitutionally deprives her of a vested interest in her married status cannot be sustained. Certainly a wife has a legitimate interest in her status as a married woman, but, separate and apart from marital property and support rights as to which Wife makes no contention, we entertain some doubt whether her interest in her status as a married woman constitutes property within the purview of the due process clauses of Article I, § 13 of the California Constitution and the Fourteenth Amendment to the United States Constitution. In any event, in view of the state's vital interest in the institution of marriage and the state's plenary power to fix the conditions under which the marital status may be created or terminated, it is clear that Wife could have no vested interest in the state's maintaining in force the grounds for divorce that existed at the time of her marriage. Her interest, however it be classified, was subject to the reserve power of the state to amend the law or enact additional laws for the public good and in pursuance of public policy. Even if Wife is said to have some constitutionally protected vested right, she has not been deprived thereof without due process of law. Vested rights, of course, may be impaired "with due process of law" under many circumstances. The state's inherent sovereign power includes the so called "police power" right to interfere with vested property rights whenever reasonably necessary to the protection of the health, safety, morals, and general well being of the people. * * *

The public policy considerations felt by the legislature to be compelling reasons for the enactment of The Family Law Act and the change in grounds for divorce from a fault standard to a marital breakdown standard are described in the Report of 1969 Divorce Reform Legislation of the Assembly Committee on Judiciary. * * *

NOTES AND QUESTIONS

1.   UMDA § 201 defines marriage as a contract. *Maynard* states that marriage is something more than a contract. Does *Maynard* mean that the parties' expectations are irrelevant? Should the law generally try to uphold the parties' expectations? What about Mrs. Walton's expectations regarding the rules applicable to the dissolution of her marriage? Is it enough to say that, by virtue of getting married, she is deemed to agree to be governed by both current marriage law and subsequent amendments?

2.   Why might the court have reached the result it did in *Walton*? If the wife had prevailed, what effect would this have had on California divorces?

3.   After New York expanded the grounds for divorce to include grounds that previously would have effected only a legal separation, N.Y. DOM. REL. L. § 170 was added:

> a.   A spouse against whom a decree of divorce has been obtained [on the 'living apart' ground], where the decree, judgment or agreement of separation was obtained or entered into prior to [January 21st, 1970], may institute an action in which there shall be recoverable, in addition to any rights under this or any other provisions of law, an amount equivalent to the value of any economic and property rights of which the spouse was deprived by virtue of such decree, except where the grounds for the separation judgment would have excluded recovery of economic and property rights.
>
> b.   In determining the value of the economic and property rights described in subdivision a hereof, the plaintiff's interest shall be calculated as though the defendant died intestate and as if the death of the defendant had immediately antedated the divorce.

Would this be a fairer way to deal with complaints like those of Mrs. Walton?

2.   VARIABILITY OF THE MARRIAGE STATUS BY AGREEMENT BEFORE MARRIAGE

Premarital agreements, also referred to as antenuptial agreements or contracts, may (try to) cover a great variety of subjects, including support, property rights, and issues related to the care of children; they may treat the spouses' rights during marriage, upon divorce, or after the death of a spouse.

Before "contaminating" your good sense with law, do you think that it would be appropriate to enforce a premarital agreement specifying: the religion in which the children of the marriage will be reared? the number and type of vacations, visits to and by in-laws, or the number of children? whether a spouse must agree to a religious divorce? in a common law state, adopting community property rules to govern the spouses' economic relationship? in a community property state, adopting common law property rules to govern the spouses' economic relationship? adopting the marital property rules of another country? restricting the grounds pursuant to which the parties could obtain a divorce? What effect would (or should) such stipulations be given at the time of divorce?

A.   VALIDITY OF PREMARITAL AGREEMENTS

Chapter 4 shows that when a marriage ends in death, in both common law states and community property states, the survivor normally has a claim to some property. If the marriage ends in divorce, Chapter 15 will outline how in all states divorce courts normally can divide the parties' property equally or "equitably." In addition, after a marriage of long duration where the spouses' incomes are unequal, post-divorce spousal support is a possibility, as discussed in Chapter 16.

Should parties be able to change these rules by contract? If so, should there be any limits to the extent to which the "normal" rules can be changed?

If you have concluded that marriage is a contract rather than a status, you have moved too fast. Marriage is a contract and a status. Marriage is a contract in that it rests on an agreement between the marriage partners and, at least to some extent, the terms of the marriage may be modified by the parties. Marriage is a status because a large set of rules is thrust upon the spouses without their specific agreement. Now we shall see that the parties' freedom to contract is limited by policy considerations, and we may be tempted to compare marriage with a form contract. Some blank lines are left for the parties to complete, but at least some of the content is prescribed by the state.

In reviewing contracts relating to marriage, courts have traditionally been concerned with three issues: (1) the presence (or more likely the absence) of contractual "consideration"; (2) the parties' so-called "fiduciary" relationship, including the duty to disclose information material to the bargain and to deal fairly; and (3) "public policy." An invocation of public policy is the open signal that a particular contract will not stand, but a great deal of judicial "policy-mongering" also has been done under the seemingly objective guise of the first two headings.

Traditionally, premarital agreements regarding property rights at death were enforceable, but premarital agreements contemplating divorce were unenforceable. *See* Charles Gamble, *The Antenuptial Contract*, 26 U. MIAMI L. REV. 692 (1972). Thus, one spouse could waive his or her rights to a share of other's assets at death, but could not waive a right to a divorce property division or alimony post-divorce. One source of this traditional approach was a concern that prospective spouses would not bargain fairly with each other regarding the financial ramifications of divorce. This fear may have stemmed both from a perception that women were less sophisticated than men and a belief that the parties' intimate relationship might undermine their ability to bargain. Another concern was that agreements fixing post-divorce obligations would encourage divorce. *See* Mulford v. Mulford, 320 N.W.2d 470, 471 (Neb. 1982).

The materials which follow show that, over the past four decades, courts and legislatures have allowed couples much greater—although not yet complete—freedom in negotiating the terms of their marriage. The new view is that a couple may, with some limits, determine property rights and support obligations at divorce as well as death.

This new view reflects a variety of factors. First, the increased rate and social acceptability of divorce has increased the acceptability of contracts that take account of the divorce possibility. If there is a significant chance a marriage will end in divorce (*see* Martin & Bumpass, *Recent Trends in Marital Disruption*, 26 DEMOGRAPHY 37, 49 (1989)), and if remarriages have a higher probability of divorce than first marriages, it seems sensible for a couple to think about and plan for the divorce possibility. Second, a higher divorce rate and increased longevity have expanded the number of remarriages where one or both spouses have children from a prior marriage; in these cases spouses often wish to ensure that their children are provided for. Third, perhaps as a result of the feminist movement and women's increased labor force participation, judges today exhibit less paternalism toward women. *See* J. Thomas Oldham, *Putting Asunder in the 1990s*, 80 CALIF. L. REV. 1091, 1106–1107 (1992); Simeone v. Simeone, 581 A.2d 162 (Pa. 1990).

Under current U.S. law, parties are free (with some limitations) to alter their marital rights via a prenuptial agreement. They are not required to make any agreements, however. Each state has enacted a default rule set of marital rights for those who have no agreement. In contrast, in many civil law countries spouses are required, before marriage, to choose the marital regime that will govern them. Although no U.S. state has such a requirement, some commentators have agreed that mandatory prenuptial agreements would be good policy. *See* Jeffery Stake, *Mandatory Planning for Divorce*, 45 VAND. L. REV. 397 (1992).

Today, all states agree that a premarital agreement is enforceable if it meets certain requirements. But no consensus has yet emerged on what those requirements should be. Nor is there consensus on whether *post*marital agreements should be enforced on the same, or different, terms.

1. Procedural Fairness

Under the original Statute of Frauds, 29 Car. II, ch. 3 (1677) and modern variants, promises made in consideration of marriage must be in writing and signed by the party to be charged. *See* Unif. Premarital Agreement Act § 2. Part performance of an oral agreement might be sufficient to satisfy the Statute of Frauds. *See* Hall v. Hall, 271 Cal. Rptr. 773 (App. 1990); Marriage of Dewberry, 62 P.3d 525 (Wash. App. 2003). However, marriage alone is not sufficient part performance. *See* Kersey v. Kersey, 802 So. 2d 523 (Fla. Dist. Ct. App. 2001).

Courts also agree that a premarital agreement must be made freely and intelligently in order to be enforceable. Courts disagree about what sort of bargaining satisfies this requirement.

Should judges apply "normal" contract principles when deciding whether to enforce a marital agreement?

ESTATE OF HOLLETT

Supreme Court of New Hampshire, 2003.
150 N.H. 39, 834 A.2d 348.

DUGGAN, J.

The petitioner, Erin Hollett, appeals an order by the Merrimack County Probate Court (Patten, J.) declaring the prenuptial agreement made between Erin and the decedent, John Hollett, to be valid. Erin argues that the agreement should be set aside because of duress, undue influence, insufficient financial disclosure, and lack of effective independent counsel. The respondents, Kathryn Hollett, the decedent's first wife, and their five children, argue that the agreement is valid and the probate court's order should be affirmed. We reverse and remand.

The following facts were found by the trial court or are evident from the record. John and Erin married on August 18, 1990. Their courtship had begun in 1984, when John was fifty-two and Erin was twenty-two. John was a successful real estate investor and developer who regularly bought and sold property in New Hampshire and Florida. He had considerable experience with attorneys and accountants because of his business dealings. Erin had dropped out of high school in the eleventh grade, and had no work or business experience aside from several low level jobs. Throughout their relationship and marriage, Erin had almost no involvement in or understanding of John's business.

John had previously been married to Kathryn C. Hollett, with whom he had five children. Under the terms of their divorce, John owed Kathryn a substantial property settlement, and still owed her millions of dollars at the time of his death. Erin was unaware of this property settlement.

In 1988, the same year that John and Erin became engaged, Erin found a newspaper article about prenuptial agreements that John had left on the kitchen counter. When Erin confronted John with the article, he explained that his first wife had given it to him, and stated that he would not get married without a prenuptial agreement. This statement provoked a "heated and unpleasant" discussion during which Erin said she would not sign such an agreement, particularly because John's first wife had insisted upon it. John said nothing to Erin about a prenuptial agreement again until several days before the August 18, 1990 wedding.

In May 1990, apparently in anticipation of the impending marriage, John sent a statement of his net worth to his attorneys in the law firm of McLane, Graf, Raulerson, and Middleton. After meeting with John on July 18, 1990, his lawyers drafted a prenuptial agreement that was sent to him on July 26. Erin testified that she did not learn about the agreement until the evening of August 16, less than forty-eight hours before the wedding. Under the original draft, Erin was to renounce any claim to alimony or a property settlement in the event of a divorce, and would receive only $25,000 and an automobile.

Several days before the wedding, John's lawyers contacted Brian Shaughnessy, a recent law school graduate, and requested that he counsel Erin regarding the prenuptial agreement. The lawyers told Shaughnessy that John would pay his fee. Shaughnessy first called Erin on August 16 to obtain her consent to act as counsel and to set up a meeting at the McLane law firm office the next day. Shaughnessy had never before negotiated a prenuptial agreement, but prior to the meeting he studied the law of prenuptial agreements and reviewed the draft agreement.

Erin, accompanied by her mother, met with Shaughnessy in person for the first and only time at the McLane law firm on August 17, the day before the wedding. At that time, all of the plans and arrangements for the elaborate wedding, at which over 200 guests were expected, had already been made and paid for; Erin's mother and father had already flown in from Thailand. During the meeting and subsequent negotiations with John's attorneys, Shaughnessy noted that Erin was under considerable emotional distress, sobbing throughout the three or four hours he was with her and at times so distressed that he was unable to speak with her. Erin testified that she remembered almost nothing about the conference. Shaughnessy, however, testified that he carefully reviewed John's financial disclosure and draft of the agreement with Erin, explained their legal significance, and asked her what she sought to obtain from the agreement. He testified that he advised her that the settlement offer in the draft was inadequate, and reminded her that the wedding could be put off if necessary.

Shaughnessy also testified that he believed the financial disclosure provided by John, which had not been audited or reviewed by any other party, was inadequate. Shaughnessy, however, had no time to independently verify any of John's finances. In any case, he believed that any failure to disclose was John's problem, as it could lead to the invalidation of the agreement.

At the end of the negotiations, the prenuptial agreement was considerably more favorable to Erin, allowing her to obtain as much as one-sixth of John's estate in the event of a divorce or John's death. John's lawyers prepared a final version of the agreement, which John and Erin signed on the morning of August 18, the day of their wedding.

The parties remained married until John's death on April 30, 2001. John was survived by Erin, his first wife, and his children from his first marriage. Erin subsequently petitioned the probate court to invalidate the prenuptial agreement, while John's first wife and children argued in favor of upholding it. After four days of hearings, the probate court concluded that the prenuptial agreement was valid and enforceable.

On appeal, Erin argues that the prenuptial agreement was invalid for three reasons: (1) the agreement was not voluntary because it was the product of duress and undue influence; (2) John's financial disclosures were inadequate; and (3) she did not have independent counsel. We need only address the issue of duress. We will defer to the findings of fact made by the probate court unless "they are so plainly erroneous that such findings could not be reasonably made." RSA 567–A:4 (1997). Although whether duress exists in a particular case is normally a question of fact, it becomes a question of law when only one valid inference can be drawn from the undisputed facts. *See Faske v. Gershman*, 30 Misc. 2d 442, 215 N.Y.S.2d 144, 148–49 (Mun. Ct. 1961). We review questions of law de novo.

RSA 460:2–a (1997) permits a man and a woman to enter into a written contract "in contemplation of marriage." A prenuptial agreement is presumed valid unless the party seeking the invalidation of the agreement proves that: (1) the agreement was obtained through fraud, duress or mistake, or through misrepresentation or nondisclosure of a material fact; (2) the agreement is unconscionable; or (3) the facts and circumstances have so changed since the agreement was executed as to make the agreement unenforceable. *See In the Matter of Yannalfo and Yannalfo*, 147 N.H. 597, 599, 794 A.2d 795 (2002).

As a practical matter, the claim of undue duress is essentially a claim that the agreement was not signed voluntarily. To establish duress, a party must ordinarily "show that it involuntarily accepted the other party's terms, that the coercive circumstances were the result of the other party's acts, that the other party exerted pressure wrongfully, and that under the circumstances the party had no alternative but to accept the terms set out by the other party." *Yannalfo*, 147 N.H. at 599, 794 A.2d 795. However, "the State has a special interest in the subject matter" of prenuptial agreements and "courts tend to scrutinize [them] more closely than ordinary commercial contracts." *MacFarlane v. Rich (MacFarlane)*, 132 N.H. 608, 613, 567 A.2d 585 (1989). Moreover, because such agreements often involve persons in a confidential relationship, "the parties must exercise the highest degree of good faith, candor and sincerity in all matters bearing on the terms and execution of the proposed agreement, with fairness being the ultimate measure." *Lutgert v. Lutgert*, 338 So. 2d 1111, 1115 (Fla. Dist. Ct. App.1976), cert. denied, 367 So. 2d 1125 (Fla.1979).

Under the heightened scrutiny afforded to prenuptial agreements, the timing of the agreement is of paramount importance in assessing whether it was voluntary. *See* 2 A. Lindey & L. Parley, *Lindey and Parley on Separation Agreements and Antenuptial Contracts* § 110.65[2] (2d ed. 2003). Fairness demands that the party presented with the agreement have "an opportunity to seek independent advice and a reasonable time to reflect on the proposed terms." *Lutgert*, 338 So. 2d at 1116. To avoid invalidation on grounds of involuntariness, it has been recommended that "[t]he contract should be presented well in advance of the ceremony, usually thirty days." 3 C. Douglas, *New Hampshire Practice, Family Law* § 1.05, at 13. Some States, in fact, automatically invalidate any prenuptial agreement signed immediately before a wedding. *See, e.g.*, MINN.STAT. § 519.11 (2002) (agreement "must be entered into and executed prior to the day of solemnization of marriage").

In arguing for the validity of the Holletts' agreement, the respondents rely upon *In the Matter of Yannalfo and Yannalfo*, 147 N.H. 597, 794 A.2d 795 (2002). In that case, the husband and wife, each of whom was employed by the United States Postal Service, signed a prenuptial agreement a "day or so" before their wedding. The agreement was limited to a house that the husband and wife had purchased one month before the wedding, for which the husband had contributed $70,000 as a down payment, and the wife had provided $5,000 for closing costs. The agreement stated that the first $70,000 of equity in the house was the property of the husband, and that in the event of a divorce, the house would be sold and $70,000 would be paid to the husband. The agreement did not concern any property other than the $70,000 contribution.

In upholding the agreement in *Yannalfo*, we rejected a per se invalidation of agreements signed immediately before the wedding. Instead, we established that each case must be decided upon the totality of its own circumstances. Citing cases from other jurisdictions, however, we suggested that "additional circumstances coupled with [such] timing" may compel a finding that a prenuptial agreement was involuntary.

Several important circumstances distinguish the present case from *Yannalfo*. First, the agreement in Yannalfo did not involve the entire estates of the parties. Rather, it only concerned money used in a transaction that both parties had participated in one month before the wedding. The agreement in this case, by contrast, involves the post-marriage disbursement of an estate that totaled over six million dollars at the time of the agreement, and the relinquishment of marital rights such as alimony. Such a complicated and important agreement will require more time for negotiation and reflection than the agreement in *Yannalfo*.

Second, unlike the parties in *Yannalfo*, Erin's bargaining position was vastly inferior to that of her husband. John was much older than Erin, and he had already been married. According to their financial disclosures, John had approximately six million dollars in assets, while Erin owned approximately five thousand dollars worth of personal property at the time of the agreement. Erin's work experience during the relationship was limited to stints as a bartender and a grocery store cashier. She had little understanding of and no real involvement in John's business ventures. According to Erin, in fact, John had encouraged Erin to stop working after they began their relationship. If Erin refused to sign the agreement, she thus not only stood to face the embarrassment of canceling a two hundred guest wedding, but also stood to lose her means of support. Prenuptial agreements that result from such a vast disparity in bargaining power must meet a high standard of procedural fairness.

Finally, John's conduct before the wedding raises serious questions regarding his good faith in dealing with Erin. John had contemplated a prenuptial agreement at least two years before the wedding, as evidenced by his argument with Erin in 1988. Despite Erin's opposition to the idea, however, he did not discuss the agreement with her again. Moreover, although John's lawyers had drafted a prenuptial agreement almost a month before the wedding, John did not obtain counsel for his wife or even inform her of the agreement until several days before the ceremony. In other words, despite having every opportunity to negotiate the agreement well before the wedding, John elected to conduct his affairs so that Erin had no time to choose her own counsel, and very little time to negotiate and reflect upon the agreement.

In upholding the agreement, the trial court cited as a factor in its reasoning Erin's failure to "repudiate or rescind" the agreement during her ten years of marriage to John. Public policy, however, limits the consideration of such evidence. As one court has stated:

> The law frowns upon litigation between husband and wife. Where their relations are friendly and affectionate, it takes account of the fact that she would be loath to institute legal proceedings against him. . . . [A]ny other policy would be apt to beget disagreements and contentions in the family fatal to domestic peace.

In re Flannery's Estate, 315 Pa. 576, 173 A. 303, 304 (1934). The *Flannery* court thus declined to permit a laches defense in a case where the wife challenged a prenuptial agreement after her husband's death. The same logic precludes us from considering the wife's delay in challenging the agreement as substantive evidence of the agreement's voluntariness or ratification. To hold otherwise would be to penalize Erin for choosing not to disrupt her marriage, which the trial court characterized as "close," "loving" and "traditional," with a lawsuit against her husband.

Finally, the trial court focused upon the assistance Erin received from Brian Shaughnessy before the execution of the agreement. The respondents, in fact, suggest that the presence of counsel should be dispositive of the issue of voluntariness. We note that the trial court itself found that the time constraints limited the quality of Shaughnessy's representation: for example, he was unable to verify the accuracy of John's disclosures. Even assuming, however, that Shaughnessy provided Erin with effective independent counsel, and that the financial representations upon which he relied were accurate, we cannot agree that his counsel by itself was sufficient to validate this agreement.

Independent counsel is useless without the ability and the time to make effective use of such counsel. As one commentator has stated:

> [M]ore recent and enlightened cases have held that the dependent party must be given sufficient time to obtain the advice of independent counsel. * * * The contract should be presented well in advance of the ceremony, usually thirty days, to allow the bride or groom a reasonable opportunity to consult with independent counsel.

3 C. Douglas, *New Hampshire Practice, Family Law* § 1.05, at 13 (emphasis added).

In this case, it would be unreasonable to conclude that Erin had "sufficient time" or a "reasonable opportunity" to make use of Brian Shaughnessy's advice. Given the complexity of John's finances and the agreement, and the disparity in the parties' bargaining power, Erin needed more than one day to negotiate and reflect upon his draft proposal. Without such time, we conclude as a matter of law that her signing of the agreement was involuntary under the heightened standard applied to prenuptial agreements.

Reversed and remanded.

DeLOREAN v. DeLOREAN

Superior Court of New Jersey, Chancery Division, 1986.
211 N.J. Super. 432, 511 A.2d 1257.

IMBRIANI, J.S.C.

This matrimonial case examines the circumstances under which an antenuptial agreement may be enforced and whether that issue may be resolved by arbitration. The intent of most marriages is to create an "indivisible union of one" in which both spouses generally contribute whatever they own prior to the marriage or acquire thereafter into a common marital fund. Upon death the survivor usually receives whatever has been accumulated but, if a divorce ensues, in the usual case they share all marital assets equally.

However, when parties enter into an antenuptial agreement their purpose is to alter that usual arrangement and enter into an economic partnership whereby many or all of the assets owned prior to the marriage or acquired thereafter are not contributed into a common marital fund but are kept segregated and, when the marriage ceases, whether by death or divorce, they are not shared equally but pursuant to a plan conceived and agreed upon before the marriage was consummated. It is important that we understand that normally the intent of most antenuptial agreements is to deny a spouse an interest in assets held in the sole name of the other which the former would ordinarily receive by operation of law when the marriage ceased.

These parties entered into an antenuptial agreement on May 8, 1973 (only a few hours before they married) which provided that: "Any and all property, income and earnings acquired by each before and after the marriage shall be the separate property of the person acquiring same, without any rights, title or control vesting in the other person." The potential assets could exceed $20 million and practically all of them are in the sole name of the husband. Absent this agreement and considering that this is a thirteen-year marriage in which there are two minor children, under New Jersey law this wife could reasonably have anticipated receiving approximately 50% of the marital assets at the time of divorce. But if this agreement is upheld she will receive relatively little. She asserts that this agreement should not be enforced because: (1) she was not provided with a full and complete disclosure of her husband's financial affairs before she signed it; and (2) undue influence was exerted upon her by her husband who possessed far greater financial knowledge and experience than she.

Initially, it is clear that antenuptial agreements fixing post-divorce rights and obligations are valid and enforceable and courts should welcome and encourage such agreements to the extent that the parties have developed comprehensive and particularized agreements responsive to their peculiar circumstances. In determining whether to enforce an antenuptial agreement, there are at least three requirements that have to be met.

First, that there was no fraud or duress in the execution of the agreement or, to put it another way, that both parties signed voluntarily. The wife alleges she did not sign voluntarily because her husband presented the agreement to her only a few hours before the marriage ceremony was performed and threatened to cancel the marriage if she did not sign. In essence, she asserts that she had no choice but to sign. While she did not have independent counsel of her own choosing, she did acknowledge that before she signed she did privately consult with an attorney selected by her husband who advised her not to sign the agreement. Yet, for whatever reasons, she rejected the attorney's advice and signed.

While her decision may not have been wise, it appears that she had sufficient time to consider the consequences of signing the agreement and, indeed, although she initially refused to sign it, after conferring with her intended spouse and an attorney, she reconsidered and decided to sign it. Concededly, the husband was 25 years older and a high-powered senior executive with General Motors Corporation, but she was not a "babe in the woods." She was 23 years old with some business experience in the modeling and entertainment industry; she had experienced an earlier marriage and the problems wrought by a divorce; and she had advice from an attorney who, although not of her own choosing, did apparently give her competent advice and recommended that she not sign. While it may have been embarrassing to cancel the wedding only a few hours before it was to take place, she certainly was not compelled to go through with the ceremony. There was no fraud or misrepresentation committed by the husband. He made it perfectly clear that he did not want her to receive any portion of the marital assets that were in his name. Under those circumstances the court is satisfied that the wife entered into the agreement voluntarily and without any fraud or duress being exerted upon her.

Second, the agreement must not be "unconscionable." This is not to say that the agreement should be what a court would determine to be "fair and equitable." The fact that what a spouse receives under an antenuptial agreement is small, inadequate or disproportionate does not in itself render the agreement voidable if the spouse was not overreached and entered into the agreement voluntarily with full knowledge of the financial worth of the other person. So long as a spouse is not left destitute or as a public charge, the parties can agree to divide marital assets in any manner they wish. Mrs. DeLorean presently enjoys substantial income from her employment as a talk-show television hostess and was given a life interest in a trust of unknown amount created by Mr. DeLorean, which he testified had assets of between $2 and $5 million dollars.[1] She will not be left destitute. The court is unaware of any public policy which requires that the division of marital assets be made in [a manner] the court believes to be fair and equitable if the parties freely and voluntarily agree otherwise. In the final analysis it is for the parties to decide for themselves what is fair and equitable, not the court. So long as a spouse had sufficient opportunity to reflect on her actions, was competent, informed, and had access to legal advice and that of any relevant experts, a court should not, except in the most unusual case, interject its own opinion of what is fair and equitable and reject the wishes of the parties. Since the wife voluntarily agreed to this division of the marital assets and she will not become destitute or a public charge, the agreement is not unconscionable.

Third, the spouse seeking to enforce the agreement [must have made] a full and complete disclosure of his or her financial wealth before the agreement was signed. Obviously, one cannot make a knowing and intelligent waiver of legal and financial rights unless fully informed of all the facts; otherwise one cannot know what is being waived. The husband

---

[1] Actually the testimony of the husband was vague, if not evasive, about the content and value of the trust fund and it appeared that the wife was unaware that she possessed a life interest in a trust fund until he disclosed that information during his testimony in court.

asserts that the wife acknowledged that she received a full and complete disclosure of his financial wealth because the agreement states:

> Husband is the owner of substantial real and personal property and he has reasonable prospects of earning large sums of monies; these facts have been fully disclosed to Wife.

However, that statement is not very meaningful and is insufficient to satisfy his obligation to make a full and complete disclosure of his financial wealth. While several states hold that a full and complete disclosure is not synonymous with a detailed disclosure, those cases can be distinguished because they impose upon each spouse a duty to inquire and investigate into the financial condition of the other. However, as far as this court can ascertain, New Jersey imposes no such duty.

not meaningful disclosure

A conflict arose as to precisely what financial information was disclosed by Mr. DeLorean. However, the court is satisfied that even if it accepted as true the testimony of Mr. DeLorean, he did not satisfy his legal obligation to make a full and complete disclosure. But we should address the question of how to avoid disputes of this nature in the future. It is clear that we can ascertain with complete certainty whether there was a full and complete disclosure only by requiring a written list of assets and income be attached to the antenuptial agreement. Anything less will encourage a plethora of plenary hearings which would frequently be contemplated by contradictory and conflicting testimony, often tainted by memory lapses. Research has disclosed, for reasons not clear to this court, several cases in which the suggestion of a written list has been rejected.

Our purpose must be to fashion a rule which will avoid litigation. * * *

While the wife was aware that Mr. DeLorean was a person of substantial wealth, there was no way that she could have known with any substantial degree of certainty the extent of his wealth. This is important because one can appreciate that while a wife might waive her legal rights to share in marital assets of $1 million, she might not be willing to do so if she knew the marital assets were worth $20 million. And the suggestion that Mrs. DeLorean had a duty to investigate to ascertain the full nature and extent of his financial wealth is both unfair and unrealistic. How many people when about to marry would consider investigating the financial affairs of their intended spouse? How many people would appreciate or tolerate being investigated by an intended spouse? And how many marriages would be canceled when one of the parties is informed of an investigation being conducted by the other? Such a requirement would cause embarrassment and impose a difficult burden. The better rule is that the

> burden is not on either party to inquire, but on each to inform, for it is only by requiring full disclosure of the amount, character, and

Rule

value of the parties' respective assets that courts can ensure intelligent waiver of the statutory [and other] rights involved.

When a spouse has a duty to fully and completely disclose his financial wealth, we would eviscerate and render meaningless that duty if we imposed upon the other spouse a duty to investigate.

The only way that Mrs. DeLorean could knowingly and intelligently waive her legal rights in Mr. DeLorean's assets was if she was fully and completely informed what they were. And for Mr. DeLorean to merely state that he had an interest in a farm in California, a large tract of land in Montana, and a share in a major league baseball club fell far short of a full and complete disclosure. If this issue were decided under New Jersey law the court would conclude that Mr. DeLorean did not make a full and complete disclosure of his financial wealth before his spouse signed the antenuptial agreement and, therefore, it would not be valid and enforceable.

However, it is argued that California, not New Jersey, law should be applied. The parties married and executed the agreement in California. It is hornbook law that when an agreement is silent as to which law should be applied, the validity and construction of a contract shall be determined by the law of the place of contracting. But this agreement is not silent and expressly provides that it

> shall be construed under the laws of the State of California and enforceable in the proper courts of jurisdiction of the State of California.

When the agreement was executed, the parties had substantial contacts with California and reasonably expected to retain many of them which, indeed, has been the case. For these reasons, the law of California must be applied in this case.

That being so, what duty does California law impose upon a party to an antenuptial agreement with regard to the disclosure of one's financial wealth? In both California and New Jersey fiduciaries are required to exercise a high degree of trust, good faith and candor in their dealings with each other.

* * *

Where California and New Jersey law part is in their determination of what constitutes a fiduciary because, unlike New Jersey, California does not treat a party to an antenuptial agreement as a fiduciary on the theory that "parties who are not yet married are not presumed to share a confidential relationship." *Marriage of Dawley*, 17 Cal. 3d 342, 355, 131 Cal. Rptr. 3, 551 P.2d 323 (1976). So long as the spouse seeking to set aside such an agreement has a general idea of the character and extent of the financial assets and income of the other, that apparently is sufficient in

California. Indeed, absent fraud or misrepresentation, there appears to be a duty to make some inquiry to ascertain the full nature and extent of the financial resources of the other. As this court reads California law, the disclosures made by John DeLorean appear to be sufficient for purposes of enforcing this agreement.

NOTES AND QUESTIONS

1. Although courts agree that a premarital agreement must be signed voluntarily, they have not construed that requirement consistently. What policy goals underlie the voluntariness requirement? Would those goals be advanced by enforcing the agreement in *DeLorean*? What is the basis of the claim that Mrs. DeLorean did not sign the agreement voluntarily?

Mrs. DeLorean had the opportunity to talk to a lawyer before she signed the agreement, and the lawyer advised her not to sign. The court appears to find this fact significant. Did she truly have the opportunity to "consult" with a lawyer? The court finds that she "had sufficient time to consider the consequences of signing the agreement." Why might Mrs. DeLorean disagree?

If Mrs. DeLorean had not talked to a lawyer before signing, should the agreement be enforced?

Why do you think Mr. DeLorean waited until a few hours before the wedding to present the agreement?

2. In *Estate of Hollett*, the bride received a draft of the agreement about a day before the intended wedding. She had the opportunity to consult with a lawyer selected by the husband's lawyer. Some financial information was exchanged, and some changes were made to the initial draft of the agreement. Presumably the *DeLorean* court would have no difficulty finding that this agreement was voluntarily signed. Why does the New Hampsuire court find that the agreement was involuntarily signed as a matter of law?

The New Hampshire court seems troubled by a number of factors. The court seems to be saying that, if the waiving party is significantly less sophisticated than the proponent of the agreement, the waiving party needs some time to understand the terms of the agreement and the financial disclosures. The court states that "independent counsel is useless without the ability and the time to make effective use of such counsel."

If Mr. Hollett had not arranged for the bride to consult with a lawyer, and she had the initial draft presented the day before the wedding, should the agreement be considered voluntarily signed? In other words, is the primary problem in *Hollett* that the bride did not have adequate time to consult with her lawyer, or was the primary problem that the draft was presented "too late"? If it was presented "too late," when does someone in Mr. Hollett's situation in New Hampshire have to first present a draft of the agreement so that it will be considered voluntarily signed?

Was it important in *Hollett* that they were expecting 200 wedding guests and that the bride's parents had flown in from Thailand?

It seems fairly clear today that most courts apply the *DeLorean* standard for voluntary execution. *See* J. Thomas Oldham, *With All my Worldly Goods I Thee Endow, or Maybe Not: A Reevaluation of the Uniform Premarital Agreement Act after Three Decades*, 19 DUKE J. GENDER L. & POL'Y 82 (2011).

3.   As *DeLorean* and *Hollett* suggest, in almost all cases a premarital agreement is desired by the wealthier party when he or she is marrying a less wealthy party. Such agreements typically are intended to limit or eliminate any financial claim the less wealthy party could make if the parties divorce. Does this frequent difference in sophistication and bargaining power suggest that additional bargaining safeguards are needed?

4.   Some courts have found involuntariness when the agreement was presented on the day of the wedding and the party waiving rights had no time to confer with genuinely independent counsel. *See generally* J. THOMAS OLDHAM, DIVORCE, SEPARATION AND THE DISTRIBUTION OF PROPERTY, § 4.03[2][d]. One concern underlying these cases is the frenzy a wedding occasions. Anyone who has experienced the hysteria produced by an imminent wedding might well conclude that this is not a good time for consulting an attorney and negotiating an important agreement. Another concern is the embarrassment occasioned by calling off the wedding at the last minute. To the extent that a court is (unlike the judge in *DeLorean*) sensitive to these concerns, when is it "too late" to enter into a premarital agreement? Is the pivotal date when out-of-town guests begin to arrive? Should it matter if the parties have previously discussed and agreed upon the general terms of the agreement? What if they had begun negotiations long before the planned wedding date, but finalized the agreement only shortly before the wedding? *See* Gardner v. Gardner, 527 N.W.2d 701 (Wis. App. 1994) (enforcing agreement signed five days before wedding where the parties had been negotiating for two months); *In re* Marriage of Adams, 729 P.2d 1151 (Kan. 1986). Is the size of the wedding party relevant, so the potential embarrassment of cancelling the wedding should be taken more seriously if it was a large wedding? *See* Fletcher v. Fletcher, 628 N.E.2d 1343 (Ohio 1994) (suggesting yes); Bonds v. Bonds, 5 P.3d 815 (Cal. 2000) (suggesting yes).

A surprising number of courts have held that an agreement was voluntarily signed even if presented a day or two before the wedding. *See generally* Oldham, *supra* note 2. Is this because these courts are treating a premarital agreement like any other commercial contract? If so, does this approach make sense? Is there a reason premarital agreements should be treated differently from a commercial contract?

5.   Most courts agree that a marital agreement is not voluntarily signed if there was duress or coercion. Therefore, if it is established that there was a pattern of violence at the time the agreement was signed, this could impact whether the agreement would be considered voluntarily signed. *See In re*

Marriage of Balcof, 47 Cal. Rptr. 3d 183 (App. 2006); *In re* Marriage of Foran, 834 P.2d 1081 (Wash. App. 1992).

6.   In addition to a voluntariness requirement, the Connecticut statute provides that a premarital agreement is not enforceable if a party was not offered a reasonable opportunity to consult with independent counsel. *See* CONN. GEN. STAT. § 46b–36g(a)(4). Would the result in *DeLorean* have been different in Connecticut? If an attorney is not provided by the spouse (as occurred in *DeLorean*), many people would have to find a lawyer and then make an appointment and consult with the lawyer. What amount of time would this normally take? In addition, did the wife in *DeLorean* have the opportunity to consult with "independent" counsel?

7.   Would it be sensible to establish a rule, or at least a presumption, that a premarital contract signed within a certain number of days before the wedding is invalid due to undue influence? The American Law Institute (ALI) has proposed that a premarital agreement must be signed at least thirty days before the wedding for there to be a presumption that the agreement was voluntarily signed. *See* AMERICAN LAW INSTITUTE, PRINCIPLES OF THE LAW OF FAMILY DISSOLUTION: ANALYSIS AND RECOMMENDATIONS § 7.04 (2002). The California legislature has concluded that the focus should be on the time between presentation and signing of the agreement. To be enforceable, the agreement must be signed at least seven days after it was presented. CAL. FAM. CODE § 1615(c)(2). What are the pros and cons of the ALI and California approaches as compared to case-by-case litigation on voluntariness? If a time-based presumption is desirable, is the California or ALI approach preferable?

8.   Circumstances other than timing may also affect the court's decision on voluntariness. For example, if previously married spouses are considering remarriage and one party presents an agreement to the other in front of the children, this could cause a court to find overreaching. *See* Ranney v. Ranney, 548 P.2d 734 (Kan. 1976). What if the woman asked to waive her rights in a premarital agreement is pregnant? Almost all courts have ruled that an agreement is not involuntarily signed if the woman is pregnant and the man states that he will marry her before the child's birth only if she signs the agreement. What if the prospective spouse asked to waive rights has already quit his or her job and moved to the planned marital domicile? *See* Holler v. Holler, 612 S.E.2d 469 (S.C. App. 2005) (concluding that a premarital agreement was involuntary where, at the time of execution, the woman was pregnant and her immigration status would have forced her to leave the U.S. in the near future if she did not marry a U.S. citizen). What if one prospective spouse threatens to call off the wedding? *See In re* Marriage of Spiegel, 553 N.W.2d 309 (Iowa 1996) (not involuntary); Mallen v. Mallen, 622 S.E.2d 812 (Ga. 2005) (same). What if one prospective spouse has greater business experience and bargaining power? *See* Estate of Hollett, 834 A.2d 348 (N.H. 2003) (relevant but not determinative).

9.   Perhaps not surprisingly, courts have not been receptive to the argument "I shouldn't be bound by the premarital agreement because I didn't

read it." *See, e.g.,* Liebelt v. Liebelt, 801 P.2d 52 (Idaho App. 1990). But what if the agreement was written in a language the prospective spouse can't understand? *See* Stein-Sapir v. Stein-Sapir, 382 N.Y.S.2d 799 (App. Div. 1976) (not a defense). What if one prospective spouse tells the other that the agreement only deals with property rights at death, when in fact the agreement also limits property rights at divorce? *See* Laird v. Laird, 597 P.2d 463 (Wyo. 1979) (not a defense).

10. Whether the prospective spouse received independent legal advice is often taken into account in determining voluntariness. Some courts have held that an agreement signed without the opportunity to consult with independent counsel will be scrutinized more closely. *See* Gant v. Gant, 329 S.E.2d 106 (W. Va. 1985); Sogg v. Nevada State Bank, 832 P.2d 781 (Nev. 1992). In Australia, a premarital agreement is enforceable *only* if each party had independent counsel. *See* Belinda Fehlberg & Bruce Smyth, *Binding Pre-Nuptial Agreements in Australia; The First Year,* 16 INT. J. L., POL'Y & FAM. 127 (2002). Few U.S. courts have adopted this view. *See* Marriage of Bonds, 5 P.3d 815 (Cal. 2000) (holding that representation was merely one of a number of factors relevant to voluntariness.) What are the advantages and disadvantages of the Australian approach?

California will enforce a contractual provision restricting the right to spousal support only if the waiving party was represented by independent counsel. CAL. FAM. CODE § 1612(c). In West Virginia, if a party waives rights in a premarital agreement, it is enforceable only if the waiving party has knowledge of its contents and its legal effect. It appears that this means the waiving party must have consulted with a lawyer. Owen v. Owen, 759 S.E.2d 468 (W. Va. 2014). In addition, an Oregon appellate court recently affirmed a finding that a premarital agreement was not enforceable where the waiving party had not consulted a lawyer and did not understand the nature of the rights being affected. *In re* Marriage of Porter, 381 P.3d 873 (Or. App. 2016).

In Missouri, a waiver of this right of a surviving spouse to take a forced share of the deceased spouse's estate is enforceable only if the waiving spouse received full disclosure of the nature and extent of the right being waived. *See* Estate of Cassidy, 356 S.W.3d 339 (Mo. App. 2011). Should something like this rule be extended to a premarital agreement where a spouse waives economic rights at divorce? For example, if the waiving party was not represented by counsel, in California a waiver of economic rights in a premarital agreement is enforceable only if the waiving party "was fully informed of the terms and basic effect of the agreement as well as the rights and obligations he or she was giving up by signing the agreement." CAL. FAM. CODE § 1615(c). Is this a good compromise between requiring independent counsel and minimum protection?

11. Almost all courts consider the poorer prospective spouse's knowledge of the other's financial situation important in determining enforceability, but they do not agree on what constitutes adequate knowledge. New Jersey requires disclosure in the form of a detailed schedule showing the prospective spouses' incomes and the net value of all their property interests. *See*

DeLorean, supra. California does not. Which policy is more sensible? If the agreement contains a waiver of the right to financial disclosures, should such a waiver be enforced? Should inadequate disclosure by itself void the agreement? (*See* Uniform Premarital Agreement Act, *infra*) (no). *Compare* Kornegay v. Robinson, 625 S.E.2d 805 (N. C. App. 2006) (concluding that the objecting spouse's information about the other's finances is a "necessary consideration" in determining whether the agreement was voluntary). Should it matter if the parties have obtained through their courtship a general familiarity with the financial situation of the other? *See* Paroly v. Paroly, 876 A.2d 1061 (Pa. Super. 2005) (yes).

12. There is a split of authority regarding whether an engaged couple should be considered in a confidential relationship. As *DeLorean* suggests, if a state (like California) does not consider an engaged couple to be in such a relationship, such states may not establish substantial bargaining safeguards regarding premarital agreements. *See also*, Mallen v. Mallen, 622 S.E.2d 812 (Ga. 2005) (engaged couple is not in a confidential relationship); McNamara v. McNamara, 40 So. 3d 78 (Fla. Dist. Ct. App. 2010) (engaged couples are in a confidential relationship); DeMatteo v. DeMatteo, 762 N.E.2d 797 (Mass. 2002) (same).

13. As *DeLorean* indicates, a governing law provision can be a very important element of premarital agreement drafting. What state's law should have been applied if there had been no choice of law provision?

14. Should a choice of forum provision be enforced? *See* Ofer v. Sirota, 984 N.Y.S.2d 312 (App. Div. 2014) (enforcing a choice of forum provision (Israel) in a dispute involving foreign nationals).

Problem 5-1:

Biff and Buffy are engaged and have planned a relatively large wedding. One week before the wedding, Biff presents Buffy with a premarital contract which would substantially limit Buffy's marital property and support rights if the marriage ends in divorce. Biff has substantial assets; Buffy does not. Buffy is quite surprised and does not want to sign the agreement. Biff suggests that she talk about the marital contract with a lawyer he knows. She immediately does this; he advises her not to sign. Biff tells her that if she does not sign the agreement, he will not marry her. Five days before the wedding, she reluctantly agrees to sign the agreement. What arguments are available to both parties? What result under *DeLorean*? Is this the right result? *See Liebelt, supra* note 9; Greenwald v. Greenwald, 454 N.W.2d 34 (Wis. App. 1990).

2.   Substantive Fairness

If an agreement is freely and intelligently signed, is there any other reason not to enforce it? Must such agreements be fair? If yes, what does "fairness" mean? Should fairness be judged at the time of signing or at the time of divorce?

RESTATEMENT (SECOND) OF CONTRACTS (1981)

§ 190. Promise Detrimental to Marital Relationship

(1) A promise by a person contemplating marriage or by a married person, other than as part of an enforceable separation agreement, is unenforceable on grounds of public policy if it would change some essential incident of the marital relationship in a way detrimental to the public interest in the marriage relationship.[1] Here a separation agreement is unenforceable on grounds of public policy unless it is made after separation or in contemplation of an immediate separation and is fair in the circumstances.

(2) A promise that tends unreasonably to encourage divorce or separation is unenforceable on grounds of public policy.

GROSS V. GROSS

Supreme Court of Ohio, 1984.
11 Ohio St. 3d 99, 464 N.E.2d 500.

HOLMES, JUDGE.

The agreement, which was in consideration of the marriage between the parties and their mutual promises, provided, in part, at § 13, that:

> Jane shall after the consummation of the marriage between the parties hereto, in the event of the separation or divorce of the parties be entitled to receive as alimony or separate maintenance the maximum sum of $200.00 per month for a period of 10 years, from the time of such separation (either by legal action or by actually living apart) or from the date of a divorce action being filed, if a court of competent jurisdiction will award Jane any alimony. This shall be the maximum amount Jane shall be entitled to receive under any and all circumstances and

---

[1] a. *Change in essential incident of marital relationship.* Although marriage is sometimes loosely referred to as a "contract," the marital relationship has not been regarded by the common law as contractual in the usual sense. Many terms of the relationship are seen as largely fixed by the state and beyond the power of the parties to modify. Two reasons support this view. One is that there is a public interest in the relationship, and particularly in such matters as support and child custody, that makes it inappropriate to subject it to modification by the parties. Another is that the courts lack workable standards and are not an appropriate forum for the types of contract disputes that would arise if such promises were enforceable. The rule stated in Subsection (1) reflects this view by making a promise unenforceable if it changes an essential incident of marriage in a way detrimental to the public interest in the relationship. This rule, however, does not prevent persons contemplating marriage or married persons from making contracts between themselves for the disposition of property, since this is not ordinarily regarded as an essential incident of the marital relationship. Nor does it prevent their making contracts for services that are not an essential incident of the marital relationship within the rule stated here. But it does, for example, preclude them from changing in a way detrimental to the public interest in the relationship the duty imposed by law on one spouse to support the other. Whether a change in the duty of support is detrimental in this way will depend on the circumstances of each case. The presence of an unenforceable promise in an otherwise enforceable antenuptial or separation agreement does not, of course, necessarily entail the unenforceability of the entire agreement. * * *

conditions, and Jane shall not be entitled to any division of the property of Thomas nor to any expense money or counsel fees in connection with any separation or divorce, and Jane agrees to waive any and all such rights or claims. Further, Jane specifically releases all her rights of dower in the property of Thomas.

Additional provisions relating to a possible divorce between the parties were the following:

16. In the event of a divorce, the personal residence of the parties shall be sold and the equity therein realized shall be divided equally between the parties.

17. In the event of a divorce, the personal property and possessions of the parties located in their residence shall be the property of Jane with the exception of Thomas' clothing, sports equipment and other purely personal items. Jane shall be entitled to the ownership of one automobile out of Thomas' property.

The antenuptial agreement also contained provisions relative to payments that would be disbursed from Thomas' estate to Ida Jane. Such provisions provided for the establishment of a trust in the principal sum of $200,000, or twenty percent of his net estate, whichever is lesser. The income derived from the trust was to be paid to Mrs. Gross for life and upon her death to provide education for her children by her previous marriage.

Attached, and made a part of the antenuptial agreement, was a statement of the assets owned by each party. At the date of the agreement, most of the appellant's assets were his interests in the family Pepsi-Cola bottling franchises located in a number of cities. There were additional stocks in other companies, as well as an interest in a real estate partnership. The value of Mr. Gross' assets at the time was listed in the proximity of $550,000. The appellee disclosed assets of household goods and effects, an automobile, and $1,000 cash for what is alleged to be a total of approximately $5,000.

The parties were married in September 1968. A son was born of the marriage in 1970. The marriage lasted nearly fourteen years when the appellant filed for divorce. However, this action was dismissed by the appellant. Subsequently, the appellee filed for a divorce, which was granted on grounds of extreme cruelty being found attributable to appellant. At trial there was evidence adduced that Mr. Gross had increased his total assets to some $8,000,000 with a net equity of $6,000,000. His gross income for the year 1980 was approximately $250,000. The trial court found the antenuptial agreement to be valid and enforceable in that it had been fairly entered into since there was no evidence of fraud, duress, or misrepresentation, and there had been a full disclosure of assets. The court entered an order in accordance with the terms of the agreement.

The court of appeals by way of a majority opinion, opted for the position that antenuptial agreements were not void per se, but that such contracts were not enforceable by a party found to be at fault in a divorce proceeding. The court ruled that such fault was a breach of the terms of the antenuptial agreement. Thus, the court of appeals held that inasmuch as the divorce had been granted upon the trial court's finding that Mr. Gross has been guilty of gross neglect of duty, he had thereby breached the antenuptial agreement and could not enforce its provisions against Mrs. Gross. Mr. Gross subsequently appealed the decision.

* * *

Historically, there has been a notable contrast between the views taken by courts in this country of provisions within antenuptial agreements setting forth the division of property and other rights and interests upon the death of one of the parties, contrasted to provisions in such agreements providing for, or affecting, property rights or conjugal and marital rights in the event of divorce. In the majority of jurisdictions, prospective spouses could contract as to the division of their property in the event of the death of one of the parties, and these agreements were generally enforced if the parties made a full disclosure of their assets and there was no showing of fraud, duress, or undue influence in the procurement of the agreement. Such provisions in an antenuptial agreement were generally recognized as being conducive to marital tranquility and thus in harmony with public policy. * * * [C]ourts throughout the country have historically taken a significantly different attitude toward provisions in antenuptial agreements providing for a division of property and sustenance alimony upon the divorce of the parties. The prevailing law in the United States was that such contracts were considered as being made in contemplation of divorce and were held to be void as against public policy.

Generally, two basic policy arguments were advanced for the invalidation of provisions in antenuptial agreements in reference to the divorce of the parties. First, provisions in such contracts which provide for one spouse to forfeit marital property or conjugal rights are potentially profitable to the other party, would encourage divorce, and, therefore, would be contrary to the state's interest in preserving the marriage. Second, the state is virtually a party to every marital contract in that it possesses a continuing concern in the financial security of divorced or separated persons.

In the last decade and a half many changes have taken place in the attitudes and mores surrounding marriage and marital relationships. These changes have altered the public policy view toward antenuptial agreements made in contemplation of a possible divorce. Some of the factors involved within this evolution of policy are the social changes which affect family law in general, such as the greater frequency of divorce and remarriage, the percentage drop in marriage generally among our citizens, the adoption by a number of states of all or a number of the provisions of the Uniform Marriage and Divorce Act and, most significantly, the widespread adoption of some manner of "no fault" divorce laws. * * *

Exemplary of this trend among the states to reconsider the common-law position or rule of law, which disfavors agreements providing for division of property and sustenance provisions under divorce, is the often cited case of *Posner v. Posner* (Fla. 1970), 233 So. 2d 381. The Florida Supreme Court held that antenuptial agreements settling alimony and property rights upon divorce should not be held *ab initio* as contrary to public policy. The court adopted the same tests which had previously been applied for the determination of the validity of antenuptial agreements containing provisions disposing of property at time of death, i.e., a showing of good faith in the entry into the agreement, and a full disclosure of assets. The court also held that upon evidence of changed circumstances, the contract would be subject to the same modification provisions that apply to all support orders in divorce proceedings.

A number of courts in other states followed the lead of *Posner* and held that this type of antenuptial agreement was valid if fairly negotiated upon a full disclosure of assets. * * *

We * * * join those other jurisdictions that have expressed the growing trend of legal thought in this country that provisions contained within antenuptial agreements providing for the disposition of property and awarding sustenance alimony upon a subsequent divorce of the parties are not void *per se* as being against public policy. We hold that such agreements are valid and enforceable if three basic conditions are met: one, if they have been entered into freely without fraud, duress, coercion, or overreaching; two, if there was a full disclosure, or full knowledge and understanding, of the nature, value and extent of the prospective spouse's property; and, three, if the terms do not promote or encourage divorce or profiteering by divorce.

The elements of the first condition may be read with their generally accepted meaning being applicable. Accordingly, the term "overreaching" is used in the sense of one party by artifice or cunning, or by significant disparity to understand the nature of the transaction, to outwit or cheat the other.

The elements of the second condition would be satisfied either by the exhibiting of the attachment to the antenuptial agreement of a listing of the assets of the parties to the agreement, or alternatively a showing that there had been a full disclosure by other means.

A hypothetical example of the type of situation which condition three seeks to avoid is where the parties enter into an antenuptial agreement which provides a significant sum either by way of property settlement or alimony at the time of a divorce, and after the lapse of an undue short period of time one of the parties abandons the marriage or otherwise disregards the marriage vows.

We are called upon to answer other important questions in this case. One is whether fault on the part of one of the parties, which occasions a divorce, invalidates the agreement, or at least vitiates the terms of the contract as to the one at fault.

* * *

As to this issue, we conclude the better view to be, and so hold, that antenuptial agreements providing for division of property and containing provisions for sustenance alimony, if otherwise found to be valid, are not abrogated as to either party for marital misconduct arising after the marriage.

Having determined the general validity of antenuptial agreements providing for the disposition and division of property and allowing for sustenance or maintenance at the time of a divorce of the parties, we must now provide for the standards of judicial review of such agreements.

At the outset it must be restated that upon a judicial review of any such agreement, it must meet the general test of fairness as referred to previously, and must be construed within the context that by virtue of their anticipated marital status, the parties are in a fiduciary relationship to one another. The parties must act in good faith, with a high degree of fairness and disclosure of all circumstances which materially bear on the antenuptial agreement.

Upon the consideration of provisions relating to the division or allocation of *property* at the time of a divorce, the applicable standards must relate back to the time of the execution of the contract and not to the time of the divorce. As to these provisions, if it is found that the parties have freely entered into an antenuptial agreement, fixing the property rights of each, a court should not substitute its judgment and amend the contract. A perfect or equal division of the marital property is not required to withstand scrutiny under this standard. This is in keeping with this court's standard of review of provisions contained in antenuptial agreements providing for the devolution of property at the time of the death of one of the parties.

In the review of provisions in antenuptial agreements regarding *maintenance or sustenance alimony*, a further standard of review must be applied—done of conscionability of the provisions at the time of the divorce or separation. Although we have held herein that such provisions in an antenuptial agreement generally may be considered valid, and even though it is found in a given case upon review that the agreement had met all of the good faith tests, the provisions relating to maintenance or sustenance may lose their validity by reasons of changed circumstances which render the provisions unconscionable as to one or the other at the time of the divorce of the parties. Accordingly, such provisions may, upon a review of all of the circumstances, be found to have become voidable at the time of the divorce or dissolution.

We believe that the underlying state interest in the welfare of the divorced spouse, when measured against the rights of the parties to freely contract, weighs in favor of the court's jurisdiction to review, at the time of a subsequent divorce, the terms in an antenuptial agreement providing sustenance alimony for one of the parties. There is sound public policy rationale for not strictly enforcing such a provision which, even though entered into in good faith and reasonable at the time of execution, may have become unreasonable or unconscionable as to its application to the spouse upon divorce. It is a valid interest of the state to mitigate potential harm, hardship, or disadvantage to a spouse which would be occasioned by the breakup of the marriage, and a strict and literal interpretation of the provisions for maintenance of the spouse to be found in these agreements.

One who, by way of a motion for modification, claims the unconscionability of a provision for maintenance within an antenuptial agreement has the burden of showing the unconscionable effect of the provision at the time of divorce or dissolution.[11] The trial court, in the determination of the issue of conscionability and reasonableness of the provisions for sustenance or maintenance of a spouse at the time of the divorce, shall utilize the same factors that govern the allowance of alimony which are set forth in R.C. 3105.18.[12]

---

[11] Unconscionability of a provision for maintenance and sustenance contained in an antenuptial agreement may be found in a number of circumstances, examples of which might be an extreme health problem requiring considerable care and expense; change in employability of the spouse; additional burdens placed upon a spouse by way of responsibility to children of the parties; marked changes in the cost of providing the necessary maintenance of the spouse; and changed circumstance of the standards of living occasioned by the marriage, where a return to the prior living standard would work a hardship upon a spouse.

[12] R.C. 3105.18(B) provides:

"In determining whether alimony is necessary, and in determining the nature, amount, and manner of payment of alimony, the court shall consider all relevant factors, including:

"(1) The relative earning abilities of the parties;

"(2) The ages and the physical and emotional conditions of the parties;

"(3) The retirement benefits of the parties;

"(4) The expectancies and inheritances of the parties;

"(5) The duration of the marriage;

"(6) The extent to which it would be inappropriate for a party, because he will be custodian of a minor child of the marriage, to seek employment outside the home;

"(7) The standard of living of the parties established during the marriage;

"(8) The relative extent of education of the parties;

"(9) The relative assets and liabilities of the parties;

Applying the law to the facts and circumstances of this case, we find that there is accord that the antenuptial agreement was entered into with all of the factors of good faith and non-overreaching as previously set forth herein. There also is no question that there was in fact a full disclosure of the assets of the parties as evidenced by the list of such assets attached to the agreement. Further, we believe that the provisions of the contract did not promote or encourage divorce, or present a profiteering device for the parties. Here, we are reviewing an antenuptial agreement entered into by the parties who married and lived together as man and wife for fourteen years, which marriage must have been a harmonious one for a considerable period of time, and one which produced an offspring.

Therefore, the basic agreement in its totality was a valid one when entered into by the parties. In accord with the principles discussed previously, the fact that a divorce was granted to the wife upon the trial court's finding that the husband had been at fault does not abrogate the contract upon which he relies, and does not prevent the husband from enforcing the provisions other than those pertaining to sustenance or maintenance which might be held voidable on behalf of the wife.

Concerning the latter point, the facts would tend to show that, although a comparatively wealthy man at the time of the execution of the antenuptial agreement, Mr. Gross became a man of considerably greater means during the years of his second marriage. Not only did his stock holdings and value thereof increase markedly, but his net income also substantially increased. The wife's standard of living has changed quite dramatically from the time of the execution of the agreement until the time of the divorce. To require the wife to return from this opulent standard of living to that which would be required within the limitations of the property and sustenance provisions of this agreement, could well occasion a hardship or be significantly difficult for the former wife.

Under the facts here, and in light of the law pronounced in this opinion, we find the provisions for maintenance within this agreement to be unconscionable as a matter of law and voidable by Mrs. Gross. Accordingly, we hold that the provisions within this agreement for the maintenance of Mrs. Gross should be reviewed by the trial court, and alternative provisions be ordered by the court.

Accordingly, the judgment of the court of appeals is reversed, and this cause is remanded to the trial court for further proceedings in accordance with this opinion.

"(10) The property brought to the marriage by either party;

"(11) The contribution of a spouse as homemaker."

NOTES AND QUESTIONS

1.   On remand, "[t]he plaintiff is awarded the sum of $2500.00 per month, not to be diminished or modified by what plaintiff may earn, so long as her earning is moderate. The alimony ordered herein is retroactive to the date of the Judgment Entry and is in addition to the child support previously referred to." Gross v. Gross, 492 N.E.2d 476 (Ohio App. 1985).

When they divorced, Mr. Gross had an annual income of $250,000, and a net worth of $6 million. They were married for about fourteen years and had one child together. The wife seemed to have quite limited career prospects at divorce. Is the award to Mrs. Gross of $30,000 in annual spousal support fair? This will be discussed in more detail in Chapter 16.

2.   How would *DeLorean* be resolved under *Gross*? How would *Gross* be resolved under *DeLorean*?

3.   *Gross* distinguishes between provisions dealing with equitable distribution and those limiting spousal support. Why might the court have been more concerned about enforcing spousal support limitations?

While a few states do not permit premarital agreements to limit spousal support (Huegli v. Huegli, 884 N.W.2d 223 (Iowa App. 2016)), most states generally enforce premarital agreements that restrict spousal support. J.T. OLDHAM, DIVORCE, SEPARATION AND THE DISTRIBUTION OF PROPERTY (2017) § 4.03A[1]. Should there be any situations where spousal support limitations should not be enforced? In California, spousal support restrictions are not enforceable if it would be unconscionable to do so. CAL. FAM. CODE § 1612. In *In re* Marriage of Facter, 152 Cal. Rptr. 3d 79 (App. 2013) the appellate court affirmed a ruling that a spousal support waiver was unconscionable, where at the time the agreement was signed the parties were in very different economic circumstances and there was significant inequality in bargaining power, and at the time of divorce the wife had significant financial needs.

4.   *Agreements "encouraging divorce":* The *Gross* decision notes that an enforceable premarital agreement must not "promote or encourage divorce." Few cases analyze in detail what types of provisions violate this limit. Of course, *all* premarital agreements encourage divorce, in the sense that they facilitate the divorce process. Some courts analyze the "promote divorce" issue in terms of whether the contract provides one or the other spouse with a financial incentive to file for divorce. For example, in *In re* Marriage of Noghrey, 215 Cal. Rptr. 153 (App. 1985):

> * * * Kambiz and Farima were married for seven and one-half months when Farima filed for divorce. * * * [T]he trial court filed the following Memorandum of Decision: It is the opinion of the Court that the petitioner and respondent entered into a written antenuptial agreement, also known as 'Katuba' [sic], prior to their marriage. The terms of the agreement were as follows: 'I, Kambiz Noghrey, agree to settle on Farima Human the house in Sunnyvale and $500,000 or one-half of my assets, whichever is greater, in the event of a divorce.'

The said agreement should be found to be a valid, binding, and enforceable agreement. * * * The agreement before us * * * is not of the type that seeks to define the character of property acquired after marriage nor does it seek to ensure the separate character of property acquired prior to marriage. This agreement is surely different and speaks to a wholly unrelated subject. It constitutes a promise by the husband to give the wife a very substantial amount of money and property, *but only upon the occurrence of a divorce.* No one could reasonably contend this agreement encourages the husband to seek a dissolution. Common sense and fiscal prudence dictate the opposite. Such is not the case with the wife. She, for her part, is encouraged by the very terms of the agreement to seek a dissolution, and with all deliberate speed, lest the husband suffer an untimely demise, nullifying the contract, and the wife's right to the money and property. * * * Farima did testify that neither she nor her parents possessed great wealth. The prospect of receiving a house and a minimum of $500,000 by obtaining the no-fault divorce available in California would menace the marriage of the best intentioned spouse.

See also Illustration 5, RESTATEMENT (SECOND) OF CONTRACTS § 190 ("A and B, who are about to be married, make an antenuptial agreement in which A promises that in case of divorce, he will settle $1,000,000 on B. A court may decide that, in view of the large sum promised, A's promise tends unreasonably to encourage divorce and is unenforceable on grounds of public policy."); Neilson v. Neilson, 780 P.2d 1264 (Utah App. 1989) (denying enforcement when premarital agreement specified that, if the wealthy spouse filed for divorce, the other would receive 50% of that spouse's assets, based on the conclusion that this provision encouraged the less wealthy spouse to goad the other to file for divorce).

Not all courts have refused to enforce marital agreements that provide for a payment of a specific sum in the event of a divorce. *See* Akileh v. Elchahal, 666 So. 2d 246 (Fla. Dist. Ct. App. 1996) (enforcing Islamic "sadaq"); Aziz v. Aziz, 488 N.Y.S.2d 123 (Sup. Ct. 1985) (enforcing "mahr" antenuptial agreement); Marriage of Bellio, 129 Cal. Rptr. 2d 556 (App. 2003) (enforcing an agreement to pay $100,000 upon divorce, when the recipient filed for divorce after one year of marriage). *Cf.*, Marriage of Dajani, 251 Cal. Rptr. 871 (App. 1988).

The "encouraging" divorce issue can also arise if one party is married to another when the agreement is being negotiated. For example, in Ludwig v. Ludwig, 693 S.W.2d 816 (Mo. App. 1985), one prospective spouse, as an inducement to the other to divorce her current husband and marry him, agreed to an equal division of his assets if they divorced. The court refused to enforce this provision because it induced the woman to divorce her first husband.

Some premarital agreements provide for a property award that varies based on the duration of the marriage. For example, in Sides v. Sides, 717 S.E.2d 472 (Ga. 2011) the parties had signed a premarital agreement. Under the agreement, the wife was entitled to a small sum if the parties divorced before their 20th anniversary, and a substantially larger sum if they divorced after being married for more than 20 years. The husband filed for divorce when the parties had been married for 19 years, and the divorce was finalized 62 days before their 20th anniversary. Should the agreement be enforced?

The "encouraging divorce" concern has been addressed primarily in the context where, under the agreement, the *poorer* spouse is given more upon divorce than he or she normally would get absent an agreement. It has been less frequently discussed in those cases where the *richer* spouse obtains an advantage. A Kansas court has concluded that a contract that gives the poorer spouse nothing at divorce is void because it encourages divorce; a Virginia court disagreed. *Compare* Ranney v. Ranney, 548 P.2d 734 (Kan. 1976) *with* Black v. Powers, 628 S.E.2d 546 (Va. App. 2006). Are provisions that benefit the poorer spouse of greater concern than those that benefit the richer one?

Is the "encouraging divorce" ground for denying enforcement a sensible one? If yes, how should it be construed?

5.   *Post-Agreement Changes in Circumstance:* In refusing to enforce the spousal-support provision of the marital agreement, the *Gross* court relied, in part, on the fact that "Mr. Gross became a man of considerably greater means during the years of his * * * marriage." In those jurisdictions willing to take account of events after the agreement is signed, a finding of unconscionability may be based on loss of spousal earning capacity due to child care responsibilities, health problems, etc., or an unexpected gain or career success. In *Newman* (*infra* UPAA n. 5), both parties had been previously married, the wife filed for divorce only thirty months after the wedding, and each party's circumstances had not changed since the wedding; although the parties' financial situations at divorce were very different, the maintenance waiver was enforced because the parties' circumstances had not substantially changed during the marriage.

Some courts have ruled that the property-division provisions of an agreement may also be invalidated when there is a substantial and unforeseen change of circumstances, but some very large shifts in net worth have not been grounds for invalidation. For example, in Blue v. Blue, 60 S.W.3d 585, 590 (Ky. App. 2001) the Court held that a property-division provision should be invalidated when "the circumstances of the parties at [divorce] are so beyond the contemplation of the parties at the time [of signing] as to cause its enforcement to work an injustice," but, nonetheless enforced the agreement despite the fact that the net worth of the wealthier spouse increased from $5 million to $77 million over the course of the marriage. *See also* Mallen v. Mallen, 622 S.E.2d 812 (Ga. 2005) (enforcing premarital agreement despite a $14 million increase in net worth during marriage). *Cf.* Lane v. Lane, 202 S.W.3d 577 (Ky. 2006) (invalidating a spousal support waiver due to a change in the parties' circumstances during the marriage).

Should a spousal-support provision be voidable based on unforeseen circumstances? A property-division provision? If yes, how much of a change should be required?

3. Construction of Premarital Agreements

If a court determines that a premarital agreement is enforceable, the effect of the agreement must be determined. What level of specificity should be required to change the parties' rights to equitable distribution at divorce? For example, in Short v. Short, 356 S.W.3d 235 (Mo. App. 2011) the parties agreed that "[in the event of a divorce] * * * each party shall keep and retain the ownership * * * of all property, real and personal * * * acquired by him on her before or during marriage." In Missouri, income received during marriage is normally considered divisible property at divorce. Does this agreement alter this normal rule? The court found that the language of the agreement was "too vague and indefinite" to reflect an intention to change this normal Missouri rule.

In contrast, another held that where parties agreed that "neither party, by virtue of the marriage, shall have, or acquire any right, title or claim in and to the real or personal estate of the other," this constituted a complete waiver of the right to property division at divorce. Brummund v. Brummund, 785 N.W.2d 182 (N.D. 2010) .

Another Texas case presents a similar problem of construction. In McClary v. Thompson, 65 S.W.3d 829 (Tex. App. 2002) the agreement provided that "[the husband] has as his separate property all benefits . . . in a retirement program * * *. If * * * the marriage is dissolved, such retirement benefits shall remain the separate property of [the husband]." At divorce, the issue was whether all funds in the retirement account at the time of divorce were the husband's separate property, or only the account balance when the parties married. The appellate court held that, because the agreements stated that the benefits would "remain" his separate property, this reflected an intention to deal with only the balance in the account when they married; the excess amount accrued during marriage was divided.

These cases show that, if a premarital agreement is perceived to be ambiguous, courts normally will construe it to maximize the size of the divisible estate. So, if you are drafting an agreement and trying to reduce the size of the divisible estate, you need to draft such a provision clearly.

UNIFORM PREMARITAL AGREEMENT ACT
9C U.L.A. 39 (2001).

§ 2. A premarital agreement must be in writing and signed by both parties. It is enforceable without consideration.

§ 3. (a) Parties to a premarital agreement may contract with respect to:

(1) the rights and obligations of each of the parties in any of the property of either or both of them whenever and wherever acquired or located;

(2) the right to buy, sell, use, transfer, exchange, abandon, lease, consume, expend, assign, create a security interest in, mortgage, encumber, dispose of, or otherwise manage and control property;

(3) the disposition of property upon separation, marital dissolution, death, or the occurrence or nonoccurrence of any other event;

(4) the modification or elimination of spousal support;

(5) the making of a will, trust, or other arrangement to carry out the provisions of this agreement;

(6) the ownership rights in and disposition of the death benefit from a life insurance policy;

(7) the choice of law governing the construction of the agreement; and

(8) any other matter, including their personal rights and obligations, not in violation of public policy or a statute imposing a criminal penalty.[1]

(b) The right of a child to support may not be adversely affected by a premarital agreement.

§ 5. After marriage, a premarital agreement may be amended or revoked only by a written agreement signed by the parties. The amended agreement or the revocation is enforceable without consideration.

§ 6. (a) A premarital agreement is not enforceable if the party against whom enforcement is sought proves that:

(1) that party did not execute the agreement voluntarily; or

(2) the agreement was unconscionable when it was executed and, before execution of the agreement, that party:

(i) was not provided a fair and reasonable disclosure of the property or financial obligations of the other party;

(ii) did not voluntarily and expressly waive, in writing, any right to disclosure of the property or financial obligations of the other party beyond the disclosure provided; and

---

[1] OFFICIAL COMMENT: * * * [S]ubject to this limitation, an agreement may provide for such matters as the choice of abode, the freedom to pursue career opportunities, the upbringing of children, and so on.

(iii) did not have, or reasonably could not have had, an adequate knowledge of the property or financial obligations of the other party.

(b) If a provision of a premarital agreement modifies or eliminates spousal support and that modification or elimination causes one party to the agreement to be eligible for support under a program of public assistance at the time of separation or marital dissolution, *a court*, notwithstanding the terms of the agreement, may require the other party to provide support to the extent necessary to avoid that eligibility.

(c) An issue of unconscionability of a premarital agreement shall be decided by the court as a matter of law.

§ 8. Any statute of limitations applicable to an action asserting a claim for relief under a premarital agreement is tolled during the marriage of the parties to the agreement. However, equitable defenses limiting the time for enforcement, including laches and estoppel, are available to either party.

NOTES AND QUESTIONS

1. How would *DeLorean* and *Gross* be resolved under the UPAA?

2. The UPAA has been adopted (with some modifications) by many states, including Arizona, Arkansas, California, Connecticut, Delaware, Florida, Hawaii, Idaho, Illinois, Indiana, Iowa, Kansas, Maine, Montana, Nebraska, Nevada, New Jersey, New Mexico, North Carolina, Oregon, Rhode Island, South Dakota, Texas, Utah, Virginia, and the District of Columbia. *See Comment*, 23 J. AM. ACAD. MAT. LAW. 355 (2010).

3. The UPAA provides that a provision "in violation of public policy" should not be enforced. The scope of this provision is unclear. Presumably, a waiver of a right to financial support during marriage would not be enforced. Painewebber v. Murray, 260 B.R. 815 (E.D. Texas 2001).

Sometimes premarital agreements contain a provision that, if the parties divorce, each party waives the right to court-awarded legal fees. An Illinois court has held that such a waiver could not extend to legal assistance regarding issues affecting minor children. Marriage of Weinrich, 7 N.E.3d 889 (Ill. App. 2014). *See also*, Gottlieb v. Gottlieb, 25 N.Y.S.3d 90 (App. Div. 2016).

4. The UPAA does not attempt to clarify what might establish involuntary execution. California has amended its version of the UPAA to provide that an agreement will be considered not voluntarily signed unless the court finds all three of the following circumstances surrounding executions were satisfied:

(1) The party against whom enforcement is sought was represented by independent legal counsel at the time of signing the agreement or, after being advised to seek independent legal counsel, expressly waived, in a separate writing, representation

by independent legal counsel and the time the agreement was signed.

(2) The party against whom enforcement is sought had not less than seven calendar days between the time that party was first presented with the agreement and advised to seek independent legal counsel and the time the agreement was signed.

(3) The party against whom enforcement is sought, if unrepresented by legal counsel, was fully informed of the terms and basic effect of the agreement as well as the rights and obligations he or she was giving up by signing the agreement, and was proficient in the language in which the explanation of the party's right was conducted and in which the agreement was written. The explanation of the rights and obligations relinquished shall be memorialized in writing and delivered to the party prior to signing the agreement. The unrepresented party shall, on or before the signing of the premarital agreement, execute a document declaring that he or she received the information required by this paragraph and indicating who provided that information. CAL FAM. CODE § 1615(c).

How would this provision have impacted the result in *DeLorean*?

5. The UPAA does not define "unconscionable," although the official comments to the UPAA do try to clarify the term's meaning.[1] How might a court determine whether an agreement was unconscionable at the time of signing? A New Jersey statute provides that an agreement is unconscionable at divorce if it would leave a party without means of reasonable support or would provide a standard of living for a party below what the party enjoyed before the marriage. N.J. STAT. ANN. § 37:2–32. Would this be a good clarification?

---

[1]   OFFICIAL COMMENT: The test of "unconscionability" is drawn from § 306 of the Uniform Marriage and Divorce Act (UMDA). The following discussion set forth in the Commissioner's Note to § 306 of the UMDA is equally appropriate here:

Subsection (b) undergirds the freedom allowed the parties by making clear that the terms of the agreement respecting maintenance and property disposition are binding upon the court unless those terms are found to be unconscionable. The standard of unconscionability is used in commercial law, where its meaning includes protection against one-sidedness, oppression, or unfair surprise (see § 302, Uniform Commercial Code), and in contract law. It has been used in cases respecting divorce settlements or awards. Bell v. Bell, 150 Colo. 174, 371 P.2d 773 (1962) ("this division of property is manifestly unfair, inequitable and unconscionable"). Hence the act does not introduce a novel standard unknown to the law. In the context of negotiations between spouses as to the financial incidents of their marriage, the standard includes protection against overreaching, concealment of assets, and sharp dealing not consistent with the obligations of marital partners to deal fairly with each other.

"In order to determine whether the agreement is unconscionable, the court may look to the economic circumstances of the parties resulting from the agreement, and any other relevant evidence such as the conditions under which the agreement was made, including the knowledge of the other party. If the court finds the agreement not unconscionable, its terms respecting property division and maintenance may not be altered by the court at the hearing."

An Indiana appellate court ruled that a premarital agreement signed by a pregnant girl who was 16 years old was unconscionable when signed. Ferris v. Fetters, 26 N.E.3d 1016 (Ind. App. 2015).

Under the UPAA, an agreement is enforceable unless it is involuntarily signed *or* the agreement was unconscionable at the time of signing *and* there was inadequate disclosure of financial information to the waiving spouse (and that spouse did not otherwise have adequate knowledge of financial information). Some states adopting the UPAA have changed these rules.

Disclosure and Unconscionability: The UPAA provides for enforcement of an unconscionable agreement if there was adequate disclosure. *Accord* Burtoff v. Burtoff, 418 A.2d 1085 (D.C. App. 1980). Connecticut has modified the UPAA so that inadequate disclosure alone is a ground for invalidating an agreement. *See* CONN. GEN. STAT. § 46b–36g(a). In addition, a few states, have adopted the UPAA but amended it to provide that a court need not enforce an unconscionable agreement. *See* N.J. STAT. ANN. § 34: 2–38; CONN. GEN. STAT. § 46b–36g(a) (both barring enforcement of a premarital agreement that is unconscionable at divorce). Some courts have taken the approach that the issue of unconscionability in a prenuptial contract should be treated as it is under general contract rules. *See* Simeone v. Simeone, 581 A.2d 162 (Pa. 1990) (court should not review the "reasonableness" of the agreement). These courts refuse enforcement only if a premarital contract is unconscionable when signed. *See* Arthur Leff, *Unconscionability and the Code*, 115 U. PA. L. REV. 485 (1967). Other courts and legislatures have required more. For example, under N.Y. DOM. REL. L. § 236B, a premarital agreement will not be enforced unless it is "fair and reasonable" when signed and "not unconscionable" at the time enforcement is sought. *Accord* Button v. Button, 388 N.W.2d 546 (Wis. 1986). While the difference between "unconscionable" and "unfair" may be somewhat vague, courts typically interpret unfairness so as to permit less deviation from the state's marital property and spousal support rules. For example, in *DeLorean, supra*, the court decided that the agreement was not unconscionable because Mrs. DeLorean did not qualify for public assistance; in contrast, the *Button* court stated that the agreement "should in some manner appropriate to the circumstances of the parties take into account that each spouse contributes to the prosperity of the marriage."

What values are promoted by the UPAA approach? by the approach of *Button* and the New York Domestic Relations Law?

6. *Fairness and Timing:* Under any fairness standard, it is important to clarify what time is chosen to determine its fairness. Some standards, such as the UPAA, look only to circumstances at the time of signing, the point at which, for purposes of general contract law, courts normally determine whether a contract is unconscionable. *See* UPAA; Martin v. Farber, 510 A.2d 608 (Md. App. 1986). Others take into account the facts at the time of enforcement. *See, e.g.*, N.Y. DOM. REL. L. § 236B; *Button, supra* n. 5; Justus v. Justus, 581 N.E.2d 1265 (Ind. App. 1991); Bassler v. Bassler, 593 A.2d 82 (Vt. 1991); McKee-Johnson v. Johnson, 444 N.W.2d 259 (Minn. 1989) (premarital agreement

unenforceable if the premises upon which [the contract was] based have so drastically changed that enforcement would not comport with the [original] reasonable expectations of the parties to such an extent that enforcement would be unconscionable). Still others look to the time of signing for property rights and the time of divorce for spousal support. *See, e.g., Gross;* Lewis v. Lewis, 748 P.2d 1362 (Haw. 1988); Newman v. Newman, 653 P.2d 728 (Colo. 1982); Rider v. Rider, 669 N.E.2d 160 (Ind. 1996).

Under which, if any, of these approaches would the agreement in *DeLorean* be unenforceable? the agreement in *Gross*? What values are promoted by each approach? Is the important issue the parties' circumstance at the time of signing? their circumstances at divorce? the extent of change between signing and divorce? the foreseeability of any such changes?

7. *Spousal Support Waivers:* No consensus has yet evolved on the enforceability of a waiver of spousal support in a premarital agreement. A few courts have enforced unfair spousal support waivers as long as the waiving spouse signed the agreement voluntarily and had the advice of independent counsel. *See* Baker v. Baker, 622 So. 2d 541 (Fla. Dist. Ct. App. 1993). The UPAA provides that such waivers are enforceable, but if a spouse qualifies for public assistance at the time of divorce, the court may require the other party to provide support to the extent necessary to avoid that eligibility. UPAA § 6(c); *accord,* MacFarlane v. Rich, 567 A.2d 585 (N.H. 1989); Cary v. Cary, 937 S.W.2d 777 (Tenn. 1996). Some states adopting the UPAA do not permit spousal support waivers. *See* S.D. COD. LAWS § 25–2–18; IOWA CODE ANN. § 596.5; N.M. STAT. ANN. § 40–3A–4. In Illinois, the UPAA was modified to provide that a spousal-support waiver will not be enforced if it causes the waiving spouse undue hardship in light of circumstances not reasonably foreseeable at the time of signing. *See* 750 ILL. COMP. STAT. ANN. § 10/7. And California modified the UPAA to provide that a spousal-support waiver is unenforceable either if (i) the waiving party was not represented by independent counsel, or (ii) the provision is unconscionable at divorce. *See* CAL. FAM. CODE § 1612(c). *See also* DeMatteo v. DeMatteo, 762 N.E.2d 797 (Mass. 2002) (an unforeseen substantial change in circumstances could warrant invalidating a premarital agreement); Unander v. Unander, 506 P.2d 719 (Or. 1973) (spousal support waiver is valid unless waiver deprives spouse of support he or she could not otherwise secure). Florida permits waivers of post-divorce spousal support but not of the right to interim support before divorce. *See* Khan v. Khan, 936 N.Y.S.2d 566 (App. Div. 2012).

What are the advantages and disadvantages of these various approaches? On balance, which one is best?

8. In *DeLorean* the parties agreed to waive completely any right to property distribution at divorce. The *DeLorean* court and the UPAA permit such an agreement but some states do not. *See* DeMatteo v. DeMatteo, 762 N.E.2d 797 (Mass. 2002). What interests are promoted by allowing such agreements? by disallowing them? On balance, which approach is preferable?

If spouses can via contract waive all the customary economic rights that flow from marriage, does this undermine or devalue marriage? Or does it merely give parties the freedom to specify what rights and obligations will arise from their relationship?

In many instances where parties sign a premarital agreement, the parties are in very different economic circumstances, and in almost all such situations the agreement is proposed (required?) by the wealthier party, and the purpose of the agreement is to substantially limit the rights of the poorer spouse if the parties divorce. *See* J. Thomas Oldham, *A Reevaluation of the Uniform Premarital Agreement Act After Three Decades,* 19 DUKE J. GENDER LAW & POL'Y 83, 89–90 n.45 (2011) (citing more than 20 appellate cases of this type). In most instances, the wealthier party is the man.

9.   *Common-Law Defenses:* Does the UPAA set forth all grounds available to challenge a premarital agreement? In Daniel v. Daniel, 779 S.W.2d 110 (Tex. App. 1989), a Texas court held that the enactment of the UPAA did not do away with "common-law defenses." The UPAA Official Comment also states that, unless a specific common-law defense is barred (like lack of consideration), ordinary contract defenses remain available.

10.   *The Uniform Premarital and Marital Agreement Act:* The Uniform Law Commission adopted a new uniform law regarding premarital and martial agreements in July 2012. The UPMAA differs from the UPAA in a few ways. An agreement can be successfully challenged either if the agreement was unconscionable when signed or financial disclosure was inadequate. In addition, before signing a party must be given "access to independent counsel", which is defined as reasonable time to (A) decide whether to retain an independent lawyer (before signing) and (B) locate an independent lawyer, obtain advice, and consider the advice provided. Uniform Premarital and Marital Agreement Act § 9(b). How should courts construe a provision like this? As of 2017, Colorado and North Dakota are the only two states that have enacted the UPMAA.

11.   *Different Approaches To Unconscionability:* In *Premarital Contracts Are Now Enforceable, Unless . . . ,* 21 HOUS. L. REV. 757, 780–81 (1984), Professor J. Thomas Oldham proposed a different test for determining whether to enforce a premarital agreement:

(a)   A written premarital or postnuptial agreement is enforceable at divorce if it is freely and intelligently executed and, considering the property and support received pursuant thereto, both spouses have adequate support at divorce under the terms of the agreement in light of the length of marriage and the wealth, needs, health, and earning capacities of the parties.

(b)   A written premarital or postnuptial agreement is enforceable at divorce if it is freely and intelligently executed, even if both spouses do not receive adequate support pursuant thereto, unless subsection (c) applies.

(c) If (i) the terms of a premarital or postnuptial agreement, considering the property and support received pursuant thereto, provide inadequate support for a spouse at divorce, in light of the length of marriage and the wealth, needs, health, and earning capacities of the parties, and (ii) there was a substantial and unforeseeable change in the parties' circumstances between the time of execution of the agreement (or the most recent amendment thereof) and divorce, the divorce court can, in its discretion, fashion a division of property and support award so that the financially dependent spouse will receive adequate support. The duration and amount of the support and property so awarded are to be based upon the length of the marriage and the wealth, needs, health, and earning capacities of the parties.[2]

(d) A premarital or postnuptial agreement may address the property division or spousal support, if any, that will result if divorce occurs.

12. The American Law Institute has proposed yet another approach for judging the substantive fairness of a premarital agreement:

§ 7.05 When Enforcement Would Work a Substantial Injustice

(1) A court should not enforce a term in an agreement if, pursuant to Paragraphs (2) and (3) of this section,

(a) the circumstances require it to consider whether enforcement would work a substantial injustice; and

(b) the court finds that enforcement would work a substantial injustice.

(2) A court should consider whether enforcement of an agreement would work a substantial injustice if, and only if, the party resisting its enforcement shows that one or more of the following have occurred since the time of the agreement's execution:

(a) more than a fixed number of years have passed, that number being set in a rule of statewide application;

---

[2] Courts desirous of establishing safeguards to protect mothers against oppressive marital contracts might adopt the following guidelines as a second paragraph of "c" of the proposal set forth above in text:

If (i) the terms of a premarital or post-nuptial agreement provide inadequate support for a spouse at divorce, in light of the length of the marriage and the wealth, needs, health, and earning capacities of the parties; (ii) the parties had one or more children together; (iii) the financially dependent spouse did not work outside the home at a full-time job for more than one-half of the duration of the marriage; (iv) the respective wealth and earning capacities of the parties are substantially different at divorce; and (v) either the marriage was of substantial duration or the financially dependent spouse will receive physical custody of one or more minor children at divorce, the court may, in its discretion, despite the agreement, fashion a division of property and support award so that the financially dependent spouse will receive adequate support, the duration and amount of which is to be based upon the length of the marriage and the wealth, needs, health, and earning capacities of the parties.

(b) a child was born to, or adopted by, the parties, who at the time of execution had no children in common;

(c) there has been a change in circumstances that has a substantial impact on the parties or their children, but when they executed the agreement the parties probably did not anticipate either the change, or its impact.

(3) The party claiming that enforcement of an agreement would work a substantial injustice has the burden of proof on that question. In deciding whether the agreement's application to the parties' circumstances at dissolution would work a substantial injustice, a court should consider all of the following:

(a) the magnitude of the disparity between the outcome under the agreement and the outcome under otherwise prevailing legal principles;

(b) for those marriages of limited duration in which it is practical to ascertain, the difference between the circumstances of the objecting party if the agreement is enforced, and that party's likely circumstances had the marriage never taken place;

(c) whether the purpose of the agreement was to benefit or protect the interest of third parties (such as children from a prior relationship), whether that purpose is still relevant, and whether the agreement's terms were reasonably designed to serve it;

(d) the impact of the agreement's enforcement upon the children of the parties.

AMERICAN LAW INSTITUTE, PRINCIPLES OF THE LAW OF FAMILY DISSOLUTION: ANALYSIS AND RECOMMENDATIONS § 7.05 (2002).

How are the Oldham and ALI tests different from that suggested in *DeLorean*? in the Uniform Premarital Agreement Act? On balance, which test is the best?

Problem 5-2:

Jeremy and Jessica married fifteen years ago just after both graduated from law school. Before marriage, they signed a premarital agreement which provided that: (1) each spouse's earnings (including all professional partnership interests) would be separate property not subject to division at divorce; and (2) each spouse waives any right to post-divorce spousal support from the other. When Jeremy and Jessica married, both earned about the same amount of money and worked at comparable legal jobs at different law firms. Jessica had a child during her first year of work and quit her job to assume the role of primary caretaker for the child; thereafter she worked only sporadically and part-time as a lawyer. Jeremy continued to work full-time as a lawyer. Jeremy has now initiated a divorce action. He is a partner in a law firm earning $200,000 annually; Jessica is working part-time, earning approximately $20,000 per year. Jeremy and Jessica have agreed that Jessica will receive custody of their child and will receive monthly child support of $500 for three years, until the child is 18 years old. Would Jeremy and Jessica's premarital agreement be enforced under the UPAA? under *Gross*? *Should* the agreement be enforced?

Problem 5-3:

Lois, a wealthy woman, is planning to marry Clark, a younger man with few assets and a small salary. Lois has consulted you about asking Clark to sign a premarital agreement whereby he would waive all rights to marital property and spousal support if the marriage ends in divorce. How would you structure the negotiations: (1) to maximize the likelihood that the agreement would be enforced; and (2) to minimize the likelihood that the contract negotiations would not undermine the relationship? If Lois were to ask whether you think she should ask Clark to sign the agreement, how would you respond?

Problem 5-4:

Two prospective spouses have asked you to draft a premarital agreement for them. What, if any, professional responsibility issues would this present?

Problem 5-5:

Helen and Walter signed a premarital agreement that complies with the UPAA. At a festive dinner on their first anniversary, they decided to revoke the agreement; to memorialize this intention they threw a copy of the agreement into the fire in the fireplace. Two years later, Helen and Walter divorce. Under the UPAA, is the agreement still valid?

Problem 5-6:

You are counsel to the state legislature's Committee on Family Law, which is considering the adoption of legislation governing premarital agreements. Case law had, by and large, followed the approach of the *Gross* decision until last year, when the state Supreme Court enforced a premarital agreement on facts similar to those in the *Gross* case. The Committee has concluded that legislation would be useful to ensure a predictable approach to the enforcement of premarital agreements.

At a public hearing, the Committee heard a number of family lawyers report anecdotal evidence that couples with a premarital agreement are more prone to divorce. The Committee also heard testimony from an expert on comparative law, who testified that, in many civil law countries, marriage partners must affirmatively elect a marital property regime (i.e., shared or separate property rights) and that some common-law countries (including England) do not permit binding premarital agreements on divorce entitlements. *See* David Leadercramer, *Prenuptial Agreements— An Idea Whose Time Has Come?*, May [2000] FAM. L. 359.

You have been asked to advise the Committee:

1.   If marriages dissolve at a higher rate when there is a premarital agreement, is this a significant public concern?

2.   Should the state permit bargaining over the financial consequences of divorce? Should it matter if the parties are already living together?

3.   If bargaining is to be permitted, how (if at all) should the state protect the poor and/or unsophisticated prospective spouse?

4.   Are there rules or entitlements so important that they should not be subject to bargaining? If yes, what are they and what limits should be imposed on bargaining?

5.   What test for determining the enforceability of premarital agreements best balances all competing concerns?

B. CONFLICTS OF LAW ASPECTS OF PREMARITAL AGREEMENTS

As you have seen, state laws on premarital agreements vary. If spouses have contacts with more than one state or country, a court must decide which law to apply.

Under current conflicts of law principles, most courts will apply the law of a state chosen by the parties to determine whether to enforce an agreement, as long as the parties have some connection with that state and its law does not violate an important policy of the forum jurisdiction. *See, e.g.*, UPAA § 3 (7) (permitting parties to select applicable law). So, in *DeLorean,* the New Jersey court applied the law of California, not New Jersey, to determine whether Mr. DeLorean's financial disclosure was adequate. But some courts have held that laws governing premarital agreements reflect state policies so important that party election should not be permitted. *See* Scherer v. Scherer, 292 S.E.2d 662 (Ga. 1982).

If the parties to a premarital agreement do not specify which state's law will govern, some courts apply the law of the state where the contract was signed. *See* Black v. Powers, 628 S.E.2d 546 (Va. App. 2006). Others apply the law of the state with which the parties have the most significant relationship. *See* RESTATEMENT, SECOND, CONFLICT OF LAWS, §§ 187, 188. If a couple marries in one state, then moves to another and divorces there, the evidence suggests that (as long as both spouses move) the forum jurisdiction will typically find that it has the most significant relationship with the couple. *See* Lewis v. Lewis, 748 P.2d 1362 (Haw. 1988). Is this unfair? If so, in what situations?

Premarital agreements made in another country raise even more difficult problems. What, for example, should a U.S. court do if foreign nationals comply with premarital agreement laws of their own country, move to the United States, and later divorce in the United States? Some civil law countries permit spouses to elect a community or separate property system to govern their rights at divorce. If the spouses elect a separate property regime, what should a court do if they later divorce in a community property state in the United States? *See In re* Marriage of Shaban, 105 Cal. Rptr. 2d 863 (App. 2001); Fernandez v. Fernandez, 15 Cal. Rptr. 374 (App. 1961). Should it matter if the election procedure followed before marriage in the foreign country complies with the forum's requirements for premarital agreements? *See* Chaudry v. Chaudry, 388 A.2d 1000 (N.J. Super. App. Div. 1978); Mehtar v. Mehtar, 1997 WL 576540 (Conn. Super. 1997).

In the United States, parties discussing a premarital agreement commonly set forth the economic terms they envision if the marriage ends in divorce. They specify what property is or is not part of the divisible marital estate, and may set forth limits on post-divorce spousal support. Another option available in some European countries gives a couple the right to choose another jurisdiction's law to govern their marital property rights. It seems unlikely that a U.S. court would enforce such a party choice of marital property law. Aside from the issue of state policy, what problems would be presented if two Americans living in the United States wanted to choose Iranian law to govern their marital property rights?

C. INCORPORATING NONECONOMIC PROVISIONS IN A PREMARITAL AGREEMENT

While premarital agreements often address property rights, some spouses (and psychotherapists) have urged that premarital agreements could usefully address a variety of other matters. Here is an example given by Professor Weitzman:

LENORE J. WEITZMAN, THE MARRIAGE CONTRACT
295 et seq. (1981).

A TRADITIONAL MARRIAGE BETWEEN A MEDICAL DOCTOR AND A
HOUSEWIFE WITH FULL PARTNERSHIP RIGHTS FOR THE WIFE

Commitment to Ourselves

1.   Absent truly extraordinary circumstances, we agree to spend at least one evening a week enjoying each other—alone together. An evening begins at 7 P.M.

2.   Absent truly extraordinary circumstances, we agree to spend at least three weekend days a month together enjoying each other.

Sex

1.   We recognize the central importance of sex in human relationships, and commit ourselves to putting time and creative energy into realizing our sexual potential.

2.   We do not intend that our love and commitment to each other shall exclude other relationships in work, friendship, or sex.

3.   We do intend that our relationship with each other shall be a primary one and that each other's feelings and needs should be a major consideration in our other actions.

4.   We will tell each other when we have sex with other people, and we will make an effort to communicate honestly about all other important relationships in our lives.

Other Responsibilities

1.   Nancy agrees to further David's career by maintaining appropriate social relationships with other doctors and their wives.

2.   Nancy agrees to participate actively in church and country club activities, to serve on medical auxiliary and hospital benefit committees, and to socialize with David's colleagues and other physicians.

3.   Nancy promises to give a dinner party or to otherwise aid David's professional advancement by entertaining at least twice a week.

4.   David agrees to accompany Nancy to the ballet at least once a month.

5.   David also agrees to schedule at least two two-week vacations with her each year, at least one of them in Europe.

Children

1.   Children will be postponed until David's education is completed.

2.   If Nancy should become pregnant prior to that time, she will have an abortion.

3.   Nancy will have full responsibility for the care of the children; financial responsibility will be fully met from the income from David's practice.

Conditions of Separation

1.   We agree to stay together, absent intense pain, for four years or until our child is three years old, whichever is earlier.

2.   After that time, we can separate at any time that we freely and mutually agree to do so.

3.   In the event that one of us wants to separate and the other does not, we agree to:

a.   Give explicit notice of the desire to separate;

b.   Work to mend our relationship for a period of six months after such notice; and

c.   Make time for each other during that period, and seek professional assistance if either of us believes it would be useful.

4.   We recognize that the process of growth is the process of change. We respect each other's freedom and separate character. We hope that we will always freely choose to grow together, but we recognize that we may not. We agree always to try to treat each other gently, politely, and with consideration. We agree that, even if we separate, we will do it in a loving way.

Termination

1.   This partnership may be dissolved by either party, at will, upon six months notice to the other party.

2.   If this partnership is terminated by either party prior to the completion of David's education, Nancy's obligation to support him will cease. Moreover, once David's career has begun, he will have the obligation of supporting Nancy at the rate of $50,000 a year (in 1979 dollars with built-in cost-of-living and inflation adjustments) for as many years as she supported him. If necessary, David will secure a loan to repay Nancy for her support. If Nancy prefers a lump-sum settlement equal to the value of this support, David will arrange a loan to provide it. Both parties agree to treat Nancy's original support of David as a loan of the value specified above. David's obligation to repay this loan has the standing of any other legal debt.

3.   Once David finishes his residency, Nancy will acquire a one-quarter vested interest in his future earnings. If the partnership is terminated after this date, Nancy will be entitled to one-fourth of his net yearly income, to be paid quarterly, for as long as he continues to practice medicine. David will purchase insurance or a bond to guarantee this payment. It is agreed that this payment is not alimony, and that it shall be continued unmodified regardless of her earning capacity or remarriage. The parties consider this Nancy's reimbursement for investing in and helping to launch David's career. It is agreed that her efforts will have been crucial to any future success that he has, and that her vested interest in his career is the consideration for that support.

4.   David agrees to pay Nancy the fixed sum of $50,000 if their marriage terminates within 15 years, as liquidated damages for the pain

and suffering she will experience from the change in her expectations and life plans.

5. David also agrees [in the event of termination of the marriage] to pay for Nancy's medical expenses or to provide her with adequate insurance at the rate of one year of coverage for every year of marriage. It is explicitly agreed that psychiatric and dental bills be included in the above.

6. Community property will be divided equally upon termination.

7. If there are children, Nancy will have custody of the children. David will have full responsibility for their support, as well as the responsibility for compensating Nancy for her services in caring for them (at the then current rate for private nurses). Suitable visiting arrangements will be made.

NOTES AND QUESTIONS

1. Would a court enforce all of these provisions? If not, is unenforceability a problem?

(a) Some of the provisions seem to reflect aspirational goals and may not be intended to be enforceable. For example, it seems unlikely that David and Nancy contemplate any legal consequences from their failure to spend at least three weekend days a month together or David's failure to attend the ballet. What purposes might such provisions have? For example, it has been reported that Mark Zuckerberg, the founder of Facebook, signed an agreement with his then girlfriend (now wife) to the effect that they would have at least one date night per week and spend 100 minutes together not in his apartment or at the Facebook office. *See* Jan Hoffman, *Just Call It a Pre-Prenup,* N.Y. TIMES, May 27, 2012, at Styles p. 9. Ms. Hoffman refers to such agreements as "a business plan for a successful romance."

(b) Other provisions seem more significant. For example, what if Nancy doesn't have an abortion if she gets pregnant and David is still in school? A court would not order specific enforcement. Does this mean it is senseless to include such a provision in a premarital agreement?

(c) UPAA § 3(a)(8) seems to endorse provisions dealing with the day-to-day aspects of married life, like those included in the Weitzman contract, as long as they are "not in violation of public policy."

Apparently some wealthy older men are asking younger prospective brides to sign a premarital agreement reflecting their understanding that they will have no children together, and that if the woman does become pregnant she will have an abortion. If the woman becomes pregnant and does not have an abortion, a financial penalty is specified. *See* Jill Brooke, *A Promise To Love, Honor and Bear No Children,* N.Y. TIMES, Oct. 13, 2002, at 9–1. Should such a provision be enforced? For example, what if the woman would lose any right to a division of marital property at divorce if she breached the agreement? *See* Joline F. Sikaitis, Comment, *A New Form of Family Planning?: The Enforceability of No-Children Provisions in Prenuptial Agreements,* 54 CATHOLIC U. L. REV. 335 (2004).

(d)   Courts agree that provisions in a premarital agreement relating to children, including those governing child custody and support, are unenforceable. *See, e.g.,* Osborne v. Osborne, 428 N.E.2d 810 (Mass. 1981) (custody); Combs v. Sherry-Combs, 865 P.2d 50 (Wyo. 1993) (support); UPAA § 3(b). Should an agreement to raise the children in a particular church be enforced? *See In re* Marriage of Weiss, 49 Cal. Rptr. 2d 339 (App. 1996) (no).

(e)   Should spouses be able to waive the right to divorce? If not, what about the more limited waiver in the Weitzman contract that the parties will not separate for four years, and will "work on the relationship" for six months before separating? *See* Coggins v. Coggins, 601 So. 2d 109 (Ala. Civ. App. 1992). What about a waiver of the right to initiate a divorce action on "no-fault" grounds, if the right to initiate a fault divorce is retained (but, of course, only if a "fault" ground is available)? Or a waiver of the right to initiate a divorce action on a "fault" ground, if the right to initiate a "no-fault" divorce is retained? *See* Massar v. Massar, 652 A.2d 219 (N.J. Super. App. Div. 1995). If such a provision is valid, should it be specifically enforced or should the breaching party be required to pay damages to the other? Would recovery on a provision not to get a divorce be comparable to recovery for breach of the contract to marry? *See generally* Theodore Haas, *The Rationality and Enforceability of Contractual Restrictions on Divorce,* 66 N.C.L. REV. 879 (1988). What policy issues are presented by this type of waiver?

2.   Some religions have divorce requirements that differ from those of the secular law. For example, a Jewish wife may not remarry unless her husband obtains a bill of divorce ("get"). Sometimes divorcing Jewish husbands have refused to obtain a get, causing significant hardship to their wives. *See* Feldman, *Jewish Women and Secular Courts: Helping a Jewish Woman Obtain a Get,* 5 BERKELEY WOMEN'S L.J. 139 (1989–90). In more recent cases, most courts have enforced agreements requiring the husband to cooperate in the get procedure. *See* Scholl v. Scholl, 621 A.2d 808 (Del. Fam. 1992); Marriage of Goldman, 554 N.E.2d 1016 (Ill. App. 1990); Avitzur v. Avitzur, 446 N.E.2d 136 (1983). *But see* Aflalo v. Aflalo, 685 A.2d 523 (N.J. Super. 1996). A New York court affirmed a trial court order which provided that the husband would pay $100 in weekly spousal support for five years, but if he didn't provide the wife a get within sixty days the support would increase to $200 per week. Mizrahi-Srour v. Srour, 29 N.Y.S.3d 516 (App. Div. 2016).

3.   A celebrity may be concerned about the possibility that a former spouse may write about intimate details of their life together. Donald Trump included a provision in his premarital agreement that prohibited his wife Ivana from writing about their marriage without his consent. Should the provision be enforced? *See* Trump v. Trump, 582 N.Y.S.2d 1008 (App. Div. 1992).

4.   What if the premarital agreement specifies that a spouse will lose all marital property rights if he or she is sexually unfaithful during marriage? *See* Laudig v. Laudig, 624 A.2d 651 (Pa. Super. 1993). In Diosdado v. Diosdado, 118 Cal. Rptr. 2d 494 (App. 2002) the parties agreed that if one spouse was sexually unfaithful during the marriage and the parties divorced, the other spouse would receive, in addition to all other marital property rights, $50,000 in liquidated damages for the infidelity. Should this provision be enforced if one spouse was unfaithful? The court ruled that this penalty was inconsistent with California's policy in favor of no-fault divorce.

3. VARIABILITY OF THE MARITAL STATUS BY AGREEMENT DURING MARRIAGE

The discussion above applies to premarital agreements. Should the rules be the same for agreements made during marriage, or are there different concerns?

BEDRICK V. BEDRICK
Supreme Court of Connecticut, 2011.
300 Conn. 691, 17 A.3d 17.

McLachlan, J.

This appeal involves a dissolution of marriage action in which the defendant, Bruce L. Bedrick, seeks to enforce a postnuptial agreement. Today we are presented for the first time with the issue of whether a postnuptial agreement is valid and enforceable in Connecticut.

The defendant appeals from the trial court's judgment in favor of the plaintiff, Deborah Bedrick. The defendant claims that the trial court improperly relied upon principles of fairness and equity in concluding that the postnuptial agreement was unenforceable and, instead, should have applied only ordinary principles of contract law. We conclude that postnuptial agreements are valid and enforceable and generally must comply with contract principles. We also conclude, however, that the terms of such agreements must be both fair and equitable at the time of execution and not unconscionable at the time of dissolution. Because the terms of the present agreement were unconscionable at the time of dissolution, we affirm the judgment of the trial court.

The record reveals the following undisputed facts and procedural history. In August, 2007, the plaintiff initiated this action, seeking dissolution of the parties' marriage, permanent alimony, an equitable distribution of the parties' real and personal property and other relief. The defendant filed a cross complaint, seeking to enforce a postnuptial agreement that the parties executed on December 10, 1977, and modified by way of handwritten addenda on five subsequent occasions, most recently on May 18, 1989.

The agreement provides that in the event of dissolution, neither party will pay alimony. Instead, the plaintiff will receive a cash settlement in an amount to be "reviewed from time to time." The May 18, 1989 addendum to the agreement provides for a cash settlement of $75,000. The agreement further provides that the plaintiff will waive her interests in the defendant's car wash business, and that the plaintiff will not be held liable for the defendant's personal and business loans.

In its memorandum of decision, the trial court stated that, although "[t]here is scant case law addressing the enforcement of postnuptial agreements in Connecticut . . . it is clear that a court may not enforce a postnuptial agreement if it is not fair and equitable. . . [C]ourts have refused to enforce postnuptial agreements for lack of consideration, failure to disclose financial information, or an improper purpose." Concluding that the agreement was not fair and equitable, the trial court declined to enforce it. The court found that the value of the parties' combined assets was approximately $927,123, and ordered, inter alia, the defendant to pay lump sum alimony in the amount of $392,372 to the plaintiff. The defendant filed a motion to reargue claiming that the court should have applied principles of contract law in determining the enforceability of the agreement.

Following reargument, the trial court issued a second written decision, again declining to enforce the postnuptial agreement, and noting that the Connecticut appellate courts have not yet addressed the issue of the validity of such agreements. The court further declined to apply Connecticut's law governing prenuptial agreements, reasoning that, unlike a prenuptial agreement, a postnuptial agreement is "inherently coercive" because one spouse typically enters into it in order to preserve the marriage, while the other is primarily motivated by financial concerns.

The trial court additionally determined that, even if postnuptial agreements were valid and enforceable under Connecticut law, the present agreement did not comply with ordinary contract principles because it lacked adequate consideration. The court explained that, because past consideration cannot support the imposition of a new obligation, continuation of the marriage itself cannot constitute sufficient consideration to support a postnuptial agreement. Moreover, the trial court emphasized that the plaintiff did not knowingly waive her marital rights because she neither received a sworn financial affidavit from the defendant nor retained independent legal counsel to review the agreement.

The trial court also opined that enforcement of the agreement would have been unjust and was "not . . . a fair and equitable distribution of the parties' assets" because the financial circumstances of the parties had changed dramatically since the agreement was last modified in 1989. Since 1989, the parties had had a child together and the defendant's car wash business had both prospered and deteriorated. This appeal followed.

I.

The defendant contends that the trial court improperly applied equitable principles in determining whether the postnuptial agreement was enforceable and, instead, should have applied only principles of contract law. Specifically, the defendant cites *Crews v. Crews*, 295 Conn. 153, 167, 989 A.2d 1060 (2010), in which we stated that "equitable considerations codified in our statutes . . . have no bearing on whether [a prenuptial] agreement should be enforced. . . In other words, whether . . . [a] court . . . thinks the agreement was a good bargain for the plaintiff does not enter into the analysis of the issue." (Internal quotation marks omitted.) The defendant claims that *Crews* precludes the consideration of factors beyond those of pure contract law in determining whether an agreement is enforceable. Although we agree with the defendant that principles of contract law generally apply in determining the enforceability of a postnuptial agreement, we conclude that postnuptial agreements are subject to special scrutiny and the terms of such agreements must be both fair and equitable at the time of execution and not unconscionable at the time of dissolution. Because the terms of the present postnuptial agreement were unconscionable at the time of dissolution, the trial court properly concluded that the agreement was unenforceable.

The standard applicable to postnuptial agreements presents a question of law, over which our review is plenary. We begin our analysis of postnuptial agreements by considering the public policies served by the recognition of agreements regarding the dissolution of marriage, including prenuptial, postnuptial and separation agreements.

Postnuptial agreements may encourage the private resolution of family issues. In particular, they may allow couples to eliminate a source of emotional turmoil—usually, financial uncertainty—and focus instead on resolving other aspects of the marriage that may be problematic. By alleviating anxiety over uncertainty in the determination of legal rights and obligations upon dissolution, postnuptial agreements do not encourage or facilitate dissolution; in fact, they harmonize with our public policy favoring enduring marriages. "Such contracts may inhibit the dissolution of marriage, or may protect the interests of third parties such as children from a prior relationship." *Ansin v. Craven-Ansin*, 457 Mass. 283, 289, 929 N.E.2d 955 (2010).

Postnuptial agreements are consistent with public policy; they realistically acknowledge the high incidence of divorce and its effect upon our population. We recognize the reality of the increasing rate of divorce and remarriage. Recent statistics on divorce have forced people to deal with the reality that many marriages do not last a lifetime. Postnuptial agreements are no different than prenuptial agreements in this regard.

Having determined that postnuptial agreements are consistent with public policy, we now must consider what standards govern their enforcement. Neither the legislature nor this court has addressed this question. To aid in our analysis of the enforceability of postnuptial agreements, we review our law on the enforceability of prenuptial agreements. Two different sets of principles govern decisions as to the enforceability of a prenuptial agreement; the date of the execution of the agreement determines which set of principles controls.

Prenuptial agreements entered into on or after October 1, 1995, are governed by the Connecticut Premarital Agreement Act, General Statutes § 46b–36a et seq. The statutory scheme provides that a prenuptial agreement is unenforceable when: (1) the challenger did not enter the agreement voluntarily; (2) the agreement was unconscionable when executed or enforced; (3) the challenger did not receive "a fair and reasonable disclosure of the amount, character and value of property, financial obligations and income of the other party" before execution of the agreement; or (4) the challenger did not have "a reasonable opportunity to consult with independent counsel."

Prenuptial agreements entered into prior to October 1, 1995, however, are governed by the common law, which we analyzed in *McHugh v. McHugh*. Summarizing, we stated: "[Prenuptial] agreements relating to the property of the parties, and more specifically, to the rights of the parties to that property upon the dissolution of the marriage, are generally enforceable where three conditions are satisfied: (1) the contract was validly entered into; (2) its terms do not violate statute or public policy; and (3) the circumstances of the parties at the time the marriage is dissolved are not so beyond the contemplation of the parties at the time the contract was entered into as to cause its enforcement to work injustice."

"To render unenforceable an otherwise valid [prenuptial] agreement, a court must determine: (1) the parties' intent and circumstances when they signed the [prenuptial] agreement; (2) the circumstances of the parties at the time of the dissolution of the marriage; (3) whether those circumstances are 'so far beyond' the contemplation of the parties at the time of execution; and (4) if the circumstances are beyond the parties' initial contemplation, whether enforcement would cause an injustice." We further note that "[i]t is additionally clear that the party seeking to challenge the enforceability of the [prenuptial] contract bears a heavy burden. . . [W]here the economic status of [the] parties has changed dramatically between the date of the agreement and the dissolution, literal enforcement of the agreement may work injustice. Absent such unusual circumstances, however, [prenuptial] agreements freely and fairly entered into will be honored and enforced by the courts as written. . . " Id.

Although we view postnuptial agreements as encouraging the private resolution of family issues, we also recognize that spouses do not contract under the same conditions as either prospective spouses or spouses who have determined to dissolve their marriage. The Supreme Judicial Court of Massachusetts has noted that a postnuptial "agreement stands on a different footing from both a [prenuptial agreement] and a separation agreement. Before marriage, the parties have greater freedom to reject an unsatisfactory [prenuptial] contract. . . "

The circumstances surrounding [postnuptial] agreements in contrast are pregnant with the opportunity for one party to use the threat of dissolution to bargain themselves into positions of advantage. . .

"For these reasons, we join many other [s]tates in concluding that [postnuptial] agreements must be carefully scrutinized." (Citations omitted; internal quotation marks omitted.) *Ansin v. Craven-Ansin*, supra, 457 Mass. at 289–90, 929 N.E.2d 955. The Appellate Division of the New Jersey Superior Court has also recognized this "contextual difference" and has noted that a wife "face[s] a more difficult choice than [a] bride who is presented with a demand for a pre-nuptial agreement. The cost to [a wife is] . . . the destruction of a family and the stigma of a failed marriage." *Pacelli v. Pacelli*, 319 N.J. Super. 185, 190, 725 A.2d 56 (App. Div.), cert. denied, 161 N.J. 147, 735 A.2d 572 (1999). Thus, a spouse enters a postnuptial agreement under different conditions than a party entering a prenuptial agreement. *Davis v. Miller*, 269 Kan. 732, 739, 7 P.3d 1223 (2000) ("[p]arties entering into a postmarital agreement are in a vastly different position than parties entering into a [prenuptial] agreement").

Other state courts have not only observed that spouses contract under different conditions; they have also observed that postnuptial agreements "should not be treated as mere 'business deals.' " *Stoner v. Stoner*, 572 Pa. 665, 672–73, 819 A.2d 529 (2003). "Ordinarily and presumptively, a confidential relation or a relationship of special confidence exists between husband and wife. It includes, but is not limited to, a fiduciary duty between the spouses, of the highest degree." 41 Am.Jur.2d 72, Husband and Wife § 69 (2005).

Because of the nature of the marital relationship, the spouses to a postnuptial agreement may not be as cautious in contracting with one another as they would be with prospective spouses, and they are certainly less cautious than they would be with an ordinary contracting party. With lessened caution comes greater potential for one spouse to take advantage of the other. This leads us to conclude that postnuptial agreements require stricter scrutiny than prenuptial agreements. In applying special scrutiny, a court may enforce a postnuptial agreement only if it complies with applicable contract principles and the terms of the agreement are both fair and equitable at the time of execution and not unconscionable at the time of dissolution.

We further hold that the terms of a postnuptial agreement are fair and equitable at the time of execution if the agreement is made voluntarily, and without any undue influence, fraud, coercion, duress or similar defect. Moreover, each spouse must be given full, fair and reasonable disclosure of the amount, character and value of property, both jointly and separately held, and all of the financial obligations and income of the other spouse. This mandatory disclosure requirement is a result of the deeply personal marital relationship.

With regard to the determination of whether a postnuptial agreement is unconscionable at the time of dissolution, "[i]t is well established that [t]he question of unconscionability is a matter of law to be decided by the court based on all the facts and circumstances of the case."

Unfairness or inequality alone does not render a postnuptial agreement unconscionable; spouses may agree on an unequal distribution of assets at dissolution. "[T]he mere fact that hindsight may indicate the provisions of the agreement were improvident does not render the agreement unconscionable." (Internal quotation marks omitted.) *Lipic v. Lipic,* 103 S.W.3d 144, 150 (Mo. App. 2003). Instead, the question of whether enforcement of an agreement would be unconscionable is analogous to determining whether enforcement of an agreement would work an injustice. *Crews v. Crews*, 295 Conn. at 163, 989 A.2d 1060. Marriage, by its very nature, is subject to unforeseeable developments, and no agreement can possibly anticipate all future events. Unforeseen changes in the relationship, such as having a child, loss of employment or moving to another state, may render enforcement of the agreement unconscionable.

II

Now that we have set forth the applicable legal standards for postnuptial agreements, we turn to the present case and address the question of whether the trial court properly concluded that the parties' postnuptial agreement should not be enforced.

We provide the following additional facts. Although the value of the parties combined assets is $927,123, the last addendum to the agreement, dated May 18, 1989, provides that the plaintiff will receive a cash settlement of only $75,000. This addendum was written prior to the initial success of the car wash business in the early 1990s, the birth of the parties' son in 1991, when the parties were forty-one years old, and the subsequent deterioration of the business in the 2000s. At the time of trial, the parties were both fifty-seven years old. Neither had a college degree. The defendant had been steadily employed by the car wash business since 1973. The plaintiff had worked for that business for thirty-five years, providing administrative and bookkeeping support, and since approximately 2001, when the business began to deteriorate, the plaintiff had managed all business operations excluding maintenance. In 2004, the plaintiff also had worked outside of the business in order to provide the family with additional income. Since approximately 2007, when the plaintiff stopped working for the business, the defendant had not been able to complete administrative or bookkeeping tasks, and had not filed taxes.

The trial court found that "[t]he economic circumstances of the parties had changed dramatically since the execution of the agreement" and that "enforcement of the postnuptial agreement would have worked injustice." It, therefore, concluded that the agreement was unenforceable. Although the trial court did not have guidance on the applicable legal standards for postnuptial agreements, which we set forth today, we previously have determined that the question of whether enforcement of a prenuptial agreement would be unconscionable is analogous to determining whether enforcement would work an injustice. Thus, the trial court's finding that enforcement of the postnuptial agreement would work an injustice was tantamount to a finding that the agreement was unconscionable at the time the defendant sought to enforce it. We review the question of unconscionability as a matter of law. The facts and circumstances of the present case clearly support the findings of the trial court that, as a matter of law, enforcement of the agreement would be unconscionable. We therefore do not need to remand this case to the trial court because its findings satisfy the test for enforceability, which we articulate today. Accordingly, we hold that the trial court properly concluded that the agreement was unenforceable.

The judgment is affirmed.

NOTES AND QUESTIONS

1. In Connecticut, for postnuptial agreements and premarital agreements signed before 1995 the court reviews whether enforcing the agreement will work a substantial injustice; if it would, the whole agreement is invalidated. In *Gross*, the Ohio court did not review the fairness of a waiver of the right to property division, but did more aggressively review whether enforcement of a restriction on the right to spousal support would be unconscionable. In *DeLorean*, the court did not review the fairness of any aspect of the agreement at divorce, unless one party would become a public charge. To what extent should a court review the fairness of an agreement at divorce? Does *Bedrick*, *Gross* or *DeLorean* seem like the best approach? Should the rule for enforcing premarital and postnuptial agreements be different?

2. Getting married is sufficient consideration for a premarital agreement; no other consideration is required. *See* UPAA § 2; J. THOMAS OLDHAM, DIVORCE, SEPARATION AND THE DISTRIBUTION OF PROPERTY, § 4.03[2][g]. In contrast, postnuptial agreements normally require consideration.

In Borelli v. Brusseau, 16 Cal. Rptr. 2d 16 (App. 1993) the parties had signed a premarital agreement that limited the wife's rights to property when the marriage ended. During marriage, the husband had health problems and was concerned that his wife would send him to a nursing home. He agreed to devise her certain property he owned if she would take care of him at home and not send him to a nursing home. She took care of him at home until he died; he did not devise her the property. When she sued his estate to enforce the agreement, the court ruled that, in light of her preexisting duty to take care of him, the agreement was unenforceable due to a lack of consideration. Does this seem to be a sensible result?

In Department of Human Resources v. Williams, 202 S.E.2d 504 (Ga. App. 1973) the court held that a wife had a preexisting duty to provide ordinary household duties, but did not have a preexisting duty to care for an incapacitated husband.

In some states postnuptial agreements are enforceable without consideration. Should the agreement in *Borelli* be enforced in those states?

3. Some states have enacted statutes analogous to the UPAA to determine the enforceability of postnuptial agreements. *See* TEX. FAM. CODE §§ 4.101, 4.105; COLO. REV. STAT. § 14–2–302. But even if one determines the enforceability of a postnuptial agreement under UPAA standards, different questions arise. Most courts agree that, if one prospective spouse presents a contract to the other a significant time before the wedding and says, "sign this or I won't marry you," this does not constitute coercion or duress. But what if one spouse presents the other with a postnuptial agreement and says, "sign this or I'll divorce you"? Should it matter whether the parties have had children together? *See* Matthews v. Matthews, 725 S.W.2d 275 (Tex. App. 1986).

In Pacelli v. Pacelli, 725 A.2d 56 (N.J. Super. App. Div. 1999), the court had to decide whether to enforce a postnuptial agreement. The parties had married in 1976. In 1986, the husband informed the wife that he would divorce her unless she signed an agreement he presented. The agreement stated that, if they divorced, she would receive $500,000 in full settlement of her rights to marital property or spousal support. At that time, the marital estate was worth about $3 million. The lawyer she consulted in 1986 estimated that, if they divorced then, she would have received about $1 million of marital property plus spousal support. The lawyer advised her not to sign; nonetheless, she signed the agreement, apparently to avoid a divorce. The husband filed for divorce in 1994 when his net worth was about $11 million. What should the court do? Is what happened here like the situation when one prospective spouse says to the other, before marriage, "sign this or I won't marry you?" Or is it somehow different?

In Borelli v. Brusseau, mentioned in note 2 above, the wife effectively told the husband "sign this or I'll send you to a nursing home." Is this sort of bargaining acceptable?

4.   In a few states, agreements signed by spouses during an ongoing marriage are not enforced. Devney v. Devney, 886 N.W.2d 61 (Neb. 2016); OHIO REV. CODE § 3103.06.

5.   While a few states seem to apply the same standards to premarital and postnuptial agreements (see Lugg v. Lugg, 64 A.3d 1109 (Pa. Super. 2013)), many states do not. For example, although Hawaii has adopted the UPAA, in Ching v. Ching, 751 P.2d 93 (Haw. App. 1988), the court held that a postnuptial agreement should be enforced only if it was "equitable" at divorce. *See also* MINN. STAT. ANN. § 519.11 (postnuptial agreements enforceable only if (i) both parties are represented by independent counsel and (ii) a divorce action is not filed within two years of signing); UNIFORM MARITAL PROPERTY ACT (UMPA) § 10(f) (employing UPAA standard for premarital agreements), but denying enforcement to postnuptial agreements if (i) the agreement was unconscionable when signed, (ii) the agreement was involuntarily signed, or (iii) there was inadequate disclosure)). In Kansas, a postmarital agreement is treated the same a separation agreement and, to be enforced, must be valid, just and equitable at the time of divorce. *In re* Marriage of Traster, 339 P.3d 778 (Kan. 2014). Louisiana requires postnuptial agreements to be approved by a judge (*see* LA. CIV. CODE art. 2329); Why would states adopt more substantial restrictions on the enforceability of postnuptial agreements?

Do you agree with *Bedrick* that postnuptial agreements "stand on a different footing" from premarital agreements? If so, does this mean a different standard should be applied to determine whether to enforce them?

6.   Spouses might sign a postnuptial agreement to address problems that have arisen during marriage. For example, in *In re* Marriage of Mehren & Dargan, 13 Cal. Rptr. 3d 522 (App. 2004), review denied, the husband had a drug problem. In the agreement, the parties agreed that he would suffer a financial penalty if he repeated this behavior. When he relapsed, the wife sued for divorce and to enforce the postnuptial agreement. The court concluded that it should not be enforced. Why might a court be reluctant to enforce such a provision?

7.   Some types of waivers may be enforceable only if made after the wedding. For example, some courts have concluded that prospective spouses may not waive certain private pension rights; only spouses can. *See* Hurwitz v. Sher, 982 F.2d 778 (2d Cir. 1992); Hagwood v. Newton, 282 F.3d 285 (4th Cir. 2002). *See generally Note*, 47 WASH. U.J. URB. & CONTEMP. L. 157 (1995).

8.   Sometimes spouses having marital difficulties might consult a leader within their spiritual community. For example, an Illinois case involved a Mulsim couple who went to see a counselor in their religious community. They signed an agreement that neither spouse would file for divorce without the conselor's written consent. If either spouse did file for divorce without the

counselor's consent, that party would automatically lose rights to custody of the spouses' minor children. The court held that these provisions violated Illinois public policy. Iqbal v. Khan, 11 N.E.3d 1 (Ill. App. 2014).

9.   States disagree about whether a prospective spouse has a fiduciary duty to the other. All states agree, however, that spouses are fiduciaries. Should this distinction impact how postnuptial agreements are reviewed by courts? When a party has claimed a spouse violated his or her fiduciary duty in connection with a postnuptial agreement, courts have looked to whether there was incomplete disclosure or a material misrepresentation. *See* Dawbarn v. Dawbarn, 625 S.E.2d 186 (N.C. App. 2006); *In re* Marriage of Pierce, 138 P.3d 889 (Or. App. 2006).

In a Florida case, during marriage the husband and wife signed an agreement whereby the wife conveyed to the husband an interest in a family business. In a later divorce, the court did not enforce the agreement, due to misrepresentations made by the husband when the agreement was signed. Kearney v. Kearney, 129 So. 3d 381 (Fla. Dist. Ct. App. 2013).

In a Georgia case, the husband asked the wife to sign a post-marital agreement. He allegedly promised to destroy the agreement after they signed it. When the husband did not destroy it and attempted to enforce it in their divorce, the court held that this was fraud and the agreement should not be enforced. Murray v. Murray, 791 S.E.2d 816 (Ga. 2016).

10.   Spouses may also seek to enforce an agreement with an in-law. For example, in Lowinger v. Lowinger, 287 A.D.2d 39, 733 N.Y.S.2d 33 (2001), the wife alleged that her mother-in-law orally promised to provide her a "wonderful house" and financial support for a "generous lifestyle" if she converted to Judaism. She converted to Judaism and sued to enforce agreement. How should the court rule?

CURRY V. CURRY

Supreme Court of Georgia, 1990.
260 Ga. 302, 392 S.E.2d 879.

WELTNER, JUSTICE.

The parties were married in 1975, divorced in 1977, and remarried "by the common law" later in 1977. The husband filed for divorce in 1981 and again in 1984. In 1984, the parties signed a reconciliation agreement that dismissed the pending action without prejudice; provided for certain payments by the husband to the wife; and barred the wife from future claims for alimony or equitable division of property. In 1989, the husband filed a new complaint for divorce, and sought an order enforcing the reconciliation agreement. A hearing was held and the trial court entered a final judgment to enforce the agreement. We granted the wife's application for discretionary appeal.

In *Scherer v. Scherer*, 249 Ga. 635, 641, 292 S.E.2d 662 (1982), we held:

[T]he trial judge should employ basically three criteria in determining whether to enforce [an antenuptial agreement in contemplation of divorce] in a particular case: (1) was the agreement obtained through fraud, duress or mistake, or through misrepresentation or nondisclosure of material facts? (2) is the agreement unconscionable? (3) have the facts and circumstances changed since the agreement was executed, so as to make its enforcement unfair and unreasonable?

We know of no reason why a reconciliation agreement should stand on a different footing from an antenuptial agreement under *Scherer, supra.* *Scherer* specifies that the trial judge shall determine whether or not to enforce the agreement. There was no error.

The wife asserts that the trial court's conclusion (that the agreement was not unconscionable) is inconsistent with its findings that:

"The terms and conditions of the reconciliation agreement were unfair and inequitable in that in any divorce proceeding in 1984, the wife had a substantial likelihood of receiving some equitable division of property despite any acts of adultery which could bar alimony * * *

"When * * * [the wife] entered into such agreement, while unfair as to specific economic benefits accruing at the time of the execution or within a reasonably foreseeable time thereafter, * * * [it] did not constitute an unconscionable agreement."

Viewing the findings in toto, there was no error. The findings are, in part, as follows:

The substantial non-marital assets and the value of the total estate of the * * * [husband] and continuing in a marriage relationship with a man who has a deteriorating health condition and a foreseeable shortened life expectancy in itself was a substantial legal benefit.

This marriage would have terminated in 1984 but for such reconciliation, which * * * [the wife] fully recognized.

There has been no change in circumstances that was not foreseeable at the time that the agreement was entered into, that the deteriorating disability of the * * * [husband] was foreseeable, the increase in the value of the non-marital assets was foreseeable, as well as her graduating from nursing school and having an independent source of earnings.

* * * [T]here has been a substantial performance under the reconciliation agreement as to the terms and conditions of said agreement such as to make the reconciliation agreement binding on the parties.

[U]nder the doctrine of equitable estoppel, since the major benefit sought by the * * * [wife] was a continuation of a marriage which but for such agreement would have terminated in divorce in 1984, and because of her intent to enter into the agreement no matter what the terms as far as immediate economic benefit to her, she achieved and received the benefit of the bargain sought and caused a substantial change in condition on the part of the * * * [husband].

* * * [Husband] had a right to rely on the agreement to his detriment. * * * [I]n entering into such agreement * * * the [husband] did not do so fraudulently or to mislead or misrepresent the facts to the * * * [wife] because he lived under said agreement from 1984 to the date of said hearing, which is a significant period of time.

* * * [S]ince the parties were represented by counsel and dealt at arm's length and bargained for what they received, this court is bound by the terms and conditions whether fair or unfair or contrary to what a court or jury would do upon a divorce proceeding.

* * * [A]bsent a showing of fraud, mistake, duress, misrepresentation of fact, unconscionability or substantial change in condition, the court does not have the authority to set aside or ignore such contract. * * * [T]he parties are both bound by those terms.

NOTES AND QUESTIONS

1.   Should premarital agreements and reconciliation agreements be treated identically? In the former context, the parties are negotiating an agreement when the relationship is going well; in the latter, substantial problems have arisen and the probabilities have increased that the marriage will end in divorce. Should this difference matter? If the wife had not had a lawyer in *Curry*, should there be a different result? *Cf.* Grover v. Grover, 276 S.W.3d 740 (Ark. App. 2008) (not enforcing a one-sided reconciliation agreement where the husband threatened to divorce the wife if she did not sign, there was little financial disclosure and the wife did not have a lawyer).

2.   Divorcing spouses sometimes sign a separation agreement, or "property settlement," setting forth their property rights and support obligations. These agreements will be discussed in Chapter 18, *infra*. In some states that subject premarital agreements to minimal requirements, separation agreements are subjected to a fairly rigorous fairness review. *See* TEX. FAM. CODE § 7.006. The rationale for this approach is that spouses are less likely to bargain fairly with each other after the relationship has broken down. Assuming the validity of the assumption, are reconciliation agreements more like premarital agreements or separation agreements?

3.   Mrs. Curry was at a substantial bargaining disadvantage. Is this situation any different from those a poor person would experience when negotiating a premarital agreement with a rich person? Mr. Curry's position apparently was "sign this or I'll divorce you." The court does not seem troubled by such bargaining. Are you?

In Pacelli v. Pacelli, 725 A.2d 56 (N.J. Super. App. Div. 1999) the parties were having marital difficulties and the husband stated he would divorce his wife unless she signed a postnuptial agreement that significantly limited her rights upon divorce. In their later divorce, the court did not enforce the agreement. Can you distinguish *Pacelli* and *Curry*?

4.   How did the *Curry* court determine whether the agreement was unconscionable? Under this view, could an agreement ever be unconscionable, absent a change in circumstances?

5.   A reconciliation agreement is often made to induce one spouse to stay married. In this context, what would make the signing involuntary? In Gilley v. Gilley, 778 S.W.2d 862 (Tenn. App. 1989), the parties signed a one-sided reconciliation agreement after the wife discovered that the husband was having an affair. When they divorced two years later, the husband challenged the agreement, arguing duress and lack of consideration. The court responded in this way:

> We find no merit to the assertion that the agreement was without consideration. Wife had several grounds upon which to prosecute a divorce, which she did not do at the husband's request, receiving promises of faithfulness secured by a property distribution, in the event of divorce, satisfactory to wife.
>
> Neither is there merit to the assertion that the agreement was obtained through coercion or duress. Duress is a condition of the mind produced by improper external pressure or influence that destroys the free will of a person causing him to make a contract not of his own volition. Husband asks us to find duress in his "willingness to sign anything" to preserve his marriage. Perhaps husband was under duress due to the discovery of his own miscreant conduct, but in order for the agreement to be defeated, we must find legal duress. Whatever perceived pressures constrained him to sign the agreement against his free will were internal and of his own making, and whatever external pressures there may have been were not improper. The wife clearly had a legal basis and right to prosecute a divorce and did nothing improper in negotiating an agreement in consideration of forgoing her claim.

6.   Did the agreement in *Curry* "encourage divorce"? In one North Carolina case, after one spouse had an affair the spouses signed an agreement that, if the unfaithful spouse left the marriage, the other would be entitled to all the parties' accumulated property. In their later divorce, this was held to be void because it gave one spouse an economic incentive to goad the other to leave. Matthews v. Matthews, 162 S.E.2d 697 (N.C. App. 1968). In another case, upon the discovery of an affair, the spouses agreed that the unfaithful spouse would immediately transfer to the other his ownership interest in all marital assets owned at the time. In a later divorce, this agreement was held not to encourage divorce. Dawbarn v. Dawbarn, 625 S.E.2d 186 (N.C. App. 2006). Does this seem to be a sensible distinction?

CHAPTER 6

NONMARITAL RELATIONSHIPS— RIGHTS AND OBLIGATIONS

■ ■ ■

Love and marriage, love and marriage, Go together like a horse and carriage, This I tell ya, brother, Ya can't have one without the other.

Sammy Cahn, 1955

*Is Marriage Really Necessary? At one time only Bohemians and socialists—people like that— asked the question. Now it has become the property of the middle class: the people who twenty years ago talked about togetherness; the people who ten years ago thought once you had her orgasm straightened out, that was that; the people who faithfully kept saying that marriage has its ups and downs, and, you know, it's a compromise and you have to work at it but, taken all in all, it's still the best shot at happiness. These are the people who are now saying, "Marriage is hell"—and maybe the hell with it. * * * Suddenly priests seem to be the only people left who really want to get married. * * * Marriage has become one of those antiquated institutions—another dirty word—that bricks people in.*

Maddocks, *Brave New Marriage*, ATLANTIC MONTHLY 230:66–69 (1972).

The only people who care about marriage today are priests and homosexuals.

Gore Vidal

1. DISPUTES BETWEEN COHABITANTS

A. THE HISTORY OF THE REGULATION OF COHABITANTS

Marriage may or may not be an "antiquated institution," but it is undeniable that nonmarital cohabitation has increased dramatically. In 2010, the U.S. Bureau of the Census found that there were 59.1 million married-couple households, (*see* Table FG1: Married Couple Family Groups, by Labor Force Status of Both Spouses, and Race and Hispanic Origin/1 of the Reference Person: 2010, U.S. Census Bureau, Housing and Household Economic Statistics Division Fertility & Family Statistics Branch, available at http://www.census.gov/population/www/socdemo/hh-fam/cps2010.html), 7.5 million heterosexual unmarried-partner households, and 620,000 households comprised of same-sex couples. *See* Rose M. Kreider, *Increase in Opposite-sex Cohabiting Couples from 2009 to 2010 in the Annual Social and Economic Supplement (ASEC) to the Current Population (CPS)*, 13 available at http://www.census.gov/population/www/socdemo/Inc-Opp-sex-2009-to-2010.pdf. Today there are more than 13 unmarried couples for every 100 married couples, compared with only one for every 100 in 1970. *See* Bureau of the Census, Unmarried-Partners Households by Sex of Partners (Census 2000 Summary File); Household Size, Household Type, and Presence of Children (Census 2000 Summary File).

While we lack detailed information on the social characteristics of nonmarital cohabitants, we do know that the explosion in nonmarital cohabitation is a worldwide phenomenon.

With the infiltration of nonmarital cohabitation into middle-class life has come increased social acceptability. But it was not so long ago that a nonmarital, or "meretricious," relationship was considered so outrageous and immoral that, even if the parties had an express written agreement, a court would not enforce it. *See* Wallace v. Rappleye, 103 Ill. 229, 249 (1882). For a more recent application of this rule, *see* Schwegmann v. Schwegmann, 441 So. 2d 316 (La. App. 1984). The harshness of this rule was ameliorated in several ways, however. The doctrine of common-law marriage, significantly more widely accepted in the early twentieth century than it is today, increased the percentage of cohabiting couples who were considered legally married. Moreover, the "illegality" rule did not apply to all dealings between cohabitants; if their agreement had nothing to do with their domestic arrangements, it was considered to be "severable" and enforceable. So, for example, if a cohabitant's legal claim related solely to a separate business arrangement, it was not barred by illegality. *See* McCall v. Frampton, 438 N.Y.S.2d 11 (App. Div. 1981). Finally, courts were sometimes willing to provide an equitable remedy for cohabitants through the use of constructive or resulting trust.

Although this summary still described the law in most states when the California Supreme Court considered Marvin v. Marvin (below), the increased rate and social acceptability of nonmarital cohabitation had substantially altered the context of such a dispute. Additionally, many states had abolished common-law marriage, causing a gradual but substantial increase in the number of cohabiting couples who were considered unmarried. And, because the common law marriage doctrine requires the couple to hold themselves out to the community as married—and most of the "new cohabitants" did not do so—they could not be considered married even in jurisdictions that retained common-law marriage. *See* Chapter 3, § 5. It was in this context that the California Supreme Court had to decide whether or not to reaffirm the traditional rule regarding cohabitants' rights.

MARVIN V. MARVIN

Supreme Court of California, 1976.
18 Cal. 3d 660, 557 P.2d 106, 134 Cal. Rptr. 815

TOBRINER, J.

During the past 15 years, there has been a substantial increase in the number of couples living together without marrying. Such nonmarital relationships lead to legal controversy when one partner dies or the couple separates. Courts of Appeal, faced with the task of determining property rights in such cases, have arrived at conflicting positions: two cases have held that the Family Law Act requires division of the property according to community property principles, and one decision has rejected that holding. We take this opportunity to resolve that controversy and to declare the principles which should govern distribution of property acquired in a nonmarital relationship.

We conclude: (1) The provisions of the Family Law Act do not govern the distribution of property acquired during a nonmarital relationship; such a relationship remains subject solely to judicial decision. (2) The courts should enforce express contracts between nonmarital partners except to the extent that the contract is explicitly founded on the consideration of meretricious sexual services. (3) In the absence of an express contract, the courts should inquire into the conduct of the parties to determine whether that conduct demonstrates an implied contract, agreement of partnership or joint venture, or some other tacit understanding between the parties. The courts may also employ the doctrine of quantum meruit, or equitable remedies such as constructive or resulting trusts, when warranted by the facts of the case.

In the instant case plaintiff and defendant lived together for seven years without marrying; all property acquired during this period was taken in defendant's name. When plaintiff sued to enforce a contract under which she was entitled to half the property and to support payments, the trial court granted judgment on the pleadings for defendant, thus leaving him with all property accumulated by the couple during their relationship. Since the trial court denied plaintiff a trial on the merits of her claim, its decision conflicts with the principles stated above, and must be reversed.

* * *

Plaintiff avers that in October of 1964 she and defendant "entered into an oral agreement" that while "the parties lived together they would combine their efforts and earnings and would share equally any and all property accumulated as a result of their efforts whether individual or combined". Furthermore, they agreed to "hold themselves out to the general public as husband and wife" and that "plaintiff would further render her services as a companion, homemaker, housekeeper and cook to * * * defendant."

Shortly thereafter plaintiff agreed to "give up her lucrative career as an entertainer [and] singer" in order to "devote her full time to defendant * * * as a companion, homemaker, housekeeper and cook"; in return defendant agreed to "provide for all of plaintiff's financial support and needs for the rest of her life."

Plaintiff alleges that she lived with defendant from October of 1964 through May of 1970 and fulfilled her obligations under the agreement. During this period the parties as a result of their efforts and earnings acquired in defendant's name substantial real and personal property, including motion picture rights worth over $1 million. In May of 1970, however, defendant compelled plaintiff to leave his household. He continued to support plaintiff until November of 1971, but thereafter refused to provide further support.

* * *

In the case before us plaintiff maintains that the trial court erred in denying her a trial on the merits of her contention. Although that court did not specify the ground for its conclusion that plaintiff's contractual allegations stated no cause of action, defendant offers some four theories to sustain the ruling; we proceed to examine them.

Defendant first and principally relies on the contention that the alleged contract is so closely related to the supposed "immoral" character of the relationship between plaintiff and himself that the enforcement of the contract would violate public policy. He points to cases asserting that a contract between nonmarital partners is unenforceable if it is "involved in" an illicit relationship, or made in "contemplation" of such a relationship. A review of the numerous California decisions concerning contracts between nonmarital partners, however, reveals that the courts have not employed such broad and uncertain standards to strike down contracts. The decisions instead disclose a narrower and more precise standard: a contract between nonmarital partners is unenforceable only to the extent that it explicitly rests upon the immoral and illicit consideration of meretricious sexual services.

* * *

Although the past decisions hover over the issue in the somewhat wispy form of the figures of a Chagall painting, we can abstract from those decisions a clear and simple rule. The fact that a man and woman live together without marriage, and engage in a sexual relationship, does not in itself invalidate agreements between them relating to their earnings, property, or expenses. Neither is such an agreement invalid merely because the parties may have contemplated the creation or continuation of a nonmarital relationship when they entered into it. Agreements between nonmarital partners fail only to the extent that they rest upon a consideration of meretricious sexual services. Thus the rule asserted by defendant, that a contract fails if it is "involved in" or made "in contemplation" of a nonmarital relationship, cannot be reconciled with the decisions.

* * *

The principle that a contract between nonmarital partners will be enforced unless expressly and inseparably based upon an illicit consideration of sexual services not only represents the distillation of the decisional law, but also offers a far more precise and workable standard than that advocated by defendant. * * *

In the present case a standard which inquires whether an agreement is "involved" in or "contemplates" a nonmarital relationship is vague and unworkable. Virtually all agreements between nonmarital partners can be said to be "involved" in some sense in the fact of their mutual sexual relationship, or to "contemplate" the existence of that relationship. Thus defendant's proposed standards, if taken literally, might invalidate all agreements between nonmarital partners, a result no one favors. Moreover, those standards offer no basis to distinguish between valid and invalid agreements. By looking not to such uncertain tests, but only to the consideration underlying the agreement, we provide the parties and the courts with a practical guide to determine when an agreement between nonmarital partners should be enforced.

Defendant secondly relies upon the ground suggested by the trial court: that the 1964 contract violated public policy because it impaired the community property rights of Betty Marvin, defendant's lawful wife. Defendant points out that his earnings while living apart from his wife before rendition of the interlocutory decree were community property under 1964 statutory law and that defendant's agreement with plaintiff purported to transfer to her a half interest in that community property. But whether or not defendant's contract with plaintiff exceeded his authority as manager of the community property, defendant's argument fails for the reason that an improper transfer of community property is not void ab initio, but merely voidable at the instance of the aggrieved spouse.

In the present case Betty Marvin, the aggrieved spouse, had the opportunity to assert her community property rights in the divorce action. The interlocutory and final decrees in that action fix and limit her interest. Enforcement of the contract between plaintiff and defendant against property awarded to defendant by the divorce decree will not impair any right of Betty's, and thus is not on that account violative of public policy.[8]

Defendant's third contention is noteworthy for the lack of authority advanced in its support. He contends that enforcement of the oral agreement between plaintiff and himself is barred by Civil Code § 5134, which provides that "All contracts for marriage settlements must be in writing." A marriage settlement, however, is an agreement in contemplation of marriage in which each party agrees to release or modify the property rights which would otherwise arise from the marriage. The contract at issue here does not conceivably fall within that definition, and thus is beyond the compass of § 5134.[9]

* * *

In summary, we base our opinion on the principle that adults who voluntarily live together and engage in sexual relations are nonetheless as competent as any other persons to contract respecting their earnings and property rights. Of course, they cannot lawfully contract to pay for the performance of sexual services, for such a contract is, in essence, an agreement for prostitution and unlawful for that reason. But they may agree to pool their earnings and to hold all property acquired during the relationship in accord with the law governing community property; conversely they may agree that each partner's earnings and the property acquired from those earnings remains the separate property of the earning partner. So long as the agreement does not rest upon illicit meretricious consideration, the parties may order their economic affairs as they choose, and no policy precludes the courts from enforcing such agreements.

* * *

---

[8] Defendant also contends that the contract is invalid as an agreement to promote or encourage divorce. The contract between plaintiff and defendant did not, however, by its terms require defendant to divorce Betty, nor reward him for so doing. Moreover, the principle on which defendant relies does not apply when the marriage in question is beyond redemption, whether or not defendant's marriage to Betty was beyond redemption when defendant contracted with plaintiff is obviously a question of fact which cannot be resolved by judgment on the pleadings.

[9] Our review of the many cases enforcing agreements between nonmarital partners reveals that the majority of such agreements were oral. In two cases the court expressly rejected defenses grounded upon the statute of frauds.

As we have noted, both causes of action in plaintiff's complaint allege an express contract; neither assert any basis for relief independent from the contract. In *In re Marriage of Cary*, 34 Cal. App. 3d 345, 109 Cal. Rptr. 862, however, the Court of Appeals held that, in view of the policy of the Family Law Act, property accumulated by nonmarital partners in an actual family relationship should be divided equally. Upon examining the *Cary* opinion, the parties to the present case realized that plaintiff's alleged relationship with defendant might arguably support a cause of action independent of any express contract between the parties. The parties have therefore briefed and discussed the issue of the property rights of a nonmarital partner in the absence of an express contract. Although our conclusion that plaintiff's complaint states a cause of action based on an express contract alone compels us to reverse the judgment for defendant, resolution of the *Cary* issue will serve both to guide the parties upon retrial and to resolve a conflict presently manifest in published Court of Appeals decisions.

Both plaintiff and defendant stand in broad agreement that the law should be fashioned to carry out the reasonable expectations of the parties.

* * *

The remaining arguments advanced from time to time to deny remedies to the nonmarital partners are of less moment. There is no more reason to presume that services are contributed as a gift than to presume that funds are contributed as a gift; in any event the better approach is to presume, as Justice Peters suggested, "that the parties intend to deal fairly with each other."

The argument that granting remedies to the nonmarital partners would discourage marriage must fail; as *Cary* pointed out, "with equal or greater force the point might be made that the pre-1970 rule was calculated to cause the income producing partner to avoid marriage and thus retain the benefit of all of his or her accumulated earnings." Although we recognize the well-established public policy to foster and promote the institution of marriage, perpetuation of judicial rules which result in an inequitable distribution of property accumulated during a nonmarital relationship is neither a just nor an effective way of carrying out that policy.

In summary, we believe that the prevalence of nonmarital relationships in modern society and the social acceptance of them marks this as a time when our courts should by no means apply the doctrine of the unlawfulness of the so-called meretricious relationship to the instant case. As we have explained, the nonenforceability of agreements expressly providing for meretricious conduct rested upon the fact that such conduct, as the word suggests, pertained to and encompassed prostitution. To equate the nonmarital relationship of today to such a subject matter is to do violence to an accepted and wholly different practice.

We are aware that many young couples live together without the solemnization of marriage, in order to make sure that they can successfully later undertake marriage. This trial period, preliminary to marriage, serves as some assurance that the marriage will not subsequently end in dissolution to the harm of both parties. We are aware, as we have stated, of the pervasiveness of nonmarital relationships in other situations.

The mores of the society have indeed changed so radically in regard to cohabitation that we cannot impose a standard based on alleged moral considerations that have apparently been so widely abandoned by so many. Lest we be misunderstood, however, we take this occasion to point out that the structure of society itself largely depends upon the institution of marriage, and nothing we have said in this opinion should be taken to derogate from that institution. The joining of the man and woman in marriage is at once the most socially productive and individually fulfilling relationship that one can enjoy in the course of a lifetime.

We conclude that the judicial barriers that may stand in the way of a policy based upon the fulfillment of the reasonable expectations of the parties to a nonmarital relationship should be removed. As we have explained, the courts now hold that express agreements will be enforced unless they rest on an unlawful meretricious consideration. We add that in the absence of an express agreement, the courts may look to a variety of other remedies in order to protect the parties' lawful expectations.[24]

The courts may inquire into the conduct of the parties to determine whether that conduct demonstrates an implied contract or implied agreement of partnership or joint venture, or some other tacit understanding between the parties. The courts may, when appropriate, employ principles of constructive trust or resulting trust. Finally, a nonmarital partner may recover in quantum meruit for the reasonable value of household services rendered less the reasonable value of support received if he can show that he rendered services with the expectation of monetary reward.[25] * * *

The judgment is reversed and the cause remanded for further proceedings consistent with the views expressed herein.

---

[24] We do not seek to resurrect the doctrine of common law marriage, which was abolished in California by statute in 1895. Thus we do not hold that plaintiff and defendant were "married," nor do we extend to plaintiff the rights which the Family Law Act grants valid or putative spouses; we hold only that she has the same rights to enforce contracts and to assert her equitable interest in property acquired through her effort as does any other unmarried person.

[25] Our opinion does not preclude the evolution of additional equitable remedies to protect the expectations of the parties to a nonmarital relationship in cases in which existing remedies prove inadequate; the suitability of such remedies may be determined in later cases in light of the factual setting in which they arise.

CLARK, JUSTICE (concurring and dissenting).

The majority opinion properly permits recovery on the basis of either express or implied in fact agreement between the parties. These being the issues presented, their resolution requires reversal of the judgment. Here, the opinion should stop.

This court should not attempt to determine all anticipated rights, duties and remedies within every meretricious relationship—particularly in vague terms. Rather, these complex issues should be determined as each arises in a concrete case.

The majority broadly indicates that a party to a meretricious relationship may recover on the basis of equitable principles and in quantum meruit. However, the majority fails to advise us of the circumstances permitting recovery, limitations on recovery, or whether their numerous remedies are cumulative or exclusive. Conceivably, under the majority opinion a party may recover half of the property acquired during the relationship on the basis of general equitable principles, recover a bonus based on specific equitable considerations, and recover a second bonus in quantum meruit.

* * *

By judicial overreach, the majority perform a nunc pro tunc marriage, dissolve it, and distribute its property on terms never contemplated by the parties, case law or the Legislature.

On April 18, 1979, the *Marvin* trial court, Case No. C23303, 5 Fam. L. Rep. (BNA) 3077 (1979), after remand decided that "no express contract was negotiated between the parties." As the court found that "the conduct of the parties * * * certainly does not reveal any implementation of any contract nor does such conduct give rise to an implied contract," the equitable remedy of resulting or constructive trust did not "in good conscience" apply, and dismissed the plaintiff's quantum meruit causes of action. It also found that there was no "mutual effort" that might support a recovery. Nevertheless, the trial court held that

> [t]he court is aware that Footnote 25 urges the trial court to employ whatever equitable remedy may be proper under the circumstances. The court is also aware of the recent resort of plaintiff to unemployment insurance benefits to support herself and of the fact that a return of plaintiff to a career as a singer is doubtful. Additionally, the court knows that the market value of defendant's property at time of separation exceeded $1,000,000. In view of these circumstances, the court in equity awards plaintiff $104,000 for rehabilitation purposes so that she may

have the economic means to re-educate herself and to learn new, employable skills or to refurbish those utilized, for example, during her most recent employment and so that she may return from her status as companion of a motion picture star to a separate, independent but perhaps more prosaic existence.

On August 11, 1981, the California Appellate Court (Marvin v. Marvin, 122 Cal. App. 3d 871, 176 Cal. Rptr. 555, 559 (1981)) reversed the trial court's $104,000 award, holding:

> * * * the special findings in support of the challenged rehabilitative award merely established plaintiff's need therefor and defendant's ability to respond to that need. This is not enough. The award, being nonconsensual in nature, must be supported by some recognized underlying obligation in law or in equity. A court of equity admittedly has broad powers, but it may not create totally new substantive rights under the guise of doing equity. The trial court in its special conclusions of law addressed to this point attempted to state an underlying obligation by saying that plaintiff had a right to assistance from defendant until she became self-supporting. But this special conclusion obviously conflicts with the earlier, more general, finding of the court that defendant has never had and did not then have any obligation to provide plaintiff with a reasonable sum for her support and maintenance and, in view of the already-mentioned findings of no damage (but benefit instead), no unjust enrichment and no wrongful act on the part of defendant with respect to either the relationship or its termination, it is clear that no basis whatsoever, either in equity or in law, exists for the challenged rehabilitative award. It therefore must be deleted from the judgment.

One day later, Michelle Marvin, 57, was fined $250 and placed on probation for shoplifting some bras and a sweater from a Beverly Hills store. TIME, Aug. 24, 1981, at p. 59; N.Y. TIMES, Aug. 13, 1981, at p. 8, col. 12.

The California Supreme Court refused Michelle's final appeal. N.Y. TIMES, Oct. 9, 1981, at p. 14, col. 4.

NOTES AND QUESTIONS

1.   Is the *Marvin* result fair? Why or why not?

2.   In some states, "lewd and lascivious cohabitation" is a crime. *See* FLA. STAT. ANN. § 798.02; MICH. STAT. § 750.335; VA. CODE § 18.2–345; MISS. STAT. § 97–29–1 (extends to all cohabitation; no "lewd and lascivious" requirement). If these statutes are constitutional after Lawrence v. Texas, 539 U.S. 558 (2003), should courts in these states continue to apply the traditional illegality rule rejected in *Marvin*? *See generally* Dr. Jo Anne Sweeney, *Undead Statutes:*

The Rise, Fall, and Continuing Uses of Adultery and Fornication Statutes, 46 LOY. CHI. L. J. 127 (2014).

3.   A number of states have adopted the *Marvin* approach toward cohabitants' disputes. *See* Carlson v. Olson, 256 N.W.2d 249 (Minn. 1977); Kozlowski v. Kozlowski, 403 A.2d 902 (N.J. 1979). *See generally* J. THOMAS OLDHAM, DIVORCE, SEPARATION AND THE DISTRIBUTION OF PROPERTY § 1.02 (2017). Marsha Garrison, *Nonmarital Cohabitation: Social Revolution and Legal Regulation*, 42 FAM. L. Q. 309, 315–316 (2008) ("twenty-six states have now approved some relational contract claims between cohabitants, although a few have disapproved recovery based on an implied contract."). Other states have accepted some, but not all, of the grounds for recovery sanctioned by *Marvin*. For example, some courts permit recovery based on an express contract (either oral or written), but not on an implied contract or quantum meruit. *See* Morone v. Morone, 413 N.E.2d 1154 (N.Y. 1980); Tapley v. Tapley, 449 A.2d 1218 (N.H. 1982).

4.   Some courts have permitted unmarried cohabitants to recover based on proof of a joint venture or partnership. *See* Martin v. Coleman, 19 S.W.3d 757 (Tenn. 2000); Estate of Thornton, 499 P.2d 864 (Wash. 1972). For example, a New Hampshire case involved a dispute between parties who had an intimate relationship for 20 years and raised a child together. During the relationship, the man purchased various parcels of real estate, normally titled in his name alone. The woman alleged that she contributed toward the down payment of some purchases, as well as toward payments of real estate taxes, utility costs, repairs and improvements. They periodically jointly took out home equity loans secured by one of the parcels. When the parties separated, two properties were titled in the man's name alone. The female sued to claim an equitable interest in the real estate and to partition their interests. The trial court characterized them as "domestic partners," and awarded the woman 40% of the equity in the real estate. This award was affirmed. Brooks v. Allen, 137 A.3d 404 (N.H. 2016). In such a situation, should the percentage given to the plaintiff be based on their relative financial contributions?

5.   A few courts have rejected all contractual and quasi-contractual bases for cohabitant obligations. Some of these courts have concluded that the legislature, not the courts, should determine the rights and obligations of unmarried parties. *See* Blumenthal v. Brewer, 69 N.E.3d 834 (Ill. 2016); Hewitt v. Hewitt, 394 N.E.2d 1204 (Ill. 1979); Carnes v. Sheldon, 311 N.W.2d 747 (Mich. App. 1981). The Illinois Supreme Court was concerned that, if it permitted unmarried partners to enforce mutual property rights, this might "encourage formation of such relationships and weaken marriage." 394 N.E.2d at 1204. The court would permit claims that were truly severable from the intimate relationship. Others have rejected *Marvin* because state law criminalized unmarried cohabitation. *See* Davis v. Davis, 643 So. 2d 931 (Miss. 1994). In Cates v. Swain, 2013 WL 1831783 (Miss.) the Mississippi Supreme Court clarified that unmarried partners, when a relationship ended, could bring a claim against the other partner for unjust enrichment based on monetary contributions.

6.   A few states enforce only written agreements between cohabitants. *See* MINN. STAT. ANN. § 513.075; TEX. FAM. CODE § 1.108; N.J. STAT. ANN. § 25:1–5(h). In contrast, almost all states that have accepted *Marvin* enforce express oral agreements between cohabitants. Why have courts accepted this rule? As was seen in Chapter 5, premarital agreements between prospective spouses need to be written to be enforceable. Although "[r]eal data on the frequency of contracting are scarce, written agreements are rare among the reported cases" and both the anecdotal and limited survey evidence suggests that the reported cases are probably typical of the larger pool. Ira M. Ellman, *"Contract Thinking" Was* Marvin's *Fatal Flaw*, 76 NOTRE DAME L. REV. 1365, 1367 n. 17 (2001); Kirsti Strom Bull, *Nonmarital Cohabitation in Norway*, 30 SCANDINAVIAN STUD. L. 31 (1986) (5% of surveyed Danish and Norwegian cohabitants had entered into contracts). Written contracts seem to be entered into more frequently by couples with committed relationships. *See* Jennifer K. Robbennolt & Monica Kirkpatrick Johnson, *Legal Planning for Unmarried Committed Partners: Empirical Lessons for a Preventative and Therapeutic Approach*, 42 ARIZ. L. REV. 417 (1999) (in a survey of 169 "committed" cohabiting couples, 29% had written agreements).

As compared to the *Marvin* approach, what are the advantages and disadvantages of confining recovery to: (a) express written contracts; or (b) express (oral or written) contracts? Why have so few states applied the statute of frauds to cohabitation contracts?

In a New Jersey case, the parties orally agreed after they broke up that the woman would have possession of their dog. The court ruled that the agreement could be subject to specific performance. *See* Houseman v. Dare, 966 A.2d 24 (N.J. Super. App. Div. 2009).

7.   In those states that permit cohabitants to enforce express oral agreements, courts have disagreed regarding how detailed and specific the terms of the agreement must be. A promise that a man would "take care of the [other party] after my death" was deemed too vague to spell out a meaningful promise in *In re* Estate of Lasek, 545 N.Y.S.2d 668 (Surr. Ct. 1989). In Friedman v. Friedman, 24 Cal. Rptr. 2d 892 (App. 1993), the court reached the same conclusion regarding a promise to "always support" another. By contrast, in Sopko v. Estate of Roccamonte, 787 A.2d 198 (N.J. Super. App. Div. 2001), affirmed 808 A.2d 838 (2002), the court held that a promise "to take care of another for the rest of her life" created an enforceable obligation.

In Dee v. Rakower, 976 N.Y.S.2d 470 (App. Div. 2013) one lesbian partner asserted a breach of contract claim against her partner when the relationship ended. She alleged that she and her partner agreed that she would quit her job outside the home to take care of the parties' children, and that both parties would share equally in the compensation received by the other partner for her work outside the home. The court ruled that an enforceable contract could result from such an alleged agreement.

8.   If rights of cohabitants are to be determined primarily based upon whether an enforceable contract can be proved, issues like consideration could

be important. For example, in William v. Ormsby, 966 N.E.2d 255 (Ohio 2012), a man began living with a woman in her house. When he paid off the outstanding mortgage loan, the woman executed a quitclaim deed conveying her interest to him. Shortly thereafter, the woman moved out. In connection with an attempt to reconcile, they signed a written agreement that they were "equal partners" regarding the house. The woman then moved back into the house and resumed their relationship. A few years later they broke up. Who owns the house? Should their agreement that they are "equal partners" regarding the house be enforced?

9.   In states that permit recovery based on quantum meruit or unjust enrichment, the plaintiff typically must show that (a) the defendant received a benefit, (b) the benefit was at the plaintiff's expense, and (c) it would be unjust to permit the defendant to retain the benefit without compensating the plaintiff. *See* Watts v. Watts, 405 N.W.2d 303 (Wis. 1987). *See also* Phillips v. Blankenship, 554 S.E. 2d 231 (Ga. App. 2001). *See generally* J. THOMAS OLDHAM, DIVORCE, SEPARATION AND THE DISTRIBUTION OF PROPERTY § 1.02[5][3] (2017); Robert C. Casad, *Unmarried Couples and Unjust Enrichment: From Status to Contract and Back Again*, 77 MICH. L. REV. 47 (1978). But quantum meruit claims are generally permitted only in those situations where it would be reasonable to expect compensation. Also, any support received by the claimant during the relationship is offset against such a claim. Thus, in Tarry v. Stewart, 649 N.E.2d 1 (Ohio App. 1994), a court refused one cohabitant's claim to be reimbursed for contributions to improvements made to the other cohabitant's house, due to the benefit the claimant had received from living in the house during the relationship. *See also* Tapley v. Tapley, 449 A.2d 1218 (N.H. 1982) (limiting quantum meruit cohabitant recovery to business services); Kitchen v. Frusher, 181 S.W.3d 467 (Tex. App. 2005) (same).

10.   *Marvin* significantly changed the test for severability, an important concept under the traditional approach. Michelle Marvin's claim would not have been severable from the sexual relationship under the traditional approach, but the *Marvin* court concludes that it is severable, distinguishing agreements that merely "contemplate" a sexual relationship (valid), from those that "rest on an unlawful meretricious consideration" (invalid). Does this mean that any contract between cohabitants is enforceable unless it is simply a prostitution arrangement? Or does it mean that an invalid agreement is one that would not have been made but for the sexual relationship? (If so, didn't the Marvin agreement fall into this category?)

Courts have not agreed how to apply the severability aspect of the *Marvin* opinion. In Jones v. Daly, 176 Cal. Rptr. 130 (App. 1981) a cohabitation relationship ended when one party died. The other sued his estate, alleging the existence of an oral agreement. The plaintiff claimed that he had agreed to devote a substantial amount of time to the defendant as his lover, companion, homemaker, traveling companion, housekeeper and cook, and that the defendant had agreed to share with him all accumulations during the relationship. The court concluded that sex was the predominant consideration and that the sexual aspect of the relationship was not severable from the agreement. But in Whorton v. Dillingham, 248 Cal. Rptr. 405 (App. 1988), the plaintiff and defendant agreed to have a sexual relationship, and the plaintiff agreed to act as the defendant's chauffeur, bodyguard, secretary, real estate counselor, confidant, and companion. The court distinguished *Jones* on the basis of the services provided. Because the *Whorton* plaintiff's services as a bodyguard, secretary, and real estate counselor would not normally be offered without payment, the court concluded that any sexual services were severable. And in Zoppa v. Zoppa, 103 Cal. Rptr. 2d 901 (App. 2001) the parties lived together and, among other things, agreed to try to conceive a child. The trial court held that, under *Marvin*, this invalidated the agreement; the court of appeals reversed. Are the *Jones, Whorton* and *Zoppa* holdings sensible constructions of *Marvin*'s rule that an agreement between cohabitants is enforceable as long as it does not rest on illicit meretricious consideration?

11. How would a court determine whether the parties had an implied agreement to share property? Although a couple may take title jointly and consistently pool resources (*see* Alderson v. Alderson, 225 Cal. Rptr. 610 (App. 1986)), in many cases the evidence will be conflicting or will reflect the fact that one party wants to share and the other does not. *See* Rissberger v. Gorton, 597 P.2d 366 (Or. App. 1979). What result would *Marvin* require in such a case?

Consider Carol Bruch, *Property Rights of De Facto Spouses Including Thoughts on the Value of Homemakers' Services*, 10 FAM. L.Q. 101, 136 (1976):

> Surely it is more sensible to place the burden upon individuals to state clearly their desire to bring about inequitable results, than to impose such results upon large numbers of people who live together without marriage with no articulated division of financial responsibility. To do otherwise is to imply in law an unconscionable contract, one in which one party may render services for a period of years only to return to the job market upon the relationship's termination with no marketable skills or financial resources while the other retains the full measure of increased wealth and increased earning power that were acquired through participation in monetarily rewarded activity outside the home.

Is Professor Bruch suggesting a presumption of equal sharing, at least in those relationships of some duration where one partner does not work outside the home? If so, how could the presumption be rebutted? How does this approach differ from the implied agreement remedy permitted by *Marvin*?

Before the legislature adopted a statute of frauds requirement for cohabitant contract claims, New Jersey courts have sometimes found an implied contract for lifetime support. For example, in Connell v. Diehl, 938 A.2d 143 (N.J. Super. 2008) a man and a woman had lived together for 30 years. When they began living together, the economically vulnerable party wanted to marry, but the other party discouraged this desire and allegedly told her that he would never abandon her. During the relationship they held themselves out to the community as a married couple. The lifetime support amount was calculated as if the court was fashioning a spousal support award at divorce.

12. *Marvin* claims have been made by gay as well as heterosexual cohabitants. *See* Vasquez v. Hawthorne, 33 P.3d 735 (Wash. 2001); Jones v. Daly, Whorton v. Dillingham; N.Y. TIMES, July 9, 1981, at p. 7 col. 3 (describing claim by Marilyn Barnett against the tennis player Billie Jean King); *Palimony Lawsuit Filed Against Pianist Cliburn,* HOUSTON CHRON., Apr. 30, 1996, at 17A. Is there any reason to treat such cohabitants differently from those who are heterosexual? Does the fact that same-sex couples could not marry in many states when they cohabited affect the analysis? If so, in what way?

13. Should *Marvin* apply regardless of the length or type of cohabitation? For example, in *In re* Marriage of Bauder, 605 P.2d 1374 (Or. App. 1980), a man cohabited with a married couple (apparently maintaining a sexual relationship with both) and alleged an agreement to share property. Should *Marvin* apply to this kind of relationship? Alternatively, should *Marvin* govern disputes between dating couples who do not share a common residence? *See Cochran, infra* p. 314.

14. Is the *Marvin* court correct that its decision does not "resurrect the doctrine of common law marriage"? What additional remedies would have been available to Ms. Triola if they had been married?

15. The dispute between Mick Jagger and Jerry Hall represents an interesting example of how the rights and responsibilities of parties are significantly affected by whether they are thought to be "married" under the traditional approach. Ms. Hall and Mr. Jagger cohabited for a substantial length of time, had three children together, and participated in what appeared to be a ceremonial marriage in Bali. However, when they "married" in Indonesia, they did not comply with all requirements of that jurisdiction (or those of England, where they lived) for a ceremonial marriage. An English court therefore determined that Ms. Hall and Mr. Jagger were cohabitants, not spouses, and that when their relationship ended Ms. Hall had no marital property rights, only a right to child support. *See* Ruth Gledhill, *The Marriage That Never Was,* THE TIMES (London), Aug. 14, 1999, Home News Section. Under *Marvin,* what, if any, rights would Ms. Hall have? Is it fair to treat long-term unmarried partners who have raised common children together essentially as roommates if they break up?

16. Approximately six states define "fornication" (sex between unmarried adults) as a criminal offense. Three criminalise cohabitation. Assuming these statutes are not unconstitutional after Lawrence v. Texas, 539 U.S. 558 (2003), should they impact whether a state should endorse *Marvin*?

17. Cohabitation claims have normally been brought when cohabiting parties break up. However, *Marvin* claims have been accepted when the cohabitation ends when one party dies. *See* Byrne v. Laura, 60 Cal. Rptr.2d 908 (App. 1997); *In re* Estate of Steffes, 290 N.W. 2d 697 (Wis. 1980). If the

survivor is not able to prove a *Marvin*-based claim, however, the surviving cohabitant is not an intestate heir. The wisdom of this rule has been challenged. *See* Jennifer Seidman, *Functional Families and Dysfunctional Laws: Committed Partners and Intestate Succession*, 75 U. COLO. L. Rev. 211 (2004).

18. Cohabitants sometimes purchase a house and take title in both names. If the parties contributed unequal amounts of money toward the house purchase, how should any equity in the house at the time of separation be allocated? *See* Hofstad v. Christie, 240 P.3d 816 (Wyo. 2010) (dividing the equity equally). If one party purchases real estate in his or her name alone, while the parties are living together, what claim should the other party have to the house, if any, if that party contributes to the (a) down payment, (b) monthly house payment, (c) real estate taxes and utilities, or (d) repairs and home improvements? *See* Brooks v. Allen, 137 A.3d 404 (N.H. 2016).

19. Assume one party purchased a home before he or she began a cohabitation relationship with another. Assume that the parties, while living together, agreed that the party who "owned" the house would pay all expenses related to the house and the other party would pay all of their other living expenses. If the house significantly increases in value while the parties live together, who should be entitled to this increase in value?

B. IS *MARVIN V. MARVIN* THE BEST WAY TO DEAL WITH COHABITATION DISPUTES TODAY?

When the California Supreme Court decided how to address Ms. Triola's claim in 1976, societal attitudes toward cohabitation were beginning to change. More than four decades later, the social context is significantly different. As we mentioned above, in 1972 there was one unmarried cohabitant couple in the United States for every 100 married couples. Now there are more than 13 for every 100 married couples. Should this societal change affect how we regulate the rights of cohabitants?

The *Marvin* court seemed to assume that cohabiting couples do not generally want to create shared property rights regarding property accumulated while the parties live together. Is this a reasonable assumption for all cohabitants today?

CONNELL V. FRANCISCO
Supreme Court of Washington, 1995.
127 Wash. 2d 339, 898 P.2d 831.

GUY, JUSTICE.

This case requires us to decide how property acquired during a meretricious relationship is distributed.

Background

[Richard Francisco and Shannon Connell met in 1983. They were both unmarried; Richard lived in Las Vegas and Shannon in New York. Richard's net worth in 1983 was $1,300,000 while Shannon owned little. At Richard's request, Shannon moved into Richard's home in November 1983. They lived together in Las Vegas for almost three years. She worked as a dancer and helped Richard some with his businesses. In 1986 she and Richard moved to Washington to manage an inn he had purchased. For more than two years, Shannon received no compensation for these management services; in 1989 and 1990 she received $400 weekly. Between 1986 and the end of 1990 Richard and a corporation controlled by him accumulated various pieces of realty. The parties separated in March 1990; all the property accumulated during their relationship was accumulated in the name of Richard or his corporation.]

Connell filed a lawsuit against Francisco in December 1990 seeking a just and equitable distribution of the property acquired during the relationship. The Island County Superior Court determined Connell and Francisco's relationship was sufficiently long term and stable to require a just and equitable distribution. The Superior Court limited the property subject to distribution to the property that would have been community in character had they been married. The trial court held property owned by each party prior to the relationship could not be distributed.

The only property characterized by the Superior Court as being property that would have been community in character had Connell and Francisco been married was the increased value of Francisco's pension plan. The increased value of the pension plan, $169,000, was divided equally, with $84,500 distributed to Connell. The Superior Court, concluding Connell did not satisfy her burden of proof with respect to the remaining property, distributed to Francisco the remainder of the pension plan and all real property.

The Court of Appeals reversed, holding both property owned by each prior to the relationship and property that would have been community in character had the parties been married may be distributed following a meretricious relationship. *Connell v. Francisco*, 74 Wash. App. 306, 317, 872 P.2d 1150 (1994).

Francisco petitioned this court for discretionary review. He argues property owned by each party prior to the relationship may not be distributed following a meretricious relationship, and a community-property-like presumption is inapplicable when a trial court distributes property following a meretricious relationship. We granted discretionary review.

Analysis

A meretricious relationship is a stable, marital-like relationship where both parties cohabit with knowledge that a lawful marriage between them does not exist. *In re Marriage of Lindsey*, 101 Wash. 2d 299, 678 P.2d 328 (1984). Relevant factors establishing a meretricious relationship include, but are not limited to: continuous cohabitation, duration of the relationship, purpose of the relationship, pooling of resources and services for joint projects, and the intent of the parties.

In *Lindsey*, this court ruled a relationship need not be "long term" to be characterized as a meretricious relationship. While a "long term" relationship is not a threshold requirement, duration is a significant factor. A "short term" relationship may be characterized as meretricious, but a number of significant and substantial factors must be present. See *Lindsey* (a less than 2-year meretricious relationship preceded marriage).

The Superior Court found Connell and Francisco were parties to a meretricious relationship. This finding is not contested.

Historically, property acquired during a meretricious relationship was presumed to belong to the person in whose name title to the property was placed. *Creasman v. Boyle*, 31 Wash. 2d 345, 356, 196 P.2d 835 (1948). This presumption is commonly referred to as "the *Creasman* presumption."

In 1984, this court overruled *Creasman*. *Lindsey, supra*. In its place, the court adopted a general rule requiring a just and equitable distribution of property following a meretricious relationship.

In *Lindsey*, the parties cohabited for less than 2 years prior to marriage. When they subsequently divorced, the wife argued the increase in value of property acquired during the meretricious portion of their relationship was also subject to an equitable distribution as if the property were community in character. We agreed, citing former RCW 26.09.080 [Ed.—The statute cited permits a divorce court to divide property acquired by a spouse before marriage.]

Francisco contends the Court of Appeals misinterpreted *Lindsey* when it applied all the principles contained in RCW 26.09.080 to meretricious relationships. We agree. A meretricious relationship is not the same as a marriage. * * * [The court cites many instances where cohabitants are not treated in the same manner as spouses.] As such, the laws involving the distribution of marital property do not directly apply to the division of property following a meretricious relationship. Washington courts may look toward those laws for guidance.

Once a trial court determines the existence of a meretricious relationship, the trial court then: (1) evaluates the interest each party has in the property acquired during the relationship, and (2) makes a just and equitable distribution of the property. *Lindsey, supra*. The critical focus is on property that would have been characterized as community property had the parties been married. This property is properly before a trial court and is subject to a just and equitable distribution.

While portions of RCW 26.09.080 may apply by analogy to meretricious relationships, not all provisions of the statute should be applied. The parties to such a relationship have chosen not to get married and therefore the property owned by each party prior to the relationship should not be before the court for distribution at the end of the relationship. However, the property acquired during the relationship should be before the trial court so that one party is not unjustly enriched at the end of such a relationship. We conclude a trial court may not distribute property acquired by each party prior to the relationship at the termination of a meretricious relationship. Until the Legislature, as a matter of public policy, concludes meretricious relationships are the legal equivalent to marriages, we limit the distribution of property following a meretricious relationship to property that would have been characterized as community property had the parties been married. This will allow the trial court to justly divide property the couple has earned during the relationship through their efforts without creating a common law marriage or making a decision for a couple which they have declined to make for themselves. Any other interpretation equates cohabitation with marriage; ignores the conscious decision by many couples not to marry; confers benefits when few, if any, economic risks or legal obligations are assumed; and disregards the explicit intent of the Legislature that RCW 26.09.080 apply to property distributions following a marriage.

Conclusion

In summary, we hold that property which would have been characterized as separate property had the couple been married is not before the trial court for division at the end of the relationship. The property that would have been characterized as community property had the couple been married is before the trial court for a just and equitable distribution. There is a rebuttable presumption that property acquired during the relationship is owned by both of the parties and is therefore before the court for a fair division.

We reverse the Court of Appeals in part, affirm in part, and remand the case to the Superior Court for a just and equitable distribution of property.

UTTER, JUSTICE (dissenting).

I disagree with the majority's conclusion that the Court of Appeals misinterpreted our decision in *In re Marriage of Lindsey*, when it applied the principles found in RCW 26.09.080 to meretricious relationships. By limiting the distribution of property following a meretricious relationship to property that would have been characterized as community property had the parties been married, the majority establishes a new rule that will be uncertain in application and will likely interfere with the ability of the courts to "make a just and equitable distribution of the property" as is required by *Lindsey*. Given the increasing number of these cases in our trial courts, what is needed in this context is a simple rule that is easy to apply. Our holding in *Lindsey*, as understood by the Court of Appeals, does just that.

The majority is correct in pointing out that a meretricious relationship is not the same as a marriage. In citing a number of cases in which this court has refused to treat them the same, however, the majority fails to realize that the question of how closely these two types of relationships are treated depends upon the context. We discussed *Lindsey* in *Davis v. Employment Sec. Dept.*, 108 Wash. 2d 272, 737 P.2d 1262 (1987), a case in which we held that an unmarried cohabitant is not eligible for benefits triggered by a "marital status" provision under our state's unemployment compensation statutes. There we noted that while *Lindsey* treated meretricious relationships like marriages in the context of property distribution, "the extension of property distribution rights of spouses to partners in meretricious relationships does not elevate meretricious relationships themselves to the level of marriages for any and all purposes."

I, therefore, would affirm the opinion of the Court of Appeals in its entirety.

NOTES AND QUESTIONS

1.   In a later case, the Washington Supreme Court replaced the term "meretricious relationship" with "committed intimate relationship." Olver v. Fowler, 168 P.3d 348 (Wash. 2007).

Unlike *Marvin*, the Washington Supreme Court holds that, if the parties had established a committed intimate relationship, they do presumptively share property accumulated while living together. If the court finds that the parties established a committed intimate relationship, should the parties share property accumulated since the beginning of the relationship, or should the shared rights begin at some other time?

If parties marry after establishing a committed intimate relationship, if they subsequently divorce the court can divide property accumulated during the cohabitation. *See In re* Neumiller, 335 P.3d 1019 (Wash. App. 2014).

2.   How would Ms. Marvin's claims be resolved under *Connell*? How would Ms. Connell's claim be resolved under *Marvin*? For a general discussion of *Connell*, *see* Gavin M. Parr, *What Is a "Meretricious Relationship"?: An Analysis of Cohabitant Property Rights Under* Connell v. Francisco, 74 WASH. L. REV. 1243 (1999).

3.   Is the *Connell* result fair? Why or why not? What are its advantages and disadvantages? One disadvantage of the *Connell* rule is its lack of clarity. This lack of clarity was not ameliorated by Marriage of Pennington, 14 P.3d 764 (Wash. 2000), where a unanimous court reversed the trial court and held that parties who had cohabited (with one brief separation) for 7 ½ years did not have a meretricious relationship. The court noted that the man was married for about 5 years of the relationship, so granting the parties meretricious relationship status during that period could complicate the divorce property division. The parties' cohabitation was characterized as "sporadic and not continuous enough to evidence a stable cohabiting relationship." It was emphasized that, after the man divorced, he refused to marry his companion when she expressed a desire to do so. Finally, the court held that, while both parties contributed to joint living expenses, they did not pool their resources.

In light of *Pennington*, the result in Long v. Fregeau, 244 P.3d 26 (Wash. App. 2010) is surprising. Here two men lived together (counting a brief separation) for almost 8 years. Each was sexually unfaithful at least once. One man was married to another woman for about 7 of the 8 years. When he divorced, he asked his male partner if the partner wanted to establish a marriage—equivalent registered domestic partnership, and the partner (who was the plaintiff in the subsequent litigation) refused. The appellate court affirmed the trial court's ruling that this was a committed intimate relationship. The only apparent difference from *Pennington* was that the parties both contributed financially to two real estate purchases.

4.   In Gormley v. Robertson, 83 P.3d 1042 (Wash. App. 2004), a Washington court adhered to the approach adopted in *Connell* and extended it to gay couples. The Washington Supreme Court has also applied *Connell* when the meretricious relationship ended when both partners died. *See* Olver v. Fowler, 168 P.3d 348 (Wash. 2007). But although a number of other countries have adopted statutory schemes consistent with *Connell* (see Section 2, *infra*), few other American jurisdictions have as yet accepted this method of determining the rights and obligations of cohabitants. Why, at least in the United States, has *Connell* proven less popular than *Marvin*?

Oregon allows cohabitants to share accumulations during the relationship if the parties "intended to pool their resources for their common benefit." A court can find an implied agreement to do this based on how they held themselves out to the community, joint acts of a financial nature, how title to property was held, and the respective financial and nonfinancial contributions of each party. The pivotal fact appears to be whether parties pooled resources and made joint investments. When this does not occur, no right to share arises, even in a long relationship. *See* Greulich v. Creary, 243 P.3d 110 (Or. App. 2010), (involving a cohabitation lasting 18 years); *In re* Baker and Andrews, 223 P.3d 417 (Or. App. 2009).

In Boulds v. Nielsen, 323 P.3d 58 (Alaska 2014) the Alaska Supreme Court authorized a "marital-like property distribution" when a marital-like cohabitation relationship ended. The court listed various factors courts should consider when deciding whether the relationship was like a marriage.

5.   The approach in *Connell*, which gives nonmarital cohabitants property rights less extensive than those of a married couple in Washington, relies on the fact that a Washington divorce court may also divide property acquired by either spouse before marriage. In those states (a substantial majority) where a divorce court may only divide property acquired during marriage, if a state supreme court wanted to adopt a similar rule, what rule would be analogous to that in *Connell*?

6.   *Public Benefits and Claims Against Third Parties:* While *Connell* goes further than any other American decision in basing rights on status as a cohabitant, it is important to keep in mind that it confers rights only against the other cohabitant. It does not convey rights to public benefits. In most states, cohabitants may not bring an action for loss of consortium if their partner is injured nor maintain a wrongful death action if the partner is killed. *See* Garcia v. Douglas Aircraft Co., 184 Cal. Rptr. 390 (App. 1982). An Indiana court did not let a fiancée sue for bystander tort recovery damages when her partner was killed in a car accident, a remedy that is available to spouses. Smith v. Toney, 656 N.E.2d 656 (Ind. 2007). The surviving cohabitant will not receive Social Security benefits available to a surviving spouse (Califano v. Boles, 443 U.S. 282 (1979)), nor inherit from the decedent cohabitant under the state's intestacy laws. Cohabitants do not enjoy the benefits of tax preferences such as the unlimited marital deduction from estate and gift tax (*see* Cory v. Edgett, 168 Cal. Rptr. 686 (App. 1980)) or the right to file a joint tax return (*see* IRS Chief Council Advice Memorandum, 32 Fam. L. Rep. (BNA) 1214 (2006)). If one cohabitant's employer provides health insurance to the other through its group health insurance plan, the value of the insurance will not be exempt from taxation as it would for a spouse. *See* Private Letter Ruling No. 9603011, 22 Fam. L. Rep. (BNA) 1144 (10/18/95). They may not jointly petition for bankruptcy. *See* Bone v. Allen, 186 B.R. 769 (Bkrtcy. N.D. Ga. 1995). If one cohabitant quits his job to follow the other to new employment in a different location, he may not be able to establish "good cause" for the move so as to obtain unemployment insurance benefits. *See* Norman v. Unemployment Insurance Appeals Board, 663 P.2d 904 (Cal. 1983).

Of course, if the partners opt into some status relationship they may obtain a variety of benefits. For example, under Maryland's domestic partner statute one partner can bring a wrongful death action if the other is killed. MD. CODE REG. 4.20.020.

Some states have deviated from the majority rule discussed above regarding cohabitant claims against third parties. The New Hampshire Supreme Court has permitted a cohabitant to bring a claim for negligent infliction of emotional distress when she witnessed the accidental death of her partner. Graves v. Easterbook, 818 A.2d 1255 (N.H. 2003). The New Mexico Supreme Court permitted a loss of consortium claim when the partners had lived together for 30 years and raised three children. Lozoya v. Sanchez, 66 P.3d 948 (N.M. 2003).

After the events of September 11, 2001, the New York State World Trade Center Relief Fund, which provided financial support for surviving spouses, children and parents, also provided benefits to some surviving domestic partners. *See* Susan J. Becker, *Tumbling Towers as Turning Points: Will 9/11 Usher in a New Civil Rights Era for Gay Men and Lesbians in the United States?*, 9 WM. & MARY J. WOMEN & L. 207, 231–232 (2003).

Problem 6-1:

Bill is a wealthy investor; Robin, an aspiring model, has few financial assets. Three years ago, Bill and Robin decided to live together and orally agreed that: (1) they would be lovers; (2) they would live in Bill's house; (3) Robin would postpone his modeling career to travel with Bill; and (4) Bill would share equally with Robin all property accumulated during the relationship and support Robin for three years after the relationship ended. The relationship recently ended. Bill has accumulated an additional $1,000,000 during the three years of the relationship. How would the *Marvin* and *Connell* courts respond to a claim by Robin against Bill?

Problem 6-2:

Twenty years ago, Melissa and Adam decided to live together. Melissa was a wealthy performer and Adam a surfer. Adam asked Melissa to marry him, but Melissa refused. Two years later they had a child, who was cared for primarily by Adam. During the relationship, Adam frequently asked Melissa to pool assets with him, but she refused. Adam and Melissa have now recently separated. Melissa had saved $500,000 prior to entering the relationship with Adam and accumulated an additional $1,000,000, in her own name, during the relationship. How would the *Marvin* and *Connell* courts respond to a claim by Adam against Melissa?

Problem 6-3:

You are a law clerk for Justice Abel, a member of the State Supreme Court. The Court has agreed to hear appeals in two cases involving claims by unmarried cohabitants.

One case involves George Smith and Amanda Martin, an unmarried couple who cohabited for twenty years and had three children before separating. George is a successful businessman with assets totaling $2 million, all titled in his name alone. Amanda has been a homemaker throughout the relationship, although before the birth of the couple's children she occasionally helped out in George's office. George and Amanda did not hold themselves out as married and did not pool assets, although George did list Amanda and the children as dependents on his income tax return. Amanda has sued George for an equal share of property accumulated during the relationship based on: (i) an alleged committed intimate relationship, (ii) an express contract (Amanda claims that George told her that "they would share everything accumulated while they lived together"; George denies any such statement), (iii) an implied contract, and (iv) quantum meruit.

The other case involves Ann Jones and Amy Barnes, who cohabited for one year and have no children. The only substantial asset owned by either is a winning lottery ticket purchased by Ann during the year's cohabitation, entitling her to $5 million over the next twenty years. Amy has sued Ann for an equal share of the lottery winnings based on claims identical to those listed by Amanda. They did not hold themselves out as a married couple. But she also has a handwritten document, dated shortly after Ann's and Amy's cohabitation began and signed by each in which both Ann and Amy promised "to share equally in all fruits of our partnership."

The Supreme Court has not heard an appeal from a claim by an unmarried cohabitant for more than thirty years, when it reaffirmed the traditional meretricious relationship rule. (A. v. B.) Conflicting lower court decisions have variously followed this approach, followed *Marvin*, or allowed claims based solely on an express agreement. The state also retains the doctrine of common law marriage.

Justice Abel has asked you to advise her on the merits of the various approaches open to the court. Specifically, she wants to know:

   a.   Is common law marriage an adequate basis for resolving claims between unmarried cohabitants? If not, what "deserving" claimants does it omit?

   b.   Which approach will produce the most litigation? the least?

   c.   Which approach will produce the most predictable outcomes? the least?

   d.   What public policy concerns are relevant to claims between cohabitants?

   e.   From a public policy perspective, what are the advantages and disadvantages of basing a cohabitant's recovery on an agreement? on his or her status as a cohabitant?

   f.   From a public policy perspective, should the length of the relationship be taken into account? If yes, which approach can best do so?

   g.   On balance, what approach should the court take?

2. COHABITATION PER STATUTE—THE FUTURE OF THE COHABITATION ALTERNATIVE?

Legislators considering the regulation of cohabitation must address a number of issues:

(1) What constitutes "cohabitation"? Must the parties share a common residence? What if the parties have separate residences but spend most evenings together?

(2) Should there be any limits on contractual freedom other than the general rules governing validity and enforcement of contracts? Should it be possible to contract expressly out of implied obligations that might arise from cohabitation? Should persons be permitted to contract into cohabitation relationships with legal effects that differ from standard marriage more than standard marriage may be modified by marital contracts?

(3) In the absence of an express contract, should a cohabitation arrangement carry (a) defined consequences imposed by law; (b) consequences depending on the parties' intent as implied in their conduct; (c) a mix of (a) and (b); or (d) no legal consequences at all?

(4) If the options remain limited to the legal status of marriage or no legal status at all, should an exception be made for the type of case in which the retroactive imposition of something like common law marriage seems "equitable"?

(5) Should the rights and obligations at the end of a cohabitation relationship be affected by whether either cohabitant was married to someone else for all or part of the time the parties lived together?

(6) Should cohabitants have the same public benefits as spouses? If yes, should they also shoulder spousal obligations? For example, should they be required to file jointly if that would be to the advantage of the IRS? Should they have support obligations to their partner, either while the relationship continues or after it ends?

(7) Is it possible to have two different legally recognized cohabitation relationships simultaneously?

The State of Nevada has recently answered these questions one way. The American Law Institute has proposed a very different approach. The main provisions of both legislative schemes follow. As you read them, try to identify their differences and the policy values on which they are based.

NEV. REV. STAT. ANN.

122A.100.   Registration: Procedure; fees; eligibility; issuance of certificate

1.   A valid domestic partnership is registered in the State of Nevada when two persons who satisfy the requirements of subsection 2:

(a) File with the Office of the Secretary of State, on a form prescribed by the Secretary of State, a signed and notarized statement declaring that both persons:

(1) Have chosen to share one another's lives in an intimate and committed relationship of mutual caring; and

(2) Desire of their own free will to enter into a domestic partnership; and [pay a filing fee].

* * *

2.   To be eligible to register pursuant to subsection 1, two persons desiring to enter into a domestic partnership must furnish proof satisfactory to the Office of the Secretary of State that:

(a) Both persons have a common residence;

(b) . . . neither person is married or a member of another domestic partnership;

(c) The two persons are not related by blood in a way that would prevent them from being married to each other in this State;

(d) Both persons are at least 18 years of age; and

(e) Both persons are competent to consent to the domestic partnership.

* * *

4.   As used in this section:

(a) "Common residence" means a residence shared by both domestic partners on at least a part-time basis, irrespective of whether:

(1) Ownership of the residence or the right to occupy the residence is in the name of only one of the domestic partners; and

(2) One or both of the domestic partners owns or occupies an additional residence.

(b) "Residence" means any house, room, apartment, tenement or other building, vehicle, vehicle trailer, semitrailer, house trailer or boat designed or intended for occupancy as a residence.

122A.110.   Solemnization ceremony not required for domestic partnership; religious faiths free to choose whether to grant religious status to domestic partnership under own rules of practice

The provisions of this chapter do not require the performance of any solemnization ceremony to enter into a binding domestic partnership contract. It is left to the dictates and conscience of partners entering into a domestic partnership to determine whether to seek a ceremony or blessing over the domestic partnership . . .

122A.200.   Rights and duties of domestic partners, former domestic partners and surviving domestic partners

(a)   Domestic partners have the same rights, protections and benefits, and are subject to the same responsibilities, obligations and duties under law, whether derived from statutes, administrative regulations, court rules, government policies, common law or any other provisions or sources of law, as are granted to and imposed upon spouses.

122A.200.   [This section provides that domestic partners will have the same rights, protections and benefits, and are subject to the same responsibilities, obligations and duties, as are granted to and imposed upon spouses.]

122A.300.   General requirements and procedures; requirements and procedure for simplified termination proceedings; fees

1.   Except as otherwise provided in subsection 2, domestic partners who wish to terminate a domestic partnership registered pursuant to NRS 122A.100 must follow the procedures set forth in [the Nevada code chapter dealing with divorce].

AMERICAN LAW INSTITUTE, PRINCIPLES OF THE LAW OF FAMILY DISSOLUTION: ANALYSIS AND RECOMMENDATIONS (2002)

§ 6.03   Determination That Persons Are Domestic Partners

(1)   For the purpose of defining relationships to which this Chapter applies, domestic partners are two persons of the same or opposite sex, not married to one another, who for a significant period of time share a primary residence and a life together as a couple.

(2)   Persons are domestic partners when they have maintained a common household, as defined in Paragraph (4), with their common child, as defined in Paragraph (5), for a continuous period that equals or exceeds

a duration, called the *cohabitation parenting period*, set in a uniform rule of statewide application.

(3) Persons not related by blood or adoption are presumed to be domestic partners when they have maintained a common household, as defined in Paragraph (4), for a continuous period that equals or exceeds a duration, called the *cohabitation period*, set in a uniform rule of statewide application. The presumption is rebuttable by evidence that the parties did not share life together as a couple, as defined by Paragraph (7).

(4) Parties "maintain a common household" when they occupy a primary residence alone or with other family members; or when, if they share a household with unrelated persons, they act jointly, rather than as individuals, with respect to management of the household.

(5) Parties have a "common child" when each party is either the child's legal parent or a parent by estoppel [as defined elsewhere].

(6) When the requirements of Paragraph (2) or (3) are not satisfied, a person asserting a claim under this Chapter bears the burden of proving that for a significant period of time the parties shared a primary residence and a life together as a couple, as defined in Paragraph (7). Whether a period of time is significant is determined in light of all the Paragraph (7) circumstances of the parties' relationship and, particularly, the extent to which those circumstances wrought change in the life of one or both parties.

(7) Whether persons shared life together as a couple is determined by reference to all the circumstances, including:

(a) the oral or written statements or promises made to one another, or representations jointly made to third partes, regarding their relationship;

(b) the extent to which the parties intermingled their finances;

(c) the extent to which their relationship fostered the parties' economic interdependence, or the economic dependence of one party upon the other;

(d) the extent to which the parties engaged in conduct and assumed collaborative roles in furtherance of their life together;

(e) the extent to which the relationship wrought change in the life of either or both parties;

(f) the extent to which the parties acknowledged responsibilities to one another, as by naming one another the beneficiary of life insurance or of a testamentary instrument, or as eligible to receive benefits under an employee benefit plan;

(g) the extent to which the parties' relationship was treated by the parties as qualitatively distinct from the relationship either party had with any other person;

(h) the emotional or physical intimacy of the parties' relationship;

(i) the parties' community reputation as a couple;

(j) the parties' participation is some form of commitment ceremony or registration as a domestic partnership;

(k) the parties' participation in a void or voidable marriage that, under applicable law, does not give rise to the economic incidents of marriage;

(*l*) the parties' procreation of, adoption of, or joint assumption of parental functions toward a child;

(m) the parties' maintenance of a common household, as defined by Paragraph (4).

Parties may opt out of or modify this system via contract, subject to the somewhat rigorous standards for such arrangements adopted by the ALI regarding premarital agreements. *Id.*, § 6.01.

The ALI proposal would give "domestic partners" the same marital property rights and spousal support rights as spouses. *Id.*, §§ 6.04, 6.06.

NOTES AND QUESTIONS

1.   How does the ALI proposal differ from the *Marvin* approach? the *Connell* approach? How does the ALI approach differ from the Nevada statute?

2.   How would Ms. Marvin and Ms. Connell fare under the ALI proposal? the Nevada approach?

3.   In about 2000, a few states provided a status other than marriage for gay couples (who could not marry). The rules relating to entering into such a status mirrored marriage. As a general rule, the status was entered into by obtaining a license and participating in some form of ceremony. In some states, parties to the "civil union," "domestic partnership" or "registered partnership" had the same rights and obligations as a married couple; in others, the parties thereby acquired fewer rights than a married couple.

More recently, some states have permitted more types of couples to choose the alternative status. For example, in California gay couples and heterosexual couples with at least one partner 62 years old can choose to be domestic partners. *See* CAL. FAM. CODE § 297(B)(5). Washington lets unmarried gay or heterosexual couples register as domestic partners if at least one party is at least 62 years old. *See* WASH. REV. CODE ANN. 26.60.030. Why might older couples be interested in a status other than marriage? Other states, like

Nevada, let any couple, straight or gay, opt into the status. *See also,* ILL. COMP. L. 75/5; 2011 HAWAII LAWS ACT 1 (S.B.232).

Most of the alternate status statutes specify the rights and obligations that will flow from the status. Although these rights could presumably be changed by agreement, the process does not encourage this. In contrast, Colorado has adopted a "designated beneficiary" status which is created by the parties signing a standard form "designated beneficiary agreement." The agreement lists a variety of potential rights the parties could confer on one another, such as the right to make medical care decisions or inherit property as an intestate heir, and, regarding each such right, the parties must initial whether they choose to grant that right. A signed copy of the agreement is to be recorded with the county clerk in the county where at least one party resides. *See* COLO. REV. STAT. § 15–22–106. Is it a good idea to invite parties in this manner to select the rights that will result from entering into a new status? What might be the advantages and disadvantages of such a system?

In France, where gay couples cannot marry, an alternate status has been created that is available to both gay and straight couples. *See* Claude Martin & Irene Thery, *The PACS and Marriage and Cohabitation in France*, 15 INT. J. L. POL'Y & FAM. 135 (2001). The status confers fewer rights and obligations than marriage and gives parties some flexibility in terms of specifying what rights will result from entering into the status. This alternate status has been surprisingly popular, particularly with younger couples. Do you think there would be significant interest in such a status in the United States?

4.   No American jurisdiction has thus far adopted the ALI approach. Internationally, both the Nevada and ALI approaches have found favor:

> (a)   *The Nevada Approach:* Many European countries have adopted some variant of the Nevada model. At least nine European countries, including Ireland, Denmark, Norway, Sweden, Iceland, Finland, and the Netherlands, have introduced a registration option that produces almost all of the rights and obligations of marriage. Most of these registry schemes are open only to gay couples. At least three other European nations, France, Belgium, and Germany, have created a registry option which confers a limited number of the rights and obligations of marriage. The French and Belgian schemes are open to heterosexual and same-sex couples; the German scheme is open only to same-sex couples. *See* Kees Waaldijk, *Others May Follow: The Introduction of Marriage, Quasi-Marriage, and Semi-Marriage for Same-Sex Couples in European Countries*, 38 NEW ENG. L. REV. 569 (2004). Canada, the Netherlands, Spain and Belgium have also made marriage available to gay partners. *See generally* Joanna Miles, *Unmarried Cohabitation in a European Perspective*, in European Family Law 82–115 (Jens M. Scherpe Ed., 2016).

> (b)   *The ALI Approach:* All of the Australian states have adopted legislation that extends certain property rights to cohabitants who have a common child or have lived together for at least two years. *See*

DOROTHY KOVACS, DEFACTO PROPERTY PROCEEDINGS IN AUSTRALIA 10–11 (1998); Lindy Wilmott et al., *De Facto Relationships Property Adjustment Law—A National Direction*, 17 AUST. J. FAM. L. 1, 2–5 (2003). And New Zealand has extended *all* of the rights and obligations of marriage to couples who have been "de facto partners" for three years. *See* http://www.legislation.govt.nz/browse_vw.asp? pal-statutes. Like the ALI approach, the New Zealand statute contains a lengthy factor list to guide the court's decision as to whether a particular pair are in fact "de facto partners." *See* PROPERTY (RELATIONSHIPS) AMENDMENT ACT 2001 § 2D2 (N.Z.) Like New Zealand, Ireland generally gives cohabitants of the same or opposite sex the rights of a divorcing couple when they break up if they lived together for at least 2 years and had a child together, or lived together for 5 years. *See* John Mee, *Cohabitation Law Reform in Ireland,* 23 CHILD & FAM. L. Q. 323 (2011). Scotland has passed a law that gives a cohabitant a remedy if the parties break up and the claimant suffered career damage due to the role assumed in the relationship. *See* Frankie McCarthy, *Cohabitation: Lessons from North of the Border?,* 23 CHILD & FAM. L. Q. 277 (2011).

Canada, too, has adopted many features of the ALI approach. Today, all Canadian provinces but Quebec impose a support obligation on cohabitants who have lived together for periods ranging from one to three years. *See* Nicholas Bala, *Controversy Over Couples in Canada: The Evolution of Marriage and Other Adult Interdependent Relationships*, 29 QUEEN'S L.J. 41, 45–49 (2003). Although a cohabitant right to share property accrued during the relationship appears to be available only to couples in the Northwest Territories (*see* Family Law Act, S.N.W.T. ch. 18 § 1), the federal MODERNIZATION OF BENEFITS AND OBLIGATIONS ACT, S.C. 2000, c. 12, made available to "common-law partners" most of the public benefits that formerly depended on marital status. These legal developments were fueled by a series of decisions by the Canadian Supreme Court. In Miron v. Trudel, [1995] 2 S.C.R. 418, the Canadian Supreme Court ruled that the exclusion of a long-term, unmarried cohabitant from the statutory definition of "spouse" was, for purposes of an automobile insurance policy, discriminatory and contrary to section 15 of the Canadian Charter of Rights and Freedoms. In M v. H., [1999] 2 S.C.R. 33, the Supreme Court ruled, on the same basis, that any support right available to heterosexual couples must also be extended to same-sex couples. However, in Nova Scotia (Attorney General) v. Walsh, [2002] 102 C.R.R. (2d) 1, the Court ruled that property-division rights available to married couples need not be extended to unmarried cohabitants. The Court noted that

> many persons in circumstances similar to those of the parties, that is, opposite sex individuals in conjugal relationships of some permanence, have chosen to avoid the institution of marriage and the legal consequences that flow from it. * * * To ignore these differences among cohabiting couples presumes a commonality of intention and understanding that simply does not exist. This effectively nullifies

the individual's freedom to choose alternative family forms and to have that choice respected and legitimated by the state.

If the fact that unmarried couples have chosen to avoid marriage is relevant to their property-division rights, should this fact also be relevant to their support rights? Their right to public benefits? Put somewhat differently, can *Walsh* be distinguished from *M. v. H.*?

Scotland has adopted a set of rules for cohabitants that differs substantially from the ALI approach. Like the ALI, the policy is descriptive; no registration is required. When the relationship ends, a judge determines whether they were "cohabitants" based on (1) the length of time the parties lived together, (2) the nature of their relationship, and (3) the nature of their financial arrangements. If the judge finds that the parties were "cohabitants" under the law, the judge can make an equitable award to an applicant from the other party, after considering (a) whether the defender party derived economic advantage from the contributions made by the applicant, and (b) whether the applicant has suffered economic disadvantage in the interests of (i) the other party or (ii) any child of the parties. *See* Richard Busby, *Learning from the Scottish Cohabitation Experience 2006–2016*, FAMILY LAW (October 2016) 1269, 1270.

5.   Some American localities have established "domestic partnership" ordinances. If parties register as partners these ordinances often enable cohabitants of municipal employees to qualify for health insurance benefits under group health insurance plans, or give a partner hospital visitation rights, but do not confer property or support rights. *See* Heidi Eischen, *For Better or Worse: An Analysis of Recent Challenges to Domestic Partner Benefits Legislation*, 31 U. TOL. L. REV. 527 (2000).

6.   Unmarried partners could very well live in more than one jurisdiction during the course of the relationship. We have seen that state law rules regarding unmarried partners are not uniform. If a couple lives initially in a state that enforces oral cohabitation agreements and then moves to another state that doesn't enforce such agreements and then they break up, what happens if one party brings suit to enforce the agreement? *See* William A. Reppy, Jr., *Choice of Law Problems Arising When Unmarried Cohabitants Change Domicile*, 55 S.M.U. L. REV. 273 (2002). In Maeker v. Ross, 99 A.3d 795 (N.J. 2014) the parties began a cohabiting relationship in New York, which enforces oral agreements between cohabitants. They later moved to New Jersey before the legislature there adopted a statute requiring cohabitants to have a written agreement to enforce a cohabitation claim based on contract. The New Jersey Supreme Court ruled that the 2010 New Jersey law did not apply to this couple and did not discuss whether New York or New Jersey law should apply. In Walsh v. Reynolds, 335 P.3d 984 (Wash. App. 2014) the Washington appellate court applied the "committed intimate relationship" principle to property accumulated by the couple while they were living in another state before they moved to Washington.

Parties that have lived in more than one country present more complicated problems. In Dion v. Rieser, 285 P.3d 678 (N.M. App (2012), a man and a woman had lived together for 20 years in Australia and New Mexico when the man died intestate. When he died, he held title to property in Australia and New Mexico. What law should govern the woman's rights?

7. In the United States, the evidence suggests that cohabitation typically delays, instead of replaces, marriage. Although 60–75% of first marriages and 80–85% of remarriages are now preceded by cohabitation, periods of cohabitation tend to be brief. 60% of cohabitants marry within five years and only about 10% of those who do not marry are still together five years later. *See generally* Daniel T. Lichter, Zhenchao Qian, & Leanna N. Mellott, *Marriage or Dissolution? Union Transitions Among Poor Cohabitating Women*, 43 DEMOGRAPHY 223 (May 2006). The median duration of U.S. cohabiting relationships is only 1.6 years.

The research data also suggest that cohabitation is a lonelier and less prosperous state than marriage. U.S. cohabitants are less healthy, wealthy, and less likely to stay together than married couples. They are much less likely than married couples to have children, demonstrate sexual fidelity, pool their resources, or feel secure and unconflicted in their relationships. They are more likely than married couples to value independence and less likely to value commitment or express commitment toward their partners. *See* Marsha Garrison, *Is Consent Necessary? An Evaluation of the Emerging Law of Cohabitant Obligation*, 52 UCLA L. REV. 815, 839–45 (2005) (surveying evidence). Children in cohabiting households thus experience more instability than those in married-couple households; some research shows that they experience worse emotional health and more abuse. The impact of cohabitation on children is of particular concern to policymakers because 40% of U.S. children are now expected to spend time in a cohabitating household. *See* Larry Bumpass & H.H. Lu, *Trends in Cohabitation and Implications for Children's Family Contexts in the United States*, 54 POPULATION STUDIES 9 (2000).

To some extent the lack of stability of cohabiting relationships is due to factors such as youth and low incomes. However, a recent study found that, after controlling for numerous factors such as race, education and economic factors, parents who were cohabiting when their child was born had two and one-half times the risk of separating as compared to parents who were married when their child was born. *See* Cynthia Osborne et al, *Married and Cohabiting Parents' Relationship Stability: A Focus on Race and Ethnicity,* 69 J. MARRIAGE & FAM. 1345 (2007). Some commentators note that it is more common for couples to have more lengthy cohabitation relationships in countries such as France or Sweden, whereas cohabitation relationships in the U.S. tend to be unstable unless the parties marry. *See* Patrick Heuveline & Jeffrey Timberlake, *The Role of Cohabitation in Family Formation: The United States in Comparative Perspective,* 66 J. MARR. & FAM. 1214, 1222 (2004). For example, when Francois Hollande was elected President of France in 2012, he moved into the French presidential palace with his unmarried partner. *See* Maia de la Baume, *First Lady Without a Portfolio (or a Ring) Seeks Her Own*

Path, N.Y. TIMES, May 16, 2012, at A9.) If European cohabitant relationships last significantly longer than U.S. cohabitation relationships, should the U.S. regulate the rights of cohabitants differently from countries like France and Sweden where longer duration cohabitation is more common?

8.   Some who have been critical of an ALI-type approach have been concerned that such an approach would discourage parties from marrying. An empirical analysis of the Australian divorce rate found that such statutes did not affect the marriage rate. *See* Kathleen Kiernan, Anne Barlow & Rosangela Merlo, *Cohabitation Law Reform and Its Impact on Marriage,* 36 FAM.L. 1074 (Dec. 2006).

9.   The Nevada approach is *elective*: the statute permits but does not require couples to assume the rights and obligations associated with a civil union. The ALI approach, by contrast, is *mandatory*: couples whose relationship satisfies the requirements for a domestic partnership assume the rights and obligations of that status whether or not they have formally elected to do so. Which approach is more consistent with the rules governing establishment of a common law marriage? The legislative trend away from recognition of common-law marriage? The expectations of the typical cohabitant?

10.   In justifying the domestic-partnership approach, the ALI has urged that "the absence of formal marriage may have little or no bearing on the character of the parties' domestic relationship and on the equitable considerations that underlie claims between lawful spouses at the dissolution of a marriage." The ALI approach thus "reflects a judgment that it is usually just to apply to both groups the property and support rules applicable to divorcing spouses, that individualized inquiries are usually impractical or unduly burdensome, and that it therefore makes more sense to require parties to contract out of these property and support rules than to contract into them." ALI, PRINCIPLES OF THE LAW OF FAMILY DISSOLUTION at § 6.03 comment b.

Commentators disagree about these claims. Professor Ellman, a reporter for the ALI project, has argued that:

> Legal claims allowed between former spouses are not based upon contract, but something else. What else? The legal duties that arise when people's lives become entwined. Relationships are themselves the source of legal duties, without the need for any assistance from contract. This is not a new idea. Landlords and tenants, employers and employees, neighbors, lawyers and clients, and doctors and patients all incur legally enforceable duties to one another arising from their relationships. They may have a contract which itself creates obligations, and we may think of their mutual decision to enter into the relationship as a kind of contract. But in all these cases, the law may impose duties upon them which are based upon the relationship itself, not upon any agreement between them.

Understanding that the law's recognition of legal obligations between husbands and wives is not based upon contract tells us that *Marvin's* focus on contract with respect to nonmarital couples missed the mark conceptually. A sensible legal rule for deciding when legal duties arise between unmarried cohabitants will not ask whether they had a contract but whether their nonmarital relationship shares with marriage those qualities which lead us to impose legal duties as between husbands and wives. What are those qualities? And how can law state an administrable rule that captures them in the nonmarital context? I believe a promising approach to them is offered by the American Law Institute's recent effort in the *Principles of the Law of Family Dissolution.*

Ira M. Ellman, *"Contract Thinking" was* Marvin's *Fatal Flaw*, 76 NOTRE DAME L. REV. 1365, 1375–77 (2001).

Professor Garrison, on the other hand, contends that:

Modern marriage * * * consistently differs from cohabitation in one large and important respect: Marriage partners have publicly assumed binding obligations to each other that restrict other marital opportunities, inhibit participation in other sexual and economic relationships, structure public and private expectations about their relationship, and burden exit from it. Cohabitants have not. This fundamental difference distinguishes marital relationships, for all their variability, from nonmarital relationships. This difference explains why marriage continues to foster "shared expectations for appropriate behavior within the partnership" while cohabitation remains an "incomplete institution" offering "no widely recognized social blueprint . . . for the appropriate behavior of cohabitors, or for the behavior of the friends, families, and other individuals and institutions with whom they interact." This difference provides a sound basis for state enforcement of both marital commitments and decisions not to make such commitments. * * *

[T]he ALI's assertion that marriage and cohabitation are equivalent relational states is unsupported by the evidence. * * * The ALI's claim that it is practical to require cohabitants to contract out of marital obligations is also unfounded. Individualized inquiry into a couple's understandings and behavior is likely to produce highly uncertain and inconsistent results that can only be determined after time-consuming and expensive litigation. Status-based rules that infer marital obligation from easily ascertained facts such as a common child or the maintenance of a common residence for a defined period avoid much of the uncertainty and expense inherent in individualized inquiry, but create serious risks of misclassification. * * *

The ALI's proposed reforms are not needed either to protect genuine marital commitments or avert unjust enrichment. Policymakers thus should affirm what is already obvious to most of the public: Marriage matters. Family law should reflect and reinforce that fundamental fact.

Marsha Garrison, *Marriage Matters: What's Wrong with the ALI's Domestic Partnership Proposal*, in RECONCEIVING THE FAMILY: PERSPECTIVES ON THE AMERICAN LAW INSTITUTE'S PRINCIPLES OF FAMILY DISSOLUTION (Robin Wilson ed. 2006). Professors Carbone and Cahn agree with Professor Garrison that there can be significant differences in commitment in unmarried-partner relationships when compared to married-couple relationships. *See* June Carbone & Naomi Cahn, *Nonmarriage*, 76 MD. L. REV. 55, 95–98 (2016).

Which view is more persuasive? Which approach, on balance, is best?

Problem 6-4:

Assume you are a legislative aide in a state where the rights of unmarried partners are governed by *Marvin*, and no alternate status is available for gay or straight couples. Your boss asks you to do a survey of regulatory approaches to unmarried partners in other states and countries, and to recommend whether state law should be changed in any way in its approach to unmarried partners. Would you recommend something like the ALI proposal or the Nevada domestic partnership? If not, what would you recommend? Is something like the Scottish approach a possible compromise?

3. DISPUTES BETWEEN DATING PARTNERS

A. ENGAGEMENT DISPUTES

1. Breach of Promise to Marry

In an earlier era, the period during which a woman was considered marriageable was quite limited and long engagements were common. If the man broke the engagement, the woman might not be able to find another marriage partner; the engagement thus was treated like a contract. If one party "breached" the contract, the innocent party could sue the other for damages. In addition to out-of-pocket losses, the innocent party could recover damages for humiliation and loss of the future economic benefit that would have resulted from the marriage. *See* Scharringhaus v. Hazen, 269 Ky. 425, 107 S.W.2d 329 (1937) (upholding award of $65,000 compensatory and $15,000 punitive damages in breach of promise action).

Over the years, many commentators—including Gilbert and Sullivan in "Trial By Jury"—argued that the breach of promise action should be abolished. Critics have argued that loss of a proposed marriage no longer produces real economic losses and that the availability of an action for breach thus encourages lawsuits based on spite and discourages withdrawal from "shaky" relationships.

About half of the states have now followed Gilbert & Sullivan's advice and abolished the action. *See* J. THOMAS OLDHAM, DIVORCE, SEPARATION AND THE DISTRIBUTION OF PROPERTY § 1.05 (2017). But some courts have been reluctant to abolish the cause of action. For example, in Stanard v. Bolin, 565 P.2d 94 (Wash. 1977), the court argued that mental and emotional harm are foreseeable consequences of a broken engagement, and concluded that the action should be retained. (Mental anguish is typically *not* compensable in other family law disputes, such as divorce, unless the other spouse has behaved outrageously.) In Maryland, a breach of promise claim may be asserted only of the plaintiff is pregnant. See MD. CODE, FAM. LAW § 3–102. In Tennessee, a breach of promise claim may be asserted only based on either (i) written evidence of an agreement to marry or (ii) the testimony of two disinterested witnesses. *See* TENN. CODE ANN. § 36–3–401. In at least one state, Illinois, the cause of action has been retained, but only to recover out-of-pocket losses (deposits, wedding clothing, wages, etc.) incurred as a result of a broken engagement. *See* 740 ILL. COMP. STAT. ANN. § 15/2. *See also,* Phillips v. Blankenship, 554 S.E. 2d 231 (Ga. App. 2001). Is this approach a sensible compromise? What would be a fair result if one party decides not to marry after the other party has incurred costs for things like dresses and nonrefundable deposits? If the party who suffered the damage is a parent of the bride, should the parent be allowed to sue the party who terminated the engagement? *See generally* Neil G. Williams, *What to Do When There's No "I Do": A Model for Awarding Damages under Promissory Estoppel*, 70 WASH. L. REV. 1019 (1995); Bruno v. Guerra, 146 Misc. 2d 206 (N.Y. Sup. Ct. 1990) ($28,000 expended by parents not recoverable).

2.   Engagement Gifts

IN RE MARRIAGE OF HEINZMAN

Supreme Court of Colorado, 1979.
198 Colo. 36, 596 P.2d 61.

GROVES, JUSTICE.

This case was commenced as an action for dissolution of a common-law marriage in the district court of Boulder County. For convenience the petitioner is referred to as "Beth" and the respondent as "William." The court found that there was no marriage, but with the consent of the parties proceeded to a determination of their respective rights in a residence property, the title to which was in their names in joint tenancy. It ordered Beth to convey her record interest to William. On review the ruling that there was no marriage was not raised. The court of appeals by a two to one majority affirmed as to the property disposition on grounds somewhat different from those of the trial court. We granted certiorari to the court of appeals and now affirm on the grounds used by the trial court.

In 1970 Beth had been occupying the residence property as a tenant. That summer it appeared that her tenancy would end as the owner intended to sell the property. William entered into a contract to purchase it in July 1970 and the real estate transaction thereunder was "closed" the following December. William moved into the residence in late September 1970, and he and Beth resided there until June 1973.

By deed executed by William on March 25, 1971 and recorded on April 16, 1971, the residence property was conveyed to William and Beth in joint tenancy. Beth was there designated as "Beth Lavato." In June 1973 Beth moved to Sparks, Nevada, and she and William did not live together thereafter. William married another on August 26, 1974. The case was tried on June 20, 1975.

At the conclusion of the trial the district court, in addition to ruling that there was no common-law marriage, found: that William intended and wished to marry Beth; that he gave her an engagement ring in the spring of 1971; that "from the acts of the parties in addition to their admitted cohabitation, it would seem to be a presumption on the side of engagement"; "that an engagement did in fact exist"; "that the gift of real estate * * * was a gift conditioned upon the subsequent ceremonial marriage"; that Beth had abandoned the home and the engagement; and that the condition was not defeated by William's actions. The court ruled that the transfer of the real estate was a gift conditioned upon a subsequent ceremonial marriage, and it ordered Beth to transfer interest in the property to William.

The majority rule appears to be that B must transfer back to A a gift received and held under the following circumstances: A and B are engaged to be married to each other. In contemplation of the formal commencement of that life of bliss A makes a gift to B. Later, through no fault of A, B breaks the engagement. The majority of courts reason that such a gift was conditioned upon a subsequent ceremonial marriage. We adopt the majority rule as applied to the facts here and affirm the trial court's conclusion that the deed was conditioned upon a subsequent ceremonial marriage.

Beth contends that recovery of the property under these circumstances is proscribed by the Statute of Frauds and the Heart Balm Statute. The Statute of Frauds does not prevent the declaration of a constructive trust. By the same reasoning it does not prevent recovery of property delivered conditionally under the particular circumstances here.

The Heart Balm Statute reads:

> All civil causes of action for breach of promise to marry, alienation of affections, criminal conversation, and seduction are hereby abolished.

No act done within this state shall operate to give rise, either within or without this state, to any of the rights of action abolished [herein]. No contract to marry made or entered into in this state shall operate to give rise, either within or without this state, to any cause or right of action for the breach thereof, nor shall any contract to marry made in any other state give rise to any cause of action within this state for the breach thereof.

We follow the rule that this statute bars actions for damages suffered from breach of promise to marry and other direct consequences of the breach, such as humiliation; but that it should not be extended to affect common-law principles governing a gift to a fiancee made on condition of marriage, with condition broken by the donee.

Judgment affirmed.

NOTES AND QUESTIONS

1.   Today some courts permit a donor to recover an engagement gift only if the donee breaks the engagement or if the engagement is broken by mutual consent. *See* Curtis v. Anderson, 106 S.W.3d 251 (Tex. App. 2003); Byam v. Jackson, 2011 WL 3035273 (Del. Com. Pl.) (engagement broken by mutual consent), citing Spinnell v. Quigley, 785 P.2d 1149 (Wash. App. 1990). "Bad behavior" (violence, an affair, etc.) that causes the broken engagement may also be taken into account. Some other states permit recovery of engagement gifts regardless of who breaks the engagement. *See, e.g.,* Fowler v. Perry, 830 N.E.2d 97 (Ind. App. 2005); Heiman v. Parrish, 942 P.2d 631 (Kan. 1997); Aronow v. Silver, 538 A.2d 851 (N.J. Super. 1987); Vigil v. Haber, 888 P.2d 455 (N.M. 1994). Which approach seems better?

2.   What, if any, recovery is appropriate when:

(a)   An engaged couple opens and jointly contributes to a bank account. The woman ends the engagement and withdraws all of the funds in the account (almost $350,000) after she learns that the man is having an affair. *See* Lee v. Yang, 3 Cal. Rptr. 3d 819 (App. 2003).

(b)   A woman becomes engaged in bad faith. Her fiancé purchases a house and titles it in her name. She thereafter breaks the engagement. *See* Nani v. Vanasse, 2006 WL 8089630 (R.I. Super. Feb. 6, 2006).

3.   For this "conditional gift" doctrine to apply, the couple needs to be engaged to be married. In Torres v. Lopez, 3 N.Y.S.3d 287 (Dist. Ct. 2014), the man gave the woman a ring while they were cohabiting. The court found that they were never "engaged," so this conditional gift theory did not apply.

4.   If a man gives an "engagement ring" to a woman still married to another, it will not be considered a conditional gift. *See* Lipschutz v. Kiderman, 905 N.Y.S.2d 247 (App. Div. 2010).

5.   In a Utah case, a man paid the couple's travel expenses to Alaska and France while engaged. The Utah court did not permit him to recover any such expenditures because it was not clear that he paid the expenses conditioned on a marriage taking place. *See* Hess v. Johnston, 163 P.3d 747 (Utah App. 2007).

Similarly, an Ohio court concluded that only engagement rings should be considered conditional gifts between engaged people. *See* Cooper v. Smith, 800 N.E.2d 372 (Ohio App. 2003).

B. APPLICABILITY OF *MARVIN* TO DATING PARTNERS

COCHRAN V. COCHRAN
California Court of Appeals, 2001.
89 Cal. App. 4th 283, 106 Cal. Rptr. 2d 899.

I.   INTRODUCTION

Plaintiff and cross-complainant Patricia A. Cochran appeals from the judgment of dismissal entered after the trial court sustained without leave to amend the demurrers which defendant and cross-defendant Johnnie L. Cochran, Jr., brought to her cross-complaint for rescission of their 1983 property settlement agreement. She also appeals from the summary judgment entered for the defendant on her complaint for breach of an alleged agreement for lifetime support. For the reasons set forth below, we reverse both judgments.

II.   PROCEDURAL HISTORY

This is the third appeal arising from two separate, but related, actions between appellant Patricia A. Cochran (appellant) and respondent Johnnie L. Cochran, Jr. (respondent) arising out of their long-term, nonmarital relationship. The first action was filed in March 1995. The operative, first amended complaint of April 1995 was primarily concerned with respondent's alleged breach of a supposed *Marvin* agreement to provide appellant with lifetime support. In *Cochran v. Cochran*, 56 Cal. App. 4th 1115, 66 Cal. Rptr. 2d 337 (1997) (*Cochran I*), we held that the statute of limitations for breach of a *Marvin* agreement did not begin to run until the defendant failed to perform as the agreement required. As a result of our decision, all that remained of the complaint in *Cochran I* were causes of action based on the alleged *Marvin* agreement.

The second action was filed in November 1996 while the appeal in *Cochran I* was still pending. The original complaint in the second action included a cause of action seeking to rescind a 1983 property settlement agreement because the agreement was induced by fraud. The operative first amended complaint omitted the rescission claim, but sought damages for intentional infliction of emotional distress based on a message left on a telephone answering machine which appellant construed as a death threat.

In *Cochran v. Cochran*, 65 Cal. App. 4th 488, 498–499, 76 Cal. Rptr. 2d 540 (1998) (*Cochran II*), we held that the message was not actionable as a death threat.

After our decision in *Cochran I* became final, that action was remanded to the trial court. On January 26, 1998, respondent cross-complained against appellant, contending she had breached the confidentiality provisions of their 1983 property settlement agreement by appearing on television to discuss their relationship. Appellant answered the cross-complaint on February 11, 1998, and filed a cross-complaint of her own ("the fraud cross-complaint"), seeking to rescind the 1983 settlement agreement because it allegedly had been induced by respondent's fraud. Respondent dismissed his cross-complaint without prejudice on March 13, 1998. He then demurred to the fraud cross-complaint, contending among other things that it was barred by the statute of limitations and was contrary to certain verified allegations in the *Cochran I* complaint concerning the validity of the settlement agreement. By minute order dated April 2, 1999, the trial court sustained the demurrers without leave to amend on two grounds: (1) the fraud cross-complaint was barred by appellant's earlier allegations; and (2) the action was also barred under the law of the case doctrine by our decision in *Cochran I*.

In November 1999 respondent moved for summary judgment on the *Cochran I* complaint, contending appellant could not prevail on her remaining *Marvin* claims because: (1) the parties were not cohabiting when the agreement was made; (2) the alleged promise of support was made under circumstances which made it unreasonable to believe the statements were a contractual offer; (3) the alleged promise to support was too uncertain to be enforced; and (4) in any event, the claim was barred by the statute of limitations. The motion was granted and judgment for respondent was entered December 21, 1999. This appeal followed.

Appellant and respondent began their relationship in 1966, at a time when respondent was still married to his first wife. Appellant later changed her surname to match respondent's. In 1973, the parties' son was born. In 1974, appellant and respondent bought a house in North Hollywood. Title was eventually placed in both their names as joint tenants. Respondent also owned a home on Hobart Street. He and appellant split their living time between the two homes. Respondent stayed with appellant and their son at the North Hollywood home from two to four nights a week. He kept clothes there and took meals at the house. Respondent held himself out to the world as appellant's husband. In 1978, respondent divorced his first wife.

In 1983, they experienced relationship troubles after appellant learned respondent was unfaithful. On October 21, 1983, they signed the property settlement agreement. Pursuant to the settlement agreement, respondent quitclaimed to appellant all his interest in their North Hollywood house. He agreed, among other things, to pay child support of $350 each month, to buy appellant a new car, to pay for construction of a swimming pool at the North Hollywood house, and to provide medical and dental insurance for their son. The agreement was expressly limited to claims then existing and included assurances of full disclosure as to all assets then owned by the parties. It did not include a waiver or release of future or unknown claims.

Within one to three weeks of signing the settlement agreement, respondent told appellant he wanted to keep things as they had been before. He also promised to care for her "financially, emotionally and legally" for the rest of her life. In return, she agreed to maintain their home and care for respondent and their son.[26] After that time, he continued to live with appellant and her son "as he had before." Appellant said respondent "wanted me to continue providing a home and continue our lifestyle and he was going to continue supporting me." The support agreement was formed as part of discussions about the future of their relationship, their continued love for each other, and their desire to eventually marry. Appellant said she wanted proof of respondent's fidelity before marriage, "so we were working on that."

Appellant said in her declaration that after the support agreement was formed, respondent "continued to live with me and our son at the [North Hollywood] house as he had done before. . . He continued to support me as he had promised until February 1995." Much of respondent's summary judgment motion centered on the form of that support, and whether it was sufficient to make the agreement enforceable or was so sporadic that it constituted a breach of the agreement which set the statute of limitations running by 1985.

In 1985, respondent married his second wife. Between 1984 and late 1992 or January 1993, appellant worked for a company named Ipson. During those years, respondent helped pay for various of appellant's expenses. He gave her cash and paid her bills as needed, including utilities and medical insurance. He twice provided her with new cars and sometimes paid for car repairs. Respondent also gave appellant credit cards issued in either her name or respondent's, with respondent paying the charges she incurred. During those years, respondent "paid child support for [their son] . . . and gave me money whenever I needed it. [Respondent] paid amounts over the $350.00 required in the [1983] Settlement Agreement because he and I understood that more was required to maintain the standard of living to which me [sic] and our son were

---

[26] Respondent's summary judgment motion did not dispute appellant's assertion that respondent made such a promise. For ease of reference, we will refer to the agreement which appellant contends she entered as "the support agreement."

accustomed. Throughout this period of time, [respondent] and I spoke on a regular basis and [respondent] knew what my financial needs were. When I needed funds he always provided funds as he promised." Cancelled checks produced by respondent showed child support payments of $1,000 were made at least as of 1991 through January 1995. A notice from appellant's bank showed that respondent wrote her a check for $4,500 in or about May 1991. However, appellant admitted that the support she received was not regular, either in amount or time of payment.

At respondent's behest, on or about January 1993, appellant left her job at Ipson. After that, in accord with the support agreement, respondent provided regular, monthly support checks for appellant. Respondent also made direct deposits to appellant's bank account. Appellant testified that the total was between $3,500 and $4,000 each month. Respondent also gave appellant cash, paid her credit card bills, car expenses, medical insurance, and cellular phone bills. Respondent concedes he provided regular support for appellant after she left her job, but contends he agreed to do so at his son's request only until appellant got another job.

Respondent produced copies of more than 200 cancelled checks in connection with payments made to appellant or their son between September 1990 and December 1998. Many were made payable to appellant, but bore notations indicating they were for child support or other expenses related to the parties' son. Several were payable to appellant herself: a July 1993 deposit of $1,500 to appellant's bank account; an August 1993 check for $375; a September 1993 check for $1,500 bearing the notation "Expenses"; and many others between January 1994 and February 1995 in amounts ranging from $1,800 to $3,557. Respondent admitted that he was unsure whether the checks he produced were all those relating to the support of either appellant or their son. He admitted that there might be other checks written on different accounts.

V.   Discussion

Respondent also contends that the support agreement is unenforceable because he and appellant did not cohabitate, or live together. Viewing the evidence in appellant's favor, it appears that before entering the 1983 settlement and support agreements, respondent stayed at the North Hollywood house two to four nights a week. Appellant and the parties' son sometimes stayed at respondent's house on Hobart Street. Appellant stated in her declaration that after respondent made his support promises, he continued to live with her as he had before. However, from her deposition testimony it is apparent that after respondent remarried in 1985, he stayed at the house less often. Appellant testified she was not sure whether respondent ever spent the night after his remarriage, although he did come for frequent visits, with appellant continuing to prepare his meals.

The *Marvin* court held "that adults who voluntarily *live together* and engage in sexual relations are nonetheless as competent as any other persons to contract respecting their earnings and property rights." So long as the agreement does not depend upon meretricious sexual relations for its consideration, or so long as that portion of the consideration may be severed from other proper forms of consideration, such agreements are enforceable.

In *Taylor v. Fields* (1986) 178 Cal. App. 3d 653, 224 Cal. Rptr. 186 (*Taylor*), the court seized upon the italicized "live together" reference in *Marvin* to hold that a dead man's mistress, who never lived with the decedent, was not entitled to enforce their purported *Marvin* agreement. Examining *Marvin* and other related decisions, the *Taylor* court held that cohabitation was a prerequisite to recovery under *Marvin*. Because the appellant's agreement in *Taylor* rested upon an illicit sexual relationship for its consideration, it was not enforceable.

Taylor was followed by *Bergen v. Wood*, 14 Cal. App. 4th 854, 18 Cal. Rptr. 2d 75 (1993) (*Bergen*). The plaintiff in *Bergen* had a long-term sexual relationship with the decedent, acting as his hostess and social companion. Though he had supposedly promised to support the plaintiff, they never lived together. In reversing a judgment for the plaintiff, the *Bergen* court noted that cohabitation was required under *Marvin* "not in and of itself, but rather, because from cohabitation flows the rendition of domestic services, which services amount to lawful consideration for a contract between the parties."

We make the additional observation that if cohabitation were not a prerequisite to recovery, every dating relationship would have the potential for giving rise to such claims, a result no one favors. Citing both *Marvin* and *Taylor*, the *Bergen* court noted that recovery under *Marvin* "requires a showing of a stable and significant relationship arising out of cohabitation." Because the plaintiff never lived with her decedent, it was impossible to sever the sexual component of their relationship from other appropriate consideration.

Citing *Taylor* and *Bergen*, respondent contends that his relationship with appellant did not involve cohabitation, since the evidence showed that he spent as little as one night a week at appellant's house after their property settlement agreement was reached in 1983. As a result, he characterizes their relationship as no more than "dating." On the other hand, appellant relies on *Bergen's* statement that cohabitation was required not in and of itself, but in order to establish lawful consideration through the performance of domestic services. Since appellant provided such services, she contends there was lawful consideration even absent cohabitation. Alternatively, she contends that there was sufficient evidence to raise a triable issue of fact as to the issue of cohabitation.

We save for another day the issue whether consenting adults need cohabit *at all* in order to enter an enforceable agreement regarding their earnings and property. Assuming for discussion's sake that cohabitation is required, we conclude that the rationale of *Marvin* is satisfied in appropriate cases by a cohabitation arrangement that is less than full-time. Here, as so construed, there was sufficient evidence to raise a triable issue of fact on the cohabitation element.

Both *Taylor* and *Bergen* considered claims by parties who served, in effect, as the mistress or girlfriend of their respective decedents. Neither plaintiff had *ever* cohabited with their respective decedents. Moreover, neither decision considered whether anything less than a full-time living arrangement was necessary to show cohabitation. By contrast, in the present case, when respondent supposedly entered the support agreement in late October or early November of 1983, he and appellant had shared a relationship for approximately 17 years. That relationship produced a son, whom they were raising together. They held themselves out to the world as husband and wife. Appellant legally changed her surname to respondent's. They had jointly owned their home until respondent quitclaimed his interest as part of their settlement agreement. Appellant performed a variety of domestic chores for respondent, including raising their son and maintaining the house. Respondent kept clothes at the house, "spent family time there" and "slept there on a regular basis."

At common law, the term "cohabitation" means to live together as husband and wife. (*People v. Ballard*, 203 Cal. App. 3d 311, 317–318, 249 Cal. Rptr. 806 (1988) (*Ballard*).) Various criminal law decisions have construed this common law meaning in the context of reviewing convictions of inflicting corporal injury on a cohabitant. (Pen. Code, §§ 273.5.) These decisions all conclude that cohabitation may exist even if the cohabitants do not live together full-time. In *Ballard*, after examining the common law definition of cohabitation, the court held that even though the defendant maintained a separate apartment, there was sufficient evidence of cohabitation. The court cited evidence that the defendant and his victim had lived together for two years, slept together in one bed, and were often together. In *People v. Holifield*, 205 Cal. App. 3d 993, 252 Cal. Rptr. 729 (1988), the defendant and his victim had seen each other "off and on" for four years. In the three months before the assault, the defendant stayed in at least three other places for weeks at a time, taking his possessions with him whenever he left. He stored clothes and personal items at three other homes and did not have a key to the victim's room. They did not share rent or make joint purchases, did not spend much free time together and had infrequent sexual relations. On those facts, the court upheld a finding that the two were cohabiting.

We find these decisions both persuasive and analogous on the issue of cohabitation in the context of a *Marvin* agreement. The purpose of *Marvin* was to permit parties to a significant and stable relationship to contract concerning their earnings and property rights. "So long as the agreement does not rest upon illicit meretricious consideration, the parties may order their economic affairs as they choose * * * " (*Marvin, supra.*) To require nothing short of full-time cohabitation before enforcing an agreement would defeat the reasonable expectations of persons who may clearly enjoy a significant and stable relationship arising from cohabitation, albeit less than a full-time living arrangement. For instance, it would exclude otherwise valid support agreements made by parties who, perhaps because their jobs are geographically far apart, maintain a part-time residence for one party, and also a second residence where at times they live jointly. Certainly the rationale of *Marvin* does not support such a result.

Here, the parties had shared a long-term, stable and significant relationship. In this context, evidence that they lived together two to four days a week both before and at the time they entered their *Marvin* agreement is sufficient to raise a triable issue of fact that they cohabitated under *Marvin*.

VI. DISPOSITION

For the reasons set forth above, we direct the trial court to enter nunc pro tunc a judgment dismissing the fraud cross-complaint based upon its orders sustaining respondent's demurrers to that pleading. To the extent appellant appeals from the order sustaining those demurrers, we deem the appeal to be taken from that judgment. The judgment of dismissal on the fraud cross-complaint and the summary judgment on the complaint are reversed. Appellant to recover her costs on appeal.

NOTES AND QUESTIONS

1.   It apparently is becoming more common for people to have a committed intimate relationship and separate residences. *See* Andrew Cherlin, *Demographic Trends in the U.S.: A Review of Research in the 2000s,* 72 J. MARR. & FAM. 403, 410 (2010); Jill Brooke, *Home Alone Together*, N.Y. TIMES, May 4, 2006 at Dl. What facts or public policies justify extending *Marvin* to part-time cohabitation? refusing to extend *Marvin* to sexual partners who don't cohabit? *See, e.g.*, Levine v. Konvitz, 890 A.2d 354 (N.J. Super. App. Div. 2006) (concluding that cohabitation is a sensible requirement because it provides notice to the parties and their families). If *Marvin* remedies exist only if parties cohabit, what does this mean? If parties spend most nights together but have separate residences, are they cohabiting? Does one have to cohabit for a certain minimum time to be able to asset a *Marvin* claim?

2.   A married man and a woman had an intimate relationship lasting 23 years where the man continually promised he would divorce his wife, marry her, and take care of her of the rest of her life. If the man does not do this and eventually ends the relationship, does the woman have a good legal claim? If

so, what remedy is appropriate? *See* Norton v. McOsker, 407 F.3d 501 (1st Cir. 2005). *See also,* M.N. v. D.S., 616 N.W.2d 284 (Minn. App. 2000).

3.   Although many courts have limited *Marvin* remedies to those who cohabit, dating partners have a full range of tort claims and defenses. For example, a number of courts have permitted recovery for misrepresentation leading to the transmission of a sexually communicable disease. *See* Kathleen K. v. Robert B., 198 Cal. Rptr. 273 (App. 1984); Meany v. Meany, 639 So. 2d 229 (La. 1994). A Massachusetts District Court has ruled that a tort claim might be possible if one dating partner accesses the other's e-mail account or social media accounts without permission. Mahoney v. DeNuzzio, 40 Fam. L. Rep. (BNA) 1152 (Mass. D. Ct. 2014).

Some Concluding Thoughts

In Chapters 1 through 6, we have seen concrete evidence of the "increasing fluidity, detachability and interchangeability of family relationships" outlined by Professor Glendon in Chapter 1. Distinctions between nonmarital cohabitation and marriage are blurring. Loosened marriage laws have reduced or eliminated many substantive and most formal restrictions on entry into marriage. Entry into marriage is nearly unrestricted, and—as we will see in Chapter 12—exit from marriage is all but unlimited. Moreover, relaxation of restrictions that traditionally governed premarital contracts has made it increasingly possible for marriage partners to individualize the terms of their marriage, typically by contracting "down" from statutory marriage. On the other side of the spectrum, cohabitants are contracting "up" from no-consequences liaisons.

Has competition from new lifestyles forced the downgrading of marriage, or has the downgrading of marriage made nonmarital cohabitation a more competitive option? Or are the decline of traditional marriage and the increase in cohabitation simply parallel developments marking a general withdrawal from traditional standards and mores? Who knows? Ironically, marriage (or a modern variant) may gain strength from the "forced marriage" concept implicit in the *Marvin* and *Connell* doctrines. This raises a question of labels: Are *Marvin* and *Connell* "reactionary" or "progressive?" Do they discourage out-of-wedlock cohabitation by making a "free union" less free? Do they resurrect the time-honored (but in this day—one might have thought—outdated) legal institution of "concubinage," conferring on the "concubine" a legal status somewhere below that of a wife?

Consider MARY ANN GLENDON, STATE, LAW AND FAMILY 85, 91 (1977):

The *union libre*, or free union, is a venerable institution in French law. Despite the fact that it is almost completely ignored by the Civil Code, and only discreetly alluded to in other legislation, it has acquired enough of a legal existence through the case law to be described in the leading treatises as comparable to the Roman *concubinatus*, a kind of qualitatively inferior marriage with legal attributes. The fact that a chapter on the *union libre* is a standard feature in French treatises on civil law is itself a sign of its established character. * * * [I]t seems to be distinctive of the French developments that the *union libre* has come to resemble legal marriage by drawing to itself many of the legal effects of marriage and by imitating others. Thus, it is possible to see the French situation as one in which the legitimate family prevails after all: "In appearance, it has certainly lost ground, but in fact it has imposed the matrimonial model on those who have declined to marry. No longer bothering to look down on its adversaries, it has transformed them in its own image."

No method of regulating nonmarital cohabitation is perfect. Cohabitation without marriage permits separation without "divorce" and without financial consequences. But cohabitation without marriage *and with Connell* will encroach (perhaps unduly) upon the personal freedom of the parties. And cohabitation without marriage *and with Marvin* may encourage frivolous litigation and lead to unpredictable, "hit-or-miss" results. *See* Ruth Deech, *The Case Against Legal Recognition of Cohabitation*, 29 INT. & COMP. L. Q. 480 (1980).

No matter what attitude a state adopts on the broad issues raised by nonmarital cohabitation, basic legal problems arising in such relationships will still have to be resolved. These inescapable problems include paternity of the unmarried woman's children [Chapter 7], the rights of the father to custody [Chapter 14] or to veto an adoption [Chapter 8] of the children, support duties to the children [Chapter 17], as well property rights in (joint?) acquisitions during the period of cohabitation.

CHAPTER 7

BECOMING A PARENT: CONTRACEPTION, ABORTION, AND PATERNITY

■ ■ ■

Paternity is a legal fiction.

JAMES JOYCE, ULYSSES (1922)

I regard sex as the central problem of life.

HAVELOCK ELLIS, STUDIES IN THE PSYCHOLOGY OF SEX

In an earlier era, becoming a parent was a relatively simple, if often accidental, matter. A man and a woman engaged in sexual intercourse and conceived a child. When a woman was married, her husband was presumed to be the child's father. With no medical tests available to disprove parentage, the presumption was rarely rebutted. When a woman was unmarried, a "shotgun" marriage was hastily arranged, an illegal (and probably unsafe) abortion was obtained, or the pregnancy was concealed to the extent possible and the baby given up for adoption at birth. In the rare event that the unmarried woman gave birth to a child and kept it, she faced scandal and the problem of establishing paternity without modern medical technology.

Technological and social changes have dramatically altered both the process of becoming a parent and the legal determination of parentage. With highly effective contraception techniques, procreation can be avoided; with access to legal abortion, pregnancy can be terminated at will; with sophisticated medical tests, paternity is relatively easy to establish or rebut. And, as a result of altered social mores, the unmarried woman who becomes pregnant no longer faces social opprobrium if she gives birth. Indeed, forty percent of U.S. births now occur out of wedlock. From an evidentiary perspective, the legal determination of parentage is now simpler; from a normative perspective, it is perhaps more complex.

1. CONTRACEPTION AND ABORTION

Although contraceptives have been known for generations, modern science has made it easier, safer, and cheaper to prevent pregnancy. The first contraceptive pills were marketed in 1960, the first intrauterine devices (IUDs) in 1963. At the time these new, highly effective means of contraception came on the market, many states and the federal government had laws, most dating from the late 19th century, that forbade their dissemination and/or use. The 1873 Comstock Law (18 U.S.C.A. §§ 1461–62) outlawed both the importation and mail transmittal of all articles designed to prevent conception. Although the law was not enforced after the 1920s, it was not repealed until 1971.

As you saw in Chapter 2, the Supreme Court struck down a state statute criminalizing the dispensing of contraceptives to a married couple in Griswold v. Connecticut, 381 U.S. 479 (1965). Although the *Griswold* court related its holding to "notions of privacy surrounding the marriage relationship," in Eisenstadt v. Baird, 405 U.S. 438 (1972), the Court relied on the Equal Protection Clause and extended its *Griswold* holding to the unmarried. Thereafter, in Carey v. Population Services International, 431 U.S. 678 (1977), the Court struck down a law forbidding: (i) sale of all contraceptives by anyone other than a licensed pharmacist; (ii) any sale of contraceptives to minors younger than sixteen; and (iii) all advertisement or display of contraceptives. The court found no compelling state interest in any of these prohibitions:

> That the constitutionally protected right of privacy extends to an individual's liberty to make choices regarding contraception does not * * * automatically invalidate every state regulation in this area. The business of manufacturing and selling contraceptives may be regulated in ways that do not infringe protected individual choices. And even a burdensome regulation may be validated by a sufficiently compelling state interest. * * *

> Restrictions on the distribution of contraceptives clearly burden the freedom to make such decisions. * * * This is so not because there is an independent fundamental "right of access to contraceptives," but because such access is essential to exercise of the constitutionally protected right of decision in matters of childbearing that is the underlying foundation of the holdings in *Griswold* [and] *Eisenstadt*. * * *

Id. at 686–688.

NOTES AND QUESTIONS

1.   *Unintended Pregnancy*: Approximately half of all U.S. pregnancies are unintended, including approximately three-quarters among women under age twenty. Unintended pregnancy is associated with increased risks for both the mother and infant. Smoking, drinking alcohol, unsafe sex practices, poor nutrition, and inadequate intake of foods containing folic acid are more common among women with unintended pregnancies. Women whose pregnancy is unintentional are also much less likely to obtain prenatal care

I take issue w/ this phrasing.

during the first trimester. If access to contraception is constitutionally guaranteed, why are 41% of children born out of wedlock? Evidence indicates that the reason is that many of the out-of-wedlock births are no longer "unintentional." The number of first births to cohabiting women tripled from 9% in 1985 to 27% in 2010. Gladys Martinez, et al. *Fertility of Men and Women Aged 15–44 Years in the United States: National Survey of Family Growth*, 51 National Health Statistics Report (April 12, 2012), available at www.cdc.gov/nchs/data/nhsr/nhsr051.pdf.

The right to contracep. is guaranteed. Access is a whole

2.   Many states and localities permit minors to obtain contraceptives without parental consent or notification. For example, COLO. REV. STAT. § 13–22–105 allows a minor to obtain birth control information and supplies when referred * * * by another physician, a clergyman, a family planning clinic, a school * * *. In 2010, the teen birth rate dropped to 34.3 per 1000, the lowest rate in decades. *Births: Preliminary Data for 2010*, 60 (2) NAT'L VITAL STAT. REP. (Nov. 17, 2011). Is access to contraceptives the major reason? Although the teen birth rate has declined nationally, it is still the highest in the developed world.

3.   Some of the newer contraceptives offer long-lasting protection against pregnancy. For example, Norplant, approved by the FDA in 1990, offers protection for up to five years after insertion of drug-releasing capsules into a woman's upper arm. Fertility is restored when the capsules are removed. The state legislature is considering the enactment of legislation that would mandate Norplant use by women receiving public assistance benefits on behalf of minor children and those convicted of child abuse or neglect. If enacted, would the legislation be constitutional? *See* David S. Coale, Note, *Norplant Bonuses and the Unconstitutional Conditions Doctrine*, 71 TEX. L. REV. 189 (1992); Stacey L. Arthur, *The Norplant Prescription Birth Control, Woman Control, or Crime Control?* 40 UCLA L. REV. 1 (1992).   *HELL   NO*

ROE V. WADE

Supreme Court of the United States,1973.
410 U.S. 113.

JUSTICE BLACKMUN delivered the opinion of the Court.

This Texas Federal appeal and its Georgia companion * * * present constitutional challenges to state criminal abortion legislation. * * *

We forthwith acknowledge our awareness of the sensitive and emotional nature of the abortion controversy, of the vigorous opposing views, even among physicians, and of the deep and seemingly absolute convictions that the subject inspires. * * * Our task, of course, is to resolve the issue by constitutional measurement, free of emotion and predilection. We seek earnestly to do this, and, because we do, we have inquired into, and * * * place some emphasis upon, medical and medical-legal history and what that history reveals about man's attitudes toward abortion procedure over the centuries. * * *

really?

I.

The Texas statutes that concern us here * * * make it a crime to "procure an abortion," as therein defined, or to attempt one, except with respect to "an abortion procured or attempted by medical advice for the purpose of saving the life of the mother." Similar statutes are in existence in a majority of the states.

* * *

VI.

It perhaps is not generally appreciated that the restrictive criminal abortion laws in effect in a majority of States today are of relatively recent vintage. * * * It is undisputed that at common law, abortion performed before "quickening"—the first recognizable movement of the fetus in *utero*, appearing usually from the 16th to the 18th week of pregnancy, was not an indictable offense. The absence of a common-law crime for pre-quickening abortion appears to have developed from a confluence of earlier philosophical, theological, and civil and canon law concepts of when life begins. * * *

VII.

Three reasons have been advanced to explain historically the enactment of criminal abortion laws in the 19th century and to justify their continued existence.

It has been argued occasionally that these laws were the product of a Victorian social concern to discourage illicit sexual conduct. Texas, however, does not advance this justification in the present case, and it appears that no court or commentator has taken the argument seriously. * * *

A second reason is concerned with abortion as a medical procedure. When most criminal abortion laws were first enacted, the procedure was a hazardous one for the woman. This was particularly true prior to the development of antisepsis. * * *

Modern medical techniques have altered this situation. * * * Mortality rates for women undergoing early abortions, where the procedure is legal, appear to be as low as or lower than the rates for normal childbirth. Consequently, any interest of the State in protecting the woman from an inherently hazardous procedure * * * has largely disappeared. * * *

The third reason is the State's interest—some phrase it in terms of duty—in protecting prenatal life. * * * Logically, of course, a legitimate state interest in this area need not stand or fall on acceptance of the belief that life begins at conception or at some other point prior to live birth. In assessing the State's interest, recognition may be given to the less rigid claim that as long as at least *potential* life is involved, the State may assert interests beyond the protection of the pregnant woman alone.

Parties challenging state abortion laws have sharply disputed in some courts the contention that a purpose of these laws, when enacted, was to protect prenatal life. Pointing to the absence of legislative history to support the contention, they claim that most state laws were designed solely to protect the woman. Because medical advances have lessened this concern, at least with respect to abortion in early pregnancy, they argue that with respect to such abortions the laws can no longer be justified by any state interest. There is some scholarly support for this view of original purpose. The few state courts called upon to interpret their laws in the late 19th and early 20th centuries did focus on the State's interest in protecting the woman's health rather than in preserving the embryo and fetus. Proponents of this view point out that in many States, * * * by statute or judicial interpretation, the pregnant woman herself could not be prosecuted for self-abortion or for cooperating in an abortion performed upon her by another. They claim that adoption of the "quickening" distinction through received common law and state statutes tacitly recognizes the greater health hazards inherent in late abortion and impliedly repudiates the theory that life begins at conception.

It is with these interests, and the weight to be attached to them, that this case is concerned.

VIII.

The Constitution does not explicitly mention any right of privacy. * * * [But] [i]n varying contexts, the Court or individual Justices have * * * found * * * the roots of that right in the First Amendment; in the Fourth and Fifth Amendments, in the penumbras of the Bill of Rights, *Griswold v. Connecticut*, 381 U.S. 479 (1965), in the Ninth Amendment, *id.;* or in the concept of liberty guaranteed by the first section of the Fourteenth Amendment (*see Meyer v. Nebraska* 262 U.S. 390 (1923)). These decisions make it clear that only personal rights that can be deemed "fundamental" or "implicit in the concept of ordered liberty," are included in this guarantee of personal privacy. They also make it clear that the right has some extension to activities relating to marriage, *Loving v. Virginia,* 388 U.S. 1, 12 (1967); procreation, *Eisenstadt v. Baird*, 405 U.S. 438 (1972); (White, J., concurring in result); family relationships, *Prince v. Massachusetts*, 321 U.S. 158, 166 (1944); and child rearing and education, *Pierce v. Society of Sisters*, 268 U.S. 510, 535 (1925); *Meyer v. Nebraska, supra.*

This right of privacy, whether it be founded in the Fourteenth Amendment's concept of personal liberty and restrictions upon state action, as we feel it is, or, as the District Court determined, in the Ninth Amendment's reservation of rights to the people, is broad enough to encompass a woman's decision whether or not to terminate her pregnancy.

The detriment that the State would impose upon the pregnant woman by denying this choice altogether is apparent. Specific and direct harm medically diagnosable even in early pregnancy may be involved. Maternity, or additional offspring, may force upon the woman a distressful life and future. Psychological harm may be imminent. Mental and physical health may be taxed by child care. There is also the distress, for all concerned, associated with the unwanted child, and there is the problem of bringing a child into a family already unable, psychologically and otherwise, to care for it. In other cases, as in this one, the additional difficulties and continuing stigma of unwed motherhood may be involved. All these are factors the woman and her responsible physician necessarily will consider in consultation.

* * * The Court's decisions recognizing a right of privacy also acknowledge that some state regulation in areas protected by that right is appropriate. A * * * State may properly assert important interests in safeguarding health, in maintaining medical standards, and in protecting potential life. At some point in pregnancy, these respective interests become sufficiently compelling to sustain regulation of the factors that govern the abortion decision. * * * We, therefore, conclude that the right of personal privacy includes the abortion decision, but that this right is not unqualified and must be considered against important state interests in regulation.

* * *

Where certain "fundamental rights" are involved, the Court has held that regulation limiting these rights may be justified only by a "compelling state interest," and that legislative enactments must be narrowly drawn to express only the legitimate state interests at stake. * * *

IX.

Texas urges that * * * life begins at conception and is present throughout pregnancy, and that, therefore, the State has a compelling interest in protecting that life from and after conception. We need not resolve the difficult question of when life begins. When those trained in the respective disciplines of medicine, philosophy, and theology are unable to arrive at any consensus, the judiciary, at this point in the development of man's knowledge, is not in a position to speculate as to the answer.

It should be sufficient to note briefly the wide divergence of thinking on this most sensitive and difficult question. There has always been strong support for the view that life does not begin until live birth. * * *

In areas other than criminal abortion, the law has been reluctant to endorse any theory that life, as we recognize it, begins before live birth or to accord legal rights to the unborn except in narrowly defined situations and except when the rights are contingent upon live birth. For example, the traditional rule of tort law denied recovery for prenatal injuries even though the child was born alive. That rule has been changed in almost every jurisdiction. In most States, recovery is said to be permitted only if the fetus was viable, or at least quick, when the injuries were sustained, though few courts have squarely so held. In a recent development, generally opposed by the commentators, some States permit the parents of a stillborn child to maintain an action for wrongful death because of prenatal injuries. Such an action, however, would appear to be one to vindicate the parents' interest and is thus consistent with the view that the fetus, at most, represents only the potentiality of life. Similarly, unborn children have been recognized as acquiring rights or interests by way of inheritance or other devolution of property, and have been represented by guardians ad litem. Perfection of the interests involved, again, has generally been contingent upon live birth. In short, the unborn have never been recognized in the law as persons in the whole sense.

X.

The Constitution does not define "person" in so many words. Section 1 of the Fourteenth Amendment contains three references to "person." The first, in defining "citizens" speaks of "persons born or naturalized in the United States." The word also appears both in the Due Process Clause and in the Equal Protection Clause. "Person" is used in other places in the Constitution * * * [b]ut in nearly all these instances, the use of the word is such that it has application only post-natally. None indicates, with any assurance, that it has any possible pre-natal application. * * *

All this, together with our observation, that throughout the major portion of the 19th century prevailing legal abortion practices were far freer than they are today, persuades us that the word "persons," as used in the Fourteenth Amendment, does not include the unborn. * * *

* * * We repeat, however, that the State does have an important and legitimate interest in preserving and protecting the health of the pregnant woman * * * and that it has still another important and legitimate interest in protecting the potentiality of human life. These interests are separate and distinct. Each grows in substantiality as the woman approaches term and, at a point during pregnancy, each becomes "compelling."

[handwritten margin note: The woman's life isn't already compelling?]

With respect to the State's important and legitimate interest in the health of the mother, the "compelling" point, in the light of present medical knowledge, is at approximately the end of the first trimester. This is so because of the now-established medical fact * * * that until the end of the first trimester mortality in abortion may be less than mortality in normal childbirth. It follows that, from and after this point, a State may regulate the abortion procedure to the extent that the regulation reasonably relates to the preservation and protection of maternal health. Examples of permissible state regulation in this area are requirements as to the qualifications of the person who is to perform the abortion; as to the licensure of that person; as to the facility in which the procedure is to be performed, that is, whether it must be a hospital or may be a clinic or some other place of less-than-hospital status; as to the licensing of the facility; and the like.

This means, on the other hand, that, for the period of pregnancy prior to this "compelling" point, the attending physician, in consultation with his patient, is free to determine, without regulation by the State, that, in his medical judgment, the patient's pregnancy should be terminated. If that decision is reached, the judgment may be effectuated by an abortion free of interference by the State.

With respect to the State's important and legitimate interest in potential life, the "compelling" point is at viability. This is so because the fetus then presumably has the capability of meaningful life outside the mother's womb. State regulation protective of fetal life after viability thus has both logical and biological justifications. If the State is interested in protecting fetal life after viability, it may go so far as to proscribe abortion during that period, except when it is necessary to preserve the life or health of the mother.

Measured against these standards, * * * the Texas Penal Code, in restricting legal abortions to those "procured or attempted by medical advice for the purpose of saving the life of the mother," sweeps too broadly. * * *

XI.

To summarize and to repeat:

1. A state criminal abortion statute of the current Texas type, that excepts from criminality only a life-saving procedure on behalf of the mother, without regard to pregnancy stage and without recognition of the other interests involved, is violative of the Due Process Clause of the Fourteenth Amendment.

(a) For the stage prior to approximately the end of the first trimester, the abortion decision and its effectuation must be left to the medical judgment of the pregnant woman's attending physician.

(b) For the stage subsequent to approximately the end of the first trimester, the State, in promoting its interest in the health of the mother, may, if it chooses, regulate the abortion procedure in ways that are reasonably related to maternal health.

(c) For the stage subsequent to viability, the State in promoting its interest in the potentiality of human life may, if it chooses, regulate, and even proscribe, abortion except where it is necessary, in appropriate medical judgment, for the preservation of the life or health of the mother. * * *

This holding, we feel, is consistent with the relative weights of the respective interests involved, with the lessons and examples of medical and legal history, with the lenity of the common law, and with the demands of the profound problems of the present day. The decision leaves the State free to place increasing restrictions on abortion as the period of pregnancy lengthens, so long as those restrictions are tailored to the recognized state interests. The decision vindicates the right of the physician to administer medical treatment according to his professional judgment up to the points where important state interests provide compelling justifications for intervention. Up to those points, the abortion decision in all its aspects is inherently, and primarily, a medical decision, and basic responsibility for it must rest with the physician. If an individual practitioner abuses the privilege of exercising proper medical judgment, the usual remedies, judicial and intra-professional, are available. * * *

JUSTICE REHNQUIST, dissenting.

* * *

I have difficulty in concluding * * * that the right of privacy is involved in this case. The fact that a majority of the States reflecting, after all the majority sentiment in those States, have had restrictions on abortions for at least a century is a strong indication, it seems to me, that the asserted right to an abortion is not "so rooted in the traditions and conscience of our people as to be ranked as fundamental." Even today, when society's views on abortion are changing, the very existence of the debate is evidence that the "right" to an abortion is not so universally accepted as the appellant would have us believe.

To reach its result, the Court necessarily has had to find within the scope of the Fourteenth Amendment a right that was apparently completely unknown to the drafters of the Amendment. * * * By the time of the adoption of the Fourteenth Amendment in 1868, there were at least 36 laws enacted by state or territorial legislatures limiting abortion * * * 21 of * * * [which] remain in effect today. There apparently was no question concerning the validity of * * * state [abortion] statutes when the Fourteenth Amendment was adopted. The only conclusion possible from this history is that the drafters did not intend to have the Fourteenth Amendment withdraw from the States the power to legislate with respect to this matter. * * * I respectfully dissent.

NOTES AND QUESTIONS

1.   Is *Roe* consistent with *Griswold* and *Eisenstadt*?

2.   Following its decision in *Roe*, the United States Supreme Court reviewed a series of state abortion restrictions:

a.   *Hospital Setting:* The Supreme Court rejected a requirement that all abortions be performed in a hospital. Doe v. Bolton, 410 U.S. 179 (1973). The Court also rejected a requirement that all abortions after the first trimester be performed in an accredited hospital instead of an outpatient clinic as imposing "a heavy and unnecessary burden on women's access to a relatively inexpensive, otherwise accessible, and safe abortion procedure." City of Akron v. Akron Center for Reproductive Health, 462 U.S. 416 (1983) (*Akron I*).

b.   *Informed Consent and Waiting Periods:* The Supreme Court struck some of Ohio's "informed" consent and waiting period provisions which, the court concluded, were designed to "persuade * * * [the woman seeking an abortion] to withhold [consent] altogether." *Akron I, supra.* In Thornburgh v. American College of Obstetricians & Gynecologists, 476 U.S. 747 (1986), the Supreme Court struck down a Pennsylvania statute requiring doctors who performed abortions to provide a detailed report on the reason the fetus was not viable. A 2011 article reported that 35 states require preabortion counseling; 26 states require written materials on abortion with some including information on fetal pain and others covering preabortion ultrasounds. *See* John A. Robertson, *Abortion & Technology, Sonograms, Fetal Pain, Viability and Early Prenatal Diagnosis*, 14 U. PA. J. CONST. L. 327 (2011).

c.   *Fetal Testing and Protection:* In Planned Parenthood Ass'n v. Ashcroft, 462 U.S. 476 (1983), the Supreme Court upheld Missouri statutes requiring a pathology report on fetal tissue removed during an abortion and the attendance of a second physician to try to preserve the life of the unborn child. Planned Parenthood of Central Missouri v. Danforth, 428 U.S. 52 (1976), sustained a statutory definition of viability and later cases upheld most state attempts to preserve the life of the fetus. *Thornburgh, supra* note b.; Webster v. Reproductive Health Services, 492 U.S. 490 (1989).

d.   *Procedure Prohibitions:* A Missouri law prohibiting abortion by saline amniocentesis after the first trimester was invalidated in *Danforth, supra* note c.

3.   *Public Funding:* The Supreme Court has consistently upheld Congressional as well as state restrictions on the use of public funding or public facilities for abortion. *See* Maher v. Roe, 432 U.S. 464 (1977); Beal v. Doe et al., 432 U.S. 438 (1977); Poelker v. Doe, 432 U.S. 519 (1977). Federal funding for abortions came to an abrupt halt with the 1976 Hyde Amendment prohibiting the use of federal funds to reimburse states for the cost of abortion under

Medicaid. The Court upheld both the Hyde amendment (Harris v. McRae, 448 U.S. 297 (1980) and a state law prohibiting the use of public employees and facilities in performing or assisting in abortions not necessary to save the life of the mother (*Webster, supra* note c). Since 1994, states may no longer deny abortion to rape or incest victims and still claim federal reimbursement. Pub. L. 103–112, 107 Stat. 1082. *See* Elizabeth Blackwell Health Center for Women v. Knoll, 61 F.3d 170 (3d Cir. 1995); Little Rock Fam. Planning Servs. v. Dalton, 60 F.3d 497 (8th Cir. 1995). The Patient Protection and Affordable Care Act (ACA), Pub. L. 111–148, 124 Stat. 119 (2010) maintains the status quo on no abortion funding and allows health plans to choose the extent they cover abortion.

PLANNED PARENTHOOD V. CASEY

Supreme Court of the United States, 1992.
505 U.S. 833.

JUSTICE O'CONNOR, JUSTICE KENNEDY, and JUSTICE SOUTER announced the judgment of the Court and delivered the opinion of the Court with respect to Parts I, II, III, V-A, V-C, and VI, an opinion with respect to Part V-E, in which JUSTICE STEVENS joins, and an opinion with respect to Parts IV, V-B and V-D.

I

Liberty finds no refuge in a jurisprudence of doubt. Yet 19 years after our holding that the Constitution protects a woman's right to terminate her pregnancy in its early stages, Roe v. Wade, that definition of liberty is still questioned. Joining the respondents as *amicus curiae*, the United States, as it has done in five other cases in the last decade, again asks us to overrule *Roe*.

At issue in these cases are five provisions of the Pennsylvania Abortion Control Act of 1982 as amended in 1988 and 1989. The Act requires that a woman seeking an abortion give her informed consent prior to the abortion procedure, and specifies that she be provided with certain information at least 24 hours before the abortion is performed. * * * For a minor to obtain an abortion, the Act requires the informed consent of one of her parents, but provides for a judicial bypass option if the minor does not wish to or cannot obtain a parent's consent. * * * Another provision of the Act requires that, unless certain exceptions apply, a married woman seeking an abortion must sign a statement indicating that she has notified her husband of her intended abortion. * * * The Act exempts compliance with these three requirements in the event of a "medical emergency," which is defined in § 3203 of the Act. In addition to the above provisions regulating the performance of abortions, the Act imposes certain reporting requirements on facilities that provide abortion services. * * * Before any of these provisions took effect, the petitioners, who are five abortion clinics and one physician representing himself as well as a class of physicians who provide abortion services, brought this suit seeking declaratory and injunctive relief. Each provision was challenged as unconstitutional on its face. The District Court entered a preliminary injunction against the enforcement of the regulations, and, after a 3-day bench trial, held all the provisions at issue here unconstitutional, entering a permanent injunction against Pennsylvania's enforcement of them. The Court of Appeals for the Third Circuit affirmed in part and reversed in part, upholding all the regulations except for the husband notification requirement. We granted certiorari.

* * *

After considering the fundamental constitutional questions resolved by *Roe*, principles of institutional integrity, and the rule of stare decisis, we are led to conclude this: the essential holding of Roe v. Wade should be retained and once again reaffirmed.

It must be stated at the outset and with clarity that *Roe's* essential holding, the holding we reaffirm, has three parts. First is a recognition of the right of the woman to choose to have an abortion before viability and to obtain it without undue interference from the State. Before viability, the State's interests are not strong enough to support a prohibition of abortion or the imposition of substantial obstacles to the woman's effective right to elect the procedure. Second is a confirmation of the State's power to restrict abortions after fetal viability, if the law contains exceptions for pregnancies which endanger a woman's life or health. And third is the principle that the State has legitimate interests from the outset of the pregnancy in protecting the health of the woman and the life of the fetus that may become a child. These principles do not contradict one another; and we adhere to each.

* * *

III

A

The obligation to follow precedent begins with necessity, and a contrary necessity marks its outer limit. With Cardozo, we recognize that no judicial system could do society's work if it eyed each issue afresh in every case that raised it. Indeed, the very concept of the rule of law underlying our own Constitution requires such continuity over time that a respect for precedent is, by definition, indispensable. At the other extreme, a different necessity would make itself felt if a prior judicial ruling should come to be seen so clearly as error that its enforcement was for that very reason doomed.

* * *

So in this case we may inquire whether *Roe's* central rule has been found unworkable; whether the rule's limitation on state power could be removed without serious inequity to those who have relied upon it or significant damage to the stability of the society governed by the rule in question; whether the law's growth in the intervening years has left *Roe's* central rule a doctrinal anachronism discounted by society; and whether *Roe's* premises of fact have so far changed in the ensuing two decades as to render its central holding somehow irrelevant or unjustifiable in dealing with the issue it addressed.

Although *Roe* has engendered opposition, it has in no sense proven "unworkable," representing as it does a simple limitation beyond which a state law is unenforceable. While *Roe* has, of course, required judicial assessment of state laws affecting the exercise of the choice guaranteed against government infringement, and although the need for such review will remain as a consequence of today's decision, the required determinations fall within judicial competence.

IV

* * *

Yet it must be remembered that Roe v. Wade speaks with clarity in establishing not only the woman's liberty but also the State's "important and legitimate interest in potential life." That portion of the decision in *Roe* has been given too little acknowledgment and implementation by the Court in its subsequent cases. Those cases decided that any regulation touching upon the abortion decision must survive strict scrutiny, to be sustained only if drawn in narrow terms to further a compelling state interest. *See e.g., Akron I.* Not all of the cases decided under that formulation can be reconciled with the holding in *Roe* itself that the State has legitimate interests in the health of the woman and in protecting the potential life within her. In resolving this tension, we choose to rely upon *Roe*, as against the later cases.

Roe established a trimester framework to govern abortion regulations. Under this elaborate but rigid construct, almost no regulation at all is permitted during the first trimester of pregnancy; regulations designed to protect the woman's health, but not to further the State's interest in potential life, are permitted during the second trimester; and during the third trimester, when the fetus is viable, prohibitions are permitted provided the life or health of the mother is not at stake. Most of our cases since *Roe* have involved the application of rules derived from the trimester framework.

* * *

We reject the trimester framework, which we do not consider to be part of the essential holding of *Roe*. Measures aimed at ensuring that a woman's choice contemplates the consequences for the fetus do not necessarily interfere with the right recognized in *Roe*, although those measures have been found to be inconsistent with the rigid trimester framework announced in that case. A logical reading of the central holding in *Roe* itself, and a necessary reconciliation of the liberty of the woman and the interest of the State in promoting prenatal life, require, in our view, that we abandon the trimester framework as a rigid prohibition on all previability regulation aimed at the protection of fetal life. The trimester framework suffers from these basic flaws: in its formulation it misconceives the nature of the pregnant woman's interest; and in practice it undervalues the State's interest in potential life, as recognized in *Roe*.

* * *

The very notion that the State has a substantial interest in potential life leads to the conclusion that not all regulations must be deemed unwarranted. Not all burdens on the right to decide whether to terminate a pregnancy will be undue. In our view, the undue burden standard is the appropriate means of reconciling the State's interest with the woman's constitutionally protected liberty.

* * *

Some guiding principles should emerge. What is at stake is the woman's right to make the ultimate decision, not a right to be insulated from all others in doing so. Regulations which do no more than create a structural mechanism by which the State, or the parent or guardian of a minor, may express profound respect for the life of the unborn are permitted, if they are not a substantial obstacle to the woman's exercise of the right to choose. Unless it has that effect on her right of choice, a state measure designed to persuade her to choose childbirth over abortion will be upheld if reasonably related to that goal. Regulations designed to foster the health of a woman seeking an abortion are valid if they do not constitute an undue burden.

Even when jurists reason from shared premises, some disagreement is inevitable. That is to be expected in the application of any legal standard which must accommodate life's complexity. We do not expect it to be otherwise with respect to the undue burden standard. We give this summary:

> (a) To protect the central right recognized by Roe v. Wade while at the same time accommodating the State's profound interest in potential life, we will employ the undue burden analysis as explained in this opinion. An undue burden exists, and therefore a provision of law is invalid, if its purpose or effect is to place a substantial obstacle in the path of a woman seeking an abortion before the fetus attains viability.

(b) We reject the rigid trimester framework of Roe v. Wade. To promote the State's profound interest in potential life throughout pregnancy, the State may take measures to ensure that the woman's choice is informed, and measures designed to advance this interest will not be invalidated as long as their purpose is to persuade the woman to choose childbirth over abortion. These measures must not be an undue burden on the right.

(c) As with any medical procedure, the State may enact regulations to further the health or safety of a woman seeking an abortion. Unnecessary health regulations that have the purpose or effect of presenting a substantial obstacle to a woman seeking an abortion impose an undue burden on the right.

(d) Our adoption of the undue burden analysis does not disturb the central holding of Roe v. Wade, and we reaffirm that holding. Regardless of whether exceptions are made for particular circumstances, a State may not prohibit any woman from making the ultimate decision to terminate her pregnancy before viability.

(e) We also reaffirm *Roe*'s holding that "subsequent to viability, the State in promoting its interest in the potentiality of human life may, if it chooses, regulate, and even proscribe, abortion except where it is necessary, in appropriate medical judgment, for the preservation of the life or health of the mother."

These principles control our assessment of the Pennsylvania statute, and we now turn to the issue of the validity of its challenged provisions.

V

A

Because it is central to the operation of various other requirements, we begin with the statute's definition of medical emergency. Under the statute, a medical emergency is

"[t]hat condition which, on the basis of the physician's good faith clinical judgment, so complicates the medical condition of a pregnant woman as to necessitate the immediate abortion of her pregnancy to avert her death or for which a delay will create serious risk of substantial and irreversible impairment of a major bodily function." 18 Pa. Cons. Stat. (1990).

We * * * conclude that, as construed by the Court of Appeals, the medical emergency definition imposes no undue burden on a woman's abortion right.

B

We next consider the informed consent requirement. Except in a medical emergency, the statute requires that at least 24 hours before performing an abortion a physician inform the woman of the nature of the procedure, the health risks of the abortion and of childbirth, and the "probable gestational age of the unborn child." The physician or a qualified nonphysician must inform the woman of the availability of printed materials published by the State describing the fetus and providing information about medical assistance for childbirth, information about child support from the father, and a list of agencies which provide adoption and other services as alternatives to abortion. An abortion may not be performed unless the woman certifies in writing that she has been informed of the availability of these printed materials and has been provided them if she chooses to view them.

* * *

Our analysis of Pennsylvania's 24-hour waiting period between the provision of the information deemed necessary to informed consent and the performance of an abortion under the undue burden standard requires us to reconsider the premise behind the decision in *Akron I* invalidating a parallel requirement. In *Akron I* we said: "Nor are we convinced that the State's legitimate concern that the woman's decision be informed is reasonably served by requiring a 24-hour delay as a matter of course." We consider that conclusion to be wrong. The idea that important decisions will be more informed and deliberate if they follow some period of reflection does not strike us as unreasonable, particularly where the statute directs that important information become part of the background of the decision. The statute, as construed by the Court of Appeals, permits avoidance of the waiting period in the event of a medical emergency and the record evidence shows that in the vast majority of cases, a 24-hour delay does not create any appreciable health risk. In theory, at least, the waiting period is a reasonable measure to implement the State's interest in protecting the life of the unborn, a measure that does not amount to an undue burden.

* * *

Our Constitution is a covenant running from the first generation of Americans to us and then to future generations. It is a coherent succession. Each generation must learn anew that the Constitution's written terms embody ideas and aspirations that must survive more ages than one. We accept our responsibility not to retreat from interpreting the full meaning of the covenant in light of all of our precedents. We invoke it once again to define the freedom guaranteed by the Constitution's own promise, the promise of liberty. * * *

NOTES AND QUESTIONS

1.   Compare *Roe* and *Casey*. On what points do the two courts agree? Disagree? What are the merits of each approach?

2.   *State Partial Birth Abortion Ban:* In *Casey*, the Supreme Court defined "undue burden" as "shorthand for the conclusion that a state regulation has the *purpose or effect* of placing a substantial obstacle in the path of a woman seeking an abortion of a nonviable fetus." By 2000, thirty states had enacted partial birth abortion bans. In Stenberg v. Carhart, 530 U.S. 914 (2000), the Court struck down a Nebraska statute that criminalized the performance of a "partial birth abortion" except when necessary "to save the life of the mother." The Court held that the statute imposed "an undue burden on a woman's ability to choose" both because it unduly burdened a woman's ability to choose a so-called "D & E" abortion (the most common late-term abortion procedure), thereby "unduly burdening the right to choose abortion itself" and because it failed to provide an exception for preservation of the mother's health. The Court found the undue burden even though the Nebraska legislative history identified "partial birth" abortion with the so called "D & X" abortion procedure and an interpretation of the law by the Nebraska Attorney General specified that only "D & X" abortions were prohibited under the statute. The Court's conclusion was based on the language of the statute itself.

3.   *The Federal Partial-Birth Abortion Ban:* Following *Stenberg*, Congress enacted the Partial-Birth Abortion Ban Act of 2003, 18 U.S.C. § 1531, which provides civil and criminal penalties applicable to a physician "who * * * knowingly performs a partial-birth abortion." A "partial birth abortion" is defined as abortion in which a physician:

> (A) deliberately and intentionally vaginally delivers a living fetus until, in the case of head-first presentation, the entire fetal head is outside the body of the mother, or in the case of breech presentation, any part of the fetal trunk past the navel is outside the body of the mother, for the purpose of performing an overt act that the person knows will kill the partially delivered living fetus; and

> (B) performs the overt act, other than completion of delivery, that kills the partially delivered fetus. * * *

Id. at § 1531(b)(1). The statute provides an exception when the woman's "life is endangered by a physical disorder, physical illness, or physical injury, including a life-endangering physical condition caused by or arising from the pregnancy itself."

Although lower courts had found the federal law unconstitutional under *Stenberg* (Carhart v. Gonzales, 413 F.3d 791 (8th Cir. 2005)), the United States Supreme Court upheld the Act in Gonzales v. Carhart, 550 U.S. 124 (2007). The Court distinguished *Stenberg*, finding "the statute at issue to be more specific concerning the instances to which it applies and more precise in its coverage." In writing for the Court, Justice Kennedy noted:

> We assume the following principles for the purposes of this opinion. Before viability, a State "may not prohibit any woman from making the ultimate decision to terminate her pregnancy." * * * It also may not impose upon this right an undue burden, which exists if a

regulation's "purpose or effect is to place a substantial obstacle in the path of a woman seeking an abortion before the fetus attains viability." * * * On the other hand, "[regulations which do no more than create a structural mechanism by which the State, or the parent or guardian of a minor, may express profound respect for the life of the unborn are permitted, if they are not a substantial obstacle to the woman's exercise of the right to choose." * * *

The Court found that the law was not void for vagueness and did not impose an undue burden on a woman's right to abortion on its overbreadth or lack of a health exception. The Act's text regulates and proscribes performing the intact D & E procedure and was not unconstitutionally vague on its face. The Act did not impose an undue burden, as a facial matter, because its restrictions on second trimester abortions are too broad. The Act does not impose a substantial obstacle to late-term, but previability, abortions, as prohibited by the *Casey* plurality.

Dissenting Justice Ginsburg, who was joined by Justices Souter, Stephens and Breyer, noted that *Stenberg* case invalidating the Nebraska statute showed fidelity to the *Roe-Casey* line of precedent:

> Today's decision is alarming. It refuses to take *Casey* and *Stenberg* seriously. It tolerates, indeed applauds, federal intervention to ban nationwide a procedure found necessary and proper in certain cases by the American College of Obstetricians and Gynecologists (ACOG). It blurs the line, firmly drawn in *Casey*, between previability and postviability abortions. And, for the first time since *Roe,* the Court blesses a prohibition with no exception safeguarding a woman's health.

> I dissent from the Court's disposition. Retreating from prior rulings that abortion restrictions cannot be imposed absent an exception safeguarding a woman's health, the Court upholds an Act that surely would not survive under the close scrutiny that previously attended state-decreed limitations on a woman's reproductive choices.

4.   *Defining Undue Burden:* In 2016, the United States Supreme Court issued its at least fiftieth abortion decision. A Texas law required all abortion doctors to have patient admission privileges at a hospital within 30 miles of the place of abortion, and required abortion clinics to meet the standards for ambulatory surgical centers. The Court's majority found that these regulations imposed an undue burden on women seeking abortions without providing sufficient health benefits. Whole Woman's Health v. Hellerstadt, 136 S. Ct. 2292 (2016).

5.   *Abortion Pill:* In 2000 the FDA approved RU486 (mifepristone), an "abortion pill" which induces the termination of a pregnancy after a fertilized ovum has implanted in the uterus. Under *Casey* and *Stenberg,* could the government ban RU486 and force women to rely on surgical abortions? Conversely, could the government ban surgical abortions and force women to

rely on RU486? *See* Planned Parenthood of Southwest Ohio Region v. Dewine, 696 F.3d 490 (6th Cir. 2012). In 2014, the United States Supreme Court held that Affordable Care Act requiring employers to pay for certain emergency contraceptives (Plan B. Ella, IUDs) that "worked" after conception violated the Religious Freedom Restoration Act. Burwell v. Hobby Lobby, 134 S. Ct. 2751 (2014).

6. *Fetal Protection Laws:* In 2004, Congress enacted the Unborn Victims of Violence Act, 18 U.S.C. § 1841, which establishes criminal liability for killing or injuring an unborn child, at any stage of gestation, during the commission of a federal crime against the pregnant woman. Several states have also enacted fetal homicide laws. *See* Amanda K. Bruchs, Note, *Clash of Competing Interests: Can the Unborn Victim of Violence Act and Over Thirty Years of Settled Abortion Law Live Peacefully?*, 55 SYRACUSE L. REV. 133 (2004). The federal government has also redefined a "child" for purposes of the State Child's Health Insurance Program (SCHIP) to include a fetus. *See* 42 C.F.R. § 457. Several states, including Mississippi and Ohio, have attempted to add a "personhood" amendment to the state constitution that would make life begin at conception. In the first six months of 2011, states enacted 162 new provisions related to reproductive health, mostly to restrict abortion. *States Enact Record Number of Abortion Restrictions in First Half of 2011*, GUTTMACHER INSTITUTE (July 13, 2011).

7. *Access to Abortion:* Obtaining an abortion has become difficult as opponents have become more visible, better organized, and more violent, resulting in a decrease in abortion providers. The Freedom of Access to Clinic Entrances Act, (FACE) (18 U.S.C. § 248) prohibits the use of force, threatened force, or physical obstruction against service providers. The law provides both criminal and civil penalties. Federal courts have upheld the constitutionality of the statute. *See* U.S. v. Gregg, 226 F.3d 253 (3d Cir. 2000). Courts have upheld state laws aimed at ensuring access to abortion clinics and granted injunctive relief to abortion clinics. *See* Schenck v. Pro-Choice Network of Western New York, 519 U.S. 357 (1997) (injunction); Hill v. Colorado, 530 U.S. 703 (2000). *But see* Scheidler v. National Organization for Women, Inc., 547 U.S. 9 (2006) (protest free zones).

8. *Abortion Facts—Who, When, and Why:* In the United States, abortions are obtained primarily by young, unmarried women. In 2008, 84.5% of women who obtained abortions were unmarried. The highest abortion rate was among women aged 20–24 years. The vast majority of abortions take place early in pregnancy. At the time of *Roe*, the abortion rate was 16.3 per 1000 women. The number doubled between 1973 and 1979, leveled off until 1990, and has declined since. Abortions declined from 29.3 per 1000 women in 1981 to 14.6 per 1000 in 2014, the lowest rate ever.

9. *Positive Procreational Liberties: Griswold, Eisenstadt, Roe* and *Casey* all deal with *negative* procreational liberties, i.e., the right to decide not to bear a child. The Supreme Court has decided only two cases addressing *positive* procreational liberties. Opining that "[t]hree generations of imbeciles are

enough," the Court long ago upheld a Virginia statute allowing for sterilization of "mental defectives." Buck v. Bell, 274 U.S. 200 (1927). But in Skinner v. Oklahoma, 316 U.S. 535 (1942), the Court struck down a criminal statute requiring sterilization of those convicted of three or more felonies involving "moral turpitude." Although the *Skinner* Court described procreation as one of the "basic civil rights of man," *(id.* at 541), it decided the case on fairly narrow equal protection grounds. However, Justice Goldberg, concurring in *Griswold*, did note the logical equivalence of laws outlawing birth control and laws mandating it (*Griswold*, 381 U.S. 479 (1965)), and both state and lower federal courts have assumed that positive procreational liberties are entitled to the same level of protection as decision making about abortion and contraception. *See* PAUL A. LOMBARDO, THREE GENERATIONS, NO IMBECILES: EUGENICS, THE SUPREME COURT AND *BUCK V. BELL* (2008).

The case law is almost entirely concerned with punitive conditions. Several federal courts have upheld prison restrictions on contact conjugal visitation. *See, e.g.*, Hernandez v. Coughlin, 18 F.3d 133 (2d Cir. 1994); Bellamy v. Bradley, 729 F.2d 416 (6th Cir. 1984). In a case involving a life-term prisoner who wanted to impregnate his wife with semen sent through the mail, the Ninth Circuit Court of Appeals ruled that loss of procreational liberty "is simply part and parcel of being imprisoned for conviction of a crime." Gerber v. Hickman, 291 F.3d 617 (9th Cir. 2002) (en banc). The Wisconsin Supreme Court upheld as a condition of probation that a father of nine avoid having another child unless he showed that he could support that child and current children despite its impact on the right to procreate. Wisconsin v. Oakley, 629 N.W.2d 200 (Wis. 2001).

Could the state constitutionally impose upon a parent convicted of child abuse and found to have seriously and repeatedly abused two different children, a probation condition requiring successful completion of drug and anger management treatment programs as a prerequisite to fathering additional children? *Compare* State v. Kline, 963 P.2d 697 (Or. App. 1998) *with* Trammell v. State, 751 N.E.2d 283 (Ind. App. 2001). Following a second conviction for child abuse, could the state mandate a parent's sterilization?

2. LEGITIMACY AND PATERNITY

A parent has a constitutional right to the care, custody and control of his or her child. A parent also has the obligation to support his or her child. Therefore, the definition of who is a child's parent is important. The determination of legal parentage has become more complex over time. At common law, marriage determined parenthood. Today, with the advent of genetic testing, children born out of wedlock, and assisted reproductive technology, it is much more difficult. The role of marriage remains important—but biology, function and intention now play a larger role.

A. THE PRESUMPTION OF LEGITIMACY

Shakespeare said, "it is a wise father that knows his own child" (Merchant of Venice, II, 2), to which might be added that the child that knows his father is fortunate. What means are provided by law to identify parents? With respect to a mother, the fact of birth, whether in or out of wedlock, has long been considered to establish their legal relationship. With respect to the father, the concept of "legitimacy" provided the principal legal nexus. A child born to a married mother is "legitimate", i.e. the child has a legal relationship with the mother's husband by the fact of birth "in wedlock," although that relationship may be defeated if the husband can prove that the child is not his. A child born out of wedlock did not start out with an automatically identified father. Until recently, even if the father is identified, the child would gain only a limited legal relationship with him.

WILLIAM BLACKSTONE, COMMENTARIES ON THE LAWS OF ENGLAND, BOOK I
Ch. 16, 454–459 (1765).

* * * A bastard, by our English laws, is one that is not only begotten, but born, out of lawful matrimony. The civil and canon laws do not allow a child to remain a bastard, if the parents afterwards intermarry: and herein they differ most materially from our law; which, though not so strict as to require that the child shall be *begotten*, yet makes it an indispensable condition that it shall be *born*, after lawful wedlock * * * The main end and design of marriage, therefore, being to ascertain and fix upon some certain person, to whom the care, the protection, the maintenance, and the education of the children should belong. * * *

* * * [C]hildren born during wedlock may in some circumstances be bastards. And if the husband be out of the kingdom of England (or, as the law somewhat loosely phrases it, *extra quatuor maria*) for above nine months, so that no access to his wife can be presumed, her issue during that period shall be bastard. But, generally, during the coverture access of the husband shall be presumed, unless the contrary can be shewn; which is such a negative as can only be proved by shewing him to be elsewhere: for the general rule is, *praesumitur pro legitimatione.* * * *

Let us next see the duty of parents to their bastard children, by our law; which principally that of maintenance. For, though bastards are not looked upon as children to any civil purposes, yet the ties of nature, of which maintenance is one, are not so easily dissolved: and they hold indeed as to many other intentions; as, particularly, that a man shall not marry his bastard sister or daughter. * * *

The incapacity of a bastard consists principally in this, that he cannot be heir to any one, neither can he have heirs, but of his own body; for, being *nullius filius*, he is therefore of kin to nobody, and has no ancestor from whom any inheritable blood can be derived.

As Blackstone notes, under the common law it was possible for a married woman to have an illegitimate child. But, under Lord Mansfield's Rule, first enunciated in Goodright v. Moss, 2 Cowp. 291, 98 Eng. Rep. 1257 (1777), neither spouse could testify to nonaccess by the husband. Without modern genetic testing and DNA analysis, the marital presumption of legitimacy was almost impossible to rebut. Because the overwhelming majority of births were to married mothers, the "marital presumption" settled the question of legal paternity in most cases. *See* HARRY D. KRAUSE, ILLEGITIMACY: LAW AND SOCIAL POLICY (1971).

Most American states incorporated the marital presumption into their statutory law and applied it even if the marriage was subsequently declared void or annulled. The strength of the presumption was justified by children's interests: illegitimacy was socially stigmatizing and deprived the child of inheritance and support rights; the presumption also prevented a putative father from interjecting himself into an intact family and disrupting the peace and stability of the marital relationship. But in an era in which nonmarital birth is common, divorce frequent, and paternity testing conclusive, courts and legislatures have been forced to evaluate whether the marital presumption continues to serve public policy objectives.

B. REMOVING THE STIGMA OF ILLEGITIMACY

Common law disabilities based on a child's illegitimacy were maintained well into the twentieth century. As late as the 1960s, in most states an illegitimate child had no right to inherit from his or her father, to bear the father's name, and to obtain public benefits for wrongful death, workers' compensation, insurance and social security; some states even denied the illegitimate child paternal support. *See* Harry Krause, *Equal Protection for the Illegitimate*, 65 MICH. L. REV. 477 (1967).

In 1968, the Supreme Court initiated a sweeping revision of the law of illegitimacy. In more than thirty decisions issued since that time, the Court has utilized the Equal Protection and Due Process Clauses to invalidate nearly all forms of legal discrimination against nonmarital children.

LEVY V. LOUISIANA

Supreme Court of the United States, 1968.
391 U.S. 68.

JUSTICE DOUGLAS delivered the opinion of the Court.

Appellant sued on behalf of five illegitimate children to recover, under a Louisiana statute for two kinds of damages as a result of the wrongful death of their mother: (1) the damages to them for the loss of their mother; and (2) those based on the survival of a cause of action which the mother had at the time of her death for pain and suffering. Appellees are the doctor who treated her and the insurance company.

We assume in the present state of the pleadings that the mother, Louise Levy, gave birth to these five illegitimate children and that they lived with her; that she treated them as a parent would treat any other child; that she worked as a domestic servant to support them, taking them to church every Sunday and enrolling them, at her own expense, in a parochial school. [The trial court's dismissal was affirmed by the Louisiana Court of Appeal which held that the "child" in Article 2315 meant "legitimate child." Denial of an action to illegitimate children was "based on morals and general welfare because it discourages bringing children into the world out of wedlock." 192 So. 2d 193, 195. The Supreme Court of Louisiana denied certiorari.]

* * *

We start from the premise that illegitimate children are not "non-persons." They are humans, live, and have their being. They are clearly "persons" within the meaning of the Equal Protection Clause of the Fourteenth Amendment.

While a State has broad power when it comes to making classifications, it may not draw a line which constitutes an invidious discrimination against a particular class. Though the test has been variously stated, the end result is whether the line drawn is a rational one.

In applying the Equal Protection Clause to social and economic legislation, we give great latitude to the legislature in making classifications. Even so, would a corporation, which is a "person," for certain purposes, within the meaning of the Equal Protection Clause, be required to forgo recovery for wrongs done its interest because its incorporators were all bastards? However that might be, we have been extremely sensitive when it comes to basic civil rights and have not hesitated to strike down an invidious classification even though it had history and tradition on its side. The rights asserted here involve the intimate, familial relationship between a child and his own mother. When the child's claim of damage for loss of his mother is in issue, why, in terms of "equal protection," should the tortfeasors go free merely because the child is illegitimate? Why should the illegitimate child be denied rights merely because of his birth out of wedlock? He certainly is subject to all the responsibilities of a citizen, including the payment of taxes and conscription under the Selective Service Act. How under our constitutional regime can he be denied correlative rights which other citizens enjoy?

Legitimacy or illegitimacy of birth has no relation to the nature of the wrong allegedly inflicted on the mother. These children, though illegitimate, were dependent on her; she cared for them and nurtured them; they were indeed hers in the biological and in the spiritual sense; in her death they suffered wrong in the sense that any dependent would.

We conclude that it is invidious to discriminate against them when no action, conduct, or demeanor of theirs is possibly relevant to the harm that was done the mother.

NOTES AND QUESTIONS

1.   In Glona v. American Guarantee & Liability Ins. Co., 391 U.S. 73 (1968), a companion case to *Levy*, the Court struck down Louisiana's wrongful death statute, which barred recovery of damages by the mother of an illegitimate child but allowed recovery by the parents of a legitimate child. In Weber v. Aetna Casualty & Surety Co., 406 U.S. 164 (1972), the Court held that a state law which denied worker's compensation benefits to nonmarital dependent children violated both the Equal Protection and Due Process clauses of the Fourteenth Amendment.

2.   *Child Support:* While most states obligated a father to pay support for an illegitimate child, a couple of states imposed no support obligation. In Gomez v. Perez, 409 U.S. 535 (1973), the Supreme Court stated:

> In Texas, both at common law and under the statutes of the State, the natural father has a continuing and primary duty to support his legitimate children. That duty extends even beyond dissolution of the marriage, and is enforceable on the child's behalf in civil proceedings and, further is the subject of criminal sanctions. The duty to support exists despite the fact that the father may not have custody of the child. * * * illegitimate children, unlike legitimate children, have no legal right to support from their fathers.

> We have held that under the Equal Protection Clause of the Fourteenth Amendment, a State may not create a right of action in favor of children for the wrongful death of a parent and exclude illegitimate children from the benefit of such a right [or keep them from sharing equally with other children in workmen's compensation benefits]. * * * We therefore hold that once a state posits a judicially enforceable right on behalf of children to needed support from their natural fathers there is no constitutionally sufficient justification for denying such an essential right to a child simply because its natural father has not married its mother.

The *Gomez* decision became extremely important for obtaining child support for the increasing number of children born out of wedlock. At the time of the *Levy* decision, less than ten percent of children were born out of wedlock. Between 1970 and 2010 the proportion of U.S. births that were nonmarital increased from 10.7 to 40.8.percent. *See Births: Preliminary Data for 2010*, 60(2) NATIONAL VITAL STATISTICS REPORT (Nov. 17, 2011).

3. *Intestate Succession:* Laws governing intestate succession have traditionally been a major source of discrimination against nonmarital children. On this issue, the Supreme Court has had more difficulty enunciating clear guidelines. In Labine v. Vincent, 401 U.S. 532 (1971), the Court upheld a Louisiana law denying a right to intestate succession to a nonmarital child whose father had acknowledged her during his lifetime. But in Trimble v. Gordon, 430 U.S. 762 (1977), the Court (5–4) utilized "intermediate scrutiny" to strike down an Illinois statute which denied nonmarital children a right to intestate succession unless the child's parents married, essentially overruling *Labine*. The Supreme Court indicated that

> * * * [f]or at least some significant categories of illegitimate children of intestate men, inheritance rights can be recognized without jeopardizing the orderly settlement of estates or the dependability of titles to property passing under intestacy laws. Because it excludes those categories of illegitimate children unnecessarily, § 12 is constitutionally flawed. * * *

A year later, Justice Powell, who wrote the opinion in *Trimble*, found himself allied with the dissenters. In Lalli v. Lalli, 439 U.S. 259 (1978), again using "intermediate scrutiny," the Court (5–4) upheld a New York statute which conditioned a nonmarital child's right to intestate succession on the judicial establishment of paternity during the father's lifetime. The court stated that:

> The primary state goal underlying the challenged aspects of § 4–1.2 is to provide for the just and orderly disposition of property at death. We long have recognized that this is an area with which the States have an interest of considerable magnitude. * * * This interest is directly implicated in paternal inheritance by illegitimate children because of the peculiar problems of proof that are involved. Establishing maternity is seldom difficult. * * * Proof of paternity, by contrast, frequently is difficult when the father is not part of a formal family unit * * *.

Unsurprisingly, the Court's "see-saw" jurisprudence on the inheritance rights of nonmarital children has been difficult for lower courts and state legislatures to apply. *See* HARRY KRAUSE, CHILD SUPPORT IN AMERICA: THE LEGAL PERSPECTIVE 119–62 (1981).

4. *Citizenship:* In Nguyen v. Immigration & Naturalization Serv., 533 U.S. 53 (2001), the Supreme Court upheld 8 U.S.C. §§ 1409, which imposes different requirements for the child's acquisition of citizenship depending upon

whether the citizen parent is the mother or the father. The Court held that the statutory distinction did not violate the Equal Protection Clause:

§ 1409(a)(4) requires one of three affirmative steps to be taken if the citizen parent is the father, but not if the citizen parent is the mother: legitimation; a declaration of paternity under oath by the father; or a court order of paternity. Congress' decision to impose requirements on unmarried fathers that differ from those on unmarried mothers is based on the significant difference between their respective relationships to the potential citizen at the time of birth. Specifically, the imposition of the requirement for a paternal relationship, but not a maternal one, is justified by two important governmental objectives. * * * The first governmental interest to be served is the importance of assuring that a biological parent-child relationship exists. In the case of the mother, the relation is verifiable from the birth itself.

* * * In the case of the father, the uncontestable fact is that he need not be present at the birth. If he is present, furthermore, that circumstance is not incontrovertible proof of fatherhood. * * *

The second important governmental interest furthered in a substantial manner by §§ 1409(a)(4) is the determination to ensure that the child and the citizen parent have some demonstrated opportunity or potential to develop not just a relationship that is recognized, as a formal matter, by the law, but one that consists of the real, everyday ties that provide a connection between child and citizen parent and, in turn, the United States. * * * In the case of a citizen mother and a child born overseas, the opportunity for a meaningful relationship between citizen parent and child inheres in the very event of birth. * * * The same opportunity does not result from the event of birth, as a matter of biological inevitability, in the case of the unwed father. Given the 9-month interval between conception and birth, it is not always certain that a father will know that a child was conceived, nor is it always clear that even the mother will be sure of the father's identity. This fact takes on particular significance in the case of a child born overseas and out of wedlock.

Paternity can be established by taking DNA samples even from a few strands of hair, years after the birth. * * * Yet scientific proof of biological paternity does nothing, by itself, to ensure contact between father and child during the child's minority.

Congress is well within its authority in refusing, absent proof of at least the opportunity for the development of a relationship between citizen parent and child, to commit this country to embracing a child as a citizen entitled as of birth to the full protection of the United States, to the absolute right to enter its borders, and to full participation in the political process. If citizenship is to be conferred by the unwitting means petitioners urge, so that its acquisition abroad bears little relation to the realities of the child's own ties and allegiances, it is for Congress, not this Court, to make that determination.

How does the opportunity to become a U.S. citizen differ from the opportunity to bring a wrongful death action or to obtain support? Is *Nguyen* consistent with *Glona, Weber,* and *Gomez? See* Lica Tomizuka, *The Supreme Court's Blind Pursuit of Outdated Definitions of Familial Relationships in Upholding the Constitutionality of 8 U.S.C. § 1409 in* Nguyen v. INS, 20 LAW & INEQ. 275 (2002). In June 2017, the United States Supreme Court held that unwed mothers and fathers may not be treated differently as to whether their children may claim American citizenship. Justice Ginsburg indicated that the law was based on the faulty assumption that "unwed fathers care little about, indeed are strangers to, their children." All children seeking citizenship should have the same time period. Sessions v. Morales-Santana, 137 S. Ct. 1678 (2017).

5. *Social Security Benefits:* A dependent nonmarital child is entitled to Social Security survivor's benefits if he or she has been formally recognized (through a written acknowledgment, paternity proceeding, or court order of support) prior to the death of the alleged father. 42 U.S.C. § 416(h)(3)(C)(i). If there has been no formal recognition of the child prior to the death of the alleged father, the Secretary may determine paternity based on: (1) the evidentiary standard contained in the relevant state intestacy law; or (2) evidence "satisfactory to the Secretary" that the deceased was the father of the applicant and lived with or contributed to the support of the child. *See* Daniels, on Behalf of Daniels v. Sullivan, 979 F.2d 1516 (11th Cir. 1992) (refusing to read Georgia intestacy law requiring paternity establishment during father's lifetime into federal law); Bennemon v. Sullivan, 914 F.2d 987 (7th Cir. 1990) (denying benefits where child had not been born when alleged father died and there was no proof of support).

Problem 7-1:

Under state law, a nonmarital child has no right to intestate succession unless paternity was established during the lifetime of the alleged father. Jane and John had a sexual relationship but did not live together. Jane became pregnant but did not get a chance to tell John before he was killed in a car accident. John came from a wealthy family and left no heirs except his parents. What, if any, constitutional arguments are available to Jane on behalf of her child? What arguments are available to the State? What result?

C. RECOGNIZING THE UNMARRIED FATHER

The presumption of legitimacy made the husband the father of a child born of the marriage. But the father of a child born out of wedlock had few enforceable legal rights. Prior to the 1960s, relatively few fathers sought a relationship and most state statutes allowed the mother alone to consent to the adoption of a the child. Before 1972, based in part on the difficulty of definitively establishing the paternity of a nonmarital child, most states did not permit an unmarried father to block an adoption. But in Stanley v. Illinois, 405 U.S. 645 (1972), the Supreme Court held that an unmarried father was entitled to a hearing on his fitness before his children could be placed in state custody. An Illinois statute conclusively presumed every father of a child born out of wedlock to be an unfit person to have custody of his children. The father in that case had lived with his children all their lives and had lived with their mother for 18 years. There was nothing in the record to indicate that Stanley had been a neglectful father who had not cared for his children. Under the statute, however, the nature of the actual relationship between parent and child was completely irrelevant. Once the mother died, the children were automatically made wards of the State. * * * [T]he Court held that the Due Process Clause was violated by the automatic destruction of the custodial relationship without giving the father any opportunity to present evidence regarding his fitness as a parent.

Following *Stanley*, the United States Supreme Court decided three other cases concerning the right of unwed fathers to withhold consent to the adoption of their child. Quilloin v. Walcott, 434 U.S. 246 (1978) involved the constitutionality of a Georgia statute that authorized the adoption, over the objection of the natural father, of a child born out of wedlock. The father had never legitimated the child. The mother remarried and her new husband filed an adoption petition after living with the child for eight years. The natural father then sought visitation rights and filed a petition for legitimation but did not ask for custody. The trial court found adoption by the new husband to be in the child's best interests. The Supreme Court unanimously held that action to be consistent with the Due Process Clause noting that the "result of the adoption . . . is to give full recognition to a family unit already in existence."

In Caban v. Mohammed, 441 U.S. 380 (1979), an unmarried couple had lived together for five years and had two children. After separating, each remarried and petitioned for stepparent adoption. The court granted the mother's petition because she could consent alone to the adoption. The father challenged the validity of the adoption relying on both the Equal Protection Clause and the Due Process Clause. The Court upheld his equal protection claim, finding that the gender-based distinction did not bear a substantial relation to the purpose of promoting adoption of illegitimate children. The court found the children had a relationship with both parents.

In Lehr v. Robertson et al., 463 U.S. 248 (1983), the mother left the hospital with the baby and did not tell the unmarried father where she went. He failed to file in the New York putative father registry. He was not listed on the child's birth certificate, had not lived openly with the mother and held himself out as father, nor had he provided financial support. The mother married and her husband wanted to adopt the child. The Court found that the state provided a way that a man who files with that registry demonstrates his intent to claim paternity of a child born out of wedlock and is therefore entitled to receive notice of any proceeding to adopt that child. Distinguishing *Stanley* and *Caban* in which there was a developed parent-child relationship, the Court stated that the mere existence of biological link does not merit equivalent constitutional protection. The significance of the biological connection was that it offered the natural father an opportunity to develop a relationship but the state could prescribe the procedures to follow. Because he did not file in the putative father registry, he was not entitled to notice and opportunity to be heard before the stepfather adopted the child. The dissent raised the question of what happens if the mother prevents the father from establishing the relationship by concealing her location. What is the extent of the father's obligation to discover the mother's deception about her location or her pregnancy? Many courts have struggled with that issue. *See In re* Adoption of Baby Girl P., 242 P.3d 1168, 1175 (Kan. 2010).

After this line of cases, fathers clearly had "opportunities" to establish a relationship with their child born out of wedlock. A more difficult question arose, however, if the mother was married to someone else at the time the child was born.

MICHAEL H. v. GERALD D.
Supreme Court of the United States, 1989.
491 U.S. 110.

JUSTICE SCALIA announced the judgment of the Court and delivered an opinion, in which THE CHIEF JUSTICE joins, and in all but note 6 of which JUSTICE O'CONNOR and JUSTICE KENNEDY join.

Under California law, a child born to a married woman living with her husband is presumed to be a child of the marriage. Cal. Evid. Code Ann. § 621 (West Supp. 1989). The presumption of legitimacy may be rebutted only by the husband or wife, and then only in limited circumstances. The instant appeal presents the claim that this presumption infringes upon the due process rights of a man who wishes to establish his paternity of a child born to the wife of another man, and the claim that it infringes upon the constitutional right of the child to maintain a relationship with her natural father.

I

The facts of this case are, we must hope, extraordinary. On May 9, 1976, in Las Vegas, Nevada, Carole D., an international model, and Gerald D., a top executive in a French oil company, were married. The couple established a home in Playa del Rey, California in which they resided as husband and wife when one or the other was not out of the country on business. In the summer of 1978, Carole became involved in an adulterous affair with a neighbor, Michael H. In September 1980, she conceived a child, Victoria D., who was born on May 11, 1981. Gerald was listed as father on the birth certificate and has always held Victoria out to the world as his daughter. Soon after delivery of the child, however, Carole informed Michael that she believed he might be the father.

In the first three years of her life, Victoria remained always with Carole, but found herself within a variety of quasi-family units. In October 1981, Gerald moved to New York City to pursue his business interests, but Carole chose to remain in California. The end of that month, Carole and Michael had blood tests of themselves and Victoria, which showed a 98.07% probability that Michael was Victoria's father. In January 1982, Carole visited Michael in St. Thomas, where his primary business interests were based. There Michael held Victoria out as his child. In March, however, Carole left Michael and returned to California, where she took up residence with yet another man, Scott K. Later that spring, and again in the summer, Carole and Victoria spent time with Gerald in New York City, as well as on vacation in Europe. In the fall, they returned to Scott in California.

In November 1982, rebuffed in his attempts to visit Victoria, Michael filed a filiation action in California Superior Court to establish his paternity and right to visitation. In March 1983, the court appointed an attorney and guardian ad litem to represent Victoria's interests. Victoria then filed a cross-complaint asserting that if she had more than one psychological or *de facto* father, she was entitled to maintain her filial relationship, with all of the attendant rights, duties, and obligations, with both. In May 1983, Carole filed a motion for summary judgment. During this period, from March through July of 1983, Carole was again living with Gerald in New York. In August, however, she returned to California, became involved once again with Michael, and instructed her attorneys to remove the summary judgment motion from the calendar.

For the ensuing eight months, when Michael was not in St. Thomas he lived with Carole and Victoria in Carole's apartment in Los Angeles, and held Victoria out as his daughter. In April 1984, Carole and Michael signed a stipulation that Michael was Victoria's natural father. Carole left Michael the next month, however, and instructed her attorneys not to file the stipulation. In June 1984, Carole reconciled with Gerald and joined him in New York, where they now live with Victoria and two other children since born into the marriage.

In May 1984, Michael and Victoria, through her guardian ad litem, sought visitation rights for Michael *pendente lite*. To assist in determining whether visitation would be in Victoria's best interests, the Superior Court appointed a psychologist to evaluate Victoria, Gerald, Michael, and Carole. The psychologist recommended that Carole retain sole custody, but that

Michael be allowed continued contact with Victoria pursuant to a restricted visitation schedule. The court concurred and ordered that Michael be provided with limited visitation privileges *pendente lite*.

On October 19, 1984, Gerald, who had intervened in the action, moved for summary judgment on the ground that under Cal. Evid. Code § 621 there were no triable issues of fact as to Victoria's paternity. This law provides that "the issue of a wife cohabiting with her husband, who is not impotent or sterile, is conclusively presumed to be a child of the marriage." * * * The presumption may be rebutted by blood tests, but only if a motion for such tests is made, within two years from the date of the child's birth, either by the husband or, if the natural father has filed an affidavit acknowledging paternity, by the wife. §§ 621(c) and (d).

On January 28, 1985, having found that affidavits submitted by Carole and Gerald sufficed to demonstrate that the two were cohabiting at conception and birth and that Gerald was neither sterile nor impotent, the Superior Court granted Gerald's motion for summary judgment, rejecting Michael's and Victoria's challenges to the constitutionality of § 621. The court also denied their motions for continued visitation pending the appeal under Cal. Civ. Code § 4601, which provides that a court may, in its discretion, grant "reasonable visitation rights * * * to any * * * person having an interest in the welfare of the child." * * * It found that allowing such visitation would "violat[e] the intention of the Legislature by impugning the integrity of the family unit."

* * *

Before us, Michael and Victoria both raise equal protection and due process challenges. *We do not reach Michael's equal protection claim, however, as it was neither raised nor passed upon below* [emphasis added by editor].

II

The California statute that is the subject of this litigation is, in substance, more than a century old. * * * In their present form, the substantive provisions of the statute are as follows:

§ 621. Child of the marriage; notice of motion for blood tests

(a) Except as provided in subdivision (b), the issue of a wife cohabiting with her husband, who is not impotent or sterile, is conclusively presumed to be a child of the marriage.

(b) Notwithstanding the provisions of subdivision (a), if the court finds that the conclusions of all the experts, as disclosed by the evidence based upon blood tests performed pursuant to Chapter 2 (commencing with § 890) of Division 7 are that the husband is not the father of the child, the question of paternity of the husband shall be resolved accordingly.

(c)   The notice of motion for blood tests under subdivision (b) may be raised by the husband not later than two years from the child's date of birth.

(d)   The notice of motion for blood tests under subdivision (b) may be raised by the mother of the child not later than two years from the child's date of birth if the child's biological father has filed an affidavit with the court acknowledging paternity of the child.

(e)   The provisions of subdivision (b) shall not apply to any case coming within the provisions of § 7005 of the Civil Code [dealing with artificial insemination] or to any case in which the wife, with the consent of the husband, conceived by means of a surgical procedure.

III

* * * Michael contends as a matter of substantive due process that because he has established a parental relationship with Victoria, protection of Gerald's and Carole's marital union is an insufficient state interest to support termination of that relationship. This argument is, of course, predicated on the assertion that Michael has a constitutionally protected liberty interest in his relationship with Victoria.

It is an established part of our constitutional jurisprudence that the term "liberty" in the Due Process Clause extends beyond freedom from physical restraint. * * * In an attempt to limit and guide interpretation of the Clause, we have insisted not merely that the interest denominated as a "liberty" be "fundamental" (a concept that, in isolation, is hard to objectify), but also that it be an interest traditionally protected by our society.

* * *

This insistence that the asserted liberty interest be rooted in history and tradition is evident, as elsewhere, in our cases according constitutional protection to certain parental rights. Michael reads the landmark case of *Stanley v. Illinois*, 405 U.S. 645 (1972), and the subsequent cases of *Quilloin v. Walcott*, 434 U.S. 246 (1978), *Caban v. Mohammed*, 441 U.S. 380 (1979) and *Lehr v. Robertson*, 463 U.S. 248, as establishing that a liberty interest is created by biological fatherhood plus an established parental relationship—factors that exist in the present case as well. We think that distorts the rationale of those cases. As we view them, they rest not upon such isolated factors but upon the historic respect—indeed, sanctity would not be too strong a term—traditionally accorded to the relationships that develop within the unitary family. In *Stanley*, for example, we forbade the destruction of such a family when, upon the death of the mother, the state had sought to remove children from the custody of a father who had lived with and supported them and their mother for 18 years. As Justice Powell stated for the plurality in *Moore v. East Cleveland*, 431 U.S. 494 (1977): "Our decisions establish that the Constitution protects the sanctity of the family precisely because the institution of the family is deeply rooted in this Nation's history and tradition."

Thus, the legal issue in the present case reduces to whether the relationship between persons in the situation of Michael and Victoria has been treated as a protected family unit under the historic practices of our society, or whether on any other basis it has been accorded special protection. We think it impossible to find that it has. In fact, quite to the contrary, our traditions have protected the marital family (Gerald, Carole, and the child they acknowledge to be theirs) against the sort of claim Michael asserts.

The presumption of legitimacy was a fundamental principle of the common law. Traditionally, that presumption could be rebutted only by proof that a husband was incapable of procreation or had had no access to his wife during the relevant period.

* * *

We have found nothing in the older sources, nor in the older cases, addressing specifically the power of the natural father to assert parental rights over a child born into a woman's existing marriage with another man. Since it is Michael's burden to establish that such a power (at least where the natural father has established a relationship with the child) is so deeply embedded within our traditions as to be a fundamental right, the lack of evidence alone might defeat his case. But the evidence shows that even in modern times—when, as we have noted, the rigid protection of the marital family has in other respects been relaxed—the ability of a person in Michael's position to claim paternity has not been generally acknowledged. For example, a 1957 annotation on the subject: "Who may dispute presumption of legitimacy of child conceived or born during wedlock," 53 A.L.R.2d 572, shows three States (including California) with statutes limiting standing to the husband or wife and their descendants, one State (Louisiana) with a statute limiting it to the husband, two States (Florida and Texas) with judicial decisions limiting standing to the husband, and two States (Illinois and New York) with judicial decisions denying standing even to the mother. Not a single decision is set forth specifically according standing to the natural father, and "express indications of the nonexistence of any * * * limitation" upon standing were found only "in a few jurisdictions."

Moreover, even if it were clear that one in Michael's position generally possesses, and has generally always possessed, standing to challenge the marital child's legitimacy, that would still not establish Michael's case. As noted earlier, what is at issue here is not entitlement to a state pronouncement that Victoria was begotten by Michael. It is no conceivable denial of constitutional right for a State to decline to declare facts unless some legal consequence hinges upon the requested declaration. What Michael asserts here is a right to have himself declared the natural father *and thereby to obtain parental prerogatives.* What he must establish, therefore, is not that our society has traditionally allowed a natural father in his circumstances to establish paternity, but that it has traditionally accorded such a father parental rights, or at least has not traditionally denied them. Even if the law in all States had always been that the entire world could challenge the marital presumption and obtain a declaration as to who was the natural father, that would not advance Michael's claim. Thus, it is ultimately irrelevant, even for purposes of determining *current* social attitudes towards the alleged substantive right Michael asserts, that the present law in a number of States appears to allow the natural father— including the natural father who has not established a relationship with the child—the theoretical power to rebut the marital presumption, see Note, *Rebutting the Marital Presumption: A Developed Relationship Test*, 88 COL. L. REV. 369, 373 (1988). What counts is whether the States in fact award substantive parental rights to the natural father of a child conceived within and born into an extant marital union that wishes to embrace the child. We are not aware of a single case, old or new, that has done so. This is not the stuff of which fundamental rights qualifying as liberty interests are made.[6]

---

[6] Justice Brennan criticizes our methodology in using historical traditions specifically relating to the rights of an adulterous natural father, rather that inquiring more generally "whether parenthood is an interest that historically has received our attention and protection." There seems to us no basis for the contention that this methodology is "nove[l]." For example, in *Bowers v. Hardwick*, 478 U.S. 186 (1986), we noted that at the time the Fourteenth Amendment was ratified all but 5 of the 37 States had criminal sodomy laws, that all 50 of the States had such laws prior to 1961, and that 24 States and the District of Columbia continued to have them: and we concluded from that record, regarding that very specific aspect of sexual conduct, that "to claim that a right to engage in such conduct is 'deeply rooted in this Nation's history and tradition' or 'implicit in the concept of ordered liberty' is, at best, facetious." In *Roe v. Wade*, 410 U.S. 113 (1973), we spent about a fifth of our opinion negating the proposition that there was a longstanding tradition of laws proscribing abortion.

We do not understand why, having rejected our focus upon the societal tradition regarding the natural father's rights vis-a-vis a child whose mother is married to another man, Justice Brennan would choose to focus instead upon "parenthood." Why should the relevant category not be even more general—perhaps "family relationships"; or "personal relationships"; or even "emotional attachments in general"? Though the dissent has no basis for the level of generality it would select, we do: We refer to the most specific level at which a relevant tradition protecting, or denying protection to, the asserted right can be identified. If, for example, there were no societal tradition, either way, regarding the rights of the natural father of a child adulterously conceived, we would have to consult, and (if possible) reason from, the traditions regarding natural fathers in general. But there is such a more specific tradition, and it unqualifiedly denies protection to such a parent.

One would think that Justice Brennan would appreciate the value of consulting the most specific tradition available, since he acknowledges that "[e]ven if we can agree * * * that 'family' and 'parenthood' are part of the good life, it is absurd to assume that we can agree on the content of those terms and destructive to pretend that we do." Because such general traditions provide

* * *

[W]e [have] observed that "[t]he significance of the biological connection is that it offers the natural father an opportunity that no other male possesses to develop a relationship with his offspring," (*Lehr, supra*) and * * * assumed that the Constitution might require some protection of that opportunity. Where, however, the child is born into an extant marital family, the natural father's unique opportunity conflicts with the similarly unique opportunity of the husband of the marriage; and it is not unconstitutional for the State to give categorical preference to the latter. * * * [A]lthough " '[i]n some circumstances the actual relationship between father and child may suffice to create in the unwed father parental interests comparable to those of the married father,' " " 'the absence of a legal tie with the mother may in such circumstances appropriately place a limit on whatever substantive constitutional claims might otherwise exist.' " *Caban, supra* at 397 (Stewart J., dissenting). In accord with our traditions, a limit is also imposed by the circumstance that the mother is, at the time of the child's conception and birth, married to and cohabitating with another man, both of whom wish to raise the child as the offspring of their union.[7] It is a question of legislative policy and not constitutional law whether California will allow the presumed parenthood of a couple desiring to retain a child conceived within and born into their marriage to be rebutted.

---

such imprecise guidance, they permit judges to dictate rather than discern the society's views. The need, if arbitrary decision-making is to be avoided, to adopt the most specific tradition as the point of reference-or at least to announce, as Justice Brennan declines to do, some other criterion for selecting among the innumerable relevant traditions that could be consulted-is well enough exemplified by the fact that in the present case Justice Brennan's opinion and Justice O'Connor's opinion, which disapproves this footnote, *both* appeal to tradition, but on the basis of the tradition they select reach opposite results. Although assuredly having the virtue (if it be that) of leaving judges free to decide as they think best when the unanticipated occurs, a rule of law that binds neither by text nor by any particular, identifiable tradition, is no rule of law at all.

Finally, we may note that this analysis is not inconsistent with the result in cases such as *Griswold v. Connecticut*, 381 U.S. 479 (1965) or *Eisenstadt v. Baird*, 405 U.S. 438 (1972). None of those cases acknowledged a longstanding and still extant societal tradition withholding the very right pronounced to be the subject of a liberty interest and then rejected it. Justice Brennan must do so here. In this case, the existence of such a tradition, continuing to the present day, refutes any possible contention that the alleged right is "so rooted in the traditions and conscience of our people as to be ranked as fundamental," or "implicit in the concept of ordered liberty."

    7   Justice Brennan chides us for thus limiting our holding to situations in which, as here, the husband and wife wish to raise her child jointly. The dissent believes that without this limitation we would be unable to "rely on the State's asserted interest in protecting the 'unitary family' in denying that Michael and Victoria have been deprived of liberty." As we have sought to make clear, however, and as the dissent elsewhere seems to understand, we rest our decision not upon our independent "balancing" of such interests, but upon the absence of any constitutionally protected right to legal parentage on the part of an adulterous natural father in Michael's situation, as evidenced by long tradition. That tradition reflects a "balancing" that has already been made by society itself. We limit our pronouncement to the relevant facts of this case because it is at least possible that our traditions lead to a different conclusion with regard to adulterous fathering of a child whom the marital parents do not wish to raise as their own. It seems unfair for those who disagree with our holding to include among their criticisms that we have not extended the holding more broadly.

We do not accept Justice Brennan's criticism that this result "squashes" the liberty that consists of "the freedom not to conform." It seems to us that reflects the erroneous view that there is only one side to this controversy—that one disposition can expand a "liberty" of sorts without contracting an equivalent "liberty" on the other side. Such a happy choice is rarely available. Here, to *provide* protection to an adulterous natural father is to *deny* protection to a marital father, and vice versa. If Michael has a "freedom not to conform" (whatever that means), Gerald must equivalently have a "freedom to conform." One of them will pay a price for asserting that "freedom"—Michael by being unable to act as father of the child he has adulterously begotten, or Gerald by being unable to preserve the integrity of the traditional family unit he and Victoria have established. Our disposition does not choose between these two "freedoms," but leaves that to the people of California. Justice Brennan's approach chooses one of them as the constitutional imperative, on no apparent basis except that the unconventional is to be preferred.

IV

We have never had occasion to decide whether a child has a liberty interest, symmetrical with that of her parent, in maintaining her filial relationship. We need not do so here because, even assuming that such a right exists, Victoria's claim must fail. Victoria's due process challenge is, if anything, weaker than Michael's. Her basic claim is not that California has erred in preventing her from establishing that Michael, not Gerald, should stand as her legal father. Rather, she claims a due process right to maintain filial relationships with both Michael and Gerald. This assertion merits little discussion, for, whatever the merits of the guardian ad litem's belief that such an arrangement can be of great psychological benefit to a child, the claim that a State must recognize multiple fatherhood has no support in the history or traditions of this country. Moreover, even if we were to construe Victoria's argument as forwarding the lesser proposition that, whatever her status vis-a-vis Gerald, she has a liberty interest in maintaining a filial relationship with her natural father, Michael, we find that, at best, her claim is the obverse of Michael's and fails for the same reasons.

Victoria claims in addition that her equal protection rights have been violated because, unlike her mother and presumed father, she had no opportunity to rebut the presumption of her legitimacy. We find this argument wholly without merit. We reject, at the outset, Victoria's suggestion that her equal protection challenge must be assessed under a standard of strict scrutiny because, in denying her the right to maintain a filial relationship with Michael, the State is discriminating against her on the basis of her illegitimacy. Illegitimacy is a legal construct, not a natural trait. Under California law, Victoria is not illegitimate, and she is treated in the same manner as all other legitimate children: she is entitled to maintain a filial relationship with her legal parents.

We apply, therefore, the ordinary "rational relationship" test to Victoria's equal protection challenge. The primary rationale underlying § 621's limitation on those who may rebut the presumption of legitimacy is a concern that allowing persons other than the husband or wife to do so may undermine the integrity of the marital union. When the husband or wife contests the legitimacy of their child, the stability of the marriage has already been shaken. In contrast, allowing a claim of illegitimacy to be pressed by the child—or, more accurately, by a court-appointed guardian ad litem-may well disrupt an otherwise peaceful union. Since it pursues a legitimate end by rational means, California's decision to treat Victoria differently from her parents is not a denial of equal protection. * * *

Affirmed.

NOTES AND QUESTIONS

1.   Is it relevant to the *Michael H.* plurality's decision that Carole was residing with Gerald when Victoria was born? What if Carole had filed for divorce? *See* Brian C. v. Ginger K., 92 Cal. Rptr. 2d 294 (App. 2000); Fish v. Behers, 741 A.2d 721 (Pa. 1999). Is it relevant that by the time of the decision Carole and Gerald has been living as a family in New York for five years and had two other children? *See* June Carbone and Naomi Cahn, *Which Ties Bind? Redefining the Parent-Child Relationship in an Age of Genetic Certainty,* 11 WM. & MARY BILL RTS. J. 1011, 1044 (2003).

2.   Justice Brennan's dissent urged that "the original reasons for the conclusive presumption of paternity are out of place in a world in which blood tests can prove virtually beyond a shadow of a doubt who sired a particular child and in which the fact of illegitimacy no longer plays the burdensome and stigmatizing role it once did." *Michael H.*, 491 U.S. at 140. What factors led common law courts to enunciate the marital presumption? Is Justice Brennan correct that *all* of the "reasons for the presumption are out of place in a world [of conclusive] * * * blood tests"? If not, which reasons survive? Are those reasons adequate to support a rule which deprives fathers like Michael H. of the opportunity to enjoy a relationship with their children?

3.   *Michael H.* is only one (but *the* one to reach the U.S. Supreme Court) of a line of cases in which unmarried fathers have challenged the presumption of legitimacy. Most of these challenges have been brought on equal protection grounds. Because the Supreme Court did not consider the equal protection argument, the precedential value of the plurality opinion in *Michael H.* is limited. In A. v. X., Y., and Z., 641 P.2d 1222 (Wyo. 1982), cert. denied 459 U.S. 1021 (1982), the equal protection issue was squarely presented:

> * * * [T]he trial court properly found that * * * the State has an interest in protecting and preserving the integrity of the family unit.
> * * * It also has an interest in protecting the best interests of the

child. Even in this era of no-fault divorce, frequent premarital sex and cohabitation and new attitudes toward child rearing, a child has a right to legitimacy and that right is one the State is bound to protect during minority.

* * *

The statute is a legitimate attempt by the legislature to protect the family unit and the children from external forces. A suit by one outside the marriage, such as in this case, could well destroy a marriage. * * * [Appellant] is concerned that the mother (actually those within the family unit-the child, the mother, and the presumed father) can bring a parentage action which would have the same deleterious effect on the marriage as would a suit by an outsider. But, the members of the family, not the outsider, are in the best position to judge whether the marriage can stand the trauma or has already failed. * * *

With *X.Y.Z.* and *Michael H.*, compare the decision in *In re* Paternity of C.A.S., 468 N.W.2d 719 (Wis. 1991):

We do not * * * suggest that a putative father may never have a constitutionally protected right to establish his parentage of an illegitimate child. Rather, we conclude that if a putative father of a child born to the wife of another man has not established an actual relationship with that child, he does not have a constitutionally protected interest in establishing his parentage of the child, or in a relationship with that child. * * * An existing marital unit is not a per se bar to a blood test, however. Ultimately, it is the manner in which this unit contributes to the best interests of the children that renders it significant. The best interests of the children are the ultimate and paramount considerations in this case, and reflect a strong public policy of this state. * * *

Is the *C.A.S.* approach likely to produce more or less litigation than that of *X.Y.Z.*? What values are served by each approach? Does the child have a stronger interest in "legitimacy" or in identifying the biological parent? *See also In re* J.W.T., 872 S.W.2d 189 (Tex. 1994) (interpreting state constitution to protect an unwed father's interest in establishing paternity, even if the mother is married).

4.   *Michael H.* is based on the assumption that a child may have only one father. Would it make sense to establish a legal relationship between the child and *both* her mother's husband and biological father? What are the pros and cons of this approach? *See* Bodwell v. Brooks, 686 A.2d 1179 (N.H. 1996). *See generally* Nancy E. Dowd, *Multiple Parents/Multiple Fathers*, 9 J. L. & FAM. STUD. 231 (2007). Ira Mark Ellman, *Thinking About Custody and Support in Ambiguous-Father Families*, 36 FAM. L Q. 49 (2002).

3.　ESTABLISHING PATERNITY

A.　PATERNITY ACTIONS AND PROCEDURES

All states provide a judicial process for establishing paternity. In some states, this process is called a "filiation" proceeding, in others a "paternity" action.

The paternity action evolved from the criminal law. From its inception, the action was designed to assist welfare authorities on whom the burden of supporting the child would fall if the father could not be held responsible. Professor Krause notes that:

> The first such statute was enacted in England in 1576 and labeled 'An Act for Setting the Poor on Work.' It provided as follows:
>
>> Concerning bastards begotten and born out of lawful matrimony (an offence against God's law and man's law) the said bastards being now left to be kept at the charges of the parish where they be born, to the great burden of the same parish, and in defrauding of the relief of the impotent and aged true poor of the same parish, and to the evil example and encouragement of the lewd life: (2) It is ordained and enacted by the authority aforesaid, That two Justices of the peace (whereof one to be of the *quorum*, in or next unto the limits where the parish church is, within which parish such bastard shall be born, upon examination of the cause and circumstance) shall and may by their discretion take order, as well for the punishment of the mother and reputed father of such bastard child, as also for the better relief of every such parish in part or in all; (3) and shall and may likewise by such discretion take order for the keeping of every such bastard child, by charging such mother or reputed father with the payment of money weekly or other sustentation for the relief of such child in such wise as they shall think meet and convenient. * * *
>
> The attitude that the paternity action is brought primarily for the benefit of the public persists. * * * Throughout most of the country, the action remains of limited scope, the primary and usually sole objective being to charge the father with a limited duty to support his illegitimate child. Only a few statutes allow the court to confer legitimate status on the child in the paternity proceeding or award inheritance rights in addition to support. * * *
>
> Paternity practice has suffered from the old saw to the effect that "maternity is a matter of fact whereas paternity is a matter of

opinion." * * * Current paternity prosecution practice in many metropolitan areas is abhorrent. Blackmail and perjury flourish, accusation is often tantamount to conviction, decades of support obligation are decided upon in minutes of court time and indigent defendants usually go without counsel or a clear understanding of what is involved.

HARRY KRAUSE, ILLEGITIMACY: LAW AND SOCIAL POLICY 105 (1971).

At the time Professor Krause wrote, state paternity laws were quite varied. A few states retained remnants of the common law bastardy action, which permitted a paternity claim to be made on behalf of the child throughout the child's minority. *See* Doughty v. Engler, 211 P. 619 (Kan. 1923). Either in addition to or in lieu of the bastardy action, several states had laws which permitted the mother to bring an action to obtain child support and recover expenses related to pregnancy and child birth. These statutes usually had statutes of limitation that required initiation of such an action within one to two years of the child's birth. Few states made provision, other than a declaratory judgment action, to allow fathers to establish their paternity. *See* Slawek v. Stroh, 215 N.W.2d 9 (Wis. 1974).

Paternity trials at this time typically turned on circumstantial evidence (dates of intercourse compared with date of birth) and the credibility of the parties. Because the defendant could escape liability by using the defense of *exception plurium concubenium* (i.e., that other men had had sexual relations with the mother during the period of conception), the mother's virtue was often a major focus of the litigation. *See* Jane L. v. Rodney B., 444 N.Y.S.2d 1012 (Fam. Ct. 1981); Stephen Sass, *The Defense of Multiple Access (Exception Plurium Concubentium) in Paternity Suits: A Comparative Analysis*, 51 TULANE L. REV. 468 (1977). Some states allowed jury trials; some treated the paternity action as quasi-criminal and required the plaintiff to prove parentage by clear and convincing evidence.

1. Paternity Actions

The National Conference of Commissioners on Uniform States Law (now called the Uniform Law Commission) promulgated a Uniform Parentage Act in 1973 UPA (1973), 9B U.L.A. 295 UPA (1973) which emphasized parentage, rather than legitimacy. It removed the legal status of illegitimacy. Section 2 stated "The parent and child relationship extends equally to every child and every parent, regardless of the marital status of the parent." At one time, nineteen states had enacted it. Revisions were made in 2000 with amendments in 2002 to reflect changes in genetic testing and assisted reproduction. The Uniform Parentage Act as revised in 2000 and amended in 2002 has been enacted in eleven states. A Revised Uniform Parentage Act passed in 2017. See www.uniformlaw.org. One of its goals is to ensure equal treatment of children born to same-sex couples in light of Obergefell v. Hodges, 135 S. Ct. 2584 (2015).

Today, the paternity action is treated as a civil action. The Uniform Parentage Act (1973) § 14(a) and UPA (2002) § 601 specify that the paternity action will be "governed by the rules of civil procedure." Federal guidelines have eliminated jury trials in paternity actions. See 42 U.S.C.A. § 666(a)(5)(I). The UPA (2002) § 632 provides that any trial shall be by the court without a jury.

The Supreme Court has ruled that the standard of proof required to prove parentage is only a preponderance of the evidence. Rivera v. Minnich, 483 U.S. 574 (1987). Some states require appointment of counsel for an indigent defendant. *See* UPA (1973) § 19.

The Uniform Parentage Act (1973) § 12 set out the type of evidence that could be admitted: (1) evidence of sexual intercourse between the mother and alleged father at time of conception; (2) an expert's opinion concerning the statistical probability of the alleged father's paternity based upon the duration of the pregnancy; (3) blood test results, weighted in accordance with evidence, if available, of the statistical probability of the alleged father's paternity; (4) medical or anthropological evidence relating to the alleged father's paternity; and (5) all other evidence relevant to the issue of paternity of the child. Some states specifically excluded evidence of sexual intercourse by the woman with a man at any time other than the time of conception. The UPA (2002) now disallows evidence related to paternity except the results of genetic tests. UPA (2002) § 621.

2.   Advent of Genetic Evidence

With the advent of exclusionary blood testing, the focus of paternity litigation shifted dramatically. The UPA (1973) § 11 provided that "The court may, and upon request of a party shall, require the child, mother, or alleged father to submit to blood tests. The tests shall be performed by an expert qualified as an examiner of blood types, appointed by the court." One of the early questions was who would pay for paternity blood testing. In Little v. Streater, 452 U.S. 1 (1981), the United States Supreme Court held that the state must pay for blood tests requested by indigent civil paternity defendants in some instances.

Courts struggled with the weight to be given to this new form of evidence which was based on the typing of the antigens found on red blood cells. They were "exclusionary" and could eliminate, but not confirm, the possibility of paternity. The results were stated in two figures. The first is a "probability of exclusion" (PE) which is computed for a particular test based on the frequency of the trait in the relevant population. The second is the "probability of paternity" which measures the likelihood that the particular combination of traits would occur in a randomly selected man. The red blood typing test yielded low PEs. See State ex rel. Hausner v. Blackman, 662 P.2d 1183 (Kan. 1983) (discussing exclusionary tests). The human leukocyte antigen (HLA) blood testing system detects markers on white blood cells. HLA testing added to the red cell blood tests could exclude a defendant as the father with 98.8% accuracy.

Today, DNA (deoxyribonucleic acid), or "genetic marker" testing offers a highly reliable method of paternity establishment that can confirm or disprove paternity at a 99% probability. *See* Paula Roberts, *Truth and Consequences: Part I, Disestablishing the Paternity of Non-Marital Children*, 37 FAM. L. Q. 35, 36 n. 5 (2003). Genetic marker testing can be done with many different types of specimens—blood, body tissue, fluid, sperm and bone—but buccal swab testing is most typical. *See* Cable v. Anthou, 699 A.2d 722 (Pa. 1997). Because genetic marker testing is so accurate and easily obtained, even after death, some questions have arisen as to whether genetic evidence should always trump. *See* Swafford v. Norton, 992 So. 2d 20 (Ala. Civ. App. 2008).

3.   Federal Government Interest in Paternity Establishment

While the early paternity actions were usually brought by mothers for support purposes, public welfare agencies began bringing actions to seek reimbursement for public funds spent on a child. The laws implementing the Aid to Families with Dependent Children (AFDC), part of the 1935 Social Security Act, required states to undertake procedures to establish paternity. When mothers were reluctant to reveal the names of fathers, states often did not push. Statutes of limitation for paternity had tradionally been short. The Supreme Court stated that the period of limitations on paternity actions must be long enough to give the child or his representative a reasonable opportunity to assert the claim and that the period of limitation must be substantially related to the state's interest in preventing the bringing of stale or fraudulent claims. The Court proceeded to invalidate a number of statutes of limitation on equal protection grounds, holding that short periods of limitation were not substantially related to the state's interest in avoiding stale or fraudulent claims. *See* Mills v. Habluetzel, 456 U.S. 91 (1982) (one year after birth); Pickett v. Brown, 462 U.S. 1 (1983) (two years); Clark v. Jeter, 486 U.S. 456 (1988) (six years).

In 1984, the Child Support Enforcement Amendments (which passed unanimously) required each state to permit paternity establishment at any time prior to a child's eighteenth birthday as a condition of federal funding. 42 U.S.C. § 666(a)(5)(A)(i). UPA (1973) § 7 provides that an action by or on behalf of a child whose paternity has not been detrmined may be brought until three years after the child reaches majority.

When background studies showed ninety percent of the beneficiaries of AFDC were mother-headed single parent families with minor children, proving paternity took on increased importance.

The Personal Responsibility and Work Opportunity Reconciliation Act of 1996 (PRWORA), Pub. L. No. 104–193, 110 Stat. 2105 (1996), imposed on the states a range of requirements aimed at early paternity establishment, including provision for voluntary acknowledgments of paternity, early genetic testing, and limitations on rebuttal of a presumption of paternity. Summarizing the shift in paternity establishment, Paul S. Legler, *The Coming Revolution in Child Support Policy: Implications of the 1996 Welfare Act*, 30 FAM. L. Q. 519 (1996) writes:

> The changes in paternity establishment law mandated by PRWORA are the result of three developments that have occurred over the past decade: a change in social perspective, in-hospital paternity establishment, and advancement in genetic testing.
>
> * * * the change in social perspective on the importance of paternity establishment. As policymakers began to pay attention to the mushrooming number of out-of-wedlock births during the 1980s, there was a growing focus on the poverty often associated with single parenthood. Establishing paternity was seen as a way to alleviate some of the poverty because it opened the door to the possible receipt of child support. * * *
>
> The second catalyst for change * * * came out of the social sciences. Esther Wattenburg published a study in 1991 focusing on the relationship of young fathers and mothers at the time of out-of-wedlock births. The findings indicated that such births were often the result of established relationships, not casual ones, and that the mothers almost always knew who the father was and where he could be found. Significantly, * * * two-thirds of fathers went to the hospital at the time of the out-of-wedlock birth. * * *
>
> The third catalyst * * * was the advancement made in scientific testing for paternity, especially the use of DNA testing. DNA testing made the identification of fathers a new certainty and suggests the possibility that fathers could be readily and confidently identified, particularly if the legal processes were to be changed to make it easier to obtain genetic tests.

Id. at 527–531.

PRWORA replaced AFDC with block grants to the states, called Temporary Assistance to Needy Families (TANF) and required states to adopt new paternity provisions to receive federal funds for child support enforcement and welfare programs. Federal law requires states to admit into evidence the results of genetic tests to establish paternity if the test is "of a type generally acknowledged as reliable by accreditation bodies designated by the Secretary [of HHS]" and performed by an accredited laboratory. 42 U.S.C. § 666(a)(5)(F). State law must create a rebuttable presumption, or at the option of the state, a conclusive presumption of paternity "upon genetic testing results indicating a threshold probability of the alleged father is the father of the child." 42 U.S.C. § 666(a)(5)(G). The UPA (2002) § 503 establishes a rebuttable presumption if the man has a 99% probability of paternity. UPA (2002) § 621 excludes all evidence related to paternity except the results of genetic tests.

As noted above, PRWORA provides that a valid, unrescinded, unchallenged acknowledgment of paternity is equivalent to a judicial determination of paternity and is entitled to full faith and credit. UPA (2002) Article 3 specifies that a voluntary affidavit represents a judgment for enforcement purposes. Today, all states have procedures for voluntary acknowledgments of paternity. They are now the most common way to establish legal parentage of children born out of wedlock. See Leslie Joan Harris, *Voluntary Acknowledgments of Parentage for Same-Sex Couples*, 20 AM. U. J. GENDER SOC. POL'Y & L. 467 (2012).

4. Presumptions of Parentage

The UPA (1973) allowed for a presumption of paternity, not only if the father was married to the mother or attempted to be married to the mother, but also based on conduct of a man who "while the child is under the age of majority, . . . receives the child into his home and openly holds out the child as his natural child." UPA (1973) § 4(a)(4). Most states amended their versions of the UPA to include a presumption if genetic testing showed probability of parentage over a certain percentage (usually over 97%), if the person has signed a voluntary acknowledgment or if a court in another jurisdiction has adjudicated the person the father. Do the presumptions of paternity have the same basis as the presumption of legitimacy?

What if there are conflicting presumptions? It is possible that there may be two presumptions, i.e. the presumption of a child born to the marriage and a genetic test result showing biological parentage in another person. Should biology always trump? The UPA 1973 § 4(b) provides that when two presumptions conflict, "the presumption which on the facts is founded on the weightier considerations of policy and logic, including the best interest of the child controls." *Id.* Does *Michael H.* present a case of conflicting presumptions? What factors should the court use in weighing conflicting presumptions? See GDK v. State, Dept of Family Services, 92 P.3d 834, 839 (Wyo 2004) (court should consider the broader sociological and psychological ramifications of its decision as to which man should be adjudicated the father); Greer ex rel. Farbo v. Greer, 324 P.3d 310 (Kan. App. 2014) (suggesting numerous factors including whether the child thinks the presumed father is the father and has a relationship with him).

The presumptions referred only to men because at the time of drafting, marriages were permitted only between a man and a woman. Can the UPA (1973) be used to recognize a same-sex partner as parent of a child born during the relationship? In Frazier v. Goudschaal, 295 P.3d 542 (Kan. 2013), the Kansas Supreme Court found that a co-parenting contract for children born of artificial insemination to one partner was not against public policy. The court enforced the agreement. The concurring opinion, however, gave perhaps the strongest, and easiest, approach to parentage using the UPA. Justice Biles in his concurring opinion notes that the Kansas Parentage Act [based on the UPA 1973] provides sufficient statutory framework to determine that the nonbiological partner was a legal parent and entitled to enforce the coparenting agreement. He stated:

> * * * we start with jurisdiction. A plain reading of K.S.A. 38–1126, which states that "[a]ny interested party may bring an action to determine the existence or nonexistence of a mother and child relationship" gives Frazier standing to present her case. And with jurisdiction established, the district court's finding that Frazier recognized maternity in writing is supported by substantial competent evidence and invokes the KPA's statutory presumptions regarding parenthood under K.S.A. 38–1114(a)(4).
>
> K.S.A. 38–1113(a) provides that a child's mother "may be established by proof of her having given birth to the child *or under this act*." (Emphasis added.) Looking further into the statutory scheme, K.S.A. 38–1114(a) provides certain statutory presumptions of paternity. And while those statutory presumptions are written in the context of a man being declared the father of a child, K.S.A. 38–1126 instructs that those presumptions are to be read in a gender-neutral manner "insofar as practicable" in an action to determine under the act the existence of a mother and child relationship. In addition to being mandated by statute, this gender-neutral reading is consistent with what this court has found to be one purpose of the KPA, which is to provide for equal and beneficial treatment of all children, regardless of their parent's marital status. See *In re Marriage of Ross*, 245 Kan. 591, 597, 783 P.2d 331 (1989); K.S.A. 38–1112. Children resulting from assisted reproductive technologies should enjoy the same treatment, protections, and support as all other children.
>
> From this juncture, we need only look to K.S.A. 38–1114(a)(4), which provides for a presumption of parentage when the child's paternity has been recognized "notoriously or in writing." * * * substantial competent evidence most certainly supports the district court's finding that the coparenting agreement and other facts were sufficient to invoke that statutory presumption.

Put simply, there is no question Goudschaal and Frazier entered into written agreements that recognized Frazier's status as a coparent and recited that Goudschaal consented to and fostered a parent and child relationship between the children and Frazier. And to the extent Goudschaal argues now that the statutory presumption in K.S.A. 38–1114(a)(4) should be rebutted due to her biological status over Frazier, K.S.A. 38–1114(c) provides the court with discretion to determine which presumptions should control within "the weightier considerations of policy and logic, including the best interests of the child." Examining the children's best interests, the district court found that it was in the children's best interests to have a parent and child relationship with Frazier. * * *

There are other cases which have used the UPA to find a same-sex partner a parent. See Chatterjee v. King, 280 P.3d 283 (N.M. 2012); Elisa B. v. Superior Court, 117 P.3d 660 (Cal. 2005).

The 2000 revisions to the Uniform Parentage Act carried over the 1973 presumptions and added an express durational requirement to the holding out presumption. The UPA (2002) has five separate classifications of parents: acknowledged, adjudicated, alleged genetic, intended and presumed. The UPA (2002) omitted the UPA (1973) provision on how to resolve cases of conflicting presumptions.

UNIFORM PARENTAGE ACT (2002)

Section 201. Establishment of Parent-Child Relationship

(a) The mother-child relationship is established between a woman and a child by:

(1) the woman's having given birth to the child [,except as otherwise provided in [Article 8][on gestational agreements" or surrogacy arrangements];

(2) an adjudication of the woman's maternity; [or]

(3) adoption of the child by the woman [; or

(4) an adjudication confirming the woman as a parent of a child born to a gestational mother if the agreement was validated under [Article] 8 or is enforceable under other law.]

(b) The father-child relationship is established between a man and a child by:

(1) an unrebutted presumption of the man's paternity of the child under Section 204,

(2) an effective acknowledgment of paternity by the man under [Article] 3,

(3) an adjudication of the man's paternity;

(4) adoption of the child by the man; [or]

(5) the man's having consented to assisted reproduction by a woman under [Article] 7 which resulted in the birth of the child [; or

(6) an adjudication confirming the man as a parent of a child born to a gestational mother if the agreement was validated under [Article] 8 or is enforceable under other law.]

9B U.L.A. 19.

Section 204. Presumption of Paternity

A man is presumed to be the father of a child if:

(1) he and the mother of the child are married to each other and the child is born during the marriage;

(2) he and the mother of the child were married to each other and the child is born within 300 days after the marriage is terminated by death, annulment, declaration of invalidity, or divorce [, or after a decree of separation];

(3) before the birth of the child, he and the mother of the child married each other in apparent compliance with law, even if the attempted marriage is or could be declared invalid, and the child is born during the invalid marriage or within 300 days after its termination by death, annulment, declaration of invalidity, or divorce [, or after a decree of separation];

(4) after the birth of the child, he and the mother of the child married each other in apparent compliance with law, whether or not the marriage is or could be declared invalid, and he voluntarily asserted his paternity of the child, and:

(A) the assertion is in a record filed with [state agency maintaining birth records];

(B) he agreed to be and is named as the child's father on the child's birth certificate; or

(C) he promised in a record to support the child as his own; or

(5) for the first two years of the child's life, he resided in the same household with the child and openly held out the child as his own.

9B U.L.A. 21.

Section 607. Limitation: Child Having Presumed Father

(a) Except as otherwise provided in subsection (b), a proceeding brought by a presumed father, the mother, or another individual to adjudicate the parentage of a child having a presumed father must be commenced not later than two years after the birth of the child.

(b) A proceeding seeking to disprove the father-child relationship between a child and the child's presumed father may be maintained at any time if the court determines that:

(1) the presumed father and the mother of the child neither cohabited nor engaged in sexual intercourse with each other during the probable time of conception; and

(2) the presumed father never openly held out the child as his own.

9B U.L.A. 46.

———————————

How would Michael H. have fared under the UPA (2002)? How do these presumptions differ from the 1973 UPA? Could there still be conflicting presumptions? Consider the Delaware presumptions of parentage.

The 2017 revisions to the Uniform Parentage Act make one additional classification of parents—de facto parents. It also has a provision for factors to consider in resolving conflicting presumptions. Among the factors in Section 613 are age of the child; length of time during which each individual assumed the role of parent; nature of the relationship between the child and each individual; the harm to the child if the relationship between the child and individual is not recognized; and other equitable factors arising from the disruption of the relationship between the child and each individual or the likelihood of harm to the child. How would Michael H. fare under the 2017 proposed UPA?

Problem 7-2:

When Ann and Robert divorced, they were granted joint custody of Susan, born during their marriage; Robert was also required to pay child support. Four years later, Ann filed a petition in which she alleged that Robert was not the biological father of Susan and sought blood tests to prove it. Under the UPA (2002), does Ann have standing? Should the judge order blood tests? *See* Dept. of Hum. Res. ex rel. Duckworth v. Kamp, 949 A.2d 43 (Md. Ct. Spec. App. 2008); Sanders v. Sanders, 558 A.2d 556 (Pa. Super. 1989); *In re* Marriage of Ross, 783 P.2d 331 (Kan. 1989).

Problem 7-3:

A year after Tom was divorced from Jenny and agreed to pay child support pursuant to a marital separation agreement, he discovered that he is now and has always been sterile. Can Tom reopen the divorce judgment? What if he found out within a year of the divorce but did not mention it until six years later when the mother brought an action for increased child support for a sixteen-year-old? *See* Wilson v. Wilson, 827 P.2d 788 (Kan. App. 1992); Anderson v. Anderson, 552 N.E.2d 546 (Mass. 1990); Gilbraith v. Hixson, 512 N.E.2d 956 (Ohio 1987).

Problem 7-4:

Ron and Sharon are in the process of obtaining a divorce. Sharon is pregnant and Ron is pretty sure it is not his child. Ron and Sharon enter into an agreement which specifies that Ron waives all parental rights to the child Sharon is carrying and is relieved of all obligations to pay support. The child is born two months later. Is the child (or the divorce court) bound by Ron and Sharon's agreement? *See* Casbar v. Dicanio, 666 So. 2d 1028 (Fla. Dist. Ct. App. 1996); *In re* Paternity of Janzen v. Janzen, 228 P.3d 425 (Kan. App. 2010).

G.E.B. v. S.R.W.

Massachusetts Supreme Judicial Court, 1996.
422 Mass. 158, 661 N.E.2d 646.

ABRAMS, JUSTICE.

The child brought an action in the Probate and Family Court Department for a judgment of paternity under G.L. c. 209C. The complaint was amended to name the mother as a plaintiff in response to the defendant's claim that the child could not litigate on her own behalf but rather only through a next friend. The putative father (defendant) moved to dismiss the child's action on the ground that the action is barred by his previous action for declaratory relief brought in June, 1982, against the mother and by the settlement agreement that followed. * * *

On November 30, 1990, a Probate Court judge ordered that the issues of paternity and support be bifurcated and that the parties proceed first on the issue of paternity. On October 10, 1991, a judgment of paternity was entered in favor of the child and, in a separate ruling, temporary child support and counsel fees were ordered. The defendant appeals * * *. [W]e affirm.

* * *

Facts. The child was born on February 22, 1982, to the mother, who was not then married and had not been married within 300 days prior the child's birth. The mother asserts that the defendant, with whom she had a sexual relationship for approximately one decade, is the child's father. The defendant disputes this.

In June, 1982, the defendant sought a declaratory judgment against the mother that he was not the child's father. The child was not a party to that action nor was she represented by counsel. Neither a guardian nor next friend was appointed to safeguard the child's interests. That case was settled by an agreement for judgment signed by counsel for the defendant and counsel for the mother. The mother and the defendant also signed a settlement agreement under which the defendant was to pay the mother $25,000 in exchange for the mother's assent to a stipulation stating that the defendant was not the child's father. The agreement purported to be signed by the mother "acting on her own behalf and on behalf of a daughter born to her on February 22, 1982," and provided that neither party would bring any further action or claim arising out of the facts giving rise to the case being settled. The agreement specifically provided that it "shall be binding upon the successors, representatives, heirs and assigns of both parties including, without limitation, the child." The child did not sign the agreement and the agreement did not provide that the money be used for child support. The stipulation was not signed by a judge of the Superior Court nor filed with the Superior Court.

On August 2, 1990, the child brought an action under G.L. c. 209C against the defendant. Genetic marker tests were performed. The plaintiff's expert, Dr. David H. Bing, opined that these tests showed the statistical probability of the defendant's paternity to be 99.8%. The paternity tests performed would have excluded 98.63% of falsely accused men as the father. The trial judge also found a physical resemblance between the defendant and the child in facial bone structure and complexion.

Res judicata effect of 1982 Adjudication under G.L. c. 273. General Laws c. 209C, § 22(d), provides: "No proceeding hereunder shall be barred by a prior finding or adjudication under any repealed sections of [c. 273] or by the fact that a child was born prior to the effective date of this chapter." The parties dispute whether the 1982 action was an adjudication under a repealed section of c. 273. A Probate Court judge found that the subject matter of the prior proceeding was similar in nature to proceedings under G.L. c. 273, § 12, and did not bar a proceeding under c. 209C. We agree. The defendant, as plaintiff in the 1982 action, relied on G.L. c. 273, § 12A, in litigating his claim. The mother, as defendant, counterclaimed for "an adjudication under G.L. c. 273, § 12, that [the defendant] is the father of [the child]." It is clear that the parties, in signing the settlement agreement, were agreeing to a legal determination of the paternity of the child. We agree with the trial judge that, "[i]f, instead of a settlement agreement, there had been an adjudication on the merits of the 1982 action in [the defendant's] favor on the question of paternity, there is no doubt that the prior adjudication would *not* have been a bar to [the child's] claim under G.L. c. 209C in the Probate Court." That the stipulation as to paternity was entered by the agreement of the parties rather than by the court is immaterial in determining whether it can be attacked collaterally.

General Laws c. 209C, § 22(*d*), specifically erodes the common law policy on finality of judgments and allows readjudication of paternity where there has been a judgment in favor of the alleged father. * * * We conclude that the 1982 Superior Court action is not a bar to the current proceeding.

Preclusive effect of 1983 judgment and agreement on the child. Even if the 1982 action could operate as a bar to subsequent proceedings, it could not have preclusive effect on the child who was not a party to that action commenced by the defendant against the mother. As a nonparty, the child's rights could not have been prejudiced by the 1982 action. * * *

The child cannot be bound by the mother's settlement of the mother's claims. We cannot conclude that the child's interests were fully protected by the mother. The child has her own, independent, interests in determining the identity of her father. She has intangible interests independent of monetary support which cannot be equated completely with her mother's interests. * * * ("At some point, the law must recognize the fact that a child's interests in paternity litigation are much greater than the mother's interest in continued support. 'In addition to the right of the child to receive support many other present as well as future rights of the child are involved, depending on the facts and circumstances of a specific case'"). The mother also has independent interests that may prevent her from fully protecting the child's sometimes competing concerns.

The defendant argues that, even if the child were not in privity with her mother and thereby bound, she should be barred from proceeding in this action because her mother was acting as "procheine amie" or "next friend" on her behalf in the 1982 action and released her rights. The child disputes that the mother can bind the child when the mother was not legally the child's representative. *See Rudow v. Fogel*, 376 Mass. 587, 589, 382 N.E.2d 1046 (1978) (policy forbids assimilation of parent litigating on his own behalf with parent litigating as representative of child). The child cannot be bound by her mother's bare assertion that she was acting on behalf of the child without a formal recognition of her status as guardian or without the child's being joined as a party to the action. * * *

Other jurisdictions are in accord. * * *

Additionally, the child has unequivocally disaffirmed her mother's purported release in the settlement agreement by instigating the instant suit. "[A] release is a type of contract which a minor may disaffirm." "A minor, in order to avoid a contract, is not obliged to use any particular words or perform any specific acts. Any acts or words showing unequivocally a repudiation of the contract are sufficient to avoid it." * * *

Even if the mother had been properly acting on behalf of the child, the agreement was subject to disaffirmance by the child who effectively disaffirmed the agreement by filing the instant suit. There is no res judicata effect from the 1982 proceedings.

* * *

The defendant also claims that to allow this suit to proceed would be an unconstitutional impairment of contracts in violation of art. I, § 10, cl. 1, of the United States Constitution. * * * [but t]he defendant's contractual rights were only against the mother, not the child. There is no impairment of contract when a State law authorizes a party not bound by that contract to act.

Estoppel and laches. The defendant argues that the mother is estopped from pursuing this action by virtue of the 1983 judgment and agreement. This argument fails because the mother is not pursuing this action, the child is. The trial judge held that "[i]n equity I don't believe the child should be barred by her mother's actions." We agree. Because, as we have previously said, the mother was not legally a representative of the child, the child cannot be barred from pursuing her legal rights by her mother's representation that she was acting on the child's behalf. The child has done nothing to induce detrimental reliance on the part of the defendant. There is no estoppel.

The defense of laches is equally inapplicable. Laches is an equitable defense. "A judge may find as a fact that laches exists if there has been unjustified, unreasonable, and prejudicial delay in raising a claim." The burden of proving laches rests with the defendant. * * * The defendant offered no proof that the child knew or should have known of her rights under G.L. c. 209C or that she unreasonably delayed after having such knowledge. "[S]o long as there is no knowledge of the wrong committed and no refusal to embrace opportunity to ascertain facts, there can be no laches." The defendant's claim of laches must fail.

* * *

Admission of [evidence]. [The trial court ruled that genetic marker tests could be admitted into evidence based on the mother's affidavit alleging sexual intercourse with the putative father during the probable period of conception.] The [trial] judge ruled that the question of whether "there was intercourse between the parties on several dates * * * is [judged] by a preponderance of the evidence." The defendant asserts that this ruling was erroneous. He contends that "sufficient evidence" required by G.L. c. 209C refers back to the burden [of proof] in G.L. c. 109C, § 7 to establish paternity by clear and convincing evidence. * * *

We decline to imply the clear and convincing standard into § 17 where it is not expressly required. * * * Evidence of intercourse between the defendant and the mother consisted of the mother's testimony. The trial judge found the mother's "testimony in this regard to be credible * * * " * * * This is legally sufficient.

[The court ruled that the trial judge had correctly excluded proffered evidence of the mother's alleged prostitution outside the period of probable conception.] * * * We conclude that the record was sufficient to support the judge's findings of fact and rulings of law. * * *

NOTES AND QUESTIONS

1. Why couldn't the mother in *G.E.B.* represent the child's interest? UPA (1973) § 9 provides that:

> [T]he child shall be made a party to the action. If he is a minor he shall be represented by his general guardian or a guardian ad litem appointed by the court. The child's mother or father may not represent the child as guardian or otherwise. The court may appoint the [appropriate state agency] as guardian ad litem for the child. The natural mother, each man presumed to be the father under § 4, and each man alleged to be the natural father, shall be made parties or, if not subject to the jurisdiction of the court shall be given notice of the action in a manner prescribed by the court and an opportunity to be heard. The court may align the parties.

UPA (2002) § 637(b) provides that a child is a permissible, but not a necessary, party to a paternity action and is not bound by the judgment unless he or she (1) was represented by a guardian ad litem; or (2) the determination of parentage was consistent with genetic tests results and this is stated in the determination. How, if at all, will representation of the child by a guardian ad litem or a child's attorney differ from representation by a parent?

2. *Post-Mortem Genetic Testing:* Because genetic marker tests can be performed on cadavers, courts have recently confronted requests for exhumation of a deceased alleged parent. Several courts have ordered exhumation or release of blood specimens. *See* Wawrykow v. Simonich, 652 A.2d 843 (Pa. Super. 1994); Batcheldor v. Boyd, 423 S.E.2d 810 (N.C. App. 1992), rev. denied. Should the court's response to such a petition depend on whether the child has a legal father or if the child has reached adulthood? *See* UPA (2002) § 606 (providing that a child who has no presumed, acknowledged or adjudicated father has a right to initiate a proceeding to determine own parentage at any time except when the defendant's estate has been closed).

B. PATERNITY DISESTABLISHMENT

HOOKS V. QUAINTANCE

Florida Appellate Court 1st District, 2011.
71 So. 3d 908.

PER CURIAM.

Appellant, Paul Hooks, appeals from the trial court's order dismissing his petition to disestablish paternity based on the finding that Appellant failed to include newly discovered evidence with his petition * * *. Appellant argues that DNA test results, which showed that he was not the biological father of the child, constituted newly discovered evidence for purposes of section 742.18(1). Because we find that Appellant did not exercise due diligence to discover whether he was the biological father of the child, we affirm the trial court's order.

On January 2, 2005, Appellee, Laytoya Quaintance, gave birth to a child. At the time of birth, no father was named on the child's birth certificate. Appellant's name was added to the child's birth certificate with his consent on September 21, 2005. Prior to Appellant's voluntary acknowledgment as the child's father, Appellee informed Appellant that there was no more than a fifty percent chance that he was the child's biological father. On the following day, September 22, 2005, Appellant married Appellee. One of Appellant's reasons for taking these steps included his express desire to provide support to the child by making the child eligible for dependent benefits arising from Appellant's enlistment in the armed forces. On November 30, 2006, the parties divorced, and without objection by either party, the divorce decree identified the child as the child of their marriage.

On January 31, 2010, Appellant filed a petition to disestablish paternity of the child * * * Section 742.18 establishes the procedure for disestablishment of paternity and provides in relevant part the following:

(1) The petition [for disestablishment of paternity] must include:

(a) An affidavit executed by the petitioner that newly discovered evidence relating to the paternity of the child has come to the petitioner's knowledge since the initial paternity determination or establishment of a child support obligation.

(b) The results of scientific tests that are generally acceptable within the scientific community to show a probability of paternity, administered within 90 days prior to the filing of such petition, which results indicate that the male ordered to pay such child support cannot be the father of the child for whom support is required, or an affidavit executed by the petitioner stating that he did not have access to the child to have scientific testing performed prior to the filing of the petition. A male who suspects he is not the father but does not have access to the child to have scientific testing performed may file a petition requesting court to order the child to be tested. *Id.*

There are seven statutory requirements which must be satisfied to prevail on a petition to disestablish paternity. Two of the statutory requirements are at issue in this case. * * * a trial court could grant relief on a petition * * * upon a finding that:

(a) Newly discovered evidence relating to the paternity of the child has come to the petitioner's knowledge since the initial paternity determination or establishment of a child support obligation.

(b) The scientific test required in paragraph (1)(b) was properly conducted. *Id.*

In the petition, Appellant asserted that the results of scientific testing ("DNA test results"), which showed that he was not the biological father of the child, constituted newly discovered evidence * * *. Appellee filed a motion to dismiss, arguing that the petition should be dismissed because Appellant failed to comply with the mandatory requirement of section 742.18 that the petition include newly discovered evidence.

The trial court granted Appellee's motion to dismiss finding that Appellant's DNA test results were not newly discovered evidence within the meaning of the statute because Appellant was fully aware of the possibility of his non-paternity and of the means to resolve any question he had in that regard. Appellant chose not to undergo DNA testing and proceeded to legitimate the child.

On appeal, Appellant seeks reinstatement of his petition, arguing that the trial court erred as a matter of law in its interpretation * * *. Appellant asserts that the trial court's interpretation * * * indicates that no male would be able to disestablish paternity when it has previously been established. Appellant also asserts that DNA test results constitute newly discovered evidence * * * as a matter of law. As support of his argument, Appellant relies upon the fact that section 742.18 requires filing a petition to disestablish paternity within ninety days from acquisition of DNA test results. Appellant asserts that after expiration of this ninety-day period, DNA test results lose "newly discovered evidence" character. We disagree with Appellant.

We review a trial court's interpretation of a statute de novo. * * * In interpreting a statute, "[l]egislative intent guides statutory analysis, and to discern that intent we must look first to the language of the statute and its plain meaning." * * * "[T]he statute's text is the most reliable and authoritative expression of the Legislature's intent." * * * Courts are "without power to construe an unambiguous statute in a way which would extend, modify, or limit, its express terms or its reasonable and obvious implications. To do so would be an abrogation of legislative power." * * * Moreover, "the Legislature does not intend to enact useless provisions, and courts should avoid readings that would render part of a statute meaningless." * * * If the meaning of the statute is clear then the court's task goes no further than applying the plain language of the statute. * * * Courts give effect to "every word, phrase, sentence, and part of the statute, if possible, and words in a statute should not be construed as mere surplusage." * * * With these principles in mind, we turn to the statute at issue in this case.

[1]   After examination of the text in section 742.18, we find that the plain language * * * requires a showing of newly discovered evidence in addition to DNA test results indicating that a male is not the father of the child. The statute treats these two requirements as separate. As a result, we interpret the requirement of newly discovered evidence as distinct from the requirement of a DNA test. Therefore, we reject Appellant's alternative construction and decline to interpret this statute in a way which would render immaterial and redundant the separate references to newly discovered evidence and DNA test results.

[2]   Florida Rule of Civil Procedure 1.540(b)(2) provides that newly discovered evidence is evidence that by due diligence could not have been discovered in time to move for a trial or rehearing. Prior to the enactment of section 742.18, the only remedy for males to challenge paternity was to bring an action pursuant to Florida Rule of Civil Procedure 1.540. * * * The Florida Legislature clearly borrowed this term from Rule 1.540 and placed it in the language of section 742.18. Courts have stated that rule 1.540(b), however, "does not have as its purpose or intent the reopening of lawsuits to allow parties to state new claims or offer new evidence omitted by oversight or inadvertence." * * * The necessary finality of litigation prohibits courts from giving parties a second chance at proof they had available in the first instance but overlooked or chose not to use. *Id.* Relief from judgment based on newly discovered evidence claim should be seldom granted and only when the party seeking relief has exercised due diligence. * * *

[3]   In this case, Appellant has provided no newly discovered evidence as defined by statute. It is undisputed that at the time Appellant voluntarily acknowledged paternity, he was well aware of the fact that there was only a fifty percent chance that he was the biological father, and he admitted that he chose not to have a DNA test. Appellant could have discovered whether he was the biological father in 2005 before he voluntarily acknowledged paternity. However, since he chose not to do so, he did not exercise due diligence to discover whether he was the biological

father. Thus, the trial court correctly found that Appellant's current DNA test results were not newly discovered evidence.

Accordingly, we affirm the trial court's order.

NOTES AND QUESTIONS

1.　Traditionally, courts were extremely reluctant to allow a presumed father to disestablish his paternity. In refusing such requests, courts often relied on the estoppel doctrine, laches, or principles of res judicata and collateral estoppel. *See* State v. R.L.C., 47 P.3d 327 (Colo. 2002); W. v. W., 779 A.2d 716 (Conn. 2001); Hubbard v. Hubbard, 44 P.3d 153 (Alaska 2002). Sometimes courts have simply cited the child's interests, without relying on any specific legal principle, as a justification for denying a disestablishment petition. Thus, in refusing a divorced man's request for genetic testing and vacation of his paternity obligation, the Vermont Supreme Court noted that the petitioner had lived with the child as her father for the first eight years of her life and continued to treat her as his daughter for six years thereafter: "It is thus readily apparent that a parent-child relationship was formed, and it is that relationship, and not the results of a genetic test, that must control." Godin v. Godin, 725 A.2d 904, 911 (Vt. 1998).

2.　What if it is the mother who is trying to disestablish a presumed father's paternity? Courts have used the same principles that work to impose paternal responsibilities on men who wish to evade them in order to protect men who wish to maintain a parental tie. Thus when a mother who has acquiesced in her husband's establishment of a paternal relationship with her child later contests his paternity, estoppel, laches, res judicata, collateral estoppel, or the child's best interest have typically led to dismissal of her petition. *See, e.g.,* Cesar C. v. Alicia L., 800 N.W.2d 249 (Neb. 2011); *In re* Gallagher, 539 N.W.2d 479 (Iowa 1995); Pettinato v. Pettinato, 582 A.2d 909 (R.I. 1990); Doe v. Doe, 52 P.3d 255 (Haw. 2002).

Because marriage does not significantly alter either the child or adult interests at stake in a paternity disestablishment proceeding, courts have relied on the same principles in cases involving nonmarital children, both when men have sought to evade parental responsibilities and when mothers have sought to disestablish paternity. *See, e.g.,* People ex rel. J.A.U. v. R.L.C., 47 P.3d 327, 333 (Colo. 2002); Paternity of Cheryl, 746 N.E.2d 488 (Mass. 2001); *In re* Nicholas H., 46 P.3d 932 (Cal. 2002).

3.　In recent years, some courts have placed greater emphasis on the interests of erroneously identified fathers. *See* M.A.S. v. Mississippi Dept. of Human Services, 842 So. 2d 527, 531 (Miss. 2003) (vacating a paternity judgment more than nine years after its entry based on DNA tests performed in an unrelated matter which revealed that the petitioner was not the child's biological father, finding it would be "profoundly unjust" to require the petitioner to continue making child support payments); Williams v. Williams, 843 So. 2d 720, 723 (Miss. 2003) (allowing the former husband's disestablishment petition after science proved it was not his). Who pays child support? *See* Paula Roberts, *Truth and Consequences: Part III, Who Pays when Paternity is Disestablished?* 37 FAM. L. Q. 69 (2003). Why have courts traditionally been reluctant to disestablish paternity? Why have some courts become less reluctant in recent years? *See* June Carbone & Naomi Cahn, *Marriage, Parentage, and Child Support*, 45 FAM. L. Q. 219 (2011).

4.   *Paternity Disestablishment Statutes:* A number of states have now enacted paternity disestablishment legislation. Some states have specified time limits within which genetic tests will invariably disestablish paternity. For example, Minnesota now permits paternity disestablishment based on genetic tests within three years after the child's birth if the man was married to or attempted to marry the child's mother and within six months of the child's birth if the man voluntarily acknowledged paternity. *See* MINN. STAT. § 257.57(b). Alaska's paternity disestablishment statute also contains a three-year statute of limitations, but the limitations period does not begin to run until the time "the petitioner knew or should have known that he might not be the child's biological father." ALASKA STAT. § 25.27.166. Other state legislatures have gone further and authorized paternity disestablishment at any time. In Maryland, a declaration of paternity may be modified or set aside "[i]f a blood or genetic test done in accordance with . . . this subtitle establishes the exclusion of the individual named as the father in the order." MD. CODE ANN. § 5–1038 (a)(2)(i)(A). And in Georgia, paternity disestablishment is now *mandatory* if genetic testing demonstrates a zero percent probability of paternity and the court finds that:

> the test was properly conducted, that the man has not adopted the child, that the child was not conceived by artificial insemination, that the man did not act to prevent the biological father from asserting his paternal rights, and that he has not done any of the following acts knowing that he is not the biological father: (1) married the child's mother; (2) acknowledged paternity in a sworn statement; (3) been named, with his consent, as the child's father on the birth certificate; (4) been required to support the child based on a written promise; (5) received notice from any agency requiring him to submit to genetic testing which he disregarded; or (6) signed a voluntary acknowledgment of paternity.

Even if a petitioner cannot obtain mandatory relief under the statute, the court invariably has discretion to "grant the motion or enter an order as to paternity, duty to support, custody, and visitation privileges as otherwise provided by law." GA. CODE ANN. § 9–7–54. *See* Melanie B. Jacobs, *When Daddy Doesn't Want to be Daddy Anymore: An Argument Against Paternity Fraud Claims*, 16 YALE J. L. & FEMINISM 193 (2004) (criticizing attempts to make disestablishing paternity with DNA similar to criminal exoneration). *See also* Alisha C. v. Jeremy C., 808 N.W.2d 875 (Neb. 2012) (allowing disestablishment based on 2008 Nebraska statute and noting legislative trend to allow judges discretion to determine if disestablishment is appropriate balancing the adjudicated father's interest and the best interest of the child).

5.   The 2002 UPA takes middle-of-the-road approach. In cases where there is a presumed father, parental status may be attacked, by any party, within two years after the child's birth. In other cases, paternity may be challenged at any time, and even when the two-year statute of limitation applies, paternity may be challenged "if the court determines that: (1) the presumed father and the mother of the child neither cohabited nor engaged in sexual intercourse with each other during the probable time of conception; and (2) the presumed father never openly held out the child as his own." UPA (2002) §§ 607, 609. In all disestablishment actions, the court is required to consider the child's best interests, including "the age of the child, length and nature of the relationship, and potential harm to the child." UPA (2002) § 608.

6.   What are the pros and cons of statutory and case law responses to the paternity-disestablishment problem? Why have statutory solutions grown in popularity? What are the pros and cons of the UPA (2002) and various state statutes described above?

7.   If paternity is disestablished, can the husband sue the biological father to recover child-raising costs of child he thought was his? *See* Fischer v. Zollino, 35 A.3d 270 (Conn. 2012) (finding public policy did not require that husband be equitably estopped from bringing action).

CHAPTER 8

ADOPTION

■ ■ ■

The beggarly question of parentage—what is it after all? What does it matter, when you come to think of it, whether a child is yours by blood or not? All the little ones of our time are collectively the children of us adults of the time, and entitled to our general care.

THOMAS HARDY, JUDE THE OBSCURE (1896).

1. THE CHANGING FACE OF ADOPTION PRACTICE

Adoption creates a legal parent-child relationship between a child and adults who are not the child's biological parents. Ordinarily, an adoption order terminates legal rights and obligations between the child and his or her biological parents, replacing them with similar rights and obligations in the adoptive parents. Adoption generally falls under the exclusive original jurisdiction of the district court, although it may be probate, family or juvenile. To grant an adoption, the child must be available for adoption (the parents have either consented to the adoption or their parental rights have been terminated); the person seeking to adopt must fall within the statutory guidelines; and adoption must be in the best interests of the child.

Historically, most ancient legal systems sanctioned adoption. The purpose of early adoption laws was to meet the needs of would-be adoptive parents. In ancient Greece and Rome, for example, adoptions were often arranged to provide an heir to perpetuate the family line. *See* Stephen B. Presser, *The Historical Background of the American Law of Adoption*, 11 J. FAM. L. 443 (1971).

The English common law did not permit formal adoption. There were informal transfers of a child as an indentured servant or apprentice but legal ties to parents remained intact. U.S. adoption laws are entirely statutory. The first American adoption statute was enacted in Massachusetts in 1851. The Massachusetts law became a model for many of the other state adoption laws passed during or shortly after the Civil War. To effect an adoption required the written consent of the child's

383

biological parent, a consent of the child if over the age of 14, a joint petition by the adoptive mother and father, and a finding by the trial judge that the adoption was "fit and proper." Once approved, the adopted child became the legal child of the petitioner and the biological parents' rights were terminated. By 1929, every state had passed adoption legislation.

In contrast to ancient adoption laws, these new statutes were designed to serve the interests of adoptive children. But the Massachusetts model, in which the propriety of the adoption order was determined based solely on a courtroom examination of the adoptive parents, was found inadequate. For example, a 1925 Commission appointed to study and revise Pennsylvania's adoption laws produced reports of cases like this one:

> Frances, aged thirteen, recently made a personal application to a social agency stating that her foster father had been having sexual relations with her for the last two years. Upon investigation living conditions were found to be very bad. The foster mother corroborated the child's statements. Frances had been legally adopted in May 1918. She was sold to her foster parents by her mother for a quart of whisky.

2 CHILDREN AND YOUTH IN AMERICA: A DOCUMENTARY HISTORY 142 (Robert H. Bremner ed. 1971).

As a result of cases like Frances', more states adopted procedures to investigate prospective adoptive parents before a judicial hearing. Minnesota passed the first law requiring pre-hearing investigation by a child welfare agency in 1917; by 1938, similar laws had been enacted in twenty-four states. State legislatures introduced other protections for the adoptive child as well, including, in some states, a trial period in the adoptive home before the adoption was legally finalized.

The Minnesota act is widely credited with having initiated sealed records in adoption proceedings, another innovation that soon became universal. The movement toward secrecy in adoption proceedings was apparently urged by social workers in child-placing agencies, who believed that parental anonymity would both foster the integration of the child into the adoptive family and prevent the stigma of illegitimacy from tainting the child's future. *See* Burton Z. Sokoloff, *Antecedents of American Adoption*, 3 FUTURE OF CHILDREN: ADOPTION 17, 22 (Spring 1993).

The trend toward anonymity in adoption was facilitated by the development of specialized adoption agencies where biological parents who wished to relinquish a child and would-be adoptive parents who wanted one could effect an exchange without personal contact. Although most states did not outlaw nonagency, or "independent" adoptions, by 1971 nearly eighty percent of nonrelative adoptions were arranged by specialized agencies. *See* VIVIANA A. ZELIZER, PRICING THE PRICELESS CHILD: THE CHANGING SOCIAL VALUE OF CHILDREN 263 (1981).

Adoption agencies often had strict requirements for adoptive parents. Many agencies refused adoption applications from would-be parents over a specified age. All stressed a stable marital relationship as a requirement to adopt. Agencies with religious affiliations typically matched the religious preferences of the birth mother with the affiliations of the prospective adoptive parents.

Adoptive parents had their own preferences, of course. Nineteenth century adoptive parents typically wanted an older child who could work, but twentieth century adoptive parents (other than those who were adopting a stepchild or relative) typically sought to adopt due to infertility. These parents wanted a healthy newborn whose appearance was not markedly different from their own.

Until the mid-1950s, the goals of adoption agencies, the pool of adoptive parents, and the supply of adoptable children were fairly well balanced. Most potential adoptive parents were infertile married couples in their child-bearing years. Due to declining rates of orphanage, most of the children available for adoption were infants placed with adoption agencies by unmarried mothers. Many of the mothers who placed children for adoption had backgrounds similar to those of the couples who sought to adopt. Unmarried motherhood was still seen as shameful and abortion was illegal, dangerous, and often unavailable. The young, unwed woman who became pregnant typically saw only two choices, marriage to the child's father or an adoption.

Although demand for adoptable infants began to exceed supply as early as the 1950s, the adoption rate moved consistently upward until 1970, when 175,000 children were adopted; about half of these adoptions were by nonrelatives. In 2007 courts approved 153,179 adoptions (133,737 domestic and 19,442 international). *See* NATIONAL COUNCIL FOR ADOPTION, ADOPTION FACTBOOK V 11–27 (2011), http://www.adoptioncouncil.org/documents/AdoptionFactbookIV.pdf. The decline in nonrelative adoptions derives largely from a reduced supply of adoptable infants resulting both from the Supreme Court's decision in Roe v. Wade, 410 U.S. 113 (1973) , which dramatically increased the availability of abortion, and a marked shift in social mores reducing the stigma associated with unwed motherhood. Before 1973, 19.3% of children born to never-married white women were placed for adoption; between 1989–1995 only 1.7% of children born to such women were placed for adoption. *See* Adoption Institute, *Overview of Adoption in the United States*, http://www.adoptioninstitute. org/FactOverview.html#head.

While the supply of adoptable infants has declined, demand has moved in the opposite direction. National surveys suggest that there are more than three adoption seekers for every actual adoption and that, at any given time, there are at least half a million Americans who want to adopt.

See CWIG, *Persons Seeking to Adopt: Numbers and Trends* (2005), http://www.childwelfare.gov/pubs/s_seek.cfm. The result of these changes in supply and demand has been a dramatic shift in the adoption "market."

First, the locus of adoption exchanges has shifted. Independent adoptions—where the birth parents either make the placement themselves or use an intermediary, such as a doctor or lawyer, to find adoptive parents—have increased. Experts estimate that one-half to two-thirds of domestic infant adoptions are now arranged independently. *See* Adoption Institute, *Private Domestic Adoption Facts*, http://www.adoptioninstitute. org/FactOverview/domestic.html.

Second, the smaller supply of healthy white infants available for adoption has increased demand for transracial adoption as well as the adoption of older and "special needs" children. One result of this shift has been a new emphasis on adoption for children who are in state foster care due to parental neglect, abuse, or incapacity. In an earlier era, these children typically remained in state-paid foster care until the age of majority if they could not be returned home. Today the state runs a domestic market on adoption which is disproportionately minorities and older children or those with special needs. *See* Chapter 10, § 5.

Third, the secrecy that traditionally characterized adoption proceedings has begun to give way. Many states now permit an adult adoptee to obtain information about his or her biological parents if those parents agree, and "open" adoption, where the biological parent(s) or family retain the right to continuing contact with the child, is permitted in a growing number of jurisdictions. These shifts have been fueled by pressure from adult adoptees who want information about their biological families, the increase in adoptions of older children who have often had ongoing relationships with their biological families, and the greater power of biological mothers resulting from the scarcity of adoptive infants and shift toward independent adoptions. The increase in divided families resulting from a higher rate of single parenthood may also have played a role. *See* Annette Ruth Appell, *Blending Families Through Adoption: Implications for Collaborative Practice*, 75 B.U. L. REV. 997, 1008–13 (1995).

State law has not always kept up with these various shifts in the adoption "market" and adoption practice. Nor have state adoption laws ever been uniform. The result is considerable variation in adoption law. Some states permit independent adoption, others do not. Many states recognize open adoption, but others do not. Standards governing the timing and revocability of parental consent also vary widely. While some experts worry that such diversity may produce both forum shopping and unfairness, attempts to unify adoption laws have thus far been unsuccessful. In 1994 the National Conference of Commissioners on Uniform State Laws made an attempt to facilitate state uniformity in adoption procedures by approving the Uniform Adoption Act. But, only Vermont used the Uniform Adoption Act as a model for changes to its adoption laws. It is now shelved as a Model Act.

Lawyers are involved with adoption as lawyers for state agencies, private agencies, birth parents or adopting parents. The basic process in all states involves termination of the natural parents' rights and obtaining a court order.

2. CONSENT TO ADOPTION

IN RE J.M.P.
Supreme Court of Louisiana, 1988.
528 So. 2d 1002.

DENNIS, JUSTICE. * * *

The facts of this case follow a sadly familiar pattern. Dawn B., an eighteen year old unmarried woman, was employed in a grocery store but remained economically dependent on her mother and stepfather, Mr. & Mrs. B., with whom she resided. She became pregnant but concealed the fact from her mother for six months. At that time, with her mother's financial assistance, she traveled by bus from her home in Zachary to consult with a doctor at an abortion clinic in Metairie. The doctor informed her that her pregnancy was too far into its term to permit an abortion. Instead, he gave her the name and phone number of an anti-abortionist attorney, Perez, who would arrange for the placement of the child for private adoption free of charge. When she returned home Dawn placed a call to Perez but had to leave her number because he was out. When Perez returned the call, Dawn's mother, Mrs. B., answered and asked him to come to Zachary to discuss surrendering the expected child for private adoption. A few days later, Perez met with Dawn and Mr. and Mrs. B. in their home and explained what he was able to do: He could find a suitable couple to adopt the baby. He would have the couple pay the hospital, OBGYN, pediatrician, anesthesiologist, and drug bills. He explained that he would not charge a fee to them or the adoptive parents because his only interest was his personal cause of preventing abortions. Everything would be handled through him confidentially so that the identities of the two families would not be disclosed to each other. He told Dawn that she could change her mind and reclaim her child at any time up until the act of surrender was signed. Dawn, her mother and her stepfather agreed to the arrangement and asked him to proceed.

Between that meeting and the birth of the child Perez said he talked with Dawn on numerous occasions over the phone. On these occasions she called him to see if checks had been mailed for drug bills that she had sent him. During this period she gave him no indication of changing her mind with respect to the adoption.

After the birth of the child on November 30, 1985, Mr. Perez met with Dawn and Mr. & Mrs. B. at the hospital. Perez testified that he reminded them that his only interest was in seeing that the baby was born and told them that he would leave immediately if they wanted to keep the child. Dawn appeared to be sad about giving up the child, but this was not unusual, he said. At his request, she readily signed the hospital release form giving him permission to take the baby from the premises. Without any objection from Dawn he removed the baby from the hospital and took it to the prospective adoptive parents in Houma.

A week later, on December 7, 1985, Perez returned to Mr. & Mrs. B's house in Zachary to have Dawn execute the act of surrender. He brought along his law partner, Roberts, to act as Dawn's attorney and to advise her of her rights. Perez and the parents stepped out on the porch while Roberts and Dawn conferred in the house. Dawn testified that Roberts read the act of surrender to her, and that she did not ask any questions. She said that she told him to change the child's name in the act, and he said that he would do so later. The act of surrender which Dawn signed before a notary and two witnesses after conferring with Roberts, declares that it was fully explained to her by the attorney and that she understood she was surrendering the child for adoption and terminating her rights as a parent of the child. We cannot consider Roberts' testimony in this regard because he was not called as a witness.

While they were on the porch, Perez again informed Mrs. B. that Dawn could still change her mind and he offered to undertake the six hour round trip to fetch the child if Dawn did not want to sign the act of surrender. Mrs. B. replied that Dawn would like to keep the child but that the only way she could raise it would be on welfare and that, since she, Mrs. B., had already raised five children, she was not going to raise another. Perez testified that he did not interpret this remark as an indication that Dawn had changed her mind.

After the act of surrender was signed, Perez continued to receive medical bills and calls about their payment from Dawn. Sometime prior to December 30, 1985, however, he received a letter from her revoking her consent to the adoption.

The testimony of Dawn, Mrs. B. and Mr. B. reveals that the young natural mother signed the act and gave up her child although she knew that she had a right to refrain from doing so. Further, the record shows she surrendered the child not because of any improper act or omission by Perez or Roberts but primarily because she did not wish to undertake the hardship of caring for the child outside of her home and without her mother's assistance.

Dawn testified that early on the morning that the act of surrender was executed her mother and stepfather told her that if she refused to sign the instrument she could not bring the baby into their house. She expressed how this affected her decision to sign the act in several ways: She signed because it was what her mother wanted; her mother wanted her to start a new life. She couldn't bring the baby into the house and she had nowhere else to go with the baby. Although she could have gone to stay with her sister in Indiana, she would have had nowhere to go with the baby for the two days it would take for her to receive transportation fare from her sister or father in Indiana. This last explanation was inconsistent with other portions of her testimony in which she admitted that she had saved an unspecified sum of money before her child was born.

Dawn contradicted Perez on one point saying that he never told her that she had the right to refuse to surrender and reclaim her child. This disagreement is, however, without consequence because her testimony and that of her parents makes it clear that she fully understood her dilemma: she could either sign the act and lose her child or refuse to sign, keep her child, and lose her home and her mother's support.

Mr. & Mrs. B. admitted that they had caused Dawn to sign the act of surrender by telling her that she could not bring the child home. They testified that they had experienced a change of heart because of the suffering Dawn had endured, that they regretted their actions which had been intended only for her own welfare, and that they now stood ready to support Dawn financially and in every other way should she recover custody of the child.

* * *

[T]he trial court concluded that the act of surrender was valid. Immediately after the trial judge's ruling, the hearing as to the best interests of the child was held. * * *

The trial court found that the adoption was in the child's best interest and entered an interlocutory decree of adoption. In his reasons for judgment the judge found it important that the P's owned a large home on which they owed only $5,000, that James P., the main wage earner, made over $40,000 a year and had substantial savings, and that the P's could provide the child a traditional family within which she could grow. He also thought it important that Dawn had originally sought an abortion, that she earned only minimum wage, that she was a single, working mother, who would have to rely on her parent's aid in raising the child and that the child would be raised in a trailer. In concluding that it would be in the best interests of the child to grant the adoption, the judge found that Dawn, as an unmarried eighteen year old, could not offer the child the stable and financially secure family unit the P's could, and that the P's were sincerely committed to providing for the welfare of the child and that they could offer the child a stable, supportive, and loving family unit. Dawn appealed the trial court's decision to the Court of Appeal, First Circuit, which affirmed for the reasons assigned by the trial court.

* * *

The Private Adoption Act of 1979 applicable to this case provides that a parent of either a natural or legitimate child may execute a voluntary surrender of custody of the child for private adoption. * * * [T]he surrendering parent must sign the surrendering document freely and voluntarily, and the parent must be informed and understand that his or her rights to the child are to be terminated. The act of surrender may not be signed before the fifth day following the child's birthday, and the surrendering parent must be represented by an attorney at the execution of the act. However, to preserve anonymity, an attorney at law may be named in the act of surrender as representative of the adopting parents.

By an act of surrender, the surrendering parent transfers legal custody of the child to the adopting parents and grants consent to their adoption of the child. However, the surrendering parent may revoke her consent to the transfer and adoption by a written declaration within 30 days after executing the act of surrender. Nevertheless, the withdrawal of consent will not prevent the adoption if the adoption is found to be in the best interests of the child. Should an interlocutory decree have been entered without opposition, the child shall not be removed from the custody of the adopting parents nor adoption denied unless the department disapproves or the court finds the adopting parents unfit.

* * *

The evidence does not establish that the plaintiff was subject to the type of duress which justifies vitiation of her consent. Dawn's decision to surrender her child for adoption was induced principally by her own desire to do what was best for the child and by her mother's refusal to allow her to rear the child in her home. * * * Mr. & Mrs. B. had a legal right to refuse to allow the adult natural mother to rear the child in their home. Therefore, their refusal was an exercise or threat to exercise a right and did not constitute duress.

* * *

The natural parent in this case timely exercised her right to revoke her consent to the surrender and to oppose the adoption. However, her action does not bar a decree of adoption if the adoption is in "the best interests of the child." La.R.S. § 9:422.11(A).

* * *

The exact scope of the standard "best interest of the child" under the private adoption statute has not been detailed by the Legislature or this court. But the policy reflected in these words is firmly established in other statutes and in the law of virtually every American jurisdiction. The basic concept underlying this standard is nothing less than the dignity of the child as an individual human being. For this reason the words of the criterion cannot be precise and their scope cannot be static. "The best interests of the child" must draw its meaning from the evolving body of knowledge concerning child health, psychology and welfare that marks the progress of a maturing society.

* * *

[The best interests of the child require t]he court * * * [to] prefer a psychological parent (i.e., an adult who has a psychological relationship with the child from the child's perspective) over any claimant (including a natural parent) who, from the child's perspective, is not a psychological parent. To award custody to a person who is a "stranger" to the child would unnecessarily risk harming the child where the other claimant has, on a continuing, day-to-day basis, fulfilled the child's psychological needs for a parent as well as his physical need.

Whether any adult becomes the psychological parent of a child is based on day-to-day interaction, companionship, and shared experiences. The role can be fulfilled either by a biological parent or by any other caring adult—but never by an absent, inactive adult, whatever his biological or legal relationship to the child. J. GOLDSTEIN, A. FREUD & A. SOLNIT, BEYOND THE BEST INTEREST OF THE CHILD (2d ed. 1979) at 18. * * *

There is little disagreement within the profession of child psychology as to the existence of the phenomenon of the child-psychological parent relationship and its importance to the development of the child. A substantial and impressive consensus exists among psychologists and psychiatrists that disruption of the parent-child relationship carries significant risks. The only disagreement among the experts appears to be over how great the significant risks are in comparison with other factors influencing a child's mental and emotional growth.

When the natural parent poses no danger to the child's physical health, and the child has not yet formed an attachment to and begun to view one of the adoptive parents as his psychological parent, the natural parent should be preferred over others. Under broadly shared social values the general rule is that the responsibility and opportunity of custody is assigned to a child's natural parents. The high value placed on family autonomy reflects a consensus that the natural parent-child relationship should be disturbed only if necessary to protect the child from physical or psychological harm. Moreover, preservation of the child's sense of lineage and access to his extended biological family can be important psychologically, as evidenced by the felt need of some adoptive children to search out their natural parents.

These guidelines are consistent with the best interests of the child principle and should dispose of most private adoption cases. * * *

Applying the best interests guidelines we conclude that the trial court fell into error by omitting any consideration of two of the most important factors in a private adoption case, viz., the natural mother-child biological relationship and the possible psychological tie of the child to one or both of the adoptive parents. Instead, the trial court based its decision primarily on the relative wealth of the parties, a factor that can have little, if any, relevance in a case of this kind. If the natural mother is fit, the broad social policy of basing custody and responsibility on the biological relationship outweighs whatever material advantages might be provided by the adoptive parents, if neither of the adoptive parents is the child's psychological parent. On the other hand, if the adoptive parents are fit, and the child has formed a psychological attachment to one or both of them, the adoptive parents should be preferred so as to avoid the grave risk of mental and emotional harm to the child which would result from a change in custody, even if the natural parent is relatively affluent.

The record does not contain sufficient evidence from which we may determine whether the child had developed a substantial psychological relationship with one of the adoptive parents. There is no psychiatrist or psychologist testimony in the record and the adoptive parents' testimony is only sketchy on this subject. The child, who was five months old at the time of the best interest hearing, is now approximately 2 1/2 years old. We can only speculate as to the child's psychological development at the time of the hearing and as to what has occurred since. It is quite possible that the child by now has acquired a strong and healthy psychological attachment to her adoptive parents. There is also the possibility that the child tragically has no psychological parent. More happily, it is possible that the child has developed a psychological tie with her natural mother if there has been regular contact between the two. We cannot decide what is in the best interest of this child on the basis of these speculations.

Accordingly, in the interest of justice we will vacate the adoption decree and remand the case for a new hearing on the best interest of the child. * * * The best interest hearing under the private adoption statute should be scheduled and conducted expeditiously in order to afford the natural mother who timely revokes her consent a real opportunity to reclaim her child. * * *

The facts of this case, which unfortunately are not atypical, illustrate the problems caused by the law's ordinary delay in adoption cases. The child was born on November 30, 1985, and surrendered for adoption on December 7, 1985 when she was one week old. The natural mother revoked her consent within thirty days of this date, at which time the child could not have been over five weeks old. The adoptive parents filed a petition for adoption on January 30, 1986 when the child was two months old. The best interest hearing was not held until April 15, 1986 by which time the child was almost 5 months old. The trial court rendered a judgment that the surrender was valid and the adoption was in the child's best interest on June 20, 1986 when the child was almost seven months old. The court of appeal affirmed the trial court's judgment on December 22, 1987 by which time the child was over two years old.

Delays of this kind cannot be tolerated under an adoption statute which was intended to (1) grant the natural parent a brief but meaningful opportunity to change her mind and to reclaim the child, provided that this may be done without psychological harm to the child, and (2) ensure that the child will not be taken from the adoptive parents after one of them has become the psychological parent of the child. * * * The basic problem is with the statute which contains no provision for expedited hearings or machinery for calling the need therefore to the courts' attention. * * *

NOTES AND QUESTIONS

1.   On remand, what is the probability that Dawn will regain her child? Was this an independent or agency adoption? Would one have protected Dawn more? *See* Elizabeth J. Samuels, *Time to Decide? The Laws Governing Mothers' Consents to the Adoption of their Newborn Infants,* 72 TENN. L. REV. 509 (2005).

2.   Cases like Dawn's represent a very small portion of non-relative adoptions because data indicates that only one percent of teens who became pregnant chose adoptive placements and because less than one percent of adoptions produce litigation. *See* V. GROZA & K. ROSENBERG, CLINICAL AND PRACTICE ISSUES IN ADOPTION: BRIDGING THE GAP BETWEEN ADOPTEES PLACED AS INFANTS AND AS OLDER CHILDREN (1998). However, when litigation does occur, the limited evidence suggests that delays like those in *J.M.P.* are still typical. *See* Theo Emery, *Tennessee Court Orders Return of Girl, 7, to Biological Parents,* N.Y. TIMES, January 24, 2007 at A11. Why haven't states provided expedited hearings in adoption cases?

3.   *Minor Parents:* In most states minority of the parent consenting to adoption will not vitiate the consent. Unemancipated teenagers younger than eighteen typically cannot enter into business contracts: should they be able to enter into adoption contracts? If yes, should the state impose additional consent requirements to take account of the teen parent's relative immaturity? What rules would be helpful? Should minors have a lawyer at the time they execute the consent? S*ee In re* Adoption of A.L.O., 132 P.3d 543 (Mont. 2006); Emily Buss, *The Parental Rights of Minors,* 48 BUFF. L. REV. 785 (2000). *See also* Malinda A. Seymore, *Sixteen and Pregnant: Minors Consent in Abortion and Adoption,* 25 YALE J. L. & FEM. 99 (2013).

4.   *Timing of Consent:* Rules governing the timing of parental consent are variable, but the trend has been toward prohibition of pre-birth consent. *See* UAA § 2–404(a). Some states additionally impose post-birth waiting

periods ranging from twelve hours (KAN. STAT. ANN. § 59–2116) to several days (*see, e.g.,* MASS. GEN. LAWS ch. 210 § 2 (fourth day after birth)). What is the purpose of these waiting periods?

5.   *Revocability of Consent:* Rules governing the revocability of parental consent also vary widely. In some states parental consent is irrevocable unless procured by fraud, undue influence or duress. *See, e.g.,* COLO. REV. STAT. § 19–5–104(7)(a). In others, consent may be revoked with court approval. *See, e.g.,* ARK. STAT. ANN. § 9–9–220 (revocation after ten days unless waived, in which case five days). In a few states, consent may be revoked until the entry of an interlocutory adoption decree. Finally, in some states, consent may be revoked, with or without cause, until the adoption becomes final.

Which of these approaches best serves the mother's interests? The interests of the adoptive parents? The interests of the child? Which approach, on balance, is the best?

6.   *Stepparent Adoptions:* Estimates are that half of all adoptions are by stepparents. Because the child is continuing to live with one parent, many states have special rules governing stepparent adoptions. The adoption terminates only the rights of the noncustodial parent. While consent of the noncustodial parent is typically required, in some states it may be waived in cases of abandonment or nonsupport. *See In re* J.J.J., 718 P.2d 948 (Alaska 1986) (statute waives consent of noncustodial parent who "failed significantly without justifiable cause * * * to communicate meaningfully with the child or * * * to provide * * * support as required by law" for at least a year; fact that father made payments after the year pursuant to court order did not preclude finding). *See also In re* J.M.D., 260 P.3d 1196 (Kan. 2011).

7.   *Technical Defects:* State law varies with respect to technical defects in the execution of an adoption consent. In a few, a parent's consent is valid if there is substantial compliance with the statutory requirements. In others, the consent is invalid. *See* Brown v. Baby Girl Harper, 766 S.E.2d 375 (S.C. 2014) (attorney witness was not present when mother signed); Bridges v. Bush, 220 S.W.3d 259 (Ark. App. 2005) (setting aside an adoption where the notary was not present when the notary signed the consent and relinquishment forms).

8.   *Child's Consent:* In most states, if the child has attained a specific age, the child must consent. A typical age is fourteen. Cf. CAL. FAM. CODE § 8602 (twelve).

ADOPTION OF KELSEY S.
Supreme Court of California, 1992.
1 Cal. 4th 816, 823 P.2d 1216, 4 Cal. Rptr. 2d 615.

BAXTER, JUSTICE.

The primary question in this case is whether the father of a child born out of wedlock may properly be denied the right to withhold his consent to his child's adoption by third parties despite his diligent and legal attempts

to obtain custody of his child and to rear it himself, and absent any showing *issue*
of the father's unfitness as a parent. We conclude that, under these
circumstances, the federal constitutional guarantees of equal protection
and due process require that the father be allowed to withhold his consent *holding*
to his child's adoption and therefore that his parental rights cannot be
terminated absent a showing of his unfitness within the meaning of Civil
Code § 221.20.

Facts

Kari S. gave birth to Kelsey, a boy, on May 18, 1988. The child's
undisputed natural father is petitioner Rickie M. He and Kari S. were not
married to one another. At that time, he was married to another woman
but was separated from her and apparently was in divorce proceedings. He
was aware that Kari planned to place their child for adoption, and he
objected to her decision because he wanted to rear the child.

Two days after the child's birth, petitioner filed an action in superior
court under Civil Code § 7006 to establish his parental relationship with
the child and to obtain custody of the child. (The petition erroneously stated
that the child had not yet been born. His birth was earlier than expected,
and petitioner had not been informed of it when he filed his action.) That
same day, the court issued a restraining order that temporarily awarded
care, custody, and control of the child to petitioner. The order also stayed
all adoption proceedings and prohibited any contact between the child and
the prospective adoptive parents.

Later that day, petitioner filed a copy of the order with law
enforcement officials. He also personally attempted to serve it on the
prospective adoptive parents at their home. He was unsuccessful.

On May 24, 1988, Steven and Suzanne A., the prospective adoptive
parents, filed an adoption petition under Civil Code § 226. Their petition
alleged that only the mother's consent to the adoption was required
because there was no presumed father under § 7004, subdivision (a). * * *
On August 26, 1988, the court found "by a bare preponderance" of the
evidence that the child's best interest required termination of petitioner's
parental rights.

* * *

Th[e] statutory scheme creates three classifications of parents:
mothers, biological fathers who are presumed fathers, and biological
fathers who are *not* presumed fathers (i.e., natural fathers). A natural
father's consent to an adoption of his child by third parties is not required
unless the father makes the required showing that retention of his parental
rights is in the child's best interest. Consent, however, is required of a *Rule*
mother and a presumed father regardless of the child's best interest. The
natural father is therefore treated differently from both mothers and

presumed fathers. With this statutory framework in mind, we now examine petitioner's contentions.

A man becomes a "presumed father" under * * * (§ 7004(a)(4)) if *"[h]e receives the child into his home* and openly holds out the child as his natural child." (Italics added.) It is undisputed in this case that petitioner openly held out the child as being his own. Petitioner, however, did not physically receive the child into his home. He was prevented from doing so by the mother, by court order, and allegedly also by the prospective adoptive parents.

* * *

The precise question before us has not been addressed by the United States Supreme Court. We are guided, however, by a series of high court decisions dealing with the rights of unwed fathers. From those decisions, we must attempt to distill the guiding constitutional principles.

In *Stanley v. Illinois (Stanley)*, the court held that under the due process clause of the Fourteenth Amendment to the federal Constitution an unmarried father was entitled to a hearing on his fitness as a parent before his children were taken from him. *Stanley* is factually distinguishable because the father in that case had lived intermittently with his children and their mother for 18 years. * * * [But] the court seemed to indicate that a father's parental rights could not be terminated absent a showing of his unfitness, and that a showing of the child's best interest would be an insufficient basis for termination of the father's rights. "What is the state interest in separating children from fathers without a hearing designed to determine *whether the father is unfit* in a particular disputed case?"

If petitioner is not a presumed parent under § 7004(a)(4), his parental rights may be terminated under § 7017, subdivision (d)(2) merely by showing that termination would be in the child's best interest. No showing of petitioner's unfitness is required under the statutes. The statutory scheme therefore appears to conflict with the emphasis in *Stanley*, on the need for *a particularized finding of unfitness*. Petitioner was never found to be unfit.

In its next case dealing with unwed fathers, *Quilloin v. Walcott, (Quilloin)*, * * * [a] unanimous court * * * found no denial of either due process or equal protection. As to due process, the court explained, "We have little doubt that the Due Process Clause would be offended '[i]f a State were to attempt to force the breakup of a natural family, over the objections of the parents and their children, *without some showing of unfitness* and for the sole reason that to do so was thought to be in the children's best interest.' But this is not a case in which the unwed father at any time had, or sought, actual or legal custody of his child. Nor is this a case in which the proposed adoption would place the child with a new set of parents with whom the child had never before lived. Rather, the result of the adoption in this case is to give full recognition to a family unit already in existence, a result desired by all concerned, except appellant [the father]. Whatever might be required in other situations, we cannot say that the State was required in this situation to find anything more than that the adoption, and denial of legitimation, were in the 'best interests of the child.' "

* * *

The present case has several of the earmarks the court found lacking in *Quilloin*, and which the court suggested might render invalid a termination of a father's rights based only on a showing of the child's best interest. Those factors are as follows:

(i) Unlike the father in *Quilloin*, petitioner asked the mother for custody of their child and, when rebuffed, immediately (as soon as the child was born) went to court seeking legal custody. He continues to seek legal recognition of his parental rights.

(ii) The mother does not seek to retain the child and have it adopted by a husband. As put by the *Quilloin* court, "the proposed adoption would place the child with a new set of parents with whom the child had never before lived." Of course, we recognize that as a result of the lower courts'. decisions the child has now been living with the prospective adoptive parents for more than three years. This fact, however, is not relevant to the analysis of whether petitioner's rights were violated *ab initio*.

(iii) The parties disagree as to the amount of care and support that petitioner provided to the child and its mother. The record is unclear as to whether and to what extent, if any, this dispute affected the trial court's decision that the adoption was barely in the child's best interest. The record is clear, however, that petitioner is not like the natural father in *Quilloin*, who avoided contact with his child until several years after its birth and came forward only when another man tried to adopt it. More important for this part of our analysis, petitioner, also unlike the father in *Quilloin*, did attempt through legal channels to shoulder full responsibility for his child.

In short, the present case is the type of case the high court emphasized it was not deciding in *Quilloin*. By implication, however, the *Quilloin* decision strongly suggests that the parental rights of a father in petitioner's position may not properly be terminated absent a showing of his unfitness as a father. On the present facts, a showing of the child's best interest would appear to be insufficient under *Quilloin*. This conclusion is reinforced by the high court's * * * decision [i]n *Caban v. Mohammed*

(Caban) * * * [where the court struck down an adoption consent statute that] "treats unmarried parents differently according to their sex." In this respect, California law is indistinguishable.

* * *

The high court again considered the rights of biological fathers only four years later in *Lehr v. Robertson (Lehr).* * * * On its face, *Lehr,* does not resolve the dilemma before us. The stated premise of the court's holding was that the equal protection clause does not prevent a state from according a child's biological father fewer rights than the mother if he has "never established a relationship" with the child. The court did not purport to decide the legal question in the present case, that is, whether the mother may constitutionally prevent the father from establishing the relationship that gives rise to his right to equal protection. The *Lehr* court, however, recognized the uniqueness of the biological connection between parent and child. "The significance of the biological connection is that it offers the natural father an opportunity that no other male possesses to develop a relationship with his offspring. If he grasps that opportunity and accepts some measure of responsibility for the child's future, he may enjoy the blessings of the parent-child relationship and make uniquely valuable contributions to the child's development." *Lehr* can fairly be read to mean that a father need only make a reasonable and meaningful attempt to establish a relationship, not that he must be successful against all obstacles.

* * * [In] *Michael H. v. Gerald D.* 491 U.S. 110 (1989) a majority of the justices were [again] solicitous of the rights of unwed biological fathers. For them, the determinative factor was whether a biological father has attempted to establish a relationship with his child.

Although the foregoing high court decisions do not provide a comprehensive rule for all situations involving unwed fathers, one unifying and transcendent theme emerges. The biological connection between father and child is unique and worthy of constitutional protection if the father grasps the opportunity to develop that biological connection into a full and enduring relationship.

* * *

Petitioner asserts a violation of equal protection and due process under the federal Constitution; more specifically, that he should not be treated differently from his child's mother. In constitutional terms, the question is whether California's sex-based statutory distinction between biological mothers and fathers serves " ' * * * important governmental objectives and [is] *substantially related* to achievement of those objectives.' " (*Caban, supra,* italics added.) * * *

There is no dispute that "The State's interest in providing for the well-being of illegitimate children is an important one." Although the legal concept of illegitimacy no longer exists in California, the problems and needs of children born out of wedlock are an undisputed reality. The state has an important and valid interest in their well-being.

* * *

Respondents do not adequately explain how an unwed mother's control over a biological father's rights furthers the state's interest in the well-being of the child. The linchpin of their position, however, is clear although largely implicit: Allowing the biological father to have the same rights as the mother would make adoptions more difficult because the consent of both parents is more difficult to obtain than the consent of the mother alone. This reasoning is flawed in several respects.

A. Respondents' view too narrowly assumes that the proper governmental objective is adoption. As we have explained, the constitutionally valid objective is the protection of the child's well-being. We cannot conclude in the abstract that adoption is itself a sufficient objective to allow the state to take whatever measures it deems appropriate. Nor can we merely assume, either as a policy or factual matter, that adoption is necessarily in a child's best interest. This assumption is especially untenable in light of the rapidly changing concept of family. As recently as only a few years ago, it might have been reasonable to assume that an adopted child would be placed into a two-parent home and thereby have a more stable environment than a child raised by a single father. The validity of that assumption is now highly suspect in light of modern adoption practice. Recent statistics show that a significant percentage of children placed for independent adoption—7.7 percent—are adopted by a single parent. The figure is even higher—21.9 percent—for children placed with agencies for adoption.

* * *

If the possible benefit of adoption were by itself sufficient to justify terminating a parent's rights, the state could terminate an unwed *mother's* parental rights based on nothing more than a showing that her child's best interest would be served by adoption. Of course, that is not the law; nor do the parties advocate such a system. We simply do not in our society take children away from their mothers—married or otherwise—because a "better" adoptive parent can be found. We see no valid reason why we should be less solicitous of a father's efforts to establish a parental relationship with his child. Respondents seem to suggest that a child is inherently better served by adoptive parents than by a single, biological father but that the child is also inherently better served by a single, biological mother than by adoptive parents. The logic of this view is not apparent, and there is no evidence in the record to support such a counterintuitive view.

B.   Nor is there evidence before us that the statutory provisions allowing the mother to determine the father's rights are, in general, *substantially* related to protecting the child's best interest. As a matter of cold efficiency, we cannot disagree that eliminating a natural father's rights would make adoption easier in some cases. That, however, begs the question because it assumes an unwed mother's decision to permit an immediate adoption of her newborn is always preferable to custody by the natural father, even when he is a demonstrably fit parent. We have no evidence to support that assumption. Moreover, the assumption has already been rejected by the United States Supreme Court: "It may be that, given the opportunity, some unwed fathers would prevent the adoption of their illegitimate children. This impediment to adoption usually is the result of a natural parental interest shared by both genders [sexes] alike; it is not a manifestation of any profound difference between the affection and concern of mothers and fathers for their children. Neither the State nor the appellees have argued that unwed fathers are more likely to object to the adoption of their children than are unwed mothers; nor is there any self-evident reason why as a class they would be." (*Caban*). * * *

* * *

Clearly, the father is treated unfairly under § 7004, subdivision (a), but equally important is the loss to the child. The child has a genetic bond with its natural parents that is unique among all relationships the child will have throughout its life. "The intangible fibers that connect parent and child have infinite variety. They are woven throughout the fabric of our society, providing it with strength, beauty, and flexibility." (*Lehr*). It therefore would be curious to conclude that the child's best interest is served by allowing the one parent (the mother) who wants to sever her legal ties to decide unilaterally that the only other such tie (the father's) will be cut as well. Absent a showing of a father's unfitness, his child is ill-served by allowing its mother effectively to preclude the child from ever having a meaningful relationship with its only other biological parent.

E.   In summary, we hold that § 7004, subdivision (a) and the related statutory scheme violates the federal constitutional guarantees of equal protection and due process for unwed fathers *to the extent that* the statutes allow a mother unilaterally to preclude her child's biological father from becoming a presumed father and thereby allowing the state to terminate his parental rights on nothing more than a showing of the child's best interest. If an unwed father promptly comes forward and demonstrates a full commitment to his parental responsibilities—emotional, financial, and otherwise—his federal constitutional right to due process prohibits the termination of his parental relationship absent a showing of his unfitness as a parent. Absent such a showing, the child's well-being is presumptively best served by continuation of the father's parental relationship. Similarly, when the father has come forward to grasp his parental responsibilities, his parental rights are entitled to equal protection as those of the mother.

A court should consider all factors relevant to that determination. The father's conduct both *before and after* the child's birth must be considered. Once he knows or reasonably should know of the pregnancy, he must promptly attempt to assume his parental responsibilities as fully as the mother will allow and his circumstances permit. In particular, the father must demonstrate "a willingness himself to assume full custody of the child—not merely to block adoption by others." A court should also consider the father's public acknowledgment of paternity, payment of pregnancy and birth expenses commensurate with his ability to do so, and prompt legal action to seek custody of the child.

We reiterate and emphasize the narrowness of our decision. The statutory distinction between natural fathers and presumed fathers is constitutionally invalid *only to the extent* it is applied to an unwed father who has sufficiently and timely demonstrated a full commitment to his parental responsibilities. * * *

NOTES AND QUESTIONS

1. Is the California Supreme Court's interpretation of *Caban* and *Quilloin* consistent with that of the *Lehr* court? Assume that the U.S. Supreme Court has agreed to hear *Kelsey S.* What arguments would you expect from the State and the father? How would you expect the Supreme Court to rule?

2. *Timing of the Unmarried Father's Objection:* Courts are generally willing to uphold the adoption veto rights of the unmarried father who comes forward promptly with both the desire and capacity to assume custody himself. But able and willing fathers who turn up *after* adoption orders have been entered have not fared well, even when their delay is excusable. *See In re Robert O. v. Russell K.*, 604 N.E.2d 99 (N.Y. 1992), the father, Robert O., and mother, Carol A., had been engaged and lived together when the baby was conceived. When Robert moved out and terminated all contact with Carol, she was pregnant. But Carol did not tell Robert about the pregnancy, apparently because she believed he would feel she was trying to coerce him into marriage. Carol made an adoption agreement with her friends Russell and Joanne K. and the child was delivered to them at the hospital where she gave birth. Carol executed an adoption consent and the adoption was finalized; she was never asked by the adoption court to identify the father, and state law did not require notice to him. Several months later, Carol and Robert reconciled and married. And nearly 18 months after the birth and 10 months after the completed adoption, Carol informed Robert that they had a child. Robert asserted that, as he had come forward to assume custody as soon as he knew about his child,

he was entitled to constitutional protection. But the New York Court of Appeals disagreed:

> To conclude that petitioner acted promptly once he became aware of the child is to fundamentally misconstrue whose timetable is relevant. Promptness is measured in terms of the baby's life not by the onset of the father's awareness. * * * The competing interests at stake in an adoption—and the complications presented by petitioner's position—are clearly illustrated here: nearly a year and a half after the baby went to live with the adoptive parents, and more than 10 months after they were told by the court that the baby was legally theirs, petitioner sought to rearrange those lives by initiating his present legal action.
>
> Petitioner's argument confuses the meaning of the constitutionally protected "opportunity" [to develop a relationship with his child.] * * * That opportunity * * * [is] protected only after the father ha[s] manifested his willingness to be a custodial parent. No one, however, let alone any State actor, prevented petitioner from finding out about Carol's pregnancy. His inaction, however regrettable and with whatever unfortunate consequences, was solely attributable to him. Nothing in * * * the Supreme Court decisions * * * suggests that the protections of constitutional due process must or should be extended to him under these circumstances.

Id. at 264–65. Is *Robert O.* consistent with *Lehr?* With *Kelsey S.? See also In re* Adoption of A.A.T., 196 P.3d 1180 (Kan. 2008) (denying biological father's attempts to set aside adoption based on his lack of knowledge of pregnancy).

3. *Thwarted Fathers:* The issue of the thwarted father creates problems. If the mother lies to the father, he does not have the opportunity to step up to assert parental responsibility. What does a father have to do to evidence responsibility? *Compare In re* Adoption of Baby Girl P., 242 P.3d 1168 (Kan. 2010) *with* O'Dea v. Olea, 217 P.3d 704 (Utah 2009). *See* Laura Oren, *Thwarted Fathers or Pop-Up Pops: How to Determine When Putative Fathers May Block the Adoption of Their Newborn Children,* 40 FAM. L. Q. 153 (2006).

4. *Putative Father Registries:* Although putative father registries exist in several states, they have widely different requirements. *In re* Baby Girl P., 802 A.2d 1192 (N.H. 2002). For a comparison of putative father registries, see NCSL, Putative Father Registries: State Legislation (2012), http.www.ncsl. org/documents/cyf/putativefatherregistries.pdf.

Would a national registry solve the problem? *See* Lisa M. Simpson, *Adoption Law: It May Take a Village to Raise a Child, But It Takes National Uniformity to Adopt One,* 3 PHOENIX L. REV. 575 (2010); Margaret Ryznar, *Two to Tango, One in Limbo: A Comparative Analysis of Father's Rights in Infant Adoptions,* 47 DUQ. L. REV. 89 (2009).

5. *Statutes of Limitation:* Some states have enacted time limits on adoption challenges. For example, under Uniform Adoption Act § 3–707, an

adoption decree "is not subject to a challenge begun more than six months after the decree or order is issued." *See also* IDAHO CODE § 16–1512 (six-month limit except in cases of fraud); NEB. REV. STAT. § 43–116 (adoptions conclusively presumed valid two years after entry of order). While few of these statutes of limitation have been tested in the courts, Virginia's highest court has ruled that its six-month limit on challenges was unconstitutional as applied to a father who could not read English and was told he was signing a release for medical treatment only. *See* F.E. v. G.F.M., 534 S.E.2d 337 (Va. App. 2000). Would the *F.E.* court have upheld the adoption in *Robert O.*? Would the *Lehr* court have struck down the six-month limit?

6.   *Tort Remedies:* Participation in a scheme to prevent an unmarried father from vetoing an adoption may be actionable in tort. A jury awarded $8 million to an unwed father who failed to learn he was a father in time to prevent his child's adoption. The West Virginia Supreme Court ruled that the mother's conduct was constitutionally protected but upheld the verdict against the mother's parents, her brother, and the adoption attorney who had advised her to give birth outside the state to avoid the statute mandating notice to the father and selected a Canadian couple to adopt the child in order to take advantage of Canadian law, which granted few rights to unmarried fathers. *See* Kessel v. Leavitt, 511 S.E.2d 720 (W. Va. 1998), *cert. denied* 525 U.S. 1142 (1999).

7.   *Adoption Annulment:* Although courts have traditionally been reluctant to permit an adoptive parent to annul an adoption order, "failed" adoptions are on the increase. An important source of failed non-relative adoptions is the increase in adoptions of older children with emotional, developmental, or physical problems. Such problems are common among both international and foster-care adoptees. As many as 90% of foster children have a physical abnormality in at least one body system, and as many as 80% need mental health services. *See* J.C. McMillen et al., *Prevalence of Psychiatric Disorders among Older Youth in the Foster Care System*, 44 J. ACAD. CHILD & ADOLESCENT PSYCHIATRY 88 (2005); Laurie Miller et al., *Health of Children Adopted from Guatemala: Comparison of Orphanage and Foster Care*, 115 PEDIATRICS e710 (2005). A few states now have statutory provisions that allow an adoption to be set aside for a developmental or mental "deficiency" existing or unknown at the time of the adoption. *See, e.g.*, CAL. FAM. CODE § 9100 (permitting action up to five years after adoption is final). In states without statutory authority for setting aside an adoption, adoptive parents must typically prove fraud, misrepresentation, or undue influence in order to set aside an adoption decree. Courts have often required proof of grounds for annulment by clear and convincing evidence, and annulment has sometimes been disallowed where the child would become a public charge.

8.   *Wrongful Adoption:* A number of courts have recognized a tort of "wrongful adoption" when an adoption agency misrepresents or withholds information relating to the adoptive child's health or psychological background. *See* Harriet Dinegar Milks, *"Wrongful Adoption" Causes of Action Against Adoption Agencies Where Children Have or Develop Mental or Physical*

Problems that Are Misrepresented or Not Disclosed to Adoptive Parents, 74 A.L.R. 5th 1 (1999).

9.   *Equitable Adoption:* Most states have recognized so-called "equitable" or "de facto" adoption, where an adoption contract is made and not performed. The equitable adoption doctrine typically cannot be used to create a parent-child relationship, but it does permit a court to treat the unadopted child as an adopted child for limited purposes. Equitable adoption relies on the equitable maxim that equity regards as done that which ought to be done. Courts require a heightened standard of proof and have typically employed the doctrine to allow recovery of statutory benefits based on a parent-child relationship such as a right to intestate succession, and to permit recovery of insurance proceeds and other contractual obligations. *See* McMullen v. Bennis, 20 So. 3d 890 (Fla. Dist. Ct. App. 2009); *In re* Scarlett Z.-D., 28 N.E.3d 776 (Ill. 2015).

Problem 8-1:

During the fall, John E., age 48, became involved in an extramarital affair with a married woman. At some point during the following spring or summer, the woman learned that she had become pregnant. Initially, she and John E. intended to live together and raise the child, but that fall the woman left John E. and resumed living with her husband. The child, Daniel, was born on December 15 and was turned over to adoptive parents four days later.

John E. had been willing to see his child raised by its mother and her husband but, when he learned in mid-January of the proposed adoption, he commenced a proceeding in Family Court to establish his paternity and seek custody; he also sought to stay the pending adoption proceeding. A genetic marker test ordered by the Court indicated the probability of John E.'s paternity to be 99.93%.

At a hearing in May, John E. indicated that he had been raised by foster parents and that, although he had no regrets about his upbringing, he believed that a certain "bonding" occurs between a biological parent and a child which is important to the child's well-being. He also told the court that, as he is divorced and employed full-time, he plans to leave Daniel during his work hours with an adult daughter, with whom he is currently living and who operates a day-care center from her home.

State law provides that the consent of the father of a child born out of wedlock who is under the age of six months at the time he or she is placed for adoption is required if: "(i) such father openly lived with the child or the child's mother for a continuous period of six months immediately preceding the placement of the child for adoption; and (ii) such father openly held himself out to be the father of such child during such period; and (iii) such father paid a fair and reasonable sum, in accordance with his means, for the medical, hospital and nursing expenses incurred in connection with the mother's pregnancy or with the birth of the child."

What result under state law? What constitutional arguments are available to John E.? Would the *Kelsey S.* court uphold the state statute? Would the U.S. Supreme Court? *See* In the Matter of John E. v. John Doe et al., 564 N.Y.S.2d 439 (App. Div. 1990).

Problem 8-2:

Ten years ago, Charlotte was born to unmarried parents, Linda and Ted. Both Linda and Ted had substance abuse problems, and Linda physically abused Charlotte. When Charlotte was two years old, Ted turned her over to her maternal grandparents (the Carrs). Charlotte has continuously lived with the Carrs since then. About a year after Charlotte came to live with the Carrs, Ted was released from jail and moved into the Carr household, too; he continued to live with the Carrs and Charlotte for the next three years.

When Charlotte was three years old, the Carrs filed a custody petition. The local Family Court appointed them as Charlotte's guardians and ordered Ted to pay $300 per month in child support. The court did not order visitation because it found that, given Ted's residence in the Carr household, he had "continuous and regular contact" with her. Ted made only one child support payment of $175.

When Charlotte was seven, the Carrs filed a domestic violence action seeking a restraining order against Ted, and the local Family Court ordered him to stay at least 200 yards away from their house. About a year later, Ted filed an application for custody of and/or reasonable visitation with Charlotte. The court ordered that the Carrs retain sole legal custody of Charlotte and approved a written visitation agreement that permitted Ted to visit Charlotte on alternate Saturdays.

About a year later, when Charlotte was eight, the Carrs filed a petition to declare Charlotte "free from the custody and control of her parents" pursuant to Probate Code § 1516, under which:

A child may be declared free from the custody and control of one or both parents if all of the following requirements are satisfied:

(1) One or both parents do not have the legal custody of the child.

(2) The child has been in the physical custody of the guardian for a period of not less than two years.

(3) The court finds that the child would benefit from being adopted by his or her guardian.

In making this determination, the court shall consider all factors relating to the best interest of the child, including but not limited to, the nature and extent of the relationship between all of the following: (A) The child and the birth parent. (B) The child and the guardian, including family members of the guardian. (C) The child and any siblings or half-siblings.

PROBATE CODE § 1516. An order declaring a minor free from the control of a parent terminates all parental rights and responsibilities with regard to the child and leaves the child eligible for adoption.

At a trial on the petition, Ted's lawyer argued that adoption would not serve Charlotte's best interests and that § 1516 was unconstitutional on its face and as applied to Ted. The trial judge found that "it is in the minor's best interest to be adopted by the guardians and it is against her best interest for the father . . . to maintain [his] parental rights." The court thus declared Charlotte "free from the custody and control of the father as provided in Probate Code § 1516." The trial judge declined to find the statute unconstitutional, although she stated on the record that, " . . . I have some significant reservations about whether it's going to survive."

On appeal, do the facts support the trial court's findings under § 1516? What constitutional arguments are available to Ted and the Carrs? Would the *Kelsey S.* court uphold the state statute? Would the U.S. Supreme Court? *See In re* Charlotte D., 39 Cal. Rptr. 3d 378 (App. 2006), rev. granted 136 P.3d 167 (Cal. 2006).

Problem 8-3:

You are counsel to the California Legislature's Committee on Family Law. The legislature is aware of the California Supreme Court's decision in *Kelsey S.* and wants to enact new standards governing the rights of unmarried fathers. Its goal is a statute that meets constitutional standards, but does not unduly delay or burden the adoption process. Draft legislation responsive to this aim. How would *Kelsey S.*, the various cases described in the notes that follow it, and Problem 8-1 be resolved under your statute?

3. ADOPTION RESTRICTIONS AND CONDITIONS

State restrictions on adoption vary substantially. The Uniform Adoption Act simply, and expansively, permits "any individual * * * [to] adopt or be adopted by another individual for the purpose of creating the relationship of parent and child between them." UAA § 1–102. But many state statutes impose restrictions on adoption.

A. WHO MAY ADOPT?

As a general rule, a married couple or a single person of legal age may adopt. A married couple must petition jointly unless the petitioner is the child's stepparent. While most adoptions used to be by married couples, increasing numbers of single persons, often women, have chosen to adopt children who are in the foster care or child welfare system. *See* W. Bradford

Wilcox & Robin Fretwell Wilson, *Bringing Up Baby: Adoption, Marriage and the Best Interests of the Child,* 14 WM. & MARY BILL OF RTS. J. 883 (2006). Should two unmarried persons be able to adopt? *See In re* Adoption of M.A., 930 A.2d 1088 (Me. 2007).

The majority of adoptions are by a child's relatives, rather than by strangers. For example, close to fifty percent of adoptions involve stepparents, primarily a stepfather adopting his wife's children. In other instances when parental rights have been terminated, some statutes give deference to grandparents or other relatives over foster parents. Some states have a preference in favor of relatives who wish to adopt. *See* Clark Cty. Dist. Att'y v. Eighth Jud. Dist. Ct., 167 P.3d 922 (Nev. 2007).

1.   Stepparent Adoption

A stepparent can adopt a stepchild if the court terminates the parental rights of the nonresidential biological or legal parent by consent or in a contested proceeding. This is called a second parent adoption. Because the adoption only terminates the rights of one parent, most states have a statutory provision that the child becomes the legal child of the adoptive stepparent, but remains the child of the biological parent. The basic test is "best interest of the child" and the procedures are often easier. *See* FLA. STAT. ANN. § 63.122(5) (eliminating the need to be a home study). If there is a divorce, most courts do not permit the former stepparent to abrogate the adoption. *See* Kathleen M. Lynch, *Adoption: Can Adoptive Parents Change Their Minds?*, 26 FAM. L.Q. 257, 260 (1992). Can (or should) the same attorney represent the biological parent and the stepparent?

2.   Gays and Lesbians

In all states a single person can adopt. Can a state ban a single person who is homosexual from adopting? *See* Florida Department of Children & Families v. Adoption of X.X.G., 45 So. 3d 79 (Fla. Dist. Ct. App. 2010) (no). Before Obergefell v. Hodges, 135 S. Ct. 2584 (2015), same-sex couples attempted to use second parent adoption statutes to legalize their relationships with children. A few states have statutes specifically allowing second parent adoption for domestic partners. CAL. FAM. CODE § 9000(b). Other states have interpreted their statutes to allow a same sex partner to adopt. *See* Adoption of Tammy, 619 N.E.2d 315 (Mass. 1993); Adoption of M.A., 930 A.2d 1088 (Me. 2007). *But see* Boseman v. Jarrell, 704 S.E.2d 494 (N.C. 2010).

3.   Grandparents and Other Relatives

Grandparents and other relatives sometimes seek to adopt a child when the biological parents have died or parental rights have been terminated. See Chapter 10. A few states give preference to grandparents and relatives, especially if the child has lived with them. Courts have been willing to honor the wishes of a parent to place the child with fit relatives. *See* FLA. STAT. 63.0425 (indicating where child has lived with grandparent for at least six months, the grandparent has priority unless deceased parent indicated other preference).

4. Foster Parents

Public and private agencies used to require foster parents to sign an agreement not to try to adopt a child placed with them. The ostensible purpose was to try to prevent the creation of bonds that would make reunification with the biological parents difficult. In recent years, however, courts have refused to enforce no-adoption agreements. New York gives a preference to foster parents with whom the child has lived for a year or more. *See* N.Y. SOC. SERVS. LAW 383(3). Other states have granted foster parent adoptions over grandparents who were not able to care adequately for the children. *See In re* Adoption of T.J.D., 186 S.W.3d 488 (Mo. App. 2006); *In re* Adoption of CF, 120 P.3d 992 (Wyo. 2005).

B. RACIAL AND ETHNIC MATCHING

Traditionally, adoption agencies attempted to place each child with adoptive parents whose biological and cultural heritage closely matched that of the child's parents. Matching was typically based on race, religion, and physical features. It was done behind the scenes in order to protect the privacy of the biological mother. As the gap between the supply of and demand for adoptable white infants widened during the 1960s, many adoption agencies reassessed matching, and some began to permit transracial adoption.

1. Transracial Adoption

Most transracial adoptions involve white parents and black or biracial children. Organized opposition quickly followed and

> by 1975 was formidable enough to bring about a reversal in policy on the part of major adoption agencies * * * The opposition was led and organized primarily by black social workers and leaders of black political organizations who saw in the practice an insidious scheme for depriving the black community of its most valuable future resource: its children. In essence, the leaders of black and Indian organizations argue that non-white children who are adopted by white parents are lost to the non-white community. * * * Both the blacks and the Indians who led and organized the opposition to transracial adoption agreed on one major point—that it is impossible for white parents to rear black or Indian children in such an environment as to permit them to retain or develop a black or Indian identity.

RITA J. SIMON & HOWARD ALTSTEIN, TRANSRACIAL ADOPTION 2–3 (1977). While Congress did not act to protect other ethnic and racial minorities, a number of states enacted or maintained race-matching requirements for adoptable children or mandated a same-race search before a transracial placement could be considered.

But during the late 1980s and early 1990s,

challenges were mounted on many fronts to the notion that children should be kept at almost all costs within their racial, ethnic, or tribal community of origin. Media stories documented * * * horrors that resulted from insisting on this priority[, including] * * * children removed from the loving foster parents who had nurtured them * * *.

Social scientists published a succession of studies demonstrating that children placed with other-race parents did just as well in all measurable respects as children placed with same-race parents. Other studies confirmed earlier evidence that delay in and denial of adoptive placement was extremely harmful to children. Yet other studies demonstrated that this kind of delay and denial was an inherent part of the race-matching regime. * * *

* * *

Critics took on the various arguments that had been made on behalf of the race-matching regime. * * * The critics pointed out that * * * there [were] so many black children in foster care, and waiting for adoption, that blacks would have to adopt at many times the rates of whites to provide homes for all of the waiting children. * * *

The critics contended that what lay behind same-race matching policies was a form of race separatism that had been rejected in other contexts and could not be justified as serving the interests of either black children or the larger black community. * * * [They noted] that polls of black people indicated no significant support for * * * the race-matching regime. * * * They argued that same-race matching policies were motivated and sustained by the commitment of certain adoption professionals, more than by any "community" commitment.

ELIZABETH BARTHOLET, NOBODY'S CHILDREN: ABUSE AND NEGLECT, FOSTER DRIFT, AND THE ADOPTION ALTERNATIVE 127–28 (1999). And by the mid-1990s, with an exploding population of former foster children "freed" for adoption—more than half of whom were African-American—the political ground shifted again. The Howard M. Metzenbaum Multiethnic Placement Act of 1994 (MEPA), Pub. L. No. 103–382, 553(a)(1), 108 Stat. 3518, 4056 (amended 1996), a federal funding statute, prohibited states from the "delay or den[ial of] the placement of a child for adoption or into foster care, on the basis of the race, color, or national origin of the adoptive or foster parent, or the child, involved." It preserved an exemption for adoptions under the Indian Child Welfare Act.

The shift in legal standards has not produced consensus on whether transracial adoption is invariably a good thing. Some critics point out that the vast majority of transracial adoptions involve infants, while most foster children who need adoptive homes are older and often have special problems. *See* Mark E. Courtney, *The Politics and Realities of Transracial Adoption*, 76 CHILD WELFARE 749, 764–65 (1997) (reporting that 87% of children of color placed by traditional adoption agencies were infants). Others argue that

> the results of the studies [demonstrating the success of transracial adoption] are overstated * * *. Many lack control groups and may be biased, either in favor of, or against transracial adoption, because of the source of their funding or their sponsorship. In some of the longitudinal studies, only a relatively small percentage of the families are still being followed years later. The families who were unsuccessful with transracial adoption may have dropped out of the studies at a greater rate than those who were successful. In addition, the objectivity of the children and their parents in assessing the transracial adoption relationship must be questioned. * * *

Twila L. Perry, *The Transracial Adoption Controversy: An Analysis of Discourse and Subordination*, 21 N.Y.U. REV. L. & SOC. CHANGE 33 (1993– 94). Finally, some commentators argue that, for African-Americans, transracial adoption is "cultural genocide":

> Forty-six percent of the children in foster care are minorities— which is more than double their proportion in the general child population. Once separated from their families, African American children are returned to their homes half as quickly as white children. African American children remain in the foster care system for disproportionately longer periods of time than white children. African American children often remain in the foster care system twice as long as do white children—an average of two years rather than one.

> The figures for displaced or outplaced African American children are almost as high as those figures reported for Native American children in the 1970's. It could be argued that, as with the Native American tribal community in the 1970's, the African American extended family community is undergoing a form of cultural genocide.

Cynthia G. Hawkins-Leon, *The Indian Child Welfare Act and the African American Tribe: Facing the Adoption Crisis,* 36 BRANDEIS J. FAM. L. 201, 212–13 (1997–98). *See also* Ruth-Arlene W. Howe, *Race Matters in Adoption*, 42 FAM. L. Q. 465 (2008); EVAN B. DONALDSON ADOPTION INSTITUTE, FINDING FAMILIES FOR AFRICAN AMERICAN CHILDREN: THE ROLE OF RACE & LAW IN ADOPTION FROM FOSTER CARE (2008) (indicating that MEPA-IEP did not open more White homes to Black children but left more Black children in foster care).

2. Indian Child Welfare Act

In 1978 Congress enacted the Indian Child Welfare Act (ICWA), 25 U.S.C. § 1902 et seq. It required the states to prefer a member of an Indian child's tribe or another Indian over other prospective adoptive parents. The Act was

> the product of rising concern * * * over the consequences to Indian children, Indian families, and Indian tribes of * * * child welfare practices that resulted in the separation of 25% to 35% of all Indian children * * * from their families [for placement] * * * in adoptive families, foster care, or institutions. Adoptive placements counted significantly in this total: in the State of Minnesota, for example, one in eight Indian children under the age of 18 was in an adoptive home, and * * * [t]he adoption rate of Indian children was eight times that of non-Indian children. Approximately 90% of the Indian placements were in non-Indian homes. A number of witnesses also testified to the serious adjustment problems encountered by such children during adolescence, as well as the impact of the adoptions on Indian parents and the tribes themselves.

Mississippi Band of Choctaw Indians v. Holyfield, 490 U.S. 30, 50 (1989). ICWA applies to all "child custody proceedings" involving an "Indian child." 25 U.S.C. § 1903 and § 1911. ICWA defines "child custody proceeding" as including foster care placements, termination of parental rights proceedings, preadoptive placements and adoptive placements. 25 U.S.C. § 1903[1][i]–[iv].

An "Indian child" is defined as "any unmarried person who is under age eighteen and is either (a) a member of an Indian tribe or (b) is eligible for membership in an Indian tribe and is the biological child of a member of an Indian tribe." 25 U.S.C. § 1903[4]. 25 U.S.C. § 1911(a) vests Indian tribal courts with exclusive jurisdiction over any child custody proceeding involving an Indian child who resides or is domiciled within the reservation of such tribe. 25 U.S.C. § 1911(b), on the other hand, creates concurrent but presumptively tribal jurisdiction in the case of an Indian child not domiciled on the reservation. In this latter case, state courts "shall" transfer any proceeding for foster care placement or termination of parental rights to the tribal court unless "good cause" to the contrary is shown, either parent objects to the transfer or the tribe declines jurisdiction. *See* Barbara Atwood, *The Voice of the Indian Child: Strengthening the Indian Child Welfare Act Through Children's Participation*, 50 ARIZ. L. REV. 127 (2008) (discussing the success of ICWA in promoting tribal family preservation programs).

Under 25 U.S.C. § 1911(c) an Indian child's tribe may intervene at any point in state court proceedings for "foster care placement" or "termination of parental rights." ICWA defines termination of parental rights as "any action resulting in the termination of the parent-child relationship." 25 U.S.C. § 1903[1][ii]. ICWA also provides substantive standards for placement of Indian children in different types of child custody proceedings. For example:

> In any adoptive placement of an Indian child under State law, a preference shall be given, in the absence of good cause to the contrary, to a placement with (1) a member of the child's extended family; (2) other members of the Indian child's tribe; or (3) other Indian families. 25 U.S.C. § 1915(a).

A few states adopted an "Existing Indian Family" exception allowing a court to use a different placement if the Indian parent did not live on the reservation and had chosen a different placement. Indeed, the United States Supreme Court appeared to use it in upholding a placement with an adoptive couple who had the child for two years over the Native American father. *See* Adoptive Couple v. Baby Girl, 133 S. Ct. 2552 (2013). The vast majority of states, however, have rejected the doctrine. *In re* Baby Boy C., 805 N.Y.S.2d 313 (App. Div. 2005); *In re* A.J.S., 204 P.3d 543 (Kan. 2009). In June 2016, new ICWA regulations were published clarifying that there is no existing Indian family exception and setting out procedures for ICWA. 81 FED. REG. 114 (June 2016).

Evaluate the possibility of an equal protection challenge to the ICWA: On what basis might the federal government attempt to justify a different adoption policy for Native American children than for all other children? What level of scrutiny would apply? What additional facts would be useful? What is the likelihood that such a challenge would prove successful? *See* David D. Meyer, *Palmore Comes of Age: The Place of Race in the Placement of Children*, 18 U. FLA. J. L. & PUB. POL'Y 183 (2007); Solangel Maldonado, *Discouraging Racial Preferences in Adoptions*, 39 U.C. DAVIS L. REV. 1415 (2006).

3.   International Adoption

Post World War II, a growing number of Americans began to adopt children from other countries, often refugee children. In 2008, the American Bar Association adopted a resolution that "supports international adoption as an integral part of a comprehensive child welfare strategy to address the worldwide problem of children without permanent homes."

The largest number of U.S. transracial adoptions are intercountry adoptions which tripled between 1992 and 2006. In 2006, four of the top five "suppliers" of international adoptees (China, Guatemala, Russia, South Korea) were non-European, supplying almost 13,000 of the 20,679 adoptive children. *See* U.S. State Dep't, *Immigrant Visas Issued to Orphans Coming to the U.S.*, http://travel.state.gov/family/adoption/stats/stats_ 451.html. Does the large number of transracial, intercountry adoptions provide support for the claims of transracial adoption advocates or critics? Consider the following from the EVAN B. DONALDSON ADOPTION INSTITUTE, FINDING FAMILIES 2008 REPORT, *supra* at 16–17, 23:

> Two international treaties established the rights of children whose families could not care for them * * * The first, the Convention on the Rights of the Child, was approved by the United Nations in 1989 and ratified by more than 175 countries; only the United States and Somalia have not ratified this treaty. Among the rights of children recognized by CRC is the right to "identity." Article 20 sets forth governmental obligations in protecting a child's identity and continuity of cultural background:
>
>> 1.   A child temporarily or permanently deprived of his or her family environment, or in whose own best interest cannot be allowed to remain in that environment, shall be entitled to special protection and assistance provided by the State.
>>
>> 2.   [While] such care could include * * * foster placement or adoption or, if necessary, placement in suitable institutions for the care of children, when considering solutions, due regard shall be paid to the desirability of continuity in a child's upbringing and to the child's ethnic, religious, cultural and linguistic background.
>
> Some opponents of international adoption use the CRC to argue against children leaving their home countries for adoption; however, research and humanitarian perspectives invariably support the position that it is better for children to be raised in permanent families than to grow up in institutions or foster care.
>
> The second treaty, the Hague Convention on Protection of Children and Cooperation in Respect of Intercountry Adoption, was adopted in 1993 * * * it has been ratified by 75 countries to date. The Hague Convention regulates international adoption practice and is designed to protect the rights of children, birthparents, and adoptive parents. Like the CRC, it recognizes the importance of a child's identity. Article 16 states that a child's

country of origin must "give due consideration to the child's upbringing and to his or her ethnic, religious and cultural background" and "determine, on the basis in particular of the reports relating to the child and the prospective adoptive parents, whether the envisaged placement is in the best interests of the child."

After the U.S. signed the Hague Convention, Congress enacted the Intercountry Adoption Act of 2000, which brings this country into compliance with the Hague Convention requirements. The Department of State, now the designated U.S. Central Authority for international adoption, has issued implementing regulations. These address * * * children's racial and ethnic needs. First, they require that prospective adoptive parents receive 10 hours of pre-adoption training which, among other topics, must address the "long-term implications for families who become multi-cultural through intercountry adoption" (Section 96.48). Second, adoption service providers are to counsel parents about the child's history, including a focus on "cultural, racial, religious, ethnic, and linguistic background" Section 96.48. The U.S. has ratified the Hague Convention, and it took effect in this country in April 2008.

The Child Citizenship Act provides automatic citizenship for many children adopted abroad by U.S. Citizens. 8 U.S.C. § 1431(b). The Hague Adoption Convention, although signed by the United States earlier, was not ratified until 2007 and was implemented in April 2008. It can be found on the home page of the Hague Conference on Private International Law, http://hcch.e-vision.nl/index_en.php.

Interestingly, the number of international adoptions has decreased. The number of intercountry adoptions began to decline after adoption of the Hague Adoption Convention. In 2001, 14% were intercountry—7% in 2012. Only 6,500 immigrant visas were issued in 2014. *See* A.P. *Foreign Adoptions by Americans Reach Lowest Mark Since 1982*, N.Y. Times, Mar. 31, 2015. The downward trend is likely to continue with the immigration policies announced by the President in 2017.

C. OPEN ADOPTION

ADOPTION OF VITO

Massachusetts Supreme Judicial Court, 2000.
431 Mass. 550, 728 N.E.2d 292.

MARSHALL, C.J.

This appeal arises from the denial of a petition to dispense with parental consent to adoption. The case concerns a child who tested positive for cocaine at the time of his birth in January, 1992, and who has lived with his foster parents (also his preadoptive parents) since he was discharged from the hospital one month after his birth. Vito [a pseudonym] has never lived with his biological mother. He is now eight and one-half years old.[4]

* * * The probate judge concluded that the mother was unfit to parent Vito, but found that the department's adoption plan was not in his best interest because it did not provide for significant postadoption contact with Vito's mother and biological siblings. She denied the petition. The judge provided that, on a timely filing of a motion for reconsideration, she might reconsider the denial and enter a new judgment should the department submit a new adoption plan that provided for postadoption contact between Vito and his biological mother and siblings, including eight yearly visits with his biological mother, as long as the mother is not abusing drugs and the contact continues to be in Vito's best interests.

The department appealed. * * *.

We vacate the judge's order denying the petition to dispense with parental consent to adoption. The judge's conclusion that the mother is unfit is not challenged. With respect to the judge's denial of the petition based on failure to provide for postadoption contact in the adoption plan, we hold that a judge may order limited postadoption contact, including visitation, between a child and a biological parent where such contact is currently in the best interests of the child. * * *

Judicial exercise of equitable power to require postadoption contact is not warranted in this case, however, because there is little or no evidence of a significant, existing bond between Vito and his biological mother, and no other compelling reason for concluding that postadoption contact is currently in his best interests. Vito has formed strong, nurturing bonds with his preadoptive family; and the record supports little more than speculation that postadoption contact will be important for his adjustment years later, in adolescence. * * *

* * * When Vito tested positive for cocaine at birth, an abuse and neglect report concerning him was filed two days after his birth, alleging his positive cocaine screen and his mother's failure to obtain prenatal care. The report was substantiated. In February, 1992, the existing care and protection petition for Vito's three older siblings was amended to include Vito, and he was placed in the temporary custody of the department.

---

[4] The department obtained permanent custody of Vito within weeks of his birth. The lengthy delay before the petition was filed may be explained by the department's efforts to place Vito permanently with a member of his biological family, by concerns raised by foster care review panels about the cultural and ethnic "inappropriateness" of his foster care placement, and his foster family's temporary change of heart regarding adoption when his foster mother was diagnosed with leukemia, later successfully treated. Nevertheless, we express our concern about any lengthy delay before a young child is placed within the secure environment of a permanent family.

Vito was discharged from the hospital one month after his birth and was placed in the home of his foster parents; his siblings had been placed in other homes. * * * From the time of his removal from his mother's care in January, 1992, while in the hospital, until January, 1995, his biological mother visited Vito only once. * * *

In 1995, while back in Massachusetts in prison on shoplifting charges, Vito's mother signed a department service plan, entered a drug rehabilitation program and began visits with Vito and his siblings. Vito's mother was released from prison in October, 1995. The judge found that the mother's visits with Vito have been generally consistent since March, 1995, and that she has attended monthly supervised visits since her release. The judge found that Vito and his biological mother have "no emotional sharing" between them and remain dissociated, despite pleasant play and conversation. The judge found that Vito did not show any genuine interest in his biological siblings and did not appear to have formed any emotional attachment to his biological mother; he did not appear to be excited to see her and separated from her with no difficulties or emotional overtones. The judge nevertheless made an ultimate finding that Vito had formed "a positive relationship" with his biological mother that has developed since visitation began when she was incarcerated. * * *

In contrast, the judge found that Vito is "fully integrated into his foster family both emotionally and ethnically." * * *

The judge concluded that, by clear and convincing evidence, Vito's mother is currently unfit to parent him. She specifically found that the biological mother "lacks the current ability, capacity, fitness and readiness" to parent Vito. Her unavailability to Vito, she concluded, resulted in Vito's "life-long placement with [his foster] family, to which he is now attached." Despite the fact that the biological mother "cares deeply for and has good intentions toward the child," however, "[g]ood intentions . . . are insufficient to establish fitness to parent a child."

The judge further determined that "racial issues may at *sometime in the future*" become a problem for Vito (emphasis added). She found that Vito's relationship with his biological mother is "crucial" for his "racial and cultural development and adjustment," that his best interests will be served by continued "significant" contact with her after any adoption, and that under the department's adoption plan Vito would have limited or no connection to his African-American family or culture. She found that the department's plan is not in Vito's "best interest so long as it does not provide for significant ongoing contact with [his m]other and [biological] siblings."

II

Despite numerous appellate decisions to the contrary, the department argues that there is no authority for the judge to enter an order requiring postadoption visitation in a termination proceeding * * *, or at least, that such an order cannot be made where there is an identified, pre-adoptive family and the child has no bond with the biological parent. Sixteen years ago we commented on whether "post-adoption visitation for the benefit of the child may be ordered" in connection with a decree dispensing with the need for a parent's consent to adoption. We said then that * * * "we see no reason why a judge dealing with a petition to dispense with parental consent may not evaluate 'the plan proposed by the department' . . . in relation to all the elements the judge finds are in the child's best interests, including parental visitation." * * *

Since our 1984 decision, numerous Appeals Court decisions have expressed an understanding that judges may effect or require postadoption visitation as an outcome of termination proceedings. That was a correct understanding of our law.

* * *

The department acknowledges that our case law has recognized that a court may utilize its equitable powers to order postadoption contact, but, in essence, asserts that the recent legislative amendments to G.L. c. 210 amount to a legislative repudiation of the view that postadoption contact may be judicially ordered. The concurrence similarly argues that the amendments "further support [the] view that the Legislature did not intend that Probate Court judges order postadoption visitation."[17] We do not agree. The amendments by their terms were not aimed at overturning the centuries-old equitable authority of courts to act in the best interests of children, when those children are properly under the courts' jurisdiction.

With the possible, narrow exception of postadoption judicial modification of voluntary contact agreements between biological parents and adoptive parents, we see nothing in the relevant, amended provisions of G.L. c. 210 that erodes this long-recognized equitable authority to act in the best interests of the child. Even where biological and prospective adoptive parents do agree on postadoption contact, the Legislature provided for judicial involvement to approve the agreement. It would be anomalous to conclude that such provisions were meant to eliminate entirely judicial involvement in other related contexts. To the contrary, various provisions of the statute mandate that the judge act in those best interests during termination and adoption proceedings. * * *

---

[17] In 1999, the Legislature amended provisions of G.L. c. 210 to allow biological parents and adoptive parents to enter into an agreement for postadoption contact. The amendment provides that "[s]uch agreement may be approved by the court issuing the termination decree under section 3; provided, however, that an agreement under this section shall be finally approved by the court issuing the adoption decree." Conditions for court approval of such an agreement include that it has been knowingly and voluntarily entered by all parties. The legislation also provides that in enforcing that agreement a court may later limit, restrict, condition, or decrease contact between the biological parents and the child, but may not increase that contact.

Where the * * * amendments address postadoption contact agreements between biological parents and preadoptive parents in the context of termination proceedings, they presuppose the identification of the prospective adoptive parents at the time the proceedings occur. These statutory postadoption contact provisions do not address those circumstances when termination proceedings occur and there is as yet no preadoptive parent identified. In such circumstances the equitable authority of the judge may be especially important in safeguarding the child's best interests. Even where preadoptive parents are identified and attempt to make an agreement with the biological parents concerning postadoption contact, an impasse may be reached between the parties, as happened in this case.[20] There, the judge's equitable intervention may also be important to move the proceedings forward toward adoption while simultaneously securing postadoption contact that will benefit the child and that all parties want, but on which they cannot quite come to terms. The best interests of a child should not be held hostage to the negotiating skills of adults.

A judge's equitable power to order postadoption contact, however, is not without limit. This equitable authority does not derive from the statutory adoption scheme, but it must necessarily be attentive to the policy directives inherent in that scheme, as well as to constitutional limitations on intrusions on the prerogatives of the adoptive family. The adoption statute contemplates, for example, that after an adoption decree, "all rights, duties and other legal consequences of the natural relation of child and parent ... shall, except as regards marriage, incest or cohabitation, terminate between the child so adopted and his natural parents." This provision strongly suggests that in ordinary circumstances adoption is meant to sever most enforceable obligations involving the biological parent with the child. This statutory language is not a bar to judicial orders for postadoption contact, however, because an order for postadoption contact is grounded in the over-all best interests of the child, based on emotional bonding and other circumstances of the actual personal relationship of the child and the biological parent, not in the rights of the biological parent nor the legal consequences of their natural relation.

Constitutional considerations also guide the exercise of this equitable power. Adoptive parents have the same legal rights toward their children that biological parents do. Parental rights to raise one's children are essential, basic rights that are constitutionally protected. "It is cardinal with us that the custody, care and nurture of the child reside first in the parents," and in most circumstances we "have respected the private realm

---

[20] According to the guardian ad litem, the foster parents expressed interest in an open adoption and did not oppose regular contacts between Vito and his biological family. The judge ordered the parties to meet to discuss * * * an open adoption agreement, but the parties could not come to an agreement.

of family life which the state cannot enter." Prince v. Massachusetts, 321 U.S. 158, 166 (1944). State intrusion in the rearing of children by their parents may be justified only in limited circumstances.

At a pragmatic level, unnecessary involvement of the courts in long-term, wide-ranging monitoring and enforcement of the numerous postadoption contact arrangements could result from too ready an application of the court's equitable power to issue contact orders. The postadoption contact arrangements contemplated by the judge in this case were both long term and wide ranging, and necessarily would have involved the court in ongoing arrangements between the biological mother and the adopting family for many years to come. But courts are not often the best place to monitor children's changing needs, particularly the needs of young children. What may be in Vito's best interest at the age of five says little about his best interests at age ten or fifteen.

We also recognize the concern raised by the department and the amici that untrammeled equitable power used to impose postadoption contact might reduce the number of prospective parents willing to adopt. Any practice that potentially reduces the pool of prospective adoptive parents raises grave concerns. * * *

Where, as here, the child has formed strong, nurturing bonds with his preadoptive family, and there is little or no evidence of a significant, existing bond with the biological parent, judicial exercise of equitable power to require postadoption contact would usually be unwarranted. On the other hand, a judicial order for postadoption contact may be warranted where the evidence readily points to significant, existing bonds between the child and a biological parent, such that a court order abruptly disrupting that relationship would run counter to the child's best interests. Cases warranting a postadoption contact order are more likely to occur where no preadoptive family has yet been identified, and where a principal, if not the only, parent-child relationship in the child's life remains with the biological parent. A necessary condition is a finding, supported by the evidence, that continued contact is currently in the best interests of the child.[25] Because an order of postadoption contact affects the rights of the adoptive parents to raise their children, the order should be carefully and narrowly crafted to address the circumstances giving rise to the best interests of the child.

* * *

---

[25] We focus here on an order requiring postadoption contact between a child and his biological parents. Similar limitations apply to postadoption contact between a child and his biological siblings. In the Appeals Court, the department did not "challenge[ ] the sibling visitation requirement." * * * While contact with siblings and contact with biological parents may * * * be governed by different statutory considerations, in terms of intrusion on the prerogatives of the adoptive family, judicial requirement of contact with biological siblings might not differ significantly from a requirement for contact with parents.

Transitional provision for posttermination or postadoption contact in the best interests of the child, however, is a far different thing from judicial meddling in the child's and adoptive family's life, based not on evidence of the emotional ties and current dynamics between the child and the biological parent, but on speculation concerning some hypothetical dynamic between parent and child several years hence, later in adolescence, for example. * * * In Vito's case the probate judge apparently favored postadoption contact because she was concerned about Vito's future racial and cultural development and adjustment, presumably based on the guardian ad litem's testimony that transracial adoptees, generally speaking, often have adjustment problems that emerge in adolescence. The judge appears to have inappropriately relied on the guardian ad litem's speculation as to the future need of Vito to have contact with his mother in order to secure his identity years later, in adolescence. That is a matter that is properly left to the wise guidance of Vito's new family.

* * *

Assuming that it was proper to use racial grounds for determining Vito's best interest, * * * [w]e discern no support for a determination that Vito's relationship with his biological mother is "crucial" for his "racial and cultural development and adjustment." Moreover, here the judge found that Vito "is a typical Latino child growing up in a Latino family . . . [and who] describe[s] himself as Latino," who was "fully integrated into his foster family both emotionally and ethnically," and whose physical appearance was not strikingly different from his foster parents. His primary language is that of his foster family, not his biological mother. The judge found Vito "did not manifest any genuine interest in his biological siblings" and did not have an "emotional attachment" to his biological mother.

We conclude, therefore, that, although the probate judge had a statutory mandate to review the department's adoption plan to determine whether the best interests of the child would be served by a termination decree with that plan, and although the judge had equitable authority to order postadoption contact, including visitation, the judge's determination that such postadoption contact was required was clearly erroneous in this case. * * *

* * *

We remand the case to the Probate and Family Court Department and direct that a decree enter granting the department's petition to dispense with parental consent to Vito's adoption. Because several years have passed since judgment was entered in the trial court [in 1997], the record is unclear as to the scope and depth of any current contact between Vito and his biological mother and siblings. The judge, in her discretion, may, but need not, determine that a further hearing would be helpful to determine whether contact between Vito and his biological mother or siblings during a circumscribed transition period currently would be in his best interests.

COWIN, J. (concurring, with whom LYNCH, J., joins).

* * *

General Laws c. 210 provides for a two-stage process: first, for dispensing with the biological parents' right to consent to an adoption; and second, for approving the adoption of a child by new parents. * * * Under § 3, the judge must consider the best interests of the child in deciding whether to order dispensation with parental consent. An order to dispense is only proper after a determination that "a parent is currently unfit to further the child's best interest."

Section 6 permits the Probate Court judge to enter a decree authorizing the adoption. Before issuing the decree, the Probate Court judge must be satisfied "that the petitioner is of sufficient ability to bring up the child and provide suitable support and education for it, and that the child should be adopted." Once the decree is entered, the adoptive parents assume all the rights and obligations of the biological parents and the rights and obligations of the biological parents terminate.

* * *

Allowing the § 3 judge to order postadoption visitation conflicts with this statutory framework. By removing the child from his biological parents and placing full parental authority with the adoptive parents, the Legislature has intended to provide a complete severance from the biological parents and a new beginning for the child. * * *

Authorizing the Probate Court judge to order postadoption visitation conflicts with the Legislature's expressed purpose of vesting all parental prerogatives in the adoptive parents because in many circumstances the adoptive parents will object to continuing contact between the child and the biological parents.

* * *

The [1999] amendments [to the adoption statute] * * * permit agreements between biological and adoptive parents that provide for postadoptive contact. The judge's power is limited to approving the agreement and reducing or conditioning the contact between the child and the biological parents. The judge is not empowered to expand the agreement. It is incongruous to believe that the Legislature would expressly deprive the court of the right to expand postadoption visitation when an agreement exists, but yet, in the absence of an agreement, grant the court broad power to order visitation.

The Legislature's decision to limit postadoption visitation to agreements between the adoptive and biological parents is consistent with the established purpose of § 6[,] * * * to assure that the adoptive parents assume full authority to make decisions on behalf of the child. By limiting postadoptive visitation to agreements entered into by adoptive parents, the Legislature, consistent with § 6, assures that the locus of visitation decision-making resides with the adoptive parents.

* * * By providing that §§ 6C and 6D do not "abrogate the right of an adoptive parent to make decisions on behalf of his child," the Legislature cautioned that these new sections should be narrowly construed with an eye toward protecting the decision-making authority of the adoptive parents. In my view, the Legislature's addition of § 6E indicates a clear intent that §§ 6C and 6D not upset the long-established purpose of § 6 to place the decision-making authority for the child with the adoptive parents. * * *

NOTES AND QUESTIONS

1. One scholar indicates that "Open adoption has now become the norm in practice for all types of adoption." Annette Ruth Appell, *Reflections on the Movement Toward a More Child-Centered Adoption*, 32 W. NEW ENG. L. REV. 1, 4 (2010). At least twenty states give courts authority to order visitation between the child and specified persons if it is in the best interests of the child. *See* CWIG, *Post-Adoption Contact Agreements Between Birth and Adoptive Families* (2005) http://www.childwelfare.gov/systemwide/laws_policies/ statutes/cooperative.cfm#states. Legal developments that permit the maintenance of a child's ties with his biological family have been spurred by two very different factors. One is a burgeoning population of foster children who, due to changes in the adoption "market," are now potentially adoptable. Many of these children, like Vito, have maintained visitation with their biological parents for years; often they have lived with their parents. Maintenance of these ongoing ties can serve the child's interests; maintenance of these ties can also convince a parent who would otherwise oppose termination of parental rights to consent to adoption. A second factor is the rise of independent adoptions, in which biological parents choose the individuals who will adopt their child and determine the terms on which the child will be relinquished. Given the dearth of adoptive infants, biological parents who want to maintain a connection with their children have considerable bargaining clout, and changed social mores have led increased numbers of parents relinquishing infants to want to exercise it.

2. Is the fact that biological parents may choose to give up children they otherwise would have refused to relinquish a benefit or a harm associated with open adoption? What are the pros and cons of judicially ordered open adoption, like that approved by the *Vito* court, as compared to an open adoption regime in which post-visitation contact can only be based on an agreement between the biological and adoptive parents? *See* Carol Sanger, *Bargaining for*

Motherhood: Postadoption Visitation Agreements, 41 HOFSTRA L. REV. 309 (2012).

3.   Does open adoption allowing for ongoing contact between the child and the birth parents help answer some of the problems with transracial adoptions? *See* Solangel Maldonado, *Permanency v. Biology: Making the Case for Post-Adoption Contact*, 37 CAP. U. L. REV. 321 (2008); Annette R. Appell, *The Endurance of Biological Connection: Heteronormativity, Same-Sex Parenting and the Lessons of Adoption*, 22 BYU J. PUB. L. 289, 305 (2008).

4.   If the court has granted an adoption, then shouldn't the adoptive parents, who are now the legal parents, have a presumption in favor of their decision of whether to allow post adoption visitation? *See* Troxel v. Granville, 530 U.S. 57 (2000), Ch. 14, sec. 5. *See In re* Adoption of Ilona, 944 N.E.2d 115 (Mass. 2011) (allowing adoption by foster parent, finding continued contact would be in child's best interests, but leaving parenting decisions to judgment of adoptive parents).

5.   Research, including one large study conducted in Minnesota and Texas, has found positive or neutral effects associated with open adoption. The Minnesota-Texas study found no significant relationship between the level of openness in the adoption and the children's socioemotional adjustment as measured by standardized inventories, either during the first point of measurement or the second, when the children were typically adolescents. Children's satisfaction with contact did not differ by level of openness at the first measurement point. However, by the second measurement, adolescents who had contact with birth mothers reported higher degrees of satisfaction with their level of adoption openness and with the intensity of their contact with birth mother than did adolescents who had no contact. *See MN/TX Adoption Research Project: Key Findings*, http://fsos.che.umn.edu/projects/mtarp/Key_Findings.html.

6.   *Adult Adoptee Access to Adoption Records:* Children raised in traditional, "closed" adoptive homes often want, after they become adults, to learn about, and even contact, their biological parents. Indeed, in one study 95% of surveyed adoptees expressed a desire to be found by their biological parents. In a survey of adolescent adoptees, 72% wanted to know why they were adopted, 65% wanted to meet their birth parents, and 94% wanted to know which biological parent they looked like. *See* Nat. Adoption Information Clearinghouse, *Searching for Birth Relatives*, www.calib.com/naic/pubs.

But based on concerns about the privacy of biological parents, most states do not permit adult adoptees to obtain information about their biological families upon demand. *See* In the Matter of Timothy AA, 899 N.Y.S.2d 433 (Sup. Ct. App. 2010) (adopting adult failed to demonstrate "good cause" for unsealing records). In 2005, only six states permitted adult adoptees to obtain their birth certificates upon demand. *See* Caroline B. Fleming, Note, *The Open-Records Debate: Balancing the Interests of Birth Parents and Adult Adoptees*, 11 WILLIAM & MARY J. WOMEN & L. 461, 461 n. 2 (2005). Although open-records laws remain rare, state legislatures in almost every state have created either a mutual consent registry, a confidential intermediary service, or both to facilitate contact between adult adoptees and members of their birth families. Some of these registry laws require consent from both birth parents; others require consent only from the registering parties. *See* COLO. REV. STAT. § 2–2–1135 (passive); OR. REV. STAT. § 109.503 (active). All states also permit adult adoptees to obtain their adoption records based on "good cause"; generally courts have been unwilling to find good cause when biological parents oppose the petition. *See* D. Marianne Brower Blair, *The Impact of Family Paradigms, Domestic Constitutions, and International Conventions on Disclosure of an Adopted Person's Identities and Heritage*, 22 MICH. J. INT'L L. 587, 602–13 nn. 74–75 (2001) (describing and categorizing state laws).

Although the justification for closed-records laws is the privacy of biological parents, recent surveys suggest that this concern is overstated. One state study found that every biological parent surveyed wanted to be found by the child he or she had placed for adoption; in another study, 86% of biological mothers supported access by adult adoptees to information identifying biological parents. *See* NAIC, *supra*, at *Searching for Birth Parents*.

Constitutional challenges to the Oregon and Tennessee open-records laws were unsuccessful. *See* Doe v. Sundquist, 2 S.W.3d 919 (Tenn. 1999); Does v. State, 993 P.2d 822 (Or. App. 1999), rev. denied 6 P.3d 1098 (Or. 2000).

4. THE BABY MARKET: GRAY AND BLACK

IN THE MATTER OF THE ADOPTION OF A CHILD BY N.P. & F.P.

New Jersey Superior Court, Probate Part, 1979.
165 N.J. Super. 591, 398 A.2d 937.

COLEMAN, J.

* * * The child herein was born on March 30, 1978 in Santiago, Chile, South America. On March 30, 1978 the natural mother delivered custody of the child for adoption to the Maternity Clinical Hospital, Social Services, Chile University. The prospective adoptive parents have no children born of their marriage. They read an article in the New York Daily News concerning children who were available for adoption from Chile. The article referred them to Pat Quinlan * * * who recommended a lawyer in Santiago, Chile, by the name of Don Eugenio Donoso. Several days later Quinlan * * * called the prospective adoptive parents to advise that a child, born March 16, 1978, was available for adoption. The prospective adoptive parents forwarded to Donoso the necessary papers to obtain a visa to bring the child to the United States. On June 9, 1978 Donoso received approval from the Fourth Judge of Letters of Courts of Minor, Santiago, Chile, to have the child brought to the United States for the purpose of adoption by the prospective adoptive parents. On June 17, 1978 the child was brought into the United States by Maria Elena Ibarra, who was hired * * * to bring the

child to Kennedy Airport in New York. The prospective adoptive parents met Maria Elena Ibarra at Kennedy Airport and took custody of the child.

The plaintiffs expended the following monies in connection with receiving the child into their home: (a) $3,000 to Don Eugenio Donoso, attorney in Santiago, Chile; (b) $1,169 to Maria Elena Ibarra for plane fare for herself and the child, clothing and passport; (c) $72 to the Consulate of Chile for legalization of documents; (d) $50 for translations; (e) $150 * * * for a home study; (f) $625 to a New Jersey attorney for services in the Union County Court, Probate Division, in connection with the instant adoption.

Donoso further itemized the disbursement of the $3,000 he received as follows: $238.79 for foster home care; $27.41 for medicine; $16.13 for doctor's bill; $9.67 for pictures; $158.85 for clothes * * *; $18 for notary on the power of attorney; $12.58 for legalization of the power of attorney and decision of the judge; $16.13 for tips to employees of the hospital; $16.13 for miscellaneous expenses; $500 for a donation to the Chile University Clinical Hospital; and $2,000 for attorney's fees.

* * *

The essential provisions of N.J.S.A. § 9:3–54 * * * provide that no person shall pay, give, or agree to give any money in connection with a placement for adoption except for fees or services of an approved agency or reimbursement of medical, hospital or other similar expenses incurred in connection with the birth or any illness of the child. It appears unmistakably clear that the payments by plaintiffs of such items as air fare for the child and escort, attorney's fee to the foreign attorney and fees paid for the foreign court proceedings and passport, were all payments of money that should subject the plaintiffs to violations of the said Statute. These payments were mailed from New Jersey and intended to pay the incidental expenses necessary to have the child placed in the plaintiff's home. Where no approved agency is involved the Legislature intended to permit payment only for medical or hospital bills related to the birth or any illness of the child. Surely the payments of air fare and the foreign attorney's fee could not qualify under the Statute. The so-called attorney's fee was more like a broker's fee or finder's fee.

The facts present a prima facie showing that plaintiffs have used international agents and large sums of money to illegally obtain a child. They have used their financial means to jump to the head of the line of those couples waiting for a placement by an approved agency.

Even though the court has concluded that plaintiffs * * * violated N.J.S.A. § 9:3–54, the court has seen no evidence indicating that plaintiffs are unfit parents with the contemplation of N.J.S.A. § 9:3–48(c)(4). The evidence does not warrant the conclusion that the possible criminal conduct of plaintiffs make them unfit parents or that the adoption would not be in the best interest of the child. However, the matter will be referred to the Union County Prosecutor in accordance with N.J.S.A. § 9:3–55(b).

NOTES AND QUESTIONS

1.   If the adoption was illegal, why didn't the court simply void it?

2.   Baby selling is a crime in all states. *See* State v. Brown, 35 P.3d 910 (Kan. 2001). Therefore, some states limit the amount that can be paid for an adoption. KAN. STAT. ANN. § 59–2121 allows:

     a.   reasonable fees for legal and other professional services rendered in connection with the placement or adoption * * *;

     b.   reasonable fees in the state of Kansas of a licensed child-placing agency;

     c.   actual and necessary expenses [in Kansas] * * * incident to placement or to the adoption proceeding;

     d.   actual medical expenses of the mother attributable to pregnancy and childbirth;

     e.   actual medical expenses of the child; and

     f.   reasonable living expenses of the mother which are incurred during or as a result of the pregnancy.

Families who pursue independent adoption in the United States report "spending $8,000 to $30,000 and more," while "[f]ees for intercountry adoption [currently] range from $7,000 to $25,000," excluding travel expenses and the child's medical expenses. Nat. Adoption Information Clearinghouse (NAIC), *Cost of Adopting*, www.calib.com/naic/ pubs/s_inter.htm. Fees for attorney or other intermediaries like those disapproved by the *N.P. & F.P.* court are almost invariable in both U.S. independent adoptions and intercountry adoptions.

3.   Although most states allow independent adoptions, they remain controversial. Some experts argue that the practice of payment for prenatal expenses may "create a sense of obligation on the part of the birth parents to the adoptive parents which may unfairly influence the birth parents' decision * * * to surrender their infant * * *." They also note that the child is often placed in the adoptive home before a home study has been completed and the birth parents have signed consents, perhaps raising the risk of later disruption. L. Jean Emery, *Agency versus Independent Adoption: The Case for Agency Adoption*, 3 FUTURE OF CHILDREN: ADOPTION 139, 144 (Spring 1993). But other experts point to evidence suggesting that birth parents often prefer independent adoption, in part because it offers them the opportunity to choose the home in which their child will reside. *See* Mark T. McDermott, *Agency versus Independent Adoption: The Case for Independent Adoption*, 3 FUTURE OF CHILDREN: ADOPTION 146 (Spring 1993).

4.   For many prospective adoptive parents, independent and intercountry adoption are attractive because of the lengthy waiting periods and

application restrictions that characterize domestic agency adoption. But these prospective parents may find themselves competing for a baby in a nebulous "gray" market where outright baby sales are clearly outlawed, but the rules governing permissible inducements—and even the origins of the baby—are unclear. For example, the U.S. government suspended intercountry adoptions from Cambodia in 2001, after concluding that:

> From 1997 to 2001, the conspirators operated a scheme to defraud U.S. citizens who adopted some 700 children from Cambodia. The conspirators received approximately $8 million dollars from adoptive parents in the United States. The conspiracy involved assorted crimes, including alien smuggling, visa fraud, and money laundering, and included schemes such as the use of baby buyers obtaining children from birth parents by informing the birth parents that they may have their child back at any time, then obtaining false Cambodian passports to enable the children to leave the country. In 2004, after a DHS investigation, a U.S. adoption facilitator pled guilty to conspiracy to commit visa fraud and conspiracy to launder money.

U.S. GOVT. ACCOUNTABILITY OFFICE, FOREIGN AFFAIRS: AGENCIES HAVE IMPROVED THE INTERCOUNTRY ADOPTION PROCESS, BUT FURTHER ENHANCEMENTS ARE NEEDED 25–26 (Gao 06–03–133, 2005), http://www.gao.gov/new.items/d06133.pdf. As of 2005, The U.S. State Department had noted "ongoing concerns" about adoptions from Nepal, Nigeria, Sierra Leone, and Guatemala, a major source of intercountry adoptees. Concerns about Guatemalan adoptions included the use of a false birth mother to create a "paper trail" for an illegally obtained child, payments to mothers to induce relinquishment, and a high incidence of document fraud. *Id.* at 26.

5.   *Should there be a legal baby market?* The existence of a gray and black market in babies led noted economists Elizabeth M. Landes and Richard A. Posner to advocate a legal baby market:

> * * * [G]overnment restrictions on the fees that may be paid in an independent adoption artificially depress the net price of providing babies through this process. The result is to reduce the number of babies supplied below the free market level while simultaneously restricting the use of price to ration the existing, and inadequate, supply. * * * In these circumstances, the economist expects a black market to emerge.

* * *

> * * * [T]here will be more fraud in a black market for babies than in a lawful market, so fear of being defrauded will further deter potential demanders. In lawful markets the incidence of fraud is limited not only by the existence of legal remedies against sellers but also by his desire to build a reputation for fair dealing. Both the clandestine mode of operation of current baby sellers and the lack of

a continuing business relationship between seller and buyer reduce the seller's market incentives to behave reputably.

* * *

[Landes and Posner note that the cost of adoption would probably go down if a free market were established and that there is no evidence that such a market would harm children's interests, as children adopted through an independent adoption appear to do just as well as others and adoption agencies] * * * after determining the pool of fit, or eligible-to-adopt, couples * * * allocate available children among them on a first-come, first-served basis. The "fittest" parents are not placed at the head of the line.

* * *

[Given these facts, t]he antipathy to an explicit market in babies may be part of a broader wish to disguise facts that might be acutely uncomfortable if widely known. Were baby prices quoted as prices of soybean futures are quoted, a racial ranking of these prices would be evident, with white baby prices higher than nonwhite baby prices. * * *

The emphasis placed by critics on the social costs of a free market in babies blurs what would probably be the greatest long-run effect of legalizing the baby market: inducing women who have unintentionally become pregnant to put up the child for adoption rather than raise it themselves or have an abortion.

Elizabeth M. Landes & Richard A. Posner, *The Economics of the Baby Shortage*, 7 J. LEGAL STUD. 323 (1978). Most of Landes and Posner's critics have concurred in their assessment of the ills associated with a black market but found their solution unpersuasive. *See, e.g., Forum: Adoption and Market Theory*, 67 B.U. L. REV. 59–175 (1987); Patricia Williams, *Spare Parts, Family Values, Old Children, Cheap*, 28 NEW ENG. L. REV. 913 (1994).

Ironically, in the years since Landes and Posner urged legalization of baby sale, the gray baby market has come to look more and more like the legal market that they envisioned. Increased demand, intercountry adoption, and the internet—which enables buyers, sellers, and middlemen to advertise and connect across wide distances—have all promoted this convergence. For example, a quick internet search now reveals any number of agencies that offer children of specified types for flat fees; one U.S. on-line agency offers a "Domestic Infant Program," involving children age "newborn to five years," which permits adoptive parents to "specify the ethnic backgrounds they are comfortable with in a child." The "flat fee" for this program is $30,000, including an initial $2,000 application fee, a "one-time" fee of $10,000 after matching with a birth mother, and final $18,000 payment "due on the date of placement of the child in the form of a Cashier's Check." Fees for the Domestic "Special Needs Program" (older, in a sibling group, African-American, or biracial) are a mere $14,000. *See* www.giftoflifeinc.org.

Are Landes and Posner right about the "greatest long-run effect" of legalizing baby sale? Are they right about the reasons most people object to such sales? Are they right that baby sale should be legalized? If baby sale should remain illegal, what steps should legislatures take to eliminate black and gray market adoption transactions?

Problem 8-4:

Twin infants were born in Missouri and placed by their mother (Mom), through an "adoption facilitator" (Tina Johnson), with a California couple, the Allens. The Allens apparently paid Johnson $6000. Two months after placement, Mom asked to see the infants and then refused to return them. She thereafter revoked her adoption consent, a revocation valid under California law. Mom's revocation of her adoption consent may have been motivated by her discovery that Mr. Allen had been accused of molesting two babysitters, a charge that ultimately led to the removal from their home of a two-year-old boy they were also seeking to adopt.

Mom then transferred the twins to a Welsh couple, the Kilgrows, who had paid Johnson $12,500. This payment was made the prior year in the hope of adopting an infant whom the Kilgrows later found out didn't exist. Unable to get their money back, the Kilgrows continued to work with Johnson.

The Allens somehow learned about the Kilgrows and a confrontation took place in the hotel lobby where the second transfer occurred. The Kilgrows thereafter filed an adoption proceeding in Arkansas, using the address of the adoption facilitator's Arkansas aunt; Arkansas law did not at that time require the adoptive parents to live in the state. The decree of adoption was granted, and the infants—with their new adoptive parents—returned to Wales.

The story of the adoption leaked out, and the Arkansas court voided the adoption because neither the adoptive parents nor the birth mother were Arkansas residents. The children were returned by the British government to Missouri, where they were then placed in foster care.

At the time of the twins' adoption, neither the U.K. nor the U.S. had ratified the Intercountry Adoption Convention. What provisions of the Convention are relevant in this case? Would ratification by both countries have altered adoption procedures and outcome? If yes, what provisions of the Convention are relevant and what changes in adoption procedure would they have required? *See In re* K.A.W., 133 S.W.3d 1 (Mo. 2004); *U.K. Couple Ends Internet Twins Fight,* http://archives.cnn.com/2001/WORLD/europe/04/12/britain.twins/index.html.

CHAPTER 9

ASSISTED REPRODUCTION

■ ■ ■

And God said unto Abraham, . . . lo, Sarah thy
wife shall have a son. And Sarah heard it in the
tent door, which was behind him. Now Abraham
and Sarah were old and well stricken in age;
and it ceased to be with Sarah after the manner
of women. Therefore Sarah laughed within
herself, saying, After I am waxed old shall I have
pleasure, my lord being old also?

Genesis 17:15; 18:10–12

The modern Sarah would not laugh at the possibility of childbirth in old age. By using artificial insemination (AI), in vitro fertilization (IVF), and employing a surrogate gestator, would-be parents can now achieve conception without sexual intercourse; they can select sperm, egg, and a human incubator for "their" baby just as they might choose a decorator and furniture for the baby's room. They can become parents post-menopause, or even post-mortem.

Use of reproductive technology has grown rapidly. AI became a recognized treatment for infertility during the 1950s. The first IVF birth did not take place until 1978. In 2008, 61,426 infants were born as a result of egg and sperm procedures, double that of 1999. *See* U.S. Centers for Disease Control & Prevention, Dep't Health & Hum. Servs. *2008 Assisted Reproductive Technology Success Rates 65* (2008), available at http://www. cdc.gov/art/ART2008/PDF/ART_2008_Full.pdf.

Current law offers little guidance on many, if not most, of the issues arising from use of reproductive technology. Laws governing the use of AI and IVF are largely nonexistent, and even the legal parentage of children born through AI and IVF is often unclear. Parentage determination is complicated by the number of actors who may be involved in the birth of a child conceived through AI or IVF. Depending on the facts of the case and the technique used, these actors may include (1) a sperm provider; (2) an ovum provider; (3) a gestator; (4) a man who has contracted with one or more of these parties with the intention of becoming a father; (5) a woman who has contracted with one or more of these parties with the intention of becoming a mother; and (6) the spouses of these various actors who may also claim, or seek to avoid, parental responsibilities. The possibilities and combinations are dizzying; the law, at least in the United States, has not yet caught up. The federal government provides information about success rates for fertility clinics, authorizes use of fertility drugs, oversees advertising, and mandates screening of donors for some communicable diseases. State law regulates the medical profession. Otherwise, there is little regulation. When an out-of-work single mother of six had IVF-conceived octuplets, calls for regulation increased, though little has happened. *See* Naomi R. Cahn and Jennifer M. Collins, *Eight is Enough*, 103 NORTHWESTERN U. L. REV. COLLOQUY 501 (2009) (concluding some form of regulation of ART is justifiable in the wake of Octomom); Deborah Spar, *As You Like It: Exploring the Limits of Parental Choice in Assisted Reproduction*, 27 LAW & INEQUALITY 481 (2009) (suggesting ART be regulated in a manner similar to adoption).

The terminology is also changing. The 2017 proposed Revised Uniform Parentage Act Section 101(4) defines assisted reproduction as a method of causing pregnancy other than sexual intercourse and includes: intrauterine or intracervical insemination; donation of gametes; donation of embryos; in vitro fertilization and transfer of embryos; and intracytoplasmic sperm injection.

1. THE STATUS OF THE PREEMBRYO

IN RE MARRIAGE OF WITTEN
Iowa Supreme Court, 2003.
672 N.W.2d 768.

TERNUS, J.

I.   BACKGROUND FACTS AND PROCEEDINGS.

The appellee, Arthur (Trip) Witten, and the appellant, Tamera Witten, had been married for approximately seven and one-half years when Trip sought to have their marriage dissolved in April 2002. One of the contested issues at trial was control of the parties' frozen embryos. During the parties' marriage they had tried to become parents through the process of in vitro fertilization. Because Tamera was unable to conceive children naturally, they had eggs taken from Tamera artificially fertilized with Trip's sperm. Tamera then underwent several unsuccessful embryo transfers in an attempt to become pregnant. At the time of trial seventeen fertilized eggs remained in storage at the University of Nebraska Medical Center (UNMC).

Prior to commencing the process for in vitro fertilization, the parties signed informed consent documents prepared by the medical center. These documents [required joint approval for] * * * transfer, release or disposition * * * except * * * "upon the death of one or both of the client depositors."

Another provision of the contract provided for termination of UNMC's responsibility to store the embryos upon several contingencies: (1) the client depositors' written authorization to release the embryos or to destroy them; (2) the death of the client depositors; (3) the failure of the client depositors to pay the annual storage fee; or (4) the expiration of ten years from the date of the agreement.

At trial, Tamera asked that she be awarded "custody" of the embryos. She wanted to have the embryos implanted in her or a surrogate mother in an effort to bear a genetically linked child. She testified that upon a successful pregnancy she would afford Trip the opportunity to exercise parental rights or to have his rights terminated. She adamantly opposed any destruction of the embryos, and was also unwilling to donate the eggs to another couple.

Trip testified at the trial that while he did not want the embryos destroyed, he did not want Tamera to use them. He would not oppose donating the embryos for use by another couple. Trip asked the court to enter a permanent injunction prohibiting either party from transferring, releasing, or utilizing the embryos without the written consent of both parties.

The district court decided the dispute should be governed by the "embryo storage agreement" between the parties and UNMC, which required both parties' consent to any use or disposition of the embryos. Enforcing this agreement, the trial court enjoined both parties "from transferring, releasing or in any other way using or disposing of the embryos * * * without the written and signed approval and authorization" of the other party. [Tamera appealed the court's order.] * * *

III. DISPOSITION OF EMBRYOS

Scope of Storage Agreement. * * * [T]he agreement * * * did not explicitly deal with

the possibility of divorce. Nonetheless, we think the present predicament falls within the general provision governing "release of embryos," in which the parties agreed that the embryos would not be transferred, released, or discarded without "the signed approval" of both Tamera and Trip. * * *

The only question, then, is whether such agreements are enforceable when one of the parties later changes his or her mind with respect to the proper disposition of the embryos. In reviewing the scarce case law from other jurisdictions on this point, we have found differing views of how the parties' rights should be determined. There is, however, abundant literature that has scrutinized the approaches taken to date. Some writers have suggested refinements of the analytical framework employed by the courts thus far; some have proposed an entirely new model of analysis.

From these various sources, we have identified three primary approaches to resolving disputes over the disposition of frozen embryos, which we have identified as (1) the contractual approach, (2) the contemporaneous mutual consent model, and (3) the balancing test.

Tamera's argument that her right to bear children should override the parties' prior agreement as well as Trip's current opposition to her use of the embryos resembles the balancing test. As for Tamera's alternative argument, we have found no authority supporting a "best interests" analysis in determining the disposition of frozen embryos. * * * We [also find] that * * * the [best interests] principles developed under th[e child-custody] statute are simply not suited to the resolution of disputes over the control of frozen embryos. * * * Moreover, it would be premature to consider which parent can most effectively raise the child when the "child" is still frozen in a storage facility. * * * For these reasons, we conclude the legislature did not intend to include fertilized eggs or frozen embryos within the scope of * * * [the child-custody law].

C. *Enforcement of Storage Agreement.* We now consider the appropriateness of the trial court's decision to allow Tamera and Trip's agreement with the medical center to control the current dispute between them. * * *

1. *Contractual approach.* The currently prevailing view—expressed in three states—is that contracts entered into at the time of in vitro fertilization are enforceable so long as they do not violate public policy. *See Kass*, 696 N.E.2d at 180; *Davis*, 842 S.W.2d at 597; *In re Litowitz*, 146 Wn. 2d 514, 48 P.3d 261, 271 (Wash. 2002). The New York Court of Appeals expressed the following rationale for this contractual approach[2]:

> [It is] particularly important that courts seek to honor the parties' expressions of choice, made before disputes erupt, with the parties' over-all direction always uppermost in the analysis. Knowing that advance agreements will be enforced underscores the seriousness and integrity of the consent process. Advance agreements as to disposition would have little purpose if they

---

[2] Application of the contractual approach in *Kass* resulted in enforcement of the parties' agreement that the fertilized eggs would be donated for research should the parties be "unable to make a decision regarding the disposition of [the] stored, frozen pre-zygotes." In *Litowitz*, the court permitted execution of the parties' previous agreement that the preembryos would be "disposed of" after five years. The resolution of the divorcing couple's dispute was more complex in *Davis* because the parties did not have a contract addressing the disposition of any unused preembryos. Noting that a "prior agreement concerning disposition should be carried out," the court concluded in the absence of such an agreement, "the relative interests of the parties in using or not using the preembryos must be weighed." The court awarded the preembryos to the husband, concluding his interest in not becoming a parent outweighed his former wife's interest in donating the preembryos to another couple for implantation. The court noted the issue might be closer if the wife had wanted to use the preembryos herself; but in view of the fact she had "a reasonable possibility of achieving parenthood by means other than use of the preembryos in question," she would not have prevailed even under those circumstances.

were enforceable only in the event the parties continued to agree. To the extent possible, it should be the progenitors—not the State and not the courts—who by their prior directive make this deeply personal life choice.

Kass, 696 N.E.2d at 180.

This approach has been criticized, however, because it "insufficiently protects the individual and societal interests at stake":

> First, decisions about the disposition of frozen embryos implicate rights central to individual identity. On matters of such fundamental personal importance, individuals are entitled to make decisions consistent with their contemporaneous wishes, values, and beliefs. Second, requiring couples to make binding decisions about the future use of their frozen embryos ignores the difficulty of predicting one's future response to life-altering events such as parenthood. Third, conditioning the provision of infertility treatment on the execution of binding disposition agreements is coercive and calls into question the authenticity of the couple's original choice. Finally, treating couples' decisions about the future use of their frozen embryos as binding contracts undermines important values about families, reproduction, and the strength of genetic ties.

Coleman, 84 MINN. L. REV. at 88–89. * * * In response to such concerns, one commentator [i.e., Coleman] has suggested an alternative model requiring contemporaneous mutual consent. We now examine that approach.

2. *Contemporaneous mutual consent.* The contractual approach and the contemporaneous mutual consent model share an underlying premise: "decisions about the disposition of frozen embryos belong to the couple that created the embryo, with each partner entitled to an equal say in how the embryos should be disposed." Departing from this common starting point, the alternative framework asserts the important question is "at what time does the partners' consent matter?" Proponents of the mutual-consent approach suggest that, with respect to "decisions about intensely emotional matters, where people act more on the basis of feeling and instinct than rational deliberation," it may "be impossible to make a knowing and intelligent decision to relinquish a right in advance of the time the right is to be exercised." Coleman, *supra. See also* Sara D. Petersen, Comment, *Dealing With Cryopreserved Embryos Upon Divorce: A Contractual Approach Aimed at Preserving Party Expectations*, 50 UCLA L. REV. 1065, 1090 & n.156 (2003) (stating "surveys of couples that have stored frozen embryos suggest that they may be prone to changing their minds while their embryos remain frozen" and citing a study that found "of the 41 couples that had recorded both a pre-treatment and post-treatment

decision about embryo disposition, only 12 (29%) kept the same disposition choice' "). One's erroneous prediction of how she or he will feel about the matter at some point in the future can have grave repercussions. "Like decisions about marriage or relinquishing a child for adoption, decisions about the use of one's reproductive capacity have lifelong consequences for a person's identity and sense of self". * * * To accommodate these concerns, advocates of the mutual-consent model propose "no embryo should be used by either partner, donated to another patient, used in research, or destroyed without the [contemporaneous] mutual consent of the couple that created the embryo." Under this alternate framework,

> * * * If either partner has a change of mind about disposition decisions made in advance, that person's current objection would take precedence over the prior consent. . .

> When the couple is unable to agree to any disposition decision, the most appropriate solution is to keep the embryos where they are—in frozen storage. Unlike the other possible disposition decisions—use by one partner, donation to another patient, donation to research, or destruction—keeping the embryos frozen is not final and irrevocable. By preserving the status quo, it makes it possible for the partners to reach an agreement at a later time.

Id. at 110–12. Although this model precludes one party's use of the embryos to have children over the objection of the other party, the outcome under the contractual approach and the balancing test would generally be the same. *See A.Z. v. B.Z.*, 725 N.E.2d 1051, 1057–58 (Mass. 2000) ("As a matter of public policy, . . . forced procreation is not an area amenable to judicial enforcement."); *J.B.*, 783 A.2d at 717 (evaluating relative interests of parties in disposition of embryos, concluding husband should not be able to use embryos over wife's objection); *Davis*, 842 S.W.2d at 604 ("Ordinarily, the party wishing to avoid procreation should prevail.")

3.   *Balancing test.* The New Jersey Supreme Court appears to have adopted an analysis regarding the disposition of frozen human embryos that incorporates the idea of contemporaneous decision-making, but not that of mutual consent. In *J.B.*, the New Jersey court rejected the *Kass* and *Davis* contractual approach, noting public policy concerns in "enforcement of a contract that would allow the implantation of preembryos at some future date in a case where one party has reconsidered his or her earlier acquiescence." The court stated:

> We believe that the better rule, and the one we adopt, is to enforce agreements entered into at the time in vitro fertilization is begun, *subject to the right of either party to change his or her mind about disposition up to the point of use or destruction of any stored preembryos.*

The court based its decision on "the public policy concerns that underlie limitations on contracts involving family relationships." *Id.*; *see also A.Z.* (refusing, in light of the same public policy concerns, to enforce an agreement that allowed the wife, upon the parties' separation, to use the couple's preembryos for implantation).

The New Jersey court did not, however, adopt the requirement for mutual consent as a prerequisite for any use or disposition of the preembryos. Rather, that court stated that "if there is a disagreement between the parties as to disposition . . . , the interests of both parties must be evaluated" by the court. This balancing test was also the default analysis employed by the Tennessee Supreme Court in *Davis* where the parties had not executed a written agreement.

The obvious problem with the balancing test model is its internal inconsistency. Public policy concerns similar to those that prompt courts to refrain from enforcement of contracts addressing reproductive choice demand even more strongly that we not substitute the courts as decision makers in this highly emotional and personal area. Nonetheless, that is exactly what happens under the decisional framework based on the balancing test because the court must weigh the relative interests of the parties in deciding the disposition of embryos when the parties cannot agree.

D.　Discussion

* * *

Tamera contends the contract at issue here violates public policy because it allows a person who has agreed to participate in an in vitro fertilization program to later change his mind about becoming a parent. While there is some question whether Trip's participation constitutes an implied agreement to become a father, we accept Tamera's assertion for purposes of the present discussion and proceed to consider whether there is any public policy against an agreement allowing a donor to abandon in vitro fertilization attempts when viable embryos remain. Tamera cites to no Iowa statute or prior case that articulates such a policy in the factual context we face here. * * * The public policy evidenced by our law relates to the State's concern for the physical, emotional, and psychological well being of children who have been born, not fertilized eggs that have not even resulted in a pregnancy.

Nor can we say that the "morals of the times" are such that a party participating in an in vitro fertilization process has the duty to use or facilitate the use of each fertilized egg for purposes of pregnancy. To the contrary, courts that have considered one party's desire to use frozen embryos over the objection of the other progenitor have held that the objecting party's fundamental right not to procreate outweighs the other party's procreative rights, even in the face of a prior agreement allowing one party to use the embryos upon the parties' divorce. Thus, we find no public policy that requires the use of the frozen embryos over one party's objection.

That brings us to the more complex issue: are prior agreements regarding the future disposition of embryos enforceable when one of the donors is no longer comfortable with his or her prior decision? We first note our agreement with other courts considering such matters that the partners who created the embryos have the primary, and equal, decision-making authority with respect to the use or disposition of their embryos. We think, however, that it would be against the public policy of this state to enforce a prior agreement between the parties in this highly personal area of reproductive choice when one of the parties has changed his or her mind concerning the disposition or use of the embryos.

Our statutes and case law evidence an understanding that decisions involving marital and family relationships are emotional and subject to change. For example, Iowa law imposes a seventy-two hour waiting period after the birth of a child before the biological parents can release parental rights. In addition, although this court has not abolished claims for breach of promise to marry, only recovery of monetary damages is permitted; the court will not force a party to actually consummate the marriage. It has also long been recognized in this state that agreements for the purpose of bringing about a dissolution of marriage are contrary to public policy and therefore void.

This court has also expressed a general reluctance to become involved in intimate questions inherent in personal relationships. In *Miller*, we refused to enforce a contract between husband and wife that required, in part, each "to behave respectfully, and fairly treat the other." * * * Certainly reproductive decisions are likewise not proper matters of judicial inquiry and enforcement.

We have considered and rejected the arguments of some commentators that embryo disposition agreements are analogous to antenuptial agreements and divorce stipulations, which courts generally enforce. Whether embryos are viewed as having life or simply as having the potential for life, this characteristic or potential renders embryos fundamentally distinct from the chattels, real estate, and money that are the subjects of antenuptial agreements. * * *

We think judicial decisions and statutes in Iowa reflect respect for the right of individuals to make family and reproductive decisions based on their current views and values. They also reveal awareness that such decisions are highly emotional in nature and subject to a later change of heart. For this reason, we think judicial enforcement of an agreement between a couple regarding their future family and reproductive choices would be against the public policy of this state.

Our decision should not be construed, however, to mean that disposition agreements *between donors and fertility clinics* have no validity at all. We recognize a disposition or storage agreement serves an important purpose in defining and governing the relationship between the couple and the medical facility, ensuring that all parties understand their respective rights and obligations. * * * Within this context, the medical facility and the donors should be able to rely on the terms of the parties' contract.

In view of these competing needs, we reject the contractual approach and hold that agreements entered into at the time in vitro fertilization is commenced are enforceable and binding on the parties, "subject to the right of either party to change his or her mind about disposition up to the point of use or destruction of any stored embryo." This decisional model encourages prior agreements that can guide the actions of all parties, unless a later objection to any dispositional provision is asserted. It also recognizes that, *absent a change of heart by one of the partners*, an agreement governing disposition of embryos does not violate public policy. * * * In fairness to the medical facility that is a party to the agreement, however, any change of intention must be communicated in writing to all parties in order to reopen the disposition issues covered by the agreement.

That brings us, then, to the dilemma presented when one or both partners change their minds and the parties cannot reach a mutual decision on disposition. * * * [W]e * * * [adopt the] contemporaneous mutual consent [model]. Under that model, no transfer, release, disposition, or use of the embryos can occur without the signed authorization of both donors. If a stalemate results, the status quo would be maintained. The practical effect will be that the embryos are stored indefinitely unless both parties can agree to destroy the fertilized eggs. Thus, any expense associated with maintaining the status quo should logically be borne by the person opposing destruction.

* * * [U]nder the principles we have set forth today, we hold there can be no use or disposition of the Wittens' embryos unless Trip and Tamera reach an agreement. Until then, the party or parties who oppose destruction shall be responsible for any storage fees. Therefore, we affirm the trial court's ruling enjoining both parties from transferring, releasing, or utilizing the embryos without the other's written consent.

SZAFRANSKI V. DUNSTON

Illinois Court of Appeals, 2015.
393 Ill. Dec. 604, 34 N.E.3d 1132.

LIU, J.

Jacob and Karla first met in 2001. Jacob is a firefighter, paramedic, and registered nurse. Karla is a physician who practices emergency medicine. The two began dating in November 2009, around the time that Jacob and his prior girlfriend, Ashley, ended their two-year relationship. Neither Jacob nor Karla expected their relationship to result in marriage. Karla testified that their relationship had no long-term prospects; Jacob agreed that he doubted their relationship when they were together, noting that they had problems and would fight.

In mid-March of 2010, Karla was diagnosed with non-Hodgkins lymphoma. Her oncologist recommended that she undergo chemotherapy, but told Karla that she would "most likely" lose her fertility as a result of the treatment.

. . . . [Jacob agreed to donate his sperm to inseminate Karla's eggs and to freeze the embryos to be stored at NMFF.]

The Informed Consent provides that "[p]atients/couples who have frozen embryos must remain in contact with NMFF on at least an annual basis in order to inform NMFF of their wishes as well as to pay fees associated with the storage of their embryos."

Pages 11 and 12 of the Informed Consent then explain Northwestern's legal rights and obligations as follows:

"Because of the possibility of you and/or your partner's separation, divorce, death or mental incapacitation, it is important, if you choose to cryopreserve your embryos, for you to decide what should be done with any of your cryopreserved embryos that remain in the laboratory in such an eventuality. Since this is a rapidly evolving field, both medically and legally, the clinic cannot guarantee what the available or acceptable avenues for disposition will be at any future date. At the present time, the options are:

1)   discarding the cryopreserved embryos

2)   donating the cryopreserved embryos for approved research studies.

3)   donating the cryopreserved embryos to another couple in order to attempt pregnancy.

Embryos are understood to be your property, with rights of survivorship. No use can be made of these embryos without the consent of both partners (if applicable).

a)   In the event of divorce or dissolution of the marriage or partnership, NMFF will abide by the terms of the court decree or settlement agreement regarding the ownership and/or other rights to the embryos.

b)   In the event of the death or legal incapacitation of one partner, the other partner will retain decision-making authority regarding the embryos.

c)   In the event both partners die or are legally incapacitated, or if a surviving partner dies or is legally incapacitated while the embryos are still stored at NMFF, the embryos shall become the sole and exclusive property of NMFF. In this event, I/we elect to: (please select and initial your choice). Note: both the patient and the partner must agree on disposition; as with other decisions relating to IVF, you are encouraged to discuss this issue."

Below this paragraph, Karla and Jacob initialed the space next to the option to "[d]onate the embryos to another couple."

Included on page 17 of the Informed Consent is an additional legal disclaimer:

"The law regarding IVF, embryo cryopreservation, subsequent embryo thaw and use, and parent-child status of any resulting child(ren) is, or may be, unsettled in the state in which either the patient, spouse, partner, or any current or future donor lives, or in Illinois, the state in which the NMFF Program is located. NMFF does not provide legal advice, and you should not rely on NMFF to give you any legal advice. You should consider consulting with a lawyer who is experienced in the areas of reproductive law and embryo cryopreservation as well as the disposition of embryos, including any questions or concerns about the present or future status of your embryos, your individual or joint access to them, your individual or joint parental status as to any resulting child, or about any other aspect of this consent and agreement."

The last page of the Informed Consent contains the signatures of Jacob, Karla, and Dr. Kazer and the date of March 25, 2010. Above their signatures is the following provision:

"After your questions have been answered to your satisfaction, please sign your names below to indicate that you have had adequate time to review the information contained in this consent form and that you are ready to begin your upcoming IVF treatment cycle."

Later that day, following their appointment at Northwestern, Jacob and Karla met with Nidhi Desai, an attorney, to discuss the IVF procedure and their options for the pre-embryos. Desai presented the couple with two possible arrangements: a co-parenting agreement or a sperm donor agreement. Desai explained that, under a co-parenting agreement, Jacob would be involved in any resulting child's life as a co-parent, including sharing financial responsibility. She also explained that, under a sperm donor agreement, Jacob would have no obligations and would be waiving his parental rights. Desai informed the parties that if they wanted to use a sperm donor agreement, each party would require independent legal representation and they would have to hire an additional attorney for this purpose. Desai did not present Jacob and Karla with any draft agreements during their initial consult; rather, they were supposed to call her afterwards to tell her which arrangement they had chosen.

On March 29, 2010, Desai received an e-mail from Karla stating that the couple had opted to proceed under a co-parenting agreement. Desai prepared and e-mailed Karla a document entitled "Co-Parent Agreement" later the same day. This proposed agreement was never signed.

On April 6, 2010, the parties went together to Northwestern, where Karla underwent the egg retrieval procedure and Jacob made his second deposit of sperm. Following the procedure, Dr. Kazer informed them that he had retrieved fewer eggs than originally anticipated and advised them that they would have a better chance of having a biological child if they fertilized all eight. Karla asked Jacob, "[W]hat should we do?" Jacob indicated to her that they should fertilize all of the eggs with his sperm. Ultimately, only three eggs were successfully fertilized.

In May, after Karla's second chemotherapy cycle, Jacob ended their relationship in a text message. Karla responded with an inquiry about the pre-embryos, but received no response.

On September 6, 2010, Jacob sent Karla another e-mail, announcing that he could not let her use the pre-embryos and that he wanted them to be donated to science or research. In her email back to Jacob that same day, Karla responded: "Those embryos mean everything to me and I will fight this to the bitter end." On September 10, 2010, Jacob sent Karla an e-mail, telling her that "if [she] could put together all the documents that [he] would need to sign over the embryos [he'll] do it." He also asked her to "mail all correspondence" to a different address and to refrain from replying to his e-mail message because "other people routinely access [his] email and will ultimately make this a harder decision for [him] to make."

Karla contacted Desai about drafting a sperm donor agreement, and Desai told her that Jacob would need to sign a waiver and obtain separate legal representation. Desai recommended an attorney for Jacob. The attorney later informed Desai that she and Jacob did not connect for a time, but when they did, Jacob said he "did not want to move forward with the arrangement."

Jacob subsequently hired an attorney, Kurt Mueller, who sent a document entitled "Sperm Donation and Confidentiality Agreement" to Karla's attorney on April 29, 2011. The proposed agreement granted Karla full custody of the pre-embryos and required, among other things, that Jacob's identity as the sperm donor remain confidential. Jacob, however, later discharged Mueller and sent his own "proposed anonymous embryo donation and confidentiality agreement" which also included a provision granting Karla full custody of the pre-embryos. Karla testified that she would have signed Jacob's proposed agreement, but Northwestern indicated that it would not abide by its terms.

Jacob testified that he responded "yes" when Karla asked him on March 24 if he would "would be willing to provide sperm to make pre[-embryos] with her." He admitted telling Karla that he wanted to help her have a child, and acknowledged that the purpose of providing his sperm was to help her have a biological child. He agreed that they never discussed any limitations on her future use of the pre-embryos. In fact, the thought of placing limitations on Karla's use of the pre-embryos "never crossed [his] mind."

Jacob acknowledged that despite the couple's initial plan to fertilize some of Karla's eggs and to cryopreserve the rest of them, he agreed that Karla should fertilize all eight eggs after Dr. Kazer indicated that there would be a better chance of creating viable pre-embryos if all the eggs were fertilized. Jacob knew that these were likely the last viable eggs Karla would ever have because of the anticipated effects of her chemotherapy treatment.

Karla testified that she believed, on March 24, that she and Jacob had reached an agreement that "Jacob was providing sperm to create embryos so [she could] have a biological child after [her] cancer treatment." She noted that Jacob agreed to donate his sperm "[w]ithout hesitation" and had expressed no doubt whatsoever about creating the pre-embryos. Karla testified that she was "relieved and so happy and so thankful" that Jacob had agreed to help her have biologically-related children.

Ashley Harris testified that she and Jacob were in a dating relationship from September 2007 to December 2012, with "a separation period for maybe five months or so" from late 2009 until April or May of 2010. She had not been aware, during their separation, that Jacob "was with someone else," i.e., Karla. A few weeks after re-kindling their relationship, Jacob told Ashley "[t]hat he donated his sperm" to help Karla create pre-embryos with her eggs. Ashley recalled that when she learned about the pre-embryos, she "wasn't happy about it." Although she "never specially asked," she "just assumed" that Karla would want to use the pre-embryos at some point. She gave Jacob an ultimatum:

"Immediately when I found out, I told him I didn't want to be with him if they had gone through with it. So I said that he would have to tell her if he wanted a relationship with me that she could not use [the pre-embryos]."

According to Ashley, that was when Jacob "realized that [neither Ashley] nor any woman would want to be with somebody who had embryos with someone else."

Following a two-day trial, on May 16, 2014, the circuit court entered a written order awarding Karla sole custody and control of the pre-embryos. First, the court found that the parties entered into an enforceable oral agreement on March 24, 2010 which "contains the offer and acceptance and meeting of the minds regarding the disposition of the embryos * * * [and] represents the intent of the parties, at that time, that Karla need not obtain Jacob's consent to use the embryos to attempt to have a child."Second, it found that the March 25, 2010 Informed Consent "specifically contemplates that another agreement between the parties may govern the future disposition of the embryos" because "[t]he form states Northwestern will abide by any agreement reached between the parties."The court ruled that the parties' "previous oral agreement * * * is not contradicted or modified by any language in the Informed Consent, or by anything else that happened between the parties."

Despite finding that the parties' interests and rights in the pre-embryos were controlled by their March 24 oral agreement, which allowed Karla to use the pre-embryos without Jacob's consent, the circuit court also considered the evidence under the balancing-of-interests analysis, presumably to provide a complete factual and legal framework for this court's benefit on review. The court held that Karla's interests in using the pre-embryos outweighed Jacob's interests in preventing their use.

An oral agreement is binding where there is an offer, an acceptance, and a meeting of the minds as to the terms of the agreement. Bruzas v. Richardson, 945 N.E.2d 1208, 1215 (Ill. App. 2011). To be enforceable, the material terms of a contract must also be definite and certain. Id. "The terms of a contract will be found to be definite and certain * * * if a court is able to ascertain what the parties agreed to, using proper rules of construction and applicable principles of equity." Id. The parties' intent in forming an oral contract and the terms of the contract are questions of fact to be determined by the trier of fact. Prignano v. Prignano, 934 N.E.2d 89, 100 (Ill. App. 2010);

The standard of review for resolving the parties' competing interpretations of their agreement of March 24 is highly deferential.

Jacob concedes that a contract was formed on March 24; as such, no dispute exists as to the existence of the parties' oral contract. The sole dispute stems from a disagreement over the scope of their agreement.

As we turn to the scope of the parties' oral contract, we note that several facts are not in dispute. Significantly, Jacob does not challenge the finding that an oral contract was created on March 24 when Karla asked him if he would be willing to donate his sperm to create pre-embryos with her, and he manifested his acceptance of Karla's offer by responding "yes." The parties both acknowledge that Jacob agreed to donate his sperm after Karla told him that she would likely become infertile after her chemotherapy treatment. Both parties further acknowledged, through trial testimony, that the purpose of the oral contract was for Jacob to provide his sperm to fertilize Karla's eggs so that she could preserve her ability to have a biologically related child of her own in the future, after her chemotherapy treatment ended. Finally, it is undisputed that the parties knew that the pre-embryos would have to be cryopreserved for later use and that they would not be transferred to Karla for implantation, at the earliest, until after she finished her chemotherapy treatment.

According to Jacob, he never agreed, on March 24, that Karla could use the pre-embryos without his consent. Conversely, Karla contends that their agreement did not include any limitation on her use of the pre-embryos and that the parties intended for Karla to use them, without condition, to have a biological child.

According to Jacob's own testimony, he never communicated a desire to have any say in Karla's future disposition of the pre-embryos; his only concern was to help her take the necessary steps to preserve her ability to create pre-embryos for that purpose.

Karla points out that he has ignored the "overwhelming" evidence that they "agreed, understood and intended that the very purpose of their agreement was to provide Karla with the ability to have her own biological child in the future with the return of her health."(Emphases in original.) Karla argues that Jacob now seeks to add a term to their oral contract that was not previously included or bargained for: namely, a right to withhold consent for transfer of the pre-embryos that would prevent Karla from using them to have a child.

[W]e see no error in the circuit court's finding that the parties intended to allow Karla to use the pre-embryos without limitation when they formed the March 24 contract.

We further find that the relief Jacob seeks—essentially, incorporating a limitation into the oral contract—would change the fundamental essence of the parties' oral contract.

Because the circuit court's judgment was not against the manifest weight of the evidence, we conclude that the court properly ruled that Karla is entitled to use the pre-embryos to have a child, without limitation.

Northwestern specifically addressed how the couple's pre-embryos will be disposed of in three different situations—divorce, death of one partner, and death of both partners—but, significantly, it did not address how their pre-embryos would be treated in the event that they separated. This can mean only one thing: that neither the couple nor Northwestern, in executing the Informed Consent, considered what would happen to the pre-embryos in that event.

In reviewing the interests of the parties, we observe that many of Jacob's cited concerns were risks that both parties faced and knowingly accepted in agreeing to undergo IVF. Jacob testified that he does not want Karla to use the pre-embryos primarily because of the impact it would have on his other relationships. He testified that he has lost a love interest—undoubtedly referring to Ashley—because of the situation with Karla; that "a lot of people" think of him differently now; and that he is worried that no one will want to have a relationship with him knowing that he has fathered a child with Karla through IVF. Jacob feels as if he is being forced to have a child; he testified that he does not "want to be a father like this" and contends that he should not be forced to procreate with a woman whom he does not love.

Karla, on the other hand, cannot have a biological child without using the pre-embryos. She suffered ovarian failure as a result of her chemotherapy treatment and cannot have a biological child without using the pre-embryos. Karla testified that she was "devastated" upon learning that she would lose her fertility and thought about how she wants to have a child "with part of" her father, who passed away when she was five years old. She maintains that she does not expect Jacob to support any child born from the pre-embryos. Before and throughout the IVF process, Karla relied on Jacob's willingness to help her have a child. Following the retrieval, she relied on Jacob's assent to fertilize all of her remaining eggs with his sperm, thereby foregoing the possibility of using an anonymous sperm donor.

We concur in the circuit court's ruling that Karla's interest in using the pre-embryos is paramount given her inability to have a biological child by any other means.

We also find no reason to disturb the circuit court's determination that Jacob's concern about not finding love in the future is "speculative." Moreover, his privacy concern is largely moot now as a result of the very public nature of this case. The record lacks evidence from which a trier of fact may reasonably infer that Jacob's act—agreeing to help a friend threatened with infertility save her last chance to have a biological child—would be considered irreconcilable or repugnant by all future romantic prospects. It seems that Jacob's regrets about his role in creating the pre-embryos developed roots at the same time that some of his friends and family members voiced their disapproval. This was evident from Jacob's and Ashley's testimony, which revealed the strain on their relationship that resulted from Karla's desire to use the pre-embryos. In his effort to save this relationship, he had to conceal his subsequent attempts to resolve the dispute. We do not discount this evidence in any way. However, without diminishing Jacob's valid concern that some may hold him in a negative light for agreeing to donate his sperm to a woman he never intended to marry and with whom he had no future, we will not give weight to the judgments of those who have no direct interest in this controversy.

Finally, we must acknowledge the remaining elephant in the room—Jacob's concern that he could be financially responsible for any child resulting from the pre-embryos. This issue has not been squarely presented for our disposition, and because we cannot render an advisory opinion, we make no findings on the matter. We note only that this decision should not be construed as a ruling on Jacob's legal status under any applicable parentage or child support statutes. We see no basis in the record why Jacob would be precluded from seeking a legal declaration of his parental status.

For the reasons stated, we affirm the order of the circuit court of Cook County granting defendant, Karla Dunston, sole custody and control of the disputed pre-embryos.

NOTES AND QUESTIONS

1.   How would the *Davis, Kass,* and *J.B.* courts have ruled in *Witten?* Is the *Witten* court's analysis persuasive? See McQueen v. Gadberry, 507 S.W.3d 127 (Mo. App. 2016) (finding the frozen preembryos to be marital property of a special character and awarding them to husband and wife jointly).

2.   What factors make the *Szafranski* case different? In Reber v. Reiss, 42 A.3d 1131 (Pa. Super. 2012), the court used a balancing test to award preembryos to a divorcing woman who had chemotherapy for breast cancer and could not achieve genetic parentage unless the court allowed her to use stored preembryos. Is there a reason to treat married couples and "friends" differently? Are there different public policy considerations?

3.   *Laws Mandating Contract Enforcement:* The *Witten* court rejected the contractual approach on public policy grounds. But some states now statutorily *require* couples undergoing IVF treatment to execute written agreements providing for the disposition of their preembryos in the event of death, divorce, or other unforeseen circumstances. *See* FLA. STAT. ANN. § 742.17. Assuming that enforcement of these required contracts is intended, is such a statute constitutional? There is an argument that parties should have a lawyer review cryopreservation contracts. *See* Cynthia E. Fruchtman, *Withdrawal of Cryopreserved Sperm, Eggs, and Embryos,* 48 FAM. L. Q. 197 (2014).

In an article quoted by the *Witten* court, Professor Coleman forcefully argues that contract enforcement violates "the right to make contemporaneous choices about how one's reproductive capacity will be used * * * and undermines important societal values about reproduction, family relationships, and the strength of genetic ties," that the liberties of both parties are entitled to equal weight, and that "the law should [thus] require the couple's mutual consent before any affirmative disposition of a frozen embryo is enforced." Carl H. Coleman, *Procreative Liberty and Contemporaneous Choice: An Inalienable Rights Approach to Frozen Embryo Disputes*, 84 Minn. L. Rev. 55, 126 (1999). Professor Robertson, on the other hand, has argued that "freedom to contract or to make directives binding in future situations enhances liberty even though it involves constraints on what may occur once the future situation comes about." John A. Robertson, *Prior Agreements for Disposition of Frozen Embryos*, 51 Ohio St. L.J. 407, 415 (1990). Which commentator has the better of this argument? Reconsider *Griswold*, *Roe*, and *Casey* and then resolve these questions:

    a.   Is the IVF implantation decision analogous to a contraception or an abortion decision? On what cases would a constitutional challenge to the new statute, based on this analogy, rely? What arguments are available to each party? On balance, how should such a claim be decided? Consider the trial court's opinion in *Kass*:

> [T]here is no legal, ethical or logical reason why an in vitro fertilization should give rise to additional rights on the part of the husband. From a propositional standpoint it matters little whether the ovum/sperm union takes place in the private darkness of a fallopian tube or the public glare of a petri dish. Fertilization is fertilization and fertilization of the ovum is the inception of the reproductive process. Biological life exists from that moment forward. The fact that an in vitro zygote does not seek to fulfill its biological destiny immediately upon such fertilization does not alter that fact. The rights of the parties are dependent upon the nature of the zygote not the stage of its development or its location. To deny a husband rights while an embryo develops in the womb and grant a right to destroy while it is in a hospital freezer is to favor situs over substance.

Kass v. Kass, 1995 WL 110368 (N.Y. Sup. Ct. 1995). Is the *Kass* trial court right that distinguishing implantation from abortion favors "situs over substance"? On what cases would this type of constitutional challenge rely? What arguments are available to each party? On balance, how should such a claim be decided?

    b.   If IVF is genuinely different from contraception and abortion, how should the reproductive liberties of the parties be evaluated?

If you were challenging the constitutionality of the Florida statute, what type of plaintiff(s) would you seek? What precedents are relevant? What arguments would you make and what counterarguments would be available to the state? How would you predict that the case would be decided?

4.   *Laws Favoring the Female Progenitor:* In the United States, would a law which confers decision-making authority on the female progenitor after ova fertilization be constitutional? What precedents are relevant? What arguments would you make in challenging such a law, and what counterarguments would be available to the state? How would you predict that the case would be decided?

5.   *Preembryo Research:* Experts estimate that U.S. IVF centers currently have about 400,000 cryopreserved preembryos in storage. *See* David I. Hoffman et al., *Cryopreserved Embryos in the United States and Their Availability for Research*, 79 FERTILITY & STERILITY 1063 (2003). In recent years, medical researchers have become interested in "left-over" preembryos that are unwanted by their creators. This interest derives from the fact that, at the stage preembryos created for IVF use are stored, their cells have not yet begun to differentiate into the various tissues and organs that may ultimately become a human being. Instead, they retain the capacity to develop into any type of human cell. This capacity, pluripotency, is lost by the end of the second week after fertilization. Cells that are pluripotent are typically called stem cells; despite their undifferentiated state, they are thought to be capable of reproducing themselves indefinitely. Many medical researchers also believe that these cells hold the key both to understanding human embryonic development and treating a wide range of currently incurable medical disorders.

Could a state or the U.S. government deny couples like Mr. and Mrs. Witten the right to donate their unused preembryos for stem cell research? Cf. MINN. STAT. § 145.422 (prohibiting the use of any living human conceptus for either research or experimentation). Could it mandate the donation of preembryos stored for a specified period without contrary instructions from the progenitors? What cases and constitutional doctrines are relevant? Does it matter how state law defines the progenitors' interests in the preembryos?

Problem 9-1:

In Louisiana, an "in vitro fertilized human ovum * * * composed of one or more living human cells and human genetic material so unified and organized that it will develop in utero into an unborn child" is a "juridical person until such time as the in vitro fertilized ovum is implanted in the womb; or at any other time when rights attach to an unborn child in accordance with law." LA. REV. STAT. §§ 9:121, 123. Under the Louisiana statute, such an in vitro fertilized ovum may not be sold or "intentionally destroyed" nor may it "be farmed or cultured solely for research purposes or any other purposes." *Id.* at §§ 9:122, 129. The statute specifies that such an ovum

> is a biological human being which is not the property of the physician which acts as an agent of fertilization * * * or the donors of the sperm and ovum. If the in vitro fertilization patients express their identity, then their rights as parents as provided under the

> Louisiana Civil Code will be preserved. If the in vitro fertilization patients fail to express their identity, then the physician shall be deemed to be temporary guardian of the in vitro fertilized human ovum until adoptive implantation can occur. A court in the parish where the in vitro fertilized ovum is located may appoint a curator, upon motion of the in vitro fertilization patients, their heirs, or physicians who caused in vitro fertilization to be performed, to protect the in vitro fertilized human ovum's rights.

LA. REV. STAT. § 9:126.

A.   Evaluate the constitutionality of the Louisiana statute.

     1.   What plaintiffs would an organization seeking to challenge the statute want to find?

     2.   What arguments would be available to those plaintiffs and to the state? Do they apply with equal force to each provision of the statute?

     3.   What is the likelihood that a constitutional challenge would be successful?

B.   Evaluate the desirability of the Louisiana approach. What problems would it resolve and what problems would it create? On balance, is this sort of legislation desirable?

2. DETERMINING THE PARENT OF AN "ART" CHILD

When a preembryo is implanted and carried to term, who are the child's parents? Where a preembryo was created with genetic material from a married couple and the wife carried the child to term, the answer is straightforward. But artificial insemination (AI), in vitro fertilization (IVF), and surrogacy may involve a much larger number of actors. Just as in the pre-implantation context, some commentators have urged that the rights and obligations of these actors should be governed by contract law. Professor Marjorie Schultz, for example, has urged that "assisted reproduction differs from ordinary reproduction" in that ordinary reproduction poses greater difficulties in "severing intention about procreation * * * from other motivations." She also argues that "the newness of the issues presented by scientific changes virtually demands consideration of new legal approaches and rules" and that coital and technological conception present "differences in moral and factual legitimacy":

> The fairness of imposing a status-based parental regime is far weaker in instances of artificial or assisted reproductive techniques. The justification for such outcomes in ongoing relationships between coital partners derives, at least in part,

from presumed intention. In * * * assisted reproduction the factual base for such presumptions about intention is often lacking.

Marjorie Schultz, *Reproductive Technology*, 1990 WIS. L. REV. 323, 324. Schultz also notes that private ordering plays a more important role in family law today than it did traditionally, and that "[o]ur society generally favors the fulfillment of individual purposes and the amplification of individual choice." *Id.* at 327. Based on these claims, she concludes that "[w]ithin the context of artificial reproductive techniques, intentions that are voluntarily chosen, deliberate, express and bargained-for ought presumptively to determine legal parenthood." *Id.* at 323. Critics of the contractual approach have urged that the extension of contract law to parentage determination poses a number of risks. Some have focused on the harms associated with introducing market norms into an aspect of life heretofore governed by personal relationships and emotions. Professor Margaret Radin, for example, has argued that reproductive capacity constitutes an attribute, like sexuality or a body part, that is so bound up with an individual's personhood that it should not be the subject of market transactions:

> Market-inalienability might be grounded in a judgment that commodification of women's reproductive capacity is harmful for the identity aspect of their personhood and in a judgment that the closeness of paid surrogacy to baby-selling harms our self-conception too deeply. There is certainly the danger that women's attributes, such as height, eye color, race, intelligence, and athletic ability will be monetized. Surrogates with "better" qualities will command higher prices by virtue of those qualities.

Margaret J. Radin, *Market-Inalienability*, 100 HARV. L. REV. 1849, 1932 (1987). Professor Elizabeth Anderson has argued that a "pregnancy contract denies mothers autonomy over their bodies and their feelings":

> Their bodies and their health are subordinated to the independent interests of the contracting parents who, through the threat of lawsuits, exercise potentially unlimited control over the gestating mother's activities. * * *

> Supporters of contract pregnancy complain that the case against it expresses paternalistic attitudes toward women that reinforce sexist stereotypes. * * * This criticism depends upon the flawed individualist, preference-based view of autonomy. * * *. But the case again surrogacy rests * * * on the claim that women are not self-sufficient bearers of autonomy. Like men, women require certain social conditions to exercise their autonomy. Among these conditions are freedom from domination, which is secured by retaining inalienable rights in one's person. Contract pregnancy

is objectionable because it undermines the social conditions for women's autonomy. It uses the norms of commerce in a manipulative way. * * * And it reinforces motivations such as self-effacing "altruism," that women have formed under social conditions inconsistent with autonomy and that reproduce these social conditions.

ELIZABETH ANDERSON, VALUE IN ETHICS AND ECONOMICS 170 (1993).

Other critics have noted that contractual determination of parental status in cases of technological conception would be inconsistent with the law now applied in cases of sexual conception:

> [B]y adopting a new ideal in one restricted case category the policymaker risks what Professor Dworkin has aptly described as "checkerboard" law:

>> Do the people of North Dakota disagree whether justice requires compensation for product defects that manufacturers could not reasonably have prevented? Then why should their legislature not impose this "strict" liability on manufacturers of automobiles but not on manufacturers of washing machines? Do the people of Alabama disagree about the morality of racial discrimination? Why should their legislature not forbid racial discrimination on buses but permit it in restaurants? * * *

> Checkerboard rulemaking violates the ethical norm that like cases receive like treatment; it denies "what is often called 'equality before the law'." * * *

> Proponents of the various approaches to technological conception have typically assumed, of course, that the new methods of baby making are sufficiently different from sexual conception to justify a novel parental status rule. And technological conception does clearly differ from sexual conception in terms of mechanics; sperm and ovum are combined in different ways. But washing machines also differ from automobiles, and restaurants from buses. We want to treat washing machines like automobiles for purposes of a manufacturer liability law because the values and policy goals that determine the choice of a liability rule apply equally to both washing machines and automobiles; we want to treat restaurants like buses for purposes of a racial discrimination law for the same reasons. * * *

> For purposes of a parental status rule, the differences between sexual and technological conception are like the differences between restaurants and buses—they are irrelevant to the values and policy goals that underlie the choice of a decision-making

standard. Parentage law regulates the formation of family relationships, not the mechanics of conception. The law has never cared whether sperm and ovum met in a fallopian tube or in the uterus; there is no obvious reason why it should care if sperm and ovum meet in a petri dish. * * * To fashion novel parental status rules for technological conception risks outcomes reliant on discordant values that have been rejected for the rest of our families.

Marsha Garrison, *Law Making for Baby Making: An Interpretive Approach to the Determination of Legal Parentage*, 113 HARV. L. REV. 835, 878–82 (2000).

Despite the wealth of commentary on the issue, legislatures have been slow to act. On many reproductive techniques—gestational surrogacy, IVF with donated sperm or ova—the majority of states have no statutory law governing a child's legal parentage. For a review of existing state ART laws, see CHARLES P. KINDREGAN, JR. & MAUREEN MCBRIEN, ASSISTED REPRODUCTIVE TECHNOLOGY: A LAWYER'S GUIDE TO EMERGING LAW AND SCIENCE (2d ed. 2011). Courts, on the other hand, have been forced to determine the enforceability of reproductive contracts that purport to govern parentage determination in a wide range of settings.

A. ARTIFICIAL INSEMINATION

Artificial insemination (AI) is the oldest and most widely used assisted reproductive technique. Although used in animal husbandry since the late 1800s, the technique became popular for human reproduction after World War II. At that time it was exclusively employed by married couples who were unable to conceive a child due to the husband's infertility. The early cases dealt with the "legitimacy" of children conceived using AI. *Compare* Gursky v. Gursky, 242 N.Y.S.2d 406 (Misc. 1963) *with* People v. Sorensen, 437 P.2d 495 (Cal. 1968). Today all states have statutes which provide that the husband who consented to the artificial insemination of his wife by a physician is the father of the child. Most states, however, provide little guidance when an unmarried woman uses AI to become a mother or when a physician is not involved.

JHORDAN C. v. MARY K.
California Court of Appeals, 1986.
179 Cal. App. 3d 386, 224 Cal. Rptr. 530.

KING, ASSOCIATE JUSTICE.

By statute in California a "donor of semen *provided to a licensed physician* for use in artificial insemination of a woman other than the donor's wife is treated in law as if he were not the natural father of a child thereby conceived." (Civ. Code, § 7005, subd. (b); emphasis added.) In this case we hold that where impregnation takes place by artificial insemination, and the parties have failed to take advantage of this statutory basis for preclusion of paternity, the donor of semen can be determined to be the father of the child in a paternity action.

Mary K. and Victoria T. appeal from a judgment declaring Jhordan C. to be the legal father of Mary's child, Devin. The child was conceived by artificial insemination with semen donated personally to Mary by Jhordan. We affirm the judgment.

II. FACTS AND PROCEDURAL HISTORY

In late 1978 Mary decided to bear a child by artificial insemination and to raise the child jointly with Victoria, a close friend who lived in a nearby town. Mary sought a semen donor by talking to friends and acquaintances. This led to three or four potential donors with whom Mary spoke directly. She and Victoria ultimately chose Jhordan after he had one personal interview with Mary and one dinner at Mary's home.

The parties' testimony was in conflict as to what agreement they had concerning the role, if any, Jhordan would play in the child's life. According to Mary, she told Jhordan she did not want a donor who desired ongoing involvement with the child, but she did agree to let him see the child to satisfy his curiosity as to how the child would look. Jhordan, in contrast, asserts they agreed he and Mary could have an ongoing friendship, he would have ongoing contact with the child, and he would care for the child as much as two or three times per week.

None of the parties sought legal advice until long after the child's birth. They were completely unaware of the existence of Civil Code § 7005. They did not attempt to draft a written agreement concerning Jhordan's status.

Jhordan provided semen to Mary on a number of occasions during a six month period commencing in late January 1979. On each occasion he came to her home, spoke briefly with her, produced the semen, and then left. The record is unclear, but Mary, who is a nurse, apparently performed the insemination by herself or with Victoria.

Contact between Mary and Jhordan continued after she became pregnant. Mary attended a Christmas party at Jhordan's home. Jhordan visited Mary several times at the health center where she worked. He took photographs of her. When he informed Mary by telephone that he had collected a crib, playpen, and high chair for the child, she told him to keep those items at his home. At one point Jhordan told Mary he had started a trust fund for the child and wanted legal guardianship in case she died; Mary vetoed the guardianship idea but did not disapprove the trust fund.

* * *

Mary gave birth to Devin on March 30, 1980. Victoria assisted in the delivery. Jhordan was listed as the father on Devin's birth certificate. Mary's roommate telephoned Jhordan that day to inform him of the birth. Jhordan visited Mary and Devin the next day and took photographs of the baby.

Five days later Jhordan telephoned Mary and said he wanted to visit Devin again. Mary initially resisted, but then allowed Jhordan to visit, although she told him she was angry. During the visit Jhordan claimed a right to see Devin, and Mary agreed to monthly visits.

Through August 1980 Jhordan visited Devin approximately five times. Mary then terminated the monthly visits. Jhordan said he would consult an attorney if Mary did not let him see Devin. Mary asked Jhordan to sign a contract indicating he would not seek to be Devin's father, but Jhordan refused.

In December 1980 Jhordan filed an action against Mary to establish paternity and visitation rights. In June 1982, by stipulated judgment in a separate action by the County of Sonoma, he was ordered to reimburse the county for public assistance paid for Devin's support. The judgment ordered him to commence payment, through the district attorney's office, of $900 in arrearages as well as future child support of $50 per month.[3]

Victoria had been closely involved with Devin since his birth. Devin spent at least two days each week in her home. On days when they did not see each other they spoke on the telephone. Victoria and Mary discussed Devin daily either in person or by telephone. They made joint decisions regarding his daily care and development. The three took vacations together. Devin and Victoria regarded each other as parent and child. Devin developed a brother-sister relationship with Victoria's 14-year old daughter, and came to regard Victoria's parents as his grandparents. Victoria made the necessary arrangements for Devin's visits with Jhordan.

In August 1983 Victoria moved successfully for an order joining her as a party to this litigation. Supported by Mary, she sought joint legal custody (with Mary) and requested specified visitation rights, asserting she was a de facto parent of Devin. Jhordan subsequently requested an award of joint custody to him and Mary.

After trial the court rendered judgment declaring Jhordan to be Devin's legal father. However, the court awarded sole legal and physical custody to Mary, and denied Jhordan any input into decisions regarding Devin's schooling, medical and dental care, and day-to-day maintenance. Jhordan received substantial visitation rights as recommended by a court-appointed psychologist. The court held Victoria was not a de facto parent,

---

[3] During the pendency of this appeal *Mary sought and obtained an increase* in Jhordan's support obligation.

but awarded her visitation rights (not to impinge upon Jhordan's visitation schedule), which were also recommended by the psychologist.

Mary and Victoria filed a timely notice of appeal, specifying the portions of the judgment declaring Jhordan to be Devin's legal father and denying Victoria the status of de facto parent.

III. DISCUSSION

We begin with a discussion of Civil Code § 7005, which provides in pertinent part: "(a) If, under the supervision of a licensed physician and with the consent of her husband, a wife is inseminated artificially with semen donated by a man not her husband, the husband is treated in law as if he were the natural father of a child thereby conceived . . . (b) The donor of semen provided to a licensed physician for use in artificial insemination of a woman other than the donor's wife is treated in law as if he were not the natural father of a child thereby conceived."

Civil Code § 7005 is part of the Uniform Parentage Act (UPA), which was approved in 1973 by the National Conference of Commissioners on Uniform State Laws. The UPA was adopted in California in 1975. Section 7005 is derived almost verbatim from the UPA as originally drafted, with one crucial exception. The original UPA restricts application of the nonpaternity provision of subdivision (b) to a *"married* woman other than the donor's wife." (emphasis added). The word "married" is excluded from subdivision (b) of § 7005, so that in California, subdivision (b) applies to all women, married or not.

Thus the California Legislature has afforded unmarried as well as married women a statutory vehicle for obtaining semen for artificial insemination without fear that the donor may claim paternity, and has likewise provided men with a statutory vehicle for donating semen to married and unmarried women alike without fear of liability for child support. Subdivision (b) states only one limitation on its application: the semen must be "provided to a licensed physician." Otherwise, whether impregnation occurs through artificial insemination or sexual intercourse, there can be a determination of paternity with the rights, duties and obligations such a determination entails.

A.   *Interpretation of the Statutory Nonpaternity Provision.*

Mary and Victoria first contend that despite the requirement of physician involvement stated in Civil Code § 7005, subd. (b), the Legislature did not intend to withhold application of the donor nonpaternity provision where semen used in artificial insemination was not provided to a licensed physician. They suggest that the element of physician involvement appears in the statute merely because the Legislature assumed (erroneously) that all artificial insemination would occur under the supervision of a physician. Alternatively, they argue the requirement of physician involvement is merely directive rather than mandatory.

We cannot presume, however, that the Legislature simply assumed or wanted to recommend physician involvement, for two reasons.

First, the history of the UPA (the source of § 7005) indicates conscious adoption of the physician requirement. The initial "discussion draft" submitted to the drafters of the UPA in 1971 did not mention the involvement of a physician in artificial insemination; the draft stated no requirement as to how semen was to be obtained or how the insemination procedure was to be performed. (H. KRAUSE, ILLEGITIMACY: LAW AND SOCIAL POLICY (1971) pp. 240, 243.) The eventual inclusion of the physician requirement in the final version of the UPA suggests a conscious decision to require physician involvement.

Second, there are at least two sound justifications upon which the statutory requirement of physician involvement might have been based. One relates to health: a physician can obtain a complete medical history of the donor (which may be of crucial importance to the child during his or her lifetime) and screen the donor for any hereditary or communicable diseases. Indeed, the commissioners' comment to the section of the UPA on artificial insemination cites as a "useful reference" a law review article which argues that health considerations should require the involvement of a physician in statutorily authorized artificial insemination. This suggests that health considerations underlie the decision by the drafters of the UPA to include the physician requirement in the artificial insemination statute.

Another justification for physician involvement is that the presence of a professional third party such as a physician can serve to create a formal, documented structure for the donor-recipient relationship, without which, as this case illustrates, misunderstandings between the parties regarding the nature of their relationship and the donor's relationship to the child would be more likely to occur.

It is true that nothing inherent in artificial insemination requires the involvement of a physician. Artificial insemination is, as demonstrated here, a simple procedure easily performed by a woman in her home. * * *

However, because of the way § 7005 is phrased, a woman (married or unmarried) can perform home artificial insemination or choose her donor and still obtain the benefits of the statute. Subdivision (b) does not require that a physician independently obtain the semen and perform the insemination, but requires only that the semen be "provided" to a physician. Thus, a woman who prefers home artificial insemination or who wishes to choose her donor can still obtain statutory protection from a donor's paternity claim through the relatively simple expedient of obtaining the semen, whether for home insemination or from a chosen donor (or both), through a licensed physician.

Regardless of the various countervailing considerations for and against physician involvement, our Legislature has embraced the apparently conscious decision by the drafters of the UPA to limit application of the donor nonpaternity provision to instances in which semen is provided to a licensed physician. The existence of sound justifications for physician involvement further supports a determination the Legislature intended to require it. Accordingly, § 7005, subdivision (b), by its terms does not apply to the present case. The Legislature's apparent decision to require physician involvement in order to invoke the statute cannot be subject to judicial second-guessing and cannot be disturbed, absent constitutional infirmity.

B. Constitutional Considerations.

* * * 1. Equal protection.

Mary and Victoria argue the failure to apply § 7005, subd. (b) to unmarried women who conceive artificially with semen not provided to a licensed physician denies equal protection because the operation of other paternity statutes precludes a donor assertion of paternity where a *married* woman undergoes artificial insemination with semen not provided to a physician.

This characterization of the effect of the paternity statutes as applied to married women is correct. In the case of the married woman her husband is the presumed father (Civ.Code, § 7004, subd. (a)(1)), and *any* outsider— including a semen donor, regardless of physician involvement—is precluded from maintaining a paternity action unless the mother "relinquishes for, consents to, or proposes to relinquish for or consent to, the adoption of the child." (Civ.Code, § 7006, subd. (d).) An action to establish paternity by blood test can be brought only by the husband or mother. * * *

But the statutory provision at issue here—Civil Code § 7005, subd. (b)—treats married and unmarried women equally. Both are denied application of the statute where semen has not been provided to a licensed physician.

The true question presented is whether a completely different set of paternity statutes—affording protection to husband and wife from any claim of paternity by an outsider—denies equal protection by failing to provide similar protection to an unmarried woman. The simple answer is that, within the context of this question, a married woman and an unmarried woman are not similarly situated for purposes of equal protection analysis. In the case of a married woman, the marital relationship invokes a long-recognized social policy of preserving the integrity of the marriage. No such concerns arise where there is no marriage at all. Equal protection is not violated by providing that certain benefits or legal rights arise only out of the marital relationship. For example, spousal support may be awarded pursuant to Civil Code § 4801 upon the breakup of a marital relationship, but not upon the breakup of a nonmarital relationship.

2. *Family autonomy.*

Mary and Victoria contend that they and Devin compose a family unit and that the trial court's ruling constitutes an infringement upon a right they have to family autonomy, encompassed by the constitutional right to privacy. But this argument begs the question of which persons comprise the family in this case for purposes of judicial intervention. Characterization of the family unit must precede consideration of whether family autonomy has been infringed.

The semen donor here was permitted to develop a social relationship with Mary and Devin as the child's father. During Mary's pregnancy Jhordan maintained contact with her. They visited each other several times, and Mary did not object to Jhordan's collection of baby equipment or the creation of a trust fund for the child. Mary permitted Jhordan to visit Devin on the day after the child's birth and allowed monthly visits thereafter. The record demonstrates no clear understanding that Jhordan's role would be limited to provision of semen and that he would have no parental relationship with Devin; indeed, the parties' conduct indicates otherwise.

We do not purport to hold that an oral or written nonpaternity agreement between the parties would have been legally binding; that difficult question is not before us (and indeed is more appropriately addressed by the Legislature). We simply emphasize that for purposes of the family autonomy argument raised by Mary, Jhordan was not excluded as a member of Devin's family, either by anonymity, by agreement, or by the parties' conduct.

In short, the court's ruling did not infringe upon any right of Mary and Victoria to family autonomy, because under the peculiar facts of this case Jhordan was not excluded as a member of Devin's family for purposes of resolving this custody dispute.

3. *Procreative choice.*

Mary and Victoria argue that the physician requirement in Civil Code § 7005, subd.(b), infringes a fundamental right to procreative choice, also encompassed by the constitutional right of privacy.

But the statute imposes no restriction on the right to bear a child. Unlike statutes in other jurisdictions proscribing artificial insemination other than by a physician, subdivision (b) of § 7005 does not forbid self-insemination; nor does the statute preclude personal selection of a donor or in any other way prevent women from artificially conceiving children under circumstances of their own choice. The statute simply addresses the perplexing question of the legal status of the semen donor, and provides a method of avoiding the legal consequences that might otherwise be dictated by traditional notions of paternity.

* * *

We wish to stress that our opinion in this case is not intended to express any judicial preference toward traditional notions of family structure or toward providing a father where a single woman has chosen to bear a child. Public policy in these areas is best determined by the legislative branch of government, not the judicial. Our Legislature has already spoken and has afforded to unmarried women a statutory right to bear children by artificial insemination (as well as right of men to donate semen) without fear of a paternity claim, through provision of the semen to a licensed physician. We simply hold that because Mary omitted to invoke Civil Code § 7005, subd. (b), by obtaining Jhordan's semen through a licensed physician, and because the parties by all other conduct preserved Jhordan's status as a member of Devin's family, the trial court properly declared Jhordan to be Devin's legal father.

The judgment is affirmed.

NOTES AND QUESTIONS

1. A California appellate court applied the reasoning in *Jhordan C.* in ruling against an unmarried father who had provided sperm to a woman through a licensed physician instead of directly. *See* Robert B. v. Susan B., 135 Cal. Rptr. 2d 785 (App. 2003). The father in *Robert B.* had also engaged in sexual intercourse to achieve a pregnancy before utilizing AID; the court found that this was irrelevant under the statute. Do you agree?

2. *Husband Consent:* State statutory standards invariably hold that a child born through AI to a married woman whose husband has consented in writing to the procedure is the child of the mother's husband, not the sperm donor. In cases where the husband's consent is at issue, courts have sometimes waived "technical" consent requirements in order to ensure the child's legitimacy, particularly when there is a basis to apply estoppel principles. *See, e.g.,* Lane v. Lane, 912 P.2d 290 (N. M. App. 1996) (waiving requirement that husband consent in writing); R.S. v. R.S., 670 P.2d 923 (Kan. App. 1983) (husband's consent presumed to continue until wife becomes pregnant unless clear and convincing evidence that consent was withdrawn). The 1973 Uniform Parentage Act (UPA) UPA § 5 provides that:

> If, under the supervision of a licensed physician and with the consent of her husband, a wife is inseminated artificially with semen donated by a man not her husband, the husband is treated in law as if he were the natural father of a child thereby conceived. The husband's consent must be in writing and signed by him and his wife. * * *

Can this provision be applied to a same-sex partner? *See In re* Madrone, 350 P.3d 495 (Or. App. 2015).

The UPA (2002) § 703 specifies:

A man who provides sperm for, or consents to, assisted reproduction by a woman, as provided for in § 704 with the intent to be the parent of her child, is a parent of the resulting child.

UPA (2002). § 704:

(a)   Consent by a woman and a man who intends to be a parent of a child born to the woman by assisted reproduction must be in a record signed by the woman and the man. The requirement does not apply to a donor.

(b)   Failure to sign a consent required by subsection (a) * * *, before or after birth of the child, does not preclude a finding of paternity if the woman and the man, during the first two years of the child's life[,] resided together in the same household with the child and openly held out the child as their own.

Why did the drafters of UPA (2002) alter the standards for AI paternity determination? Is the new standard constitutionally required? What policy arguments support the new standard? What arguments can be used to oppose it?

3.   *Unmarried Women:* Legislatures initially did not see the need to extend AI law to unmarried women because of the perception that the stigma attached to unwed motherhood was sufficiently great that none would want to use the procedure. Much has changed over the past fifty years, and courts increasingly confront cases in which an unmarried woman, with or without a partner, has used AI to bear a child.

Virtually all of the reported cases involve semen donors who, like Jhordan C., personally made a sperm-donation arrangement with the mother. On either statutory or policy grounds, most courts have ruled that such a known semen donor is the legal father of a child born to an unmarried woman. *See* C.M. v. C.C., 377 A.2d 821 (N.J. Super. 1977) ("[I]f an unmarried woman conceives a child through artificial insemination from semen from a known man, that man cannot be considered to be less a father because he is not married to the woman"). *See* Bruce v. Boardwine, 70 S.E.2d 774 (Va. App. 2015). Some courts have gone further and refused to enforce contracts limiting the sperm donor's rights. Tripp v. Hinckley, 736 N.Y.S.2d 506 (App. Div. 2002). However, some courts have enforced rights-limiting agreements. *See* Leckie v. Voorhies, 875 P.2d 521 (Or. App. 1994).

As you learned in Chapter 7, contracts voiding the paternity or limiting the parental rights of the father of a sexually conceived child are unenforceable. What arguments support different treatment for sperm-donor fathers? *See* Ferguson v. McKiernan, 940 A.2d 1236 (Pa. 2008). What arguments support similar treatment? Does the strength of these arguments vary depending on whether the donor is known to the mother? Given that parenthood, like marriage, is a constitutionally protected "fundamental right," could a sperm-donor father whose rights were limited by contract successfully maintain an equal protection action? The Kansas Supreme Court found that a statute barring presumption of paternity for a sperm donor absent a written agreement to the contrary did not violate equal protection or due process. *See In re K.M.H.*, 169 P.3d 1025 (Kan. 2007). *See* Elizabeth E. McDonald, *Sperm Donor or Thwarted Father? How Written Agreement Statutes Are Changing the Way Courts Resolve Legal Parentage Issues in Assisted Reproduction Cases*, 47 FAM. CT. REV. 340 (2009).

4.   *The UPA (2002) and Unmarried Women:* The revised UPA (2002) § 702 explicitly provides that "[a] donor is not a parent of a child conceived by means of assisted reproduction." Comments to the section make it clear that "[t]he donor can neither sue to establish parental rights, nor be sued and required to support the resulting child. In sum, donors are eliminated from the parental equation." The drafters describe the basis of the change as follows:

> This section of UPA (2002) * * * opts not to limit nonparenthood of a donor to situations in which the donor provides sperm for assisted reproduction by a married woman. This requirement is not realistic in light of present practices in the field of assisted reproduction. Instead, donors are to be shielded from parenthood in all situations in which either a married woman or a single woman conceives a child through assisted reproduction. * * * This provides certainty of nonparentage for prospective donors. * * * Under th[e]se circumstances—called a "relatively rare situation" in [a] * * * 1988 Comment—"the child would have no legally recognized father." This result is retained in UPA (2002), although the frequency of unmarried women using assisted reproduction appears to have grown significantly since 1988.

On the merits, are the drafters' arguments in favor of new § 702 convincing?

Under the UPA (2002), should Jhordan C. be classified as a sperm donor under § 702 or as an intended father under § 703? Assuming that UPA (2002) § 702 applies to a father like Jhordan C., what constitutional arguments would be available to Jhordan C.? What arguments would be available to the state? On what cases would each party rely? On balance, what is the likelihood that § 702 would survive a constitutional challenge as applied to Jhordan C.?

B. IVF AND SURROGACY

Surrogacy involves one woman carrying a child to term to be reared by another. Surrogacy involves either traditional or gestational surrogacy. With traditional surrogacy, the married woman cannot produce a healthy egg. Her husband's sperm is used to fertilize a surrogate's egg and the surrogate carries the baby to term. In gestational surrogacy, the married woman may be able to produce healthy eggs which may be fertilized by her husband's sperm and implanted into a gestational surrogate. Public attention was first focused on the issues posed by surrogacy contracts as a result of the case of *In re* Baby M., 537 A.2d 1227 (N.J. 1988). William Stern and Mary Beth Whitehead entered into a contract whereby Mary Beth would bear Stern's child (by AI). The New Jersey Supreme Court found that an agreement by a "traditional" surrogate mother (i.e., one who is also the child's biological mother) to relinquish the child she had conceived through artificial insemination to the sperm donor and his wife in return for $10,000 "conflict[ed] with existing statutes and * * * with the public policies of this State":

> The surrogacy contract * * * is based upon[ ] principles that are directly contrary to the objectives of our laws. It guarantees the separation of a child from its mother; it looks to adoption regardless of suitability; it totally ignores the child; it takes the child from the mother regardless of her wishes and her maternal fitness; and it does all of this, it accomplishes all of its goals, through the use of money.

The New Jersey Supreme Court thus declared the contract void. *Baby M.* was widely publicized and was a major factor in turning the tide of public opinion against traditional surrogacy. California, however, has taken a different approach to surrogacy.

JOHNSON V. CALVERT
Supreme Court of California, 1993.
5 Cal. 4th 84, 851 P.2d 776, 19 Cal. Rptr. 2d 494.

PANELLI, J.

* * *

Mark and Crispina Calvert are a married couple who desired to have a child. Crispina was forced to undergo a hysterectomy in 1984. Her ovaries remained capable of producing eggs, however, and the couple eventually considered surrogacy. In 1989 Anna Johnson heard about Crispina's plight from a coworker and offered to serve as a surrogate for the Calverts.

On January 15, 1990, Mark, Crispina, and Anna signed a contract providing that an embryo created by the sperm of Mark and the egg of Crispina would be implanted in Anna and the child born would be taken into Mark and Crispina's home "as their child." Anna agreed she would relinquish "all parental rights" to the child in favor of Mark and Crispina. In return, Mark and Crispina would pay Anna $10,000 in a series of installments, the last to be paid six weeks after the child's birth. Mark and Crispina were also to pay for a $200,000 life insurance policy on Anna's life.

The zygote was implanted on January 19, 1990. Less than a month later, an ultrasound test confirmed Anna was pregnant.

Unfortunately, relations deteriorated between the two sides. Mark learned that Anna had not disclosed she had suffered several stillbirths and miscarriages. Anna felt Mark and Crispina did not do enough to obtain the required insurance policy. She also felt abandoned during an onset of premature labor in June.

In July 1990, Anna sent Mark and Crispina a letter demanding the balance of the payments due her or else she would refuse to give up the child. The following month, Mark and Crispina responded with a lawsuit, seeking a declaration they were the legal parents of the unborn child. Anna filed her own action to be declared the mother of the child, and the two cases were eventually consolidated. The parties agreed to an independent guardian ad litem for the purposes of the suit.

The child was born on September 19, 1990, and blood samples were obtained from both Anna and the child for analysis. The blood test results excluded Anna as the genetic mother. The parties agreed to a court order providing that the child would remain with Mark and Crispina on a temporary basis with visits by Anna.

* * *

Anna, of course, predicates her claim of maternity on the fact that she gave birth to the child. The Calverts contend that Crispina's genetic relationship to the child establishes that she is his mother. Counsel for the minor joins in that contention and argues, in addition, that several of the presumptions created by the Act dictate the same result. As will appear, we conclude that presentation of blood test evidence is one means of establishing maternity, as is proof of having given birth, but that the presumptions cited by minor's counsel do not apply to this case.

* * *

We see no clear legislative preference in Civil Code § 7003 as between blood testing evidence and proof of having given birth.[8] * * * It is arguable that, while gestation may demonstrate maternal status, it is not the *sine qua non* of motherhood. Rather, it is possible that the common law viewed genetic consanguinity as the basis for maternal rights. Under this latter interpretation, gestation simply would be irrefutable evidence of the more fundamental genetic relationship. This ambiguity, highlighted by the problems arising from the use of artificial reproductive techniques, is nowhere explicitly resolved in the Act.

---

[8] We decline to accept the contention of amicus curiae the American Civil Liberties Union (ACLU) that we should find the child has two mothers. Even though rising divorce rates have made multiple parent arrangements common in our society, we see no compelling reason to recognize such a situation here. The Calverts are the genetic and intending parents of their son and have provided him, by all accounts, with a stable, intact, and nurturing home. To recognize parental rights in a third party with whom the Calvert family has had little contact since shortly after the child's birth would diminish Crispina's role as mother.

Because two women each have presented acceptable proof of maternity, we do not believe this case can be decided without enquiring into the parties' intentions as manifested in the surrogacy agreement. Mark and Crispina are a couple who desired to have a child of their own genes but are physically unable to do so without the help of reproductive technology. They affirmatively intended the birth of the child, and took the steps necessary to effect in vitro fertilization. But for their acted-on intention, the child would not exist. Anna agreed to facilitate the procreation of Mark's and Crispina's child. The parties' aim was to bring Mark's and Crispina's child into the world, not for Mark and Crispina to donate a zygote to Anna. Crispina from the outset intended to be the child's mother. Although the gestative function Anna performed was necessary to bring about the child's birth, it is safe to say that Anna would not have been given the opportunity to gestate or deliver the child had she, prior to implantation of the zygote, manifested her own intent to be the child's mother. No reason appears why Anna's later change of heart should vitiate the determination that Crispina is the child's natural mother.

We conclude that although the Act recognizes both genetic consanguinity and giving birth as means of establishing a mother and child relationship, when the two means do not coincide in one woman, she who intended to procreate the child—that is, she who intended to bring about the birth of a child that she intended to raise as her own—is the natural mother under California law.

Our conclusion finds support in the writings of several legal commentators. Professor Hill, arguing that the genetic relationship per se should not be accorded priority in the determination of the parent-child relationship in the surrogacy context, notes that "while all of the players in the procreative arrangement are necessary in bringing a child into the world, the child would not have been born but for the efforts of the intended parents. * * * [T]he intended parents are the first cause, or the prime movers, of the procreative relationship." Similarly, Professor Shultz * * * argues [that] "intentions that are voluntarily chosen, deliberate, express and bargained-for ought presumptively to determine legal parenthood."

* * *

Moreover, as Professor Shultz recognizes, the interests of children, particularly at the outset of their lives, are "[un]likely to run contrary to those of adults who choose to bring them into being." Thus, "[h]onoring the plans and expectations of adults who will be responsible for a child's welfare is likely to correlate significantly with positive outcomes for parents and children alike." Under Anna's interpretation of the Act, by contrast, a woman who agreed to gestate a fetus genetically related to the intending parents would, contrary to her expectations, be held to be the child's natural mother, with all the responsibilities that ruling would entail, if the intending mother declined to accept the child after its birth. In what we must hope will be the extremely rare situation in which neither the gestator nor the woman who provided the ovum for fertilization is willing to assume custody of the child after birth, a rule recognizing the intending parents as the child's legal, natural parents should best promote certainty and stability for the child.

* * *

Anna urges that surrogacy contracts violate several social policies. Relying on her contention that she is the child's legal, natural mother, she cites the public policy embodied in Penal Code § 273, prohibiting the payment for consent to adoption of a child. She argues further that the policies underlying the adoption laws of this state are violated by the surrogacy contract because it in effect constitutes a prebirth waiver of her parental rights.

We disagree. Gestational surrogacy differs in crucial respects from adoption and so is not subject to the adoption statutes. The parties voluntarily agreed to participate in *in vitro* fertilization and related medical procedures before the child was conceived; at the time when Anna entered into the contract, therefore, she was not vulnerable to financial inducements to part with her own expected offspring. As discussed above, Anna was not the genetic mother of the child. The payments to Anna under the contract were meant to compensate her for her services in gestating the fetus and undergoing labor, rather than for giving up "parental" rights to the child. Payments were due both during the pregnancy and after the child's birth. We are, accordingly, unpersuaded that the contract used in this case violates the public policies embodied in Penal Code § 273 and the adoption statutes. For the same reasons, we conclude these contracts do not implicate the policies underlying the statutes governing termination of parental rights.

* * *

Finally, Anna and some commentators have expressed concern that surrogacy contracts tend to exploit or dehumanize women, especially women of lower economic status. Anna's objections center around the psychological harm she asserts may result from the gestator's relinquishing the child to whom she has given birth. Some have also cautioned that the practice of surrogacy may encourage society to view children as commodities, subject to trade at their parents' will. * * *

We are unpersuaded that gestational surrogacy arrangements are so likely to cause the untoward results Anna cites as to demand their invalidation on public policy grounds. * * * The argument that a woman cannot knowingly and intelligently agree to gestate and deliver a baby for intending parents carries overtones of the reasoning that for centuries prevented women from attaining equal economic rights and professional status under the law. To resurrect this view is both to foreclose a personal and economic choice on the part of the surrogate mother, and to deny intending parents what may be their only means of procreating a child of their own genes. Certainly in the present case it cannot seriously be argued that Anna, a licensed vocational nurse who had done well in school and who had previously borne a child, lacked the intellectual wherewithal or life experience necessary to make an informed decision to enter into the surrogacy contract.

Constitutionality of the Determination That Anna Johnson Is Not the Natural Mother

Anna argues at length that her right to continued companionship of the child is protected under the federal Constitution. * * * Anna relies principally on the decision of the United States Supreme Court in *Michael H. v. Gerald D.*, 491 U.S. 110 (1989) to support her claim to a constitutionally protected liberty interest in the companionship of the child, based on her status as "birth mother." In that case, a plurality of the Court held that a state may constitutionally deny a man parental rights with respect to a child he fathered during a liaison with the wife of another man, since it is the marital family that traditionally has been accorded a protected liberty interest, as reflected in the historic presumption of legitimacy of a child born into such a family. The reasoning of the plurality in *Michael H.* does not assist Anna. Society has not traditionally protected the right of a woman who gestates and delivers a baby pursuant to an agreement with a couple who supply the zygote from which the baby develops and who intend to raise the child as their own; such arrangements are of too recent an origin to claim the protection of tradition. To the extent that tradition has a bearing on the present case, we believe it supports the claim of the couple who exercise their right to procreate in order to form a family of their own, albeit through novel medical procedures.

Moreover, if we were to conclude that Anna enjoys some sort of liberty interest in the companionship of the child, then the liberty interests of Mark and Crispina, the child's natural parents, in their procreative choices and their relationship with the child would perforce be infringed. Any parental rights Anna might successfully assert could come only at Crispina's expense. As we have seen, Anna has no parental rights to the child under California law, and she fails to persuade us that sufficiently strong policy reasons exist to accord her a protected liberty interest in the companionship of the child when such an interest would necessarily detract from or impair the parental bond enjoyed by Mark and Crispina.

Amicus curiae ACLU urges that Anna's rights of privacy embodied in the California Constitution (Cal. Const., art. I, § 1), requires recognition and protection of her status as "birth mother." We cannot agree. * * *

Amicus curiae appears to assume that the choice to gestate and deliver a baby to its genetic parents pursuant to a surrogacy agreement is the equivalent, in constitutional weight, of the decision whether to bear a child of one's own. We disagree. A woman who enters into a gestational surrogacy arrangement is not exercising her own right to make procreative choices; she is agreeing to provide a necessary and profoundly important service without (by definition) any expectation that she will raise the resulting child as her own. * * *

The judgment of the Court of Appeal is affirmed.

IN RE BUZZANCA

California Court of Appeals, 1998.
61 Cal. App. 4th 1410, 72 Cal. Rptr. 2d 280.

SILLS, P.J.

Jaycee was born because Luanne and John Buzzanca agreed to have an embryo genetically unrelated to either of them implanted in a woman— a surrogate—who would carry and give birth to the child for them. After the fertilization, implantation and pregnancy, Luanne and John split up, and the question of who are Jaycee's lawful parents came before the trial court.

Luanne claimed that she and her erstwhile husband were the lawful parents, but John disclaimed any responsibility, financial or otherwise. The woman who gave birth also appeared in the case to make it clear that she made no claim to the child.

The trial court then reached an extraordinary conclusion: Jaycee had no lawful parents. First, the woman who gave birth to Jaycee was not the mother; the court had—astonishingly—already accepted a stipulation that neither she nor her husband were the "biological" parents. Second, Luanne was not the mother. According to the trial court, she could not be the mother because she had neither contributed the egg nor given birth. And John could not be the father, because, not having contributed the sperm, he had no biological relationship with the child.

We disagree. Let us get right to the point: Jaycee never would have been born had not Luanne and John both agreed to have a fertilized egg implanted in a surrogate.

The trial judge erred because he assumed that legal motherhood, under the relevant California statutes, could only be established in one of two ways, either by giving birth or by contributing an egg. He failed to consider the substantial and well-settled body of law holding that there are times when fatherhood can be established by conduct apart from giving birth or being genetically related to a child. * * *

John Is the Lawful Father of Jaycee

The same rule which makes a husband the lawful father of a child born because of his consent to artificial insemination should be applied here— by the same parity of reasoning that guided our Supreme Court in the first surrogacy case, Johnson v. Calvert—to both husband and wife. Just as a husband is deemed to be the lawful father of a child unrelated to him when his wife gives birth after artificial insemination, so should a husband and wife be deemed the lawful parents of a child after a surrogate bears a biologically unrelated child on their behalf. In each instance, a child is procreated because a medical procedure was initiated and consented to by intended parents. The only difference is that in this case—unlike artificial insemination—there is no reason to distinguish between husband and wife. We therefore must reverse the trial court's judgment and direct that a new judgment be entered, declaring that both Luanne and John are the lawful parents of Jaycee.

* * *

As noted in *Johnson*, "courts must construe statutes in factual settings not contemplated by the enacting legislature." So it is, of course, true that application of the artificial insemination statute to a gestational surrogacy case where the genetic donors are unknown to the court may not have been contemplated by the Legislature. Even so, the two kinds of artificial reproduction are exactly analogous in this crucial respect: Both contemplate the procreation of a child by the consent to a medical procedure of someone who intends to raise the child but who otherwise does not have any biological tie.

If a husband who consents to artificial insemination under Family Code § 7613 is "treated in law" as the father of the child by virtue of his consent, there is no reason the result should be any different in the case of a married couple who consent to in vitro fertilization by unknown donors and subsequent implantation into a woman who is, as a surrogate, willing to carry the embryo to term for them. The statute is, after all, the clearest expression of past legislative intent when the Legislature did contemplate a situation where a person who caused a child to come into being had no biological relationship to the child.

Indeed, the establishment of fatherhood and the consequent duty to support when a husband consents to the artificial insemination of his wife is one of the well-established rules in family law. * * * Indeed, in the one case we are aware of where the court did not hold that the husband had a support obligation, the reason was not the absence of a biological relationship as such, but because of actual lack of consent to the insemination procedure. (*See In re* Marriage of Witbeck-Wildhagen, 667 N.E.2d 122, 125–126 (1996) [it would be "unjust" to impose support obligation on husband who never consented to the artificial insemination].)

It must also be noted that in applying the artificial insemination statute to a case where a party has caused a child to be brought into the world, the statutory policy is really echoing a more fundamental idea—a sort of *grundnorm* to borrow Hans Kelsen's famous jurisprudential word— already established in the case law. That idea is often summed up in the legal term "estoppel." Estoppel is an ungainly word from the Middle French (from the word meaning "bung" or "stopper") expressing the law's distaste for inconsistent actions and positions—like consenting to an act which brings a child into existence and then turning around and disclaiming any responsibility.

While the Johnson v. Calvert court was able to predicate its decision on the Act rather than making up the result out of whole cloth, it is also true that California courts, prior to the enactment of the Act, had based certain decisions establishing paternity merely on the common law doctrine of estoppel. * * * There is no need in the present case to predicate our decision on common law estoppel alone, though the doctrine certainly applies. The estoppel concept, after all, is already inherent in the artificial insemination statute. In essence, Family Code § 7613 is nothing more than the codification of the common law rule. * * * By consenting to a medical procedure which results in the birth of a child * * * a husband incurs the legal status and responsibility of fatherhood.

John argues that the artificial insemination statute should not be applied because, after all, his wife did not give birth. But for purposes of the statute with its core idea of estoppel, the fact that Luanne did not give birth is irrelevant. The statute contemplates the establishment of lawful fatherhood in a situation where an intended father has no biological relationship to a child who is procreated as a result of the father's (as well as the mother's) consent to a medical procedure.

Luanne is the Lawful Mother of Jaycee, Not the Surrogate, and Not the Unknown Donor of the Egg

In the present case Luanne is situated like a husband in an artificial insemination case whose consent triggers a medical procedure which results in a pregnancy and eventual birth of a child. Her motherhood may therefore be established "under this part," by virtue of that consent. In light of our conclusion, John's argument that the surrogate should be declared the lawful mother disintegrates. The case is now postured like the Johnson v. Calvert case, where motherhood could have been "established" in either of two women under the Act, and the tie broken by noting the intent to parent as expressed in the surrogacy contract. The only difference is that this case is not even close as between Luanne and the surrogate. Not only was Luanne the clearly intended mother, no bona fide attempt has been made to establish the surrogate as the lawful mother.

We should also add that neither could the woman whose egg was used in the fertilization or implantation make any claim to motherhood, even if she were to come forward at this late date. Again, as between two women who would both be able to establish motherhood under the Act, the *Johnson* decision would mandate that the tie be broken in favor of the intended parent, in this case, Luanne.

Our decision in *In re* Marriage of Moschetta, relied on by John, is inapposite and distinguishable. * * * There is a difference between a court's enforcing a surrogacy agreement and making a legal determination based on the intent expressed in a surrogacy agreement. By the same token, there is also an important distinction between enforcing a surrogacy contract and making a legal determination based on the fact that the contract itself sets in motion a medical procedure which results in the birth of a child.

* * *

Family Code § 7570, subdivision (a) states that "There is a compelling state interest in establishing paternity for all children." The statute then goes on to elaborate why establishing paternity is a good thing: It means someone besides the taxpayers will be responsible for the child. * * * Family Code § 7570 necessarily expresses a legislative policy applicable to maternity as well. It would be lunatic for the Legislature to declare that establishing paternity is a compelling state interest yet conclude that establishing maternity is not. The obvious reason the Legislature did not include an explicit parallel statement on "maternity" is that the issue almost never arises except for extraordinary cases involving artificial reproduction.

* * *

* * * [T]he *Johnson* court had occasion, albeit in dicta, to address "pretty much the exact situation before us." THE LANGUAGE BEARS QUOTING AGAIN: "In what we must hope will be the extremely rare situation in which neither the gestator nor the woman who provided the ovum for fertilization is willing to assume custody of the child after birth, a rule recognizing the intending parents as the child's legal, natural parents should best promote certainty and stability. . . " This language quite literally describes precisely the case before us now: neither the woman whose ovum was used nor the woman who gave birth have come forward to assume custody of the child after birth.

John now argues that the Supreme Court's statement should be applied only in situations, such as that in the *Johnson* case, where the intended parents have a genetic tie to the child. The context of the *Johnson* language, however, reveals a broader purpose, namely, to emphasize the intelligence and utility of a rule that looks to intentions.

* * *

In the case before us, there is absolutely no dispute that Luanne caused Jaycee's conception and birth by initiating the surrogacy arrangement whereby an embryo was implanted into a woman who agreed to carry the baby to term on Luanne's behalf. In applying the artificial insemination statute to a gestational surrogacy case where the genetic donors are unknown, there is, as we have indicated above, no reason to distinguish between husbands and wives. Both are equally situated from the point of view of consenting to an act which brings a child into being. Accordingly, Luanne should have been declared the lawful mother of Jaycee.

John Is the Lawful Father of Jaycee Even If Luanne Did Promise to Assume All Responsibility for Jaycee's Care

The same reasons which impel us to conclude that Luanne is Jaycee's lawful mother also require that John be declared Jaycee's lawful father. Even if the written surrogacy contract had not yet been signed at the time of conception and implantation, those occurrences were nonetheless the direct result of actions taken pursuant to an oral agreement which envisioned that the fertilization, implantation and ensuing pregnancy would go forward. Thus, it is still accurate to say, as we did the first time this case came before us, that for all practical purposes John caused Jaycee's conception every bit as much as if things had been done the old-fashioned way.

When pressed at oral argument to make an offer of proof as to the "best facts" which John might be able to show if this case were tried, John's attorney raised the point that Luanne had (allegedly, we must add) promised to assume all responsibility for the child and would not hold him responsible for the child's upbringing. However, even if this case were returned for a trial on this point (we assume that Luanne would dispute the allegation) it could make no difference as to John's lawful paternity. It is well established that parents cannot, by agreement, limit or abrogate a child's right to support.

* * *

The rule against enforcing agreements obviating a parent's child support responsibilities is also illustrated by Stephen K. v. Roni L., 105 Cal. App. 3d 640, 164 Cal. Rptr. 618 (1980), a case which is virtually on point about Luanne's alleged promise. In *Stephen K.*, a woman was alleged to have falsely told a man that she was taking birth control pills. In "reliance" upon that statement the man had sexual intercourse with her. The woman became pregnant and brought a paternity action. While the man did not attempt to use the woman's false statement as grounds to avoid paternity, he did seek to achieve the same result by cross-complaining against the woman for damages based on her fraud.

The trial court dismissed the cross-complaint on demurrer and the appellate court affirmed. The cross-complaint was "nothing more than asking the court to supervise the promises made between two consenting adults as to the circumstances of their private sexual conduct."

There is no meaningful difference between the rule articulated in *Stephen K.* and the situation here—indeed, the result applies a fortiori to the present case: If the man who engaged in an act which merely opened the possibility of the procreation of a child was held responsible for the consequences in *Stephen K.*, how much more so should a man be held responsible for giving his express consent to a medical procedure that was intended to result in the procreation of a child. Thus, it makes no difference that John's wife Luanne did not become pregnant. John still engaged in "procreative conduct." In plainer language, a deliberate procreator is as responsible as a casual inseminator.

Conclusion

Even though neither Luanne nor John are biologically related to Jaycee, they are still her lawful parents given their initiating role as the intended parents in her conception and birth. * * *

Again we must call on the Legislature to sort out the parental rights and responsibilities of those involved in artificial reproduction. No matter what one thinks of artificial insemination, traditional and gestational surrogacy (in all its permutations), and—as now appears in the not-too-distant future, cloning and even gene splicing—courts are still going to be faced with the problem of determining lawful parentage. A child cannot be ignored. * * * These cases will not go away.

NOTES AND QUESTIONS

1.   Most states still lack legislative solutions to the problems posed in *Johnson* and *Buzzanca*. A few states have extended their AI husband-consent rules to ova donation. *See, e.g.,* FLA. STAT. ANN. § 742.11. North Dakota, Oklahoma and Virginia have adopted similar provisions. Sieglein v. Schmidt, 136 A.3d 751 (Md. 2016) (finding husband was the father of child conceived through IVF via donated egg and sperm).

2.   How does the estoppel doctrine described in *Buzzanca* differ from the intention-based approach to parenthood determination outlined in *Johnson*? Why did the *Buzzanca* court rely on estoppel to find that John was Jaycee's legal father and intention to find that Luanne was her legal mother? Could the court have relied on the same doctrine to determine both motherhood and fatherhood?

3.   The *Buzzanca* court states that "[t]here is a difference between a court's enforcing a surrogacy agreement and making a legal determination based on the intent expressed in a surrogacy agreement." But wouldn't enforcement of a surrogacy contract simply make a legal determination based

on the contracting parties' intentions? If so, how can *Buzzanca* be distinguished from *Moschetta*? Put somewhat differently, is "legal determination based on * * * intent" simply contract enforcement with another label? If not, how does legal determination based on intent differ from contract enforcement?

4. Both *Johnson* and *Buzzanca* rely on the parties' intentions in determining parental status. But if intention is irrelevant to parental obligation, why should it be relevant to parental status? Put somewhat differently, is it possible to successfully distinguish *Stephen K.* from *Johnson* and *Buzzanca*?

5. How does gestational surrogacy differ from adoption and termination of parental rights? Why was the court unwilling to recognize two legal mothers? CAL. FAM. CODE § 7612 allows the court to accord parental rights to a third person based on finding that recognizing only two parents would be detrimental to the child.

6. *Surrogacy Legislation:* The Connecticut Supreme Court found that intended parents who are parties to a valid gestational agreement acquire parental status and are entitled to be placed on the birth certificate, without respect to the biological relationship. The court summarized the statutory regulation of assisted reproduction. Twenty states still have no statutory guidance on gestational surrogacy; six states bar gestational surrogacy agreements; ten states prohibit compensation, two (Florida and Texas) limit recognition to married intended parents, and others have other requirements. *See* Raftopol v. Ramey, 12 A.3d 783 (Conn. 2011).

7. UPA (2002) § 801 contains an "optional" section authorizing enforceable surrogacy agreements between "intended parents" and a "gestational" surrogate. The drafters note that "thousands of children are born each year pursuant to gestational agreements" and argue that about one-half [of the states have] recognized such agreements, and the other half rejected them. * * * In states rejecting gestational agreements, the legal status of children born pursuant to such an agreement is uncertain. If gestational agreements are voided or criminalized, individuals determined to become parents through this method will seek a friendlier legal forum. This raises a host of legal issues. For example, a couple may return to their home state with a child born as the consequence of a gestational agreement recognized in another state. This presents a full faith and credit question if their home state has a statute declaring gestational agreements to be void or criminal.

Confusingly, however, the UPA (2002) "gestational" surrogacy provisions apply to both gestational and "traditional" surrogate mothers who are genetically related to the children they bear:

> Article 8's replacement of the * * * term[ ] "surrogate mother[ ]" by "gestational mother" is important. First, labeling a woman who bears a child a "surrogate" does not comport with the dictionary definition of the term under any construction, to wit: "a person appointed to act

in the place of another" or "something serving as a substitute." The term is especially misleading when "surrogate" refers to a woman who supplies both "egg and womb," that is, a woman who is a genetic as well as gestational mother. That combination is now typically avoided by the majority of ART practitioners in order to decrease the possibility that a genetic/gestational mother will be unwilling to relinquish her child to unrelated intended parents. Further, the term "surrogate" has acquired a negative connotation in American society, which confuses rather than enlightens the discussion.

In contrast, the term "gestational mother" is both more accurate and more inclusive. It applies to both a woman who, through assisted reproduction, performs the gestational function without being genetically related to a child, and a woman is both the gestational and genetic mother. The key is that an agreement has been made that the child is to be raised by the intended parents. The latter practice has elicited disfavor in the ART community, which has concluded that the gestational mother's genetic link to the child too often creates additional emotional and psychological problems in enforcing a gestational agreement.

Id. at Article 8 Prefatory Comment. Are the reasons the drafters offer for the new UPA standard convincing? What arguments support different treatment of gestational and "traditional" surrogacy? On balance, should gestational and "traditional" surrogacy be governed by the same or different rules?

K.M. v. E.G.

California Supreme Court, 2005.
37 Cal. 4th 130, 117 P.3d 673, 33 Cal. Rptr. 3d 61.

MORENO, J.

We granted review in this case * * * to consider the parental rights and obligations, if any, of a woman with regard to a child born to her partner in a lesbian relationship. * * *

Facts

On March 6, 2001, petitioner K.M. filed a petition to establish a parental relationship with twin five-year-old girls born to respondent E.G., her former lesbian partner. K.M. alleged that she "is the biological parent of the minor children" because "[s]he donated her egg to respondent, the gestational mother of the children." E.G. moved to dismiss the petition on the grounds that, although K.M. and E.G. "were lesbian partners who lived together until this action was filed," K.M. "explicitly donated her ovum under a clear written agreement by which she relinquished any claim to offspring born of her donation."

On April 18, 2001, K.M. filed a motion for custody of and visitation with the twins. A hearing was held at which E.G. testified that she first considered raising a child before she met K.M., at a time when she did not have a partner. She met K.M. in October 1992 and they became romantically involved in June 1993. E.G. told K.M. that she planned to adopt a baby as a single mother. E.G. applied for adoption in November 1993. K.M. and E.G. began living together in March 1994 and registered as domestic partners in San Francisco.

E.G. visited several fertility clinics in March 1993 to inquire about artificial insemination and she attempted artificial insemination, without success, on 13 occasions from July 1993 through November 1994. K.M. accompanied her to most of these appointments. K.M. testified that she and E.G. planned to raise the child together, while E.G. insisted that, although K.M. was very supportive, E.G. made it clear that her intention was to become "a single parent."

In December 1994, E.G. consulted with Dr. Mary Martin at the fertility practice of the University of California at San Francisco Medical Center (UCSF). E.G.'s first attempts at in vitro fertilization failed because she was unable to produce sufficient ova. In January 1995, Dr. Martin suggested using K.M.'s ova. E.G. then asked K.M. to donate her ova, explaining that she would accept the ova only if K.M. "would really be a donor" and E.G. would "be the mother of any child," adding that she would not even consider permitting K.M. to adopt the child "for at least five years until [she] felt the relationship was stable and would endure." E.G. told K.M. that she "had seen too many lesbian relationships end quickly, and [she] did not want to be in a custody battle." E.G. and K.M. agreed they would not tell anyone that K.M. was the ova donor.

K.M. acknowledged that she agreed not to disclose to anyone that she was the ova donor, but insisted that she only agreed to provide her ova because she and E.G. had agreed to raise the child together. K.M. and E.G. selected the sperm donor together. K.M. denied that E.G. had said she wanted to be a single parent and insisted that she would not have donated her ova had she known E.G. intended to be the sole parent.

On March 8, 1995, K.M. signed a four-page form on UCSF letterhead entitled "Consent Form for Ovum Donor (Known)." The form states that K.M. agrees "to have eggs taken from my ovaries, in order that they may be donated to another woman." After explaining the medical procedures involved, the form states on the third page: "It is understood that I waive any right and relinquish any claim to the donated eggs or any pregnancy or offspring that might result from them. I agree that the recipient may regard the donated eggs and any offspring resulting therefrom as her own children." The following appears on page 4 of the form, above K.M.'s signature and the signature of a witness: "I specifically disclaim and waive any right in or any child that may be [**8] conceived as a result of the use of any ovum or egg of mine, and I agree not to attempt to discover the identity of the recipient thereof." E.G. signed a form entitled "Consent Form for Ovum Recipient" that stated, in part: "I acknowledge that the child or children produced by the IVF procedure is and shall be my own legitimate child or children and the heir or heirs of my body with all rights and privileges accompanying such status."

E.G. testified she received these two forms in a letter from UCSF dated February 2, 1995, and discussed the consent forms with K.M. during February and March. E.G. stated she would not have accepted K.M.'s ova if K.M. had not signed the consent form, because E.G. wanted to have a child on her own and believed the consent form "protected" her in this regard.

K.M. testified to the contrary that she first saw the ovum donation consent form 10 minutes before she signed it on March 8, 1995. K.M. admitted reading the form, but thought parts of the form were "odd" and did not pertain to her, such as the part stating that the donor promised not to discover the identity of the recipient. She did not intend to relinquish her rights and only signed the form so that "we could have children." despite having signed the form, K.M. "thought [she] was going to be a parent."

Ova were withdrawn from K.M. on April 11, 1995, and embryos were implanted in E.G. on April 13, 1995. K.M. and E.G. told K.M.'s father about the resulting pregnancy by announcing that he was going to be a grandfather. The twins were born on December 7, 1995. The twins' birth certificates listed E.G. as their mother and did not reflect a father's name. As they had agreed, neither E.G. nor K.M. told anyone K.M. had donated the ova, including their friends, family and the twins' pediatrician. Soon after the twins were born, E.G. asked K.M. to marry her, and on Christmas Day, the couple exchanged rings.

Within a month of their birth, E.G. added the twins to her health insurance policy, named them as her beneficiary for all employment benefits, and increased her life insurance with the twins as the beneficiary. K.M. did not do the same.

E.G. referred to her mother, as well as K.M.'s parents, as the twins' grandparents and referred to K.M.'s sister and brother as the twins' aunt and uncle, and K.M.'s nieces as their cousins. Two school forms listed both K.M. and respondent as the twins' parents. The children's nanny testified that both K.M. and E.G. "were the babies' mother."

The relationship between K.M. and E.G. ended in March 2001 and K.M. filed the present action. In September 2001, E.G. and the twins moved to Massachusetts to live with E.G.'s mother.

The superior court granted the motion to dismiss finding, in a statement of decision, "that [K.M.] . . . knowingly, voluntarily and intelligently executed the ovum donor form, thereby acknowledging her understanding that, by the donation of her ova, she was relinquishing and waiving all rights to claim legal parentage of any children who might result from the *in vitro* fertilization and implantation of her ova in a recipient (in this case, a known recipient, her domestic partner [E.G.]). . . [K.M.]'s testimony on the subject of her execution of the ovum donor form was contradictory and not always credible." * * *

The Court of Appeal affirmed the judgment. * * * We granted review.

Discussion

K.M. asserts that she is a parent of the twins because she supplied the ova that were fertilized in vitro and implanted in her lesbian partner, resulting in the birth of the twins. As we will explain, we agree that K.M. is a parent of the twins because she supplied the ova that produced the children, and Family Code § 7613 (b) (hereafter § 7613(b)), which provides that a man is not a father if he provides semen to a physician to inseminate a woman who is not his wife, does not apply because K.M. supplied her ova to impregnate her lesbian partner in order to produce children who would be raised in their joint home.

The determination of parentage is governed by the Uniform Parentage Act (UPA). * * *

In *Johnson v. Calvert*, we determined that a wife whose ovum was fertilized in vitro by her husband's sperm and implanted in a surrogate mother was the "natural mother" of the child thus produced. We noted that the UPA states that provisions applicable to determining a father and child relationship shall be used to determine a mother and child relationship "insofar as practicable." We relied, therefore, on the provisions in the UPA regarding presumptions of paternity and concluded that "genetic consanguinity" could be the basis for a finding of maternity just as it is for paternity. Under this authority, K.M.'s genetic relationship to the children in the present case constitutes "evidence of a mother and child relationship as contemplated by the Act."

The Court of Appeal in the present case concluded, however, that K.M. was not a parent of the twins, despite her genetic relationship to them, because she had the same status as a sperm donor. Section 7613(b) states: "The donor of semen provided to a licensed physician and surgeon for use in artificial insemination of a woman other than the donor's wife is treated in law as if he were not the natural father of a child thereby conceived." In *Johnson*, we considered the predecessor statute to § 7613(b). * * * We did not discuss whether this statute applied to a woman who provides ova used to impregnate another woman, but we observed that "in a true 'egg donation' situation, where a woman gestates and gives birth to a child formed from the egg of another woman with the intent to raise the child as her own, the birth mother is the natural mother under California law." We held that the statute did not apply under the circumstances in *Johnson*, because the husband and wife in *Johnson* did not intend to "donate" their sperm and ova to the surrogate mother, but rather "intended to procreate a child genetically related to them by the only available means."

The circumstances of the present case are not identical to those in *Johnson*, but they are similar in a crucial respect; both the couple in *Johnson* and the couple in the present case intended to produce a child that would be raised in their own home. In *Johnson*, it was clear that the married couple did not intend to "donate" their semen and ova to the surrogate mother, but rather permitted their semen and ova to be used to impregnate the surrogate mother in order to produce a child to be raised by them. In the present case, K.M. contends that she did not intend to donate her ova, but rather provided her ova so that E.G. could give birth to a child to be raised jointly by K.M. and E.G. E.G. hotly contests this, asserting that K.M. donated her ova to E.G., agreeing that E.G. would be the sole parent. It is undisputed, however, that the couple lived together and that they both intended to bring the child into their joint home. Thus, even accepting as true E.G.'s version of the facts (which the superior court did), the present case, like *Johnson*, does not present a "true 'egg donation'" situation. K.M. did not intend to simply donate her ova to E.G., but rather provided her ova to her lesbian partner with whom she was living so that E.G. could give birth to a child that would be raised in their joint home. Even if we assume that the provisions of § 7613(b) apply to women who donate ova, the statute does not apply under the circumstances of the present case. * * *

Although the predecessor to § 7613 was based upon the Model UPA, the California Legislature made one significant change; it expanded the reach of the provision to apply to both married and unmarried women. * * *

This * * * was purposeful. * * * California intended to expand the protection of the model act to include unmarried women so that unmarried women could avail themselves of artificial insemination. But there is nothing to indicate that California intended to expand the reach of this provision so far that it would apply if a man provided semen to be used to impregnate his unmarried partner in order to produce a child that would be raised in their joint home. It would be surprising, to say the least, to conclude that the Legislature intended such a result. The Colorado Supreme Court considered a related issue and reached a similar conclusion.

In *In Interest of R.C.*, the Colorado Supreme Court addressed a Colorado statute identical to § 7613(b), which applied to both married and unmarried women. At issue were the parental rights, if any, of a man who provided semen to a physician that was used to impregnate an unmarried friend of the man. The man claimed that the woman had promised that he would be treated as the child's father. The court recognized that the Model UPA addressed only the artificial insemination of a woman married to someone other than the semen donor, adding that the parental rights of a semen donor are "least clearly understood when the semen donor is known and the recipient is unmarried." The court concluded that the statute did not apply when a man donated semen to an unmarried woman with the understanding that he would be the father of the resulting child. * * *

* * * We are faced with an even more compelling situation, because K.M. and E.G. * * * lived together and were registered domestic partners. Although the parties dispute whether both women were intended to be parents of the resulting child, it is undisputed that they intended that the resulting child would be raised in their joint home. Neither the Model UPA, nor § 7613(b) was intended to apply under such circumstances.

As noted *ante*, K.M.'s genetic relationship with the twins constitutes evidence of a mother and child relationship under the UPA and, as explained *ante*, § 7613(b) does not apply to exclude K.M. as a parent of the twins. The circumstance that E.G. gave birth to the twins also constitutes evidence of a mother and child relationship. Thus, both K.M. and E.G. are mothers of the twins under the UPA.

It is true we said in *Johnson* that "for any child California law recognizes only one natural mother." But as we explain in the companion case of *Elisa B. v. Superior Court*, this statement in *Johnson* must be understood in light of the issue presented in that case; "our decision in *Johnson* does not preclude a child from having two parents both of whom are women. . ."

Justice Werdegar's dissent argues that we should determine whether K.M. is a parent using the "intent test" we developed in *Johnson v. Calvert*. * * * [But] this case differs from *Johnson* in that both K.M. and E.G. can be the children's mothers. Unlike in *Johnson*, their parental claims are not mutually exclusive. K.M. acknowledges that E.G. is the twins' mother. K.M. does not claim to be the twins' mother *instead of* E.G., but *in addition to* E.G., so we need not consider their intent in order to decide between them. Rather, the parentage of the twins is determined by application of the UPA. E.G. is the twins' mother because she gave birth to them and K.M. also is the twins' mother because she provided the ova from which they were produced.

* * * Nothing in *Johnson* suggests that the intent test applies in cases not involving surrogacy agreements, and the dissent agrees that the linchpin of the decision in *Johnson*—that a child cannot have two mothers—does not apply here. We simply hold that § 7613(b), which creates an exception to the usual rules governing parentage that applies when a man donates semen to inseminate a woman who is not his wife, does not apply under the circumstances of this case in which K.M. supplied

ova to impregnate her lesbian partner in order to produce children who would be raised in their joint home. Because the exception provided in § 7613(b) does not apply, K.M.'s parentage is determined by the usual provisions of the UPA. As noted above, under the UPA, K.M.'s genetic relationship to the twins constitutes "evidence of a mother and child relationship."

It would be unwise to expand application of the *Johnson* intent test * * * beyond the circumstances presented in *Johnson*. Usually, whether there is evidence of a parent and child relationship under the UPA does not depend upon the intent of the parent. For example, a man who engages in sexual intercourse with a woman who assures him, falsely, that she is incapable of conceiving children is the father of a resulting child, despite his lack of intent to become a father.

* * * Justice Werdegar's dissent concludes that K.M. did not intend to become a parent, because the superior court "found on the basis of conflicting evidence that she did not," noting that "[w]e must defer to the trial court's findings on this point because substantial evidence supports them." Had the superior court reached the opposite conclusion, however, the dissent presumably again would defer to the trial court's findings and reach the opposite conclusion that K.M. is a parent of the twins. Rather than provide predictability, therefore, using the intent test would rest the determination of parentage upon a later judicial determination of intent made years after the birth of the child. * * *

The superior court in the present case found that K.M. signed a waiver form, thereby "relinquishing and waiving all rights to claim legal parentage of any children who might result." But such a waiver does not affect our determination of parentage. Section 7632 provides: "Regardless of its terms, an agreement between an alleged or presumed father and the mother or child does not bar an action under this chapter." (*See In re Marriage of Buzzanca* ["It is well established that parents cannot, by agreement, limit or abrogate a child's right to support."] A woman who supplies ova to be used to impregnate her lesbian partner, with the understanding that the resulting child will be raised in their joint home, cannot waive her responsibility to support that child. Nor can such a purported waiver effectively cause that woman to relinquish her parental rights.

In light of our conclusion that * * * K.M. is the twins' parent (together with E.G.), based upon K.M.'s genetic relationship to the twins, we * * * do not, consider whether K.M. is presumed to be a parent of the twins under § 7611(d), which provides that a man is presumed to be a child's father if "[h]e receives the child into his home and openly holds out the child as his natural child."

The judgment of the Court of Appeal is reversed.

WERDEGAR, J., dissenting.

* * *

I find the majority's reasons for not applying the *Johnson* intent test unpersuasive. The majority criticizes the test as basing "the determination of parentage upon a later judicial determination of intent made years after the birth of the child." But the task of determining the intent of persons who have undertaken assisted reproduction is not fundamentally different than the task of determining intent in the context of disputes involving contract, tort or criminal law, something courts have done satisfactorily for centuries. The expectation that courts will in most cases accurately decide factual issues such as intent is one of the fundamental premises of our judicial system. Indeed, the majority itself expresses willingness to continue applying the *Johnson* intent test to determine whether gestational surrogacy agreements are enforceable. This position leaves no plausible basis for refusing to apply the same test to determine whether ovum donation agreements are enforceable. Ovum donation and gestational surrogacy agreements are two sides of the same coin * * *. * * *

No more persuasive is the majority's suggestion that to respect the formally expressed intent of the parties to an ovum donation agreement is prohibited by the rule that parental obligations may not be waived by contract. We expressly rejected a similar argument directed against a gestational surrogacy agreement in *Johnson*. * * * *Johnson*'s intent test does not *enforce* ovum donation and gestational surrogacy agreements; it merely directs courts to consider such documents, along with all other relevant evidence, in determining preconception intent.

* * * [T]he majority [also] suggests that to apply the test outside the context of *Johnson* might shield from the obligations of fatherhood, contrary to existing law, a man who, lacking the intent to become a father, "engages in sexual intercourse with a woman who assures him, falsely, that she is incapable of conceiving children. . . " But no one * * * proposes to apply the intent test to determine the parentage of children conceived through ordinary sexual reproduction. * * *

The new rule the majority substitutes for the intent test entails serious problems. First, the rule inappropriately confers rights and imposes disabilities on persons because of their sexual orientation. * * * Although the majority denies that its rule depends on sexual orientation, the opinion speaks for itself. The majority has chosen to use the term "lesbian" no less than six times in articulating its holding. Moreover, the majority prevents future courts from applying its holding automatically to persons other than lesbians by stating that it "decide[s] only the case before us, which involves a lesbian couple who registered as domestic partners." I see no rational basis—and the majority articulates none—for permitting the enforceability of an ovum donation agreement to depend on the sexual orientation of the parties. Indeed, lacking a rational basis, the rule may well violate equal protection. *See Romer v. Evans,* (1996) 517 U.S. 620. Why should a lesbian not have the same right as other women to donate ova without becoming a mother, or to accept a donation of ova without accepting the donor as a coparent, even if the donor and recipient live together and both plan to help raise the child? * * *

Perhaps the most serious problem with the majority's new rule is that it threatens to destabilize ovum donation and gestational surrogacy agreements. * * * *Johnson*'s intent test * * * permit[ted] persons who made use of reproductive technology to create, before conception, settled and enforceable expectations about who would and would not become parents. *Johnson,* thus gave E.G. a right at the time she conceived to expect that she alone would be the parent of her children—a right the majority now retrospectively abrogates. * * * We cannot recognize K.M. as a parent without diminishing E.G.'s existing parental rights. In light of the majority's abrogation of *Johnson* and apparent willingness to ignore preconception manifestations of intent, at least in some cases, women who wish to donate ova without becoming mothers, serve as gestational surrogates without becoming mothers, or accept ovum donations without also accepting the donor as a coparent would be well advised to proceed with the most extreme caution. * * *

* * * Only legislation defining parentage in the context of assisted reproduction is likely to restore predictability and prevent further lapses into the disorder of ad hoc adjudication.

NOTES AND QUESTIONS

1.   In a companion case to *K.M.,* Elisa B. v. Superior Court, 117 P.3d 660 (Cal. 2005), the California Supreme Court held that a same-sex cohabitant who had treated her partner's twins, one of whom had Down's Syndrome, as her own, was legally obligated to support the twins despite the absence of a biological or adoptive relationship or any written support agreement. The biological mother

> agreed to have children with Respondent, and relied on her promise to raise and support her children. She would not have agreed to impregnation but for this agreement and understanding * * * The need for the application of this doctrine is underscored by the fact that the decision of Respondent to create a family and desert them has caused the remaining family members to seek county assistance * * * The child was deprived of the right to have a traditional father to take care of the financial needs of this child. Respondent chose to step in those shoes and assume the role and responsibility of the 'other' parent. This should be her responsibility and not the responsibility of the taxpayer.

Id. at 115.

The trial court concluded that the cohabitant was obligated to support the twins under the doctrine of equitable estoppel. The California Supreme Court relied on the same interpretation of the California Family Code that it utilized in *K.M.* instead of the estoppel doctrine. Its decision was unanimous.

In another companion case to *K.M.*, the California Supreme Court relied on the estoppel doctrine instead of the statute; this decision, too, was unanimous. Kristine H. v. Lisa R., 117 P.3d 690 (Cal. 2005), involved a same-sex couple who had stipulated to the parentage of the child that they planned to raise together during the biological mother's pregnancy. The couple separated two years after the child's birth and the nonparent sought to vacate the judgment. The California Supreme Court held that, because Kristine, the parent, "stipulated to the issuance of a judgment, and enjoyed the benefits of that judgment for nearly two years, it would be unfair both to Lisa and the child to permit Kristine to challenge the validity of that judgment." *Id.* at 166.

Why did the California Supreme Court rely on estoppel in *Kristine H.* and not in *Elisa B.*?

2. Under *Johnson, Buzzanca, K.M., Kristine H.,* and *Elisa B.,* what result in a case in which husband and wife utilize what they believe to be a donated preembryo and IVF to produce "their" child and it later develops that the preembryo was misappropriated by the fertility clinic? *See* Alice M. Noble-Allgire, *Switched at the Fertility Clinic: Determining Maternal Rights When a Child is Born from Stolen or Misdelivered Genetic Material*, 64 MO. L. REV. 417 (1999).

3. How do preembryo and ova donation differ from the case of a pregnant woman who has contracted to relinquish her child to an adoption agency? If the state permits the pregnant woman to change her mind after the child's birth (and all states do), does consistency require that the ova and preembryo donor also have the right to change her mind after the child's birth?

4. How do the agreements at issue in *Johnson, Buzzanca, K.M., Elisa B.* and *Kristine H.* differ from nonpaternity contracts? If nonpaternity contracts are unenforceable, does consistency require that these other reproductive agreements also be unenforceable?

5. How do the agreements at issue in *Johnson, Buzzanca, K.M., Elisa B.* and *Kristine H.* differ from an IVF agreement like that at issue in *Witten*? In a state that has adopted the *Witten* approach, does consistency require that these other reproductive agreements also be unenforceable?

6. Reconsider the arguments for and against contract as a method of parentage determination in light of the developing case law. On balance, are contracts the best means of resolving questions of parental rights and responsibilities?

3. TOWARD A LEGISLATIVE FRAMEWORK

One way to deal with the parentage issues that arise from technological conception is simply to prohibit practices likely to produce litigation. Gestational surrogacy, for example, could simply be banned. Such a prohibition would be relatively easy to enforce because IVF cannot be performed except in a hospital setting by medical personnel who will rarely be willing to risk jobs and licenses by breaking the law.

With the exception of surrogacy, however, neither the states nor the federal government have attempted to limit access to and use of reproductive technology. Given that U.S. fertility clinics are often for-profit entities, the result is access and use criteria determined largely by the whims of the marketplace: even the infertile octogenarian might find a clinic willing to assist her in becoming pregnant with donated ova.

Many other countries have taken a much more activist regulatory stance. For example, a large number of European nations require sperm banks to make AI available only to married women and those with a long-term, heterosexual cohabitant who has consented to the procedure. *See* Kathryn Venturatos Lorio, *The Process of Regulating Assisted Reproductive Technologies: What We Can Learn from Our Neighbors— What Translates and What Does Not*, 45 LOYOLA L. REV. 247 nn. 40–41 & 254–55 (1999). These laws are typically grounded in child-centered family policies and the fact that—in contrast to the case of a woman whose husband or cohabitant has consented to the procedure—use of sperm from an anonymous donor by an unmarried, noncohabiting woman virtually ensures that the child she conceives will have no legal father. Again on child-centered grounds, some countries additionally ban IVF for post-menopausal women, or post-mortem AI, or IVF with a preembryo unrelated to either prospective parent—or all of the above.

The U.K. has the most comprehensive regulatory scheme. The Human Fertilisation and Embryology Act of 1990 was drafted "to ensure that * * * sensitive issues of moral and legal complexity and dealt with in a clear framework," to "balance what are the sometimes conflicting interests of the involuntarily childless and the children of the reproduction resolution * * * [and] to mediate between the families who may benefit from research into the causes of genetically inherited disease * * * and the human embryo or foetus." DEREK MORGAN & ROBERT G. LEE, BLACKSTONE'S GUIDE TO THE HUMAN FERTILISATION & EMBRYOLOGY ACT 1990 26 (1991). The Act specifies the parental status of AI, IVF, and surrogacy participants; it contains detailed access and consent criteria; it established a governmental agency to license providers and resolve issues not dealt with in the statute itself. Although few nations as yet have regulation as comprehensive as that of the U.K., many have legislative or regulatory standards governing some aspects of IVF and AI practice; most have at least established national commissions to formulate such standards.

One factor in explaining the relative paucity of reproductive technology regulation in the United States is U.S. health care financing, reliant entirely on private insurance except in the case of the elderly and very poor. Nations that extensively regulate reproductive technology typically have more centralized health care systems that extensively regulate other aspects of medical practice as well. It thus should not surprise us that it is the United Kingdom, with arguably the most centralized European health care delivery and financing system, that has enacted the most comprehensive regulatory regime.

A. CONSTITUTIONAL REQUIREMENTS

Could the states or federal government restrict access to or use of reproductive technology? Some commentators have argued that the U.S. Constitution would preclude many of the regulatory measures adopted in other countries. The best-known advocate of this position is Professor John Robertson, who has argued that,

> if bearing, begetting, or parenting children is protected as part of personal privacy or liberty, those experiences should be protected whether they are achieved coitally or noncoitally. In either case they satisfy the basic biologic, social, and psychological drive to have a biologically related family. * * * [Thus o]nly substantial harm to tangible interests of others should * * * justify restriction [on use of reproductive technologies].

> * * *

> A main reason for presumptively enforcing the preconception agreement for rearing is procreative liberty. * * * If the couple lacks the gametes or gestational capacity to produce offspring, a commitment to procreative liberty should * * * permit them the freedom to enlist the assistance of willing donors and surrogates.

> Reliance on preconception agreements [is] * * * necessary to give the couple—as well as the donors and surrogates—the assurance they need to go forward with the collaborative enterprise.

JOHN A. ROBERTSON, CHILDREN OF CHOICE 32, 39–40, 125–26 (1994). In recent years, Professor Robertson has extended his constitutional claim, arguing that even some forms of cloning are constitutionally protected:

> The strongest case for human reproductive cloning is for persons who are not able to reproduce sexually, and who thus face the prospect of having no genetically-related children to rear. * * * Based on prevailing conceptions of procreative freedom, persons who opt for reproductive cloning in order to establish an otherwise

unavailable genetic connection with offspring should have a presumptive right to use that technique. That right should be denied them only if substantial harm from cloning to have genetically-related children for rearing could be shown.

That argument assumes that reproduction is an important source of value and meaning for individuals, and that state efforts to limit reproduction require compelling justification. It assumes that reproduction is valued because rearing and genetic transmission occur together (even though each may have personal importance separately). On this view, * * * reproduction without rearing * * * should not be protected to the same extent that genetic transmission and rearing combined are. Conversely, rearing a child with whom one has no genetic or biologic kinship connection may be important and meaningful, but it is not reproductive, and is not included at the present time in the category of rights or values that are distinctively "reproductive."

Homosexual Cloning

* * * The normative question presented by a lesbian's choice to clone rather than reproduce sexually is whether her desire to reproduce without male involvement should be respected as much as any desire to have and rear genetically-related children. If a woman's wish to have children without male gametes is valued as an essential part of her procreation, then the need to clone herself, whether she is alone or with a partner, can plausibly be viewed as a case of reproductive failure. * * * If the choice to eschew male involvement deserves respect, then the situation is very much like that of an infertile heterosexual couple who clones the husband to provide him with a genetic connection to the child whom he rears, and not because of a desire per se to replicate another individual. Lesbian cloning to avoid male involvement might then be perceived as * * * the equivalent of reproductive failure because sexual reproduction is not feasible.

It is much harder to view gay male cloning as [reproductive failure]. * * * No man, whether gay or straight, can reproduce sexually or by cloning without the assistance of a woman to provide an egg and gestate. Nor is it possible for each male partner to contribute biologically to the child in the way that each lesbian partner could, with one partner providing mtDNA and cytoplasm and gestating, and the other providing nuclear DNA. If a woman's cooperation must in any case be obtained to provide an egg and gestation, cloning alone will not enable a man to produce a child who has no alternative feasible way to have a genetic child to rear. If so, he cannot claim that cloning is necessary for him to have and rear genetically-related children because sexual reproduction also requires that help. * * *

John A. Robertson, *Two Models of Human Cloning*, 27 HOFSTRA L. REV. 609, 617 et seq. (1999).

Unsurprisingly, Robertson's view of the procreative liberties doctrine is controversial. Other commentators have argued that the Constitution imposes only modest restraints on state regulation of reproductive technology:

> * * * Robertson fails to note that the Supreme Court has never * * * required a showing of "substantial harm to tangible interests" to justify state regulation in th[e] area [of reproduction]. Indeed, in recent years, the Court has retreated from the position that "compelling" interests are required to justify government restrictions on procreational choice, holding that state abortion limitations will be upheld unless they impose an "undue burden" on a woman's right to terminate an unwanted pregnancy.

* * *

Although the evidence is scanty, it seems probable that the procreative liberties doctrine would preclude explicit state restrictions on family size; the Court has itself noted that a birth control requirement and a birth control ban were logically equivalent. A complete state ban on access to reproductive technology thus would also be constitutionally suspect, as it would deprive the infertile of their only chance at genetic parenthood. And gender-based access restrictions * * * might well constitute impermissible gender discrimination.

But given that traditional restrictions on choice of a sexual partner—prohibitions on prostitution, incest, fornication, statutory rape, adultery—all appear to be valid, there is no obvious reason why restrictions on choice of a technological "partner" would not also be valid. * * * Nor does the procreative liberties doctrine pose any apparent bar to state rules defining parental status. * * *

Our tradition of deference to individual decisions about coital procreation and parenting undeniably argues in favor of equivalent deference to individual choice in the use of technological conception. But deference does not imply abdication of any regulatory role. Indeed, parents who want to adopt, the "traditional" method of achieving parenthood noncoitally, face a maze of state regulations—imposing waiting periods before an adoption is finalized, voiding parental consents obtained prenatally, permitting rescission of parental consent within stated time limits, requiring adoption through an intermediary agency. Under Robertson's view of the procreative liberties doctrine, all of these rules should fail. Baby selling prohibitions would also be unconstitutional under Robertson's proposed standard, as it is unlikely that children whose parents want to sell them are better off remaining in parental custody.

Given the range of public values evident in this small sample of rules imposing restrictions on access to parentage * * * it is not obvious that * * * [Robertson's] perspective is preferable to the more moderate approach that our legal tradition has thus far followed, and which allows states considerable latitude both in regulating technological conception and defining the status of participants.

Marsha Garrison, *Law Making for Baby Making: An Interpretive Approach to the Determination of Legal Parentage*, 113 HARV. L. REV. 835, 855–58 (2000).

Problem 9-2:

Consider whether the state could constitutionally prohibit use of reproductive technology by men and women who do not have a consenting spouse or cohabitant. The policy basis for such a prohibition was described by Professor Krause more than twenty years ago:

> Throughout this area, the overriding social concern—in my view— is to safeguard the best interests of children. Our law emphasizes that point of view wherever children are in the picture, even in derogation of parental rights, once there is a clear conflict.

> * * *

> Let us look now at * * * the question whether artificial insemination (or fertilized egg donation) should be available to single women. * * * Having worked for the rights of the child to have two parents [in the area of child support and paternity] * * *, I am strongly opposed to single mother fertilization—and I have good company. Each child is entitled to the social and financial support of two parents—and so is the taxpayer who has quite enough single mothers and one-parent children to support. It seems ironic that the illegitimacy battle—waged and won on the idea that each child is entitled to two legal parents—may have to be refought * * * on this new territory.

> The analogy to the reality of single, divorced, or widowed mothers is—by the way—wholly inappropriate. These are real-life tragedies. It is not good practice to manufacture tragedies.

Harry D. Krause, *Artificial Conception: Legislative Approaches*, 19 FAM. L.Q. 185, 192–96 (1985).

Assume that the state legislature has adopted legislation providing that

> [n]o sperm bank shall provide sperm to a woman unless: i) she has applied for services jointly with a man who has, in writing, agreed to become the legal father of any child born as a result of the woman's artificial insemination; or ii) the sperm donor is her husband.

PARENTAGE ACT § 1210. The Act further specifies that the father "of a child born through artificial insemination shall be the man who has consented to become the legal father under Parentage Act § 1210" and provides that, in the event that no man has so consented, the "child's legal father is the donor of sperm used for conception." *Id.* at §§ 1211–12.

Parallel provisions of the Act apply to fertility clinics and disallow use of IVF unless the clinic has received written statements from a prospective mother and father, both of whom have consented to serve as the legal parents of any child born as a result of the IVF procedure. The Act also requires license revocation for sperm banks and fertility clinics that violate its provisions.

The prefatory statement to the legislation quotes Professor Krause's comments and specifies that the legislative proscription is aimed at "ensuring that each child born in this state can claim the support, care, inheritance rights, and other privileges contingent upon a parent-child relationship from two legal parents. Children conceived sexually are entitled to establish the paternity of their biological fathers; the same opportunity should be available to children conceived through reproductive technology."

A.   You are a summer associate at Reproductive Rights, a public interest organization devoted to the goal of "advancing reproductive autonomy through legislation and litigation." You have been asked to evaluate the advisability of a constitutional challenge to the new law, if the governor signs it.

1.   What constitutional arguments might RR use to challenge the Act? What arguments would be available to the government defendants? On what cases would both parties' arguments rely?

2.   What sort of plaintiffs should RR seek? What practical and evidentiary problems would each party face in litigating such a case?

3.   What is the likelihood that RR could successfully challenge the legislation?

B. You are counsel to the governor, who is trying to decide whether to sign the new legislation. What considerations support signing the legislation? Not signing it? What advice will you give the governor?

B. POSTMORTEM USE OF REPRODUCTIVE TECHNOLOGY

Most states have statutes declaring a child born to the wife of a decedent within 300 days of his death to be his legal child. These statutes are aimed at parentage determination when a child was conceived before, but born after, the biological father's death. But courts increasing confront cases involving postmortem conception with AI—or cases in which such conception is sought. One well-known case involved a testator who bequeathed his cryopreserved sperm to his girlfriend before he committed suicide. His adult children urged the court to rule that the bequest violated public policy. But the appellate court refused to do so and the girlfriend got the sperm. Kane v. Superior Court (Hecht), 44 Cal. Rptr. 2d 578 (App. 1995).

Interpreting their intestacy statutes, state courts have reached varying conclusions on whether a posthumously conceived child can inherit from the deceased parent. *Compare* Woodward v. Commissioner of Social Security, 760 N.E.2d 257, 261 (Mass. 2002) (posthumously conceived twin girls born two years after their father's death from leukemia could inherit if they could establish a genetic tie and the evidence showed that their deceased parent had consented "clearly and unequivocally * * * not only to posthumous reproduction but also to the support of any resulting child.") *with* Gillett-Netting v. Barnhart, 231 F. Supp. 2d 961 (D. Ariz. 2002) (posthumously conceived child could not inherit from deceased parent under Arizona law). *See also In re* Estate of Kolacy, 753 A.2d 1257 (N.J. Super. Ch. Div. 2000).

The United States Supreme Court unanimously upheld the Social Security Administration's denial of Social Security survivor benefits to Florida twins conceived through in vitro fertilization eighteen months after their father died of cancer. According to SSA, children are entitled to benefits from a wage earner who dies if they qualify for inheritance under state law. Florida does not allow a child to inherit unless the child was conceived while the deceased parent was alive. So the twins did not qualify. Astrue v. Capato ex rel. B.N.C., 132 S. Ct. 2021 (2012).

The litigated cases represent only the tip of the postmortem conception iceberg. Both medical journals and the popular press report requests for postmortem sperm retrieval in increasing numbers. But in contrast to *Hecht* and *Woodward*, most requests follow the decedent's sudden death; they thus do not rely on his written, or even explicit, consent. Because there is no federal or state law on postmortem sperm retrieval, individual physicians and hospitals are now free to honor such a request—or to deny it. Some medical institutions have adopted policies against "sperm harvesting" without explicit consent from the decedent:

> The ethics committee (EC) at the University of Washington has addressed posthumous reproduction in the context of requests for gamete harvesting after death. The EC felt that * * * it was essential to confirm that the deceased clearly wanted to have his sperm or her eggs harvested and a child conceived after his/her death. The EC required that this desire be demonstrated in the form of an explicit written consent. Although it was recognized that written consent would rarely, if ever, be present in the event of accidental death, the issues seemed grave enough that these restrictions were considered reasonable by the medical providers.

> What may seem like a simple and altruistic request has many complex ramifications. A conservative stance limiting this practice seems reasonable when all the considerations are examined. The ultimate result of these activities could be the creation of a new life, and the potential for misunderstanding and harm appears to be too great where the deceased has not specifically expressed the desire to procreate after death.

Michael R. Soules, *Commentary: Posthumous Harvesting of Gametes—A Physician's Perspective*, 27 J. L. MED & ETHICS 362, 363 (1999). But other institutions have acceded to relative request without any indication of the decedent's wishes. *See* Carson Strong, *Ethical and Legal Aspects of Sperm Retrieval after Death or Persistent Vegetative State*, 27 J. L. MED. & ETHICS 347, 348–50 (1999) (noting that "at least twenty-six sperm retrievals after death or PVS have been performed without explicit prior or reasonably inferred consent; and with the publicity this issue is receiving, we can expect this number to increase").

> Outside the United States, many countries have prohibited postmortem sperm retrieval without decedent consent:

> Most of the legislation * * * prohibits the use of the sperm of a deceased man. However, some countries also address the newer issue of use of the eggs of a deceased woman or the use of embryos when one member of the couple dies. The Law Reform Commission of Canada in its Medically Assisted Procreation Working Paper recommended that any children born as a result of post-mortem use of gametes or embryos not be permitted to inherit unless the decedent contributor specifically so provided in his or her will.

Lorio, *supra*, at 264–65.

UPA (2002) takes no position on postmortem sperm retrieval but does provide that a deceased individual is not a parent of * * * [a] child [conceived postmortem using reproductive technology] unless the deceased spouse consented in a record that if assisted reproduction were to occur after death, the deceased individual would be a parent of the child.

UPA (2002) § 707.

Problem 9-3:

Evaluate the constitutionality of laws forbidding postmortem sperm and ova retrieval without explicit written consent: What arguments would be available to a widow or widower who wished to challenge such a prohibition? What arguments would be available to the government defendants? On what cases would both parties' arguments rely? What practical and evidentiary problems would each party face in litigating such a case? On balance, what is the likelihood that such a challenge would be successful?

CHAPTER 10

CHILD, PARENT, AND STATE: RIGHTS AND OBLIGATIONS

■ ■ ■

The Power, then, that Parents have over their Children, arises from that Duty which is incumbent on them, to take care of their Offspring, during the imperfect state of Childhood. To inform the Mind, and govern the Actions of their yet ignorant Nonage, till reason shall take its place, and ease them of that Trouble, is what the Children want, and the Parents are bound to.

JOHN LOCKE, THE SECOND TREATISE ON GOVERNMENT § 58

I'm a goddamned minor.

Holden Caulfield, J.D. SALINGER, THE CATCHER IN THE RYE

1. CHILDREN'S RIGHTS AND LEGAL STATUS

Consider the case of Gregory Kingsley, twelve years of age, the oldest child of Ralph and Rachel Kingsley. Gregory's parents separated when he was four. For most of the next five years, Gregory lived with his father, who suffered from a severe substance abuse problem. After investigation led the State Department of Health and Human Resources (HRS) to conclude that Gregory was being neglected, he was removed from his father's care and placed with his mother. But only five months later, when Gregory was still nine, his mother voluntarily placed him and his brother Jeremiah in foster care. Gregory remained in foster care for almost a year, then was returned to his mother. Less than three months later, Gregory was returned to foster care after Mrs. Kingsley told state authorities that she could no longer cope with her children. Mrs. Kingsley, like her husband, suffered from a substance abuse problem; she was also involved in abusive adult relationships and paid little attention to her children.

After returning to foster care, HRS placed Gregory at the Lake County Boys Ranch. His mother executed a performance agreement requiring her to take steps to cure the problems that had led to Gregory's placement. But Mrs. Kingsley failed to comply with the agreement and requested that her visits with Gregory cease. Accordingly, HRS transferred the case to its adoption unit. Later that year, Gregory, now eleven, was placed with the Russ family. Mr. Russ was an attorney who specialized in the representation of children; Mrs. Russ was a homemaker. They had several children of their own.

Three months later, HRS informed Mr. and Mrs. Russ that it would soon file a petition to terminate Gregory's parents' rights so that they could adopt him. Gregory was elated. But six weeks later, without explanation, HRS reversed its decision and decided to attempt another reunification with Gregory's parents. Gregory reacted to the new plan by threatening to run away. Mr. Russ suggested to Gregory that he might have "certain legal and Constitutional rights which, although not fully recognized presently under the law, may be obtainable for children." Gregory then consulted Jerri Blair, an attorney and acquaintance of Mr. Russ, who agreed to sue on Gregory's behalf to terminate his parents' rights; Mr. Russ agreed to serve as co-counsel.

Shortly after Ms. Blair filed an action seeking termination of Mr. and Mrs. Kingsley's parental rights, Gregory's father agreed to voluntarily relinquish his rights. Gregory's mother did not. HRS entered the case and argued that Gregory had no right either to select his own attorney or to file an action to terminate his parents' rights.

The decision of the appellate court follows. As you read it, consider the larger questions: What are the rights of parents and children? What is the source of these rights and how are they forfeited? When should the state intervene on behalf of the child or to support parental authority? These are the questions with which this chapter is concerned.

KINGSLEY V. KINGSLEY

Florida Court of Appeals, 1993.
623 So. 2d 780.

DIAMANTIS, JUDGE.

Rachel Kingsley, the natural mother of Gregory, a minor child, appeals the trial court's final orders terminating her parental rights based upon findings of abandonment and neglect, and granting the petition for adoption filed by Gregory's foster parents, George and Elizabeth Russ.

* * *

1. Capacity: Rachel contends that the trial court erred in holding that Gregory has the capacity to bring a termination of parental rights

proceeding in his own right. Specifically, Rachel argues that the disability of nonage prevents a minor from initiating or maintaining an action for termination of parental rights. We agree.

Capacity to sue means the absence of a legal disability which would deprive a party of the right to come into court. * * * Courts historically have recognized that unemancipated minors do not have the legal capacity to initiate legal proceedings in their own names. * * *

The necessity of a guardian ad litem or next friend * * * to represent a minor is required by the orderly administration of justice and the procedural protection of a minor's welfare * * *. [T]he fact that a minor is represented by counsel, in and of itself, is not sufficient.

* * *

This disability of nonage has been described as procedural, rather than jurisdictional, in character because if a minor mistakenly brings an action in his own name such defect can be cured by the subsequent appointment of a next friend or guardian ad litem. Thus, the concept of capacity determines the procedure which a minor must invoke in order to pursue a cause of action. * * *

As a general rule, states "may require a minor to wait until the age of majority before being permitted to exercise legal rights independently." *Bellotti v. Baird*, 443 U.S. 622, 650 (1979). Objective criteria, such as age limits, although inevitably arbitrary, are not unconstitutional unless they unduly burden the minor's pursuit of a fundamental right. Gregory's lack of capacity due to nonage is a procedural, not substantive, impediment which minimally restricts his right to participate as a party in proceedings brought to terminate the parental rights of his natural parents; therefore, we conclude that this procedural requirement does not unduly burden a child's fundamental liberty interest to be "free of physical and emotional violence at the hands of his . . . most trusted caretaker."

Although we conclude that the trial court erred in allowing Gregory to file the petition in his own name because Gregory lacked the requisite legal capacity, this error was rendered harmless by the fact that separate petitions for termination of parental rights were filed on behalf of Gregory by the foster father, the guardian ad litem, HRS, and the foster mother. * * *

HARRIS C.J., concurring in part, dissenting in part.

* * * I concur with the majority holding that so long as the parents do nothing to forfeit their fundamental liberty interest in the care, custody and management of their child, no one (including the child) can interfere with that interest. While the child has the right not to be abused, neglected or abandoned, there is no right to change parents simply because the child

finds substitutes that he or she likes better or who can provide a better standard of living.

Florida does not recognize "no-fault" termination of parental rights. That is why the focus in a termination case is (and must be), at least in the first analysis, on the alleged misconduct of the biological parent or parents which would authorize termination of parental rights. Termination of parental rights requires a two step analysis. First, did the parents do something that the State has determined to be sufficiently egregious to permit forfeiture of their right to continue as parents (abuse, neglect, abandonment, voluntary consent to adoption). Unless the answer to this first question is affirmative, the second step in the analysis (the best interest of the child) is unnecessary. Because of the trial strategy employed by the attorneys for the child in this case, the trial court failed to keep these steps separated.

One artful maneuver which attracted the attention of the media (and distracted the court) was the filing of this cause as a declaratory action * * * in the name of the child (as opposed to next friend, etc.) and joining the proposed adoptive parents as parties in interest in the action for declaratory relief. * * * [T]he focus was shifted to a comparison of this troubled biological mother (a single parent) with the prospective adoptive parents (a lawyer and his wife) to determine which could provide the child a better life. The mother could not win this contest. The alleged misconduct of the biological mother ceased to be an issue independent of (except as a condition precedent to) any consideration of the best interest of the child; instead it became an issue inextricably intertwined with the best interest of the child—and even this issue was improperly influenced by the presence and active participation of the proposed adoptive parents as parties—and with the proposed adoptive father acting as one of the child's attorneys.

I concur with the majority that there is sufficient evidence in the record to support the court's finding of abandonment. But I also urge that there is sufficient evidence in the record (and precedent) to support the court had it found no abandonment. That is why I am unable to agree that the numerous errors in this case, and the cumulative effect of them, can be disregarded as merely harmless error. * * * [T]he "best interest" factors * * * should not have been considered by the court until after the court first determined that there was abandonment. * * * Was the mother prejudiced by the manner in which this trial was conducted? It is possible that the court might have given more consideration to the mother's belated showing of interest in her son, her strong desire to accept her parenting obligations as evidenced by her willingness to expose all her blemishes to full media scrutiny, her apparent successful substantial completion of her HRS performance agreement and the recommendation by the Missouri counterpart of our HRS to return the child to his mother, if it had not been subjected to the confusion and pressures caused by the procedural irregularities of this case. It is not clear what the court would have done if the case had been presented in the proper manner. Because the procedural errors may well have affected the outcome of this case, I submit that the mother is entitled to a new hearing on the issue of abandonment under proper pleadings and confronted only by the proper parties.

The mother might lose again. But even if she did, she (and all those who have closely followed this case) would at least know that she lost on a level playing field.

NOTES AND QUESTIONS

1.   Would you classify Gregory's claimed rights as procedural or substantive? Would granting Gregory the right to bring an action in his own name affect his legal relationship with his biological and foster parents? Would it affect his social relationship with his biological and foster parents?

2.   If Gregory were granted the right to party status and empowered to choose his own attorney, who would have the obligation to pay the attorney fees and court costs he would incur?

3.   Legal capacity to sue or to retain an attorney is based on a child's emancipation. Emancipation has two aspects: it removes a minor from parental authority and ends parental obligations; it may also make the minor capable of transacting business with outsiders. Under the Restatement of Contracts, for example, "[u]nless a statute provides otherwise, a natural person has the capacity to incur only voidable contractual duties until the beginning of the day before the person's eighteenth birthday." RESTATEMENT OF CONTRACTS § 14. The most common emancipating event is attaining the age of majority (eighteen in most states). A child may also become emancipated before attaining the age of majority by getting married, enlisting in the armed forces, or becoming self-supporting. The issue of emancipation arises most often in cases where a parent's support obligation is at issue and requires judicial action. *See* Chapter 17, Section 2.

4.   The United States Supreme Court in *In re Gault*, 387 U.S. 1 (1967), found that due process required the appointment of counsel for a child in a delinquency case. The federal Child Abuse Prevention and Treatment Act provides that the states, as a condition of receiving federal child welfare funds, must implement "procedures requiring that in every case involving an abused or neglected child which results in a judicial proceeding, a guardian ad litem, who has received training appropriate to the role, and who may be an attorney or a court appointed special advocate who has received training appropriate to that role (or both), shall be appointed to represent the child in such proceedings—(I) to obtain first-hand, a clear understanding of the situation and needs of the child; and (II) to make recommendations to the court concerning the best interests of the child * * *." 42 U.S.C.A. § 5106a(b)(2)(A)(viii). In some states, the courts have held that the appointment of a lawyer for an abused or neglected child is constitutionally

required. *See, e.g., In re* Orlando F., 351 N.E.2d 711 (N. Y. 1976). But many states rely on volunteer court appointed special advocates (CASAs).

The spotty empirical evidence suggests that these children's representatives play a powerful role in determining the outcome of child protection litigation. For example, one group of researchers found that the recommendation of the child's representative is "commonly the eventual order of the court" both in settled and litigated cases and that representatives' recommendations in emergency hearings almost always determine the outcome. *See* Patricia S. Curley & Gregg Herman, *Representing the Best Interests of Children: The Wisconsin Experience*, J. AM. ACAD. MATRIMONIAL L. (1996). In a more recent study of CASA volunteers, the researchers found that, in four out of five cases, "all or almost all CASA volunteer recommendations" were accepted by the court. Michael S. Piraino, *Evaluation Research on the Effectiveness of CASA/GAL Volunteer Advocacy*, http://www.nationalcasa.org/ JudgesPage/Article_CASAevaluation_10–04.htm.

The spotty empirical evidence also suggests that children's representatives often reinforce the recommendations of child welfare officials.

> One author noted that 'in several of our site visits staff observed a tendency for the child's counsel to side with the position of the attorney for the petitioning agency.' This observation [is] * * * supported by a 1983 study of attorney GALs in North Carolina, which showed that in 88% of the cases the attorney GAL's recommendation matched that of the agency social worker. This finding prompted the authors to conclude that '[r]epresentation seemed to be a token affair, a mere procedural requirement with attorneys serving as a rubber stamp for the recommendation of the department of social services.'

Bridget Kearns, Comment, *A Warm Heart But a Cool Head: Why a Dual Guardian Ad Litem System Best Protects Families Involved in Abused and Neglected Proceedings*, 2002 WIS. L. REV. 699, 729. In Kenny A. ex rel. Winn v. Perdue, 356 F. Supp. 2d 1353 (N.D. Ga. 2005), the federal district court held as a matter of state constitutional law that children in dependency and termination proceedings have a constitutional right to counsel.

5. The appropriate role of a children's lawyer is controversial. Some commentators argue that the lawyer should *not* simply advocate the child's views:

> Children['s] * * * primary right is to remain in their parents' custody unless their parents have been inadequate. * * * If, and only if, a parent is inadequate, should the state interfere with the parents' and child's right to familial integrity. * * *

> * * * In the real world, judges rely on the advocacy of a child's lawyer. It is impossible to know, however, whether the lawyer's views advance or hinder the child's rights. Because the child's right to secure state protection is conditional, that right is wrongfully invoked when the predicate facts justifying it do not exist. If a parent abused

her child, the child has the right to be protected. But if a parent has not, the child has the right to have the case dismissed without additional intervention. When a young child's lawyer argues that the court should remove the child from her home based on the lawyer's incorrect conclusion that the parent is unfit, the lawyer has breached the child's right not to be removed.

In addition, * * * the lawyer's views on the proper result unavoidably will be the product of a host of factors that will never be the subject of review by anybody. Finally, liberating lawyers for children to advocate results they believe are best for their clients will ensure the randomness and chaos that a rational legal system would avoid whenever possible. It is eminently possible to avoid such chaos in child protective proceedings by the simple device of barring lawyers from advocating an outcome. We should be particularly willing to impose this restriction precisely because there is no assurance in the first place that the lawyer will seek the correct result. * * *

Martin Guggenheim, *A Paradigm for Determining the Role of Counsel for Children*, 64 FORDHAM L. REV. 1399, 1428–31 (1996). Had Gregory K.'s lawyer followed Professor Guggenheim's advice, what role would she have played in the termination of parental rights proceeding? If lawyers for children don't advocate an outcome, what should they do in a litigated proceeding?

6. The American Bar Association in 1996 adopted *Standards for Lawyers Who Represent Children in Abuse and Neglect Cases* (ABA Standards). The ABA Standards expressed a clear preference for appointing a lawyer who takes the role of the child's attorney. The child's attorney is "a lawyer who provides legal services for a child and who owes the same duties of undivided loyalty, confidentiality and competent representation to the child as [are] due an adult client." ABA Standards, A-1, A-2. This approach was endorsed by National Association of Counsel for Children, by a 1995 Fordham Conference on Ethical Issues and Representation of Children and a 2006 UNLV Conference on Representing Children in Families. If the child is unable or does not want to express a preference, the ABA Standards provide that the lawyer is to advocate for the child's legal interests. B-4(1) & (2).

In 2006, the Uniform Law Commission proposed the Uniform Representation of Children in Abuse Neglect and Custody Proceedings Act (URCANCPA) and amended it in 2007. The judge was given discretion to appoint either an attorney for the child or a best interest attorney who can argue for the child's best interests even if contrary to the child's wishes. A heated debate followed between those favoring the child's attorney model versus the best interests attorney approach. *Compare* Barbara Ann Atwood, *The Uniform Representation of Children in Abuse Neglect and Custody Proceedings Act: Bridging the Divide Between Pragmatism and Idealism*, 42 FAM. L. Q. 63 (2008) *with* Katherine Hunt Federle, *Righting Wrongs: A Reply to the Uniform Law Commission's Uniform Representation of Children in Abuse Neglect and Custody Proceedings Act*, 42 FAM. L. Q. 103 (2008). The

American Bar Association did not endorse the URCANCPA. Instead in August 2011, the American Bar Association passed the *Model Act on Child Representation in Abuse and Neglect Cases*. It is based on the 1996 *ABA Standards* and incorporates several provisions of the now shelved proposed URCANCPA. The most significant provision requires a judge to appoint a lawyer who "acts like a lawyer," not a best interest advocate, for every child in an abuse and neglect case. The lawyer is bound by the ABA Model Rules of Professional Conduct as is any other lawyer.

7.   Representing children in abuse and neglect cases requires lawyers to maintain a child focus. Jean Koh Peters stresses that lawyers must individualize the representation to allow maxium participation by the child. Peters has proposed a list of questions for children's lawyers to ask themselves to maintain the child focus:

a.   Am I making the best effort to see the case from my client's subjective point of view?

b.   Does the child understand as much as I can explain about what is happening?

c.   If my client were an adult, would I be taking the same actions, making the same decisions, and treating her the same way?

d.   If I treat my client differently [from adult], in what ways will my client concretely benefit? Can I explain the benefit to the client?

e.   Is it possible I am making decisions for the gratification of adults, not the child?

f.   Is it possible I am making decisions for my own gratification?

g.   Does the representation as a whole, reflect what is unique about the child?

See JEAN KOH PETERS, REPRESENTING CHILDREN IN CHILD PROTECTIVE PROCEEDINGS: ETHICAL AND PRACTICAL DIMENSIONS (3d ed. 2007). *See also* Ann M. Haralambie, *Humility and Child Autonomy in Child Welfare and Custody Representation of Children*, 28 HAMLINE J. PUB. L. & POL'Y 177 (2006).

8.   Lawyers are increasingly being appointed for children who are the subject of custody litigation. *See* Chapter 14. How, if at all, does the task of a child's lawyer in a custody contest differ from that of a child's lawyer in a child protective proceeding? Is a lawyer more or less desirable? Is a lawyer more or less likely to determine case outcome?

The notion of children's rights is a modern innovation. Under the English common law—as well as the traditional laws of most other legal systems— unemancipated minors had no rights whatsoever; parents were accorded virtually unlimited power over their child's care, education, and well-being.

Blackstone, writing in the late eighteenth century, describes the rationale for parental power and its extent.

WILLIAM BLACKSTONE, COMMENTARIES ON THE LAWS OF ENGLAND, BOOK I
Ch. 16 (1765).

2.   The *power* of parents over their children is derived from the former consideration, their duty; this authority being given them, partly to enable the parent more effectually to perform his duty, and partly as a recompence for his care and trouble in the faithful discharge of it. And upon this score the municipal laws of some nations have given a much larger authority to the parents, than others. The ancient Roman laws gave the father a power of life and death over his children; upon this principle, that he who gave had also the power of taking away. * * * The power of a parent by our English laws is much more moderate; but still sufficient to keep the child in order and obedience. He may lawfully correct his child, being under age, in a reasonable manner; for this is for the benefit of his education. The consent or concurrence of the parent to the marriage of his child under age, was also *directed* by our ancient law to be obtained; but now it is absolutely *necessary*; for without it the contract is void. And this also is another means, which the law has put into the parent's hands, in order the better to discharge his duty; first, of protecting his children from the snares of artful and designing persons; and, next, of settling them properly in life, by preventing the ill consequences of too early and precipitate marriages. A father has no other power over his son's *estate*, than as his trustee or guardian; for, though he may receive the profits during the child's minority, yet he must account for them when he comes of age. He may indeed have the benefit of his children's labour while they live with him, and are maintained by him; but this is no more than he is entitled to from his apprentices or servants. The legal power of a father (for a mother, as such, is entitled to no power, but only to reverence and respect) * * * over the persons of his children ceases at the age of twenty one: for they are then enfranchised by arriving at years of discretion, or that point which the law has established (as some must necessarily be established) when the empire of the father, or other guardian, gives place to the empire of reason. Yet, till that age arrives, this empire of the father continues even after his death; for he may by his will appoint a guardian to his children. He may also delegate part of his parental authority, during his life, to the tutor or schoolmaster of his child: who is then *in loco parentis*, and has such a portion of the power of the parent committed to his charge, viz. that of restraint and correction, as may be necessary to answer the purposes for which he is employed.

The policies described by Blackstone were successfully challenged during the late nineteenth century by the child protection movement. As the movement's name suggests, child protectionists were concerned with ensuring that children received care, not rights. Their efforts led to the first White House Conference on Children, which proclaimed that, in order to ensure a productive economy and citizenry, government should ensure each child "humane treatment, adequate care, and proper education." Proceedings of the White House Conference on the Care of Dependent Children, S. Doc. 721, 60th Cong. 2d Sess. 192 (1909). The protection movement ultimately succeeded in altering many of the legal systems and rules that affect children: child labor laws, compulsory schooling, the juvenile court, and the modern child welfare system are all products of protectionism.

The child protection movement was linked with a bold new optimism about both the human condition and state intervention. Protectionists believed that the state could—and should—play the role of a beneficent educator both toward wayward children and wayward parents. Allied with the new social work profession, protectionists argued that, when a child committed a criminal act, the state should provide rehabilitation; the goal was to help the child, not to punish him. The same approach was applied to parents. Those who could not adequately care for their children were to receive rehabilitative services while the children were in temporary placements; the goal was to reunite parent and child in a stable, caring family environment.

Children's advocates did not talk in terms of rights for children until the 1960s, a period when distrust of legal authority was high. By this point, a growing body of evidence had also established that the reality of state intervention was often far removed from the rehabilitative ideal. For example, the landmark *Gault* decision (387 U.S. 1 (1967)), in which the Supreme Court required juvenile courts to accord minors various due process protections, involved a fifteen-year-old boy who had been sentenced to an indefinite stay in a state "school" (i.e. kiddie prison) for having made a couple of phone calls "of the irritatingly offensive, adolescent, sex variety" to a neighbor. And a landmark study of the foster care system revealed that, once placed in "temporary" state care, children frequently remained there until adults while the state made no serious effort either to cure the problems that had led to placement or to sever parental rights. *See* HENRY S. MAAS & RICHARD E. ENGLER, JR, CHILDREN IN NEED OF PARENTS (1959).

Like their protectionist predecessors, children's rights advocates were initially bold and optimistic. Educator A.S. Neill argued that "children should be free to do exactly as they like as long as they don't interfere with the freedom of others" and that such "self-regulated" children would "not [be] haters; they could not possibly be anti-Semitic or racialists." A.S. Neill, *Freedom Works*, in CHILDREN'S RIGHTS: TOWARD THE LIBERATION OF THE

CHILD 127, 137–38 (1971). The Bill of Rights for Children set out by Henry Foster and Doris Jonas Freed in 1972 evidences the same bold spirit.

HENRY FOSTER & DORIS FREED, A BILL OF RIGHTS FOR CHILDREN
6 FAM. L.Q. 343, 347 (1972).

A child has a moral right and should have a legal right:

1.   To receive parental love and affection, discipline and guidance, and to grow to maturity in a home environment which enables him to develop into a mature and responsible adult;

2.   To be supported, maintained, and educated to the best of parental ability, in return for which he has the moral duty to honor his father and mother;

3.   To be regarded as a *person*, within the family, at school, and before the law;

4.   To receive fair treatment from all in authority;

5.   To be heard and listened to;

6.   To earn and keep his own earnings;

7.   To seek and obtain medical care and treatment and counseling;

8.   To emancipation from the parent-child relationship when that relationship has broken down and the child has left home due to abuse, neglect, serious family conflict, or other sufficient cause, and his best interests would be served by the termination of parental authority;

9.   To be free of legal disabilities or incapacities save where such are convincingly shown to be necessary and protective of the actual best interests of the child; and

10. To receive special care, consideration, and protection in the administration of law or justice so that his best interests always are a paramount factor.

NOTES AND QUESTIONS

1.   Legal rights may be either negative or affirmative; they may apply against one or many duty-bearers. Thus, according to one classic formulation:

> If B owes A a thousand dollars, A has an *affirmative* right *in personam* * * * that B shall do what is necessary to transfer to A the legal ownership of that amount of money. * * * If A owns and occupies Whiteacre, not only B but also a great many other persons—not necessarily all persons—are under a duty, e.g., not to enter on A's land. The latter right is a multital one, for it is one of A's class of similar, though separate rights, actual and potential, against very

many persons. The same points apply as regards A's right that B shall not commit a battery on him, and A's right that B shall not manufacture a certain article as to which A has a so-called patent.

WESLEY N. HOHFELD, FUNDAMENTAL LEGAL CONCEPTIONS AS APPLIED IN JUDICIAL REASONING AND OTHER ESSAYS 73–74 (Walter W. Cook ed. 1923).

What do Foster and Freed mean when they say the child "should have a legal right"? Affirmative or negative? In personam or multital? Against whom? In tort, contract, equity or through the criminal law? As you think about children's rights, keep these questions in mind!

2.   In 1989 the U.N. General Assembly adopted the U.N. Convention on the Rights of the Child (UNCRC), which sets out 41 articles providing rights for children. U.N.Doc. A/Res/44/25, 28 I.L.M. 1456 (1989). Among other requirements, the Convention provides that signatory states must:

3.   [i]n all actions concerning children, whether undertaken by public or private * * * authorities * * *, [make] the best interests of the child * * * a primary consideration. * * *

9.   * * * ensure that a child shall not be separated from his or her parents against their will, except when competent authorities subject to judicial review determine, in accordance with applicable law and procedures, that such separation is necessary for the best interests of the child. * * *

12.   * * * assure to the child who is capable of forming his or her own views the right to express those views freely in all matters affecting the child, the views of the child being given due weight in accordance with the age and maturity of the child. [T]he child shall * * * be provided the opportunity to be heard in any judicial and administrative proceedings affecting the child, either directly, or through a representative or an appropriate body * * *;

19.   * * * take all appropriate legislative, administrative, social and educational measures to protect the child from all forms of physical or mental violence, injury or abuse, neglect or negligent treatment, maltreatment or exploitation, including sexual abuse, while in the care of parent(s), legal guardian(s) or any other person who has the care of the child. * * *

27.   * * * recognize the right of every child to a standard of living adequate for the child's physical, mental, spiritual, moral and social development. [ ] The parent(s) or others responsible for the child have the primary responsibility to secure, within their abilities and financial capacities, the conditions of living necessary for the child's development. States Parties, in accordance with national conditions and within their means, shall take appropriate measures to assist parents and others responsible for the child to implement this right and shall in case of need provide material assistance and support

programmes, particularly with regard to nutrition, clothing and housing.

U.N. CONVENTION ON THE RIGHTS OF THE CHILD, *supra.* What, if any, arguments would the convention offer Gregory Kingsley? Would the adoption of the Convention mandate a different outcome in *Kingsley*?

The possible impact of the Convention on *Kingsley* is a theoretical inquiry because the United States is the only U.N. member that has not adopted it. Professor Krause predicted this outcome early on:

> The Convention asks * * * the State[ ] to recognize the child as an independent actor, breaking with a past that put children under the sole control of their parents. In that sense, the Convention mirrors developments in social programmes, tax policies and protective legislation of leading countries. * * *

> Ironically, the high rate of international acclaim that has accompanied the Convention may be due to the acceptability in many countries of a wide gulf between public, especially international, pronouncements and their realization in practical terms. In the United States, by contrast, a ratification of the Convention would force real change because a federal treaty would supersede state laws in an area traditionally reserved to the latter. Since that would strike at the heart of U.S. federalism, chances for ratification are not great.

Harry D. Krause, *Child Law, in* 13 INT. LIBRARY OF ESSAYS IN LAW AND LEGAL THEORY xix–xx (1992). Are there reasons beyond federalism why the United States would be reluctant to adopt the Convention? Consider this question as you read the balance of this chapter. Even though the United States has not ratified the UNCRC, it has been cited in state and federal courts, including by the United States Supreme Court in Roper v. Simmons, 543 U.S. 551, 576 (2005).

3.   Commentators disagree on the utility of children's rights as a means of advancing children's interests. Some argue that "[r]ights * * * offer the possibility of improving children's experiences by recognizing and remedying their powerlessness":

> * * * Rights have an empowering effect for they limit what we may do to others and what others may do to and for us. By empowering children, rights have the potential to minimize the victimization of the youngest members of society, even when that harm occurs privately within the family. There is a fundamental difference between respecting children because they are powerful and protecting children because they are vulnerable. Although it would be naive to think that if children had such rights they would no longer experience victimization, it is nevertheless realistic to believe that the nature and frequency of the harms inflicted upon children would change substantially if we envision children as powerful beings. Rethinking the construct of child as dependent and disabled through

a coherent account of rights would enable us to see the ways in which we have disempowered and harmed children. * * * The value of rights, therefore, relates not only to its practical worth but also to its empowering effects.

* * *

The experiences of children within the child welfare system * * * reflect the disadvantaging effects of an impoverished rights theory. Because prevention and early intervention programs are virtually nonexistent in most jurisdictions, a typical case begins with an allegation that neglect has already occurred. If the allegation is substantiated, the child can be removed from her home and placed in foster care. However, financial constraints and programmatic limitations created by policy decisions limit the nature and kind of services available to the child and her family as well as the quality of the personnel in the child welfare system. The child, therefore, is likely to experience a number of foster care placements over a period of years and may never be reunited with her parents. Her views and preferences as to her placement also are unlikely to be heard because the child is seldom represented by independent counsel. From an empowerment rights perspective, however, the child would be a respected and powerful participant in the child welfare system. Under this view, one would expect the victimization of children to decrease as they come to be seen as powerful, rights-bearing individuals. Moreover, the emphasis would be on the vindication of children's rights rather than on their vulnerabilities and dependence. This would require a commitment to improving the economic conditions of children and their families through a reallocation of our financial resources. In turn, this may reduce opportunities for the neglect and abuse of children. * * *

Katherine Hunt Federle, *Looking Ahead: An Empowerment Perspective on the Rights of Children*, 68 TEMPLE L. REV. 1585, 1596–97 (1995).

But other commentators argue that, for children, "the perspective of rights is not merely indirect, but blurred and incomplete":

Appeals to children's rights might have political and rhetorical importance if children's dependence on others is like that of oppressed social groups whom the rhetoric of rights has served well. However, the analogy between children's dependence and that of oppressed groups is suspect. When colonial peoples, or the working classes or religious and racial minorities or women have demanded their rights, they have sought recognition and respect for capacities for rational and independent life and action that are demonstrably there and thwarted by the denial of rights. * * *

* * *

The crucial difference between (early) childhood dependence and the dependence of oppressed social groups is that childhood is a stage of life, from which children normally emerge and are helped and urged to emerge by those who have most power over them. Those with power over children's lives usually have some interest in ending childish dependence. Oppressors usually have an interest in maintaining the oppression of social groups. Children have both less need and less capacity to exert "pressure from below," and less potential for using the rhetoric of rights as a political instrument. Those who urge respect for children's rights must address not children but those whose action may affect children; they have reason to prefer the rhetoric of obligations to that of rights, both because its scope is wider and because it addresses the relevant audience more directly.

* * *

* * * The great disanalogies between children's dependence and that of members of oppressed social groups suggest that the rhetoric of rights can rarely empower children. * * * Nothing is lost in debates about the allocation of obligations to children between families and public institutions if we do not suppose that fundamental rights are the basis of those obligations.

Onora O'Neill, *Children's Rights and Children's Lives*, 98 ETHICS 455, 460–63 (1988).

Reconsider the case of Gregory Kingsley. Gregory confronted parental abandonment and neglect, ineffectual attempts by state child welfare officials to cure the problems that led to his placement in foster care, and refusal by those officials to initiate parental rights termination proceedings at the point when Gregory wished. With respect to which problems are Professor O'Neill's views on children's rights more persuasive? Professor Federle's? On balance, does Gregory's case suggest that conferring rights on neglected children would benefit them? If yes, what specific rights would be helpful?

4. Why do you think the United States has been slow to recognize children's "rights?" *See* Linda D. Elrod, *Client-Directed Lawyers for Children: It Is the Right Thing To Do*, 27 PACE L. REV. 869, 875 (2007) (suggesting several reasons for lack of recognition).

2. EDUCATION

The United State Supreme Court has described education as "perhaps the most important function of state and local governments":

Compulsory school attendance laws and the great expenditures for education both demonstrate our recognition of the importance of education to our democratic society. It is required in the performance of our most basic public responsibilities, even service in the armed forces. It is the very foundation of good citizenship. Today it is a principal instrument in awakening the child to cultural values, in preparing him for later professional training, and in helping him to adjust normally to his environment.

Brown v. Board of Education, 347 U.S. 483 (1954). In Plyler v. Doe, 457 U.S. 202, 220–24 (1982), the Court noted that, while "[p]ublic education is not a 'right' granted to individuals by the Constitution[,] * * * neither is it merely some governmental 'benefit' indistinguishable from other forms of social welfare legislation":

> The stigma of illiteracy will mark * * * [children] for the rest of their lives. By denying * * * children a basic education, we deny them the ability to live within the structure of our civic institutions, and foreclose any realistic possibility that they will contribute in even the smallest way to the progress of our Nation.

See if you can reconcile these lofty pronouncements with the Court's decision in Wisconsin v. Yoder.

WISCONSIN V. YODER

Supreme Court of the United States, 1972.
406 U.S. 205.

CHIEF JUSTICE BURGER delivered the opinion of the Court.

* * *

Respondents Jonas Yoder and Adin Yutzy are members of the Old Order Amish Religion, and respondent Wallace Miller is a member of the Conservative Amish Mennonite Church. They and their families are residents of Green County, Wisconsin. Wisconsin's compulsory school attendance law required them to cause their children to attend public or private school until reaching age 16 but the respondents declined to send their children, ages 14 and 15, to public school after completing the eighth grade. The children were not enrolled in any private school, or within any recognized exception to the compulsory attendance law, and they are conceded to be subject to the Wisconsin statute.

On complaint of the school district administrator for the public schools, respondents were charged, tried and convicted of violating the compulsory attendance law in Green County Court and were fined the sum of $5 each. Respondents defended on the ground that the application of the compulsory attendance law violated their rights under the First and Fourteenth Amendments. The trial testimony showed that respondents believed, in accordance with the tenets of Old Order Amish communities generally, that their children's attendance at high school, public or private, was contrary to the Amish religion and way of life. They believed that by sending their children to high school, they would not only expose themselves to the danger of the censure of the church community, but, as found by the county court, endanger their own salvation and that of their children. The State stipulated that respondents' religious beliefs were sincere.

In support of their position, respondents presented as expert witnesses scholars on religion and education whose testimony is uncontradicted. They expressed their opinions on the relationship of the Amish belief concerning school attendance to the more general tenets of their religion, and described the impact that compulsory high school attendance could have on the continued survival of the Amish communities as they exist in the United States today. * * * Old Order Amish communities today are characterized by a fundamental belief that salvation requires life in a church community separate and apart from the world and worldly influence. This concept of life aloof from the world and its values is central to their faith. * * *

* * *

Formal high school education beyond the eighth grade is contrary to Amish beliefs, not only because it places Amish children in an environment hostile to Amish beliefs with increasing emphasis on competition in class work and sports and with pressure to conform to the styles, manners, and ways of the peer group, but also because it takes them away from their community, physically and emotionally, during the crucial and formative adolescent period of life. During this period, the children must acquire Amish attitudes favoring manual work and self-reliance and the specific skills needed to perform the adult role of an Amish farmer or housewife. They must learn to enjoy physical labor. * * * And, at this time in life, the Amish child must also grow in his faith and his relationship to the Amish community if he is to be prepared to accept the heavy obligations imposed by adult baptism. In short, high school attendance with teachers who are not of the Amish faith—and may even be hostile to it—interposes a serious barrier to the integration of the Amish child into the Amish religious community. Dr. John Hostetler, one of the experts on Amish society, testified that the modern high school is not equipped, in curriculum or social environment, to impart the values promoted by Amish society. * * * On the basis of such considerations, Dr. Hostetler testified that compulsory high school attendance could not only result in great psychological harm to Amish children, because of the conflicts it would produce, but would also, in his opinion, ultimately result in the destruction of the Old Order Amish church community as it exists in the United States today. * * *

There is no doubt as to the power of a State, having a high responsibility for education of its citizens, to impose reasonable regulations for the control and duration of basic education. *See e.g., Pierce v. Society of Sisters,* 268 U.S. 510, 534 (1925). Providing public schools ranks at the very apex of the function of a State. Yet even this paramount responsibility was, in *Pierce*, made to yield to the right of parents to provide an equivalent education in a privately operated system. There the Court held that Oregon's statute compelling attendance in a public school from age eight to age 16 unreasonably interfered with the interest of parents in directing the rearing of their offspring including their education in church-operated schools. As that case suggests the values of parental direction of the religious upbringing and education of their children in their early and formative years have a high place in our society. Thus, a State's interest in universal education, however highly we rank it, is not totally free from a balancing process when it impinges on other fundamental rights and interests, such as those specifically protected by the Free Exercise Clause of the First Amendment and the traditional interest of parents with respect to the religious upbringing of their children so long as they, in the words of *Pierce*, "prepare [them] for additional obligations." * * *

* * *

The impact of the compulsory attendance law on respondents' practice of the Amish religion is not only severe, but inescapable, for the Wisconsin law affirmatively compels them, under threat of criminal sanction, to perform acts undeniably at odds with fundamental tenets of their religious beliefs. Nor is the impact of the compulsory attendance law confined to grave interference with important Amish religious tenets from a subjective point of view. It carries with it precisely the kind of objective danger to the free exercise of religion which the First Amendment was designed to prevent. As the record shows, compulsory school attendance to age 16 for Amish children carries with it a very real threat of undermining the Amish community and religious practice as it exists today; they must either abandon belief and be assimilated into society at large, or be forced to migrate to some other and more tolerant region. In sum, the unchallenged testimony of acknowledged experts in education and religious history, almost 300 years of consistent practice, and strong evidence of a sustained faith pervading and regulating respondents' entire mode of life support the claim that enforcement of the State's requirement of compulsory formal education after the eighth grade would gravely endanger if not destroy the free exercise of respondents' religious beliefs.

* * *

We turn, then to the State's broader contention that its interest in its system of compulsory education is so compelling that even the established religious practices of the Amish must give way. Where fundamental claims of religious freedom are at stake, however, we cannot accept such a sweeping claim; despite its admitted validity in the generality of cases, we must searchingly examine the interests which the State seeks to promote * * *.

The State advances two primary arguments in support of its system of compulsory education. It notes, as Thomas Jefferson pointed out early in our history, that some degree of education is necessary to prepare citizens to participate effectively and intelligently in our open political system if we are to preserve freedom and independence. Further, education prepares individuals to be self-reliant and self-sufficient participants in society. We accept these propositions.

However, the evidence adduced by the Amish in this case is persuasively to the effect that an additional one or two years of formal high school for Amish children in place of their long established program of informal vocational education would do little to serve those interests. Respondents' experts testified at trial, without challenge, that the value of all education must be assessed in terms of its capacity to prepare the child for life. It is one thing to say that compulsory education for a year or two beyond the eighth grade may be necessary when its goal is the preparation of the child for life in modern society as the majority live, but it is quite another if the goal of education be viewed as the preparation of the child for life in the separated agrarian community that is the keystone of the Amish faith.

The State attacks respondents' position as one fostering "ignorance" from which the child must be protected by the State. No one can question the State's duty to protect children from ignorance but this argument does not square with the facts disclosed in the record. Whatever their idiosyncrasies as seen by the majority, this record strongly shows that the Amish community has been a highly successful social unit within our society even if apart from the conventional "mainstream." Its members are productive and very law-abiding members of society; they reject public welfare in any of its usual modern forms. The Congress itself recognized their self-sufficiency by authorizing exemption of such groups as the Amish from the obligation to pay social security taxes.

* * *

Contrary to the suggestion of the dissenting opinion of Mr. Justice Douglas, our holding today in no degree depends on the assertion of the religious interest of the child as contrasted with that of the parents. It is the parents who are subject to prosecution here for failing to cause their children to attend school, and it is their right to free exercise, not that of their children, that must determine Wisconsin's power to impose criminal penalties on the parent. The dissent argues that a child who expresses a desire to attend public high school in conflict with the wishes of his parents should not be prevented from doing so. There is no reason for the Court to consider that point since it is not an issue in the case. The children are not parties to this litigation. The State has at no point tried this case on the theory that respondents were preventing their children from attending school against their expressed desires, and indeed the record is to the contrary. The State's position from the outset has been that it is empowered to apply its compulsory attendance law to Amish parents in the same manner as to other parents—that is, without regard to the wishes of the child. That is the claim we reject today.

Our holding in no way determines the proper resolution of possible competing interests of parents, children, and the State in an appropriate state court proceeding in which the power of the State is asserted on the theory that Amish parents are preventing their minor children from attending high school despite their expressed desires to the contrary. Recognition of the claim of the State in such a proceeding would, of course, call into question traditional concepts of parental control over the religious upbringing and education of their minor children recognized in this Court's past decisions. It is clear that such an intrusion by a State into family decisions in the area of religious training would give rise to grave questions of religious freedom comparable to those raised here and those presented in *Pierce v. Society of Sisters*. On this record we neither reach nor decide those issues.

* * *

* * * [I]t seems clear that if the State is empowered, as *parens patriae*, to "save" a child from himself or his Amish parents by requiring an additional two years of compulsory formal high school education, the State will in large measure influence, if not determine, the religious future of the child. * * * [T]his case [thus] involves the fundamental interest of parents, as contrasted with that of the State, to guide the religious future and education of their children. The history and culture of Western civilization reflect a strong tradition of parental concern for the nurture and upbringing of their children. This primary role of the parents in the upbringing of their children is now established beyond debate as an enduring American tradition. * * *

* * *

* * * And when the interests of parenthood are combined with a free exercise claim of the nature revealed by this record, more than merely a "reasonable relation to some purpose within the competency of the State" is required to sustain the validity of the State's requirement under the First Amendment. To be sure, the power of the parent, even when linked to a free exercise claim, may be subject to limitation * * * if it appears that parental decisions will jeopardize the health or safety of the child, or have a potential for significant social burdens. But in this case, the Amish have introduced persuasive evidence undermining the arguments the State has advanced to support its claims in terms of the welfare of the child and society as a whole. The record strongly indicates that accommodating the religious objects of the Amish by forgoing one, or at most two, additional years of compulsory education will not impair the physical or mental health of the child, or result in an inability to be self-supporting or to discharge the duties and responsibilities of citizenship, or in any other way materially detract from the welfare of society. * * *

For the reasons stated we hold * * * that the First and Fourteenth Amendments prevent the State from compelling respondents to cause their children to attend formal high school to age 16. Our disposition of this case, however, in no way alters our recognition of the obvious fact that courts are not school boards or legislatures, and are ill-equipped to determine the "necessity" of discrete aspects of a State's program of compulsory education. This should suggest that courts must move with great circumspection in performing the sensitive and delicate task of weighing a State's legitimate social concern when faced with religious claims for exemption from generally applicable educational requirements. It cannot be over-emphasized that we are not dealing with a way of life and mode of education by a group claiming to have recently discovered some "progressive" or more enlightened process for rearing children for modern life. * * *

JUSTICE DOUGLAS, dissenting in part.

* * * If the parents in this case are allowed a religious exemption, the inevitable effect is to impose the parents' notions of religious duty upon their children. When the child is mature enough to express potentially conflicting desires, it would be an invasion of the child's rights to permit such an imposition without canvassing his views. * * * As the child has no other effective forum, it is in this litigation that his rights should be considered. And, if an Amish child desires to attend high school, and is mature enough to have that desire respected, the State may well be able to override the parents' religiously motivated objections.

Religion is an individual experience. It is not necessary, nor even appropriate, for every Amish child to express his views on the subject in a prosecution of a single adult. Crucial, however, are the views of the child whose parent is the subject of the suit. Frieda Yoder has in fact testified that her own religious views are opposed to high-school education. I therefore join the judgment of the Court as to respondent Jonas Yoder. But Frieda Yoder's views may not be those of Vernon Yutzy or Barbara Miller. I must dissent, therefore, as to respondents Adin Yutzy and Wallace Miller as their motion to dismiss also raised the question of their children's religious liberty.

* * *

These children are "persons" within the meaning of the Bill of Rights. We have so held over and over again. * * * While the parents, absent dissent, normally speak for the entire family, the education of the child is a matter on which the child will often have decided views. He may want to be a pianist or an astronaut or an ocean geographer. To do so he will have to break from the Amish tradition. * * * The views of the two children in question were not canvassed by the Wisconsin courts. The matter should be explicitly reserved so that new hearings can be held on remand of the case.

NOTES AND QUESTIONS

1. The trend has been to raise the age of required school attendance. Wisconsin now requires school attendance until eighteen or high school graduation.

2. *Amish Life Style and Education:* Amish life style has changed significantly since the *Yoder* decision. As recently as 1970, 61% of Amish were farmers; by 1988, only 37% were. "[T]he high cost and shortage of land and Amish proximity to urban areas and suburban development have forced many Amish, particularly the young, to take off-farm jobs, even if the eventual goal is to get a farm. In some communities less than half the Amish are now engaged in farming." Michael L. Yoder, *Occupations, in* Global Anabaptist Mennonite Encyclopedia Online, http://www.gameo.org/encyclopedia. Only a third of young Amish men under the age of 30 are now engaged in agriculture. *See* DONALD B. KRAYBILL, THE RIDDLE OF AMISH CULTURE 245 (REV. ED. 2001). The Amish who have left agriculture typically work in factories or own small businesses, which are Amish-owned but cater to non-Amish customers. As a result of this occupational shift, more and more Amish have regular contact with mainstream American culture.

Survey evidence nonetheless supports the Amish claim that education outside the community is an important factor in determining the defection decisions of Amish youth. One researcher found that defection was about 75% higher (21% as compared to 12%) for Amish youth who went to public schools as compared to those who went to Amish schools. "Marital status has the greatest impact on the younger defectors," however, among defectors under age 46, more than a third were unmarried. Thomas J. Meyers, *The Old Order Amish: To Remain in the Faith or to Leave*, MENNONITE Q. REV. at 8, tbl. 10 (1993). Other significant predictors of defection were birth order (older children were more likely to defect than younger ones), residence (those living near a mainstream American town were more likely to defect than those who did not), and the strictness of a congregation's discipline (those that were most conservative had the fewest defections). *Id.* at tbl. 9.

What new arguments would the recent alterations in Amish life style, either alone or in combination with the changed compulsory education law, offer the parties in *Yoder*? Would these new arguments likely alter the outcome? *See* Lisa Biedrzycki, Comment, *"Conformed to This World": A Challenge to the Continued Justification of the* Wisconsin v. Yoder *Education Exception in a Changed Old Order Amish Society*, 79 TEMPLE. L. REV. 249 (2006).

3.　In a concurring opinion in *Yoder*, Justice White wrote that the state has a legitimate interest in "seeking to prepare * * * [its children] for a lifestyle which they may later choose." Can this viewpoint be reconciled with the result in *Yoder*? Is it consistent with the Court's statement that "[i]t is one thing to say that compulsory education for a year or two beyond the eighth grade may be necessary when its goal is the preparation of the child for life in modern society as the majority live, but it is quite another if the goal of education be viewed as the preparation of the child for life in the separated agrarian community that is the keystone of the Amish faith?"

4.　Was the *Yoder* decision more influenced by the fact that the Amish are law-abiding, productive citizens or by the free exercise claims that they raised? In Duro v. District Attorney, 712 F.2d 96 (4th Cir. 1983), a federal appeals court upheld North Carolina's compulsory education law against a challenge by Pentecostalist parents who objected to the use of physicians and opposed "the unisex movement where you can't tell the difference between boys and girls and the promotion of secular humanism." Because of these beliefs, the parents wished to educate their children at home, using the Alpha Omega Christian Curriculum; instruction was to be offered by the mother, who lacked both a teaching certificate and teacher training. In upholding the law, the Court stressed that:

> [t]he Duros, unlike their Amish counterparts, are not members of a community which has existed for three centuries and has a long history of being a successful, self-sufficient, segment of American society. Furthermore, in *Yoder*, the Amish children attended public school through the eighth grade and then obtained vocational training to enable them to assimilate into the self-contained Amish community. However, * * * Duro refuses to enroll his children in a public or nonpublic school for any length of time, but still expects them to * * * live normally in the modern world upon reaching the age of 18.

Is there language in *Yoder* to support the *Duro* court's interpretation? To oppose it? On balance, is the *Duro* court's interpretation of *Yoder* convincing? If yes, what additional limitations on parental rights should be added to those explicitly stated in *Yoder*?

5.　Under *Yoder*, does a parent have the right to withdraw her child, on religious grounds, from sex education classes? *See* Leebaert v. Harrington, 332 F.3d 134 (2d Cir. 2003); Brown v. Hot, Sexy and Safer Productions, Inc., 68 F.3d 525, 539 (1st Cir. 1995), cert. denied, 516 U.S. 1159 (1996). From a school project requiring students to design and make a representation of a Hindu god? *See* Altman v. Bedford Central School District, 45 F. Supp. 2d 368 (S.D. N.Y. 1999). From a community service requirement? *See* Immediato v. Rye Neck School District, 73 F.3d 454 (2d Cir. 1996). From reading books about homosexual families? *See* Parker v. Hurley, 514 F.3d 87 (8th Cir. 2008). From taking surveys about sexual attitudes, alcohol use and relations between children and parents? *See* C.N. v. Ridgewood Board of Education, 430 F.3d 159

(3d Cir. 2005); Maxine Eichner, *School Surveys and Children's Education: The Argument for Shared Authority Between Parents and the State*, 38 J.L. & EDUC. 459 (2009). If *Yoder* entitles parents to withdraw their children from a particular activity, would—and should—it make a difference to the outcome if parental objections are based on educational philosophy and family values that are not religiously motivated?

6. In a series of decisions the Supreme Court has held that the Establishment Clause forbids the state from introducing religion into its educational curriculum. *See* Engel v. Vitale, 370 U.S. 421 (1962) (holding that Establishment Clause prohibits a state from authorizing prayer in the public schools); Edwards v. Aguillard, 482 U.S. 578 (1987) (invalidating Louisiana law requiring equal time for creation science); Lee v. Weisman, 505 U.S. 577 (1992) (banning nonsectarian benedictions and prayers in public school graduation ceremonies).

The most recent Establishment Clause problem involves educational voucher programs that permit, but do not require, parents to send their children to private, religious schools at state expense. State and federal courts had disagreed on the propriety of such programs. The Supreme Court, reviewing the constitutionality of a program in which 96% of voucher recipients chose sectarian schools, found no constitutional violation. Writing for the majority, Justice Rehnquist emphasized that the program "provides benefits to a wide spectrum of individuals, defined only by financial need and residence * * *. It permits such individuals to exercise genuine choice among options public and private, secular and religious." Zelman v. Simmons-Harris, 536 U.S. 639 (2002). Some states prohibit public funding of religious institutions which may preclude voucher programs that support children in religious schools. *See* Bush v. Holmes, 919 So. 2d 392 (Fla. 2006). Arizona enacted legislation allowing a tax credit for donation to school tuition organizations which used the money to give scholarships to students attending private schools. The Supreme Court found that a taxpayer group lacked standing to challenge the tax credit program. Arizona Christian School Tuition Organization v. Winn, 131 S.Ct. 1436 (2011).

7. Article 28 of the U.N. Convention on the Rights of the Child recognizes a right to primary education that is "free and compulsory." Can a child's right to education be reconciled with the parental right recognized by *Yoder*?

8. In his dissenting opinion, Justice Douglas suggests that each Amish child should be asked to "express his views." What factors might color the children's expressed preferences? Should a child have the right to decide whether to continue her education? Can such a right be reconciled with the right to a free and compulsory education? If not, how should the child's rights be balanced? How would Professors Federle and O'Neill likely respond to these questions?

Problem 10-1: Home Schooling

You are counsel to the Joint Legislative Committee on Education, which is currently considering the issue of home schooling. The state Education Law was recently amended to require all children to attend either a public school or "a state-certified private educational institution." Until the amendment, parents were free to home school their children as long as they submitted a curricular plan to local school authorities that covered subjects required in the applicable grade. The amendment has produced both a constitutional challenge and an intense lobbying effort by home-schooling families seeking its repeal.

Most states continue to permit home schooling. Indeed, a federal survey conducted in 2007 found that 1.5 million students are being home-schooled in the United States. This represented a 74% increase from the estimated 850,000 students who were being home-schooled in 1999 and a 36% increase from 2003. In 2007, parents gave as their most common reason for home schooling their desire to impart religious and moral instruction followed by concerns with the school environment. *See* Nat. Center for Education Statistics, Issue Brief, 1.5 Million Homeschooled Students in the United States in 2007 (Dec. 2008), available at http://nces. ed.gov/pubsearch/pubsinfo.asp?pubid=2009030.

There is no consensus on whether home schooling is good or bad. As a group, home schoolers tend to outperform publicly educated students at their grade level on standardized tests. *See Academic Statistics on Home Schooling*, http://www.hslda.org/docs/nche/000010/200410250.asp. However, we do not know the extent to which these differences are due to home schooling or the characteristics of the families who choose to home school. Some experts also argue that home schooling interferes with the goal of ensuring that children develop the capacity to become responsible, deliberative citizens who understand the values of a pluralistic society and have the capacity to engage in critical thinking. *See* AMY GUTMANN, DEMOCRATIC EDUCATION 1–70 (1987); Ira C. Lupu, *Home Education, Religious Liberty, and the Separation of Powers*, 67 B.U.L. REV. 971 (1987). Other experts contend that allowing parents to reject schooling that promotes values contrary to their own fosters the democratic aim of achieving a diverse and pluralistic society. *See* Stephen G. Gilles, *On Educating Children: A Parentalist Manifesto*, 63 U. CHI. L. REV. 937 (1996); Stephen Macedo, *Liberal Civic Education and Religious Fundamentalism: The Case of God v. John Rawls*, 105 ETHICS 468 (1995).

Nor is there consensus on appropriate state standards for home-schooling families. State home schooling standards thus vary widely. Ten states impose no regulations on home schooling. *See* Kimberly A. Yuracko, *Education Off the Grid: Constitutional Constraints on Homeschooling*, 96 CAL. L. REV. 123 (2008) (criticizing states with little to know regulation).

Fourteen states require parents to notify school officials that the child is being home-schooled. Sixteen states require that parents provide test scores or other evaluations. N.Y. EDUCATION LAW § 3204(2) provides that private or home education must be "equivalent" to that received in the public schools while Mississippi exempts from the compulsory education law all "legitimate home instruction programs," defined as "those not operated or instituted for the purpose of avoiding or circumventing the compulsory attendance law." MISS. STAT. § 37–13–91. While courts have recognized the authority of the state to take steps to ensure that home schooling meets minimum standards, the Supreme Court has not ruled on any aspect of home schooling and the state case law is both sparse and nonuniform. *See* Combs v. Homer-Center School Dist., 540 F.3d 231 (3d Cir. 2008) (requiring curriculum and rejecting parents' arguments that regulations unconstitutionally invaded their right of free exercise of religion); Battles v. Anne Arundel County Bd. of Education, 904 F. Supp. 471 (D. Md. 1995) (state monitoring of home-schooling program content); Brunelle v. Lynn Public Schools, 702 N.E.2d 1182 (Mass. 1998) (home visits); Crites v. Smith, 826 S.W.2d 459 (Tenn. App. 1991) (qualifications of teachers for high school age students); State v. Rivera, 497 N.W.2d 878 (Iowa 1993) (annual reports); Texas Education Agency v. Leeper et al., 893 S.W.2d 432 (Tex. 1994) (standardized achievement tests). *See also* Jack MacMullan, *The Constitutionality of State Home Schooling Statutes*, 39 VILL. L. REV. 1309 (1994); Robin Cheryl Miller, Annot., *Validity, Construction, and Application of Statute, Regulation, or Policy Governing Home Schooling or Affecting Rights of Home-Schooled Students*, 70 A.L.R.5th 169 (1999). The California Court of Appeals found that the statutory permission to home school may be constitutionally overridden to protect the child's safety when the child has been declared dependent. *See* Jonathan L. v. Superior Court, 81 Cal. Rptr. 3d 571 (Ct. App. 2008).

In 2006, the European Court of Human Rights upheld a German law forbidding home schooling. The plaintiffs, who opposed public schooling on religious grounds, argued that the German law violated their rights, guaranteed under the European Convention on Human Rights, to religious freedom and to "respect for * * * private and family life * * * "; under the Convention, public authorities may not interfere "with the exercise of this right except as is in accordance with the law and as necessary in a democratic society in the interests of national security, public safety or the economic well-being of the country, for the prevention of disorder or crime, for the protection of health or morals, or for the protection of the rights and freedoms of others." The plaintiffs also argued that the German law violated a provision of the Convention providing that "[n]o person shall be denied the right to education" and specifying that, "[i]n the exercise of any functions which it assumes in relation to education and to teaching, the State shall respect the right of parents to ensure such education and teaching in conformity with their own religious and philosophical convictions." The Court rejected all of these claims:

> * * * [T]here appears to be no consensus among the Contracting States with regard to compulsory attendance of primary schools. While some countries permit home education, other States provide for compulsory attendance of its State or private schools.
>
> In the present case, the Court notes that the German authorities and courts have carefully reasoned their decisions and mainly stressed the fact that not only the acquisition of knowledge, but also the integration into and first experience with society are important goals in primary school education. The German courts found that those objectives cannot be equally met by home education even if it allowed children to acquire the same standard of knowledge as provided for by primary school education. The Court considers this presumption as not being erroneous and as falling within the Contracting States' margin of appreciation which they enjoy in setting up and interpreting rules for their education systems. The Federal Constitutional Court stressed the general interest of society to avoid the emergence of parallel societies based on separate philosophical convictions and the importance of integrating minorities into society. The Court regards this as being in accordance with its own case-law on the importance of pluralism for democracy.
>
> Moreover, the German courts have pointed to the fact that the applicant parents were free to educate their children after school and at weekends. Therefore, the parent's right to education in conformity with their religious convictions is not restricted in a disproportionate manner. The compulsory primary school attendance does not deprive the applicant parents of their right to "exercise with regard to their children natural parental functions as educators, or to guide their children on a path in line with the parents' own religious or philosophical convictions."

Konrad v. Germany, No. 35504103, [2006] ECHR.

The Committee has heard testimony from a number of religious organizations that urge their members to engage in home schooling as well as a range of parents who want to engage in home schooling. Many of these parents are fundamentalist Christians who wish to shield their children from teaching that conflicts with their religious values. But others wish to withdraw their children from public school because of the perceived inadequacy of the curriculum or because of their child's special needs; the Committee has heard, for example, from parents of children who are particularly gifted, who have learning disabilities, who have been subject to bullying, or who have developed a school phobia.

You have been asked to advise the Committee:

A. Under the U.S. Constitution and *Yoder*, what constitutional arguments are available to home-schooling parents who challenge the current law? What arguments are available to the state? What is the likely outcome of the litigation?

B. From a legislative perspective, should the amendment be retained or abandoned: what goals does a ban on home schooling serve? What goals are served by a permissive approach? Is there some way of accommodating both sets of goals?

3. MEDICAL DECISION MAKING

A. CONSTITUTIONAL STANDARDS

PARHAM V. J.R.

Supreme Court of the United States, 1979.
442 U.S. 584.

CHIEF JUSTICE BURGER delivered the opinion of the Court.

The question presented in this appeal is what process is constitutionally due a minor child whose parents or guardian seek state administered institutional mental health care for the child and specifically whether an adversary proceeding is required prior to or after the commitment.

I.

Appellee sought a declaratory judgment that Georgia's voluntary commitment procedures for children under the age of 18 violated the Due Process Clause of the Fourteenth Amendment . . . After considering expert and lay testimony and extensive exhibits and after visiting two of the State's regional mental health hospitals, the District Court held that Georgia's statutory scheme was unconstitutional because it failed to protect adequately the appellees' due process rights. * * *

[Plaintiff] J. L. * * * was admitted in 1970 at the age of 6 years to Central State Regional Hospital in Milledgeville, Ga. Prior to his admission, J. L. had received out-patient treatment at the hospital for over two months. J. L.'s mother then requested the hospital to admit him indefinitely. The admitting physician interviewed J. L. and his parents. He learned that J. L.'s natural parents had divorced and his mother had remarried. He also learned that J. L. had been expelled from school because he was uncontrollable. He accepted the parents' representation that the boy had been extremely aggressive and diagnosed the child as having a "hyperkinetic reaction of childhood." J. L.'s mother and stepfather agreed to participate in family therapy during the time their son was hospitalized.

Under this program, J. L. was permitted to go home for short stays. Apparently his behavior during these visits was erratic. After several months, the parents requested discontinuance of the program.

In 1972, the child was returned to his mother and stepfather on a furlough basis, i.e., he would live at home but go to school at the hospital. The parents found they were unable to control J. L. to their satisfaction, and this created family stress. Within two months, they requested his readmission to Central State. J. L.'s parents relinquished their parental rights to the county in 1974. Although several hospital employees recommended that J. L. should be placed in a special foster home with "a warm, supported, truly involved couple," the Department of Family and Children Services was unable to place him in such a setting. * * * J. L. (with J. R.) filed this suit requesting an order of the court placing him in a less drastic environment suitable to his needs.

Appellee J. R. was declared a neglected child by the county and removed from his natural parents when he was three months old. He was placed in seven different foster homes in succession prior to his admission to Central State Hospital at the age of 7. * * * [At Central State] [i]t was determined that he was borderline retarded, and suffered an "unsocialized, aggressive reaction of childhood." It was recommended unanimously that he would "benefit from the structured environment" of the hospital and would "enjoy living and playing with boys of the same age." J.R.'s progress was re-examined periodically. In addition, unsuccessful efforts were made by the Department of Family and Children Services during his stay at the hospital to place J. R. in various foster homes.

Georgia Code § 88–503.1 (1975) provides for the voluntary admission to a state regional hospital of children such as J. L. and J. R. * * * [A]dmission begins with an application for hospitalization signed by a "parent or guardian." Upon application, the superintendent of each hospital is given the power to admit temporarily any child for "observation and diagnosis." If, after observation, the superintendent finds "evidence of mental illness" and that the child is "suitable for treatment" in the hospital, then the child may be admitted "for such period and under such conditions as may be authorized by law." * * * [T]he superintendent . . . has an affirmative duty to release any child "who has recovered from his mental illness or who has sufficiently improved that the superintendent determines that hospitalization of the patient is no longer desirable". * * * There is substantial variation among the institutions with regard to their admission [and review] procedures. * * * [None involve formal pre-admission hearings.]

III.

* * * It is not disputed that a child, in common with adults, has a substantial liberty interest in not being confined unnecessarily for medical

treatment and that the state's involvement in the commitment decision constitutes state action under the Fourteenth Amendment. * * *

Appellees argue that the constitutional rights of the child are of such magnitude and the likelihood of parental abuse is so great that the parents' traditional interests in and responsibility for the upbringing of their child must be subordinated at least to the extent of providing a formal adversary hearing prior to a voluntary commitment.

Our jurisprudence historically has reflected Western civilization concepts of the family as a unit with broad parental authority over minor children. Our cases have consistently followed that course; our constitutional system long ago rejected any notion that a child is "the mere creature of the State" and, on the contrary, asserted that parents generally "have the right, coupled with the high duty, to recognize and prepare [their children] for additional obligations." *Pierce v. Society of Sisters*, 268 U.S. 510, 535 (1924). *See also Wisconsin v. Yoder* [p. 510]. Surely, this includes a "high duty" to recognize symptoms of illness and to seek and follow medical advice. The law's concept of the family rests on a presumption that parents possess what a child lacks in maturity, experience, and capacity for judgment required for making life's difficult decisions. More important, historically it has recognized that natural bonds of affection lead parents to act in the best interests of their children. 1 W. Blackstone, Commentaries 447.

* * *

Simply because the decision of a parent is not agreeable to a child or because it involves risks does not automatically transfer the power to make that decision from the parents to some agency or officer of the state. The same characterizations can be made for a tonsillectomy, appendectomy, or other medical procedure. Most children, even in adolescence, simply are not able to make sound judgments concerning many decisions, including their need for medical care or treatment. Parents can and must make those judgments. Here, there is no finding by the District Court of even a single instance of bad faith by any parent. * * * The fact that a child may balk at hospitalization or complain about a parental refusal to provide cosmetic surgery does not diminish the parents' authority to decide what is best for the child. Neither state officials nor federal courts are equipped to review such parental decisions.

* * *

* * * [W]e conclude that our precedents permit the parents to retain a substantial, if not the dominant, role in the decision, absent a finding of neglect or abuse, and that the traditional presumption that the parents act in the best interests of their child should apply.

* * * The State in performing its voluntarily assumed mission also has a significant interest in not imposing unnecessary procedural obstacles that may discourage the mentally ill or their families from seeking needed psychiatric assistance. The parens patriae interest in helping parents care for the mental health of their children cannot be fulfilled if the parents are unwilling to take advantage of the opportunities because the admission process is too onerous, too embarrassing, or too contentious. * * *

The State also has a genuine interest in allocating priority to the diagnosis and treatment of patients as soon as they are admitted to a hospital rather than to time-consuming procedural minuets before the admission. One factor that must be considered is the utilization of the time of psychiatrists, psychologists, and other behavioral specialists in preparing for and participating in hearings rather than performing the task for which their special training has fitted them. Behavioral experts in courtrooms and hearings are of little help to patients.

* * *

We now turn to consideration of what process protects adequately the child's constitutional rights by reducing risks of error without unduly trenching on traditional parental authority and without undercutting "efforts to further the legitimate interests of both the state and the patient that are served by" voluntary commitments. We conclude that the risk of error inherent in the parental decision to have a child institutionalized for mental health care is sufficiently great that some kind of inquiry should be made by a "neutral factfinder" to determine whether the statutory requirements for admission are satisfied. That inquiry must carefully probe the child's background using all available sources, including, but not limited to, parents, schools, and other social agencies. Of course, the review must also include an interview with the child. It is necessary that the decisionmaker have the authority to refuse to admit any child who does not satisfy the medical standards for admission. Finally, it is necessary that the child's continuing need for commitment be reviewed periodically by a similarly independent procedure. We are satisfied that such procedures will protect the child from an erroneous admission decision in a way that neither unduly burdens the states nor inhibits parental decisions to seek state help.

Due process has never been thought to require that the neutral and detached trier of fact be law trained. * * * Surely, this is the case as to medical decisions. * * * Thus, a staff physician will suffice, so long as he or she is free to evaluate independently the child's mental and emotional condition and need for treatment.

It is not necessary that the deciding physician conduct a formal or quasi-formal hearing. A state is free to require such a hearing, but due process is not violated by use of informal traditional medical investigative techniques. Since well-established medical procedures already exist, we do not undertake to outline with specificity precisely what this investigation must involve. * * * We do no more than emphasize that the decision should represent an independent judgment of what the child requires and that all sources of information that are traditionally relied on by physicians and behavioral specialists should be consulted.

* * *

Another problem with requiring a formalized, factfinding hearing lies in the danger it poses for significant intrusion into the parent-child relationship. Pitting the parents and child as adversaries often will be at odds with the presumption that parents act in the best interests of their child. It is one thing to require a neutral physician to make a careful review of the parents' decision in order to make sure it is proper from a medical standpoint; it is a wholly different matter to employ an adversary contest to ascertain whether the parents' motivation is consistent with the child's interests.

Moreover, it is appropriate to inquire into how such a hearing would contribute to the long range successful treatment of the patient. Surely, there is a risk that it would exacerbate whatever tensions already existed between the child and the parents. Since the parents can and usually do play a significant role in the treatment while the child is hospitalized and even more so after release, there is a serious risk that an adversary confrontation will adversely affect the ability of the parents to assist the child while in the hospital. Moreover, it will make his subsequent return home more difficult. These unfortunate results are especially critical with an emotionally disturbed child; they seem likely to occur in the context of an adversary hearing in which the parents testify. A confrontation over such intimate family relationships would distress the normal adult parents and the impact on a disturbed child almost certainly would be significantly greater.

It has been suggested that a hearing conducted by someone other than the admitting physician is necessary in order to detect instances where parents are "guilty of railroading their children into asylums" or are using "voluntary commitment procedures in order to sanction behavior of which they disapprov[e]." Curiously, it seems to be taken for granted that parents who seek to "dump" their children on the state will inevitably be able to conceal their motives and thus deceive the admitting psychiatrists and the other mental health professionals who make and review the admission decision. It is elementary that one early diagnostic inquiry into the cause of an emotional disturbance of a child is an examination into the environment of the child. * * * It is unrealistic to believe that trained psychiatrists, skilled in eliciting responses, sorting medically relevant facts, and sensing motivational nuances will often be deceived about the family situation surrounding a child's emotional disturbance. Surely a lay, or even law-trained, factfinder would be no more skilled in this process than the professional.

* * *

Some members of appellees' class, including J. R., were wards of the State of Georgia at the time of their admission. Obviously their situation differs from those members of the class who have natural parents. While the determination of what process is due varies somewhat when the state, rather than a natural parent, makes the request for commitment, we conclude that the differences in the two situations do not justify requiring different procedures at the time of the child's initial admission to the hospital.

Reversed and remanded.

JUSTICE BRENNAN, with whom JUSTICE MARSHALL and JUSTICE STEVENS join, concurring in part and dissenting in part.

* * * In the absence of a voluntary, knowing, and intelligent waiver, adults facing commitment to mental institutions are entitled to full and fair adversary hearings in which the necessity for their commitment is established to the satisfaction of a neutral tribunal. At such hearings they must be accorded the right to "be present with counsel, have an opportunity to be heard, be confronted with witnesses against [them], have the right to cross-examine, and to offer evidence of [their] own."

These principles also govern the commitment of children. * * * Indeed, it may well be argued that children are entitled to more protection than are adults. The consequences of an erroneous commitment decision are more tragic where children are involved. Children, on the average, are confined for longer periods than are adults. Moreover, childhood is a particularly vulnerable time of life and children erroneously institutionalized during their formative years may bear the scars for the rest of their lives. Furthermore, the provision of satisfactory institutionalized mental care for children generally requires a substantial financial commitment that too often has not been forthcoming. Decisions of the lower courts have chronicled the inadequacies of existing mental health facilities for children. *See, e. g.,* New York State Assn. for Retarded Children v. Rockefeller, 357 F. Supp. 752, 756 (E.D.N.Y. 1973) (conditions at Willowbrook School for the Mentally Retarded are "inhumane," involving "failure to protect the physical safety of [the] children," substantial personnel shortage, and "poor" and "hazardous" conditions).

In addition, the chances of an erroneous commitment decision are particularly great where children are involved. Even under the best of circumstances psychiatric diagnosis and therapy decisions are fraught with uncertainties. * * * These * * * uncertainties often lead to erroneous commitments since psychiatrists tend to err on the side of medical caution and therefore hospitalize patients for whom other dispositions would be more beneficial. The National Institute of Mental Health recently found that only 36% of patients below age 20 who were confined at St. Elizabeths Hospital actually required such hospitalization. Of particular relevance to this case, a Georgia study Commission on Mental Health Services for Children and Youth concluded that more than half of the State's institutionalized children were not in need of confinement if other forms of care were made available or used.

Notwithstanding all this, Georgia denies hearings to juveniles institutionalized at the behest of their parents * * * on the theory that * * * [c]hildren incarcerated because their parents wish them confined * * * are really voluntary patients. I cannot accept this argument.

In our society, parental rights are limited by the legitimate rights and interests of their children. * * * This principle is reflected in the variety of statutes and cases that authorize state intervention on behalf of neglected or abused children and that, *inter alia*, curtail parental authority to alienate their children's property, to withhold necessary medical treatment, and to deny children exposure to ideas and experiences they may later need as independent and autonomous adults.

This principle is also reflected in constitutional jurisprudence. * * *

* * * The presumption that parents act in their children's best interests, while applicable to most child-rearing decisions, is not applicable in the commitment context. Numerous studies reveal that parental decisions to institutionalize their children often are the results of dislocation in the family unrelated to the children's mental condition. Moreover, even well-meaning parents lack the expertise necessary to evaluate the relative advantages and disadvantages of in-patient as opposed to out-patient psychiatric treatment. Parental decisions to waive hearings in which such questions could be explored, therefore, cannot be conclusively deemed either informed or intelligent. In these circumstances, * * * it ignores reality to assume blindly that parents act in their children's best interests when making commitment decisions and when waiving their children's due process rights.

This does not mean States are obliged to treat children who are committed at the behest of their parents in precisely the same manner as other persons who are involuntarily committed. The demands of due process are flexible and the parental commitment decision carries with it practical implications that States may legitimately take into account. * * * [But] the special considerations that militate against preadmission commitment hearings when parents seek to hospitalize their children do not militate against reasonably prompt postadmission commitment hearings. In the first place, postadmission hearings would not delay the commencement of needed treatment. Children could be cared for by the State pending the disposition decision.

Second, the interest in avoiding family discord would be less significant at this stage since the family autonomy already will have been fractured by the institutionalization of the child. In any event, postadmission hearings are unlikely to disrupt family relationships. At later hearings, the case for and against commitment would be based upon the observations of the hospital staff and the judgments of the staff psychiatrists, rather than upon parental observations and recommendations. The doctors urging commitment, and not the parents, would stand as the child's adversaries. As a consequence, postadmission commitment hearings are unlikely to involve direct challenges to parental authority, judgment, or veracity. To defend the child, the child's advocate need not dispute the parents' original decision to seek medical treatment for their child, or even, for that matter, their observations concerning the child's behavior. The advocate need only argue, for example, that the child had sufficiently improved during his hospital stay to warrant outpatient treatment or outright discharge. Conflict between doctor and advocate on this question is unlikely to lead to family discord. * * *

[Nor can t]he rule that parents speak for their children, even if it were applicable in the commitment context, * * * be transmuted into a rule that state social workers speak for their minor clients. The rule in favor of deference to parental authority is designed to shield parental control of child rearing from state interference. * * * The social worker-child relationship is not deserving of the special protection and deference accorded to the parent-child relationship, and state officials acting in loco parentis cannot be equated with parents.

NOTES AND QUESTIONS

1.   Is *Parham* based on parental rights or the belief that parents will act in the best interest of their child? Put somewhat differently, could the state adopt more formal commitment procedures without violating parents' constitutional rights? How does the court use the *Mathews v. Eldridge* test? What is the nature of the child's interest?

2.   Is *Parham* consistent with *Yoder*?

3.   During the 1970s, the Supreme Court ruled that a mentally ill adult could not be confined for involuntary treatment except on clear and convincing evidence that he was dangerous to himself or others. O'Connor v. Donaldson, 422 U.S. 563 (1975); Addington v. Texas, 441 U.S. 418 (1979). As noted by dissenting Justice Brennan, the Supreme Court also held that the grounds for commitment must be established at a full adversarial hearing at which proposed patients have the right to "be present with counsel, have an opportunity to be heard, be confronted with witnesses against [them], have the

right to cross-examine, and to offer evidence of [their] own." Can *Parham* be reconciled with *O'Connor-Addington?*

4. Under *Parham* and *O'Connor-Addington,* are admission procedures like those at issue in *Parham* constitutionally adequate for the admission of a mentally retarded adult to a state treatment facility? *See* Porter v. Knickrehm, 457 F.3d 794 (8th Cir. 2006).

5. Over time, many states have statutorily provided what *Parham* refused to recognize as constitutionally required; more than half now provide greater due process protection to juveniles than *Parham* mandates. In 1998, three states prohibited all third-party commitments of juveniles, instead requiring involuntary commitment civil proceedings like those required for adults. Eleven states followed the approach urged by the *Parham* dissent and required post-admission review of all voluntary admissions. Six states required the consent of older children and two required judicial review if a child of any age objects to commitment. At least fifteen states had laws, covering both public and private psychiatric hospitals, requiring the minimal *Parham* procedures for younger children and providing older children with "additional procedural safeguards, such as consent requirements and evaluations before and after admission." Frances J. Lexcen & N. Dickon Reppucci, *Psychology and the Law: Effects of Psychopathology on Adolescent Medical Decision-Making,* 5 U. CHI. L. SCH. ROUNDTABLE 63, 73 (1998). In spite of stricter admission requirements, the proportion of children admitted to private inpatient psychiatric facilities increased substantially in the 1980s and 1990s while admission to public facilities decreased. *See* Lois A. Weithorn, *Envisioning Second-Order Change in America's Responses to Troubled and Troublesome Youth,* 33 HOFSTRA L. REV. 1305 (2005).

IN RE GREEN

Supreme Court of Pennsylvania, 1972.
448 Pa. 338, 292 A.2d 387.

JONES, CHIEF JUSTICE.

The Director of the State Hospital for Crippled Children at Elizabethtown, Pennsylvania, filed a "petition to initiate juvenile proceedings" under the Juvenile Court Law which sought a judicial declaration that Ricky Ricardo Green (hereinafter "Ricky") was a "neglected child" within the meaning of the Act and the appointment of a guardian. After an evidentiary hearing, the [Trial] Court * * * dismissed the petition. On appeal, the Superior Court unanimously reversed and remanded the matter * * *. We granted allocatur.

Ricky was born on September 10, 1955, to Nathaniel and Ruth Green. He lives with his mother as his parents are separated and the father pays support pursuant to a court order. Ricky has had two attacks of poliomyelitis which have generated problems of obesity and, in addition, Ricky now suffers from paralytic scoliosis (94% curvature of the spine).

Due to this curvature of the spine, Ricky is presently a "sitter," unable to stand or ambulate due to the collapse of his spine; if nothing is done, Ricky could become a bed patient. Doctors have recommended a "spinal fusion" to relieve Ricky's bent position, which would involve moving bone from Ricky's pelvis to his spine. Although an orthopedic specialist testified, "there is no question that there is danger in this type of operation," the mother did consent conditionally to the surgery. The condition is that, since the mother is a Jehovah's Witness who believes that the Bible proscribes any blood transfusions which would be necessary for this surgery, she would not consent to any blood transfusions. Initially, we must recognize that, while the operation would be beneficial, there is no evidence that Ricky's life is in danger or that the operation must be performed immediately. Accordingly, we are faced with the situation of a parent who will not consent to a dangerous operation on her minor son requiring blood transfusions solely because of her religious beliefs.

By statute, a "neglected child"—"a child whose parent * * * neglects or refuses to provide proper or necessary * * * medical or surgical care"—may be committed "to the care, guidance and control of some respectable citizen of good moral character * * *" appointed by the court. The guardian appointed by the court may, with the court's approval, commit the child to a "crippled children's home or orthopaedic hospital or other institution" for treatment. Thus, it has been held that a child whose parent views smallpox vaccination as "harmful and injurious" may be considered a "neglected child." On the other hand, *In re Tuttendario*, 21 Pa. Dist. 561 (Q.S. Phila. 1912), held that surgery on a seven-year-old male to cure rachitis would not be ordered over the parents' refusal due to fear of the operation. While these statutes could be construed to cover the facts of this appeal, we cannot accept the Commonwealth's construction if it abridges the Free Exercise clause of the First Amendment. * * *

In our view, the penultimate question presented by this appeal is whether the state may interfere with a parent's control over his or her child in order to enhance the child's physical well-being when the child's life is in no immediate danger and when the state's intrusion conflicts with the parents' religious beliefs. Stated differently, does the State have an interest of sufficient magnitude to warrant the abridgment of a parent's right to freely practice his or her religion when those beliefs preclude medical treatment of a son or daughter whose life is not in immediate danger? We are not confronted with a life or death situation * * * [in this case]. Nor is there any question in the case at bar of a parent's omission or neglect for non-religious reasons. * * *

Our research disclosed only two opinions on point; both are from the New York Court of Appeals but the results differ. In *Matter of Seiferth*, 309 N.Y. 80, 127 N.E.2d 820 (1955), the State of New York sought the appointment of a guardian for a "neglected child", a fourteen-year-old boy with a cleft palate and harelip. The father's purely personal philosophy, "not classified as religion," precluded any and all surgery as he believed in mental healing; moreover, the father had "inculcated a distrust and dread of surgery in the boy since childhood." The boy was medically advised and the Children's Court judge interviewed both the boy and his father in chambers. The trial judge concluded that the operation should not be performed until the boy agreed. After reversal by the Appellate Division, Fourth Department, the Court of Appeals, by a four-to-three vote, reinstated the order of the Children's Court. The primary thrust of the opinion was the child's antagonism to the operation and the need for the boy's cooperation for treatment; since the Children's Court judge saw and heard the parties involved and was aware of this aspect, the Court of Appeals decided that the discretion of the Children's Court judge should be affirmed.

On facts virtually identical to this appeal, the Family Court of Ulster County ordered a blood transfusion. *In re Sampson*, 65 Misc. 2d 658, 317 N.Y.S.2d 641 (1970). Kevin Sampson, fifteen years old, suffered from Von Recklinghausen's disease which caused a massive disfigurement of the right side of his face and neck. While the incurable disease posed no immediate threat to his life, the dangerous surgery requiring blood transfusions would improve "not only the function but the appearance" of his face and neck. It should also be noted that all physicians involved counseled delay until the boy was old enough to decide since the surgical risk would decrease as the boy grew older. The Family Court judge ruled in an extensive opinion that the State's interest in the child's health was paramount to the mother's religious beliefs. That court further decided not to place this difficult decision on the boy and to order an immediate operation, thereby preventing psychological problems. On appeal, the Appellate Division, Third Department, unanimously affirmed the order [and] * * * rejected the argument that "State intervention is permitted only where the life of the child is in danger by a failure to act [as] a much too restricted approach." * * * [T]he Court of Appeals * * * affirmed per curiam * * * but added two observations: (1) the *Seiferth* opinion turned upon the question of a court's discretion and not the existence of its power to order surgery in a non-fatal case, and (2) religious objections to blood transfusions do not "present a bar at least where the transfusion is necessary to the success of the required surgery."

With all deference to the New York Court of Appeals, we disagree with the second observation in a non-fatal situation and express no view of the propriety of that statement in a life or death situation. If we were to describe this surgery as "required," like the Court of Appeals, our decision would conflict with the mother's religious beliefs. Aside from religious considerations, one can also question the use of that adjective on medical grounds since an orthopedic specialist testified that the operation itself was dangerous. Indeed, one can question who, other than the Creator, has the right to term certain surgery as "required." This fatal/non-fatal distinction also steers the courts of this Commonwealth away from a medical and philosophical morass: if spinal surgery can be ordered, what about a hernia or gall bladder operation or a hysterectomy? The problems created by *Sampson* are endless. We are of the opinion that as between a parent and the state, the state does not have an interest of sufficient magnitude outweighing a parent's religious beliefs when the child's life is *not immediately imperiled* by his physical condition.

Unlike *Yoder* and *Sampson*, our inquiry does not end at this point since we believe the wishes of this sixteen-year-old boy should be ascertained; the ultimate question, in our view, is whether a parent's religious beliefs are paramount to the possibly adverse decision of the child. * * * While the record before us gives no indication of Ricky's thinking, it is the child rather than the parent in this appeal who is directly involved which thereby distinguishes *Yoder's* decision not to discuss the beliefs of the parents vis-a-vis the children. In *Sampson*, the Family Court judge decided not to "evade the responsibility for a decision now by the simple expedient of foisting upon this boy the responsibility for making a decision at some later day." While we are cognizant of the realistic problems of this approach * * *, we believe that Ricky should be heard.

It would be most anomalous to ignore Ricky in this situation when we consider the preference of an intelligent child of sufficient maturity in determining custody. Moreover, we have held that a child of the same age can waive constitutional rights and receive a life sentence. Indeed, minors can now bring a personal injury action in Pennsylvania against their parents. We need not extend this litany of the rights of children any further to support the proposition that Ricky should be heard. The record before us does not even note whether Ricky is a Jehovah's Witness or plans to become one. We shall, therefore, reserve any decision regarding a possible parent-child conflict and remand the matter for an evidentiary hearing similar to the one conducted in *Seiferth* in order to determine Ricky's wishes.

The order of the Superior Court is reversed and the matter remanded to the Court of Common Pleas * * * for proceedings consistent with the views expressed in this opinion. * * *

EAGEN, JUSTICE (dissenting).

* * * I would affirm the order of the Superior Court. * * *

I * * * do not agree with the emphasis the majority places on the fact this is not a life or death situation. The statute with which we are dealing does not contain any such language, nor do I find support for this position in the case law (note the use of the word health in the *Yoder* and *Prince* opinions). The statute in pertinent part states:

"A child whose parent * * * neglects or refuses to provide *proper or necessary* subsistence, education, *medical or surgical care, or other care necessary for his or her health * * *.*"

The statute only speaks in terms of "health", not life or death. If there is a substantial threat to health, then I believe the courts can and should intervene to protect Ricky. By the decision of this Court today, this boy may never enjoy any semblance of a normal life which the vast majority of our society has come to enjoy and cherish.

Lastly, * * * I do not believe that sending the case back to allow Ricky to be heard is an adequate solution. We are herein dealing with a young boy who has been crippled most of his life, consequently, he has been under the direct control and guidance of his parents for that time. To now presume that he could make an independent decision as to what is best for his welfare and health is not reasonable. Moreover, the mandate of the Court presents this youth with a most painful choice between the wishes of his parents and their religious convictions on the one hand, and his chance for a normal healthy life on the other hand. We should not confront him with this dilemma.

On the basis of the foregoing, I would affirm the Order of the Superior Court.

NOTES AND QUESTIONS

1.   Is the *Green* majority or dissent right about constitutional standards? What cases are controlling?

2.   Should a parent's religious objection to medical care be treated differently than an objection based on the risks and benefits of the proposed treatment? This question is complicated by "religious accommodation" statutes that, in more than forty states, establish a defense to a neglect action and/or criminal prosecution for parental failure to provide medical treatment based on a good-faith religious objection. *See* Eric W. Treene, Note, *Prayer-Treatment Exemptions to Child Abuse and Neglect Statutes*, 30 HARV. J. LEGIS. 135, 140–141. Some courts have upheld criminal prosecutions despite such laws; others have set aside convictions on due process grounds. *Compare* Walker v. Superior Court, 763 P.2d 852 (Cal. 1988), cert. denied 491 U.S. 905 (1989) (upholding prosecution) *with* Commonwealth v. Twitchell, 617 N.E.2d 609 (Mass. 1993) (setting aside involuntary manslaughter conviction).

Based on the "belie[f] that all children deserve effective medical treatment that is likely to prevent substantial harm or suffering or death," the American Academy of Pediatrics has called for the repeal of religious accommodation laws. *See* Am. Academy of Pediatrics Committee on Bioethics, *Religious Objections to Medical Care*, 99 PEDIATRICS 279 (1997). Could a religious accommodation law withstand a challenge under the equal protection clause? What arguments would be available to the state and to children contesting the law? Which arguments are more persuasive? *See* State v. Miskimens, 490 N.E.2d 931 (Ohio 1984); James G. Dwyer, *The Children We Abandon: Religious Exemptions to Child Welfare and Education Laws as Denials of Equal Protection to Children of Religious Objectors*, 75 N.C. L. REV. 1321 (1996).

3.   A survey of published opinions dealing with parent-physician disagreement over the appropriate medical treatment of a child found 50 opinions dealing with 66 children in 20 states. Overall, physicians prevailed at the trial level in 44 of the 50 disputes studied (88%). Physicians were more likely to prevail in religion-based disputes than in other cases (27 of 30). *See* Derry Ridgway, *Court-Mediated Disputes Between Physicians and Families over the Medical Care of Children,* 158 ARCH. PEDIATRIC ADOLESCENT MED. 891 (2004).

4.   Article 24 of the U.N. Convention on the Rights of the Child requires states to "recognize the right of the child to the enjoyment of the highest attainable standard of health and to facilities for the treatment of illness and rehabilitation of health. States Parties shall strive to ensure that no child is deprived of his or her right of access to such health care services." Would the Convention permit the *Green* holding?

5.   *Green and the Parent-Child Tie:* The most prominent theoretical argument for the decision-making standard utilized in *Green* was developed by law professor Joseph Goldstein, psychoanalyst Anna Freud, and psychiatrist Albert Solnit, relying on the "psychological parent" concept you read about in *J.M.P.* [Chapter 8]. Goldstein, Freud, and Solnit argue that the risks inherent in state intervention are sufficiently grave that a parent's medical decisions should be overruled only when:

a.   Medical experts agree that treatment is nonexperimental and appropriate for the child; and

b.   Denial of that treatment will result in the Child's death; and

c.   The treatment can reasonably be expected to result in a chance for the Child to have normal healthy growth or a life worth living.

JOSEPH GOLDSTEIN, ANNA FREUD, ALBERT J. SOLNIT, BEFORE THE BEST INTERESTS OF THE CHILD 194 (1979). Freedom from state intrusion, Goldstein et al. urge, is essential both to "provide parents with an uninterrupted opportunity to meet the developing physical and emotional needs of their child" and to "safeguard the continuing maintenance of these family ties—of psychological parent-child relationships—once they have been established." *Id.* at 10. Goldstein et al. also argue that state child protection policy should focus on safeguarding the psychological parent-child relationship because such a relationship is the crucial element necessary to ensure the child's "healthy growth and development":

[O]ngoing interactions between parents and children become for each child the starting point for an all-important line of development that leads toward adult functioning. What begins as the experience of physical contentment or pleasure that accompanies bodily care develops into a primary attachment to the person who provides it. This again changes into the wish for a parent's constant presence irrespective of physical wants. Helplessness requires total care and over time is transformed into the need or wish for approval and love. It fosters the desire to please by compliance with a parent's wishes. It provides a developmental base upon which the child's responsiveness to educational efforts rests. Love for the parents leads to identification with them, a fact without which impulse control and socialization would be deficient. Finally, after the years of childhood comes the prolonged and in many ways painful adolescent struggle to attain a separate identity with physical, emotional, and moral self-reliance.

These complex and vital developments require the privacy of family life under the guardianship by parents who are autonomous. * * * When family integrity is broken or weakened by state intrusion, * * * [the child's] needs are thwarted and his belief that his parents are omniscient and all-powerful is shaken prematurely. The effect on the child's developmental progress is invariably detrimental.

* * *

* * * [T]he law does not have the capacity to supervise the fragile, complex interpersonal bonds between child and parent. * * * The legal system has neither the resources nor the sensitivity to respond to a growing child's ever-changing needs and demands. It does not have the capacity to deal on an individual basis with the consequences of its decisions, or to act with the deliberate speed that is required by a child's sense of time.

Id. at 8–9, 11–12.

Critics of Goldstein, Freud, and Solnit have noted that there is no research evidence showing that children's developmental progress is invariably harmed by state intrusion into family life. *See* Marsha Garrison, *Child Welfare Decision Making: In Search of the Least Drastic Alternative*, 75 GEO. L.J. 1745, 1762–66 (1987). To the contrary, intrusion is most likely when children are at risk of removal from their homes due to parental abuse or neglect, and a number of studies have found that, when families receive intensive preservation services, children experience fewer days in placement, more case closings, and shorter times in placement. *See* Jacquelyn McCroskey & William Meezan, *Family-Centered Services: Approaches and Effectiveness*, 8 FUTURE OF CHILDREN 54, 63–64 (Spring, 1998).

Despite the skimpy evidentiary basis for their conclusions, Goldstein, Freud, and Solnit's concept of the "psychological parent" has had a major impact on both judicial and legislative decision making in the area of child custody and visitation. But their proposal to narrow the statutory grounds for medical neglect has not been widely adopted. Can you think of any reasons why?

6.   *Green and the Child's Right to an "Open Future":* Some commentators have argued that the state has an obligation to protect the child's "open future." *See* Joel Feinberg, *The Child's Right to an Open Future, in* WHOSE CHILD? CHILDREN'S RIGHTS, PARENTAL AUTHORITY, AND STATE POWER 124 (WILLIAM AIKEN & HUGH LAFOLLETT, EDS., 1980). Ensuring the child's open future requires overruling parental judgments that would deprive the child of rights that would be available to her as an adult but which are not available to her as a child:

> A striking example is the right to reproduce. A young child cannot physically exercise that right, and a teenager might lack the legal and moral grounds on which to assert such a right. But clearly the child, when he or she attains adulthood, will have that right, and therefore the child now has the right not to be sterilized, so that the child may exercise that right in the future. * * * [M]orally the child is first and foremost an end in herself. * * * Parental practices that close exits virtually forever are insufficiently attentive to the child as end in herself. By closing off the child's * * * open future, they define the child as an entity who exists to fulfill parental hopes and dreams, not her own.

Dena Davis, *Genetic Dilemmas and the Child's Right to an Open Future,* 27 HASTINGS CTR. RPT. 7, 9, 12 (Mar. 1997). Like Goldstein et al., Professor Davis does not offer an empirical basis for the proposition that the state should protect the child's open future; the claim simply assumes that harm comes from "practices that close exits virtually forever." Not only is the evidence lacking, but it is not altogether obvious which parental actions "close exits." Reconsider Wisconsin v. Yoder, for example. Schooling undeniably has a major impact on life prospects; but given that it would be possible for the child to make up the lost schooling later on, is it possible to fairly describe a parental decision to end schooling as one that "close[s] exits virtually forever"?

7.   *Open Future v. Parent-Child Tie:* How (if it is possible to predict) would Davis and Goldstein et al. resolve these cases:

a.   *Green;*

b.   *Sampson;*

c.   *Parham;*

d.   Parental refusal to treat a three-year-old child's ear infection with antibiotics.

Can the state both protect the parent-child relationship, as suggested by Goldstein et al., and protect the child's open future, as suggested by Professor Davis? If not, how should the two goals be balanced?

Problem 10-2:

You are an associate counsel to the Children's Rights Project (CRP) and have been asked to evaluate the possibility of a lawsuit challenging religion-based exemptions to state vaccination requirements. In 2002, forty-eight states provided religion-based exemptions to vaccinations and sixteen provided exemptions for philosophical reasons. *See* Janna C. Merrick, *Spiritual Healing, Sick Kids and the Law: Inequities in the American Healthcare System*, 29 AM. J. L. & MED. 269 (2003). Janna Merrick reports that studies of infectious disease transmission suggest that "children who are exempted based on their parents' philosophical or religious preferences put others in the community at risk":

> A retrospective national study of measles for the years 1985 through 1992 showed that children ages five to nineteen years, who were exempted for religious or philosophical reasons, were thirty-five times more likely to contract measles than children who were vaccinated. A subsequent study of both measles and pertussis outbreaks in Colorado showed that day care and elementary age children who were exempted for religious or philosophical reasons were sixty-two times more likely to become infected with measles and sixteen times more likely to become infected with pertussis than children who were vaccinated. * * *

> Of the 179 cases of measles studied in Colorado, forty-five (twenty-five percent) were known to be among children exempted for religious or philosophical reasons. This figure does not include children who did not receive conventional medical care, were not reported to health officials and, as a result, not included in the study. Thus, the actual number of cases among philosophical and religious exemptors may be higher. The rest of the cases were children who had been vaccinated or had been medically exempted from the vaccine. Of the vaccinated children who became infected, at least eleven percent contracted measles from someone with a religious or philosophical exemption. The authors point out that the source of infection was unknown in sixty-seven percent of the vaccinated children, and therefore the number of vaccinated children infected by someone with a philosophical or religious vaccination exemption is probably higher than eleven percent. * * *

Merrick, *supra*, at 275–76.

In a lawsuit challenging a religious-exemption law, what plaintiffs should CRP seek? What arguments might CRP make in challenging such a law, and on what cases do those arguments rely? What arguments would be available to the state in defending the statute and on what cases do those arguments rely? On balance, should CRP bring a constitutional challenge?

Problem 10-3:

You are a local superior court judge. This morning you received an emergency petition from University Hospital regarding the medical treatment of Phillip Venable. At a bedside hearing, you learned the following facts:

Phillip, age 10, was admitted to University Hospital from the Emergency Room the day before yesterday. Preliminary tests indicated that his blood was being broken down and that in all likelihood he would require a blood transfusion. Phillip's parents refused to consent to the transfusion, citing their membership in a Protestant religious sect, the Church of God. They did consent to CAT scans and, the next morning, to a needle biopsy and bone marrow analysis.

The CAT scans showed an extensive mass involving the back part of the abdomen with fluid on both sides of the chest. The bone marrow analysis revealed malignant cells in the bone marrow; the needle biopsy showed that Phillip had rhabdomyosarcoma, a form of pediatric cancer of the tissue that is to become muscle. By the time the analysis results were available early yesterday afternoon, Phillip's blood counts had further deteriorated.

Dr. Peter Land, Chief of Pediatric Hemotology and Oncology, testified at the hearing. He indicated that there is a large mass infiltrating the abdominal cavity, with spread to the vertebrae and the area of the right buttock; the cancer has also metastasized to the bone marrow and there is also pulmonary effusion in both lungs. The recommended treatment for rhabdomyosarcoma is chemotherapy and radiation; with such treatment, 75 percent of patients go into remission for a period from several months to years and 25–30 percent of these patients are "cured". Dr. Land testified that, without treatment, Phillip will die, probably within a month, during which time he will experience a great deal of pain. He indicated that, because of the dropping hemoglobin and low blood pressure, blood transfusions would have to be administered before chemotherapy treatment could be undertaken; he urged that immediate action was necessary, noting that an unmanageable emergency could arise at any moment and that any delay was harmful to Phillip. In response to questions, Dr. Land admitted that the chemotherapy did have side effects, including hair loss, nausea, neurological problems, and reduced immunological function creating a serious risk of infection.

Theodore Venable, the patient's father, testified that he was unalterably opposed to Phillip receiving chemotherapy, radiation, or even blood transfusions. He indicated that Church of God members are forbidden to use medicine, undergo vaccinations, or obtain any form of medical treatment; instead, they are taught by the Church to live with, and be healed by, faith. Joan Venable concurred in her husband's refusal to consent to treatment, citing the same beliefs described by her husband. In response to questions, Mrs. Venable also indicated that the family, which includes four children younger than Phillip, joined the Church of God approximately ten years ago. Phillip testified briefly. He noted his faith in the Church of God and his wish not "to die in sin." Outside Phillip's room after the formal hearing had concluded, Mr. and Mrs. Venable stated that they believed that "Phillip will die or be unable to live a normal life, regardless of what is done" and that they did not want "to simply prolong his suffering."

You have never decided a case like this one, but do recall reading about two other cases involving religiously motivated parental refusal to consent to treatment for pediatric cancer. In Newmark v. Williams, 588 A.2d 1108 (Del. 1991), parents refused to consent to chemotherapy treatment for Burkitt's Lymphoma offering "at best" a 40% chance of "curing" the illness. Without treatment, the three-year-old patient's life expectancy was six to eight months. Although doctors put the chance of "survival" at 40%, they admitted that the term survival described "only * * * the probability that the patient will live two years after chemotherapy without a recurrence of cancer." Doctors also testified that "there was no available medical data to conclude that Colin could survive to adulthood." On these facts, the court declined to order treatment:

> Applying * * * the "best interests standard" here, the State's petition must be denied. The egregious facts of this case indicate that Colin's proposed medical treatment was highly invasive, painful, involved terrible temporary and potentially permanent side effects, posed an unacceptably low chance of success, and a high risk that the treatment itself would cause his death. The State's authority to intervene in this case, therefore, cannot outweigh the Newmarks' parental prerogative and Colin's inherent right to enjoy at least a modicum of human dignity in the short time that was left to him.

In *In re* Hamilton, 657 S.W.2d 425 (Tenn. App. 1983) , parents refused to consent to chemotherapy treatment for Ewings Sarcoma. Without treatment, the twelve-year-old patient's life expectancy was six to nine months; with treatment she was believed to have a 25–50% of chance of long-term survival. The court ordered treatment; it did not discuss the risks of treatment or the treatment setting.

A.   Write a decision either consenting to treatment for Phillip or upholding Mr. and Mrs. Venable's treatment refusal.

B.   Reflect on your decision. Should treatment invariably be ordered if it offers a 51% chance of long-term survival? A 49% chance? Are cases like *Newmark* and *Hamilton* easier to resolve:

> if, as in *Green*, parental rights are controlling unless "the child's life is not immediately imperiled by his physical condition"?

    if, as suggested by Goldstein, Freud, and Solnit, parental judgment is controlling unless "[t]he treatment can reasonably be expected to result in a chance for the Child to have normal healthy growth or a life worth living."

    if, as suggested by Professor Davis, the state is committed to protecting the child's right to an open future?

B. THE "MATURE" MINOR

What weight should be given to the wishes of an older child like Ricky Green? Advocates of deference to older children's decisions, like Justice Douglas in *Yoder*, urge that older adolescents are just as capable of understanding health care decisions as are adults:

> Numerous studies can be cited to make the basic point. Almost twenty years ago, a comprehensive analysis of the literature in developmental psychology by Thomas Grisso and Linda Vierling indicated that "generally minors below the ages of 11–13 do not possess many of the cognitive capacities one would associate with the psychological elements of intelligent consent." By contrast, the authors stated that there "is little evidence that minors of age 15 and above as a group are any less competent to provide consent than are adults". On the basis of their literature analysis, they concluded that "minors are entitled to have some form of consent or dissent regarding the things that happen to them in the name of assessment, treatment, or other professional activities that have generally been determined unilaterally by adults in the minor's interest" * * * [Many o]ther writers agree. Several groups of professionals concur about adolescents in research settings. For example, the Committee on Child Psychiatry from the Group for the Advancement of Psychiatry has produced a lengthy study on children and adolescents in which they examine the question, "How Old Is Old Enough?" In their study they assess adolescent decision-making capacity by saying that "we would expect that by 14, most children would be ready to participate meaningfully in the consent process in regard to research * * * [and] there is little disagreement that above 14, all potential subjects must give their informed consent separate from their parents." Other professional groups agree.

Robert F. Weir & Charles Peters, *Affirming the Decisions Adolescents Make About Life and Death*, 27 HASTINGS CTR. RPT. 29, 31–32 (Nov. 1997).

But those who oppose adolescent decision making can also cite an impressive body of evidence. This evidence, some of which comes from the medical literature on various chronic disorders, suggests that adolescents' cognitive capacities are not matched by a similar level of emotional maturity. For example, the literature on diabetes—one of the most common chronic diseases of adolescence—contains literally dozens of articles dealing with the special difficulties of treating teenage patients. As a group, adolescents are less adherent to a diabetes regimen than are younger children. *See, e.g.,* A.M. Thomas et al., *Problem Solving and Diabetes Regimen Adherence by Children and Adolescents with IDDM in Social Pressure Situations: A Reflection of Normal Development,* 22 J. PEDIATRIC PSYCHOLOGY 541 (1997). Both glucose control and psychosocial adjustment to diabetes also tend to worsen as children age. And many experts have suggested that the normal developmental needs of adolescents are incompatible with good diabetes management. Researchers have often reported that adolescents with diabetes are prone to high-risk behaviors such as staying away from home, drinking, and smoking; they have also noted that these behavioral patterns may represent a "deliberate lifestyle choice on the part of the adolescent that reflects the short-term priority of enjoying life over valuing tight glycemic control." Beverly Faro, *The Effect of Diabetes on Adolescents' Quality of Life,* 25 PEDIATRIC NURSING 247 (1999). Similar themes emerge in the literature dealing with management of other chronic conditions of adolescence, such as asthma. *See, e.g.,* Pauline Ladebauche, *Managing Asthma: A Growth and Development Approach,* 23 PEDIATRIC NURSING 37 (1997). And even among those without chronic impairments, experts agree that "the main threats to adolescents' health are predominantly the health-risk behaviors and choices they make." Michael D. Resnick et al., *Protecting Adolescents from Harm: Findings from the National Longitudinal Study on Adolescent Health,* 278 JAMA 823 (1997).

So, how much weight should Ricky's views on his treatment receive? The Supreme Court has dealt with adolescent health-care decision making primarily in one context, abortion. But in this context the case law is extensive. In Planned Parenthood of Central Missouri v. Danforth, 428 U.S. 52 (1976), the Court noted that the abortion decision was both constitutionally protected and impossible to postpone. It accordingly held that, "the State may not impose a blanket provision * * * requiring the consent of a parent or person in loco parentis as a condition for abortion of an unmarried minor during the first 12 weeks of her pregnancy." In later cases, the Court has required the state to provide a judicial "bypass" procedure at which the minor can show that: i) "she is mature enough and well enough informed to make her abortion decision, in consultation with her physician, independently of her parents' wishes"; or ii) "even if she is not able to make this decision independently, the desired abortion would be in her best interests." Bellotti v. Baird, 443 U.S. 622 (1979). *See also* City of Akron v. Akron Center for Reproductive Health, Inc., 462 U.S. 416 (1983) (striking down statute without bypass procedure); Planned Parenthood v. Ashcroft, 462 U.S. 476 (1983) (upholding one-parent consent requirement after construing statute to permit minor to avoid consent provision with showing of maturity or best interests).

NOTES AND QUESTIONS

1.   What significant difference justifies the constitutional requirement of individualized determination of a minor's maturity in the case of abortion and the rigid age limits the law prescribes for other important events, such as the achievement of majority, drinking alcoholic beverages, driving, and marriage? Assuming that abortion can be distinguished from marriage, driving, etc., do the factors that distinguish abortion also apply to contraception?

2.   Could the state require parental consent before an abortion is performed on a minor under the age of 13 (i.e., presume such a minor not to be mature)? Could the state proscribe the sale of contraceptives to minors under the age of 13?

3.   The Court has had considerable difficulty with state laws mandating parental notification as a precondition to abortion. In H.L. v. Matheson, 450 U.S. 398 (1981), the Court held that a Utah statute requiring a physician to "notify, if possible" the parents of an unmarried minor prior to performing an abortion was constitutional at least as applied to "immature and dependent minors." But in Hodgson v. Minnesota, 497 U.S. 417 (1990), five members of the Court upheld a forty-eight hour waiting period following parental notification, while a different five-member majority struck down the same statute's requirement that both of the minor's parents receive the required notification.

4.   Under the judicial "bypass" procedure required by the Supreme Court in *Bellotti II*, a judge must grant a minor's petition for permission to obtain an abortion without parental consent if: (1) he finds that the minor is sufficiently mature to make an abortion decision independently of her parents; or (2) even if she is too immature to make the decision independently, the desired abortion would be in her best interests. Research in Massachusetts on the impact of the new procedure revealed that, during the first twenty-two months the bypass procedure was available, approximately 1300 pregnant minors sought judicial authorization. In about 90% of the cases, the Court found that the minor was mature and allowed her to decide for herself. In the cases where the minor was found to be immature, the judge decided that an abortion would be in her best interests in all but five cases. Even in these cases, all of the girls obtained abortions. Four did so on appeal or through another judge; one went out of state rather than appeal the decision. The researchers concluded that "[t]he explanation for this result is that the superior court judges realize that it would be impossible as a legal proposition to justify a finding that a pregnant minor was too immature to decide whether to have an abortion for herself, but that it was in her best interests to bear a child. 'There is no way you could substantiate such a decision,' John J. Irwin, Jr., a judge who strongly opposes abortion, told the Boston Globe. 'I can't see any abortion that wouldn't be

ordered or sanctioned by the courts under this law.' In the words of another Superior Court judge who indicated that he once gave permission for an abortion to an eleven year-old, '[t]he law puts judges in the ridiculous position of being rubber stamps.'" Robert H. Mnookin, *Bellotti v. Baird: A Hard Case,* *in* IN THE INTEREST OF CHILDREN: ADVOCACY, LAW REFORM, AND PUBLIC POLICY 150, 240 (Robert H. Mnookin ed. 1985). Studies conducted during the 1990s suggest similar percentages of successful bypass applicants. *See In re* Doe, 19 S.W.3d 346, 353 (Tex. 2000).

5.   *Is Abortion Unique?* If the Constitution requires states to afford minors the opportunity to demonstrate their maturity in the abortion context, does the Constitution demand a similar opportunity in the context of treatment decisions like that faced by Ricky Green? The Supreme Court has not confronted this issue, but what arguments would be available to an adolescent who had been denied the right to make his own medical decision by the state? What arguments would be available to the state? How does the type of medical decision (i.e., life-and-death, treatment A vs. treatment B) affect the strength of each party's arguments? On balance, who should win?

6.   *The "Mature Minor" Doctrine:* A few states have statutorily adopted a "mature minor" doctrine applicable to medical treatment decisions. For example, Arkansas authorizes consent to treatment by "any unemancipated minor of sufficient intelligence to understand and appreciate the consequences of the proposed surgical or medical treatment or procedures * * *." ARK. CODE § 20–9–602(7). Try applying the Arkansas statute to the *Green* case. In an evidentiary hearing after remand, Ricky Green indicated that he did not wish to submit to the proposed surgery. Ricky did not stress religious factors; instead, he said that he had been going to the hospital for a long time and no one had told him that " 'it is going to come out right.' " *In re* Green, 452 Pa. 373, 307 A.2d 279, 280 (Pa. 1973). Under the Arkansas statute, should Ricky Green be considered a mature minor: What evidence would be relevant? On balance, does that evidence support a mature minor finding?

7.   Are mature minor statutes a good idea? Professor Scott has argued that:

> there is little evidence that, in most contexts, the interests of adolescents are harmed by a regime of binary classification. Creating a separate legal category for adolescents would add complexity, but generally with little promised payoff. Indeed, the effect of a legal regime that includes a series of legislative bright line rules is to extend adult rights and responsibilities over an extended period of time into early adulthood, without incurring the costs of establishing an intermediate category, or of undertaking a case-by-case inquiry into maturity. * * * Occasionally, to be sure, useful exceptions to the binary classification scheme are introduced. For example, under recent statutory reforms, young drivers are accorded the adult privilege of operating motor vehicles, subject to special restrictions as they gain experience and learn responsibility. In this setting, youth

welfare and social welfare are both served by the creation of an intermediate category.

Elizabeth S. Scott, *The Legal Construction of Adolescence,* 29 HOFSTRA L. REV. 547, 577 (2000). Could a case-by-case mature minor principle be recast as a bright-line rule? What costs and benefits would flow from such a conversion? Would the benefits and costs be comparable to those provided by the restricted driver rules Scott mentions? On balance, do the benefits of establishing is a mature minor category—rule or case-based—outweigh the costs? For listings of the state laws on minor consents, *see* GUTTMACHER INSTITUTE, AN OVERVIEW OF MINORS' CONSENT LAWS (Sept. 1, 2011).

Problem 10-4: Condom Distribution in Public Schools

Last month, following numerous public meetings at which the problems of teenage sexuality, venereal disease, and AIDS were discussed and debated, the local School Committee voted to make condoms available in the district's junior and senior high schools. Under the plan, junior high school students can obtain free condoms from the school nurse after receiving counseling and informational pamphlets on AIDS and other sexually transmitted diseases. Students at the high school can request free condoms from the nurse or buy them for $.75 from vending machines in the restrooms; counseling for high school students is optional. The plan does not allow parents to exclude their children from the program, nor does it provide for parental notification after a child requests condoms.

A group of parents has brought an action in which they allege that the condom availability program violates their rights to direct the upbringing of their children and infringes their religious liberties. You are the law clerk of the trial court judge to which the case has been assigned. What Supreme Court precedents are relevant? What arguments can be expected from the parents and the state? How should the Court rule? *See* Alfonso v. Fernandez, 606 N.Y.S.2d 259 (App. Div. 1993), app. dismissed, 637 N.E.2d 279 (N. Y. 1994); Curtis v. School Committee, 652 N.E.2d 580 (Mass. 1995), cert. denied, 516 U.S. 1067 (1996); Parents United for Better Schools v. Philadelphia Bd. of Educ., 148 F.3d 260 (3d Cir. 1998). *See also* Doe v. Irwin, 615 F.2d 1162 (6th Cir. 1980); Comment, 109 HARV. L. REV. 687 (1996).

C. THE NEONATE

MILLER V. HCA, INC.
Supreme Court of Texas, 2003.
118 S.W.3d 758.

ENOCH, JUSTICE.

The narrow question we must decide is whether Texas law recognizes a claim by parents for either battery or negligence because their premature infant, born alive but in distress at only twenty-three weeks of gestation, was provided resuscitative medical treatment by physicians at a hospital without parental consent. * * *

We hold that circumstances like these provide an exception to the general rule imposing liability on a physician for treating a child without consent. That exception eliminates the Millers' claim for battery. We further conclude that the Millers' negligence claim—premised not on any physician's negligence in treating the infant but on the hospital's policies, or lack thereof, permitting a physician to treat their infant without parental consent—fails as a matter of law for the same reasons. * * *

I.   FACTS

The unfortunate circumstances of this case began in August 1990, when approximately four months before her due date, Karla Miller was admitted to Woman's Hospital of Texas (the "Hospital") in premature labor. An ultrasound revealed that Karla's fetus weighed about 629 grams or 1 1/4 pounds and had a gestational age of approximately twenty-three weeks. Because of the fetus's prematurity, Karla's physicians began administering a drug designed to stop labor.

Karla's physicians subsequently discovered that Karla had an infection that could endanger her life and require them to induce delivery. Dr. Mark Jacobs, Karla's obstetrician, and Dr. Donald Kelley, a neonatologist at the Hospital, informed Karla and her husband, Mark Miller, that if they had to induce delivery, the infant had little chance of being born alive. The physicians also informed the Millers that if the infant was born alive, it would most probably suffer severe impairments, including cerebral palsy, brain hemorrhaging, blindness, lung disease, pulmonary infections, and mental retardation. Mark testified at trial that the physicians told him they had never had such a premature infant live and that anything they did to sustain the infant's life would be guesswork.

After their discussion, Drs. Jacobs and Kelley asked the Millers to decide whether physicians should treat the infant upon birth if they were forced to induce delivery. At approximately noon that day, the Millers informed Drs. Jacob and Kelley that they wanted no heroic measures performed on the infant and they wanted nature to take its course. Mark testified that he understood heroic measures to mean performing resuscitation, chest massage, and using life support machines. Dr. Kelley recorded the Millers' request in Karla's medical notes, and Dr. Jacobs informed the medical staff at the Hospital that no neonatologist would be needed at delivery. Mark then left the Hospital to make funeral arrangements for the infant. In the meantime, the nursing staff informed other Hospital personnel of Dr. Jacobs' instruction that no neonatologist would be present in the delivery room when the Millers' infant was born. An afternoon of meetings involving Hospital administrators and physicians followed. Between approximately 4:00 p.m. and 4:30 p.m. that day, Anna Summerfield, the director of the Hospital's neonatal intensive care unit, and several physicians, including Dr. Jacobs, met with Mark upon his return to the Hospital to further discuss the situation. Mark testified that Ms. Summerfield announced at the meeting that the Hospital had a policy requiring resuscitation of any baby who was born weighing over 500 grams. Although Ms. Summerfield agreed that she said that, the only written Hospital policy produced described the Natural Death Act and did not mention resuscitating infants over 500 grams. Moreover, the physicians at the meeting testified that they and Hospital administrators agreed only that a neonatologist would be present to evaluate the Millers' infant at birth and decide whether to resuscitate based on the infant's condition at that time. * * *

Although Dr. Eduardo Otero, the neonatologist present in the delivery room when Sidney was born, did not attend that meeting, he confirmed that he needed to actually see Sidney before deciding what treatment, if any, would be appropriate:

> Q.   Can you . . . tell us from a worst case scenario to a best case scenario, what type of possibilities you've seen in your own personal practice?

> A.   Well, the worst case scenario is . . . the baby comes out and it's dead, it has no heart rate. . . Or you have babies that actually go through a rocky start then cruise through the rest and go home. And they may have small handicaps or they may have some problems but—learning disabilities or something like that, but in general, all babies are normal children or fairly normal children.

> Q.   And is there any way that you could have made a prediction, at the time of Sidney's birth, where she would fall in that range of different options?

> A.   No, Sir. * * *

Mark testified that, after the meeting, Hospital administrators asked him to sign a consent form allowing resuscitation according to the Hospital's plan, but he refused. Mark further testified that when he asked how he could prevent resuscitation, Hospital administrators told him that he could do so by removing Karla from the Hospital, which was not a viable option given her condition. Dr. Jacobs then noted in Karla's medical charts that a plan for evaluating the infant upon her birth was discussed at that afternoon meeting.

That evening, Karla's condition worsened and her amniotic sac broke. * * * At 11:30 p.m. that night, Karla delivered a premature female infant weighing 615 grams, which the Millers named Sidney. Sidney's actual gestational age was twenty-three and one-seventh weeks. And she was born alive. Dr. Otero noted that Sidney had a heart beat, albeit at a rate below that normally found in full-term babies. He further noted that Sidney, although blue in color and limp, gasped for air, spontaneously cried, and grimaced. Dr. Otero also noted that Sidney displayed no dysmorphic features other than being premature. He immediately "bagged" and "intubated" Sidney to oxygenate her blood; he then placed her on ventilation. * * * Neither Karla nor Mark objected at the time to the treatment provided.

Sidney initially responded well to the treatment * * *, [b]ut at some point during the first few days after birth, Sidney suffered a brain hemorrhage—a complication not uncommon in infants born so prematurely.

* * * [T]he hemorrhage caused Sidney to suffer severe physical and mental impairments. At the time of trial, Sidney was seven years old and could not walk, talk, feed herself, or sit up on her own. The evidence demonstrated that Sidney was legally blind, suffered from severe mental retardation, cerebral palsy, seizures, and spastic quadriparesis in her limbs. She could not be toilet-trained and required a shunt in her brain to drain fluids that accumulate there and needed care twenty-four hours a day. The evidence further demonstrated that her circumstances will not change. * * *

The Millers' claims stemmed from their allegations that despite their instructions to the contrary, the Hospital not only resuscitated Sidney but performed experimental procedures and administered experimental drugs, without which, in all reasonable medical probability, Sidney would not have survived. * * * [At trial, t]he jury found that the Hospital, without the consent of Karla or Mark Miller, performed resuscitative treatment on Sidney. The jury also found that the Hospital's * * * negligence "proximately caused the occurrence in question." The jury concluded that * * * the Hospital [and other defendants] were grossly negligent and that the Hospital acted with malice. * * * The trial court rendered judgment jointly and severally against the HCA defendants on the jury's verdict of $29,400,000 in actual damages for medical expenses, $17,503,066 in prejudgment interest, and $13,500,000 in exemplary damages. * * * [The Court of Appeal reversed.] We granted the Millers' petition for review to consider this important and difficult matter. * * *

II. ANALYSIS

This case requires us to determine the respective roles that parents and healthcare providers play in deciding whether to treat an infant who is born alive but in distress and is so premature that, despite advancements in neonatal intensive care, has a largely uncertain prognosis. * * * [W]e conclude that neither the Texas Legislature nor our case law has addressed this specific situation. We accordingly begin our analysis by focusing on what the existing case law and statutes do address.

Generally speaking, the custody, care, and nurture of an infant resides in the first instance with the parents. As the United States Supreme Court has acknowledged, parents are presumed to be the appropriate decision-makers for their infants:

> Our jurisprudence historically has reflected Western civilization concepts of the family as a unit with broad parental authority over minor children. Our cases have consistently followed that course; our constitutional system long ago rejected any notion that a child is "the mere creature of the State" and, on the contrary, asserted that parents generally "have the right, coupled with the high duty, to recognize and prepare [their children] for additional obligations." (Meyer v. Nebraska; Pierce v. Society of Sisters) . . .

Surely, this includes a "high duty" to recognize symptoms of illness and to seek and follow medical advice. The law's concept of the family rests on a presumption that parents possess what a child lacks in maturity, experience, and capacity for judgment required for making life's difficult decisions. More important, historically it has recognized that natural bonds of affection lead parents to act in the best interests of their children. *See* Parham v. J.R., [p. 522].

The Texas Legislature has likewise recognized that parents are presumed to be appropriate decision-makers, giving parents the right to consent to their infant's medical care and surgical treatment. A logical corollary of that right * * * is that parents have the right not to consent to certain medical care for their infant, i.e., parents have the right to refuse certain medical care.

Of course, this broad grant of parental decision-making authority is not without limits. The State's role as parens patriae permits it to intercede in parental decision-making under certain circumstances. * * *

* * *

With respect to consent, the requirement that permission be obtained before providing medical treatment is based on the patient's right to receive information adequate for him or her to exercise an informed decision to accept or refuse the treatment. Thus, the general rule in Texas is that a physician who provides treatment without consent commits a battery. But there are exceptions. For example, in Gravis v. Physicians & Surgeons Hospital, this Court acknowledged that "consent will be implied where the patient is unconscious or otherwise unable to give express consent and an immediate operation is necessary to preserve life or health."

In Moss v. Rishworth, the court held that a physician commits a "legal wrong" by operating on a minor without parental consent when there is "an absolute necessity for a prompt operation, but not emergent in the sense that death would likely result immediately upon the failure to perform it." But the court in *Moss* expressly noted that "it [was] not contended [there] that any real danger would have resulted to the child had time been taken to consult the parent with reference to the operation." *Moss* therefore implicitly acknowledges that a physician does not commit a legal wrong by operating on a minor without consent when the operation is performed under emergent circumstances—i.e., when death is likely to result immediately upon the failure to perform it.

Moss guides us here. We hold that a physician, who is confronted with emergent circumstances and provides life-sustaining treatment to a minor child, is not liable for not first obtaining consent from the parents. * * * Though in situations of this character, the physician should attempt to secure parental consent if possible, the physician will not be liable under a battery or negligence theory solely for proceeding with the treatment absent consent. * * *

Following these guiding principles, we now determine whether the Millers can maintain their battery and negligence claims against HCA. The jury found that the Hospital, through Dr. Otero, treated Sidney without the Millers' consent. The parties do not challenge that finding. Thus, we only address whether the Hospital was required to seek court intervention to overturn the lack of parental consent—which it undisputedly did not do—before Dr. Otero could treat Sidney without committing a battery. The Millers acknowledge that numerous physicians at trial agreed that, absent an emergency situation, the proper course of action is court intervention when health care providers disagree with parents' refusal to consent to a child's treatment. And the Millers contend that, as a matter of law, no emergency existed that would excuse the Hospital's treatment of Sidney without their consent or a court order overriding their refusal to consent. The Millers point out that before Sidney's birth, Drs. Jacobs and Kelley discussed with them the possibility that Sidney might suffer from the numerous physical and mental infirmities that did, in fact, afflict her. And some eleven hours before Sidney's birth, the Millers indicated that they did not want any heroic measures performed on Sidney. The Millers note that these factors prompted the dissenting justice in the court of appeals to conclude that "[a]nytime a group of doctors and a hospital administration ha[ve] the luxury of multiple meetings to change the original doctors' medical opinions, without taking a more obvious course of action, there is no medical emergency."

We agree that a physician cannot create emergent circumstances from his or her own delay or inaction and escape liability for proceeding without consent. But the Millers' reasoning fails to recognize that, in this case, the evidence established that Sidney could only be properly evaluated when she was born. * * *

* * * The evidence further reflected that Sidney was born alive but in distress. At that time, Dr. Otero had to make a split-second decision on whether to provide life-sustaining treatment. While the Millers were both present in the delivery room, there was simply no time to obtain their consent to treatment or to institute legal proceedings to challenge their withholding of consent, had the Millers done so, without jeopardizing Sidney's life. Thus, although HCA never requested a jury instruction, nor challenged the absence of a jury instruction, on whether Dr. Otero treated Sidney under emergent circumstances, the evidence conclusively established that Dr. Otero was faced with emergent circumstances when he treated Sidney. Those circumstances resulted from not being able to evaluate Sidney until she was born, not because of any delay or inaction by * * * the Hospital, or Dr. Otero. * * *

* * * We agree that, whenever possible, obtaining consent in writing to evaluate a premature infant at birth and to render any warranted medical treatment is the best course of action. And physicians and hospitals should always strive to do so. But if such consent is not forthcoming, or is affirmatively denied, we decline to impose liability on a physician solely for providing life-sustaining treatment under emergent circumstances to a new-born infant without that consent. * * *

HCA [also] argues that the federal "Baby Doe" regulations, 42 U.S.C. §§ 5101 et seq.; 45 C.F.R. §§ 1340.1 et seq., are part of Texas law and forbid any denial of medical care based on quality-of-life considerations. While we do not disagree with HCA's assertion as a general proposition, * * * [these regulations] state[ ] that Texas must provide a mechanism by which the child protective services system can initiate legal proceedings to prevent the withholding of medical treatment from infants. * * * But it is undisputed that neither the Hospital nor HCA initiated or requested child protective services to initiate legal proceedings to override the Millers' "withholding of medical treatment" by refusing to consent to Sidney's treatment. Thus, the federal funding regulations appear to contemplate legal proceedings to override the lack of parental consent, and they do not answer the question of whether Dr. Otero committed a battery by providing treatment without doing so. * * *

III. CONCLUSION

Dr. Otero provided life-sustaining treatment to Sidney under emergent circumstances as a matter of law. Those circumstances provide an exception to the general rule imposing liability on a physician for providing treatment to a minor child without first obtaining parental consent. Therefore, Dr. Otero did not commit a battery. And HCA cannot be held liable for the Millers' battery and negligence claims. * * * We affirm the court of appeals' judgment.

NOTES AND QUESTIONS

1.   Is the *HCA* decision consistent with *Green*? Does it meet constitutional standards?

2.   *The Origin of the "Baby Doe" Regulations:* The federal "Baby Doe" regulations mentioned in *HCA* were enacted in response to a series of highly publicized cases in which physicians acceded to parental requests to forgo life-saving treatment for handicapped infants. In one case, doctors at Johns Hopkins University Hospital did not operate on a Down's syndrome baby with an intestinal blockage who died 15 days later of starvation. The parents had decided that they did not want to be burdened with a child who would be retarded and incapable of full human development; the physicians acquiesced in their decision, even though allowing the baby to starve to death created a good deal of anguish among the staff. And in a famous article published in 1973, two physicians reported that 43 of 299 infants who died at the special-care nursery at Yale-New Haven Hospital over a 2½ year period did so after parents and doctors jointly decided to discontinue medical treatment. *See* Raymond Duff & A.G.M. Campbell, *Moral and Ethical Dilemmas in the Special Care Nursery*, 289 NEW ENG. J. MED. 890 (1973).

Duff and Campbell argued that parents and physicians should have discretion to decide whether an impaired newborn should live or die:

> We believe the burdens of decisionmaking must be borne by families and their professional advisers because they are most familiar with the respective situations. Since families primarily must live with and are most affected by the decisions, it therefore appears that society and the health professions should provide only general guidelines for decision making. Moreover, since variations between situations are so great, and the situations themselves so complex, it follows that much latitude in decisionmaking should be expected and tolerated.

Id. But many readers—and government regulators—were horrified by what they saw as cavalier acceptance of parental decisions to kill infants whom they did not want.

3.   *The Federal Response:* In 1984, in response to the Johns Hopkins case and others like it, Congress amended the Child Abuse Prevention and Treatment Act (CAPTA) and required the states to establish programs for responding to reported cases of "withholding of medically indicated treatment." 42 U.S.C. § 5103(b)(2)(K). The term "withholding of medically indicated treatment" is defined to mean

> failure to respond to the infant's life threatening conditions by providing treatment (including appropriate nutrition, hydration, and medication) which, in the treating physician's or physicians' reasonable medical judgment, will be most likely to be effective in ameliorating or correcting all such conditions, except that the term does not include the failure to provide treatment (other than appropriate nutrition, hydration, or medication) to an infant when,

> in the treating physician's or physicians' reasonable medical judgment, (A) the infant is chronically ill and irreversibly comatose, (B) the provision of such treatment would (i) merely prolong dying, (ii) not be effective in ameliorating or correcting all of the infant's life-threatening conditions, or (iii) otherwise be futile in terms of survival of the infant; or (C) the provision of such treatment would be virtually futile in terms of the survival of the infant and the treatment itself under such circumstances would be inhumane.

42 U.S.C. § 5106(g). The federal Department of Health and Human Services also requires state programs to be in writing and to include an independent medical examination of the infant.

What did CAPTA require in *HCA*? How does the CAPTA standard differ from the decision-making approach outlined in *Green*? What justifications support unique standards for the treatment of newborns? Are those justifications convincing?

4.   *The Impact of CAPTA:* Physician surveys suggest that CAPTA has had an effect on medical decision making. A 1988 survey of Massachusetts pediatricians, for example, found that doctors were more inclined to treat babies with problematic prognoses and were paying less heed to parents' wishes than they did when surveyed in 1977. *See* Gina Kolata, *Parents of Tiny Infants Find Care Choices Are Not Theirs*, N. Y. TIMES, Sept. 30, 1991, at A1. But the U.S. Commission on Civil Rights nonetheless reported in 1989 that the CAPTA requirements were not having their intended effect. According to the Commission, state child welfare authorities tended to defer to hospitals rather than conducting independent evaluations. While hospitals are encouraged under the federal regulations to set up infant care review committees to make recommendations in specific cases, the Commission did not find them effective. *See* U.S. COMMISSION ON CIVIL RIGHTS, MEDICAL DISCRIMINATION AGAINST CHILDREN WITH DISABILITIES (1989).

Although more recent survey data are unavailable, one expert has suggested that the primary effect of CAPTA has been to shift the area of controversy. He reports that, as a result of CAPTA,

> [i]t is difficult to find a single case of withholding life-sustaining treatment from an infant based on a diagnosis of Down syndrome or spina bifida since 1985. While neonatologists continued to recommend withholding or withdrawing life-sustaining treatment based on expectations of quality of life, such decisions shifted to extremely low-birth-weight infants, * * * infants whose prospects for meaningful life were considerably more bleak than those with Down syndrome or spina bifida.

Norman Fost, *Decisions Regarding Treatment of Seriously Ill Newborns*, 281 JAMA 2041 (1999). Does Professor Fost's assessment suggest that CAPTA been a success or a failure?

5.   Although the prospects for extremely low-birth-weight infants remain poor, they are improving. A recent examination of survival and outcome data for such births showed a significant increase in survival and a significant decrease in neurodevelopmental impairment. *See* Betty R. Vohr et al., *Neurodevelopmental Outcomes of Extremely Low Birth Weight Infants 32 Weeks' Gestation Between 1993 and 1998*, 116 PEDIATRICS 635 (2005). A study of extremely premature Swedish children at age 11 found that significantly more extremely immature children than full-term controls had chronic conditions, including functional limitations (64% vs. 11%, respectively), compensatory dependency needs (59% vs. 25%), and services above those routinely required by children (67% vs. 22%). Specific diagnoses or disabilities with higher rates in extremely immature children than in controls included neurosensory impairment (15% vs. 2%), asthma (20% vs. 6%), poor motor skills of 2 SDs above the mean (26% vs. 3%), poor visual perception of 2 SDs above the mean (21% vs. 4%), poor learning skills of 2 SDs above the mean (27% vs. 3%), poor adaptive functioning with T scores of 40 (42% vs. 9%), and poor academic performance with T score 40 (49% vs. 7%). However, the authors of the survey also report that, although "[c]hildren born extremely immature have significantly greater health problems and special health care needs at 11 years of age[,] * * * few children have severe impairments that curtail major activities of daily living." Aijaz Farooqi et al., *Chronic Conditions, Functional Limitations, and Special Health Care Needs in 10- to 12-year-old Children Born at 23 to 25 Weeks' Gestation in the 1990s: A Swedish National Prospective Followup Study*, 118 PEDIATRICS E1466 (2006). Most doctors are "reluctant to initiate potentially life-sustaining medical care for neonates born below twenty-three weeks." Sadath A. Sayeed, *The Problem of Non-Identity in Valuing Newborn Human Life*, 25 GA. ST. U. L. REV. 865, 874 (2009).

6.   *Should* parents have the right to decide against treatment of an extremely premature infant like Sidney?

Problem 10-5:

Linda Ames is 23; her husband Dan is 30. Linda entered St. Charles Hospital last week, three weeks past due with her first child. The baby was born by Caesarian section. When Linda awakened in the recovery room, Dan told her that their child was seriously handicapped.

The baby's handicaps are multiple: She has a damaged kidney, microcephaly (an abnormally small head), a cleft palate, spina bifida with meningomyelocele (a defect of skin, vertebral arches and neural tube evident at birth as a skin defect over the back, bordered laterally by bony prominences of the unfused neural arches of the vertebrae), and hydrocephalus (a disorder in which fluid fails to drain from the cranial areas).

Doctors told Mr. and Mrs. Ames that, with her combination of birth defects, chances that the baby could lead a relatively normal life were "a long shot." According to the doctors, it is fairly certain that the baby will be unable to walk, incontinent, incapable of normal speech, and mentally retarded. It is possible that she will also be bedridden and sufficiently retarded that she will be unable even to experience emotions such as sadness or joy. But it is also possible that she would be able to sit in a wheelchair, communicate, and learn at some level. At this point, doctors simply cannot predict the exact degree of impairment.

Doctors have also told Mr. and Mrs. Ames that the most common treatment for spina bifida and hydrocephalus is surgery to insert a "shunt" and repair the spinal lesion. Although surgery entails risks, there are also risks from nontreatment. Untreated, hydrocephalus results in grossly distorted skull growth and mental retardation. Where a baby shows evidence of hydrocephalus at birth, some mental retardation is ensured, but insertion of a shunt, which provides a drain for the excess fluid, can minimize skull distortion and reduce the level of future retardation. Untreated, spina bifida entails a serious danger of infection, such as spinal meningitis, and death. It is possible to treat the condition with sterile dressings and antibiotics until the skin grows over the opening, but this treatment entails higher risks of infection. According to Dr. Albert Butler, the hospital's chief neurosurgeon, "surgery is preferable because of the lower risk of infection, but in a case like this one, both procedures are medically acceptable."

Mr. and Mrs. Ames were asked if they would consent to surgery to insert a shunt and repair the spinal lesion. Mr. and Mrs. Ames spent the next few hours consulting with more neurological experts, family members, a hospital social worker, and their priest. In the end, they refused to consent to the operation.

While doctors and hospital officials were willing to abide by Mr. and Mrs. Ames' treatment decision, an aide in the pediatric intensive care unit was not. Believing that Baby Ames was not receiving the best possible treatment, she called Larry Washburn, an attorney and children's advocate, about Baby Ames. Washburn immediately brought an action against St. Charles Hospital and Mr. and Mrs. Ames alleging medical neglect and requesting the appointment of a guardian ad litem to consent to surgery for Baby Ames.

You are the law clerk of Judge Smith, to whom the case has been assigned, and have been asked to determine: (1) whether Baby Ames is a neglected child within the meaning of the state's neglect law, which specifies that a child is neglected if its "parent * * * neglects or refuses to provide necessary, medically appropriate, health or surgical care;" (2) what result is required under CAPTA; and (3) what, if any, weight federal law should receive in this proceeding. *See* Weber v. Stony Brook Hospital, 467 N.Y.S.2d 685, *aff'd*, 456 N.E.2d 1186 (N. Y. 1983), cert. denied 464 U.S. 1026 (1983).

4. CHILD ABUSE AND NEGLECT

A. AN OVERVIEW OF THE CHILD WELFARE SYSTEM

The primary reason for state intervention into the family results from the abuse or neglect of children. States generally have four types of laws that deal with abuse and neglect of children: reporting statutes; child protective statutes; criminal statutes; and social services statutes.

MARSHA GARRISON, CHILD WELFARE DECISIONMAKING: IN SEARCH OF THE LEAST DRASTIC ALTERNATIVE
75 GEO. L. J. 1745, 1750–58 (1987).

* * * The American child welfare system traces its descent from an early public assistance scheme, the Elizabeth Poor Laws. Under the Poor Laws, destitute children were placed in apprenticeship until the age of majority. Such placements could be accomplished without parental consent and divested the parent of both legal custody and the right to obtain the child's return. The Poor Laws aided only the destitute, however; except for the potential reach of the criminal law, abuse and neglect did not provoke state intervention.

The Poor Laws were transported to the American colonies along with other English legal institutions. During the colonial era, child welfare administration remained largely synonymous with public assistance administration, and apprenticeship until the age of majority remained the preferred form of aid. During the nineteenth century, as changing economic and social conditions made the indenture of young children increasingly difficult to arrange, the poorhouse, specialized children's institutions, foster care, and adoption came to supplement apprenticeship as methods of relieving childhood destitution. It was not until the latter half of the century, however, that the jurisdiction of child welfare authorities was redefined to include the prevention of harm due to parental abuse or neglect as well as poverty. Even then, abuse and neglect were poorly differentiated from mere need, and permanent placement was almost invariably the only service made available to children and their parents.

Not until the dawn of this century did enlightened opinion conclude that financial aid, rather than placement, was the most appropriate service for children of poor but competent parents. Only incompetents should lose their children to the state, reformers argued, and even then should not lose their children permanently. With proper diagnosis and individualized treatment by trained child welfare workers, the reformers claimed, parental inadequacies could be rectified so as to rehabilitate the family and save the state the cost of permanent placement. * * * The enactment of state and federal welfare programs for needy children, along with the introduction of social work techniques and personnel into child welfare administration, seemed to ensure that the[se] new goals could be met. * * *

By mid-century it was apparent that the goals of the new child welfare system had not been realized. * * * The system continued to serve substantial public assistance functions in addition to protecting children from parental incompetence. The most comprehensive study of foster care undertaken during this period determined that only 14.6% of the children surveyed were in foster care due to abuse or neglect, while problems associated with poverty—poor health, inadequate housing, and insufficient resources—were still responsible for many placements.

* * * Poor families could seldom obtain the kind of help—daycare, for example, or temporary placement with a boarding school, friend or relative—that enabled wealthier families to cope with their children when an emergency occurred and were thus disproportionately forced to turn to the child welfare system. Moreover, as a result of the high stress levels and substandard living conditions associated with long-term indigence, poor parents were more likely to confront childcare crises, and more prone to other serious problems that impeded their ability to cope with them.

The system had also been less than totally successful in its goal of rehabilitating families and thus reducing the length of time children were wards of the state. Although most children did go home within a year or two, long-term placement continued to be fairly common, and some children still stayed in placement until the age of majority. Those parents who did regain their children apparently did so, in most cases, through their own efforts; rehabilitative services to parents were seldom provided, and many agencies did not even stay in touch with parents. During placement, children frequently lost touch with their own parents altogether. A few also suffered frequent shifts from one home to the next, thus depriving them of any meaningful familial relationships. * * *

In analyzing what had gone wrong, researchers discovered a system in which discretion was largely unbounded and frequently abused. * * * Although the rationale for * * * [officials'] broad discretionary powers was the need for individualized treatment in accordance with the specific needs of the child and his family, agencies tended instead to follow uniform practices based on bureaucratic convenience, custom, and funding priorities. Discretion was seldom exercised to meet the individual needs of the child or family. Many parents, for example, reported that daycare or housekeeping assistance could have averted foster care placement, but that agencies seldom offered such alternatives. Foster homes were typically selected with little attempt to match a child with adults who would be sensitive to the child's particular needs, or who lived in a location conducive to retaining ties with the child's natural parents, family, and friends. Frequently, foster parents were not even advised of a child's special problems prior to receiving the child. Rehabilitative efforts were also standardized, with little or no individualized treatment of the parental and family problems that had occasioned placement.

Moreover, agency practices had the effect of systematically discouraging parent-child contact or reunion. Visiting privileges, for example, were usually inflexible and infrequent. Parents were also given no role in the selection of the foster family and were not involved in decisions about the child's discipline or daily care.

Many factors contributed to the child welfare system's failure to exercise its discretion in accordance with the therapeutic ideal. Legislatures frequently failed to give adequate funding to services other than foster care and thus limited agency options. Agencies themselves also suffered from poor funding and from massive personnel problems. Bureaucratic inertia—unchecked by any review mechanisms—also kept alive the rigid, placement-oriented practices of the poor law era. The net result of these varied problems was that some poor children were unnecessarily placed in foster care and some stayed in foster care too long. The hopes of the turn of the century reformers had not been realized.

Mounting evidence of the inadequacies of the child welfare system produced a range of state initiatives aimed at foster care "permanency planning," as well as the federal Adoption Assistance and Child Welfare Act of 1980 (AACWA), Pub. L. 96–272, which set out a range of requirements that state child welfare agencies must meet as a condition of receiving federal foster care funds. More specifically, the Act requires a judicial finding that the state child welfare agency has made "reasonable efforts" to solve the problem in the home, the institution of case planning, periodic case review, and the provision of services to reunite children with their parents or ensure that they are placed in another permanent home. 42 U.S.C. §§ 671(a)(15)–(16), 672(a)(1)–(2), 675(5)(B). NATIONAL ASSOCIATION OF COUNSEL FOR CHILDREN, CHILD WELFARE LAW AND PRACTICE (Donald N. Duquette, Ann M. Haralambie, & Vivek S. Sankaran, eds. 3rd ed. 2016). As you read the cases that follow, assess the success of the AACWA in remedying the deficiencies in child welfare practice at which it was aimed.

B. WHAT CONSTITUTES NEGLECT?

IN RE T.G., C.G., D.G., AND D.G., D.F., AND E.G.

District of Columbia Court of Appeals, 1996.
684 A.2d 786.

MACK, SENIOR JUDGE.

The mother and father of four young children challenge, in separate appeals, the findings of a trial court that the children were "neglected" within the meaning of D.C. Code §§ 16–2301(9)(B) and (F) as well as the court's order committing the children to the Department of Human Services (DHS) for placement in foster homes. Basically, the parents attack the sufficiency of the evidence to support a finding of neglect. In the circumstances of this case, viewing, as we must, the evidence in the light most favorable to the government, we agree with the parents that the evidence supporting the finding that the children were "neglected" was insufficient as a matter of law. The government did not meet its burden of proof * * * of showing that any failure of proper care was not due to the parents' lack of financial means. On this record, we are disturbed at the rush to judgment exhibited by DHS, which on September 13, 1992, took the children into protective custody (and the following day sought the finding of neglect) based on a single visit to the home of the children. Finally, on the basis of a transcript of an October 1993, dispositional hearing which was requested, but not made a part of this record until after oral argument in this court, we conclude that DHS has not acted adequately to further the basic aim of society's interest in reunification of the family.

I.   This family came to the attention of city officials for the first time on September 13, 1992. On that morning, the children's maternal grandmother died at her residence. An officer, responding to the report of death, found the two older children, T.G. And D.G., in their grandmother's house. The officer later described the house as being in a deplorable state and the children dirty and in need of clean clothes and baths. Shortly thereafter, the children's mother arrived with the two younger children. The officer drove the mother and the four children to the residence of the mother and father; he found that house likewise to be in a deplorable state. The two younger children were also dirty and in need of baths. the officer took all four children into protective custody and carried them to DHS. A social worker visited the two houses the same afternoon and thereafter corroborated the officer's description of the children and their living conditions. The next day, September 14, 1992, DHS filed neglect petitions. The court ordered that all four children be placed in the custody of DHS, pending further action, basing its finding on the inadequacy of the children's living arrangements and their then ages (approximately eight, four, two, and one).

The following year, on September 8, 1993, the trial court conducted a factfinding hearing with regard to the neglect petitions, heard and credited the testimony of the officer and social worker who discovered the family on September 13, 1992, and based its finding of neglect . . . on the deplorable living conditions. The court did not adopt the reasoning of DHS that the mother and father were unable to discharge their parental responsibilities because of physical or mental disabilities, specifically stating that it did not find respondents to be neglected children pursuant to D.C. Code § 16–2301(9)(C). The mother and father were present at the hearing, did not testify, but moved through counsel for dismissal on the ground that a finding of neglect could not be based upon a lack of financial means * * *, and that, therefore, DHS had failed to meet its burden. The trial court rejected the argument of DHS that the burden of showing that the deplorable living conditions resulted from the lack of financial means shifted to respondents; it nevertheless denied the motion to dismiss, holding that DHS had met its burden of proof. On October 26, 1993, the court held a dispositional hearing, indicated its intent to order a home-study and continued the placement of the children under the custody of DHS (with the boys remaining at St. Ann's Infant Home and the girls in foster care of a paternal aunt).

II.   The term "neglect," warranting the protective intervention of the state, is by its very nature the equivalent of "negligence"—i.e., implying habits or omissions of duty, patterns of neglect, etc. Thus, we have held that a trial court's inquiry in neglect proceedings must go beyond "simply examining the most recent episode . . . The judge must be apprised of the entire mosaic." Quite obviously, the "entire mosaic" includes an examination of any history of, but also the reasons for, neglect—i.e., chronic indifference, carelessness, dereliction, inability to perform, etc.

We have also held that "The purpose of the child neglect statute is to promote the best interests of allegedly neglected children." These "interests are presumptively served by being with a parent, provided that the parent is not unfit." Viewed against this backdrop, the circumstances of the instant case give us cause for concern. All four children were taken into protective custody on the same day (September 13, 1992), that their ailing grandmother died, and that their living quarters were first observed. They were taken into protective custody because they were dirty and their living quarters were dirty. All of the evidence as to parental housekeeping or child care was gathered on that one day in September 1992, and a neglect petition was filed on the following day. It was not until the following year, on October 12, 1993, that the children, on this evidence, were found to be neglected. Meanwhile, it appears that it was not until 1993 that DHS, in preparing for an October 26 disposition hearing, sought to contact these parents to inquire about reunification. At this time, no assessment of the parents' current living conditions had been made and no case plan had been developed. During this period, the parents had visited the two boys at St. Ann's Infant Home on a regular basis (and, presumably, the two girls who were in the care of a paternal aunt).

We are dealing here with parents who have not been found to be "unfit." While the neglect petition alleged incapacity because of physical or mental disabilities, the trial court did not find neglect on these grounds. Moreover, we have recognized that the "relevant focus" for the court in neglect proceedings is the children's condition, not parental culpability. State intervention is justified only after it is demonstrated that the need arises from some act or failure to act on the part of the parent "which endangers the welfare of the child." * * *

The problem in this case arises as a result of DHS's immediate focus on the conditions in two residences on a particular day. One could find empathy for the plight of social workers who, charged with the protection of children, must face the stark realities of poverty in an urban dwelling. One could also argue that constant exposure to filthy living conditions creates the risk of physical deterioration. Not enough focus, however, was centered on the physical or emotional condition of the children overall. There was testimony about some skin rash, but also the testimony of a social worker that she had seen many dirty children. There was testimony that there was no edible food in the residences, and that at the time the children appeared to be hungry. Yet, the children bore no signs of malnourishment or abuse requiring medical attention. In fact, there was testimony that the mother had explained that the father used borrowed funds to bring home food every day. There was testimony that the only family income came from a social security check, payable to the mother's father, who in turn gave the mother a certain amount of the funds for her use.

It may well be, as counsel for DHS argued (in opposing the motion to dismiss on the ground that a finding of neglect could not be based upon a lack of financial means), that society cannot bear the burden of funneling massive or minor amounts of money into deplorable housing to permit children to live there. True, also, as counsel argued, "you don't need a lot of money to clean up." It also may well be that overburdened service agencies and court systems are ill-equipped to meet certain problems of society. Nevertheless, here a sympathetic trial court, aware of the problems of substandard housing, rejecting the argument that the father and mother had the burden of proving the lack of financial means, but drawing inferences (on a "close issue") from the government's evidence of filthy conditions, found neglect, noting:

> We're talking about a bar of soap, we're talking about a washing of clothes, we're talking about changing of clothes, and even if

there is one pair of clothes, these clothes can be washed out overnight.

There is a point, however, when decision-makers may be called upon to draw a balance between a bar of soap and love, and although we are loathe to second-guess the trial court's findings on this score, we nevertheless feel compelled to reverse the finding of neglect because of the failure of the government to meet its burden of proof.

We are also here disturbed by how little DHS did in seeking reunification of this family. It is beyond dispute that even if the parents were less than perfect, DHS has not lived up to its obligations in these proceedings. Although the allegations were made that the mother was learning disabled, and that the father had some substance abuse problems, the trial court's order of neglect made no findings as to unfitness. The court's findings reflected mostly the almost unspeakable poverty in which the family subsisted without the assistance of aid payments from the District. But DHS did not immediately seek to help the parents do what they had to do to reunite their family, according to the record before us. Indeed, in a report prepared in connection with the dispositional hearing scheduled for October 26, 1993, more than a year after the children were removed, DHS noted that it had not called the parents until recently. Although it may have been the parents' failings that brought DHS into the matter in the first place, DHS should not have been satisfied to document that the parents were imperfect. Instead, DHS should have taken an active role in spurring repair of the family by, for example, calling the parents immediately—and repeatedly, if necessary—to develop a strategy for reunification.

That the parents desired to be reunited with their children is evident from a reading of the transcript of the 1993 dispositional hearing. The father, mother, paternal grandparents, and paternal aunt (caretaker of the two girls) were present. Indeed, the father requested a short delay in proceedings to make certain that his wife, who walked slowly because of a weight problem, would arrive in time. The father sought custody of the boys because "it was better for children to be with relatives than [in an institution]." He told the court that the parents had a home available, but that no one from DHS had come to inspect it. Counsel explained that the mother was living at her father's house and was in the process of "fixing that home up" but had not been contacted by DHS. The children's father spoke of having to stop work in order to help his wife apply for public assistance and his desire to return to work. He indicated that he and his wife customarily visited the boys at St. Ann's twice a week. The trial court, in setting a date for further review, indicated that it would order a home-study before releasing the boys and it ordered that the continued visitation be preserved. In view of our holding that the evidence was not sufficient to support the drastic separation of parent from child in the first instance, it follows that (at least as to the DHS commitment) the question of disposition may be a moot one.

* * *

Because of the failure of the government to meet its burden of proof that any neglect was not due to the lack of financial needs, we are required to reverse the order with respect to neglect. In so doing, we recognize that the Superior Court, in the ordinary course of events, would order the release of the children from custody. In view of the intervening lapse of time since the children were taken into custody, however, we reverse the order of neglect, but stay the mandate of termination, to permit the court to review "the need for detention or shelter care" or to allow time for the parties to effect the children's transition to the parents' home or for the District to take such other action as the family's current circumstances and the children's best interest may require. * * * So ordered.

KING, ASSOCIATE JUDGE, dissenting.

Because I disagree with the majority's conclusion that the trial court erred in finding neglect * * *, I respectfully dissent. * * *

In my view, the majority has * * * ma[de] its own findings of fact based on its interpretation of the evidence. At the evidentiary hearing the court heard from two witnesses presented by the government, a police officer and a social worker. Neither the father nor the mother testified. The trial judge made the following findings of fact:

1. After hearing the testimony, the Court credits the testimony of the two government witnesses. Based upon this persuasive testimony, this Court finds that the children were residing in deplorable living conditions, which were not the function or product of the parents' lack of financial means. 2. Officer Mathis testified that the grandparent's home was in a deplorable condition. Upon entering the house, he noticed a powerful stench which burned his nose with every breath. This odor emanated around the entire house. He observed piles of clothes and trash strewn about the home. The rug was filthy. There were holes in the floor and ceiling, and there were electrical wires hanging from the ceiling and walls. The officer stated that the entire kitchen was cluttered with trash, and there was the sound of mice in the corner. 3. Officer Mathis further testified that the children were unkempt. The children were not washed and one child's hair was completely matted. Both children were wearing clothes that had the appearance of not being washed for over a period of time. Their bodies emitted a foul odor. The children's room was filled with trash and scattered clothing. There was also one double-sized mattress on which all of the children slept. 4. Officer Mathis proceeded to visit the home of the parents. This house was found to be in the same deplorable condition as the grandmother's house. Two of the children found in this house suffered

from skin rashes, which are consistent with dirt irritation. Furthermore, all of the children were hungry. Upon inspection of the kitchen, Officer Mathis noted only one item in the freezer and one half-gallon of sour milk in the refrigerator. 5. The Court heard the testimony of Joan Mallory, Department of Human Services Social Worker, who accompanied Officer Mathis into the grandparent's home. Ms. Mallory also had the opportunity to observe the clothing and hygiene of the children. She too stated that each child emitted a strong foul odor. The children slept on a single mattress, which smelled of urine and had no sheets. Upon examination of the home, she observed spoiled food, dirty utensils and stagnant water in the tub. She further stated that the carpeting and floor were so dirty that it was difficult to distinguish one from the other. The house was in a complete unsanitary condition. 6. The Court also concludes that the condition of the children and the home in which they were living was not caused by parents' lack of financial means. The evidence demonstrated that the family received Social Security Income benefits. The fact that the children were not malnourished further indicated that sufficient food was provided to the children. Whether the family lived in substandard housing is of no significance because it is not the cause of the aforementioned deplorable conditions. The cost of cleaning the home, washing the children, and bathing a child is minimal. Therefore, the filthy conditions of the children and the home were the result of neglect, rather than lack of financial means.

I submit that these findings of fact are supported by the record and this court has no basis for concluding otherwise.

* * * The majority seems to be saying that neglect was not established because it was only shown that the children and their homes were filthy on a single day in their lives. Setting aside the point that no such argument was ever made to the trial judge, it would not be unreasonable to infer, as the trial judge undoubtedly could and did, that the conditions described had existed for some time before the day they were observed. For example, the social worker testified that the children's clothes were so filthy that they had to be thrown away, and the trial court found that the clothing of at least two of the children "had the appearance of not being washed over a period of time." The social worker also testified that the odor given off by the children was so overwhelming that she had to air-out the office where the children had been taken. Finally, there was testimony that trash was strewn around the homes, the stove and utensils in one of the kitchens were "very very dirty," and both homes emitted a foul odor. This evidence strongly suggests that the condition of the children and the homes was a problem of long standing.

Moreover, the finding on financial ability is supportable based on the testimony regarding the mother's access to the proceeds of a Social Security Income ("SSI") benefits check. The majority places reliance on testimony that the proceeds of the check went to the mother's father who "gave [the mother] a certain amount of money to [take] care of herself," thus implying that the mother only received that portion of the proceeds that her father chose to give her. * * * There was also testimony, however, that the beneficiary of the SSI check was the mother, and that her father was the designated payee on her behalf and the proceeds were "solely for her." From this testimony the trial court could conclude that all of the funds from the SSI check went to the mother. * * * Therefore, because the findings of the trial court are supported by the record, I would affirm its ruling that the government had met its burden of proof in establishing neglect. * * *

I take no position with respect to the majority's decision to stay the mandate. * * * I note, however, that on this record it is safe to say that the children's future can only be described as precarious. For example, at the disposition hearing * * *, the trial judge had before him a disposition report that stated that the "mother is unable to discharge her parental responsibilities to and for the children. The father is unable to discharge his responsibilities to and for the children because of a physical incapacity [and] drug use. . . " At the time of the hearing, the two daughters were placed with their paternal aunt and the two sons were in St. Anne's home. The father had no objection to the continued placement of the two girls with the aunt, but sought reunification with the two boys. Counsel for the mother represented that the mother "thought" she was capable of caring for two of the children. The trial judge committed all of the children to the custody of DHS, ordering that the two girls remain with the aunt and the two boys be placed in foster care. Because the majority has reversed the finding of neglect, however, that commitment must be set aside.

NOTES AND QUESTIONS

1. Why, according to the majority, has the state failed to show neglect? What additional facts would be required? What should child welfare officials have done?

2. In *In re* A.H., 842 A.2d 674, 685–86 (D.C. 2004), the District of Columbia Court of Appeals upheld a neglect finding based on "deplorable home conditions much like those found in [*T.G.*]." According to the *A.H.* court, "[t]he majority in *T.G.* did not dispute * * * that 'we don't need to leave children in deplorable conditions until they get hurt. . . ' The *T.G.* majority simply was troubled by the fact that the neglect petitions before it were predicated on nothing more than a single snapshot of the family's existence—the deplorable living conditions at issue in the case had been observed on only one, possibly uncharacteristic, day, and there was no evidence (or so the majority concluded) that those conditions were other than temporary or that the parents tolerated them." Is this an accurate characterization of the *T.G.* majority's conclusion?

A number of other courts have found conditions like those in *T.G.* are adequate to sustain a neglect finding. *See, e.g., In re* Interest of N.M.W., 461

N.W.2d 478 (Iowa App. 1990) (upholding neglect determination based on "chronic unsanitary conditions" of home despite lack of evidence of adverse health effects). Nor are cases like *T.G.* atypical. One survey found that "environmental neglect"—i.e., "lack of adequate food, clothing, or shelter * * * or poor environmental conditions" was the basis for 8.7% of child maltreatment allegations; "lack of supervision" or "risk of harm" each accounted for 12% of allegations, parental substance abuse 10%, physical abuse 9%, and sexual abuse 6%. Another 40% of cases lacked an indicated allegation, sometimes because the allegation related to another child in the home and sometimes because the reason for child welfare involvement was lack of a parent willing or able to care for her. *See* Kristin Shook, *Assessing the Consequences of Welfare Reform for Child Welfare*, POVERTY RES. NEWS (1998).

3.   The *T.G.* decision offers a vivid portrayal of the situations which child welfare workers confront. Most maltreated children live in poverty. *See* N.J. Div. Youth & Fam. Servs. v. P.W.R., 11 A.3d 844 (N.J. 2011) (not finding abuse and neglect and noting most of the allegations were the product of the family's tight financial situation).

> All forms of child maltreatment are strongly associated with poverty, and neglect—the most common form of maltreatment—is linked with poverty to a startling extent. A U.S. national incidence study of maltreatment found that children from families with annual incomes below $15,000 were *60 times* more likely to die from maltreatment and *22 times* more likely to be seriously harmed by it than were children from families with annual incomes above $30,000. Extreme poverty also tends to be associated with more extreme abuse and neglect. As a result of these patterns, foster children are overwhelming from our poorest families. In 1999, approximately 55% of U.S. foster children were eligible for federal funding—funding derived from eligibility rules for the defunct Aid to Families with Dependent Children (AFDC) program without adjustments for inflation.

Marsha Garrison, *Reforming Child Protection: A Public Health Perspective*, 12 VA. J. SOC. POL'Y & L. 590, 612–13 (2005).

The Fourth National Incidence Study of Child Abuse and Neglect reported that the rate of child maltreatment in low-income households (less than $15,000 a year) was five times higher than for all children and seven times higher for cases of neglect. It also found that Black children are maltreated at higher rates than White children for several types of abuse and neglect. *See* Andrea J. Sedlak et al., *Fourth National Incidence Study of Child Abuse and Neglect, Executive Summary* § 5.2.1 (2010).

The families of maltreated children are also overwhelmed with problems. In one often-cited survey, 33% of the children's main caretakers suffered from "severe" mental or emotional problems, 60% of families included an adult member who used alcohol excessively, 20% had at least one member who had been a heroin user, 53% of main caretakers had a severe physical illness or condition, and 76% of families had at least one child with a serious health problem. *See* Horowitz & Wolock, *Material Deprivation, Child Maltreatment and Agency Interventions Among Poor Families, in* THE SOCIAL CONTEXT OF CHILD ABUSE AND NEGLECT 137, 146 (Leonard Pelton ed. 1981). The various problems that afflict the families of maltreated children tend to be linked and geographically concentrated. Thus a judge in British Columbia charted, between poor western and well-off eastern Vancouver, a six-fold difference in income to basic needs, a five-fold difference in the proportion of children under twelve living with a single parent, a ten-fold difference in adult education levels and access to child care, and an *83 fold* difference in neglect rates. *See* Garrison, *supra*, at 615–16.

The environmental conditions that promote child maltreatment are also strongly linked with an extraordinarily broad spectrum of serious risks to childhood development and adult well-being. In the Vancouver survey, for example, between West and East Vancouver, there was a 50-fold difference in children's language and cognitive development, a 17-fold difference in emotional maturity, an 8-fold difference in emotional maturity, and a 60-fold difference in nursing bottle decay. *Id.*

The American Academy of Pediatrics has estimated that 30% of foster children have severe emotional, behavioral, or developmental problems. *See* Am. Acad. Pediatrics, *Developmental Issues for Young Children in Foster Care*, 106 PEDIATRICS 1145 (2000).

4.　　*T.G.* also offers a vivid portrait of a large, urban child welfare system. Before 1992, a number of federal courts held that the various provisions of the federal Adoption Assistance and Child Welfare Act of 1990 were enforceable through a private action brought under 42 U.S.C. § 1983; law reform actions based on the law were brought in many parts of the country—including the District of Columbia. In 1991, a federal district court ruled that the District of Columbia Department of Human Services had consistently evaded its responsibilities under local and federal law. Among the agency's failures were the "failure * * * to initiate timely investigations into reports of abuse or neglect, the failure to provide services to families to prevent the placement of children in foster care, the failure to place those who may not safely remain at home in appropriate foster homes and institutions, the failure to develop case plans for children in foster care, and the failure to move children into a situation of permanency, whether by returning them to their homes or freeing them for adoption." LaShawn A. v. Dixon, 762 F. Supp. 959, 960 (D.D.C. 1991). After the District Court's findings were upheld on appeal (990 F.2d 1319 (D.C. Cir. 1993)), the district court judge, as part of a settlement, took control of a large part of the District's foster care system and announced that he was appointing the Center for the Study of Social Policy as a monitor to ensure that the District complied with strict deadlines concerning improved staffing and procedures, reducing the backlog of children in foster care, and establishing a procedure for reviewing the deaths of children in its care. In a later order, the judge extended the receivership order to child protective services as well as foster care. *See* Tony Lacy, *Court Tightens Grip on D.C. Foster Care*,

WASHINGTON POST, Nov. 19, 1994, at B1. The D.C. system was under court receivership from 1995 to 2001, and during this period the city hired more social workers, speeded investigations, and reduced the number of children in group homes. But as late as 2005, the Washington Post reported that, "[a]fter years of delay, D.C. officials are *beginning* to tackle the cases of hundreds of children who have been in the city's foster care system for years but are not actively being considered for adoption because the rights of their biological parents have not been terminated." Theola S. Labbe, *D.C. Tackles Case Backlog in Foster Care*, WASHINGTON POST, May 15, 2005, at B1 (emphasis added). On September 30, 2010, 408,000 children were in foster care in the United States. On average, the children had been in foster care for more than two years; one fourth were waiting for adoption. *See* U.S. Dep't of Health & Hum. Serv., Children's Bureau, Administration for Children, Youth and Families, *The AFCARS Report: Preliminary FY 2010, Estimates as of June 2011.*

To what extent does the Court's decision in *T.G.* appear to be influenced by the systemic inadequacies of the District's child welfare system?

5.   In Suter et al. v. Artist M. et al., 503 U.S. 347 (1992), an action brought on behalf of children against the director of the Illinois child abuse and neglect agency based on the agency's alleged failure to comply with the "reasonable efforts" requirements of the Adoption Assistance and Child Welfare Act of 1980, the Supreme Court held that the Act does *not* confer on its intended beneficiaries a private right that is enforceable in a 42 U.S.C. § 1983 action. *See* Carson P. v. Heineman, 240 F.R.D. 456 (D. Neb. 2007); Foster Children v. Bush, 329 F.3d 1255 (11th Cir. 2003). However, courts have found other sections of AACWA and ASFA enforceable by private action but the action may be barred by the Eleventh Amendment or by federal abstention requirements. *See* Sam v. Chafee, 800 F. Supp. 2d 363 (D.R.I. 2011); Connor B. v. Patrick, 771 F. Supp. 2d 142 (D. Mass. 2011).

6.   *Damages for Failure to Protect:* In the United States, state child welfare officials are often insulated against damages actions by sovereign immunity, and the Supreme Court has held that their misfeasance is not actionable under the Fourteenth Amendment. *See DeShaney v. Winnebago County Dept. of Social Services*, 489 U.S. 189 (1989). By contrast, the European Court of Human Rights has held that the failure of state child welfare workers to protect children from serious harm represents a violation of Convention Article 3, prohibiting inhuman or degrading treatment or punishment. The Court has also held that such a protection failure, unless it results in adequate compensation to the affected children, violates Article 13, providing for "an effective remedy before a national authority notwithstanding that the violation has been committed by persons acting in an official capacity" for rights secured by the Convention:

> * * * [T]he remedy required by Article 13 must be "effective" in practice as well as in law. In particular its exercise must not be unjustifiably hindered by the acts or omissions of the authorities of

the respondent State. Where alleged failure by the authorities to protect persons from the acts of others is concerned, Article 13 may not always require that the authorities undertake the responsibility for investigating the allegations. There should however be available to the victim or the victim's family a mechanism for establishing any liability of State officials or bodies for acts or omissions involving the breach of their rights under the Convention. Furthermore, in the case of a breach of Articles 2 and 3 of the Convention, which rank as the most fundamental provisions of the Convention, compensation for the non-pecuniary damage flowing from the breach should in principle be available as part of the range of redress.

E and others v. United Kingdom, [2002] ECHR 763. In *E and others,* the Court found that the failure to provide "full compensation for the severe [sexual and physical] abuse which took place over many years" was actionable under Article 13 despite the fact that three of the plaintiffs had already received some compensation from the U.K. Criminal Injuries Board. The Court awarded additional damages ranging from EUR 16,000—32,000 to each plaintiff as well as EUR 64,000 in costs and expenses.

In *DeShaney,* the state defendants had received complaints that the child was being abused by his father and took various steps to protect him. But they did not remove the child from his father's custody. The child was eventually beaten so severely that he suffered permanent brain damage and became profoundly retarded. The child and his mother sued under 42 U.S.C. § 1983, alleging a deprivation of the child's liberty interest in bodily integrity; the Supreme Court held that the State's failure to protect an individual against private violence generally does not constitute a violation of the Due Process Clause. In the Court's view, "[t]he Clause is phrased as a limitation on the State's power to act, not as a guarantee of certain minimal levels of safety and security; while it forbids the State itself to deprive individuals of life, liberty, and property without due process of law, its language cannot fairly be read to impose an affirmative obligation on the State to ensure that those interests do not come to harm through other means." *DeShaney, supra.*

Under the European Convention, did Joshua DeShaney have a claim to compensation? Under the European Convention, did the children in *T.G.* have a claim to compensation? Did Gregory K.? Would the state have an obligation to protect Joshua had he been placed in foster care instead of with his father? *See* Doe v. S.C. Dep't Soc. Servs., 597 F.3d 163 (4th Cir. 2010).

7.   *The Adoption and Safe Families Act of 1997 (ASFA):* ASFA limited the "reasonable efforts" requirement of the AACWA. Under ASFA, reasonable efforts at reunification need not be made: (1) if the parent has subjected the child to "aggravated circumstances," as defined by state law; (2) if the parent has committed or aided in, conspired in, or attempted the commission of murder or voluntary manslaughter of another of that parent's children, or has committed a felony assault resulting in serious bodily injury to the child or another child of the parent; and (3) if the parent's rights have been terminated

with regard to a sibling of the child whose case is proceeding. 42 U.S.C. § 671(a)(15)(D). ASFA also requires that states file a petition to terminate the parental rights of the parent(s) of any child who has been in foster care for fifteen of the most recent twenty-two months and shortened the time frame within which states must schedule a permanency hearing. For children whose parents are not entitled to reasonable efforts, ASFA requires a permanency hearing within 30 days. For others the time frame was shortened from eighteen to twelve months from the time a child enters foster care; an exception is provided in cases where parents have not received services required by the reasonable efforts clause. 42 U.S.C. §§ 675(5)(C)–(E). ASFA also created an adoption incentive program by which states will receive $4,000 to $6,000 per child for any increase in the annual number of adoptions over a "baseline" year.

ASFA, enacted with broad bipartisan support but little new funding, reflected growing disillusionment with the efficacy of reunification efforts and a sharp increase in the foster care population: in 1984, there were 276,000 children in foster care and 20,000 adoptions; in 1996 there were 502,000 children in foster care and 27,000 adoptions. *See* Robert M. Gordon, *Drifting Through Byzantium: The Promise and Failure of the Adoption and Safe Families Act of 1997*, 83 MINN. L. REV. 637, 650 n. 73 (1999). Surveys also showed that children who remained in foster care until the age of majority often fared poorly. For example, a national study of the Title IV-E foster care independent living program, which is supposed to assist foster children in the transition to self-sufficiency, found that, 21/2 to 4 years after aging out of the system, 46% of those surveyed had not completed high school; 38% had not held a job for longer than one year; 25% had been homeless for at least one night; 60% of women had given birth to a child; and 40% had been on public assistance, incarcerated, or a cost to the community in some other way. *See* U.S. GEN. ACCT'ING OFFICE, FOSTER CARE: EFFECTIVENESS OF INDEPENDENT LIVING SERVICES UNKNOWN 3–4 (1999). In another study, 27% of males and 10% of females were incarcerated within 18 months, 50% were unemployed, 37% had not finished high school, 33% received public assistance, and 19% of females had given birth to children. Before leaving care, 47% were receiving counseling or medication for mental health problems. *See* M. Courtney & I. Pilavin, *Struggling in the Adult World*, WASH. POST, July 21, 1998 (describing Wisconsin research).

But can ASFA succeed where the AACWA failed? ASFA does seem to have had an impact on the adoption of foster children; in 1999 alone, the number of finalized adoptions of children in foster care increased 28%. Over the past few years, however, adoptions from foster care have leveled off. Between 1998 and 2001, adoptions jumped from 37,000 to 47,000; in 2002, 53,000 children were adopted from foster care and in 2005, preliminary estimates show that 51,000 were adopted. *See AFCARS Reports 1998–2002, Preliminary Estimates for 2005,* http://www.acf.hhs.gov/programs/cb/stats_research/afcars/tar/report12. htm. These results suggest that ASFA has had a definite, but modest impact on adoptions from foster care. More recent data suggests increase in adoptions.

Many experts question whether ASFA can produce significantly more adoptions. Foster children awaiting adoption are *not*, it is important to keep in mind, healthy white infants. Nationally, in 2005, only 40% of children waiting to be adopted from foster care were white, and only 18% were age two or younger. *See* AFCARS, *supra.* A majority of these children also have what are euphemistically described as "special needs." *See* U.S. GEN. ACC'TING OFFICE, FOSTER CARE: STATES FOCUSING ON FINDING PERMANENT HOMES FOR CHILDREN, BUT LONG-STANDING BARRIERS REMAIN 42 (GAO–03–626T, 2003) (describing states' difficulties in finding adoptive homes for special needs children). Those who do adopt challenging children may also return them, subjecting these children to yet another form of impermanency. *See* James A. Rosenthal, *Outcomes of Adoption of Children with Special Needs, in* 3 FUTURE OF CHILDREN: ADOPTION 77, 78–84 (Spr. 1993) (reporting that, as special needs adoptions increased during 1970s and 80s, so did rate of disruption; studies report highly disparate findings on disruption rates, ranging from 2% to 53%).

Most foster children live with unrelated adults. There may be relatives, however, who could provide the needed care. The Fostering Connections to Success and Increasing Adoptions Act of 2008, Pub. L. 110–351, requires child welfare agencies to exercise due diligence to identify and notify all adult relatives within 30 days of a child's placement in state care. The Act also requires states to provide enhanced financial assistance and other help to relative caregivers. Approximately 24–26 percent of foster children live with relatives. AFCARS report.

8.   While the D.C. neglect statute is a fairly typical one, during the 1970s and early 80s, a number of commissions and panels recommended that state neglect statutes be redrawn so as to specify the grounds for state intervention with greater particularity and thus prevent unwarranted state intervention. Standards drafted under the auspices of the Institute for Judicial Administration and American Bar Association (IJA-ABA), for example, authorize state intervention for neglect only when:

    a.   A child has suffered, or there is a substantial risk that a child will imminently suffer, a physical harm, inflicted nonaccidentally upon him/her by his/her parents, which causes, or creates a substantial risk of causing disfigurement, impairment of bodily functioning, or other serious physical injury;

    b.   A child has suffered, or there is a substantial risk that a child will imminently suffer, physical harm causing disfigurement, impairment of bodily functioning, or other serious physical injury as a result of conditions created by his/her parents or by the failure of the parents to adequately supervise or protect him/her;

    c.   A child is suffering serious emotional damage, evidenced by severe anxiety, depression, or withdrawal, or untoward aggressive behavior toward self or others, and the child's parents are not willing to provide treatment for him/her;

d. A child has been sexually abused by his/her parent or a member of his/her household * * * where the parent know or should have known and failed to take appropriate action. * * *

e. A child is in need of medical treatment [for a serious medical condition] * * * and his/her parents are unwilling to provide or consent to the medical treatment;

f. A child is committing delinquent acts as a result of parental encouragement, guidance, or approval.

JOINT COMM'N ON JUVENILE JUSTICE STANDARDS, INST. OF JUDICIAL ADMIN., ABA STANDARDS RELATING TO ABUSE AND NEGLECT, STANDARD 2.1 (1981). Would the Standards permit intervention in *T.G.*?

9. The minimal state intervention philosophy that underlies the IJA-ABA standards rests in part on Goldstein, Freud, and Solnit's "psychological parenting" theory. Unsurprisingly, Goldstein, Freud, and Solnit urge extremely limited grounds for state intervention to protect the child against physical and emotional neglect just as they urge limited grounds for medical neglect; specifically, they propose that intervention by child welfare authorities be limited to cases of: "[s]erious bodily injury inflicted by parents upon their child, or an attempt to inflict such harms, or repeated failure of the parents to prevent the child from suffering such injury"; conviction of a sexual offense against the child; or abandonment. *See* JOSEPH GOLDSTEIN ET AL., BEFORE THE BEST INTERESTS OF THE CHILD 193–95 (1979). Goldstein et al. find intervention for neglect particularly troublesome because of the high risk that it will lead to the child's removal from the home, thus disrupting "[c]ontinuity of relationships, surroundings and environmental influences [that] are essential for a child's normal development" and creating the risk of multiple placements which interfere with the "attachments that are essential for an individual's growth." Goldstein et al. argue that even the child's return to his parents when he has formed attachments elsewhere is risky because it "causes distress and harm[s] * * * [the child's] psychological development." JOSEPH GOLDSTEIN ET AL., BEYOND THE BEST INTERESTS OF THE CHILD 31–32 (2d ed. 1979); JOSEPH GOLDSTEIN ET AL., BEFORE THE BEST INTERESTS OF THE CHILD 46, 49, 136 (1979).

Although the minimum-intervention philosophy influenced the federal Adoption Assistance and Child Welfare Act of 1980, state legislatures have not heeded the call to narrow the grounds for abuse and neglect intervention. Can you think of any reasons why? What are the pros and cons of narrow vs. open-ended neglect standards?

10. Assuming that the state should protect the child's "right" to an "open future," should it intervene in a case like *T.G.?* What are the arguments in favor of intervention? Against? On balance, is intervention desirable? *See* Howard Davidson, *Federal Law and State Intervention When Parents Fail: Has National Guidance of Our Child Welfare System Been Successful?*, 42 FAM. L. Q. 481 (2008).

Problem 10-6:

You are counsel to the Joint Legislative Committee on Child Protection, which is considering amendment of current state law to explicitly authorize state intervention to protect unborn children. You have been asked to write a memorandum addressing both the constitutionality and advisability of such an amendment.

A. Constitutionality

The impetus for the legislature's move is a recent decision of the state Supreme Court interpreting the current legislation as excluding unborn children. This decision is consistent with the judicial trend; most state courts have interpreted the meaning of "child" in state child protection legislation to exclude unborn fetuses. *See In re* Unborn Child of Julie Starks, 18 P.3d 342 (Okla. 2001); Arkansas Dept. of Human Services v. Collier, 95 S.W.3d 772 (Ark. 2003); *In re* H., 74 P.3d 494 (Colo. App. 2003); Wisconsin ex. rel. Angela M.W. v. Kruzicki, 561 N.W.2d 729 (Wis. 1997).

Some state legislatures have responded to these decisions by revising child-protection laws to include the unborn. For example, following the *Angela M.W.* decision, the Wisconsin legislature revised its Children's Code to create a new category of "unborn child" abuse. *See* WIS. STAT. ANN. §§ 48.01(1)(2), 48.02(1)(a). The revised law permits the state to intervene to protect an "unborn child" from

> [s]erious physical harm inflicted on the unborn child, and the risk of serious physical harm to the child when born, caused by the habitual lack of self control of the expectant mother of the unborn child in the use of alcohol beverages, controlled substances or controlled substance analogs, exhibited to a severe degree.

The statute defines "unborn child" as a "human being from the time of fertilization to the time of birth" and authorizes confinement of the pregnant "abuser" in a treatment facility. The states of Minnesota and South Dakota have also adopted legislation authorizing the confinement of pregnant alcohol or drug users in treatment centers; the South Dakota statute explicitly permits confinement for as long as nine months. *See* MINN. STAT. § 626.5562; S.D. COD. L. § 34–20A–63.

The proposed law would permit confinement for as long as nine months; it would define "unborn child abuse" and "unborn child" in the same manner as the Wisconsin statute. Its advocates argue that the proposed change in the state's child protection law would harmonize it with criminal and tort law. Your state, like eighteen others, has enacted fetal homicide legislation that protects the unborn child from the point of conception onward. It has also enacted legislation allowing recovery for the wrongful death of an unborn fetus no matter what its stage of gestation. *See* Amy Lotziero, Comment, *The Unborn Child: A Forgotten Interest:*

Reexamining Roe in Light of Increased Recognition of Fetal Rights, 79 TEMP. L. REV. 279 (2006) (categorizing state laws).

The constitutionality of laws like those adopted in Wisconsin, Minnesota, and South Dakota has not been addressed by the Supreme Court, and the limited state case law reaches inconsistent results. In Whitner v. State, 492 S.E.2d 777 (S. C. 1997), cert. denied 523 U.S. 1145 (1998), the Court sustained a criminal conviction for child neglect based on prenatal use of illegal drugs:

> Whitner[, the defendant,] argues that prosecuting her for using crack cocaine after her fetus attains viability unconstitutionally burdens her right of privacy, or, more specifically, her right to carry her pregnancy to term. We disagree.
>
> * * * It strains belief for Whitner to argue that using crack cocaine during pregnancy is encompassed within the constitutionally recognized right of privacy. Use of crack cocaine is illegal, period. No one here argues that laws criminalizing the use of crack cocaine are themselves unconstitutional. If the State wishes to impose additional criminal penalties on pregnant women who engage in this already illegal conduct because of the effect the conduct has on the viable fetus, it may do so. We do not see how the fact of pregnancy elevates the use of crack cocaine to the lofty status of a fundamental right.
>
> Moreover, as a practical matter, we do not see how our interpretation of * * * [the child neglect statute] imposes a burden on Whitner's right to carry her child to term. * * * [D]uring her pregnancy after the fetus attained viability, Whitner enjoyed the same freedom to use cocaine that she enjoyed earlier in and predating her pregnancy—none whatsoever. * * * The State's imposition of an additional penalty when a pregnant woman with a viable fetus engages in the already proscribed behavior does not burden a woman's right to carry her pregnancy to term; rather, the additional penalty simply recognizes that a third party (the viable fetus or newborn child) is harmed by the behavior.

The dissenting judge in *Angela M.W.*, *supra*, reached a similar conclusion on the constitutionality of confining the pregnant drug abuser:

> Angela * * * contends that the custodial effect of the protective order violated her due process liberty interest under the United States Constitution. * * * The test for violation of a fundamental liberty interest is two pronged. First, in order to restrict a fundamental liberty interest, a challenged statute must further a compelling state interest. Second, the statute must be narrowly tailored to serve that compelling state interest.

In regard to the state interest implicated here, the United States Supreme Court has determined:

> With respect to the State's important and legitimate interest in potential life, the "compelling" point is at viability. This is so because the fetus then presumably has the capability of meaningful life outside the mother's womb. State regulation protective of fetal life after viability thus has both logical and biological justifications. . . (*Casey v. Planned Parenthood*).

The *Casey* Court further emphasized: " . . . Roe v. Wade speaks with clarity in establishing not only the woman's liberty but also the State's 'important and legitimate interest in potential life.' "

* * * Thus, as determined by the United States Supreme Court, the state's interest in protecting the life and health of an unborn child becomes compelling and dominant once the fetus reaches viability.

* * * [T]his court's decision in State v. Black is also relevant. In *Black*, the petitioner allegedly caused the death of a fetus due to be born in five days by assaulting the unborn child's mother. * * * [T]he Black court concluded that the state may enact legislation to protect a viable fetus in areas other than simply abortion, and, therefore, implicitly determined that the state has a compelling interest in the welfare of a viable fetus in other contexts.

In the present case, there is no dispute that Angela's child was a viable fetus when the petition was filed, that Angela was actively using cocaine, and that the use of cocaine put the child at substantial risk of great bodily harm or possibly death. As such, the state has a compelling state interest to protect Angela's fetus under *Roe, Casey*, and *Black*.

The next issue therefore is whether the infringement on Angela's liberty is narrowly tailored to further the compelling state interest. I conclude that [the due process protections contained in t]he Children's Code * * * [, which require] a hearing within 24 hours of the time the decision was made to hold the child in protective custody [and a] * * * determin[ation] whether there is probable cause to believe the child is within the jurisdiction of the court, and that the child will be subject to injury if he or she is not taken into protective custody * * * [ensure that] the state's compelling interest is served are narrowly tailored to "attain the purposes and objectives of the legislation" to protect children. * * *

In re Angela M.W., supra.

However, in *In re* Tanya P., N.Y.L.J., Feb. 28, 1995, at 26, col. 6 (Sup. Ct. N.Y. Co., 1995), the court denied a commitment petition that would have permitted a state mental hospital to retain an inmate who was eight months pregnant and had been a serious crack abuser prior to her hospital admission. Although the patient was "no longer delusional or hallucinating," her doctors believed she would resume drug use and a life on the streets when she left the hospital, with consequent risk to the viable fetus she was carrying. The Court held that:

> [the] right to determine one's medical treatment and to make reproductive choices is, and must be superior to any interest which the state may have in an unborn fetus. * * * In addition to implicating the right to refuse medical treatment, involuntary commitment based on fetal endangerment infringes the right to privacy also protected by the Fourteenth Amendment by penalizing the woman for being pregnant. * * *

> Since involuntary commitment based upon fetal endangerment infringes on the constitutionally protected rights of liberty and privacy, the * * * proponent of the policy must demonstrate that such confinement serves a compelling interest, and that the policy is narrowly tailored to achieve its goals. * * * In order to justify its draconian violation of liberty and privacy interests, the petitioner * * * would have to show that * * * retention [of the pregnant woman] was the sole means to preserve the fetus. * * * If the fetus likely would, or even might, survive without involuntary confinement of the pregnant woman, there is no "compelling" interest. * * *

Evaluate the positions of the *Whitner* and *Tanya P.* courts and the *Angela M.W.* dissent. On which Supreme Court decisions does each rely? Which position is more persuasive? On balance, would the proposed constitutional amendment pass constitutional muster? Why?

B. Advisability

The Effects of Prenatal Substance Abuse: While the majority of pregnant substance abusers experience an uncomplicated labor and delivery, prenatal exposure to addictive substances is associated with a higher risk of premature birth and morbidity as well as low birth weight, short-term withdrawal symptoms, and long-term developmental, behavioral, and learning problems. *See* Am. Acad. Pediatrics Committee on Drugs, *Neonatal Drug Withdrawal*, 101 PEDIATRICS 1079 (1998). But research on the consequences of prenatal substance abuse is complicated by the fact that women who use one addictive substance during pregnancy often use several. In one survey, 76% of adult women who reported smoking during their first trimester of pregnancy said that they also drank alcohol during that period. And a national study found that 74% of women who used illicit drugs during pregnancy also reported either smoking, drinking, or both. *See* Marie D. Cornelius, *The Effects of Tobacco Use During and*

After Pregnancy on Exposed Children, 24 ALCOHOL RES. & HEALTH 242 (2000).

Although the evidence is inconclusive, illegal drugs do not appear to pose greater risks than legal drugs. For example, although cocaine abuse has not been conclusively linked with specific physical abnormalities, alcohol abuse has. The most serious long-term consequence of prenatal exposure to large quantities of alcohol is fetal alcohol syndrome (FAS). FAS is characterized by prenatal growth retardation, a pattern of specific minor anomalies that include characteristic facial abnormalities, and central nervous system manifestations, including microcephaly or delayed mental development, hyperactivity, attention deficiencies, learning disabilities, intellectual deficits, visual impairment, and seizures. Children exposed to alcohol in utero who have some manifestations of FAS but not enough for a firm FAS diagnosis are considered to have fetal alcohol effects (FAE). The available data indicate that the behavioral and mental manifestations of FAS do not typically diminish during childhood. *See* E.L. ABEL, FETAL ALCOHOL ABUSE SYNDROME (1998).

Tobacco use during pregnancy has also been linked to fetal harm, particularly premature and low-birth-weight deliveries. Women who smoke during pregnancy are almost twice as likely to have a low-birth-weight infant; as a result smoking is "the most significant risk factor" for low birth weight—a leading cause of infant mortality and disability. *See* Anne D. Walling, *Which Risks Are Most Significant Predictors of SGA Births?*, 64 AM. FAM. PHYSICIAN 11892 (2001); Nat. Center for Health Statistics Dataline, *Latest U.S. Birth Statistics Show Progress in Maternal and Infant Health*, 113 PUB. HEALTH RPTS. 475 (1998). Studies of low-birth-weight children have shown that approximately 20% have severe disabilities; among those weighing less than 750 grams at birth, 50% exhibit functional impairments. A recent study that followed these very small infants to school showed that up to 50% of them scored low on standardized intelligence tests, including 21% who were mentally retarded. In addition, 9% had cerebral palsy and 25% had severe vision problems. As a result, 45% ended up enrolling in special-education programs. *See* Ezekiel J. Emanuel, *The Case Against Octuplets*, NEW REPUBLIC, Jan. 25, 1999, at 8.

By contrast, a meta-analysis of controlled studies analyzing the impact of prenatal cocaine exposure found no clear evidence that even heavy use of cocaine during pregnancy had any persistent effect on the child's physical growth and development, motor skills, intellectual capacity, language, or behavior up to the age of six. There were small effects on birth weight and the physiological regulation and motor performance of newborns. Some studies also found continuing delays in motor development, but only until the age of seven months. Nor did parents and teachers report any special behavior problems, although a few sophisticated experiments and statistical interpretations of standard test scores suggested some effects on attention and impulse control. *See* Deborah A. Frank et al., *Growth, Development, and Behavior in Early Childhood Following Prenatal Cocaine Exposure: A Systematic Review*, 285 JAMA 1613 (2001). *See also* L.T. Singer et al., *Cognitive Outcomes of Preschool Children with Prenatal Cocaine Exposure*, 291 JAMA 2448 (2004) (finding no significant association between prenatal cocaine exposure and cognitive functioning).

Voluntary vs. Coerced Treatment: There is little research on the relative efficacy of coerced vs. voluntary substance abuse treatment among pregnant women. However, researchers who analyzed the impact of coercion on the drug treatment success of post-partum women recently reported that their findings "lend support for the argument in favor of coercion for treatment":

> First, women who were coerced to come to treatment via the criminal justice system (i.e., mandated by the child dependency court and welfare system) and who had custody of their children remained in treatment longer. Second, an interaction effect was found between type of treatment and having custody of one's child. In particular, women who had custody and were in the gender sensitive, more structured, and intensive day treatment program completed treatment at substantially higher rates than those in the traditional male-based, less structured outpatient treatment program with minimal hours of attendance.

Robert H. Nishimoto et al., *Coercion and Drug Treatment for Postpartum Women*, 27 AM. J. DRUG & ALCOHOL ABUSE 161 (2001). But coercion was not significantly correlated with treatment success among women who did not have custody; for pregnant women, it is thus unclear whether this study's findings are relevant. Studies correlating motivation and coercion with treatment retention and outcomes in broader or different populations also show decidedly mixed results; several studies have found that coerced treatment produced results equal to or better than voluntary treatment, but other studies have found pressure to be negatively correlated with case outcome. *See id.*

The Impact of Race and Social Class on State Intervention: Tobacco use during pregnancy appears to be more common among poor women than their wealthier counterparts, but use of illegal drugs does not appear to be strongly correlated with racial background or socioeconomic status. These factors do appear to be significantly related to intervention decisions, however. A six-month study of women seeking prenatal care at five public health clinics and twelve private obstetrical offices in Pinellas County, Florida found that 14% of the African-American mothers tested positive for drug and alcohol use, compared to 15% of the Caucasian women. But only

1% of Caucasian women testing positive were reported to the health authorities, compared to 11% of the African-American women. *See* Ira Chasnoff et al., *The Prevalence of Illicit Drug or Alcohol Use During Pregnancy and Discrepancies in Mandatory Reporting in Pinellas County, Florida*, 322 NEW ENG. J. MED. 1202 (1990).

How might proponents of the proposed amendment use the research data? How might opponents? On balance, do the data support or undermine the case for involuntary prenatal intervention?

C. TERMINATION OF PARENTAL RIGHTS

IN THE INTEREST OF M.M.L.

Supreme Court of Kansas, 1995.
258 Kan. 254, 900 P.2d 813.

HOLMES, C.J.

[Michael, t]he natural father of M.M.L., a minor, appeals in a child in need of care case from an order of the district court placing M.M.L. in long-term foster care. He argues the best interests of the child standard in K.S.A. § 38–1563(d) violates his constitutional right to custody of his child absent a finding of unfitness.

* * *

Michael and [M.M.L.'s mother] J.C. were married in 1974, and one son, now an adult, was born to the marriage. The couple was divorced in 1979; however, they reestablished a relationship and lived together until sometime in 1984, apparently as residents of the Kansas City, Missouri, area. M.M.L. was born during this period on January 4, 1981. In mid-1984 M.M.L. and her mother left the home, and at some later date J.C. married M.C., whose name is also Michael. The coincidence of both the father and stepfather having the same first name, Michael, creates some confusion in attempting to get a clear picture of some of the events described in the record. In an attempt to avoid further confusion, we will refer to the father of M.M.L. as Michael and the stepfather as M.C.

In 1985 Michael filed a proceeding in Missouri to obtain custody of both children. Soon thereafter M.M.L. alleged she had been sexually abused by "Michael" or by one of her mother's boyfriends. As it eventually turned out, Michael, the father, was absolved of any sexual abuse of M.M.L., although expert testimony did establish that she had, in all probability, been abused by someone, either M.C. or one of the other friends of J.C. Sometime in 1985 Michael moved to the state of Washington and lost track of his children. His custody suit was dismissed when he failed to show up for the hearing. Thereafter M.M.L. and her mother moved to Great Bend. Despite his efforts to obtain information about M.M.L from her maternal grandmother, Michael was unable to obtain any information about her whereabouts or about her welfare. Michael moved back to Kansas City in 1988 or 1989, to Georgia in 1989, and back to Kansas City in late 1991 or 1992. In late 1990 or early 1991 Michael learned by chance that J.C. and M.M.L. were in Great Bend. He has been attempting to gain custody ever since.

On September 6, 1990, M.M.L. was placed in the temporary custody of the Department of Social and Rehabilitation Services (SRS) based on allegations that she had been sexually abused by M.C. She was placed by SRS in a foster home in Great Bend, where she has remained since. On January 17, 1991, the trial court found by clear and convincing evidence that M.M.L. had been sexually abused by her stepfather and adjudicated her a child in need of care. At that point Michael had not had contact or a relationship with M.M.L. for approximately five years. At a dispositional hearing held March 12, 1991, the court found that placing M.M.L. with her father was not a viable option at that time and denied him visitation rights so that M.M.L.'s therapist could prepare her for future visitation. It was at about this time that J.C. moved to Texas and apparently abandoned any interest in M.M.L. or in any further court proceedings in her behalf.

As the case progressed, review hearings were held and, in early 1992 Michael was granted visitation rights. Initially the visits were limited to supervised visits in Great Bend, but eventually Michael was granted unsupervised visits at his home in Kansas City for several days at a time. Throughout the proceedings, Michael did everything requested of him by the court. Various examinations indicated (1) he does not portray sexual offender characteristics; (2) he has never sexually abused M.M.L.; (3) he exhibits no psychological problems impairing his ability to care for his daughter; and (4) he shows no signs of alcoholism or drug abuse. He has attended alcohol information school, effective parenting classes, anger-control counseling, counseling for parents of sexually abused children, individual counseling, and joint counseling with M.M.L. Home studies have been performed and the latest done in July 1994 recommended M.M.L. be placed in Michael's home with supervision.

Despite Michael's efforts, M.M.L. maintained throughout the proceedings that she did not want to live with him. Although she was initially excited and hopeful about a relationship with her father, she became frightened and disillusioned as the visits progressed. From the outset of the case, M.M.L. saw a psychologist, Dr. Kohrs. M.M.L. repeatedly expressed two concerns about her father's behavior to Dr. Kohrs, which Dr. Kohrs believed were based on M.M.L.'s observations and not on any "predictions" given to M.M.L. as a child by her mother. First, M.M.L. described "a pattern of arbitrary and provocative hostility" by her father, such as verbally abusing and continually provoking arguments with his mother to whom M.M.L. is attached, making exaggerated and hostile complaints in public places, teasing her cousins unnecessarily, and having conflicts with her aunts and foster mother. Michael's mother and his sisters (the aunts) deny these allegations. M.M.L. does not trust him and is afraid he will sexually abuse her because he gets so " 'pushy and mad.' " * * * M.M.L. was [also] concerned with her father's use of alcohol. Although he acknowledges occasional use of alcohol, he denies any problem, and various psychological tests and counseling bear that out. M.M.L.'s emotional and psychological concerns about sexual abuse and excessive use of alcohol appear to be a result of her early childhood experiences with her stepfather and one or more of her mother's other male companions.

M.M.L. seems to have established a good relationship with her paternal grandmother and her aunts, all of whom reside near Michael in the Kansas City area. The grandmother lives next door to Michael, and she and Michael's sisters are supportive of his efforts to obtain custody of M.M.L. They are also available to assist Michael in caring for M.M.L. Dr. Kohrs believed M.M.L. tried to focus on the positive aspects of the relationship, and M.M.L. likes it when Michael is nice to her and takes her bowling. She feels good about herself when she cooks meals for him and has appreciated getting to know her relatives in the Kansas City area. However, based on M.M.L.'s concerns, Dr. Kohrs recommended that M.M.L. remain in the foster home in Great Bend and continue visitation with her father and relatives in Kansas City. She was concerned "that if the situation is this problematic while being monitored by SRS and the Court, what the quality of home life would be if there were no scrutiny by the Court."

In contrast, M.M.L. was firmly attached to the foster care home, describing it as a place where she was safe, secure, and part of a family. At an earlier hearing, a counselor testified M.M.L. would suffer grief, loss, and confusion about her identity if she had to move away from the foster home and that moving her would add to the confusion and chaos in her life. Also, at this hearing, Dr. Kohrs testified the optimum placement was in the foster home because the children were involved in school and community activities and the relationship was not filled with conflict like the one with Michael.

On the other hand, professionals in the Kansas City area who have counseled with Michael over the years of these proceedings and with both Michael and M.M.L. on the occasions when she visits in Kansas City reach a diametrically opposite conclusion. They recommend that M.M.L. be placed in her father's custody. From their reports and the testimony of Michael, M.M.L. seems to be happy and well adjusted when with her father. She voiced no serious complaints to the Kansas City counselors and professionals. However, upon returning to Great Bend she apparently tells a totally different story and has consistently maintained she will not live with her father. The record includes several letters written by M.M.L. to the court in which she voices her desire to stay with her foster parents and complains bitterly about her father's actions and appearance.

* * * Michael moved for an order placing M.M.L. in his custody. He alleged that despite his compliance with all court orders, SRS had refused to prepare a reintegration plan with measurable objectives and time schedules and the only reason articulated for not placing M.M.L. with him was her desire not to live with him. * * * At a dispositional hearing on August 15, 1994, the district court concluded * * * that although Michael was not an unfit parent, no close bond existed between Michael and M.M.L. despite his tremendous efforts. While reasonable efforts had been made to reintegrate M.M.L., the efforts had not been successful largely due to M.M.L.'s attitude and fears. The court believed forcing M.M.L. to live with her father could cause more emotional damage. Because a close bond existed between M.M.L. and her foster family, the court continued placement in long-term foster care with visitation to be worked out by the parties. At the * * * hearing the court * * * [heard] conflicting testimony of the various therapists, counselors, psychologists, and other professionals * * * [and] made the following findings.

1. That the natural father is not an unfit parent.

2. That the Court recognizes that a parent has a fundamental right to have custody of his or her child. * * *

5. That the Court finds that reasonable efforts have been made to reintegrate the child into the home of the natural father.

6. That said efforts have not been successful due mainly to the attitude of the minor child.

7. That a close daughter-father bond does not exist despite the efforts of the father to re-establish that bond.

8. That placement of the child with the natural father could cause more emotional damage to the minor child.

9. That a close bond between the foster family and the child exists.

10. That placement therefore should continue in long term foster care with continuing visitation as agreed to by the parties between the father and the minor child.

There have been literally dozens of hearings held by the court and hundreds of hours devoted to this case by dedicated judges, counsel, and professional workers in an attempt to arrive at an acceptable solution to the apparent legal and emotional conflict between Michael and M.M.L. and/or SRS. While the legal principles, applicable statutes, and constitutional arguments are not extremely difficult to resolve, it is doubtful any good solution to the dilemma facing the trial court and this court exists. * * *

* * * K.S.A. § 38–1563 provides [that]

(d) If the court finds that placing the child in the custody of a parent will not assure protection from physical, mental or emotional abuse or neglect or sexual abuse or will not be in the best interests of the child, the court shall enter an order awarding custody of the child * * * to one of the following:

(1) A relative of the child or a person with whom the child has close emotional ties;

(2) any other suitable person;

(3) a shelter facility or * * * [the state].

* * * In the instant case all parties concede that Michael is not unfit to have the care and custody of M.M.L. It is also apparent that he has gone to great lengths to improve his parenting capabilities and educate himself in the skills necessary to raise his daughter. He has adequate physical and residential facilities for her care and also has the support of his sisters and mother, who are available to furnish family support.

* * *

Michael contends that K.S.A. § 38–1563(d) is either unconstitutional on its face or unconstitutional as applied to the facts of this case because the best interests of the child test, contained in the statute, violates his right to due process under the Fourteenth Amendment to the United States Constitution. He asserts that the parental preference rule is the proper test and that failure to apply it denies his fundamental right to custody of M.M.L.

* * * The United States Supreme Court [has] * * * recognized the fundamental nature of the relationship between parent and child. * * * The State argues at length that Michael's fundamental constitutional rights must give way to the best interests of the child * * * because actions under the Code are deemed to be taken and done under the parens patriae doctrine or parental power of the State. It also argues that because M.M.L. was found to be a child in need of care by clear and convincing evidence, Michael's due process rights were adequately protected.

* * *

A review of the numerous Kansas and United States Supreme Court cases involving the powers of the State under the parens patriae doctrine clearly indicates that the courts must assert a balancing test between the fundamental constitutional right of parents to the care, custody, and control of their children and the power of the State to ensure the protection and welfare of children. In balancing the interests of all parties, the best interests of the child is a factor to be considered and must be given appropriate weight. However, absent a showing that the parent is unfit or that there are highly unusual or extraordinary circumstances mandating the State's exercise of its parens patriae powers, the rights of the parent must prevail.

* * * We therefore construe the best interests of the child language contained in K.S.A. § 38–1563(d) to be constitutional when applied in a child in need of care case in which the court has found by clear and convincing evidence that the parent or parents are unfit or that highly unusual or extraordinary circumstances exist which substantially endanger the child's welfare. Absent such findings the long-standing parental preference doctrine controls.

Here * * * the primary basis of the trial court's holding was that M.M.L. does not want to leave her friends and comfortable foster home surroundings in Great Bend, coupled with her professed dislike of her father. Such feelings are not unusual in children who have become attached to, and feel comfortable with, their peers, school, and other surroundings. Such feelings and wishes do not, in our opinion, constitute the highly unusual or extraordinary circumstances necessary to deprive a parent, who is not unfit and who is capable and desirous of providing the necessary care, control, and guidance of his or her child, of the custody of the child. We conclude that under the facts of this case, K.S.A. § 38–1563(d), as applied, violated Michael's constitutional rights. * * * We recognize that M.M.L. will need continued counseling and Michael must make such provisions for further counseling with qualified personnel in the Kansas City area as may be directed by the trial court.

In conclusion, we hold that the best interests of the child test contained in K.S.A. § 38–1563(d) is constitutional [only] when the court has determined by clear and convincing evidence that the parent is unfit or that highly unusual or extraordinary circumstances exist which substantially endanger the child's welfare. * * *. We further order that the custody of M.M.L. be placed with her father, Michael, subject to appropriate continued counseling in the father's residential area and under such conditions of reporting and monitoring as may be directed by the court. * * *

IN THE MATTER OF THE GUARDIANSHIP OF
J.C., J.C., AND J.M.C., MINORS

Supreme Court of New Jersey, 1992.
129 N.J. 1, 608 A.2d 1312.

HANDLER, J.

* * * The Court in this case * * * is required to determine whether the parental rights of a natural mother should be terminated based on the need to protect children from potential harm that may result from being separated from foster parents with whom the children may have formed parental bonds. * * *

A.C., who was born in Colombia and came to this country as a teenager, is the natural mother of three children. Two girls, J.C. and J.M.C., were born in July 1983 and in January 1985, respectively, and J.C., a boy, was born in August 1986. A.C. voluntarily placed her two girls in foster care with the Division of Youth and Family Services (DYFS, Division, or Agency) in August 1985. The children were returned to her after three months. Almost a year later, in October 1986, A.C. again placed the two girls, along with her new child, J.C., in foster care, where they have remained for the past five and a half years. A.C. began unsupervised weekend visits with her children soon after their placement in foster care, seeing them regularly twice a month during the following year. Although DYFS had intended to reunite the family, in November 1987 the agency stopped unsupervised visits out of concern that the children were not being properly cared for. DYFS also came to believe that A.C. was addicted to drugs and was being abused by her husband (who, she claims, was not the father of any of the children). However, bi-monthly visits at the DYFS office continued. In April of the following year, A.C. entered drug treatment. By November 1988 the agency concluded that the children could not be returned successfully and that preparation should be initiated for their permanent placement and adoption. The agency transferred the case to its Adoption Resources Center (A.R.C.), which subsequently terminated visitation.

DYFS filed a petition * * * on July 7, 1989 [seeking] * * * termination of A.C.'s parental rights on the grounds that A.C. was unable and unwilling to stop causing the children harm and that to delay permanent placement would add to the harm facing the children.

At the time that DYFS moved for guardianship, the oldest child, J.C., had lived with at least two foster families. She was moved to her current pre-adoptive parents a week later, on July 13, 1989. J.M.C. had been living with her current foster parents since October or November 1988. A.C. has since consented to the adoption of her youngest child, J.C., and his status is not an issue in the case.

The case was initially tried on November 9, 1989, and December 15, 1989. Following a remand and additional hearings held in March 1991, the trial court concluded that termination of A.C.'s parental rights was necessary in the best interests of the children. It determined that A.C. had not, as a matter of law, abandoned her children even though she had placed them in foster care and had failed to achieve the requisite fitness to secure their return. However, it did find that the children would suffer serious psychological harm if they were removed from their foster or pre-adoptive homes and returned to A.C., and that the harm in part was attributable to A.C.'s own inability to plan for their future and her failure to rehabilitate herself. The Appellate Division affirmed.

* * *

[A] trial court should make [specific findings] before it terminates parental rights. The first finding is that the child's health and development have been or will be seriously impaired by the parental relationship. * * * Secondly, the court must conclude that the parents are unable or unwilling to eliminate the harm and that a delay in permanent placement will add to the harm. * * * Third, the court should be convinced that alternatives to terminating parental rights have been thoroughly explored and exhausted, including sufficient efforts made to help the parents cure the problems that led to the placement. * * * Fourth, all of those considerations must inform the determination that termination of parental rights will not do more harm than good.

* * *

Termination of parental rights permanently cuts off the relationship between children and their biological parents. * * * The burden falls on the State to demonstrate by clear and convincing evidence that the natural parent has not cured the initial cause of harm and will continue to cause serious and lasting harm to the child. * * *

In this case[,] * * * [t]he evidence strongly indicated that A.C. showed an interest in her children while they were in foster care, visiting them regularly and frequently. DYFS recognized that interest but stopped short of returning the children to A.C. on several occasions due to concerns about her housing situation and drug and alcohol addiction. Toward the end of 1987, after the two girls had been in foster care for more than a year, DYFS made plans to return the children, one by one, to A.C. Those plans were cancelled after reports of domestic violence in A.C.'s home, as well as renewed concerns over her continuing drug and alcohol abuse.

* * * Based on the trial testimony and the subsequent report the trial court on May 22, 1990, the court ordered that parental rights be terminated and guardianship transferred to DYFS. * * * The Appellate Division remanded [and] * * * [o]n remand, beginning in March 1991, the court heard six days of * * * testimony from Ms. Johnson as well as from other experts. First, the parties stipulated to several facts about A.C.'s rehabilitation. With respect to her housing situation, they agreed that she was living in the same apartment in which she had been living since December 1989. Concerning her work, they agreed that she had a steady job, that she had been working there for the previous two years, and that there was on-site after school child care at her workplace. Finally the parties "stipulated" that A.C. asserted that she was drug and alcohol free and that DYFS had no evidence to suggest otherwise.

In addition to the testimony of Ms. Johnson, the court-appointed counselor, DYFS produced its own expert, Dr. Martha Page. Dr. Page testified only with respect to J.C., with whom she had a counseling relationship. Dr. Page stated that when she met with J.C. in November 1990, she "was having a great deal of difficulty in school" and "[h]er behavior was very uneven" and "she was extremely hard to handle." She described J.C. as an "emotionally disturbed child" with special needs and a low resiliency to change, one who "needs stability . . . [and] a sense of identity." According to Dr. Page, separating J.C. from her foster parents would "reinforce her notion that she's somehow failed again." She mentioned J.C.'s fear of being rejected and emphasized her need for consistent care and permanency in planning for placement. Dr. Page also believed that if the child were returned to A.C. and the placement did not work out, the result would be particularly damaging to the emotional health of the child. She also concluded that any visitation with A.C. and delay in J.C.'s permanent placement would be "disastrous" and result in "transplant shock."

Dr. Matthew Johnson testified on behalf of A.C. He found a strong and enduring bonded relationship between J.C. and A.C. He believed "erasing" the biological mother from the child's life would cause the child serious emotional harm, particularly regarding the child's identity and development in adolescence. Thus, although he recognized potential danger in moving J.C. out of her current foster home, he also felt that terminating her relationship with her natural mother could also cause serious long-term harm. Dr. Johnson expressed concerns about A.C.'s ability to care for the children, mentioning among other things that she might have "residual emotional difficulty" in caring for the children and that she appeared to lack social networks necessary to support her in times of crisis. On the other hand, he noted that she had a number of strengths, that she was intelligent, had largely cleaned up her life, and had maintained contact with the children. Nevertheless, when asked on direct examination whether he believed A.C. could "assume custodial care of [J.C.]," Dr. Johnson again said that "to be frank there are concerns," and emphasized that "this child [J.C.] had emotional disturbance."

There was much less focus during the second trial on the younger child, J.M.C. Dr. Johnson found that she had significant relationships with both her foster mother and her natural mother. However, he was not able to say conclusively that there was bonding in either case. * * * Dr. Johnson made no recommendation on who should have final custody over the two children, but suggested continued visitation and, at least at that time, the preservation of parental rights in A.C.

* * * The trial court found that the children had bonded to their foster parents, and that this bonding had been caused by or exacerbated by A.C.'s conduct. * * * It based its decision to terminate parental rights on the substantial psychological harm * * * that would result from severing [those] * * * relationship[s]. * * *

* * * [W]e are compelled by the record as it currently stands to conclude that there is not clear and convincing evidence to support the findings necessary to terminate parental rights. Although a significant amount of testimony has been taken in this case, much of the evidence was either flawed or insufficient to answer the central question of serious psychological harm. * * *

In cases in which DYFS seeks termination of parental rights, not on grounds of current unfitness but because of potential harm to the child based on separation from a foster parent with whom the child has bonded, the quality of the proof adduced must be consistent with the interests at stake. To the extent that the quality of the child's relationship with foster parents may be relevant to termination of the natural parents' status, that relationship must be viewed not in isolation but in a broader context that includes as well the quality of the child's relationship with his or her natural parents.

* * *

[P]rolonged inattention by natural parents that permits the development of disproportionately stronger ties between a child and foster parents may lead to a bonding relationship the severing of which would cause profound harm—a harm attributable to the natural parents. * * * To show that the child has a strong relationship with the foster parents or might be better off if left in their custody is not enough. DYFS must prove by clear and convincing evidence that separating the child from his or her foster parents would cause serious and enduring emotional or psychological harm. *Santosky v. Kramer*, 455 U.S. at 768. * * * Such proof should include the testimony of a well qualified expert who has had full opportunity to make a comprehensive, objective, and informed evaluation of the child's relationship with the foster parent. In hearing a petition for termination in which the fitness of natural parents is neither relied on nor disputed by the agency, the trial court must also consider parallel proof relating to the child's relationship with his or her natural parents in assessing the existence, nature, and extent of the harm facing the child.

As the contrasting opinions of the experts in this case illustrate, there are competing psychological theories of the effects of parental bonding. In large measure, the variances in their recommendations derive from different assumptions concerning the fragility versus resiliency of the child psyche. *Compare* JOSEPH GOLDSTEIN, ANNA FREUD, & ALBERT SOLNIT, BEYOND THE BEST INTERESTS OF THE CHILD (1973) *with* Everett Waters & Donna Noyes, *Psychological Parenting vs. Attachment Theory: The Child's Best Interests and the Risks of Doing the Right Things for the Wrong Reasons*, 12 N.Y.U.REV.L. & SOC. CHANGE 505, 513 (1983–84). Those who, like Dr. Page, urge the wider use of psychological parenting theory see children as highly vulnerable and fragile. Their psyches are easily injured by traumatic events and those injuries can adversely shape their subsequent development. *See* GOLDSTEIN, FREUD & SOLNIT, *supra*, at 33. In contrast, others, presumably like Dr. Johnson, posit more flexibility in children, arguing that attachments "support[ ] the development of independence." Waters & Noyes, *supra*, at 509–10. Change under the right circumstances can play a positive role in children's development. Indeed, a good deal of recent literature on the subject argues that psychological parenting theory overestimates the importance of continuity in care in relation to other factors that affect child development, such as the quality of care children receive. In addition, experts and commentators differ over the importance of ongoing relationships between children and their natural parents. Although natural parents can be a disruptive influence for children who have been adopted, some commentators and psychologists believe that trying to eliminate the natural parents from the children's lives and memory is impossible, and therefore wrong. * * * Parents with few resources rely on foster care to protect their children during difficult periods, including but not limited to experiences of homelessness and domestic violence. A single-minded focus on continuity in care can result in parents who rely temporarily on foster care for needed assistance, finding it impossible to regain custody over their children. * * *

* * * The tangles and snares that surround bonding theory are evident in this case. * * * The primary support for the trial court's decision came from Ms. Regina Johnson, whose report was initially requested by the trial court. * * * However, her testimony revealed that she had little or no formal training in conducting bonding evaluations or comprehensive knowledge of the relevant scientific literature. Nor did she have an opportunity to evaluate A.C. or her relationship with the children. Her conclusion that bonding had occurred and that harm would result if those bonds were severed lacked the support and cogency that should surround an expert's opinion in this kind of case.

A.C.'s expert, Dr. Johnson was qualified * * * [but] we are unable to say here that Dr. Johnson's conclusion that there was a strong relationship between the children and their adoptive parents demonstrated that serious harm would ensue if the children were returned to their mother. That is particularly so in light of the expert's own inability to reach a firm conclusion with respect to custody. * * *

Consequently, we remand to the trial court in order that additional evidence may be adduced directly addressing whether the two children have bonded with their foster parents and if so whether breaking such bonds would cause the children serious psychological or emotional harm. * * * [W]e recognize that A.C.'s parental rights may ultimately be terminated even though her contact with the children, in contrast to her custody over them, exposes them to no harm. The risk to children stemming from the deprivation of the custody of their natural parent is one that inheres in the termination of parental rights and is based on the paramount need the children have for permanent and defined parent-child relationships. * * * In this case there is expert testimony indicating a significant relationship between A.C. and J.C. and a potential for harm to J.C. if contact does not continue. This evidence raises the question of whether the welfare of children under certain circumstances reasonably requires continued contact with natural parents subsequent to guardianship being granted to DYFS or an adoption. We note that this question may arise at some future time but do not address it here. * * *

CLIFFORD, J., concurring in judgment.

* * * In addressing the intricate and painful issue before us, one can be forgiven for seeing ghosts; but I have a nagging concern that absent strict enforcement of the Child Placement Review Act, DYFS can unilaterally abandon plans for reunifying biological families in favor of pre-adoptive placement. Once that decision is implemented and the child is placed in the pre-adoptive home, bonding with that family begins. Until that time, bonding with the foster family, although ultimately relevant in the trial court's termination proceeding under N.J.S.A. § 30:4C–20, is an inevitable side effect of a temporary plan whose purpose is to promote stability in the relationship between biological parent and child. * * *

* * * [T]he dearth of adequate and safe rehabilitation residences and the premium placed on stability in a child's home life force troubled parents to confront a harrowing choice between two alternatives, each of which equally damages the child and therefore compromises parental rights. A.C. could have chosen to forego seeking invaluable professional help in order to continue to live and bond with J.M.C., although she might thereby have risked exposing the child to an unrehabilitated lifestyle; or she could have attempted to avail herself of one of the scarce spots in a State rehabilitation facility, thereby assuming the very real risk that bonding during her

rehabilitation would thwart reunification with her offspring. Notwithstanding its conclusion that A.C.'s temporary placement of J.M.C. with DYFS had averted damage to that child, the trial court terminated her parental rights to J.M.C. based solely on the bonding that had occurred during the pendency of that placement. A more graphic illustration of the parent's Catch-22 bind is difficult to imagine.

* * * Neither fundamental notions of justice nor the Constitution permits termination based solely on the psychological bonding that takes place while the mother complies with the visitation provisions of a plan that purportedly has been designed—by DYFS—to foster eventual reunification. * * * I would disallow termination of A.C.'s parental rights in respect of both J.C. and J.M.C. if the trial court concludes on remand that DYFS has not produced clear and convincing evidence of full compliance with the Child Placement Review Act. * * *

NOTES AND QUESTIONS

1. In *J.C.*, Judge Clifford notes his "nagging concern" that, once the agency has decided to proceed with termination and placed the child in a pre-adoptive home, "bonding with that family begins. Until that time, bonding with the foster family, although ultimately relevant in the trial court's termination proceeding under N.J.S.A. § 30:4C–20, is an inevitable side effect of a temporary plan whose purpose is to promote stability in the relationship between biological parent and child." Do the facts of *J.C.* support Judge Clifford's concern? If so, how (if at all) should the court take account of this factor?

2. How would the Kansas Supreme Court have decided *J.C.*? How would the New Jersey Supreme Court have decided *M.M.L.*? How would each court have decided the case of Gregory Kingsley? What are the pros and cons of each approach from the child's perspective? the agency's? the parent's?

3. Is the holding in *J.C.* constitutional? What arguments would you expect from each side?

4. Recall that ASFA requires the states, with certain stated exceptions, to "file a petition to terminate the parental rights of [a] child's parents" when the child "has been in foster care under the responsibility of the State for 15 of the most recent 22 months" to retain eligibility for federal funding. 42 U.S.C. § 675(5)(E). In order to comply with ASFA, many states have revised their parental rights termination standards. Illinois, for example, enacted legislation providing that a parent may be found unfit (the statutory basis for termination) if his child

> has been in foster care for 15 months out of any 22 month period * * * unless the child's parent can prove by a preponderance of the evidence that it is more likely than not that it will be in the best interests of the child to be returned to the parent within 6 months of

the date on which a petition for termination of parental rights is filed.
* * *

750 ILL. COMP. L § 50/1(D)(m-1). The 15-month time limit is tolled during any period for which there is a court finding that the appointed custodian or guardian failed to make reasonable efforts to reunify the child with his or her family. Does the new termination standard meet constitutional requirements? What cases are relevant and what arguments would you expect from each party? How would you expect the *J.C.* and *M.M.L.* courts to rule? *See In re H.G.*, 757 N.E.2d 864 (Ill. 2001); Kurtis A. Kemper, *Construction and Application by State Courts of the Federal Adoption and Safe Families Act and Its Implementing State Statutes*, 10 A.L.R.6th 173 (2006).

5.   The Supreme Court has not yet ruled on the minimum circumstances that justify termination of parental rights, although it has ruled on a variety of procedural issues. The Court has held that the importance of the interests at stake mandate clear and convincing evidence as a basis for parental rights termination (Santosky v. Kramer, 455 U.S. 745 (1982)) and that the state may not constitutionally condition appeal from a trial court's termination of parental rights order on advance payment of record preparation fees (M.L.B. v. S.L.J., 519 U.S. 102 (1996)). But, in Lassiter v. Department of Social Services, 452 U.S. 18 (1981), the Court held that the Due Process Clause did not require the appointment of counsel for indigent parents in every parental termination case. And in Baltimore City Dept. of Social Serv. v. Bouknight, 493 U.S. 549 (1990), it held that the Fifth Amendment privilege against self-incrimination did not apply to a Juvenile Court order requiring a mother to produce a child under the supervision of state child welfare authorities.

6.   The *J.C.* court notes the possibility of maintaining the child's relationship with her biological parent after termination of parental rights, a possibility that you have already seen in *In re* Adoption of Vito, 728 N.E.2d 292 (Mass. 2000). [Chapter 8]. But another state supreme court refused to terminate the biological parents' rights based on the child's bonds with her foster parents, with whom she had lived for all but six months of her life. Instead, the Court ordered reunification with the biological parents and "provisions * * * to ease the transition for everyone concerned. The foster family has earned a special place in Kristina's life, and its role cannot be forgotten. It should continue to be a part of the child's life." *In re* Kristina L., 520 A.2d 574 (R.I. 1987). What are the advantages and disadvantages of the approaches in *M.M.L.*, *Kristina L.*, and *J.C.*?

Problem 10-7: Reforming Child Welfare Practice

Professor Clare Huntington argues that "[t]he child welfare system is caught in the trap of ever greater emphasis on competing rights, at the expense of the very parents and children who are meant to be helped by the system. No amount of more careful calibration of those rights will solve the problems facing families in the child welfare system. We need to shift our focus away from rights and toward problems. * * * A problem-solving model can deliver what a solely rights-based system never will." Clare

Huntington, *Rights Myopia in Child Welfare*, 53 UCLA L. REV. 637, 699 (2006).

Professor Huntington advocates shifting the child welfare system away from adjudication and toward a system based on "family group conferencing":

> * * * [U]nder the current system, after the state agency receives a credible report of child abuse or neglect sufficient to warrant removal, a caseworker goes to the home and assesses the danger to the child. Assuming the caseworker finds sufficient evidence of such danger, the caseworker removes the child and places her in foster care pending a more thorough investigation. The state agency then files a petition in court seeking temporary custody of the child. The child is assigned a guardian ad litem to represent her interests. The caseworker then develops a case plan for the parents, requiring the parents to, for example, obtain drug treatment and attend parenting classes. If the parents do not comply with this case plan within the specified period, generally twelve to eighteen months, then the state agency files for a petition for the termination of parental rights. If the court agrees that parental rights should be terminated, the child is freed for adoption. The majority of decisions in this model are made by professionals: caseworkers, therapists, guardians ad litem, and judges.
>
> * * * In a * * * family group conferencing case, * * * [i]f the social worker concludes there is evidence of abuse or neglect, she refers the case to a coordinator, who has the authority to convene a family group conference. The coordinator contacts the parents, the child, extended family members, and significant community members who know the family. Before the conference, each potential conference participant meets separately with the coordinator to learn about the process. In these meetings, the coordinator screens for potentially complicating factors, such as a history of domestic violence, to determine whether the case is appropriate for family group conferencing and, if so, what additional supports may be needed for the participants.
>
> There are three stages of the conference. In the first stage, the coordinator and any professionals involved with the family, such as therapists, teachers, and the investigating social worker, explain the case to the family. In the second stage, the coordinator and professionals leave the room while the family and community members engage in private deliberation. During the private deliberation, the participants acknowledge that the child was abused or neglected and develop a plan to protect the child and

help the parents. After the participants reach an agreement, they present the plan to the social worker and coordinator, who likely have questions for the participants. Parents, custodians, social workers, and coordinators can veto the plan produced by the conference and refer the case to court. In practice, this rarely occurs: The participants come to a decision, and the social worker and coordinator accept the plan (perhaps with a few changes) if it meets predetermined criteria. The coordinator writes up the plan, sends it to all participants, and then sets a time for a subsequent conference to assess developments in the case.

Id. at 675–76.

Consider the various child welfare cases you have read in this chapter:

1. Do these cases offer evidence to support or oppose Professor Huntington's claim that parents' and children's rights impede the solution of family problems?

2. How would adoption of a family-conferencing system like that advocated by Professor Huntington likely alter current child-welfare outcomes? Would these altered outcomes serve the interests of children? Parents? The state?

3. Would a family-conferencing system meet constitutional requirements?

4. On balance, is adoption of a family-conferencing system a good idea?

CHAPTER 11

THE LAWYER'S ROLE IN
FAMILY DISPUTES

■ ■ ■

The practice of family law is as intellectually demanding as mergers and acquisitions or intellectual property.

Monroe L. Inker, *Changes in Family Law: A Practitioner's Perspective*, 33 FAMILY LAW QUARTERLY 515, 516 (1999)

Discourage litigation. Persuade your neighbors to compromise whenever you can. Point out to them how the nominal winner is often a real loser—in fees, expenses and waste of time. As a peace-maker, the lawyer has a superior opportunity of being a good man. There will still be business enough.

Abraham Lincoln (1846)

1. FAMILY LAW AS A SPECIALTY

This chapter examines the tasks that family lawyers perform, the ethical rules governing lawyer conduct, issues related to malpractice, and the new field of "collaborative" lawyering. It also discusses alternatives to litigation—mediation and arbitration.

Family law cases have become both more numerous and more complex. Domestic relations cases are the largest and fastest-growing segment of state court civil caseloads making up 16% of the nontraffic cases. *See* NAT'L CTR. FOR STATE COURTS, EXAMINING THE WORK OF STATE COURTS 7 (2015). Family law is also one of the largest areas of unmet legal needs. DEBORAH J. RHODE, THE TROUBLE WITH LAWYERS 47 (2016). New family forms and new laws at the state, federal, and international level make family law practice increasingly complex. Even a "simple" divorce may involve alimony or pension valuation and division issues. The family law specialist engages in a wide range of "lawyering" activities, including counseling, drafting agreements (premarital, cohabitation or separation), negotiating, and litigating. A family lawyer may also be a mediator, arbitrator, guardian ad litem, parent coordinator or parent educator.

Family law clients differ from litigants in other areas of law in that the parties have often had an intimate relationship. In a divorce action, for example, they will have lived and slept together, sometimes for a long time. Because family disputes involve important personal relationships, they are often emotionally charged and highly stressful. As one family lawyer stated, "Divorce is the most difficult experience a person goes through alive. I often think that neurosurgeons have it easier because their patients are anesthetized. I have to keep clients not only conscious, but functioning." Ira Lurvey, *in* EMILY COURIC, THE DIVORCE LAWYERS 39, 291 (1992).

The family lawyer will often meet the divorce client at one of the worst times in the client's life. In one study, divorce was ranked second of 42 stressful life events. *See* Thomas H. Holmes & Richard H. Rakke, *The Social Readjustment Rating Scale*, 11 J. PSYCHOSOMATIC RES. 213 (1967). The lawyer can best serve the client if she understands that divorce involves social, moral, emotional, and economic issues as well as a legal claim. *See* SHEILA KESSLER. THE AMERICAN WAY OF DIVORCE: PRESCRIPTION FOR CHANGE (1975) (describing stages of divorce as disillusionment or disenchantment; erosion or disengagement; disinterest or detachment; physical separation; mourning; second adolescence; hard work and resolution). The lawyer must respond appropriately to these nonlegal aspects of family law litigation or the client's representation will suffer. "Client's emotions, their fear, their anger and vulnerability, [can] distort communication, obstruct prediction, and paralyze planning. * * * " Gary Skoloff and Robert J. Levy, *Custody Doctrines and Custody Practice: A Divorce Practitioner's View*, 36 FAM. L. Q. 79 (2002). These same emotions can lead to unhappy clients (or their spouses) filing ethical complaints. The good news is that ninety percent are dismissed. Even with all the emotions, surveys find that family lawyers have one of the highest job satisfaction scores. Lawrence R. Richard, *Psychological Type & Job Satisfaction Among Producing Lawyers in the United States*, 29 CAP. U. L. REV. 979 (2002).

One of the lawyer's tasks is to clarify the legal process. Much client frustration results from the divorce process and a client's unrealistic expectations:

> [Clients] expect the legal process to take their problems seriously, and they usually seek vindication of the positions that they have adopted. They expect the legal process to follow its own rules, to proceed in an orderly manner, and to be fair and error-free.* * *
> [M]ost litigants begin with a fairly strong belief in 'formal justice.' By the time a problem has become serious enough to warrant bringing it to a lawyer and mobilizing the legal process, the grievant wants vindication, protection of his or her rights, an

advocate to help in the battle or a third party who will uncover the 'truth' and declare the other party wrong. Observations suggest that courts rarely provide this * * * but inexperienced plaintiffs do not know this.

Lawyers believe that part of their job is to bring these expectations and images of law and legal justice closer to the "reality" that they experience daily by constructing new meanings and new understandings. The legal process provides an arena where compromises are explored, settlements are reached, and, if money is at issue, assets are divided. Because lawyers' experience is so much more extensive than that of clients, lawyers attempt to "teach" their clients about the requirements of the legal process and to socialize them into the role of the client. As a result, some of the client's problems and needs will be translated into legal categories and many more will have legal labels attached to them. Yet, in the end, the fit between the legal categories through which lawyers see the world of divorce and the social and personal meanings that divorce holds for most clients is rarely very good.

AUSTIN SARAT & WILLIAM L.R. FELSTINER, DIVORCE LAWYERS AND THEIR CLIENTS: POWER AND MEANING IN THE LEGAL PROCESS 150 (1995).

A report on the status of family law education demonstrates how family disputes differ from other litigation and suggests that a family law curriculum should:

teach * * * that the family court of the early twenty-first century is often an interdisciplinary enterprise, where psychologists, social workers, non-lawyer mediators, and others may wield extraordinary power. At times, these professionals may work as partners with the attorney, providing both help and insight into the resolution of the family law dispute. In other cases, the attorney's role is to help the client navigate the often bewildering world of mandatory mediation, mandatory divorce education, court-appointed custody evaluation, parenting coordination, and more.

Mary E. O'Connell & J. Herbie DiFonzo, *The Family Law Education Reform Project Final Report*, 44 FAM. CT. REV. 524, 525 (2006). These interdisciplinary aspects of family law practice mean that "family law is—and must be—a collaborative enterprise." Former Justice Sandra Day O'Connor, *Remarks: The Supreme Court and the Family*, 3 U. PA. J. CONST. L. 573 (2001).

2. REGULATING THE LAWYER-CLIENT RELATIONSHIP

Family lawyers face complex ethical issues in their relationships with clients, the courts and opposing counsel. All states have ethical rules to guide lawyers generally. All, except California, have patterned their ethical rules after the American Bar Association (ABA) Model Rules of Professional Conduct (Model Rules), most recently amended in 2016. The ABA Standing Committee on Ethics and Professionalism as well as state and local bar association ethics committees issue opinions on ethical questions. A lawyer's failure to follow applicable rules and ethical considerations can lead to public censure, license suspension, or disbarment. It may also lead to a malpractice claim.

Because the ethical rules are crafted for all lawyers, usually in adversary proceedings, they often do not provide enough guidance for the unique issues that arise in family law. Many states have supplemented the Model Rules with special court rules or guidelines. For example, in 1993, the New York Court of Appeals issued binding rules to supplement its Model Code in divorce actions. *See* 22 N.Y.C.R.R. § 1200.1. States with specialty certification in family law also typically have additional ethical rules. National organizations, such as the ABA, have endorsed standards of practice for attorneys representing children, representing welfare agencies, and representing parents in abuse and neglect cases. The ABA, as well as the American Academy of Matrimonial Lawyers (AAML), have adopted standards for lawyers who represent children in custody cases.

There are also unofficial rules that influence the practice of family law. The Restatement (Third) of the Law Governing Lawyers (2000 & Supp. 2016) establishes practice standards that apply across specialties. The AAML has also promulgated standards of conduct called the "Bounds of Advocacy" specifically tailored to family law practice. http://www.aaml.org/library/publications/19/bounds-advocacy. While the AAML's standards apply only to its members, the standards provide more guidance and some state bar associations have incorporated parts of them.

A. AVOIDING CONFLICTS OF INTEREST

Conflict of interests issues often arise in family law cases because the parties may seek to save money by hiring only one lawyer. In addition to loss of privilege between commonly represented clients, there are other problems. ABA Model Rule 2.1 states: "In representing a client, a lawyer shall exercise independent professional judgment and render candid advice." ABA Model Rule 1.7 says a lawyer cannot represent a client if there is a "concurrent conflict of interest." A concurrent conflict of interest exists if (1) the representation of one client will be directly adverse to another client; or (2) there is a significant risk that the representation of one or more clients will be materially limited by the lawyer's responsibilities to another client, a former client, or a third person or by a personal interest of the lawyer.

Subsection (b) allows the lawyer to represent in spite of the conflict if

(1) the lawyer reasonably believes that the lawyer will be able to provide competent and diligent representation to each affected client;

(2) the representation is not prohibited by law;

(3) the representation does not involve the assertion of a claim by one client against another client represented by the lawyer in the same litigation or proceeding before a tribunal; and

(4) each affected client gives informed consent, confirmed in writing.

The temptation to help parties who claim just want someone to "look over" their agreement or "submit it to the court" can get a lawyer into conflict situations.

IN RE MARRIAGE OF EGEDI

California Court of Appeals, 2001.
88 Cal. App. 4th 17, 105 Cal. Rptr. 2d 518.

YEGAN, J.

Parties contemplating dissolution of marriage may choose a "friendly divorce" or they can engage in the emotional and financial turmoil of protracted litigation. Some parties electing a "friendly divorce" will seek the help of a single attorney to assist them in putting their settlement agreement in proper legal form.[1] In this situation, there is a problem but not an insurmountable one, i.e., the attorney draftsperson has a potential conflict of interest because he or she cannot simultaneously represent adverse parties. As we shall explain, where a single attorney obtains an informed written waiver of the potential conflict of interest and acts only as a scrivener of the parties' marital settlement agreement (MSA), such agreement is enforceable.

Wife appeals from the judgment challenging the trial court's refusal to enforce the MSA freely and voluntarily entered into by the parties without fraud, duress, or undue influence. The MSA was typed by an attorney who

---

[1] "Requests for 'dual representation' are common in domestic relations matters. Many couples contemplating marriage dissolution believe they share common interests and/or can amicably come to terms on support obligations, child custody and visitation and a fair property settlement. For convenience—and, especially, to save money—they want to hire a single attorney to draft the necessary documents and obtain an uncontested judgment of dissolution at minimal expense." * * * This situation is to be contrasted to that where the parties to a dissolution seek the assistance of an attorney to mediate their dispute.

informed the parties of the potential conflict of interest caused by his acting as a scrivener of the agreement. The parties signed a waiver of the conflict. Nevertheless, the trial court invalidated the MSA on the theory that the attorney's disclosures were insufficient to enable the parties to give an informed consent to dual representation. We reverse. * * *

FACTS

In July 1998, the parties filed a joint petition for summary dissolution of their marriage.

Thereafter the parties asked an attorney to formalize their MSA. He had previously represented wife in a criminal matter and husband in a paternity action. He told the parties that he did not want to prepare the MSA because of a potential conflict of interest. He advised them to obtain independent counsel. However, the parties had extreme confidence in the attorney and insisted that he prepare the MSA. He ultimately agreed to serve as the scrivener of their agreement. He told them that he would not render legal advice but would merely set out the terms that the parties had agreed to and add standard provisions normally found in an MSA. In August 1998, the parties faxed to the attorney their signed agreement, drafted by husband, specifying the terms to be included in the MSA. Husband testified that, during the interval between the fax and the signing of the MSA, the attorney would not discuss the terms with him because of the potential conflict of interest: The attorney "told me that there was a huge potential conflict of interest and that he * * * wanted to remain as neutral as possible.* * *" The attorney testified that he spoke to both parties on the telephone only to confirm the terms they wanted included in the final MSA. In September 1998, the parties met with the attorney at his office to sign the MSA. The attorney again discussed the potential conflict of interest. The parties signed a waiver which provided:

> This will confirm that Angela Egedi and Paul Egedi have been advised that * * * [attorney's] mere typing of an agreement made between the parties may be a potential conflict of interest, despite the fact that he was not in the advisory capacity, nor involved in the negotiation of the agreement. Each party knowingly waives any potential conflict of interest in the preparation of the parties' agreement. In addition, each party has been advised to seek independent legal counsel and advice with respect to this letter and the agreement.

The MSA provided, inter alia, for $750 monthly spousal support to wife until a new lease was signed by the tenant of husband's separate property. After the signing of the new lease, monthly spousal support would increase to $2,000 or one-half of the net monthly lease income, whichever was greater. In addition, wife would receive one-half of the "yearly percentage income" paid by the tenant. Spousal support would terminate after five years or when wife became self-supporting, whichever occurred first. The MSA allocated responsibility for the attorney's past due attorney's fees, required husband to pay a $100,000 loan secured by his separate property in Texas, and provided that the parties would keep whatever property was in their possession. The agreement recited that "the parties intend to effect a complete and final division of their assets and debts, and to resolve all rights and obligations relating to spousal support." It also recited: "The parties agree that: (1) each of the parties has read and reviewed this Agreement; (2) each of the parties is fully aware of the contents, legal effect and consequences of this agreement and its provisions; (3) each of the parties has read this Agreement and understands and accepts its contents and acknowledges that there have been no promises or agreements by either party to the other, except as set forth here, that were relied on by either party as inducement to enter into this Agreement; and (4) this Agreement has been entered into voluntarily, free from duress, fraud, undue influence, coercion, or misrepresentation of any kind."

Thereafter wife fully performed her MSA obligations but husband elected not to pay spousal support as agreed. Wife sought judicial enforcement of the MSA. Husband contended that the MSA should be set aside on various grounds, i.e., failure of consideration, unfairness, improper conduct by attorney, fraud, duress, undue influence and mistake.

TRIAL COURT RULING

The court found that "the MSA was in fact the free and voluntary agreement of the parties. * * * " It rejected "the claim that [husband] was forced to consent to [the MSA's] terms as a result of fraud, duress, or undue influence." The court credited the attorney's testimony that he had "observed nothing that suggested the agreement was anything other than what the parties freely and genuinely 'wanted' and consented to at the time it was signed." The court found the attorney's "testimony on this issue clear, credible and convincing." Furthermore, it concluded that, if husband's allegations of mistake were true, the mistake was insufficient to invalidate the MSA.

Nevertheless, the trial court ruled that the MSA "may not be enforced because the conflict disclosures made by [attorney] were inadequate to permit his dual representation of the parties. * * * " Despite the attorney's role as a "scrivener," the trial court found that "he was effectively rendering legal advice to both [parties]" because he added "standard provisions" to the MSA. It concluded that "he could do so only after making full disclosure of all facts and circumstances necessary to enable both parties to make a fully informed decision regarding such representation." The trial court also said that the attorney failed to disclose "all facts and circumstances necessary to enable both parties to make a fully informed decision regarding [his] representation." It did not, however, specify the "facts and circumstances" that should have been disclosed.

MSA SET ASIDE RULES

"Property settlement agreements occupy a favored position in the law of this state. * * * " Courts are reluctant to disturb them "except for equitable considerations. A property settlement agreement, therefore, that is not tainted by fraud or compulsion or is not in violation of the confidential relationship of the parties is valid and binding on the court. * * * " Here the trial court found that the MSA was not tainted by fraud, duress, or undue influence. Nor was the MSA in violation of the parties' confidential relationship. The trial court found that the parties had voluntarily entered into the agreement, which reflected "what the parties freely and genuinely 'wanted' and consented to at the time it was signed."

The trial court may set aside an MSA on traditional contract law. "An MSA is governed by the legal principles applicable to contracts generally. [citations omitted]" These other grounds include mistake, failure of consideration, unlawfulness of the contract, and prejudice to the public interest. The trial court also had the power to invalidate the MSA if it was inequitable. Family law cases "are equitable proceedings in which the court must have the ability to exercise discretion to achieve fairness and equity." " 'Equity * * * will assert itself in those situations where right and justice would be defeated but for its intervention.' * * * " Thus, marital settlement agreements may be set aside where the court finds them inequitable even though not induced through fraud or compulsion.

CONFLICT DISCLOSURE

While the trial court mentioned its equitable powers, it is clear that it set aside the MSA solely because the attorney did not adequately disclose the potential conflict of interest. The trial court relied on Klemm v. Superior Court, 75 Cal. App. 3d 893, 142 Cal. Rptr. 509 (1977). This case, however, does not hold that an MSA may be invalidated because of a potential inadequate disclosure of a conflict of interest. The issue before us is a matter of first impression.

Klemm concluded that the same counsel may represent both husband and wife in an uncontested dissolution proceeding if the conflict of interest is potential, not actual, and the parties give an informed, intelligent consent in writing after full disclosure. A conflict is potential in the absence of an "existing dispute or contest between the parties. * * * " In dicta, the *Klemm* court noted that counsel "who undertake to represent parties with divergent interests owe the highest duty to each to make a full disclosure of all facts and circumstances which are necessary to enable the parties to make a fully informed decision regarding the subject matter of the litigation, including the areas of potential conflict and the possibility and desirability of seeking independent legal advice." The court went on to observe that "the validity of any agreement negotiated without independent representation of each of the parties is vulnerable to easy attack as having been procured by misrepresentation, fraud and overreaching."

But here the trial court factually found that the MSA was not procured by misrepresentation, fraud, or overreaching. *Klemm* does not suggest that an MSA may be invalidated solely for lack of informed consent to dual representation where the parties have freely and voluntarily entered into an agreement to which the attorney adds "standard MSA provisions." In fact, *Klemm* says: "The California cases are generally consistent with rule 5–102 [now rule 3–310 of the Rules of Professional Conduct] permitting dual representation where there is a full disclosure and informed consent by all the parties, at least insofar as a representation pertains to agreements and negotiations prior to a trial or hearing. As to the 'standard provisions' added by the attorney, it is sufficient to observe that not only did the parties agree thereto, these terms were not and are not in dispute."

Here, even if there was dual representation, there was informed consent within the meaning of rule 3–310 which, in pertinent part provides:

Avoiding the Representation of Adverse Interests.

(A) For purposes of this rule:

  (1) 'Disclosure' means informing the client or former client of the relevant circumstances and of the actual and reasonably foreseeable adverse consequences to the client or former client;

  (2) 'Informed written consent' means the client's or former client's written agreement to the representation following written disclosure[.]

* * *

(C) A member shall not, without the informed written consent of each client:

  (1) Accept representation of more than one client in a matter in which the interests of the clients potentially conflict; or

  (2) Accept or continue representation of more than one client in a matter in which the interests of the clients actually conflict. * * * "

Other than telling the parties what the attorney did tell them, the trial court did not articulate, husband does not suggest, and we cannot think of any further advisement which could have been made save telling the parties, consistent with the rule drafter's comment, that in the event of future litigation, there would be a waiver of the attorney-client privilege. A single attorney acting as a scrivener should not advise the parties of the pros and cons of their agreement so that they might "unagree." This would defeat the very purpose for which they sought assistance.

Advisement and waiver of a potential conflict of interest in typing a MSA should not be equated with the admonitions and waivers required when a guilty plea is entered to a criminal charge. * * * A fortiori, spouses in a marital proceeding can waive a potential conflict of interest in writing to settle property and support issues.

Finally, nothing that the attorney did or did not do caused the parties to enter into the faxed agreement which was incorporated into the September 1998 MSA. As indicated, the trial court expressly credited the attorney's testimony to this effect. Phrased otherwise, the parties both orally or in writing agreed to the essential terms of the September 1998 MSA on their own. Husband may not seize upon the subsequent conduct of the attorney to invalidate the MSA.

DISPOSITION

The judgment is reversed. The matter is remanded for enforcement of the September 1998 MSA. Wife shall recover her costs and reasonable attorney fees on appeal * * *

NOTES AND QUESTIONS

1. Is being a scrivener providing "representation"? How can a lawyer exercise "independent professional judgment" when being a scrivener? Will the fact of joint representation affect the level or type of review a court will undertake? *See* Vandenburgh v. Vandenburgh, 599 N.Y.S.2d 328 (App. Div. 1993). If there is dual representation, is an agreement more likely to be overturned for overreaching? See Logiudice v. Logiudice, 889 N.Y.S.2d 164 (App. Div. 2009). If the dual representation breaks down, what happens? *See,* Lawyer Discip. Bd. v. Frame, 479 S.E.2d 676 (W. Va. 1996) (after lawyer filed petition for husband and answer for wife, she called to report husband was abusing her).

2. AAML Standard 3.1 provides that "[a]n attorney should not represent both husband and wife even if they do not wish to obtain independent representation." Some state ethics codes provide that a lawyer should never "represent" both parties to a divorce. *See* Utah State Bar Op. 116 (6/25/92). What about a premarital agreement? *See* Ware v. Ware, 687 S.E.2d 382 (W. Va. 2009) (no).

3. In states that permit joint representation, the lawyer is required to withdraw if joint representation becomes "objectively unreasonable." Model Rule 1.7, Comment 5. Is joint representation "inherently unethical"? *See* Mary E. Chester, *Comment, Joint Representation in Friendly Divorce: Inherently Unethical?*, 27 J. LEGAL PROF. 155 (2002–2003). *But see* Russell G. Pearce,

Family Values and Legal Ethics: Competing Approaches To Conflicts in Representing Spouses, 62 FORDHAM L. REV. 1253 (1994).

4.   *Unbundling*? Would an ethical rule allowing limited representation be a solution to the *Egedi* problem?

5.   Potential conflicts of interest often arise when a lawyer is asked to represent the spouse of a prior client. ABA Model Rule 1.9 states:

a.   A lawyer who has formerly represented a client in a matter shall not thereafter represent another person in the same or a substantially related matter in which that person's interests are materially adverse to the interests of the former client unless the former client gives informed consent, confirmed in writing.

b.   A lawyer shall not knowingly represent a person in the same or a substantially related matter in which a firm with which the lawyer formerly was associated had previously represented a client,

(1)   whose interests are materially adverse to that person; and

(2)   about whom the lawyer has acquired information protected by Rule 1.6 and 1.9(c) that is material to the matter; unless the former client gives informed consent, confirmed in writing.

c.   A lawyer who has formerly represented a client in a matter or whose present or former firm has formerly represented a client in a matter shall not thereafter:

(1)   use information relating to the representation to the disadvantage of the former client except as these Rules would permit or require with respect to a client, or when the information has become generally known; or

(2)   reveal information relating to the representation except as these Rules would permit or require with respect to a client.

In determining whether interests are "materially adverse," courts typically consider whether information pertinent to the present representation was also pertinent in the prior representation. *See* Bjorgen v. Kinsey, 466 N.W.2d 553 (N.D. 1991); State ex rel. Oklahoma Bar Assoc. v. Katz, 733 P.2d 406 (Okla. 1987). There are also problems with representing one spouse after having a consultation with the other. Model Rule 1.18. *See In re* Marriage of Newton, 955 N.E.2d 572 (Ill. App. 2011).

6.   If one party refuses to get representation, what is the lawyer's duty to an unrepresented party? ABA Model Rule 4.3 requires that when the lawyer knows or reasonably should have known that the unrepresented person misunderstands the lawyer's role, the lawyer shall "make reasonable efforts to correct the misunderstanding." The Comment to this rule provides that, "[d]uring the course of a lawyer's representation of a client, the lawyer should not give advice to an unrepresented person other than the advice to obtain

counsel." AAML Standard 3.2 recommends that the lawyer inform the opposing party, in writing, that:

- I am your spouse's lawyer.

- I do not and will not represent you.

- I will at all times look out for your spouse's interests, not yours.

- Any statements I make to you about this case should be taken by you as negotiation or argument on behalf of your spouse and not as advice to you as to your best interest.

- I urge you to obtain your own lawyer.

Is this enough?

7. Representation involving a conflict of interest may lead to disciplinary action, fee forfeiture, or a malpractice action. *See In re* Wilder, 764 N.E.2d 617 (Ind. 2002) (suspending attorney where he represented an unmarried couple in various business matters and then with the consent of one party represented the other in the dissolution of their legal affairs); *In re* Houston, 985 P.2d 752 (N.M. 1999) (suspending lawyer when he represented the wife in an "uncontested" divorce giving husband unsupervised visitation with the children while representing the husband on charges of criminal sexual penetration of the couple's child and domestic violence against the wife). Success in a malpractice action based on the attorney's conflict of interest requires proof that the conflict caused the injury. *See* Bevan v. Fix, 42 P.3d 1013 (Wyo. 2002).

Problem 11-1:

Lara Lawyer drafted Wanda's will and represented her in a custody, visitation and support action against Harry. A few years later, Harry hires Lara to bring a partition action against Wanda. Is Lara's representation of Harry permissible? *See* Lawyer Disciplinary Board v. Printz, 452 S.E.2d 720 (W. Va. 1994). If Lara had represented Wanda in negotiating a premarital agreement with Harry before the marriage, could Lara represent Harry in a subsequent divorce action against Wanda? *See* Sargent v. Buckley, 697 A.2d 1272 (Me. 1997). If Lara had represented both parties in buying a business or other commercial transaction, could Lara then represent one of the parties in a divorce? Florida Bar v. Dunagan, 731 So. 2d 1237 (Fla. 1999).

Problem 11-2:

Larry Lawyer represented two business partners, Jake and Jim, in a bankruptcy action in which he listed both of their wives as creditors. Larry subsequently represented Jake's wife, Jane, and Jim's wife, Maria, in their divorce actions against Jake and Jim. Jim and Jake both consented to the representation of their wives. Did Larry violate any ethical obligation? *In re* Hockett, 734 P.2d 877 (Or. 1987).

Problem 11-3:

Larry Lawyer was appointed to represent the children of Tom and Jane in their custody dispute. The judge subsequently appointed Larry to mediate the financial issues in the divorce case. Jane asked to have Larry disqualified. Should he be? Isaacson v. Isaacson, 792 A.2d 525 (N.J. Super. App. Div. 2002).

B. FEE ISSUES

The Model Rules, which apply to lawyers in all types of practices, includes a provision on what constitutes a reasonable fee. Model Rule 1.5(a) lists eight factors for determining whether a lawyer's fee was reasonable, including (1) the time and labor required, the novelty and difficulty of the questions involved, and the skill requisite to perform the legal service properly; (2) the likelihood, if apparent to the client, that the acceptance of the particular employment will preclude other employment by the lawyer; (3) the fee customarily charged in the locality for similar legal services; (4) the amount involved and the results obtained; (5) the time limitations imposed by the client or by the circumstances; (6) the nature and length of the professional relationship with the client; (7) the experience, reputation, and ability of the lawyer or lawyers performing the services; and (8) whether the fee is fixed or contingent. In family law cases, however, courts do not allow contingency fees, except in enforcement of judgments. Consider the next case.

V.W. v. J.B.

Supreme Court, New York County, 1995.
165 Misc. 2d 767, 629 N.Y.S.2d 971.

LEWIS R. FRIEDMAN, JUSTICE.

Plaintiff seeks summary judgment on the fifth cause of action, for rescission. The application raises serious questions under the Code of Professional Responsibility ("CPR"), not previously addressed in the New York cases, concerning retainer agreements and "bonuses" in matrimonial cases.

In July 1992 plaintiff retained defendant to represent her in a matrimonial matter. The written retainer called for plaintiff to pay a fee determined solely by multiplying the number of hours expended on the case times the hourly rate charged for the service. Negotiations proceeded for over two years until a settlement was reached. Plaintiff's Husband ultimately agreed to pay her more than 20 times his original offer. Plaintiff has stated in her pleadings that defendant's legal work was "fabulous." On August 18, 1994 plaintiff, in New York, executed the separation agreement. The document was shipped by Federal Express to plaintiff's husband who was in California; he executed it on August 19. The parties were divorced by judgment entered August 30, 1994.

Defendant and her former firm were paid about $300,000 based on their time charges. On August 18, allegedly after plaintiff had executed the Separation Agreement, plaintiff and defendant executed the Performance Fee Agreement ("PFA") which is at issue here. In the PFA, plaintiff "in light of the results achieved by [defendant] * * * has graciously and generously agreed to pay a performance fee of $2,000,000" in three installments. Defendant agreed to waive her outstanding bill for $41,000 in fees and expenses. The first installment of the performance fee $1,000,000, was due "upon transfer to [plaintiff] of the equitable distribution payment" in the separation agreement. That part of the fee was paid on August 29, 1994. Plaintiff retained new counsel in early January 1995, refused to pay the second installment, due January 15, and demanded repayment of the $1,000,000 already paid. This action for rescission and restitution followed. Defendant counterclaimed for the balance of her fee.

In the fifth cause of action plaintiff contends that the PFA violated the CPR. There is no doubt that a retainer agreement with counsel is invalid if it violates the CPR. Specifically plaintiff alleges a violation of DR 2–106[C][2] which at the relevant time provided that an attorney "shall not enter into an arrangement for, charge or collect: [2] any fee in a domestic relations matter (i) the payment or amount of which is contingent upon the securing of a divorce or upon the amount of maintenance, support, equitable distribution or property settlement * * *."

The rule against contingent fees in domestic relations cases in this state is deep-seated and well established. * * *

When New York adopted the CPR it modified the Model Code of Professional Responsibility promulgated by the American Bar Association to adopt the clear prohibition on contingent fees in domestic relations cases contained in DR 2–106[C][2]. The original ABA Ethical Consideration [EC 2020] as adopted in 1970 by the New York State Bar Association did not contain a flat prohibition on contingent fees in matrimonial cases but noted that "because of the human relationships involved and the unique character of the proceedings contingent fee arrangements in domestic relations cases are rarely justified."

The policy reasons for the restrictions in matrimonial cases on the use of fees which are contingent on the outcome has been that this kind of fee might induce lawyers to discourage reconciliation and encourage bitter and wounding court battles. Another often expressed policy reason to preclude contingent fees in matrimonial actions is that they are not necessary. Since the court may award attorney's fees to a non-monied spouse, any party should be able to retain counsel.

The question whether the PFA violates the CPR requires analysis of *issue* whether the payment or amount was "contingent" on the result. Plaintiff correctly notes that DR 2–106[C][2] does not use the term "contingent fee," which is used in DR 2–106[C][1] banning those fees in criminal cases. Clearly the fee here could not be called a "contingent fee" in its traditional sense. The CPR does not define "contingent." One common definition of a "contingent fee" between attorney and client is an agreement express, or implied, for legal services * * * under which compensation, contingent in whole or in part upon the successful accomplishment or disposition of the subject matter of the agreement, is to be in an amount which either is fixed or is to be determined under a formula.

* * *

That is consistent with the definition in Black's Law Dictionary, 553 [5th ed. 1979]. The usual meaning of a "contingent fee" is that the attorney will be paid only if the case is won. There is no doubt that by its terms the PFA was a fixed, binding agreement that did not turn on the outcome of the case or on the amount received by plaintiff. The attorney had no risk that the fee would not be paid if the case was lost.

Plaintiff suggests that because the first payment of the fee was to be paid from a specified equitable distribution payment it was "contingent" for payment on the completion of the case. In *Shanks v. Kilgore*, 589 S.W.2d 318, 321 [Mo. Ct. App. 1979] the court found that since the $60,000 fee was to be paid partially from each equitable distribution installment it was based on a prohibited contingency, the receipt of payment. This court rejects that analysis; once the fee has been firmly fixed the uncertainty of actual payment does not make it invalid. It has long been an accepted practice in this jurisdiction, even where the entire fee is fixed at an hourly rate, for counsel to agree to await payment until the ultimate resolution of the case. Neither the fee nor the obligation to pay it turn on the outcome. Only the timing of the payment is uncertain. Bar Ethics Committees appear to support that view. The court cannot conclude that such a provision makes a fixed fee into a "contingent fee."

A more troubling question is presented because the language of DR6–102[C][2] uses the term "contingent * * * upon the amount of * * * equitable distribution." "Contingent" means "possible, but not assured; doubtful or uncertain; conditional upon the occurrence of some future event which is itself uncertain, or questionable." [citing Black's Law Dictionary]. The PFA based the fee on "the results achieved." The CPR, following well established New York law provides that one of the "factors to be considered as guides in determining the reasonableness of a fee * * * [is] the amount involved and the results obtained." DR 2–106[B][4]. Thus the question before this court becomes whether the use of the "results obtained" to set the final fee necessarily makes the fee "contingent" on the ultimate amount. The answer to that question has divided the courts which have considered it.

In Head v. Head, [505 A.2d 868 (Md. App. 1986)], the court found no violation of DR 2–106[C][2]. In that case there had been a judicial determination by the lower court of a legal fee which included a "bonus" based on the result. The fee was held not to be contingent because "the fee was not directly related by percentage or formula to the amount recovered or protected." The court supported its conclusion by noting that the fee did not serve the usual purpose of a contingent fee since the parties could afford counsel and no res was created since the party involved was the monied spouse. In *In re Marriage of Malec*, the court simply agreed with *Head's* conclusion and observed that a fee to be determined based on performance would not be contingent. However, in *Malec* the fee arrangement was actually invalidated as "contingent" because a $1 million bonus was tied to counsel's achievement of a specific result. *Wilson*, [597 A.2d 696 (Pa. Super. 1991)], after reviewing the cases, concluded that a fee based on a minimum hourly rate with the final fee to be based on the reasonable value of the services, including whether a favorable result was reached, is not a fee grounded on a prohibited contingency. The court reasoned that since the attorney would be paid regardless of the outcome, the risk of nonpayment in case of an unfavorable result, characteristic of a contingent fee, was missing. The court found that the agreement was the equivalent of a quantum meruit fee based on the factors permitted by the Rules of Practice.

On the other hand a number of courts have found "result" based fees to be prohibited contingencies. In *Salerno v. Salerno*, [575 A.2d 532 (N.J. Super. 1990)], the retainer provided for hourly billing and a final fee "premium" based, inter alia, on "the result accomplished." The court held that a charge based on a percentage of the equitable distribution to the client clearly has all the aspects of a contingent fee. Although a fee contingent on the amount of equitable distribution was held valid under the New Jersey Rules, which are based on the Model Rules, the fee was invalidated for violation of Rule 1.5[c] which requires that the agreement be in writing and set the exact percentage of recovery which the attorney sought as a fee.

* * *

This court concludes that where the parties enter into a fee agreement prior to the completion of the matter where a legal fee turns on the "result obtained," that of necessity is a fee based on a prohibited contingency of the amount of the award. * * *

Defendant argues that this case differs from those where "bonuses" or "tips" have been invalidated because the PFA was not referred to in the retainer but was only agreed to after the case was "completed" and there was a "final resolution of the matrimonial matter." Defendant notes that plaintiff had also executed the documents necessary for an uncontested divorce prior to signing the PFA. Plaintiff, however, relies on the undisputed fact that on August 18, when the settlement agreement, other documents and the PFA were signed by her, her husband had not yet executed the settlement agreement, nor had Husband's counsel concluded that the other documents were "in acceptable form" as was required. * * *

This court's experience is that, despite the sense of counsel that a deal has been struck and that a separation agreement is final, there are often last minute disagreements and proposed changes by the client. This matter was obviously not final, at least until signed by plaintiff's then husband. That uncertainty meant that, at the time of its execution, the PFA was contingent; it was contingent on the husband's execution of the separation agreement and his counsel's approval of certain documents. If the husband had raised any issues, defendant's self interest in the result would have created the conflicted loyalty to the client that DR 2–106[C][2] was designed to prevent. Defendant counters by claiming that the PFA is for a fixed "unconditional" fee, final and binding on plaintiff. Yet that position is belied by the use of the phrase "results achieved" in the PFA. If the husband did not sign or had demanded substantive changes there would have been no "results." Defendant's papers continuously justify the fee by the size of the equitable distribution settlement. Of course, a $2,000,000 "bonus" for an unexecuted separation agreement, with no results, would be patently excessive * * * warranting invalidation of the PFA for that reason alone. Thus, this court concludes that the PFA when executed by plaintiff was invalid pursuant to DR 2–106[C][2]. Of course, this decision does not express any view on the propriety of a truly voluntary agreement for a "bonus" to counsel entered into after completion of the entire proceeding.

Plaintiff concedes that in light of the invalidity of the PFA defendant would be entitled to the $41,000 of her time charges which she waived. This court agrees. Plaintiff's motion for summary judgment on the fifth cause of action is granted. The counterclaim is dismissed.

[On appeal, the Supreme Court Appellate Division found that there was a material issue of fact as to whether the separation agreement between the husband and wife was complete at the time the performance agreement was entered so the case was remanded. Weinstein v. Barnett, 640 N.Y.S.2d 103 (App. Div. 1996).]

NOTES AND QUESTIONS

1.   The bonus in *V.W.* was large. Is it appropriate to ban all bonus billing? Would a ban simply lead to higher quoted fees at the beginning of the representation? *See* May v. Sessums & Mason, 700 So. 2d 22 (Fla. Dist. Ct. App. 1997) (invalidating a $1,000,000 bonus based on vague language in the fee agreement). For a discussion of "results" billing, *see generally* Linda J. Ravdin & Kelly J. Capps, *Alternative Pricing of Legal Services in Domestic*

Relations Practice: Choices and Ethical Considerations, 33 FAM. L.Q. 387 (1999).

2. *Contingency Fees*: Although contingency fees in tort actions are common, they have long been disfavored in family law matters. *See* Maxwell Schuman & Co. v. Edwards, 663 S.E.2d 329 (N.C. App. 2008). If the case involves more than a divorce and custody, such as proving the existence of a common law marriage, a court might be willing to allow a contingency fee. *See* Ballesteros v. Jones, 985 S.W.2d 485 (Tex. App. 1998). AAML Standard 4.5 provides that an attorney should not charge a contingency fee for (a) obtaining a divorce; (b) custody or visitation provisions; or (c) the amount of alimony or child support awarded but allow one for other matters as long as the client is informed of the right to have the fee based on a hourly rate and has the opportunity to seek independent legal advice concerning desirability of such an arrangement. Why do the AAML Standards distinguish divorce from other forms of family litigation? Is the distinction sound? Is such a ban warranted? *See* GEOFFREY C. HAZARD, JR. & W. WILLIAM HODES, THE LAW OF LAWYERING § 8.14, at 8–35 (4th ed. 2014) (suggesting maybe not).

3. *Retainer Fees*: Some family law practitioners charge an up-front retainer fee to offset the cost of the initial interview and related expenses. Among lawyers who charge such a retainer, some deposit the fee in a trust account and utilize it to pay the client's bills; others do not utilize the retainer unless the client fails to pay monthly bills. *See* Leonard Loeb, *Hourly Charges in Divorce Cases are Archaic*, 1 AM. J. FAM. L. 1 (1987). Some states have found that nonrefundable retainer fees are unethical. *See* Wright v. Arnold, 877 P.2d 616 (Okla. App. 1994). In addition to outlawing the nonrefundable retainer, the New York Court of Appeals has mandated, in all divorce actions, written explanations of retainer fees and itemized bills issued at least every two months. *See* Jan Hoffman, *New York's Chief Judge Imposes Strict Rules for Divorce Lawyers,* N.Y. TIMES, Aug. 17, 1993, at A1, A9. *See* In the Matter of Snow, 677 N.Y.S.2d 829 (App. Div. 1998).

4. *Fee Agreements*: Many fee disputes arise because the lawyer and client did not have a clear agreement on how the fee would be determined. Neither the Model Rules nor the Model Code mandate a written fee agreement (*see* Model Rule 1.5(b)); the AAML Standards do (4.1). Is a written fee agreement desirable? Why?

5. What if there is a dispute over the fee? In 1996, the ABA adopted Model Rules for Fee Arbitration and recommended that all states adopt mandatory, nonbinding fee arbitration.

6. *Award of Attorney Fees*: As a general rule in civil litigation, each party pays his or her own attorney fees. In divorce actions, however, the court has the equitable power to order one party to pay the other's fees. *See* TEX. FAM. CODE ANN. § 6.708. State rules on fee allocation and reasonableness vary. *See* FLA. STAT. ANN. § 61.16 (after considering the financial resources of both parties); KAN. STAT. ANN. § 23–2715 ("as justice and equity require"). The trial court can determine the reasonableness of the fees. *See* Edinger v. Edinger, 724

N.W.2d 852 (S.D. 2006). Is there a sound basis for permitting fee reallocation in divorce cases when it is not permitted in other forms of civil litigation? Florida determined while the trial court has inherent authority to award fees against a lawyer for bad faith conduct, there must be an express finding of bad faith before the award is justified. *See* Diaz v. Diaz, 826 So. 2d 229 (Fla. 2002) (invalidating an award that was imposed against a lawyer for litigating a divorce rather than accepting a generous settlement). Can the threat of a court award of attorney's fees to the other party prevent an attorney from litigating a frivolous claim or bad faith refusal to settle?

C. DUTIES TO THE CLIENT

1. Competence, Communication and Diligence

Communication, diligence, and competency issues go together. ABA Model Rule 1.1 requires that lawyers possess the "legal knowledge, skill, thoroughness and preparation reasonably necessary" to the representation undertaken. Whether the case is settled or litigated, the client is entitled to the same level of skill, knowledge and diligence. *See* LOUIS PARLEY, THE ETHICAL FAMILY LAWYER: A PRACTICAL GUIDE TO AVOIDING PROFESSIONAL DILEMMAS chs. 3 & 5 (1995); McMahon v. Shea, 657 A.2d 938 (Pa. Super. 1995). This means that a lawyer must know or learn all laws that apply to every aspect of the case. A lawyer should at least know how to calculate child support in the jurisdiction. Att'y Grievance Comm'n v. Kreamer, 946 A.2d 500 (Ind. 2008).

Model Rule 1.3 mandates that a lawyer act with reasonable diligence and promptness. The lawyer should show up for scheduled hearings and meet filing deadlines. *See In re* Hawkins, 373 P.3d 718 (Kan. 2016). It also means informing the client of necessary requirements, such as attending a parenting class. *See In re* Nichols, 45 So. 3d 603 (La. 2010). A client's agreement or instruction to limit the scope of representation to save money does not excuse the lawyer from the responsibility to be competent and diligent.

Model Rule 1.4 requires attorneys to keep a client "reasonably informed" about that status of their case and to comply with reasonable requests for information. The single biggest complaint against family lawyers is the failure to return phone calls. *See* Office of Lawyer Regulation v. Christnot, 685 N.W.2d 788 (Wis. 2004) (suspending lawyer for failing to respond for two years to divorce client who repeatedly tried to make contact). AAML Standard 2.6 adds that the lawyer should "promptly respond to letters and telephone calls." *See* Tucker v. Virginia State Bar, 357 S.E.2d 525 (Va. 1987) (disbarring a lawyer because he failed to return his clients' phone calls, closed his office and disconnected his phone without notifying clients).

2. Deference to the Client's Decisions

Model Rule 1.2 requires that a lawyer abide by the client's objectives in the representation and consult with the client as to the means to pursue those objectives. The client, not the lawyer, has the right to accept or reject a settlement offer. *See* Tsavaris v. Tsavaris, 244 So. 2d 450 (Fla. Dist. Ct. App. 1971); Jones v. Feiger, Collison & Killmer, 903 P.2d 27 (Colo. App. 1994).

FLORIDA BAR V. SUSAN K. GLANT

Supreme Court of Florida, 1994.
645 So. 2d 962.

PER CURIAM.

Attorney Susan K. Glant petitions this Court for review of the referee's recommendation that she receive a public reprimand for her handling of a child custody case. * * *

We agree that Glant violated Florida Rule of Professional Conduct 4–1.2(a), which requires a lawyer to abide by a client's decision regarding the objectives of representation,[1] and find that a public reprimand is the appropriate sanction.

The Bar filed a complaint against Glant over her handling of a child custody case at Central Florida Legal Services (CFLS). Glant was asked to resign from CFLS because of her actions.

The referee made these findings of fact: When Glant began working at CFLS in 1991, she was assigned to represent a mother with four minor children (two boys and two girls) in a custody action against the father. The mother wanted to end the Department of Health and Rehabilitative Services' (HRS) supervision of the children and to retain custody of her two girls. At one point, all four children had been removed from the father's home after allegations of sexual abuse. The record reflects that HRS did not litigate those allegations because of insufficient evidence.

Glant knew the mother did not want custody of all four children. She was to attend a hearing in June 1991 and present the court with a recommendation that HRS terminate its supervision and retain the current custody status (two girls living with the mother and two boys living

---

[1]   Florida Rule of Professional Conduct 4–1.2(a) provides in relevant part:

A lawyer shall abide by a client's decisions concerning the objectives of representation, subject to subdivisions (c), (d), and (e), and shall consult with the client as to the means by which they are to be pursued.

Paragraph (c) allows a lawyer to limit the objectives of representation if the client consents. Paragraph (d) prohibits a lawyer from counseling a client to engage, or assisting a client, in conduct the lawyer knows or reasonably should know is criminal or fraudulent. Paragraph (e) requires a lawyer to consult with a client about limitations if the client expects assistance not permitted by law or the Rules of Professional Conduct.

with the father). After the hearing, based on her belief that the father was sexually abusing the girls, Glant sent a letter to HRS in Tallahassee requesting further investigation.[2] She included a copy of an unfiled motion for custody modification which asked that the mother be given custody of all four children.

Glant testified that she felt obligated to send the letter and unfiled motion to HRS because of rule 4–1.2(d), which prohibits a lawyer from assisting a client in criminal or fraudulent conduct.[3] She also relied on rule 4–1.6(b).[4]

Glant challenges the referee's recommendations, arguing that: (1) there is no substantial, competent evidence in the record to support the referee's finding that she violated rule 4–1.2; (2) the referee erred as a matter of fact and law in refusing to direct a verdict in her favor; (3) the referee erred as a matter of law in finding Glant guilty of violating rule 4–1.2. * * *

Initially, we address the three issues dealing with rule 4–1.2(a). A referee's findings of fact are presumed correct and will be upheld unless "clearly erroneous or lacking in evidentiary support." *The Florida Bar v. Hayden*, 583 So. 2d 1016, 1017 (Fla. 1991). The record is undisputed that Glant sent the letter and documents to Bob Williams, who was then the Secretary of HRS, even though she knew her client did not want custody of all four children. Glant testified:

> In my opinion, there's really only two things an attorney can do when a client says the children are being sexually molested and you're faced with this type—with this type of, what I consider, solid evidence. * * * If I withdrew, those children would have been buried—been buried in paperwork, so I did the best thing that I thought in my opinion as an attorney—the next thing was that I wrote HRS whose [sic] got access to all those documents. I said, you better take a look at this case. You better take a look at what the local HRS attorney is doing to those children. Okay? I sent the Motion to—to Bob Williams. He knew, according to my letter, that I had not filed that Motion, and that's basically why I sent the letter. * * * The mother would have said no, and Jonathan Hewett would have told me no, and why would they have told me no. The mother would have told me no because she did not care that the children were being sexually molested by her ex-husband.

---

[2] Glant also mailed the letter to the U.S. Attorney General's office in Washington, Governor Lawton Chiles and the State Attorney's office for the Eight Judicial District.

[3] A lawyer shall not counsel a client to engage, or assist a client, in conduct that the lawyer knows or reasonably should know is criminal or fraudulent.

[4] A lawyer shall reveal such information to the extent the lawyer believes necessary: (1) to prevent a client from committing a crime; or (2) to prevent a death or substantial bodily harm to another.

Glant also testified that she did the right thing in sending the letter.

THE COURT: Do you believe you should have disclosed to your client what you were going to do?

Ms. Glant: No

THE COURT: Why not?

Ms. Glant: She would have said no.

THE COURT: No—in that you had made a decision—my understanding is that you made a decision regardless of what your client said to send the letter.

Ms. Glant: That's right.

THE COURT: My question is—you said—my question is do you believe you should have disclosed what you're about to do, that is, in the letter and the Motion to HRS and to the Governor, you believe you should not have disclosed—

Ms. Glant: Her opinion meant nothing to me at that point in time because this is a mother who knows that sexual abuse is happening to her children and is not doing a single thing to prevent it. I don't care if she said yes or no, your honor. I would have sent the letter anyway.

THE COURT: All right. And in sending the letter, you realized it could have subjected you to a violation or alleged violation—

Ms. Glant: Certainly.

THE COURT:—of the Code of Conduct for Attorneys.

Ms. Glant: Certainly.

THE COURT: All right.

Ms. Glant: But Your Honor, you know, I still—today, I still would have done it. I still would have done the same thing as I did then.

Glant was the only person who testified that the father had abused his children. The mother never testified that she knew her daughters were being molested; she told the grievance committee it was possible, but "I can't say that I know because I don't know, you know." It was Glant's opinion that the mother was engaging in criminal conduct, but the referee did not accept this opinion—or Glant's reliance on rule 4–1.2(a). We rely on the referee, as the fact-finder, to resolve any conflicts in the evidence. The record supports the referee's finding that Glant violated rule 4–1.2(a). Thus, the referee did not err in refusing to grant Glant's motion for a directed verdict, and we approve the finding that Glant violated rule 4–1.2(a).

We find that a public reprimand is the appropriate sanction for Glant. Florida Standard for Imposing Lawyer Sanctions 7.3 says a public reprimand is appropriate when a lawyer negligently engages in conduct that violates a duty owed as a professional and causes injury or potential injury to the client, the public, or the legal system. In deciding the appropriate sanction, a bar disciplinary action must serve three purposes: the judgment must be fair to society, it must be fair to the attorney, and it must sufficiently deter other attorneys from similar misconduct. Glant was admitted to the Bar in 1984 and has no disciplinary history. A public reprimand, followed by six months on probation, serves the purposes of attorney disciplinary action.

NOTES AND QUESTIONS

1. At what point did the lawyer err? Could she have corrected the error? (Perhaps she should have read STEVE COMINSKY'S SECRETS A GOOD LAWYER [AND THEIR BEST CLIENTS] ALREADY KNOW (1997): "Know who your client is; remember who your client is; only represent your client; don't surprise your client.")

2. How, if at all, would the outcome in *Glant* be affected if state law required lawyers to report sexual abuse of children? *See, e.g.* North Carolina Op. 120, at ABA/BNA 1001:6603 (no obligation to report but can report to stop future abuse). *See also* Robin A. Rosencrantz, *Rejecting "Hear No Evil Speak No Evil": Expanding the Attorney's Role in Child Abuse Reporting*, 8 GEO. J. LEGAL ETHICS 327 (1995).

3. What is the lawyer's role in assisting the client to make decisions on case strategy? What should the lawyer do if he or she feels that the client's decisions are improvident? Model Rule 2.1 provides that "[i]n representing a client, a lawyer shall exercise independent professional judgment and render candid advice. In rendering advice, a lawyer may refer not only to law but to other considerations such as moral, economic, social and political factors, that may be relevant to the client's situation." Although a lawyer must generally defer to the client's decisions on case strategy, Model Rule 3.1 prohibits a lawyer from bringing or defending a proceeding or controverting an issue without a nonfrivolous basis.

4. Does the lawyer representing a parent have any obligation to the client's child? The AAML Standards provide: "An attorney representing a parent should consider the welfare of, and seek to minimize the adverse impact of the divorce on, the minor children" and that "[a]n attorney should not permit a client to contest child custody, contact or access for either financial leverage or vindictiveness." Standards 6.1, 6.2. How do these obligations affect a lawyer's zealous representation of his or her parent client? Consider the statement by the Massachusetts Supreme Court: "The attorney's ethical duty to zealously represent the client in a custody or visitation matter is not a license to adopt strategies and tactics reasonably likely to create a situation of

prolonged destabilization and uncertainty in contravention of the child's best interests." A.H. v. M.P., 857 N.E.2d 1061, n. 14 (Mass. 2006).

3. Confidentiality

Confidentiality lies at the heart of the attorney-client relationship because it encourages honest communication. ABA Model Rule 1.6 provides:

> (a) A lawyer shall not reveal information relating to the representation of a client unless the client gives informed consent, the disclosure is impliedly authorized in order to carry out the representation or the disclosure is permitted by paragraph (b).

> (b) A lawyer may reveal information relating to the representation of a client to the extent the lawyer reasonably believes necessary:

>> (1) to prevent reasonably certain death or substantial bodily harm;

>> (2) to prevent the client from committing a crime or fraud that is reasonably certain to result in substantial injury to the financial interests or property of another and in furtherance of which the client has used or is using the lawyer's services;

>> (3) to prevent, mitigate or rectify substantial injury to the financial interests or property of another that is reasonably certain to result or has resulted from the client's commission of a crime or fraud in furtherance of which the client has used the lawyer's services;

>> (4) to secure legal advice about the lawyer's compliance with these Rules;

>> (5) to establish a claim or defense on behalf of the lawyer in a controversy between the lawyer and the client, to establish a defense to a criminal charge or civil claim against the lawyer based upon conduct in which the client was involved, or to respond to allegations in any proceeding concerning the lawyer's representation of the client; or

>> (6) to comply with other law or a court order.

Social media offers new opportunities to violate confidentiality rules. For example, a couple of lawyers have been disciplined for breaching confidentiality by posting information on the internet. *See In re* Skinner, 758 S.E.2d 788 (Ga. 2014) (attorney posted personal client information); People v. Isaac, 2016 WL 6124510 (Colo. O.P.D.J. 2016) (after two negative client reviews, attorney posted online responses which included confidential information).

4. Sex with Clients

Model Rule 1.8(j) prohibits a lawyer from having sex with a client unless a consensual sexual relationship existed prior to the start of the professional representation. AAML Standard 3.3 provides that an attorney should not have a sexual relationship with a client, opposing counsel, or a judicial officer involved in the case during the time of the representation.

In several states ethical opinions have imposed sanctions on lawyers who have engaged in sexual relations with clients. *See* State ex rel. Oklahoma Bar Association v. Sopher, 852 P.2d 707 (Okla. 1993); Iowa Supreme Court Attorney Disciplinary Bd. v. McGrath, 713 N.W.2d 682 (Iowa 2006); Attorney Grievance Comm'n of Maryland v. Culver, 849 A.2d 423 (Md. 2004). An Indiana court provided an explanation for the ban on sex with clients:

> * * * In their professional capacity, lawyers are expected to provide emotionally detached, objective analysis of legal problems and issues for clients who may be embroiled in sensitive or difficult matters. Clients, especially those who are troubled or emotionally fragile, often place a great deal of trust in the lawyer and rely heavily on his or her agreement to provide professional assistance. Unfortunately, the lawyer's position of trust may provide opportunity to manipulate the client for the lawyer's sexual benefit. Where a lawyer permits or encourages a sexual relationship to form with a client, that trust is betrayed and the stage is set for continued unfair exploitation of the lawyer's fiduciary position. Additionally, the lawyer's ability to represent effectively the client may be impaired. Objective detachment, essential for clear and reasoned analysis of issues and independent professional judgment, may be lost.

In the Matter of Grimm, 674 N.E.2d 551, 554 (Ind. 1996).

Can you think of other harms that can come from an attorney-client sexual relationship?

NOTES AND QUESTIONS

1. Should it matter if the client, rather than the lawyer, initiates a sexual relationship? Can a sexual relationship between attorney and client be consensual? Disciplinary Counsel v. Detweiler, 989 N.E.2d 41 (Ohio 2013) (yes). Should consent be a defense? Iowa S. Ct. Atty. Disciplinary Bd. v. Moothart, 860 N.W.2d 598 (Iowa 2015) (no). *See* Jennifer Tuggle Crabtree, *Does Consent Matter? Relationships Between Divorce Attorneys and Clients*, 23 J. LEGAL PROF. 221 (1998). *See also* Rhoda Feinberg & James Tom Greene,

Transference and Countertransference Issues in Professional Relationships, 29 FAM. L. Q. 111 (1995).

2.   What, if any, remedies are available to a client who has had a sexual relationship with his or her lawyer? If damages are available, how should they be calculated? *See* McDaniel v. Gile, 281 Cal. Rptr. 242 (App. 1991); *Woman Wins Suit on Coerced Affair with Lawyer,* N.Y. TIMES, Nov. 29, 1992, at 38 (reporting award of $20,000 compensatory and $200,000 punitive damages in action against male lawyer alleged to have coerced his female client into having sex 200 times over 18 month period).

3.   Social media has increased opportunities for lawyers to communicate with their clients in sometimes inappropriate ways. Think Anthony Weiner. *See* Disciplinary Matter Involving Stanton, 376 P.3d 693 (Alaska 2016) (attorney violated ethical rules by sending lewd text messages and nude photographs to client); Disciplinary Counsel v. Bartels, 2016 WL 3344953 (Ohio, June 14, 2016) (two years probation where lawyer sent hundreds of voluntary sexually explicit text messages and photos with divorce client).

D. DUTIES TO OPPOSING PARTIES, COUNSEL AND THE COURT

1.   Communication with Other Parties

A lawyer may not communicate about the subject of representation with a person known to be represented by counsel unless the other lawyer consents or is authorized by law or court order. *See* ABA Model Rule 4.2. Some courts have also held that a lawyer may not communicate with children for whom a guardian ad litem has been appointed. *See In re* Disciplinary Proceedings Against Frank X. Kinast, 530 N.W.2d 387 (Wis. 1995); *ABA Standards of Conduct for Lawyers Who Represent Children in Abuse and Neglect Cases,* 29 FAM. L. Q. 175 (1995). Can an attorney handle his own divorce case and talk to his wife who is not represented by counsel? *See* Barrett v. Virginia State Bar, 611 S.E.2d 375 (Va. 2005); Louis Parley, *Lawyers, Their Divorces and Legal Ethics,* 30 FAM. L. Q. 661 (1996).

2.   Fair Bargaining

ABA Model Rule 4.1 prohibits a lawyer from making a false statement of a material fact or law to a third person or failing to disclose a material fact when necessary to avoid assisting a criminal or fraudulent act by the client. *See also* AAML Standard 3.2 ("An attorney should never deceive or intentionally mislead opposing counsel"); AAML Standard 2.13 (attorney should not encourage the client to hide or dissipate assets); AAML Standard 3.3 (attorney should not rely on a mistake by opposing counsel to obtain an unfair benefit for the client).

Although there is no duty to volunteer information which opposing counsel has not requested except to prevent fraud, many courts require counsel to provide information on a change in property value occurring between pre-trial discovery and trial. *See In re* Marriage of Wilson, 223 P.3d 815 (Kan. App. 2010) (imposing $30,000 fine on husband for not reporting income had increased from $472,498 in 2006 to over two million dollars in 2007 and reporting his lawyer to the disciplinary board). Some courts have also held that the spousal relationship entails fiduciary obligations. *See* CAL. FAM. CODE § 2100(c); Billington v. Billington, 595 A.2d 1377 (Conn. 1991); Miller v. Miller, 700 S.W.2d 941 (Tex. App. 1985).

The lawyer must use fairness in gathering evidence. The lawyer cannot use improperly obtained information. For example, an attorney was suspended indefinitely for using emails that his client had obtained from his wife's personal email account without her permission. *In re* Eisenstein, 485 S.W.3d 759 (Mo. 2016). *See* Barbara Glesner Fines, *The Changing Landscape of Disciplinary Risks in Family Law Practice*, 50 FAM. L. Q. 367, 371 (2016).

3. Duty of Candor

A lawyer may not engage in conduct involving "dishonesty, fraud, deceit or misrepresentation." ABA Model Rule 8.4(c). ABA Model Rule 1.2(d) prohibits a lawyer from counseling a client to engage in or assist a client in conduct that the lawyer knows is criminal or fraudulent. Model Rule 3.3(a)(1) provides that "a lawyer shall not knowingly (1) make a false statement of fact or law * * * or (3) offer evidence that the lawyer knows to be false. If a lawyer, the lawyer's client or a witness called by lawyer, has offered material evidence and the lawyer comes to know its falsity, the lawyer shall take reasonable remedial measures, including, if necessary, disclosure to the tribunal." Model Rule 3.3(b) provides that a lawyer " * * * who knows that a person intends to engage, is engaging or has engaged in criminal or fraudulent conduct related to the proceeding shall take reasonable remedial measures * * *." *See In re* Whitney, 120 P.3d 550 (Wash. 2005) (disbarring an attorney who lied while testifying as a guardian ad litem in a custody case).

Some states impose more stringent reporting requirements than do the Model Rules and require an attorney to reveal a client's intention to commit a crime. *See* Opinion No. 87–9, Ill. State Bar Comm. on Prof. Resp., 14 Fam. L. Rep. (BNA) 1363 (1988). *See also* Nix v. Whiteside, 475 U.S. 157 (1986).

Problem 11-4:

Jerry, a family law attorney, unhappy with the judge's rulings in a child custody case involving alleged sexual abuse, posted comments on Twitter about the judge. In an attempt to influence the family court judge, Jerry urged readers to contact the judge and other judicial officers to communicate their displeasure. Has Jerry violated any ethical rules? *See In re* McCool, 172 So. 3d 1058 (La. 2015).

3. CRITICISMS OF THE DIVORCE PROCESS

Divorce lawyers and the judicial system have been criticized for being too adversarial, too expensive and too lengthy. In reforming the Oregon family law system, the report summarized the problems:

> The divorce process in Oregon, as elsewhere, was broken and needed fixing. Lawyers, mediators, judges, counselors and citizens . . . agreed that the family court system was too confrontational to meet the human needs of most families undergoing divorce. The process was adversarial where it needn't have been: All cases were prepared as if going to court, when only a small percentage actually did. The judicial system made the parties adversaries, although they had many common interests.

> * * *

> . . . the sheer volume of cases was causing the family court system to collapse. Too often, children were treated like property . . . . The combative atmosphere made it more difficult for divorcing couples to reach a settlement and develop a cooperative relationship once the divorce was final.

OREGON TASK FORCE ON FAMILY LAW, FINAL REPORT TO GOVENOR JOHN A. KITZHABER AND THE OREGON LEGISLATIVE ASSEMBLY 2 (1997).

A. THE PROCESS IS TOO ADVERSARIAL

Many critics argue that the divorce process is too adversarial. Divorce litigation can escalate hostilities, reduce the possibility of compromise and, in extreme cases, harm both the litigants and their children. One does not have to look too far to find a report like this one:

> Port St. Joe, Fla., July 28 (AP)—A man in court for an alimony hearing today shot and killed his ex-wife's lawyer, a witness and the judge hearing the case, the authorities said. The man, Clyde Melvin, also wounded his former wife before he was hit by a sheriff's bullet, the officials said. * * * A .357-caliber Magnum and .22-caliber Derringer were found on Mr. Melvin when he was taken into custody.

N.Y. TIMES, July 29, 1987, at 13, col. 4.

One complaint centers on "bombers," i.e., lawyers who engage in "dirty tricks" such as prolonging discovery by taking depositions of unneeded witnesses, excessively interfering with questioning of witnesses, making burdensome requests for unnecessary documents, denying allegations everyone knows are true, filing unnecessary paperwork, failing to return phone calls, making personal attacks on opposing counsel, and generally using delay or nasty tactics to drag the case along and make it unpleasant for all involved.

How should a lawyer respond to dirty tricks by the other side? The two predominant means of disciplining bombers are through sanctions and seeking an award of attorney fees. A court may also impose nonmonetary sanctions, such as requiring the attorney to attend educational seminars. AAML Standard 3 specifies that "overzealous, discourteous, abrasive, 'hard ball' conduct by matrimonial lawyers is inconsistent with both their obligation to effectively represent their clients and their duty to improve the process of dispute resolution."

The American Bar Association Family Law Section adopted Standards of Civility in 2006 which emphasize the nature of the lawyer's obligations to clients, opposing lawyers and the court. Among, other things, lawyers should:

1.   Act with complete honesty; show respect for the court by proper demeanor; and act and speak civilly to the judge, court staff and adversaries.

2.   Avoid frivolous litigation and non-essential pleading in litigation.

3.   Explore settlement possibilities at the earliest reasonable date, and seek agreement on procedural and discovery matters.

4.   Avoid delays not dictated by a competent and justified presentation of a client's claims or defenses.

5.   Strive to protect the dignity and independence of the judiciary, particularly from unjust criticism and attack.

See www.abanet.org/family/reports/home.shtml. Would these Standards make divorce less adversarial?

CHARLES B. CRAVER, NEGOTIATION ETHICS: HOW TO BE DECEPTIVE WITHOUT BEING DISHONEST/HOW TO BE ASSERTIVE WITHOUT BEING OFFENSIVE
38 S. TEX. L. REV. 713 (1997).

* * *

Many practicing attorneys seem to think that competitive/adversarial negotiators—who use highly competitive tactics to maximize their own client returns—achieve more beneficial results for their clients than their cooperative/problem-solving colleagues—who employ more cooperative techniques designed to maximize the joint return to the parties involved. An empirical study, conducted by Professor Gerald Williams, of legal practitioners in Denver and Phoenix contradicts this notion. Professor Williams found that sixty-five percent of negotiators are considered cooperative/problem-solvers by their peers, twenty-four percent are viewed as competitive/adversarial, and eleven percent did not fit in either category. When the respondents were asked to indicate which attorneys were "effective," "average," and "ineffective" negotiators, the results were striking. While fifty-nine percent of the cooperative/problem-solving lawyers were rated "effective," only twenty-five percent of competitive/adversarial attorneys were rated effective. On the other hand, while a mere three percent of cooperative/problem-solvers were considered "ineffective," thirty-three percent of competitive/adversarial bargainers were rated "ineffective."

In this study, Professor Williams found that certain traits were shared by both effective cooperative/problem-solving negotiators and effective competitive/adversarial bargainers. Successful negotiators from both groups are thoroughly prepared, behave in an honest and ethical manner, are perceptive readers of opponent cues, are analytical, realistic, and convincing, and observe the courtesies of the bar. The proficient negotiators from both groups also sought to *maximize* their *own client's* return. Since this is the quintessential characteristic of competitive/adversarial bargainers, it would suggest that a number of successful negotiators may be adroitly masquerading as sheep in wolves' clothing. They exude a cooperative style, but seek competitive objectives.

Most successful negotiators are able to combine the most salient traits associated with the cooperative/problem-solving and the competitive/adversarial styles. They endeavor to maximize client returns, but attempt to accomplish this objective in a congenial and seemingly ingenuous manner. They look for shared values in recognition of the fact that by maximizing joint returns, they are more likely to obtain the best settlements for their own clients. Although successful negotiators try to manipulate opponent perceptions, they rarely resort to truly deceitful tactics. They know that a loss of credibility will undermine their ability to achieve beneficial results. Despite the fact successful negotiators want as much as possible for their own clients, they are not "win-lose" negotiators who judge their results, not by how well they have done, but by how poorly they think their opponents have done. They realize that the imposition of poor terms on opponents does not necessarily benefit their own clients. All factors being equal, they want to maximize opponent satisfaction. So long as it does not require significant concessions on their part, they acknowledge the benefits to be derived from this approach. The more satisfied opponents are, the more likely those parties will accept proposed terms and honor the resulting agreements.

These eclectic negotiators employ a composite style. They may be characterized as competitive/problem-solvers. They seek competitive goals (maximum client returns), but endeavor to accomplish these objectives through problem-solving strategies. They exude a cooperative approach and follow the courtesies of the legal profession. They avoid rude or inconsiderate behavior, recognizing that such openly adversarial conduct is likely to generate competitive/adversarial responses from their opponents. They appreciate the fact that individuals who employ wholly inappropriate tactics almost always induce opposing counsel to work harder to avoid exploitation by these openly opportunistic bargainers. Legal negotiators who are contemplating the use of offensive techniques should simply ask themselves how they would react if similar tactics were employed against them.

* * *

Lawyers must remember that they have to live with their own consciences, and not those of their clients or their partners. They must employ tactics they are comfortable using, even in those situations in which other people encourage them to employ less reputable behavior. If they adopt techniques they do not consider appropriate, not only will they experience personal discomfort, but they will also fail to achieve their intended objective due to the fact they will not appear credible when using those tactics. Attorneys must also acknowledge that they are members of a special profession and owe certain duties to the public that transcend those that may be owed by people engaged in other businesses. Even though ABA Model Rule 1.3 states that "[a] lawyer shall act with reasonable diligence," Comment One expressly recognizes that "a lawyer is not bound to press for every advantage that might be realized for a client. A lawyer has professional discretion in determining the means by which a matter [shall] be pursued."

Popular negotiation books occasionally recount the successful use of questionable techniques to obtain short-term benefits. The authors glibly describe the way they have employed highly aggressive, deliberately deceptive, or equally opprobrious bargaining tactics to achieve their objectives. They usually conclude these stories with parenthetical admissions that their bilked adversaries would probably be reluctant to interact with them in the future. When negotiators engage in such questionable behavior such that they would find it difficult, if not impossible, to transact future business with their adversaries, they have usually transcended the bounds of propriety. No legal representatives should be willing to jeopardize long-term professional relationships for the narrow interests of particular clients. Zealous representation should never be thought to require the employment of personally compromising techniques.

Lawyers must acknowledge that they are not guarantors—they are only legal advocates. They are not supposed to guarantee client victory no matter how disreputably they must act to do so. They should never countenance witness perjury or the withholding of subpoenaed documents. While they should zealously endeavor to advance client interests, they should recognize their moral obligation to follow the ethical rules applicable to all attorneys.

Untrustworthy advocates encounter substantial difficulty when they negotiate with others. Their oral representations must be verified and reduced to writing, and many opponents distrust their written documents. Their negotiations become especially problematic and cumbersome. If nothing else moves practitioners to behave in an ethical and dignified manner, their hope for long and successful legal careers should induce them to avoid conduct that may undermine their future effectiveness.

Attorneys should diligently strive to advance client objectives while simultaneously maintaining their personal integrity. This philosophy will enable them to optimally serve the interests of both their clients and society. Legal practitioners who are asked about their insistence on ethical behavior may take refuge in an aphorism of Mark Twain: "Always do right. This will gratify some people, and astonish the rest[!]"

WINGSPREAD REPORT AND ACTION PLAN, HIGH CONFLICT CUSTODY CASES: REFORMING THE SYSTEM FOR CHILDREN
34 FAMILY LAW QUARTERLY 589, 595 (2001).

* * *

1. The Lawyer's Responsibility to Promote Conflict Resolution

   a. Lawyers should diligently exercise their counseling function in assisting their clients to avoid inappropriate conflict in dealing with custody-related issues, including the ways in which the parties and counsel pursue litigation. Lawyers should discuss with client parents the negative consequences of custody conflicts and disputes on their children and should advise parents about the availability of resources to reduce conflict.

   b. Lawyers should discuss alternatives to litigation, such as mediation, with their clients.

   c. As a general rule, lawyers should encourage their clients to cooperate with forensic custody and mental health evaluations.

    d.   Lawyers have a duty to realistically evaluate their client's case and not raise false expectations.

    e.   Lawyers should encourage early court interventions to identify issues in high-conflict cases and should refer clients to available resources and processes to help them resolve their conflicts outside the courtroom.

    f.   Lawyers should assist one another and the court in expeditiously determining the best interests of the child by cooperating in defining and limiting the issues, procedures, and evidence necessary to determine the best interest of the child.

    g.   Lawyers should maintain a civil demeanor and encourage their clients to follow their example.

    h.   Lawyers and parties should not use the media, child protective services, or other means to create or exacerbate conflict and should be sensitive to the child's need for privacy.

    i.   Lawyers should be trained in child development, child abuse and neglect, domestic violence, family dynamics, and alternative conflict resolution and be knowledgeable about cross-disciplinary issues affecting their high-conflict custody cases, such as competencies of other professionals and available community resources.

    j.   Lawyers should develop and participate in special continuing legal education programs for high-conflict custody cases and encourage law schools to incorporate interdisciplinary training in mental health and dispute resolution into the family law curriculum to improve lawyers' ability to reduce conflict in custody cases.

NOTES AND QUESTIONS

    1.   Negotiation has traditionally been the primary means of resolving family law disputes. Studies have confirmed that cooperative lawyers get better results than adversarial. *See* JULIE MACFARLANE, THE NEW LAWYER: HOW SETTLEMENT IS TRANSFORMING THE PRACTICE OF FAMILY LAW (2008); Forrest S. Mosten, *Lawyer as Peacemaker: Building a Successful Law Practice Without Ever Going to Court*, 43 FAM. L. Q. 489 (2009). *See also* Andrea Kupfer Schneider, *Shattering Negotiation Myths: Empirical Evidence on Effectiveness of Negotiation Style*, 7 HARV. NEG. L. REV. 143 (2002).

    2.   Would adoption of the Wingspread recommendations for lawyers require changes to the Model Rules?

    3.   Family courts have become more interdisciplinary and problem solving. Family lawyers have more resources to help them negotiate, especially

the emotional dynamics. *See* ROGER FISHER & DANIEL SHAPIRO, BEYOND REASON: USING EMOTIONS AS YOU NEGOTIATE (2006). Some think this is the proper direction. JANE C. MURPHY & JANA B. SINGER, DIVORCED FROM REALITY: RETHINKING FAMILY DISPUTE RESOLUTION (2015). Others, however, think the adversary system is best suited to protect the vulnerable. Glenna Goldis, *When Family Courts Shun Adversarialism*, 18 U.C. DAVIS J. JUV. L. & POL'Y 195 (2014).

B. THE PROCESS IS TOO EXPENSIVE

Divorce lawyers have sometimes been criticized for charging excessive fees. The lawyer's fee, however reasonable, is not the only divorce expense. The client may also be billed for court costs, such as filing fees and court reporter charges; photocopying, faxing, and mailing costs; fees for investigation, discovery, and travel; expert fees, including accountants, investigators, appraisers for real estate, business, art or antiques, pension actuaries, psychologists or psychiatrists, and business or tax experts. The divorce will also entail hidden costs, including the time the client has to take off from work to attend depositions, hearings and to meet with his or her lawyer.

The perception that divorce lawyers are expensive is one reason that many divorces involve one (or even two) unrepresented parties. In many areas, a minority of divorces involves two-party representation. INST. OF THE AM. LEGAL SYSTEM, CASES WITHOUT COUNSEL: EXPERIENCES OF SELF-REPRESENTATION IN U.S. FAMILY COURT 19–22 (2016).

Courts have found that processing pro se cases is more difficult and time-consuming. Increased rates of pro se representation have thus led some states to enact simplified divorce procedures, adopt standard forms and pleadings, or provide some form of assistance (self help packets, clinics) for unrepresented litigants. Maricopa County, Arizona, for example, initiated a range of reforms, including guidelines and printed forms, model pleadings, courthouse assistance, night court, client libraries, and child care. *See* Jessica Pearson, *Court Services: Meeting the Needs of Twenty-first Century Families,* 33 FAM. L. Q. 617 (1999). Do-it-yourself divorce kits have become popular. Many lawyers feel that these kits mislead the lay public and result in serious problems that may not be recognized for several years. *See* Jona Goldschmidt, *The Pro Se Litigant's Struggle for Access to Justice: Meeting the Challenge of Bench and Bar Resistance*, 40 FAM. CT. REV. 36 (2002).

Nonlawyers who provide legal advice in connection with a divorce may be subject to prosecution for the unauthorized practice of law. *See* State Bar v. Cramer, 249 N.W.2d 1 (Mich. 1976); Florida Bar v. Furman, 451 So. 2d 808 (Fla. 1984). The proliferation of divorce kits has led some states, like Arkansas and Ohio, to strengthen their unauthorized practice of law provisions. Other states, however, like Arizona, California, Oregon and

Washington, have created programs to allow nonlawyers ("legal technicians") who meet state-established educational and ethical requirements to sell legal forms or help clients in certain situations. *See* Lori W. Nelson, *LLLT—Limited License Legal Technician: What It Is, What It Isn't, and the Grey Area in Between*, 50 FAM. L. Q. 447 (2016).

ABA Model Rule 1.2(c) allows a lawyer to limit the scope of representation. Some states have approved "Limited Representation" for lawyers which would allow a lawyer to handle part of a case with client consent.

C. THE PROCESS TAKES TOO LONG

Divorce cases can take literally years to resolve. The case of Wolfe v. Wolfe, 389 N.E.2d 1143 (Ill. 1979), for example, was originally filed as a divorce action by the wife, consumed eight years, cost more than $100,000, required 113 hearings, and involved 35 judges and 25 lawyers before concluding in an annulment granted to the husband. The vast majority of divorce cases are resolved in less than eight years but, in some urban courts, delays of nine to ten months are not uncommon in uncontested divorces; it may take years to resolve a contested divorce.

What, if anything, can be done to minimize delay? Would a speedy trial requirement, like that applicable to criminal cases, be desirable?

One suggestion is to use differentiated case management (DCM). DCM is based on the assumption that the "amount and type of court intervention will vary from case to case." Judith S. Kaye & Jonathan Lippman, *New York State Unified Court System Family Justice Program*, 36 FAM. & CONCIL. CTS. REV. 144, 163 (1998). "Under this model * * * a case is assessed at its filing stage for its level of complexity and management needs and placed on an appropriate 'track.' Firm deadlines and time frames are established according to case classification." *Id.*

DCM has been used in criminal and other civil cases and is starting to be used in high conflict divorce and custody cases. DCM utilizes time tracks that vary based on the complexity of the case, need for discovery, need for services, need for protection and other factors. Procedures are simplified for the cases in which parents cooperate and are able to resolve their issues. A type of summary dissolution expedites the process. *See* Lynda B. Munro, Johanna S. Katz, & Meghan M. Sweeney, *Administrative Divorce Trends and Implications*, 50 FAM. L. Q. 427 (2016). A more rigid structure with strict time lines is imposed on feuding parents. *See* Andrew Schepard, *The Evolving Judicial Role in Child Custody Disputes: From Fault Finder to Conflict Manager to Differential Case Management*, 22 U. ARK. LITTLE ROCK L. J. 395, 412–427 (2000).

4. MEDIATION

The adversarial nature of divorce disputes, slow dockets, prohibitive costs, and unpredictable judges increased enthusiasm for alternatives to the traditional litigation and settlement process. Many experts have noted the need for mechanisms to resolve family disputes without litigation.

Los Angeles offered the first "alternate dispute resolution" program in the 1930s; its "conciliation" program provided marriage counseling aimed at reconciliation. California later established a conciliation program in each court with principal jurisdiction over divorce cases involving child custody and visitation. *See* Henry Foster & Doris Jonas Freed, *Divorce Reform: Brakes on Breakdown*, 13 J. FAM. L. 443 (1973–74). Few courts have conciliation programs today although some believe that reconciliation is still a worthy goal. *See e.g.* American Academy of Matrimonial Lawyers Standards of Conduct 2.2 provides: "An attorney should advise the client of the emotional and economic impact of divorce and possibility or advisability of reconciliation."

Alternative dispute resolution (ADR) mechanisms today encompass negotiation, mediation, arbitration, and combinations of these techniques. There is a growing consensus that lawyers should have to advise clients of ADR options. ABA Model Rule 2.4, cmt. 1 (2015) notes that alternative dispute resolution has become a substantial part of the domestic justice system.

Mediation is the most widely used ADR method in child custody cases. Mediation is:

> * * * a process in which a mediator, an impartial third party, facilitates the resolution of family disputes by promoting the participants' voluntary agreement. The family mediator assists communication, encourages understanding and focuses the participants on their individual and common interests. The family mediator works with the participants to explore options, make decisions and reach their own agreements.

American Bar Association Model Standards of Practice for Family and Divorce Mediation, 35 FAM. L. Q. 27 (2001).

A lawyer may be involved in the mediation process in a number of roles. The lawyer may be a mediator who helps the parties reach agreement without representing either of them. The lawyer may represent one of the parties who is in the mediation process or the child whose parents are in mediation. The lawyer may be a participant/observer helping the client make reasoned decisions. The lawyer may be a reviewer of a mediated agreement for one of the parties. Forrest S. Mosten, *Lawyer as Peacemaker: Building a Successful Law Practice Without Ever Going to Court*, 43 FAM. L. Q. 489 (2009).

A. THE MEDIATION PROCESS

JAY FOLBERG, DIVORCE MEDIATION: A WORKABLE ALTERNATIVE

American Bar Association, Alternative Means of Dispute Resolution 12, 13–15, 41
(Howard Davidson et al. eds., 1982).

The subjects of divorce mediation include, but are not limited to, those that would be resolved by a judge in court, but for the mediated settlement. It can thus be seen as an alternative or, at least, a complement to the court process. Divorce mediation is defined here as a non-therapeutic process by which the parties together, with the assistance of a neutral resource person or persons, attempt to systematically isolate points of agreement and disagreement, explore alternatives and consider compromises for the purpose of reaching a consensual settlement of issues relating to their divorce or separation. Mediation is a process of conflict resolution and management that gives back to the parties the responsibility for making their own decisions about their own lives. It is usually conducted in private without the presence of the parties' attorneys. It has identifiable stages and divisible tasks, but no universal pattern.

In order to better distinguish and isolate mediation from other interventions, we might look at what it is not. It is not, as above defined, a therapeutic process. * * * It is not focused on insight to personal conflict or in changing historically set personality patterns. It is much more an interactive process than an interpsychic one. Mediation is task-directed and goal-oriented. It looks at resolution and results between the parties rather than the internalized causes of conflict behavior. It discourages dependence on the professional provider rather than promoting it. * * *

Mediation is not arbitration. In arbitration, the parties authorize a neutral third person or persons to *decide* upon a binding resolution of the issues. The process used in arbitration is adjudicatory, but is typically less formal than that utilized in court and is usually conducted in private. Other than its informality and privacy, arbitration is much like the judicial process, except the "judge" is chosen or agreed upon by the parties and derives his or her authority from the agreement to arbitrate. In mediation the parties may choose the mediator, but do not authorize the mediator to make the decisions for them. Arbitration may follow mediation, either as a separate proceeding or as part of the same "med-arb" process.

Mediation is not the same as traditional negotiation of divorce disputes. Negotiation is generally a "sounding out" process to aid dispute resolutions but is not accomplished through any established framework and may be pursued through representatives, most often attorneys. Negotiation does not normally utilize a neutral resource person and is premised on an adversary model. Private negotiation may, however, precede mediation, follow unsuccessful mediation, or in some settings go on simultaneously.

Mediation is not conciliation, though the two terms are often used interchangeably. The two can be distinguished by looking at their historical development and application to the field of family law. California first offered court-connected conciliation services in 1939. The initial focus of these services was on providing marriage counseling aimed at effecting a reconciliation of spouses. With the adoption of no-fault divorce and the increase in the divorce rate, the focus of conciliation has shifted from marriage counseling aimed at reconciling parties to separation counseling and evaluation services for purposes of assisting the domestic relations judges in making child custody and visitation orders. Indeed, in California, where mandatory custody mediation is usually performed by conciliation personnel, the distinction between conciliation and mediation has become somewhat obfuscated.

* * *

Divorce mediation has been touted as a replacement for the adversary system and a way of making divorce less painful. Though it may serve as an alternative for those that choose to use it, it is neither a panacea that will create love where there is hate, nor will it totally eliminate the role of the adversary system in divorce. It may, however, reduce acrimony by promoting cooperation and it may lessen the burden of the courts in deciding many cases that can be diverted to less hostile and costly procedures. Divorce mediation does appear to be a rational alternative attracting considerable interest. It is still in its infancy in the United States and, therefore, along with its promises, it has raised substantial issues. The resolution of these issues will require additional empirical research, experience and dialogue.

NOTES AND QUESTIONS

1.   When Folberg wrote in 1982, mediation was a relatively new idea. Today, mediation is available in all states, and mandatory in some. Nancy Ver Steegh, *Family Court Reform and ADR: Shifting Values and Expectations Transform Divorce Process*, 42 FAM. L. Q. 659 (2008). Mediation is also utilized outside the United States. In 2011 England required parties to participate in mandatory mediation in most divorce cases before going to court.

2.   Mediation may take place at any point in the litigation process— before filing, after filing and before discovery, after discovery, after failed negotiations, or post-divorce. Typically, divorce mediation starts after a divorce petition and answer are filed; at that point, it may help resolve discovery problems, focus the parties on unresolved issues, and provide a forum in which to decide issues of temporary support, custody and visitation. Complex equitable distribution problems may require the parties to have completed

extensive discovery or at the least have agreed upon appraisals and valuations on property. Custody contests may require medical or psychological reports. For more thorough discussions of the mediation process, *see* DIVORCE AND FAMILY MEDIATION: MODELS, TECHNIQUES, AND APPLICATIONS (Jay Folberg, et al. eds 2004); FORREST S. MOSTEN, THE COMPLETE GUIDE TO MEDIATION: HOW TO EFFECTIVELY REPRESENT YOUR CLIENTS AND EXPAND YOUR LAW PRACTICE (2d ed. 2015).

3.   Mediation began as a voluntary alternative for couples wishing to resolve custody and visitation issues amicably, but the trend has been toward mandated pre-trial custody mediation. *See, e.g.,* CAL. FAM. CODE § 3170; FLA. STAT. ANN. § 44.102(c); NEV. REV. STAT. ANN. § 3.500. In some states, the court may order mediation of *any* contested issue, including property division and even child neglect. What are the advantages of voluntary versus court-ordered mediation? *See* Holly A. Streeter-Schaefer, Note, *A Look at Court Mandated Civil Mediation*, 49 DRAKE L. REV. 367 (2001) (discussing advantages and disadvantages of mandated mediation).

4.   Should children be involved in custody mediation? *See* Rebecca Hinton, Comment, *Giving Children a Right to be Heard: Suggested Reforms to Provide Louisiana Children a Voice in Child Custody Disputes*, 65 LA. L. REV. 1539 (2005). *See also* Cassandra W. Adams, *Children's Interest—Lost in Translation: Making the Case for Involving Children in Mediation of Child Custody Cases*, 36 U. DAYTON L. REV. 353 (2011). In England and Wales, a child over nine is expected to attend custody mediation. *See* Nigel V. Lowe, *The Allocation of Parental Rights and Responsibilities—The Position of England and Wales*, 39 FAM. L. Q. 267, 277 (2005).

B. ETHICAL CONSIDERATIONS

Both lawyers and mental health professionals mediate divorce disputes. Lawyers tout their superior knowledge of the law and court processes. Mental health professionals and social workers tout their communication skills and expertise in working with people. Ideally, a mediator should be familiar with both the law and the emotional aspects of divorce. When mediation first began, almost anyone could hang up a shingle as a mediator. Several states now have established educational and training qualifications for mediators; some require additional specialized training to mediate family disputes. Mediators who receive court referrals often must possess an advanced degree in law, social work, mental health or accounting. *See* Joan B. Kelly, *Issues Facing the Family Mediation Field*, 1 PEPP. DISP. RESOL. L.J. 37 (2000) (contending that certification of mediators will be one of the major challenges as professionals struggle to define "competency" in the context of mediation).

Lawyers who mediate face unique ethical issues: Does confidentiality or privilege attach to mediation if the mediator is a lawyer? Can the unhappy party subpoena the mediator to testify at trial? Can a lawyer mediator ever represent one of the parties to the mediation in any other forum? Is the lawyer acting as an intermediary? Can a law firm offer both adversary and conciliatory services? *See* Carrie Menkel-Meadow, *Ethics in ADR: The Many "Cs" of Professional Responsibility and Dispute Resolution*, 28 FORDHAM URBAN L. J. 979, 981 (2001) (identifying the "Four Cs of Ethics and ADR"—counseling about ADR, confidentiality, conflicts of interest, and conciliation). *See also* Loretta M. Moore, *Lawyer Mediators: Meeting the Ethical Challenges*, 30 FAM. L. Q. 679 (1996).

The American Bar Association adopted Standards of Practice for Lawyer Mediators in 1984 and revised them in 2001. *See* Model Standards of Practice for Family and Divorce Mediation, 35 FAM. L. Q. 27 (2001). In 1994, the ABA Section of Dispute Resolution, the American Arbitration Association and the Association for Conflict Resolution promulgated Model Standards of Conduct for Mediators which covers nonlawyer mediators as well as lawyers. They were revised in 2005.

NOTES AND QUESTIONS

1.   What type of training should a mediator obtain? The commentary to the 2001 ABA Standards of Practice Standard II suggests that the family mediator should have knowledge of family law; have knowledge of and training in the impact of family conflict on parents, children and other participants, including knowledge of child development, domestic abuse and child abuse and neglect; have education and training specific to the process of mediation; and be able to recognize the impact of culture and diversity. Would you add anything else?

2.   Who determines if a mediator is qualified? For court-ordered mediation, many states require mediators to meet certain criteria and register to be placed on an approved list. The parties may select a person from the list. If the parties are unable to select a mediator, the court appoints one. If the mediation is voluntary, the parties are free to select whomever they choose, regardless of the qualifications. What qualifications would you look for if the mediation involved complex financial issues? Parenting time issues?

3.   Why is confidentiality so important? *See* Powell v. Fackler, 891 N.E.2d 1091 (Ind. App. 2009) (noting ADR rules prohibit parties from waiving confidentiality). The 2002 Uniform Mediation Act proposes that most communications in mediation not be subject to discovery or admissible in most legal proceedings. For a discussion of the Uniform Mediation Act from a family law perspective, *see* Gregory Firestone, *An Analysis of Principled Advocacy in the Development of the Uniform Mediation Act*, 22 N. ILL. U. L. REV. 265 (2002).

VITAKIS-VALCHINE V. VALCHINE

Florida District Court of Appeals, 4th Dist., 2001.
793 So. 2d 1094.

STEVENSON, J.

This is an appeal from a final judgment of dissolution which was entered pursuant to a mediated settlement agreement. The wife argues that the trial court erred in affirming the recommendations of the general master and in denying her request to set aside the settlement agreement on the grounds that it was entered into under duress and coercion. We affirm the order to the extent that the trial court concluded that the wife failed to meet her burden of establishing that the marital settlement agreement was reached by duress or coercion on the part of the husband and the husband's attorney. The wife also alleges that the mediator committed misconduct during the mediation session, including but not limited to coercion and improper influence, and that she entered into the settlement agreement as a direct result of this misconduct. For the reasons which follow, we hold that mediator misconduct can be the basis for a trial court refusing to enforce a settlement agreement reached at court-ordered mediation. Because neither the general master nor the trial court made any findings relative to the truth of the allegations of the mediator's alleged misconduct, we remand this case for further findings.

Procedural background

By August of 1999, Kalliope and David Valchine's divorce proceedings to end their near twelve-year marriage had been going on for one and a half to two years. On August 17, 1999, the couple attended court-ordered mediation to attempt to resolve their dispute. At the mediation, both parties were represented by counsel. The mediation lasted seven to eight hours and resulted in a twenty-three page marital settlement agreement. The agreement was comprehensive and dealt with alimony, bank accounts, both parties' IRAs, and the husband's federal customs, postal, and military pensions. The agreement also addressed the disposition of embryos that the couple had frozen during *in vitro* fertilization attempts prior to the divorce. The agreement provided in this regard that "[t]he Wife has expressed her desire to have the frozen embryos, but has reluctantly agreed to provide them to the husband to dispose of."

A month later, the wife filed a *pro se* motion seeking to set aside the mediated settlement agreement, but by the time of the hearing, she was represented by new counsel. The wife's counsel argued two grounds for setting aside the agreement: (1) coercion and duress on the part of the husband, the husband's attorney and the mediator; and (2) the agreement was unfair and unreasonable on its face. The trial court accepted the general master's findings which rejected the wife's claim on both grounds. On appeal, the wife attacks only the trial court's refusal to set aside the couple's settlement agreement on the ground that it was reached through duress and coercion.

Third party coercion

As a general rule under Florida law, a contract or settlement may not be set aside on the basis of duress or coercion unless the improper influence emanated from one of the contracting parties—the actions of a third party will not suffice. In this case, the record adequately supports the finding that neither the husband nor the husband's attorney was involved in any duress or coercion and had no knowledge of any improper conduct on the part of the mediator. Because there was no authority at the time holding that mediator misconduct, including the exertion of duress or coercion, could serve as a basis for overturning the agreement, the general master made no findings relative to the wife's allegations. The mediator's testimony was presented prior to that of the wife, and, consequently, her allegations of potential misconduct were not directly confronted. Here, we must decide whether the wife's claim that the mediator committed misconduct by improperly influencing her and coercing her to enter into the settlement agreement can be an exception to the general rule that coercion and duress by a third party will not suffice to invalidate an agreement between the principals.

The former wife's claims

The wife testified that the eight-hour mediation, with Mark London as the mediator, began at approximately 10:45 a.m., that both her attorney and her brother attended, and that her husband was there with his counsel. Everyone initially gathered together, the mediator explained the process, and then the wife, her attorney and her brother were left in one room while the husband and his attorney went to another. The mediator then went back and forth between the two rooms during the course of the negotiations in what the mediator described as "Kissinger-style shuttle diplomacy."

With respect to the frozen embryos, which were in the custody of the Fertility Institute of Boca Raton, the wife explained that there were lengthy discussions concerning what was to become of them. The wife was concerned about destroying the embryos and wanted to retain them herself. The wife testified that the mediator told her that the embryos were not "lives in being" and that the court would not require the husband to pay child support if she were impregnated with the embryos after the divorce. According to the wife, the mediator told her that the judge would *never* give her custody of the embryos, but would order them destroyed. The wife said that at one point during the discussion of the frozen embryo issue, the mediator came in, threw the papers on the table, and declared "that's it, I give up." Then, according to the wife, the mediator told her that if no agreement was reached, he (the mediator) would report to the trial judge that the settlement failed because of her. Additionally, the wife testified that the mediator told her that if she signed the agreement at the mediation, she could still protest any provisions she didn't agree with at the final hearing—including her objection to the husband "disposing" of the frozen embryos.

With respect to the distribution of assets, the wife alleges that the mediator told her that she was not entitled to any of the husband's federal pensions. She further testified that the mediator told her that the husband's pensions were only worth about $200 per month and that she would spend at least $70,000 in court litigating entitlement to this relatively modest sum. The wife states that the mediation was conducted with neither her nor the mediator knowing the present value of the husband's pensions or the marital estate itself. The wife testified that she and her new attorney had since constructed a list of assets and liabilities, and that she was shortchanged by approximately $34,000—not including the husband's pensions. When asked what she would have done if Mr. London had told her that the attorney's fees could have amounted to as little as $15,000, the wife stated, "I would have took [sic] it to trial."

Finally, the wife testified that she signed the agreement in part due to "time pressure" being placed on her by the mediator. She testified that while the final draft was being typed up, the mediator got a call and she heard him say "have a bottle of wine and a glass of drink, and a strong drink ready for me." The wife explained that the mediator had repeatedly stated that his daughter was leaving for law school, and finally said that "you guys have five minutes to hurry up and get out of here because that family is more important to me." The wife testified that she ultimately signed the agreement because "[I] felt pressured. I felt that I had no other alternative but to accept the Agreement from the things that I was told by Mr. London. I believed everything that he said."

Court-ordered mediation

Mediation is a process whereby a neutral third party, the mediator, assists the principals of a dispute in reaching a complete or partial voluntary resolution of their issues of conflict. Mandatory, court-ordered mediation was officially sanctioned by the Florida legislature in 1987, and since then, mediation has become institutionalized within Florida's court system. All twenty judicial circuits in Florida utilize some form of court-connected mediation to assist with their caseloads. The process is meant to be non-adversarial and informal, with the mediator essentially serving as a facilitator for communications between the parties and providing assistance in the identification of issues and the exploration of options to resolve the dispute. Ultimate authority to settle remains with the parties. Mediation, as a method of alternative dispute resolution, potentially saves both the parties and the judicial system time and money while leaving the power to structure the terms of any resolution of the dispute in the hands of the parties themselves.

Mediation, pursuant to chapter 44, is mandatory when ordered by the court. Any court in which a civil action, including a family matter, is pending may refer the case to mediation, with or without the parties' consent. Communications during the mediation sessions are privileged and confidential. During court-ordered mediation conducted pursuant to the statute, the mediator enjoys "judicial immunity in the same manner and to the same extent as a judge." The mediation must be conducted in accordance with rules of practice and procedure adopted by the Florida Supreme Court.

Comprehensive procedures for conducting the mediation session and minimum standards for qualification, training, certification, professional conduct, and discipline of mediators have been set forth by the Florida Supreme Court in the Florida Rules for Certified and Court Appointed Mediators, Rule 10 * * *. One of the hallmarks of the process of mediation is the empowerment of the parties to resolve their dispute on their own, agreed-upon terms. While parties are required to attend mediation, no party is required to settle at mediation.

(a) Decision-making. Decisions made during a mediation are to be made by the parties. A mediator shall not make substantive decisions for any party. A mediator is responsible for assisting the parties in reaching informed and voluntary decisions while protecting their right of self-determination. Fla. R. Med. 10.310(a).

The committee notes to the rule provide in part that

While mediation techniques and practice styles may vary from mediator to mediator and mediation to mediation, a line is crossed and ethical standards are violated when any conduct of the mediator serves to compromise the parties' basic right to agree or not to agree. Special care should be taken to preserve the party's right to self-determination if the mediator provides input to the mediation process.

In keeping with the notion of self-determination and voluntary resolution of the dispute at court-ordered mediation, any improper influence such as coercion or duress on the part of the mediator is expressly prohibited:

(b) Coercion Prohibited. A mediator shall not coerce or improperly influence any party to make a decision or unwillingly participate in a mediation. Fla. R. Med. 10.310(b).

Likewise, a mediator may not intentionally misrepresent any material fact in an effort to promote or encourage an agreement:

(c) Misrepresentation Prohibited. A mediator shall not intentionally or knowingly misrepresent any material fact or circumstance in the course of conducting a mediation. Fla. R. Med. 10.310(c).

Other sections of Rule 10 address the rendering of personal or professional opinions by the mediator, and one section specifically provides that a mediator shall not offer a personal or professional opinion as to how the court in which the case has been filed will resolve the dispute. Fla. R. Med. 10.370(c). Under this section, the committee notes caution that while mediators may call upon their own qualifications and experience to supply information and options, the parties must be given the opportunity to freely decide upon any agreement. Mediators shall not utilize their opinions to decide any aspect of the dispute or to coerce the parties or their representatives to accept any resolution option.

The question we are confronted with in this case is whether a referring court may set aside an agreement reached in court-ordered mediation if the court finds that the agreement was reached as a direct result of the mediator's substantial violation of the rules of conduct for mediators. We believe that it would be unconscionable for a court to enforce a settlement agreement reached through coercion or any other improper tactics utilized by a court-appointed mediator. When a court refers a case to mediation, the mediation must be conducted according to the practices and procedures outlined in the applicable statutes and rules. If the required practices and procedures are not substantially complied with, no party to the mediation can rightfully claim the benefits of an agreement reached in such a way. During a court-ordered mediation, the mediator is no ordinary third party, but is, for all intent and purposes, an agent of the court carrying out an official court-ordered function. We hold that the court may invoke its inherent power to maintain the integrity of the judicial system and its processes by invalidating a court-ordered mediation settlement agreement obtained through violation and abuse of the judicially-prescribed mediation procedures.

"Every court has inherent power to do all things that are reasonably necessary for the administration of justice within the scope of its jurisdiction, subject to valid existing laws and constitutional provisions." *Rose v. Palm Beach County*, 361 So. 2d 135, 137 (Fla. 1978). In a variety of contexts, it has been held that the courts have the inherent power to protect the integrity of the judicial process from perversion and abuse. * * * While the doctrine of inherent power should be invoked "cautiously" and "only in situations of clear necessity," we have little trouble deciding that the instant case presents a compelling occasion for its use.

We hasten to add that no findings were made as to whether the mediator actually committed the alleged misconduct. Nevertheless, at least some of the wife's claims clearly are sufficient to allege a violation of the applicable rules. On remand, the trial court must determine whether the mediator substantially violated the Rules for Mediators, and whether that misconduct led to the settlement agreement in this case.

Affirmed in part, reversed in part, and remanded.

NOTES AND QUESTIONS

1.   As *Valchine* shows, mediation may not reduce the need for legal assistance. The wife alleged that neither she nor the mediator knew the present value of the husband's pensions or of the marital estate. It would seem that before a party could make an informed decision in this situation, the party needs to know the value of the assets to be distributed and have advice on legal issues and rights, including how to terminate mediation. Mrs. Valchine's new lawyer put together a list of assets and values. Shouldn't that have been done before the first mediation? How could the wife have received a more accurate estimate of the costs of litigation—there is a big difference between $15,000 and $70,000! Should parties see a lawyer before mediating? *See* Amy G. Applegate & Connie J.A. Beck, *Self-Represented Parties in Mediation: Fifty Years Later It Remains the Elephant in the Room*, 51 FAM. CT. REV. 87 (2013).

2.   Once the parties have signed the mediation agreement, it may be enforceable under contract law. *See In re* Lovell-Osburn, 448 So. 2d 616, 620 (Tex. App. 2014). The mediated agreement is submitted to the court for incorporation into a judgment or decree. Should the court play the same role in reviewing a mediated agreement that it plays in reviewing a negotiated agreement? Why? *See In re* Marriage of Kirk, 941 P.2d 385 (Kan. App. 1997) (requiring parties to provide valuations of property so the court can fulfill the obligation to review the agreement of the parties to see if it is valid, just and equitable); Feliciano v. Feliciano, 674 So. 2d 937 (Fla. Dist. Ct. App. 1996) (noting that trial court may set aside provisions of a mediated agreement dealing with child support, custody and visitation, if they are not in the best interest of the children).

3.   May a judge order the mediation of future nonemergency disputes? The Maine Supreme Court held that it was a denial of access to the court for a judge to require mediation before parties could go to court. Karamanoglu v. Gourlaouen, 140 A.3d 1249 (Me. 2016). *Compare In re* Marriage of Aleshire, 652 N.E.2d 383 (Ill. App. 1995) (finding no statutory or common law authority for court to order mediation of prospective visitation disputes in the absence of a preliminary finding that the issues are proper for mediation) *with* Bauer v. Bauer, 28 S.W.3d 877 (Mo. App. 2000) (allowing court to require the parties to mediate before seeking modification). Does it matter if the parties have entered into a parenting agreement to mediate first? *See* Gould v. Gould, 523 S.E.2d 106 (Ga. App. 1999) (enforcing provision in parties' separation agreement requiring mediation before litigating a post-divorce custody dispute).

C. THE PROMISE AND RISKS OF MEDIATION

STEPHEN W. SCHLISSEL, A PROPOSAL FOR FINAL AND BINDING ARBITRATION OF INITIAL CUSTODY DETERMINATIONS

26 FAM. L. Q. 71, 74–76 (1992).

* * *

First, "our judicial system continues to intervene in divorce with the same confrontational format that existed prior to the no-fault revolution." The system is premised, in part, on the idea that the court should have ongoing supervision over custody arrangements between the spouses because those arrangements result from an adversarial confrontation between the divorcing parties. The concept seems to be that judicial control is necessary in light of the parties' determination to resort to the judiciary for problem resolution in the first instance. Thus, the courts get their power to control due to the inability of the parents to agree.

* * * Because the present method for resolution of custody disputes is decidedly an adversarial one, the parents are almost required to dig up the dirt on the other. Although the standard most often used in an initial custody determination is the "best interests of the child," each of the parents tries to prove the other less fit. "This adversarial emphasis is directly contrary to the child's interests in stability of environment and minimum civility and cooperation between his or her parents."

Litigation fosters the process where the parents use the children as bait to get what they want financially and emotionally; it often creates adjustment problems for the children, if not a tug-of-war between their parents. The New York Law Revision Commission has noted these adjustment problems and has stated that:

> The available evidence points almost without equivocation to the conclusion that children are better off if both parents are meaningfully involved in their lives after their separation. . . Therefore, the challenge for the custody dispute resolution system is now to organize itself so as to maximize the number of families in which both parents are involved in the child's post-separation life. Available evidence suggests that reliance on adversary litigation controlled by the parents and their lawyers as a primary technique for dispute resolution does not further this goal and, indeed, works against it.

The Commission concluded that the adversarial process exacerbated the harmful effects of divorce on the children.

Second, custody litigation is very costly from the perspective of both the court and the divorcing or separating couple. Matrimonial cases occupy a great deal of scarce judicial time and money. Moreover, a typical divorce case consumes a substantial part of the wealth available to the parties, often reducing each party's future standard of living.

Third, "bitterly contested cases often produce court orders which are resented and violated, leading to repeated rounds of litigation." Many custody cases seem to almost outlive the parents or go on for more years than necessary for the children to reach majority. Litigation is best suited for situations where a judgment must be made concerning present consequences of past behavior. It doesn't work well where the goal is to provide some finality to a dispute, and the parties must thereafter remain in constant contact with each other. "Unlike a settlement in a tort case, where the parties usually never see each other again, parents in a divorce need to maintain a continuing relationship." In domestic relations cases, and especially in custody cases, there are, more often than not, hosts of future problems that must be resolved.

All of the above suggests that we should consider nonlitigation alternatives to resolving custody disputes.

MARTHA FINEMAN, DOMINANT DISCOURSE, PROFESSIONAL LANGUAGE, AND LEGAL CHANGE IN CHILD CUSTODY DECISION MAKING
101 HARV. L. REV. 727, 728, 756 (1988).

* * *

Social workers view divorce as occasioning the birth of an ongoing, albeit different, relationship, with mediators and social workers as its midwives and monitors. "Let's talk about it" seems to be the ideal, and the talk is envisioned as continuing for decades. The continued involvement is not only with each other but with the legal system as well. This ideal is obviously very different from the traditional legal system, which seeks an end or termination of a significant interaction at divorce: a division, distribution, or allocation of the things acquired during marriage—an emancipatory model—and with its "ending," the permission for a "new life" for the participants and the withdrawal of active legal interference in their relationship.

The helping professions' ideal process "avoids" or "reduces" conflict and is typified by mediation. Helping professionals believe that mediation, employing a therapeutic process, is within their exclusive domain because lawyers, unlike social workers, ignore the underlying causes of divorce and give little regard to the "real reason" for the split-up. Therapeutic skills can facilitate acceptance of the divorce and foster a positive approach to the crisis.

Lawyers' skills are downgraded and social workers' and mediators' skills are mystified and reified.

* * *

The adoption of the mediators' image has important substantive implications with significant political and social ramifications. One of the most harmful assumptions underlying social workers' discourse is that a parent who seeks sole custody of a child has some illegitimate motivation. Mediators may acknowledge exceptions to this generalization in situations in which one parent is a drunkard or drug addict or in which a child is abused, but the general assumption is that the parent who is willing to live up to the ideal of shared custody and control is the one with the child's real interests at heart.

Mediation advocates often characterize opposition to shared custody as pathological. The assumption in the social workers' discourse is that the parent who rejects the shared parenting ideal and seeks sole custody of his or her child has an illegitimate motive. A mother who resists sharing her child with her ex-husband is characterized as having "issue overlay"; she protests too much. Such women may be characterized as clinging and overly dependent on the role identification as wife and mother; social workers and mediators assert that these women can be helped through the mediation process only if they are cooperative. Other women are seen as greedy, merely using the children in order to get larger property settlements; it is claimed that an "effective" mediator can block these women from achieving their evil ends. A third stereotype focuses on vindictive mothers who use the children to get back at their ex-husbands; it is perceived that these are the type of women who should be punished by having their children taken away and sole custody awarded to the fathers.

Lost in the rhetoric of the social worker are real concerns. There is little or no appreciation of the many real problems that joint custody and the ideal of sharing and caring can cause. The prospect of a continued relationship with an ex-spouse may be horrifying to contemplate, but the sharing ideal assumes that a relationship between the noncustodial parent and the child cannot proceed without it. Also unsettling is the extent to which allegations of mistreatment, abuse, or neglect on the part of husbands toward either their wives or children are trivialized, masked, or lost amid the psychological rhetoric that reduces mothers' desires to have custody and control of their children to pathology.

We should be deeply skeptical of these views of women and mothers. They are most accurate and the visions they present are deeply misogynous. Most mothers love their children and would not willfully deprive them of contact with a caring and responsible father. In fact, if the children are old enough to assert their own interests, it is unlikely that mothers could deprive them of contact with their fathers even if they wanted to. By making these observations, I do not mean to suggest that abuses never occur, but rather to point out that they are not typical, or even common, and that it is irrational to base custody policy on the deviant rather than the typical post-divorce situation.

Because social workers and others sympathetic to mediation have created and controlled the presentation of both narratives, the real nature of the competition between the legal and therapeutic models has been hidden. Notably, there are no parallel scenarios involving vindictive or greedy husbands in the mediation literature. No alternative narrative, sympathetic to single parent or sole custody and control, has gained any credibility in the literature. Nor do many stories assign different characters to the stock "victim" and "villain" roles.

Further, by branding opposition to mediation and joint custody as the manifestation of a psychological problem to which mediation is itself the solution, mediation rhetoric forecloses any effective expression of women's legitimate concerns. As things now stand, the cries of protest over the imposition of a joint custody or shared parenting solution from mothers who will be assuming primary care for their children (but sharing control) are attributed to the fact that these mothers have not accomplished an "emotional divorce." As soon as they are able to get over "their issues" they will be able to begin "rational problem solving" and will cooperate agreeably.

The social workers' discourse accepts without criticism the superiority of "rational decisionmaking" within the new, reconstructed family structure. Through this method, the "vindictive" woman is thwarted, the "victimized" man allowed to continue to operate as *paternal familius* (in an altered form, of course) by being given "equal rights" without the formal imposition of responsibility. The helping professionals believe this approach remedies the pro-mother imbalance that has existed in custody decisionmaking.

* * *

The mediation movement's strong bias against anything morally "judgmental" has led to an ideological belief that you can compromise anything. This means meeting halfway some propositions that may be not only unspeakable, but plainly irrational.

NOTES AND QUESTIONS

1.   Mediation's proponents claim that it can resolve disputes, make divorce less painful, promote better communication, reduce costs, and produce better parent-child and parent-parent relationships. Mediation does appear to produce a high level of user satisfaction. *See* Robert E. Emery, David Sbarra & Tara Grover, *Divorce Mediation: Research and Reflections*, 43 FAM. CT. REV. 22 (2005) (reporting research that mediation settles a large percentage of cases

with less time and money, higher client satisfaction and improved parental communication).

2. Some critics of mediation express concern about the lack of public scrutiny in the mediation process. "Mediation may risk second-class private justice that further disadvantages the poor or powerless." Judith L. Maute, *Public Values and Private Justice: A Case for Mediator Accountability*, 4 GEO. J. LEG. ETHICS 503 (1991). *See also* Trina Grillo, *The Mediation Alternative: Process Dangers for Women*, 100 YALE L. J. 1545 (1991). Carol Bohmer & Marilyn L. Ray, *Effects of Different Dispute Resolution Methods on Women and Children After Divorce*, 28 FAM. L.Q. 223, 227–28, 232 (1994).

On the other hand, there is little systematic empirical evidence that women fare worse in mediation than litigation or negotiation. In Trowbridge v. Trowbridge, 674 So. 2d 928 (Fla. Dist. Ct. App. 1996), the court noted that mediation offers more public scrutiny than many negotiated settlements, including prenuptial and postnuptial agreements:

> Mediation agreements are reached under court supervision, before a neutral mediator. The mediation rules create an environment intended to produce a final settlement of the issues with safeguards against the elements of fraud, overreaching, etc., in the settlement process.

3. The presence of domestic violence complicates the mediation picture because of the need to protect the victim from further abuse and to empower the victim to participate "equally" in the mediation. Among the special concerns are the increased risk posed to victims before and after mediation sessions; mediated agreements which give the abuser more access to the victim than a litigated result; mediators who are not trained to recognize abusive relationships or to counteract the power imbalance. Mediators should screen for domestic violence. *See* Amy Holtzworth-Munroe et al., *The Mediator's Assessment of Safety Issues and Concerns (MASIC): A Screening Interview for Intimate Partner Violence and Abuse Available in the Public Domain*, 48 FAM. CT. REV. 646 (2010); Jane Murphy & Robert Rubinson, *Domestic Violence and Mediation: Responding to the Challenges of Crafting Effective Screens*, 39 FAM. L. Q. 53 (2005). Some critics go farther and argue that cases involving domestic violence are inherently unsuitable for mediation. *See* Fiona Raitt, *Domestic Violence and Divorce Mediation*, 18 J. SOC. WELF. & FAM. L. 11 (1996); Holly Joyce, *Mediation and Domestic Violence: Legislative Responses*, 14 J. AM. ACAD. MATRIM. LAW. 447 (1997) (surveying the arguments for and against the use of mediation in domestic violence cases). Nancy Ver Steegh et al., *Look Before You Leap: Court System Triage of Family Law Cases Involving Intimate Partner Violence*, 95 MARQ. L. REV. 955 (2012).

A mediator can structure mediation to protect a victim of domestic violence (and the mediator) by holding separate sessions with the participants even without the agreement of all participants; allowing a friend, representative, advocate, counsel or attorney to attend the mediation sessions; encouraging the participants to be represented by an attorney, counsel or an advocate throughout the mediation process; referring the participants to appropriate community resources; suspending or terminating the mediation sessions, with appropriate steps to protect the safety of the participants; and having the parties arrive and leave at different times.

4.   Does mediation save time and money? Research reports from the United States indicate that mediation is significantly less expensive than traditional litigation. In 2007, the Boston Law Collaborative analyzed 199 divorce cases. They found that divorces resolved by mediation had a median cost of $6,600. Collaborative divorces cost on average $19,723. Divorces settled by counsel through traditional negotiation cost an average of $26,830. Divorces resolved by a judge at trial cost on average $77,746. Although mediation clients appear to reach agreement 50% to 85% of the time, it is unclear how many would also have reached agreement through the traditional negotiation process. Nor is it clear whether mediation produces a "better" process or outcome. *See* Connie J. A. Beck & Bruce D. Sales, *A Critical Reappraisal of Divorce Mediation Research and Policy*, 6 PSYCHOL. PUB. POL'Y & L. 989 (2000) (critically reviewing role of mediation in divorce and finding that expectations may have been overly optimistic).

Problem 11-5:

Your client has received a notice that she is required to attend court-ordered custody mediation. What, if any, preparation is advisable? What advice should you give her? *See* Kimberlee K. Kovach, *New Wine Requires New Wineskins: Transforming Lawyer Ethics for Effective Representation in a Non-Adversarial Approach to Problem Solving: Mediation*, 28 FORDHAM URBAN L. J. 935 (2001).

Problem 11-6:

Mary comes to see you with a handwritten agreement that she and her husband reached with the help of a court-appointed mediator. She wants you to prepare the agreement in proper legal form and present it to the court for her. The agreement divides property and settles the residency of the children. Are you required to do additional discovery or any investigation? Can you add "boilerplate" language, such as a "severability" clause? How do you protect yourself in the event the husband did not fully disclose everything? *See* Lerner v. Laufer, 819 A.2d 471 (N.J. Super. App. Div. 2003).

5. ARBITRATION

Arbitration is a consensual process in which the parties to a dispute agree to submit some or all disputed issues to a neutral third party, the arbitrator who makes a final and binding decision. The parties may jointly select the arbitrator. The arbitrator may conduct the hearing in a private informal setting; at the hearing, evidence may be submitted in any form to which the parties agree, without regard to the rules of evidence. The arbitration decision is submitted to the court for confirmation; if it has been property reached, it will be affirmed by the court as part of its judgment.

The roots of arbitration are ancient. Modern arbitration developed in the early twentieth century through judicial and legislative action, particularly in the labor context. The Uniform Arbitration Act, 7 U.L.A. 1 (1985), promulgated in 1955, has been adopted in thirty states and the District of Columbia. The Revised Uniform Arbitration Act, which contains substantial due process provisions, has been enacted in nineteen states. Today, arbitration is a routine feature of labor law and collective bargaining; it is increasingly common in commercial disputes as well. Arbitration's advocates argue that it should be used more frequently in family law disputes After a three year drafting process, the Uniform Law Commission promulgated a Uniform Family Law Arbitration Act in July 2016. It was endorsed by the American Bar Association in February 2017.

What can be arbitrated? The Uniform Family Law Arbitration Act defines a family law dispute as a contested issue arising under the family or domestic relations law of a state. UFLAA, Definition 2(5). In most states, a family law dispute would include the interpretation and enforcement of premarital and other agreements, the characterization, evaluation and division of property and allocation of debt; awards of alimony; parenting time; child support; award of attorney's fees. If a state enacts the UFLAA, the parties can choose to have an arbitrator decide any family law dispute that could be decided by a judge, except status determinations. The arbitrator cannot divorce the parties, grant an adoption, terminate parental rights, or adjudicate a child in need of care or the like. The UFLAA brackets "child-related dispute" which includes custody and child support which means that a state may choose to enact the UFLAA but exclude children's issues. Sec. 3.

ALLAN R. KORITZINSKY ET AL., THE BENEFITS OF ARBITRATION
14 FAM. ADVOC. 45 (1992).

ARBITRATION'S BENEFITS

Some of the benefits of arbitration in family law are:

1. *Selection of Decision Maker:* The parties and their attorneys can choose as the arbitrator a family law specialist * * * In many court systems, judges are assigned to family law cases without regard to their background, training, interest, or experience.

2. *Convenient Forum for Hearing:* The arbitration hearing can be scheduled at the convenience of the participants, with none of the interruptions or delays that are so frequent in the courts. * * *

3. *Procedural Flexibility:* The parties and their attorneys can agree to * * * [use] telephone [submissions], sworn affidavits, reports, or any other agreed-upon method.

4. *Speedy and Less Costly:* Arbitration is likely to cost significantly less than a trial. * * *

5. *Final and Binding*: The parties can stipulate that the decision * * * is final and binding, with limited rights of review and appeal. * * *

ARBITRATION'S DETRIMENTS

1. *Lack of Discovery:* The parties generally are not protected by discovery rules and have to resort to the courts to compel discovery when items are not produced. * * *

2. *Nonapplicability of Evidentiary and Other Rules:* * * * To resolve these issues, the parties may provide in the arbitration agreement that some or all of the rules of evidence and other procedural rules apply. * * * However, this may be counterproductive to the arbitration process itself * * *

3. *Nonbinding Nature of Certain Issues:* Court decisions indicate that custody and possibly child support may not be subject to final and binding arbitration, with resulting limited court review and appeal rights. * * *

4. *Lack of Enforcement:* An arbitrator does not have the power to enforce the arbitration award or enter a decree of divorce. * * * [but] the Uniform Arbitration Act specifically provides that the decision or award *shall* be confirmed by the court in a judgment or decree unless vacated or changed by that court.

HARVEY V. HARVEY

Michigan Supreme Court, 2004.
470 Mich. 186, 680 N.W.2d 835.

PER CURIAM.

In this divorce proceeding, the parties agreed that the friend of the court would determine the custody of their children and that the circuit court could not review the decision. Honoring this, the circuit court entered the friend of the court's recommended order awarding sole custody of the children to defendant and denied plaintiff's motion for a hearing to review the matter.

The Court of Appeals vacated the circuit court's order and remanded the case for a hearing de novo. We affirm that opinion, but write to provide clarification. Regardless of the type of alternative dispute resolution that parties use, the Child Custody Act requires the circuit court to determine independently what custodial placement is in the best interests of the children. * * *

I. BACKGROUND

A. Trial Court Proceedings

Two daughters were born during the parties' marriage, one in 1994 and the other in 1996. In February 2000, plaintiff filed a complaint for divorce with the Family Division of the Oakland Circuit Court. A variety of issues were disputed, including custody of the children. Instead of proceeding directly to trial, the parties opted for a form of alternative dispute resolution. On May 15, 2001, the circuit court entered a consent order, approved by both parties' counsel, for binding arbitration. Its object was to resolve all property matters and provide for an evidentiary hearing and binding decision by the friend of the court referee regarding custody, parenting time, and child support issues. The order stated that the referee's decision could not be reviewed by the circuit court * * *

Following an evidentiary hearing, the friend of the court submitted findings to the circuit court with a recommended order awarding legal and physical custody of the children solely to defendant. Plaintiff filed timely written objections to the order.

The circuit court entered the recommended order, over plaintiff's objection, changing the existing custodial arrangement. The court denied her motion for an evidentiary hearing de novo and refused to set aside the order when defendant argued that the parties' stipulation restricted its authority to review the order. [Plaintiff appealed.]

* * *

III. ANALYSIS

The Child Custody Act is a comprehensive statutory scheme for resolving custody disputes. With it, the Legislature sought to "promote the best interests and welfare of children." The act applies to all custody disputes and vests the circuit court with continuing jurisdiction. The act makes clear that the best interests of the child control the resolution of a custody dispute between parents, as gauged by the factors set forth at MCL 722.23. It places an affirmative obligation on the circuit court to "declare the child's inherent rights and establish the rights and duties as to the child's custody, support, and parenting time in accordance with this act" whenever the court is required to adjudicate an action "involving dispute of a minor child's custody." Taken together, these statutory provisions impose on the trial court the duty to ensure that the resolution of any custody dispute is in the best interests of the child.

Thus, we * * * remand this case to the circuit court for a hearing de novo * * * The Child Custody Act *required* the circuit court to determine the best interests of the children before entering an order resolving the custody dispute.

Our holding should not be interpreted, where the parties have agreed to a custody arrangement, to require the court to conduct a hearing or otherwise engage in intensive fact-finding. Our requirement under such circumstances is that the court satisfy itself concerning the best interests of the children. When the court signs the order, it indicates that it has done so. A judge signs an order only after profound deliberation and in the exercise of the judge's traditional broad discretion.

However, the deference due parties' negotiated agreements does not diminish the court's obligation to examine the best interest factors and make the child's best interests paramount .. Nothing in the Child Custody Act gives parents or any other party the power to exclude the legislatively mandated "best interests" factors from the court's deliberations once a custody dispute reaches the court.

Furthermore, neither the Friend of the Court Act nor the domestic relations arbitration act relieves the circuit court of its duty to review a custody arrangement once the issue of a child's custody reaches the bench. The Friend of the Court Act states that the circuit court "shall" hold a hearing de novo to review a friend of the court recommendation if either party objects to that recommendation in writing within twenty-one days.

Likewise, MCL 600.5080 authorizes a circuit court to modify or vacate an arbitration award that is not in the best interests of the child. It requires the circuit court to review the arbitration award in accordance with the requirements of other relevant statutes, including the Child Custody Act. The court retains authority over custody until the child reaches the age of majority. Thus, even when parties initially elect to submit a custody dispute to an arbitrator or to the friend of the court, they cannot waive the authority that the Child Custody Act confers on the circuit court. As the Court of Appeals has previously explained, parties "cannot by agreement usurp the court's authority to determine suitable provisions for the child's best interests." Permitting the parties, by stipulation, to limit the trial court's authority to review custody determinations would nullify the protections of the Child Custody Act and relieve the circuit court of its statutorily imposed responsibilities.

IV. CONCLUSION

* * * [P]arties cannot stipulate to circumvent the authority of the circuit court in determining the custody of children. In making its determination, the court must consider the best interests of the children. Child custody determinations or agreements are not binding until entered by court order.

KELM V. KELM

Supreme Court of Ohio, 2001.
92 Ohio St. 3d 223, 749 N.E.2d 299.

SWEENEY, J.

On October 1, 1993, the Franklin County Court of Common Pleas, Division of Domestic Relations, granted appellant, Russell A. Kelm, and appellee, Amy K. Kelm, a judgment of divorce. The judgment incorporated the parties' shared parenting plan, which provided, *inter alia,* that any future disputes between the parties regarding child custody or visitation would be submitted to arbitration.

* * *

We are asked to decide whether, in a domestic relations case, matters relating to child custody and visitation may be resolved through arbitration. For the reasons that follow, we hold that these matters cannot be resolved through arbitration. Only the courts are empowered to resolve disputes relating to child custody and visitation.

The parties' divorce has a long and convoluted history. It has already produced one decision from this court, (*"Kelm I"*). In *Kelm I,* we were asked to decide whether an arbitration clause in the parties' antenuptial agreement was enforceable as to matters relating to spousal and child support. We held that these support matters could be made subject to an agreement to arbitrate. * * * In so holding, we recognized that, under the doctrine of *parens patriae,* courts are entrusted to protect the best interests of children. We concluded, however, that permitting parents to arbitrate child support does not interfere with the judicial protection of the best interests of children. In short, we saw "no valid reason why the arbitration process should not be available in the area of child support; the advantages of arbitration in domestic disputes outweigh any disadvantages." Appellant urges us to extend our holding in *Kelm I* to allow matters of child custody and visitation to be resolved through arbitration. We decline to do so.

While we recognize the important impact that monetary support can have upon a child's life, we believe that custody and visitation have a much greater impact upon the child in terms of both the child's daily life and his or her long-term development. Custody and visitation have the potential to affect countless aspects of a child's life, including the child's relationships with his or her parents, the child's relationships with extended family, the child's social and cultural upbringing, and even, in some unfortunate cases, the child's physical and emotional security. More than support determinations, " 'determinations of custody go to the very core of the child's welfare and best interests.' " * * * "[T]he process of arbitration, useful when the mundane matter of the amount of support is in issue, is less so when the delicate balancing of the factors composing the best interests of a child is at issue." * * * For this reason, we are less inclined than we were in *Kelm I* to permit arbitration to encroach upon the trial court's traditional role as *parens patriae.*

As appellant points out, there are decisions from a number of jurisdictions upholding the use of arbitration to settle disputes over child custody and visitation. Typically, these decisions protect the courts' role as *parens patriae* by making the arbitrator's decision subject to *de novo* review and modification by the courts. * * *. While this approach preserves the court's role as *parens patriae,* we believe that, ultimately, it advances neither the children's best interests nor the basic goals underlying arbitration. A two-stage procedure consisting of an arbitrator's decision followed by *de novo* judicial review "is certain to be wasteful of time and expense and result in a duplication of effort." Clearly, it does not seem advantageous to the best interests of children that questions of custody be postponed "while a rehearsal of the decisive inquiry is held." * * * The protracted two-stage process adopted by some courts also frustrates the very goals underlying arbitration. "Arbitration is favored because it provides the parties thereto with a relatively expeditious and economical means of resolving a dispute * * * [and] * * * has the additional advantage of unburdening crowded court dockets." *Kelm* I. A two-stage process consisting of both arbitration and judicial review achieves none of these goals. Furthermore, "[i]f an issue is to be arbitrated, the expectation [of the parties] is that an award will not be disturbed." *De novo* review destroys this expectation. Thus, there is an inevitable tension between the court's traditional responsibility to protect the best interests of children and the parties' expectation that an arbitration award will be final.

Appellant argues that because the shared parenting plan contained an agreement to arbitrate any future custody and visitation disputes, and because this agreement was, by consent of both parties, incorporated into the trial court's judgment of divorce, appellee could not subsequently challenge the arbitration agreement. Essentially, appellant argues that by agreeing to arbitrate custody and visitation matters, appellee has waived her right to challenge the agreement. We disagree.

The law permits parties to voluntarily waive a number of important legal rights, and in the interest of finality, courts are usually quite reluctant to relieve parties of the consequences of these choices. * * * However, a waiver of rights will be recognized only when the waiver does not violate public policy. A fundamental flaw in appellant's argument is its assumption that arbitration of custody and visitation matters does not violate public policy. We have already concluded, for the reasons set forth above, that it does. To hold that appellee has waived her right to challenge the arbitration agreement and to permit arbitration of the parties' child custody and visitation disputes would prevent the trial court from fulfilling its role as *parens patriae.* Because this is contrary to public policy, we conclude that appellee has not, by virtue of her acquiescence to the original shared parenting plan, waived her right to challenge that plan's provision for arbitration of custody and visitation matters.

There is an even more fundamental flaw in appellant's waiver analysis. With respect to matters of custody and visitation, the central focus is not, as appellant suggests, the rights of the parents but is, rather, the best interests of the children. The duty owed by the courts to children under the doctrine of *parens patriae* cannot be severed by agreement of the parties. It stands to reason that "[i]f parents cannot bind the court by an agreement affecting the interests of their children, they cannot bind the court by agreeing to let someone else, an arbitrator, make such a decision for them." "As the representative of the State, the [court's] responsibility to ensure the best interests of the children supersedes that of the parents."

Finally, appellant argues that because appellee could have mounted a challenge to the arbitration clause in a previous action, she is now barred from bringing this challenge under the doctrine of *res judicata.* This argument, too, lacks merit. * * * In many states, including Ohio, an allocation of custody and visitation rights remains subject to future modification by the trial court. For this reason, a number of courts have held that the doctrine of *res judicata* should not be applied strictly in cases involving child custody and visitation. * * * We find these decisions persuasive. * * * in the area of custody and visitation, we sacrifice finality and some of our limited judicial resources in order to secure a higher value—the best interests of children.

For the foregoing reasons, we hold that in a domestic relations case, matters of child custody and parental visitation are not subject to arbitration. The authority to resolve disputes over custody and visitation rests exclusively with the courts. Any agreement to the contrary is void and unenforceable.

NOTES AND QUESTIONS

1. How do the holdings in *Harvey* and *Kelm* differ? Does *Harvey* restrict the ability of parties to use alternative dispute resolution? If the court reserves the power to conduct a de novo review on matters relating to children, is there any point in arbitration? As *Kelm* illustrates, many courts disallow binding arbitration of child custody and support matters because of the court's interest in protecting children. Cohoon v. Cohoon, 770 N.E.2d 885 (Ind. App. 2002) (finding agreement to arbitrate child support, custody, and visitation inconsistent with public policy). On the other hand, New Jersey finds that the decision to arbitrate child custody and parenting time rather than litigate or mediate is within the decision-making prerogative of fit parents. *See* Fawzy v. Fawzy, 973 A.2d 347 (N.J. 2009). Is there a distinction between child custody and child support? *See In re* Marriage of Bereznak, 2 Cal. Rptr. 3d 351 (App. 2003). How about arbitration of a specific term, such as which school a child

will attend? *See* Schulberg v. Schulberg, 883 So. 2d 352 (Fla. Dist. Ct. App. 2004).

2.   In 2016, the Uniform Law Commission approved a Uniform Family Law Arbitration Act (UFLAA). A state may choose to enact the UFLAA but exclude a child-related dispute (chid custody or support). Sec. 3. Agreements to arbitrate child-related disputes must be made contemporaneously with the dispute. Sec. 5(c).

3.   If the arbitration proceeding produces appeals, what is gained by arbitration? Consider Warren Burger, *Isn't There A Better Way*, 68 A.B.A.J. 274, 276 (1982):

> We must, however, be cautious in setting up arbitration procedures to make sure they become a realistic alternative rather than an additional step in an already prolonged process. For this reason, if a system of voluntary arbitration is to be truly effective, it should be final and binding, without a provision for *de novo* trial or review. This principle was recognized centuries ago by Demosthenes, who, in quoting the law, told the people of Athens: "[W]hen [the parties] have mutually selected an arbiter, let them stand fast by his decision and by no means carry on appeal from him to another tribunal; but let the arbiter's [decision] be supreme."

What then should be the standard of review of an arbitrator's award? The American Academy of Matrimonial Lawyers approved a Model Family Law Arbitration Act in 2005 which allows a party to ask a court to vacate an award for child support or child custody if not in the best interest of the child, or if there is misconduct by an arbitrator.

Consider the New Jersey approach in Johnson v. Johnson, 9 A.3d 1003 (N.J. 2010):

> * * * As a matter of practice * * * When a child custody or parenting time arbitration award issues, one party will ordinarily move for confirmation. If there is no challenge, the award will be confirmed. If there is a challenge that does not implicate harm to the child, the award is subject to review under the limited standards in the relevant arbitration statute or as agreed by the parties. If a party advances the claim that the arbitration award will harm the child, the trial judge must determine whether a prima facie case has been established. In other words, is there evidence which if not controverted, would prove harm? If that question is answered in the negative, for example, where a claim of harm is insubstantial or frivolous (e.g., not enough summer vacation), the only review available will be that provided in the relevant arbitration act or as otherwise agreed. If, on the other hand, the claim is one that, if proved, would implicate harm to the child, the judge must determine if the arbitration record is an adequate basis for review. If it is, the judge will evaluate the harm claim and, if there is a finding of harm,

the parents' choice of arbitration will be overcome and it will fall to the judge to decide what is in the children's best interests. If the arbitration record is insufficient, the judge will be required to conduct a plenary hearing. *Id.* at 545–6.

Is this a high enough standard to both protect the child and prevent appeals? The Uniform Family Law Arbitration Act requires the arbitrator to cause a verbatim record to be made of any part of an arbitration hearing concerning a child-related dispute. Sec. 14(b). An award determining a child related dispute must state the reasons on which it is based as required by the law of the state in family law cases—this means findings of fact and conclusions of law in most states. To confirm an award with a child-related dispute, the court must determine that the award complies with the law of the state and is in the best interests of the child. Sec. 16(c).

4.   How would an arbitrator handle the domestic violence issue? The Uniform Family Law Arbitration Act Section 12 provides that if a party is subject to an order of protection or if the arbitrator otherwise finds that a party's safety or ability to participate effectively in the arbitration is at risk, the arbitration is suspended unless the party who is at risk reaffirms the desire to arbitrate and a court allows it. If an arbitrator finds that a child is abused or neglected, the arbitrator must report it, and the arbitration is terminated.

5.   Religious arbitration has existed for centuries. Should courts recognize arbitration awards from a religious tribunal. *See* Michael A. Helfand, *Religious Arbitration and the New Multiculturalism: Negotiating Conflicting Legal Orders*, 86 NYU L. REV. 1231 (2011) (indicating that if the arbitration is conducted pursuant to a valid agreement, parties of the same religion could have religious authorities decide their disputes in accordance with religious law). Are there concerns as we saw in Chapter 1 about importing religious law into the American system?

6.   Mediation-arbitration, "med-arb," in which the parties agree to submit to arbitration whatever they fail to work out in mediation, is one of the newest versions of dispute resolution. *See* Fla. R. Civ. Pro. Rule 1.800 (court can order any child dispute to arbitration or arbitration in conjunction with mediation, where the court determines that the dispute is of such nature the parties or the court could benefit). Is med-arb preferable to a trial? to mediation or arbitration alone? *See* Barry Bartel, *Med-Arb as a Distinct Method of Dispute Resolution: History, Analysis, and Potential*, 27 WILLIAMETTE L. REV. 661 (1991).

7.   *Parent Coordination:* The role of parent coordinator (special master, case manager) combines aspects of mediation and arbitration. After the parents have failed to cooperate by either filing repeated motions or engaging in destructive behaviors, the court may appoint a third party neutral who generally has mediation training and is a social worker, psychologist or lawyer. The parent coordinator assists the parties in creating, maintaining, and monitoring compliance with judicial orders and parenting plans. Parent coordinators handle minor decisions but cannot make binding decisions unless

the attorneys file a detailed stipulation with the court or the court approves the decision after a judicial review. Parent coordination appears to work. *See* Wilma Henry et al, *Parenting Coordination and Court Relitigation: A Case Study*, 47 FAM. CT. REV. 682, 690 (2011) (showing 60% of couples filed fewer motions in first year parenting coordination).

Problem 11-7:

Marsha is a former judge who mediated a dispute between Amanda and James over their daughter's custody. Several months after the divorce, Amanda and James had a dispute over property division issues. The court appointed Marsha to act as arbitrator in the dispute. You represent Amanda. What objections do you have to Marsha serving as arbitrator? *See In re* Cartwright, 104 S.W.3d 706 (Tex. App. 2003).

Problem 11-8:

The administrator of your local court is interested in setting up some alternate dispute resolution programs in divorce cases, which represent approximately 30% of the court's very crowded docket. The administrator wants a program that will "resolve cases without using judicial resources, and do it well enough that the litigants won't come back to court later." You have been asked to structure a program. Should it involve mediation, arbitration, or both? In what types of cases does arbitration appear to be preferable to mediation? to judicial decision making? In what types of cases and at what stage of the litigation process will the various forms of ADR be most cost-effective?

6. COLLABORATIVE LAW

"Collaborative law" aims to reduce divorce litigation, expense, and delay by encouraging the parties and their counsel to work together to reach an efficient, fair, and comprehensive settlement of all issues. In collaborative representation, each party is represented by counsel, but the retainer agreements specify that the scope of representation is limited to assistance in reaching a fair agreement; litigation is not permitted during the collaborative period. If the parties cannot agree, new "adversarial" counsel handle post collaboration litigation. *See* PAULINE H. TESLER, COLLABORATIVE LAW (ABA 3d ed. 2017). The North Carolina statute is illustrative:

N.C. GEN. STAT. ANN. § 50–71: As used in this article, the following terms mean:

(1) Collaborative law.—A procedure in which a husband and wife who are separated and are seeking a divorce, or are contemplating separation and divorce, and their attorneys agree to use their best efforts and make a good faith attempt to resolve their disputes arising from the marital relationship on an agreed basis. The

procedure shall include an agreement by the parties to attempt to resolve their disputes without having to resort to judicial intervention, except to have the court approve the settlement agreement and sign the orders required by law to effectuate the agreement of the parties as the court deems appropriate. The procedure shall also include an agreement where the parties' attorneys agree not to serve as litigation counsel, except to ask the court to approve the settlement agreement.

(2) Collaborative law agreement.—A written agreement, signed by a husband and wife and their attorneys, that contains an acknowledgement by the parties to attempt to resolve the disputes arising from their marriage in accordance with collaborative law procedures.

(3) Collaborative law procedures.—The process for attempting to resolve disputes arising from a marriage as set forth in this Article.

(4) Collaborative law settlement agreement.—An agreement entered into between a husband and wife as a result of collaborative law procedures that resolves the disputes arising from the marriage of the husband and wife.

(5) Third-party expert.—A person, other than the parties to a collaborative law agreement, hired pursuant to a collaborative law agreement to assist the parties in the resolution of their disputes.

NOTES AND QUESTIONS

1.   How does collaborative law differ from traditional negotiation? *See* Pauline H. Tesler, *Collaborative Family Law*, 4 PEPP. DISP. RESOL. L.J. 317 (2004) (discussing the differences from conventional settlement negotiations and mediation). How does it discourage litigation? How does collaborative law differ from the practice of hiring one lawyer to act as a scrivener? What is the difference between mediation and collaborative lawyering? Cooperative lawyering? *See In re* Mabray, 355 S.W.3d 16 (Tex. App. 2010) (upholding parties' agreement provision not requiring lawyers to resign if no agreement). *See* John Lande & Gregg Herman, *Fitting the Forum to the Family Fuss: Choosing Mediation, Collaborative Law, or Cooperative Law for Negotiating Divorce Cases*, 42 FAM. CT. REV. 280 (2004).

2.   How is collaborative law likely to alter the lawyer-client relationship? New Jersey Supreme Court Advisory Committee on Professional Ethics, Op. 699 (2006) indicates that before agreeing to represent a client in a collaborative process, the lawyer must determine that it will serve the client's interests and advise the client of the risks involved. What are the potential benefits and risks of agreeing to a collaborative process? *See* John Lande, *The Promise and Perils*

of Collaborative Law, 12 DISP. RESOL. MAG. 29 (Fall 2005). The collaborative agreement requires that each party be represented by his or her own counsel. The process may also involve mental health professionals as child specialists, coaches or advisors and financial experts to help the parties reach reasoned agreements. Will collaborative law help reduce the delays or the costs of divorce? Are there potential problems with confidentiality?

3.   States are beginning to allow for collaborative law by statute or court rule. *See* Utah Code Jud. Admin. R. 4–510(1)(D) (2006). One proponent says that "collaborative law is a revolutionary approach to divorce." Sherri Goren Slovin, *The Basics of Collaborative Family Law: A Divorce Paradigm Shift*, 18 AM. J. FAM. L. 74 (2004). Is it likely that collaborative law will become the norm in divorce actions? Why or why not? *See* Ted Schneyer, *The Organized Bar and the Collaborative Law Movement: A Study in Professional Change*, 50 ARIZ. L. REV. 289 (2008).

4.   The Uniform Collaborative Law Act passed the Uniform Law Commission in 2010. It requires that lawyers screen for domestic violence. *See* Nancy VerSteegh, *The Uniform Collaborative Law Act and Intimate Partner Violence: A Roadmap for Collaborative (and Non-Collaborative) Lawyers*, 38 HOFSTRA L. REV. 699 (2009). The UCLA failed to gain approval of the American Bar Association or the Academy of Matrimonial Lawyers but by 2017, the UCLA had been enacted in fifteen states.

5.   Not everyone thinks that collaborative law is a panacea. Professor Penelope Bryan criticizes collaborative law for "retard[ing] meaningful reform * * * by allegedly offering a procedural cure for substantive ills." Penelope E. Bryan, *"Collaborative Divorce": Meaningful Reform or Another Quick Fix?*, 5 PSYCH., PUB. POL. & L. 1001 (1999). *See also* Susan B. Apel, *Collaborative Law: A Skeptic's View*, Vt. B. J., Spring 2004, at 41, 43. A Colorado Ethics Opinion found that collaborative law violates Rule 1.7(b) insofar as it requires a lawyer to enter into a contractual agreement with opposing counsel to withdraw if not successful. The opinion noted the difference between Cooperative Law which does not require withdrawal and Collaborative Law. Colo. Ethics Op. 115 (Feb. 24, 2007). In 2007 the American Bar Association Standing Committee on Ethics and Professional Responsibility stated: "Before representing a client in a collaborative law process, a lawyer must advise the client of the benefits and risks of participation in the process. If the client has given his or her informed consent, the lawyer may represent the client in the collaborative process. ABA Formal Op. #07–447 (Aug. 9, 2007).

7. MALPRACTICE

Family law claims comprise close to 10% of total malpractice claims. *See* ABA PROFILE OF LEGAL MALPRACTICE CLAIMS 2000–2003. In a malpractice action, the plaintiff must establish an attorney-client relationship giving rise to a duty of care, a breach of the attorney's duty that was the proximate cause of injury to the client, and actual damages. An attorney must exercise that degree of learning, skill and experience which is ordinarily possessed by other attorneys in the community practicing in the relevant area of law. *See* RONALD E. MALLEN & JEFFREY M. SMITH, LEGAL MALPRACTICE (2016 ed.). Expert testimony is generally required to establish the standard of care applicable to the attorney's conduct; an attorney is not answerable for every error or mistake based upon an honest exercise of professional judgment. Woodruff v. Tomlin, 616 F.2d 924, 930 (6th Cir. 1980), *cert. denied*, 449 U.S. 888 (1980).

A. LIABILITY TO THE CLIENT

GRAYSON V. WOFSEY, ROSEN, KWESKIN AND KURIANSKY

Supreme Court of Connecticut, 1994.
231 Conn. 168, 646 A.2d 195.

PALMER, ASSOCIATE JUSTICE.

The principal issue raised by this appeal is whether a client who has agreed to the settlement of a marital dissolution action on the advice of his or her attorney may then recover against the attorney for the negligent handling of her case. The plaintiff, Elyn K. Grayson, brought this action against the defendants * * * and their law firm, Wofsey, Rosen, Kweskin and Kuriansky, alleging that they had committed legal malpractice in the preparation and settlement of her dissolution action. After trial, a jury returned a verdict in the amount of $1,500,000 against the defendants. The trial court, Ballen, J., rendered judgment for the plaintiff in accordance with the jury verdict, and this appeal followed. The defendants claim that: (1) the plaintiff failed to establish, as a matter of law, that she was entitled to a recovery against them; (2) the evidence was insufficient to support the jury's verdict; (3) the trial court's rulings on certain evidentiary issues constituted an abuse of discretion; and (4) the trial court's instructions to the jury were improper. We affirm the judgment of the trial court.

The relevant facts and procedural history are as follows. In 1981, Arthur I. Grayson (husband) brought an action against the plaintiff for the dissolution of their marriage. On May 28, 1981, the third day of the dissolution trial before Hon. William L. Tierney, Jr., state trial referee, the plaintiff, on the advice of the defendants, agreed to a settlement of the case that had been negotiated by the defendants and counsel for her husband. The agreement provided, inter alia, that the plaintiff would receive lump sum alimony of $159,000 and periodic alimony of $12,000 per year. Judge Tierney found that the agreement was fair and reasonable and, accordingly, rendered a judgment of dissolution incorporating the agreement.[3]

---

[3] "The stipulated judgment ordered the [husband] to pay to the [plaintiff] lump sum alimony of $150,000, payable in installments of $50,000 by June 28, 1981, $50,000 by August 28, 1981 * * * and $50,000 by February 28, 1982 * * * together with nonmodifiable periodic alimony of $12,000 per year. The [husband] was also ordered to pay $15,000 as part of the [plaintiff's] attorney's fees

On September 23, 1981, the plaintiff moved to open the judgment on the ground that the settlement agreement had been based on a fraudulent affidavit submitted to the court and to the plaintiff by her husband. The trial court, Jacobson, Jr. denied the plaintiff's motion to open the judgment and the plaintiff appealed to the Appellate Court, which affirmed the judgment. * * *

The plaintiff also brought this legal malpractice action against the defendants. Her complaint alleged that she had agreed to the settlement of the dissolution action on the advice of the defendants who, she claimed, had failed properly to prepare her case. The plaintiff further alleged that as a result of the defendants' negligence, she had agreed to a settlement that "was not reflective of her legal entitlement" and that she had "thereby sustained an actual economic loss."

At trial, the plaintiff introduced evidence concerning her thirty year marriage, its breakdown due to her husband's affair with another woman, and the couple's financial circumstances. After a detailed recounting of the history of the divorce litigation, the plaintiff presented the testimony of two expert witnesses, Thomas Hupp, a certified public accountant, and Donald Cantor, an attorney who specialized in the practice of family law.

Hupp testified that the defendants had failed properly to value the marital estate and, in particular, the husband's various business interests. Cantor gave his opinion that the defendants' representation of the plaintiff fell below the standard of care required of attorneys in marital dissolution cases. Specifically, Cantor testified that: (1) the defendants had not conducted an adequate investigation and evaluation of the husband's business interests and assets; (2) they had not properly prepared for trial; (3) as a result of the defendants' negligence, the plaintiff had agreed to a distribution of the marital estate and an alimony award that were not fair and equitable under the law; (4) the plaintiff would have received a greater distribution of the marital estate and additional alimony had she been competently represented. The trial court, Ballen, J., denied the defendants' motion for a directed verdict at the close of the plaintiff's case.

In their case in defense, the defendants testified concerning their handling of the plaintiff's case, and they also presented the expert

and to maintain a $50,000 life insurance policy on his life owned by the [plaintiff] and payable to her. The [plaintiff] was ordered to transfer her one half interest in a business building at 636 Kings Highway, Fairfield, to the [husband], the equity in which he claimed was $50,000. The [plaintiff] was required to relinquish her claim in the amount of $27,000 to a certificate of deposit managed by the [husband]. The [plaintiff] was awarded full ownership of Daniel Oil [Company], which the [husband's] affidavit claimed produced an income of $18,000 per year. Works of art valued by the [husband] at $64,700 were ordered divided between the parties. Otherwise, each was to retain substantial other assets shown on their affidavits. The principal asset shown by the [husband's] affidavit [was] the valuation, after taxes due on liquidation, of his pension plan in Grayson Associates, Inc., at $340,152 and the principal asset shown by the [plaintiff's] affidavit [was] the former family residence at 15 Berkeley Road, Westport, in which the claimed equity was $167,000." *Grayson v. Grayson*, 4 Conn. App. 275, 277–78, 494 A.2d 576 (1985).

testimony of two attorneys, James Stapleton and James Greenfield. These experts expressed the opinion that the defendants' representation of the plaintiff comported with the standard of care required of attorneys conducting dissolution litigation.

The jury returned a verdict for the plaintiff in the amount of $1,500,000. The defendants thereafter filed motions to set aside the verdict and for judgment notwithstanding the verdict. The trial court denied those motions and rendered judgment in accordance with the verdict. Additional facts are set forth as relevant.

I

The defendants first claim that the trial court improperly denied their motions for a directed verdict and for judgment notwithstanding the verdict on the ground that the plaintiff was barred from recovering against them, as a matter of law, due to her agreement to settle the marital dissolution action. We conclude that the plaintiff was not so barred.

The defendants urge us to adopt a common law rule whereby an attorney may not be held liable for negligently advising a client to enter into a settlement agreement. They argue that, as a matter of public policy, an attorney should not be held accountable for improperly advising a client to settle a case unless that advice is the product of fraudulent or egregious misconduct by the attorney. The defendants contend that the adoption of such a rule is necessary in order to promote settlements, to protect the integrity of stipulated judgments, and to avoid the inevitable flood of litigation that they claim will otherwise result. They claim that such a rule is particularly appropriate if, as here, the court has reviewed and approved the settlement agreement.

* * * At a time when our courts confront an unprecedented volume of litigation, we reaffirm our strong support for the implementation of policies and procedures that encourage fair and amicable pretrial settlements.

We reject the invitation of the defendants, however, to adopt a rule that promotes the finality of settlements and judgments at the expense of a client who, in reasonable reliance on the advice of his or her attorney, agrees to a settlement only to discover that the attorney had failed to exercise the degree of skill and learning required of attorneys in the circumstances. "Although we encourage settlements, we recognize that litigants rely heavily on the professional advice of counsel when they decide whether to accept or reject offers of settlement, and we insist that the lawyers of our state advise clients with respect to settlements with the same skill, knowledge, and diligence with which they pursue all other legal tasks." Therefore, when it has been established that an attorney, in advising a client concerning the settlement of an action, has failed to "exercise that degree of skill and learning commonly applied under all the circumstances in the community by the average prudent reputable member of the [legal] profession * * * [and that conduct has] result[ed in] injury, loss, or damage to the [client]"; the client is entitled to a recovery against the attorney. Accordingly, like the majority of courts that have addressed this issue, we decline to adopt a rule that insulates attorneys from exposure to malpractice claims arising from their negligence in settled cases if the attorney's conduct has damaged the client. * * *

Furthermore, we do not believe that a different result is required because a judge had approved the settlement of the plaintiff's marital dissolution action. Although in dissolution cases "[t]he presiding judge has the obligation to conduct a searching inquiry to make sure that the settlement agreement is substantively fair and has been knowingly negotiated"; the court's inquiry does not serve as a substitute for the diligent investigation and preparation for which counsel is responsible. Indeed, the dissolution court may be unable to elicit the information necessary to make a fully informed evaluation of the settlement agreement if counsel for either of the parties has failed properly to discover and analyze the facts that are relevant to a fair and equitable settlement.

Finally, we do not share the concern expressed by the defendants about the impact that our resolution of this issue will have on settlements, stipulated judgments, and the volume of litigation. Indeed, the defendants do not suggest that attorneys have heretofore been unwilling to recommend settlements out of concern over possible malpractice suits, for attorneys in this state have never been insulated from negligence claims by the protectional rule urged by the defendants. Because settlements will often be in their clients' best interests, we harbor no doubt that attorneys will continue to give advice concerning the resolution of cases in a manner consistent with their professional and ethical responsibilities.

The defendants contend that the evidence does not support a determination that they were deficient in their representation of the plaintiff. They also claim that the plaintiff's evidence was so speculative that a jury reasonably could not have concluded that the defendants' conduct was the proximate cause of any economic harm to the plaintiff. We disagree.

The following evidence, which the jury could have credited, is relevant to these claims. At the time of the trial of the marital dissolution action, the plaintiff and her husband had been married for thirty years. The plaintiff, fifty-three years old, was a graduate of Simmons College, and for eight years had owned and operated her own real estate business. Prior to opening her real estate office, the plaintiff had remained at home to raise the couple's three daughters. Her husband, a fifty-six year old graduate of Wharton School of Finance and Columbia Law School, was a successful entrepreneur.

Among her husband's business interests were several bowling alleys. He held a 20 percent general partnership interest in Nutmeg Bowl, Colonial Lanes and Laurel Lanes, and was in charge of their management. In addition, he owned 100 percent of the stock in three lounges that served food and beverages to patrons of the bowling alleys. The husband also had a beneficial interest in the Grayson Associate Pension and Profit Sharing Plan, which in turn was a limited partner in the three bowling alleys.

Grayson Associates, Inc., a management company in which the husband was the sole shareholder, received management fees from the three bowling alleys. Although Grayson Associates had a fair market value of $487,000, the husband's financial affidavit listed only its book value of $14,951. The husband's financial affidavit also listed a $46,080 limited partnership interest in Georgetown at Enfield Associates (Georgetown partnership), and a future general partnership interest in that partnership of $959.76. The husband's affidavit failed to disclose, however, that he intended to take a $185,000 partnership distribution from the Georgetown partnership and that he was entitled to $45,000 in management fees from that partnership. To the contrary, the affidavit affirmatively represented that the husband would receive no future income from the Georgetown partnership. Finally, the husband's affidavit indicated an annual income of approximately $62,000.

The plaintiff's financial affidavit, which was prepared by the defendants in consultation with the plaintiff, indicated that she had no income. The plaintiff had testified at her deposition prior to the dissolution trial, however, that she earned approximately $25,000 annually from her real estate business, and that she expected to receive commissions in excess of $34,000 in 1981.

The plaintiff's expert witness Cantor expressed his opinion that the defendants had been negligent in failing properly to discover and evaluate certain assets of the marital estate. Specifically, Cantor testified that the defendants had improperly failed to: (1) ascertain the full value of the Georgetown partnership; (2) discover the $165,000 anticipated distribution to the husband by that partnership; and (3) discover the $45,000 management fee owed to the husband by the partnership. Cantor also testified that because the defendants had failed to obtain appraisals for several of the assets, including 636 Kings Highway and Grayson Associates, Inc., the defendants were unable to challenge various inconsistencies in the husband's financial affidavit. Cantor further testified that the defendants had failed properly to establish the husband's "residual interest in the bowling alleys * * * as a general partner," an asset not expressly valued in the husband's affidavit.

Cantor also explained that, in his opinion, the defendants had failed to exercise due care in the preparation of the plaintiff's financial affidavit.

In Cantor's judgment, the plaintiff's credibility had been seriously and unnecessarily compromised because her financial affidavit did not include the income from her real estate business. Cantor also noted that the plaintiff's credibility may have been further undermined by virtue of the defendants' submission of three separate documents containing three different valuations of another marital asset, the Daniel Oil Company.

Cantor expressed his opinion that at the end of the two days of trial, there was not enough financial information available to the lawyers to permit them to responsibly recommend settlement to the plaintiff. He further concluded that the defendants' failure to satisfy the standard of skill and care required of attorneys in such cases was the cause of economic damage to the plaintiff because, in his view, she would have received a larger distribution of the marital estate had the defendants represented her competently.

Finally, Cantor testified to his opinion that the plaintiff reasonably could have anticipated receiving 40 to 60 percent of the total marital estate, which, according to the plaintiff's witnesses, had a value of approximately $2,400,000. Cantor also opined that the plaintiff reasonably could have anticipated receiving periodic modifiable alimony of approximately 35 to 50 percent of the parties' combined incomes.

We conclude that the evidence adduced at trial was sufficient to support the jury's determination that the defendants were negligent in their representation of the plaintiff. The jury reasonably could have determined, on the basis of the testimony of the plaintiff's expert, that the defendants had negligently failed to discover and value the husband's business interests and related assets, and that the terms of the settlement agreement did not represent a fair and equitable distribution of the true marital estate. Moreover, the jury was entitled to credit Cantor's testimony that the defendants' advice to accept the settlement agreement was the product of their inadequate investigation and preparation.

We further conclude that the evidence supported the jury's determination that the defendants' negligence was the proximate cause of economic damage to the plaintiff.

The defendants further claim that the jury's verdict was excessive as a matter of law. We do not agree.

The jury could have credited the testimony of the plaintiff's witnesses that the value of the marital estate, at the time of the divorce, was approximately $2,400,000, and that the value of the plaintiff's distribution, under the terms of the stipulated judgment, was approximately $450,000. Because the jury could have concluded, as Cantor testified, that the plaintiff reasonably could have expected to receive up to 60 percent of the value of the marital estate, namely, $1,400,000, the jury also could have determined that the plaintiff, had she been competently represented, would have received approximately $1,000,000 more of the estate's assets than she had been awarded pursuant to the stipulated judgment. In addition, on the basis of Cantor's testimony that the plaintiff could have expected to receive alimony of between 35 and 50 percent of the parties' combined annual income, the jury reasonably could have concluded that the plaintiff would have received alimony of up to $35,000 more per year than she had agreed to in settlement of the marital dissolution action. Furthermore, the jury was free to have calculated the economic damage to the plaintiff in lost alimony from the date of the marital dissolution action in 1981 indefinitely into the plaintiff's future. Viewed in the light most favorable to the plaintiff, therefore, the evidence supported the jury's verdict of $1,500,000.

NOTES AND QUESTIONS

1.　Must an attorney obtain appraisals in every case, regardless of their cost and the value of the marital estate? *See* William C. Lhotka, *Woman Wins $6.8 Million From Her Divorce Attorney*, ST. LOUIS POST DISPATCH, March 9, 1993, at 1. *See also* Meyer v. Wagner, 709 N.E.2d 784 (Mass. 1999).

2.　In giving advice about a proposed settlement, a lawyer must act with the same level of skill, knowledge, and diligence applicable to litigation. *See* Ziegelheim v. Apollo, 607 A.2d 1298 (N.J. 1992).

Problem 11-9:

Larry Lawyer represented Tom in drafting a premarital agreement which did not include an "alimony waiver" because, at the time the agreement was drafted, such a waiver was contrary to public policy. A few years later, a statute is enacted specifically allowing such a waiver. Does Tom have a viable malpractice against Larry if, following a divorce, he is ordered to pay his ex-wife alimony? *See* Vande Kop v. McGill, 528 N.W.2d 609 (Iowa 1995).

Problem 11-10:

Larry Lawyer represented a wife in a divorce action. Husband owned some unvested stock options. The state has neither determined whether unvested stock options are marital property nor whether unvested stock options should be valued without deducting potential capital gains tax. The parties reached a settlement which excluded the options and took into account the potential capital gains tax. Wife later discovered that the majority of other states have found unvested stock options to be part of the marital estate and have valued them without accounting for capital gains. Can Larry be sued for malpractice? *See* Wood v. McGrath, North, et al., 589 N.W.2d 103 (Neb. 1999).

B. LIABILITY TO THIRD PARTIES

RUCKER V. SCHMIDT

Supreme Court of Minnesota, 2011.
794 N.W.2d 114.

PAGE, JUSTICE.

Respondent Katherine M. Rucker successfully sued her ex-husband, Robert Rucker, for fraud on the court committed during a dissolution of marriage action. The trial court found that in the dissolution action Robert Rucker engaged in an intentional course of material misrepresentation and non-disclosure concerning the value of his business interest in The Tile Shop that resulted in a "grossly unfair" property settlement. Katherine Rucker subsequently sued Robert Rucker's dissolution attorney and the law firm that employed him, appellants Steven B. Schmidt and Rider Bennett, LLP, based primarily on the same facts asserted in her suit against Robert Rucker. Katherine Rucker accused Schmidt and Rider Bennett of fraud, fraud on the court, and aiding and abetting fraud in the marriage dissolution action. The district court granted summary judgment to Schmidt and Rider Bennett, holding that due to the attorney-client relationship, Robert Rucker and his attorneys were in privity for purposes of the application of the doctrine of res judicata, and therefore, Katherine Rucker's separate action against Schmidt and Rider Bennett was barred. The court of appeals reversed and remanded, concluding that the attorney-client relationship, by itself, did not create privity between Robert Rucker and his attorneys for purposes of res judicata. * * * [W]e affirm.

The material facts in this case are not in dispute. During their marriage dissolution action, the Ruckers agreed to use an independent appraiser to establish the value of Robert Rucker's 50% interest in The Tile Shop. Robert Rucker was represented in the dissolution action by Schmidt, who was employed by the Rider Bennett law firm. Based on documents provided by Robert Rucker and employees of The Tile Shop, the independent appraiser valued Robert Rucker's interest in The Tile Shop at $7.125 million. Based on this valuation, the Ruckers signed a marriage termination agreement, drafted by Schmidt, that involved a property settlement award of $2.4 million to Katherine Rucker. Robert Rucker represented in the agreement that he had made full disclosure of his business interests. The Ruckers' marriage was dissolved by a judgment and decree entered on October 1, 2001.

Katherine Rucker subsequently sued Robert Rucker for fraud on the court, asserting that Robert Rucker intentionally provided deceptive, misleading, and incomplete information to the independent appraiser and to the district court about his interest in The Tile Shop that resulted in the undervaluation of that interest. In that litigation, the district court concluded that Katherine Rucker had established her claim that Robert Rucker committed fraud on the court regarding the value of his interest in The Tile Shop. The district court found that the actual value of Robert Rucker's 50% interest in the Tile Shop was $15,367,200 and that Robert Rucker had engaged in an intentional course of material misrepresentation and non-disclosure during the marital dissolution action. Based on those findings, the court awarded Katherine Rucker an additional $3,285,864. After factoring in prejudgment interest, costs, and disbursements, the judgment entered against Robert Rucker was $4,215,673.49.

Robert Rucker appealed, but before his appeal was final, the Ruckers settled Katherine Rucker's claim. The settlement agreement, which specifically reserved Katherine Rucker's right to pursue an action against Schmidt and Rider Bennett, released and discharged Robert Rucker, The Tile Shop, and certain individuals and entities related to The Tile Shop from all further claims in exchange for a payment of $2,600,000.

On September 15, 2006, Katherine Rucker sued Schmidt and Rider Bennett, asserting fraud and deceit, fraud on the court, and aiding and abetting fraud. Katherine Rucker sought treble damages under Minn. Stat. § 481.07 and 481.071 (2010). The complaint alleges that Schmidt held a meeting with Robert Rucker and other senior management of The Tile Shop to discuss creating two sets of business projections: one of growth and new stores, to be used internally by The Tile Shop for actual business purposes, and one of no growth and no new stores to be given to the independent appraiser for use in the dissolution action. Schmidt and Rider Bennett denied this allegation and eventually moved for summary judgment on several grounds, including res judicata.

The district court, noting that "the alleged fraud arose out of Schmidt's representation of [Robert] Rucker in the underlying divorce proceeding" and that precedent establishes—and the federal and state courts of the Eighth Circuit consistently hold—that an attorney is in privity with his client for purposes of res judicata, held that privity existed between Robert Rucker, Schmidt, and Rider Bennett. As a result of that privity, the court granted summary judgment to Schmidt and Rider Bennett based on res judicata. The court of appeals reversed and remanded, holding that an attorney-client relationship alone is insufficient to establish privity as a matter of law. * * * The court of appeals further held that before res judicata can be applied, the district court is required to analyze whether its application would work an injustice on the party against whom it is urged, and because the district court did not make such a determination, remand was necessary even if the finding of privity was appropriate. *Id.* at 417–18.

Schmidt and Rider Bennett concede that a party is free to sue joint tortfeasors separately, * * * but argue that because they are in privity with

Robert Rucker, Katherine Rucker's claims against them are barred. According to Schmidt and Rider Bennett, they are in privity with Robert Rucker because the facts underlying Katherine Rucker's claims against them are the same facts underlying her claims in her fraud action against Robert Rucker and the conduct at issue arose out of Schmidt's and Rider Bennett's representation of Robert Rucker in the dissolution action. They also argue, by analogy, that to the extent that the attorney-client relationship is akin to a principal-agent relationship, privity can be found on a principal-agent basis.

Summary judgment is appropriate when there are no genuine issues of material fact and either party is entitled to a judgment as a matter of law. * * * We review the application of res judicata de novo. * * * Res judicata applies as an absolute bar to a subsequent claim when: (1) the earlier claim involved the same set of factual circumstances; (2) the earlier claim involved the same parties or their privies; (3) there was a final judgment on the merits; and (4) the estopped party had a full and fair opportunity to litigate the matter. * * * "All four prongs must be met for res judicata to apply."

For purposes of determining whether the judgment in the fraud action bars Katherine Rucker's claims against Schmidt and Rider Bennett based on res judicata, the parties agree that: (1) Katherine Rucker's claims against Robert Rucker in the fraud action involved the same set of factual circumstances that are involved in her action against Schmidt and Rider Bennett; (2) there was a final judgment on the merits in Katherine Rucker's fraud action against Robert Rucker; and (3) Katherine Rucker had a full and fair opportunity to litigate the matter asserted in her fraud action against Robert Rucker. The dispute here is over the privity prong of the res judicata test—that is, whether Schmidt's and Rider Bennett's actions in representing Robert Rucker and their attorney-client relationship are sufficient to establish privity for purposes of res judicata.

Privity " 'expresses the idea that as to certain matters and in certain circumstances persons who are not parties to an action but who are connected with it in their interests are affected by the judgment with reference to interests involved in the action, as if they were parties.' " * * * " 'Privies' to a judgment are those who are so connected with the parties in estate or in blood or in law as to be identified with them in interest, and consequently to be affected with them by the litigation." * * * According to the Restatement of Judgments, courts will find privity to exist for " 'those who control an action although not parties to it,' " " 'those whose interests are represented by a party to the action,' " and " 'successors in interest to those having derivative claims.' " * * * However, privity may also be found in other circumstances, beyond those categories noted in the Restatement, when a person is otherwise " 'so identified in interest with another that he represents the same legal right.' " * * * Because the circumstances in which privity will be found cannot be precisely defined, we have held that determining whether parties are in privity requires a careful examination of the circumstances of each case. * * *.

Thus, the dispositive question is whether Schmidt and Rider Bennett are so identified in interest with Robert Rucker that they represent the same legal right. * * * A careful examination of the circumstances of this case leads us to conclude that Schmidt and Rider Bennett are not so identified in their interests with Robert Rucker, based on the attorney-client relationship, that they represent the same legal right.

We first examine the relationship in the context of the fraud action. Schmidt and Rider Bennett concede that they did not have a "controlling participation" or an "active self-interest" in the fraud action, so privity cannot be found on that basis.* ** Schmidt and Rider Bennett similarly concede that they are not successors in interest to a derivative claim of a party involved in the fraud action. * * *. Finally, Schmidt and Rider Bennett do not claim that any party represented their interests in the fraud action against Robert Rucker. * * * Therefore, none of the categorical circumstances in which the Restatement recognizes that privity may be found are asserted to exist in the fraud action. Nevertheless, the question remains whether Schmidt's and Rider Bennett's interests are so identified with Robert Rucker that they represent the same legal right with respect to Katherine Rucker's fraud claims. Schmidt and Rider Bennett contend that the required identity of interest is found in their attorney-client relationship with Robert Rucker and Schmidt's conduct as Robert Rucker's attorney in the dissolution action.

As is true of the fraud action, Schmidt and Rider Bennett do not assert that any of the categorical circumstances in which privity has been found existed with respect to the dissolution proceeding. That is, they do not claim that they had a "controlling participation" or an "active self-interest" in the dissolution proceeding, that they are successors in interest to a derivative claim of a party involved in the dissolution proceeding, or that any party represented their interests in the dissolution proceeding. Instead, Schmidt and Rider Bennett claim that they are in privity with Robert Rucker in the fraud action because the attorney conduct on which the fraud claim against them is based was taken in the context of their attorney-client relationship with Robert Rucker in the dissolution action. But that is not sufficient to establish an identity of legal interests.

An attorney is professionally obligated to advocate on behalf of his client. Therefore, the attorney and client necessarily have a common interest—more accurately, a common objective—in obtaining a favorable outcome for the client. Here, Schmidt and Rider Bennett had the common objective with Robert Rucker of obtaining a favorable outcome for him in the marriage dissolution proceeding. But that level of common interest in obtaining a favorable outcome in the dissolution action is not the kind of estate, blood, or legal interest that would give rise to privity for purposes of the fraud action. * * * Something more than the common objective of attorney and client in obtaining an outcome favorable to the client is necessary to establish privity. That something more—here, a mutuality of legal interest in the outcome of the dissolution action—is missing in this case. Therefore, we conclude that the attorney-client relationship and Schmidt's actions taken on behalf of Robert Rucker in the dissolution proceeding did not establish an identity of legal interests and therefore Schmidt and Rider Bennett were not in privity with Robert Rucker in the fraud action.

We further conclude that Schmidt's and Rider Bennett's reliance, by analogy, on agency principles to establish privity fails. In support of this argument, Schmidt points to several opinions by federal circuit courts of appeal that have held that when the relationship between two parties is analogous to that of principal and agent, a judgment in favor of either, in an action brought by a third party, rendered upon a ground equally applicable to both, is a bar to the plaintiff's right of action against the other. * * *

We have not had occasion to address whether the attorney-client relationship is analogous to that of principal and agent and therefore sufficient to establish privity. We now conclude that it does not. The instant lawsuit arises out of Schmidt's and Rider Bennett's actions in representing Robert Rucker in the dissolution proceeding. Although a client hires an attorney and that attorney has a fiduciary duty to act on behalf of the client, the attorney-client relationship is not tantamount to an agent-principal relationship. The principal and agent relationships where privity is found involve a mutuality of legal interests. That is, the legal interests of the principal and agent, or the corporation and its officers, are similarly affected by the outcome of a legal proceeding. That common legal interest is substantively different than the common objective shared by attorney and client of an outcome favorable to the client.

Further, although attorneys in the discharge of their professional duties are, in a restricted sense, agents of their clients, this agency is distinguishable from other agency relationships in that attorneys are also quasi-judicial officers of the court charged with a definite responsibility to the administration of justice in the interest of the public welfare. *Hoppe v. Klapperich,* 224 Minn. 224, 240, 28 N.W.2d 780, 791 (1947). Out of an attorney's status as an officer of the court arise duties that are public as distinguished from the purely private duties owed to one's client. * * *

In Hoppe, we described an attorney's dual obligation by saying:

An attorney at law is an officer of the court. The nature of his obligations is both public and private. His public duty consists in his obligation to aid the administration of justice; his private duty, to faithfully, honestly, and conscientiously represent the interests of his client. In every case that comes to him in his professional capacity he must determine wherein lies his obligations to the public and his obligations to his client, and to discharge this duty properly requires the exercise of a keen discrimination; and *wherever the duties to his client conflict with those he owes to the public as an officer of the court in the administration of justice, the former must yield to the latter.* He therefore occupies what may be termed a *quasi*-judicial office.

Id. at 240–41, 28 N.W.2d at 791. Thus, while in the principal and agent relationship the agent's duty is to act on behalf of the principal, the attorney, acting on behalf of the client, has a duty not only to the client, but also to "the public as an officer of the court in the administration of justice." Given the lack of mutuality of interest in the outcome of the legal proceeding between the attorney and his client and the attorney's duty to the public, we conclude that Schmidt's and Rider Bennett's analogy to agency principles does not lead to a finding of privity in this case.

We recognize that a number of courts from other jurisdictions have concluded that when an attorney is sued based upon his or her actions in representing a client, the attorney and the client are in privity. Because our long-established test for determining whether privity exists between parties has served us well in varying situations over the years, we decline to adopt such a per se rule now. Applying our traditional test for determining whether privity exists in this case leads us to the conclusion that Schmidt and Rider Bennett are not in privity with Robert Rucker for purposes of res judicata and therefore res judicata does not bar Katherine Rucker's claims against Schmidt and Rider Bennett. As a result, we affirm the court of appeals.

Affirmed and remanded * * *

NOTES AND QUESTIONS

1. Often the persons seeking to sue are the children of one of the parties. Scholler v. Scholler, 462 N.E.2d 158 (Ohio 1984). Does *Scholler* mean that children need their own lawyer(s) in every divorce action? *See* Miller v. Miller, 677 A.2d 64 (Me. 1996).

Problem 11-11:

Larry Lawyer represented Mary in a divorce action against Tom. The divorce was granted on November 4. Because of some delays and vacations, Larry did not get the divorce journal entry filed until December 1st at 8:00 a.m. Tom, however, had died at 3:00 a.m. that morning. Because the journal entry was not filed, the divorce was not final and Mary inherited Tom's property as a surviving spouse. Do Tom's children have a cause of action against Larry for failure to file the journal entry? *See* Strait v. Kennedy, 13 P.3d 671 (Wash. App. 2000); Wilson-Cunningham v. Meyer, 820 P.2d 725 (Kan. App. 1991).

CHAPTER 12

DIVORCE AND DIVORCE SUBSTITUTES

■ ■ ■

[Divorce probably originated at nearly] the same date as marriage. I believe, however, that marriage is some weeks more ancient.

Voltaire

A divorce is like an amputation: you survive it, but there is less of you.

Margaret Atwood

We have examined the requirements our society imposes on those who want to marry as well as the entitlements and disabilities with which it endows those who enter the married state. Now we must examine the rules applicable when one or both spouses want to terminate the relationship.

In modern America, marital termination is a frequent event. In 2005, there were approximately a million divorces. *See* Paul Sutton & Martha Munson, *Births, Marriages, Divorces and Deaths: Provisional Data for 2005*, 54 NAT. VITAL STATISTICS RPTS. 6, tbl. 3 (2006). Domestic relations cases represented about one-third of all civil cases filed in U.S. courts of general jurisdiction in 1990. *See* Paula M. DeWitt, *Breaking Up Is Hard to Do*, AMERICAN DEMOGRAPHICS, Oct. 1992, at 53.

Divorce is highly concentrated in the early years of marriage. Nationally, in 2001, the median age of men and women divorcing for the first time was less that thirty-two; the median marital duration at divorce was eight years. *See* Rose M. KREIDER, NUMBER, TIMING AND DURATION OF MARRIAGE AND DIVORCE: 2001 8–10 tbls. 5–6 (U.S. Census Bureau Current Pop. Rpt. 70–97, 2005). These data are based on the national Survey of Income Programs and Participation and thus represent weighted estimates. *Id.* at 16. Many of these marriages appear to have been doomed from the start. "Almost 40% of divorced respondents to a Gallup poll reported that problems were present when they married or early in marriage." DeWitt, *supra*.

While the sources of today's high divorce rate are controversial, unprecedented prosperity and a remarkable increase in women's paid employment has reduced the likelihood that a dissatisfied spouse will remain married for purely economic reasons. Longer life expectancies have also dramatically increased the amount of time a married couple may expect to spend in the "bonds of matrimony." At the same time (whether as cause or effect or both), popular opinion on divorce has shifted dramatically. Many Americans do not remember—and cannot imagine— the time when a durable marriage was seen as a virtue per se, divorce was considered a disgraceful event, and divorce law was aimed at fettering the inclination to stray from the married state:

> [I]t must be carefully remembered that the general happiness of the married life is secured by its indissolubility. When people understand that they must live together, except for a very few reasons known to the law, they learn to soften by mutual accommodation that yoke which they know they cannot shake off; they become good husbands and good wives from the necessity of remaining husbands and wives; for necessity is a powerful master in teaching the duties which it imposes. If it were once understood that upon mutual disgust married persons might be legally separated, many couples who now pass through the world with mutual comfort, with attention to their common offspring and to the moral order of civil society, might have been at this moment living in a state of mutual unkindness, in a state of estrangement from their common offspring, and in a state of the most licentious and unreserved immorality. In this case, as in many others, the happiness of some individuals must be sacrificed to the greater and more general good.

Evans v. Evans, 161 Eng. Rep. 466, 1 Hag. Con. 35 (1790).

Today, there is skepticism that "mutual disgust" can be transformed by indissolubility into "mutual comfort," and that restrictions on the legal termination of a marriage can play a meaningful role in preventing the factual termination of a relationship through abandonment or consensual separation. Nor is there widespread agreement that "the happiness of some * * * must be sacrificed to the greater good." This shift is linked (but without a clear causal relationship) to our relatively high divorce rate and relatively "lax" divorce laws.

1. A BRIEF HISTORY OF DIVORCE

Most cultures have established procedures to terminate marital relationships if one or both parties desired it. In Europe during the early Christian era, both Roman and Jewish law permitted divorce; somewhat later, Germanic and Anglo-Saxon law permitted either unilateral or mutual-consent divorce. But, as we saw in Chapter 3, to the Roman Catholic Church marriage represented a sexual union blessed and sanctified by God. Under Roman Catholic canon law, "what God has joined together, let no man put asunder." In 1563, the Council of Trent officially reaffirmed the church's prohibition on divorce, a prohibition maintained to the present day.

Canon law had a "safety valve," however, in annulment, which voided the marriage *ab initio*. The evidence suggests that annulment was freely obtainable for the right inducement:

> Practically speaking, it cannot be doubted that there existed a very wide liberty of divorce in the Middle Ages, though it existed mainly for those who were able to pay the ecclesiastical judge for finding a way through the tortuous maze of forbidden degrees [of consanguinity]. In a divorce procedure masquerading under the guise of an action for nullifying spurious marriages lurked the germs of perjury and fraud. When both persons were willing to separate, the matter must have been easy enough by collusion; and when one consort was tired of the other, the ecclesiastical court for money would be able to find good reasons for effecting his release. Spouses who had quarreled began to investigate their pedigrees and were unlucky if they could discover no "impedimentum dirimens" or cause which would have prevented the contraction of a valid marriage. The canons prescribing the prohibited degrees of relationship were marvels of ingenuity. Spiritual relationships, those gained in baptism, were recognized no less than natural relationships, and equally with them served as barriers to legal marriage. Marriage was prohibited within seven degrees of relationship and affinity; and none but the astutest students of the law were able to unravel so complicated a system. The annulling of marriages, which has been contracted within the prohibited degrees, became a flourishing business of the Church. No exercise of its power yielded more money, or caused more scandal. So tangled was the casuistry respecting marriage, at the beginning of the sixteenth century, that it might be said that, for a sufficient consideration, a canonical flaw could be found in almost any marriage.

G. HOWARD, II A HISTORY OF MATRIMONIAL INSTITUTIONS 56–60 (1904).

Martin Luther and John Calvin criticized the Catholic church's brisk business in annulments as well as its views on marital indissolubility; both took the position that divorce should be permitted, at least for adultery. Their views influenced sixteenth-century marriage law in Scandinavia, Switzerland, the Netherlands, Scotland, and parts of Germany. *See generally* RODERICK PHILLIPS, PUTTING ASUNDER: A HISTORY OF DIVORCE IN WESTERN SOCIETY (1988).

Other European nations, particularly those where most of the population was Catholic, continued to forbid divorce up to the modern era.

Spain, Italy, and Ireland did not permit divorce until the twentieth century; in France, divorce was briefly available during the Revolution and Napoleonic era, then forbidden until 1884. Despite Henry VIII's break with the Roman Catholic Church over its unwillingness to annul his first marriage, in England absolute divorce was unobtainable except by a special act of Parliament until 1857. The Church of England's ecclesiastical courts did grant divorces *"a mensa et thoro"* (from bed and board), that authorized legal separation but did not constitute an absolute divorce that would permit remarriage.

In keeping with the diverse geographic origins and religious views of the American colonists, colonial divorce laws were quite varied. In New England, many Puritans believed that divorce was preferable to a highly dysfunctional marriage. The Massachusetts divorce law thus dates from 1692. As early as 1620, Plymouth's officials declared marriage to be a civil rather than an ecclesiastical matter. Southern states typically agreed that marriage was a civil matter but refused to countenance divorce; South Carolina had no divorce law until the 1940s. *See* GLENDA RILEY, DIVORCE: AN AMERICAN TRADITION 8–29 (1991).

Any discussion of divorce history must, of course, acknowledge the possibly huge gulf between law and behavior. Even without divorce, in an era without computers or social security numbers, desertion and separation were facts of life, and it was not uncommon for a separated spouse to resettle, and remarry, in a new locale. (This option was, however, probably more open to men than women.)

During the nineteenth century, the demand for divorce increased. A system of legislative divorce was incapable of processing divorce petitions in quantity. Professor Friedman notes this frustrated remark made by a delegate to the Kentucky Constitutional Convention of 1849:

> [Y]ear after year a great portion of the time of the general Assembly has been consumed with the passage of [private divorce] acts, [which] gave rise to 'universal complaint' because of the 'unnecessary' consumption of time and * * * expense." The remedy, of course, was to abolish legislative divorce. The statutes were never simple, facilitative laws. To begin with, the law recognized no such thing as consensual divorce. Divorce was a privilege granted to an innocent spouse. It was in the form of an adversary lawsuit: Plaintiff had to allege and prove "grounds" for divorce against defendant. In some states, only innocent plaintiffs were allowed to marry again. Guilty parties were left to stew in their juices.

In other words, legislatures recognized the need for an efficient way to dissolve a marriage, but the enacted statutory schemes were never *too* efficient. There were, in short, compromises between two genuine social demands, which were in hopeless conflict. One was a demand that the law lend moral and physical force to the sanctity and stability of marriage. The other was a demand that the law permit people to choose and change their legal relations.

The moral goals of divorce law were reflected in the statutory lists of "grounds." Adultery was always on the list. A few strict states, such as New York, hardly went further. Other states had longer lists. Desertion was commonly included. Other grounds included fraud, impotence, conviction of a felony, or habitual drunkenness.

Lawrence Friedman, *Rights of Passage: Divorce Law in Historical Perspective*, 63 OR. L. REV. 649, 652–53 (1984). By the dawn of the twentieth century, judicial divorce laws had been enacted by almost all American states and the vast majority of European nations.

The enactment of judicial divorce laws was accompanied by a rapid increase in the divorce rate. Between 1885 to 1910 the number of French divorces tripled; between 1867 and 1910, the number of English divorces increased fivefold. The same trend was seen in the United States.

Immediately following both World War I and World War II, the divorce rate climbed rapidly. The trend was widespread, but was most evident among young people directly affected by the War. In both instances, the abrupt post-war increase in the divorce rate was succeeded by a period of relative stability. In the 1960s, however, the divorce rate again began to rise sharply. In the United States and most European countries, the divorce rate doubled during the period from about 1960 to 1985. In the period since 1985, the divorce rate has, again, been relatively stable.

Across the "up and down" pattern in divorce rates, two trends, both evident in the graph reprinted below, are consistent. One, applicable to each country represented, is a higher divorce rate over time; while in all nations the divorce rate has gone up and down, overall the ups outweigh the downs. The other, applicable across nations, is in favor of a comparatively high U.S. divorce rate. In 1910, there were four times as many divorces in the United States as in England, Scotland, France, the Netherlands, Belgium, and the Scandinavian countries combined, despite the fact that the U.S. population was smaller than the total population of these other nations. In 1980, at 5 divorces per 1,000 population, the U.S. divorce rate was about twice that of England and Canada. In the late 1970s, for the first time in U.S. history more marriages were ended each year by divorce than by death.

Comparative Divorce Rates—1950 to 1985

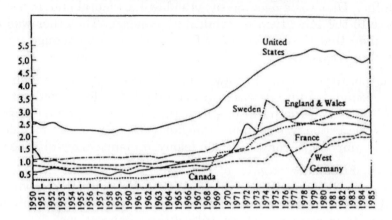

Divorces per 1,000 population

Source: RODERICK PHILLIPS, UNTYING THE KNOT 213 (1991).

Recent divorce data show that the U.S. divorce rate is falling. In 1999, 2000, and 2001 the U.S. divorce rate per 1000 population was 4.1, 4.2 and 4.0, respectively. *See Births, Marriages, Divorces, and Deaths: Provisional Data for 2001,* tbl. 1, 50 Nat. Vital Statistics Rpts., No. 14 (2002). By 2005, the U.S. divorce rate had fallen to 3.6 divorces per 1000 population. *See* Sutton & Munson, *supra,* at 1, tbl. A (2006). By contrast, in 2000, the average divorce rate in the European Union was 1.9. Finland and Denmark had the highest rate, both 2.7 per 1000 in 2000. *See Italy Considers a Proposal to Cut the Time to Complete a Divorce,* N.Y. TIMES, March 31, 2003, at A7, col. 1. One commentator has found that, of all marriages, the percent that end in separation or divorce in various countries within 5 years of the wedding is 23% in the United States, 12% in Germany, 8% in France and Great Britain, and 10% in Canada. *See* ANDREW J. CHERLIN, THE MARRIAGE GO-ROUND at 206 (2010). While the divorce rate in the United States remains significantly higher than a number of other countries in Western Europe, the United States divorce rate has been declining for decades. *See* Betsey Stevenson & Justin Wolfers, *Marriage and Divorce: Changes and Their Driving Forces,* 21 J. ECON. PERSP. 27 (2007); Claire Can Miller, *The Divorce Surge Is Over, But the Myth Lives On,* N.Y. TIMES, Dec. 2, 2014, A3.

Divorce rates are also impacted by the parties' ages and incomes. One study found that the risk of divorce is 30% lower for couples whose annual income exceeds $50,000, compared to couples whose family income is less than $25,000. Those who marry after age 25 have a 24% lower divorce rate than those whose who are younger than 18. NATIONAL MARRIAGE PROJECT, STATE OF OUR UNIONS; MARRIAGE IN AMERCIA 67, 74 (2012).

One recent change in the United States relating to divorce rates pertains to the relationship between education and divorce rates. While women with a college degree have had a lower divorce rate for some time, the difference in divorce rates based on the woman's educational level is growing. For example, of all women marrying for the first time from 1975–1979, those women with a college degree had a 28% chance of permanent separation or divorce within 10 years, whereas those without a college degree had a 37% chance. Fifteen years later, this gap widened substantially. Of those women marrying from 1990–1994, women with a college degree had a 16% chance of a permanent separation or divorce within 10 years. In contrast, women who had graduated from high school and possibly had attended some college had a 37% chance of the relationship ending within 10 years; women who had not graduated from high school had a 46% chance of their relationship ending within 10 years. *See* ANDREW J. CHERLIN, *Demographic Trends in the United States: A Review of Research in the 2000s,* 72 J. MARR. & FAM. 403, 405 (2010). Can you think of any reason why divorce rates might be linked to educational level?

The judicial divorce laws enacted during the nineteenth century made divorce available to a victimized spouse who could show, in a judicial proceeding, that the defendant spouse was guilty of one or another form of statutorily defined wrongdoing. While these laws were written with the idea that divorce would be denied if the plaintiff spouse could not show that the defendant spouse was guilty of conduct constituting a ground for divorce, the fact that the statutes permitted judgments on default opened the possibility of spousal collusion. The evidence suggests that collusion was common throughout the fault era. The proportion of divorce actions that were contested was 15.4% for the 1887–1906 period, 14.8% in 1922, declining to 11.9% in 1929, and increasing to 14.1% after the Depression began. U.S. DEP'T OF H.E.W., 100 YEARS OF MARRIAGE AND DIVORCE STATISTICS, UNITED STATES, 1867–1967 p. 19 (DHEW Publication No. (HRA) 74–1902 (1973)). In 1969, the Illinois Family Commission found that, in Cook County, Illinois, 97% of the 16,068 divorce decrees entered were uncontested. STATE OF ILLINOIS, FAMILY STUDY COMMISSION, REPORT AND RECOMMENDATIONS TO THE MEMBERS OF THE 76TH GENERAL ASSEMBLY 12 (1969). The evidence also suggests that divorce lawyers were sometimes knowing participants in sham proceedings. For example, in New York, where until 1966 adultery was the sole ground for divorce, researchers discovered that "the other woman" named in a number of cases was the secretary of a prominent divorce lawyer. *See, e.g.,* Richard H. Wels, *New York: The Poor Man's Reno,* 35 CORNELL L.Q. 303 (1950); *Note, Collusive and Consensual Divorce and the New York Anomaly,* 36 COLUM. L. REV. 1121 (1936).

Despite widespread acknowledgment of collusion and the law's inability to control it, the fault-based system of divorce survived, more or less intact, until the 1960s. In the late 1960s and 1970s

the dam seemed to burst in divorce law. * * * The old system collapsed completely; no-fault rushed into the vacuum. California was a pioneer state, but no-fault is now the rule almost everywhere. * * * Why did this happen? With regard to this legal change, it certainly makes sense to note changing attitudes and ideologies about family, sex, and marriage, and push economic motives into the background. Many people have an economic interest in cheap divorce; but they always did. What stood in the way was an ethical opposition, which has gradually but definitely crumbled.

Lawrence Friedman, *Rights of Passage: Divorce Law in Historical Perspective*, 63 OR. L. REV. 649, 666–67 (1984).

When support for fault divorce finally began to crumble, "no-fault" divorce spread rapidly across the Western industrialized world. Consistently, states and nations have moved from divorce based on fault toward at least limited acceptance of divorce based on demand. But today, no-fault divorce is also under attack. Some state legislatures have recently considered limiting or abolishing no-fault divorce; it is thus possible that fault divorce may become more important in the near future.

2. GROUNDS FOR DIVORCE

A. FAULT DIVORCE

Although all states have now accepted some form of no-fault divorce, fault-based divorce remains significant. First, most states merely added no-fault divorce as an additional divorce ground; in these states a spouse may elect a "fault" or "no-fault" divorce process. Second, because many no-fault divorce statutes require a minimum period of separation but fault grounds do not, a fault divorce is often quicker to obtain. Third, divorce entitlements to spousal support and property may be affected by whether the divorce is obtained on fault grounds. In a number of states, a court may consider the relative fault of both spouses when dividing marital property (*see* Chapter 15); in some states spousal support may not be awarded to a spouse whose marital fault provided the basis of the divorce (*see* Chapter 16). Finally, in a few states, no-fault divorce is available only if both spouses agree; absent such consent, divorce requires a showing of fault. *See* MISS. CODE § 93–5–2; TENN. CODE § 36–4–103.

Fault divorce grounds typically include adultery, desertion or abandonment, and cruelty. Adultery has been a basis for divorce in all American fault-based divorce statutes; while proof is not always easy, courts have interpreted adultery in a fairly consistent manner. Desertion invariably means a separation to which one spouse does not consent. But, in some courts, one spouse's departure will not be considered desertion if it was necessitated by the other's misconduct. Some courts have also held that, even if both spouses remain within the marital household, unjustified refusal to have sexual relations constitutes "constructive" desertion. *See* HOMER H. CLARK, JR., THE LAW OF DOMESTIC RELATIONS IN THE UNITED STATES 496–527 (2d ed. 1988); HARRY D. KRAUSE & DAVID D. MEYER, FAMILY LAW IN A NUTSHELL 247 (5th ed. 2007).

As you can see from the chart below, adultery, cruelty and desertion were consistently the most common grounds for divorce during the period between the 1860s and 1960s. But the proportion of cases falling into each category changed dramatically over this period, with allegations of adultery declining from 25% of the total to 1.4%, and allegations of cruelty rising from 16% to 42%. Can you think of any reasons for such a shift?

U.S. DEPT. OF H.E.W. 100 YEARS OF MARRIAGE AND
DIVORCE STATISTICS, UNITED STATES, 1867–1967

DHEW Publication No. (HRA) 74–1902 (1973), p. 49

Table 20

DIVORCES AND PERCENT DISTRIBUTION BY LEGAL
GROUNDS: UNITED STATES, SELECTED YEARS
1867–1965

Legal grounds	1965[1]	1960[2]	1950[3]	1930	1916	1887–1906	1867–1886
	Percent Distribution						
All grounds	100.0	100.0	100.0	100.0	100.0	100.0	100.0
Adultery	1.4	1.8	1.7	8.5	11.5	18.8	24.6
Bigamy and fraud	0.5	(4)	0.5	0.2	(4)	0.2	0.5
Conviction of crime	0.5	(4)	0.5	0.8	(4)	0.9	0.9
Cruelty	41.7	60.7	57.5	43.4	28.3	21.2	16.3
Desertion or abandonment	13.8	28.0	23.9	31.3	36.8	43.3	44.1
Drunkeness	0.3	(4)	2.5	2.5	3.4	5.7	7.8
Incompatibility	0.7	0.8	0.0	1.6	(4)	0.0	0.5
Indignities	15.5	(5)	9.9	(4)	(5)	1.2	(5)
Neglect or nonsupport	18.0	5.6	2.2	12.4	4.7	8.3	4.6
Separation or absence	3.5	0.6	0.2	0.5	(6)	0.1	0.0
Other grounds	4.1	2.5	1.1	0.4	15.3[7]	0.4	0.6

[1] Total of 22 reporting States.

[2] Total of 18 reporting States.

[3] Total of 20 reporting States.

[4] Included with "other grounds."

[5] Decrees granted for indignities included with decrees granted for cruelty.

[6] Decrees granted for separations or absence included with decrees granted for desertion or abandonment.

[7] Including 9,332 decrees granted for combinations of listed grounds—8.3 percent of the total.

LYNCH V. LYNCH

Massachusetts Court of Appeals, 1973.
1 Mass. App. 589, 304 N.E.2d 445.

KEVILLE, JUDGE.

This is an appeal by the libellant from a decree dismissing his libel for divorce brought on grounds of cruel and abusive treatment and desertion.

* * *

The parties have been married for fifty years and have not lived together since 1931. After finding that there was no evidence that the libellant had been deserted, the judge found, on admissions of the libellee, whose testimony he stated was "entirely credible," two isolated instances of her alleged cruel and abusive treatment toward the libellant. The first was an exchange of epithets between the parties in the libellant's barber shop in 1965 where the libellee had gone to ask him for money for her support. The second occurred in 1967 when she called him "a faker" after a court hearing to which he had been summoned for failure to obey an order of ten dollars a week for her support. There are instances in which verbal abuse may constitute cruel and abusive treatment. However, the facts found here do not as a matter of law require a different decree from that which had been entered.

NOTES AND QUESTIONS

1. In *Lynch*, the parties had not been living together for more than 40 years. What is the point of prohibiting a divorce in this situation?

2. In what circumstances do you think verbal abuse could constitute cruel and abusive treatment?

CAPPS V. CAPPS

Supreme Court of Virginia, 1975.
216 Va. 382, 219 S.E.2d 898.

PER CURIAM.

* * * The only questions properly presented on this appeal are whether the chancellor erred in awarding the wife a divorce on the ground of the physical cruelty alleged in her cross-bill and in denying the husband a divorce on the ground of desertion.

The parties were married on October 9, 1969. One child was born to them, and the husband adopted the wife's daughter by a former marriage. Prior to the marriage the husband had been seriously wounded while serving in the armed forces in Vietnam and, as a result, his left arm is paralyzed, he is forced to wear a leg brace for support, and he has a plate in his head.

The husband testified that his wife willfully deserted him on October 23, 1973. He admitted that he argued with her on the date of the alleged desertion and that, when she remarked that he "wasn't half the man Gary was," he became angry and struck her one time. He testified, however, that he immediately attempted to apologize to his wife, but was rebuffed. She then left their home, taking the two children with her, and they have not lived together as husband and wife since the date of the desertion. The husband admitted that there had been numerous separations and arguments in the past, but denied that he had ever been cruel to his wife.

The husband's father testified that the wife left his son on October 23, 1973, and that the parties have not lived together as husband and wife since that date.

The wife testified that on October 23, 1973, she had been physically abused by her husband. On that occasion, she said that an argument arose because he refused help from Child Protective Services to save their marriage. During the argument her husband struck her and choked her "in the bend of his arm." She testified that after she broke free from his hold, he said, "You and your bastard get out of here." She stated that immediately thereafter she left the home, taking with her the two children.

The wife's mother testified that on the evening of October 23, 1973, her daughter came to her home "hurting" and "crying." She noticed a "big knot" behind her daughter's ear, and she drove her to a hospital for x-rays.

* * *

In her cross-bill and proof, the wife relied on a single instance of physical abuse by her husband to support her claim of cruelty. Her testimony tended to show that during the October 23rd argument her husband struck and choked her, and ordered her to leave their home. There was no corroboration of the wife's testimony that her husband told her to "get out." Code § 20–99. While her testimony of physical injury is sufficiently corroborated by her mother's observation of a "big knot" on her head following the incident, we hold that this one instance of physical cruelty is insufficient to establish a ground for divorce.

In *DeMott v. DeMott*, 198 Va. 22, 92 S.E.2d 342 (1956), the wife established that during an argument her husband grabbed her, threw her against the wall, and threatened her with a knife. We held there that a divorce grounded on cruelty was properly denied the wife in that:

> * * * [A] single act of physical cruelty does not constitute ground for divorce, unless it is so severe and atrocious as to endanger life, or unless the act indicates an intention to do serious bodily harm or causes reasonable apprehension of serious danger in the future, or the precedent or attendant circumstances show that the acts are likely to be repeated. 198 Va. at 28, 92 S.E.2d at 346.

* * *

Although we hold that the wife is not entitled to a divorce, it does not necessarily follow that the husband must be granted a divorce on the ground of desertion. * * *

Here the wife proved, by corroborated testimony, that her husband physically abused her and that this conduct was the provoking cause for her leaving the marital abode. Under these circumstances, we find that the husband's conduct did not entitle him to a divorce on the ground of willful desertion since his wife left the home without legal fault. Therefore the husband's prayer for a divorce was properly denied by the chancellor.

For the reasons stated the decree appealed from, insofar as it awarded the wife a divorce, is reversed.

NOTES AND QUESTIONS

1.   The courts in *Lynch* and *Capps* attempted to articulate a distinction between relatively trivial marital misbehavior, insufficient to justify a divorce, and serious misbehavior, sufficient to justify a divorce. Can you articulate a clearer or more sensible test? Under your rule, how, if at all, would the results change?

2.   Should the test for cruelty justifying a divorce vary based upon the gender, race, class and cultural background of the petitioner? Consider Pochop v. Pochop, 233 N.W.2d 806, 807 (S.D. 1975):

> Any definition of extreme cruelty in a marital setting must necessarily differ according to the personalities of the parties involved. What might be acceptable and even commonplace in the relationship between rather stolid individuals could well be extraordinary and highly unacceptable in the lives of more sensitive or high-strung husbands and wives. Family traditions, ethnic and religious backgrounds, local customs and standards, and other cultural differences all come into play when trying to determine what should fall within the parameters of a workable marital relationship and what will not.

3.   During the four decades since *Capps*, U.S. courts have become much less tolerant of family violence, and now seem much more willing to grant a fault divorce when violence is shown. *See* Rogers v. Rogers, 2002 WL 1335694 (Ark. App.) (unpublished); Das v. Das, 754 A.2d 441 (Md. App. 2000). This trend is not universal, however. In S.K. v. I.K., 2010 WL 131943 (N.Y. Sup. Ct. 2010) (unpublished), despite the fact that the husband testified that the wife had initiated "at least forty instances of violence" against him, this was insufficient to establish "cruel and inhuman treatment" because the husband did not require medical treatment after any of the instances of violence.

If instances of violence should be grounds for a divorce, what if it is established that the wife slapped the husband numerous times? *See* Evans v.

Evans, 610 S.E.2d 264 (N.C. App. 2005) (divorce granted). What if the husband cursed and yelled at the wife repeatedly? *See* Harmon v. Harmon, 141 So. 3d 37 (Miss. App. 2014) (divorce granted).

What constitutes "cruel and inhuman treatment"? The Mississippi Supreme Court has said that "more is required than mere unkindness, rudeness or incompatibility." Robinson v Robinson, 722 So. 2d 601, 603 (Miss. 1998). Another case suggests the petitioner must establish that the actions of the other spouse rendered continued cohabilitation impossible. *See* Kergosien v. Kergosian, 471 So. 2d 1206 (Miss. 1985).

4.   Adultery is accepted as a fault ground in a number of states. It is customarily proved by circumstantial evidence. What proof should be sufficient to prove adultery? What if it is shown that the parties frequently met for lunch and that the woman was observed leaving the man's apartment at about 8 a.m.? *See* Spence v. Spence, 930 So. 2d 415 (Miss. App. 2005) (held, insufficient evidence). What if the husband is observed kissing another woman and staying late at her home? *See* Watts v. Watts, 581 S.E.2d 224 (Va. App. 2003) (held, sufficient evidence).

5.   Some states define adultery as sexual intercourse between a married person and someone not his or her spouse. *See* Marcotte v. Marcotte, 886 So. 2d 671, 673 (La. App. 2004). According to this view, sexual activity between members of the same sex could not constitute adultery. *See In re* Blanchflower, 834 A.2d 1010, 1011 (N.H. 2003). Some other states have broadened the definitions to include oral sex. *See* S.B. v. S.J.B, 609 A.2d 124, 126 (N.J. Super 1992). Should adultery be limited to acts of sexual intercourse? If not, should kissing and fondling another constitute adultery? *See* Brown v. Brown, 665 S.E.2d 174, 178 (S.C. App. 2008) (yes). *See* also N.Y. DOM. REL. L. § 170(4), which defines adultery to include oral sexual conduct. Should a sexual relationship began after the parties separated and agreed to divorce constitute adultery? *Compare* Barnett v. Barnett, 908 So. 2d 833 (Miss. App. 2005) (yes) *with* Smith v. Smith, 964 So. 2d 663 (Ala. App. 2005) (no).

Can an online "affair" constitute adultery? In Beckwith v. Beckwith, 2013 WL 4726691 (W. Va. 2013), the West Virginia Supreme Court ruled that this did not constitute adultery.

6.   During the 1950s a highly respected sociologist conducted a survey and asked divorced wives to describe the cause of the divorce. He found that

> [s]ome sophisticated respondents attempted to present a personality diagnosis of their husbands in superficially objective terms. Others felt that the husband personally betrayed them, or suddenly became a drunkard. A few never guessed that a divorce was impending until it happened, while others felt from an early period in the marriage that it would not last. It was not possible to classify each answer on several levels of meaning, as we wanted to do, because each respondent varied in her grasp of these levels. * * *

The answers were varied, but almost all responses fell into these categories: *1. Personality, 2. Authority or Cruelty, 3. "Complex," 4. Desertion, 5. Triangle, 6. Home Life, 7. Consumption, 8. Value, 9. Nonsupport, 10. Drinking, 11. Relatives.*

WILLIAM J. GOODE, WOMEN IN DIVORCE 115–116 (1969) (originally titled AFTER DIVORCE (1956)).

7.   Does fault-based divorce encourage or discourage marriage? What, if any, effect should the possibility of a fault-based divorce have on marital behavior?

B. FAULT DIVORCE DEFENSES

HOLLIS V. HOLLIS
Virginia Court of Appeals, 1993.
16 Va. App. 74, 427 S.E.2d 233.

BARROW, JUDGE.

In this appeal from a final decree of divorce, we . . . hold that a finding of connivance, the prior consent of one spouse to the misconduct of another, was sufficiently supported by the evidence. We further hold that the defense of connivance need not be expressly asserted in the pleadings.

Responding to the wife's allegation of the husband's adultery, the husband admitted that he was engaged in an adulterous relationship with another woman before the husband and wife separated. The wife asserted in her cross-bill for divorce that the husband's adultery began "on or about May 24, 1990." The husband acknowledged that he had lived together with another woman since March 22, 1990, and had had sexual relations with the other woman. The nature of the relationship was corroborated by the testimony of the other woman and the testimony of a private investigator.

The husband, however, asserted that his wife had urged him to date the other woman and that he had entered into a relationship only after his wife encouraged it. He introduced into evidence a handwritten letter from the wife dated February 4, 1990, which he received before an intimate relationship with the other woman began. The wife wrote that she wished to be free from her marriage but was afraid that the husband would "marry some bimbo." She wrote that she had seen the husband talking to the other woman at a Christmas party and hoped that the husband would fall in love with the other woman so that the wife could get out of her marriage. She said, "I want so badly for [the husband] to fall in love and share the rest of his life with someone who really loves him; someone like [the other woman], or even [the other woman]."

The husband and the other woman testified that they first had sexual relations at the Greenbrier Hotel the third weekend in February 1990.

While there, they received flowers and a card from the wife. The card said, "My very best wishes to you both today, to your new beginning."

Finally, the husband and wife signed a document dated May 23, 1990, stating that the wife "consent[ed] to [the husband] moving out of our home." In it she also said that she was "aware that this could entail his moving in and living with another female." She agreed that she would not "use this against him as grounds for divorce or punitive action."

The trial court found that the husband's adultery resulted from the wife's "connivance and procurement" and granted the husband a divorce on no-fault grounds. The wife contends that the evidence does not support this finding and that the husband's failure to plead connivance barred his assertion of it.

Connivance has been defined as "the plaintiff's consent, express or implied, to the misconduct alleged as a ground for divorce." *Greene v. Greene*, 15 N.C. App. 314, 316, 190 S.E.2d 258, 260 (1972). Connivance denotes "direction, influence, personal exertion, or other action with knowledge and belief that such action would produce certain results and which results are produced." *Id*. The defense of connivance is based on "the maxim 'volenti non fit injuria,' or that one is not legally injured if he has consented to the act complained of or was willing that it should occur." *Id*. Other courts have similarly defined connivance.

Condonation, on the other hand, is one spouse's forgiveness of the other spouse's adulterous misconduct, usually evidenced by resumption and continuation of apparently normal matrimonial relations. Knowledge of the misconduct is necessary before condonation may occur. Condonation, it follows, may only occur after the occurrence of the misconduct and differs from connivance in when the act of consent or, in the case of connivance, influence occurs. While condonation occurs after the misconduct, connivance occurs before the misconduct.

* * *

The evidence supported the trial court's finding of the wife's connivance in the husband's misconduct. Her letters and the note accompanying the flowers amply support the finding that she encouraged, as well as consented to, the husband's adulterous relationship.

NOTES AND QUESTIONS

1.   Another traditional defense to a fault divorce (in addition to connivance and condonation) is *recrimination*, applicable when the misconduct of the plaintiff spouse constitutes a justification for the defendant spouse's misconduct. *See* Chastain v. Chastain, 559 S.W.2d 933 (Tenn. 1977). Even during the fault era, the defense was widely criticized:

When both parties have committed material offenses, it is generally obvious that the marriage is beyond salvage; yet the rule that recrimination is an absolute defense leaves the parties legally bound to each other. This situation produces many evils: it promotes adulterous relationships; it increases the danger of giving birth to illegitimate children; it encourages collusive and uncontested divorces; it exerts a corrupting influence on the negotiations that precede a default divorce case, including the exaction of an unfair property settlement or alimony arrangement; and in community property states it leaves the management of the community property in the hands of the husband.

24 AM. JUR. 2D DIVORCE AND SEPARATION § 226 (1966). In many states today, the recrimination defense has been expressly abolished by statute. *See* HOMER H. CLARK, JR., THE LAW OF DOMESTIC RELATIONS IN THE UNITED STATES 527–28 (2d ed. 1988). The defense does still exist in some states. *See In re* Ross, 146 A.3d 1232 (N.H. 2016) (ruling that a sexual relationship initiated after the spouses permanently separated could constitute grounds for a recrimination defense).

Condonation at most excuses prior acts. So if a wife commits adultery and the husband agrees to continue the marriage, that does not mean he condones future adultery. Brewer v. Brewer, 919 So. 2d 135 (Miss. App. 2005).

C. NO-FAULT DIVORCE

1. No-Fault Grounds

UNIFORM MARRIAGE AND DIVORCE ACT
9A U.L.A. 147 (1987).

§ 302.

(a) The [_____] court shall enter a decree of dissolution of marriage if:

(1) the court finds that one of the parties, at the time the action was commenced, was domiciled in this State, or was stationed in this State while a member of the armed services, and that the domicil or military presence has been maintained for 90 days next preceding the making of the findings;

(2) the court finds that the marriage is irretrievably broken, if the finding is supported by evidence that (i) the parties have lived separate and apart for a period of more than 180 days next preceding the commencement of the proceeding, or (ii) there is serious marital discord adversely affecting the attitude of one or both of the parties toward the marriage;

(3) the court finds that the conciliation provisions of Section 305 either do not apply or have been met;

(4) to the extent it has jurisdiction to do so, the court has considered, approved, or provided for child custody, the support of any child entitled to support, the maintenance of either spouse, and the disposition of property; or has provided for a separate later hearing to complete these matters.

(b) If a party requests a decree of legal separation rather than a decree of dissolution of marriage, the court shall grant the decree in that form unless the other party objects.

§ 303.

* * *

(e) Previously existing defenses to divorce and legal separation, including but not limited to condonation, connivance, collusion, recrimination, insanity, and lapse of time, are abolished.

§ 305.

(a) If both of the parties by petition or otherwise have stated under oath or affirmation that the marriage is irretrievably broken, or one of the parties has so stated and the other has not denied it, the court, after hearing, shall make a finding whether the marriage is irretrievably broken.

(b) If one of the parties has denied under oath or affirmation that the marriage is irretrievably broken, the court shall consider all relevant factors, including the circumstances that gave rise to filing the petition and the prospect of reconciliation, and shall:

(1) make a finding whether the marriage is irretrievably broken; or

(2) continue the matter for further hearing not fewer than 30 nor more than 60 days later, or as soon thereafter as the matter may be reached on the court's calendar, and may suggest to the parties that they seek counseling. The court, at the request of either party shall, or on its own motion may, order a conciliation conference. At the adjourned hearing the court shall make a finding whether the marriage is irretrievably broken.

(c) A finding of irretrievable breakdown is a determination that there is no reasonable prospect of reconciliation.

* * *

NOTES AND QUESTIONS

1. After prolonged discussion with the Family Law Section of the American Bar Association (ABA), the new subsection (2) of § 302(a) was substituted for an earlier version which had simply read "the court finds that the marriage is irretrievably broken." The Family Law Section was not satisfied, however, and, in February 1974, recommended that the American Bar Association (ABA) House of Delegates withhold approval of the UMDA:

> [T]he grounds of objection include, but are not necessarily limited to, the fact that the alternative provision for divorce in § (a)(2) of the amended act 'or (ii) there is serious marital discord adversely affecting the attitude of one or both of the parties toward the marriage' makes possible a dissolution of marriage of however long duration by the whim of one party and, in practical effect, vitiates the 180 days separation period provided for in § 302(a)(2)(i). * * *

The Family Law Section recommended the following language:

> (2) * * * [A] marriage is irretrievably broken, which finding shall be established by proof (a) that the parties have lived separate and apart for a period of more than one year; * * * (b) that such serious marital misconduct has occurred which has so adversely affected the physical or mental health of the petitioning party as to make it impossible for the parties to continue the marital relation, and that reconciliation is improbable * * * or (3) The court finds that the conciliation provisions of § 305 have been met and that past efforts at reconciliation have failed or that further attempts at reconciliation would be impracticable or not in the best interests of the family.

What are the pros and cons of: (1) the original UMDA; (2) the ABA proposal; and (3) the amended UMDA?

2. Only a minority of states have followed the UMDA approach and adopted irretrievable breakdown (or irreconcilable differences or incompatibility or some other similar term) as the sole ground for divorce. *See* Linda D. Elrod & Robert Spector, *A Review of the Year in Family Law*, 44 FAM. L. Q. 469, 514, Chart 4 (2011). Some have added an irretrievable breakdown ground to fault grounds for divorce (*see, e.g.,* TEX. FAM. CODE § 6.001; GA. CODE § 19–5–3). A large number of states have added to their fault grounds a provision permitting no-fault divorce after a minimum period of separation. The period of separation required ranges from six months in Vermont (*see* VT. STAT. ANN. tit. 15 § 551), to three years in Utah (*see* UTAH CODE ANN. § 30–3–1–(3)(j)).

Should parties have to establish that they have been separated for a certain period before a no-fault divorce is possible? What is the purpose of a rule like this?

3. A study in 1996 found that Germany, the Netherlands, England, and all of the Scandinavian countries except Denmark accepted unilateral no-fault divorce (when only one spouse believes the marriage should be ended); a number of other European nations permitted no-fault divorce, but only if both spouses want the divorce. *See* JEAN MILLAR & ANDREA WARMAN, FAMILY OBLIGATIONS IN EUROPE 14 (1996).

4. For a discussion of divorce law in other parts of the world, *see* MARIANNE BLAIR, ET AL., FAMILY LAW IN THE WORLD COMMUNITY 170–179 (Ireland); 179–184 (Western Europe), 184–189 (East Asia) (2d ed. 2009).

Problem 12-1:

You represent Henry in a divorce action against his wife, Wendy. Henry initiated the divorce action alleging adultery by Wendy. Wendy has counterclaimed for divorce based on irreconcilable differences; she has also requested permanent maintenance and equitable property distribution. Would it make sense to consent to the entry of a divorce decree on a no-fault basis? Why might it be advantageous for your client to obtain a fault divorce? *See* Ebbert v. Ebbert, 459 A.2d 282 (N.H. 1983). This will be discussed in more detail in Chapters 15 and 16.

2. What Constitutes Irretrievable Breakdown

HAGERTY V. HAGERTY
Supreme Court of Minnesota, 1979.
281 N.W.2d 386.

MAXWELL, JUSTICE.

* * * Claire, after unsuccessfully urging William to seek treatment for alcoholism, asked him in the summer of 1976 to leave the home. William moved out in August and filed for divorce in September. He made several unsuccessful attempts at reconciliation, but testified that no hope of reconciliation remained at the time of the proceedings. Claire claimed the marriage could be saved if William were treated for alcoholism, but she had not otherwise been willing to take him back.

Prior to the hearing on the dissolution petition, Claire had unsuccessfully sought a court order dismissing the petition unless her husband completed treatment for his alcoholism within 6 months and agreed to a one-year after-care program; if thereafter he wanted the dissolution, she would not resist.

On April 6, 1978, the trial court dissolved the marriage after finding, among other things, that William suffered from alcoholism, a treatable disease; that it was a principal cause of marital discord which adversely affected his attitude towards the marriage; and that the marriage was irretrievably broken.

The pithy statement in appellant's brief that she "simply suggests that the alcoholism is the culprit and that Petitioner's assessment of the marriage is deluded," sets the scene. She then asks: (1) how lucid are the perceptions of an alcoholic about the marriage; (2) whether the same perception would exist after recovery from alcoholism; and (3) whether the petitioner proved that the marriage was irretrievable broken.

The record amply supports the finding of serious marital discord, and Minn. St.1976, § 518.06, subd. 2, expressly permits a finding of irretrievable breakdown upon such evidence.

Since the record also amply supports the findings of alcoholism as a principal cause of the discord and as a treatable disease, the issue is whether the petitioner's untreated alcoholism can or should defeat findings of discord and breakdown. The "can" issue is one of statutory construction; the "should" issue is one of public policy.

Statutory Construction: Although irretrievable breakdown was the only ground for dissolution in the 1976 statute, several former grounds were retained in altered form in Minn. St.1976, § 518.06, subd. 2, as evidentiary guidelines for establishing that ground, and the guideline of serious marital discord was added. There was no requirement for reconciliation attempts or stay of dissolution for any specified, limited period. Without requirements indicating a legislative policy of affirmatively encouraging a possibility of reconciliation, the statute contemplates that the likelihood of reconciliation be considered in the determination of irretrievable breakdown along with the evidentiary guidelines.

Commentators and cases in other jurisdictions which have interpreted the grounds in no-fault dissolution statutes generally agree that the underlying concern is whether a meaningful marriage exists or can be rehabilitated. With that concern as the central issue, irretrievable breakdown is a fact which can be shown where both parties acknowledge that a breakdown exists at the time of the proceedings and one sees no reconciliation possibility. It can also be shown by evidence of only one party's belief that it is the existing state, particularly where the parties have been living apart.

Where one party urged that the marriage situation was remediable but the other refused to pursue counseling or reconciliation, the subjective factor proving irretrievable breakdown was established and dissolution was granted. In situations where statutes authorize counseling or continuance and the testimony of the party alleging breakdown might be impeachable or doubtful, a continuance is favored over a denial, with dissolution following in the event reconciliation is not accomplished.

Because the courts look at the existing subjective attitude, evidence of cause is no more determinative than evidence of fault. * * *

Upon the evidence introduced, . . . and under the prevailing view of the single ground for dissolution in no-fault statutes, the husband's untreated alcoholism cannot defeat findings of serious marital discord and irretrievable breakdown.

NOTES AND QUESTIONS

1.   Most courts have followed the *Hagerty* approach, finding irretrievable breakdown even if one spouse wants to continue the marriage. *See* Desrochers

v. Desrochers, 347 A.2d 150 (N.H. 1975); Eversman v. Eversman, 496 A.2d 210 (Conn. App. 1985); *Note,* 7 LOYOLA L. A. L. REV. 453 (1974). Is this sensible?

2.   In an Oklahoma case, the court found that, because the wife was diagnosed with multiple sclerosis, the parties decided to divorce and give the husband all of their assets, so the wife would qualify for social security and Medicaid benefits relating to her illness. Should the court grant a divorce? *See* Vandervort v. Vandervort, 134 P.3d 892 (Okla. App. 2005) (no).

3.   Even before no-fault divorce, it was possible to get a divorce if both parties desired it. What is new about the acceptance of no-fault divorce in most states, as *Hagerty* shows, is that one spouse can now get a divorce even if the other spouse does not want a divorce. A few states such as Mississippi do not permit no-fault divorce if one party objects to the divorce. *See* MISS. CODE § 93–5–2. Is this wise? The impact of such a law is that a party in a dead marriage could not get a divorce regardless of the length of separation if the other spouse objected. *See* Bowen v. Bowen, 688 So. 2d 1374 (Miss. 1997). French law used to give a judge the power to deny a divorce if it was shown that granting a divorce would impose mental or physical hardship on an objecting spouse or a minor child. *See* FAMILY LAW IN THE WORLD COMMUNITY, *supra,* at 180. This restriction upon the right to divorce was abolished in 2005. Alternatively, should divorce be more difficult (but not barred forever) if one party wants the divorce but the other does not? In Maryland, if one party does not want a divorce the mandatory period of separation is lengthened from a period of one year to two years. *See* Aronson v. Aronson, 691 A.2d 783 (Md. App. 1997). Is this a good compromise?

3.   What Constitutes Separation

A number of states require a minimum period of separation to obtain a no-fault divorce. This requires courts to establish standards for what constitutes "separation."

FREY V. FREY

Pennsylvania Superior Court, 2003.
821 A.2d 623.

Opinion by STEVENS, J.

The relevant facts and procedural history are as follows: On August 28, 1993, the parties were married in Fayette County, and, on August 6, 1999, Husband filed a complaint in divorce alleging that the parties separated on March 1, 1999, and the marriage was irretrievably broken. On September 12, 1999, Wife filed an answer to the complaint with counterclaims for, *inter alia,* equitable distribution, alimony *pendente lite,* spousal support, alimony, and child support for the parties' minor daughter.

On August 10, 2001, Husband filed a petition for bifurcation seeking to separate the parties' divorce from the economic claims. Husband also filed a petition requesting equitable distribution. On August 15, 2001, the trial court granted Husband's request for equitable distribution and ordered his complaint so amended. On August 22, 2001, Wife filed a counter-affidavit opposing the entry of a divorce decree on the grounds that the parties had not lived separate and apart for at least two years and the marriage was not irretrievably broken.

On November 27, 2001, a hearing was held, during which Husband and Wife testified regarding the date of separation. On direct examination, Husband testified that he filed a complaint in divorce on August 6, 1999, and when he filed the complaint, he and Wife were living in the same residence with their daughter. Husband testified that, prior to this time, he occasionally ate meals with Wife and his daughter, but he and Wife had not slept together in the same bed since March 23, 1998. Husband testified that he remembered this date well because it was his daughter's birthday, he had the flu, and he and Wife had an argument. Husband testified that from March 23, 1998 to August 6, 1999, when he filed for divorce, he and Wife had sexual intercourse a few times, however, after he filed for divorce, he and Wife had no sexual contact whatsoever. Husband testified that, on occasion, prior to filing for divorce, he and Wife went out for dinner to discuss their problems and the distribution of their estate. Husband indicated that he was "tired of fighting [and] want[ed] out of the marriage." Husband testified that, as of the time of the hearing, he was still physically present in the marital residence. Husband indicated that he refused to move because he had no other house, he had built the house, his daughter lived in the house, and his lumber company was located next to the house. Husband testified that he and Wife have attempted to reconcile, but the discussions have always turned into arguments. As for the eating of meals after the divorce was filed, Husband testified that he usually ate at his mother's house, but on occasion he would eat with his daughter at the marital residence. Husband testified that he could not remember the last time he and Wife had a meal together, and, for the most part, he used the marital residence for sleeping purposes only, although he did not always sleep at the marital residence. Husband testified that he got home from work sometime after dark, and he left for work at approximately 6:00 a.m. Many times after coming home from work, Husband would leave again to prepare for the next day's work. Husband admitted that, following the filing of the divorce complaint, he, Wife, and their daughter went on vacations to Walt Disney World and Myrtle Beach. However, Husband testified that he and Wife did not sleep together while on vacation, and the sole purpose for the trips was to benefit their daughter. Husband spoke to his attorney prior to both vacations, and he specifically informed Wife that he was going solely for the benefit of their daughter. Husband testified that Wife knew he was going on vacations for the benefit of their daughter.

Wife testified that she believes the parties separated in October 2001 because that is when she and Husband first met with attorneys and Wife came to realize that the parties would not reconcile. Wife testified that from 1999 to October 2001, she, Husband, and their daughter attended school activities and holidays, went to the movies and dinner, and went on vacations together. Wife admitted that Husband generally eats with his mother, but she indicated that she washed all of his clothes, with the exception of his shirts. Wife testified that from 1999 to 2001 she and Husband had sexual intercourse on a regular basis, and the last time they had sexual intercourse was the weekend of October 28, 2001. Wife also testified that she and Husband had sexual contact during the summer of 2001 while they were at Myrtle Beach, and they saw a marriage counselor in March and June of 2000.

Following the hearing, the trial court filed an opinion and order on January 22, 2002, concluding that the parties separated on August 6, 1999, and the marriage was irretrievably broken. On January 31, 2002, Husband filed a motion to schedule a hearing regarding his petition for bifurcation, and on February 12, 2002, Wife filed a motion for reconsideration of the trial court's January 2002 order. Specifically, Wife contended that the trial court erred in determining the parties' date of separation and in concluding that the marriage was irretrievably broken. Wife requested a hearing on her motion for reconsideration. On February 20, 2002, the trial court denied Wife's motion for reconsideration without a hearing.

On April 1, 2002, following a bifurcation hearing, the trial court granted Husband's petition for bifurcation and ordered that all economic issues be preserved. Husband filed a request for a final decree in divorce, and on May 10, 2002, the trial court issued a final divorce decree. This timely appeal followed.

Wife first contends that the trial court erred in concluding that the parties' date of separation was August 6, 1999, and not October 2001, and, therefore, the statutory period for a no-fault divorce was not met. Essentially, Wife challenges whether there was sufficient, credible evidence to support the trial court's finding regarding the date of separation.

Subsection 3301(d)(1) provides that the court may grant a no-fault divorce where a complaint has been filed alleging that the marriage is irretrievably broken and an affidavit has been filed alleging that the parties have lived separate and apart for a period of at least two years. When considering a challenge to the trial court's determination of the date of separation, we have applied the following standard:

> The Divorce Code defines 'separate and apart' as follows: 'Complete cessation of any and all cohabitation, whether living in the same residence or not.' 23 Pa.C.S.A. § 3103. In *Thomas v.*

Thomas, 335 Pa.Super. 41, 483 A.2d 945 (1984), this [C]ourt held that 'cohabitation' means 'the mutual assumption of those rights and duties attendant to the relationship of husband and wife.' Thus, the gravamen of the phrase 'separate and apart' becomes the existence of separate lives not separate roofs. This position follows the trend of Pennsylvania case law in which a common residence is not a bar to showing that the parties live separate and apart.

"The ties that bind two individuals in a marital relationship involve more than sexual intercourse." *Miller v. Miller*, 352 Pa.Super. 432, 508 A.2d 550, 553 (1986).

Applying the foregoing, we conclude that the trial court did not err when it determined the date of separation to be August 6, 1999, as the date is supported by sufficient, credible evidence. For example, Husband testified that, as of August 6, 1999 to the time of the hearing, he did not sleep in the same room as Wife, and, in fact, he used the marital residence for sleeping purposes only. Husband testified that he remained in the house for reasons other than those relating to Wife. As for the eating of meals, Husband testified that, after August 6, 1999, he usually ate meals at his mother's house and that, when he did eat at the marital residence, it was with his daughter only. Husband testified that Wife washes his work jeans sometimes, but he takes all of his shirts to his mother and he sometimes washes his own jeans. With regard to vacations and other outings, Husband admitted that he went on vacations and other outings with Wife and his daughter after August 6, 1999; however, Husband specifically testified that such activities were for the benefit of his daughter only and Wife was aware of this fact. Husband did not engage in sexual intercourse or sleep in the same bed as Wife during the vacations, and as Husband testified, he and Wife gave the appearance that everything was fine for the sake of their daughter. Based on the aforementioned, we conclude that the evidence supported the August 6, 1999 separation date.

We specifically disagree with Wife's contention that the fact she attended the lumber company's 1999 Christmas party, the parties sought counseling twice in 2000, and the parties had dinner together in October 2001 requires a finding that the date of separation should be after August 6, 1999. This Court has held that isolated attempts at reconciliation do not begin running anew the marital relationship. Moreover, the fact Wife's testimony differed from Husband's in many respects is not determinative in this case. Husband testified that, after August 6, 1999, he and Wife did not have sexual relations, however, Wife testified that they regularly had sexual relations. Apparently finding neither spouse to be totally forthcoming, the trial court concluded that occasional sexual relations occurred between Husband and Wife following August 6, 1999. The trial court was free to make its credibility determination, and we will not disturb this determination on appeal.

In sum, the evidence in this case reveals that Husband and Wife led separate lives, even though the parties generally slept under the same roof, and their activities together were knowingly performed solely for the benefit of their daughter. Husband should not be penalized for attempting to make life for his daughter more pleasurable and his isolated, unsuccessful attempts at reconciliation. We believe that "cohabitation" contemplates more of a martial relationship than what occurred in this case after August 6, 1999. As such, we conclude that the trial court did not err in this regard.

Affirmed.

NOTES AND QUESTIONS

1. In most states where no-fault divorce is available based on a period of separation, consensual separation is not required. *See* HOMER H. CLARK, THE LAW OF DOMESTIC RELATIONS IN THE UNITED STATES 517–18 (2d ed. 1988).

2. Some courts have held that the separation must be coupled with the intention of dissolving the marital relationship. For example, in Sinha v. Sinha, 526 A.2d 765 (Pa. 1987), the husband moved from India to New Jersey to begin a graduate program. Due to visa problems, the wife stayed in India. The husband did not communicate to his wife that there were marital problems until he filed for divorce in Pennsylvania three years after he moved to the United States. The Pennsylvania Supreme Court concluded that, to satisfy the statutory requirement that the spouses have lived separately for three years, at least one spouse must have "a clear intent * * * to dissolve the marital ties at the beginning of the three-year period." Because the husband did not prove such intent, the divorce was not granted.

3. A number of courts have held that separation entails residence in separate dwellings. Thus, in Barnes v. Barnes, 280 S.E.2d 538 (S.C. 1981), the court denied a divorce petition when the parties claimed that they had lived in separate rooms of the marital home and had had no sexual relations during the required separation period. The court held that "[t]his situation encourages collusion between the dissatisfied partners of the marriage." *See also,* Viator v. Miller, 900 So. 2d 1135, 1138 n.1 (La. App. 2005); Marriage of Norviel, 126 Cal. Rptr.2d 148 (App. 2002). *But see In re* Marriage of Kenik, 536 N.E.2d 982 (Ill. App. 1989); *In re* Marriage of A. J. H., 2002 WL 31454020 (Del. Fam. Ct. 2002). What if people cannot afford two separate households? Would they effectively be barred from getting a divorce? Would that be constitutional? *Cf.* Boddie v. Connecticut, 401 U.S. 371 (1971). *See also* Bchara v. Bchara, 563 S.E.2d 398 (Va. App. 2002) (treating a couple living in the same house as "separated" where they slept in separate bedrooms, kept their finances separate, and did not attend church or family functions together). In another Virginia case where the parties slept in separate bedrooms, the court found that they were not

living "separate and apart," where the parties continued to go to social gatherings and church together, and the wife continued to do the cooking, cleaning and laundry for the family. *See* Catalano v. Catalano, 2005 WL 1154251 (Va. Cir. Ct. 2005).

In states where a couple needs to live "separate and apart" for a certain period to obtain a "no-fault" divorce, the question has arisen whether parties are living "separate and apart" if they are living in separate residences but occasionally "date" and sometimes have sex. In Pearson v. Vanlowe, 2005 WL 524597 (Va. App. 2005), the court held that a couple in this circumstance was living separate and apart. In contrast, in Bergeris v. Bergeris, 90 A.3d 553 (Md. App. 2014), the court denied the divorce because, while the parties were living in separate residences, they continued to have sexually explicit telephone conversations.

What is the policy reason for requiring a couple to live separately for a certain period before a no-fault divorce will be granted?

4. The utility of a minimum separation period to deter hasty divorce will depend, in large part, on whether other divorce grounds that do not require such a separation are available. For example, England still has fault grounds in addition to no-fault divorce based on separation; in 1986, three-fourths of all divorces were granted on fault grounds. *See* Law Commission, "Facing the Future: A Discussion Paper on the Ground for Divorce," Law. Com. 170 (1988). An Ohio study reports an even larger percentage of divorcing couples choosing fault divorce rather than utilizing no-fault divorce, which required a two-year separation. *See* Robert E. McGraw et al., *A Case Study in Divorce Law Reform and Its Aftermath*, 20 J. FAM. L. 443, 464 (1982).

4. Summary Divorce Procedures

A few states have adopted summary dissolution (i.e., nonjudicial) divorce procedures for cases in which public policy concerns are minimal. For example, in California, summary dissolution is available if the parties have not had a child (and the wife is not pregnant), the marriage has lasted fewer than five years, neither party owns realty other than a leasehold interest, the community estate does not exceed $25,000 and the family debts do not exceed $4,000, the parties have signed a settlement agreement regarding their rights and liabilities, and no spousal support is sought. *See* CAL. FAM. CODE § 2400. The Oregon provision is similar. *See* OR. REV. STAT. § 107.485.

5. When a Spouse Dies Before a Divorce Action Is Completed

As discussed in Chapter 4, rules applicable to determining the spouses' respective property and support rights differ depending upon whether a marriage is dissolved by death or divorce. Sometimes a spouse dies after a divorce action is initiated and before it is finalized. When this occurs, in most states the divorce action abates, and the marriage is treated as dissolved by death. *See* Camp v. Camp, 128 P.3d 351 (Haw. App. 2006); *In re* Marriage of Rettke, 696 N.W.2d 846 (Minn. App. 2005). This rule was applied, for example, when, after the parties had signed a mediated settlement agreement, the husband died a day or two before a divorce decree was signed. *See In re* Mortner, 130 A.3d 584 (N.H. 2015).

Should the divorce action be abated if one spouse kills the other? *Compare* Simpson v. Simpson, 473 So. 2d 299 (Fla. Dist. Ct. App. 1985) *with* Howsden v. Rolenc, 360 N.W.2d 680 (Neb. 1985).

6. The Possibility of a Bifurcated Divorce

In some states, a couple cannot be "divorced" until all matters in dispute are resolved. In others, the process can be "bifurcated" in that the parties can be "divorced" before the other matters in dispute are resolved. This distinction can be significant, for example, if spouses continue to accumulate marital property until they are divorced.

In *In re* Marriage of Breashears, 65 N.E.3d 955 (Ill. App. 2016), a terminally ill husband had filed for divorce. He wanted to marry another before he died, so the court granted his petition for bifurcated divorce.

7. Impact of Divorce upon Beneficiary Designations

A spouse during marriage almost always designates the other spouse as beneficiary of various benefits; these beneficiary designations are often not changed in connection with divorce. A number of states have enacted statutes which provide that a divorce presumptively revokes any designations during marriage of the other spouse as a beneficiary. If the party desires the beneficiary designations to remain effective after divorce, the designation must be repeated after divorce. *See* COLO. REV. STAT. § 15–11–804; N.M. STAT. ANN § 45–2–804; Estate of Lamparella, 109 P.3d 959 (Ariz. App. 2005) (citing various statutes). If the beneficiary designation is made regarding a fringe benefit received by a spouse as an employee of a private employer, the U.S. Supreme Court has held that, due to ERISA, the benefit needs to be paid to the named beneficiary. *See* Kennedy v. Plan, Adm'r for Dupont Sav. and Inv. Plan, 555 U.S. 285 (2009). It is not yet clear whether, if the recipient has waived the right to the benefit in the divorce, after the benefit is distributed to the beneficiary the decedent's estate could sue the beneficiary and recover the amount distributed. *See* Flesner v. Flesner, 845 F. Supp. 2d 791 (S.D. Tex. 2012) (permitting such a recovery). *Cf.,* Vassil v. Office of Personnel Management, 43 Fam. L. Rep. (BNA) 1147 (E.D. Mich. 2017) (ex-wife is entitled to life insurance proceeds).

3. THE CURRENT DEBATE: WHAT DIVORCE LAW DO WE WANT?

THE LAW COMMISSION (LONDON), FACING THE FUTURE: A DISCUSSION PAPER ON THE GROUND FOR DIVORCE
29–30, 32, 45 (Law Com. No. 170, 1988).

4.3 The move away from pure fault systems seems to reflect an almost universal recognition by legislators that restricting divorce to cases where a particular fault-based ground has been satisfied does not buttress the stability of marriage and does not ensure justice between the spouses, as was originally thought. Thus, provision is made for divorce either on the ground of breakdown or separation in addition to fault-based grounds. The retention of fault-based grounds in the mixed systems would seem to reflect the view that the law must provide a moral framework for marriage. Principally, it is thought that an innocent spouse must always be able to obtain an immediate divorce against a guilty one on the basis of the offence. The fault-based grounds define what behaviour is acceptable and what is not. However, as has been shown above, this view is based on the dubious assumptions that commission of a particular marital offence causes breakdown of marriage and that the victim of that offence is completely innocent. It is recognition that neither assumption is necessarily correct, * * * that has prompted a number of legal systems to remove the element of fault from their divorce laws entirely.

4.7 * * * [I]t would seem that although breakdown is a widely accepted *principle*, experience elsewhere bears out the Commission's earlier view that it is not a justiciable issue. Any attempt at adjudication is likely to reintroduce an element of fault or at least of bitter recrimination. A logical application of the breakdown principle requires divorce on unilateral demand, at least if that demand is persisted in for any length of time. * * *

* * *

4.14 There are two main criticisms [of unilateral divorce on demand]. The first is that it represents the abdication of the State from any responsibility for determining whether a divorce should be granted. Yet, as we have seen, this may be the only logical application of the breakdown principle, which has been so widely accepted as the basis of modern divorce law. If breakdown is not justiciable and any fact chosen to prove breakdown is arbitrary, the only true judges of whether the marriage can continue are the parties themselves. This criticism also fails to address the difficult question of the nature of the State's interest. Once breakdown is accepted as the proper rationale for divorce, it is difficult to devise any logical basis for protecting a spouse who does not wish to be divorced even though the marriage has clearly broken down. The State's real interest may then be in protecting that spouse's financial position (and with it that of the State itself) and the interests of any minor children.

4.15 A second criticism is that if divorce is available immediately on unilateral demand, then parties may be tempted to divorce without having considered the implications thoroughly. The mere fact of requiring a court hearing does not necessarily solve this problem, as the court will not always be able to identify a possibility of reconciliation. The Swedish requirement that in cases involving minor children or lack of consent, the divorce is delayed for a six month "reconsideration period" (unless there has been a two years' separation) is clearly designed to meet the problem of precipitate divorce, although it may be thought too limited. It may, however, be more effective to use the divorce *process*, rather than the ground for divorce, as a means of identifying cases where there is a realistic possibility of reconciliation.

* * *

5.36 Under the present system, in * * * [contested] cases a decree can be refused altogether if this would result in grave financial or other hardship to the respondent and it would in all the circumstances be wrong to dissolve the marriage. This has been restrictively applied, partly because any hardship has usually already resulted from five years' separation [required to obtain a contested no-fault divorce] and will not be materially increased by the divorce itself, save where substantial widow's benefits are at stake, and partly because a liberal application of the provision would circumvent the very policy which led to the 1969 reforms.

5.37 The rationale for this provision was to safeguard the position of the innocent spouse who did not wish to be divorced * * * [but] the implication that only respondents in these cases are wholly innocent and worthy of protection whereas respondents in other cases are not, is unfounded. * * * If we were to move to a wholly no-fault divorce law, there would obviously be a case for extending the protection of a hardship bar to all who wished to invoke it.

5.38 There are considerable attractions in doing so. There is still a substantial economic imbalance between the spouses in most marriages which have lasted for any length of time, particularly where there are children. We cannot conclude from the fact that the hardship bar is hardly ever invoked at present that it is totally ineffective. The * * * hardship bar at the end may well have an effect upon the bargaining of couples * * * To remove all the obstacles to divorce by the economically more powerful spouse, without giving any protection to the weak, might well be thought objectionable.

5.39 However, there are objections to using a hardship bar to supply that protection. If divorce were impossible in cases where hardship could not be avoided, it would defeat the object of enabling dead marriages to be dissolved in due course. * * * [I]t would deny divorce to the poor or not-so-poor who were unable to make proper provision. It might well be necessary to reintroduce notions of fault in order to ensure that divorces were not denied to deserving spouses in such cases. There clearly will be cases in which to deny one spouse a divorce on the ground that it will cause hardship to the other will be to cause as much if not more hardship to the first.

* * *

6.2 We suggest that the principle that divorce should be available when, but only when, a marriage has irretrievably broken down should be retained. Several methods of establishing this are discussed. * * *

6.3 Two proposals * * * emerge as the most realistic. These are:

(a) divorce after a period of separation; and

(b) divorce after a period of transition in which the parties are given time and encouragement to reflect and make the necessary arrangements for the future.

Following the Commission report, the English Parliament adopted legislation that retained fault grounds and added two no-fault grounds: separation for two years with mutual consent, and separation for five years. This legislation retained the "grave hardship" divorce defense described in sections 5.36–5.39 of the Law Commission Report.

In 1996, Parliament adopted a new Family Law Act. The 1996 Act retained the earlier "grave hardship" defense to divorce, but replaced the prior mix of fault and no-fault divorce grounds with one ground. The new ground was "irretrievable breakdown" coupled with a compulsory nine-month "period for reflection and consideration" and attendance at an "information meeting" aimed at educating the divorce applicant about:

a. marriage counselling and other marriage support services;

b. the importance to be attached to the welfare, wishes and feelings of children;

c. how the parties may acquire a better understanding of the ways in which children can be helped to cope with the breakdown of a marriage;

d. the nature of the financial questions that may arise on divorce or separation, and services which are available to help the parties;

> e.   protection available against violence, and how to obtain support and assistance;
>
> f.   mediation;
>
> g.   the availability to each of the parties of independent legal advice and representation;
>
> h.   the principles of legal aid and where the parties can get advice about obtaining legal aid;
>
> i.   the divorce and separation process.

1996 Act 8. Under the Act, a spouse could file a "statement of marital breakdown" three months after attending an information meeting; a nine-month "period of reflection and consideration" to permit the parties to "reflect on whether the marriage can be saved[,] . . . to have an opportunity to effect a reconciliation, and consider what arrangements should be made for the future" commenced fourteen days after filing of a marital-breakdown statement. 1996 Act 7. If one spouse opposed the divorce and requested an extension or if the couple had a child under the age of six months, the reflection period would be extended for another six months unless a domestic violence order had been entered. 1996 Act 5, 7.

After passage of the 1996 Act, the government initiated a number of pilot projects to determine the best type of informational meeting. In 2001, the government announced that it had abandoned this effort:

> Different types of information meetings have been tested in pilot schemes for two years. But the research concludes that none of the six models of meeting was good enough for the implementation * * * on a nationwide basis. * * * Six models of information meeting were piloted. * * * The research showed that, although those attending valued the provision of information, the information meetings were not effective in helping most people to save their marriages, as these meetings came too late. The evidence showed that the meeting tended to incline those who were uncertain about their marriage towards divorce. They were too inflexible to provide people with information tailored to their personal needs. In addition, in the great majority of cases, only the person petitioning for divorce attended the meeting, but marriage counselling, conciliatory divorce and mediation depend for their success on the willing involvement of both parties.

Lord Chancellor's Dep't, *Press Release, Divorce Law Reform—Government Proposes to Repeal Part II of the Family Law Act,* http://www.gnn.gov.uk/ Content/51fDetail.asp?ReleaseID=25847&NewsAreaID=2. Based on these disappointing results and fear that the Act's "complex procedures . . . would be likely to lead to significant delay and uncertainty . . . over the divorce process which will be unhelpful for families at what is always a difficult and emotional time," the Government declined to proceed with implementation of the 1996 Act and urged "Parliament to repeal it once a suitable legislative opportunity occurs." *Id.*

Throughout the English no-fault experiment, the older fault grounds for divorce have remained in effect. A British solicitor's divorce-information website thus advises prospective clients that, "[a]lthough divorces based on * * * [no-fault] grounds are by no means uncommon, in practice most divorces are based either on unreasonable behaviour or adultery. The reason for this is that neither of these two grounds involve the wait which the other grounds involve. When a marriage breaks down it is not usually too difficult to find some instances of unreasonable behaviour on either or both sides and so this is, not unnaturally, seen as a route to a quick divorce * * * " http://www.terry.co.uk/divorce.html.

Perhaps ironically given the high U.S. divorce rate, American critics of no-fault divorce have been more willing than their British counterparts to abandon no-fault divorce in at least some situations. Their criticisms of no-fault divorce fall into several diverse categories.

1.   Divorce Bargaining under Fault and No-Fault Divorce.

Some critics have focused on the divorce bargaining process. Fault divorce provided the virtuous spouse a very large bargaining chip; he or she could block the guilty spouse's ability to obtain a divorce. Professor Allen Parkman has argued that, because of the loss of the fault bargaining chip, unilateral divorce enables one spouse to obtain a divorce without adequately compensating the other for sacrifices made during marriage; mutual consent divorce, he asserts, would enhance the bargaining power of the spouse who is not seeking a divorce, increasing the probability that he or she would receive adequate compensation in the divorce. *See* ALLEN PARKMAN, NO-FAULT DIVORCE: WHAT WENT WRONG? (1992). Alternatively, Professor Mary Ann Glendon has suggested that the potential for economic hardship occasioned by unilateral no-fault divorce could be lessened by granting judges the power to deny a divorce based on a showing of exceptional hardship. *See* MARY ANN GLENDON, ABORTION AND DIVORCE IN WESTERN LAW 74 (1987); MARY ANN GLENDON, THE TRANSFORMATION OF FAMILY LAW 192 (1989).

Similar criticisms of no-fault divorce were made earlier by Professor Lenore Weitzman, who undertook a pioneering study of California's no-fault divorce law. Weitzman found that the likelihood of receiving alimony, the duration of alimony awards, and the proportion of marital property awarded women all decreased following the introduction of no-fault and thus argued that "[t]he major economic result of the divorce law revolution is the systematic impoverishment of divorced women and their children." *See* LENORE J. WEITZMAN, THE DIVORCE REVOLUTION 74, 164–67 (1985).

The available data fail to support Weitzman's claims. First, Weitzman's assertion assumes that the spouse who will typically wish to resist divorce is the wife. While that assertion may well have been true in 1970 when women had fewer economic opportunities outside marriage, by the early 1990s more than half of the divorced women interviewed by the Gallup Organization said that it was their idea to separate, as compared with only 44 per cent of men. Paul M. DeWitt, *Breaking Up is Hard to Do*, AMERICAN DEMOGRAPHICS, Oct. 1992, at 53. *See also* Sanford L. Braver et al., *Who Divorced Whom? Methodological and Theoretical Issues*, 20 J. DIVORCE & REMARRIAGE 1 (1993). This pattern is evident even in China, where a government study found that women had initiated 70% of divorce applications in Guangdong Province in 2004. *See* Jim Yardley, *Women in China Embrace Divorce as Stigma Eases*, N.Y. TIMES, Oct. 4, 2005, at A1.

Weitzman's assertion also neglects the fact that California, like many other states that adopted no-fault divorce, contemporaneously overhauled its rules governing alimony and property distribution. Professor Marsha Garrison reviewed research on divorce outcomes in a number of states before and after no-fault divorce was adopted and compared them to her own research results in New York, which changed its alimony and property distribution rules but did not adopt unilateral no-fault divorce. She found that divorced wives in New York who retained their fault bargaining chips were no more likely to receive an alimony award than were divorced wives in no-fault states. *See* Marsha Garrison, *The Economics of Divorce: Changing Rules, Changing Results, in* DIVORCE REFORM AT THE CROSSROADS 90–100 (Stephen D. Sugarman & Herma H. Kay eds. 1990).

2. The "Message" of No-Fault.

Other critics of no-fault divorce have been less troubled by bargaining endowments than by no-fault's message about marital commitment:

> The error of treating romantic love as the necessary condition for entering into marriage, and, more importantly, for continuing marriage has been by far the more harmful * * * As a social matter * * * the problem is not that love drives us only temporarily insane and that we eventually discover that our mate is not whom or what we thought. It is, rather, that we accept the belief that taking on, and adhering to, the life-long responsibility of marriage and children should be tied to the continuance of so ephemeral a thing as romantic love. This flawed notion has enticed millions of people to abandon marriage when romantic love faded, and, perhaps more importantly, it has led the rest of society to assent and to treat the absence of romantic love as an excuse, even a justification, for abandoning a marriage. Societal acceptance in turn encourages people to act toward their spouses without love, honor or respect, knowing that they can leave should they discover

that they have "grown apart." That the law has assented to this cultural change by permitting divorce willy-nilly is independently harmful. But the liberalization of divorce laws was less the cause, and more the effect, of a widespread cultural acceptance of men and women renouncing their marriage vows.

Lloyd Cohen, *Rhetoric, The Unnatural Family, and Women's Work,* 81 VA. L. REV. 2275, 2291 (1995).

A related claim relates to marriage incentives:

[Unilateral no-fault divorce] creates [incentives] for marriages designed from the outset to end in divorce. A poor young woman marries a rich old man, knowing that every year his income exceeds his expenses and produces substantial savings. At the end of five years, pursuant to her original intention, she dissolves the marriage and claims one half of the savings built up during it. Unilateral divorce * * * fosters the symmetrical incentive for unscrupulous poor women to marry rich men.

RICHARD POSNER, ECONOMIC ANALYSIS OF LAW 134 (3d ed. 1986).

Finally, some commentators argue that divorce *should* be about fault:

Under * * * [no-fault] a wrongdoing husband can come home every Saturday night for five years, drunk and penniless because of skirt-chasing, gambling, or some other misdeeds; then, he may beat, bruise and abuse his wife because he is unhappy with himself, and then he will be permitted to go down and get a divorce on printed forms purchased at a department store and tell the trial judge that the marriage is "irretrievably broken." Or, the offending wife, after jumping from bed to bed with her new found paramours, chronically drunk, and when at home nagging, brawling and quarreling, all against the wishes of a faithful husband who remains at home nurturing the children, is permitted to divorce her husband who does not desire a divorce, but rather, has one forced upon him, not because of anything he has done, but because the offending wife tells the trial court that her marriage is "irretrievably broken." In my opinion, the offending spouse should not have standing to obtain a divorce if the innocent one invokes the doctrine that, "He who comes into equity must come with clean hands."

Ryan v. Ryan, 277 So. 2d 266, 278 (Fla. 1973) (Roberts, J., dissenting).

These claims are difficult to evaluate. Undeniably, no-fault divorce sends a different message about marital commitment than does fault divorce. But there is evidence to suggest that a shift in public attitudes toward marital commitment set the stage for no-fault divorce, rather than the reverse. And it is quite unclear what role, if any, divorce grounds play in determining divorce behavior; certainly the message of fault divorce did not suffice to prevent widespread fraud and collusion. Finally, the message of fault may hinder reconciliation and make it more difficult for a couple to work together after divorce. *See* GWYNN DAVIS & MERVYN MURCH, GROUNDS FOR DIVORCE (1988) (arguing in favor of no-fault divorce).

3.   The Impact of No-Fault Divorce on the Divorce Rate.

Other critics have focused on the divorce rate, claiming that no-fault divorce increased the number of couples who divorce. Researchers have been analyzing this claim for the past generation, but the answer is still unclear. It is clear that divorce rates rose following the introduction of no-fault in the late 1960s and 1970s. It is also clear that divorce rates had been rising for the entire century that preceded this legal innovation. Did the advent of no-fault contribute significantly to the preexisting trend? Most observers of the U.S. data have found that it did in the short-run, but over the long run, there is no agreement whatsoever; some researchers argue in favor of independent effects while others argue that the divorce reforms had no long-term impact and were themselves the product of a longer-term cultural shift. *Compare* Norval Glenn, *Further Discussion of the Effects of No-Fault Divorce on Divorce Rates,* 59 J. MARRIAGE & FAM. 800 (1999) and Ira Ellman & Sharon Lohr, *Dissolving the Relationship Between Divorce Rates and Divorce Laws,* 18 INT'L J. ECON. 341 (1998) *with* Douglas W. Allen, *The Impact of Legal Reforms on Marriage and Divorce, in* THE LAW AND ECONOMICS OF MARRIAGE AND DIVORCE 191 (Antony W. Dnes & Robert Rowthorn eds., 2002) & Rogers et al., *Did No-Fault Divorce Legislation Matter? Definitely Yes and Sometimes No,* 61 J. MARRIAGE & FAM. 803 (1999). One recent research report concludes that the data do not permit rejection of "either moderately positive or moderately negative [long-term] changes," but that none of the estimates "suggest that unilateral divorce laws can explain much of the rise in the divorce rate over the past half century". JUSTIN WOLFERS, DID UNILATERAL DIVORCE LAWS RAISE DIVORCE RATES? A RECONCILIATION AND NEW RESULTS (2005), http://bpp. wharton.upenn.edu/jwolfers/Papers/ Divorce.pdf.

There is less research on the impact of no-fault divorce outside the United States, but one recent report which analyzed divorce trends across 18 European nations between 1950 and 2003 found that reforms which "made divorce easier" were followed by significant increases in divorce rates. The researchers concluded that the "effect of no-fault legislation was strong and permanent, while unilateral reforms only had a temporary effect on divorce rates." Overall, they estimate that the legal reforms account for about 20% of the increase in divorce rates in Europe between 1960 and 2002. *See* Libertad Gonzalez & Tarja K. Vitanen, *The Effect of Divorce Laws on Divorce Rates in Europe,* IZA Discussion Paper No. 2023 (2006), http://papers.ssrn.com/sol3/papers.cfm?abstract_id=892354.

4.   The Impact of No-Fault Divorce on Children.

An argument related to the claim that no-fault divorce has increased divorce rates is that it is bad for children. Children's standard of living tends to fall after divorce, and in all nations single-parent households are more vulnerable to poverty than are two-parent households. Some nations provide child-related benefits that offset much of this advantage; other nations—and particularly the United States—do not. In addition to the economic disadvantage of divorce, accumulating research data demonstrates that *except in high-conflict marriages*, children in single-parent households are comparatively disadvantaged in many other ways. Researcher after researcher has documented the fact that children in single-parent households are more likely to experience poor health, behavioral problems, delinquency, and low educational attainment than their peers in intact families. Although lower socioeconomic status explains about half of these differences, the other half appears to result from differences in care and parental investment.

The advantage of being raised with and by both biological parents appears to extend into a child's adulthood and even to his or her children. Researchers have documented a strong link between growing up in a single-parent household and adult income, health, and emotional stability. A number of studies have also found that both men and women who experience a single-parent household as children are more likely, as adults, to experience marital discord and to divorce or separate. *See* SARA MCLANAHAN & GARY SANDEFUR, GROWING UP WITH A SINGLE PARENT: WHAT HURTS, WHAT HELPS 39–63 (1994)*;* Wendy Sigle-Rushton & Sara McLanahan, *Father Absence and Child Well-Being: A Critical Review, in* THE FUTURE OF THE FAMILY 116, 120–22 (Daniel P. Moynihan et al., eds., 2004). And researchers who examined links between child outcomes and divorce in the grandparent generation have reported that grandparental divorce is significantly associated with less education, more marital discord, more divorce, and greater tension in early parent-child relationships. *See* Paul R. Amato & Jacob Cheadle, *The Long Reach of Divorce: Divorce and Child Well-Being Across Three Generations*, 67 J. MARRIAGE & FAM. 191, 193 (2005).

Two-parent care is associated with advantages to children at all income levels and across national boundaries. Even in Sweden, where public support ensures a child poverty rate of less than 3%, single parenthood remains a serious risk factor for children. The most compelling study, which analyzed almost a million cases and took account of possibly confounding factors such as socioeconomic status and parental mental health, found that Swedish children in single-parent households showed significantly increased risks of "all adverse outcomes analyzed, including psychiatric disease, suicide or suicide attempt, injury, and addiction." Gunilla Ringback Weitoft et al., *Mortality, Severe Morbidity, and Injury in*

Children Living with Single Parents in Sweden: A Population-Based Study, 361 LANCET 289 (2003).

Given this evidence, one prominent pair of researchers has argued that parents in low-conflict marriages should stay together for their children's benefit:

> Although maintaining an unhappy but low conflict marriage entails a degree of sacrifice from spouses, this situation may not be as onerous as some might think. Most adults live more than two-thirds of their lives without children in the household. Spending one-third of one's life living in a marriage that is less than satisfactory in order to benefit children—children that parents elected to bring into the world—is not an unreasonable expectation. This idea is especially compelling, given that many people who divorce and remarry find that their second marriage is no happier than their first. Furthermore, such an arrangement provides an important benefit for parents that helps to balance the cost: parents—especially fathers—are able to maintain continuous relations with coresident children. Given the pain experienced by most noncustodial parents following separation from their children, this should be an incentive to invest extra effort in the marital relationship.

PAUL R. AMATO & ALAN BOOTH, A GENERATION AT RISK: GROWING UP IN AN ERA OF FAMILY UPHEAVAL 238 (1997).

Whatever the merits of the arguments against no-fault divorce, within the past few years, legislators in some states have taken them seriously. Laws making divorce more difficult for couples with minor children have been introduced in several states. *See* Vobejda, *Breaking Up Called Far Too Easy To Do,* HOUS. CHRON., March 12, 1996, at 7A. col. 1. Although none of these proposals have been enacted, in 1997, Louisiana enacted a divorce law which allows a couple to choose at the time of marriage what grounds for divorce will be available. If both spouses sign, before marriage, an affidavit that their marriage is a "covenant marriage" it may be dissolved only if a fault ground is proved or if the parties have been separated for two years (three and a half years in the case of minor children). LA. REV. STAT. §§ 9: 273, 9: 307.

Arizona adopted a similar measure in 1998, although the Arizona law permits couples who opt for covenant marriage to nonetheless divorce on no-fault grounds if both spouses consent at the time divorce is sought. *See* ARIZ. REV. STAT. § 25–901. Arkansas also adopted a covenant marriage law in 2001. The statute permits divorce based on a two-year separation as well as fault grounds.

The covenant marriage option did not initially appeal to a large segment of the marrying public. In Louisiana, of 4,148 marriage license applications filed in 2000, only 115 sought covenant marriage. *See Covenant Marriages on Decline*, SUNDAY ADVOC. (Baton Rouge, La.). Feb. 4, 2001, at 23.

Whatever the merits of the arguments against no-fault divorce, the trend in favor of easy divorce thus seems irresistible: despite a lot of talk, no nation has reversed its no-fault enactments and returned to a fault regime. Instead, they have moved toward shorter waiting periods and less time-consuming and expensive procedures.

Problem 12-2:

Evaluate the merits of the following divorce regimes:

1.   Pure fault-based divorce;

2.   Fault-based divorce plus divorce based on mutual consent;

3.   Fault-based divorce plus divorce based on a period of separation;

4.   Divorce based solely on mutual consent;

5.   Divorce based solely on a period of separation;

6.   Divorce based either on mutual consent or a period of separation;

7.   Divorce based on a period of separation, with a "hardship" exception;

8.   Pure no-fault divorce (i.e., divorce at the request of either spouse);

9.   A "private choice" divorce rule, like that adopted in Louisiana.

What are the advantages of each approach in terms of fairness, judicial economy, and promoting marital stability? the disadvantages? Which approach, on balance, should the legislature adopt?

4. ALTERNATIVES TO DIVORCE

A. SEPARATE MAINTENANCE AND DIVORCE FROM BED AND BOARD

When judicial divorce became available, many states continued to permit courts to grant divorces *a mensa et thoro* (i.e., from bed and board) which provided legal separation without the right to remarry. Other states abolished divorce *a mensa et thoro* and enacted "separate maintenance" statutes that permitted a judge to compel support for a spouse living separately.

Technically, divorce *a mensa et thoro* requires the spouses to live apart and nullifies the marital obligation of cohabitation, while separate maintenance enforces the spouse's support obligation and favors a resumption of cohabitation. Under a decree of divorce *a mensa et thoro*, the court may settle the property interests of the parties; under a separate maintenance decree, marital property rights may continue to accrue. Divorce *a mensa et thoro* thus provides a potentially valuable alternative to full divorce where the parties (1) want to settle the full range of their economic affairs, (2) do not intend to remarry, (3) want to preserve entitlements available to spouses under public or private benefit plans, such as social security insurance, survivors' benefits or state or private pensions, worker's compensation or health care plans or (4) are religiously or emotionally opposed to full divorce. For example, in D.L.J. v. B.R.J., 887 So. 2d 242 (Ala. App. 2003), the parties sought a legal separation so the wife could retain health insurance through the husband's employer. And in Estate of Carlisle, 653 N.W.2d 368 (Iowa 2002), the wife was treated as the surviving spouse with a forced share right when the husband died after a separate maintenance decree had been entered.

The two remedies have different tax consequences. Under the Internal Revenue Code, a divorce *a mensa et thoro* is treated as a dissolution of the marital status while a separate maintenance decree is interpreted as maintaining it. While Internal Revenue Code § 143(a) (*cf.* § 71) specifies that an individual "shall not be considered as married" if "legally separated from his spouse under a decree of divorce or of separate maintenance," court decisions have interpreted this language to mandate a decree that *requires* the parties to live apart. Under a separate maintenance decree, one spouse thus may demand that the other participate in filing a joint return. Separate maintenance also does not allow filing separately under the "singles" tax tables, nor is the payor entitled to deduct support paid as alimony.

THEISEN V. THEISEN
Supreme Court of South Carolina. 2011.
716 S.E.2d 27.

HEARN, JUDGE.

This case presents the novel issue of whether an action for separate maintenance and support can be pursued when the parties are still living together. We hold that it cannot and affirm the family court's decision to dismiss this action. Due to our conclusion that this action fails a matter of law, we further hold that the family court did not err in cancelling the *lis pendens* and request for attorney's fees filed in conjunction with this suit.

Wife argues the family court erred in dismissing her complaint because she failed to allege she was living separate and apart from Husband. We disagree.

Section 20–3–130(B)(5) of the South Carolina Code . . . contains the following provisions regarding separate maintenance:

> Alimony and separate maintenance and support awards may be granted *pendente lite* and permanently in such amounts and for periods of time subject to conditions as the court considers just including, but not limited to: . . .
>
> > (5) Separate maintenance and support to be paid periodically, but terminating upon the continued cohabitation of the supported spouse, upon divorce of the parties, or upon the death of either spouse . . . and terminable and modifiable based upon changed circumstances in the future. The purpose of this form of support may include, but is not limited to, circumstances where a divorce is not sought, but it is necessary to provide for support of the supported spouse by way of separate maintenance and support when the parties are living separate and apart.

Initially, we note that section 20–3–130(B)(5) does not specifically state whether the parties must live separate and apart prior to petitioning the court for separate maintenance. However, the very name *separate* maintenance and support connotes separation between the parties. "Separate" means "to set or keep apart" or "become divided or detached." Merriam-Webster Dictionary, http://www.merriam-webster.com/dictionary/separate. Thus, the purpose of separate maintenance is to provide support for a spouse when he or she is living apart from the other spouse. The statute also specifically states that it applies when the parties are living separate and apart but a divorce is not sought. The fact that separate maintenance terminates upon the continuous cohabitation of the supported spouse with another is more evidence of the same; the supported spouse cannot cohabitate with another unless he has already separated from the payor spouse. Furthermore, Wife's emphasis that she sleeps in a different room than Husband appears to be a tacit recognition on her part that at least some degree of separation is required.

We implicitly have recognized for years that living separate and apart is a requirement for separate maintenance. Under South Carolina law, a spouse does not need grounds that would merit a divorce in order to receive separate maintenance. We have thus refused to define any specific grounds and instead have left this decision to the discretion of the family court. However, we have often searched for whether there was justification—whatever that justification may be—for the supported spouse to *leave* the marital home.

While we have never specifically addressed the precise question presented here, we have addressed whether a spouse must leave the marital home when seeking a divorce, despite no statutory language directly on point. If the parties are seeking a no-fault divorce based on one year's continuous separation, they must live in separate domiciles during that time. Our rationale was that otherwise, evidence of the actual separation, which is the gravamen of a no-fault divorce, would exist only "behind the closed doors of the matrimonial domicile," thus encouraging collusion between the parties. The same rule applies if the parties seek a divorce on the fault ground of desertion.

On the other hand, citing public policy concerns and the diminished threat of collusion or condonation, we refused to extend that rule to parties seeking a fault-based divorce on any other ground. In those fault-based situations it is better to permit the separating spouse to remain in the home at the time of filing, and have custody and other living arrangements dealt with at a temporary hearing, than to require that spouse to vacate the home and potentially cause more disruption in the family's life at the time of filing.

The public policy concerns that drove our decision in *Watson* are not present here. Therefore, in order to state a claim for separate maintenance, the complaint must allege that the parties are living separate and apart. To hold otherwise would permit spouses to inundate the family court with claims following relatively minor disputes and quarrels. Because there are no defined grounds for this relief, parties could bring an action in the family court for almost any reason absent some threshold requirement. Requiring spouses to separate stems this tide by helping guarantee that court intervention into the marital relationship actually is truly necessary because the grounds underlying the complaint will at least be enough to warrant leaving the marital home.

We affirm the order of the family court dismissing Wife's complaint for separate maintenance because she failed to allege that she and Husband were living separate and apart at the time of filing. Furthermore, because Wife's *lis pendens* and claim for attorney's fees hinge on the validity of her complaint, we find no error in the family court's denial of that relief to Wife.

B. ANNULMENT

In the strict sense, an annulment is a judicial declaration that, by reason of a defect in its inception, a purported marriage does not now and has never existed. Annulment stems from the same canonical roots that gave us divorce and separate maintenance, and religious annulment remains important within the Catholic Church; a judicial annulment is not necessary to obtain a religious annulment. Religious annulments are separate proceedings that have no impact upon state divorce law. For example, if a tribunal of the Roman Catholic Church concluded that a marriage was void and granted an annulment, this would have no impact upon the parties' prior divorce decree. *See* Age v. Age, 340 S.W.3d 88 (Ky. App. 2011).

Typical grounds for judicial annulment—reflecting the restrictions on marriage described in Chapter 2—include youth, mental incapacity, impotence, insanity, and lack of consent. A ground for annulment must have existed at the time of marriage; a ground arising later might serve as the basis for a divorce, but not an annulment. In the absence of an applicable annulment statute (Illinois, for example, did not have one until 1977), courts have asserted jurisdiction in equity to annul a marriage.

Equitable doctrines, including variants of the clean hands doctrine, estoppel, ratification and laches, are often defenses to an annulment action, especially where the defect is primarily of interest to the partners. For instance, the underage "defrauder" of the adult spouse may be estopped from attacking the marriage; or the adult "victim" may be held to have ratified the marriage (but only after obtaining knowledge of the fraud or after the proper age for marriage has been reached). Of course, the partners may not ratify a marriage that offends an important public policy, such as the prohibition on incest. In the case of bigamy, however, UMDA § 207(b), where adopted, validates a void marriage upon divorce from or the death of the "surplus" spouse, but only as of the time the impediment is removed.

Although some case law permits annulment based on a "material misrepresentation," *(see* Kober v. Kober, 211 N.E.2d 817 (N.Y. 1965) (annulment granted where husband concealed his Nazi past and fanatical anti-Semitism)), traditionally courts required fraud going to the "essentials of the marriage." *See* Reynolds v. Reynolds, 85 Mass. (3 Allen) 605 (1862); Bilowit v. Dolitsky, 304 A.2d 774 (N.J. Super. Ch. Div. 1973) (husband misrepresented that he was practicing Orthodox Jew). The line of distinction between fraud going to the "essentials" and lesser misrepresentation is not always easy to discern. Nor is the case law necessarily consistent. States with narrow divorce grounds (New York, New Jersey) often tended toward a liberal view of fraud; some courts have taken the position that an unconsummated marriage should be annulled more readily.

Couples today often marry in one state and then move to another. If they marry in a state with a "liberal" annulment standard, and move to another state with a "strict" standard, and an annulment action is filed in the second state, which state's annulment law should be applied? *See In re* Geraghty, 150 A.3d 386 (N.H. 2016) (applying forum annulment law).

A question sometimes arises regarding who has standing to assert an annulment claim. Sometimes a person's executor or another family member attempts to seek an annulment of a marriage of the party who has died. For example, a daughter of Richard Pryor, after he died, attempted to annul his marriage to a caregiver celebrated shortly before he died. The court ruled that the daughter did not have standing to seek an annulment. *See* Pryor v. Pryor, 99 Cal. Rptr. 3d 853 (App. 2009); Morris v. Goodwin, 148 A.3d 63 (Md. App. 2016). The majority rule is that only the parties themselves can petition for an annulment.

In some cases the litigant will have a choice between annulment and divorce. Depending on the litigant's circumstances and state law, the weight of advantages may lie with either choice. Annulment traditionally did not permit the grant of alimony or a division of property rights but did revive the alimony obligation of an earlier marriage. This result flowed from the fact that an annulment voids the marriage from its inception. Carried to its logical conclusion, children born during the annulled marriage are illegitimate and rights based on marital status (for example, a divorced wife's entitlement to Social Security benefits based on her husband's Social Security contributions) must be cancelled.

Because this "logical" approach would often produce inequitable results, today children of an annulled marriage are considered legitimate; alimony and property rights may be granted after an annulment; alimony generally is not revived after the nullification of any attempted later marriage; government benefits typically do not hinge on whether the marriage was annulled or terminated through divorce. *See generally* Carla M. Venkoff, *Divorce or Death, Remarriage and Annulment: The Path Toward Reinstating Financial Obligations from a Previous Marriage,* 37 BRANDEIS L. J. 435 (1998). However, while joint income tax returns filed during a voidable marriage survive an annulment, this is *not* so in the case of a void marriage.

The UMDA goes further and treats void and voidable marriages alike in terms of (1) legal consequences, (2) the circle of persons permitted to attack a defective marriage, and (3) the need for a formal "declaration of invalidity." The UMDA also provides flexibility on the question of retroactivity. Declarations of invalidity are retroactive "unless the court finds, after a consideration of all relevant circumstances, including the effect of a retroactive decree on third parties, that the interests of justice would be served by making the decree not retroactive." In that case, "the provisions * * * relating to property rights of the spouses, maintenance, support, and custody of children on dissolution of marriage are applicable" (UMDA § 208(e)). In terms of outcome, the non-retroactive declaration of invalidity turns into the equivalent of divorce. Of course, in dividing property and awarding support the court will consider equitable factors. So, in *In re* Marriage of Joel and Roohi, 2012 WL 3127305 (Colo. App.), the court held that where a woman fraudulently induced a man to marry her so she could get a green card, the court held the marriage invalid, no spousal support should be awarded, and that the woman should be awarded property only to the extent she financially contributed.

Some cases have involved the situation where spouses believe they are married, and then discover that one of the parties have a prior marriage that was not dissolved. For example, in Splawn v. Splawn, 429 S.E.2d 805 (S.C. 1993) the wife filed for divorce. She then discovered that the husband's prior marriage had not been dissolved, (He apparently had retained a lawyer and instructed him to obtain a divorce but this did not occur). She contended that the marriage was therefore void and the parties should be treated like cohabitants. The divorce court granted an annulment and also equitably divided the parties' property; the South Carolina Supreme Court affirmed. (Note that in states that accept the concept of "putative spouse", (see Chapter 3), a remedy could be provided in such cases on this basis as well.)

C. DISSOLVING CIVIL UNIONS AND DOMESTIC PARTNERSHIPS

Before same-sex marriage was recognized in 2015, a number of states created some sort of new status other than marriage for gay couples. The rights and responsibilities resulting from entering into this new status, sometimes called a "civil union" or a "domestic partnership," were not uniform. Some states created a status that was intended to be the equivalent of the rights and responsibilities of a married couple.

After gay marriage was accepted, different states have responded in different ways. For example, in 2013 Delaware enacted a law providing that all civil unions not dissolved by 2013 would be converted to marriages. In some states, however, civil union status continues as a separate status. This creates the question of how parties can dissolve the separate status. Not all states accept or recognize civil unions. In states that recognize civil unions, most have established residency requirements for dissolutions. Parties might live in a state that does not recognize their relationship status and want to dissolve their relationship. The Vermont Supreme Court has ruled that those who have established a Vermont civil union may dissolve it in Vermont even if both parties are non-residents, if they establish that their current state of residence does not permit a civil union. *See* Soloman v. Guidry, 2016 WL 5338492 (Vermont 2016). A Pennsylvania court has held that it could dissolve a Vermont civil union. *See* Neyman v. Buckley, 43 Fam. L. Rep. (BNA) 1107 (Pa. Super. 2016).

5. ACCESS TO DIVORCE

BODDIE V. CONNECTICUT

Supreme Court of the United States, 1971.
401 U.S. 371.

JUSTICE HARLAN delivered the opinion of the Court.

Appellants, welfare recipients residing in the State of Connecticut, brought this action in the Federal District Court for the District of Connecticut on behalf of themselves and others similarly situated, challenging, as applied to them, certain state procedures for the commencement of litigation, including requirements for payment of court fees and costs for service of process, that restrict their access to the courts in their effort to bring an action for divorce. * * *

As this Court on more than one occasion has recognized, marriage involves interests of basic importance in our society. See, e.g., *Loving v. Virginia*, 388 U.S. 1 (1967); *Skinner v. Oklahoma*, 316 U.S. 535; *Meyer v. Nebraska*, 262 U.S. 390 (1923). It is not surprising, then, that the States have seen fit to oversee many aspects of that institution. Without a prior judicial imprimatur, individuals may freely enter into and rescind commercial contracts, for example, but we are unaware of any jurisdiction where private citizens may covenant for or dissolve marriages without state approval. Even where all substantive requirements are concededly met, we know of no instance where two consenting adults may divorce and mutually liberate themselves from the constraints of legal obligations that go with marriage, and more fundamentally the prohibition against remarriage, without invoking the State's judicial machinery.

Prior cases establish, first, that due process requires, at a minimum, that absent a countervailing state interest of overriding significance, persons forced to settle their claims of right and duty through the judicial process must be given a meaningful opportunity to be heard.

* * *

Our cases further establish that a statute or a rule may be held constitutionally invalid as applied when it operates to deprive an individual of a protected right although its general validity as a measure enacted in the legitimate exercise of state power is beyond question. Thus, in cases involving religious freedom, free speech or assembly, this Court has often held that a valid statute was unconstitutionally applied in particular circumstances because it interfered with an individual's exercise of those rights. * * *

Just as a generally valid notice procedure may fail to satisfy due process because of the circumstances of the defendant, so too a cost requirement, valid on its face, may offend due process because it operates to foreclose a particular party's opportunity to be heard. The State's obligations under the Fourteenth Amendment are not simply generalized ones; rather, the State owes to each individual that process which, in light of the values of a free society, can be characterized as due.

Drawing upon the principles established by the cases just canvassed, we conclude that the State's refusal to admit these appellants to its courts, the sole means in Connecticut for obtaining a divorce, must be regarded as the equivalent of denying them an opportunity to be heard upon their claimed right to a dissolution of their marriages, and, in the absence of a sufficient countervailing justification for the State's action, a denial of due process.

The arguments for this kind of fee and cost requirement are that the State's interest in the prevention of frivolous litigation is substantial, its use of court fees and process costs to allocate scarce resources is rational, and its balance between the defendant's right to notice and the plaintiff's right to access is reasonable.

In our opinion, none of these considerations is sufficient to override the interest of these plaintiff-appellants in having access to the only avenue open for dissolving their allegedly untenable marriages. Not only is there no necessary connection between a litigant's assets and the seriousness of his motives in bringing suit, but it is here beyond present dispute that appellants bring these actions in good faith. Moreover, other alternatives exist to fees and cost requirements as a means for conserving the time of courts and protecting parties from frivolous litigation, such as penalties for false pleadings or affidavits, and actions for malicious prosecution or abuse of process, to mention only a few. In the same vein we think that reliable alternatives exist to service of process by a state-paid sheriff if the State is unwilling to assume the cost of official service. This is perforce true of service by publication which is the method of notice least calculated to bring to a potential defendant's attention the pendency of judicial proceedings. We think in this case service at defendant's last known address by mail and posted notice is equally effective as publication in a newspaper.

We are thus left to evaluate the State's asserted interest in its fee and cost requirements as a mechanism of resource allocation or cost recoupment. Such a justification was offered and rejected in *Griffin v. Illinois*, 351 U.S. 12 (1956). In *Griffin* it was the requirement of a transcript beyond the means of the indigent that blocked access to the judicial process. While in *Griffin* the transcript could be waived as a convenient but not necessary predicate to court access, here the State invariably imposes the costs as a measure of allocating its judicial resources. Surely, then, the rationale of *Griffin* covers this case.

Very narrow application of decision

In concluding that the Due Process Clause of the Fourteenth Amendment requires that these appellants be afforded an opportunity to go into court to obtain a divorce, we wish to re-emphasize that we go no further than necessary to dispose of the case before us, a case where the *bona fides* of both appellants' indigency and desire for divorce are here beyond dispute. We do not decide that access for all individuals to the courts is a right that is, in all circumstances, guaranteed by the Due Process Clause of the Fourteenth Amendment so that its exercise may not be placed beyond the reach of any individual, for, as we have already noted, in the case before us this right is the exclusive precondition to the adjustment of a fundamental human relationship. The requirement that these appellants resort to the judicial process is entirely a state-created matter. Thus we hold only that a State may not, consistent with the obligations imposed on it by the Due Process Clause of the Fourteenth Amendment, preempt the right to dissolve this legal relationship without affording all citizens access to the means it has prescribed for doing so.

Reversed.

JUSTICE DOUGLAS, concurring in the result.

* * * The power of the States over marriage and divorce is, of course, complete except as limited by specific constitutional provisions. But could a State deny divorces to domiciliaries who were Negroes and grant them to whites? Deny them to resident aliens and grant them to citizens? Deny them to Catholics and grant them to Protestants? Deny them to those convicted of larceny and grant them to those convicted of embezzlement?

* * * While Connecticut has provided a procedure for severing the bonds of marriage, a person can meet every requirement save court fees or the cost of service of process and be denied a divorce. * * *

Thus, under Connecticut law divorces may be denied or granted solely on the basis of wealth. * * * Affluence does not pass muster under the Equal Protection Clause for determining who must remain married and who shall be allowed to separate.

NOTES AND QUESTIONS

1.   Does *Boddie* imply that there is a constitutional right to divorce? Could a state prohibit absolute divorce if it permitted legal separation? Could it bar divorce based on hardship? Could it allow divorce based only on fault?

2.   Is there a constitutional right *not* to be divorced? *See* Walton v. Walton 104 Cal. Rptr. 471 (App. 1972) (see Chapter 5).

3.   If there is a right to divorce (or at least a right not to be excluded from obtaining a divorce due to poverty), is there also a right to counsel in a divorce case? Most courts have not thought so. *See In re* Smiley, 330 N.E.2d 53 (N.Y. 1975) (legal counsel is not required to obtain a divorce, so court-ordered counsel

is not required by *Boddie*). *See also* Kiddie v. Kiddie, 563 P.2d 139 (Okla. 1977). *Cf.*, Peter Van Runkle, *Lassiter v. Dept. of Social Services: What It Means for the Indigent Divorce Litigant*, 43 OHIO ST. L. J. 969 (1982). The Alaska Supreme Court has held that there is a right to court-appointed counsel for an indigent party in a child custody dispute where the other parent is represented by counsel provided by a public agency. *See* Flores v. Flores, 598 P.2d 893 (Alaska 1979).

4.   Under Jewish religious law, a wife may not remarry unless her husband has given her a *get*. Some Jewish wives unable to obtain *gets* from their former husbands have brought actions based on the marriage contract executed during a traditional Jewish wedding; some courts have granted wives contractual relief and others have not. *Compare* Goldman v. Goldman, 554 N.E.2d 1016 (Ill. App. 1990) (finding husband contractually bound to provide a *get* and ordering specific performance) *with* Victor v. Victor, 866 P.2d 899 (Ariz. App. 1993) (standard marriage contract not sufficiently specific with respect to the husband's *get* obligation to support an order requiring specific performance). In response to the *get* problem, New York enacted a statute under which a final judgment of divorce or annulment may not be granted until the plaintiff files "a verified statement that he or she has taken all steps solely with his or her power to remove all barriers to the defendant's remarriage * * *." N.Y. DOM. REL. L. § 253. The statute's exclusive focus on divorce plaintiffs apparently stems from the legislature's fear that a statute applicable to defendants would violate the Establishment Clause. At least one appellate court has refused, based on Establishment Clause concerns, to require a defendant husband to obtain a *get*, because he claimed that he wanted to reconcile with his wife. *See* Aflalo v. Aflalo, 685 A.2d 523 (N.J. Super. Ch. Div. 1996).

5.   Some courts have attempted to create financial incentives to provide a *get*. In Mizrahi-Srour v. Srour, 29 N.Y.S.3d 516 (App. Div. 2016) , the court awarded the woman monthly post-divorce spousal support of $100 per week for 5 years. If this man did not provide a get within 60 days, this amount increased to $200 per week.

MASSAR V. MASSAR

Superior Court of New Jersey, 1995.
279 N.J. Super. 89, 652 A.2d 219.

CUFF, J.S.C.

This appeal arises from an order enforcing an agreement between a husband and wife which limited the grounds for a complaint for divorce to eighteen months continuous separation.

This is the second marriage for both parties. Prior to their marriage on November 25, 1988, Jacqueline Massar and Cyril Massar signed a prenuptial agreement. In April 1993, the marriage had deteriorated to the point that the parties discussed separation and eventual divorce. In an agreement signed April 30, 1993, Mr. Massar agreed to vacate the marital home, and Mrs. Massar agreed not to seek termination of the marriage for any reason other than eighteen months continuous separation. Pursuant to this agreement, Mr. Massar moved out of the marital home.

However, contrary to the agreement, on October 1, 1993, Mrs. Massar filed a complaint for divorce on the grounds of extreme cruelty. Mr. Massar filed a motion to dismiss the complaint and to enforce the prenuptial agreement. After oral argument, Hon. Thomas Dilts, J.S.C. upheld the agreement and dismissed the complaint. An order reflecting these rulings was entered on December 14, 1993. Mrs. Massar appeals from that portion of the order enforcing the agreement to seek a divorce solely on "no fault" grounds.

In enforcing this agreement, Judge Dilts found that the agreement was clear, unequivocal and supported by consideration. He also found that Mrs. Massar had failed to present facts which would lead him to conclude that the agreement was executed under duress. At most, she submitted facts to support that she wanted Mr. Massar out of the house. Furthermore, Mrs. Massar was represented by an attorney who was representing solely her interests. Moreover, Judge Dilts found that public policy did not prohibit such agreements. In fact, he concluded that public policy requires that agreements which restrict the grounds on which a divorce shall be obtained to the no-fault eighteen months continuous separation should be recognized. He reasoned that such an agreement should be encouraged by the State since it can give a couple a period of time to assess their relationship and determine whether a reconciliation is possible.

On appeal, Mrs. Massar argues that a complaint for divorce on the grounds of extreme cruelty does not violate the intent of the agreement. She further argues that the agreement violates public policy and is unenforceable. Finally, she argues that a plenary hearing was required. We disagree and affirm the order entered by Judge Dilts substantially for the reasons set forth in his oral decision of December 10, 1993 as supplemented by his letter opinion dated December 13, 1993. We add only the following comments.

This State has a strong public policy favoring enforcement of agreements. Marital agreements are essentially consensual and voluntary and as a result, they are approached with a predisposition in favor of their validity and enforceability. Marital agreements, however, are enforceable only if they are fair and equitable. Any marital agreement which is unconscionable or is the product of fraud or overreaching by a party with power to take advantage of a confidential relationship may be set aside. In fact, the law affords particular leniency to agreements made in the domestic arena and similarly allows judges greater discretion when interpreting these agreements. Such discretion is based on the premise that, although marital agreements are contractual in nature, "contract principles have little place in the law of domestic relations." Citing *Lepis v. Lepis,* 83 N.J. 139, 148, 416 *A.*2d 45 (1980). Nevertheless, the contractual nature of such agreements has long been recognized and principles of contract interpretation have been invoked particularly to define the terms of the agreement and divine the intent of the parties.

In this case, Mr. Massar agreed to vacate the marital home. Mrs. Massar agreed as follows:

> [W]aives any claim that she may have against the husband in any action to dissolve, nullify, or terminate their marriage for desertion *or any other cause of action, except no-fault divorce based upon living separate and apart for a period of 18 months or more* based upon the husband's vacating the marital premises pursuant to this agreement. (emphasis added).

We agree with Judge Dilts that this language is clear and unequivocal and that Mrs. Massar surrendered her right to seek a divorce on any other than a no-fault basis. We also agree that the certifications submitted by Mrs. Massar establish nothing more than that she wished Mr. Massar out of the house; they certainly did not create a fact issue concerning duress. Similarly, we concur that this agreement is supported by consideration. Not only did Mr. Massar leave a house in which he had as much right to reside as Mrs. Massar, but also he had to undertake the additional expense of establishing a separate residence. Finally, we also agree with Judge Dilts that there is insufficient evidence to suggest that this waiver was not a knowing and voluntary act by Mrs. Massar, and a plenary hearing was not warranted.

Mrs. Massar urges us to adopt a per se rule that agreements confining a spouse to a particular cause of action for dissolution of a marriage are against public policy and are unenforceable. We have declined, however, to adopt a per se rule of enforceability of negotiated provisions in agreements between spouses. Rather, we have reviewed the enforceability of these provisions on a case-by-case basis to determine if the application of the provision is fair and just according to the circumstances of the particular case.

The State has certainly adopted a public policy through *N.J.S.A.* 2A:34–1 *et seq.* that the citizens of this state shall have liberal grounds to disengage themselves from marriages which are not viable. *See Babushik v. Babushik,* 157 N.J.Super. 128, 130, 384 *A.*2d 574 (Ch. Div.1978). On the other hand, this State does not promote divorce and has always had a strong public interest in promoting marriage. Indeed, the no-fault provision requiring an eighteen-month continuous separation was adopted in part to allow divorcing spouses the time to reflect and discern if divorce is the appropriate action for them. *The Final Report of the Divorce Law*

Study Commission (1970) at 70, 128–29. As observed by Judge Dilts, there is good reason to encourage a cooling off period for spouses to assess their relationship and calmly reflect whether dissolution of their marriage is the course they wish to take.

Accordingly, we decline to adopt a per se rule. We can envision many circumstances where it may be in the best interests of the parties and any children born of the marriage to dissolve a marriage without the assertion of allegations of emotional or physical abandonment, substance abuse, or certain allegations that pass for extreme cruelty. Similarly, we can envision many instances in which such an agreement may not be enforceable because it may serve to hide from the court actions of an abusive spouse or substance dependent spouse which may endanger the physical and emotional welfare of the other spouse and any children.

But that is not the situation in this case. Indeed, based on the certifications before Judge Dilts it appears that Mr. Massar realized that a physical separation was appropriate given the state of his marriage. However, he was concerned that such a separation might be interpreted as a financial abandonment of his wife. Similarly, he was concerned about his continuing ability to function as a deacon in his church. These concerns became real because upon the filing of the complaint for divorce alleging extreme cruelty he was temporarily suspended from his position in his church. Furthermore, the record before Judge Dilts suggests that Mrs. Massar filed the complaint for divorce only when her initial proposal for equitable distribution was not instantly embraced by Mr. Massar.

We emphasize that there is no suggestion in this record of any physical or mental abuse. The certifications submitted by Mrs. Massar reveal no more than a couple engaging in verbal confrontations in the context of a disintegrating marriage. Two intelligent adults should be able to agree concerning the framework and timetable for the dissolution of their troubled marriage and have that agreement enforced, if that agreement is fair and equitable to both parties under the unique circumstances of their case.

Accordingly, the December 14, 1993 Order entered by Judge DILTS is affirmed.

NOTES AND QUESTIONS

1.   In Allen v. Allen, 789 S.E.2d 787 (Va. App. 2016), the spouses signed a postnuptial agreement providing that the husband would not file for divorce for 20 years from the date the agreement was signed. In consideration of this commitment, the wife waived any interest in the husband's pension. The goal apparently was to make sure the wife would contine to be covered by the husband's health insurance. Despite the agreement, shortly thereafter the

husband filed for divorce. The trial court granted the divorce, but ruled that the husband was liable for the wife's medical expenses for 20 years.

Problem 12-3:

Hilda and Walter married in Louisiana in 2005, satisfying the requirements for creating a "covenant marriage." They later moved to California (which does not recognize such a thing as a "covenant marriage"), where Hilda filed for a no-fault divorce. Walter argues that he and Hilda may be divorced only for reasons permitted under the Louisiana code provisions governing a covenant marriage. What arguments are available to Hilda? What should the California court do? *See* Blackburn v. Blackburn, 180 So. 3d 16 (Ala. App. 2015).

Problem 12-4:

Before Helen and William married, they signed a premarital agreement including a waiver of the right to obtain a no-fault divorce. William later filed for divorce based on a no-fault ground permitted under state law. The state has adopted the UPAA (see Chapter 5). Is a waiver of the right to obtain a no-fault divorce different from the wavier of a right to pursue a fault-based divorce discussed in *Massar*? What arguments are available to William? to Helen? What result should the court reach?

Problem 12-5:

Heinrich and Wilhelmina, who are citizens of a country in which divorce is only permitted based on mutual consent, established a legal residence in the United States. Wilhelmina filed for divorce on a no-fault ground permitted under the divorce code of their state of residence. Heinrich argues that the marriage may be terminated only based on consent. What arguments are available to Wilhelmina? What should the court do? *See* Sharma v. Sharma, 667 P.2d 395 (Kan. App. 1983).

Problem 12-6:

The legislature has decided to adopt legislation inspired by Amato and Booth's notion of parental self-sacrifice. Struck by the fact that Amato and Booth found that less than a third of divorcing couples were highly conflicted, the legislature plans to adopt legislation that would require all divorcing couples with children under the age of 16 to undertake mandatory counseling and conciliation for a six-month period. That counseling will aim at conflict reduction and parental education; only those who complete the program will be eligible to divorce *and even those who complete the program will be prohibited from divorce if the counseling team finds that, on balance, it is in the interests of the children to preserve the marriage.*

Would this legislative scheme pass constitutional muster? Is it a good idea?

CHAPTER 13

JURISDICTION OVER FAMILY DISPUTES

■ ■ ■

*** *[J]urisdictional rules relating to marriage and divorce are unusual and combine in such a way as almost to make certain that no public policy can be coherently served.*

Brian Bix, Choice of Law and Marriage: A Proposal, 36 FAMILY LAW QUARTERLY 255, 256 (2002)

1. JURISDICTION OVER DIVORCE

Jurisdictional rules in family law matters are quite complex. There are different standards for determining whether a court can grant a divorce, order a support award, divide property, or decide a custody dispute.

PETER HAY, CONFLICT OF LAWS
127–31 (West Blackletter Series, 3rd ed. 2000).

* * *

An *"ex parte"* divorce is one in which *only the petitioner* was before and was subject to the jurisdiction of the divorce court.

THE *WILLIAMS* CASES

The early case law was restrictive (and uncertain) concerning a court's power to grant a divorce in the absence of personal jurisdiction (presence or domicile) over both spouses. The landmark decisions in *Williams v. North Carolina* addressed this problem but did not resolve it completely. 317 U.S. 287 (1942) ("Williams I"); 325 U.S. 226 (1945) ("Williams II").

In *Williams* the husband and the wife of two different marriages respectively had gone to Nevada, complied with that state's six-weeks' residence requirement, divorced their respective spouses, married each other, and returned to North Carolina. The Nevada court did not have personal jurisdiction over the North Carolina stay-at-home spouses, but they had received notice in North Carolina of the Nevada divorce proceedings. Upon their return to North Carolina, the Nevada newlyweds faced criminal charges for bigamous cohabitation, on the ground that their

Nevada divorces were invalid and that their subsequent marriage to each other was therefore bigamous.

The United States Supreme Court held in the first *Williams* decision that the *domicile of the plaintiff* suffices for divorce jurisdiction. The Court likened an ex parte divorce proceeding (i.e., a proceeding in which the plaintiff who is before the court seeks divorce from a spouse who is not) to a proceeding *in rem*. The *res* before the court is the *marital status* of the parties, and that *status is localized at the domicile of each spouse*. With jurisdiction over the *res*, the court then has power to affect the marital status, for instance to dissolve the marriage.

Williams I thus established that the state of the plaintiff's domicile has jurisdiction to grant a divorce. Whether it was the state of domicile, however, is a *question of fact*. Since the absent spouse, by definition, did not have an opportunity to litigate this jurisdictional fact, he or she cannot be precluded by the F-1 decision with respect to this issue. The Supreme Court therefore held in the second *Williams* decision that F-2 may reexamine the existence of the plaintiff's domicile in F-1 and, with it, F-2's jurisdiction. In *Williams II*, the Supreme Court upheld North Carolina's finding that the parties had not established proper domicile, that their divorces were therefore invalid, and that their subsequent marriage was bigamous.

The *Williams* decisions raise a number of problems. They are outlined in the following subsections.

THE DEFINITION OF DOMICILE FOR DIVORCE JURISDICTION

The Supreme Court said in *Williams II* that the definition of domicile for divorce jurisdiction raises a federal question. This is so because *Williams I* involves the Constitutions's Full Faith and Credit mandate and it, in turn, applies when the F-1 court exercised jurisdiction in accordance with Constitutional standards. Jurisdiction exists (due process is satisfied) *Williams I* had held—when the plaintiff-spouse has his or her domicile in the forum state. If domicile is required to satisfy due process, it follows that a state cannot define domicile by itself. Otherwise it could decide for itself whether it has complied with the due process requirement. Nevertheless, the Court concluded in *Williams II* that North Carolina's view with respect to the defendants' Nevada domicile was not unreasonable. Thus, rather than providing a federal definition, the Court merely reviewed the reasonableness of the state court's determination.

A few states have adopted the *Uniform Divorce Recognition Act*, which contains the presumption that a person, domiciled in the enacting state, who obtains a divorce in another state and returns to the enacting state thereafter, was domiciled in the enacting state at the time of the divorce. Applying the *Williams* decisions, the out-of-state divorce would therefore be invalid. The constitutional validity of the presumption in the Uniform Act, in light of due process considerations, has not been tested.

THE *IN REM* APPROACH AND "MINIMUM CONTACTS"

In *Shaffer v. Heitner*, 433 U.S. 186 (1977), the U.S. Supreme Court said that all assertions of state court jurisdiction, including those based on *in rem* jurisdiction, must satisfy the "minimum contacts" test of *International Shoe*. The question is: are minimum contacts an additional requirement for *ex parte* divorce jurisdiction?

The answer is probably "no" **if** *ex parte* divorce jurisdiction is based on the plaintiff's domicile. By definition, domicile is the closest connection a person can have to a state; it therefore far exceeds any required "minimum" contacts. The Court also noted in *Shaffer* that its decision in that case was not meant to address traditional bases for jurisdiction in status matters.

The answer is of course less clear whether it should be permissible for a court to assert ex parte divorce jurisdiction on a basis *short* of the plaintiff's domicile.

PARTIES TO COLLATERAL ATTACK

The defendant spouse may collaterally attack the *ex parte* divorce on jurisdictional grounds because he or she is not bound by the determination of the underlying jurisdictional facts in an action to which he or she was not a party. Similarly, any other interested party, for instance an heir, may collaterally attack the F-1 decree.

IS DOMICILE REALLY NEEDED?

Several authorities, including the Restatement 2d § 72, suggest that a state may exercise ex parte divorce jurisdiction when the plaintiff has a close connection with the state but does not maintain his or her domicile there. In order to meet the needs of military personnel who may lack the capacity to establish a local domicile, several states have enacted statutes providing for divorce jurisdiction on the basis of specified periods of residence. The court in *Lauterbach v. Lauterbach*, 392 P.2d 24 (Alaska 1964) upheld such a statute on the ground that "domicile is not the sole jurisdictional basis for divorce." More broadly, Arkansas law bases divorce jurisdiction solely on residence and not on domicile. *Wheat v. Wheat*, 229 Ark. 842, 318 S.W.2d 793 (1958).

The *Williams* decisions are not necessarily inconsistent with a wider view of *ex parte* divorce jurisdiction. In *Williams*, Nevada law itself had equated six weeks' residence in Nevada with Nevada domicile. Nevada law therefore required domicile, and the question before the Supreme Court was only whether domicile was a sufficient basis, not whether it was the *only* basis for ex parte divorce jurisdiction.

* * *

DIVISIBLE DIVORCE

In *ex parte* divorces, the granting court's jurisdiction extends only to the status of the parties' marriage. Absent personal jurisdiction over the defendant, *the court lacks power to affect the incidents of the marriage, such as support and custody rights.* Its decree will be entitled to recognition in so far as it had jurisdiction (dissolution of the marriage) but not in so far as it attempted to affect the incidents of marriage without proper jurisdiction to do so. The divorce decree is thus "divisible," *Estin v. Estin,* 334 U.S. 541 (1948). When the divorcing court lacks jurisdiction to deal with the incidents of marriage, these must be litigated in a subsequent proceeding in which there is personal jurisdiction over the defendant.

* * *

THE *SHERRER* DOCTRINE

When both parties participated in the divorce, ordinary principles of preclusion apply: unless raised by appeal, defects underlying the F-1 decree (except perhaps for certain species of fraud), *including an erroneous finding of jurisdiction,* are lost when that decree becomes final; they cannot be raised collaterally. Thus, even though a party's domicile may be required for the court's jurisdiction to grant a divorce, the absence of domicile cannot be raised collaterally: since it could have been raised in the F-1 proceeding, it has now become res judicata. *Sherrer v. Sherrer,* 334 U.S. 343 (1948). "Participation" in this context means that the defendant has entered an appearance which afforded him or her an opportunity to be heard, *Cook v. Cook,* 342 U.S. 126 (1951), or was subject to personal jurisdiction in the forum state by long arm statute or otherwise. Note that the Uniform Divorce Recognition Act, which establishes a presumption against domicile in the divorcing state, *cannot* be invoked by parties who, as a result of *Sherrer,* are bound by the F-1 determination.

THIRD PARTIES

Parties who are in privity with a former spouse are bound by the decree, such as children, will be barred from a collateral attack the same as the spouses themselves. *Johnson v. Muelberger,* 340 U.S. 581 (1951) (daughter). Persons not in privity with the former spouse(s) have sometimes also been barred from a collateral attack. See *Cook v. Cook,* 342 U.S. 126 (1951) (second husband). The Supreme Court has not addressed the question whether the former home state of the parties, such as in *Williams,* may collaterally attack the divorce when it was procured bilaterally and not *ex parte* (as in *Williams*). Since it was not in privity, the home state technically is not precluded. The suggested answer, however, is that the home state is not a "third party to the marriage relationship" and thus has *no standing* to raise jurisdictional defects. Decisions like *Williams* must therefore be restricted to their context: the home state protecting the societal interest of the home state in and on behalf of the resident spouse.

EFFECT OF COLLATERAL DETERMINATIONS OF INVALIDITY

Assume that F-1 has granted an *ex parte* divorce, and has even done so upon the express jurisdictional finding that the plaintiff spouse was domiciled there. Since the absent spouse was not bound by the jurisdictional determination in the *ex parte* proceeding, she collaterally attacked the F-1 decree in F-2 in a proceeding with personal jurisdiction over the F-1 plaintiff. F-2 finds that F-1 lacked jurisdiction and holds the F-1 divorce to be invalid. What is the effect of the F-2 determination on the validity of the F-1 decree in F-1? The F-1 decree is invalid *everywhere* including in F-1.

SOSNA V. IOWA
Supreme Court of the United States, 1975.
419 U.S. 393.

JUSTICE REHNQUIST delivered the opinion of the Court.

Appellant Carol Sosna married Michael Sosna on September 5, 1964, in Michigan. They lived together in New York between October 1967 and August 1971, after which date they separated but continued to live in New York. In August 1972, appellant moved to Iowa with her three children, and the following month she petitioned the District Court of Jackson County, Iowa, for a dissolution of her marriage. Michael Sosna, who had been personally served with notice of the action when he came to Iowa to visit his children, made a special appearance to contest the jurisdiction of the Iowa court. The Iowa court dismissed the petition for lack of jurisdiction, finding that Michael Sosna was not a resident of Iowa and appellant had not been a resident of the State of Iowa for one year preceding the filing of her petition. In so doing the Iowa court applied the provisions of Iowa Code § 598.6 requiring that the petitioner in such an action be "for the last year a resident of the state."

* * *

The durational residency requirement under attack in this case is a part of Iowa's comprehensive statutory regulation of domestic relations, an area that has long been regarded as a virtually exclusive province of the States. Cases decided by this Court over a period of more than a century bear witness to this historical fact. In *Barber v. Barber*, 62 U.S. (21 How.) 582, 584 (1859), the Court said that "[w]e disclaim altogether any jurisdiction in the courts of the United States upon the subject of divorce * * *." In *Pennoyer v. Neff*, 95 U.S. 714, 734–735 (1877), the Court said: "The State * * * has absolute right to prescribe the conditions upon which the marriage relation between its own citizens shall be created, and the causes for which it may be dissolved," and the same view was reaffirmed in *Simms v. Simms*, 175 U.S. 162, 167 (1899).

The statutory scheme in Iowa, like those in other States, sets forth in considerable detail the grounds upon which a marriage may be dissolved and the circumstances in which a divorce may be obtained. Jurisdiction over a petition for dissolution is established by statute in "the county where either party resides," * * * and the Iowa courts have construed the term "resident" to have much the same meaning as is ordinarily associated with the concept of domicile. * * * Iowa has recently revised its divorce statutes, incorporating the no-fault concept, but it retained the one-year durational residency requirement.

The imposition of a durational residency requirement for divorce is scarcely unique to Iowa, since 48 States impose such a requirement as a condition for maintaining an action for divorce. As might be expected, the periods vary among the States and range from six weeks to two years. The one-year period selected by Iowa is the most common length of time prescribed.

Appellant contends that the Iowa requirement of one year's residence is unconstitutional for two separate reasons: *first*, because it establishes two classes of persons and discriminates against those who have recently exercised their right to travel to Iowa, thereby contravening the Court's holdings in *Shapiro v. Thompson*, 394 U.S. 618 (1969), *Dunn v. Blumstein*, 405 U.S. 330 (1972), and *Memorial Hospital v. Maricopa County*, 415 U.S. 250 (1974); and *second*, because it denies a litigant the opportunity to make an individualized showing of bona fide residence and therefore denies such residents access to the only method of legally dissolving their marriage. *Vlandis v. Kline*, 412 U.S. 441 (1973); *Boddie v. Connecticut*, 401 U.S. 371 (1971).

State statutes imposing durational residency requirements were of course invalidated when imposed by States as a qualification for welfare payments, *Shapiro*, supra, for voting, *Dunn*, supra, and for medical care, *Maricopa County*, supra. * * * What those cases had in common was that the durational residency requirements they struck down were justified on the basis of budgetary or record-keeping considerations which were held insufficient to outweigh the constitutional claims of the individuals. * * *

Iowa's residency requirement may reasonably be justified on grounds other than purely budgetary considerations or administrative convenience. A decree of divorce is not a matter in which the only interested parties are the State as a sort of "grantor," and a plaintiff such as appellant in the role of "grantee." Both spouses are obviously interested in the proceedings, since it will affect their marital status and very likely their property rights. Where a married couple has minor children, a decree of divorce would usually include provisions for their custody and support. With consequences of such moment riding on a divorce decree issued by its courts, Iowa may insist that one seeking to initiate such a proceeding have the modicum of attachment to the State required here.

Such a requirement additionally furthers the State's parallel interests in both avoiding officious intermeddling in matters in which another State has a paramount interest, and in minimizing the susceptibility of its own divorce decrees to collateral attack. * * * The State's decision to exact a one-year residency requirement as a matter of policy is therefore buttressed by a quite permissible inference like this requirement not only effectuates state substantive policy but likewise provides a greater safeguard against successful collateral attack than would a requirement of bona fide residence alone. This is precisely the sort of determination that a State in the exercise of its domestic relations jurisdiction is entitled to make.

We therefore hold that the state interest in requiring that those who seek a divorce from its courts be genuinely attached to the State, as well as a desire to insulate divorce decrees from the likelihood of collateral attack, requires a different resolution of the constitutional issue presented than was the case in *Shapiro, Dunn*, and *Maricopa County*, supra.

Nor are we of the view that the failure to provide an individualized determination of residency violates the Due Process Clause of the Fourteenth Amendment. * * * An individualized determination of physical presence plus the intent to remain, which appellant apparently seeks, would not entitle her to a divorce even if she could have made such a showing. For Iowa requires not merely "domicile" in that sense, but residence in the State for a year in order for its courts to exercise their divorce jurisdiction.

In *Boddie v. Connecticut*, 401 U.S. 371 (1971) this Court held that Connecticut might not deny access to divorce courts to those persons who could not afford to pay the required fee. Because of the exclusive role played by the State in the termination of marriages, it was held that indigents could not be denied an opportunity to be heard "absent a countervailing state interest of overriding significance." But the gravamen of appellant Sosna's claim is not total deprivation, as in *Boddie*, but only delay.

* * *

Affirmed.

NOTES AND QUESTIONS

1.   In 2015, nine states required a divorce petitioner to have been a resident of the forum for at least one year. The most common residency requirement is six months; more than ten states have a residency requirement of no more than ninety days. *See* Linda D. Elrod & Robert G. Spector, *A Review*

of the Year in Family Law: 2014–2015: Family Law Continues to Evolve as Marriage Equality Is Attained, 49 FAM. L. Q. 545, 600–604 (2016).

2.   Does satisfaction of a state's residency requirement establish domicile? In *In re* Marriage of Amezquita & Archuleta, 124 Cal. Rptr. 2d 887 (Ct. App. 2002), the California Court of Appeals noted that:

> Courts and legal writers usually distinguish 'domicile' and 'residence,' so that 'domicile' is the one location with which for legal purposes a person is considered to have the most settled and permanent connection, the place where he intends to remain and to which, whenever he is absent, he has the intention of returning, but which the law may also assign to him constructively; whereas 'residence' connotes any factual place of abode of some permanency, more than a mere temporary sojourn. 'Domicile' normally is the more comprehensive term, in that it includes both the *act* of residence and an *intention* to remain; a person may have only one domicile at a given time, but he may have more than one physical residence separate from his domicile, and at the same time. But statutes do not always make this distinction in the employment of those words. They frequently use 'residence' and 'resident' in the legal meaning of 'domicile' and 'domiciliary,' and at other times in the meaning of factual residence or in still other shades of meaning. * * * In the context of jurisdiction to enter a judgment dissolving a marriage, [i]t is well settled in California that the term 'residence' is synonymous with 'domicile.'

Is *Amezquita & Archuleta* consistent with *Williams I* and *II?* Does it make sense to base divorce jurisdiction on the domicile of one of the parties? *See* Rhonda Wasserman, *Divorce and Domicile: Time to Sever the Knot,* 39 WM. & MARY L. REV. 1 (1997). Some courts have concluded that if a party satisfies the residency requirement, nothing more is needed. *See* Kar v. Nanda, 805 N.W. 2d 609 (Mich. App. 2011).

3.   Whether "residence" or "domicile" is required, the court must determine if one of the parties has met the durational residency requirement. *See* Bridgeman v. Bridgeman, 63 S.W.3d 686 (Mo. App. 2002) (finding wife still a "resident" for purposes of Missouri's 90 day residency requirement to file for divorce because she maintained a home there even though she and children had lived with husband in Wisconsin for eight months).

4.   Sometimes courts are asked to dismiss a divorce action based on forum non conveniens. In Marriage of Townley and Carraz, 2014 WL 2158993 (Ill. App. 2014) (unpublished), a former Illinois domiciliary who had moved to Ireland with his wife some time before the divorce filing petitioned for a divorce in Illinois. The court granted the motion to dismiss based on forum non conveniens. In contrast, in Spies v. Carpenter, 765 S.E.2d 340 (Ga. 2014) a married couple living in Georgia separated, and the wife moved to California with her children. The husband later filed for divorce in Georgia, and the court granted the wife's motion to dismiss the action based on forum non conveniens.

The Georgia Supreme Court reversed, ruling that the husband had a constitutional right to litigate the divorce (but not custody) where he lived, citing Holtsclaw v. Holtsclaw, 496 S.E.2d 262 (Ga. 1998).

2. PERSONAL JURISDICTION

KULKO V. SUPERIOR COURT OF CALIFORNIA
Supreme Court of the United States, 1978.
436 U.S. 84.

JUSTICE MARSHALL delivered the opinion of the Court.

The issue before us is whether, in this action for child support, the California state courts may exercise *in personam* jurisdiction over a nonresident, nondomiciliary parent of minor children domiciled within the State. For reasons set forth below, we hold that the exercise of such jurisdiction would violate the Due Process Clause of the Fourteenth Amendment.

Appellant Ezra Kulko married appellee Sharon Kulko Horn in 1959, during appellant's three-day stopover in California en route from a military base in Texas to a tour of duty in Korea. At the time of this marriage, both parties were domiciled in and residents of New York State. Immediately following the marriage, Sharon Kulko returned to New York, as did appellant after his tour of duty. Their first child, Darwin, was born to the Kulkos in New York in 1961, and a year later their second child, Ilsa was born, also in New York. The Kulkos and their two children resided together as a family in New York City continuously until March 1972, when the Kulkos separated.

Following the separation, Sharon Kulko moved to San Francisco, California. A written separation agreement was drawn up in New York; in September 1972, Sharon Kulko flew to New York City in order to sign this agreement. The agreement provided that the children would remain with their father during the school year but would spend their Christmas, Easter and summer vacations with their mother. While Sharon Kulko waived any claim for her own support or maintenance, Ezra Kulko agreed to pay his wife $3,000 per year in child support for the periods when the children were in her care, custody and control. Immediately after execution of the separation agreement, Sharon Kulko flew to Haiti and procured a divorce there; the divorce decree incorporated the terms of the agreement. She then returned to California, where she remarried and took the name Horn.

The children resided with appellant during the school year and with their mother on vacations, as provided by the separation agreement, until December 1973. At this time, just before Ilsa was to leave New York to spend Christmas vacation with her mother, she told her father that she wanted to remain in California after her vacation. Appellant bought his daughter a one-way plane ticket, and Ilsa left, taking her clothing with her. Ilsa then commenced living in California with her mother during the school year and spending vacations with her father. In January 1976, appellant's other child, Darwin, called his mother from New York and advised her that he wanted to live with her in California. Unbeknownst to appellant, appellee Horn sent a plane ticket to her son, which he used to fly to California where he took up residence with his mother and sister.

Less than one month after Darwin's arrival in California, appellee Horn commenced this action against appellant in the California Superior Court. She sought to establish the Haitian divorce decree as a California judgment; to modify the judgment so as to award her full custody of the children; and to increase appellant's child support obligations. Appellant appeared specially and moved to quash service of the summons on the ground that he was not a resident of California and lacked sufficient "minimum contacts" with the State under *International Shoe Co. v. Washington*, 326 U.S. 310, 316 (1945), to warrant the State's assertion of personal jurisdiction over him.

The trial court summarily denied the motion to quash, and appellant sought review in the California Court of Appeal by petition for a writ of mandate. Appellant did not contest the court's jurisdiction for purposes of the custody determination, but, with respect to the claim for increased support, he renewed his argument that the California courts lacked personal jurisdiction over him. The appellate court affirmed the denial of appellant's motion to quash, reasoning that, by consenting to his children's living in California, appellant had "caused an effect in th[e] state" warranting the exercise of jurisdiction over him.

The California Supreme Court granted appellant's petition for review, and in a 4–2 decision sustained the rulings of the lower state courts. * * * [It noted first that the California Code of Civil Procedure demonstrated an intent that the courts of California utilize all bases of *in personam* jurisdiction "not inconsistent with the Constitution."] Agreeing with the court below, the Supreme Court stated that, where a nonresident defendant has caused an effect in the State by an act or omission outside the State, personal jurisdiction over the defendant in causes arising from that effect may be exercised whenever "reasonable." It went on to hold that such an exercise was "reasonable" in this case because appellant had "purposely availed himself of the benefits and protections of the laws of California" by sending Ilsa to live with her mother in California. While noting that appellant had not, "with respect to his other child, Darwin, caused an effect in [California]"—since it was appellee Horn who had arranged for Darwin to fly to California in January 1976—the court concluded that it was "fair and reasonable for defendant to be subject to personal jurisdiction for the support of both children, where he has committed acts with respect to one child which confers personal jurisdiction and has consented to the permanent residence of the other child in California."

We have concluded that jurisdiction by appeal does not lie, but, treating the papers as a petition for a writ of certiorari, we hereby grant the petition and reverse the judgment below.

The Due Process Clause of the Fourteenth Amendment operates as a limitation on the jurisdiction of state courts to enter judgments affecting rights or interests of nonresident defendants. See *Shaffer v. Heitner*, 433 U.S. 186, 198–200 (1977). It has long been the rule that a valid judgment imposing a personal obligation or duty in favor of the plaintiff may be entered only by a court having jurisdiction over the person of the defendant. *Pennoyer v. Neff*, 95 U.S. 714, 732–733 (1878); *International Shoe Co. v. Washington, supra*, 326 U.S., at 316, at 158. The existence of personal jurisdiction, in turn, depends upon the presence of reasonable notice to the defendant that an action has been brought. *Mullane v. Central Hanover Trust Co.*, 339 U.S. 306, 313–314 (1950), and a sufficient connection between the defendant and the forum State as to make it fair to require defense of the action in the forum. In this case, appellant does not dispute the adequacy of the notice that he received, but contends that his connection with the State of California is too attenuated, under the standards implicit in the Due Process Clause of the Constitution, to justify imposing upon him the burden and inconvenience of defense in California.

The parties are in agreement that the constitutional standard for determining whether the State may enter a binding judgment against appellant here is that set forth in this Court's opinion in *International Shoe Co. v. Washington, supra*: that a defendant "have certain minimum contacts with [the forum state] such that the maintenance of the suit does not offend 'traditional notions of fair play and substantial justice.'"

Like any standard that requires a determination of "reasonableness," the "minimum contacts" test of *International Shoe* is not susceptible of mechanical application; rather, the facts of each case must be weighed to determine whether the requisite "affiliating circumstances" are present. *Hanson v. Denckla*, 357 U.S. 235, 246 (1958). We recognize that this determination is one in which few answers will be written "in black and white. The greys are dominant and even among them the shades are innumerable." *Estin v. Estin*, 334 U.S. 541, 545 (1948). But we believe that the California Supreme Court's application of the minimum contacts test in this case represents an unwarranted extension of *International Shoe* and would, if sustained, sanction a result that is neither fair, just, nor reasonable.

In reaching its result, the California Supreme Court did not rely on appellant's glancing presence in the State some 13 years before the events that led to this controversy, nor could it have. Appellant has been in California on only two occasions, once in 1959 for a three-day military stopover on his way to Korea, and again in 1960 for a 24-hour stopover on his return from Korean service. To hold such temporary visits to a State a basis for the assertion of *in personam* jurisdiction over unrelated actions arising in the future would make a mockery of the limitations on state jurisdiction imposed by the Fourteenth Amendment. Nor did the California court rely on the fact that appellant was actually married in California on one of his two brief visits. We agree that where two New York domiciliaries, for reasons of convenience, marry in the State of California and thereafter spend their entire married life in New York, the fact of their California marriage by itself cannot support a California court's exercise of jurisdiction over a spouse who remains a New York resident in an action relating to child support.

Finally, in holding that personal jurisdiction existed, the court below carefully disclaimed reliance on the fact that appellant had agreed at the time of separation to allow his children to live with their mother three months a year and that he had sent them to California each year pursuant to this agreement. As was noted below, to find personal jurisdiction in a State on this basis, merely because the mother was residing there, would discourage parents from entering into reasonable visitation agreements. Moreover, it could arbitrarily subject one parent to suit in any State of the Union where the other parent chose to spend time while having custody of their offspring pursuant to a separation agreement. As we have emphasized,

> The unilateral activity of those who claim some relationship with a nonresident defendant cannot satisfy the requirement of contact with the forum State. * * * [I]t is essential in each case that there be some act by which the defendant purposefully avails [him]self of the privilege of conducting activities within the forum State. * * * *Hanson v. Denckla, supra*, 357 U.S., at 253.

The "purposeful act" that the California Supreme Court believed did warrant the exercise of personal jurisdiction over appellant in California was his "actively and fully consent[ing] to Ilsa living in California for the school year * * * and * * * sen[ding] her to California for that purpose." We cannot accept the proposition that appellant's acquiescence in Ilsa's desire to live with her mother conferred jurisdiction over appellant in the California courts in this action. A father who agrees, in the interests of family harmony and his children's preferences, to allow them to spend more time in California than was required under a separation agreement can hardly be said to have "purposefully availed himself" of the "benefits and protection" of California's laws. See *Shaffer v. Heitner, supra*, 433 U.S., at 216.[7]

Nor can we agree with the assertion of the court below that the exercise of *in personam* jurisdiction here was warranted by the financial benefit appellant derived from his daughter's presence in California for nine months of the year. This argument rests on the premise that, while appellant's liability for support payments remained unchanged, his yearly expenses for supporting the child in New York decreased. But this circumstance, even if true, does not support California's assertion of jurisdiction here. Any diminution in appellant's household costs resulted, not from the child's presence in California, but rather from her absence from appellant's home. Moreover, an action by appellee Horn to increase support payments could now be brought, and could have been brought when Ilsa first moved to California, in the State of New York; a New York court would clearly have personal jurisdiction over appellant and, if a judgment were entered by a New York court increasing appellant's child support obligations, it could properly be enforced against him in both New York and California. Any ultimate financial advantage to appellant thus results not from the child's presence in California but from appellee's failure earlier to seek an increase in payments under the separation agreement. The argument below to the contrary, in our view, confuses the question of appellant's liability with that of the proper forum in which to determine that liability.

In light of our conclusion that appellant did not purposefully derive benefit from any activities relating to the State of California, it is apparent that the California Supreme Court's reliance on appellant's having caused an "effect" in California was misplaced. This "effects" test is derived from the American Law Institute's Restatement (Second) of Conflicts § 37 (1971), which provides:

> A state has power to exercise judicial jurisdiction over an individual who causes effects in the state by an act done elsewhere with respect to any cause of action arising from these effects unless the nature of the effects and of the individual's relationship to the state make the exercise of such jurisdiction unreasonable.

While this provision is not binding on this Court, it does not in any event support the decision below. As is apparent from the examples accompanying § 37 in the Restatement, this section was intended to reach wrongful activity outside of the State causing injury within the State, *see,*

---

[7]   The court below stated that the presence in California of appellant's daughter gave appellant the benefit of California's "police and fire protection, its school system, its hospital services, its recreational facilities, its libraries and museums. * * * " 19 Cal. 3d, at 522, 138 Cal. Rptr., at 589, 564 P.2d, at 356. But, in the circumstances presented here, these services provided by the State were essentially benefits to the child, not the father, and in any event were not benefits that appellant purposefully sought for himself.

e.g. Comment a, p. 157 (shooting bullet from one State into another), or commercial activity affecting state residents, ibid. Even in such situations, moreover, the Restatement recognizes that there might be circumstances that would render "unreasonable" the assertion of jurisdiction over the nonresident defendant.

The circumstances in this case clearly render "unreasonable" California's assertion of personal jurisdiction. There is no claim that appellant has visited physical injury on either property or persons within the State of California. The cause of action herein asserted arises, not from the defendant's commercial transactions in interstate commerce, but rather from his personal, domestic relations. * * * Furthermore, the controversy between the parties arises from a separation that occurred in the State of New York; appellee Horn seeks modification of a contract that was negotiated in New York and that she flew to New York to sign. * * *

Finally, basic considerations of fairness point decisively in favor of appellant's State of domicile as the proper forum for adjudication of this case, whatever the merits of appellee's underlying claim. It is appellant who has remained in the State of the marital domicile, whereas it is appellee who has moved across the continent.

In seeking to justify the burden that would be imposed on appellant were the exercise of *in personam* jurisdiction in California sustained, appellee argues that California has substantial interests in protecting the welfare of its minor residents and in promoting to the fullest extent possible a healthy and supportive family environment in which the children of the State are to be raised. These interests are unquestionably important. But while the presence of the children and one parent in California arguably might favor application of California law in a lawsuit in New York, the fact that California may be the "center of gravity" for choice of law purposes does not mean that California has personal jurisdiction over the defendant. And California has not attempted to assert any particularized interest in trying such cases in its courts by, e.g., enacting a special jurisdictional statute.

California's legitimate interest in ensuring the support of children resident in California without unduly disrupting the children's lives, moreover, is already being served by the State's participation in the Uniform Reciprocal Enforcement of Support Act of 1968. This statute provides a mechanism for communication between court systems in different States, in order to facilitate the procurement and enforcement of child-support decrees where the dependent children reside in a State that cannot obtain personal jurisdiction over the defendant. California's version of the Act essentially permits a California resident claiming support from a nonresident to file a petition in California and have its merits adjudicated in the State of the alleged obligor's residence, without either party having to leave his or her own State. * * * New York State is a signatory to a similar act. Thus, not only may plaintiff-appellee here vindicate her claimed right to additional child support from her former husband in a New York court, but the uniform acts will facilitate both her prosecution of a claim for additional support and collection of any support payments found to be owed by appellant.[15]

It cannot be disputed that California has substantial interests in protecting resident children and in facilitating child-support actions on behalf of those children. But these interests simply do not make California a "fair forum," *Shaffer v. Heitner, supra*, 433 U.S., at 215, in which to require appellant, who derives no personal or commercial benefit from his child's presence in California and who lacks any other relevant contact with the State, either to defend a child-support suit or to suffer liability by default.

* * *

Accordingly, we conclude that the appellant's motion to quash service, on the ground of lack of personal jurisdiction, was erroneously denied by the California courts. The judgment of the California Supreme Court is, therefore, reversed.

NOTES AND QUESTIONS

1. In Burnham v. Superior Court, 495 U.S. 604 (1990), the Supreme Court held that a state may exercise personal jurisdiction over a party if the party was personally served in the state, even though the forum lacks contacts sufficient to satisfy the *International Shoe* requirements. *See also* In the Interest of Gonzalez, 993 S.W.2d 147 (Tex. App. 1999) (finding that father was properly served on a plane when it landed in the state for refueling). At least one court has held that trickery will not divest a court of personal jurisdiction under *Burnham*. *See* Rutherford v. Rutherford, 971 P.2d 220 (Ariz. App. 1998) (finding Arizona had jurisdiction even though Ohio father alleged the mother had withheld visitation to get him to Arizona where he was served in action to modify child support).

In addition to personal jurisdiction based on *International Shoe* or *Burnham*, a court may acquire personal jurisdiction over a party by consent. *See* Harris v. Harris, 31 N.E.3d 991 (Ind. App. 2015).

2. In early 2017, all states except Massachusetts had enacted the Uniform Child Custody Jurisdiction and Enforcement Act (UCCJEA), 9 U.L.A. (Part 1A) 649 (1999), which states that:

---

[15] Thus, it cannot here be concluded, as it was in *McGee v. International Life Insurance Co.*, 355 U.S., at 223–224, with respect to actions on insurance contracts, that resident plaintiffs would be at a "severe disadvantage" if *in personam* jurisdiction over out-of-state defendants were sometimes unavailable.

a party to a child-custody proceeding, including a modification proceeding, or a petitioner or respondent in a proceeding to enforce or register a child custody determination, is not subject to personal jurisdiction in this State for another proceeding or purpose solely by reason of having participated, or having been physically present for the purpose of participating in the proceeding.

UCCJEA § 109. *See* Harrison v. Harrison, 706 S.E.2d 905 (Va. App. 2011).

3.   To divide property outside the forum state, the court must have personal jurisdiction over both spouses. *See* Ennis v. Ennis, 725 S.E.2d 311 (Ga. 2012) (Georgia court did not have personal jurisdiction over the wife because she had not lived there for seven years, owned no property in Georgia and did not transact business there); Mock v. Mock, 400 S.E.2d 543 (Va. App. 1991). There is some question whether a court in State A must enforce a divorce decree from State B that purports to affect title to realty in A. *See* Fall v. Eastin, 215 U.S. 1 (1909) (affirming Nebraska's refusal to recognize a Washington decree awarding title to Nebraska realty); Breitenstine v. Breitenstine, 62 P.3d 587 (Wyo. 2003) (finding Wyoming court decree could not directly impact title to out of state property). The safest practice is to have the State A court order the title-holding spouse to sign the appropriate title instrument (quitclaim deed, grant deed, etc.), and then record that instrument in the appropriate office in State B. *See* William Dorsaneo, *Due Process, Full Faith and Credit, and Family Law Litigation*, 36 Sw. L. J. 1085 (1983).

4.   Even when the forum lacks a basis for personal jurisdiction, most courts have concluded that the forum state's tribunal may divide property within the state. *See, e.g.,* Abernathy v. Abernathy, 482 S.E.2d 265 (Ga. 1997); Bechtold v. Bechtold, 588 So. 2d 321 (Fla. Dist. Ct. App. 1991). *But see* Dawson-Austin v. Austin, 968 S.W.2d 319 (Tex. 1998) (finding no jurisdiction to divide property where the forum did not have personal jurisdiction over both spouses and the spouse who filed for divorce moved the property to the forum after separation, apparently without the consent of the other spouse).

5.   Special jurisdictional rules apply to military personnel. For example, under the Uniformed Services Former Spouses' Protection Act (USFSPA), 10 U.S.C. § 1408(c)(4), a divorce court may exercise jurisdiction over a military person only if (1) the forum state is the domicile of the member of the uniformed services; *or* (2) the member consents to the exercise of jurisdiction by taking an affirmative action; *or* (3) the member resides there for reasons other than military assignment in that state or territory. *See* Walters v. Walters, 586 S.E.2d 663 (Ga. 2003) (finding military husband could be sued in Georgia because it was his domicile before entering the military). In addition to more specific jurisdictional rules, a service member on active duty can obtain a stay of civil proceedings under certain circumstances. The stated purpose of the Servicemembers Civil Relief Act, 50 U.S.C.A. App. § 501 et seq. (2003), is to "strengthen, and expedite the national defense" by enabling service members of the United States "to devote their entire energy to the defense needs of the Nation." *In re* Marriage of Bradley, 137 P.3d 1030 (Kan. 2006) (finding that a

stay was not mandatory, but discretionary, where the servicemember fails to comply with the conditions of the SCRA).

6.   Personal jurisdiction over a party is a prerequisite to some other family law remedies. In Mannise v. Harrell, 791 S.E.2d 653 (N.C. App. 2016) the court ruled that a court cannot enter a protective order against someone if the court did not have personal jurisdiction over him. In Ex Parte J.B., 2016 WL 6836349 (Ala. App. 2016) the court held that a paternity action against a non-resident should be dismissed due to a lack of personal jurisdiction over the non-resident.

7.   Citizens of other countries live in the United States for substantial periods. U.S. courts are being asked with increasing frequency whether divorces obtained in other countries should be enforced in the United States. Many courts will enforce such divorces if both parties had the opportunity to participate, at least one party was a resident of the country when the divorce was issued, and the substantive law does not offend an important state policy. *See* Badawi v. Alesawy, 24 N.Y.S.3d 683 (App. Div. 2016). Divorces obtained by a spouse in another country will not be recognized if neither party was a resident when the divorce was issued. *See* Baze-Sif v. Sif, 2016 WL 101687 (Ohio App.).

3.   INTERSTATE MODIFICATION AND ENFORCEMENT OF SUPPORT AWARDS

Separated parents frequently live in different states. The result, all too frequently, has been conflicting support orders. The typical pattern involves a divorce and support order entered in State A, a move by the noncustodial parent to State B, a modification proceeding in State B, and a new State B order. Which order controls?

One of the first uniform laws that aimed to resolve the problem of conflicting support decrees was the 1950 Uniform Reciprocal Enforcement of Support Act (URESA). Under URESA, a custodial parent could initiate a support action in her own state, to be "forwarded" to another state where the obligor lived or owned property. A government attorney—usually a local prosecutor—appeared on behalf of the custodial parent in the distant forum, avoiding the necessity of an expensive personal appearance. If the court in the distant forum concluded that the obligor had a support obligation, it entered a support order and forwarded payments to the obligee. Even though all states enacted one or another version of URESA, it proved inadequate to resolve the problem of conflicting state support decrees. The inadequacies of URESA produced the 1968 Revised Uniform Reciprocal Enforcement of Support Act (RURESA); its inadequacy led to the Uniform Interstate Family Support Act.

The central problem under both URESA and RURESA was that all proceedings were de novo; support orders entered under the statute had no effect on other support orders and thus did not prevent a new forum state from issuing a conflicting support decree. To resolve this problem, Congress enacted the Full Faith and Credit for Child Support Orders Act (FFCCSOA), 28 U.S.C. § 1738B. Under the FFCCSOA, the state that issues a support order retains continuing, exclusive jurisdiction over support as long as it is the residence of the child or any party. FFCCSOA requires state courts to enforce all child support orders made in accordance with its provisions and prohibits them from modifying such orders unless: (1) the new forum has jurisdiction to make a child support order; and (2) the State that originally issued the support order no longer has jurisdiction or each contestant has filed a written consent to the new forum's modification and continuing, exclusive jurisdiction over the order.

In 1996, Congress required the states to adopt the Uniform Interstate Family Support Act (UIFSA), 9 U.L.A. (Pt 1B) 177 (2005). UIFSA employs the same concept of continuing, exclusive jurisdiction as the FFCCSOA. It also contains long-arm jurisdiction provisions designed to ensure that the forum state will maximize its jurisdiction over nonresident obligors and procedures designed to speed up interstate case processing, transmission of information and documents, interstate telephone conferencing, and standardized forms. 2001 amendments to UIFSA further limit the ability of the parties to modify orders in states other than the issuing state.

UNIFORM INTERSTATE FAMILY SUPPORT ACT
9 U.L.A. (Pt. 1B) 177.

Section 201. Bases for Jurisdiction.

(a) In a proceeding to establish, or enforce, or modify a support order or to determine parentage of a child, a tribunal of this State may exercise personal jurisdiction over a nonresident individual * * * if:

(1)   the individual is personally served * * * within this State;

(2)   the individual submits to the jurisdiction of this State by consent, by entering a general appearance, or by filing a responsive document having the effect of waiving any contest to personal jurisdiction;

(3)   the individual resided with the child in this State;

(4)   the individual resided in this State and provided prenatal expenses or support for the child;

(5)   the child resides in this State as a result of the acts or directives of the individual;

(6)   the individual engaged in sexual intercourse in this State and the child may have been conceived by that act of intercourse;

(7)   the individual asserted parentage of a child in the [putative father registry] * * *; or

(8) there is any other basis consistent with the constitutions of this State and the United States for the exercise of personal jurisdiction.

(b) The bases of personal jurisdiction set forth in subsection (a) or in any other law of this State may not be used to acquire personal jurisdiction for a tribunal of the State to modify a child support order of another State unless the requirements of Section 611 or, in the case of a foreign support order, unless the requirements of section 615 are met.

Section 205. Continuing, Exclusive Jurisdiction.

(a) A tribunal of this State that has issued a child-support order consistent with the law of this State has and shall exercise continuing, exclusive jurisdiction to modify its child-support order if its order is the controlling order and

(1) at the time of the filing of a request for modification this State is the residence of the obligor, the individual obligee, or the child for whose benefit the support order is issued; or

(2) even if this State is not the residence of the obligor, the individual obligee, or the child for whose benefit the support order is issued, the parties consent in a record or in open court that the tribunal of this State may continue to exercise jurisdiction to modify its order.

(b) A tribunal of this State that has issued a child support order consistent with the law of this State may not exercise continuing, exclusive jurisdiction to modify the order if:

(1) all of the parties who are individuals file consent in a record with the tribunal of this State that a tribunal of another State that has jurisdiction over at least one of the parties who is an individual or that is located in the State of residence of the child may modify the order and assume continuing exclusive jurisdiction; or

(2) its order is not the controlling order.

(c) If a tribunal of another State has issued a child-support order * * * which modifies a child-support order of a tribunal of this State, tribunals of this State shall recognize the continuing exclusive jurisdiction of * * * the other State.

(d) A tribunal of this State that lacks continuing, exclusive jurisdiction to modify a child-support order may serve as an initiating tribunal to request a tribunal of another State to modify a support order issued in that State.

(e) A temporary support order issued ex parte or pending resolution of a jurisdictional conflict does not create continuing, exclusive jurisdiction in the issuing tribunal.

Section 206. Continuing Jurisdiction to Enforce Child-Support Order.

(a) A tribunal of this State that has issued a child-support order consistent with the law of this State may serve as an initiating tribunal to request a tribunal of another state to enforce:

(1) the order if the order is the controlling order and has not been modified by a tribunal of another State that assumed jurisdiction pursuant to [the Uniform Interstate Family Support Act]; or

(2) a money judgment for arrears of support and interest on the order accrued before a determination that an order of another State is the controlling order.

(b) A tribunal of this State having continuing jurisdiction over a support order may act as a responding tribunal to enforce the order.

[Section 207 provides the procedure for determining which is the controlling support order].

Section 211. Continuing, Exclusive Jurisdiction to Modify Spousal-Support Order.

(a) A tribunal of this State issuing a spousal-support order consistent with the law of this State has continuing exclusive jurisdiction to modify the spousal-support order throughout the existence of the support obligation. * * *

Section 601. Registration of Order for Enforcement.

A support order or income-withholding order issued in another state or a foreign support order may be registered in this State for enforcement.

Section 603. Effect of Registration for Enforcement.

(a) A support order or income-withholding order issued in another state or a foreign support order is registered when the order is filed in the registering tribunal of this State.

(b) A registered order issued in another state or a foreign country is enforceable in the same manner and is subject to the same procedures as an order issued by a tribunal of this State.

(c) Except as otherwise provided in this act, a tribunal of this State shall recognize and enforce, but may not modify, a registered order if the issuing tribunal had jurisdiction.

Section 604. Choice of Law.

(a) Except as otherwise provided in subsection (d), the law of the issuing state or foreign country governs:

(1) the nature, extent, amount, and duration of current payments under a registered support order.

(2) the computation and payments of arrearages and accrual of interest on the arrearages under the support order; and

(3) the existence and satisfaction of other obligations under the support order.

(b) In a proceeding for arrears under a registered support order, the statute of limitation of this State or of the issuing State or foreign country, whichever is longer, applies.

Section 605. Notice of Registration Order.

(a) When a support order or income-withholding order issued in another state or a foreign support order is registered, the registering tribunal shall notify the nonregistering party. The notice must be accompanied by a copy of the registered order and the documents and relevant information accompanying the order.

(b) A notice must inform the nonregistering party:

(1) that a registered order is enforceable as of the date of registration in the same manner as an order issued by a tribunal of this State;

(2) that a hearing to contest the validity or enforcement of the registered order must be requested within [20] days after the date of mailing or personal service of the notice unless the registered order is under section 707;

(3) that failure to contest the validity or enforcement of the registered order in a timely manner will result in confirmation of the order and enforcement of the order and the alleged arrearages; and

(4) of the amount of any alleged arrearages.

(c) If the registering party asserts that two or more orders are in effect, a notice must also:

(1) identify the two or more orders and the order alleged by the registering party to be the controlling order and the consolidated arrears, if any;

(2) notify the nonregistering party of the right to a determination of which is the controlling order;

(3) state that the procedures provided in subsection (b) apply to the determination of which is the controlling order; and

(4) state that failure to contest the validity or enforcement of the order alleged to be the controlling order in a timely manner may result inn confirmation that the order is the controlling order.

(d) Upon registration of an income-withholding order for enforcement, the support enforcement agency or the registering tribunal shall notify the obligor's employer pursuant to [the income-withholding law of this State].

[Section 606 spells out the procedure for contesting the validity or enforcement of registered orders.]

* * *

Section 607. Contest of Registration or Enforcement.

(a) A party contesting the validity or enforcement of a registered support order or seeking to vacate the registration has the burden of proving one or more of the following defenses:

(1) the issuing tribunal lacked personal jurisdiction over the contesting party;

(2) the order was obtained by fraud;

(3) the order has been vacated, suspended, or modified by a later order;

(4) the issuing tribunal has stayed the order pending appeal;

(5) there is a defense under the law of this State to the remedy sought;

(6) full or partial payment has been made;

(7) the statute of limitation under § 604 precludes enforcement of some or all of the alleged arrearages; or

(8) the alleged controlling order is not the controlling order.

(b) If a party presents evidence establishing a full or partial defense under subsection (a), a tribunal may stay enforcement of a registered support order, continue the proceeding to permit production of additional relevant evidence, and issue other appropriate orders. An uncontested portion of the registered support order may be enforced by all remedies available under the law of this State.

Section 611. Modification of Child Support Order of Another State

(a) * * * upon [petition] a tribunal of this State may modify a child-support order issued in another state which is registered in this State if, after notice and hearing, the tribunal finds that:

* * *

(1) (A) neither the child, nor the obligee who is an individual, nor the obligor resides in the issuing state;

(B a [petitioner] who is a nonresident of this State seeks modification; and

(C) the [respondent] is subject to the personal jurisdiction of the tribunal of this State; or

(2) this State is the State of residence of the child or a party who is an individual is subject to the personal jurisdiction of the tribunal of this State, and all of the parties who are individuals have filed consents in a record in the issuing tribunal for a tribunal of this State to modify the support order and assume continuing, exclusive jurisdiction.

(b) Modification of a registered child support order is subject to the same requirements, procedures, and defenses that apply to the modification of an order issued by a tribunal of this State and the order may be enforced and satisfied in the same manner.

(c) A tribunal of this State may not modify any aspect of a child support order that may not be modified under the law of the issuing state, including the duration of the obligation of support. If two or more tribunals have issued child-support orders for the same obligor and the same child, the order that controls and must be so recognized under Section 207 established the aspects of the support order which are nonmodifiable.

(d) In a proceeding to modify a child-support order, the law of the State that is determined to have issued the initial controlling order governs the duration of the obligation of support. The obligor's fulfillment of the duty of support established by that order precludes imposition of a further obligation of support by a tribunal of this State.

(e) On issuance of an order by a tribunal of this State modifying a child support order issued in another state, the tribunal of this State becomes the tribunal of continuing, exclusive jurisdiction.

(f) Notwithstanding subsections (a) through (e) and Section 201(b), a tribunal of this state retains jurisdiction to modify an order issued by a tribunal of this state if:

(1) one party resides in another state; and

(2) the other party resides outside the United States.

NOTES AND QUESTIONS

1. These examples summarize how UIFSA handles some common child support problems:

a. Henry and Winnie live in State A with their child, Carl. After their separation but before Winnie has obtained a child support order, Henry moves to State B. Under UIFSA, Winnie may obtain a support order in State A, based on the law of State A, or in State B, based on the law of State B, or she may initiate a two-state procedure that would result in an order in State B, based on the law of State B. The State in which she obtained the original order will have exclusive continuing jurisdiction.

b.   Harold and Wanda live in State A with their child, Carla. Harold and Carla go to State B. Harold cannot initiate a support action in State B unless Wanda has sufficient B contacts to satisfy the *International Shoe* standard. He may initiate a support action in State A, based on the law of State A or initiate a two-state procedure that would result in an order in State A, based on State A's law.

2.   Do UIFSA's long-arm provisions (§ 201) conform to the standards established in *Kulko? See* John J. Sampson & Barry J. Brooks, *Uniform Interstate Family Support Act (with Prefatory Notes and Comments—and Still More Annotations),* 36 FAM. L. Q. 329, 357–362 (2002).

3.   Section 205 provides that the rendering state retains exclusive continuing jurisdiction to modify the child support order as long as it is the "residence" of one party. A number of courts have interpreted this term to mean domicile. *See* Lilly v. Lilly, 250 P.3d 994 (Utah App. 2011); Lattimore v. Lattimore, 991 So. 2d 239 (Ala. App. 2008). *Cf.* Deazle v. Miles, 908 N.Y.S. 2d 716 (App. Div. 2010).

The constitutionality of this provision has been unsuccessfully challenged by parties who had been living in another state for a significant period. *See* Barker v. Barker, 757 S.E.2d 42 (Ga. 2014); Hornblower v. Hornblower, 94 A.3d 1218 (Conn. App. 2014).

4.   Under UIFSA, when everyone has moved from the rendering state, and the parents live in two different states, the person who wants to modify the child support order must sue where the other parent lives. Courts have disagreed whether, due to the FFCCSOA (and its arguable preemptive effect), the parent desiring modification once everyone has moved from the initial rendering state could sue where he or she lives, if personal jurisdiction could be obtained over the other parent. *Compare* Pulkkinen v. Pulkkinen, 127 So. 3d 738 (Fla. Dist. Ct. App. 2013) (no); Jackson v. Holiness, 961 N.E.2d 48 (Ind. App. 2012) (no); Roberts v. Bedard, 359 S.W.3d 554 (Ky. App. 2011) (no); Trissler v. Trissler, 987 So. 2d 209 (Fla. Dist. Ct. App. 2008) (no) *with* Bowman v. Bowman, 917 N.Y.S. 2d 379 (App. Div. 2011) (yes); Draper v. Burke, 881 N.E.2d 122 (Mass. 2008) (yes).

5.   Parties have attempted to change by contract certain UIFSA rules. For example, UIFSA provides that, if a court has jurisdiction to modify an order of another state the court should apply its child support guidelines. If the parties agreed that the amount of child support should always be determined based on the law of the initial rendering state, should such an agreement be enforced? *Compare* Prisco v. Stroup, 3 A.3d 316 (D.C. App. 2010) (enforcing the agreement) *with* Crosby v. Grooms, 10 Cal. Rptr. 3d 146 (App. 2004) (not enforcing).

6.   There is a distinction between the power to modify a child support order and the power to enforce one. For example, in Sidell v. Sidell, 18 A.3d 499 (R.I. 2011) all the parties had moved away from Rhode Island, which

issued the original order. While the court therefore lost exclusive jurisdiction to modify the order, the court ruled it still had the power to enforce it.

7.   Under UIFSA, if the initial rendering state loses jurisdiction to modify, the state with jurisdiction to modify generally applies its law to govern the modification. *See* Adams-Smyrichinsky v. Smyrichinsky, 2013 WL 6037306 (Ky. App. 2013). One exception is the duration of the order. In Spencer v. Spencer, 882 N.E.2d 886 (N.Y. 2008), the initial Connecticut child support order terminated when the child turned 18. The wife then filed a new action in New York, where child support continues until age 21. Although the trial court granted the new order, the New York Court of Appeals concluded that by doing so New York was effectively modifying the duration of the initial order, in violation of UIFSA and the FFCCSOA. *See also In re* Jones, 48 N.E.3d 700 (Ill. App. 2016). This principle has also been applied to determine whether support can be awarded to a disabled adult child. The law of the initial rendering state governs. *See In re* Martinez, 450 S.W.3d 157 (Tex. App. 2014); Studer v. Studer, 131 A.3d 240 (Conn. 2016).

8.   Unlike orders for child support, UIFSA § 211 provides that the issuing state always retains exclusive jurisdiction over modification of spousal support. In light of this provision, the appellate court in O'Neil v. O'Neil, 724 S.E.2d 247 (Va. App. 2012) held that a court that issued the initial spousal support order could not transfer a petition to modify to another state based on forum non conveniens.

Problem 13-1:

Henry and Wilma lived as a married couple in New Jersey and later in Florida. While resident in Florida, Henry and Wilma separated and Wilma returned to New Jersey. Henry filed for divorce in Florida. Shortly thereafter, Wilma filed for divorce in New Jersey. Henry made a special appearance to challenge the jurisdiction of the New Jersey divorce court. The New Jersey court ruled that it had jurisdiction and enjoined Henry from proceeding with his Florida divorce. But Henry did not withdraw the Florida action. Wilma neither contested the jurisdiction of the Florida divorce court nor appeared in the action; the Florida court entered a default divorce judgment and divided the marital estate. After the Florida decree had been entered, the New Jersey divorce court also issued a divorce decree and divided the marital estate. The New Jersey decree granted Wilma spousal maintenance, which the Florida decree did not; it also awarded her a larger share of the marital property.

Henry has brought an action in federal court under the Declaratory Judgment Act challenging the validity of the New Jersey decree. What arguments are available to Henry? To Wilma? Which decree is entitled to full faith and credit? *See* Rash v. Rash, 173 F.3d 1376 (11th Cir. 1999).

Problem 13-2:

Herman and Wanda married in Michigan and lived there for thirteen years. In 1993, they moved to the United Kingdom (U.K.) with their children. In 1995, Herman filed for divorce in the U.K. Four days later, Wanda filed for divorce in Michigan. Shortly before filing the divorce petition, Herman received a distribution of several million dollars from a family trust. Wanda has consulted you for advice: Would a Michigan divorce court have jurisdiction to issue a divorce decree? To decide issues of custody, support, and property division? Assuming that U.K. residency and other jurisdictional requirements are met, would a U.K. divorce judgment be recognized in Michigan? Should Wanda appear in the U.K. divorce action? *See* Dart v. Dart, 597 N.W.2d 82 (Mich. 1999). What can you guess about British vs. Michigan divorce law from the fact that Herman filed his action in the U.K.?

Problem 13-3:

Mary and Al Jones were married in California and have lived there throughout their marriage; both of their children were born in California and have lived there at all times. They have a house in California.

    a.   Mary and Al decide to divorce. Mary moves to Kansas and files for divorce, custody, and support in Kansas. Does Kansas have jurisdiction over the divorce? Over property located in California? Over child support under UIFSA? *See* Alley v. Parker, 707 A.2d 77 (Me. 1998); Snider v. Snider, 551 S.E.2d 693 (W. Va. 2001).

    b.   Mary and Al obtain a divorce in California; Mary is awarded custody and child support. Al moves to New Mexico and files a petition to modify his support obligation. Mary also moves to New Mexico. Under UIFSA, does New Mexico have jurisdiction to modify the support order?

    c.   Mary and Al obtain a divorce in California; Mary is awarded custody and child support. Al moves to New Mexico. Mary and the two children move to Florida. Mary files a petition to modify the support order. Under UIFSA, does Florida have jurisdiction to modify? If not, how should Mary proceed? *See* Groseth v. Groseth, 600 N.W.2d 159 (Neb. 1999); *In re* Marriage of Erickson, 991 P.2d 123 (Wash. App. 2000).

Problem 13-4:

George and Karen live in State A and obtain a divorce there; the divorce decree requires Karen to pay support for their child Eric until he turns 21. Karen moves to State B, where the obligation to support a child ends at age 18. Under UIFSA, if Karen stops paying support when the child turns 18 and George registers the order in State B for enforcement, will

Karen be ordered to continue to pay support? *See* UIFSA § 611(c), (d); Robdau v. Commonwealth, Va. Dept. Social Serv., 543 S.E.2d 602 (Va. App. 2001); State ex rel. Harnes v. Lawrence, 538 S.E.2d 223 (N.C. App. 2000). What if Karen moves to State B and registers the support order there? *See In re* Marriage of Doetzl, 65 P.3d 539 (Kan. App. 2003).

Problem 13-5:

Sam and Jane divorced in State A. Under the State A decree, Sam was ordered to pay Jane $500.00 a month in spousal support for fifteen years. Thereafter, Jane moved to State B, which does not allow an award of spousal support for more than ten years and Sam moved to State C. Under UIFSA, can Sam register the support order in State B and seek to modify its term to ten years? *See* UIFSA § 211; *In re* Marriage of Rassier, 118 Cal. Rptr. 2d 113 (App. 2002).

Problem 13-6:

Wilma and Harry were divorced in California, and a California court issued a divorce judgment. Wilma and Harry agreed at that time to reserve the issue of child support. After Harry established residency in Maryland and Wilma established residency in Utah, Wilma filed a petition in a Utah court to modify the California divorce judgment by establishing a child support order. May the Utah court modify the California judgment? *See* Case v. Case, 103 P.3d 171 (Utah App. 2005).

4. INTERSTATE CHILD CUSTODY JURISDICTION

In order to make a decision regarding adoption, custody, child abuse/neglect, or termination of parental rights, the court must have jurisdiction over the child. Historically, the states exercised jurisdiction over custody disputes based either on personal jurisdiction over the parents or the child's physical presence in the state. Under the latter approach, the child is treated like a marriage. But there is no equivalent to the *Williams'* decisions in the area of child custody; the Supreme Court has never expressly ruled that the child's physical presence in a state is constitutionally sufficient to confer jurisdiction over a custody action. In a concurring opinion in May v. Anderson, 345 U.S. 528 (1953), Justice Frankfurter did state that, while personal jurisdiction was necessary for application of the Full Faith and Credit Clause to a custody decree, the due process clause did not bar a state from adjudicating a custody dispute when it lacked personal jurisdiction. But no other member of the *May* court addressed the issue and the Supreme Court has not revisited it.

Under the traditional approach to child custody jurisdiction, the Full Faith and Credit issue was of marginal importance because, given that a child custody decree is always subject to modification (*see* Ch. 14), no custody decree was final; even a decree clearly entitled to full faith and credit was subject to relitigation in another forum state. If a custodial parent, resident in State A, allowed the child to visit the other parent in State B, he or she thus risked the possibility that the noncustodial parent would bring another custody proceeding based on the child's presence in State B and that the State B court would award custody to the (formerly) noncustodial parent. In this situation, State B courts, typically without the presence of the custodial parent and perhaps biased toward its own residents, did often award custody to the home litigant parent; even parents who kidnapped their children were often able to find a friendly forum.

A. THE UNIFORM CHILD CUSTODY JURISDICTION ACT (UCCJA) AND THE PARENTAL KIDNAPPING PREVENTION ACT (PKPA)

In 1968, the National Conference of Commissioners on Uniform State Laws (NCCUSL) proposed the Uniform Child Custody Jurisdiction Act (UCCJA), 9 U.L.A. (Pt. I) 115 (1988). With the Act, the Commissioners hoped to discourage continued controversies over child custody, to deter child abductions, to promote interstate cooperation and communication in adjudicating child custody matters, and to facilitate the enforcement of custody decrees of sister states. The UCCJA provided four alternative bases for jurisdiction:

(1) th[e] State (i) is the home state [i.e., the state where the child had lived for the six months immediately preceding filing of the petition] of the child at the time of commencement of the proceeding, or (ii) had been the child's home state within 6 months before commencement of the proceeding and the child is absent from this State because of his removal or retention by a person claiming his custody or for other reasons, and a parent or person acting as parent continues to live in this State; *or*

(2) it is in the best interest of the child that a court of th[e] State assume jurisdiction because (i) the child and his parents, or the child and at least one contestant, have a significant connection with this State, and (ii) there is available in this State substantial evidence concerning the child's present or future care, protection, training, and personal relationships; or

(3) the child is physically present in this State and (i) the child has been abandoned or (ii) it is necessary in an emergency to protect the child because he has been subjected to or threatened with mistreatment or abuse or is otherwise neglected [or dependent]; or

(4)(i) it appears that no other state would have jurisdiction under prerequisites substantially in accordance with paragraphs (1), (2), or (3), or another state has declined to exercise jurisdiction on the ground that this State is the more appropriate forum to determine the custody of the child, and (ii) it is in the best interest of the child that this court assume jurisdiction.

The drafters of the UCCJA made some assumptions that turned out to be incorrect. First, they assumed that if two states exercised jurisdiction over a child using different grounds, the courts would communicate to reach a decision as to which state would be the better forum and the other state would dismiss its action. Second, they assumed that forum shopping would be reduced. Both of these assumptions proved wrong. The lack of any priority regarding the grounds for jurisdiction coupled with little or no communication between courts created a "race to the courthouse" for custody matters. A parent would be encouraged to file first in the desired state and then move to dismiss any later action filed in another state.

The UCCJA's custody modification rules also created problems. The UCCJA drafters intended that once a court made a custody determination, it would retain exclusive jurisdiction to modify as long as the court retained jurisdiction under its law and did not decline to assume jurisdiction. Courts, however, interpreted the UCCJA to allow concurrent modification jurisdiction in the child's new home state and in the original decree state based on significant connection jurisdiction. This resulted in competing custody modification proceedings in the child's new home state and the original decree state which led to confusion about which order should be recognized and enforced. *See* Patricia M. Hoff, *The ABC's of the UCCJEA: Interstate Child Custody Practice Under the New Act*, 32 FAM. L. Q. 267, 281 (1998).

In 1980, Congress enacted the Parental Kidnapping Prevention Act, Pub. L. No. 96–611, 94 Stat. 3568 (1980) in order to cure the problems which the UCCJA had failed to resolve. As a federal statute, the PKPA preempts state law, including the UCCJA. Despite its somewhat confusing name, it applies to *all* interstate custody disputes. The PKPA mandates full faith and credit to a sister state custody order that substantially complies with the PKPA provisions.

PARENTAL KIDNAPPING PREVENTION ACT
28 U.S.C. § 1738A (2000).

(a) * * * Every State shall enforce * * * and shall not modify except as provided in subsections (f), (g), and (h) of this section any custody * * * or visitation determination made consistently with the provisions of this section by a court of another state.

* * *

(c)   A child custody or visitation determination made by a court of a State is consistent with the provisions of this section only if—

(1)   such court has jurisdiction under the law of such State; and

(2)   one of the following conditions is met:

(A)   such State (i) is the home State of the child on the date of the commencement of the proceeding, or (ii) had been the child's home State within six months before the date of the commencement of the proceeding and the child is absent from such State because of his removal or retention by a contestant or for other reasons, and a contestant continues to live in such State;

(B)(i) it appears that no other State would have jurisdiction under subparagraph (A), and (ii) it is in the best interest of the child that a court of such State assume jurisdiction because (I) the child and his parents, or the child and at least one contestant, have a significant connection with such State other than mere physical presence in such State, and (II) there is available in such State substantial evidence concerning the child's present or future care, protection, training, and personal relationships;

(C)   the child is physically present in such State and (i) the child has been abandoned, or (ii) it is necessary in an emergency to protect the child because the child, a sibling, or parent of the child has been subjected to or threatened with mistreatment or abuse;

(D)(i) it appears that no other State would have jurisdiction under subparagraph (A), (B), (C), or (E), or another State has declined to exercise jurisdiction on the ground that the State whose jurisdiction is in issue is the more appropriate forum to determine the custody or visitation of the child, and (ii) it is in the best interest of the child that such court assume jurisdiction; or

(E)   the court has continuing jurisdiction pursuant to subsection (d) of this section.

(d)   The jurisdiction of a court of a State which has made a child custody or visitation determination consistently with the provisions of this section continues as long as the requirement of subsection (c)(1) of this section continues to be met and such State remains the residence of the child or of any contestant.

(e)   Before a child custody or visitation determination is made, reasonable notice and opportunity to be heard shall be given to the contestants, any parent whose parental rights have not been previously terminated and any person who has physical custody of a child.

(f)   A court of a State may modify a determination of the custody of the same child made by a court of another State, if—

(1) it has jurisdiction to make such a child custody determination; and

(2) the court of the other State no longer has jurisdiction, or it has declined to exercise such jurisdiction to modify such determination.

(g) A court of a State shall not exercise jurisdiction in any proceeding for a custody or visitation determination commenced during the pendency of a proceeding in a court of another State where such court of that other State is exercising jurisdiction consistently with the provisions of this section to make a custody determination.

(h) A court of a State may not modify a visitation determination made by a court of another State unless the court of the other State no longer has jurisdiction to modify such determination or has declined to exercise jurisdiction to modify such determination.

NOTES AND QUESTIONS

1.   In Thompson v. Thompson, 484 U.S. 174 (1988), the Supreme Court held that the PKPA did not create a private right of action in federal court. The context in which the PKPA was enacted—the existence of jurisdictional deadlocks among the States in custody cases and a nationwide problem of interstate parental kidnapping—suggests that Congress' principal aim was to extend the requirements of the Full Faith and Credit Clause to custody determinations and not to create an entirely new cause of action. The court also noted that the PKPA's legislative history provides an unusually clear indication that Congress did not intend the federal courts to play the enforcement role. To date, Congress has not created a private right of action under the PKPA.

2.   Under the PKPA a state should not exercise "significant connection" jurisdiction if another state is the child's home state. If a state does exercise custody jurisdiction in such a situation, and the home state also renders a custody order, the home state order would be the one entitled to full faith and credit. Others are not. By itself, the PKPA does not preclude the possibility of conflicting *initial* custody decrees. *See, e.g., In re* Glanzner, 835 S.W.2d 386 (Mo. App. 1992).

B. THE UNIFORM CHILD CUSTODY JURISDICTION AND ENFORCEMENT ACT (UCCJEA)

In 1997, the National Commissioners of Uniform State Laws approved the Uniform Child Custody Jurisdiction and Enforcement Act (UCCJEA), 9 U.L.A. (Part I A) 649 (1999), which has, by 2017, been adopted in 49 states. Only Massachusetts still uses the UCCJA. Unlike the UCCJA, the UCCJEA is consistent with the PKPA and adopts home-state preference. The UCCJEA specifies that its provisions apply to *all* proceedings in which legal custody, physical custody, or visitation is an issue, including a proceeding for divorce, separation, neglect, abuse, dependency, guardianship, paternity, termination of parental rights, and protection from domestic violence. *See* UCCJEA § 102(4); *Uniform Child-Custody Jurisdiction and Enforcement Act (with Prefatory Note and Comments by Robert G. Spector)* 32 FAM. L. Q. 301 (1998). For a comparison of the UCCJA and UCCJEA, *see* Ron W. Nelson, *The UCCJA and the UCCJEA: A Side-by-Side Comparison,* 10/12 DIVORCE LITIG. 233 (1998).

UNIFORM CHILD CUSTODY JURISDICTION
AND ENFORCEMENT ACT

9 U.L.A. (Part IA) 649 (1999).

§ 201. Initial Child-Custody Jurisdiction.

(a) * * * [A] court of this State has jurisdiction to make an initial child-custody determination only if:

(1) this State is the home State of the child on the date of the commencement of the proceeding, or was the home State of the child within six months before the commencement of the proceeding and the child is absent from this State but a parent or person acting as a parent continues to live in this State;

(2) a court of another State does not have jurisdiction under paragraph (1), or a court of the home State of the child has declined to exercise jurisdiction on the ground that this State is the more appropriate forum under Section 207 or 208, and:

(A) the child and the child's parents, or the child and at least one parent or a person acting as a parent, have a significant connection with this State other than mere physical presence; and

(B) substantial evidence is available in this State concerning the child's care, protection, training, and personal relationships;

(3) all courts having jurisdiction under paragraph (1) or (2) have declined to exercise jurisdiction on the ground that a court of this State is the more appropriate forum to determine the custody of the child under Section 207 or 208; or

(4) no court of any other State would have jurisdiction under the criteria specified in paragraph (1), (2), or (3).

(b) Subsection (a) is the exclusive jurisdictional basis for making a child-custody determination by a court of this State.

(c) Physical presence of, or personal jurisdiction over, a party or a child is not necessary or sufficient to make a child-custody determination.

§ 202. Exclusive Continuing Jurisdiction.

(a)   Except as otherwise provided in Section 204, a court of this State which has made a child-custody determination consistent with Section 201 or 203 has exclusive, continuing jurisdiction over the determination until:

(1)   a court of this State determines that neither the child, the child and one parent, nor the child and a person acting as a parent have a significant connection with this State and that substantial evidence is no longer available in this State concerning the child's care, protection, training, and personal relationships; or

(2)   a court of this State or a court of another State determines that the child, the child's parents, and any person acting as a parent do not presently reside in this State.

(b)   A court of this State which has made a child-custody determination and does not have exclusive, continuing jurisdiction under this section may modify that determination only if it has jurisdiction to make an initial determination under Section 201.

§ 204. Temporary Emergency Jurisdiction.

(a)   A court of this State has temporary emergency jurisdiction if the child is present in this State and the child has been abandoned or it is necessary in an emergency to protect the child because the child, or a sibling or parent of the child, is subjected to or threatened with mistreatment or abuse. * * *

§ 206. Simultaneous Proceedings.

(a)   * * * [A] court of this State may not exercise its jurisdiction * * * if, at the time of the commencement of the proceeding, a proceeding concerning the custody of the child has been commenced in a court of another State having jurisdiction substantially in conformity with the [Act], unless the proceeding has been terminated or is stayed by the court of the other State. * * *

§ 207. Inconvenient Forum.

(a)   A court of this State which has jurisdiction * * * may decline to exercise its jurisdiction at any time if it determines that it is an inconvenient forum under the circumstances and that a court of another State is a more appropriate forum. The issue of inconvenient forum may be raised upon motion of party, the court's own motion, or request of another court. * * *

(b)   * * * the court shall * * * consider all relevant factors, including:

(1)   whether domestic violence has occurred and is likely to continue in the future and which State could best protect the parties and the child;

(2) the length of time the child has resided outside this State;

(3) the distance between the court in this State and the court in the State that would assume jurisdiction;

(4) the relative financial circumstances of the parties;

(5) any agreement of the parties as to which State should assume jurisdiction;

(6) the nature and location of the evidence required to resolve the pending litigation, including testimony of the child;

(7) the ability of the court of each State to decide the issue expeditiously and the procedures necessary to present the evidence; and

(8) the familiarity of the court of each State with the facts and issues in the pending litigation.

§ 208. Jurisdiction Declined by Reason of Conduct.

(a) * * * if a court of this State has jurisdiction under this [Act] because a person invoking the jurisdiction has engaged in unjustifiable conduct, the court shall decline to exercise its jurisdiction unless:

(1) the parents and all persons acting as parents have acquiesced in the exercise of jurisdiction;

(2) a court of the State otherwise having jurisdiction * * * determines that this State is a more appropriate forum * * *; or

(3) no other State would have jurisdiction * * *.

§ 303. Duty to Enforce.

(a) A court of this State shall recognize and enforce a child-custody determination of a court of another State if the latter court exercised jurisdiction that was in substantial conformity with this [Act] or the determination was made under factual circumstances meeting the jurisdictional standards of this [Act]. * * *

§ 305. Registration of Child-Custody Determination.

(a) A child-custody determination issued by a court of another State may be registered in this State, with or without a simultaneous request for enforcement * * *

§ 306. Enforcement of Registered Determination.

(a) A court of this State may grant any relief normally available under the law of this State to enforce a registered child-custody determination made by a court of another State.

(b) A court of this State shall recognize and enforce, but may not modify, except in accordance with [Article] 2, a registered child-custody determination of a court of another State.

IN RE MARRIAGE OF MYRLAND

Supreme Court of Montana, 2010.
359 Mont. 1, 248 P.3d 290.

LEAPHART, JUSTICE.

Carl Myrland (Carl) appeals from the 2009 Order dismissing his Petition for Dissolution and Parenting Plan for lack of subject matter jurisdiction. We address the following issues:

2.   Was the District Court correct in setting aside the Parenting Plan for lack of subject matter jurisdiction?

3.   Did the District Court abuse its discretion in declining to exercise jurisdiction over the custody of ANM?

We remand for further proceedings consistent with this opinion.

FACTUAL AND PROCEDURAL BACKGROUND

Carl and Heather were married March 28, 1998, in Helena, Montana. Heather and Carl had one child (ANM), born in Lewiston, Montana. Thereafter, Carl and Heather moved to North Carolina for work. Then, Heather moved to Las Vegas, leaving ANM and Carl in North Carolina. Carl and ANM moved back to Montana and remained in the state from 2002–2006. Heather made no attempt to contact ANM during this time period and alleges that she was living in Texas.

In March, 2006, Heather came to Helena along with her partner whom she introduced as her common law husband. They were living in the cab of a semi truck that they parked in front of the house where Carl and ANM were living in Helena, Montana. Heather requested to take ANM "for her Birthday" and offered to return her in a month. Heather took ANM and never returned. Heather filed an action for dissolution of marriage in Texas on May 26, 2006.

Carl claims that he was unaware of the whereabouts of Heather and ANM. Carl filed for a dissolution action in Montana on October 2, 2006. Carl attempted to serve Heather in Nevada, but to no avail. Carl effectively served Heather in Texas on about March 23, 2009.

Carl moved for default on the Petition for Dissolution filed in Montana. Heather made an appearance in the Montana dissolution action by mail at the Lewis and Clark County Courthouse on April 20, 2009. The court granted Carl's petition for default and issued a Decree of Dissolution. The Decree included a Parenting Plan.

The court issued the Decree on April 30, 2009, without actual knowledge of Heather's appearance on file at the courthouse. Heather then, through counsel, moved to have the default and dissolution set aside. Heather's motion was granted. A hearing was scheduled on the default decree and jurisdiction. The District Court determined that the dissolution of Carl and Heather's marriage and custody of ANM should be resolved in Texas. Carl appeals.

Was the District Court correct in setting aside the Parenting Plan for lack of subject matter jurisdiction?

Both Montana and Texas have adopted the Uniform Child Custody Jurisdiction and Enforcement Act (UCCJEA), which outlines the jurisdictional requirements for custodial determinations:

> A court of this state has jurisdiction to make an initial child custody determination only if . . . this state is the home state of the child on the date of the commencement of the proceeding or was the home state of the child within 6 months before the commencement of the proceeding and the child is absent from this state but a parent or person acting as a parent continues to live in this state.
>
> . . .
>
> Physical presence of . . . a party or a child is not necessary or sufficient to make a child custody determination.

Section 40–7–201, MCA. Therefore, the pertinent date for purposes of determining jurisdiction is the date of commencement, that is, the date the first pleading was filed. The Commissioners' Note explains how the UCCJEA should address potential jurisdictional conflicts by reason of conduct:

> [I]f a parent takes the child from the home State and seeks an original custody determination elsewhere, the stay-at-home parent has six months to file a custody petition under the extended home state jurisdictional provision of Section 201 [§ 40–7–201, MCA], which will ensure that the case is retained in the home State.

Commissioners' Note, § 40–7–109, MCA.

The facts in this case are identical to the scenario described in the Commissioners' Note. Heather left Montana with ANM and immediately sought an original custody determination elsewhere. ANM had resided in Montana for four years when Heather removed her from the State on or about April 24, 2006. Therefore, Montana was ANM's home state for purposes of jurisdiction until at least October 24, 2006. When Heather filed in Texas on May 26, 2006, ANM could have been in Texas for a few weeks.

A few weeks are clearly insufficient to establish Texas as the home state. When Carl filed in Montana, on October 2, 2006, Montana was still the home state of ANM and his petition was filed within six months of Heather's petition. Despite a delay in service and subsequent judicial proceedings, Montana is the only home state of ANM for purposes of jurisdiction.

The District Court determined that "the state in which the child has been living for the last six months is deemed the home state under Montana law." The court goes on to reason that under any of the facts asserted by the parties, the child had been in Texas "close enough" to the six months necessary to establish jurisdiction in Texas when Carl filed on October 2, 2006. The court further supported its analysis with the fact that ANM and Heather have been living in Texas for the past three years.

We disagree with the District Court's interpretation of the statute.

The District Court has first mischaracterized the jurisdictional requirements. The home state for purposes of jurisdiction is the home state of the child within six months before commencement of the proceeding. Section 40–7–201(1)(a), MCA. The home state is not, as the District Court's logic would suggest, any state where the child has resided for six months or for "the last" six months. Next, the District Court states that since ANM had been in Texas for nearly six months by the time Carl filed, the time ANM was in Texas is "close enough" to establish jurisdiction. However, this interpretation disregards that the pertinent date is the filing of the first pleading. The first pleading in this case was Heather's May 26, 2006, petition. At the time that Heather filed, ANM may have been in Texas for a few weeks. A few weeks are not at all "close enough" to the six month minimum requirement for home state jurisdiction. Finally, the fact that ANM has been in Texas for the last three years is not at all significant to our jurisdictional inquiry because according to § 40–7–201(3), MCA, physical presence of the child is neither necessary nor sufficient to establish jurisdiction.

Dismissing the case for lack of subject matter jurisdiction does not comport with the purpose of the UCCJEA to "deter abductions of children" and is a misapplication of the statute. The District Court incorrectly applied § 40–7–201, MCA, in setting aside the Parenting Plan for lack of subject matter jurisdiction. Montana was the only home state of ANM at the time Heather filed her Petition for Dissolution and thus is the only State with jurisdiction over the custody of ANM.

Under the UCCJEA, even where Montana is the home state, a district court may decide to decline jurisdiction at any time if it determines that it is an inconvenient forum.

The District Court set aside the Parenting Plan and dismissed Carl's petition for lack of subject jurisdiction. The court supported its conclusion with the fact that ANM has resided in Texas for approximately three years. Although the time the child has spent in another state is one of the many factors outlined in § 40–7–108(2), the District Court has not considered whether Montana is an inconvenient forum for that reason or any of the other reasons established in § 40–7–108(a)–(h), MCA.

CONCLUSION

Since Montana is the home state of ANM, the court had to either exercise its jurisdiction of the custody proceedings or determine that Montana is not a convenient forum for those proceedings. In the event the court determines that Montana is an inconvenient forum, the court must stay the proceedings so that custody proceedings may be promptly commenced in another state. Accordingly, we reverse and remand for the court to address the inconvenient forum factors under § 40–7–108(2)(a)–(h), MCA.

NOTES AND QUESTIONS

1.   UIFSA and the UCCJEA differ in some important respects. A state must have personal jurisdiction over the obligor to render a support order, while the UCCJEA assumes personal jurisdiction over the parents is not required. Under the UCCJEA, there is a "home state preference" for initial custody jurisdiction. This preference applies regardless whether an action has been filed in the home state, and as *Myrland* shows, a state remains the home state for six months after the child leaves if one parent stays there. Under UIFSA, there is a home state preference only if an action is filed in the home state shortly after an action is filed elsewhere, and a state stops being the home state when the child leaves (unless it is a temporary absence).

2.   UCCJEA includes a comprehensive definition of a "child custody proceeding" because there were some differences between states under the UCCJA. The section 102(a)(4) definition of a child custody proceeding "includes a proceeding for divorce, separation, neglect, abuse, dependency, guardianship, paternity, termination of parental rights, and protection from domestic violence, in which the issue may appear." The UCCJEA excludes juvenile delinquency proceedings as not custody and excludes adoption because its jurisdiction is covered in the Uniform Adoption Act, 9 U.L.A. 11 (1999).

3.   UCCJEA Section 204 expanded emergency jurisdiction to allow a court to assume jurisdiction without the home state or significant connection requirements if the child is subjected to or threatened with abuse as well as when the child has been abandoned. The jurisdiction is limited to temporary orders which protect the child until a state with initial or continuing jurisdiction enters an order. *See In re* Salminen, 492 S.W.3d 31 (Tex. App. 2016) (temporary emergency jurisdiction requires proof of extraordinary circumstances); South Carolina Dept. of Social Services v. Tran, 792 S.E.2d 254 (S.C. App. 2016) (parental rights cannot be terminated based on the exercise of emergency jurisdiction). If there is no home state or other state with

jurisdiction, the emergency custody determination can become final when the issuing state becomes the home state. The Uniform Child Abduction Prevention Act, adopted by the National Conference of Commissioners on Uniform State Laws, found at www.nccusl.org, allows for temporary emergency provision if there is "a credible risk of abduction." UCAPA § 5(b).

4.   The UCCJEA eliminates the UCCJA requirement that clerks of court maintain a registry for filing out of state custody decrees and documents and substitutes a registration procedure. Should this help with enforcement of child custody orders across state lines? *See* Patricia M. Hoff, *The ABC's of the UCCJEA: Interstate Child-Custody Practice Under the New Act*, 32 FAM. L. Q. 267, 290–291 (1998) (contending that deletion of the registry provision is a mistake in light of the advent of child support and domestic violence registries).

5.   *Foreign Country Orders:* UCCJEA § 105(b) provides: "Except as otherwise provided in (c), a child-custody determination made in a foreign country under factual circumstances in substantial conformity with the jurisdictional standards of this [Act] must be recognized and enforced." Subsection (c) provides that a court need not apply the UCCJEA if the child custody law of a foreign country violates fundamental principles of human rights.

6.   For purposes of calculating whether a child has been in a state for six months, periods of "temporary absence" are to be ignored. The statute does not clarify what this term means. Presumably it means absences from the state where, when the child leaves, both parents intend the child to return. So, in one case when the parents moved from Louisiana to Texas with the child and listed their Louisiana house for sale, and the mother changed her mind and returned to Louisiana with the child four months later, the court concluded this did not constitute a "temporary absence." *See In re* Marriage of Marsalis, 338 S.W.3d 131 (Tex. App. 2011).

In a Georgia case, the parents and their young child moved to Georgia in January 2014. In April 2014, the mother and the child went to Texas. In July 2014, the father filed an action in Georgia seeking custody, arguing that the mother's trip with the child to Texas was a temporary absence. In determining whether the absence was temporary, the appellate court noted that the mother had established that she had obtained a job in Texas, received public benefits in Texas, had found a doctor for the child there and attended church there. The appellate court found that this was not a temporary absence from Georgia. *See* Kogel v. Kogel, 786 S.E.2d 518 (Ga. App. 2016). If a child leaves the state to spend a short period of time with the other parent while planning to return, this is a temporary absence. *See* Felty v. Felty, 882 N.Y.S.2d 504, 509–510 (App. Div. 2009). If a child leaves the state with an initial understanding that the absence will be temporary, but then the parents later decide that the absence will be permanent, the absence ceases to be temporary when the parents' intention changes. *See In re* Marriage of Doolan, 682 N.W.2d 83 (Iowa App. 2004); Ogawa v. Ogawa, 221 P.3d 699, 704–705 (Nev. 2009).

In Drexler v. Bornman, 92 A.3d 628 (Md. App. 2014) the court proposed that courts should consider all surrounding circumstances when evaluating what is a temporary absence. In this case, after the parent had lived in Indiana for a year, she made what the court characterized as an impulsive decision to move to Maryland. She returned to Indiana 8 days later. This was held to be a temporary absence in Maryland.

Work assignments can sometimes be considered a temporary absence. In Garba v. Ndiaye, 132 A.3d 908 (Md. App. 2016) a couple married in Maryland. The wife took a job with the U.N. and primarily worked outside the U.S. She returned to Maryland to give birth. She then moved with the child to various international assignments for the next few years. She and the child sporadically returned to Maryland for visits during this period, sometimes for significant periods. The wife then filed an action for divorce in Maryland. Applying the "totality of the circumstances" test, the court found that the child's home state was Maryland, and that the trips abroad were temporary absences.

7.   Standards for determining whether a state has jurisdiction to make a custody award are different than those governing support. So, a court may find itself with custody jurisdiction but with no power to order support. *See* Ketteman v. Ketteman, 347 S.W.3d 647 (Mo. App. 2011).

8.   For a newborn, the UCCJEA defines the home state as "the state in which the child lived from birth with a parent." A state cannot obtain jurisdiction based on a pregnant woman living in the state before the child is born. *See* Arnold v. Price, 365 S.W.3d 455 (Tex. App. 2011).

For newborns, the question has arisen regarding how long the newborn must live in the state before that state becomes the home state. In *In re* R.L., 208 Cal. Rptr. 3d 523 (App. 2016) the California court held that, to establish home state status, the mother must live with the infant for a period of time. Merely giving birth in a California hospital did not create home state status. In Ocegueda v. Perreira, 181 Cal. Rptr. 3d 845 (App. 2015), the mother took a leave of absence from her California job so she could give birth to her child in Hawaii. Forty one days after the child's birth, she returned to California with the child. The day after she arrived in California, the father filed a custody action in California. Shortly thereafter, the mother filed an action in Hawaii. The California court ruled that, on the day the father filed the action in California, the child's home state was Hawaii. The fact that the mother always intended to return to California was not relevant. *See also,* Baker v. Tunny, 201 So. 3d 1235 (Fla. Dist. Ct. App. 2016) (living in Florida for two weeks after the birth creates home state). In Blanchette v. Blanchette, 476 S.W.3d 273 (Mo. 2015), the pregnant mother and father were living in West Virginia with one child when the father filed for divorce there. The mother and her son then moved to Missouri, where she gave birth to a daughter. If she files a custody action in Missouri after the daughter's birth, what state has jurisdiction to make a custody determination? Would the Missouri court have to enforce a West Virginia custody award regarding either or both children? (The Missouri court ruled that it did need to enforce the West Virginia custody decree as to both children).

IN RE FORLENZA

Supreme Court of Texas, 2004.
140 S.W.3d 373.

O'NEILL, JUSTICE.

After the trial court in this case made an initial child-custody determination, the children lived with their custodial parent in four different states over a five and one-half year period while the non-custodial parent remained in Texas. In this modification suit, we must decide whether significant connections with Texas exist or substantial evidence is available here such that the initial trial court retained exclusive continuing jurisdiction * * *. Based on the record presented, we hold that the trial court retained exclusive continuing jurisdiction over the modification proceedings and the court of appeals erred in concluding otherwise. * * *

I

Ann Marie and Robert Joseph Forlenza were divorced in Collin County, Texas, on March 1, 1996. On July 23, 1997, the trial court signed an agreed modification order, modifying the original divorce decree, that granted Robert primary custody of their two children, now ten and fourteen years old, and the exclusive right to establish their primary physical residence. That same month, the children moved with Robert to Issaquah, Washington. Over the next five years, Robert moved with the children three more times—on August 30, 1998, they moved to Ohio, on February 19, 1999, they moved to Virginia, and on August 27, 2002, they moved to Colorado where they now reside.

The current dispute arose in 2001 when Robert lost his job in Virginia and was offered a two-year contract job in Taipei, Taiwan. Claiming that she had experienced difficulty in exercising her possession rights, Ann filed this suit on September 10, 2001, seeking to modify the prior agreed possession order. She also requested a restraining order prohibiting Robert from relocating the children outside the United States, which the trial court granted. * * *

Robert filed a * * * motion to dismiss alleging that the court did not have exclusive continuing jurisdiction * * * to modify its previous child-custody order. The trial court conducted an[ ] evidentiary hearing and denied the motion. The court of appeals * * * concluded that the trial court had abused its discretion and granted Robert's petition for writ of mandamus, ordering the trial court to vacate its prior order and dismiss the case. We granted Ann's petition to determine whether the trial court retained exclusive continuing jurisdiction under the Uniform Child Custody Jurisdiction Enforcement Act (UCCJEA).

II

* * *

Article 2 of the UCCJEA specifically grants exclusive continuing jurisdiction over child-custody disputes to the state that made the initial custody determination and provides specific rules on how long this jurisdiction continues. * * * Rules that prevent another state from modifying a child-custody determination while exclusive continuing jurisdiction remains in the original-decree state complement these provisions. Texas adopted Article 2 without substantial variation from the UCCJEA.

Robert's challenge involves the proper interpretation of section 152.202(a), which governs the duration of the decree-granting state's exclusive continuing jurisdiction. That section provides that a court of this state that has made an initial child-custody determination consistent with section 152.201 has exclusive continuing jurisdiction over the determination until

> (1) a court of this state determines that *neither the child, nor the child and one parent,* nor the child and a person acting as a parent, *have a significant connection with this state and* that *substantial evidence is no longer available in this state* concerning the child's care, protection, training, and personal relationships; or

> (2) a court of this state or a court of another state determines that the child, the child's parents, and any person acting as a parent do not presently reside in this state. (emphasis added).

* * * [S]ection 152.202(a)(2) does not apply because Ann continues to reside in Texas. Therefore, we must decide whether the trial court properly applied section 152.202(a)(1) in deciding that it had exclusive continuing jurisdiction over these modification proceedings. Statutory construction is a question of law that we review de novo.

* * * By alleging that the court's prior orders conferred exclusive continuing jurisdiction, Ann satisfied her initial statutory burden. The statute specifically provides that a court *retains* exclusive continuing jurisdiction *until* it determines that the significant-connection and substantial-evidence requirements are no longer met. Robert may challenge whether the statutory elements are satisfied, or the court may consider them sua sponte, but Ann has satisfied her initial jurisdictional burden under the statute.

Robert contends that the children no longer have a significant connection with Texas because (1) the children visited here only five times in the four-year period preceding this action, and (2) Ann's residence in Texas is not sufficient, as the commentary to section 152.202 specifically notes that the presence of one parent remaining in the state is not determinative. But Ann does not rely on her mere presence in Texas to establish a significant connection under the statute. Contrary to Robert's briefing, the record indicates that the children actually visited Texas six times in the relevant period. On four of these occasions the children lived with Ann for considerable periods, each lasting approximately one month during the summer. *See Fish v. Fish,* 596 S.E.2d 654, 656 (Ga. Ct. App. 2004) (pointing to extended custodial visitation in state to support court's finding of a significant connection); *Ruth v. Ruth,* 32 Kan. App. 2d 416, 83 P.3d 1248, 1254 (2004) (same). Moreover, we presume that the trial court accepted as true Ann's testimony that more visitation would have occurred in Texas but for Robert's actions and the fact that the children were not allowed to fly to Texas.

Other courts commonly consider visitation within the state as evidence of a significant connection. In addition, numerous relatives, including Ann's mother and sister and Robert's sister and sister-in-law, live in Texas and maintain a relationship with the children.

Moreover, the evidence in this case clearly indicates that Ann maintained a significant relationship with her children. * * * To accommodate the children's schedule over the years, Ann repeatedly flew to Washington, Ohio, and Virginia to see them. Robert admits that Ann made at least fifteen such trips in the four-year period under review. Because the record establishes that the children visited Texas on a number of occasions and maintained a close relationship with their mother and other relatives residing in Texas, all important considerations under the UCCJEA, we hold that the children have a significant connection with Texas sufficient to support the trial court's exclusive continuing jurisdiction over the modification proceedings. * * *

Robert claims that no other court has exercised exclusive continuing jurisdiction over children who have resided out of state for more than five years. We disagree. In *Fish,* the Georgia Court of Appeals determined that the trial court had exclusive continuing jurisdiction pursuant to a prior divorce decree even though the mother and the children had lived in Florida for seven years. Similarly, in *Ruth,* the Kansas Court of Appeals determined that the trial court had jurisdiction pursuant to a prior divorce decree after the mother and children had lived in Missouri for approximately six years. And in *Heath v. Heath,* a Connecticut court exercised exclusive continuing jurisdiction even though the children had lived in California for eight years. Moreover, contrary to Robert's argument, the UCCJEA does not premise the exclusive continuing jurisdiction determination on which state has the *most* significant connection with the child. *See In re Dale McCormick,* 87 S.W.3d at 750 (stating that "[a]lthough evidence was admitted which establishes that [the child] has significant ties with the state of Kansas, that fact does not necessarily mean that there is no significant connection with Texas or that substantial evidence cannot be found here"). This relative type of inquiry is appropriate under section 152.207, which allows a court with exclusive continuing jurisdiction to decline it in favor of a more convenient forum, but it does not affect the initial section 152.202 jurisdictional analysis. Importantly, the only issue before us is whether the Texas court retained jurisdiction; the court could still decline to exercise that jurisdiction if another forum was more convenient. In this case, though, the children's almost continual change of residence supports the trial court's conclusion that the children had a significant connection with Texas based on their visits here and their personal relationships maintained in this state.

Finally, Robert argues that substantial evidence does not exist in Texas regarding the children's care, protection, training, and personal relationships, and section 152.202(a)(1) requires the trial court to find *both* a significant connection with Texas *and* that substantial evidence exists here before it can exercise exclusive continuing jurisdiction. * * * We disagree.

Robert's * * * [claim] ignores section 152.202(a)(1)'s plain language. That section specifically states that jurisdiction continues until the court determines that there is not a significant connection with Texas *and* that substantial evidence concerning the children's care, protection, training, and personal relationships is no longer available here. Clearly, exclusive jurisdiction continues in the decree-granting state as long as a significant connection exists *or* substantial evidence is present. * * * Because we conclude that the trial court did not err in concluding that the children had a substantial connection with Texas on September 10, 2001, we need not address whether substantial evidence existed here as well.

For the foregoing reasons, we hold that the trial court had exclusive continuing jurisdiction over this modification proceeding and that mandamus relief is justified. Accordingly, we conditionally grant the writ of mandamus and direct the court of appeals to vacate its order directing the trial court to dismiss the case for lack of jurisdiction. The writ will issue only if the court of appeals does not comply.

NOTES AND QUESTIONS

1.   Under the UCCJEA, the rendering state loses its jurisdiction to modify if at the time a modification action is filed no party continues to reside in the rendering state. In Sidell v. Sidell, 18 A.3d 499 (R.I. 2011) the parties agreed in their marital settlement agreement that the courts of Rhode Island would have continuing exclusive jurisdiction over custody and visitation matters regardless if everyone left Rhode Island. The Rhode Island Supreme Court concluded that, despite this agreement, Rhode Island courts lacked

subject matter jurisdiction to hear a motion to modify custody once all parents had moved from the state. *See also* Friedman v. District Court, 264 P.3d 1161 (Nev. 2011). Similarly, in *In re* Ruff, 275 P.3d 1175 (Wash. App. 2012) the court held that the parties could not by agreement change the court with exclusive continuing jurisdiction to modify.

2.   One of the many differences between UIFSA and the UCCJEA is that the latter gives the court with jurisdiction the right to defer to another forum that is more convenient, while the former does not. *See* O'Neil v. O'Neil, 724 S.E.2d 247 (Va. App. 2012); Ervin v. Ervin, 265 P.3d 1272 (Mont. 2011). Similarly, while the UCCJEA gives the court hearing a petition for an initial custody order the discretion to decline jurisdiction based on the petitioner's conduct, there is no comparable provisions in UIFSA. *See In re* M.I.M., 370 S.W.3d 94 (Tex. App. 2012).

3.   The rendering state can lose exclusive continuing jurisdiction to modify custody if it is determined that neither the child nor any parent "presently resides" in this state. In Brandt v. Brandt, 268 P.3d 406 (Colo. 2012) the Colorado Supreme Court construed this term as referring to domicile, not physical presence.

4.   In Kar v. Kar, 378 P.3d 1204 (Nev. 2016) after a Nevada court rendered a custody decree, both parents moved out of the country. When the father filed a motion to modify the custody decree in Nevada two months after the mother had moved to England with the child, the trial court dismissed the petition because neither parent resided in Nevada. The Nevada Supreme Court ruled that, while Nevada courts may have lost the exclusive jurisdiction to modify, it might still have jurisdiction. The Nevada court held that, because there was no home state when the father filed his motion, because the Nevada action was filed first the Nevada court could exercise jurisdiction based on a significant connection between Nevada and the child and a parent.

Problem 13-7:

Harry and Wanda lived in Maine with their child Sam. Harry took Sam without Wanda's permission and absconded; Wanda did not know where they were. If Wanda files an action in Maine, could the court determine custody while Sam and Harry are out of state? *See* Lyons v. Lyons, 314 S.E.2d 362 (Va. 1984). If she does not file an action, does the state to which Harry has taken Sam become the home state after six months? *See* Sams v. Boston, 384 S.E.2d 151 (W. Va. 1989).

Problem 13-8:

Mary and Tom have always lived in Florida with their two children, ages 6 and 9. Mary and Tom decide to divorce and Mary and the children moved to Kansas, which requires residency for sixty days before filing for divorce. Three months after the move, Mary filed for divorce and custody in Kansas. The children were enrolled in school and doing well. Five months after the move, Tom filed for divorce and custody in Florida. Does

Kansas have jurisdiction over the divorce? over child custody under the PKPA? the UCCJEA?

Problem 13-9:

Carol and Jake have lived in Colorado throughout their marriage; both of their two children, now ages 8 and 12, have lived there throughout their lives. Carol moved to Kansas in June with the children. In October, of the same year she filed for divorce and custody in Kansas. Two months later, the Kansas court awards Carol a divorce and custody of the two children with Jake have specified visitation. The children went to visit Jake in June, of the following year; he refused to return them and filed a petition to modify the Kansas custody decree in Colorado. Under the PKPA and UCCJEA, must the Colorado court enforce the Kansas decree? Must it *not* enforce the decree?

Problem 13-10:

Winnie filed for divorce in Texas. At that time, Winnie, her husband Henry, and their two children were all living in Germany because Henry was stationed there. Winnie filed suit in Texas because Henry was legally domiciled in Texas for the six months the divorce filing and was a "resident" of Dallas County. In her petition, Winnie did not request the trial court to enter orders regarding custody or support of their children. Instead, she alleged the children were under the jurisdiction of a German court. Henry answered the divorce petition and filed a counterpetition requesting the Texas court to make custody and support orders. Winnie filed a motion to dismiss the counterpetition, asserting that the Texas court did not have jurisdiction over custody issues under the Uniform Child Custody Jurisdiction Enforcement Act (UCCJEA) because Texas was not the "home state" of the children and because there was a "pending custody matter" before a German court. The trial court conducted a hearing on the motion to dismiss. At the hearing, Winnie established that a German court had entered orders regarding the children, but only with respect to Winnie's right to establish the children's residence. After the hearing, the trial court denied the motion.

Winnie and Henry subsequently entered into a settlement agreement regarding custody, visitation, child support, and division of property. They agreed they would cooperate to have the decree registered in Germany with the intent that it be enforced as permitted by law. Pursuant to the settlement, the trial court entered an agreed final decree.

Winnie has now appealed from the decree. She claims that the trial court did not have jurisdiction under the UCCJEA to include in its decree provisions regarding child custody because Texas is not the "home state" of the children. What ruling should the appellate court make? Why? *See* Seligman-Hargis v. Hargis, 186 S.W.3d 582 (Tex. App. 2006).

5. THE HAGUE CONVENTION

International child abduction has become a serious problem because of the increasing number of international marriages and the ease of international travel and communication. In 1980 the Hague Conference on Private International Law adopted the Hague Convention on the Civil Aspects of International Child Abduction to secure the return of children wrongfully removed from the country of their "habitual residence." The Convention generally requires that, subject to certain exceptions, if a child is found to have been wrongfully removed from the child's habitual residence, a court in the country where the child has been taken is obligated to order the child returned to the child's habitual residence. In 1986, the United States Congress passed the implementing legislation: International Child Abduction Remedies Act (ICARA), 42 U.S.C. §§ 11601–11610. In early 2017, 94 countries had adopted this convention. *See* Hague Conference on Private International Law: Status Sheet Convention #28 http://www.hcch.net/e/status/abdshte.html.

FRIEDRICH V. FRIEDRICH
United States Court of Appeals, Sixth Circuit, 1996.
78 F.3d 1060.

BOGGS, CIRCUIT JUDGE.

For the second time, we address the application of the Hague Convention on the Civil Aspects of International Child Abduction ("the Convention") and its implementing legislation, the International Child Abduction Remedies Act ("the Act"), 42 U.S.C. §§ 11601–11610, to the life of Thomas Friedrich, now age six. We affirm the district court's order that Thomas was wrongfully removed from Germany and should be returned.

I

Thomas was born in Bad Aibling, Germany, to Jeana Friedrich, an American service-woman stationed there, and her husband, Emanuel Friedrich, a German citizen. When Thomas was two years old, his parents separated after an argument on July 27, 1991. Less than a week later, in the early morning of August 2, 1991, Mrs. Friedrich took Thomas from Germany to her family home in Ironton, Ohio, without informing Mr. Friedrich. Mr. Friedrich sought return of the child in German Family Court, obtaining an order awarding him custody on August 22. He then filed this action for the return of his son in the United States District Court for the Southern District of Ohio on September 23.

We first heard this case three years ago. *Friedrich v. Friedrich*, 983 F.2d 1396 (6th Cir. 1993) ("*Friedrich I*"). At that time, we reversed the district court's denial of Mr. Friedrich's claim for the return of his son to Germany pursuant to the Convention. We outlined the relevant law on what was then an issue of first impression in the federal appellate courts, and remanded with instructions that the district court determine whether, as a matter of German law, Mr. Friedrich was exercising custody rights to Thomas at the time of removal. We also asked the district court to decide if Mrs. Friedrich could prove any of the four affirmative defenses provided by the Convention and the Act. Thomas, meanwhile, remained with his mother and his mother's parents in Ohio.

On remand, the district court allowed additional discovery and held a new hearing. The court eventually determined that, at the time of Thomas's removal on August 1, 1991, Mr. Friedrich was exercising custody rights to Thomas under German law, or would have been exercising such rights but for the removal. The court then held that Mrs. Friedrich had not established any of the affirmative defenses available to her under the Convention. The court ordered Mrs. Friedrich to return Thomas to Germany "forthwith," but later stayed the order, upon the posting of a bond by Mrs. Friedrich, pending the resolution of this appeal.

Mrs. Friedrich's appeal raises two issues that are central to the young jurisprudence of the Hague Convention. First, what does it mean to "exercise" custody rights? Second, when can a court refuse to return a child who has been wrongfully removed from a country because return of the abducted child would result in a "grave" risk of harm?

In answering both these questions, we keep in mind two general principles inherent in the Convention and the Act, expressed in *Friedrich I*, and subsequently embraced by unanimous federal authority. First, a court in the abducted-to nation has jurisdiction to decide the merits of an abduction claim, but not the merits of the underlying custody dispute. Hague Convention, Article 19; 42 U.S.C. § 11601(b)(4) * * * Second, the Hague Convention is generally intended to restore the pre-abduction status quo and to deter parents from crossing borders in search of a more sympathetic court. * * *

II

The removal of a child from the country of its habitual residence is "wrongful" under the Hague Convention if a person in that country is, or would otherwise be, exercising custody rights to the child under that country's law at the moment of removal. Hague Convention, Article 3. The plaintiff in an action for return of the child has the burden of proving the exercise of custody rights by a preponderance of the evidence. 42 U.S.C. § 11603(e)(1)(A). We review the district court's findings of fact for clear error and review its conclusions about American, foreign, and international law *de novo*.

The district court held that a preponderance of the evidence in the record established that Mr. Friedrich was exercising custody rights over Thomas at the time of Thomas's removal. Mrs. Friedrich alleges that the district court improperly applied German law. Reviewing *de novo*, we find no error in the court's legal analysis. Custody rights "may arise in particular by operation of law or by reason of a judicial or administrative decision, or by reason of an agreement having legal effect under the law of the State." Hague Convention, Article 3. German law gives both parents equal *de jure* custody of the child, German Civil Code 1626(1), and, with a few exceptions, this *de jure* custody continues until a competent court says otherwise.

Mrs. Friedrich argues that Mr. Friedrich "terminated" his custody rights under German law because, during the argument on the evening of July 27, 1991, he placed Thomas's belongings and hers in the hallway outside of their apartment. The district court properly rejected the claim that these actions could end parental rights as a matter of German law. We agree. * * *

Mrs. Friedrich also argues that, even if Mr. Friedrich had custody rights under German law, he was not *exercising* those custody rights as contemplated by the Hague Convention. She argues that, since custody rights include the care for the person and property of the child, Mr. Friedrich was not exercising custody rights because he was not paying for or taking care of the child during the brief period of separation in Germany.

The Hague Convention does not define "exercise." As judges in a common law country, we can easily imagine doing so ourselves. One might look to the law of the foreign country to determine if custody rights existed *de jure*, and then develop a test under the general principles of the Hague Convention to determine what activities—financial support, visitation—constitute sufficient exercise of *de jure* rights. The question in our immediate case would then be: "was Mr. Friedrich's single visit with Thomas and plans for future visits with Thomas sufficient exercise of custodial rights for us to justify calling the removal of Thomas wrongful?" One might even approach a distinction between the exercise of "custody" rights and the exercise of "access" or "visitation" rights. If Mr. Friedrich, who has *de jure* custody, was, not exercising sufficient *de facto* custody, Thomas's removal would not be wrongful.

We think it unwise to attempt any such project. Enforcement of the Convention should not to be made dependent on the creation of a common law definition of "exercise." The only acceptable solution, in the absence of a ruling from a court in the country of habitual residence, is to liberally find "exercise" whenever a parent with *de jure* custody rights keeps, or seeks to keep, any sort of regular contact with his or her child.

We see three reasons for this broad definition of "exercise." First, American courts are not well suited to determine the consequences of parental behavior under the law of a foreign country. It is fairly easy for the courts of one country to determine whether a person has custody rights under the law of another country. It is also quite possible for a court to determine if an order by a foreign court awards someone "custody" rights, as opposed to rights of "access." Far more difficult is the task of deciding, prior to a ruling by a court in the abducted-from country, if a parent's custody rights should be ignored because he or she was not acting sufficiently like a custodial parent. A foreign court, if at all possible, should refrain from making such policy-oriented decisions concerning the application of German law to a child whose habitual residence is, or was, Germany.

Second, an American decision about the adequacy of one parent's exercise of custody rights is dangerously close to forbidden territory: the merits of the custody dispute. The German court in this case is perfectly capable of taking into account Mr. Friedrich's behavior during the August 1991 separation, and the German court presumably will tailor its custody order accordingly. A decision by an American court to deny return to Germany because Mr. Friedrich did not show sufficient attention or concern for Thomas's welfare would preclude the German court from addressing these issues—and the German court may well resolve them differently.

Third, the confusing dynamics of quarrels and informal separations make it difficult to assess adequately the acts and motivations of a parent. An occasional visit may be all that is available to someone left, by the vagaries of marital discord, temporarily without the child. Often the child may be avoided, not out of a desire to relinquish custody, but out of anger, pride, embarrassment, or fear, vis a vis the other parent. Reading too much into a parent's behavior during these difficult times could be inaccurate and unfair. Although there may be situations when a long period of unexplainable neglect of the child could constitute non-exercise of otherwise valid custody rights under the Convention, as a general rule, any attempt to maintain a somewhat regular relationship with the child should constitute "exercise." This rule leaves the full resolution of custody issues, as the Convention and common sense indicate, to the courts of the country of habitual residence.

We are well aware that our approach requires a parent, in the event of a separation or custody dispute, to seek permission from the other parent or from the courts before taking a child out of the country of its habitual residence. Any other approach allows a parent to pick a "home court" for the custody dispute *ex parte*, defeating a primary purpose of the Convention. We believe that, where the reason for removal is legitimate, it will not usually be difficult to obtain approval from either the other parent or a foreign court. Furthermore, as the case for removal of the child in the custody of one parent becomes more compelling, approval (at least the approval of a foreign court) should become easier to secure. * * *

We therefore hold that, if a person has valid custody rights to a child under the law of the country of the child's habitual residence, that person cannot fail to "exercise" those custody rights under the Hague Convention short of acts that constitute clear and unequivocal abandonment of the child. Once it determines that the parent exercised custody rights in any manner, the court should stop—completely avoiding the question whether the parent exercised the custody rights well or badly. These matters go to the merits of the custody dispute and are, therefore, beyond the subject matter jurisdiction of the federal courts.

In this case, German law gave Mr. Friedrich custody rights to Thomas. The facts before us clearly indicate that he attempted to exercise these rights during the separation from his wife. Mr. and Mrs. Friedrich argued during the evening of July 27, 1991, and separated on the morning of July 28. Mrs. Friedrich left with her belongings and Thomas. She stayed on the army base with the child four days. Mr. Friedrich telephoned Mrs. Friedrich on July 29 to arrange a visit with Thomas, and spent the afternoon of that day with his son. Mr. and Mrs. Friedrich met on August 1 to talk about Thomas and their separation. The parties dispute the upshot of this conversation. Mrs. Friedrich says that Mr. Friedrich expressed a general willingness that Thomas move to America with his mother. Mr. Friedrich denies this. It is clear, however, that the parties did agree to immediate visitations of Thomas by Mr. Friedrich, scheduling the first such visit for August 3. Shortly after midnight on August 2, Mrs. Friedrich took her son and, without informing her husband, left for America by airplane.

Because Mr. Friedrich had custody rights to Thomas as a matter of German law, and did not clearly abandon those rights prior to August 1, the removal of Thomas without his consent was wrongful under the Convention, regardless of any other considerations about Mr. Friedrich's behavior during the family's separation in Germany.

III

Once a plaintiff establishes that removal was wrongful, the child must be returned unless the defendant can establish one of four defenses. Two of these defenses can be established by a preponderance of the evidence, 42 U.S.C. § 11603(e)(2)(B): the proceeding was commenced more than one year after the removal of the child and the child has become settled in his or her new environment, Hague Convention, Article 12; or, the person seeking return of the child consented to or subsequently acquiesced in the removal or retention, Hague Convention, Article 13a. The other two defenses must be shown by clear and convincing evidence, 42 U.S.C. § 11603(e)(2)(A): there is a grave risk that the return of the child would expose it to physical or psychological harm, Hague Convention, Article 13b; or, the return of the child "would not be permitted by the fundamental principles of the requested State relating to the protection of human rights and fundamental freedoms," Hague Convention, Article 20.

All four of these exceptions are "narrow." They are not a basis for avoiding return of a child merely because an American court believes it can better or more quickly resolve a dispute. In fact, a federal court retains, and should use when appropriate, the discretion to return a child, despite the existence of a defense, if return would further the aims of the Convention.

Mrs. Friedrich alleges that she proved by clear and convincing evidence in the proceedings below that the return of Thomas to Germany would cause him grave psychological harm. Mrs. Friedrich testified that Thomas has grown attached to family and friends in Ohio. She also hired an expert psychologist who testified that returning Thomas to Germany would be traumatic and difficult for the child, who was currently happy and healthy in America with his mother.

> [Thomas] definitely would experience the loss of his mother * * * if he were to be removed to Germany. That would be a considerable loss.

> And there then would be the probabilities of anger both towards his mother, who it might appear that she has abandoned him [sic], and towards the father for creating that abandonment. [These feelings] could be plenty enough springboard for other developmental or emotional restrictions which could include nightmares, antisocial behavior, a whole host of anxious-type behavior.

Blaske Deposition at 28–29.

If we are to take the international obligations of American courts with any degree of seriousness, the exception to the Hague Convention for grave harm to the child requires far more than the evidence that Mrs. Friedrich provides. Mrs. Friedrich alleges nothing more than *adjustment* problems that would attend the relocation of most children. There is no allegation that Mr. Friedrich has ever abused Thomas. The district court found that the home that Mr. Friedrich has prepared for Thomas in Germany appears adequate to the needs of any young child. The father does not work long hours, and the child's German grandmother is ready to care for the child when the father cannot. There is nothing in the record to indicate that life in Germany would result in any permanent harm or unhappiness.

Furthermore, even *if* the home of Mr. Friedrich were a grim place to raise a child in comparison to the pretty, peaceful streets of Ironton, Ohio, that fact would be irrelevant to a federal court's obligation under the Convention. We are not to debate the relevant virtues of Batman and *Max und Mortiz,* Wheaties and *Milchreis.* The exception for grave harm to the child is not license for a court in the abducted-to country to speculate on where the child would be happiest. That decision is a custody matter, and reserved to the court in the country of habitual residence.

Mrs. Friedrich advocates a wide interpretation of the grave risk of harm exception that would reward her for violating the Convention. A removing parent must not be allowed to abduct a child and then—when brought to court—complaint that the child has grown used to the surroundings to which they were abducted. Under the logic of the Convention, it is the *abduction* that causes the pangs of subsequent return. The disruption of the usual sense of attachment that arises during most long stays in a single place with a single parent should not be a "grave" risk of harm for the purposes of the Convention.

In thinking about these problems, we acknowledge that courts in the abducted-from country are as ready and able as we are to protect children. If return to a country, or to the custody of a parent in that country, is dangerous, we can expect that country's courts to respond accordingly. And if Germany really is a poor place for young Thomas to grow up, as Mrs. Friedrich contends, we can expect the German courts to recognize that and award her custody in America. When we trust the court system in the abducted-from country, the vast majority of claims of harm—those that do not rise to the level of gravity required by the Convention—evaporate.

The international precedent available supports our restrictive reading of the grave harm exception. * * * Finally, we are instructed by the following observation by the United States Department of State concerning the grave risk of harm exception:

> This provision was not intended to be used by defendants as a vehicle to litigate (or relitigate) the child's best interests. Only evidence directly establishing the existence of a grave risk that would expose the child to physical or emotional harm or otherwise place the child in an *intolerable* situation is material to the court's determination. The person opposing the child's return must show that the risk to the child is grave, not merely serious.

> A review of deliberations on the Convention reveals that "intolerable situation" was not intended to encompass return to a home where money is in short support, or where educational or other opportunities are more limited than in the requested State. An example of an "intolerable situation" is one in which a custodial parent sexually abuses the child. If the other parent removes or retains the child to safeguard it against further victimization and the abusive parent then petitions for the child's return under the Convention, the court may deny the petition. Such action would protect the child from being returned to an

"intolerable situation" and subjected to a grave risk of psychological harm.

Public Notice 957, 51 FR 10494, 10510 (March 26, 1986) (emphasis added).

For all of these reasons, we hold that the district court did not err by holding that "[t]he record in the instant case does not demonstrate by clear and convincing evidence that Thomas will be exposed to a grave risk of harm." Although it is not necessary to resolve the present appeal, we believe that a grave risk of harm for the purposes of the Convention can exist in only two situations. First, there is a grave risk of harm when return of the child puts the child in imminent danger *prior* to the resolution of the custody dispute—*e.g.,* returning the child to a zone of war, famine, or disease. Second, there is a grave risk of harm in cases of serious abuse or neglect, or extraordinary emotional dependence, when the court in the country of habitual residence, for whatever reason, may be incapable or unwilling to give the child adequate protection. Psychological evidence of the sort Mrs. Friedrich introduced in the proceeding below is only relevant if it helps prove the existence of one of these two situations.

IV

Mrs. Friedrich also claims that the district court erred in ordering Thomas's return because Mrs. Friedrich proved by a preponderance of the evidence that Mr. Friedrich (i) consented to, and (ii) subsequently acquiesced in, the removal of Thomas to America.

Mrs. Friedrich bases her claim of consent to removal on statements that she claims Mr. Friedrich made to her during their separation. Mr. Friedrich flatly denies that he made these statements. The district court was faced with a choice as to whom it found more believable in a factual dispute. There is nothing in the record to suggest that the court's decision to believe Mr. Friedrich, and hold that he "did not exhibit an intention or a willingness to terminate his parental rights," was clearly erroneous. In fact, Mr. Friedrich's testimony is strongly supported by the circumstances of the removal of Thomas—most notably the fact that Mrs. Friedrich did not inform Mr. Friedrich that she was departing. * * * The deliberately secretive nature of her actions is extremely strong evidence that Mr. Friedrich would not have consented to the removal of Thomas. For these reasons, we hold that the district court did not abuse its discretion in finding that Mrs. Friedrich took Thomas to America without Mr. Friedrich's consent.

Mrs. Friedrich bases her claim of subsequent acquiescence on a statement made by Mr. Friedrich to one of her commanding officers, Captain Michael Farley, at a cocktail party on the military base after Mrs. Friedrich had left with Thomas. Captain Farley, who cannot date the conversation exactly, testified that:

> During the conversation, Mr. Friedrich indicated that he was not seeking custody of the child, because he didn't have the means to take care of the child.

Farley Deposition at 13. Mr. Friedrich denies that he made this statement. The district court made no specific finding regarding this fact.

We believe that the statement to Captain Farley, even if it was made, is insufficient evidence of subsequent acquiescence. Subsequent acquiescence requires more than an isolated statement to a third-party. Each of the words and actions of a parent during the separation are not to be scrutinized for a possible waiver of custody rights. Although we must decide the matter without guidance from previous appellate court decisions, we believe that acquiescence under the Convention requires either: an act or statement with the requisite formality, such as testimony in a judicial proceeding, a convincing written renunciation of rights; or a consistent attitude of acquiescence over a significant period of time.

By August 22, 1991, twenty-one days after the abduction, Mr. Friedrich had secured a German court order awarding him custody of Thomas. He has resolutely sought custody of his son since that time. It is by these acts, not his casual statements to third parties, that we will determine whether or not he acquiesced to the retention of his son in America. Since Mrs. Friedrich has not introduced evidence of a formal renunciation or a consistent attitude of acquiescence over a significant period of time, the judgment of the district court on this matter was not erroneous.

V

The district court's order that Thomas be immediately returned to Germany, is affirmed, and the district court's stay of that order pending appeal is vacated. Because Thomas's return to Germany is already long-overdue, we order, pursuant to Fed. R. App. P. 41(a), that our mandate issue forthwith.

NOTES AND QUESTIONS

1. Under the Convention, federal and state courts in the jurisdiction where the child is located have concurrent jurisdiction to hear actions. There has been an increasing number of reported Hague cases in federal court. *See* Merle H. Weiner, *Navigating the Road Between Uniformity and Progress: The Need for Purposeful Analysis of the Hague Convention on the Civil Aspects of International Child Abduction*, 33 COLUM. HUMAN RIGHTS L. REV. 275 (2002) (noting 300% increase in number of cases between July 2000 and January 2001 over 1993). How would you determine whether to file in state or federal court? See Robert G. Spector, *International Child Abduction of Children: Why the UCCJEA is Usually a Better Remedy Than the Abduction Convention*, 49 FAM. L. Q. 385 (2015).

2.   If an action under the Convention is brought within one year of a wrongful taking or retention, the court must return the child unless a defense to return under article 13 or 20 is found. These defenses are: (a) parental consent or subsequent acquiescence to the removal; (b) a "grave risk" that return will expose the child to physical or psychological harm or place the child in an intolerable situation; or (c) an objection to return by a child of "suitable age." As *Friedrich* indicates, courts have construed all of these defenses narrowly. *See* Habrzyk v. Habrzyk, 775 F. Supp. 2d 1054, 1065 (N.D. Ill. 2011); March v. Levine, 249 F.3d 462 (6th Cir. 2001); Miller v. Miller, 240 F.3d 392 (4th Cir. 2001).

If a petition is filed more than one year after the wrongful removal, the court does not have to order the child's return if the child is now "settled" in its new environment. Hague Convention, Art. 12. *See* Aranda v. Serna, 911 F. Supp. 2d 601 (M.D. Tenn. 2013); *In re* D.T.J., 956 F. Supp. 2d 523 (S.D. N.Y. 2013). There is no tolling of the one year even if one parent has concealed the child. Lozano v. Montoya Alvarez, 134 S. Ct. 1224 (2014).

3.   What factors constitute "grave risk of harm" under the Convention?

a.   Proven abuse of child? *See* Ortiz v. Martinez, 789 F.3d 722 (7th Cir. 2015) (finding abuse and refusing return); Danaipour v. McLarey, 286 F.3d 1 (1st Cir. 2002) (ordering forensic evaluation); Blondin v. Dubois, 238 F.3d 153 (2d Cir. 2001) (denying request to return children to France where judge found that children would suffer post-traumatic stress syndrome). Cf. Vale v. Avila, 538 F.3d 581 (7th Cir. 2008) (one incident of striking with video game chord was not sufficient showing of "abuse").

b.   Child's fear of abuse? *See* Rodriguez v. Rodriguez, 33 F. Supp. 2d 456 (D. Md. 1999) (finding that grave risk of harm to children came from their well-founded fear of physical abuse, whether or not actual abuse occurred).

c.   One parent's abuse of the other parent? *See* Walsh v. Walsh, 221 F.3d 204 (1st Cir. 2000) (allowing defense where mother was domestic violence victim and father had a history of violating court orders); Acosta v. Acosta, 725 F.3d 868 (8th Cir. 2013) (grave risk because evidence showed the petitioner had verbally and physically abused the other in front of the children); Miltiadous v. Tetervak, 686 F. Supp. 2d 544 (E.D. Pa. 2010) (not returning children where father had physically abused wife, but not children).

d.   One parent's temper and alcohol usage? Baran v. Beaty, 526 F.3d 1340 (11th Cir. 2008) (finding grave risk of harm in light of father's temper and alcohol abuse).

e.   Child's need for particular therapy? Ermine v. Vittori, 738 F.3d 153 (2d Cir. 2014) (autistic child brought to the United States to receive therapy not available in Italy should not be returned to Italy).

f. Psychological harm resulting from the proposed return? *See* England v. England, 234 F.3d 268 (5th Cir. 2000) (no).

4. Studies show that, contrary to expectations at the time of enactment, many international child abductors are mothers, many of whom are seeking protection from domestic violence. Seven of the nine cases decided in federal courts between July 2000 and July 2001 involved an abductor who alleged she was a victim of domestic violence. *See* Merle H. Weiner, *Navigating the Road Between Uniformity and Progress: The Need for Purposeful Analysis of the Hague Convention on the Civil Aspects of International Child Abduction*, 33 COLUM. HUM. RTS. L. REV. 275, 277 (2002) (citing reports showing that 70% of abductors are mothers who are primary caregivers fleeing from domestic violence).

5. The Hague Abduction Convention applies to "rights of custody" not "rights of access" or visitation. Therefore the inquiry is whether the law of the habitual residence gives the parent rights of "custody." *See* Bromley v. Bromley, 30 F. Supp. 2d 857 (E.D. Pa. 1998) (finding no authority to enforce father's right of access); Kufner v. Kufner, 519 F.3d 33 (1st Cir. 2008). A difficult issue arises when the parent with rights of access also has the right to prevent the child from being removed from the jurisdiction, called a *ne exeat* clause. Although several lower courts had found the ne exeat clause did not convert a right of access into rights of custody, the United States Supreme Court disagreed and found that a ne exeat clause did create a "right of custody." *See* Abbott v. Abbott, 560 U.S. 1 (2010). This is consistent with the views of other Hague countries. *See* Linda Silberman, *Patching Up the Abduction Convention: A Call for a New International Protocol and a Suggestion for Amendments to ICARA,* 33 TEX. INT'L L. J. 41 (2003).

6. The International Parental Kidnapping Act of 1993 (IPKA), 18 U.S.C.A. § 1204, makes it a federal felony to remove or retain a child outside of the United States with intent to obstruct the lawful exercise of parental rights. The term "parental rights" means joint or sole physical custody, including visitation rights. *See* United States v. Fazal-Ur-Raheman-Fazal, 355 F.3d 40 (1st Cir. 2004). There are three defenses: the defendant acted pursuant to a lawful court order; was fleeing an incident of domestic violence; or was unable to return the child for circumstances beyond the defendant's control, defendant tried to notify the person entitled to custody and did return the child as quickly as possible. The IPKA has been upheld as a constitutional exercise of Congress' power to regulate foreign commerce. United States v. Cummings, 281 F.3d 1046 (9th Cir. 2002). State parental kidnapping laws vary with some recognizing the plight of victims of domestic violence and others failing to acknowledge the victim's situation. National Clearinghouse for the Defense of Battered Women, The Impact of Parental Kidnapping Laws and Practice on Domestic Violence Survivors 3, Appendix A & B (August 2005) (listing state parental kidnapping statutes).

7. "Habitual residence" is not defined in either the Hague Abduction Convention or in the implementing legislation but is one of the most important

questions. Murphy v. Sloan, 754 F.3d 1144 (9th Cir. 2014). In a widely cited decision, (Mozes v. Mozes, 239 F.3d 1067 (9th Cir. 2001), the Ninth Circuit Court of Appeals analyzed this definitional issue:

> [T]he first step toward acquiring a new habitual residence is forming a settled intention to abandon the one left behind. Otherwise, one is not habitually residing; one is away for a temporary absence of long or short duration. Of course, one need not have this settled intention at the moment of departure; it could coalesce during the course of a stay abroad originally intended to be temporary. Nor need the intention be expressly declared, if it is manifest from one's actions; indeed, one's actions may belie any declaration that no abandonment was intended. * * * Whether there is a settled intention to abandon a prior habitual residence is a question of fact * * *.

> While the decision to alter a child's habitual residence depends on the settled intention of the parents, they cannot accomplish this transformation by wishful thinking alone. First, it requires an actual "change in geography." Second, home isn't built in a day. It requires the passage of "an appreciable period of time," one that is "sufficient for acclimatization." When the child moves to a new country accompanied by both parents, who take steps to set up a regular household together, the period need not be long. On the other hand, when circumstances are such as to hinder acclimatization, even a lengthy period spent in this manner may not suffice.

> * * * Most agree that, given enough time and positive experience, a child's life may become so firmly embedded in the new country as to make it habitually resident even though there be lingering parental intentions to the contrary. The question is how readily courts should reach the conclusion that this has occurred. * * * [W]e conclude that, in the absence of settled parental intent, courts should be slow to infer from such contacts that an earlier habitual residence has been abandoned.

> * * * The function of a court applying the Convention is not to determine whether a child is happy where it currently is, but whether one parent is seeking unilaterally to alter the status quo with regard to the primary locus of the child's life.

The *Mozes* children and their mother had gone to the United States from Israel. The mother "had long wanted to live in the United States, and both parents agreed that the children would profit from a chance to here, learn English, and partake of American culture." The parties agreed that the father "had consented to the children's remaining in the United States for fifteen months and disagreed as to their understanding beyond that." On these facts, the *Mozes* court concluded that the Mozes children's habitual residence was still Israel.

Many courts have followed the *Mozes* approach in determining habitual residence. *See, e.g.*, Gitter v. Gitter, 396 F.3d 124 (2d Cir. 2005); Ruiz v. Tenorio, 392 F.3d 1247 (11th Cir. 2004); Whiting v. Krassner, 391 F.3d 540, 548–550 (3d Cir. 2004), cert. denied, 545 U.S. 1131 (2005); Silverman v. Silverman, 338 F.3d 886 (8th Cir. 2003), cert. denied 540 U.S. 1107 (2004); Koch v. Koch, 450 F.3d 703 (7th Cir. 2006). *Cf.* Robert v. Tesson, 507 F.3d 981 (6th Cir. 2007) (defining habitual residence as a place where, at the time of removal, the child has been present long enough to allow acclimatization). Other circuits have focused both on the parents' shared intent and whether the child is settled into the new place of residence. For a general discussion of how U.S. courts have determined a child's habitual residence, *See generally* Stephen I. Winter, *Home Is Where the Heart Is: Determining "Habitual Residence" under the Hague Convention on the Civil Aspects of International Child Abduction*, 33 WASH. U. J. L. & POL'Y 351 (2010); JEREMY D. MORLEY, THE HAGUE ABDUCTION CONVENTION 84–86 (2d Ed. 2016).

8. *Maturity*: The Hague Convention does not apply to children older than 16. *See* Custodio v. Samillan, 842 F.3d 1084 (8th Cir. 2016) (child turned 16 while case was on appeal). Article 13 of the Hague Convention allows courts to refuse to return an objecting child who has "attained an age and degree of maturity at which it is appropriate to take account of its views." Rodriguez v. Yanez, 817 F.3d 466 (5th Cir. 2016) discusses this defense. One commentator, comparing the U.S. and U.K. case law on maturity, argues that the U.K. decisions are "more exhaustive and consistent with the Hague Convention" while the U.S. decisions are "arguably inconsistent with the Hague Convention":

> U.S. courts tend to "assume" when a child is mature enough or old enough to have his/her views considered with very little, if any, supporting analysis. For example, in *Tahan v. Duquette*, a New Jersey state court acknowledged that the Hague Convention does not suggest * * * any threshold determination on age, but then makes the blanket statement that the maturity and views exception simply does not apply to a nine year-old. In *In re Nicholson v. Nicholson*, a federal court judge in Kansas at least afforded a ten year-old the opportunity for an in-camera interview, but * * * added that the child had no "valid" objection * * * [and] failed to explain why. Likewise, in New York's first Hague Convention case, the court refused to consider the views of a nine year-old child stating simply: "he is only nine years old." * * * [And in] England v. England * * * the [appellate] court overruled the lower court's finding that the thirteen year-old, who had clearly objected to being returned to Australia, was old enough and mature enough for the court to consider her views * * * [because] child was adopted, [had] * * * Attention Deficit Disorder (ADD), possessed certain learning disabilities, and had prior parental figures in her life, [reasoning] that she must be confused by her present situation. * * *

* * * [By contrast,] U.K. courts [use] * * * a two-step process. The first step is determining whether the child objects to being returned. * * * [T]he second step is determining whether the child is of an age and maturity level for which it is appropriate to consider the child's views. [Both of these inquiries are made by a "court welfare officer" who reports findings to the court.] * * * If the child is old enough or mature enough to have his/her views considered, then the court must exercise its discretion in determining whether to still order the child's return. Some factors the court will consider are: whether the child's views are unduly influenced by the abducting parent * * * and whether the child's objections are valid. * * * [T]he court * * * balance[s] the child's objections against the interests and policies set forth by the Hague Convention. * * *

[I]n Re M [offers an example of this approach. T]he parents had two children, ages nine and eight, and were married and resided in Greece until their marriage fell apart. * * * [T]he mother [had previously] * * * removed the children from Greece and had Hague Convention proceedings commenced against her. The court * * * [found that] the children * * * object[ed] to being returned and were mature enough to understand their situation. * * * Given the children's deep attachments to their mother and their unquestionable objections to returning to Greece, the court concluded that a "return at this stage to Greece is of greater consequence than the importance of the court marking its disapproval of the behaviour of the mother by refusing to allow her to benefit from it." * * *

Brian S. Kenworthy, Note, *The Un-Common Law: Emerging Differences Between the United States and the United Kingdom on the Children's Rights Aspects of the Hague Convention on International Child Abduction*, 12 IND. INT'L & COMP. L. REV. 329, 352–62 (2002).

What facts and Convention policies support Kenworthy's claim that the U.S. approach is inconsistent with the Convention? What facts and Convention policies suggest that he is wrong?

For a comparative discussion of how the Hague Convention has been applied, *see* Nigel V. Lowe, *The Operation of the 1980 Hague Abduction Convention—A Global View,* 41 FAM. L. Q. 59 (2007).

9.   Anyone who helps someone abduct a child can be sued in a number of states. This can include lawyers. *See* Kibert Marcos, *Law Firm Hit with $950,000 Judgment in Passport Case,* THE RECORD (Bergen County New Jersey) May 11, 2011 at L 02.

10. A parent who abducts a child to the United States can be awarded legal fees in connection with court procedings to return the child. *See* Raps v. Zaparta, 2017 WL 74739 (S. D. N. Y. 2017).

Problem 13-11:

Tuulikki, a citizen of Finland, and Frank, a citizen of the United States, were married in California in 1989. Their two children were also born (in 1990 and 1991) in California. In April 1992, the family moved to Kentucky where Frank hoped to find work. But Tuulikki did not like Kentucky and, in June of 1992, the family moved to Finland, where they remained until April 1995, when they returned to the United States. This time the family located in the Houston area, where Tuulikki had lived when she first came to the U.S. Prior to their arrival, they investigated job opportunities in South Texas, obtained information from the local Chamber of Commerce, and contacted a realtor; upon arrival, they leased two automobiles and rented a condominium; Frank also prepared a resume. But in late May 1995, Frank and Tuulikki had a violent argument that culminated in Tuulikki's arrest; thereafter, Frank took the two children and left for northern Kentucky to stay with his sister. On May 30, 1995, Frank filed a custody petition in Kentucky; on the same date, Tuulikki filed a custody petition in Texas, alleging that she was a Texas resident. At the same time, Tuulikki filed a custody petition in Finland. On June 13, the Finnish court issued an order granting custody to Tuulikki; neither Tuulikki nor Frank appeared in the Finnish court. Shortly thereafter, Tuulikki sought to enforce the Finnish order in Kentucky.

What, if any, U.S. court(s) have jurisdiction under the UCCJEA? the PKPA? Under the Hague Convention, is the Kentucky court required to enforce the Finnish decree? *See* Harsacky v. Harsacky, 930 S.W.2d 410 (Ky. App. 1996); Cassie M.D. v. Othmar D., 22 Fam. L. Rep. (BNA) 1313 (N.Y. Fam. 1996).

Problem 13-12:

Wim lived in Belgium but visited New York frequently. On one such trip he met Christina, and a romantic relationship developed. A few months later, Christina moved into Wim's New York apartment. While continuing to live in Belgium, Wim spent about a quarter of his time in New York. A few months later, Christina learned that she was pregnant and began prenatal care in New York. Christina had no medical insurance. Because Wim refused to pay for delivery of the baby in the United States and Belgium offered free medical services, Christina agreed to have the baby in Belgium. Three months into her pregnancy, Christina traveled to Belgium on a three-month tourist visa, bringing along only one or two suitcases. She left the rest of her belongings, including her non-maternity clothes, in the New York apartment. When her visa expired she did not extend it. The baby was born six months after her arrival in Belgium. By then the relationship between the parties had deteriorated. After initially resisting, two months after the baby's birth, Wim signed the consent form that enabled Christina to get an American passport for the baby and agreed to her return to the United States. Over the next two months, Wim made several trips to the United States and the couple made several attempts to reconcile. When those efforts failed, Wim filed a petition under the Hague Convention. Must a U.S. court order the baby's return to Belgium? *See* Delvoye v. Lee, 329 F.3d 330 (3d Cir. 2003).

Problem 13-13:

Fritz, a German citizen, and Marj, an American citizen, were married in Germany where they resided for five years and where their son was born. They moved to Chicago with their son when he was two years old. They separated two years later and entered into an agreement which provided for joint custody of their son. Four months later, Franz's employer transferred him back to Germany. During the months when Franz had joint custody pursuant to the separation agreement, he returned to Germany and enrolled the child in school. Four months after Franz's move to Germany, Marj took the child back to Chicago without Franz's permission. Franz promptly filed a proceeding under the Hague Convention seeking return of the child. Must a U.S. court order the child's return? *See* Whiting v. Krassner, 391 F.3d 540 (3d Cir. 2004).

CHAPTER 14

CHILD CUSTODY

■ ■ ■

We are allowing our children to bear the psychological, economic, and moral brunt of divorce.

JUDITH S. WALLERSTEIN & SANDRA BLAKESLEE, SECOND CHANCES: MEN, WOMEN AND CHILDREN A DECADE AFTER DIVORCE (1989)

What's done to children, they will do to society.

Karl A. Menninger, M.D.

VENTURA, Calif. (UPI)—The only California condor egg known to have been laid this breeding season was knocked off a cliff by the parents, who were fighting. A team of specialists trying to save the huge endangered birds, watched from half a mile away as the four-inch egg smashed on the rocks below the condors' cave and the embryo was eaten by ravens. The condors, the specialists said, were apparently battling over which of them should take care of the egg. * * * "One of them would sit down on the egg and the other would come in and try to push the first one off. They would jab each other in the face and really get physical. This went on for hours. They were so absorbed, no one was incubating." N.Y. TIMES, March 6, 1982, at 6, col. 13.

GRAND RAPIDS, Mich. (UPI)—In a ruling reminiscent of Solomon, a judge says a divorced couple should have the body of their son cremated and each claim half the ashes unless they can agree who has the right to bury him. * * * "I just want to take him home," a weeping Mrs. Simmons said when the judgment was delivered Wednesday. "We didn't want him to be alone." [Judge] Cook said Thursday his opinion was one of the most difficult he ever had to make. "We are asked to play God, a role we are neither trained nor prepared for." * * * Cook said he saw no other solution to the dilemma unless the parents could decide out of court which of them should have custody of Greg's body. CHICAGO DAILY L. BULL., July 21, 1978, at 1, col. 7.

Child custody disputes are difficult for parents, their lawyers, and the judges who must decide them. Custody is the term used to denote the right to decide where and how a child will be raised. Parents in an intact family share the custody of their child. In a separated family, parents may share *legal* custody, the right to make decisions about the child's care, education, health and religion; they may also share *physical custody* or residency if the child spends a substantial amount of time living in each parent's household. Even if one parent obtains sole legal custody and physical residency, the other will typically retain the right to "parenting time" or visitation with the child. *See generally* LINDA D. ELROD, CHILD CUSTODY PRACTICE AND PROCEDURE (REV. ED. 2017).

More than a million children experience their parents' divorce each year. It is not only divorcing parents, but also unwed parents and former same-sex couples who may not be able to agree on custody of the child. Approximately one-quarter of all children lived with only one parent in 2008 with over 80% living with their mothers. *See* Custodial Mothers and Fathers and Their Child Support: 2007 2 (U.S. Census Bureau 2009). Most of these divorcing parents settle custody arrangements for their children without the need for judicial intervention. But when a custody dispute does go to court, it is often bitterly fought. In battling over their own rights, it is easy for parents to lose track of their children's needs and interests.

1. WHAT RIGHTS FOR CHILDREN?

THE LAW COMMISSION (LONDON), FACING THE FUTURE: A DISCUSSION PAPER ON THE GROUND FOR DIVORCE
24–26 (Law. Com. No. 170, May 1988).

* * *

3.39 Several studies have indicated that most children whose parents have separated would have preferred them to have stayed together. Children of parents who have separated are more likely to suffer from at least temporary social and behavioural problems during and in the aftermath of the separation. Although the findings are less clear, research has also linked marital separation with various longer-term problems. As marital separation frequently leads to downward social mobility and economic hardship such findings are not surprising, but once again may be attributed to the consequences of separation rather than divorce as such. Perhaps the most significant research finding is that adjustment to separation depends on the quality of the relationships with and between both parents *after* the separation. Thus good continuing relationships with both parents seem to be protective against the problems associated with children from broken marriages. Conversely, post-divorce conflict between the parents is more damaging than marital conflict.

3.40 The implications from this research are that, although divorce law is powerless to prevent prejudice to the children caused by marital breakdown, it can help to minimize that prejudice in two ways. First, since the children are most vulnerable in the immediate aftermath of the separation which often coincides with the timing of the divorce process, nothing should be involved in that process which makes it more difficult for the children to cope with the separation. Secondly, every effort should be made to encourage good post-divorce relationships with both parents and between the parents themselves. The Booth Committee, expressing the view that divorcing or separating parents should be encouraged and advised to maintain their joint responsibility for the children and to co-operate in this respect, recommended that provision should be made for joint statement of arrangements to be filed. Such co-operation may only be possible where there has not been irretrievable harm to the spouses' own relationship.

NOTES AND QUESTIONS

1.   Many researchers have investigated the effects of divorce on children. One of the most publicized studies is Judith Wallerstein's twenty-five year study of sixty families in Marin County, California. As a result of that research "[t]he earlier view of divorce as a short-lived crisis * * * has given way to a more sober appraisal, accompanied by rising concern that a significant number of children suffer long-term, perhaps permanent detrimental effects from divorce, and that others experience submerged effects that may appear years later." Judith Wallerstein, *The Long-Term Effects of Divorce on Children: A Review*, 30 J. CHILD ADOLESCENCE & PSYCHIATRY 349, 358 (1991). *See also* JUDITH WALLERSTEIN, JULIA M. LEWIS, & SANDRA BLAKESLEE, THE UNEXPECTED LEGACY OF DIVORCE: A 25 YEAR LANDMARK STUDY 298 (2000). Experts agree that divorce poses serious risks to long-term childhood development:

> Overall, most children of divorce experience dramatic declines in their economic circumstances, abandonment (or the fear of abandonment) by one or both of their parents, the diminished capacity of both parents to attend meaningfully and constructively to their children's needs (because they are preoccupied with their own psychological, social, and economic distress as well as stresses related to the legal divorce), and diminished contact with familial or potential sources of psychosocial support (friends, neighbors, teachers, schoolmates, etc.), as well as familiar living settings. As a consequence, the experience of divorce is a psychological stressor and a significant life transition for most children, with long-term repercussions for many. Some children from divorced homes show

long-term behavior problems, depression, poor school performance, acting out, low self-esteem, and (in adolescence and young adulthood) difficulties with intimate heterosexual relationships.

Michael E. Lamb et al., *The Effects of Divorce and Custody Arrangements on Children's Behavior, Development, and Adjustment*, 35 FAM. & CONCIL. CTS. REV. 393, 395–396 (1997). *See also* Sol R. Rappaport, *Deconstructing the Impact of Divorce on Children*, 47 FAM. L. Q. 353 (2013).

Experts also agree, however, that the long-term effects of divorce are highly variable and that effects are mediated by psychological, social and economic factors:

> Children who experience parental divorce, compared with children in continuously intact two-parent families, exhibit more conduct problems, more symptoms of psychological maladjustment, lower academic achievement, more social difficulties, and poorer self-concepts. Similarly, adults who experienced parental divorce as children, compared with adults raised in continuously intact two-parent families, score lower on a variety of indicators of psychological, interpersonal, and socioeconomic well-being.

> However, the overall group differences between offspring from divorced and intact families are small, with considerable diversity existing in children's reactions to divorce. Children's adjustment to divorce depends on several factors, including the amount and quality of contact with noncustodial parents, the custodial parents' psychological adjustment and parenting skills, the level of interparental conflict that precedes and follows divorce, the degree of economic hardship to which children are exposed, and the number of stressful life events that accompany and follow divorce. These factors can be used as guides to assess the probable impact of various legal and therapeutic interventions to improve the well-being of children of divorce.

Paul R. Amato, *Life-Span Adjustment of Children to Their Parents' Divorce, in* THE FUTURE OF CHILDREN: CHILDREN AND DIVORCE 143 (1994). *See also* E. MAVIS HETHERINGTON & JOHN KELLY, FOR BETTER OR FOR WORSE: DIVORCE RECONSIDERED 7–8 (2003) (thirty-year longitudinal study revealed that about 25% of children whose parents divorced suffered long-term harm; the long term effects correlate with the child's individual resilience and support systems). For an account from a child's perspective, *see* ELIZABETH MARQUARDT: BETWEEN TWO WORLDS: THE INNER LIVES OF CHILDREN OF DIVORCE (2005).

Michael Lamb's review of more than one thousand studies of childhood adjustment summarized the most important factors that promote healthy development and adjustment in children:

> a.   the quality of the child's relationships with parents or parent figures;

b.   the quality of the relationships between the parents and other significant adults (conflict associated with maladjustment); and

c.   the availability of adequate economic, social and physical resources. See Michael E. Lamb, *Mothers, Fathers, and Circumstances: Factors Affecting Children's Development*, 16 APPLIED DEVELOPMENTAL SCIENCE 98 (2012).

2.   A number of studies have found that parental conflict is strongly associated with childhood behavioral problems and other negative symptoms. *See* Joan B. Kelly, *Children's Adjustment in Conflicted Marriage and Divorce: A Decade Review of Research*, 39 J. AM. ACAD. CHILD & ADOLESCENT PSYCHIAT. 963 (2000) (reviewing studies); John H. Grych, *Interparental Conflict as a Risk Factor for Child Maladjustment*, 43 FAM. CT. REV. 97 (2005). A growing number of states and courts have tried various ways to reduce parental conflict. *See* Nancy VerSteegh, *Family Court Reform and ADR: Shifting Values and Expectations Transform the Divorce Process*, 42 FAM. L.Q. 659 (2008). *See also* Milfred D. Dale, *Don't Forget the Children: Court Protection from Parental Conflict Is in the Best Interests of Children*, 52 FAM. CT. REV. 648 (2014).

Prior to separation the two most important risk factors are intense marital conflict and problematic parenting. Age and gender of the children, father absence and a parent's remarriage are also risk factors. Researchers have found that risk can be reduced through protective buffers—shielding children from the conflict and at least one caring, authoritative and involved parent. *See* Joan B. Kelly, *Risk and Protective Factors Associated with Child and Adolescent Adjustment Following Separation and Divorce: Social Science Applications in* PARENTING PLAN EVALUATIONS: APPLIED RESEARCH FOR THE FAMILY COURT 49, 59, 68 (KATHRYN F. KUEHNLE & LESLIE M. DROZD, EDS. 2012).

Many courts require parents of minor children to attend educational programs as a condition of obtaining a divorce. For example, New Jersey requires couples with children who file for divorce to take a Parent Education and Family Stabilization Course that covers the legal and emotional impact of divorce on adults and children, financial responsibility, laws regarding child abuse and neglect and conflict resolution skills. *See* N.J. STAT. ANN. § 2A:34–12.1–2A:34–12.8. The impact of these programs is still being assessed. *See generally* Linda D. Elrod, *Reforming the System to Protect Children in High Conflict Custody Cases,* 28 WM. MITCHELL L. REV. 495, 531–532 (2001).

Evaluations of parent-education programs suggest that these programs are worthwhile. *See* Shelley Kierstead, *Parent Education Programs in Family Courts: Balancing Autonomy and State Intervention,* 49 FAM. CT. REV. 140 (2011) (reporting that attendance at a parent-education program is positively associated with lower relitigation rates and parents report they are better able to shield their children from conflict and promote a strong relationship with the other parent as a result of participating in the program).

MILLER V. MILLER

Supreme Judicial Court of Maine, 1996.
677 A.2d 64.

LIPEZ, JUSTICE.

This case is before us on report * * * of an interlocutory order entered in the Superior Court, granting the motion of three minor children to intervene as parties in the divorce action between their parents and be represented by legal counsel independently of the guardian ad litem appointed previously to represent their interests. We vacate the order of the Superior Court.

Eileen and Clark Miller were married on October 25, 1975. In December 1992, Eileen filed a complaint for a divorce. * * * Both parties * * * [sought physical custody of] their three children: Carissa Noel Miller, age 14; Nicholas Russell Miller, age 11; and Dylan Patrick Miller, age 9. Following a contested hearing in June 1993, the court issued its order pending divorce and awarded the primary residence of all three children to Eileen.

Prior to its order pending the divorce, and by an agreement of the parties, the court appointed a guardian ad litem for the three children.[1] Pursuant to the terms of the order appointing the guardian, Charles L. Robinson, a psychologist, prepared a psychological evaluation of the parties and the children. In preparing his evaluation, Robinson had a joint ninety minute meeting with Clark and Eileen; one-time individual meetings with Clark and Eileen; one visit each at the homes of Clark and Eileen when the children were present; and finally, two meetings with each of the children individually, in the presence of the guardian. All three children rejected the opportunity to speak with Robinson or the guardian alone. In January 1994, Robinson submitted a report recommending that all three children's primary residence be with Clark. Robinson noted in his report Eileen's

---

[1] The terms of the court's order provided, in relevant part: ORDERED that the guardian *ad litem* shall act in pursuit of the best interest of the children and shall investigate the circumstances concerning the children's welfare as it relates to the disposition of parental rights and responsibilities under 19 M.R.S.A. § 752. The guardian *ad litem* shall have the authority to undertake any or all of the following action [sic] which the guardian, in her discretion, deems appropriate including: (1) Review of relevant mental health records and materials of the parents and children; (2) Review of relevant medical records of the parents and children; (3) Review of relevant school records and other pertinent materials of the parents and children; (4) Interviews with the children with or without other persons present; (5) Interviews with parents, grandparents, teachers, daycare providers, psychologists and other persons who have been involved in caring for or treating the children or parents, or who may have knowledge of the children or family; (6) Request and arrange for psychological evaluations and/or counseling for the parents and/or children; (7) Appearance at any and all future proceedings, including pretrial conferences and trial; (8) Submission to the Court of a report in writing summarizing her position on behalf of the children with regard to the issues before the Court, provided that the guardian *ad litem* furnish copies to all parties reasonably in advance of hearing; and (9) Any other further and necessary authority as may be required to carry out her responsibilities.

stated intention to move to Connecticut. He also noted that Nicholas had expressed a preference to live with his mother.

Less than one month after Robinson submitted his report, the guardian submitted her report, which also recommended that all three children maintain their primary residence with Clark. The guardian's investigation consisted of one interview separately with Clark and Eileen, and two interviews with each of the children in the presence of either Dr. Robinson or Clark. The guardian also accompanied Robinson on each of the home visits mentioned above. The guardian noted in her report Eileen's stated intention to move to Connecticut, and Nicholas's expressed desire to move to Connecticut with his mother. According to the guardian's report, Dylan did not express a discernible preference about where he wished to reside.

Subsequent to the recommendations of Robinson and the guardian, Clark filed a motion to alter and amend the order pending the divorce to provide that the children's primary residence be with him. The motion was based primarily on his belief that Eileen was considering moving from Maine to Connecticut. At the hearing on Clark's motion, Eileen admitted that she was planning to move to Connecticut, and Carissa expressed a clear preference to live with Eileen.

In May 1994, attorney Margaret Semple received a phone call from Nicholas Miller seeking legal representation for himself and his siblings in his parents' pending divorce. Semple agreed to represent all three children on a pro bono basis. In July 1994, the Miller children filed a motion to intervene in their own names and to be represented by legal counsel. Clark opposed the children's motion, as did the guardian.

In August 1994, the court granted Clark's motion to amend the order pending divorce by providing that the children's primary residence be with him. In September 1994, the children's motion to intervene [and to be represented by attorney Semple] was granted. * * *

The claim of the children pursuant to the common law.

There is no basis in the common law for the intervention of minor children as parties in the divorce action of their parents with an attorney of their choice. Although at common law minor children have a right to sue and be sued, children do not possess the requisite legal capacity to participate in litigation in their own names. This incapacity is premised on age, inexperience, and immaturity. Due to their incapacity, children must bring or defend a legal proceeding through an adult representative, such as a next friend or a guardian ad litem. 43 C.J.S. *Infants* § 215. Similarly, intervention of minor children in an action may only be commenced by a guardian ad litem or a next friend. A person acting as either a next friend or a guardian ad litem is only a nominal party to the litigation; the child is the real party in interest. The next friend or guardian ad litem brings the minor child's claim or interest to the attention of a court.

The Maine Rules of Civil Procedure reflect this common law tradition. * * * Pursuant to Rule 17(b), a minor child may only sue if the child has a representative, next friend, or guardian ad litem. The court is empowered to appoint such a representative for a child whenever protection of the child's interests demands it. * * *

There is another obstacle to the claim of the Miller children that they have a right to intervene as parties in this divorce action with an attorney of their choice. Pursuant to Maine law, children have "no authority to appoint an attorney." * * * "Even should the infant employ counsel, who procures the suit dismissed, the entry would be void, because the infant could not appear by attorney as the employment would be null." * * *

Although the law imposes procedural imitations on children, it does so to protect their interests. In the realm of divorce and other family litigation, this protective purpose finds expression in the best interest standard. In Maine, as in the multitude of other states which have adopted the best interest standard, courts faced with the task of rearranging parental rights and responsibilities must strive for an outcome that will maximize the best interest of children. This standard protects children who lack the ability because of youth, inexperience, and immaturity to protect themselves. The protective purpose of this standard is also important in analyzing the constitutional claim of the Miller children.

The constitutional claim of the children.

The remaining issue is whether the intervention of the children as parties in the divorce action of their parents with an attorney of their choice is constitutionally required. Relying on the procedural due process guarantees of the Fourteenth Amendment of the United States Constitution, the Miller children contend that they have a significant liberty interest in the outcome of their parents' divorce because of the custodial issues involved. Assuming, *arguendo*, that the Miller children have a liberty interest in the outcome of their parents' divorce, we must determine whether representation by a court-appointed guardian ad litem responsible for advocating for their best interests satisfies the requirements of procedural due process.

The test we use for evaluating procedural due process claims was set forth by the United States Supreme Court in *Mathews v. Eldridge*, 424 U.S. 319 (1976). It consists of three factors which must be balanced against each other: (1) the private interests affected by the chosen procedure; (2) the risk of erroneous deprivation of those interests by the chosen procedure and the probable value, if any, of additional or substitute procedural safeguards; and (3) the countervailing state interest(s) supporting use of the challenged procedure.

The interests involved in a divorce case include those of the divorcing parties and, if they have children, those of the children. The interests of the divorcing parents are financial, custodial, and emotional. As a result of divorce, financial and custodial rights and obligations are reconfigured. In addition, divorce terminates a legal partnership. For the children, there is an emotional fallout from the divorce, and an interest in the financial bargain struck by the divorcing parties, especially on child support. The most immediate interest of the children, however, is in the custodial outcome. The position of the Miller children confirms this immediacy. They do not want to intervene in their parents' divorce because of the potential impact on them of the property, alimony, or child support bargains that will be struck. Rather, the Miller children wish to participate in the reconfiguration of their family and advocate their preferences because their custody is at stake. They argue that this interest is not and cannot be met by the guardian ad litem, who is duty-bound to represent their best interests as *she* sees them. They emphasize that the guardian ad litem's recommendations on custody are directly contrary to their wishes.

In making this point, the Miller children link their custodial interest in the outcome of the divorce to forceful advocacy of their preference by independent counsel representing them as parties, and cite the absence of such advocacy as increasing the likelihood of an erroneous deprivation of their custodial interest. Implicit in that argument is the further contention that the preference of the children should have primacy when the court makes its custody determination. We reject that proposition. The best interest standard set forth in 19 M.R.S.A. § 752(5) appropriately makes the preference of the child only one of many factors that the court must consider. The exclusion of children as parties in the divorce of their parents, and the related possibility that there will be no forceful advocacy for the custodial preference of the children, does not increase the risk of erroneous custody determinations that deserve the best interests of children. The guardian ad litem is already an advocate for the best interest of the children in all of its complex dimensions. The narrow focus of an attorney for the children, who would be obligated to carry out their preferences regardless of the wisdom of such a course, might well increase the likelihood of a custody determination that is not in the best interest of the children.

Finally, the State has a substantial interest in divorce proceedings that do not include children as parties represented by counsel. Divorce litigation would be complicated exponentially by the involvement of children as parties. Children could object to any settlement offer. They would have the right to participate in discovery and at hearings to present witnesses on their own behalf and cross-examine witnesses called by the other parties. Multiple children could insist on multiple representation. The occurrence of any or all of these probabilities would protract divorce litigation beyond current bounds, and result in a substantial additional financial burden on both the parties and our court system.

In our view, the use of guardians ad litem to protect the best interests of children in divorce proceedings fully satisfies any federal constitutional requirements. Accordingly, the Miller children are not entitled to intervene in the divorce action of their parents and be represented by independent legal counsel.

NOTES AND QUESTIONS

1.   Most courts have agreed with the *Miller* court's conclusion that a divorcing couple's children are not "parties" in the divorce action. *See, e.g., In re* Marriage of Osborn, 135 P.3d 199 (Kan. 2006). Does lack of party status necessarily mean that the children should not be represented? Or heard? Reconsider Professor Guggenheim's argument against the child's lawyer being a "full participant" in a child protection proceeding. See Chapter 10. Do the same arguments apply equally to a custody contest? If yes, are Guggenheim's arguments convincing?

2.   Consult footnote 1 in *Miller* and determine how, if at all, the role of a guardian ad litem differs from that of an attorney. Would a lawyer submit a written report? Testify in court? *See* Schult v. Schult, 699 A.2d 134 (Conn. 1997) (noting that child's attorney could advocate a position different from that of child's guardian ad litem). *See* Linda D. Elrod, *Client-Directed Lawyers for Children: It Is the Right Thing To Do*, 27 PACE L. REV. 869 (2007).

3.   Why does the *Miller* court believe that appointment of a guardian ad litem for the children is preferable to appointment of an attorney? The Alaska Supreme Court summarized arguments for appointment of counsel for children in a divorce action in Veazey v. Veazey, 560 P.2d 382 (Alaska 1977):

> Appellee here urges that advocacy of the child's interest be left to the attorney for one or the other of the competing claimants, because there is only one ultimate issue in a custody case—the custody of the child—and * * * adding an additional advocate [will merely increase] the cost and complexity of custody litigation without shedding any additional light on the facts and issues.
>
> The attorney for a claimant has a professional duty to exercise his judgment "solely for the benefit of his client and free of compromising influences and loyalties. * * * [T]he desires of third persons should [not] be permitted to dilute his loyalty to his client." Code of Prof. Responsibility, EC 5–1. In a number of instances, that attorney cannot assert the interests of the child without creating a conflict of interest.
>
>   * * *
>
> Furthermore, to say there is only one ultimate issue in a custody case oversimplifies the matter. The terms of custody, visitation, and

support may vary greatly. None of those issues is of an "either-or" nature, and they are all of interest to the child. Shared or joint custody is sometimes awarded.

* * *

Unfortunately the custody of children is often merely another bargaining point between the divorcing parents, along with the questions of property division, spousal support, child support, and visitation. Divorcing parents seek, or decide not to seek, custody of their children for many different reasons, many of which may have little correlation with the best interests of the child.

On balance, should the divorce court appoint a guardian ad litem for the children or a lawyer? *See* Richard Ducote, *Guardians Ad Litem in Private Custody Litigation: The Case for Abolition,* 32 LOYOLA J. PUBLIC INT. LAW 106 (2002).

4.   When should a court appoint an attorney for a child who is the subject of a custody dispute? Under UMDA § 310, "[t]he court may appoint an attorney to represent the interests of a minor or dependent child with respect to his support, custody, and visitation." Commissioners' Note. In Connecticut, in any divorce action, a judge may " * * * appoint counsel for any minor child * * * if the court deems it to be in the best interests of the child * * * [or] when the court finds that the custody, care, education, visitation or support of a minor child is in actual controversy." *See* CONN. GEN. STAT. § 46b–54(a)–(b). Experts disagree on the appropriate standard. *Compare* Linda D. Elrod, *Counsel for the Child in Custody Disputes: The Time is Now,* 26 FAM. L. Q. 53 (1992) (any time there is a dispute over custody) *with* American Academy of Matrimonial Lawyers, REPRESENTING CHILDREN: STANDARDS FOR ATTORNEYS AND GUARDIANS AD LITEM IN CUSTODY OR VISITATION PROCEEDINGS 11 (when both parties request or the court finds after a hearing that appointment is necessary in light of the particular circumstances). What are the pros and cons of these approaches?

5.   Should the age of the child determine whether a lawyer is appointed and what role that lawyer should play? As a general rule, the older the child, the more likely their wishes will be ascertained and weighed. *See* D.A. v. R.C., 105 A.3d 1103 (N.J. Super. App. Div. 2014) (court was required to consider preference of fourteen year old); Kubicki v. Sharpe, 858 N.W.2d 57 (Mich. App. 2014) (reversing where court failed to consider wishes of ten year old child). But see Addison v. Addison, 463 S.W.3d 755 (Ky. 2015) (upholding judge's refusal to interview young children where there was abundant information for the court).

The ABA and AAML Standards both take the position that the child's counsel should be a "full participant" in the proceedings and that the child should determine the goals of representation if he or she has the capacity to do so. *See also* Model Rules of Professional Conduct 1.2, 1.14. Assuming that a children's lawyer was appointed in *Miller* and the AAML Standards governed his role, could the lawyer represent all of the children? Why? *See* Barbara A. Atwood, *Representing Children Who Can't or Won't Direct Counsel: Best Interest Lawyering or No Lawyer at All?*, 53 ARIZ. L. REV. 381 (2011). *See* Ruth Bettelheim, *In Whose Best Interests?* N.Y. TIMES, May 19, 2012, at SR-9.

6.   Studies indicate that children want to be heard. *See* Judith Cashmore & Patrick Parkinson, *Children's and Parent's Perceptions on Children's Participation in Decision Making After Parental Separation and Divorce*, 46 Fam. CT. REV. 91 (2008). Most state statutes include the voice of the child as a factor to consider. *See* LINDA D. ELROD, CHILD CUSTODY PRACTICE AND PROCEDURE 468–500 (REV. ED. 2017). One way to incorporate the voice of the child is for the judge to interview the child. *See* Nicholas Bala, et al., *Children's Voices in Family Court: Guidelines for Judges Meeting Children*, 47 FAM. L. Q. 379 (2013).

7.   Article 12 of the U.N. Convention on the Rights of the Child, 28 I.L.M. 1448 (Nov. 20, 1989), provides that a child of sufficient age and maturity should be heard in all cases involving his or her custody. Would adoption mandate the provision of lawyers for children involved in custody contests? What other ways are there to hear the child's voice? *See* Melissa L. Berger, *Against the Dilution of a Child's Voice in Court*, 20 IND. INT'L & COMP. L. REV. 175 (2010) (suggesting adoption of child-centered rules about roles of all).

8.   If a lawyer is appointed for the children, must the parents pay his or her fees? If yes, must the state pay if the parents are financially unable to do so? *See In re* Marriage of Metzger, 169 Cal. Rptr. 3d 382 (App. 2014); Marlin v. Marlin, 808 A.2d 707 (Conn. App. 2002) (ordering father who requested attorney's appointment to pay bulk of fees).

2.   PARENT V. PARENT—DETERMINING THE BEST INTERESTS OF THE CHILD

Under the common law, the child's father was entitled to custody. According to Blackstone, the mother was "entitled to no power [over her children], but only to reverence and respect." 1 WILLIAM BLACKSTONE, COMMENTARIES ON THE LAW OF ENGLAND 453 (1765). The paternal custody entitlement was not absolute—the poet Percy Bysshe Shelley, for example, was denied custody of his children based on his immorality, atheism, and denial of the Christian religion (Shelley v. Westbrooke, 37 Eng. Rep. 850 (Ch. 1817))—but absent unusual circumstances, the father's rights were paramount.

Over the course of the nineteenth century, "growing concern with child nurture and the acceptance of women as more legally distinct individuals, ones with a special capacity for moral and religious leadership and for child rearing, undermined the primacy of paternal custody rights.* * *" MICHAEL GROSSBERG, GOVERNING THE HEARTH: LAW AND THE FAMILY IN NINETEENTH CENTURY AMERICA 239 (1985). By the late nineteenth century, American courts universally awarded custody based on the "best interests of the child." The best interests standard was augmented by the "tender years doctrine," which established a rebuttable presumption that a young child belonged with its mother. *See generally* MARY ANN MASON, FROM FATHER'S PROPERTY TO CHILDREN'S RIGHTS (1994).

The tender years doctrine survived until the 1960s when courts and legislatures universally moved toward gender-neutral application of the best interests standard. Without a presumption to simplify the process of determining a child's best interests, a court must assess information on a wide range of issues. The Uniform Marriage and Divorce Act § 402, 9A U.L.A. (Part 2) 282, for example, provides as follows:

§ 402. Best Interest of Child

The court shall determine custody in accordance with the best interest of the child. The court shall consider all relevant factors including:

(1)   the wishes of the child's parent or parents as to his custody;

(2)   the wishes of the child as to his custodian;

(3)   the interaction and interrelationship of the child with his parent or parents, his siblings, and any other person who may significantly affect the child's best interest;

(4)   the child's adjustment to his home, school, and community; and

(5)   the mental and physical health of all individuals involved.

The court shall not consider conduct of a proposed custodian that does not affect his relationship to the child.

ROBERT H. MNOOKIN, CHILD CUSTODY ADJUDICATION: JUDICIAL FUNCTIONS IN THE FACE OF INDETERMINACY
39 LAW & CONTEMPORARY PROBLEMS 227 (1975).

* * * Custody disputes under the best-interests principle require "person-oriented," not "act-oriented," determinations. Most legal rules require determination of some event and are thus "act-oriented." A "person-oriented" rule, on the other hand, requires an evaluation of the "whole person viewed as a social being." * * *

* * * In a divorce custody fight, a court must evaluate the attitudes, dispositions, capacities, and shortcomings of each parent to apply the best-interest standard. * * * Adjudication usually requires the determination of past acts and facts, not a prediction of future events. Applying the best-interests standard requires an individualized prediction: with whom will this child be better off in the years to come? Proof of what happened in the past is relevant only insofar as it enables the court to decide what is likely to happen in the future.

* * *

Because custody disputes involve relationships between people, a decision affecting any one of the parties will often necessarily have an effect on the others. The resolution of a custody dispute may permanently affect—or even end—the parties' legal relationship; but the social and psychological relationships will usually continue. The best-interests principle requires a prediction of what will happen in the future, which, of course, depends in part on the future behavior of the parties. * * *

A determination that is person-oriented and requires predictions necessarily involves an evaluation of the parties who have appeared in court. This has important consequences for the roles of both precedent and appellate review in custody cases. The result of an earlier case involving different people has limited relevance to a subsequent case requiring individualized evaluations of a particular child and the litigants. * * * All of this makes the scope of appellate review extremely limited. Because the trial court's decision involves an assessment of the personality, character, and relationship of people the judge has seen in court, appellate courts are extremely loath to upset the trial court's determination on the basis of a transcript. * * *

NOTES AND QUESTIONS

1. Before your views have been "corrupted" by the remainder of this chapter, evaluate the UMDA factor list. Are there additional factors that should be added? Are there factors that should be subtracted? Should some factors receive more weight than others? If yes, which factors should receive more weight and how much weight should they receive? *See* Margaret M.C. v. William J.C., 972 N.Y.S.2d 396 (Sup. 2012) (no one factor is determinative).

2. Many custody statutes include factors in addition to those contained in the UMDA factor list. For example, Colorado requires the court to additionally consider "the economic situation of the parents; educational needs and opportunities; necessities; stable, consistent supervision; ability of each parent to promote a continuing relationship between the child and the other parent; age and sex of parent and child; religious needs; presence of domestic violence; and recommendations of professionals." COLO. REV. STAT. § 14–10–124(1.5). What are the pros and cons of lengthy and relatively brief factor lists? *See* Linda D. Elrod & Mildred D. Dale, *Paradigm Shifts and Pendulum Swings in Child Custody: The Best Interests of Children in the Balance*, 42 FAM. L. Q. 381 (2008).

3. Most states encourage custody agreements. If the parents agree on a custody arrangement, the court will typically presume that the agreement is in the child's best interests. *See, e.g.*, KAN. STAT. ANN. § 23–3202. Even with an agreement, however, the judge has a duty to determine if the agreement is in the best interests of the child. *See* Stone v. Stone, 991 N.E.2d 992 (Ind. App. 2013), reh'g granted. *See also* Kimberly C. Emery & Robert E. Emery, *Who*

Knows What is Best for Children? Honoring Agreements and Contracts Between Parents Who Live Apart, 77 LAW & CONTEMP. PROBS. 151 (2014).

A. PROHIBITED FACTORS: GENDER AND RACE

EX PARTE DEVINE

Supreme Court of Alabama, 1981.
398 So. 2d 686.

MADDOX, JUSTICE.

* * * By the middle of the 19th century, the courts of England began to question and qualify the paternal preference rule. This was due, in part, to the "hardships, not to say cruelty, inflicted upon unoffending mothers by a state of law which took little account of their claims or feelings." W. FORSYTH, A TREATISE ON THE LAW RELATING TO THE CUSTODY OF INFANTS IN CASES OF DIFFERENCE BETWEEN PARENTS OR GUARDIANS 66 (1850). Courts reacted by taking a more moderate stance concerning child custody, a stance which conditioned a father's absolute custodial rights upon his fitness as a parent. Ultimately, by a series of statutes culminating with Justice Talfourd's Act, 2 and 3 Vict. c. 54 (1839), Parliament affirmatively extended the rights of mothers, especially as concerned the custody of young children. Justice Talfourd's Act expressly provided that the chancery courts, in cases of divorce and separation, could award the custody of minor children to the mother *if the children were less than seven years old.* This statute marks the origin of the tender years presumption in England.

In the United States the origin of the tender years presumption is attributed to the 1830 Maryland decision of *Helms v. Franciscus*, 2 Bland Ch. (Md.) 544 (1830). In *Helms*, the court, while recognizing the general rights of the father, stated that it would violate the laws of nature to "snatch" an infant from the care of its mother:

> The father is the rightful and legal guardian of all his infant children; and in general, no court can take from him the custody and control of them, thrown upon him by the law, not for his gratification, but on account of his duties, and place them against his will in the hands even of his wife. * * * Yet even a court of common law will not go so far as to hold nature in contempt, and snatch helpless, puling infancy from the bosom of an affectionate mother, and place it in the coarse hands of the father. The mother is the softest and safest nurse of infancy, and with her it will be left in opposition to this general right of the father.

Thus began a "process of evolution, perhaps reflecting a change in social attitudes, [whereby] the mother came to be the preferred custodian of young children and daughter. * * * " Foster, *Life with Father: 1978*, 11 FAM. L. Q. 327 (1978).

* * *

At the present time, the tender years presumption is recognized in Alabama as a rebuttable factual presumption based upon the inherent suitability of the mother to care for and nurture young children. All things being equal, the mother is presumed to be best fitted to guide and care for children of tender years. To rebut this presumption the father must present clear and convincing evidence of the mother's positive unfitness. Thus, the tender years presumption affects the resolution of child custody disputes on both a substantive and procedural level. Substantively, it requires the court to award custody of young children to the mother when the parties, as in the present case, are equally fit parents. Procedurally, it imposes an evidentiary burden on the father to prove the positive unfitness of the mother.

In recent years, the tender years doctrine has been severely criticized by legal commentators as an outmoded means of resolving child custody disputes. Several state courts have chosen to abandon or abolish the doctrine, noting that the presumption "facilitates error in an arena in which there is little room for error." * * *

It is safe to say that the courts of this state, like the courts of sister states, have come full circle in resolving the difficult questions surrounding child custody. At common law, courts spoke of the natural rights of the father. Now they speak of the instinctive role of the mother.

The question we are confronted with is not dissimilar to the question confronting the English courts over 150 years ago: Is it proper to deny a parent the custody of his or her children on the basis of a presumption concerning the relative parental suitability of the parties? More specifically, can the tender years presumption withstand judicial scrutiny under the Fourteenth Amendment to the United States Constitution as construed in recent decisions by the Supreme Court of the United States? * * *

Having reviewed the historical development of the presumption as well as its modern status, and having examined the presumption in view of * * * [recent Supreme Court decisions], we conclude that the tender years presumption represents an unconstitutional gender-based classification which discriminates between fathers and mothers in child custody proceedings solely on the basis of sex. * * *

The trial court's custody decree conclusively shows that the tender years presumption was a significant factor underlying the court's decision. Confronted with two individuals who were equally fit (i.e., all things being equal), the trial court awarded custody to the mother.

Accordingly, the judgment of the Court of Civil Appeals affirming the lower court decree and affirming the constitutionality of the tender years presumption is hereby reversed. The cause is due to be remanded to the trial court with directions that the court consider the individual facts of the case. The sex and age of the children are indeed very important considerations; however, the court must go beyond these to consider the characteristics and needs of each child, including their emotional, social, moral, material and educational needs; the respective home environments offered by the parties; the characteristics of those seeking custody, including age, character, stability, mental and physical health; the capacity and interest of each parent to provide for the emotional, social, moral, material and educational needs of the children; the interpersonal relationship between each child and each parent; the interpersonal relationship between the children; the effect on the child of disrupting or continuing an existing custodial status; the preference of each child, if the child is of sufficient age and maturity; the report and recommendation of any expert witnesses or other independent investigator; available alternatives; and any other relevant matter the evidence may disclose. Only in this way will the court truly consider the best interests of the Devine children.

TORBERT, CHIEF JUSTICE (dissenting).

* * * The well-being of the child is the paramount consideration in determining its custody. The focus in a child custody hearing is on the child's welfare and best interest, not on the parents or their personal rights. Custody of one's child is not a prize to be fought for; rather it is a responsibility imposed by the court under appropriate conditions or restrictions the court sees fit to impose. Therefore, *Orr v. Orr,* 440 U.S. 268 (1979) [holding that a statute restricting alimony eligibility to women, and other cases involving gender-based eligibility barriers] * * * [and other gender discrimination cases cited by the majority] have no relevance in the field of child custody. Gender may be an inappropriate factor to consider in bestowing a benefit, but it should be a factor in determining which parent will have primary custody of a very small child.

We are not faced here with * * * a rule by which one gender was given absolute preference over the other. The tender years doctrine, as the majority correctly stated, has evolved over the years into a factor to be considered in child custody determinations, rather than a compelling presumption. I believe it is valid as such, and should be retained in its present form. I therefore respectfully dissent.

NOTES AND QUESTIONS

1. Gender-based classifications are now subject to so-called "intermediate" scrutiny. Using that approach, is the *Devine* court's holding sound?

2.   Most states, by statute or case law, prohibit use of the tender years doctrine. *See* FLA. STAT. § 61.13(2)(b)(1); Hubbell (Gault) v. Hubbell, 702 A.2d 129 (Vt. 1997); Giffin v. Crane, 716 A.2d 1029 (Md. 1998). A few states continue to permit use of the tender years doctrine only as a tie-breaking factor. *See* Copeland v. Copeland, 904 So. 2d 1066 (Miss. 2004).

3.   Some feminist scholars have argued for a return to a maternal preference standard. Consider Mary Becker, *Maternal Feelings: Myth, Taboo and Child Custody,* 1 S. CAL. REV. L. & WOMEN'S STUDIES 133, 223–24 (1992):

> I assess custody standards against their ability to protect the greater emotional commitments of women to children. I reject the best interest standard, joint custody, and deference to the mature child because they do not protect adequately the strong emotional bonds between children and their mothers. * * * At divorce, judges should defer to the fit mother's decision with respect to custody.

Others contend that a gender-neutral best interest standard discriminates against women. *See* Penelope Bryan, *Reasking the Woman Question at Divorce,* 75 CHI.-KENT L. REV. 713 (2000); Martha Fineman, *Fatherhood, Feminism and Family Law,* 32 MCGEORGE L. REV. 1031 (2001); Katharine T. Bartlett, *Comparing Race and Sex Discrimination in Custody Cases,* 28 HOFSTRA L. REV. 877 (2000). Which position is more convincing?

4.   Has the demise of the tender years doctrine made a difference in custody outcomes? Researchers who reviewed a hundred appellate opinions in each of three time periods—the 1920s, the 1960s and the 1990s—reported that

> * * * in spite of * * * outward change, mothers and fathers in 1920, 1960, and 1990–95 are each still favored close to half the time. This remarkable continuity in the face of what appears to be massive discontinuity, both in rhetoric and procedure, is not easily explained. One possible explanation is that mothers, not fathers, want custody in the vast majority of cases, but when fathers fight for custody they have always had about a 50 percent chance of winning, no matter what arguments or what experts they employ. * * * Mothers' preference and moral fitness have given way to gender-neutral criteria, such as stability and time spent with the child. There are those who argue that such criteria * * * translates to maternal preference. That * * * [is another possible] explanation of why fathers have not gained more. [But] others have claimed that judges consider mothers more critically today. * * * Seen in * * * historical context, however, it is apparent that rhetoric alone cannot predict custody outcomes. It is not clear that the factors judges claim are most important in determining custody have much to do with the ultimate result. * * * The continuity of decision making may mean that divorcing families look much as they always have, and judges exercise the same judicial discretion to achieve similar results.

Mary Ann Mason & Ann Quirk, *Are Mothers Losing Custody? Read My Lips: Trends in Judicial Decision-Making in Custody Disputes—1920, 1960, 1990, and 1995*, 31 FAM. L. Q. 215 (1997). *See also* Stephen J. Bahr et al., *Trends in Child Custody Awards: Has the Removal of Maternal Preference Made a Difference?*, 28 FAM. L. Q. 247 (1994) (finding Utah fathers were no more likely to obtain sole custody in 1993 than in 1970, although joint custody awards increased significantly).

PALMORE V. SIDOTI

Supreme Court of the United States, 1984.
466 U.S. 429.

CHIEF JUSTICE BURGER delivered the opinion of the Court.

* * *

When petitioner Linda Sidoti Palmore and respondent Anthony J. Sidoti, both Caucasians, were divorced in May 1980 in Florida, the mother was awarded custody of their three-year old daughter.

In September 1981 the father sought custody of the child by filing a petition to modify the prior judgment because of changed conditions. The change was that the child's mother was then cohabiting with a Negro, Clarence Palmore, Jr., whom she married two months later. * * *

After hearing testimony from both parties and considering a court counselor's investigative report, * * * the court made a finding that "there is no issue as to either party's devotion to the child, adequacy of housing facilities, or respect[a]bility of the new spouse of either parent."

The court then addressed the recommendations of the court counselor, who had made an earlier report "in [another] case coming out of this circuit also involving the social consequences of an interracial marriage." From this vague reference to that earlier case, the court turned to the present case and noted the counselor's recommendation for a change in custody because "[t]he wife [petitioner] has chosen for herself and for her child, a life-style unacceptable to her father *and to society*. * * * The child * * * is, or at school age will be, subject to environmental pressures not of choice."

The court then concluded that the best interests of the child would be served by awarding custody to the father. The court's rationale is contained in the following:

> The father's evident resentment of the mother's choice of a black partner is not sufficient to wrest custody from the mother. It is of some significance, however, that the mother did see fit to bring a man into her home and carry on a sexual relationship with him without being married to him. Such action tended to place gratification of her own desires ahead of her concern for the child's future welfare. *This Court feels that despite the strides that have*

> *been made in bettering relations between the races in this country,
> it is inevitable that Melanie will, if allowed to remain in her
> present situation and attains school age and thus more vulnerable
> to peer pressures, suffer from the social stigmatization that is sure
> to come.*

App. to Pet. for Cert. 26–27 (emphasis added)

* * *

The judgment of a state court determining or reviewing a child custody decision is not ordinarily a likely candidate for review by this Court. However, the court's opinion, after stating that the "father's evident resentment of the mother's choice of a black partner is not sufficient" to deprive her of custody, then turns to what it regarded as the damaging impact on the child from remaining in a racially-mixed household. This raises important federal concerns arising from the Constitution's commitment to eradicating discrimination based on race.

The Florida court did not focus directly on the parental qualifications of the natural mother or her present husband, or indeed on the father's qualifications to have custody of the child. The court found that "there is no issue as to either party's devotion to the child, adequacy of housing facilities, or respectability of the new spouse of either parent." *Id.*, at 24. This, taken with the absence of any negative finding as to the quality of the care provided by the mother, constitutes a rejection of any claim of petitioner's unfitness to continue the custody of her child.

The court correctly stated that the child's welfare was the controlling factor. But that court was entirely candid and made no effort to place its holding on any ground other than race. Taking the court's findings and rationale at face value, it is clear that the outcome would have been different had petitioner married a Caucasian male of similar respectability.

A core purpose of the Fourteenth Amendment was to do away with all governmentally-imposed discrimination based on race. * * *

The State, of course, has a duty of the highest order to protect the interests of minor children, particularly those of tender years. In common with most states, Florida law mandates that custody determinations be made in the best interests of the children involved. The goal of granting custody based on the best interests of the child is indisputably a substantial governmental interest for purposes of the Equal Protection Clause.

It would ignore reality to suggest that racial and ethnic prejudices do not exist or that all manifestations of those prejudices have been eliminated. There is a risk that a child living with a step-parent of a different race may be subject to a variety of pressures and stresses not present if the child were living with parents of the same racial or ethnic origin.

The question, however, is whether the reality of private biases and the possible injury they might inflict are permissible considerations for removal of an infant child from the custody of its natural mother. We have little difficulty concluding that they are not. The Constitution cannot control such prejudices but neither can it tolerate them. Private biases may be outside the reach of the law, but the law cannot, directly or indirectly, give them effect. "Public officials sworn to uphold the Constitution may not avoid a constitutional duty by bowing to the hypothetical effects of private racial prejudice that they assume to be both widely and deeply held." *Palmer v. Thompson*, 403 U.S. 217, 260–261 (1971) (WHITE, J., dissenting).

* * *

Whatever problems racially-mixed households may pose for children in 1984 can no more support a denial of constitutional rights than could the stresses that residential integration was thought to entail in 1917. The effects of racial prejudice, however real, cannot justify a racial classification removing an infant child from the custody of its natural mother found to be an appropriate person to have such custody.

The judgment of the District Court of Appeal is reversed.

NOTES AND QUESTIONS

1. On remand in *Palmore*, the trial court relinquished jurisdiction to the Texas courts, citing the child's more than two year residence in Texas with her father and stepmother. The appellate court affirmed. *See* Palmore v. Sidoti, 472 So. 2d 843 (Fla. Dist. Ct. App. 1985).

2. Does *Palmore* preclude all consideration of race? *Compare* Henggeler v. Hanson, 510 S.E.2d 722 (S.C. App. 1998) (finding mother's sensitivity to the adopted children's interest in understanding their Korean heritage and having ethnic diversity in their environment were appropriately taken into account by the trial court) *with* Ebirim v. Ebirim, 620 N.W.2d 117 (Neb. App. 2000) (finding trial court did not err in refusing to consider child's biracial heritage). Fifteen percent of marriages in 2010 involved persons of different racial or ethnic backgrounds. *See* PAUL TAYLOR, ET AL., THE RISE OF INTERMARRIAGE: RATES, CHARACTERISTICS VARY BY RACE AND GENDER 1 (Pew Research Center 2012). Even more cohabitants are of different races. *See* Zhenchao Qian & Daniel T. Lichter, *Changing Patterns of Interracial Marriage in a Multiracial Society*, 73 J. MARR. & FAM. 1065, 1073 (2011). Do you think race is an important element of personal identity? If so, should courts consider whether placement with a minority parent would be beneficial to the child?

3. Does *Palmore* preclude racial matching in adoption? *See* Chapter 8, Section 3. *See also* Indian Child Welfare Act, 25 U.S.C. § 1903(1); Jones v. Jones, 542 N.W.2d 119 (S.D. 1996) (distinguishing *Palmore* and awarding custody of three children to Native American father).

B. THE ROLE OF RELIGION AND PARENTAL LIFESTYLE

OSIER V. OSIER

Supreme Court of Maine, 1980.
410 A.2d 1027.

[The trial court granted custody to the father based primarily on the mother's testimony that she would not consent to a blood transfusion for her son even if necessary to safeguard his health.]

* * * [I]n approaching a case of this sort, the divorce court should make a preliminary determination of the child' best interest, without giving any consideration to either parent's religious practices, in order to ascertain which of them is the preferred custodial parent. Where that preliminary determination discloses that the religious practices of only the nonpreferred parent are at issue, any need for the court to delve into a constitutionally sensitive area is avoided.

If, on the other hand, that preliminary determination discloses a preference for the parent whose religious practices have been placed in issue, the divorce court, in fashioning an appropriate custody order, may take into account the consequences upon the child of that parent's religious practices. Because of the sensitivity of the constitutional rights involved, however, any such inquiry must proceed along a two-stage analysis, designed to protect those rights against unwarranted infringement. To summarize that analysis briefly: first, in order to assure itself that there exists a factual situation necessitating such infringement, the court must make a threshold factual determination that the child's temporal well-being is immediately and substantially endangered by the religious practice in question and, if that threshold determination is made, second, the court must engage in a deliberate and articulated balancing of the conflicting interests involved, to the end that its custody order makes the least possible infringement upon the parent's liberty interests consistent with the child's well-being. * * *

If and only if the court is satisfied that an immediate and substantial threat to the child's well-being is posed by the religious practice in question, need it proceed to the second stage of the inquiry, requiring it to engage in an explicit balancing of the conflicting interests. In fashioning the appropriate order, the court should adopt a means of protecting the best interests of the child that makes the least possible intrusion upon the constitutionally protected interests of the parent. This balancing process requires the judge to conduct an evidentiary hearing on the alternative remedies available. * * *

NOTES AND QUESTIONS

1.   *Osier* states the majority rule that a parent's religious practices are relevant to the custody determination only if the practices are illegal, immoral, or pose a substantial threat of imminent harm to the child as a direct result of exposure to the practice. *See* Harrison v. Tauheed, 256 P.3d 851 (Kan. 2011) (leaving primary residency with Jehovah Witness mother over Muslim father where no showing of harm from mother's religious beliefs). The court, however, may consider that child has developed ties to a particular religion in awarding custody to the parent who would foster that religion. *See* Gribeluk v. Gribeluk, 991 N.Y.S.2d 117 (App. Div. 2014) (here Hasidic Judaism). For additional discussion, *see* Carolyn Wah, *Religion in Child Custody and Visitation Cases: Presenting the Advantage of Religious Participation*, 28 FAM. L. Q. 269 (1994); Carl E. Schneider, *Religion and Child Custody*, 25 U. MICH. J. L. REF. 879 (1992).

2.   How would the *Osier* analysis apply in a case in which one parent belongs to a church that performs exorcisms? Believes that a wife should be subservient to her husband? Shuns nonbelievers? *See In re* Marriage of Wang, 896 P.2d 450 (Mont. 1995); *In re* Marriage of Hadeen, 619 P.2d 374 (Wash. App. 1980).

3.   As a general rule, the custodial parent has the right to determine the child's religious upbringing "unless the court after hearing finds, upon motion by the noncustodial parent, that in the absence of a specific limitation of the custodian's authority, the child's physical health would be endangered or his emotional development significantly impaired." MONT. CODE ANN. § 40–4–218(1). What if one parent's religion leads her to not believe in vaccinations? *See* Winters v. Brown, 50 So. 3d 656 (Fla. Dist. Ct. App. 2011) (awarding medical decision making to father).

4.   Absent a clear showing of substantial harm to the child, a parent who does not have decision-making authority with respect to religion nevertheless retains a constitutional right to educate the child in that parent's religion. *See In re* Marriage of McSoud, 131 P.3d 1208 (Colo. App. 2006) (finding that "harm to the child from conflicting religious instructions or practices, which would justify a limitation, should not be simply assumed or surmised; it must be demonstrated in detail."); Feldman v. Feldman, 874 A.2d 606 (N.J. Super. App. Div. 2005) (holding that secondary caretaker could take children to religious services of her choice but could not enroll them in Catholic training and education classes over Jewish father's objections).

5.   Is a premarital agreement regarding children's future religious upbringing enforceable during marriage? at divorce? *See* Abbo v. Briskin, 660 So. 2d 1157 (Fla. Dist. Ct. App. 1995); Scialdo v. Kernan, 788 N.Y.S.2d 473 (App. Div. 2005) (modifying custody order to grant custody to father based in part on mother's violation of an agreement that the parties' child would be brought up Roman Catholic).

6.   Does the child have First Amendment rights that must be balanced against those of his or her parent(s)? *See* Susan Higginbotham, *"Mom, Do I Have to Go to Church?"—The Noncustodial Parent's Obligation to Carry Out the Custodial Parent's Religious Plans*, 31 FAM. L. Q. 585, 594–595 (1997).

Problem 14-1:

At the time of marriage, Harry was Roman Catholic and Wilma was Jewish. They agreed that their children would be raised in the Jewish faith. Joshua was born five years ago and circumcised in a traditional Jewish ceremony. Two years after Joshua's birth, Harry joined a fundamentalist Christian church and, a year later, Wilma joined an Orthodox synagogue. Unsurprisingly, the parties filed for divorce soon thereafter. At the time the divorce action was filed, Joshua attended a Jewish religious school in accordance with the parents' agreement. At trial, Harry testified that he believes that those who don't accept Jesus Christ are "damned to go to hell" and that he would like Joshua to accept Jesus Christ. He also stated that "he will never stop trying to save his child." Wilma testified that she does not accept Jesus Christ, does not want Joshua to believe in Jesus Christ, and that she wants Joshua to grow up in the Jewish religion. She also expressed fear that Harry will try to undermine not only Joshua's religious education, but also his feelings about her. A court-appointed psychiatrist testified that Joshua thinks of himself as Jewish, was deeply troubled by the conflict between his parents, and was deeply attached to both parents. The psychiatrist also testified that both parents were sincere, loving, and capable. You are the trial court judge; what custody decision will you make? How will you justify it? *See* Kendall v. Kendall, 687 N.E.2d 1228 (Mass. 1997).

FULK V. FULK
Mississippi Court of Appeals, 2002.
827 So. 2d 736.

BRIDGES, J.

* * * The polestar consideration in child custody cases is the best interest and welfare of the child. *Albright v. Albright,* 437 So. 2d 1003, 1005 (Miss. 1983). The *Albright* case provided Mississippi courts with guidelines for determining the best placement of the child after custody disputes. These factors include: (1) age, health and sex of the child; (2) determination of the parent that had the continuity of care prior to the separation; (3) which has the best parenting skills and which has the willingness and capacity to provide primary child care; (4) the employment of the parent and responsibilities of that employment; (5) physical and mental health and age of the parents; (6) emotional ties of parent and child; (7) moral fitness of parents; (8) the home, school and community record of the child; (9) the preference by law; (10) stability of home environment and employment of each parent; and (11) other factors relevant to the parent-child relationship. * * * Marital fault should not be used as a sanction in the custody decision, nor should differences in religion, personal values and lifestyles be the sole basis for custody decisions.

* * * Rhonda argues that the chancellor erred by placing too much emphasis on the fact that Rhonda had an adulterous affair with another woman. Jeffery counters that the chancellor was not concerned that the affair was of the lesbian nature but that the person Rhonda had the affair with was a severely emotionally unstable person who testified that she would still be a part of Rhonda's life as a friend and, consequently, be around the baby. Jeffery argues that the chancellor, in determining what was best for the baby, ruled that this unstable person would not be a good influence or provide a good environment for raising a small child.

Albright dictates that "difference in religion, personal values and lifestyles" would not be the sole basis for custody decisions. Our supreme court addressed a similar issue in 2001 and held that too much weight was placed upon the "moral fitness" factor based upon the mother's homosexual affair and reversed the decision of the chancery court. *Hollon v. Hollon*, 784 So. 2d 943, 949–50 (Miss. 2001). The chancellor in the case at bar stated that although both Rhonda and her female counterpart in the affair testified that the sexual relationship was over, it was her opinion and that of the court, that the sexual relationship was indeed not over. Furthermore, the chancellor found that it was "unacceptable for any child to be around this type of behavior." Apparently, Chancellor Weathersby forgot that the father was the instigator in the triangle relationship, not the mother. All three parties testified that Jeffery was involved in the affair and Jeffery even testified that he had oral sex with the second woman involved. As our supreme court has previously held, "it is of no consequence that a mother was having an affair with a woman rather than a man."

Therefore, it was error for the chancellor to have relied so heavily on the affair, as it was not just Rhonda's affair due to Jeffery's willingness to be an eager participant.

The facts in this case are unusual, as skeletons are in both parties' closets. The record indicates that Rhonda and Jeffery's relationship was unsteady during their entire courtship and marriage. To say that Jeffery and his father-in-law are not friendly with one another is an understatement. Rhonda is a young mother who does not have a source of income. She lives with her parents and a younger sibling. Both of her parents are unemployed and rely on "checks" as means for survival. As we have previously mentioned, Rhonda and Jeffery had a sexual relationship with one of Rhonda's female friends. Jeffery admits to having used drugs and alcohol heavily, although he claims to have now stopped using the addictive toxins. However, Rhonda entered into evidence photographs of marijuana and other drug paraphernalia located inside Jeffery's dresser drawers which were taken on the first day of February, the day of the final separation.

Two incidents are very disturbing to this Court in our review of the record. Specifically, the time when Jeffery "forgot" his wife was in his home and padlocked her inside the house since it was his habit to padlock the door. At that time, Rhonda was pregnant and trapped inside the home. Her father had to come and take the door off of the hinges to allow his daughter out of the house. Secondly, we view the domestic disturbance call which ended when the police arrested Jeffery for threatening to kill Rhonda and her family with a claw hammer. Jeffery was charged with resisting arrest and domestic violence. Jeffery proceeded to plead guilty to all charges against him and was sentenced to anger management classes. It is not clear from the chancellor's opinion that she considered these incidents. Her bench ruling states, "I find that the father may have done some things in the past he is not proud of, but the Court thinks that the responsibility of fatherhood has matured him. As the Court said before, I view the marital troubles as being part of his violent temper troubles." We are of the opinion these incidents should have been addressed and considered in making the *Albright* findings. It was error for the chancellor to ignore such matters. * * *

NOTES AND QUESTIONS

1.   Why do you suppose the chancellor placed more emphasis on the mother's sexual conduct than the father's abusive conduct? At one time some courts considered a parent's homosexuality to be a per se unfitness factor. Even before Obergefell v. Hodges, 135 S. Ct. 2584 (2015), most courts had moved to the nexus test concluding that a parent's homosexuality is not by itself sufficient to deny a parent custody. *See, e.g.,* T.C.H. v. K.M.H., 784 S.W.2d 281, 284 (Mo. App. 1989) ("the rule appears to be that there must be a nexus between harm to the child and the parent's homosexuality," before the parent's homosexuality is a relevant factor). Courts still may prefer the more "conventional" parent. *See* Adams v. Adams, 432 S.W.3d 49 (Ark. App. 2014); *In re* Marriage of Magnuson, 170 P.3d 65 (Wash. App. 2007) (placing child with mother over transgendered father).

2.   Today, the *Fulk* appellate court's approach to parental misconduct is typical. The trial judge who decides a custody contest based on parental conduct not shown to adversely affect the child is inviting reversal:

> [T]o deprive a parent of custody [based on allegation of sale of drugs in the home], the evidence must support a logical inference that some specific, identifiable behavior or conduct of the parent will probably cause significant physical or emotional harm to the child. This link between parent's conduct and harm to the child, moreover, may not

be based on evidence which raises a mere surmise or speculation of harm.

May v. May, 829 S.W.2d 373, 377 (Tex. App. 1992). *See also* Ford v. Ford, 65 S.W.3d 432 (Ark. 2002) (mother was properly awarded custody despite her alcoholism and use of marijuana in children's presence). This does not mean that courts will not consider moral fitness if it impacts on the child. See Heinen v. Heinen, 753 N.W.2d 891 (S.D. 2008) (mother's infidelity in post marital relationship related to moral fitness and stability).

The rise of legalized marijuana in several states has led to some issues about how much emphasis judges can put on marijuana use. Arizona's Medical Marijuana Act states that "No person may be denied custody or visitation or parenting time with a minor, and there is no presumption of neglect or child endangerment . . . unless the person's behavior creates an unreasonable danger to the safety of the minor as established by clear and convincing evidence. ARIZ. REV. STAT. § 36–2813. Can the use of legal marijuana be considered? *See* Daggett v. Sternick, 109 A.3d 1137 (Me. 2015) (awarding custody to the mother and allowing her to move where the father used large amounts of marijuana which he kept all over the house and his capacity to parent was impaired by his marijuana use).

Problem 14-2:

Rexayne and Wes are divorced and Rexayne has primary residential custody of their two sons. About six months ago, Kellie, an acknowledged lesbian, moved in with Rexayne and began to pay rent. There is no proof of any sexual relationship between Rexayne and Kellie, and they both deny one. Wes has requested custody based on the claim that the boys will be harmed because people will conclude that Rexayne and Kellie have a sexual relationship and tease the boys. Should Wes's motion be granted? *See* Taylor v. Taylor, 110 S.W.3d 731 (Ark. 2003).

C. THE ROLE OF DOMESTIC VIOLENCE

OWAN V. OWAN
Supreme Court of North Dakota, 1996.
541 N.W.2d 719.

MESCHKE, JUSTICE.

Rayann Owan appeals from a divorce decree placing custody of her daughter Danika with Stephen Owan. We reverse and remand for findings about domestic violence and for reconsideration of custody accordingly.

Rayann and Stephen lived together for two years before their marriage in 1990. Their daughter Danika was born in 1991. They moved several times, going from Williston to Minnesota, back to Williston, to Arizona, and again back to Williston. The relationship between Rayann and Stephen was often turbulent.

Rayann testified that Stephen had kicked through a locked bathroom door in their apartment, had thrown a cordless phone into a wall near her, and often would put Rayann "up against the wall and hit the wall above me and scare me," while calling her names: "tramp, bitch, whore * * * " Rayann testified about other controlling and domineering behavior by Stephen: "he'd go through my purse and rip my purse open and take all my credit cards, and take all my money." According to Rayann, Stephen threatened to kill her if she left him, and several times threatened suicide. There was also evidence that Rayann had slapped and scratched Stephen sometimes.

Rayann sued for divorce in February 1994 and received temporary custody of Danika. Before trial in December 1994, Stephen had moved back to Arizona to be close to his family, and Rayann was pregnant by a man she intended to marry. The trial court granted the divorce, divided the marital property, and placed custody of Danika with Stephen, with Rayann to pay child support. Rayann appealed.

We conclude that the dispositive aspect of this appeal is the lack of adequate attention to the statutory presumption against placing custody with a parent who has committed domestic violence. Part of NDCC § 14–09–06.2(1)(j) directs:

> The court shall cite specific findings of fact to show that the custody or visitation arrangement best protects the child and the parent or other family or household member who is the victim of domestic violence. * * * The fact that the abused parent suffers from the effects of the abuse may not be grounds for denying that parent custody.

"Domestic violence" is defined in NDCC § 14–07.1–01(2):

> "Domestic violence" includes physical harm, bodily injury, sexual activity compelled by physical force, assault, or the infliction of fear of imminent physical harm, not committed in self-defense, on the complaining family or household members.

* * * The effect of the statutory presumption makes domestic violence the paramount factor in a custodial placement when there is credible evidence of it. To rebut the presumption, the violent parent must prove by clear and convincing evidence that other circumstances require that the child be placed with the violent parent rather than the non-violent parent. * * * [W]hen there is evidence of domestic violence, the trial court must make specific findings about it.

On this record, the trial court made only a single finding from the opinion of Stephen's social-worker witness to minimize Stephen's violent conduct:

The Court gives [Stephen's social-worker witness's] testimony and opinion a great deal of credibility. The Court has reviewed North Dakota Century Code § 14–09–06.2 and does concur with Mr. Yockim's findings as follows: the allegations of Stephen's physical altercations appear to be minor. In most cases, [Rayann] has acted and [Stephen] has reacted.

This finding is unsatisfactory for several reasons.

First, the trial court improperly relied upon Stephen's social-worker witness to assess trial testimony as an expert on Stephen's violent conduct. To justify the trial court's abbreviated analysis about violence, Stephen's brief in this court also relied on testimony by that witness, Jim Yockim:

I was aware of the allegation, the verbal allegations, the abuse, the breaking the door in, the whole thing. Again it seemed to be situational in nature, situational in terms of the marital discord rather than a pattern, I guess, in Stephen's life. There were allegations on the other side in terms of scratching and those kinds of things, too, and I did not think that—again, I dealt with him in terms of being situational in the marital discord.

* * *

Q. Did you analyze that violent behavior in light of the presumption in the Century Code that absent other factors, the non-violent party is given a nod so to speak under the categories that are analyzed? how did you weigh that, if at all?

A. I guess I did not feel that it met the same level of violent behavior that I would, I guess I—

Q. You didn't apply the presumption basically, is that fair?

A. I don't think that I held that what had happened in that case as meeting that standard that the court is looking for as a determining factor.

Stephen principally urges here that we affirm the trial court's finding because Mr. Yockim's written home study makes no finding or suggestion of credible evidence of domestic violence by either party.

Rayann responds, "If one * * * *assumes* the Court intended by its statement as to Yockim's credibility to *adopt* the findings of Stephen's expert, more is required." We agree.

The trial court cannot delegate its specific statutory responsibility to weigh the evidence and make findings on domestic violence. Generally, a "court cannot make the report of an independent investigator the conclusive basis of its decision regarding the custody of the children. The reason for this rule is usually expressed by the phrase that the trial court cannot delegate to anyone the power to decide questions of child custody." That concept is particularly important for domestic violence. Here, the statute directs the trial court itself to weigh the testimony about domestic violence, to make specific findings about it, and to "show" that the custodial arrangement "protects the child and the parent * * * who is the victim of domestic violence." NDCC § 14–09–06.2(1)(j). Those duties cannot be delegated by the trial court.

Nor does the trial court's finding permit adequate review of the reason for minimizing the extensive evidence of Stephen's violent conduct in this record. * * * [T]he extent of the evidence of physical abuse in a case like this must be specifically addressed and dealt with in the findings.

The trial court also failed to make findings about the slapping and scratching that Stephen alleged Rayann did. * * *

> [I]f domestic violence has been committed by both parents, the trial court [must] measure the amount and extent of domestic violence inflicted by both parents. If the amount and extent of domestic violence inflicted by one parent is significantly greater than that inflicted by the other, the statutory presumption against awarding custody to the perpetrator will apply only to the parent who has inflicted the greater domestic violence, and will not apply to the parent who has inflicted the lesser. However, if the trial court finds that the amount and extent of the violence inflicted by one parent is roughly proportional to the violence inflicted by the other parent, and both parents are otherwise found to be fit parents, the presumption against awarding custody to either perpetrating parent ceases to exist. In such a case, the trial court is not bound by any presumption, but may consider the remaining customary best-interests factors in making its custody decision.

Krank v. Krank, 529 N.W.2d at 850. If the violence between parents is proportional, the trial court should also consider, together with the other usual factors for custody, which parent is least likely to continue to expose the child to violence. Here, though, the trial court failed to measure or weigh the violent conduct described in the testimony, nor did it measure the propensity of each of these parents for continued violence.

The trial court's findings on domestic violence are insufficient for us to review its decision to place custody with Stephen. Accordingly, we reverse and remand for further findings and reconsideration of the custodial placement.

SANDSTROM, JUSTICE, dissenting.

* * *

This is a child custody case. Yet, nowhere does the majority even discuss "the best interests of the child." * * * Domestic violence is unacceptable. The goal of punishing perpetrators of domestic violence, however, cannot justify a child-custody award that is, in fact, not in the best interests of the child. Certainly domestic violence should be considered as it affects the best interests of the child. To the extent the majority analysis fails to limit child-custody-case consideration of domestic violence to the extent it in fact affects the best interests of the child, it is constitutionally infirm.

If the majority is saying, under the current law, a finding of domestic violence preempts consideration of all other factors relating to the best interests of the child, the legislation is remarkably parallel to that struck down as unconstitutional in *Stanley v. Illinois,* 405 U.S. 645 (1972). * * *

> Procedure by presumption is always cheaper and easier than individualized determination. But when, as here, the procedure forecloses the determinative issues of competence and care, when it explicitly disdains present realities in deference to past formalities, it needlessly risks running roughshod over the important interests of both parent and child. It therefore cannot stand.

Stanley at 656–57, 92 S. Ct. at 1215.

Because the majority ignores the fundamental need to determine the best interests of the child *in fact,* I dissent.

NOTES AND QUESTIONS

1. How, if at all, does the North Dakota domestic violence presumption at issue in *Owan* differ from the presumption at issue in Stanley v. Illinois? Is the dissent correct that the presumption fails to meet constitutional standards? *See* Opinion of the Justices to the Senate, 691 N.E.2d 911 (Mass. 1998) (concluding that presumption against awarding custody to a parent who had engaged in domestic violence would not violate either the state or federal constitutions). For a review of issues in custody cases involving domestic violence, see Dana Harrington Connor, *Abuse and Discretion: Evaluation, Judicial Discretion in Custody Cases Involving Violence Against Women*, 17 AM. U. J. GENDER SOC. POL'Y & L. 163 (2009).

2. Researchers have uniformly found that a child's exposure to domestic violence is associated with a range of harmful consequences. First, child abuse is far more common in homes where domestic violence is present. Second, children exposed to domestic violence typically exhibit emotional and physical symptoms similar to those of abused children, as well as decreased empathy,

increased aggression, tolerance of the use of violence, and victim blaming. Third, exposure to parental violence has been found to increase the risk of becoming violent—or victimized—in adult relationships. Finally, recent brain research indicates that children are at risk of brain damage from witnessing domestic violence as well as being the victim of it. Exposure to domestic violence triggers a "flight or fight" stress reaction in children. Repeated episodes causes "the biologic embedment of stress." This can cause long term negative harm. *See* Lynn Hecht Shafran, *Domestic Violence, Developing Brains and the Life Span: New Knowledge from Neuroscience*, 53 JUDGES J. 32 (2014). *See also* Nancy Ver Steegh, *Differentiating Types of Domestic Violence: Implications for Child Custody*, 65 LA. L. REV. 1379 (2005). In Schechter v. Schechter, 37 N.E.3d 632 (Mass. App. 2015), the mother was awarded custody and father's visitation suspended for a year because of his abusive and degrading conduct toward mother in the presence of the child.

3.   All fifty states and the District of Columbia now require the court to consider domestic violence or spousal abuse when making a custody or visitation determination. *See* Leslie Joan Harris, *Failure to Protect from Exposure to Domestic Violence in Private Custody* Contests, 44 FAM. L. Q. 169 (2010). Some states have established a rebuttable presumption against the award of custody or unsupervised visitation with the perpetrator of domestic violence. *See* Nancy K. D. Lemon, *Statutes Creating Rebuttable Presumptions Against Custody to Batterers: How Effective Are They?*, 28 WM. MITCHELL L. REV. 601 (2001). Other states have created custody preclusions. *See, e.g.* 23 PA. CONS. STAT. ANN. § 5303 (precluding custody or visitation award to parent convicted of designated domestic violence or child abuse crimes unless qualified professional testifies that parent has participated in specialized counseling and does not pose risk of harm to child). In 2000 the American Bar Association recommended that states address the safety of adult and child domestic violence victims during visitation exchanges.

4.   The opinion of the social worker who testified at the *Owan* custody trial is consistent with research showing that "experts" tend to ignore or minimize domestic violence. *See* Linda D. Elrod & Mildred D. Dale, *Paradigm Shifts and Pendulum Swings in Child Custody: The Interests of Children in the Balance*, 42 FAM. L. Q. 381, 395 (2008). Not recognizing or minimizing violence can be harmful to children. *See* Allen Bailey, *Prioritizing Child Safety as the Prime Best Interest Factor*, 47 FAM. L. Q. 35 (2013); Fernanda S. Rossi, et al., *Intimate Partner Violence and Child Custody in* PARENTING PLAN EVALUATIONS: APPLIED RESEARCH FOR THE FAMILY COURT 346 (LESLIE M. DROZD, ET AL., EDS. 2ND ED. 2016) (noting that failure to adequately screen and account for intimate partner violence in custody disputes create opportunities for the abuser to continue victimizing the other parent and expose the children to abusive behavior). *See also* Sarah M. Buel, *Domestic Violence and the Law: An Impassioned Exploration for Family Peace*, 33 FAM. L. Q. 719, 737–738 (1999).

5.   Is it possible that a victim parent trying to protect the child (and herself) would engage in behavior that might appear to be alienating? *See* Joan

S. Meier, *Getting Real About Abuse and Alienation: A Critique of Drozd and Olesen's Decision Tree*, 7 J. CHILD CUSTODY 219 (2010); Leslie Drozd & Nancy Olesen, *Abuse and Alienation are Each Real—A Response to a Critique by Joasn Meier*, 7 J. CHILD CUSTODY 253 (2010).

6. Over the last twenty years, there has been a seeming increase in allegations of domestic violence, sometimes child sexual abuse, in custody litigation. Although some commentators have alleged that many of these allegations are made falsely in order to obtain a litigation advantage, research fails to bear that out. *See* Kathleen Coulborn Faller & Ellen DeVoe, *Allegations of Sexual Abuse in Divorce*, 4 J. CHILD SEXUAL ABUSE (1996) (reporting that 72.6% of allegations are substantiated). In some cases, courts have relied on false allegations of abuse as a basis for awarding custody to the accused parent. *See In re* John T., 695 S.E.2d 868 (W. Va. 2010) (granting father full custody and ordering mother to pay father's legal fees for having to defend himself for years against two baseless abuse complaints during and after divorce); Handrahan v. Malenko, 12 A.3d 79 (Me. 2011) (mother failed to show father abused the child by a preponderance of the evidence); *In re* Wedemeyer, 475 N.W.2d 657 (Iowa App. 1991). *But see* Renaud v. Renaud, 721 A.2d 463 (Vt. 1998) (mother awarded sole custody even though allegations turned out to be false and her factual support was "weak at best" because she acted appropriately in seeking guidance from experts, including the child's pediatrician and therapist, before making the allegations).

D. THE ROLE OF THE "EXPERT"

In most litigated custody contests, the court cannot rely on a presumption. Instead, it must weigh and measure the advantages to the child of conferring custody on each parent. Almost invariably, each parent will offer a combination of strengths and weaknesses. Because both parents are typically "fit," the custody award will hinge on the court's decision as to which parent is better able to meet the child's needs.

If the parents can afford to do so, each will typically obtain and present expert testimony regarding his or her parenting skills and relationship with the children. This phase of the custody trial will closely resemble any other "battle of experts" in civil litigation. In about half of the states, the court is also authorized to order its own investigation and report, either by a guardian ad litem, a social services agency, or a private organization. These court-appointed investigators typically have, or may obtain from the court, the authority to obtain records, talk to witnesses, consult with other experts, and have the child evaluated. Judges have

> enthusiastically relied upon out-of-court caseworker custody investigations in divorce cases for a complex of reasons * * *: custody decisions are too important to be treated in the same fashion as ordinary adversary litigation—in which the parties have uncontrolled discretion as to what testimony is presented to

the decision maker; a neutral expert, removed from the emotional turmoil of the dispute and the partisan advocacy of the lawyers, can provide more reliable information to the judge than the embattled spouses are likely to provide; the information essential to custody decision making tends to be more psychological than in other litigation contexts and therefore more suited to written reports by psychological experts than to testimony in a courtroom.

Robert J. Levy, *Custody Investigations as Evidence*, 21 FAM. L.Q. 149, 150–51 (1987).

JONES V. JONES

Supreme Court of South Dakota, 1996.
542 N.W.2d 119.

JOHNS, CIRCUIT JUDGE.

Dawn R. Jones (Dawn) appeals from a decree of divorce awarding custody of the parties' three minor children to Kevin Mark Jones (Kevin). We affirm.

FACTS

Dawn and Kevin Jones were married on March 11, 1989 in Britton, South Dakota. Kevin was thirty years old at time of trial and is an enrolled member of the Sisseton-Wahpeton Dakota Nation. He was adopted at age seven by Maurice and Dorothy Jones. Dawn was twenty-five years old at time of trial and is Caucasian. The parties have three children, Lyndra, Elias and Desiree. * * *

During the marriage, the parties resided in a trailer house on the farm of Kevin's parents. Kevin is a minority shareholder in and works for Penrhos Farms. Penrhos is a close family farm corporation, owned primarily by Kevin's father and his three uncles. The Joneses are an extremely close-knit and supportive family. In fact, Kevin often takes the children to work with him, as this is a family tradition. However, farm safety is very important and is stressed by all members of the family.

Kevin works predominantly in construction and in the feeding of the cattle on the Penrhos Farms. His net earnings for child support purposes are approximately $1,880.00 a month. During the marriage, Dawn was a homemaker for a time and also held various jobs. She is currently enrolled in a nursing program at the Sisseton-Wahpeton Community College

Kevin is a recovering alcoholic who, while drinking, exhibited a behavior of violence towards Dawn and a somewhat casual indifference to the children. He has been sober since December 1992 and regularly attends and presents Alcoholics Anonymous meetings. Dawn suffers from depression and low self-esteem but is seeking counseling at this time.

Deterioration of the marriage is attributed to Kevin's alcoholism, Dawn's depression, financial problems and a lack of communication. Both parties were granted a divorce based upon mental cruelty. They were also granted joint legal custody of the children with primary physical custody being awarded to Kevin. * * *

Dawn contends that the trial court erred in finding as a matter of fact that Kevin is a fit person to have care, custody and control of his children. She also contends that even if the trial court did not err in finding that Kevin is fit to parent the children, the trial court abused its discretion when it chose Kevin over herself as the parent who would have primary physical custody of the children.

The paramount consideration for the trial court in deciding the issue of child custody is the temporal, mental and moral welfare of the child. The trial court exercises broad discretion in awarding custody and its discretion will be reversed only upon a clear showing of an abuse of that discretion * * * In determining whether there has been an abuse of discretion, this court does not decide whether it would have made the same ruling, but must determine if a judicial mind could have made a similar decision in view of the law and that particular case's circumstances.

Dawn contends that because Kevin sometimes verbally and physically abused her when he was drinking, he is not a fit person to have charge of the care and education of his children. The trial court's finding that Kevin is fit is based, in part, on a home study completed by Mr. Thomas L. Price, a licensed psychologist. His home study included clinical interviews with the parties, meetings with the children, and his observations of the parents and children together at the respective homes of the parties and his office. Mr. Price also administered to both parties the Minnesota Multiphasic Personality Inventory, the Millon Clinical Multiphasic Inventory—II, The Custody Quotient, the Child Access to Parental Strength Questionnaire, and the Access to Adult Strength: Parental Self-Report Data. After considering the effect of Kevin's alcoholism and domestic violence on his parental capacity, Mr. Price rendered the following conclusions and recommendations:

> Both Kevin and Dawn Jones were found to demonstrate adequate parental capacities. Dawn Jones obtained a higher score on the Custody Quotient. [Kevin obtained a CQ score of 112 which is in the High Average Parent Classification Range. Dawn obtained a CQ score of 120 which is at the low end of the Superior Parent Classification Range.] Her personality test findings were less suggestive of psychological difficulties and Lyndra's rating on the BPS [Bricklin Perceptual Scales: Child Perception of Parent] tended to favor her mother. Parent-child interactions and home

visitations failed to reveal significant difference between the parents.

The preponderance of information gathered by this examiner favors Dawn Jones as the custodial parent. The court is encouraged to afford liberal visitation rights to Kevin Jones, however.

Based on the home study of Mr. Price along with his testimony and all of the other evidence in the record, we are unable to say that the trial court's finding of Kevin's fitness is clearly erroneous. Thus, we affirm the trial court on this issue.

Contrary to the recommendations of Mr. Price and his associate, Ms. Judi Muessigmann, a clinical social worker, that primary custody of the children be placed with Dawn, the trial court determined that it should go to Kevin. In its findings of fact and conclusions of law, the court relied heavily upon the stability and continuity that Kevin could provide through his relationship with the Jones family. Specifically, the court stated in finding of fact number 52 that "the children have always known Penrhos Farms as their home, and granting primary physical custody to Father will allow the children to remain on the farm, and give them access to the numerous family support systems of the large and close Jones family." The trial court also stressed that, while Dawn may well be the preferable custodial parent at the immediate time, he was of the opinion that Kevin was the preferable parent over the "long haul." In doing so, he recognized * * * that stability is a very desirable factor in child rearing.

The trial court made its custody decision after hearing the testimony of the parties at the interim custody hearing and after nearly three days of trial testimony. It is apparent that the trial court wrestled long and hard with its decision as evidenced by the 20-page memorandum opinion, 15 pages of which dealt with the custody issue. After reviewing the testimony, along with the trial court's findings of fact and conclusions of law, we cannot say that its decision to award Kevin primary custody was an abuse of discretion. We affirm the trial court on this issue.

NOTES AND QUESTIONS

1. Would the *Owan* court uphold the trial court's decision in *Jones*? Why?

2. *Child Custody Evaluations:* Judges adjudicating complex child custody cases and family law attorneys may turn to mental health experts for help, especially if there are allegations of physical or sexual abuse of a parent or child, substance abuse, high conflict, alienation or lack of compliance with court orders. A mental health professional may perform a child custody evaluation or parenting assessment.

How much judges rely upon child custody evaluations varies and can be controversial. In the best circumstances, judges, attorneys, and the parties collaboratively develop psycholegal questions for the evaluator to investigate and provide opinions about. Forensic assessments in contested custody cases are often pivotal documents that can have a dramatic effect on the trajectory of the litigation. Courts and lawyers value the recommendation about the ultimate custody and parenting plan arrangements. Some mental health professionals, however, feel that experts should not make opinions on the ultimate issue, claiming the empirical scientific foundation is "tenuous or nonexistent." *See* Timothy T. Tippins & Jeffrey P. Wittmann, *Empirical and Ethical Problems with Custody Recommendations: A Call for Clinical Humility and Judicial Vigilance*, 43 FAM. CT. REV. 193 (2005). Indeed, all courts agree that a judge cannot delegate its obligation to independently weigh evidence in determining the children's best interests to the evaluator. In the Matter of Nold, 304 P.3d 1093 (Ariz. App. 2013).

Because of the importance of the custody evaluation, family law attorneys need to be familiar with the social science literature on child custody issues. They also need to know how jurisdiction-specific and profession-specific ethical principles for different mental health professionals fit into individualizing case plans and trial strategies. Attorneys who are familiar with social science and ethical rules are better able to evaluate, examine, and critique the quality of mental health reports and testimony. *See* Milfred D. Dale & Jonathan W. Gould, *Science, Mental Health Consultants, and Attorney-Expert Relationships in Child Custody*, 48 FAM. L. Q. 1, 2–3 (2014).

Family attorneys use the rules of evidence, professional guidelines, and help from mental health consultants to challenge adverse expert reports. The rules of evidence for experts provide tools for assessing the scientific foundation for an expert's report or testimony. *See* Daubert v. Merrell Dow Pharmaceuticals, 509 U.S. 579 (1993) (outlining a list of factors judges can use to determine the reliability of expert testimony). The court's focus on the reliability and relevance of evidence is designed to insure experts utilize the "same intellectual rigor that characterizes the practice of an expert in the relevant field." Kumho Tire Co. v. Carmichael, 526 U.S. 137, 152 (1999). *See* JEFFREY WITTMAN, EVALUATING EVALUATIONS: AN ATTORNEY'S HANDBOOK FOR ANALYZING CHILD CUSTODY REPORTS (2013).

3. *Criticisms of Custody Evaluations:* A number of commentators have raised concerns about court-ordered child custody evaluations, including issues of confidentiality, hearsay, and bias. An evaluation of custody investigations in Minnesota, for example, concluded that "[s]ome of the reports * * * were modest, thoughtful and, insofar as it was possible to check their facts, careful and accurate. But such conclusions could not be drawn about all, or even most, of the reports." Robert J. Levy, *Custody Investigations as Evidence*, 21 FAM. L. Q. 149, 160 (1987). The researcher found some instances in which facts about one or another parent were suppressed. In other cases there was clear evidence that the caseworker had "shaped" the report to produce a work product favorable to a judge or referee who had already made up his mind. *Id.* at 163.

And "[i]n some of the cases, the investigators obviously imposed upon the divorcing spouses their own personal and idiosyncratic child care and personal behavioral values in making custodial recommendations." *Id. See also* Janet M. Bowermaster, *Legal Presumptions and the Role of Mental Health Professionals in Child Custody Proceedings,* 40 DUQUESNE L. REV. 265, 306–307 (2002).

4. *Are Custody Evaluations Useful?* Some commentators have questioned the utility of all expert testimony in custody cases.

> Testifying about how the best interests of a particular child will be served by a particular custodial arrangement entails making a prediction, as contrasted with providing the court with information about the parties that would otherwise be unavailable. * * * While there is much well-grounded * * * research relevant to family law decisions, there is often an inverse correlation between its legal relevance and scientific grounding. The best research is likely to be of general application and is unlikely to be useful in predicting outcomes in particular cases. Nonetheless, there is an understandable natural inclination for lawyers and judges to want mental health professionals to go beyond the data to predict outcomes in particular cases. And a natural belief on the part of mental health professionals that because of their qualifications they are capable of doing so, even when they can point to no research to support that belief.

Daniel W. Shuman, *What Should We Permit Mental Health Professionals to Say About "The Best Interests of the Child"? An Essay on Common Sense,* Daubert *and the Rules of Evidence,* 31 FAM. L.Q. 551 (1997). *See also* Daniel W. Shuman, *The Role of Mental Health Experts in Custody Decisions: Science, Psychological Tests, and Clinical Judgment,* 36 FAM. L.Q. 135 (2002).

Did the custody evaluation in *Jones* evidence bias or inaccurate fact-finding? Why do you think the *Jones* trial judge did not adopt the evaluator's conclusions? On balance, was the evaluation in *Jones* useful?

5. *Improving Custody Evaluations:* The use (and abuse) of child custody evaluations has resulted in several suggestions for improving the practice. An ABA-sponsored conference on high conflict custody cases made several recommendations for improving custody evaluations: evaluators should follow national guidelines; evaluate both parents and children; distinguish their clinical judgments from research-based opinions and philosophical positions; and write their reports in plain, accessible English. They also urged the adoption of uniform evaluator qualifications and routine use of neutral evaluators. *See* Wingspread Conferees, *High Conflict Custody Cases: Reforming the System for Children-Conference Report and Action Plan,* 34 FAM. L. Q. 589, 592–3 (2001).

Aspirational guidelines for child custody evaluations have been developed by numerous professional organizations. Association of Family and

Conciliation Courts, *Model Standards of Practice for Child Custody Evaluation*, 45 FAM. CT. REV. 70 (2007). For a discussion of the history and role of custody evaluations, *see* Linda D. Elrod & Mildred D. Dale, *Paradigm Shifts and Pendulum Swings in Child Custody: The Interests of Children in the Balance*, 42 FAM. L. Q. 381, 410–417 (2008).

Surveys outlining the practices of evaluators also help identify appropriate methods and procedures used by evaluators. State statutes generally reflect methodologies to be used and what constitutes a complete evaluation. *See* CAL. CT. R. 5.220; COLO. REV. STAT. § 14–10–127; FLA. ADMIN. CODE ANN. R. 64B19–18.007; MONT. ADMIN. R. 24.219.12; 22 TEX. ADMIN. CODE § 465.18. The trend is towards holding evaluators more accountable for the scientific basis and reliability of their procedures.

3. ALTERNATIVES TO THE BEST INTERESTS STANDARD—SOLVING OR COMPOUNDING THE DILEMMA?

A. THE PRIMARY CARETAKER PRESUMPTION

GARSKA V. MCCOY
Supreme Court of West Virginia, 1981.
167 W. Va. 59, 278 S.E.2d 357.

J. NEELY:

[The mother appealed from trial court's award of custody to the father based on the court's findings that the father was "better educated," "more intelligent," "better able to provide financial support," "has a somewhat greater command of the English language," "can provide a better social and economic environment," "has a better appearance and demeanor," and "is very highly motivated in his desire to have custody."]

* * *

In setting the child custody law in domestic relations cases we are concerned with three practical considerations. First, we are concerned to prevent the issue of custody from being used in an abusive way as a coercive weapon to affect the level of support payments and the outcome of other issues in the underlying divorce proceeding. Where a custody fight emanates from this reprehensible motive the children inevitably become pawns to be sacrificed in what ultimately becomes a very cynical game. Second, in the average divorce proceeding intelligent determination of relative degrees of fitness requires a precision of measurement which is not possible given the tools available to judges. Certainly it is no more reprehensible for judges to admit that they cannot measure minute gradations of psychological capacity between two fit parents than it is for a physicist to concede that it is impossible for him to measure the speed of an electron. Third, there is an urgent need in contemporary divorce law for a legal structure upon which a divorcing couple may rely in reaching a settlement.

While recent statutory changes encourage private ordering of divorce upon the "no-fault" ground of "irreconcilable differences," our legal structure has not simultaneously been tightened to provide a reliable framework within which the divorcing couple can bargain intelligently. Nowhere is the lack of certainty greater than in child custody. * * *

Since the Legislature has concluded that private ordering by divorcing couples is preferable to judicial ordering, we must insure that each spouse is adequately protected during the out-of-court bargaining. Uncertainty of outcome is very destructive of the position of the primary caretaker parent because he or she will be willing to sacrifice everything else in order to avoid the terrible prospect of losing the child in the unpredictable process of litigation.

This phenomenon may be denominated the "Solomon syndrome", that is that the parent who is most attached to the child will be most willing to accept an inferior bargain. In the court of Solomon, the "harlot" who was willing to give up her child in order to save him from being cleaved in half so that he could be equally divided was rewarded for her sacrifice, but in the big world out there the sacrificing parent generally loses necessary support or alimony payments. This then must also be compensated for "in the best interests of the children." Moreover, it is likely that the primary caretaker will have less financial security than the nonprimary caretaker and, consequently, will be unable to sustain the expense of custody litigation, requiring as is so often the case these days, the payments for expert psychological witnesses.

Therefore, in the interest of removing the issue of child custody from the type of acrimonious and counter-productive litigation which a procedure inviting exhaustive evidence will inevitably create, we hold today that there is a presumption in favor of the primary caretaker parent, if he or she meets the minimum, objective standard for being a fit parent * * * regardless of sex. Therefore, in any custody dispute involving children of tender years it is incumbent upon the circuit court to determine as a threshold question which parent was the primary caretaker parent before the domestic strife giving rise to the proceeding began.

While it is difficult to enumerate all of the factors which will contribute to a conclusion that one or the other parent was the primary caretaker parent, nonetheless, there are certain obvious criteria to which a court must initially look. In establishing which natural or adoptive parent is the primary caretaker, the trial court shall determine which parent has taken primary responsibility for, inter alia, the performance of the following caring and nurturing duties of a parent: (1) preparing and planning of meals; (2) bathing, grooming and dressing; (3) purchasing, cleaning, and care of clothes; (4) medical care, including nursing and trips to physicians; (5) arranging for social interaction among peers after school, i.e. transporting to friends' houses or, for example, to girl or boy scout meetings; (6) arranging alternative care, i.e. babysitting, day-care, etc.; (7) putting the child to bed at night, attending to child in the middle of the night, waking child in the morning; (8) disciplining, i.e. teaching general manners and toilet training; (9) educating, i.e. religious, cultural, social, etc.; and, (10) teaching elementary skills, i.e., reading, writing and arithmetic.

In those custody disputes where the facts demonstrate that child care and custody were shared in an entirely equal way, then indeed no presumption arises and the court must proceed to inquire further into relative degrees of parental competence. However, where one parent can demonstrate with regard to a child of tender years that he or she is clearly the primary caretaker parent, then the court must further determine only whether the primary caretaker parent is a fit parent. Where the primary caretaker parent achieves the minimum, objective standard of behavior which qualifies him or her as a fit parent, the trial court must award the child to the primary caretaker parent.

Consequently, all of the principles enunciated in [the tender years doctrine] are reaffirmed today except that wherever the words "mother," "maternal," or "maternal preference" are used in that case, some variation of the term "primary caretaker parent," as defined by this case should be substituted. In this regard we should point out that the absolute presumption in favor of a fit primary caretaker parent applies only to children of tender years. Where a child is old enough to formulate an opinion about his or her own custody the trial court is entitled to receive such opinion and accord it such weight as he feels appropriate. When, in the opinion of the trial court, a child old enough to formulate an opinion but under the age of 14 has indicated a justified desire to live with the parent who is not the primary caretaker, the court may award the child to such parent.

NOTES AND QUESTIONS

1.   Is the primary caretaker presumption another version of the maternal preference? Justice Neely, author of the *Garska* opinion, has noted that "West Virginia law does not permit a maternal preference. But it does accord an explicit and almost absolute preference to the 'primary caretaker parent' * * *. This list of criteria usually, but not necessarily, spells 'mother.' That fact reflects social reality; the rule itself is neutral on its face and in its application." Richard Neely, *The Primary Caretaker Parent Rule: Child Custody and the Dynamics of Greed*, 3 YALE LAW & POL'Y REV. 167 (1984).

2. *Caretaking Activities as a Factor in Custody Decision Making*: Although no state currently has a statutory presumption in favor of the primary caretaker, many statutes explicitly require *consideration* of past caretaking roles. *See, e.g.,* LA. CIV. CODE ANN. art. 1334(12); N.J. STAT. ANN. § 9:2–4(c). Several states, either under the relevant custody statute or case law, require the court to give *priority* to past caretaking roles. *See* WASH. REV. CODE ANN. § 26.09.187(3)(a)(i) (requiring court to give "greatest weight" to "[t]he relative strength, nature, and stability of the child's relationship with each parent, including whether a parent has taken greater responsibility for performing caretaking functions related to the daily needs of the child"); Davis v. Davis, 749 P.2d 647, 648 (Utah 1988) ("considerable weight" should be given to the primary caretaking role). What are the pros and cons of these various methods of taking parental caretaking into account? Why do no states now utilize a primary caretaker presumption? Is giving priority to past caretaking roles different from a primary caretaker presumption? *See* Katherine T. Bartlett, *Prioritizing Past Caretaking in Child Custody*, 77 LAW & CONTEMP. PROBS. 29 (2014).

3. The primary caregiver is rooted in attachment theory. Experts find that attachment, is only one of several factors that should be considered. Some authors have proposed five factors to consider when the court is determining custody, residency, and parenting time for young children, with specific questions and guidance on each:

(1) The parent's relationship history with the child.

(2) The child's relationship with each parent and others.

(3) The parent's future commitment to rearing the child, including specific plans for supporting this commitment.

(4) The level of family violence and abuse.

(5) The nature of the coparenting relationship.

Pamela S. Ludolf and Milfred D. Dale, *Attachment in Child Custody: An Additive Factor, Not a Determinative One*, 46 FAM. L. Q. 34, 36 (2012).

4. *Custody Bargaining*: The *Garska* court describes the need to "insure that each spouse is adequately protected during out-of-court bargaining" as one basis for a primary caretaker presumption. Some family law experts have theorized that the indeterminacy of the best interests standard encourages fathers who are in reality uninterested in obtaining custody to threaten a custody fight in order to obtain economic concessions from mothers. *See* LENORE J. WEITZMAN, THE DIVORCE REVOLUTION: THE UNEXPECTED SOCIAL AND ECONOMIC CONSEQUENCES FOR WOMEN AND CHILDREN IN AMERICA 242–43 (1985); ELEANOR E. MACCOBY & ROBERT H. MNOOKIN, DIVIDING THE CHILD: SOCIAL AND LEGAL DILEMMAS OF CUSTODY 44–56 (1992).

5. Should it matter that the primary caretaker parent will be placing the child in daycare? *See* Ireland v. Smith, 547 N.W.2d 686 (Mich. 1996) (child care arrangements may be a proper consideration but there is no preference

for one form of child care over another); West v. West, 21 P.3d 838 (Alaska 2001) (finding that the fact that father's new wife would care for child instead of babysitters and extended family should not have been the determining factor in award of custody). *See* D. Kelly Weisberg, *Professional Women and the Professionalization of Motherhood: Marcia Clark's Double Bind*, 6 HASTINGS WOMEN'S L.J. 295 (1995). Instability in employment, however, may be a factor. See Hughes v. Rogusta, 830 N.E.2d 898 (Ind. App. 2005).

B. JOINT CUSTODY TO SHARED PARENTING

For centuries, sole custody in one parent was the norm. As more mothers worked outside the home and more fathers actively participated in parenting, sole custody failed to reflect family parenting styles. Joint legal custody emerged during the 1970s to preserve both parents' rights to make decisions regarding their child's care. By the end of the 1980s, more than two-thirds of the states had statutes specifically authorizing an award of joint custody. While some awards were for joint legal custody only; others included joint physical custody which would establish a residence pattern in which the child spends substantial periods of time in each parent's household. Even without explicit statutory authorization, most courts have held that they have inherent authority to grant joint custody. *See* LINDA D. ELROD, CHILD CUSTODY PRACTICE AND PROCEDURE, ch. 5 (Rev. ed. 2017).

As you read the following materials, consider the advantages and disadvantages of joint custody.

BECK V. BECK
Supreme Court of New Jersey, 1981.
86 N.J. 480, 432 A.2d 63.

CLIFFORD, J.

The parties to this matrimonial action have been granted joint legal and physical custody of their two adopted female children. Although neither party requested joint custody, the trial court nevertheless found such an arrangement to be in the best interests of the children.

* * *

In recent years the concept of joint custody has become topical, due largely to the perceived inadequacies of sole custody awards and in recognition of the modern trend toward shared parenting in marriage. Sole custody tends both to isolate children from the noncustodial parent and to place heavy financial and emotional burdens on the sole caretaker, usually the mother, although awards of custody to the father, especially in households where both parents are employed outside the home, are more common now than in years past. Moreover, because of the absolute nature of sole custody determinations, in which one parent "wins" and the other "loses," the children are likely to become the subject of bitter custody contests and post-decree tension. The upshot is that the best interests of the child are disserved by many aspects of sole custody.

Joint custody attempts to solve some of the problems of sole custody by providing the child with access to both parents and granting parents equal rights and responsibilities regarding their children. Properly analyzed, joint custody is comprised of two elements—legal custody and physical custody. Under a joint custody arrangement legal custody—the legal authority and responsibility for making "major" decisions regarding the child's welfare—is shared at all times by both parents. Physical custody, the logistical arrangement whereby the parents share the companionship of the child and are responsible for "minor" day-to-day decisions, may be alternated in accordance with the needs of the parties and the children.

At the root of the joint custody arrangement is the assumption that children in a unified family setting develop attachments to both parents and the severance of either of these attachments is contrary to the child's best interest. Through its legal custody component joint custody seeks to maintain these attachments by permitting both parents to remain decision-makers in the lives of their children. Alternating physical custody enables the children to share with both parents the intimate day-to-day contact necessary to strengthen a true parent-child relationship.

Joint custody, however, is not without its critics. The objections most frequently voiced include contentions that such an arrangement creates instability for children, causes loyalty conflicts, makes maintaining parental authority difficult, and aggravates the already stressful divorce situation by requiring interaction between hostile ex-spouses. * * * Although these same problems are already present in sole custody situations, some courts have used these objectives either to reject or strictly limit the use of joint custody.

Because we are persuaded that joint custody is likely to foster the best interests of the child in the proper case, we endorse its use as an alternative to sole custody in matrimonial actions. We recognize, however, that such an arrangement will prove acceptable in only a limited class of cases.

* * *

At the conclusion of the plenary hearing the trial court reiterated its prior findings and modified its original decision. Viewing the issue in terms of the importance of fatherhood in the lives of the two girls, it concluded that the lack of real contact with the father would have negative developmental effects, particularly because the girls are adopted.

* * *

The trial court stressed that although defendant's care of the girls was more than adequate, she is limited by an inability to be both a mother and a father. It found Mrs. Beck to be a "sensible" person, but also somewhat bitter and "stiff lipped" and more partisan than plaintiff, whom he described as "a rather * * * relaxed type of man." Noting that Mrs. Beck "honestly objects to the plan because she contends she cannot cooperate with her former husband," the court concluded, based on the testimony of Dr. Greif, that an amicable relationship between the parties is "comparatively unimportant and not essential" as long as the parties "are looking out for the best interests of the children."

Referring to this state's policy of seeking maximum visitation by the non-custodial parent in sole custody cases and to N.J.S.A. § 9:2–4, which gives both parents equal rights to custody, the trial court concluded that "there is a real purpose of fatherhood as well as motherhood." Furthermore, it distinguished between custodial time and visitation, describing the former as "meaningful contact" and the latter as "entertainment time." It saw the contact and involvement of the girls with two fit, concerned parents as "going to be what's good for the girls." Finally, it reiterated that this case is uniquely suitable to joint custody and ordered that the parents share "joint control and supervision" of the children with alternating physical custody for four month periods. It also provided for counseling services for the family.

The Appellate Division reversed, ruling that Mr. Beck, as the party seeking to change the status quo, had failed to satisfy the burden of proving that "the potentiality for serious psychological harm accompanying [implementation of the plan] will not become a reality."

* * *

We find the determination of the Appellate Division to be fundamentally flawed. * * * The question of whether a trial court may make a *sua sponte* custody determination need not long detain us. The paramount consideration in child custody cases is to foster the best interests of the child. This standard has been described as one that protects the "safety, happiness, physical, mental and moral welfare of the child." It would be incongruous and counterproductive to restrict application of this standard to the relief requested by the parties to a custody dispute. Accordingly, a *sua sponte* custody determination is properly within the discretion of the trial court provided it is supported by the record. However, we emphasize again the desirability of the trial court giving the parties an opportunity to address any new issues raised by the court.

The factors to be considered by a trial court contemplating an award of joint custody require some elaboration. * * *

First, before embarking on a full-blown inquiry into the practicability of a joint custody arrangement, the court must determine whether the children have established such relationships with both parents that they would benefit from joint custody. For such bonds to exist the parents need not have been equally involved in the child rearing process. Rather, from the child's point of view it is necessary only that the child recognize both parents as sources of security and love and wish to continue both relationships.

Having established the joint custody arrangement's potential benefit to the children, the court must focus on the parents in order to determine whether they qualify for such an arrangement. At a minimum both parents must be "fit"—that is, physically and psychologically capable of fulfilling the role of parent. In addition, they must each be willing to accept custody, although their opposition to *joint* custody does not preclude the court from ordering that arrangement. Rather, even if neither parent seeks joint custody, as long as both are willing to care for the children joint custody is a possibility.

The most troublesome aspect of a joint custody decree is the additional requirement that the parent exhibit a potential for cooperation in matters of child rearing. This feature does not translate into a requirement that the parents have an amicable relationship. Although such a positive relationship is preferable, a successful joint custody arrangement requires only that the parents be able to isolate their personal conflicts from their roles as parents and that the children be spared whatever resentment and rancor the parents may harbor. Moreover, the potential for cooperation should not be assessed in the "emotional heat" of the divorce.

If the parents outside of the divorce setting, have each demonstrated that they are reasonable and are willing to give priority to the best interest of their child, then the judge need only determine if the parents can separate and put aside any conflicts between them to cooperate for the benefit of the child. The judge must look for the parents' ability to cooperate and if the potential exists, encourage its activation by instructing the parents on what is expected of them.

The necessity for at least minimal parental cooperation in a joint custody arrangement presents a thorny problem of judicial enforcement in a case such as the present one, wherein despite the trial court's determination that joint custody is in the best interests of the child, one parent (here, the mother) nevertheless contends that cooperation is impossible and refuses to abide by the decree. Traditional enforcement techniques are singularly inappropriate in a child custody proceeding for which the best interests of the child is our polestar. Despite the obvious unfairness of allowing an uncooperative parent to flout a court decree, we are unwilling to sanction punishment of a recalcitrant parent if the welfare of the child will also suffer. However, when the actions of such a parent deprive the child of the kind of relationship with the other parent that is deemed to be in the child's best interests, removing the child from the custody of the uncooperative parent may well be appropriate as a remedy of last resort. * * * Although an award of sole custody to Mr. Beck in this case may be a closer question, * * * it cannot be ruled out as a potential enforcement tool, albeit one to be considered only after all other measures have failed.

In addition to the factors set forth above, the physical custody element of a joint custody award requires examination of practical considerations such as the financial status of the parents, the proximity of their respective homes, the demands of parental employment, and the age and number of the children. Joint physical custody necessarily places an additional financial burden on the family. Although exact duplication of facilities and furnishings is not necessary, the trial court should insure that the children can be adequately cared for in two homes. The geographical proximity of the two homes is an important factor to the extent that it impinges on school arrangements, the children's access to relatives and friends (including visitation by the non-custodial parent), and the ease of travel between the two homes. Parental employment is significant for its effect on a parent's ability properly to care for the children and maintain a relationship with them. The significance of the ages and number of the children is somewhat unclear at present, and will probably vary from case to case, requiring expert testimony as to their impact on the custody arrangement.

If joint custody is feasible except for one or more of these practical considerations, the court should consider awarding legal custody to both parents with physical custody to only one and liberal visitation rights to the other. Such an award will preserve the decision-making role of both parents and should approximate, to the extent practicable, the shared companionship of the child and non-custodial that is provided in joint physical custody.

Finally, as in all custody determinations, the preference of the children of "sufficient age and capacity" must be accorded "due weight." This standard gives the trial court wide discretion regarding the probative value of a child's custody preference.

Our review of the record indicates that the trial court gave proper consideration to the preference expressed by the children, eight and ten years old at the time of trial. After interviewing them privately, the court stated for the record that the children were sincere and honest in their desire to remain with their mother. However, observing that they expressed love for both parents and wanted to continue visitation with their father, the court concluded that they had been "persuaded" to make their statements of preference and that the defendant's negative attitude toward joint custody had "consciously or unconsciously spilled over" to the children. Given this conclusion that the tender years of the children, a determination that did not fully accommodate their express wishes was not unreasonable.

Having found the decision of the trial court to be based on sufficient credible evidence, we would ordinarily reinstate it. However, in child custody cases we are always mindful that our task is to act in the best interests of the child as presently situated. Over two years have elapsed since the original decree of joint custody. Although we uphold that decree as originally made, we recognize that the facts and relationships upon which it was based may have changed dramatically. Therefore, we remand this case to the trial court for further fact-finding and a determination consonant with this opinion. We admonish the court to make a speedy but thorough investigation into the present circumstances of the parties and their children—using whatever procedural mechanism and hearing what further testimony, if any, is deemed necessary—so that this matter may be expeditiously and properly laid to rest.

The judgment of the Appellate Division is reversed and the case remanded to the trial court.

MARTHA A. FINEMAN, DOMINANT DISCOURSE, PROFESSIONAL LANGUAGE, AND LEGAL CHANGE IN CHILD CUSTODY DECISIONMAKING
101 HARV. L. REV. 727, 734–735, 768–769 (1988).

The helping professions' discourse has presented shared parenting as the only truly acceptable custody policy. This is because they view joint custody as the only "fair" result. Ironically, although they might question the capacity of legal processes and institutions to resolve custody disputes in accordance with this ideal, they view law itself as possessing vast power to transform people's behavior. The helping professions therefore have little hesitation in resorting to law for the implementation of their social policies.

The merits of shared parenting as a legal and social ideal have not been critically debated in political and legal forums in any meaningful way. Although there has been limited criticism of the feasibility of the ideal, these criticisms do not challenge the degree to which presumptive shared parenting actually reflects pre-or post-divorce family structures. Similarly, there has been uncritical acceptance of the empirical proposition that women and men make undifferentiated, exchangeable contributions to parenting. By focusing on the importance of the father/child relationship, the helping professions' discourse undervalues a mother's real life role, assuming it to be no different than a father's. The extreme presentation of this view is that at times a mother's "mothering" may be characterized as pathological and harmful to children. The creation of such a stereotype has gone largely unchallenged.

* * *

In focusing on ideal sex roles and equalitarian marriage, the helping professions' literature emphasized that traditional custody policy discriminated against men by unjustifiably favoring sole maternal custody. Not unlike the emerging fathers' rights discourse, their rhetoric asserted that there was no basis for maternal preference, which was grounded in the sexist assumption that men could not nurture but that women could. In real life, according to the helping profession, parents shared parenting and "parents are forever." * * * [But] [i]n most marriages, one parent, normally the mother, assumes day-to-day primary care. Shared parenting in these situations seldom means equally divided responsibility and control; typically one parent sacrifices more than the other in order to care for the child. The sense of sharing in this context is not based on the actual assumption of divided responsibilities by the parents. Rather, the shared parenting can be viewed as based on the relationship between the parents who, because of the intimacy of their situation, share the potential for jointly exercising important decisionmaking responsibility for their children. Yet an unrealistic and idealized vision of shared parenting *independent* of the relationship (or lack thereof) between parents is now imposed on couples after divorce. This vision assumes that they will work out their relationship to make shared parenting successful. It is one thing for divorcing parents voluntarily to choose the shared parenting ideal, but quite another to impose it on parents who do not or cannot live up to its demands. There may be substantial costs to treating the deviant as the norm and fashioning rights outside the context of responsibility. In the divorce context, this amounts to furthering the interests of non-caretaking fathers over the objections and, in many instances, against the interests of caretaking mothers.

NOTES AND QUESTIONS

1.   Why, from a judge's perspective, might joint custody be an attractive option? Does a joint custody award represent an abdication of judicial responsibility to determine the child's best interests? What constitutes a joint physical custody award? Is 50/50 shared parenting time required? Or can other arrangements constitute joint physical custody? *See* Rivero v. Rivero, 216 P.3d 213 (Nev. 2009) (joint physical custody means custody "is shared by the parents in such a way to ensure the child * * * of frequent associations and a continuing relationship with both parents).

2. *Criteria for Awarding Joint Custody*: Many judges believe that the most important factors in awarding joint custody are that the parties agree to it, have shared values as to child rearing, and are able to cooperate in reaching shared decisions about their child. In Wright v. Kaura, 964 N.Y.S.2d 573 (App. Div. 2013), the New York court awarded sole custody to the mother noting that joint custody is encouraged for relatively stable, amicable parents who can behave in a mature, civilized fashion. When shared decision making is not possible, imposing joint custody often results in litigation. See Gray v. Gray, 239 S.W.3d 26, 30 (Ark. App. 2006); *In re* Marriage of Hansen, 733 N.W.2d 683, 695 (Iowa 2007). *See also* Herbie DiFonzo, *From the Rule of One to Shared Parenting: Custody Presumptions in Law and Policy*, 52 FAM. CT. REV. 213 (2014).

3. *The Benefits of Joint Custody*: Successful joint physical custody arrangements are strongly associated with high income, education, and past cooperative parenting. Some research suggests that the positive outcomes associated with joint custody arrangements may result, in part, from preexisting attributes of the parents who make joint custody arrangements. Researchers have reported that joint physical custody is associated with higher levels of father contact, involvement, and payment of child support than is traditional mother custody. *See, e.g.*, Judith A. Seltzer, *Father by Law: Effects of Joint Legal on Nonresident Fathers' Involvement with Children*, 35 DEMOGRAPHY 135, 141 (1998) (finding positive effect on visits but no significant effect on payment of child support). Some studies also show that children in joint physical custody are more satisfied than those in the custody of one parent. One comparative longitudinal study found that children in father-custody, mother-custody, and joint custody households "were quite similar in their self-reported levels of adjustment * * * and most appeared to be functioning well within the normal range." The researchers also found that child satisfaction was highest with dual residence custodial arrangements. *See* Eleanor E. Maccoby et al., *Postdivorce Roles of Mothers and Fathers in the Lives of Their Children*, 7 J. FAM. PSYCH. 24, 25–27, 34 (1993). *See also* Robert Bauserman, *Child Adjustment in Joint-Custody versus Sole-Custody Arrangements: A Meta-Analytic Review*, 16 J. FAM. PSYCHOL. 91 (2002) (reviewing research). Moreover, a meta-analysis of more than thirty studies comparing outcomes in joint and sole custody arrangements found that

> children in joint custody are better adjusted, across multiple types of measures, than children in sole (primarily maternal) custody. This difference * * * appears robust * * * [and] is consistent with the hypothesis that joint custody can be beneficial to children in a wide range of family, emotional, behavioral, and academic domains.

Bauserman, at 97–98.

Several studies have documented the harm to children from absent fathers. *See* Judith S. Wallerstein & Julia M. Lewis, *Divorced Fathers and Their Adult Offspring: Report from a Twenty-five Year Longitudinal Study*, 42 FAM. L. Q. 695 (2009). Will joint custody keep fathers engaged? The answer is unknown. One report showed that while the number of stay-at-home fathers has doubled since 1989, one-fourth of fathers who do not live with their children had not seen them in more than one year. *See* Gretchen Livingston & Kim Parker, Pew Research Ctr, *A Tale of Two Fathers: More Are Active, But More Are Absent* 4 (2011).

4.   *The Dangers of Joint Custody:* Shared custody tends to restrict the autonomy of the primary residential parent, who is still often the mother. One author indicates that the primary residential parent is "doubly disadvantaged * * * by the dissolution of the couple's economic partnership and then by the decision-making restrictions that accompany judicially-mandated post-divorce coparenting." See Jana B. Singer, *Dispute Resolution and the Postdivorce Family: Implications of a Paradigm Shift*, 47 FAM. CT. REV. 363, 366 (2009). When joint or shared residential custody is coupled with high levels of parental conflict, some researchers have reported negative effects on child well-being. *See* Janet R. Johnston, *High Conflict Divorce, in* 4 FUTURE OF CHILDREN 165, 174 (Spring, 1994). Others have found that a substantial percentage of high-conflict joint custody arrangements simply break down, producing de facto sole custody. *See* ELEANOR MACCOBY & ROBERT MNOOKIN, DIVIDING THE CHILD: SOCIAL AND LEGAL DILEMMAS OF CUSTODY 159 (1992) (finding that about half of high-conflict joint physical custody cases produced de facto mother custody). Still others have found high levels of post-divorce litigation. *See* Amy Koel et al., *Patterns of Relitigation in the Post Divorce Family*, 56 J. MARRIAGE & FAM. 265 (1994). When both parents had initially sought sole custody, both the level of parental conflict and the likelihood of joint custody increased. Thirty-six percent of joint physical custody cases involved "substantial or intense legal conflict." MACCOBY & MNOOKIN, *supra,* at 150–51, tbl. 7.6 & 159.

Overall, however, the available evidence suggests that high level of conflict between separated parents is rare. *See* Juliana M. Sobolewski & Valarie King, *The Importance of the Coparental Relationship for Nonresident Fathers' Ties to Children*, 67 J. MARRIAGE & FAM. 1196, 1202–03 (2005) (only 4% of surveyed custodial mothers reported a "great deal of conflict" over how the child was raised). The relative rarity of high conflict may explain why cooperative joint custody is associated with better child outcomes overall. A recent compilation of studies indicates that overall children benefitted more from shared parenting than from sole residence even if the parents had a conflicted relationship. *See* Linda Nielson, *Shared Physical Custody: Does It Benefit Most Children?*, 28 J. AM. ACAD. MATRIMONIAL LAWYERS 79, 94 (2015).

One big danger of joint physical custody may be the reduction in child support going to the lower income earning parent who may need the money to keep a roof overhead. *See* Karen Syma Czapanskiy, *The Shared Custody Child Support Adjustment: Not Worth the Candle*, 49 FAM. L. Q. 409 (2015).

5.   *State Rules on Joint Custody*: All states now permit an award of joint custody, but most do not allow the imposition of joint custody on reluctant parents. *See* OR. REV. STAT. § 107.169(3) (joint custody prohibited "unless both parties agree to the terms and conditions of the order."); VT. STAT. ANN. tit. 15

§ 665 (*accord*); *In re* Marriage of McCoy, 650 N.E.2d 3 (Ill. App. 1995) (upholding award of sole custody to mother even though parents had been using an alternate-week custody schedule for more than two years based on mother's contention that the father had a violent temper and that they could not agree on child care issues).

A few states have enacted some type of presumption or preference in favor of joint custody. In some jurisdictions, the presumption operates only when the parents agree to joint custody. In others, the preference in favor of joint custody may be overcome based on the child's best interests. *See generally* Kimberly C. Emery & Robert E. Emery, *Who Knows What is Best for Children? Honoring Agreements and Contracts Between Parents Who Live Apart*, 77 LAW & CONTEMP. PROBS. 151 (2014). What if domestic violence is present? *See* Judith G. Greenberg, *Domestic Violence and the Danger of Joint Custody Presumptions*, 25 N. ILL. U. L. REV. 403 (2005). Even if there is a statute presuming joint custody, the court may refuse to order it in cases of high conflict because of the potential for harm to the child. *See In re* Marriage of Hansen, 733 N.W.2d 683 (Iowa 2007).

6.   What if the parents have joint legal custody and cannot agree on a major child care issue, such as where the child will go to school? Consider Lombardo v. Lombardo, 507 N.W.2d 788 (Mich. App. 1993):

> Parties to a divorce judgment cannot by agreement usurp the courts authority to determine suitable provisions for the child's best interest. Similarly, the court should not relinquish its authority to determine the best interests of the child to the primary physical custodian. Accordingly, we conclude that a trial court must determine the best interests of the child in resolving disputes concerning "important decisions affecting the welfare of the child" that arise between joint custodial parents.

In *In re* Kurowski, 20 A.3d 306 (N.H. 2011), parents sharing legal and physical custody disagreed over the mother homeschooling the daughter. The court ordered the mother to send the child to public school. *See also In re* Marriage of Debenham, 896 P.2d 1098 (Kan. App. 1995) (schools); *In re* Doe, 418 S.E.2d 3 (Ga. 1992) (medical treatment); Elk Grove v. Newdow, 542 U.S. 1 (2004) (pledge of allegiance). Sometimes the judge will give tie breaking power to one of the parents to prevent relitigation.

7.   *Parenting Plans*: Several states require parents to consent to a "parenting plan" before the court grants a divorce. See WASH. REV. CODE ANN. § 26.09.181(1). For example, OR. REV. STAT. § 107.102 requires that:

> (1) In any proceeding to establish or modify a judgment providing for parenting time with a child * * * there shall be developed and filed with the court a parenting plan to be included in the judgment. * * *

> (2) A general parenting plan may include a general outline of how parental responsibilities and parenting time will be shared and may allow the parents to develop a more detailed agreement on an

informal basis. However, a general parenting plan must set forth the minimum amount of parenting time and access a noncustodial parent is entitled to have.

(3)   A detailed parenting plan may include, but need not be limited to, provisions relating to:

(a)   Residential schedule;

(b)   Holiday, birthday and vacation planning;

(c)   Weekends, including holidays, and school in-service days preceding or following weekends;

(d)   Decision-making and responsibility;

(e)   Information sharing and access;

(f)   Relocation of parents;

(g)   Telephone access;

(h)   Transportation; and

(i)   Methods for resolving disputes. * * *

How does a parenting plan differ from an award of joint legal custody? If the parents agree to a parenting plan, should the judge always approve it? *See* PARENTING PLAN EVALUATIONS: APPLIED RESEARCH FOR THE FAMILY COURT (Kathryn Juehnle & Leslie Drozd, eds. 2012). If the parents cannot agree on a parenting plan, the judge may substitute a standard plan generated by statute, court rule or bench-bar guidelines. *See e.g.* ARIZ. REV. STAT. ANN. § 25–403.02.D.

Problem 14-3:

You are counsel to the state legislature's joint Committee on Family Law. The Committee has scheduled public hearings on whether current state custody standards (identical to UMDA § 402) should be revised. Various women's organizations have proposed that current law be replaced with a primary caretaker presumption; various father's groups have proposed that current law be replaced with a presumption in favor of joint custody. The chair of the Committee has suggested standards recently proposed by the American Law Institute (ALI) as a model for reform. The ALI proposal requires a court to make a custody decision based on the child's best interests, subject to certain limiting factors. AMERICAN LAW INSTITUTE PRINCIPLES OF THE LAW OF FAMILY DISSOLUTION (2002).

Under § 2.12, the court should *not* consider any of the following factors:

(a)   the race or ethnicity of the child, a parent or other member of the household;

(b)   the sex of a parent or of the child;

(c)   the religious practices of a parent or of the child, except to the minimum degree necessary to protect the child from severe and almost certain harm or to protect the child's ability to practice a religion that has been a significant part of the child's life;

(d)   the sexual orientation of a parent;

(e)   the extramarital sexual conduct of a parent, except upon a showing that it causes harm to the child;

(f)   the parents' relative earning capacities or financial circumstances, except the court may take account of the degree to which the combined financial resources of the parents set practical limits on the custodial arrangements.

Under § 2.11, if either of the parents so requests or upon receipt of credible information that such conduct has occurred, the court should determine promptly whether a parent who would otherwise be allocated responsibility under a parenting plan has done any of the following:

(a)   abused, neglected, or abandoned a child;(b)   inflicted domestic abuse, or allowed another to inflict domestic abuse;

(c)   abused drugs, alcohol, or another substance in a way that interferes with the parent's ability to perform caretaking functions; or

(d)   interfered persistently with the other parent's access to the child, except in the case of actions taken in the reasonable, good faith belief that they are necessary to protect the safety of the child or the interfering parent or another family member.

Under § 2.08, unless otherwise resolved by agreement of the parents * * * the court should allocate custodial responsibility so that the proportion of custodial time the child spends with each parent approximates the proportion of time each parent spent performing caretaking functions for the child prior to the parents' separation * * *, except to the extent required under § 2.11 or necessary to achieve one or more of the following objectives:

(a)   to permit the child to have a relationship with each parent which, in the case of a legal parent or a parent by estoppel who has performed a reasonable share of parenting functions, should be not less than a presumptive amount of custodial time determined through a uniform rule of statewide application;

(b)   to accommodate the firm and reasonable preferences of a child who has reached a specific age, as set forth in a uniform rule of statewide application;

(c)   to keep siblings together when the court finds that doing so is necessary to their welfare;

(d)   to protect the child's welfare when the presumptive allocation under this section would harm the child because of a gross disparity in the quality of the emotional attachment between each parent and the child or in each parent's demonstrated ability or availability to meet the child's needs;

(e)   to take into account any prior agreement * * * that would be appropriate to consider in light of the circumstances as a whole, including the reasonable expectations of the parties, the extent to which they could have reasonably anticipated the events that occurred and their significance, and the interests of the child;

(f)   to avoid an allocation of custodial responsibility that would be extremely impractical or that would interfere substantially with the child's need for stability in light of economic, physical, or other circumstances, including the distance between the parents' residences, the cost and difficulty of transporting the child, each parent's and the child's daily schedules, and the ability of the parents to cooperate in the arrangement;

(g)   to apply the Principles set forth in § 2.17(4) if one parent relocates or proposes to relocate at a distance that will impair the ability of a parent to exercise the presumptive amount of custodial responsibility under this section;

(h)   to avoid substantial and almost certain harm to the child.

* * *

Section 2.03(5) defines "caretaking functions" as "tasks that involve interaction with the child or that direct, arrange, and supervise the interaction and care provided by others." They include, but are not limited to, * * *

(a)   satisfying the nutritional needs of the child, managing the child's bedtime and wake-up routines, caring for the child when sick or injured, being attentive to the child's personal hygiene needs including washing, grooming, and dressing, playing with the child and arranging for recreation, protecting the child's physical safety, and providing transportation;

(b)   directing the child's various developmental needs, including the acquisition of motor and language skills, toilet training, self-confidence and maturation;

(c)   providing discipline, giving instruction in manners, assigning and supervising chores, and performing other tasks that attend to the child's needs for behavioral control and self-restraint;

(d)   arranging for the child's education, including remedial or special services appropriate to the child's needs and interests, communicating with teachers and counselors, and supervising homework;

(e) helping the child to develop and maintain appropriate interpersonal relationships with peers, siblings, and other family members;

(f) arranging for health care providers, medical follow-up, and home health care;

(g) providing moral and ethical guidance;

(h) arranging alternative care by a family member, babysitter, or other child care provider or facility, including investigation of alternatives, communication with providers, and supervision of care.

Under § 2.09, unless otherwise agreed to by the parents, the court should allocate responsibility for making significant life decisions on behalf of the child to one parent or two parents jointly, in accordance with the child's best interests, in light of the following:

(a) the allocation of custodial responsibility;

(b) the level of each parent's participation in past decisionmaking on behalf of the child;

(c) the wishes of the parents;

(d) the level of ability and cooperation the parents have demonstrated in past decision making on behalf of the child;

(e) a prior agreement that would include reasonable expectations of parents and the interests of their child; and

(f) the existence of any limiting factors.

You have been asked to determine:

1. How, if at all, does the ALI approach differ from the "traditional" best interests test? To the extent that there are differences, in what type(s) of cases would adoption of the ALI standard alter the case outcome?

2. What are the advantages and disadvantages of each approach to custody decision making?

3. Which approach is most likely to promote settlement of custody disputes?

4. Which approach is most likely to produce consistent and predictable case outcomes?

5. Which approach, on balance, is most likely to advance children's interests post-divorce?

See generally Herma Hill Kay, *No-Fault Divorce and Child Custody: Chilling Out the Gender Wars*, 36 FAM. L. Q. 27 (2002); Katharine T. Bartlett, *Preference, Presumption, Predisposition, and Common Sense: From Traditional Custody Doctrines to the American Law Institute's Family Law Dissolution Project*, 36 FAM. L. Q. 11 (2002).

4. PARENTING TIME RIGHTS OF THE NONRESIDENTIAL PARENT

UNIFORM MARRIAGE AND DIVORCE ACT § 407(a)

(a) A parent not granted custody of a child is entitled to reasonable visitation rights unless the court finds after a hearing, that visitation would endanger seriously the child's physical, mental, moral or emotional health.

(b) The court may modify an order granting or denying visitation rights whenever the modification would serve the best interest of the child; but the court shall not restrict a parent's visitation rights unless it finds that the visitation could endanger seriously the child's physical, mental, moral or emotional health.

For decades, the parent not awarded "custody" was awarded "visitation." A parent does not become a nonparent by not being designated as primary residential parent. Additionally, more courts are awarded shared residential custody. In recent years, states have changed the terminology from custody and visitation to parenting time or parental access. The court may restrict a parent's parenting time or access if there is a showing of harm to the child.

IN RE MARRIAGE OF KIMBRELL

Kansas Court of Appeals, 2005.
34 Kan. App. 2d 413, 119 P.3d 684.

GREEN, J.

William David Kimbrell (David) appeals the trial court's decision regarding parenting time with his 16-year-old son Evan Kimbrell. The issue in this case is whether the trial court can condition a noncustodial parent's right to parenting time with his or her minor child upon the desires of the child. We determine that this cannot be done. K.S.A.2004 Supp. § 60–1616(a) makes it clear that a parent has a right to reasonable parenting time with his or her minor child "unless the court finds, after a hearing, that the exercise of parenting time would seriously endanger the child's physical, mental, moral or emotional health." Conditioning parenting time on the wishes of a minor child improperly gives the child the authority to determine a noncustodial parent's rights to parenting time and visitation and can have the effect of completely denying the noncustodial parent's rights to parenting time. * * *

The parties, David Kimbrell and Janet Bouley * * * divorced in April 1996, after nearly 16 years of marriage. The parties had three children together * * * At present, Evan is the only minor child involved in this case.

At the time of their divorce, David and Janet entered into a mediated agreement, where they agreed to joint custody of their children and a shared parenting time arrangement. * * * In July 2001, David moved to modify the 1996 divorce decree and for an emergency change of placement for Dylan and Evan. In his motion, David asked that he be given residential custody of Dylan and Evan, that the trial court order strict supervision of Janet's contact with the boys, and that the trial court order a psychological evaluation of Janet, Dylan, and Evan to determine whether Janet was alienating the children from him. David maintained that Janet had "commenced a program and concerted effort to alienate the three children" from him and that she had interfered with his visitations and the parenting time and visitation schedule. At David's request, these motions were dismissed in March 2002.

For summer 2001, the parties agreed to a split parenting arrangement where the children would essentially spend alternating weeks with each parent. In addition, the parties agreed to participate in psychological evaluations and testing. The agreed parenting plan was to continue until psychological evaluations and reports were completed.

Upon agreement by the parties, the trial court appointed Susan Vorhees, Ph.D., to conduct evaluation and testing of the parties and their minor children. Although David later moved for a protective order to prohibit the dissemination of Dr. Vorhees' proposed report, the trial court ordered that Dr. Vorhees' evaluation be provided to the court. Dr. Vorhees' report, which was filed in December 2002, indicated that * * * "[David] is alienated from the[ ] [children] by his own inability to accept that they and their mother are independent individuals, that they need and want a relationship with both parents, and that he cannot be in control of either of these relationships." Dr. Vorhees indicated that David's alienation from the children could be resolved by David trying to accept his children for who they are and by listening to his children.

The trial court, on its own motion, appointed retired District Court Judge James Buchele as the case manager in January 2002. * * * Judge Buchele recommended in January 2002 that the children reside with Janet and that David's parenting time be "as approved by the Case Manager or as ordered by the Court." * * * In his report, Judge Buchele addressed David's allegations that Janet had alienated Dylan and Evan. Judge

Buchele's opinion was that Dylan's and Evan's alienation from David was caused by David's own conduct. * * * Judge Buchele [also] indicated that the brief attempt to expand David's parenting time with Evan had been disastrous. Judge Buchele concluded that the problems in this case could not be resolved by additional time being spent between Evan and his father. * * *

In November 2002, upon David's motion, the trial court appointed Dr. Richard Gardner, M.D., to conduct a parental alienation syndrome (PAS) evaluation of the family. * * * Moreover, the trial court ordered that the contact between Evan and David continue under the current arrangement and that the contact between Dylan and David be as Dylan desired.

Dr. Gardner completed the PAS evaluation and filed a written report in January 2003. Dr. Gardner found no evidence that the children were suffering from PAS or that Janet was a PAS alienator. Instead, Dr. Gardner indicated that the primary source of the children's alienation from David was David's own psychiatric problems, especially his obsessive-compulsive personality disorder and paranoid trends. Dr. Gardner recommended that Janet continue to have primary parenting time with Dylan and Evan, that Janet have primary legal custody, and that the court rescind the order requiring Dylan and Evan to participate in therapy. * * *

[After more motions, in 2004, the court appointed a special master whose duties included recommending therapy for the parties and their children as well as preparing findings of fact and conclusions of law for the trial court to review if the parties could not agree on child-rearing decisions or therapy. The master also found that Dylan, then age 18, was no longer under the jurisdiction of the court and that:]

"3. Evan, DOB 10/09/88, is almost sixteen. His parenting time with his father, given his maturity and the history of this case, should be as is mutually requested."

* * *

David first argues that the trial court's decision infringes upon his parental rights without any showing that he is an unfit parent or that he presents any threat or danger to his child. David maintains that the trial court's decision results in a denial of due process.

* * *

It is well established that parents have fundamental rights in the custody and control of their children under the Due Process Clause of the Fourteenth Amendment of the United States Constitution. * * *

It is unclear whether parents have a specific due process right under the United States Constitution regarding parenting time and visitation with their children. * * * Nevertheless, Kansas law * * * makes it clear that parents have a right to parenting time and visitation with their children, absent exceptional circumstances, such as a threat to the children's welfare. This is in line with other jurisdictions which recognize that noncustodial parents have a natural right to visitation with their children. [citations omitted].

* * *

In his brief, David has informed us that he has not had any parental contact with Evan since late 2002. If this is in fact the case, David has been effectively denied any parenting time with Evan. With no statutory finding that David's parenting time would seriously endanger Evan, the trial court should have ordered certain and reasonable parenting and visitation times in order to ensure that David would have the opportunity to exercise his parenting time rights. The trial court improperly made David's parenting time with Evan contingent on Evan's desires or requests to see his father.

We wish to make clear that the above analysis does not preclude the trial court from considering a child's desires when setting a parenting time and visitation schedule. In fact, K.S.A. 2004 Supp. § 60–1610(a)(3)(B) states that "[i]n determining the issue of child custody, residency, and parenting time, the court shall consider all of the relevant factors, including but not limited to: * * * (iii) the desires of the child as to the child's custody or residency." Under our applicable statutes, a child's desires is only one of the factors to be considered when determining the issue of parenting time and visitation. Noting that a court may consider a child's wishes concerning visitation but that such wishes are not controlling even in jurisdictions that afford great weight to an older child's preference, Professor Linda Henry Elrod, in Rutkin, 3 Family Law and Practice, Child Custody and Visitation § 32.09[3][c], pp. 32–278 to 32–279, cautioned:

> As with awarding custody, the court may consider the child's wishes as to visitation. The court must balance its *parens patriae* role with its recognition of the importance of respecting the child's wishes. The weight to be given the child's preference depends upon the child's age and maturity. Even in jurisdictions that give great weight to the preferences of older children, the children's wishes are not controlling. Courts are reluctant to put too much weight on the child's desires as to visitation because the child's immature emotions or the custodial parent's disparaging comments about the other parent may form the basis for the child's feelings.

Here, the trial court should consider Evan's wishes when setting a parenting time schedule. Nevertheless, this cannot be the exclusive factor. In pointing out that children are more interested in their momentary desires than the long-range needs for developing a healthy relationship with both parents, the Mississippi Court of Appeals stated: " 'While there is nothing wrong with the children being heard regarding their wishes, our law proceeds on the assumption that they are nevertheless children and, thus, more interested in the desire of the moment than in considering the long range needs for the development of a healthy relationship with both parents where that is possible.'" [citation omitted] Consequently, in the absence of a finding under K.S.A. 2004 Supp. 60–1616(a) that "the exercise of parenting time would seriously endanger the child's physical, mental, moral or emotional health," the trial court should have set forth certain and reasonable times for David's parenting time with Evan. * * *. The trial court should not have conditioned David's parenting time with Evan upon Evan's desires or requests to see his father. * * *

NOTES AND QUESTIONS

1.   No one doubts that some children become alienated from a parent after divorce, but there is widespread disagreement on the role played by parents in inducing such reactions. Many experts have found that children's alienation often occurs without parental inducement. *See* Janet R. Johnston, *The Alienated Child, A Reformulation of Parental Alienation Syndrome,* 39 FAM. CT. REV. 249, 251 (2001). Some also contend that "alienation syndrome" is not a meaningful diagnostic concept. *See* Carol S. Bruch, *Parental Alienation Syndrome and Parental Alienation: Getting It Wrong in Child Custody Cases,* 35 FAM. L. Q. 527 (2001) (describing parental alienation syndrome or parental alienation as "junk science."). *See also* Barbara Jo Fidler & Nicholas Bala, *Children Resisting Postseparation Contact With a Parent: Concepts, Controversies, and Conundrums,* 48 FAM. CT. REV. 10 (2010); Peter G. Jaffe, et al, *Early Identification and Prevention of Parent-Child Alienation: A Framework for Balancing Risks and Benefits of Intervention,* 48 FAM. CT. REV. 136 (2010).

2.   In *Kimbrell,* the Court of Appeals remanded the case either for a determination of a visitation schedule or a finding that visitation would harm the child. How should a court assess visitation risk? MICH. COMP. LAWS ANN. § 722.27a requires the court to consider, *inter alia,* * * *

(c)   The reasonable likelihood of abuse or neglect of the child during parenting time.

(d)   The reasonable likelihood of abuse of a parent resulting from the exercise of parenting time.

* * *

(h)   The threatened or actual detention of the child with the intent to retain or conceal the child from the other parent or from a third person who has legal custody. A custodial parent's temporary residence with the child in a domestic violence shelter shall not be construed as evidence of the custodial parent's intent to retain or conceal the child from the other parent.

Would any of these types of "harms" apply to Evan?

3. Psychoanalyst Anna Freud, law professor Joseph Goldstein, and psychiatrist Albert J. Solnit have urged that "the noncustodial parent should have no legally enforceable right to visit the child, and the custodial parent should have the right to decide whether it is desirable for the child to have such visits." JOSEPH GOLDSTEIN ET AL., THE BEST INTERESTS OF THE CHILD 24 (1996). The basis of Goldstein, Freud and Solnit's position is the view that:

> * * * it is beyond the capacity of courts to help a child establish or maintain positive relationships to two people who are at cross-purposes with each other; * * * by forcing visits, courts are more likely to prevent the child from developing a reliable tie to either parent; and * * * children who are shaken, disoriented, and confused by the breakup of their family need an opportunity to settle down in the privacy of their reorganized family, with one person in authority upon whom they can rely for answers to their questions and for protection from external interference. * * *
>
> A child develops best if she can trust the adults who are responsible for her to be the arbiters of her care and control as she moves toward the full independence of adulthood, and gradually comes to rely upon herself as her own caregiver. A court undermines that trust when it subjects her custodial parent to special rules about raising her by ordering (even scheduling) visits with the noncustodial parent. In the child's eyes, the court, by directing her to visit against the express wishes of her custodial parent, casts doubt on that parent's authority and capacity to parent. Particularly for the younger child, this undermines her confidence in her parent's omnipotence. It invites the older child to pit one parent against the other rather than to learn to work things out with her custodial parent. The continuity guideline means that the already-stressed relationship between child and custodial parent should not be plagued with the never-ending threat of disruption by the impersonal authority of the court.
>
> We did not and do not oppose visits. We oppose only *forced* visits—court-ordered visits. Indeed, other things being equal, courts, in order to accord with the continuity guideline, could award custody to the parent who is most willing to provide opportunities for the child to see the other parent. * * * [But v]isits that are meaningful for the child can occur only if both the custodial and the noncustodial parents are of a mind to make them work. If parents agree, a court order is both unnecessary and undesirable; if they do not agree, such an order and the threat or actual attempt to enforce it can do the child no good. The child needs a parent who can help her to resolve her wishes to see and not to see the other parent and who can help her to deal with her joys and sorrows following visits, and her hurts when the noncustodial parent refuses to maintain contact or fails to show up.

What practical problems would the Goldstein, Freud, and Solnit approach solve? What practical problems would it create? On balance, is their position persuasive? Why? For critical commentary on Goldstein, Freud, and Solnit's argument that severance of "secondary" attachments serves children's interests, *see* Peggy C. Davis, *The Good Mother: A New Look at Psychological Parent Theory*, 22 N.Y.U. REV. L. & Soc. CHANGE 295 (1996); Pamela S. Ludolph & Milfred D. Dale, *Attachment in Child Custody: An Additive Factor, Not a Determinative One*, 46 FAM. L. Q. 1 (2012).

4.   What if the court had ordered Evan to visit but he refused to go? Could he be held in contempt for refusal to visit? *See In re* Marriage of Marshall, 663 N.E.2d 1113 (Ill. App. 1996) (holding two children in direct civil contempt for refusing to go to North Carolina to visit their father even though one daughter testified she was afraid of him). *See generally* Janet R. Johnston, *Children of Divorce Who Reject a Parent and Refuse Visitation: Recent Research and Social Policy Implications for the Alienated Child*, 38 FAM. L. Q.757 (2005). Would more time with David have helped Evan? A psychologist who did longitudinal research on 2,500 children over 30 years, "It is the quality of the relationship between the non-residential parent and child rather than sheer frequency of visitation that is most important * * * Moreover, visits from an alcoholic, abusive, depressed, or conflict-prone parent do nothing for a troubled child, except possibly make the child more troubled." *See* E. MAVIS HEATHERINGTON AND JOHN KELLY, FOR BETTER OR FOR WORSE: DIVORCE RECONSIDERED 134 (2002).

5.   Courts have the authority to order supervised visitation where the noncustodial parent poses a risk of harm to the child. The risk of harm may be prior abuse, threats of abduction, mental illness or substance abuse. Supervisors can be friends, relatives, or licensed professionals such as social workers. Complete denial of visitation is rare, but does occur. *See* Allen v. Farrow, 611 N.Y.S.2d 859 (App. Div. 1994); Allen v. Farrow, 626 N.Y.S.2d 125 (App. Div. 1995) (upholding subsequent denial of supervised visitation with son based on independent expert's view that "therapeutic visitation" was not in the child's best interests while the father (Woody Allen) continued to maintain a sexual relationship with his sister).

6.   *Enforcement:* Visitation can be enforced through several means, including a contempt order, injunctive relief, posting of a bond, "make-up" visitation, and modification of the custody order to more clearly specify visitation times. In extreme cases, a court may also modify the custody order by changing the primary custodian. *See* Begins v. Begins, 721 A.2d 469 (Vt. 1998); *In re* Marriage of Cobb, 988 P.2d 272 (Kan. App. 1999). Some courts permit the award of civil damages. *See In re* Marriage of Myers, 99 P.3d 398 (Wash. App. 2004); ALASKA STAT. § 25.24.300; COLO. REV. STAT. ANN. § 14–10–129.5. Most courts do not allow a parent to withhold or suspend child support for interference with visitation. Stancill v. Stancill, 408 A.2d 1030, 1034 (Md. 1979); Ira Mark Ellman, *Should Visitation Denial Affect the Obligation to Pay Child Support?*, 36 ARIZ. ST. L. J. 661 (2004).

5. NONPARENT CUSTODY AND VISITATION

The United States Supreme Court has long recognized that the "custody, care and nurture of the child reside first in the parents." Prince v. Massachusetts, 321 U.S. 158, 166 (1944). Custody law has traditionally followed the *Prince* approach. State courts have often held that a parent may not be deprived of custody without a showing of abandonment or unfitness.

Starting in the 1970s, this traditional emphasis on parental rights began to give way. The Uniform Marriage and Divorce Act § 401(d)(2) gives nonparents standing to file a petition for custody only when the child is not in the physical custody of a parent. Some legislatures have enacted even more liberal standing rules. HAW. REV. STAT. § 571–46(2), for example, authorizes a custody award "to persons other than the father or mother whenever the award serves the best interest of the child."

Grandparent visitation statutes date from the 1960s and 70s, a time when both the divorce rate and the number of elderly Americans rose quite dramatically. Their rationale was eloquently described by the New Jersey Supreme Court in Mimkon v. Ford, 332 A.2d 199 (N. J. 1975):

> * * * It is common human experience that the concern and interest grandparents take in the welfare of their grandchildren far exceeds anything explicable in purely biological terms. A very special relationship often arises and continues between grandparents and grandchildren. The tensions and conflicts which commonly mar relations between parents and children are often absent between those very same parents and their grandchildren. Visits with a grandparent are often a precious part of a child's experience and there are benefits which devolve upon the grandchild from the relationship with his grandparents which he cannot derive from any other relationship. Neither the Legislature nor this Court is blind to human truths which grandparents and grandchildren have always known. In view of this, we can only say that it is proper that in the unfortunate case of parental separation or death, grandparents should sometimes have privileges of visitation even over the objections of the adoptive parents. It is not only the ordinary devotion to the grandchild that merits the grandparent's continued right to be with him, but also the fact that in such cases, the continuous love and attention of a grandparent may mitigate the feelings of guilt or rejection, which a child may feel at the death of or separation from a parent, and ease the painful transition.

PAINTER V. BANNISTER

Supreme Court of Iowa, 1966.
258 Iowa 1390, 140 N.W.2d 152, cert. denied 385 U.S. 949 (1966).

STUART, J.

We are here setting the course for Mark Wendell Painter's future. Our decision on the custody of this 7 year old boy will have a marked influence on his whole life. The fact that we are called upon many times a year to determine custody matters does not make the exercising of this awesome responsibility any less difficult. Legal training and experience are of little practical help in solving the complex problems of human relations. However, these problems do arise and under our system of government, the burden of rendering a final decision rests upon us. It is frustrating to know we can only resolve, not solve, these unfortunate situations.

The custody dispute before us in this habeas corpus action is between the father, Harold Painter, and the maternal grandparents, Dwight and Margaret Bannister. Mark's mother and younger sister were killed in an automobile accident on December 6, 1962 near Pullman, Washington. The father, after other arrangements for Mark's care had proved unsatisfactory, asked the Bannisters to take care of Mark. They went to California and brought Mark to their farm home near Ames in July, 1963. Mr. Painter remarried in November, 1964 and about that time indicated he wanted to take Mark back. The Bannisters refused to let him leave and his action was filed in June, 1965. Since July 1965 he has continued to remain in the Bannister home under an order of this court staying execution of the judgment of the trial court awarding custody to the father until the matter could be determined on appeal. For reasons hereinafter stated, we conclude Mark's better interests will be served if he remains with the Bannisters.

Mark's parents came from highly contrasting backgrounds. His mother was born, raised and educated in Rural Iowa. Her parents are college graduates. Her father is agricultural information editor for the Iowa State University Extension Service. The Bannister home is in the Gilbert Community and is well kept, roomy and comfortable. Mr. Bannisters has served on the school board and regularly teaches a Sunday school class at the Gilbert Congregational Church. Mark's mother graduated from Grinnell College. She then went to work for a newspaper in Anchorage, Alaska, where she met Harold Painter.

Mark's father was born in California. When he was 2 1/2 years old, his parents were divorced and he was placed in a foster home. Although he has kept in contact with his natural parents, he considers his foster parents, the McNelly's as his family. He flunked out of a high school and a trade school because of a lack of interest in academic subjects, rather than any lack of ability. He joined the Navy at 17. He did not like it. After receiving an honorable discharge, he took examinations and obtained his high school diploma. He lived with the McNelly's and went to college for 2 1/2 years under the G.I. bill. He quit college to take a job on a small newspaper in Ephrata, Washington in November 1955. In May 1956, he went to work for the newspaper in Anchorage which employed Jeanne Bannister.

Harold and Jeanne were married in April, 1957. Although there is a conflict in the evidence on the point, we are convinced the marriage, overall, was a happy one with many ups and downs as could be expected in the uniting of two such opposites.

We are not confronted with a situation where one of the contesting parties is not a fit or proper person. There is no criticism of either the Bannisters or their home. There is no suggestion in the record that Mr. Painter is morally unfit. It is obvious the Bannisters did not approve of their daughter's marriage to Harold Painter and do not want their grandchild raised under his guidance. The philosophies of life are entirely different. As stated by the psychiatrist who examined Mr. Painter at the request of Bannisters' attorneys: "It is evident that there exists a large difference in ways of life and value systems between the Bannisters and Mr. Painter, but in this case, there is no evidence that psychiatric instability is involved. Rather, these divergent life patterns seem to represent alternative normal adaptations."

It is not our prerogative to determine custody upon our choice of one of two ways of life within normal and proper limits and we will not do so. However, the philosophies are important as they relate to Mark and his particular needs.

The Bannister home provides Mark with a stable, dependable, conventional, middle-class, mid-west background and an opportunity for a college education and profession, if he desires it. It provides a solid foundation and secure atmosphere. In the Painter home, Mark would have more freedom of conduct and thought with an opportunity to develop his individual talents. It would be more exciting and challenging in many respects, but romantic, impractical and unstable.

Little additional recitation of evidence is necessary to support our evaluation of the Bannister home. It might be pointed out, however, that Jeanne's three sisters also received college educations and seem to be happily married to college graduates.

Our conclusion as to the type of home Mr. Painter would offer is based upon his Bohemian approach to finances and life in general. We feel there is much evidence which supports this conclusion. His main ambition is to be a freelance writer and photographer. He has had some articles and picture stories published, but the income from these efforts has been negligible. At the time of the accident, Jeanne was willingly working to support the family so Harold could devote more time to his writing and photography. In the 10 years since he left college, he has changed jobs seven times. He was asked to leave two of them; two he quit because he didn't like the work; two because he wanted to devote more time to writing and the rest for better pay. He was contemplating a move to Berkeley at the time of trial. His attitude toward his career is typified by his own comments concerning a job offer:

> About the Portland news job, I hope you understand when I say it took guts not to take it; I had to get behind myself and push. It was very, very tempting to accept a good salary and settle down to a steady, easy routine. I approached Portland, with the intention of taking the job, I began to ask what, in the long run, would be the good of this job: 1, it was not *really* what I wanted; 2, Portland is just another big farm town, with none of the stimulation it takes to get my mind sparking. Anyway, I decided Mark and myself would be better off if I went ahead with what I've started and the hell with the rest, sink, swim or starve.

There is general agreement that Mr. Painter needs help with his finances. Both Jeanne and Marilyn, his present wife, handled most of them. Purchases and sales of books, boats, photographic equipment and houses indicate poor financial judgment and an easy come easy go attitude. He dissipated his wife's estate of about $4300, most of which was a gift from her parents and which she had hoped would be used for the children's education.

The psychiatrist classifies him as "a romantic and somewhat of a dreamer." An apt example are the plans he related for himself and Mark in February 1963: "My thought now is to settle Mark and myself in Sausilito, near San Francisco; this is a retreat for wealthy artists, writers, and such aspiring artists and writers as can fork up the rent money. My plan is to do expensive portraits ($150 and up), sell prints ($15 and up) to the tourists who flock in from all over the world * * *."

The house in which Mr. Painter and his present wife live, compared with the well kept Bannister home, exemplifies the contrasting ways of life. In his words "it is a very old and beat up and lovely home * * * ". They live in the rear part. The interior is inexpensively but tastefully decorated. The large yard on a hill in the business district of Walnut Creek, California, is of uncut weeds and wild oats. The house "is not painted on the outside because I do not want it painted. I am very fond of the wood on the outside of the house."

The present Mrs. Painter has her master's degree in cinema design and apparently likes and has had considerable contact with children. She is anxious to have Mark in her home. Everything indicates she would provide a leveling influence on Mr. Painter and could ably care for Mark.

Mr. Painter is either an agnostic or atheist and has no concern for formal religious training. He has read a lot of Zen Buddhism and "has been very much influenced by it." Mrs. Painter is Roman Catholic. They plan to send Mark to a Congregational Church near the Catholic Church, on an irregular schedule.

He is a political liberal and got into difficulty in a job at the University of Washington for his support of the activities of the American Civil Liberties Union in the university news bulletin.

There were "two funerals" for his wife. One in the basement of his home in which he alone was present. He conducted the service and wrote her a long letter. The second at a church in Pullman was for the gratification of her friends. He attended in a sport shirt and sweater.

These matters are not related as a criticism of Mr. Painter's conduct, way of life or sense of values. An individual is free to choose his own values, within bounds, which are not exceeded here. They do serve, however, to support our conclusion as to the kind of life Mark would be exposed to in the Painter household. We believe it would be unstable, unconventional, arty, Bohemian, and probably intellectually stimulating.

Were the question simply which household would be the most suitable in which to raise a child, we would have unhesitatingly chosen the Bannister home. We believe security and stability in the home are more important than intellectual stimulation in the proper development of a child. There are, however, several factors which have made us pause.

First, there is the presumption of parental preference, which though weakened in the past several years, exists by statute. We have a great deal of sympathy for a father, who in the difficult period of adjustment following his wife's death, turns to the maternal grandparents for their help and then finds them unwilling to return the child. There is no merit in the Bannister claim that Mr. Painter permanently relinquished custody. It was intended to be a temporary arrangement. A father should be encouraged to look for help with the children, from those who love them without the risk of thereby losing the custody of the children permanently. This fact must receive consideration in cases of this kind. However, as always, the primary consideration is the best interest of the child and if the return of custody to the father is likely to have a seriously disrupting and disturbing effect upon the child's development, this fact must prevail. * * *

Second, Jeanne's will named her husband guardian of her children and if he failed to qualify or ceased to act, named her mother. The parent's wishes are entitled to consideration.

Third, the Bannisters are 60 years old. By the time Mark graduates from high school they will be over 70 years old. Care of young children is a strain on grandparents and Mrs. Bannister's letters indicate as much.

We have considered all of these factors and have concluded that Mark's best interest demands that his custody remain with the Bannisters. Mark was five when he came to their home. The evidence clearly shows he was not well adjusted at that time. He did not distinguish fact from fiction and was inclined to tell "tall tales" emphasizing the big "I". He was very aggressive toward smaller children, cruel to animals, not liked by his classmates and did not seem to know what was acceptable conduct. As stated by one witness: "Mark knew where his freedom was and he didn't know where his boundaries were." In two years he made a great deal of improvement. He now appears to be well disciplined, happy, relatively secure and popular with his classmates, although still subject to more than normal anxiety.

We place a great deal of reliance on the testimony of Dr. Glenn R. Hawks, a child psychologist. The trial court, in effect, disregarded Dr. Hawks' opinions stating: "The court has given full consideration to the good doctor's testimony, but cannot accept it at full face value because of exaggerated statements and the witness' attitude on the stand." We, of course, do not have the advantage of viewing the witness' conduct on the stand, but we have carefully reviewed his testimony and find nothing in the written record to justify such a summary dismissal of the opinions of this eminent child psychologist.

Dr. Hawks is head of the Department of Child Development at Iowa State University. However, there is nothing in the record which suggests that his relationship with the Bannisters is such that his professional opinion would be influenced thereby. Child development is his specialty and he has written many articles and a textbook on the subject. He is recognized nationally, having served on the staff of the 1960 White House Conference on Children and Youth and as consultant on a Ford Foundation program concerning youth in India. He is now education consultant on the project "Head Start". He has taught and lectured at many universities and belongs to many professional associations. He works with the Iowa Children's Home Society in placement problems. Further detailing of his qualifications is unnecessary.

Between June 15th and the time of trial, he spent approximately 25 hours acquiring information about Mark and the Bannisters, including appropriate testing of and "depth interviews" with Mark. Dr. Hawks' testimony covers 70 pages of the record and it is difficult to pinpoint any bit of testimony which precisely summarizes his opinion. He places great emphasis on the "father figure" and discounts the importance of the "biological father." "The father figure is a figure that the child sees as an authority figure, as a helper, he is a nutrient figure, and one who typifies maleness and stands as maleness as far as the child is concerned."

His investigation revealed: " * * * the strength of the father figure before Mark came to the Bannisters is very unclear. Mark is confused about the father figure prior to his contact with Mr. Bannister." Now, "Mark used Mr. Bannister as his father figure. This is very evident. It shows up in the depth interview, and it shows up in the description of Mark's life given by Mark. He has a very warm feeling for Mr. Bannister."

Dr. Hawks concluded that it was not for Mark's best interest to be removed from the Bannister home. He is criticized for reaching this conclusion without investigating the Painter home or finding out more about Mr. Painter's character. He answered:

> I was most concerned about the welfare of the child, not the welfare of Mr. Painter, not about the welfare of the Bannisters. In as much as Mark has already made an adjustment and sees the Bannisters as his parental figures in his psychological makeup, to me this is the most critical factor. Disruption at this point, I think, would be detrimental to the child even though Mr. Painter might well be a paragon of virtue. I think this would be a kind of thing which would not be in the best interest of the child. I think knowing something about where the child is at the present time is vital. I think something about where he might go, in my way of thinking is essentially untenable to me, and relatively unimportant. It isn't even helpful. The thing I was most concerned about was Mark's view of his own reality in which he presently lives. If this is destroyed I think it will have rather bad effects on Mark. I think then if one were to make a determination whether it would be to the parents' household, or the McNelly household, or X-household, then I think the further study would be appropriate.

Dr. Hawks stated: "I am appalled at the tremendous task Mr. Painter would have if Mark were to return to him because he has got to build the relationship from scratch. There is essentially nothing on which to build at the present time. Mark is aware Mr. Painter is his father, but he is not very clear about what this means. In his own mind the father figure is Mr. Bannister. I think it would take a very strong person with everything in his favor in order to build a relationship as Mr. Painter would have to build at this point with Mark."

It was Dr. Hawks' opinion "the chances are very high (Mark) will go wrong if he is returned to his father." This is based on adoption studies which "establish that the majority of adoptions in children who are changed, from ages six to eight will go bad, if they have had a prior history of instability, some history of prior movement. When I refer to instability I am referring to where there has been no attempt to establish a strong relationship." Although this is not an adoption, the analogy seems appropriate, for Mark who had a history of instability would be removed from the only home in which he has a clearly established "father figure" and placed with his natural father about whom his feelings are unclear.

We know more of Mr. Painter's way of life than Dr. Hawks. We have concluded that it does not offer as great a stability or security as the Bannister home. Throughout his testimony he emphasized Mark's need at this critical time is stability. He has it in the Bannister home.

Other items of Dr. Hawks' testimony which have a bearing on our decision follow. He did not consider the Bannisters' age any way disqualifying. He was of the opinion that Mark could adjust to a change more easily later on, if one became necessary, when he would have better control over his environment.

He believes the presence of other children in the home would have a detrimental effect upon Mark's adjustment whether this occurred in the Bannister home or the Painter home.

The trial court does not say which of Dr. Hawks' statements he felt were exaggerated. We were most surprised at the inconsequential position to which he relegated the "biological father." He concedes "child psychologists are less concerned about natural parents than probably other professional groups are." We are not inclined to so lightly value the role of the natural father, but find much reason for his evaluation of this particular case.

Mark has established a father-son relationship with Mr. Bannister, which he apparently had never had with his natural father. He is happy, well adjusted and progressing nicely in his development. We do not believe it is for Mark's best interest to take him out of this stable atmosphere in the face of warnings of dire consequences from an eminent child psychologist and send him to an uncertain future in his father's home. Regardless of our appreciation of the father's love for his child and his desire to have him with him, we do not believe we have the moral right to gamble with this child's future. He should be encouraged in every way possible to know his father. We are sure there are many ways in which Mr. Painter can enrich Mark's life.

For the reasons stated, we reverse the trial court and remand the case for judgment in accordance herewith. * * *

NOTES AND QUESTIONS

1.   Two years after the *Painter* opinion was issued (and following publication of a book by Mark's father entitled, MARK, I LOVE YOU), the grandparents allowed Mark to visit his father in California. The father obtained a California custody order in his favor. Mark wanted to stay with his father and the Bannisters did not appeal the order. *See* CIVIL LIBERTIES No.

258, October 1968, page 12, col. 3. Had the PKPA (or UCCJEA) been in effect, could Mr. Painter have obtained a custody order in California?

2.   The *Painter* opinion reflected a movement away from the parental preference rule. Many commentators have viewed a child's "psychological parent" as equally deserving of protection as a legal parent. The term "psychological parent" was coined by Joseph Goldstein, Anna Freud, and Albert Solnit, who defined the psychological parent as the adult "who, on a continuing, day-to-day basis, through interaction, companionship, interplay, and mutuality, fulfills the child's psychological needs for a parent, as well as the child's physical needs."JOSEPH GOLDSTEIN, ET AL, BEYOND THE BEST INTERESTS OF THE CHILD 98 (1973). They also stressed stability and continuity of care, the child's sense of time and the least detrimental alternative placement. Although Goldstein, Freud, and Solnit's proposals regarding parental visitation rights have had no discernable effect on statutory standards or case law, their emphasis on a relational, rather than status-based, approach to custody disputes has had a profound and long-lasting impact. Oregon's statute governing standing in a custody dispute, for example, defines a "child-parent relationship" by paraphrasing Goldstein, Freud, and Solnit. Under the statutory standard, a child-parent relationship is one existing "within the six months preceding the filing of an action * * * and in which relationship a person having physical custody of a child or residing in the same household as the child supplied * * * food, clothing, shelter, * * * and provided the child with necessary care, education and discipline, and which relationship continued on a day-to-day basis, through interaction, companionship, interplay and mutuality, that fulfilled the child's psychological needs for a parent as well as the child's physical needs." OR. REV. STAT. § 109.119.

Why would Goldstein, Freud and Solnit's thinking on psychological parenthood have had a profound impact when their proposals on visitation have had no impact at all?

3.   In writing about *Painter*, Anna Freud provides some sense of how an emphasis on psychological parenting would alter traditional custody adjudication:

> In disagreement with the trial judge and in agreement with his expert Dr. Hawks, we discount the importance of the "biological father" as such * * * Psychologically speaking, the child's "father" is the adult man to whom the child attaches a particular, psychologically distinctive set of feelings. When this type of emotional tie is disrupted, the child's feelings suffer. When such separations occur during phases of development in which the child is particularly vulnerable, the whole foundation of his personality may be shaken * * *

> We place less emphasis than Mr. Justice Stuart on benefits such as a "stable dependable background" with educational and professional opportunities. Important as such external advantages are, we have

seen too often that they can be wasted unless they are accompanied by the internal emotional constellations which enable the children to profit from them. * * *

It is not possible at this point to foretell whether, after investigation, our advice will be in line with the judgment of the trial court or with Mr. Justice Stuart. What can be promised is that it will be based not on external facts but on internal data. We shall advise that Mark had better stay with his grandparents provided that the following facts can be ascertained:

> that the transfer of his attachment from the parents to the grandparents is fairly complete and promises to be permanent during his childhood; * * * that, given this new attachment, a further change is not advisable * * *; that the grandparents cherish Mark for his own sake, not only as a replacement for the daughter who was killed, nor as a pawn in the battle with their son-in-law.

Conversely, we shall advise that Mark had better be returned to his father if the following facts emerge:

> that Mr. Painter still retains his place as "father" in Mark's mind and that in spite of separation and new experiences the child's feelings and fantasies continue to revolve around him; that anger about the "desertion" and perhaps blame for the mother's death have not succeeded in turning this relationship into a predominantly hostile one; that the father cherishes Mark for his own sake; that it can be shown that Mr. Painter's using the child for publicity purposes was not due to lack of paternal consideration on his part but happened owing to the bitterness and resentment caused by the fight for possession of his son.

> Provided that Mr. Painter, Mr. and Mrs. Bannister, and Mark would allow the clinic two or three weeks' time for investigation, I am confident that we should be able to guide them toward a potentially helpful solution of their difficult problem.

Anna Freud, *Painter v. Bannister: Postscript by a Psychoanalyst*, 7 WRITINGS OF ANNA FREUD 250–55 (1966–70).

4.   Some commentators have seen *Painter* as an example of the ease with which the best interests standard can be manipulated to emphasize the personal values of the trial judge. Does application of the psychological parenting concept substantially reduce the risk that a parent will be denied custody of his child because his household is " * * * unconventional, arty, Bohemian, and probably intellectually stimulating" or in some other way offensive to the judge?

TROXEL V. GRANVILLE

Supreme Court of the United States, 2000.
530 U.S. 57.

JUSTICE O'CONNOR, joined by THE CHIEF JUSTICE, and JUSTICES GINSBURG and BREYER.

Section 26.10.160(3) of the Revised Code of Washington permits "[a]ny person" to petition a superior court for visitation rights "at any time," and authorizes that court to grant such visitation rights whenever "visitation may serve the best interest of the child." Petitioners Jenifer and Gary Troxel petitioned a Washington Superior Court for the right to visit their grandchildren, Isabelle and Natalie Troxel. Respondent Tommie Granville, the mother of Isabelle and Natalie, opposed the petition. The case ultimately reached the Washington Supreme Court, which held that § 26.10.160(3) unconstitutionally interferes with the fundamental right of parents to rear their children.

Tommie Granville and Brad Troxel shared a relationship that ended in June 1991. The two never married, but they had two daughters, Isabelle and Natalie. Jenifer and Gary Troxel are Brad's parents, and thus the paternal grandparents of Isabelle and Natalie. After Tommie and Brad separated in 1991, Brad lived with his parents and regularly brought his daughters to his parents' home for weekend visitation. Brad committed suicide in May 1993. Although the Troxels at first continued to see Isabelle and Natalie on a regular basis after their son's death, Tommie Granville informed the Troxels in October 1993 that she wished to limit their visitation with her daughters to one short visit per month.

In December 1993, the Troxels commenced the present action by filing, in the Washington Superior Court for Skagit County, a petition to obtain visitation rights with Isabelle and Natalie. The Troxels filed their petition under two Washington statutes, Wash. Rev. Code §§ 26.09.240 and 26.10.160(3). Only the latter statute is at issue in this case. Section 26.10.160(3) provides: "Any person may petition the court for visitation rights at any time including, but not limited to, custody proceedings. The court may order visitation rights for any person when visitation may serve the best interest of the child whether or not there has been any change of circumstances." At trial, the Troxels requested two weekends of overnight visitation per month and two weeks of visitation each summer. Granville did not oppose visitation altogether, but instead asked the court to order one day of visitation per month with no overnight stay. In 1995, the Superior Court issued an oral ruling and entered a visitation decree ordering visitation one weekend per month, one week during the summer, and four hours on both of the petitioning grandparents' birthdays.

Granville appealed, during which time she married Kelly Wynn. Before addressing the merits of Granville's appeal, the Washington Court of Appeals remanded the case to the Superior Court for entry of written findings of fact and conclusions of law. On remand, the Superior Court found that visitation was in Isabelle and Natalie's best interests: "The Petitioners [the Troxels] are part of a large, central, loving family, all located in this area, and the Petitioners can provide opportunities for the children in the areas of cousins and music." The court took into consideration all factors regarding the best interest of the children and considered all the testimony before it. The children would be benefitted from spending quality time with the Petitioners, provided that that time is balanced with time with the children's nuclear family. The court finds that the children's best interests are served by spending time with their mother and stepfather's other six children.

Approximately nine months after the Superior Court entered its order on remand, Granville's husband formally adopted Isabelle and Natalie. The Washington Court of Appeals reversed the lower court's visitation order and dismissed the Troxels' petition for visitation, holding that nonparents lack standing to seek visitation * * * unless a custody action is pending. In the Court of Appeals' view, that limitation on nonparental visitation actions was "consistent with the constitutional restrictions on state interference with parents' fundamental liberty interest in the care, custody, and management of their children." Having resolved the case on the statutory ground, however, the Court of Appeals did not expressly pass on Granville's constitutional challenge to the visitation statute.

The Washington Supreme Court granted the Troxels' petition for review and, after consolidating their case with two other visitation cases, affirmed. * * * The court rested its decision on the Federal Constitution, holding that § 26.10.160(3) unconstitutionally infringes on the fundamental right of parents to rear their children. * * * First, according to the Washington Supreme Court, the Constitution permits a State to interfere with the right of parents to rear their children only to prevent harm or potential harm to a child. Section 26.10.160(3) fails that standard because it requires no threshold showing of harm. Second, by allowing "any person" to petition for forced visitation of a child at "any time" with the only requirement being that the visitation serve the best interest of the child, the Washington visitation statute sweeps too broadly. "It is not within the province of the state to make significant decisions concerning the custody of children merely because it could make a 'better' decision." The Washington Supreme Court held that "[p]arents have a right to limit visitation of their children with third persons," and that between parents and judges, "the parents should be the ones to choose whether to expose their children to certain people or ideas." * * *

We granted certiorari and now affirm the judgment.

II

The demographic changes of the past century make it difficult to speak of an average American family. The composition of families varies greatly from household to household. While many children may have two married parents and grandparents who visit regularly, many other children are raised in single-parent households. In 1996, children living with only one parent accounted for 28 percent of all children under age 18 in the United States. Understandably, in these single-parent households, persons outside the nuclear family are called upon with increasing frequency to assist in the everyday tasks of child rearing. In many cases, grandparents play an important role. For example, in 1998, approximately 4 million children, or 5.6 percent of all children under age 18, lived in the household of their grandparents.

The nationwide enactment of nonparental visitation statutes is assuredly due, in some part, to the States' recognition of these changing realities of the American family. * * * The extension of statutory rights in this area to persons other than a child's parents, however, comes with an obvious cost. For example, the State's recognition of an independent third-party interest in a child can place a substantial burden on the traditional parent-child relationship. * * *

The Fourteenth Amendment provides that no State shall "deprive any person of life, liberty, or property, without due process of law." We have long recognized that the Amendment's Due Process Clause, like its Fifth Amendment counterpart, "guarantees more than fair process." Washington v. Glucksberg, 521 U.S. 702, 719 (1997). The Clause also includes a substantive component that provides heightened protection against government interference with certain fundamental rights and liberty interests.

The liberty interest at issue in this case, the interest of parents in the care, custody, and control of their children, is perhaps the oldest of the fundamental liberty interests recognized by this Court. More than 75 years ago, in Meyer v. Nebraska, we held that the "liberty" protected by the Due Process Clause includes the right of parents to "establish a home and bring up children" and "to control the education of their own." Two years later, in Pierce v. Society of Sisters, we again held that the "liberty of parents and guardians" includes the right "to direct the upbringing and education of children under their control." We explained in *Pierce* that "[t]he child is not the mere creature of the State; those who nurture him and direct his destiny have the right, coupled with the high duty, to recognize and prepare him for additional obligations." We returned to the subject in Prince v. Massachusetts, and again confirmed that there is a constitutional dimension to the right of parents to direct the upbringing of their children. "It is cardinal with us that the custody, care and nurture of the child reside first in the parents, whose primary function and freedom include preparation for obligations the state can neither supply nor hinder."

In subsequent cases also, we have recognized the fundamental right of parents to make decisions concerning the care, custody, and control of their children. [*See Stanley v. Illinois*, 405 U.S. 645 (1972); *Wisconsin v. Yoder*, 406 U.S. 205 (1972); *Quilloin v. Walcott*, 434 U.S. 246 (1978); *Parham v. J.R.*, 442 U.S. 584 (1979); *Santosky v. Kramer*, 455 U.S. 745 (1982); *Washington v. Glucksberg*, 521 U.S. 702 (1997)]. In light of this extensive precedent, it cannot now be doubted that the Due Process Clause of the Fourteenth Amendment protects the fundamental right of parents to make decisions concerning the care, custody, and control of their children.

Section 26.10.160(3), as applied to Granville and her family in this case, unconstitutionally infringes on that fundamental parental right. The Washington nonparental visitation statute is breathtakingly broad. According to the statute's text, "[a]ny person may petition the court for visitation rights at any time," and the court may grant such visitation rights whenever "visitation may serve the best interest of the child." That language effectively permits any third party seeking visitation to subject any decision by a parent concerning visitation of the parent's children to state-court review. Once the visitation petition has been filed in court and the matter is placed before a judge, a parent's decision that visitation would not be in the child's best interest is accorded no deference. Section 26.10.160(3) contains no requirement that a court accord the parent's decision any presumption of validity or any weight whatsoever. Instead, the Washington statute places the best-interest determination solely in the hands of the judge. Should the judge disagree with the parent's estimation of the child's best interests, the judge's view necessarily prevails. Thus, in practical effect, in the State of Washington a court can disregard and overturn any decision by a fit custodial parent concerning visitation whenever a third party affected by the decision files a visitation petition, based solely on the judge's determination of the child's best interests. The Washington Supreme Court had the opportunity to give § 26.10.160(3) a narrower reading, but it declined to do so.

Turning to the facts of this case, the record reveals that the Superior Court's order was based on precisely the type of mere disagreement we have just described and nothing more. The Superior Court's order was not founded on any special factors that might justify the State's interference with Granville's fundamental right to make decisions concerning the rearing of her two daughters. To be sure, this case involves a visitation petition filed by grandparents soon after the death of their son, the father of Isabelle and Natalie, but the combination of several factors here compels our conclusion that § 26.10.160(3), as applied, exceeded the bounds of the Due Process Clause.

First, the Troxels did not allege, and no court has found, that Granville was an unfit parent. That aspect of the case is important, for there is a presumption that fit parents act in the best interests of their children. * * * Accordingly, so long as a parent adequately cares for his or her children (i.e., is fit), there will normally be no reason for the State to inject itself into the private realm of the family to further question the ability of that parent to make the best decisions concerning the rearing of that parent's children.

The problem here is not that the Washington Superior Court intervened, but that when it did so, it gave no special weight at all to Granville's determination of her daughters' best interests. More importantly, it appears that the Superior Court applied exactly the opposite presumption. In reciting its oral ruling after the conclusion of closing arguments, the Superior Court judge explained:

> The burden is to show that it is in the best interest of the children to have some visitation and some quality time with their grandparents. I think in most situations a commonsensical approach [is that] it is normally in the best interest of the children to spend quality time with the grandparent, unless the grandparent, [sic] there are some issues or problems involved wherein the grandparents, their lifestyles are going to impact adversely upon the children. That certainly isn't the case here from what I can tell.

The judge's comments suggest that he presumed the grandparents' request should be granted unless the children would be "impact[ed] adversely." In effect, the judge placed on Granville, the fit custodial parent, the burden of disproving that visitation would be in the best interest of her daughters. * * *

The decisional framework employed by the Superior Court directly contravened the traditional presumption that a fit parent will act in the best interest of his or her child. In that respect, the court's presumption failed to provide any protection for Granville's fundamental constitutional right to make decisions concerning the rearing of her own daughters. In an ideal world, parents might always seek to cultivate the bonds between grandparents and their grandchildren. Needless to say, however, our world is far from perfect, and in it the decision whether such an intergenerational relationship would be beneficial in any specific case is for the parent to make in the first instance. And, if a fit parent's decision of the kind at issue here becomes subject to judicial review, the court must accord at least some special weight to the parent's own determination.

Finally, we note that there is no allegation that Granville ever sought to cut off visitation entirely. Rather, the present dispute originated when Granville informed the Troxels that she would prefer to restrict their visitation with Isabelle and Natalie to one short visit per month and special holidays. In the Superior Court proceedings Granville did not oppose visitation but instead asked that the duration of any visitation order be shorter than that requested by the Troxels. While the Troxels requested two weekends per month and two full weeks in the summer, Granville asked the Superior Court to order only one day of visitation per month (with no overnight stay) and participation in the Granville family's holiday celebrations. The Superior Court gave no weight to Granville's having assented to visitation even before the filing of any visitation petition or subsequent court intervention. The court instead rejected Granville's proposal and settled on a middle ground, ordering one weekend of visitation per month, one week in the summer, and time on both of the petitioning grandparents' birthdays. Significantly, many other States expressly provide by statute that courts may not award visitation unless a parent has denied (or unreasonably denied) visitation to the concerned third party.

Considered together with the Superior Court's reasons for awarding visitation to the Troxels, the combination of these factors demonstrates that the visitation order in this case was an unconstitutional infringement on Granville's fundamental right to make decisions concerning the care, custody, and control of her two daughters. * * * Accordingly, we hold that § 26.10.160(3), as applied in this case, is unconstitutional.

Because we rest our decision on the sweeping breadth of § 26.10.160(3) and the application of that broad, unlimited power in this case, we do not consider the primary constitutional question passed on by the Washington Supreme Court, whether the Due Process Clause requires all nonparental visitation statutes to include a showing of harm or potential harm to the child as a condition precedent to granting visitation. We do not, and need not, define today the precise scope of the parental due process right in the visitation context. * * * Because much state-court adjudication in this context occurs on a case-by-case basis, we would be hesitant to hold that specific nonparental visitation statutes violate the Due Process Clause as a per se matter.

* * *

Accordingly, the judgment of the Washington Supreme Court is affirmed.

JUSTICE STEVENS, dissenting.

* * *

* * * [T]the Washington Supreme Court's holding "that the Federal Constitution requires a showing of actual or potential 'harm' to the child before a court may order visitation continued over a parent's objections" finds no support in this Court's case law. While, as the Court recognizes, the Federal Constitution certainly protects the parent-child relationship

from arbitrary impairment by the State, * * * we have never held that the parent's liberty interest in this relationship is so inflexible as to establish a rigid constitutional shield, protecting every arbitrary parental decision from any challenge absent a threshold finding of harm. * * *

* * *

A parent's rights with respect to her child have thus never been regarded as absolute, but rather are limited by the existence of an actual, developed relationship with a child, and are tied to the presence or absence of some embodiment of family. These limitations have arisen, not simply out of the definition of parenthood itself, but because of this Court's assumption that a parent's interests in a child must be balanced against the State's long-recognized interests as parens patriae and, critically, the child's own complementary interest in preserving relationships that serve her welfare and protection.

While this Court has not yet had occasion to elucidate the nature of a child's liberty interests in preserving established familial or family-like bonds, it seems to me extremely likely that, to the extent parents and families have fundamental liberty interests in preserving such intimate relationships, so, too, do children have these interests, and so, too, must their interests be balanced in the equation. At a minimum, our prior cases recognizing that children are, generally speaking, constitutionally protected actors require that this Court reject any suggestion that when it comes to parental rights, children are so much chattel. * * * The constitutional protection against arbitrary state interference with parental rights should not be extended to prevent the States from protecting children against the arbitrary exercise of parental authority that is not in fact motivated by an interest in the welfare of the child.

This is not, of course, to suggest that a child's liberty interest in maintaining contact with a particular individual is to be treated invariably as on a par with that child's parents' contrary interests. Because our substantive due process case law includes a strong presumption that a parent will act in the best interest of her child, it would be necessary, were the state appellate courts actually to confront a challenge to the statute as applied, to consider whether the trial court's assessment of the "best interest of the child" incorporated that presumption. * * *

But presumptions notwithstanding, we should recognize that there may be circumstances in which a child has a stronger interest at stake than mere protection from serious harm caused by the termination of visitation by a "person" other than a parent. The almost infinite variety of family relationships that pervade our ever-changing society strongly counsel against the creation by this Court of a constitutional rule that treats a biological parent's liberty interest in the care and supervision of her child as an isolated right that may be exercised arbitrarily. It is indisputably the business of the States, rather than a federal court employing a national standard, to assess in the first instance the relative importance of the conflicting interests that give rise to disputes such as this. Far from guaranteeing that parents' interests will be trammeled in the sweep of cases rising under the statute, the Washington law merely gives an individual with whom a child may have an established relationship the procedural right to ask the State to act as arbiter, through the entirely well-known best-interests standard, between the parent's protected interests and the child's. It seems clear to me that the Due Process Clause of the Fourteenth Amendment leaves room for States to consider the impact on a child of possibly arbitrary parental decisions that neither serve nor are motivated by the best interests of the child.

Accordingly, I respectfully dissent.

NOTES AND QUESTIONS

1.   In addition to the plurality decision and Justice Stevens' dissent, there were four other opinions in *Troxel*. Justice Souter, concurring, argued that the Court should affirm the Washington Supreme Court's conclusion that the statute was facially unconstitutional. Justice Thomas, also concurring in the judgment, stated that he would apply strict scrutiny to the Washington statute. Justice Scalia dissented on the basis that the Court should not further extend the substantive due process rights of parents, saying "The sheer diversity of today's opinions persuades me that the theory of unenumerated parental rights has small claim to stare decisis protection." Justice Kennedy also dissented contending that the Washington Supreme Court was wrong when it held that third parties could not constitutionally be awarded visitation unless they could prove harm to the child. He noted, "Cases are sure to arise—perhaps a substantial number of cases—in which a third party by acting in a caregiving role over a significant period of time has developed a relationship with a child which is not necessarily subject to absolute parental veto." *See* Emily Buss, *"Parental" Rights*, 88 VA. L. REV. 635 (2002).

2.   Under *Troxel*, what standard should a court use in evaluating the constitutionality of a statute governing the award of custody or visitation to a nonparent? *See* David D. Meyer, *Constitutional Pragmatism for a Changing American Family*, 32 RUTGERS L. J. 711 (2001) (arguing in favor of flexible, discretionary mode of review); Janet L. Dolgin, *The Constitution as Family Arbiter: A Moral in the Mess?*, 102 COLUM. L. REV. 337 (2002).

3.   Does *Troxel* preclude use of a best interests test in custody or visitation litigation between a parent and nonparent? In Rubano v. DiCenzo, 759 A.2d 959 (R.I. 2000), the Rhode Island Supreme Court said no. *Rubano* involved a visitation action by a lesbian coparent whose name was listed on the child's birth certificate along with that of the biological mother and who lived with the child and mother for four years. After an "informal visitation schedule" collapsed due to opposition by the biological mother, the coparent went to court to establish a legal relationship with the child under R.I. STAT.

§§ 15–8–26, providing that "[a]ny interested party may bring an action to determine the existence or nonexistence of a mother and child relationship." The Supreme Court ruled that the statute did not violate the constitutional standard enunciated in *Troxel*:

> * * * Rubano was an "interested party" because she claimed that she had a de facto mother and child relationship with the child and because she claimed that the child's biological mother had agreed to allow her reasonable visitation with the child. Whether her claims had any merit was a factual matter for the Family Court to decide, but the plain language of [the Rhode Island statute] * * * vests the Family Court with jurisdiction to declare the existence *vel non* of a mother and child relationship in these limited circumstances. Thus, in contrast to the situation in the United States Supreme Court's recent decision of *Troxel v. Granville,* * * * we construe §§ 15–8–26's "[a]ny interested party" language much more narrowly, requiring an alleged parent-like relationship with the child before a party who is neither the child's biological parent nor a legal representative of the child can seek relief under §§ 15–8–26. Rubano's alleged close involvement with the child's conception and upbringing for as long as she and DiCenzo cohabited (approximately four years) and her alleged visitation agreement with DiCenzo when the couple separated endowed her with the requisite parent-like relationship and standing to obtain a judicial determination under this section. * * * [T]he Family Court * * * has the power to determine the existence of a de facto parent-child relationship despite the absence of any biological relationship between the putative parent and the child.

The New Jersey Supreme Court reached a similar conclusion in a case decided before *Troxel*, holding that a nonparent could obtain visitation over a parent's objection when: (1) the biological or adoptive parent consented to, and fostered, the establishment of a parent-like relationship between the petitioner and the child; (2) the petitioner lived in the same household with the child; (3) the petitioner fulfilled obligations of parenthood by taking responsibility for the child's care, education and development, without expecting financial compensation; and (4) the petitioner has been in a parental role for a length of time sufficient to have established a bond with the child. *See* V.C. v. M.J.B., 748 A.2d 539 (N.J. 2000).

     4. *Nonparent Visitation Post-*Troxel*:* Since *Troxel*, many state high courts have examined the constitutionality of their grandparent visitation statutes. Courts have agreed that a fit parent's visitation decision is entitled to significant weight and that the party seeking visitation bears the burden of proof. Where courts differ is whether the evidence must show harm to the child or merely best interest to visit. *See* David D. Meyer, *Who Gets the Children? Parental Rights after* Troxel v. Granville: *Constitutional Pragmatism for a Changing American Family*, 32 RUTGERS L.J. 711, 714 (2001). *See also* Jeff Atkinson, *Shifts in the Law Regarding the Rights of Third Parties to Seek*

Visitation and Custody of Children, 47 FAM. L. Q. 1 (2013); Rebecca L. Scharf, *Psychological Parentage,* Troxel, *and the Best Interests of the Child*, 13 GEO. J. GENDER & L. 615 (2012).

State legislatures have also been active but the statutory amendments do not follow a uniform pattern in interpreting *Troxel*'s mandate. North Dakota, for example, retained the best interests test but mandated a showing that visitation would not interfere with parent-child relationship. N.D. CENT. CODE § 14–09–05.1). Tennessee and Utah adopted a rebuttable presumption that a parental visitation decision was in the child's best interest. TENN. CODE ANN § 30–5–2; UTAH CODE ANN. § 30–5–2.

5.   Consider the following fact patterns and determine how a legislature should respond to *Troxel*'s mandate:

a.   a father who has lost custody of his children concurs with the children's mother that the paternal grandparents should not visit the children.

b.   a father and mother with joint custody concur that grandparents should not visit the children.

c.   the parent (and child of the petitioning grandparents) has been deprived of access to the child because of past physical abuse.

d.   the grandparents are divorced and *both* want visitation.

In which cases should a court have the authority to overrule a parental visitation decision? In those cases in which a parental decision may be overruled, what evidentiary showing should be required as a precondition to court-ordered visitation? Courts strictly construe the statutes so if a person is not listed, the person has no standing. Lott v. Alexander, 134 So. 3d 369 (Miss. App. 2014) (greatgrandparent was not listed in statute).

6.   *Stepparent Custody and Visitation:* While the common law did not recognize a right to stepparent visitation, occasionally courts allowed a stepparent to visit where he or she had acted in loco parentis. Today, with 45 million stepparents in the United States, the law is changing. Many states now have statutes which permit stepparent visitation. *See, e.g.,* CAL. FAM. CODE § 3101 (authorizing "reasonable visitation to a stepparent" when "in the best interest of the minor child"). Even in states where there is no such statutory authorization, some courts have granted stepparents visitation based on their inherent equitable powers.

After *Troxel*, is the California stepparent visitation statute constitutional? If no, what standard would meet constitutional requirements?

7.   *Sibling Visitation:* Under *Troxel*, what standard should apply to a sibling visitation dispute? *See* M.B.B. v. E.R.W., 100 P.3d 415 (Wyo. 2004) (finding that only grandparents and caretakers listed in statute had standing to seek visitation); Frank v. Frank, 833 A.2d 194 (Pa. Super. 2003); *In re* Victoria C., 88 A.3d 749 (Md. 2014) (teenage girl in foster care was a third party

seeking visitation with younger siblings). Should siblings be treated differently than grandparents, stepparents, and other nonparents?

Problem 14-4:

Sara married Tom, the father of a one-month-old boy, Sam. During the marriage, Sara gave birth to a daughter, Susan. When the parties divorced a few years later, Sara was awarded custody of Susan. For four years after the divorce, Tom allowed Sara to visit Sam twice a month. Tom then discovered that Susan was not his biological child and cut off her visits with Sam. What arguments can Sara make for continued visitation? *See In re* Marriage of Engelkens, 821 N.E.2d 799 (Ill. App. 2004); *In re* Marriage of Riggs and Hem, 129 P.3d 601 (Kan. App. 2006).

Problem 14-5:

Usha K. was born in India. She is an only child whose father died when she was 12. When she was 14 years old she began working full time and attended secretarial school at night so that she might eventually earn enough money to come to this country for a college education. She arrived in the United States at the age of eighteen and began to study agriculture and nutrition. Two years later she obtained an associate degree from the State University system. That same year her mother died in India.

While in New York Usha met an Indian student who apparently agreed to marry her; but when she later became pregnant, he deserted her. She dropped out of school and gave birth to her daughter, Sanjivini. Unwed and temporarily unable to support the child, she agreed to place her in the custody of the Department of Social Services. She refused, however, to surrender the child for adoption and would only consent to temporary foster care. After the child's birth, Usha obtained a job to reimburse the department for medical expenses and to contribute to the support of her daughter. When Sanjivini was about eighteen months old, Usha returned to school after reimbursing the department $800 for her medical expenses. With the aid of a scholarship and part-time employment, she attended a university in Maryland and then in North Carolina, which apparently were the only schools within her means which offered the necessary courses. She still continued to visit her child when able, generally once every two or three months. When her education was completed, she returned to New York. At that point Sanjivini was four years old and had lived with her foster parents for two years. Usha requested help from the Department in finding employment; she also asked for the return of her child. The agency worker assigned to the case furnished Usha with the names and addresses of two potential employers selected from the telephone book but did nothing more even though Usha informed her that she had already been denied employment at those locations. She also refused to return Sanjivini in view of Usha's "current financial and residential instability." Because of her immigrant status, Usha was unable to obtain employment in Rockland

County where Sanjivini lived. Finally she obtained clerical employment in New York City. She contributed monthly to the child's support and once every other week travelled from New York City to Rockland County to visit the girl. But the Department refused to give her Sanjivini. Instead, when Sanjivini was seven, it filed a petition to award permanent custody to the foster parents, who had by then cared for the child for five years. In its petition, the Department alleged that "while the mother was furthering her own education, the child still needed parents. Mr. and Mrs. Ames [the foster parents] have fulfilled that role and are the child's psychological parents. To return Sanjivini to her mother at this point would pose grave risks to her psychological development." State case law permits an award of custody to a nonparent in a case of parental unfitness, abandonment, or "extraordinary circumstances." What arguments would you make on behalf of Usha K.? the State and Mr. and Mrs. Ames? If you were the judge assigned to the case, what decision would you make and how would you justify it? *See In re* Sanjivini K., 391 N.E.2d 1316 (N.Y. 1979); Bessette v. Saratoga County Comm'r, 619 N.Y.S.2d 359 (App. Div. 1994).

Problem 14-6:

In 2006, Christine Titchenal and Diane Dexter began an intimate relationship. They purchased a home together, held joint bank accounts, and jointly owned their automobiles. They both contributed financially to their household, and each regarded the other as a life partner. They also decided to have a child together. When their attempts to conceive via a sperm donor failed, they decided to adopt a child. In July 2013, Diane adopted a newborn baby girl, who was named Sarah Ruth Dexter-Titchenal. Christine and Diane described themselves to Sarah and all others as her parents. The child called one parent "Mama Chris" and the other parent "Mama Di." For the first three and one-half years of Sarah's life, Christine cared for the child approximately 65% of the time. Christine did not seek to adopt Sarah because the parties believed that the then-current adoption statute would not allow her to do so. In November 2015, Diane moved out of the couple's home, taking Sarah with her. For the first five months following separation, Sarah stayed with Christine between Wednesday afternoons and Friday evenings. By the spring of 2016, however, Diane had severely curtailed plaintiff's contact with Sarah and had refused her offer of financial assistance; Christine filed a petition for visitation. The state has a grandparent visitation statute, but no other statutory authority for nonparental visitation. The courts have construed the grandparent visitation provision narrowly, but has construed both the adoption and divorce laws quite expansively. *See, e.g., In re* B.L.V.B., 628 A.2d 1271 (Vt. 1993) (construing adoption statute to permit adoption by same-sex partner). What arguments would you make on behalf of Christine? Diane? If you were the judge assigned to the case, what decision would you make and how would you justify it? *See* Titchenal v. Dexter, 693

A.2d 682 (Vt. 1997). *See* Jones v. Boring Jones, 884 A.2d 915 (Pa. Super. 2005); A.H. v. M.P., 857 N.E.2d 1061 (Mass. 2006).

Problem 14-7:

After Amanda married Doris' son John, Doris began to care for Amanda's baby Christopher (Amanda's son from a prior relationship) while Amanda was at work; typically Doris cared for Christopher between 8:00 a.m. and 6:00 p.m. on weekdays. When Amanda and John had their own child, Jill, Doris continued to care for them both. When Christopher was about four years old, John and Amanda separated. Thereafter, Amanda found other child care arrangements and refused to permit Doris to visit with either Jill or Christopher. State law authorizes a grandparent to petition for visitation "following the death or divorce of the grandparent's child who has given birth to the child who is the subject of the petition." Doris seeks visitation with both Jill and Christopher. What arguments would you make on behalf of Doris? Amanda? If you were the judge assigned to the case, what decision would you make and how would you justify it? *See In re* Hood, 847 P.2d 1300 (Kan. 1993). *See also* P.B. v. T.H., 851 A.2d 780 (N.J. Super. App. Div. 2004).

6. MODIFYING A CUSTODY ORDER

Because of the need to protect the best interests of a child, custody and visitation orders are subject to modification throughout the child's minority. But because stability and finality are also important values in child custody litigation, most states permit modification only when there has been a substantial change of circumstances since the original custody and visitation decree. In evaluating whether such a change has occurred, courts typically look at events occurring after the decree was entered and which were unanticipated by the parties. *See, e.g.*, Lizzio v. Jackson, 640 N.Y.S.2d 330 (App. Div. 1996) (finding asthmatic son's allergy to mother's smoking was not a change of circumstances because mother smoked before the divorce). *But see In re* Marriage of Kiister, 777 P.2d 272 (Kan. 1989) (finding *all* evidence on the welfare of the child, whether predecree or not, can be considered if not presented to court because child's welfare is paramount); K.J.B. v. C.M.B., 779 S.W.2d 36 (Mo. App. 1989) (allowing consideration of father's predissolution abusive conduct toward the children because not known to the court at the time of the original custody decree).

In a number of states, even a substantial change in circumstances will not provide a basis for modification if a petition is brought too quickly after entry of the original custody decree. In these states, a petitioner for modification within a statutorily specified time period must meet more demanding criteria, such as a showing of harm to the child. Most of these statutory time limits on modification are for one or two years following the last custody order. *See, e.g.* DEL. CODE ANN. tit. 13, § 729(c) (two years); MINN. STAT. ANN. § 518.18(a), (b) (one year after order, or within two years from disposition of prior motion).

If the proposed modification would entail a change in physical custody of the child, some states require more than a showing of a substantial change in circumstances. The UMDA § 409(b), for example, specifies that such a modification is permissible only when: (1) the current custodian agrees to the modification; (2) the child has been integrated into the family of the petitioner with consent of the custodial; or (3) the child's present environment seriously endangers his physical, mental, moral, or emotional health, and the harm likely to be caused by a change of environment is outweighed by its advantages.

In contrast, some jurisdictions require less than a showing of a substantial change in circumstances in some cases. For example, a joint custody order may be modified more easily than a sole custody order. *See, e.g.,* WIS. STAT. ANN. § 767.325(2) (restrictions on modification do not apply when parents have substantially equal physical custody); OKLA. STAT. ANN. tit. 43, § 109(F) (joint custody order modifiable under best interests test). Some states also permit easier modification of an order based on an agreement of the parties. And a few jurisdictions do not require a change of circumstances in any modification context. *See, e.g.,* CONN. GEN. STAT. ANN. § 46b–56(b); NEV. REV. STAT. ANN. § 125.510.

A substantial change in circumstances or other threshold showing must typically be established by a preponderance of the evidence before the court will consider whether modification would serve the child's best interests. As the court noted in Wagner v. Wagner, 674 A.2d 1 (Md. Spec. Ct. App. 1996):

> A change of custody resolution is most often a chronological two-step process. First, unless a material change of circumstances if found to exist, the court's inquiry ceases. In this context, the term "material" relates to a change that may affect the welfare of a child. Moreover, the circumstances to which change would apply would be the circumstances known to the trial court when it rendered the prior order. If the actual circumstances extant at that time were not known to the court because evidence relating thereto was not available to the court, then the additional evidence of actual (but previously unknown) circumstances might also be applicable in respect to a court's determination of change. If a material change of circumstance is found to exist, then the court, in resolving the custody issue, considers the best interest of the child as if it were an original custody proceeding. Certainly, the very factors that indicate that a material change in circumstances has occurred may also be extremely relevant at the

second phase of the inquiry—that is, in reference to the best interest of the child. If not relevant to the best interest of the child, the changes would not be material in the first instance. Because of the frequency with which it occurs, this two-step process is sometimes considered concurrently, in one step, i.e., the change in circumstances evidence also satisfies—or does not—the determination of what is in the best interest of the child. Even if it alone does not satisfy the best interest standard, it almost certainly will afford evidentiary support in the resolution of the second step. Thus, both steps may be, and often are, resolved simultaneously.

While a "substantial" or "material" change in circumstances is difficult to define or quantify, courts will ordinarily look for a change that is ongoing and which significantly affects the welfare of the child. For example, a father who alleged in his affidavit that the mother had changed residence several times, was on welfare, and had exposed the children to physically and sexually abusive relationships met his burden of showing a substantial change in circumstances and was permitted to proceed. *In re* Marriage of Morazan, 772 P.2d 872 (Mont. 1989). A number of courts have held that significant interference with parental visitation constitutes a substantial change in circumstances. *See* Ready v. Ready, 906 P.2d 382 (Wyo. 1995). *See also* KAN. STAT. ANN. § 23–3221(b) ("Repeated unreasonable denial of or interference with visitation rights or parenting time * * * may be considered a material change of circumstances which justifies modification of a prior order of legal custody, residency, visitation or parenting time.") Many requests for modification arise when one parent wishes to move.

O'CONNOR V. O'CONNOR

Appellate Division, 2002.
349 N.J. Super. 381, 793 A.2d 810.

FALL, J.

In this post-judgment matrimonial matter, we again address the troubling issue of a parent's application to remove the child of the dissolved marriage to another state as a result of that parent's need to relocate. Justice Long succinctly posed the dilemma as follows: Ideally, after a divorce, parents cooperate and remain in close proximity to each other to provide access and succor to their children. But that ideal is not always the reality. In our global economy, relocation for employment purposes is common. On a personal level, people remarry and move away. Noncustodial parents may relocate to pursue other interests regardless of the strength of the bond they have developed with their children. Custodial parents may do so only with the consent of the former spouse. Otherwise, a court application is required.

Inevitably, upon objection by a noncustodial parent, there is a clash between the custodial parent's interest in self-determination and the noncustodial parent's interest in the companionship of the child. There is rarely an easy answer or even an entirely satisfactory one when a noncustodial parent objects. If the removal is denied, the custodial parent may be embittered by the assault on his or her autonomy. If it is granted, the noncustodial parent may live with the abiding belief that his or her connection to the child has been lost forever.

When relocation of one parent is certain, the ultimate dilemma facing the court is the vexatious reality that there is no result that satisfactorily meets the needs of the parties or the child. In circumstances where the parent has a healthy, meaningful relationship and bond with the child, there are few circumstances where the judicial determination will not adversely affect the parties and the child. If removal is granted, the nature of the relationship and bond between the parent left behind and the child changes and is at risk. The same result occurs as to the relationship and bond between the relocated parent and the child if removal is denied. Additionally, removal actions often create, or fortify, walls of animosity between the parents, furthering the negative impact to all concerned. The result is hard and predetermined; no one wants it, yet the consequences are inevitable. It is against this dreary context that we consider this appeal.

Plaintiff, Kathleen M. O'Connor, appeals from an order entered on September 25, 2001, after a plenary hearing, denying her application to remove and relocate the parties' child to the State of Indiana and designating defendant, William J. O'Connor, as the child's primary residential custodian. We hold that in determining the standard to be applied to a parent's removal application, the focus of the inquiry is whether the physical custodial relationship among the parents is one in which one parent is the "primary caretaker" and the other parent is the "secondary caretaker." If so, the removal application must be analyzed in accordance with the criteria outlined in [our decision in] *Baures*.

If, however, the parents truly share both legal and physical custody, an application by one parent to relocate and remove the residence of the child to an out-of-state location must be analyzed as an application for a change of custody, where the party seeking the change in the joint custodial relationship must demonstrate that the best interests of the child would be better served by residential custody being primarily vested with the relocating parent.

In determining whether the parties truly share joint physical custody, although the division of the child's time with each parent is a critical factor, the time each parent spends with the child must be analyzed in the context of each parent's responsibility for the custodial functions and duties normally reposed in a primary caretaker.

Here, we conclude the findings and conclusions of the trial court that the parties truly share jointly both legal and physical custody of their child is supported by substantial, credible evidence in the record. We affirm the court's rejection of plaintiff's application for removal.

* * *

[The trial judge made the following findings:]

* * * [T]here was a shared parenting relationship * * *. [T]here is a good faith reason for the move. * * * There is no need for the plaintiff to relocate for business purposes or for her job[.] * * * [T]he move will not be [inimical] to the child's interest * * *.

* * * [T]he agreement that was originally executed at the time of the divorce certainly had changed. * * * The Court finds that [the child's residential time] * * * is 50/50 and the Court finds that there's a shared parenting relationship.

* * *[T]his is the child's home state. * * * This is where his friends are, where his cousins are. He's acknowledged to the Court that this is where his grandmother and grandfather [are] and where his cousins are. That he has spent considerable quality time with his father, that it is 50 percent, that it is meaningful time, * * * he did acknowledge to the Court that the father only missed one of his sporting events and that the father worked with him.

* * *

That—with regard to comparable educational health and leisure opportunities, the Court finds there's no difference. * * * The child has no * * * special needs or talents. * * * He's a very normal well adjusted good student, a wonderful young man, and therefore, can take advantage of any opportunities.

Whether a visitation and communication schedule can be developed that will allow the non-custodial parent to maintain a full continuous relationship with the child, well, I don't find there's a non-custodial person here. I find that there's a shared parenting. That the father would be willing to maintain that relationship, and that the mother certainly could maintain the relationship. That even if the child comes to New Jersey that she has flexibility in her work schedule, that she can come to New Jersey. She can maintain relationships through the Internet, et cetera, with the child if he is housed in New Jersey, and that she can still maintain her relationship with Mr. Love. That Mr. Love could relocate. I'm not even going to force him to do that, but certainly, she has that flexibility.

The likelihood that the custodial parent will continue to foster the relationship of the child with the non-custodial parent, I have some serious problems whether I think the plaintiff can do that if she moves to Indianapolis. * * *

[T]here is going to be an adverse effect on the extended family relationships. Not with plaintiff's family. She has no family in Indianapolis or Indiana or the Midwest at all that we heard of * * * but that there is a substantial relationship with the * * * relatives in New Jersey. That Ryan, when he spoke to the Court, indicated his substantial relationship with his cousins and his grandparents, and how valuable they were to him.

* * * [H]is [i.e., Ryan's] preference is to stay in New Jersey. * * *

[Defendant has] worked 20 years for the same company, and he has worked out an arrangement * * * to have substantial parenting time with his child. However, the mother can [live] anywhere she wants to. She doesn't have to relocate to Indianapolis. She has the ability to be wherever she wants to be. Apparently, * * * she can work and tele-commute, and that she, in fact, has an office in New Jersey. * * *

[The child] * * * doesn't want to be going back and forth on airplanes. The mother's arrangement that the father is going to live in her house to stay out there seems somewhat farfetched, to say the least. How comfortable the father would be living in someone else's house, especially his ex-wife's house and her fiancée's strains credibility. But the mother, in fact, could maintain two residences if she so wishes.

She has an economic ability to do that. She can travel back and forth and she could maintain residence here in New Jersey if she so wished. She testified to her high economic status, and certainly adjustments could be made to do that[.]

* * *

The father * * * offer[s] a stable home environment for that child, and that's what the child is seeking, and that the extent and quality of the time spent with the child prior to and subsequent to the separation, or in this case prior to * * * and since the decision to relocate, the father has spent quality time with this child and sufficient time. * * *

So, the Court is going to require that the child stay in the State of New Jersey with his father, but is going to require the father to enroll the child in the Mahwah School District immediately and will pay for that if he doesn't relocate, if there's a charge, because he is not in Mahwah right now, but I'll accept his word that he's going to do so, and he'll pay for any kind of tuition for that.

* * *

In a removal application, the party seeking the relocation has the initial burden to "produce evidence to establish *prima facie* that (1) there is a good faith reason for the move and (2) that the move will not be inimical to the child's interest. Included within that *prima facie* case should be a visitation proposal. By *prima facie* is meant evidence that, if unrebutted, would sustain a judgment in the proponent's favor." *Baures, supra* * * * Once the proponent of the removal application establishes a *prima facie* case, "the burden devolves upon the noncustodial parent who must produce evidence opposing the move as either not in good faith or inimical to the child's interest." *Id.* The Court held that in assessing whether to permit removal, the court should look to the following factors relevant to the plaintiff's burden of proving good faith and that the move will not be inimical to the child's interest: (1) the reasons given for the move; (2) the reasons given for the opposition; (3) the past history of dealings between the parties insofar as it bears on the reasons advanced by both parties for supporting and opposing the move; (4) whether the child will receive educational, health and leisure opportunities at least equal to what is available here; (5) any special needs or talents of the child that require accommodation and whether such accommodation or its equivalent is available in the new location; (6) whether a visitation and communication schedule can be developed that will allow the noncustodial parent to maintain a full and continuous relationship with the child; (7) the likelihood that the custodial parent will continue to foster the child's relationship with the noncustodial parent if the move is allowed; (8) the effect of the move on extended family relationships here and in the new location; (9) if the child is of age, his or her preference; (10) whether the child is entering his or her senior year in high school at which point he or she should generally not be moved until graduation without his or her consent; (11) whether the noncustodial parent has the ability to relocate; (12) any other factor bearing on the child's interest.

However, the Court made it clear that the removal analysis is entirely inapplicable to a case in which the noncustodial parent shares physical custody either *de facto* or *de jure* or exercises the bulk of custodial responsibilities due to the incapacity of the custodial parent or by formal or informal agreement. In those circumstances, the removal application effectively constitutes a motion for a change in custody and will be governed initially by a changed circumstances inquiry and ultimately by a simple best interests analysis. * * * Obviously then, the preliminary question in any case in which a parent seeks to relocate with a child is whether it is a removal case or whether by virtue of the arrangement between the parties, it is actually a motion for a change of custody. * * *

Accordingly, the initial inquiry centers on the nature of the custodial relationship between the parents and the child. Where the parents truly share both legal and physical custody, an application by one parent to relocate with the child to an out-of-state location is analyzed as an application for a change of custody. Under such circumstances, the party seeking the change in the custodial relationship must demonstrate that the best interests of the child would be better served by residential custody being vested primarily with the relocating parent. * * * Where the relocating parent is the "custodial parent" or "primary caretaker" in relation to the physical custody of the child, the removal application is analyzed in accordance with the criteria outlined in *Baures, supra.* * * *

The focus here is not on "joint legal custody." The parties clearly share joint legal custody. In determining the applicable standard to apply to plaintiff's removal application, the primary inquiry is whether the physical custodial relationship between plaintiff and defendant is one where plaintiff is the "primary caretaker" and defendant is the "secondary caretaker," or, whether these parties truly share both legal and physical custody. * * *

* * *

* * * Here, the trial judge made specific and detailed findings concerning the custodial relationship between plaintiff and defendant that centered not only upon the division of the child's time with each parent, but also on the division of key custodial responsibilities, such as bringing the child to and picking the child up from school; helping the child with his homework assignments; bringing the child to and attending his sports and school activities; preparing and planning the child's meals; caring for the child overnight; and attending to the child's medical and other health needs. The judge found both parties shared these primary custodial responsibilities. The scope of appellate review of a trial court's fact-finding function is limited; the factual findings of the trial court are binding on appeal when supported by adequate, substantial, credible evidence. * * * Here, the factual findings of the judge are fully supported by substantial, credible evidence contained in the record.

The judge's conclusion that the custodial relationship of the parties evolved over the years into one of shared physical custody, where neither parent could be considered as the primary caretaker, is fully supported by those factual findings. The record is clear that not only did Ryan physically spend approximately half of his time with each parent, the parties also equally shared those custodial responsibilities that related to Ryan's day-to-day health, education and welfare. As such, the judge's conclusion that the traditional * * * removal analysis was inapplicable, was correct.

* * *

* * * Based upon the findings of Judge Wilson, it is clear that plaintiff's application to remove Ryan from the State of New Jersey was properly rejected as an unwarranted change of custody.

NOTES AND QUESTIONS

1.   *Parental Relocation as a Substantial Change in Circumstances:* Some jurisdictions treat the relocation of a custodial parent as a substantial change of circumstances warranting reevaluation of the current custody/visitation arrangement. *See, e.g.,* MO. ANN. STAT. § 452.411; OR. STAT. § 107.159; Gietzen v. Gietzen, 575 N.W.2d 924 (N.D. 1998).

Other courts do not treat relocation as a per se basis for a best interests reexamination of the custody decree. *See, e.g.,* KAN. STAT. ANN. § 23–3222(c) (may be a change of circumstances); Hanson v. Belveal, 280 P.3d 1186 (Wyo. 2012) (finding no change of circumstances even with a travel restriction in the decree); Arnott v. Arnott, 293 P.3d 440 (Wyo. 2012) (relocation not always a change of circumstances but may be). See Theresa Glennon, *Still Partners? Examining the Consequences of Post-Dissolution Parenting,* 41 FAM. L. Q. 105 (2007) (noting that the relocation disputes are an area where the emphasis on co-parenting conflicts with the clean break and move on with one's life approach).

2.   *What Standard Must the Relocating Parent Meet to Obtain Permission to Take the Child?* Not only have numerous standards been applied to this issue, but

> [t]his area of law has been unusually unstable, with some states having undergone rather significant shifts in their standards over recent years. The clear trend has been that of increasing leniency toward the parent with whom the child has been primarily living. One reason for this trend may be the frustration some appellate courts have experienced with the restrictive way courts have applied prior law.

AM. LAW INSTITUTE, PRINCIPLES OF THE LAW OF FAMILY DISSOLUTION § 2.17 Comment d. (2002) (describing standard shifts in some states and variation across states). The most liberal approach allows the custodial parent and child to move unless the motives for moving are vindictive. *See* Aaby v. Strange, 924 S.W.2d 623 (Tenn. 1996). Other states require the relocating parent to establish that the move is in the child's best interests. *See* Pollock v. Pollock, 889 P.2d 633 (Ariz. App. 1995). Yet others have focused on whether the move will be detrimental to the child. *See In re* Marriage of Pape, 989 P.2d 1120 (Wash. 1999); Ireland v. Ireland, 717 A.2d 676 (Conn. 1998); Hayes v. Gallacher, 972 P.2d 1138 (Nev. 1999); Tropea v. Tropea, 665 N.E.2d 145 (N.Y. 1996) ("all the relevant facts and circumstances" be balanced).

Some type of best interests approach appears to be the current trend. *See* FLA. STAT. § 61.13001 (no presumption shall arise in favor or against a relocation by primary residential parent); *In re* Marriage of Ciesluk, 113 P.3d 135 (Colo. 2005); Fohey v. Knickerbocker, 130 S.W.3d 730 (Mo. App. 2004). *See* Linda D. Elrod, *A Move in the Right Direction?—Best Interests of the Child Emerging as Standard for Relocation Cases*, 3 J. CHILD CUSTODY 29 (2006) (concluding that the best interests standard has become the most popular approach). *See also* Linda D. Elrod, *National and International Momentum Builds for More Child Focus in Relocation Disputes*, 44 FAM. L. Q. 341 (2010) (discussing the proposed ABA Family Law Section Model Relocation Act and the 2010 Washington Declaration on International Family Relocation).

What are the advantages of a liberal approach to relocation? a strict approach? On balance, what approach seems best?

3. *The Right to Travel:* Protection of the custodial parent's constitutionally protected right to travel requires a standard that does not place the burden of proof on the moving custodial parent. *See, e.g.,* Jaramillo v. Jaramillo, 823 P.2d 299 (N.M. 1991). Other courts have rejected this analysis. See Baxendale v. Raich, 878 N.E.2d 1252 (Ind. 2008); *In re* Marriage of Cole, 729 P.2d 1276 (Mont. 1986) (assuring the maximum opportunities for the love, guidance and support of both natural parents, may constitute a compelling state interest worthy of reasonable interference with the right to travel interstate). Even if there is a right to travel, a court may impose reasonable travel restrictions if there is a credible risk that a parent may abduct the child or keep the child in a foreign country. Katare v. Katare, 283 P.3d 546 (Wash. 2012) . A Maine court ordered that custody would change to the father if the mother moved to Italy. Light v. D'Amato, 105 A.3d 447 (Me. 2014).

4. Does a child's newly formed preference to live with the other parent constitute a substantial change of circumstances? What about the child's maturation? A significant increase or decrease in parental income? Remarriage of one or both parents? The birth of additional children? *See* Walker v. Chatfield, 553 N.E.2d 490 (Ind. App. 1990) ("mere changes that occur as life goes on do not, standing alone, justify a modification of custody").

5. "Virtual" visitation has received some discussion in the last couple of years. *See* McCoy v. McCoy, 764 A.2d 449 (N.J. Super. App. Div. 2001); Chen v. Heller, 759 A.2d 873 (N.J. Super. App. Div. 2000) (parenting plan provided for unlimited phone calls, computer access and video imaging to maintain contact between parent and child who lived in different states). Will the ability to teleconference make it easier for custodial parents to move? *See* Kimberly R. Shefts, *Virtual Visitation: The Next Generation of Parent-Child Communication,* 36 FAM. L. Q. 303 (2002).

6. The ALI Principles provide:

The court should allow a parent who has been exercising the clear majority of custodial responsibility to relocate with the child if the parent shows that the relocation is for a valid purpose, in good faith, and to a location that is reasonable in light of the purpose.

AM. LAW INST., PRINCIPLES OF THE LAW OF FAMILY DISSOLUTION, § 2.17(4)(a)(2002). Relocation constitutes a change of circumstances only when it "significantly impairs" either parent's ability to exercise responsibilities under the parenting plan. *Id.* at § 2.17(1). Does the ALI approach represent an improvement on current statutory standards?

CHAPTER 15

PROPERTY DIVISION AT DIVORCE

■ ■ ■

*I've always been a good housekeeper. Every time
I get divorced, I keep the house.*

Zsa Zsa Gabor

1. AN OVERVIEW

In Chapter 4, we examined the common law and community property systems that govern property rights during marriage and at the death of a spouse. Now it is time to consider spousal property rights at divorce.

In an earlier era, the same rules that governed property rights during marriage generally governed property rights at divorce. A spouse in a common law state was typically entitled to that property to which he or she held title, plus a share of any assets held in joint tenancy or tenancy by the entireties. In cases where one spouse held title to most of the assets, the common law system often produced inequitable results. For example, in Wirth v. Wirth, 326 N.Y.S.2d 308 (App. Div. 1971), the husband began a "crash" savings program in 1956, telling his wife that the savings were "for the two of us" and "for our latter days." From that point on, the wife's earnings and money from a rental apartment were used to pay the household expenses; most of the husband's salary was invested. All of these investment assets were titled in the husband's name alone, as was the husband's life insurance, his retirement fund, and even the marital home, purchased in 1949 with a down payment of $6500 supplied by the husband's mother. When husband and wife divorced in 1970, all of these assets were considered the husband's property. The wife, who held title to no assets, left the marriage with nothing. The wife appealed, arguing that the husband was able to acquire property in his own name because his legal obligation to support her and their two children was fulfilled out of her earnings rather than his: "What * * * [the wife] seeks," the court noted, "is a community property division in the guise of equitable relief." But such a division was not available in a common law property state. While "[t]here may be a moral judgment that can be made on the basis of respondent's conduct and the imperfectly expressed intention of some possible future benefit to appellant," the court held, " * * * that is not enough to set the court in motion." *Id.* at 613.

Because of inequities like that in *Wirth*, none of the common law states still determine property rights at divorce on the basis of title. States have adopted different systems regarding property division at divorce, but each must respond to two questions: (1) What property is subject to division at divorce? and (2) What share of that property should each spouse receive? The property system must, in short, provide a basis both for the *definition* and *division* of the marital estate.

On the definitional issue, two basic systems have been adopted. A minority of states follow a "universal community" approach (sometimes more descriptively called a "hotchpot" or "kitchen sink" system). Under this approach, *all* property owned by either or both spouses at divorce is subject to division. *See, e.g.*, McMurry v. McMurry, 245 P.3d 316 (Wyo. 2010) (court divided equally $18 million in property titled on husband's name that derived from gifts from his father). The majority of states follow a "marital property" or "deferred community" approach, under which property is subject to division, *but only if acquired during the marriage by means other than gift, bequest, or inheritance.* This approach, as the tag "deferred community" suggests, is more or less like a community property system except that it comes into play only at the point the marriage terminates through divorce. A few states, sometimes called "hybrid" states, combine these two systems. In these states, marital property alone is subject to division unless the court finds that hardship would result; in such a case, division of separate property is also permitted. Finally, seven community property states follow a community property approach to defining property subject to division at divorce. (The other two community property states, Washington and Wisconsin, are hybrid states.) For a state-by-state summary, *see* J. THOMAS OLDHAM, DIVORCE, SEPARATION AND THE DISTRIBUTION OF PROPERTY § 3.03 (2017).

On the divisional issue, a few states—California, for example—mandate an equal division of the pool of property subject to division. One would expect all community property states to follow this approach; the central concept of community property is, after all, that each spouse is an equal owner of community assets. But some community property states, like most common law states, follow an "equitable distribution" approach, under which the judge is charged with the task of achieving a fair, rather than an equal, division of the marital estate. *See* TEX. FAM. CODE § 7.001. Finally, a few states employ a presumption of equal division, from which the judge may deviate if he or she finds (again based on a factor list) that equal division would be inequitable.

Some who generally accept a marital property system have argued that, as a marriage continues, separate property should gradually become marital. These commentators contend that, as a marriage continues, it becomes more reasonable for spouses to assume they will share all resources either has, not just accumulations during marriage due to work.

Would this be a sensible modification to the marital property system? *Compare* Carolyn J. Frantz & Hanoch Dagan, *Properties of Marriage,* 104 COLUM. L. REV. 75, 113–14 (2004) (yes) *with* J. Thomas Oldham, *Should Separate Property Gradually Become Community Property As a Marriage Continues?* 72 LA. L. REV. 127 (2011) (no). If so, after what length of marriage should separate property begin to become marital?

In a "kitchen sink" state, the court can divide all property "owned" by either spouse at divorce. In Pfannenstiehl v. Pfannenstiehl, 55 N.E.3d 933 (Mass. 2016), at the time of divorce the husband was a beneficiary of a discretionary trust created by his father. The Massachusetts Supreme Court ruled that the husband's rights under the trust were too remote and speculative to be included in the marital estate.

As you read the material that follows, it is important to keep in mind that, for a majority of divorcing couples, property division rules are of marginal relevance. The divorce rate for couples living below the poverty line is double that of the general U.S. population; half of all U.S. divorces occur when husband and wife are in their early thirties or younger. *See* Chapter 12. Because of the relative youth and low incomes of the divorce population, many couples have almost nothing to divide. Divorce surveys show that probably half of divorcing couples have a net worth of $30,000 or less. A substantial number have *negative* net worth (*i.e.*, their debts exceed their assets). *See* Marsha Garrison, *The Economic Consequences of Divorce,* 32 FAM. & CONCILIATION CTS. REV. 10 (1994) (surveying reports).

The rules detailed in this chapter govern particular types of assets—tort and disability claims, pensions, employment benefits, professional degrees and licenses, business goodwill—and the determination of what is separate and what is marital. But the typical asset pool is significantly more limited—it includes home equity (encumbered with a substantial mortgage obligation), a car (encumbered by an auto loan), household goods, and a small bank account. Less than 10% of divorcing couples own business assets. *See* LENORE J. WEITZMAN, THE DIVORCE REVOLUTION: THE UNEXPECTED SOCIAL AND ECONOMIC CONSEQUENCES FOR WOMEN AND CHILDREN IN AMERICA 63 (1985). Professional degrees and licenses are sufficiently rare that divorce surveys rarely bother to tabulate the percentage of couples possessing one. And less than half of divorcing couples divorcing in a "marital property" state possess separate property. *See* Marsha Garrison, *Good Intentions Gone Awry: The Impact of New York's Equitable Distribution Law upon Divorce Outcomes,* 57 BROOKLYN L. REV. 621, 660 (1991). Moreover, the value of individually-owned assets (whether marital or separate) is typically low. In one survey, the median value of the husband's net worth (i.e., the total value of husband's individual property minus his individual debts) was $50. *See* Garrison, *supra,* at 656 tbl. 7.

The scarcity of valuable marital assets at divorce does not, of course, mean that the rules in this chapter are unimportant. Couples with little to divide are disproportionately likely to forgo legal representation; they cannot afford it! Divorcing couples who consult family lawyers are typically wealthier and need legal representatives who are well-versed in the rules governing property distribution at divorce.

If divorcing spouses have lived in two or more states during the marriage, this presents the court with a conflict of laws issue. As was mentioned above, the property division rules in various states differ significantly. Should the court apply its law to all property owned by the parties at divorce, or should the court apply the law of the state in which the parties were living when a particular item of property was acquired? While some states have done the latter (Anderson v. Anderson, 449 A.2d 334 (D.C. App. 1982)), most courts have applied forum law to divide all property owned by the couple at divorce. *See* Dority v. Dority, 645 P.2d 56 (Utah 1982); Zeolla v. Zeolla, 908 A.2d 629 (Me. 2006); Marriage of Day, 904 P.2d 171 (Or. App. 1995); Savello v. Savello, 650 So. 2d 476 (Miss. 1995); Kirilenko v. Kirilenko, 505 S.W.3d 766 (Ky. 2016). This is true even regarding foreign nationals divorcing in the United States. *See* Ismail v. Ismail, 702 S.W.2d 216 (Tex. App. 1985).

2. DEFINING AND VALUING MARITAL PROPERTY

A. SEPARATE V. MARITAL: WHEN AND HOW WAS THE PROPERTY ACQUIRED?

In almost all marital property and hybrid states, property interests acquired by one spouse before marriage, during marriage by gift, bequest, or devise, and after termination of the marriage generally are separate property not subject to division at divorce. Courts therefore must still determine how to characterize property acquired by a spouse after the divorce action has been initiated but before a final decree has been entered.

GIHA V. GIHA
Supreme Court of Rhode Island, 1992.
609 A.2d 945.

FAY, CHIEF JUSTICE.

This matter is before the Supreme Court on appeal by the defendant, Nelly Giha (the wife), from a judgment of the Family Court dismissing her complaint for post final judgment relief. The wife urged the Family Court to vacate its final judgment of divorce, arguing that the Massachusetts State Lottery (lottery) prize acquired by the plaintiff, Nagib Giha (the husband), is a marital asset and is subject to equitable distribution. The trial justice dismissed the wife's complaint and determined that the parties' property rights were finally adjudicated upon the issuance of the interlocutory order. For the reasons discussed herein, we reverse that portion of the trial justice's decision concerning the lottery prize.

On October 7, 1987, the husband filed a complaint for divorce on the grounds of irreconcilable differences. The trial began on May 20, 1988. During a recess on the first day of trial the parties reached an agreement for the disposition of their property. Both parties testified that the husband would retain the future income from his medical practice from May 20, 1988, the date of the trial. The parties also agreed to divide equally the net proceeds from the sale of their marital assets. On May 31, 1988, the Family Court entered a decision pending entry of final judgment confirming the parties' agreement reached at trial.

On December 25, 1988, the husband learned that he had won the MEGABUCKS game. His winning lottery ticket was worth approximately $2.4 million, payable over twenty years at $120,000 per year. The husband waited until October 6, 1989, to claim his prize from the Massachusetts State Lottery Commission. He testified that he delayed claiming his prize for health reasons and because he was trying to liquidate his medical practice.

On April 27, 1989, six months prior to the husband's claiming his prize, the Family Court entered its final judgment severing the parties' marriage. The wording of the final judgment was slightly different from the interlocutory order. The final judgment stated that "[c]ommencing as of May 20, 1988, all income of Plaintiff shall be the sole property of Plaintiff."

In December 1990 the wife filed a complaint for post final judgment relief pursuant to Rule 64A of the Rules of Procedure for Domestic Relations. She argued that the husband committed fraud by failing to disclose his lottery prize to her and to the Family Court. The wife asserted that the $2.4 million lottery prize was a marital asset since the husband won the prize during their marriage and that the prize should be divided equally between the parties.

The wife argues that the trial justice erred in dismissing her complaint. She contends that the husband's lottery prize, won prior to the entry of the final judgment, is a marital asset subject to equitable distribution. The husband argues that the equitable-distribution statute contemplates assignment of only those assets that existed at the time of trial. We disagree with the husband's argument.

General Laws 1956 (1988 Reenactment) § 15–5–16.1 governs the distribution of marital assets by the Family Court. The statute is intended "to provide a fair and just assignment of the marital assets * * * on the basis of the joint contribution of the spouses to the marital enterprise." *Stanzler v. Stanzler*, 560 A.2d 342, 345 (R.I. 1989). § 15–5–16.1, with the exception of several statutory exemptions, provides for an equitable distribution of all property owned or acquired by either spouse during the marriage.

Although this court has not previously had the opportunity to address the issue presented by this case, we have established that the "parties to a divorce action remain as husband and wife until the entry of the final decree of divorce." *Alix v. Alix*, 497 A.2d 18, 20 (R.I. 1985); *see Vanni v. Vanni*, 535 A.2d 1268, 1270 (R.I. 1988); *Centazzo v. Centazzo*, 509 A.2d 995, 998 (R.I. 1986). In both *Vanni* and *Centazzo* we concluded that assets acquired by a spouse after the parties had separated or after a complaint for divorce had been filed were subject to equitable distribution. "[T]he acquisition of assets after the irremediable breakdown of a marriage or after a valid complaint for divorce is filed *or at any time before final decree for divorce is granted* will not have any effect on the applicability of the equitable-distribution statute." (Emphasis added.) *Vanni*, 535 A.2d at 1270.

In the present case the husband won the lottery prize four months before the Family Court entered its final judgment. The parties remained as husband and wife until the entry of the final judgment in 1989. The mere fact that the husband won the lottery prize after the Family Court issued an interlocutory order does not affect the applicability of the equitable-distribution statute. The interlocutory order did not sever either the matrimonial or the economic ties between the husband and the wife. Because the parties' marriage remained in effect throughout the waiting period, so did the property rights each spouse had in the property acquired by the other spouse during that period. Therefore, since the husband won the $2.4 million lottery prize during the existence of the parties' marriage, we conclude that the prize is a marital asset and is subject to the equitable-distribution statute. Because we hold that all property acquired prior to the entry of the final judgment, which property is not excluded in § 15–5–16.1, is subject to equitable distribution, we conclude that the parties to a divorce action have a continuing duty to provide information about changes in their financial condition until the entry of a final judgment of divorce.

In his decision the trial justice noted that "as of the May hearing date, all income received by Dr. Giha thereafter would be his sole property." However, at the time the husband obtained the right to the payment of the lottery prize the interlocutory order was still in effect. The interlocutory order stated that the husband retained only the future income from his medical practice. The $2.4 million lottery prize cannot be classified as income from his medical practice.

The trial justice also suggested that "public policy requires that there must be an end to litigation once the court adjudicates the [parties'] property rights * * * [t]o do otherwise would subject our [judicial] system to chaos by a continual uncertainty of judgments." We disagree with the notion that our decision in the present case will cause "continual uncertainty." Litigation ends, and the parties' property rights in marital assets become final and conclusive upon the issuance of the final judgment. When considering whether to enter a final judgment, the trial justice will determine if the parties have acquired marital assets during the statutory waiting period. If the parties have acquired such marital assets, the trial justice will decide whether to alter the alimony or the equitable assignment established by the interlocutory order. The judge will then enter a final judgment, thereby severing the matrimonial and economic ties of the spouses.

For the reasons stated herein, the wife's appeal is sustained. The judgment appealed from is reversed. For purposes of re-examination of the equitable distribution, the papers in the case are remanded to the Family Court with our decision endorsed thereon.

NOTES AND QUESTIONS

1.   Can a stream of income to be received *after* divorce be included in the marital estate? As *Giha* suggests, most courts include such income in the marital estate if the right to receive it was acquired during the marriage without an investment of separate property, the payments do not compensate the recipient spouse for lost post-divorce earning capacity, and post-divorce effort by the recipient spouse is not required to obtain the payments. Issues of apportionment may arise. For example, in Garrett v. Garrett, 683 P.2d 1166 (Ariz. App. 1983) and in McDermott v. McDermott, 986 S.W.2d 843 (Ark. 1999), the courts concluded that part of any contingency fee to be received by a lawyer spouse after divorce on cases begun during marriage was partially marital property; the marital portion was determined by dividing the time the lawyer devoted to the case during marriage by the total time expended. (The problem with this approach, of course, is that it requires knowledge of the total time eventually devoted to the case). *See also In re* Marriage of Monslow, 912 P.2d 735 (Kan. 1996) (awarding nontitled spouse a share of future income generated after divorce from a patent developed during marriage); Canisius v. Morganstern, 35 N.E.3d 385 (Mass. App. 2015) (including in the marital estate money to be generated after divorce from copyrighted work created during the marriage).

Disability insurance benefits received after divorce based on an injury during marriage present a similar classification problem. If the court views the benefits as replacing post-divorce lost wages, the post-divorce benefits will be considered the separate property of the injured spouse. *See* TEX. FAM. CODE § 3.008. If the court views the benefits as insurance proceeds made possible by payments of marital property, they will be treated as marital property. *See* Metz v. Metz, *infra.*

2.   When does the accrual of marital property cease? *Giha* again follows the majority view that marital property continues to accrue until the final divorce decree is entered. But, in some states, marital property ceases to accrue

after the date of permanent separation (CAL. FAM. CODE § 771; N.C. GEN. STAT. § 50–20; WASH. REV. CODE ANN. § 26.09.080; VA. CODE ANN. § 20–107.3) or the date of divorce filing (N.Y. DOM. REL. L. § 236B; Warner v. Warner, 859 So. 2d 146 (La. App. 2003); FLA. STAT. ANN. § 61.075). What are the advantages and disadvantages of each approach? What should the court do if the separated spouses are domiciled, at divorce, in two different states with different rules about when spouses stop acquiring marital property? *See* Seizer v. Sessions, 940 P.2d 261 (Wash. App. 1997) (the court applied the law of the forum).

If spouses stop accruing marital property when they separate, this can have a signficiant impact on the divorce property division. For example, the lottery winnings in *Giha* would not have been marital property under such a rule. North Carolina has adopted this rule. In Robbins v. Robbins, 770 S.E.2d 723 (N.C. App. 2013), the spouses bought a house during marriage. After the parties separated, the husband continued to pay homeowner's insurance premiums. When the house was damaged in a tornado before the divorce was final, the husband received $16,572 from the insurance company for the damage to the house. The appellate court ruled that the insurance proceeds were husband's separate property because the right to the proceeds arose after separation due to the payment of premiums after separation with his separate property.

In most states, spouses continue to accrue marital property until the divorce is final. In addition, a spouse in need of support can receive interim spousal support until the divorce is final. If you are representing a person with a substantially lower income than his or her spouse, how might these rules impact your desire to finalize the divorce quickly?

3.   When should the marital property be valued? In many urban areas, a contested divorce action can take years to complete. In such a situation, the choice of a date on which to value marital assets will be significant. Most states give the divorce court discretion in selecting a valuation date. *See In re Marriage of Cray*, 867 P.2d 291 (Kan. 1994) (surveying jurisdictions). In most instances, the court will choose a date fairly close to the date of the final decree. *See* MINN. STAT. ANN. § 518.58 [p. 955]; Zern v. Zern, 544 A.2d 244 (Conn. App. 1988). *See* Comment, 21 J. AM. ACAD. MAT. LAW. 747 (2008). In some states, marital property is normally valued as of the filing date if the property increased in value after the filing date due to the efforts of one of the spouses; in contrast, marital property is valued when the divorce is finalized if the property has changed in value due to market forces. This approach reflects marital partnership theory, under which the marital estate should obtain the benefit of a passive, but not an "active" (i.e., due to spousal effort) increase in the value of the marital estate during the time the divorce action is pending. *See* Mahoney-Buntzman v. Buntzman, 824 N.Y.S.2d 755 (Sup. Ct. 2006); Burch v. Burch, 717 S.E.2d 757 (S.C. 2011).

4.   Before a court can determine what is an "equitable" division of property, it must determine the value of each item. When valuing marital assets, should taxes and sale expenses be deducted from asset values? Most

courts have made such deductions in cases where a sale is imminent (*see* Oberhansly v. Oberhansly, 798 P.2d 883 (Alaska 1990); Flynn v. Flynn, 402 N.W.2d 111 (Minn. App. 1987)) and rejected them as too speculative when a sale is not contemplated. *See* Solomon v. Solomon, 857 A.2d 1109 (Md. 2004); Anzalone v. Anzalone, 835 A.2d 773 (Pa. Super. 2003); *In re* Wolters, 123 A.3d 1008 (N.H. 2015); *In re* Marriage of Perino, 587 N.E.2d 54 (Ill. App. 1992). *See generally* Comment, 21 J. AM. ACAD. MAT. LAW. 697 (2008).

5.   Even if a lottery prize is included in the marital estate in a situation like *Giha,* it doesn't mean the court will divide it equally. In *In re* Marriage of Perez, 7 N.E.3d 1009 (Ind. App. 2014), the husband won the lottery after he and his wife had been living separately for more than five years.. The divorce court awarded the wife 2.5% of the $2 million lottery prize.

6.   *Giha* considers when spouses stop accumulating marital property. The opposite issue is when spouses start acquiring marital property. In most states, this is when the marriage begins. In some states, however, courts have concluded that if property (like a house) is purchased before the marriage, but in contemplation of marriage, it can be marital. *See* Stidham v. Stidham, 136 S.W.3d 74 (Mo. App. 2004); Winer v. Winer, 575 A.2d 518 (N.J. Super. 1990).

7.   Gay couples dissolving their relationships have encountered some complex issues regarding when they began to accumulate divisible property. In *In re* Civil Union of Hamlin and Vasconcellos, 42 N.E.3d 866 (Ill. App. 2015) a lesbian couple living in Illinois had gone to Vermont in 2002 to enter into a civil union. The next year they went to Canada and married. They filed to dissolve their civil union in Illinois in 2011 shortly after Illinois enacted legislation recognizing civil unions. The court held that all property accumulated by the efforts of either after their 2002 civil union was divisible. In a similar New York case, a lesbian couple living in New York entered into a civil union in Vermont in 2003. They later married in Canada in 2006. In 2011, actions were filed in New York for divorce or dissolution of the civil union. The court ruled that it could divide only the marital estate accumulated by the parties after they married. *See* O'Reilly-Morshead v. O'Reilly-Morshead, 19 N.Y.S.3d 689 (Sup. 2015).

8.   Until 2015, some states recognized same-sex marriage and some did not. In a number of cases, parties living in states that did not recognize gay marriage traveled to a state that did, ceremonially married, and shortly thereafter returned to their state of residence. After the U.S. Supreme Court recognized the right to gay marriage in 2015, it is unclear whether such parties will be considered married (regarding, for example, when they began to accumulate marital property) beginning in 2015, or beginning when they ceremonially married.

A Texas case involved two women who had lived in a same-sex romantic relationship until one of the women was killed in a car accident in March 2015, before the U.S. Supreme Court ruled in Obergefell v. Hodges, 135 S. Ct. 2584 (2015). The surviving partner brought a wrongful death action as a surviving spouse against the negligent driver. The District Court ruled that *Obergefell* should be given retroactive effect, and the partner should be considered to have established a common-law marriage as of March, 2015. *See* Ranolls v. Dewling, 223 F.Supp. 3d 613 (E.D. Tex. 2016).

IN RE MUNSON AND BEAL

Supreme Court of New Hampshire, 2016.
169 N.H. 274, 146 A.3d 153.

HICKS, J.

The respondent, Coralee Beal, argues that the court erred by failing to consider the parties' approximately fifteen-year period of premarital cohabitation when it determined the provisions of the decree. We hold that the trial court may consider premarital cohabitation when formulating an equitable distribution of marital property. Accordingly, we vacate both the property distribution and alimony award and remand for further proceedings.

The trial court found, or the record supports, the following facts. Munson and Beal met in 1992. The following year, they began living together in Munson's home in Chester. Approximately fifteen years later, on October 8, 2008, the parties entered into a civil union, and, on January 1, 2011, their civil union converted to a marriage by operation of law. On March 28, 2012, Munson filed a petition for divorce.

At trial, Munson took the position that the parties' marriage was a short-term marriage. Beal challenged that position in her trial memorandum:

> Prior to the legalization of gay marriage, [Beal] and [Munson] did what the law allowed them to do as any other married couple to provide for the other, including, but not limited to executing estate plans that left respective estates to the other, [Munson] providing life and health insurance for her partner's benefit, having joint accounts, commingling bank and credit card accounts, sharing duties within the home and finally joining together in a civil union and legal marriage.

Beal argued that "[t]he Court must consider the parties['] lengthy twenty-one year relationship . . . when ordering [a] . . . distribution of the marital property in this matter." (Underlining and bolding omitted.)

The trial court granted the parties a divorce based upon irreconcilable differences. In its decree, the court made extensive findings of fact concerning the parties' premarital relationship; however, it determined that "the effect of the civil union between [the parties] on October 8, 2008 started their marriage and the issues in their divorce will be determined using that as the start date." It then found that the parties' marriage was "short-term" and concluded that "this is a special circumstance wherein distribution of the assets is not equal." Based upon these findings, the court ordered the distribution of approximately twelve percent of the marital estate to Beal and that Munson pay $500 per month in alimony to Beal for a term of five years.

We first address the trial court's division of the marital property. Under RSA 458:16–a, the marital estate includes "*all* tangible and intangible property and assets, real or personal, belonging to either or both parties, whether title to the property is held in the name of either or both parties." The statute does not classify property based upon when or by whom it was acquired, but rather assumes that all property is susceptible to division.

[The statute] grants the trial court the authority to equitably divide the marital estate: The statute requires the court to "presume that an equal division is an equitable distribution of property." We have interpreted the statute to require that, "[a]bsent special circumstances, the court must make the distribution as equal as possible."

However, RSA 458:16–a, II also permits the court to find "that an equal division would not be appropriate or equitable after considering one or more of" fifteen enumerated factors. The factors include "the length of the marriage, the ability of the parties to provide for their own needs, the needs of [a] custodial parent, the contribution of each party during the marriage and the value of property contributed by each party." The statute also permits the court to "consider any other factor it deems relevant in equitably distributing the parties' assets."

In discussing the length of the marriage, we have noted that "[a] marriage of only one or two years may be considered differently than a long-term marriage of ten, twenty, or thirty years." We have observed that, "[i]n a short-term marriage, it is easier to give back property brought to the marriage and still leave the parties in no worse position than they were in prior to it." However, we have explained that "[t]he duration of a marriage is but one of the factors for a court to consider when equitably dividing the parties' property," and that it may not always be equitable "to treat a short-term marriage differently from a long-term marriage." We have also emphasized the general principle that, "[i]n a divorce proceeding, marital property is not to be divided by some mechanical formula but in a manner deemed 'just' based upon the evidence presented and the equities of the case."

Here, the trial court focused its analysis almost entirely upon the duration of the parties' marriage. The court acknowledged Beal's arguments about the parties' lengthy period of premarital cohabitation, but ruled that the "issues in [the parties'] divorce will be determined using" the date when the parties entered into a civil union, October 8, 2008, "as the start date." Based upon that "start date," the court concluded that the parties' marriage was "a short-term marriage," and ordered an unequal distribution of the marital property. The court also noted that it "decline[d] [Beal's] invitation to declare the parties married upon their cohabitation in the 1990s." Thus, it appears that the court did not consider the parties' period of premarital cohabitation when it divided their marital estate.

Beal argues that the "parties' lengthy cohabitation and commingling of assets, along with all the many legal steps they took to solidify their commitment . . . compel a finding that their relationship was in effect a long-term marriage." Alternatively, she argues that, "at a minimum, the [trial] court should have applied equitable principles to consider the commingling of assets before 2008." She asserts that, by focusing "primarily on one . . . factor[ ], the length of the parties' legal marriage, . . . the [trial] court ignored the substantial and uncontroverted evidence developed at trial that the parties had a committed romantic and financial partnership long before 2008."

Munson counters that "[t]here is no need to fashion a new rule as [Beal] urges that would label periods of cohabitation as a marriage because the trial court already has the discretion to consider it." According to her, the "court weighed the parties' testimony and evidence, the statutory factors, and each parties' [sic] financial situation[ ] before constructing an equitable division of the property." She argues that, "[b]ased on the totality of the circumstances, including the parties' lengthy cohabitation, the trial court reasonably concluded that each party should keep [her] own assets and debts except for a portion . . . of . . . [Munson's] retirement accounts and pension to be transferred to [Beal]."

The parties appear to agree that, under RSA 458:16–a, II, premarital cohabitation is a permissible factor for the court to consider when dividing marital property. Their principal disagreement concerns whether the trial court erred in not doing so.

We have twice found it unnecessary to decide whether the trial court may consider premarital cohabitation under RSA 458:16–a, II. In *Hoffman v. Hoffman*, 143 N.H. 514, 727 A.2d 1003 (1999), the trial court took into account the parties' five-year cohabitation period along with their twelve-year marriage, concluded that the parties' relationship was long-term, and awarded the plaintiff, among other things, nearly half of the marital estate. We declined to decide whether the trial court erred by "tack[ing] the five-year cohabitation period onto the twelve-year marriage period" because, we concluded, "[e]ven without considering the five-year premarital relationship, the court could have regarded the [parties'] twelve-year marriage as long-term." In *In the Matter of Crowe and Crowe*, we decided against "fashion[ing] a specific rule regarding premarital cohabitation as it relates to the division of property." *In the Matter of Crowe & Crowe*, 148 N.H. at 222, 804 A.2d 455. We rejected the petitioner's argument that the trial court "erroneously subsumed the period of premarital cohabitation into the duration of the marriage and treated as marital assets property acquired during that time period," because, we observed, "RSA 458:16–a, I, makes no distinction between property brought to the marriage by the parties and that acquired during marriage; thus, all property owned by each spouse, regardless of the source, may be included in the marital estate,"

Courts in several other jurisdictions, however, have held that premarital cohabitation is a factor that the trial court may consider when dividing marital property or awarding alimony. For instance, in reviewing an alimony award under a statute containing language similar to that in RSA 458:16–a, the Court of Appeals of Oregon noted:

> Although we agree with husband that the statute plainly refers to "duration of the marriage" as one factor that the court may consider in determining an award of spousal maintenance, we note that the statute's final subsection gives the court broad discretion to consider other factors that "the court deems just and equitable."

Lind and Lind, 207 Or. App. 56, 139 P.3d 1032, 1040 (2006). The court could "see no reason why that discretion necessarily excludes considering the length of the parties' premarital cohabitation." Moreover, addressing a factual scenario that was similar to the one in this case, the Court of Appeals of Michigan rejected the defendant's argument "that he and [the] plaintiff had a short-term marriage," and held that the trial court did not err in its consideration of "all of the factors which [were] relevant to the equitable division of the parties' property," including a fifteen-year period of premarital cohabitation. *Nielsen v. Nielsen*, 179 Mich. App. 698, 446 N.W.2d 356, 357 (1989). Several other courts have reached similar conclusions. *See, e.g., Chen v. Hoeflinger*, 279 P.3d 11, 25 (Haw. Ct. App. 2012) ("In this case, it does not contravene a just and equitable division of property to consider the parties' premarital cohabitation, even though one of the parties might have been legally married to someone else at that time."); *Bertholet v. Bertholet*, 725 N.E.2d 487, 495 (Ind. Ct. App.2000) ("[A] trial court may consider periods of cohabitation followed by marriage in determining a proper distribution of the marital estate." (quotation omitted)); *In re Marriage of Clark*, 316 Mont. 327, 71 P.3d 1228, 1231 (2003) ("[I]t would be inequitable to disregard [the parties'] premarital cohabitation when considering [the wife's] contributions to the marital estate.").

We have identified only one court—the Connecticut Supreme Court—that has declined to permit the trial court to consider premarital cohabitation. In *Loughlin v. Loughlin*, 280 Conn. 632, 910 A.2d 963 (2006), the court concluded that "consideration of a period of cohabitation that precedes a marriage as part of the statutory factor of 'length of the marriage' in a dissolution action is improper" because Connecticut "draw[s] a clear distinction between marriage and cohabitation, and . . . award[s] greater rights and protections to persons who make the formal legal commitment of marriage." However, the court acknowledged that "events that occur during a period of cohabitation" may "indirectly bear[ ] on <u>other</u> statutory criteria, such as the health, station, occupation, amount and sources of income, vocational skills . . . [and] employability."

The *Loughlin* court was interpreting a statutory provision similar to RSA 458:16–a, II(a). Consistent with *Loughlin*'s reasoning, we conclude that the "duration of the marriage," RSA 458:16–a, II(a), plainly refers to the period during which the parties were married, which, as a matter of law, does not include premarital cohabitation. Accordingly, we reject Beal's assertion that the "parties' lengthy cohabitation and commingling of assets . . . compel a finding that their relationship was in effect a long-term marriage."

However, we note that, like the statute analyzed in *Lind*, RSA 458:16, II permits the trial court to consider, apart from the enumerated factors, "[a]ny other factor that [it] deems relevant." And, as both the *Lind* and *Loughlin* courts recognized, premarital cohabitation may be relevant to the distribution of marital property. For instance, a couple living together may commingle their finances or jointly acquire property in anticipation of marriage. Their marriage may not occur for several years, and after it occurs, it may be short in duration. Still, the couple may have become dependent upon the assets that they shared prior to marriage, such that it may not be just for a court in divorce proceedings to ignore their cohabitation period when determining what constitutes an equitable property division. As the *amici* explain, when a divorcing couple's relationship has included "years of economically interdependent cohabitation followed by a 'short' marriage, the notion of returning the parties to their original pre-marital position is unrealistic" because "the relationship was not, in any relevant way, short-term."

Thus, we see no reason why RSA 458:16–a, II(*o*), which broadly permits the trial court to consider "[a]ny other factor that [it] deems relevant," would not permit the court to consider premarital cohabitation. We therefore hold that premarital cohabitation is a factor that the court may consider in divorce proceedings when determining whether to depart from the presumption that "an equal division is an equitable distribution of property."

Here, the trial court found that, prior to entering into a civil union, the parties had lived together since 1993; "shared a joint account into which most of [their] funds were deposited and out of which the bills were paid"; "obtained personal property, decorated the home and acquired additional debt"; and filed with Munson's employer two "Affidavit[s] of Life Partnership . . . to establish their rights as a couple"; among other things. However, the court apparently ignored these findings when it decided to depart from the statutory presumption, which suggests that it believed that it had no discretion to consider them. Although, until now, we have not expressly held that premarital cohabitation may be considered a factor under RSA 458:16–a, II, we conclude that, by not taking these findings into account, the court did not exercise the full breadth of its discretion under the statute.

The "[f]ailure to exercise discretion constitutes an [unsustainable exercise] of discretion." *DeButts v. LaRoche*, 142 N.H. 845, 847, 711 A.2d 877 (1998); *see State v. Lambert*, 147 N.H. 295, 296, 787 A.2d 175 (2001) (explaining "unsustainable exercise of discretion"). Having concluded that the court has the discretion to consider premarital cohabitation under RSA 458:16–a, II, we hold that the court's failure to do so in this case rendered its division of the parties' marital property unsustainable. Accordingly, we vacate that portion of the court's decree.

We now turn to the court's alimony award. RSA 458:19 grants the trial court the authority to "make orders for the payment of alimony to the party in need of alimony, either temporary or permanent, for a definite or indefinite period of time." When "determining the amount of alimony," the court must consider *all* of the factors that the statute enumerates. RSA 458:19, IV(b); *see In the Matter of Crowe & Crowe*, 148 N.H. at 225, 804 A.2d 455 (listing the statutory factors that the trial court *"must* consider." One of those factors is "the property awarded under RSA 458:16–a." We conclude that the court's division of the marital property under RSA 458:16–a was unsustainable; thus, the court could not have adequately considered it in determining the amount of alimony under RSA 458:19, IV(b). We therefore vacate the court's alimony award.

We remand for further proceedings consistent with this opinion.

SHEA V. SHEA
California Court of Appeals, 1980.
111 Cal. App. 3d 713, 169 Cal. Rptr. 490.

BROWN, PRESIDING JUSTICE.

Thomas M. Shea appeals an interlocutory judgment dissolving his marriage to Sandra E. Shea. The appeal concerns only the trial court's finding Thomas' veteran's education benefits received during marriage were community property, and the court's method of computing the community interest in the parties' residence.

Thomas served in the United States Navy from January 1969 to January 1973. In May 1973 he began receiving veteran's education benefits

(38 U.S.C. § 1651 *et seq.*) which continued with a few interruptions during the summer months when he was not in school, until December 1978. In June 1974, he bought a house, taking title in his own name. He made a down payment of $3,000, paid almost $1,500 in "points" and closing costs, and obtained a loan for the balance of the purchase price. He then began making monthly payments on the loan. Each installment included interest, taxes and insurance, as well as reduction of the loan principal. Sandra and Thomas were married November 27, 1974, and separated May 17, 1979.

At trial Thomas contended the veteran's benefits were his separate property and he sought to introduce evidence showing he had used these funds for most of the house payments made during the marriage. The trial court found the benefits received during marriage were community property and calculated the community interest in the house accordingly. The court did not permit Thomas to offer evidence showing the source of money used for house payments during the marriage.

Where one spouse has served in the armed forces before marriage, are veteran's education benefits received during marriage community property?

Congress has enacted a comprehensive program of veteran's education benefits to make service in the armed forces more attractive to prospective recruits and to make educational opportunities available to veterans who otherwise would not be able to afford them, or whose educations have been interrupted by military service (38 U.S.C. § 1651). To receive the benefits, a veteran must meet eligibility requirements, including a minimum of 180 days of service (§ 1652); a veteran must have served at least 18 months on active duty to be eligible to receive benefits for the maximum period of 45 months (§ 1661(a)). A veteran must apply for the benefits, but the Veterans Administration "shall" approve the application unless the veteran or his planned course of study is ineligible (§ 1671). Benefits are payable only while the veteran is enrolled and making satisfactory progress in an approved educational program (§§ 1674, 1683, 1772). The benefits are "an educational subsistence allowance to meet, in part, the expenses of the veteran's subsistence, tuition, fees, supplies, books, equipment, and other education costs" (§ 1681), but the statute does not expressly limit the purposes for which the veteran may use the funds. A veteran with dependents receives an increased allowance, based on the number of dependents (§ 1682).

The veteran's educational allowances provided by this statutory scheme are a form of employee benefits, similar in nature to the wide variety of fringe benefits—for example, employer-paid life insurance, tuition reimbursement programs, and pensions—furnished by public and private employers. Like other types of employee benefits, the veteran's education allowance is designed to attract prospective employees, and entitlement to these benefits can be attained only by service with the employer. Consequently, the general principles governing characterization of fringe benefits flowing from the employment relationship determine whether veteran's education benefits are community property.

Under the community property system, each spouse's time, skill, and labor are community assets, and whatever each spouse earns from them during marriage is community property. Fringe benefits are not a gift from the employer but are earned by the employee as part of the compensation for his services. Accordingly, fringe benefits are community property to the extent they are earned by employment during marriage. Conversely, where a fringe benefit is earned by employment before marriage, it is the separate property of the employee even if received after marriage.

Here Thomas' military service occurred entirely before marriage, and his veteran's education benefits are his separate property unless the parties expressly or impliedly agreed these funds would be community property. Since the record contains no evidence of such an agreement, the trial court's finding the benefits community property is not supported by the evidence.

The judgment is reversed.

NOTES AND QUESTIONS

1.   A person sometimes receives a payment or benefit at a different time from when the services are rendered that earned the right to receive the payment or benefit. Pensions are common examples of this. In marital property states, a payment or benefit is marital to the extent that the right was earned as a result of services rendered during the marriage.

2.   In a New Jersey case, the parties cohabitated for eight years before they married. The female gave birth to and raised their child for seven years before they married, while the man devoted himself to a very demanding job. His employer made a written commitment to him before the marriage that the man would receive a substantial bonus if the company was ever sold to a third party. The female did not work outside the home after she became pregnant. Fourteen months after the parties married the man filed for divorce. Three months after they divorced, the husband's employer sold the company and paid the husband a bonus of $2,250,000. The wife sued to obtain half of this bonus. The trial court concluded that the husband had earned this bonus from all his time he worked at the company, and allocated it as additional monthly compensation of $14,453 for every month he worked. Because the parties were married for 14 months, the court held that $201,923 constituted marital property and awarded the wife $109,961. The New Jersey Supreme Court affirmed the ruling that compensation earned during premarriage cohabitation could not be divided in a New Jersey divorce, but ruled that the wife should obtain a larger share of the bonus in this case based on the principle of unjust enrichment. The court remanded the case to the trial court

to determine what portion of the bonus should be awarded the wife to avoid unjust enrichment. *See* Thieme v. Aucoin-Thieme, 151 A.3d 545 (N.J. 2016).

Problem 15-1:

You are employed as a law clerk to an appellate judge. The judge instructs you to write a memorandum regarding a matter recently appealed to the court. In this case, the parties had divorced and resolved all financial claims that they were aware of at the time. After the divorce, however, the U.S. government awarded the former husband a "fishing quota." This quota was a valuable right, and the size of the huband's quota was determined based on his fishing activity conducted while the parties were married. The former wife has sued the husband to obtain 50% of the value of the quota. What arguments could the wife make that the quota is marital property? Should she prevail? *See* McGee v. McGee, 974 P.2d 983 (Alaska 1999).

O'NEILL V. O'NEILL

Kentucky Court of Appeals, 1980.
600 S.W.2d 493.

HOGGE, JUSTICE.

The marriage of Richard and Susan O'Neill has been dissolved. Dr. O'Neill appeals from a portion of the decree of the Fayette circuit court dividing the marital property which he and his former wife acquired during their marriage. Dr. O'Neill contends that the trial court erred by excluding from the marital property certain items which Mrs. O'Neill describes as gifts from Dr. O'Neill.

The issue in this case is whether the trial court erred by failing to consider as marital property certain jewelry and other items of personal property which Dr. O'Neill presented to Mrs. O'Neill on her birthday, at Christmas and other occasions. The items were purchased out of Dr. O'Neill's salary, and included a ring with an appraised value of $35,000.00 and other jewelry with an appraised value of $15,900.00. The circuit court held that these items were gifts to Mrs. O'Neill and should not be included in the marital property.

This issue involves the interpretation of KRS 403.190, which excludes from marital property items acquired by gift.

Under the statute, we start with the premise that all property acquired by either spouse subsequent to marriage is marital property. Without reading the statute further, there is no doubt that the property transferred to Mrs. O'Neill was marital property as it was acquired by her subsequent to marriage. Then the statute excepts from marital property that which is acquired by "gift." The issue, at this point, is whether this property given to Mrs. O'Neill by Dr. O'Neill were "gifts" within the meaning of the statute as intended by the legislature.

In determining this issue, the court's decision would necessarily have to be based on the pertinent facts of each case. In each case, consideration should be given to the source of the money with which the "gift" was purchased, the intent of the donor at that time as to intended use of the property, status of the marriage relationship at the time of the transfer, and whether there was any valid agreement that the transferred property was to be excluded from the marital property.

Further, we note that Dr. O'Neill testified that the jewelry and certain other items were purchased as an investment. He hoped that the purchases would appreciate in value, and that they could be converted into cash in the event money was needed for the children's education. This is evidence of probative value that he intended that the transfer of possession of this property would not divest him of this marital property and that, if necessary, the property could be reconverted into cash, at a future time, at an appreciated price, for a purpose of mutual benefit to the parties, the education of their children. Further, we find no evidence at all that there was any agreement that the property so transferred herein was to be excluded or be treated as the separate property of Mrs. O'Neill. Under these circumstances, we hold that these transfers were not a gift within the meaning of the statute and that the trial court erred in so determining.

As to the "gifts" the judgment of the circuit court is reversed and remanded for further proceedings consistent with this opinion.

NOTES AND QUESTIONS

1.   The categorization of spousal gifts varies. In some states (like Kentucky), marital property can become separate if one spouse makes a gift to the other; therefore categorization depends on whether a gift occurred. In others, spousal gifts are always categorized as marital property. *See, e.g.*, N.Y. DOM. REL. L. § 236B(1)(d)(1). In California, a spousal gift does not become the separate property of the recipient if it is "substantial in value" in light of the circumstances of the parties. *See* CAL. FAM. CODE § 852. In South Carolina, items received as spousal gifts remain marital property. *See* McMillan v. McMillan, 790 S.E.2d 2016 (S.C. App. 2016). Why might a state decide to treat spousal gifts differently from a gift from a third party?

2.   In addition to issues relating to gifts between spouses, gifts from other family members can present classification issues at divorce. If a parent makes a gift during marriage, it can be significant whether the gift is to one spouse or both spouses. In addition, sometimes a parent will claim that an advance of money during marriage was a loan and not a gift. How should a court resolve such a claim? *See* Barrow v. Barrow, 716 S.E.2d 302 (S.C. App. 2011) (finding it relevant that the alleged loan was never documented).

3.   In most marital property states, an amount inherited by a spouse during marriage is that spouse's separate property. In Strauss v. Strauss, 27 A.3d 233 (Pa. Super. 2011) the court held that an amount received during marriage by the husband in settlement of a will contest relating to his father's estate was separate property.

B. SEPARATE V. MARITAL: APPORTIONMENT OF APPRECIATION, COMMINGLING, TRACING, AND TRANSMUTATION

In a marital property state, a spouse contending that certain property is his or her "separate" property must prove that it was acquired before marriage or received during marriage by gift or inheritance, and also must show that this property still exists and is identifiable at the time of divorce. Separate property may become marital property in a few ways. If, for example, one spouse receives a gift of money during marriage from a parent and deposits it into a bank account where she also deposits her earnings, the gift will likely become hopelessly mixed, or "commingled" with marital assets and, as a result, all the account will be treated as marital property. For discussions of commingling, see Carol Bruch, *The Definition and Division of Marital Property in California: Towards Parity and Simplicity*, 33 HASTINGS L. J. 769, 782 (1982); J. Thomas Oldham, *Tracing, Commingling and Transmutation*, 23 FAM. L.Q. 219 (1989).

Separate property may be used to buy something else during marriage. That newly purchased item is separate property if the spouse can show he used separate property to buy it. See Crawford v. Crawford, 358 S.W.3d 16 (Ky. App. 2011).

A spouse may change separate property into marital property or the other party's separate property by agreement or the spouse's action. One common example of this arises when a spouse receives a gift during marriage and deposits the funds in a joint account, or buys property with the gift and takes title jointly with the other spouse. By doing this, in many states a presumption will arise that the owner intended to make a gift to the marital estate and the funds will be "transmuted" from separate to marital property. See Chotiner v. Chotiner, 829 P.2d 829 (Alaska 1992); Robertson v. Robertson, 593 So. 2d 491 (Fla. 1991); Verrilli v. Verrilli, 568 N.Y.S.2d 495 (App. Div. 1991).

This presumption of gift can be rebutted. For example, in Douglas v. Douglas, 2016 WL 4198434 (Tenn. App. 2016) the wife successfully argued that, when she deposited inherited funds into a joint bank account with her husband, this was done solely for estate planning purposes.

In addition to transmutation of separate property due to joint title or joint accounts, in some states property is considered transmuted into marital property if the parties used it during the marriage. *See* Harris v. Harris, 59 So. 3d 731 (Ala. App. 2010).

BROWN V. BROWN

Supreme Court of New York, Appellate Division, 1994.
203 A.D.2d 912, 611 N.Y.S.2d 65.

Before DENMAN, P.M., and BALIO, LAWTON, DOERR and DAVIS, J.J.

* * *

Supreme Court erred in awarding plaintiff 25% of the appreciation in defendant's Investment Management Account at Chase Lincoln First Bank. The account was defendant's separate property and the appreciation in the account during the marriage was not due to defendant's efforts but, rather, was due to the bank's management of the account, market forces, and the 1984 deposit of an inheritance from defendant's father. Consequently, plaintiff has no claim to a share of the appreciation. We modify the judgment, therefore, to reduce plaintiff's distributive award from $96,989.50 to $47,039.50 and otherwise affirm.

COCKRILL V. COCKRILL

Supreme Court of Arizona, 1979.
124 Ariz. 50, 601 P.2d 1334.

GORDON, JUSTICE.

Appellant, Robert Cockrill, and Rose Cockrill, appellee, were married on June 15, 1974. At the time of the marriage, appellant owned, as his separate property, a farming operation known as Cockrill Farms. There seems to be no dispute that the net worth increase of the farm, during the two year and ten month marriage, after some credits, was $79,000. The trial court found that this increase was attributable primarily to the efforts of Mr. Cockrill and was, therefore, community property. Appellant contends that the net worth increase was primarily due to the inherent nature of his separate property, the farm, and was, therefore, also his separate property.

The profits of separate property are either community or separate in accordance with whether they are the result of the individual toil of a spouse or the inherent qualities of the business itself.

Seldom will the profits or increase in value of separate property during marriage be exclusively the product of the community's effort or exclusively the product of the inherent nature of the separate property. Instead, as in the instant case, there will be evidence that both factors have contributed to the increased value or profits. In Arizona, these "hybrid profits" have been governed by what can be labeled the "all or none rule." Pursuant to this rule, the profits or increase in value will be either all community property or all separate property depending on whether the increase is primarily due to the toil of the community or primarily the result of the inherent nature of the separate property.

This Court has also become disenchanted with the all or none rule. To implement the all or none rule and determine the primary source of the profits, the portion of the profits that resulted from each source must be calculated. Once this has been done, it is only logical to apportion the profits, or increased value, accordingly. To do otherwise will either deprive the property owner of a reasonable return on the investment or will deprive the community of just compensation for its labor.

We, therefore, also depart from the all or none rule and hold that profits, which result from a combination of separate property and community labor, must be apportioned accordingly.

There are several approaches to the problem of apportionment: "In making such apportionment between separate and community property our courts have developed no precise criterion or fixed standard, but have endeavored to adopt a yardstick which is most appropriate and equitable in a particular situation." *Beam v. Bank of America*, 6 Cal. 3d 12, 18 (1971).

In the case of real estate, the owner of the real property can be awarded its rental value, with the community being entitled to the balance of the income produced from the lands by the labor, skill and management of the parties. Another approach is to determine the reasonable value of the community's services and allocate that amount to the community, and treat the balance as separate property attributable to the inherent nature of the separate estate. *Van Camp v. Van Camp*, 53 Cal. App. 17, 199 P. 885 (1921). Finally, the trial court may simply allocate to the separate property a reasonable rate of return on the original capital investment. Any increase above this amount is community property. *Pereira v. Pereira*, 156 Cal. 1, 103 P. 488 (1909).

All of these approaches have merit, with different circumstances, requiring the application of a different method of apportionment. We, therefore, hold that the trial court is not bound by any one method, but may select whichever will achieve substantial justice between the parties.

The judgment of the Superior Court is reversed and the case remanded for the trial court to apportion the profits or increase in value of appellant's separate property between separate and community property.

NOTES AND QUESTIONS

1. Although there are a few exceptions (*see, e.g.*, COLO. REV. STAT. § 14–10–113), most marital property and hybrid states provide, as in *Brown,* that any increase in the value of separate property during marriage due solely to market forces is separate property. *See* Langschmidt v. Langschmidt, 81

S.W.3d 741 (Tenn. 2002). This follows from the "marital economic partnership" concept that the spouses should share only those assets that result from the efforts of either spouse.

2.   In most states, an increase in the value of separate property due to spousal efforts will be categorized as marital. *See* Robertson v. Robertson, 78 So. 3d 76 (Fla. Dist. Ct. App. 2012). All community property states employ one of the two valuation approaches described in *Cockrill*. Under the *Pereira* approach, the value of the community's interest in the separate asset is computed by adding a "reasonable" annual rate of return to the value of the separate asset at the beginning of the marriage; this sum is subtracted from the value of the asset at dissolution to determine the amount of the community property claim. Under the *Van Camp* approach, the value of community property interest is determined by computing the reasonable value of the owner-spouse's services to the business during marriage; any salary actually received by the spouse during marriage from the business is deducted from this amount. *See generally* J. Thomas Oldham, *Separate Property Businesses That Increase in Value During Marriage*, 1990 WIS. L. REV. 585. Under either approach, the value of the title-holding spouse's separate property expended for community living expenses is offset against any community claim. *See* Beam v. Bank of America, 490 P.2d 257 (Cal. 1971).

3.   The distinction drawn in *Cockrill* between enhanced value resulting from "individual toil" and that due to "the inherent qualities of the business" is more typically characterized as "active" vs. "passive" appreciation. Under this widely-utilized approach, an increase in the value of separate property due to the effort of a spouse or the expenditure of marital funds creates marital property, while increased value resulting from inflation, market forces, or other factors outside the control of the spouses remains separate.

4.   In a number of states, spousal effort invested in a separate business will not create marital property unless that effort is substantial. *See* Vallone v. Vallone, 644 S.W.2d 455 (Tex. 1982); *In re* Marriage of Tatham, 527 N.E.2d 1351 (Ill. App. 1988); *In re* Marriage of Boehlje, 443 N.W.2d 81 (Iowa App. 1989). In Florida, courts have ruled that there can be active appreciation of a separate property business interest only if the spouse has a significant management role. *See* Witt-Bahls v. Bahls, 193 So. 3d 35 (Fla. Dist. Ct. App. 2016). Why would courts adopt a rule that only substantial effort contributed to separate property creates a marital claim?

5.   Perhaps because they have had less experience in apportioning separate and marital property, common law states are more variable (and, to be blunt, confused) in their treatment of the *Cockrill* problem. Some ostensibly require effort by the spouse who is *not* the owner of the separate business to create marital property. *See* N.Y. DOM. REL. L. § 236B; S.C. CODE ANN. § 20–7–473. This position is, of course, inconsistent with the partnership theory (that all fruits of marital effort belong to the marriage) that underlies the marital property concept. Such inconsistency may explain the New York Court of Appeal's decision in Price v. Price, 503 N.E.2d 684 (N.Y. 1986), holding that

homemaking services by a non-owner spouse are sufficient to establish a marital claim to business assets that are the separate property of the other spouse; if taken literally, the *Price* directive would mean that the marital estate might have a claim to a separately held business when the owner-spouse had expended no effort in the business whatsoever. *See also* Zelnik v. Zelnik, 573 N.Y.S.2d 261 (App. Div. 1991) (holding that, where any of the increase in value stems from the nonowner spouse's efforts, all of the increase in value during marriage is marital property). For a general discussion of apportionment problems, *see* Mary M. Wenig, *Increase in Value of Separate Property During Marriage: Examination and Proposals*, 23 FAM. L. Q. 301 (1989); Suzanne Reynolds, *Increases in Separate Property and the Evolving Marital Partnership*, 24 WAKE FOREST L. REV. 239 (1989).

6. This issue of active appreciation of separate property can arise if a spouse devotes substantial time during marriage to managing stock investments. *See* David v. David, 767 S.E.2d 241 (Va. App. 2015).

7. Marital property and hybrid states have reached conflicting conclusions on the categorization of *income* from separate property generated during marriage. Because marital property represents the fruits of marital effort and income from a nonbusiness asset is typically determined by market forces, the majority of states have concluded that income from separate property remains separate. *See* Thomas Andrews, *Income from Separate Property: Towards a Theoretical Foundation,* 1993 L. & CONTEMP. PROB. 171. But the decision to invest in a savings account or stocks, gold, commodities futures, or oil wells may involve spousal effort. Perhaps for this reason, a minority of states have concluded that income from separate property received during marriage should be categorized as marital property. *See id.* In these states, an interest-bearing account containing premarital savings may, over time, become a commingled asset. *See, e.g.,* W. VA. CODE § 48–2–1. When determining the character of income generated in a separate property investment account, a North Carolina appellate court has suggested a hybrid approach, holding that the characterization of income from a separate-property investment account should take into account: (i) whether investment decisions were made exclusively by the parties, in consultation with a broker, or exclusively by a broker; (ii) the frequency with which the parties made investment decisions consistent with a broker's recommendations; and (iii) whether the parties conducted their own investment research. *See* O'Brien v. O'Brien, 508 S.E.2d 300 (N.C. App. 1998). Under *O'Brien,* what should be the result if a spouse sometimes, but not always, follows her broker's recommendation? On balance, is the *O'Brien* approach preferable to a black-letter rule on income? If not, which black-letter rule is preferable?

It is not always clear whether something should be classified as income from separate property. In a Minnesota case, the wife was a member of a certain Native American tribe, and therefore was entitled to substantial payments of profits from the casino operations conducted by the tribe. At divorce, how should any monies saved from such payments during marriage be classified? *See* Zander v. Zander, 720 N.W.2d 360 (Minn. App. 2006) (income from separate property). If, during marriage, a spouse's parents create a trust, and the spouse is given the right to receive all income generated from the corpus until he dies, how should these distributions be classified? *See* Marriage of Guinn, 93 P.3d 568 (Colo. App. 2004) (not income from separate property).

8.   In Mayhew v. Mayhew, 519 S.E.2d 188 (W. Va. 1999), the husband received, during marriage, a gift of stock in a family business. The stock was worth $113,000 when given to the husband and $457,000 when the divorce action was filed. The husband worked full-time in the business and, after the gift, owned a controlling share of the stock. The trial court held that $29,600 in unpaid stock dividends and $147,000 in unpaid salary were marital property but discounted these values to take account of taxes that would have been due had the dividends and salary been paid. The Supreme Court upheld the trial court's decision on asset characterization but reversed on discounting; finding the full value of the unpaid income was marital property. Was the Supreme Court's decision on discounting sound?

In a decision consistent with *Price* (note 5), the Supreme Court also found that the *Mayhew* trial court had erred in ignoring the wife's homemaking and community service. Based on expert testimony that the wife's activities increased the value of the business by $90,000, the Court held that the wife's efforts created $90,000 of marital property. Thus, of the $334,000 appreciation in value occurring during the marriage, the Court concluded that $266,600— $29,600 (unpaid dividends), $147,000 (unpaid salary), and $90,000 (value created by wife's efforts) were marital property.

Evaluate the *Mayhew-Price* approach to homemaker services: On what basis might the wife's expert have concluded that her homemaking and community activities created $90,000 worth of marital property? (The *Mayhew* court does not explain the expert's methodology.) Assume that Mr. Mayhew engaged in homemaking and community activities instead of his wife; which, if any, methodologies would also permit characterizing his activities as a source of marital property? If Mr. Mayhew's homemaking and community activities cannot be characterized as a source of marital property, is it fair to treat Mrs. Mayhew's activities as a source of marital property? Does the *Mayhew-Price* approach unfairly advantage homemakers whose spouses own businesses over those whose spouses own more conventional assets like stocks and bonds? On balance, is this a fair and useful approach?

C. ACQUISITIONS OVER TIME

BRANDENBURG V. BRANDENBURG
Kentucky Court of Appeals, 1981.
617 S.W.2d 871.

[The parties here dispute how to calculate the marital claim when a spouse purchases realty before marriage with borrowed money and continues to make payments during marriage with marital funds.]

GANT, JUDGE.

The guidelines for apportionment between marital and nonmarital property were issued in *Newman v. Newman*, Ky., 597 S.W.2d 137 (1980). The court therein approved the formula utilized by the lower court, saying that the interests of the parties were "the same percentages as their respective contributions to the total equity in the property." In other words, there is to be established a relationship between the nonmarital contribution and the total contribution, and between the marital contribution and the total contribution. These relationships, reduced to percentages, shall be multiplied by the equity in the property at the time of distribution to establish the value of the nonmarital and marital properties.

With this basis established, we provide the following definitions:

Nonmarital contribution (nmc) is defined as the equity in the property at the time of marriage, plus any amount expended after marriage by either spouse from traceable nonmarital funds in the reduction of mortgage principal, and/or the value of improvements made to the property from such nonmarital funds.

Marital contribution (mc) is defined as the amount expended after marriage from other than nonmarital funds in the reduction of mortgage principal, plus the value of all improvements made to the property after marriage from other than nonmarital funds.

Total contribution (tc) is defined as the sum of nonmarital and marital contributions.

Equity (e) is defined as the equity in the property at the time of distribution. This may be either at the date of the decree of dissolution, or, if the property has been sold prior thereto and the proceeds may be properly traced, then the date of the sale shall be the time at which the equity is computed.

[Ed. Note: For the mathematically challenged, equity at the time of marriage can be computed by subtracting the principal balance due on any secured loans (such as a mortgage) from the value of the property at the time of the marriage; equity at the divorce valuation date is computed by subtracting the principal balance due on any secured loans from the value of the property on the valuation date.]

The formula to be utilized is:

nmc/tc x e = nonmarital property

mc/tc x e = marital property

The contribution of either spouse of other than marital or nonmarital funds shall not be considered in the increase of equity of the property, and any dicta or other language to the contrary in *Robinson v. Robinson*, 569

S.W.2d 178 (Ky. App. 1978), is specifically overruled. For example, the contribution of one spouse as homemaker, etc., shall be considered only in affixing the percentage of the marital property to be assigned to that spouse.

Ilhardt Property

This property was purchased by the husband for $15,900 on December 16, 1968, $900 being the down payment and the husband executing a mortgage of $15,000. Prior to marriage, the husband reduced the mortgage principle by $352.80, the court below finding the value of the property at marriage to be $15,900 and the nonmarital equity to be $1,252.80. After marriage and before sale on July 18, 1975, the mortgage principal was further reduced by $1,176.00. This sum was realized from rents on this property, which rents are marital funds under *Brunson v. Brunson*, Ky. App., 569 S.W.2d 173 (1978). The sale price was $32,500, which was applied in the following manner: $13,471.20 was applied to extinguish the mortgage on this property, leaving a balance of $19,028.80. Of the latter sum, $13,800 was applied on the husband's mortgage on the Wilmore property, extinguishing that mortgage; $963,43 was applied on the husband's mortgage on the Glen Cove property; $3,717 was paid on a joint mortgage on property with which we are not concerned; and the balance was put by the husband in his lock box.

Applying the formula, we find:

nmc = $1,252.80 (the equity at marriage)

mc = $1,175.00 (mortgage principal reduction during marriage)

tc = $2,428.80

e = $19.028.80

1,252.80/2,428.80 = 51.6% x 19,028.80 = 9,815.25–Value of nonmarital property

1,175.00/2,428.80 = 48.4% x 19,028.80 = 9,213.55–Value of marital property

NOTES AND QUESTIONS

1.   Valuable assets, such as cars and houses, are typically purchased with borrowed money. Most states follow the *Brandenburg* approach, under which installment payments on a separate asset made with marital funds will create a fractional marital property interest in the separate asset. In a minority of states, installment payments made with marital funds create only a marital lien against the separate asset; at divorce, marital funds must be repaid, without interest, by the title-holding spouse. For a general discussion of approaches used in different states, *see* J. THOMAS OLDHAM, DIVORCE, SEPARATION AND THE DISTRIBUTION OF PROPERTY § 7.05 (2017). What are the

pros and cons of each approach? Which is more consistent with the partnership theory that underlies the marital property concept? In an age of inflation, which approach is most likely to enhance the marital estate?

2. Under the *Brandenburg* approach, equity derived from payment of indebtedness is not distinguished from equity derived from inflationary appreciation, nor is premarital appreciation distinguished from marital appreciation. The result is that marital equity, as defined by the formula, may bear little relation to the value of marital contributions; during a period of high inflation, the approach will probably yield a marital equity figure that exceeds the value of marital contributions. What other valuation methods are available? What are the pros and cons of each?

3. Should a court employ the *Brandenburg* approach when a couple uses separate property to make a down payment on a home purchased jointly during the marriage? If yes, should the marital contribution be valued based on total mortgage indebtedness or equity acquired through reduction of the mortgage principal with marital funds? What arguments support each approach? *See* Smith v. Smith, 503 S.W.3d 178 (Ky. App. 2016); Keeling v. Keeling, 624 S.E.2d 687 (Va. App. 2006).

D. INSURANCE PROCEEDS AND TORT CLAIMS

TRAHAN V. TRAHAN
Louisiana Court of Appeals, 1980.
387 So. 2d 35.

CUTRER, JUSTICE.

[In this action, the trial court characterized proceeds paid during marriage under a homeowner's insurance policy as H's separate property. W appeals.]

The residence in which [H and W] lived was owned by John Trahan before his marriage to Betty Trahan. It was clearly his separate property.

During the marriage a homeowner's insurance policy covering the residence was purchased in the name of John Trahan. Three or four months later, the home burned and John Trahan received $46,560.00 in insurance proceeds. We conclude that the proceeds from the fire insurance policy were the separate property of John Trahan. The object of the insurance policy was the residence belonging to the separate estate of John Trahan. When that residence burned, the estate, consisting of the residence, was transformed into the insurance proceeds.

We base our conclusion on the case of *Thigpen v. Thigpen*, 91 So. 2d 12 (La. 1956), in which our Supreme Court faced a similar situation. In that case, the parties, Mr. and Mrs. Thigpen, had a number of disputes regarding their community property settlement which was being settled as a result of a divorce proceeding.

During the existence of a previous marriage, Mr. Thigpen and his wife purchased several buildings. Sometime later, the first wife died and the property then became jointly owned by the deceased wife's heirs and Mr. Thigpen. Later, Mr. Thigpen remarried. Clearly the interest in the property purchased during the existence of his first marriage was separate property of the husband as to the second marriage. During the existence of the second marriage, Thigpen purchased a fire insurance policy to cover the buildings. Shortly thereafter the buildings burned and the loss was replaced with funds from the insurance proceeds. The Supreme Court held that these insurance proceeds did not become community property. The court noted that since the premiums were paid out of the community funds, there may have been a justifiable claim for reimbursement for the wife's contributions to the premiums, but this did not make the proceeds themselves community property.

METZ V. METZ

Supreme Court of Wyoming, 2003.
61 P.3d 383.

[The husband purchased a disability insurance policy and was injured during marriage. As a result of his injury, he became entitled to receive a monthly disability benefit until he reached age 65. The court addressed whether the portion of these benefits to be received after divorce was divisible marital property.]

* * *

We consider next whether disability payments which the insurance policy will provide the husband until he turns sixty-five were properly included in the property division. In concluding that such payments should be included, the trial court said:

> 14. Due to the length of the marriage, the fact that . . . the parties['] assets were accrued exclusively during the marriage, and the fact that both parties are, for all practical purposes, retired, the Court finds that the parties' incomes should be made as nearly equal as possible in a property division so that they will be left in similar economic circumstances after the marriage.

In light of the evidence presented, dividing the benefits of the disability policy yet to be received provided the means for leaving the parties in similar economic circumstances after the divorce.

Despite the trial court's stated purpose, the husband argues the future disability payments were not subject to division because they were not received during the marriage. The husband likens the benefits to money a spouse earns subsequent to divorce. The husband's analysis fails to take into account the fact that these payments will be derived from an insurance policy paid for by his professional corporation during the marriage from funds which otherwise could have been used for family living expenses or invested for the family's benefit. In this sense, the disability benefits are not like earnings post-divorce, which have no relation to the marriage.

Considering all the facts and circumstances of this case, the parties' respective education and employment back-grounds, the length of their marriage, their respective contributions—both economic and noneconomic—to their home and family during the marriage, and their age and current financial circumstances, we cannot say the result reached by the trial court in this case was clearly unjust and inequitable. We, therefore, affirm the property distribution, including the division of disability benefits.

NOTES AND QUESTIONS

1.   *Metz* categorizes insurance proceeds based on the character of the premiums used to pay for the policy; *Trahan* categorizes them based on the character of what the policy proceeds will replace. Which approach yields the fairest results?

2.   Most courts follow the *Trahan* approach in categorizing disability benefits to be received after divorce; unless the benefits include a component representing a marital pension or lost marital wages, the benefits are the recipient's separate property. *See, e.g.*, TEX. FAM. CODE § 3.008; Holland v. Holland, 337 P.3d 562 (Ariz. App. 2014); Marriage of Saslow, 710 P.2d 346 (Cal. 1985); Marriage of Kittleson, 585 P.2d 167 (Wash. 1978); Fleitz v. Fleitz, 606 N.Y.S.2d 825 (App. Div. 1994); Marriage of Walker, 137 Cal. Rptr. 3d 611 (App. 2012).

To determine the character of casualty insurance proceeds, some states focus on the character of the property that was insured. *See* TEX. FAM. CODE § 3.008. Other states characterize the proceeds based on the money used to pay the premium. *See* Locklear v. Locklear, 374 S.E.2d 406 (N.C. App. 1988); Robbins v. Robbins, 770 S.E.2d 723 (N.C. App. 2015).

3.   Personal injury and workers' compensation awards present characterization problems similar to those presented by disability benefits. Some divorce statutes specify how damages for a personal injury should be categorized; many do not. When the statute does not specify how such an award should be categorized, the majority of courts have followed an "analytical" approach. Courts applying this approach attempt to determine what the benefit is intended to replace. If the benefit replaces something that would have been marital, the benefit should also be marital. To the extent the benefit replaces something that would have been separate, it is considered separate. *See* Grace v. Peterson, 269 P.3d 663 (Alaska 2012); Ward v. Ward, 453 N.W.2d 729 (Minn. App. 1990); Everhardt v. Everhardt, 602 N.E.2d 701 (Ohio App. 1991). Under this "analytic" approach, that portion of a personal injury award intended to compensate for lost marital wages is categorized as marital

property while the pain and suffering component and any award for post-divorce lost wages are categorized as separate property. Under the alternate "mechanical" approach, only property specifically defined as separate by the legislature will be categorized as separate. Because most statutes do not expressly address such awards, courts following this approach usually characterize the benefit as marital property. *See, e.g.*, Drake v. Drake, 725 A.2d 717 (Pa. 1999) (utilizing mechanistic approach and characterizing full value of award as marital property because it was received during marriage); Marsh v. Marsh, 437 S.E.2d 34 (S.C. 1993) (same).

In those states that apply the analytical approach to personal injury settlements, if a claim is settled for a lump sum during the marriage it will constitute a commingled fund. The pain and suffering damages would be the injured spouse's separate property, while the damages for lost wages during marriage and medical expenses reimbursement would be marital. Before any of the settlement could be treated as separate property, the injured spouse would need to show what portion of the settlement was separate. *See* Kyles v. Kyles, 832 S.W.2d 194 (Tex. App. 1992). If both spouses jointly sue regarding the injury, this would further complicate the tracing. *See* Rizzo v. Rizzo, 993 N.Y.S.2d 104 (App. Div. 2014).

The difference between the analytic and mechanical approach can be seen in two cases arising from wrongful conviction recoveries. In *In re* Marriage of Rivera and Sanders-Rivera, 2016 WL 5700158 (Ill. App. 2016), the man was convicted of murder in 1992. He married in 2000. In 2011, his conviction was reversed on the grounds that his confession was coerced. He then sued for wrongful conviction and won. The court ruled that his eventual $11.36 million recovery was marital property because his wrongful conviction claims arose during marriage. In Phillips v. Tucker, 442 S.W.3d 543 (Tex. App. 2014), a married man was convicted in 1982 of various crimes and was then incarcerated for a substantial period. The parties divorced in 1992. In 2008, the man was exonerated based on DNA evidence. He therefore qualified for a Texas governmental benefit that provided all wrongfully imprisoned people with compensation of $80,000 for each year wrongfully imprisoned. The wife then sued to obtain a portion of the payment. The appellate court ruled that, because the recovery was not tied to the claimant's lost wages, the recovery was solely to compensate for the wrongful imprisonment and was the man's separate property. If the Illinois court had applied this analytic approach, would the result have been different?

E. PENSION BENEFITS AND OTHER EMPLOYEE COMPENSATION

1. Basic Terminology

Pension rights are often the most valuable asset at divorce. Most pension plans are *"defined benefit"* or *"defined contribution"* types.

Under a *defined benefit plan*, the employer agrees to pay an employee who has satisfied the minimum plan requirements (*e.g.*, length of employment, age, etc.) a monthly retirement payment based on a formula set forth in the plan. The formula might, for example, specify that:

Monthly payment = .03 x last monthly salary x number of years of service with the employer.

Under this particular formula, a retiree would receive 90% of his last monthly salary post-retirement if he had worked for the employer for thirty years. With a defined benefit plan, contributions are not made to employees' individual pension accounts; instead, the employer makes deposits to a general retirement fund in an amount estimated to satisfy all retirement obligations. Defined benefit plans typically are funded by the employer.

Defined benefit plan rights are always initially "unvested"; if the employee dies, quits, or is fired before the specified "vesting date," he or she has no rights under the plan. An employee holding unvested pension rights thus possesses only a contingent interest in plan benefits; he or she may ultimately receive full benefits, or no benefits.

Each defined benefit plan specifies a date or event at which the employee's pension benefits will "vest." After vesting, the employee will receive benefits, even if he is fired or quits, as long as he survives until retirement age. Under some, but not all, plans, his estate may be entitled to death benefits should he die before retirement.

When the employee has the right, under the plan, to retire, the benefits "mature." (Many employees choose to work after the maturity date and do not elect to take early retirement.) When the employee retires and begins to receive benefits, the pension is "in pay status."

Under a *"defined contribution plan,"* a separate account is maintained for each employee. Contributions, based on a formula (i.e., percentage of salary, percentage of company profits), are periodically made to each employee's account. A defined contribution plan may be funded solely by the employer or by the employer and employee (by payroll deduction). Employee contributions must vest immediately; employer contributions will vest based on a plan schedule. When an employee with a defined contribution plan interest retires, his retirement benefit equals whatever annuity can be purchased with his pension account balance.

Some government pension benefits combine features of defined contribution and defined benefit plans. The employee makes contributions to a pension account and has the right to withdraw any balance if he or she quits before retirement. If the employee remains at his job until retirement, benefits are calculated under the plan based on a formula rather than the value of the annuity that could be purchased with the account balance.

For a good general reference on pension issues, *see* William Troyan, *Pension Evaluation for Marriage Dissolutions Actions: A Pension Evaluator's Perspective*, 3 VALUATION & DISTRIBUTION OF MARITAL PROPERTY ch. 45 (1986). *See also* William Troyan, *An Update on Pension Evaluation*, 31 FAM. L.Q. 5 (1997); Marvin Snyder, *Challenges in Valuing Pension Plans*, 35 FAM. L. Q. 235 (2001).

2. Apportionment

If an employee is married for a portion of his or her career and has a pension, the pension will be partly separate and partly marital. Each state needs to establish rules regarding how to calculate the marital portion.

TAGGART V. TAGGART
Supreme Court of Texas, 1977.
552 S.W.2d 422.

POPE, JUSTICE.

Ann Taggart instituted this suit against George Taggart for the partition of military retirement benefits that were not divided when the parties were divorced. The trial court, upon a finding that the parties were married during the time that eight-ninths of the retirement benefits accumulated, rendered judgment that plaintiff was entitled to four-ninths of all retirement pay received by her former husband. The court ordered defendant George Taggart to receive plaintiff's share in trust for the plaintiff and make monthly disbursement to her of her share. The court of civil appeals reversed that judgment and rendered judgment that plaintiff take nothing. 540 S.W.2d 823. We reverse the judgment of the court of civil appeals and reform that of the trial court.

On June 5, 1943, George Taggart entered the United States Navy. Ann and George Taggart were married on October 7, 1947, and they were divorced on January 5, 1968. The divorce proceedings made no mention of retirement benefits.

On July 1, 1964, three and one-half years before the divorce, George completed the equivalent of twenty years of active duty. George did not retire but elected to be placed in the Fleet Reserve. As an enlisted man in the regular Navy, he had to complete thirty years of active duty before he was eligible for retirement based on years of service. Mr. Taggart was retired from the Navy on April 1, 1974. Ann Taggart instituted this suit for the recovery of her share of the retirement benefits since April 1, 1974. She did not seek any part of the retainer pay that George Taggart earned for his service in the Fleet Reserve, nor was there any plea of limitations urged in this case.

The court of civil appeals decided this case in August, 1976, at which time the supreme court had granted a writ of error but had not written its opinion in *Cearley v. Cearley*, 544 S.W.2d 661 (Tex. 1976). We decided in *Cearley* that retirement benefits are subject to division as vested contingent community property rights even though the present right has not fully matured. We refused to follow the California case of *French v. French*, 17 Cal. 2d 775, 112 P.2d 235 (1941), which treated an unmatured pension right as a nonvested expectancy instead of a vested right. In *Cearley*, we held that military benefits were community property even though the benefits at the time of the divorce "had not matured and were not at the time subject to possession and enjoyment." There is no necessity to again analyze the relevant Texas decisions or the opinion of the California court in *Brown v. Brown*, 15 Cal. 3d 838, 126 Cal. Rptr. 633, 544 P.2d 561 (1976), which rejected the rule of *French v. French, supra*, and recognized a present contingent right subject to divestment.

Since *Cearley* controls this case, we hold that Ann Taggart owned as her part of the community estate a share in the contingent right to military benefits even though that right had not matured at the time of the divorce. It appears, however, that the trial court did not make the correct computation of her fractional interest.

The trial court computed Ann Taggart's one-half interest in George Taggart's retirement benefits upon the basis of his twenty years of service as a member of the regular Navy. At the end of the twenty years, he was not entitled to receive any retirement benefits based upon his term of service because he had to serve in the Fleet Reserve for an additional ten years. It was, therefore, his three hundred and sixty months of service that entitled him to the retirement benefits. According to the undisputed evidence Ann and George Taggart's marriage coincided with his service in the Navy for a period of two hundred and forty-six months. The correct computation of Ann Taggart's vested interest is that she was entitled only to one-half of 246/360th's of the retirement pay.

The judgment of the court of civil appeals is reversed; the judgment of the trial court is reformed to adjudge the correct fractional interest to Ann Taggart and as reformed is affirmed.

JOHNSON V. JOHNSON

Supreme Court of Utah, 2014.
330 P.3d 704.

ASSOCIATE CHIEF JUSTICE NEHRING.

Petitioner Mark Lawrence Johnson and Respondent Elizabeth Ann Johnson, nee Zoric, married in 1974 and divorced in 1984. During the parties' ten-year marriage, Mr. Johnson accrued approximately ten years of service in the United States Air Force. At the time of the divorce, he was a staff sergeant with a pay grade of E-5. Because Mr. Johnson's pension required twenty years to vest, at the time of the divorce the district court was unable to determine a specific monetary amount that would be owed to Ms. Zoric as her marital property portion of Mr. Johnson's potential future retirement benefit. The district court's decree instead awarded Ms. Zoric "1/2 of 10 years of [Mr. Johnson]'s retirement." Here the trial court, when dividing the husband's defined benefit pension, utilized the approach used by the Texas Supreme Court in the prior *Taggart* case. Under this approach, the marital property pension claim is calculated based on the amount of the actual pension benefit the employee receives. In this case, the Utah Supreme Court considers whether this is always appropriate.

The Court of Appeals Erred when It Affirmed the District Court's Award Granting Ms. Zoric Her Marital Fraction of Mr. Johnson's Actual Retirement Benefit

The district court in this case was faced with the issue of how to determine the appropriate portion of Mr. Johnson's pension benefits to award Ms. Zoric. Specifically, the parties disagreed as to whether the district court should include postdivorce increases to Mr. Johnson's pension benefits when calculating Ms. Zoric's pension benefit award. The district court, relying on our precedent in *Woodward v. Woodward,* held that Ms. Zoric was entitled to an award that included the postdivorce increases in Mr. Johnson's pension benefits. A divided panel of the court of appeals affirmed that decision. As discussed below, the district court's reliance solely on *Woodward* was misplaced. As such, the district court applied the wrong legal standard, and in so doing, abused its discretion. On this issue, we reverse the court of appeals and remand to the district court.

On certiorari, Mr. Johnson argues that Ms. Zoric's share of his retirement benefit should be based on his pay grade at the time of the parties' divorce or the present-day salary for his pay grade at the time of divorce, rather than his pay grade and salary at the time of his retirement. We begin by noting that a former spouse is entitled to an equitable distribution of an employee spouse's retirement or pension benefits that "accrue[ ] in whole or in part during the marriage."

We have established that a nonemployee spouse is entitled to receive "a portion of the retirement benefits represented by the number of years of the marriage divided by the number of years of the [employee spouse's] employment." This has become known as the "time rule" formula. A number of jurisdictions have adopted this time rule formula to determine the "marital fraction," which determines the martial interest in pension benefits. The marital fraction is calculated by dividing the number of years (or months) that the employee spouse has earned toward the pension during the marriage by the number of years (or months) of total service toward the pension. The marital fraction is then multiplied by the employee spouse's monthly benefit that is subject to equitable distribution. Each spouse is then awarded one-half of the marital interest in the pension that is subject to equitable distribution.

When a court invokes this formula, there are two unknowns at the time of divorce: the years of total service and the amount of the monthly benefit. Once the employee spouse retires, the years of total service factor is known and can be plugged into the equation to determine the marital fraction. In the present case, the parties were married for ten years, during which time Mr. Johnson accrued ten years of qualifying service. Mr. Johnson retired after twenty-four years of qualifying service. Using the time rule formula above, the parties were married for 41.6 percent of the time Mr. Johnson was employed by the Air Force, and Ms. Zoric's half of that portion is 20.8 percent. The parties agree on this calculation. The remaining unknown factor at the time of divorce, and what the parties dispute in this case, is the amount of the monthly benefit that is to be multiplied by the marital fraction. Though our decision in *Woodward* established the time rule formula as the appropriate method for calculating the marital fraction, we were not presented with the question of how to properly determine the amount of the employee spouse's monthly benefit subject to equitable distribution. That question is squarely presented here. Thus, we must determine whether postdivorce increases in pension benefits that are predicated on increases in the employee spouse's rank and pay grade following the parties' divorce are properly part of the monthly benefit subject to equitable distribution. The district court had several alternatives from which to choose.

At one end of the spectrum is the bright line approach—the approach advocated by Mr. Johnson. The bright line approach "likens post-divorce pension enhancements to post-divorce earnings and characterizes all such increases as the separate property of the employee spouse." Under this approach, "pension benefits accruing as compensation for services rendered after a divorce are not part of the [marital] estate . . . subject to division on divorce." This approach treats any subsequent advancement (and the resulting pay increase) as the separate property of the employee spouse because any such advances or increases result solely from the labors of the employee spouse. A court applying this approach uses the employee spouse's pay grade at the time of the parties' divorce, instead of the pay grade at the time of retirement to calculate the monthly pension benefits. The bright line approach comports with the long-established notion that property acquired after the marriage is generally considered separate property and is, therefore, not subject to distribution along with the martial estate. This approach is also aligned with our precedent that marital property should be valued at the time of the divorce decree, absent compelling circumstances.

At the other end of the spectrum is the marital foundation approach, which acknowledges that postdivorce *earnings* are separate property, but treats *all* postdivorce *increases* in pension benefits as marital property. The marital foundation approach is easy to apply, as a district court need only apply the time rule formula to the employee spouse's monthly pension benefit at retirement, with no need to "parse out the 'marital' portion of the post-dissolution enhancement from the 'separate' portion . . . attributable solely to the efforts of the employee spouse." Furthermore, the marital foundation approach seeks to offset the "risk of forfeiture, delay in receipt, and lack of control over the timing of the receipt of benefits" suffered by the nonemployee spouse by permitting the nonemployee spouse to share in postdivorce enhancements to benefits.

The bright line and marital foundation approaches can be thought of as anchoring each end of a spectrum of approaches available to district courts. Judge Davis, in dissenting from the result adopted by the court of appeals, advocated an approach between these two extremes. Judge Davis disagreed with both the bright line approach and the marital foundation approach as used in the context of this case. Judge Davis would have awarded Ms. Zoric 20.8 percent of the monthly benefit Mr. Johnson would have received had he remained at the E-5 pay grade he attained during the parties' marriage. This would have included normal cost of living increases, but not the increases attributable to Mr. Johnson's promotion to the E-7 pay grade he attained prior to retirement. Judge Davis reasoned that "there is no evidence of any specific contribution made by [Ms.] Zoric to [Mr.] Johnson's earning capacity apart from the fact that she was married to him while he was employed at the E-5 rank." Accordingly, Judge Davis found no reason to award Ms. Zoric the benefit of "all future improvements in [Mr. Johnson's] financial situation merely by virtue of their having been married for some period of time."

Like Judge Davis, we believe that a context-specific approach leads to the most equitable distribution of pension benefits. District courts are charged with making an equitable distribution of marital property, including pension benefits. In making such distribution, the presumptive value of marital property is determined at the time of the divorce, absent compelling circumstances. District courts should also consider a variety of factors when making equitable distributions, including whether the property was acquired during the marriage, the source of the property, and the parties' respective financial conditions. "The appropriate distribution of property var[ies] from case to case, [but] [t]he overriding consideration is that the ultimate division be equitable—that the property be fairly divided between the parties, given their contribution during the marriage and their circumstances at the time of the divorce." Thus, our precedent has endorsed a context-specific approach that recognizes the various ways marital property can be acquired and then distributed equitably.

When determining the most equitable distribution of the employee spouse's pension benefits, a district court should consider the pension benefits much like it does other marital property. That is, the district court should consider the extent to which the property was acquired during the marriage and the ultimate source of the property. In the context of pension benefits, this will require the district court to consider how the trajectory of the employee spouse's career intersected with the marriage and the extent to which the marriage contributed to the employee spouse's pay grade at retirement. For example, if the parties were married only briefly early in the employee spouse's career, it is highly unlikely that the nonemployee spouse contributed significantly to the employee spouse's ultimate pay grade at retirement. In such a scenario, there would be no reason to award the nonemployee spouse the benefit of all of the employee spouse's subsequent pay raises, whether they result from promotions, renegotiations of union contracts, or job changes.

On the other hand, if the parties are married for a significant portion of the employee spouse's career, it is much more likely that the nonemployee spouse's contributions impacted the trajectory of the employee spouse's career in a way the court should credit. This would be especially true in circumstances in which the parties were married while the employee spouse underwent specialized training or schooling that would further his or her career. To the extent such training or education led to increases in rank or pay grade, the court could see fit to award the nonemployee spouse credit for the resulting increase in pension benefits. Even in this circumstance, however, it does not stand to reason that the nonemployee spouse would then be entitled to *all* subsequent increases. The district court should, in its discretion, determine what contribution the nonemployee spouse made to the subsequent increases, if any, and award credit only for those fairly attributable to that contribution.

Therefore, the district court is not bound by a specific prescribed approach in determining the most equitable distribution of pension benefits following the dissolution of a marriage, but should evaluate all relevant factors and circumstances in making such a determination.

Based on our review of the record in this case, we find that it is insufficient to determine the extent to which Mr. Johnson's career trajectory was impacted by his marriage to Ms. Zoric. There is no question that Ms. Zoric's efforts during the marriage helped Mr. Johnson attain the E-5 rank that he held at the time of the parties' divorce. And had Mr. Johnson remained at this rank and merely received his anticipated cost of living increases, Ms. Zoric would have been entitled to share in his monthly pension benefits as they were awarded. But, Mr. Johnson did not remain at the E-5 rank. Mr. Johnson was promoted from Staff Sergeant to Master Sergeant following his divorce from Ms. Zoric, and consequently, his rank and pay were elevated to E-7. The record is unclear as to the extent Mr.

Johnson's postdivorce promotion and career trajectory can be fairly attributed to Ms. Zoric's efforts during the marriage. As such, we remand to the district court for further fact-finding with the understanding that the district court is not limited to the marital foundation approach when determining the amount of monthly benefits to insert in to the time rule formula. Rather, the district court is authorized to use any approach it deems necessary to come to the most equitable outcome.

CONCLUSION

The district court abused its discretion when it erroneously concluded that it was bound by the marital foundation approach to determine that Ms. Zoric's marital fraction should be applied to Mr. Johnson's actual retirement benefit, and as such, we reverse and remand to the district court for further fact-finding regarding the equitable distribution of marital property.

NOTES AND QUESTIONS

1.   Until the mid-1970s, divorce courts applied a restrictive definition of "property" that precluded the division of contingent benefits or expectancies such as unvested pension rights. A few states still apply this rule. *See* Harris v. Harris, 31 N.E.3d 991 (Ind. App. 2015). Because contingent rights can eventually be valuable, most courts today follow the *Taggart* approach and permit the division of unvested pension rights. Because a divorcing spouse with an unvested pension right may never receive benefits, many courts apply a "wait and see" or "deferred sharing" approach, like that utilized in *Taggart*.

Other types of contingent rights at divorce can be marital property, based on the more expansive concept of "property" applied in *Taggart*. For example, there can be a marital claim to a lawsuit pending at divorce.

2.   Pension plans often pose apportionment problems. If, as in *Taggart*, the spouse with pension rights accrued some of those rights before marriage or after marital termination, in a marital property state the rights not earned during marriage will be categorized as separate property. The *Taggart* court computed the marital component of the pension by calculating the portion of the employee's career during which the employee was married; because the employee was married for 246 of 360 months of employment, 246/360 of the pension benefits was marital property.

Note that *Taggart* assumes each month of employment was of the same value. Most courts have adopted this assumption when dealing with defined benefit pensions. *See In re* Marriage of Hunt, 909 P.2d 525 (Colo. 1995); Stiel v. Stiel, 348 S.W.3d 879 (Tenn. App. 2011). Some courts have been persuaded that later years of employment are more valuable than early years of employment. In these states, if the employee divorces while still working and can show that post-divorce work will be more valuable than service during marriage, some means of valuation is needed that bars the marital estate from sharing in the value of the work after divorce. *See* Koelsch v. Koelsch, 713 P.2d 1234 (Ariz. 1986); Berry v. Berry, 647 S.W.2d 945 (Tex. 1983). The *Johnson* court gives the divorce court discretion regarding whether the marital claim should include pension increases that occur after divorce.

3.   Early retirement incentives generally permit an employee to retire with a higher payment than the employee had earned under the basic plan. For example, under defined benefit plans, to encourage an employee to retire the employer may offer the employee a pension calculated based on more years of service than the employee had actually served (thereby qualifying for a larger pension payment). This presents a difficult apportionment issue if a court divides the pension benefits based on a time formula. For example, imagine an employee who is married for the first 20 years of her career. If she works for 10 more years after divorce and then accepts an early retirement offer to give her credit for 35 years of work, should the marital portion of the pension she receives be 20/35 or 20/30? *See* Eisenhardt v. Eisenhardt, 740 A.2d 164 (N.J. Super. App. Div. 1999).

4.   A time-based approach to pension apportionment will not make sense unless the pension benefits are based on years of employment. Thus, in *In re Marriage of Poppe*, 158 Cal. Rptr. 500 (App. 1979), the appellate court reversed the trial court's decision to divide the husband's naval reserve pension on a "time" basis when the value of the pension was based on "points" accumulated during active duty and naval reserve service. The husband retired with 5,002 points, of which only 1,632 were accumulated due to naval reserve service during the marriage. Most of the points were earned before marriage when the husband was on active duty. The court held that "[i]n this case * * * the amount of the pension is not a function of the number of years of service; the number of years of service during the marriage is not a fair gauge of the community contribution; and the court's apportionment of the pension on the basis of the number of "qualifying" years served as compared to the number of years of service during the marriage must be said to be unreasonable, arbitrary and an abuse of discretion." In Whorrall v. Whorrall, 691 S.W.2d 32 (Tex. App. 1985), the appellate court upheld the trial court's determination that the entire value of an early retirement "special payment" was community property, even though the employee spouse was married during only 65 of his 252 months of employment (but was married at the time of payment). The court's determination was based on evidence that the special payment represented a "unique" and "strictly discretionary" incentive designed to coax an unproductive employee into early retirement. "The fact that such payment is purely discretionary," the court held, " * * * negates the notion that it is earned or accrued over the employee's tenure," so it wasn't be characterized for marital property purposes as a pension.

5.   In addition to pension benefits, courts have held that a range of other employment benefits are divisible at divorce:

a.   Some courts have held that vacation time earned during marriage may be treated as a divisible asset, particularly when the employee had the option of receiving cash at retirement for unused vacation time. *See In re* Moore, 171 Cal. Rptr. 3d 762 (App. 2014); *In re* Marriage of Cardona and Castro, 316 P.3d 626 (Colo. 2014); (emphasizing that the holding was limited to situations where the employee had an enforceable right to be paid for unused vacation time or sick leave); Schober v. Schober, 692 P.2d 267 (Alaska 1984), *In re* Marriage of Williams, 927 P.2d 679 (Wash. App. 1996); Forrester v. Forrester, 953 A.2d 175 (Del. 2008); Dye v. Dye, 17 So. 3d 1278 (Fla. Dist. Ct. App. 2009); Lesko v. Lesko, 457 N.W.2d 695 (Mich. App. 1990); Ryan v. Ryan, 619 A.2d 692 (N.J. Super. 1992). In a marital property state, any vacation time accrued but unused before marriage should be subtracted from the employee's accrued vacation time at the end of the marital property accrual period. *See* Everette v. Everette, 620 So. 2d 1115 (Fla. Dist. Ct. App. 1993); Cole v. Roberts, 661 So. 2d 370 (Fla. Dist. Ct. App. 1995). Other courts have disagreed and have not considered vacation time accrued during marriage as marital property. *See In re* Marriage of Abrell, 923 N.E.2d 791 (Ill. 2010); Bratcher v. Bratcher, 26 S.W.3d 797 (Ky. App. 2000); Thomasian v. Thomasian, 556 A.2d 675 (Md. App. 1989); Akers v. Akers, 729 N.E.2d 1029 (Ind. App. 2000).

b.   Stock options and bonuses have generally been held divisible to the extent they represent compensation for marital employment. *See, e.g.,* Davidson v. Davidson, 578 N.W.2d 848 (Neb. 1998) (holding that a time rule should be used to determine extent to which stock options and retention shares were earned during marriage); DeJesus v. DeJesus, 687 N.E.2d 1319 (N.Y. 1997) (same); *In re* Marriage of Valence, 798 A.2d 35 (N.H. 2002) (same).

c.   Most courts have concluded that the right to a maintain a term life insurance policy post-divorce is valueless and thus not subject to division. *But see In re* Marriage of Logan, 236 Cal. Rptr. 368 (App. 1987) (term life insurance right could be valuable if employee had become uninsurable during marriage).

d.   Some courts have ruled that if an employee during retirement will receive health insurance benefits from the employer, the portion of the value of these benefits earned from working during marriage can be marital property. *See* Engstrom v. Engstrom, 350 P.3d 766 (Alaska 2015); *In re* Marriage of Moore, 171 Cal. Rptr. 3d 762 (App. 2014).

6.   For defined contribution plans, the marital component is typically computed by subtracting the balance in the account when the marriage began from the balance at divorce. The main complication here is how to treat interest

accruing during marriage on premarital contributions. Some courts treat all interest accruing during marriage as marital property (*see, e.g.,* Jones v. Jones, 2016 IL App. (2d) 160065-U; Maslen v. Maslen, 822 P.2d 982 (Idaho 1991)), while others treat interest on premarital contributions as the pension owner's separate property. *See, e.g.,* White v. White, 521 N.W.2d 874 (Minn. App. 1994). Most courts do not apply the time rule to determine the marital portion of a defined contribution account. *See* Prizzia v. Prizzia, 707 S.E.2d 461 (Va. App. 2011).

Problem 15-2:

William has been married for 14 years; he has worked for Widget Corp. for approximately 21 years. Under the terms of the Widget defined benefit pension plan, employees do not accrue any pension rights until they have five years of service; thereafter, each year of service counts equally. Pension rights vest at 20 years of service. The normal retirement age is 65; William is now 60. If he retires at age 65 (as he currently intends to do), William will receive $1000 per month. What, if any, fraction of the pension is marital? *See In re* Marriage of Joiner, 755 S.W.2d 496 (Tex. App.) reh'g granted, 766 S.W.2d 263 (Tex. App. 1988).

Problem 15-3:

George began work at Widget Corp. 30 years ago. Seven years ago he married Mary. During his marriage to Mary, he was promoted to a position that qualified him for a special "executive" pension in addition to his normal defined benefit pension. The defined benefit pension was vested at the time of George and Mary's marriage. Both pensions are based on years of service. George is now 60; normal retirement age is 65. If George retires at age 65 (as he now intends), he will receive $1000 per month in "regular" benefits and $500 per month in "executive" benefits. What, if any, fraction of each pension is marital? *See* Hudson v. Hudson, 763 S.W.2d 603 (Tex. App. 1989).

3. Payment

1. There are two methods of paying the nontitled spouse his or her share of the marital component of a pension:

> a. Under the *"reserved jurisdiction"* or *"deferred payment"* approach, the nontitled spouse is paid if and when the titled spouse receives benefits. The primary disadvantage of this approach is delay, a particular problem if the nontitled spouse needs money at the time of divorce. *See* Bulicek v. Bulicek, 800 P.2d 394 (Wash. App. 1990). Another problem arises if, post-divorce, the value of the pension increases due to a promotion or merit pay increase. Some courts have held that a former spouse is not entitled to a share of any post-divorce increase in a retirement fund derived from post-divorce effort, education or achievement

by the employee spouse; if the value of the pension is increased post-divorce by, for example, a merit raise or an extraordinary promotion, the employee spouse may request the court to adjust the community fraction to credit his or her separate property with that increment. *See, e.g.*, Hare v. Hodgins, 586 So. 2d 118 (La. 1991); Gemma v. Gemma, 778 P.2d 429 (Nev. 1989). Others have rejected this approach and do not permit post-divorce challenges to the pension award even if post-divorce raises or promotions have enhanced its value. *See, e.g., In re* Marriage of Judd, 137 Cal. Rptr. 318 (App. 1977); Bulicek v. Bulicek, 800 P.2d 394 (Wash. App. 1990); *In re* Marriage of Hunt, 909 P.2d 525 (Colo. 1995); Seifert v. Seifert, 346 S.E.2d 504, 508 (N.C. 1986). A third group of states avoids the problem by requiring the divorce court to assume for valuation purposes that the employee spouse has retired on the date marital property ceases to accrue; post-divorce service must be ignored. *See* Berry v. Berry, 647 S.W.2d 945 (Tex. 1983). What are the advantages and disadvantages of each approach? Which seems fairest?

b.   Under the *"present value"* approach, the nontitled spouse receives the value of his or her share of the pension at the time of the divorce. This approach has two disadvantages. The first problem is finding funds to pay the nontitled spouse. Because a defined benefit pension interest is not like a bank account from which funds can be immediately withdrawn, the titled spouse must have enough cash to pay the nontitled spouse his or her share or the couple must have other property which can be awarded the nontitled spouse to "offset" the pension. The second problem is computational. Determining the present value of a defined contribution pension is fairly straightforward. If all pension contributions were made during marriage, the present value is the account balance at the cut-off date for marital property accrual. (An offset for future taxes is not generally accepted, probably because the tax rate then applicable is speculative). If some, but not all, contributions were made during the marriage, apportionment will be necessary. But determining the present value of a defined benefit pension is a more complicated process. The first step is to determine the aggregate value of expected payments by subtracting the employee's expected retirement age from his life expectancy. If the pension is vested but the employee spouse has not yet retired, the aggregate value must be adjusted to reflect the fact that the employee may die before retirement and never collect; if the pension is also unvested, an additional adjustment is required to reflect the fact that the employee may quit or be fired before obtaining a right to receive benefits. Finally, the expected aggregate value of the pension rights must be discounted to "present value." Discounting to present value reflects the fact that the right to receive money in the future is worth less than the right to receive money immediately because of forgone investment opportunities. In light of these complexities, it is fairly easy to see why many family lawyers have close relationships with accountants and actuaries. For a more detailed discussion of present value calculation approach, *see* WILLIAM TROYAN ET AL., 3 VALUATION & DISTRIBUTION OF MARITAL PROPERTY § 45.23 *et seq.* (1986).

2. A number of courts have held that, when there is enough marital property to "offset" an award of the entire pension to the employee spouse, the present value approach should be utilized. *See, e.g.,* Dewan v. Dewan, 506 N.E.2d 879 (Mass. 1987); Bishop v. Bishop, 440 S.E.2d 591 (N.C. App. 1994).

3. *The Qualified Domestic Relations Order ("QDRO"):* When courts first began to utilize the deferred payment approach with defined benefit plans, they ordered the employee spouse to pay the other spouse a specified fraction of payments to be received when he or she retired. This approach entailed several disadvantages: it required continuing contact between spouses, thus inviting future disputes; the employee spouse had to pay taxes on the whole pension payment; and the nonemployee spouse could not obtain payment until the employee spouse actually retired. In 1984, Congress enacted legislation permitting a qualified pension plan administrator to pay benefits directly to an "alternate payee" in compliance with a "qualified domestic relations order." *See* Retirement Equity Act of 1984, 29 U.S.C.A. § 1056. Such an order may require payment when the employee's rights mature, regardless of when he or she actually retires. All payments made pursuant to a QDRO are taxed to the recipient, not the employee. (If an attorney prepares an order that does not qualify as a QDRO, payments are taxed to the employee, a tax (and malpractice) disaster. *See* Hawkins v. Commissioner, 102 T.C. 61 (1994)).

A QDRO must specify:

(1) The name and the last known mailing address of the participant and the name and mailing address of each alternate payee;

(2) The amount or percentage of the participant's benefits to be paid to each alternate payee or the manner in which the amount or percentage is to be determined;

(3) The number of payments of the period to which the order applies; and

(4) Each plan to which the order applies.

A QDRO may not:

(5) Provide any type or form of benefit, or any option, not otherwise provided by the plan;

(6) Provide any increased benefits (determined on the basis of actuarial value); or

(7) Pay benefits to an alternate payee that must be paid to another alternate payee under a previous QDRO.

For a defined contribution plan, a QDRO normally specifies the amount or percentage of benefits the alternate payee is to receive. For a defined benefit plan, a QDRO specifies either a percentage or a formula to be used by the plan administrator to determine the percentage of benefit to be paid. Government pension plans are not subject to the Retirement Equity Act of 1984. For more on QDROs, *see* GALE S. FINLEY, ASSIGNING RETIREMENT BENEFITS IN DIVORCE: A PRACTICAL GUIDE TO NEGOTIATING AND DRAFTING QDROS (2d Ed. 1999); DAVID CLAYTON CARRAD, THE COMPLETE QDRO HANDBOOK (3d ed. 2009).

4. Federal Retirement Benefits and Other Federal Preemption Issues

Because federal law "preempts" state law, a state court may not divide a federal pension if division is prohibited by federal law. (Federal preemption normally does not prohibit an agreement by the parties to divide benefits that would otherwise be indivisible. *See* Owen v. Owen, 419 S.E.2d 267 (Va. App. 1992). *Cf. In re* Marriage of Anderson, 252 P.3d 490 (Colo. App. 2010) (husband's agreement that he would pay his former wife a portion of his Social Security benefits was void.).) Some federal pension systems clearly specify that plan benefits may be divided. All federal civil service retirement benefits, for example, are subject to division at divorce. *See* Naydan v. Naydan, 800 S.W.2d 637 (Tex. App. 1990). Some, but not all, railroad retirement benefits are subject to division. *See* 45 U.S.C.A. § 231m; Kamel v. Kamel, 721 S.W.2d 450 (Tex. App. 1986); Harris v. Harris, 42 N.E.3d 1010 (Ind. App. 2015). Statutes that do not specify whether benefits are divisible require court interpretation as to Congressional intent; all courts, for example, have found that Congress did not intend division of Social Security benefits. *See* Pongonis v. Pongonis, 606 A.2d 1055 (Me. 1992); Pleasant v. Pleasant, 632 A.2d 202 (Md. App. 1993); Depot v. Depot, 893 A.2d 995 (Me. 2006); Olsen v. Olsen, 169 P.3d 765 (Utah App. 2007); *In re* Marriage of Brane, 908 P.2d 625 (Kan. App. 1995) (Social Security benefits not divisible, but may be taken into account in dividing other property); *In re* Herald and Steadman, 322 P.3d 546 (Or. 2014) (same); Smith v. Smith, 358 P.3d 171 (Mont. 2015) (same). While all states agree that Social Security benefits cannot be divided at divorce, courts have disagreed regarding the appropriate response if one divorcing spouse will receive Social Security benefits and the other will not, and the spouse who will not receive Social Security benefits has earned pension benefits in a program that replaces Social Security benefits. This is common for school teachers, for example. Some courts have ruled that, in this situation, it is appropriate to consider the hypothetical value of Social Security benefits the spouse without Social Security benefits would have earned, and to subtract that value from the value of the spouse's pension rights to determine what portion is divisible. *See* Cornbleth v. Cornbleth, 580 A.2d 369 (Pa. Super. 1990); Kelly v. Kelly, 9 P.3d 1046 (Ariz. 2000). In contrast, some courts have concluded that divorce courts may not consider the existence of Social Security benefits when fashioning financial remedies at divorce. *See* Manning v. Schultz, 93 A.3d 566 (Vt. 2014); Wolff v. Wolff, 929 P.2d 916 (Nev. 1996); Olson v. Olson, 445 N.W.2d 1 (N.D. 1989); *In re* Mueller, 34 N.E.3d 538 (Ill. 2015). The majority view is that a divorce court may consider the existences of Social Security benefits when dividing the marital estate. *See In re* Herald and Steadman, 322 P.3d 546 (Or. 2014); Jackson v. Sollie, 141 A.3d 1122 (Md. 2016); *In re* Marriage of Zahm, 978 P.2d 498 (Wash. 1999); Pongonis v. Pongonis, 606 A.2d 1055 (Me. 1992); *In re* Marriage of Boyer, 538 N.W.2d 293 (Iowa 1995); Smith v. Smith, 358 P.3d 171 (Mont. 2015).

Lawyers should be aware that, if the marriage lasted at least 10 years before divorce, the spouse with the least amount of earned income during the marriage has a right, as an alternative to Social Security retirement benefit based on their own wages, unless he or she remarries, to a Social Security retirement benefit based on the other spouse's income history, if that would be desired. *See* Sarah R. Boonin, *Ten Years Too Long— Reforming Social Security's Marriage Duration Requirement in Cases of Domestic Violence*, 39 HARV. J.L. & GENDER 369 (2016).

Congressional intent regarding military retirement benefits has produced a long history of litigation and legislation. In June 1981, the U.S. Supreme Court held that Congress did not intend that military retirement benefits should be divisible at divorce, and that no offsetting award to compensate the non-employee spouse for the value of the benefits was permissible. McCarty v. McCarty, 453 U.S. 210 (1981). Congress responded to *McCarty* by enacting the Uniformed Services Former Spouse's Protection Act (USFSPA), 10 U.S.C.A. § 1408. USFSPA, which became effective February 1, 1983, permitted, but did not require, divorce courts to divide "disposable retired pay" of a military employee. This does not include amounts of retirement pay waived in order to receive disability benefits. See Mansell v. Mansell, 490 U.S. 581 (1989).

In *Mansell*, the military spouse had waived a right to some military retirement pay before the parties divorced. The *Mansell* court held that the divorce court could divide only the amount of retirement pay being received by the miliarty spouse. Disability benefits could not be divided. In Howell

v. Howell, 2017 WL 2039158 (U.S. 2017) the Supreme Court extended the *Mansell* rule to situations where, after divorce, the military spouse waives retirement pay to receive disability benefits. Only the amount of retirement pay could be divided, and the Family Court could not order the military spouse to "reimburse" the former spouse for the share of retirement pay waived.

In addition to pension benefits, the former spouse of a government employee may also qualify for certain privileges, such as medical coverage and commissary privileges, if the marriage was of sufficient duration. A divorce court may also require the employee spouse to elect a survivor annuity and designate the non-employee as the recipient.

For nongovernmental employees, Congress has adopted ERISA, a broad regulatory framework that governs benefits paid to employees of most private employers. The U.S. Supreme Court has held that, in some instances, state family law rules are preempted by ERISA. For example, in Egelhoff v. Egelhoff, 532 U.S. 141 (2001) the Court reviewed a Washington statute creating a presumption that, when a spouse divorces, he intends to revoke the designation of a former spouse as a life insurance beneficiary. The Court held that ERISA required the company to pay the proceeds to the named beneficiary. *See also* Boggs v. Boggs, 520 U.S. 833 (1997); Kennedy v. Plan Adm'r for DuPont Sav. and Inv. Plan, 555 U.S. 285 (2009).

Problem 15-4:

Margaret and John married thirty-five years ago and separated three years ago. John was employed as a pilot with Arrow Airlines from approximately one year after his marriage to Margaret, until about two years before their separation, when he joined a strike called by the Air Line Pilots Association, International (ALPA).

Following the strike, Arrow filed a bankruptcy petition. The bankruptcy court in essence ordered that: (1) the strike be terminated; (2) no recrimination or retaliation be taken against striking pilots; (3) the parties to dismiss all litigation between them pending in federal courts; and (4) striking pilots be given the option of being recalled and reinstated or severance pay.

The severance pay option provided that active pilots on Arrow's seniority list as of the strike date could elect severance pay in exchange for waiving the right to recall and waiving the right to claims against the company connected with the strike. The amount of severance pay was to be computed by multiplying $4,000 times the number of years of active service with Arrow as of the strike date.

John opted for the severance pay option and his severance pay was calculated at $126,800. According to the set schedule, John receives 10 percent in an initial payment this year, 15 percent next year, and the remainder in 20 quarterly payments, with 10 percent interest to be paid on amounts due after the first eight quarterly payments.

John and Margaret worked out a division of their marital estate with the exception of the severance pay, which John claimed was his separate property and Margaret claimed was a community asset.

You are the law clerk of the California divorce court judge who will decide whether the severance pay is divisible. The judge has asked you to research the problem, tell her the right answer, *and* explain the basis for that answer. The following precedents are relevant:

In *In re* Marriage of Skaden, 566 P.2d 249 (Cal. 1977), the California Supreme Court found termination benefits paid to an insurance agent under an employment agreement to be community property. The benefits consisted of a percentage of insurance premiums collected on insurance policies sold by the agent. The *Skaden* court held the benefits were community property because they were deferred compensation for the agent's previous endeavors.

Following *Skaden*, the issue of whether termination or severance benefits were community or separate property was raised in four published cases: In *In re* Marriage of Flockhart, 173 Cal. Rptr. 818 (App. 1981), a federal employee whose job was adversely affected by expansion of Redwood National Park received "weekly lay-off" benefits. The *Flockhart* court held that the benefits were separate property, as they were intended to presently compensate the employee for loss of earnings. In *In re* Marriage of Wright, 189 Cal. Rptr. 336 (App. 1983), the court also held that the lay-off benefits were separate property as they were designed to ease the employee's transition back into the work force, a need arising from his involuntary termination. In *In re* Marriage of Kuzmiak, 222 Cal. Rptr. 644 (App. 1986), the court reached the same result based on similar facts and the same reasoning. The most recent case to consider the issue is *In re* Marriage of Horn, 226 Cal. Rptr. 666 (App. 1986).

In *Horn*, the court concluded that the important issue in cataloging termination or severance benefits is "whether the benefits constitute (a) deferred compensation for past services or (b) present compensation for loss of earnings. If the benefits are deferred compensation for past earnings, the benefits are community property; if they are present compensation for loss of earnings, they are separate property." *Horn* also states that the character of the benefits is to be determined by considering all relevant circumstances.

At issue in *Horn* was the severance pay received by the husband from the National Football League (NFL) on his retirement from football. During the husband's playing days, the management of the NFL and the National Football League Players Association added a severance pay provision to the collective bargaining agreement, which provided that any player with two or more seasons with the NFL was entitled to a lump sum of severance pay, the amount to be based on the player's number of NFL seasons. In finding the severance pay to be community property, the *Horn* court noted these characteristics:

> * * * (a) it is derived from a contract right; (b) it is based on the number of seasons worked; (c) it must be paid back to the NFL if the player returns to professional football within one year of receipt; (d) it will be paid back to him when he again leaves football, but no additional amount will have accrued for the seasons worked after his return; (e) it is given to the player's stated beneficiary or estate if he dies; (f) it is received in a lump sum after a certain period of time has passed following the player's notification to the club of his intent to permanently retire from professional football.

The *Horn* court characterized the severance pay as community property because the husband had an absolute right to it based on his eight seasons with the NFL and the contractual agreement. The court noted that in *In re* Marriage of Flockhart, *supra*, *In re* Marriage of Wright, *supra*, and *In re* Marriage of Kuzmiak, *supra*, there were no absolute rights to receive severance pay; the husband in each case received severance pay only because a loss of work was forced upon him. The *Horn* court also noted that the three cases did not involve a contractual right to a payment.

1.   Margaret and John's lawyers have not yet filed briefs in the case. What arguments would you expect each to make?

2.   What decision should the judge reach? Why? *See In re* Marriage of DeShurley, 255 Cal. Rptr. 150 (App. 1989); Biddlecom v. Biddlecom, 495 N.Y.S.2d 301 (App. Div. 1985); Ryan v. Ryan, 619 A.2d 692 (N.J. Super. Ch. Div. 1992).

F.   PROFESSIONAL DEGREES AND LICENSES

FRAUSTO V. FRAUSTO
Texas Court of Appeals, 1980.
611 S.W.2d 656.

KLINGEMAN, JUSTICE.

This is a divorce action but the appeal herein pertains to the trial court's division of the properties between the parties. Appellant, Manuel Jesus Frausto, complains only of an order in the divorce decree which requires him to pay to appellee, Maria Lourdes Frausto, the sum of $20,000, payable in the amount of $200 per month, "as a part of the division of the estate of the parties and as reimbursement for petitioner's share of the community expense for respondent's education."

By a number of points of error appellant asserts that the trial court erred in holding that (1) the husband's education preparing him for the practice of medicine was community property and a property right divisible on divorce; and (2) appellee was entitled to such sum as reimbursement for her share of the community expense for appellant's education. We agree.

Degree isn't property

During the early part of the marriage, appellant and appellee were both school teachers. It was agreed by both that the husband would enter medical school. The wife continued to work while the husband was obtaining his medical education, and it is clear that during such period a considerable portion of all expenses of such marriage came from the wife's earnings. After the husband obtained his doctor's license to practice medicine, his earnings at times were substantial, but his work record is spotty, at times he was unemployed, and at other times his earnings were not large by medical standards. The husband testified that he had sustained injuries to both of his legs and that this made it difficult for him to work at times, and that he had quit some jobs because of this problem. There is evidence that at times the husband was a heavy spender. Despite whatever earnings the husband and wife had, no large community estate was accumulated. Both the husband and wife had college degrees, and the wife had taught school for many years and has continued to work as a school teacher. Two children were born of such marriage, one born in 1973 and the other in 1975. This case is somewhat typical of what sometimes happens when one spouse continues to work while the other spouse is obtaining a degree resulting in high potential earnings for the degreed spouse, and a divorce thereafter ensues.

From the plain language of the decree it is apparent that the award of $20,000 to the wife was an attempt by the trial judge to divide the medical education of appellant as a part of the community estate, or to reimburse appellee for expenditures made by the community for appellant's medical education.

There are no Texas cases directly in point. Two community property states, California and Colorado, have passed on the questions here involved. In Todd v. Todd, 78 Cal. Rptr. 131, 272 Cal. App. 2d 786 (1969), the California court held that a spouse's education preparing him for the practice of law is not of such a character that a monetary value for division can be placed on it for a division between the spouses in a divorce proceeding.

This rule was reaffirmed in *In re* Marriage of Aufmuth, 152 Cal. Rptr. 668, 89 Cal. App. 3d 446 (1979), wherein it was held that a determination that a legal education is community property would require a division of post-dissolution earnings, even though such earnings are the separate property of the acquiring spouses. A Colorado court in *In re* Marriage of

Graham, 38 Colo. App. 130, 555 P.2d 527 (1976), found that education is not a property item capable of division.

We agree with the jurisdictions that have held a professional educational degree is not divisible upon divorce.

In Nail v. Nail, 486 S.W.2d 761 (Tex. 1972), it was contended that professional good will was an asset capable of being divided upon dissolution of the marriage. The supreme court rejected this contention and stated that the professional good will of a doctor does not "possess value or constitute an asset separate and apart from his person or from his individual ability to practice his profession. It would be extinguished in the event of his death, or retirement, or disablement, as well as in the event of the sale of his practice or the loss of his patients, whatever the cause." Although Nail does not involve a spouse's education, we regard it as comparable and persuasive.

The trial court, upon divorce, is authorized to divide the "estate of the parties" which has been interpreted to refer to community property alone. Further, the trial court cannot divest spouses of rights to separate property whether real or personal.

An award of future monthly payments which is specifically referable to an education received by spouses during marriage, as we have in the case before us, violates the rules and authorities hereinbefore set forth, and an award of monthly payments to be made in the future that is based on future earnings is an award of separate property, property not acquired during the marriage relationship.

We recognize there are inequities which may result from the failure to compensate the spouse who supports the other spouse through college or professional school. *See*, Castleberry, Constitutional Limitations on the Division of Property Upon Divorce, 10 ST. MARY'S L.J. 37, 56 (1978). However, in an attempt to overcome such difficulties the trial court has wide discretion in dividing the estate of the parties in a divorce decree and may consider many factors including the difference in earning capacity, education and ability of the parties; probable future need for support; fault in breaking up the marriage; and the benefits an innocent spouse may have received from a continuation of the marriage. However, the trial court is limited by our basic community property laws in making a division as hereinbefore outlined.

We hold that a professional education acquired during marriage is not a property right and is not divisible upon divorce.

We must now consider whether the award of $20,000 can be justified on the basis of reimbursement. It is clear from the language of the decree that to whatever extent it is reimbursement, it is reimbursement for appellee's share of community expenses for appellant's education. This is not a typical reimbursement which ordinarily pertains to payments or contributions made by one spouse out of separate property to the community or by the community to one of the spouse's separate property. Reimbursement is ordinarily allowed where money is spent by one estate to pay off a debt of another estate, or where improvements are made from one estate to the other estate. The rule is sometimes stated that on dissolution of the marriage, if one party has contributed separate property, or if community funds have been applied to the enhancement of the property of the other, reimbursement is allowed. We do not have this here. Any reimbursement here is referable only to the education of one of the spouses, which we have held is not a property right, and which was admittedly paid for from community funds. Moreover, there are no pleadings seeking reimbursement. Ordinarily, an award for reimbursement is not allowable in the absence of an allegation of liability of such a nature or anything in the pleading to support such a judgment. Under the pleadings and the record we find no justification for such award on the theory of reimbursement.

The trial court's award of $20,000 to appellee as a part of the division of the estate of the parties and as a reimbursement for appellee's share of community expenses for appellant's education constitutes error and is an abuse of the trial court's discretion.

Where an appellate court finds that the trial court abused its discretion in a divorce suit, ordinarily, the proper order is a reversal and remand. As hereinbefore pointed out, it is not possible for us to determine exactly what portion of the community estate was awarded to the husband, and what portion to the wife. Consequently, it is not possible for us to tell to what extent the trial court considered the professional education and degree and substantially higher earning capacity of the husband, in making a division of the community estate between the parties. The interests of justice will best be served by a remand as to that portion of the divorce decree making a division of the property between the parties.

NOTES AND COMMENTS

1.   This is an instance where two basic principles of equitable distribution conflict. On one hand, the marital estate should share in the value of all property acquired by either spouse during marriage from effort. On the other hand, a spouse's post-divorce earnings are separate property. In 1985, the New York Court of Appeals ruled that a professional degree obtained during marriage was marital property, and should be valued in terms of the extent the degree enhanced the educated spouse's lifetime earnings. *See* O'Brien v. O'Brien, 489 N.E.2d 712 (N.Y. 1985). Every other state high court that has considered the issue has rejected the *O'Brien* approach. *See, e.g.,* Nelson v. Nelson, 736 P.2d 1145 (Alaska 1987); Wisner v. Wisner, 631 P.2d 115 (Ariz. App. 1981); *In re* Marriage of Sullivan, 184 Cal. Rptr. 796 (App. 1982);

vacated, 691 P.2d 1020 (Cal. 1984) (statute amended to provide for the community to be reimbursed for community contributions to education of a party); *In re* Marriage of Olar, 747 P.2d 676 (Colo. 1987); Hughes v. Hughes, 438 So. 2d 146 (Fla. Dist. Ct. App. 1983); *In re* Marriage of Weinstein, 470 N.E.2d 551 (Ill. App. 1984); Archer v. Archer, 493 A.2d 1074 (Md. 1985); Drapek v. Drapek, 503 N.E.2d 946 (Mass. 1987); Ruben v. Ruben, 461 A.2d 733 (N.H. 1983); Mahoney v. Mahoney, 453 A.2d 527 (N.J. 1982); Hodge v. Hodge, 520 A.2d 15 (Pa. 1986); Wehrkamp v. Wehrkamp, 357 N.W.2d 264 (S.D. 1984); Petersen v. Petersen, 737 P.2d 237 (Utah App. 1987). Here are some of the reasons other courts were hesitant to adopt the holding of the New York Court of Appeals in *O'Brien*:

> a.   *Consistency:* Under either a marital or community property regime, post-divorce wages are separate property; *O'Brien* is inconsistent with this approach. Most courts have failed to see a logical basis for distinguishing between cases where enhanced post-divorce wages result from acquisition of a degree or license and cases where enhanced post-divorce wages result from work experience, nondegree training, and promotions obtained during marriage:

> The termination of a marriage represents, if nothing else, the disappointment of expectations, financial and nonfinancial, which were hoped to be achieved by and during the continuation of the relationship. It does not, in our view, represent a commercial loss.

> If the plan fails by reason of the termination of the marriage, we do not regard the supporting spouse's consequent loss of expectation by itself as any more compensable or demanding of solicitude than the loss of expectations of any other spouse who, with the hope and anticipation of the endurance of the relationship * * * has invested a portion of his or her life, youth, energy and labor in a failed marriage.

> Mahoney v. Mahoney, 442 A.2d 1062 (N.J. Super. App. Div. 1982).

> b.   *Modifiability:* We do not know where Dr. O'Brien will practice, whether he will in fact pursue his chosen specialty, or how successful he will be. Yet, as Judge Meyer points out in *O'Brien*, property division awards are not modifiable due to changed circumstances. If the court's guess on the value of Dr. O'Brien's degree is inaccurate, no recourse is available to either party.

> c.   *Valuation:* The *O'Brien* court held that the degree should be valued by comparing the average lifetime earnings of a college graduate and those of a medical doctor practicing in Dr. O'Brien's chosen field of specialization. This approach ignores the fact that those admitted to medical school are a highly credentialed group of college graduates who likely have better than average career prospects whether they attend medical school or not. The *O'Brien* approach thus may substantially overvalue the degree. Further valuation problems arise if the couple divorces after the degree has

matured into a professional practice. In many states (including New York) professional goodwill in a practice established during marriage is marital property subject to division. Should the degree "merge" into the practice to avoid double-counting? Must the degree and practice be valued separately? If so, how is it possible to avoid double-counting? The New York Court of Appeals has attempted to answer these questions, holding that both the degree and practice are marital property; the court noted that overlapping awards should be avoided, but does not specify a valuation method to ensure such a result. *See* McSparron v. McSparron, 662 N.E.2d 745 (N.Y. 1995). For a valiant attempt by a trial court to apply the *McSparron* approach, *see* Rochelle G. v. Harold M.G., 649 N.Y.S.2d 632 (Misc. 1996).

d.   *Allocation:* The first Mrs. O'Brien has a claim to $188,000 of Dr. O'Brien's post-divorce earnings, wages that would traditionally be considered the marital property of Dr. O'Brien and any second Mrs. O'Brien. Is the $188,000 Dr. O'Brien's separate property with respect to his second spouse? Or is it the property of both marriages? The first approach seems unfair to the second Mrs. O'Brien; the second approach seems unfair to Dr. O'Brien. In New York, a marital property state, income from separate property received during marriage is separate property. *See* Sauer v. Sauer, 459 N.Y.S.2d 131 (App. Div. 1983). But no New York court has as yet dealt with this allocation issue.

e.   *Inflexibility:* Mrs. O'Brien was a very sympathetic plaintiff who not only supported her husband for years, but also sacrificed her own career goals and moved to another country, only to be dumped when the degree (but no property to compensate her) was in hand. The *O'Brien* holding, however, applies in all cases in which a degree is earned during marriage, even if there is other property, even if the spouses' living expenses were paid by the educated spouse's parents, even if the claimant spouse has higher earning capacity than the educated spouse, even if the claimant spouse has actively discouraged attainment of the degree.

In 2016, the New York legislature passed a statute providing that a professional degree or license should not be considered a marital asset in a divorce. *See* N.Y. DOM. REL. LAW § 236 (B)(5)(d)(7).

2.   As an alternative to treating a professional degree or license as property subject to division, many courts have granted the supporting spouse other remedies such as a rehabilitative or reimbursement alimony award. *See* Drapek v. Drapek, 503 N.E.2d 946 (Mass. 1987); Forristall v. Forristall, 831 P.2d 1017 (Okla. App. 1992); OR. REV. STAT. § 107.105; Ashby v. Ashby, 227 P.3d 246 (Utah 2010). California, for example, has statutorily adopted a reimbursement approach in the degree cases. CAL. FAM. CODE § 2641 requires reimbursement to the marital community "for community contributions to education or training of a party that substantially enhances the earning

capacity of the party. The amount reimbursed shall be with interest at the legal rate, accruing from the end of the calendar year in which the contributions were made." Reimbursement "shall be reduced or modified to the extent circumstances render such a disposition unjust," including, but not limited to, any of the following:

a.   The community has substantially benefitted from the education, training, or loan incurred for the education or training of the party. There is a rebuttable presumption, affecting the burden of proof, that the community has not substantially benefitted from community contributions to the education or training made less than 10 years before the commencement of the proceeding, and that the community has substantially benefitted from community contributions to the education or training made more than 10 years before the commencement of the proceeding.

b.   The education or training received by the party is offset by the education or training received by the other party for which community contributions have been made.

c.   The education or training enables the party receiving the education or training to engage in gainful employment that substantially reduces the need of the party for support that would otherwise be required.

The statute also excludes educational loans from community liabilities, assigning these debts to the spouse whose education the loan financed. What are the pros and cons of the California approach as compared to *O'Brien*? Other states with remedies like the California approach include IND. CODE ANN § 31–15–7–6; Bold v. Bold, 574 A.2d 552 (Pa. 1990). Oregon has adopted a more expansive system of "compensatory spousal support." *See In re* Marriage of Harris, 244 P.3d 801 (Or. 2010).

3.   The Utah Supreme Court has held that the spouse who supported the other while he or she attended school could have a remedy based on the couple's premarital or postnuptial contract. See Ashby v. Ashby, 227 P.3d 246 (Utah 2010).

4.   Some courts have said that, in the *O'Brien* situation, the non-educated spouse does not support the other with the "expectation of compensation." *See* Sullivan v. Sullivan, 184 Cal. Rptr. 796 (App. 1982). But undeniably the spouse would *hope* to share in the fruits from the education. Does this mean that some remedy should be provided? If so, what type of remedy?

5.   A spouse's earning capacity normally increases as he or she gains more experience. Are the professional degree cases different? If a professional degree is divisible property, would the earning capacity at divorce of all spouses be divisible property? Should a special remedy be created for the situation where a spouse's earning capacity increases during marriage due to education?

If a special remedy should be created when a spouse goes to graduate school, should it apply to all instances? Should it matter whether the spouse goes to day school or works and goes to night school? Should it make any difference if the living expenses and school expenses of the spouse going to school are paid by that spouse's parents or by the other spouse? Should an art history degree be treated differently from a law degree?

6.   If a spouse attends school during marriage and borrows money, if the parties divorce before these loans are repaid, who should have to repay these loans after divorce?

G. BUSINESS GOODWILL

"Goodwill" refers to the portion of a business's value derived from its reputation. In computing the value of a marital business, almost all courts have concluded that the value of *commercial goodwill*, that associated with the business rather than the owner spouse, should be included in the marital estate. *Cf.* Lewis v. Lewis, 54 So. 3d 216 (Miss. 2011) (the value of goodwill of any type should not be included when valuing a business at divorce). There is less agreement on *personal goodwill*, the portion of the goodwill that derives from the personal reputation of the owner spouse. Some courts have held that, if earned during marriage, it is a marital asset subject to division. Other courts, troubled by the fact that personal goodwill is an intangible (and often nonmarketable) asset much like earning capacity, have held that it should not be treated as a marital asset. For a general discussion of this problem, *see* THEODORE P. ORENSTEIN & GARY N. SKOLOFF, WHEN A PROFESSIONAL DIVORCES (ABA, 2d ed. 1994). For a general discussion of business valuation methods, *see* SHANNON PRATT, THE LAWYER'S BUSINESS VALUATION HANDBOOK: UNDERSTANDING FINANCIAL STATESMENTS, APPRAISAL REPORTS, AND EXPERT TESTIMONY (2D ED. 2010).

PRAHINSKI V. PRAHINSKI
Maryland Court of Appeals, 1990.
321 Md. 227, 582 A.2d 784.

COLE, JUDGE.

In this case we must determine whether the goodwill of a solo law practice is a value includable as marital property for purposes of calculating a monetary award upon divorce.

The facts are neither complicated nor in dispute. Margaret and Leo F. X. Prahinski were married on March 20, 1965. Margaret discontinued her education after her freshman year in college in order to maintain the family home. Leo continued his formal education and eventually obtained a law degree. In 1971, Leo started his own law practice. Margaret became his secretary, and as the law practice grew, so did Margaret's responsibilities in the office. Gradually, the focus of the practice shifted to real estate settlements and Margaret's position evolved into that of office manager.

Leo became involved with another woman in 1983. The parties separated thereafter, and Margaret filed for divorce on November 14, 1986. The Circuit Court for Prince George's County granted an absolute divorce, and on July 10, 1987, the court filed a written order determining what was marital property, providing for distribution of marital assets, and granting both a monetary award and indefinite alimony. Included in the monetary award was one-half of the value of the law practice.

Leo appealed to the Court of Special Appeals claiming that the trial court erred in considering his law practice to be marital property consisting totally of goodwill and dividing the value thereof equally between the parties. Leo also questioned the propriety of setting the amount of alimony at a time far in advance of when the alimony payments were to commence.

The Court of Special Appeals, 75 Md. App. 113, 540 A.2d 833 (1988), held that the value of the practice consisted entirely of the reputation of Leo F. X. Prahinski, Attorney-at-Law, and was therefore personal to him. As such, the value of the practice was not marital property and could not be subject to distribution as part of the monetary award. The intermediate appellate court left open the possibility that goodwill in a solo practice could be marital property if it could be shown that the goodwill was severable from the reputation of the practitioner.

Margaret argues that the value of the practice should be considered marital property, and therefore subject to a monetary award to compensate her for her contributions thereto. She insists that the majority of the work handled by the practice did not require an attorney, and that she contributed the overwhelming majority of the time and effort which made the practice successful. To deny her an equitable share of the goodwill inherent in the practice, she claims, would frustrate the purpose of the monetary award statute, which seeks to adjust the rights of the parties based upon their contributions during the marriage.

Specifically, Margaret contends that goodwill is a form of property which the practice acquired during the marriage; hence it fits the definition of marital property, no matter whose name is on the business. She further urges this Court to adopt the position that the professional goodwill of a sole proprietorship is valuable property to be included in the marital estate.

Leo maintains that his vocation has always been a solo law practice. As such, any intangible value assigned to the business is a result of his personal reputation as an attorney. The only way that goodwill could be considered marital property, he argues, is if the goodwill had a value independent of the continued presence or reputation of the sole practitioner. He contends that he is the only person who can practice under the name "Leo F. X. Prahinski, Attorney-at-law." He claims he could not sell his practice and its intangible assets to anyone; therefore, he concludes that the goodwill is personal to him and should not be considered marital property.

The characterization of goodwill and its relationship to a business is crucial to the determination of this issue. In *Hagan v. Dundore*, 187 Md. 430, 50 A.2d 570 (1947), we examined the sale of a partnership interest. In so doing, we took notice of the definitions of goodwill applied by other jurisdictions. One such definition states: "The goodwill of a business comprises those advantages which may inure to the *purchaser* from holding himself out to the public as succeeding to an enterprise which has been identified in the past with the name and repute of his *predecessor.*" *Id.* at 442, 50 A.2d at 576 (emphasis added). According to this definition, goodwill can exist in those situations in which a business has successive owners, each one benefitting from the management of the business by the preceding owners.

Goodwill exists, however, in businesses that are still in the hands of their founders and which may never be sold. We took notice of such a situation in *Brown v. Benzinger*, 118 Md. 29, 84 A. 79 (1912), where we quoted Lord Eldon's definition of goodwill as "the probability that the old customers will resort to the old place." *Id.* at 35, 84 A. at 81 (quoting *Cruttwell v. Lye*, 34 Eng.Rep. 129, 134 (Ch. 1810)). Such a definition provides for the presence of goodwill in a business even if no monetary value has ever been placed on it.

In *Brown*, the Court was confronted with the sale of a "business conducted by [the vendor] as surgeon chiropodist." 118 Md. at 31, 84 A. at 79. That opinion makes it that as long ago as 1912, this Court considered the goodwill involved in a profession to be different from the goodwill involved in a commercial business. Examining the decisions from other jurisdictions, the *Brown* court noted that in the context of a non-competition agreement in the sale of a business, the goodwill of a professional practice had been held to be personal to the practitioner. The Court specifically observed that there was a distinction between the sale of the goodwill of a trade or business of a commercial character where the location is an important feature of the business, and the sale of an established practice and goodwill of a person engaged in a profession or calling where the income therefrom is the immediate or direct result of his labor and skill and where integrity, skill, ability and other desirable personal qualities follow the person and not the place.

Having recognized the existence of goodwill in the above noted situations, we must now determine whether goodwill can exist in the particular circumstances of the instant case. Although the trial court found that the business was predominantly a title company and treated it as such, both parties' arguments to this Court are based on the Court of

Special Appeals' holding that the business was a sole proprietorship, and in particular a solo law practice. It should be noted that neither party is contesting the status of the license to practice law. What is being contested is the existence of goodwill in a practice established once the professional license has been obtained.

Because the question of whether professional goodwill is marital property is one of first impression in Maryland, we found it beneficial to review the decisions of the courts of other states which have addressed the issue. This review revealed three positions. The view most often followed treats goodwill as marital property in all cases. The next largest group considers goodwill to be personal to the practitioner, and therefore not marital property. Finally, a small group of states requires a case-by-case examination to determine how goodwill should be treated. It is interesting to note that the classification of a jurisdiction as a community property state or an equitable distribution state is not determinative of its treatment of goodwill.

The view that the goodwill of a solo practice should be considered as marital property was early on set forth in the California decisions of *Mueller v. Mueller*, 144 Cal. App. 2d 245, 301 P.2d 90 (1956) and *Golden v. Golden*, 270 Cal. App. 2d 401, 75 Cal. Rptr. 735 (1969).

In *Mueller*, the husband was the sole owner of a dental laboratory which employed six people. The wife sought to have the value of the business divided at the time of the divorce. The husband argued that the goodwill of the business was wholly dependent upon his personal skill and ability. The court examined the business and concluded that the business was too old and too large to be dependent solely upon the owner for its goodwill, 144 Cal. App. 2d at 251, 301 P.2d at 95, and held that the value of this business was to be divided between the parties. Furthermore, the *Mueller* court examined the argument that goodwill cannot arise in a professional business depending upon the personal skill and ability of a particular person. Even though unnecessary to its decision, the court stated that this argument was based on the definition of goodwill set forth by Lord Eldon, and the better, more modern, view is that the skill and learning acquired by a professional has intangible value which may be transferred. *Id.* at 251, 301 P.2d at 94–95. This left open the possibility that professional goodwill could also be divided upon divorce.

The court in *Golden* used the opening left by *Mueller* to hold that professional goodwill was marital property. The husband in *Golden* was a sole practicing physician. The wife sought a division of the value of the practice when the couple was divorced. The court, looking to *Mueller*, 270 Cal. App. 2d at 405, 75 Cal. Rptr. at 737, set forth the holding that "the better rule is that, in a divorce case, the goodwill of the husband's professional practice as a sole practitioner should be taken into consideration in determining the award to the wife." *Id.*

The *Golden* court distinguished a divorce from the dissolution of a partnership, in which it might be difficult to determine the correct share upon distribution.

> [I]n a matrimonial matter, the practice of the sole practitioner husband will continue, with the same intangible value as it had during the marriage. *Under the principles of community property law, the wife, by virtue of her position of wife, made to that value the same contribution* as does a wife to any of the husband's earnings and accumulations during marriage. She is as much entitled to be recompensed for that contribution as if it were represented by the increased value of stock in a family business.

Id. at 405, 75 Cal. Rptr. at 738 (emphasis added).

Although the California court used community property law to give the wife credit for the increase in the goodwill value during the marriage, the non-monetary contribution aspect of equitable distribution principles tends to accomplish the same result. Note, *Treating Professional Goodwill as Marital Property in Equitable Distribution States*, 58 N.Y.U. L. Rev. 554, 558 (1983).

The New Jersey case of *Dugan v. Dugan*, 92 N.J. 423, 457 A.2d 1 (1983) presents a situation which is quite similar to the instant case, but in that case the court held that the goodwill of a solo law practice was marital property. The husband was an attorney who operated his practice as a wholly-owned professional corporation. New Jersey and Maryland both place the following limitations on the practice of law: (1) sole practitioners cannot sell their law practices, (2) restrictive covenants prohibiting competition by the transferor of the practice are not allowed, and (3) clients may not be sold between practices. Regarding domestic relations law, both Maryland and New Jersey are equitable distribution states, and neither treats a professional degree or license to practice as property.

The New Jersey court began its analysis by looking at the various definitions of goodwill used in other states. Its conclusion was that goodwill exists and is a legally protected interest. Next the court examined the relationship between goodwill and "going concern value." Goodwill was found to be closely related to reputation, and the definition settled on by the New Jersey court was that goodwill "is equivalent to the excess of actual earnings over expected earnings based on a normal rate of return on investment." *Id.* at 431, 457 A.2d at 5.

Examining the relationship between goodwill and earning capacity (as that relates to a medical degree), the court found a difference between the two:

Future earning capacity *per se* is not goodwill. However, when that future earning capacity has been enhanced because reputation leads to probable future patronage from existing and potential clients, goodwill may exist and have value. When that occurs the resulting good will is property subject to equitable distribution.

Id. at 433, 457 A.2d at 6.

Having distinguished goodwill from earning capacity and having found goodwill subject to equitable distribution, the court went on to state its rationale for the decision:

After divorce, the law practice will continue to benefit from that goodwill as it had during the marriage. Much of the economic value produced during an attorney's marriage will inhere to the goodwill of the law practice. *It would be inequitable to ignore the contribution of the non-attorney spouse to the development of that economic resource.* An individual practitioner's inability to sell a law practice does not eliminate existence of goodwill and its value as an asset to be considered in equitable distribution. Obviously, equitable distribution does not require conveyance or transfer of any particular asset. The other spouse, in this case the wife, is entitled to have that asset considered as any other property acquired during the marriage partnership.

Id. at 434, 457 A.2d at 6 (emphasis added).

The view that professional goodwill is personal to the practitioner and is not marital property is articulated by the Texas court in *Nail v. Nail*, 486 S.W.2d 761 (Tex. 1972). Despite the fact that Texas, like California, is a community property state, the *Nail* court held that the goodwill built up by a medical practice was personal to the husband doctor. The court determined that the goodwill was based on the husband's personal skill, experience, and reputation. Because the goodwill was not an asset separate and apart from the doctor, it would be extinguished if he died, retired, or became disabled. Because of the personal nature of this asset, it was not considered by the court as an earned or vested property right at the time of the divorce, and did not qualify as property subject to division in a divorce proceeding.

Taylor v. Taylor, 222 Neb. 721, 386 N.W.2d 851 (1986), sets forth the middle ground between the two extremes. The trial court found that the husband's professional medical corporation contained no goodwill which was subject to distribution upon divorce. On appeal, the Nebraska Supreme Court affirmed that finding. In so doing, however, the appellate court noted that in proper circumstances, professional goodwill might exist as a salable or marketable business asset. Whether such a situation existed would be a question of fact. If the goodwill was found to be saleable or marketable, the court could divide that goodwill as a marital asset. The court stated that the essential factor which would determine the goodwill to be personal would be its dependence upon the continued presence of the individual.

Taylor, therefore, provides for a case-by-case analysis to determine whether goodwill in a particular situation should be considered marital property. Unlike the Texas court, *Taylor* does not rule out the possibility that a professional solo practice might contain such goodwill. And unlike the California cases, it allows for distinctions between those situations where goodwill is truly personal and where it is indeed marital property. It was this rationale which the Court of Special Appeals found persuasive.

After reviewing these three alternatives and the rationale of their respective supporting cases, we are of the opinion that the goodwill of a solo law practice is personal to the individual practitioner. Goodwill in such circumstances is not severable from the reputation of the sole practitioner regardless of the contributions made to the practice by the spouse or employees. In order for goodwill to be marital property, it must be an asset having a separate value from the reputation of the practitioner.

We are not convinced that the goodwill of a solo law practice can be separated from the reputation of the attorney. It is the attorney whose name, whether on the door or stationery, is the embodiment of the practice. We are cognizant that in this computer age many law practices, and in Leo's practice in particular, much of the research and "form" work is done by non-lawyers. In the final analysis, however, it is the attorney alone who is responsible for the work that comes out of the office. Rule of Professional Conduct 5.3(c). In the instant case, the responsibility is solely Leo's, and no amount of work done by Margaret will shift the responsibility to her. The attorney's signature or affidavit places his seal of approval on the work being done and makes the attorney liable for its accuracy and authenticity. This professional assurance is what might have convinced some clients to use Leo F. X. Prahinski, Attorney-at-Law, instead of going to a title company to have their settlements completed. The assurance would end should Leo somehow remove himself from the practice. Therefore, the goodwill generated by the attorney is personal to him and is not the kind of asset which can be divided as marital property.

Because the instant case involves the practice of law, special considerations arise which might not be present in other professional practices. In *Brown v. Benzinger*, 118 Md. 29, 84 A. 79 (1912), we quoted with approval from *Yeakley v. Gaston*, 50 Tex. Civ. App. 405, 111 S.W. 768 (1908) where the court said, "the sale of goodwill be a professional carries with it the obligation that he will abstain from practice in the future in the territory from which he binds himself to withdraw." It is clear that an attorney, as distinguished from other professionals, may not covenant to abstain from the practice of law, and therefore, may not sell his or her goodwill.

Other professions do not have the prohibition against the sale of goodwill. *Brown v. Benzinger, supra* (sale of her practice "including goodwill" by a "surgeon chiropodist"); *Warfield v. Booth*, 33 Md. 63 (1870) (sale of a physician's practice including goodwill); *Spaulding v. Benenati*, 57 N.Y.2d 418, 456 N.Y.S.2d 733, 442 N.E.2d 1244 (1982) (goodwill of a dentist is a saleable asset); *Dwight v. Hamilton*, 113 Mass. 175 (1873) (goodwill of a physician is a saleable asset).

Since a lawyer's goodwill is not a saleable asset, it has no commercial value. The methods for valuing the marketable goodwill of a profession or business would not be applicable to an attorney's nonmarketable goodwill. The fact that a lawyer's goodwill cannot be sold by the lawyer is another factor in our determination that it is not marital property.

We have noted, as did the Court of Special Appeals, that the circuit court included the value of the goodwill of the legal practice of Leo F. X. Prahinski as a part of the marital property. The alimony and the monetary award were both calculated with the value being a factor. This was error. Therefore, the entitlements of the spouse must be recalculated.

Judgment of the Court of Special Appeals Affirmed.

Notes and Questions

1.   *Prahinski* summarizes the various approaches to professional goodwill developed during marriage. What are the pros and cons of each? Which seems the fairest?

2.   How a court values a professional practice at divorce varies depending on the position the state has taken toward professional goodwill. Washington, for example, has adopted a relatively expansive definition of divisible goodwill which permits Washington courts to use any of a number of methods to value a practice. In *In re* Marriage of Hall, 692 P.2d 175, 179–80 (Wash. 1984) the court summarized the possible approaches:

> In valuing goodwill five major formulas have been articulated. There are three accounting formulas. Under the straight capitalization accounting method the average net profits of the practitioner are determined and this figure is capitalized at a definite rate, as, for example, 20 percent. This result is considered to be the total value of the business including both tangible and intangible assets. To determine the value of goodwill the book value of the business assets are subtracted from the total value figure.

Average net earnings	$ 60,000
Capitalize at 2	× 5
Total business tangible and intangible assets	300,000
Less current net tangible assets	−30,000
Goodwill	$270,000

The second accounting formula is the capitalization of excess earnings method. Under the pure capitalization of excess earnings the average net income is determined. From this figure an annual salary of average employee practitioner with like experience is subtracted. The remaining amount is multiplied by a fixed capitalization rate to determine the goodwill.

Average net earnings	$ 60,000
Less comparable net salary	−40,000
Average earnings on intangible assets	20,000
Capitalize at 20%	× 5
Goodwill	$100,000

The IRS variation of capitalized excess earnings method takes the average net income of the business for the last 5 years and subtracts a reasonable rate of return based on the business' average net tangible assets. From this amount a comparable net salary is subtracted. Finally, this remaining amount is capitalized at a definite rate. The resulting amount is goodwill.

Average net earnings	$ 60,000
Less rate of return on average tangible assets	−2,500
Subtotal	57,500
Less comparable net salary	40,000
Average Earnings on intangible assets	17,500
Capitalize at 20%	x 5
Goodwill	$ 87,500

The fourth method, the market value approach, sets a value on professional goodwill by establishing what fair price would be obtained in the current open market if the practice were to be sold. This method necessitates that a professional practice has been recently sold, is in the process of being sold or is the subject of a recent offer to purchase. Otherwise, the value may be manipulated by the professional spouse.

The fifth valuation method, the buy/sell agreement method, values goodwill by reliance on a recent actual sale or an unexercised existing option or contractual formula set forth in a partnership agreement or corporate agreement. Since the professional spouse may have been influenced by many factors other than fair market value in negotiating the terms of the agreement, courts relying on this method should inquire into the presence of such factors, as well as the arm's length nature of the transaction.

These five methods are not the exclusive formulas available to trial courts in analyzing the evidence presented. Nor must only one method be used in isolation. One or more methods may be used in conjunction with the *Fleege* factors to achieve a just and fair evaluation of the existence and value of any professional's goodwill.

The danger of using any one method without regard to the *Fleege* factors is apparent in the present case where appellant's expert witnesses used only the capitalized excess earnings approach. Under this approach the experts testified that Phillip had no goodwill. Further testimony, however, indicated that Phillip's comparatively low earnings were a result of office expansion expenses, a deliberate decision to limit hours of practice and failure to compare Phillip with cardiologists in the same age and experience group doing similar procedures in Seattle. Consideration of the appellant's reputation, associations, referrals, location and trade name indicate the existence of goodwill.

This case also exemplifies the need for caution in the use of the buy/sell agreement. The Northwest Cardiology Clinic buy/sell agreement does not include a goodwill factor. When the third doctor became a shareholder, no value was assigned to goodwill. The trial court must, however, inquire whether the omission in the agreement was the result of other factors or deliberations on the part of the shareholders, particularly when the particular agreement is made in close proximity in time to the divorce.

3.   States employing a less expansive definition of divisible goodwill may restrict valuation methods accordingly. For example, the Missouri Supreme Court concluded that only goodwill separate from the professional's individual reputation should be divisible; as a result it "state[d] a strong preference" for the fair market value approach to valuation:

First, the fair market value approach "does not take explicitly into consideration the future earning capacity of the professional goodwill or the post-dissolution efforts of the professional spouse." Comment, *Professional Goodwill in Louisiana: An Analysis of Its Classification, Valuation and Partition*, 43 LA. L. REV. 139, 142 (1982).

Second, fair market value evidence appears to us to be the most equitable and accurate measure of both the existence and true value of the goodwill of an enterprise. Evidence of a recent actual sale of a similarly situated practice, an offer to purchase the subject or a similar practice, or expert testimony and testimony of members of the subject profession as to the present value of goodwill of a similar practice in the open, relevant, geographical and professional market is the best evidence of value.

Third, the fair market value method is most likely to avoid the "disturbing inequity in compelling a professional practitioner to pay a spouse a share of intangible assets at a judicially determined value that could not be realized by a sale or another method of liquidating value."

We reject the use of capitalization formulae as a substitute for fair market value evidence of the value of goodwill in a professional practice. The very purpose of capitalization formulae is to place a present value on the future earnings of the business entity being valued. The formulae draw no distinction between the future earning capacity of the individual and that of the entity in which he or she practices. And as we have said previously, the future earning capacity of the individual professional is not, *per se*, an item of marital property subject to division in a dissolution proceeding.

Hanson v. Hanson, 738 S.W.2d 429, 434–35 (Mo. 1987) (citations omitted).

4.   The *Hall* approach (note 2, *supra*) would seem to require division of all increased earning capacity acquired during marriage as a result of enhanced reputation. But neither the *Hall* court nor others utilizing an expansive definition of goodwill have in fact gone this far. In *Hall*, for example, both spouses were medical doctors. The husband was a partner in a clinic and had gross yearly earnings of about $52,000. The wife was a professor at the University of Washington Medical School; she earned $42,000 annually and, as a well-known expert in pediatric genetics, had received offers to teach elsewhere at salaries of up to $60,000 annually. The court concluded that employees, as a matter of law, could not have goodwill; thus the value of the husband's professional reputation was divisible, while the wife's was not. States accepting the expansive Washington/California view of professional goodwill frequently distinguish goodwill from earning capacity in this manner.

In *In re* Marriage of McTiernan and Dubrow, 35 Cal. Rptr. 3d 297 (App. 2005) the husband during marriage became a successful movie director. The trial court concluded that, due to his personal skill and reputation, he had an "expectation of future patronage" after divorce, and that the marital estate should share this; the trial court valued his enhanced reputation at $1.5 million. The court of appeals reversed, holding that the marital estate can only share in the personal goodwill of a business. Mr. McTiernan's enhanced personal earning capacity was personal to him, not a business, and could not be sold.

5.   In valuing goodwill, most courts have concluded that a value specified in a partnership agreement (for purposes of buyout) is relevant, but not binding. *See, e.g.*, Burns v. Burns, 643 N.E.2d 80 (N.Y. 1994). A minority of courts treats the agreement valuation as determinative if made in good faith. *See* McDiarmid v. McDiarmid, 649 A.2d 810 (D.C. App. 1994) (citing other cases). Should it matter whether the practice can be sold? If it does matter, should it also matter whether the seller would have to agree not to compete with the practice in order to make a sale?

6.   In those states that do not consider "personal" professional goodwill divisible, should "personal" goodwill in other types of marital businesses be divisible? *See* Rathmell v. Morrison, 732 S.W.2d 6 (Tex. App. 1987) (no); Marriage of Talty, 652 N.E.2d 330 (Ill. 1995) (no).

7.   In Cesar v. Sundelin, 967 N.E. 2d 171 (Mass. App. 2012) the court held that, in connection with the award of a family business to one spouse, the court had the power to enjoin the other from operating a competing business.

H. VALUING AN INTEREST IN A BUSINESS OR PRACTICE

Before a court divides the marital estate, it must determine the value of each item in the estate. In many states, the standard is the item's "fair market value," what a willing buyer would pay a willing seller. When determining the fair market value of an interest in a small business or practice, courts encounter a few difficult issues.

First, an appraiser of a business would discount the value of an ownership interest due to the lack of a ready market for the interest. This "marketability discount" has been accepted by a number of courts when valuing business interests in a divorce. *See In re* Marriage of Thornhill, 200 P.3d 1083 (Colo. App. 2008); Erp v. Erp, 976 So. 2d 1234 (Fla. App. 2008). *But see* Caveney v. Caveney, 960 N.E.2d 331 (Mass. App. 2012) (marketability discount should not be applied when valuing a business interest at divorce if a sale of the interest is not planned). In addition, if the interest is a minority ownership interest, some courts have accepted that the value should be reduced for this factor as well. *See In re* Marriage of Heroy, 895 N.E.2d 1025 (Ill. App. 2008); Thompson v. Thompson, 978 So. 2d 509 (La. App. 2008). In Schickner v. Schickner, 348 P.3d 890 (Ariz. App. 2015), the court held that a court should decide whether to apply a minority discount when valuing a business interest at divorce on a case-by-case basis.

A few courts have argued that such discounts are inappropriate if there is no evidence the spouse plans to sell the interest. *See* Bernier v. Bernier, 873 N.E.2d 216 (Mass. 2007); Caveney v. Caveney, 960 N.E.2d 231 (Mass. App. 2012).

Finally, when valuing an interest in a business or professional practice some courts would consider any contractual restrictions impeding the owner's ability to sell the interest.

I.　DEBTS

Few state divorce statutes expressly address debts. In a marital property state, premarital and post-divorce debts will be the separate obligations of the debtor spouse, while debts incurred during marriage may be assigned to either spouse, regardless of who incurred the debt. *See* Marriage of Stewart, 757 P.2d 765 (Mont. 1988). (The divorce court's order does not, of course, affect the right of a creditor to sue the spouse who incurred the debt.)

There is consensus on some recurring cases. Although not typically required under state law, courts generally agree that student loans should be assigned to the spouse who attended school (*see* Tasker v. Tasker, 395 N.W.2d 100 (Minn. App. 1986)) and that the spouse who receives property encumbered by a secured debt takes it subject to that debt. (Of course, the value of the debt is subtracted to determine the asset's net value. *See* Daniels v. Daniels, 726 S.W.2d 705 (Ky. App. 1986); Talent v. Talent, 334 S.E.2d 256 (N.C. App. 1985)). Debts or fines incurred as a result of criminal activity are generally assigned to the spouse who violated the law. *See* Thompson v. Thompson, 105 P.3d 346 (Okla. App. 2004); Curda-Derickson v. Derickson, 668 N.W.2d 736 (Wis. App. 2003). If one spouse incurs a debt when the marriage is breaking down with the intention of depleting the marital estate, it will be allocated to the spouse who incurred it. And debts incurred after separation are typically, but not invariably, assigned to the spouse who incurred the debt. *See* Zecchin v. Zecchin, 386 N.W.2d 652 (Mich. App. 1986); Gelb v. Brown, 558 N.Y.S.2d 934 (App. Div. 1990).

There is less agreement on other debt allocation issues. If a spouse incurs an investment loss during marriage, should this debt be subtracted from the value of the divisible marital estate, to determine the net divisible estate? *See* Marriage of Hauge, 427 N.W.2d 154 (Wis. App. 1988) (yes). *Cf.* note 2, page 961. Should the recklessness of the investment have an effect on the answer? If one spouse was much more frugal than the other during marriage, should this affect how the debts (or property) are divided?

J.　PETS

Pets today are treated at divorce like any other type of personal property. So, for example, in a marital property state if one party acquired a pet before marriage, he or she should keep it after divorce. *See* Isbell v. Willoughby, 2005 WL 1744468 (Cal. App.). In addition, a pet acquired during marriage needs to be awarded to one party. In a Florida case, the court reversed an award that gave the wife "visitation" rights with the family dog. *See* Bennett v. Bennett, 655 So. 2d 109 (Fla. Dist. Ct. App. 1995). Another court considering a similar issue reached the same conclusion, noting that "just as a divorce court lacked the power to grant visitation regarding a table or lamp, it does not have the power to make such an order regarding a pet." *See* Desanctis v. Pritchard, 803 A.2d 230, 231 (Pa. Super. 2002). *See also*, Hamert v. Baker, 97 A.3d 461 (Vt. 2014) (holding that a pet is personal property and may not be the subject of a visitation order).

Is this a good approach? Or should courts be more amenable to "shared custody" of pets after divorce? For a general discussion, *see generally* Ann Hartwell Britton, *Bones of Contention: Custody of Family Pets*, 20 J. AM. ACAD. MAT. LAW. 1 (2006). In March, 2017 Alaska became the first state to enact a statute which allows a judge to consider the animal's well-being.

Problem 15-5:

Harry and Wilma married in September 2005. Wilma filed for divorce in September 2007. Following a reconciliation, the divorce petition was voluntarily dismissed in September 2008. After the reconciliation failed, Wilma filed another divorce petition in September 2014; the divorce trial took place in October 2016. What valuation date should be used for Harry's pension, worth $100,000 in September, 2005; $115,000 in September, 2007; $130,000 in September 2008; $150,000 in September 2014; and $172,000 in October 2016. What factors are relevant?

Problem 15-6:

Ernest and Maggie May were married approximately twelve years ago, when Ernest was 26 and Maggie 22. At the time they married, Maggie had just graduated from college with a B.A. in Early Childhood Education; Ernest had obtained a Ph. D. in Linguistics.

Following their marriage, Ernest and Maggie moved into a home Ernest had purchased with a small inheritance from his grandmother. Ernest took a job as an Assistant Professor of Linguistics; Maggie took a job as a kindergarten teacher. The following year, Ernest and Maggie's first child (Polly) was born. Maggie quit her job and so did Ernest. In his spare time, Ernest started a language school, Lingua Lab.

Two years after Polly's birth, Maggie and Ernest had twins (Jeff and Jane). Ernest worked approximately 40 hours per week at his university job and 15–20 hours at his school. Maggie ran the household and performed virtually all child care tasks until the twins were in kindergarten, when she began to teach again.

Maggie has consulted your law firm for legal advice. She and Ernest have had increasingly bitter arguments over the last couple of years; she wants to terminate the relationship. But she is worried about money and wants to know how much property she would obtain at divorce. Last year, Ernest earned $70,000 from his University position and $35,000 from

Lingua Lab; Maggie earns $30,000 per year. She and Ernest own the following assets:

1.   Marital home: Purchased by Ernest for $125,000 around the time of his marriage to Maggie with a down payment ($25,000) inherited from his grandmother. Maggie believes that the house is now worth about $250,000. Ernest is the sole owner of the house. The note has been paid down to a balance owing of $80,000.

2.   Lingua Lab: Solely owned by Ernest, Lingua Lab now has two employees in addition to Ernest and serves approximately 500 clients per year. Lingua rents space; its tangible assets (books, desks, computers, etc.) are worth approximately $50,000. Last year, Ernest received a salary of $35,000 from the company's net profits of $50,000. (The other teachers (all part-time), who perform fewer administrative functions than Ernest but teach the same number of classes, earned $25,000 last year.) The remaining $15,000 was used to pay for new computer equipment. Last year's profit picture was typical of the company's profitability over the past few years; in each of the prior five years, Lingua had average net earnings of approximately $50,000. Ernest is the most popular teacher at the school; his classes are always sold out. Maggie thinks that Ernest would have a hard time finding a buyer for the school; he has never received an offer.

3.   Pension: Ernest is a participant in a defined contribution plan; his account is currently worth $130,000.

4.   Mutual Fund: The shares were originally purchased with money inherited from Ernest's grandmother ($100,000). The account balance ($250,000) represents appreciation and reinvestment of capital gains.

State law permits division of all "marital assets," defined as "property acquired by either spouse during marriage, except for property acquired by gift, inheritance, or bequest." Separate property ("all property acquired by gift, inheritance, or bequest and all property acquired before marriage; income and appreciation from such property; and property acquired in exchange for such property") is not divisible. What assets are marital property? What assets are separate property? What value (or range of values) would you place on each marital asset?

3.   DIVIDING THE DIVISIBLE ESTATE

Once the divisible estate has been determined and valued, it must be divided. A few states, like California, require equal division. *See* CAL. FAM. CODE § 2550. A few others, like Arkansas, have established a rebuttable presumption in favor of equal division:

ARK. STAT. ANN. § 9–12–315 Division of property.

(a) At the time a divorce decree is entered:

(1)(A)   all marital property shall be distributed one-half (1/2) to each party unless the court finds such a division to be inequitable. In that event the court shall make some other division that the court deems equitable taking into consideration:

(i)   The length of the marriage;

(ii)   Age, health, and station in life of the parties;

(iii)   Occupation of the parties;

(iv)   Amount and sources of income;

(v)   Vocational skills;

(vi)   Employability;

(vii)   Estate, liabilities, and needs of each party and opportunity of each for further acquisition of capital assets and income;

(viii) Contribution of each party in acquisition, preservation, or appreciation of marital property, including services as a homemaker; and

(ix)   The federal income tax consequences of the court's division of property.

(B) When property is divided pursuant to the foregoing considerations the court must state its basis and reasons for not dividing the marital property equally between the parties, and the basis and reasons should be recited in the order entered in the matter.

Most statutes (or court decisions, if no statute has been enacted) merely instruct the court to divide the marital estate equitably, after considering a number of factors. For a discussion of the various factors applicable in different states, *see Comment*, 50 FORDHAM L. REV. 415 (1981). The Minnesota statute is typical:

MINN. STAT. ANN. § 518.58 Division of marital property

Subdivision 1. Upon a dissolution of a marriage * * * the court shall make a just and equitable division of the marital property of the parties without regard to marital misconduct, after making findings regarding the division of the property. The court shall base its findings on all relevant factors including the length of the marriage, any prior marriage of a party, the age, health, station, occupation, amount and sources of income, vocational skills, employability, estate, liabilities, needs, opportunity for future acquisition of capital assets, and income of each party. The court shall also consider the contribution of each in the acquisition, preservation, depreciation or appreciation in the amount or value of the marital property, as well as the contribution of a spouse as a homemaker. It shall be conclusively presumed that each spouse made a substantial contribution to the acquisition of income and property while they were living together as husband and wife. The court may also award to either spouse the household goods and furniture of the parties, whether or not acquired during the marriage. The court shall value marital assets for purposes of division between the parties as of the day of the initially scheduled prehearing settlement conference, unless a different date is agreed upon by the parties, or unless the court makes specific findings that another date of valuation is fair and equitable. If there is a substantial change in value of an asset between the date of valuation and the final distribution, the Court may adjust the valuation of that asset as necessary to effect an equitable distribution.

Although many statutes set forth a long list of factors, three central themes—need, contribution and fault—predominate. These themes often lead in conflicting directions. For example, one spouse will often have contributed the majority of the marital assets (although many statutes explicitly recognize nonmonetary contributions), while the other will have greater post-divorce financial need. Which factor should predominate?

In situations where the spouses have accumulated a very large marital estate, this is usually due to the unusual business skills of one spouse. What should happen if spouses like those divorce? Should the spouse who generated the wealth receive substantially more than 50% of the accumulated estate, due to his or her extraordinary constibutions? *See generally* David N. Hofstein, et al. *Equitable Distributions Involving Large Marital Estates*, 26 J. AM. ACAD. MAT. LAW. 311 (2014).

In practice, judges appear to tend strongly toward fifty-fifty division. *See* Marsha Garrison, *How Do Judges Decide Divorce Cases? An Empirical Analysis of Discretionary Decision Making*, 74 N.C. L. REV. 401, 454 tbl. 8 (1996) (judges divided net worth relatively equally in 48% of surveyed New York cases); Suzanne Reynolds, *The Relationship of Property Division and Alimony: The Division of Property to Address Need*, 54 FORDHAM L. REV. 827, 854–55 (1988) (judges in six states seldom deviated from equal division except in "extraordinary circumstances"). But when judges do deviate from an equal division, their decision making appears to be relatively unpredictable. In a survey of divorce decision-making by New York judges, Professor Garrison found that indications of the wife's need—poor health, unemployment, low income, low occupational status, and income representing a small fraction of family income, were all *negatively* correlated with the wife's percentage award. So were the husband's ownership of a marital business or degree, the percentage of marital property owned by the husband, and the net value of marital assets. The wife's income and the value of the husband's separate property, on the other hand, were *positively* correlated with the wife's percentage award. But the predictive value of these factors was slight; a decision-making model utilizing all of these factors could predict no more than 14% of the variation in net worth outcomes. Garrison, *supra* at 456–64. Outcomes in settled cases were somewhat more predictable, but the important predictive variable was the percentage of property to which each spouse held title—the very factor that equitable property distribution was supposed to make unimportant. *Id.* at 466. The relative unpredictability of outcomes under equitable distribution schemes has led Professor Mary Ann Glendon to call them "discretionary," rather than "equitable," distribution systems. *See* MARY ANN GLENDON, THE NEW FAMILY AND THE NEW PROPERTY 64 (1981).

Some courts have stated, that if the parties have been married a short time, the divorce court should seek to return the parties to their pre-martial economic circumstances. *See* James v. James, 344 S.W.2d 915 (Tenn. App. 2010). Is this a sensible rule?

In those divorces involving very large marital estates, additional complexities arise. If one believes that a primary purpose of equitable distribution is to try to assure that, to the extent possible, both spouses should have adequate post-divorce support, when the marital estate is quite large this adequate support function could be accomplished by awarding a spouse significantly less than 50% of the marital estate. When the marital estate is quite large, and was accumulated due to the extraordinary business success of one of the spouses, should the marital estate be divided equally, or should the spouse who generated the wealth get a larger share of the estate? *See* David N. Hofstein et al, *Update to Equitable Distribution in Large Marital Estate Cases*, 21 J. AM. ACAD. MAT. LAW. 439 (2008).

GASTINEAU V. GASTINEAU
Supreme Court of New York, Suffolk County, 1991.
151 Misc. 2d 813, 573 N.Y.S.2d 819.

LEIS, J.

* * * The Plaintiff, Lisa Gastineau, is represented by counsel. The Defendant, Marcus Gastineau appeared pro se. * * * The parties were married in December of 1979. This action was commenced in September 1986. Consequently, this is a marriage of short duration. The Plaintiff is thirty-one years old and the Defendant is thirty-four. The parties have one child, Brittany, born on 11/6/82. * * * The parties married just after Marc

Gastineau had been drafted by the New York Jets to play professional football. The Plaintiff, at that time, was a sophomore at the University of Alabama. The Plaintiff never completed her college education, nor did she work during the course of the marriage.

In 1982, when Britanny was born, the parties purchased a house in Huntington, New York for $99,000.00. In addition to the purchase price, the Plaintiff and Defendant spent another $250,000.00 for landscaping and other renovations. This money came from the Defendant's earnings as a professional football player.

According to the uncontroverted testimony of the Plaintiff, in 1979 (the Defendant's first year in professional football) the Defendant earned a salary of $55,000.00. In his second year, 1980, the Defendant's salary was approximately $75,000.00. In 1981 it was approximately $95,000.00 and in 1982 he earned approximately $250,000.00. The Defendant's tax returns (which were not available for the years 1979 through 1982) indicate that the Defendant earned $423,291.00 in 1983, $488,994.00 in 1984, $858,035.00 in 1985, $595,127.00 in 1986, $953,531.00 in 1987 and in 1988, his last year with the New York Jets, his contract salary was $775,000.00 plus $50,000.00 in bonuses. It must be noted that in most years the Defendant earned monies in excess of his contract salary as a result of promotions, advertisements and bonuses.

In 1985 the parties purchased a home in Scottsdale, Arizona for $550,000.00. During the course of the parties' marriage Plaintiff and Defendant acquired many luxury items including a power boat, a BMW, a Corvette, a Rolls Royce, a Porsche, a Mercedes and two motorcycles. They continually had a housekeeper who not only cleaned the house but prepared the parties' meals. In addition, the parties frequently dined out at expensive restaurants. The Plaintiff testified that as a result of this life style she has become accustomed to buying only the most expensive clothes and going to the best of restaurants.

In 1988 the Defendant began an illicit relationship with Brigitte Nielsen. When Ms. Neilsen was diagnosed as having cancer the Defendant testified that he could no longer concentrate on playing football. At that time the Defendant was under contract with the New York Jets at a salary of $775,000.00. He left professional football in October 1988 (breaking his contract) after the sixth game of the 1988 season. The Defendant went to Arizona and remained with Ms. Nielsen while she underwent treatment for cancer.

Regardless of whether the Defendant wanted to be with his girl friend while she underwent treatment for cancer, he had a responsibility to support his wife and child. The Court cannot condone Mr. Gastineau's walking away from a lucrative football contract when the result is that his wife and child are deprived of adequate support.

According to the testimony adduced at trial, there are sixteen games per season in the NFL. Players are paid one-sixteenth of their contract salary at the end of each game. Based on the Defendant's salary for 1988 ($775,000.00), he received $48,437.00 per game. The Defendant played six games in the 1988 season and received approximately $290,622.00 plus $50,000.00 in bonuses. He was entitled to an additional $484,437.00 for the ten games remaining in the season. This Court finds that by walking away from his 1988–89 contract with the NFL the Defendant dissipated a marital asset in the amount of $484,437.00.

Whether or not the Defendant would have been offered a contract by the New York Jets for the 1989/90 football season if he had not broken his 1988/89 contract is pure speculation. In professional football there are no guarantees. * * * It must also be noted that there has been no testimony offered by the Plaintiff to establish that the Defendant would have been re-signed by the New York Jets for the 1989/90 season had he not broken his contract.

The speculative nature of the Defendant's future in professional football is highlighted by the fact that in 1989 he tried out for the San Diego Chargers, the LA Raiders and the Minnesota Vikings, without success. The New York Jets also refused to offer him a contract. In 1990 the Defendant did acquire a position with the British Colombia Lions in the Canadian Football League at a salary of $75,000.00. He was cut, however, less than half way through the season. The Defendant played five of the 18 scheduled games and was paid approximately $20,000.00. The Defendant's performance in the Canadian Football League lends credence to his claim that he no longer has the capacity to earn the monies that he once made as a professional football player. Under these circumstances the Court is limited to considering the dissipation of a marital asset valued at $484,437.00, to wit: the remaining amount of money that the Defendant was eligible to collect pursuant to his 1988/89 contract.

While Defendant admits that he has name recognition, he claims that his name has a negative rather than a positive connotation. The Defendant testified that because of his antics on the field (such as his victory dance after sacking a quarterback), the fact that he crossed picket lines during the NFL player's strike and because he walked away from his professional football career, his name has no value for promotions or endorsements. There has been no evidence presented to the contrary by the Plaintiff.

The Defendant testified that his chances of obtaining employment with a professional football team are almost nil. Although he is presently attempting to obtain a position at a Jack LaLanne Health Spa he could not provide details as to the potential salary. * * * Since the Defendant left professional football he has not worked or earned any money (except for the $20,000.00 that he earned when he played football in Canada).

According to the Defendant, Ms. Nielsen paid for all of the Defendant's expenses during the period of time that they lived together.

* * *

With all of the money that the Defendant earned throughout the course of his professional football career he has retained only three significant marital assets. (1) The Huntington house, which has been valued at approximately $429,000.00 and has an outstanding mortgage of $150,000.00. (2) A house located in the state of Arizona which was purchased for approximately $550,000.00 and has a $420,000.00 mortgage (which in all probability will be sold at foreclosure [and which the court determines has no net value]); (3) The Defendant's severance pay from the NFL of approximately $83,000.00.

It is clear that the Defendant has also dissipated a marital asset worth approximately $324,573.00 (to wit: $484,437.00 the Defendant was entitled to receive pursuant to his 1988/89 contract tax effected by 33%, reflecting approximate federal and state income tax). Although neither the Plaintiff nor the Defendant attempted to tax effect this dissipated marital asset, it is clear that the Defendant would not have actually received $484,437.00 had he finished the 1988/89 season. The Court therefore, on its own, has tax effected this amount by 33%, approximately what the Defendant would have paid in federal and state taxes had he actually received the $484,437.00. * * *

* * *

It is a guiding principle of equitable distribution that parties are entitled to receive equitable awards which are proportionate to their contributions, whether direct or indirect, to the marriage. In this case, the Plaintiff testified that during the course of the marriage she supervised the renovations made on the Huntington house, traveled with the Defendant wherever he trained and, with the assistance of a full-time nanny, raised and cared for their child.

This is not a long term marriage, and there has been minimal testimony elicited concerning the Plaintiff's direct or indirect contributions to the Defendant's acquisition of marital assets. Although it was the Defendant's own athletic abilities and disciplined training which made it possible for him to obtain and retain his position as a professional football player, equity dictates, under the facts of this case, that the Plaintiff receive one-third of the marital assets. The Defendant's decision to voluntarily terminate his contract with The New York Jets, depriving Plaintiff and the parties' child of the standard of living to which they had become accustomed, his failure to obtain meaningful employment thereafter and the indirect contributions made by the Plaintiff during the course of the marriage warrants an award to the Plaintiff of one third of the parties' marital assets. The court is also mindful of the fact that during the years of the Defendant's greatest productivity, the Plaintiff enjoyed the fruits of Defendant's labors to the fullest.

There are only two marital assets to be considered in granting Plaintiff her one-third distributive award, (1) the Huntington house, and (2) the $324,573.00 dissipated marital asset. The Arizona house has no equity. The Huntington house is valued at $429,000.00. It has a $150,00.00 mortgage with $15,000.00 owed in back mortgage payments. It thus has an equity of $264,000.00. One third of the equity would entitle the Plaintiff to $87,120.00. when one adds $107,109.00 (1/3 of the $324,573.00 tax effected marital asset which was dissipated), the Plaintiff would be entitled to $194,229.00. This would encompass Plaintiff's 1/3 distributive award of the parties' sole remaining marital asset (the Huntington house) and her 1/3 share of the marital asset dissipated by the Defendant. If one adds this $194,229.00 to the arrears owed by the Defendant on the pendente lite order ($71,707.00) Plaintiff could be awarded the total equity ($264,000.00) in the Huntington house in full satisfaction of her one-third distributive award of the parties' marital assets and still have approximately $1,936.00 remaining as a credit. The Court awards Plaintiff the Huntington house and grants her a Judgment for $1,936.00 for the remaining arrears owed to her.

NOTES AND QUESTIONS

1.   *Gastineau* raises a number of questions: Should the court have taken Gastineau's mental condition into account in judging the dissipation issue? If not, why should the wife receive only one-third of the marital assets?

2.   *Economic Fault:* Most states agree that economic fault or "dissipation" should be considered at divorce. *See generally* J. Thomas Oldham, *Romance without Finance Ain't Got No Chance,* 21 J. AM. ACAD. MAT. LAW. 501 (2008). If, after the marriage has broken down, a spouse destroys, wastes, or sells marital property for less than fair market value, the divorce court will typically divide the marital estate as if the dissipating spouse still owned the property dissipated or, if the property was sold for less than fair market value, allocate to the dissipating spouse the amount lost by the marital estate. *See* Reynolds v. Reynolds, 109 S.W.3d 258 (Mo. App. 2003); Blackman v. Blackman, 517 N.Y.S.2d 167 (App. Div. 1987); Talent v. Talent, 334 S.E.2d 256 (N.C. App. 1985); Dahl v. Dahl, 406 N.W.2d 639 (Neb. 1987). Illusory transfers will be disregarded. *See* Marriage of Frederick, 578 N.E.2d 612 (Ill. App. 1991). Common examples of dissipation include gifts to a girlfriend or boyfriend (*see* Zeigler v. Zeigler, 530 A.2d 445 (Pa. Super. 1987)); intentionally trying to destroy marital property (*see* Hunt v. Hunt, 791 N.W.2d 164 (N.D. 2010)); and a sale of marital property for less than adequate consideration when the marriage is breaking down (*see* Halvorson v. Halvorson, 482 N.W.2d 869 (N.D. 1992) (conveyance to children); *In re* Marriage of Pahlke, 507 N.E.2d 71 (Ill. App. 1987) (transfer to girlfriend); Kasinski v. Questel, 472 N.Y.S.2d 807 (App.

Div. 1984) (same); Thomas v. Thomas, 974 N.E.2d 679 (Ohio App. 2012) (same); Watson v. Watson, 607 A.2d 383 (Conn. 1992)). The dissipation doctrine forces the spouse dissipating property to bear the full amount of the loss; it is intended to deter spouses from wasting or misappropriating marital assets, particularly while the marriage is breaking down.

Should an unsuccessful speculative investment made when the marriage is breaking down constitute dissipation? What about an expenditure for cosmetic surgery?

In Lesko v. Stanislaw, 86 A.3d 14 (Me. 2014), the husband during marriage was charged with and convicted of sexually abusing young girls. As a result, the parties spent substantial marital assets for legal fees, the husband was incarcerated for a period and could not work, and the wife lost patients at her medical practice. The court awarded the wife 73% of the marital assets.

The dissipation doctrine does not extend to the payment of legitimate debts. *See. e.g.*, Tummings v. Francois, 82 So. 3d 955 (Fla. Dist. Ct. App. 2011); Hunt v. Hunt, 952 S.W.2d 564 (Tex. App. 1997) (child support paid from marital funds was not dissipated). Nor does it extend to expenditures ratified by both spouses or losses resulting from spousal negligence. *See, e.g.*, Fountain v. Fountain, 559 S.E.2d 25 (N.C. App. 2002) (cost of wife's plastic surgery was not dissipated asset when husband was "very pleased with results of wife's first * * * operation and urged her to have the second"); Booth v. Booth, 371 S.E.2d 569 (Va. App. 1988) (speculative investment did constitute dissipation). Of course, in many instances, the distinction between intentional and negligent conduct is thin. A number of courts have found that gambling losses may be treated as a dissipated asset. *See, e.g.*, Marriage of Hagshenas, 600 N.E.2d 437 (Ill. App. 1992) (gambling losses could constitute dissipation if significant in amount and the other spouse objected to the gambling). *Cf.* Zambuto v. Zambuto, 76 So. 3d 1044 (Fla. Dist. Ct. App. 2011) (gambling losses were not dissipation where they were incurred while the marriage had not begun to break down, the husband gambled while entertaining clients, and the wife also gambled). Some have treated losses incurred as a result of criminal misconduct as dissipation. *See, e.g.*, *In re* Marriage of Rodriguez, 969 P.2d 880 (Kan. 1998) ($56,000 in legal fees, fines, and property forfeited as a result of husband's drug sale conviction was a dissipated asset). And some have found dissipation when, after the break-up of the marriage, a spouse's failure to repair or sell property in a timely manner results in a significant loss to the marital estate. *See* Marriage of Hokanson, 80 Cal. Rptr. 2d 699 (App. 1998) (treating difference between market value of house when wife should have placed it on market and sale price as dissipated asset); Grossnickle v. Grossnickle, 935 S.W.2d 830 (Tex. App. 1996) (wife charged with the cost of roof damage incurred as a result of failure to repair leak). In evaluating whether dissipation has occurred, the court may consider the impact of the expenditure on the couple's overall finances and the extent to which the complainant spouse was aware of the expenditure. *See, e.g.,* Kittredge v. Kittredge, 803 N.E.2d 306 (Mass. 2004); Salten v. Ackerman, 836 N.E.2d 323 (Mass. App. 2005).

Even if the divorce court does not find dissipation and hold the wrongdoer spouse accountable for the entire loss, it can, in many states, take economic misconduct into account in dividing marital assets. *See, e.g.,* Keathley v. Keathley, 61 S.W.3d 219 (Ark. App. 2001) (spouse's gambling was an appropriate factor to consider when dividing marital estate); Sands v. Sands, 497 N.W.2d 493 (Mich. 1993) (attempt to conceal marital asset should affect division); Marriage of Rossi, 108 Cal. Rptr. 2d 270 (App. 2001) (attempt to conceal marital asset should result in forfeiture of that asset).

In California, if a spouse is convicted of attempting to murder the other spouse, the convicted spouse forfeits all of his or her marital interest in any pension plan. *See* CAL FAM. CODE § 782.5.

3.   If, when the marriage is breaking down, a spouse controls liquid marital assets of substantial value and these assets no longer exist at trial, a presumption of dissipation arises in many states. The presumption stems from the common-sense notion that, when a marriage breaks down, a party might well be tempted to hide marital assets. If a spouse can show that the assets were used for reasonable living expenses, this will ordinarily be sufficient to rebut the presumption. *See* Marriage of Randall, 510 N.E.2d 1153 (Ill. App. 1987); Reaney v. Reaney, 505 S.W.2d 338 (Tex. Civ. App. 1974); Contino v. Contino, 529 N.Y.S.2d 14 (App. Div. 1988); Rock v. Rock, 587 A.2d 1133 (Md. App. 1991). To determine reasonableness, a court might look to the standard of living before the marital breakdown. *See In re* Marriage of Stallworth, 237 Cal. Rptr. 829 (App. 1987); *In re* Marriage of Ryman, 527 N.E.2d 18 (Ill. App. 1988); Zecchin v. Zecchin, 386 N.W.2d 652 (Mich. App. 1986).

4.   *Noneconomic Misconduct:* There is less agreement among the states about the relevance of noneconomic (i.e. marital) misconduct. Professor Ira Ellman conducted a state-by-state survey on the role of marital fault in divorce decision making. In 1996, twenty-three states disallowed consideration of marital misconduct in connection with property division or alimony. Twelve allowed consideration of fault in connection with an alimony award, but not in connection with property division. Fifteen states permitted consideration of marital misconduct in both property division and alimony awards. *See* AMERICAN LAW INSTITUTE, PRINCIPLES OF THE LAW OF FAMILY DISSOLUTION: ANALYSIS AND RECOMMENDATIONS 45–47 (2002). In New York, marital fault may be considered but only if "outrageous." In interpreting this test, courts have found outrageous conduct in cases of serious criminal misconduct such as attempted murder, kidnapping, rape, and assault, but have found that lesser misconduct does not meet the test. *See* McCann v. McCann, 593 N.Y.S.2d 917, 920–22 (Sup. Ct. 1993) (reviewing cases). What are the pros and cons of each approach? Which, on balance, is the best? If noneconomic fault can be considered when dividing the martial estate, how significantly should it impact the property division?

5.   *Tort Actions as a Remedy for Spousal Misconduct:* Another way to take account of spousal misconduct is through a tort action. With the demise of spousal immunity, intentional tort actions (assault, battery, false

imprisonment) between current and former spouses have proliferated. But courts do not agree on whether the dissipation of marital assets is an appropriate basis for a tort action. *Compare* Beers v. Beers, 724 So. 2d 109 (Fla. Dist. Ct. App. 1998) (reversing $200,000 punitive damages award and holding that dissipation could not be the basis for a tort claim) *with In re* Gance, 36 P.3d 114 (Colo. App. 2001) (tort action could be based on dissipation). Nor do courts agree whether a spouse's divorce and tort actions should be joined. *Compare* Chen v. Fischer, 843 N.E.2d 723 (N.Y. 2005) (permitting joinder); Twyman v. Twyman, 855 S.W.2d 619 (Tex. 1993) (same) *with* Heacock v. Heacock, 520 N.E.2d 151 (Mass. 1988) (disallowing joinder); Simmons v. Simmons, 773 P.2d 602, 605 (Colo. App. 1988) (same). In those states that permit joinder of the tort and divorce actions, double recovery is not permitted. *See Twyman, supra.* Of course, even if the tort action is tried separately, the prospect of double recovery exists. *See* S.A.V. v. K.G.V., 708 S.W.2d 651, 653 (Mo. 1986) (noting that "to the extent that conduct of the spouses is taken into account in division of marital property, the dissolution decree might be admissible in the subsequent tort action. The same may hold true for the dissolution proceeding if that action follows trial of the tort claim.").

If damages are awarded before divorce, the court must determine which estate is entitled to the damage award. While courts typically distinguish between damages for personal injury pain and suffering (separate) and lost pre-divorce earnings (marital) [*see* note 3 p. 914], some courts (unsurprisingly) have held that the tortfeasor should not share in any portion of the victimized spouse's damages award. *See* Freehe v. Freehe, 500 P.2d 771 (Wash. 1972).

Finally, in a community property state, the court may also have to decide which estate should bear the cost of any damage award. Most state statutes do not address this issue; TEX. FAM. CODE § 3.203 gives the court discretion to determine which estate, or combination, should bear the loss.

6. *Ramifications of Frustrating the Other Spouse's Ability to Remarry:* In some religious traditions, a divorcing husband must do some affirmative act to facilitate the ability of his former wife to remarry. In Mojdeh M. v. Jamshid A., a divorce in New York, the husband was unwilling to accompany his wife to a mosque so she could obtain a religious divorce. The judge ordered him, within 45 days, to take any necessary steps to remove any barriers to the wife's remarriage, or he would forfeit his right to equitable distribution. *See* Andrew Keshner, *Failure to Get Islamic Divorce Could Impact Distribution*, N.Y.L.J., June 13, 2012.

7. *Post-Divorce Economic Misconduct:* In some states, a spouse can be held financially responsible for actions after divorce. For example, in Collins v. Collins, 746 N.E.2d 201 (Ohio App. 2000) the husband was in the military at the time of divorce, but had not served sufficient time to qualify for retirement benefits. The divorce court awarded the other spouse a fraction of any military retirement benefits he eventually received. After divorce, the man did not re-enlist, and never qualified for any benefits. When the ex-wife sued, the court found that, because he lost his benefits by the voluntary act of choosing not to

re-enlist, he owed his former spouse the amount of the benefits she lost as a result. Particularly in a time of war, is this fair to a spouse in the military?

Problem 15-7:

The state legislature is considering replacing its current property division law (identical to the Minnesota statute on p. 955). The legislature is concerned that "equitable" distribution may, in practice, mean unpredictable and inconsistent distribution. It is also concerned that "equitable distribution may be too complex for most divorcing couples, who have little to divide."

As a replacement for the current system, the legislature is particularly interested in two new ideas. One is the system currently in effect in Germany. This system requires a comparison of each spouse's net worth at marriage and divorce; any gain during the marriage is divided equally. *See* MARY ANN GLENDON, THE TRANSFORMATION OF FAMILY LAW: STATE, LAW, AND FAMILY IN THE UNITED STATES AND WESTERN EUROPE 217–18 (1989). No American state has adopted a system like this one.

The other system in which the legislature is interested was recently adopted by the American Law Institute; it, again, has currently been adopted by no American state. *See* AMERICAN LAW INSTITUTE, PRINCIPLES OF THE LAW OF FAMILY DISSOLUTION: ANALYSIS AND RECOMMENDATIONS (2002) (hereinafter "ALI Principles"). For a critical overview of the ALI Principles, *see* J. Thomas Oldham, *ALI Principles of Family Dissolution: Some Comments*, 1997 ILL. L. REV. 801. This system is more complex.

The ALI definition of marital and separate property is fairly traditional. Marital property includes pension rights earned during marriage (whether vested or unvested), personal injury or disability benefits that replace lost marital wages, and professional goodwill; personal injury or disability benefits that compensate for pain and suffering, earning capacity, and professional degrees and licenses are excluded. Sec. 4.07. Separate property—premarital acquisitions and property acquired during marriage by gift, descent, and devise—includes appreciation of and income from separate property, as well as property acquired after the divorce action is filed.

The ALI approach to division is quite novel, however. Marital property is to be divided equally, except in cases of asset dissipation; also, *separate property gradually becomes marital property*. After a minimum "waiting period" specified in the state statute, a state-specified percentage of separate assets is annually recharacterized as marital; once converted to marital property, separate property is also subject to the equal division rule. For example, a state might specify that 4% of separate property would be recharacterized annually after five years of marriage. Under this approach, all property would be marital property after thirty years of marriage; each spouse (except in a case of dissipation) would obtain fifty percent of all property.

Perhaps because it is an unusual system (hotchpot states permit, but do not require, division of separate assets), the ALI Principles also contain an "opt-out" provision. If one spouse gives the other written notice of his or her intention to maintain separate assets as separate, it is binding from that date forward; the other spouse need not agree.

The drafters of the ALI Principles argue that recharacterization is appropriate because spouses, over time, tend to view all assets as "ours" rather than "yours" and "mine." (They cite no empirical evidence for this proposition.) They also note that the new Uniform Probate Code provisions on spousal rights at death similarly employ an accrual type approach.

You have been asked to evaluate the ALI and German systems in light of the legislature's concerns:

1.   How does each differ from a community property approach? a hotchpot approach? an equitable distribution of marital property approach? a presumption of equal division?

2.   Which approach will produce the most certain results?

3.   Which approach is most responsive to the needs of couples with few marital assets? with many marital assets?

4.   Which approach achieves the fairest results?

5.   Which approach, on balance, should the legislature adopt?

Problem 15-8:

Harry and Wilma divorce. In connection with the divorce, Wilma agrees to waive the right to spousal support in exchange for a substantial property award, which is paid to her when the decree is entered. A few years later, the husband is sued by the SEC for fraud, and the SEC sues Wilma to recover the divorce property award, which the SEC contends represented money stolen from others. Should the SEC be able to recover the money? *See* Commodity Futures Trading Commission v. Walsh, 951 N.E.2d 369 (N.Y. 2011).

Problem 15-9:

Harry and Wilma divorce. In connection with the divorce, Harry receives a brokerage account with Bernard Madoff apparently worth $5.4 million, and wife receives a cash award of $6,250,000. Shortly after the divorce, Harry discovers Madoff has been operating a fraudulent scheme and that his account is worthless. He sues his wife to revise the divorce property division. What should happen? Property division at divorce normally can't be reopened based on changes in value after the divorce. Is this somehow different? *See* Simkin v. Blank, 968 N.E.2d 459 (N.Y. 2012).

CHAPTER 16

SPOUSAL SUPPORT

■ ■ ■

1. AN INTRODUCTION TO SPOUSAL SUPPORT

In all states, divorce courts divide property accumulated during marriage. However, many divorcing parties don't have much property. And, even if they do have some property, Chapter 15 shows that a party's earning capacity at divorce is not considered "property" to be divided. When spouses divorce, they may have very different incomes. When, if ever, should one party have to make periodic payments to the other to reduce differences in their post-divorce household income?

HOMER H. CLARK, JR., THE LAW OF DOMESTIC RELATIONS IN THE UNITED STATES
619–21 (2d ed. 1988).

American law imported the practice of granting alimony as an incident to divorce from the English ecclesiastical law as it existed before the reform of the English court system in 1857. As with other rules borrowed from England, those relating to alimony were applied in a different context. In England the ecclesiastical courts gave only divorces *a mensa et thoro*, authorizing husband and wife to live apart, but not freeing them from the marriage bond. The alimony which was awarded by the ecclesiastical courts under those circumstances merely constituted a recognition and enforcement of the husband's duty to support the wife which continued after the judicial separation. The wife's need was the greater in those days because of the control over her property which the law gave to her husband. This was reflected in the courts' willingness to take into account in fixing the amount of alimony the value of the property which the wife brought into the marriage. Alimony was further made necessary by the lack of employment opportunities for married women. In addition to these factors the English courts gave consideration to the degree of the husband's fault in making the award. Where the wife was at fault, she was entitled to no alimony. Thus, even in the English law alimony was not solely measured by the wife's need for support.

* * *

When the English institution of alimony, which served the plain and intelligible purpose of providing support for wives living apart from their husbands, was utilized in America in suits for absolute divorce, however, its purpose became less clear. As a result of absolute divorce the marriage is entirely dissolved. It is harder to justify imposing on the ex-husband a continuing duty to support his former wife than after a divorce a mensa which does not dissolve the marriage. This difficulty is not obviated by labelling alimony a "substitute" for the wife's right to support. Why should there be such a substitute? Would it not be more logical to say that when the marriage is dissolved all rights and duties based upon it end?

* * *

Notwithstanding the logical objection to alimony, as an incident to absolute divorce, it has been granted in the United States from the earliest colonial times to the present. * * * Although nearly all states have statutes authorizing alimony in appropriate cases,[1] there is a lack of agreement on just what purpose alimony serves. In the opinion of some judges alimony continues the support which the wife was entitled to receive while the marriage existed. Others look on alimony as furnishing damages for the husband's wrongful breach of the marriage contract. Still others speak as if it were a penalty imposed on the guilty husband. * * * It is notable that the Uniform Marriage and Divorce Act is framed with the purpose of providing for the spouses by means of a division of property rather than by an award of alimony. Of course it is clear that only a small proportion of divorces involve enough property to be of any benefit to the spouses.

―――――――――

Although the Supreme Court has held that an alimony statute may not discriminate based on gender (Orr v. Orr, 440 U.S. 268 (1979)), the debate on the basis and scope of alimony,[2] now often described as spousal maintenance or support, continues: Should the award serve the primary purpose of providing support for a needy spouse after divorce? Or should the award serve the purpose of compensating a spouse for career damage incurred due to marital responsibilities, such as child care? Or should it compensate a spouse for expectations that a divorce has shattered? Should alimony be denied based on fault? Should it be used to compensate for a "marital wrong"? If yes, what fault should suffice and what marital wrongs should be compensated? Should the award be paid for a fixed term or indefinitely (and perhaps for the remainder of the recipient's life)? Should

―――――――――

[1] Ed. Note: Since Texas accepted a limited version of post-divorce spousal support in 1995, all U.S. states have permitted the award of alimony.

[2] Ed. Note: The word alimony comes from the Latin "alimonia," meaning sustenance. See BLACK'S LAW DICTIONARY 67 (5th ed. 1979).

the award be in an amount sufficient to lift the recipient out of poverty or should it be based on the marital standard of living?

Unsurprisingly, no consensus has been reached on any of these questions. One reason for the lack of agreement is simply that alimony has never had a unitary basis. As Professor Clark notes, the English ecclesiastical courts awarded alimony to protect against need *and* to compensate for property brought into the marriage *and* to punish marital fault. Nor does consensus on basic principles ensure agreement on how principles should be applied. Consider these appellate decisions:

> A woman is not a breeding cow to be nurtured during her years of fecundity, then conveniently and economically converted to cheap steaks when past her prime. If a woman is able to do so, she certainly should support herself. If, however, she has spent her productive years as a housewife and mother and has missed the opportunity to compete in the job market and improve her job skills, quite often she becomes, when divorced, simply a "displaced homemaker." In the case at bench we are faced with a woman who, during the last 25 years, has borne 2 children and confined her activities to those of a mother and housewife. * * * Assuming she does not become blind, her experience as a homemaker qualifies her for either of two positions, charwoman or babysitter. A candidate for a well paying job, she isn't. * * * [In such a case] the husband simply has to face up to the fact that his support responsibilities are going to be of extended duration—perhaps for life. This has nothing to do with feminism, sexism, male chauvinism or any other trendy social ideology. It is ordinary common sense, basic decency and simple justice.

In re Marriage of Brantner, 136 Cal. Rptr. 635 (App. 1977).

> The law should provide both parties with the opportunity to make a new life on this earth. Neither should be shackled by the unnecessary burdens of an unhappy marriage. This is not to suggest that women of no skills, or those who suffer a debilitating infirmity, or who are of advanced age (whatever that may be) should be denied alimony for as long as needed. But such women are the exception, not the rule.

Turner v. Turner, 385 A. 2d 1280 (N.J. Super. 1978).

Both the *Brantner* and *Turner* courts seem to agree that need and work skills are key issues in an alimony inquiry. But the *Brantner* court sees need where the alimony claimant is qualified for low-wage employment, while the *Turner* court sees need only where there are "no skills," a "debilitating infirmity," or "advanced age." The two courts also seem to have very different attitudes toward the alimony payor, with one sympathetically focused on the shackles "of an unhappy marriage," the other concerned that one spouse may wish to "economically convert [the other] to cheap steaks when past her prime."

State alimony statutes evidence no more consensus than the judicial opinions. But it is important to keep in mind that in most states alimony is not awarded frequently. If alimony is awarded, it generally would not be an award of high value. The average annual alimony award in 1985 was $3730. U.S. BUREAU OF THE CENSUS, CHILD SUPPORT AND ALIMONY, 1985 (Current Pop. Rpts., Series P-60, No. 152). State surveys of alimony awards conducted during the 1980s show anywhere from 7% to 30% of divorced women receiving alimony awards. *See* Marsha Garrison, *The Economics of Divorce: Changing Rules, Changing Results* 91 tbl. 3.11 *in* DIVORCE REFORM AT THE CROSSROADS (Herma H. Kay & Stephen D. Sugarman eds. 1991) (surveying reports). While these surveys also show declines in the proportion of women obtaining alimony between the 1970s and 1980s, approximately 15% of surveyed divorced women reported to the Census Bureau that they had been awarded alimony during the late 1970s and early 1980s, while 17% did so in 1989, the last year the Census Bureau collected alimony data. U.S. BUREAU OF THE CENSUS, CHILD SUPPORT AND ALIMONY, 1989 (Current Pop. Rpts., Series P-60, No. 173 (1990)) (showing alimony rate but not values). Nor do earlier reports show a higher alimony rate; census data from the turn of the century indicate that 9.3% of divorces included alimony awards. *See* PAUL H. JACOBSON, AMERICAN MARRIAGE AND DIVORCE 127–28 (1959). Debate over alimony principles thus has not substantially altered the relatively low—and constant—*likelihood* of an alimony award.

There has been a recent, marked shift in the typical *duration* of an alimony award. Until the no-fault divorce movement of the 1960s and 70s, the spouse who was at fault in causing the dissolution of the marriage was barred from obtaining alimony. But, once granted, an alimony award typically extended until the recipient's death or remarriage. With the advent of no-fault divorce, some states began to permit a "guilty" spouse to obtain alimony; many states also revised their alimony rules to permit short-term, "rehabilitative" alimony. Divorce surveys suggest that these statutory reforms were typically followed by a substantial reduction—in some states as high as 50%—in the proportion of alimony awards awarded permanently (i.e., until death or remarriage). For example, Professor Garrison found that, in the 1970s, about 80% of surveyed New York alimony awards were permanent; less than ten years later, only about 40% were. *See* Marsha Garrison, *Good Intentions Gone Awry: The Impact of New York's Equitable Distribution Law on Divorce Outcomes*, 57 BROOKLYN L. REV. 621, 700 (1991); Mary Kay Kisthardt, *Re-Thinking Alimony: The AAML's Considerations for Calculating Alimony, Spousal Support or Maintenance,* 21 J. AM. ACAD. MAT. LAW. 61 (2008). *See also* Heather Wishik, *Economics of Divorce: An Exploratory Study*, 20 FAM. L. Q. 79

(1986); James B. McClindon, *Separate But Unequal: The Economic Disaster of Divorce for Women and Children*, 21 FAM. L. Q. 351 (1987).

Anecdotal evidence suggests that, during the past few decades, there has been, in some states, a reevaluation of whether short-term "rehabilitative" awards are appropriate when parties divorce after a marriage of some significant duration.

Some states have "resolved" the alimony debate by granting judges broad discretionary powers; the Pennsylvania alimony statute exemplifies this approach. Other state legislatures have taken a strong position on the alimony question and limited judicial discretion accordingly; the Texas statute provides an example. The Uniform Marriage and Divorce Act takes an intermediate approach.

23 PA. CONS. STAT. ANN. § 3701. Alimony

(a) General rule.—Where a divorce decree has been entered, the court may allow alimony, as it deems reasonable, to either party only if it finds that alimony is necessary.

(b) Factors relevant.—In determining whether alimony is necessary and in determining the nature, amount, duration and manner of payment of alimony, the court shall consider all relevant factors, including:

(1) The relative earnings and earning capacities of the parties.

(2) The ages and the physical, mental and emotional conditions of the parties.

(3) The sources of income of both parties, including, but not limited to, medical, retirement, insurance or other benefits.

(4) The expectancies and inheritances of the parties.

(5) The duration of the marriage.

(6) The contribution by one party to the education, training or increased earning power of the other party.

(7) The extent to which the earning power, expenses or financial obligations of a party will be affected by reason of serving as the custodian of a minor child.

(8) The standard of living of the parties established during the marriage.

(9) The relative education of the parties and the time necessary to acquire sufficient education or training to enable the party seeking alimony to find appropriate employment.

(10) The relative assets and liabilities of the parties.

(11) The property brought to the marriage by either party.

(12) The contribution of a spouse as homemaker.

(13) The relative needs of the parties.

(14) The marital misconduct of either of the parties during the marriage. * * *

(15) The Federal, State and local tax ramifications of the alimony award.

(16) Whether the party seeking alimony lacks sufficient property, including, but not limited to, property distributed [in the divorce action] * * * to provide for the party's reasonable needs.

(17) Whether the party seeking alimony is incapable of self-support through appropriate employment.

(c) Duration.—The court in ordering alimony shall determine the duration of the order, which may be for a definite or an indefinite period of time which is reasonable under the circumstances.

TEX. FAM. CODE

§ 8.051. Eligibility for Maintenance

The court may order maintenance for either spouse only if the spouse seeking maintenance will lack sufficient property, including the spouse's separate property, on dissolution of the marriage to provide for the spouse's minimum reasonable needs and:

(1) the spouse from whom maintenance is requested was convicted of or received deferred adjudication for a criminal offense that also constitutes an act of family violence, as defined by Section 71.004, committed during the marriage against the other spouse or the other spouse's child and the offense occurred:

(A) within two years before the date on which a suit for dissolution of the marriage is filed; or

(B) while the suit is pending; or

(2) the spouse seeking maintenance:

(A) is unable to earn sufficient income to provide for the spouse's minimum reasonable needs because of an incapacitating physical or mental disability;

(B) has been married to the other spouse for 10 years or longer and lacks the ability to earn sufficient income to provide for the spouse's minimum reasonable needs; or

(C) is the custodian of a child of the marriage of any age who requires substantial care and personal supervision because of a physical or mental disability that prevents the spouse from earning sufficient income to provide for the spouse's minimum reasonable needs.

§ 8.054. Duration of Maintenance Order

(a) Except as provided by Subsection (b), a court:

(1) may not order maintenance that remains in effect for more than:

(A) five years after the date of the order, if:

(i) the spouses were married to each other for less than 10 years and the eligibility of the spouse for whom maintenance is ordered is established under Section 8.051(1); or

(ii) the spouses were married to each other for at least 10 years but not more than 20 years;

(B) seven years after the date of the order, if the spouses were married to each other for at least 20 years but not more than 30 years; or

(C) 10 years after the date of the order, if the spouses were married to each other for 30 years or more; and

(2) shall limit the duration of a maintenance order to the shortest reasonable period that allows the spouse seeking maintenance to earn sufficient income to provide for the spouse's minimum reasonable needs, unless the ability of the spouse to provide for the spouse's minimum reasonable needs is substantially or totally diminished because of:

(A) physical or mental disability of the spouse seeking maintenance;

(B) duties as the custodian of an infant or young child of the marriage; or

(C) another compelling impediment to earning sufficient income to provide for the spouse's minimum reasonable needs.

(b) The court may order maintenance for a spouse to whom Section 8.051(2)(A) or (C) applies for as long as the spouse continues to satisfy the eligibility criteria prescribed by the applicable provision .

(c) On the request of either party or on the court's own motion, the court may order the periodic review of its order for maintenance under Subsection (b).

§ 8.055. Amount of Maintenance

(a) A court may not order maintenance that requires an obligor to pay monthly more than the lesser of:

(1) $5,000; or

(2) 20 percent of the spouse's average monthly gross income.

UNIFORM MARRIAGE AND DIVORCE ACT § 308

9A U.L.A. 347–48 (1987).

(a)   * * * [T]he court may grant a maintenance order for either spouse, only if it finds that the spouse seeking maintenance:

(1)   lacks sufficient property to provide for his reasonable needs; and

(2)   is unable to support himself through appropriate employment or is the custodian of a child whose condition or circumstances make it appropriate that the custodian not be required to seek employment outside the home.

(b)   the maintenance order shall be in amounts and for periods of time the court deems just, without regard to marital misconduct, and after considering all relevant factors including:

(1)   the financial resources of the party seeking maintenance, including marital property apportioned to him, his ability to meet his needs independently, and the extent to which a provision for support of a child living with the party includes a sum for that party as custodian;

(2)   the time necessary to acquire sufficient education or training to enable the party seeking maintenance to find appropriate employment;

(3)   the standard of living established during the marriage;

(4)   the duration of the marriage;

(5)   the age and physical and emotional condition of the spouse seeking maintenance; and

(6)   the ability of the spouse from whom maintenance is sought to meet his needs while meeting those of the spouse seeking maintenance.

Problem 16-1:

Harold, age 33, and Winona, age 30, have been married for nine years and have three children, ages 7, 5, and 2. For the first two years of the marriage, Winona worked as a beautician; during these years Harold completed his law school education and worked part-time as a paralegal. Since Harold's graduation from law school, he has been employed as an attorney. Winona has been a full-time homemaker. Her beautician's license lapsed two years ago; she is a high school graduate and has completed one year of college in addition to beautician training. Harold is now employed by the Maxit Corp. at an annual salary of $130,000. Harold has been having an affair with another attorney at Maxit and has asked Winona for a divorce. Harold and Winona own a house, in which they have equity totalling $60,000. They have other liquid assets worth $30,000. Harold has only recently come to work for Maxit and is not yet covered by the company's pension plan. Neither spouse has separate assets. What arguments related to the award of alimony are available to Harold and Winona: (a) in Pennsylvania; (b) in Texas; (c) under the UMDA?

Problem 16-2:

Herman, age 60, and Wendy, age 58, have been married for thirty-four years and have one child, age 30. Herman has for many years been a self-employed businessman. For the past ten years, Wendy has sold real estate part-time. Before that time she was a full-time homemaker. Wendy is also actively involved in community affairs; she is a member of the local school board and a trustee of the town library. Herman's business is very successful; he has earned, on average, $250,000 per year for the past five years. Wendy, during the same period, has averaged $25,000. Marital assets total approximately $750,000. Harold has separate assets totalling $2,000,000. Both spouses completed two years of college. Both wish to end the marriage due to feelings of incompatibility. What arguments related to the award of alimony are available to Herman and Wendy: (a) in Pennsylvania; (b) in Texas; (c) under the UMDA?

How, if at all, would your analysis change if marital assets totalled $10,000, neither spouse had separate assets, Herman was a mechanic earning $23,000 and Wendy a custodian earning $5,000?

Problem 16-3:

Harvey and Willa have been married for 10 years; both are 38 years old. Willa earns $120,000 annually; Harvey earns $40,000. The ratio of their salaries at the time of the marriage was approximately the same. Marital assets total $30,000; there are no children. Both have had affairs and wish to end the marriage. What arguments related to the award of alimony are available to Harvey and Willa: (a) in Pennsylvania; (b) in Texas; (c) under the UMDA?

Problem 16-4:

Henry, age 50, and Winifred, age 45, have been married for eight years. At the time of the marriage, both earned about $50,000 per year. Two years ago, Henry had a heart attack that left him unable to work; he receives $700 monthly in Social Security benefits. Winifred is in good health and earns $60,000 annually. Marital assets total $40,000. Winifred wishes to end the marriage. What arguments related to the award of alimony are available to Henry and Winifred: (a) in Pennsylvania; (b) in Texas; (c) under the UMDA?

NOTES AND QUESTIONS

1. Which of the three statutes appears to yield, on average, the "fairest" results?

2. How easy is it to assess: (a) the likelihood; (b) duration; and (c) value of alimony under the three statutes?

3. Highly discretionary standards are "largely based on the assumption that the infinite variety of circumstances is such that the attempt to lay down general rules is bound to lead to injustice. Justice can only be done by the individualized, ad hoc approach." P.S. ATIYAH, FROM PRINCIPLES TO PRAGMATISM: CHANGES IN THE FUNCTION OF THE JUDICIAL PROCESS AND THE LAW 11 (1978). What are the pros and cons of an ad hoc approach to alimony determination?

2. FACTORS IN DETERMINING THE AWARD OF ALIMONY

A. NEED AND MARITAL DURATION

A 2001 survey revealed that the vast majority of alimony statutes include one or more need-related criteria: thirty-eight states (95%) listed the parties' physical health or disabilities, over four-fifths (87.5%) listed the standard of living established during the marriage or the parties' economic status, and twenty-nine states (72.5%) listed the needs of the recipient or the earning (or income) potential of the parties (65%). 72.5% of the states listed the spouses' financial resources and means, 62.5% the time needed for rehabilitative education, and 72.5% the presence of a child in the home whose care precludes or limits employment as a significant factor. *See* Robert Kirkman Collins, *The Theory of Marital Residuals: Applying an Income Adjustment Calculus to the Enigma of Alimony,* 24 HARVARD WOMEN'S L.J. 23, 34 (2001). These assorted need-related criteria pose—but do not themselves resolve—the same basic question: what does "need" mean? Assume that one spouse earns $75,000 annually and the other $40,000, that both are in decent health, and that they enjoyed a middle-class standard of living during the marriage and have no minor children. Does the lower-earning spouse "need" support?

MORGAN V. MORGAN

Supreme Court Trial Term, New York County, 1975.
81 Misc. 2d 616, 366 N.Y.S.2d 977.

BENTLEY KASSAL, JUDGE.

The parties were married on January 27, 1967 when the husband was in his third year pre-law course at the University of North Carolina and the wife, a sophomore, studying biology, at the Florida State University.

Recognizing that both could not simultaneously continue their education and be self-supporting, they agreed it would be preferable for him to finish his undergraduate and law school education while she worked. She commenced working full time, earning a monthly salary of $328.00 until the day before she gave birth to a son, on August 9, 1967. She resumed working a few months later, in January 1968, on a part-time basis, took care of her own and other children, on an exchange basis, and did typing at home for students, as well as her husband's theses. This continued until she and her husband separated in October 1972.

In the interim, Mrs. Morgan has become very proficient at shorthand and typing and also worked as a data analyst. I am satisfied that she is very skilled and, as an executive secretary or technician, could probably command an annual salary of at least $10,000 in normal economy and, very possibly, even in the present employment market.

In February 1973, she returned to the campus to pursue a full time educational career by undertaking a pre-medical course at Hunter College and her grades have been exceptional—a 3.83 general average (out of a 4.0 maximum) and an A score in the organic chemistry course, ranking 5th in a class of 70.

For his part, the husband has progressed well in his profession, having graduated from Columbia Law School after being selected for its Law Journal. His career started, as planned, with a one year stint as a law clerk to a Federal Circuit Judge and he immediately thereafter became an associate at a prominent Wall Street law firm. His starting salary, in August 1972 was $18,000 per annum with $500 increases on November 1, 1972, March 1, 1973, April 1, 1973, a $3,500 increase on November 1, 1973, a $1,500 increase on May 1, 1974 with the most recent increase of $3,000 on November 1, 1974, to a present salary level of $27,500. In all, he has done well and his future appears very promising. * * *

At a time when some call for treating the marriage contract as any other contract, it is particularly appropriate to speak of the wife's duty to mitigate the damages to the husband upon breach. I agree that "when she can, she should also be required to mitigate the husband's burden either by her own financial means or earning potential or both." But it is a corollary to the rule of mitigation that the injured party may also recover for the expenses reasonably incurred in an effort to avoid or reduce the damages. In this case, any possible short-term economic benefit which would result from the wife's returning to a position similar to the one she held over two years ago, is far outweighed by the potential benefit, economic, emotional, and otherwise, of her pursuing her education.

In coming to the conclusion I do, I am seeking to effect a balancing of many factors—the parties' financial status, their obligations, age, station in life and opportunities for development and self-fulfillment. Times have changed, owing not alone to the co-equal status which a married woman shares with her husband, but also to the increase in the number of married women working in gainful occupations.

* * * The provisions of § 236 of the Domestic Relations Law direct, *inter alia*, that the Court consider the "ability of the wife to be self-supporting," as well as "the circumstances of the case and of the respective parties." "Self-supporting," in my judgment, does not imply that the wife shall be compelled to take any position that will be available when her obvious potential in life, in terms of "self-support," will be greatly inhibited.

Cognizance must also be taken of other language in the very same section, namely, " * * * the court *may* direct the husband to *provide suitably* for the support of the wife, *as, in the court's discretion, justice requires * * * *" (emphasis added). This has been interpreted to vest broad discretion in the court, "unfettered by" literal readings of the law. Obviously two households cannot be maintained as cheaply as one and we therefore encounter the threshold issue of whether the wife—a very capable woman, probably able to earn at least $10,000 annually as a secretary or office worker—shall be compelled to contribute this sum or a fair share thereof, to her own support, at this time, or shall she have an opportunity to achieve a professional education based upon her potential, which will be comparable to the one her husband received as a result of her assistance by working during their marriage.

In my opinion, the answer to this issue is that under these circumstances, the wife is also entitled to equal treatment and a "break" and should not be automatically relegated to a life of being a well-paid, skilled technician laboring with a life-long frustration as to what her future might have been as a doctor, but for her marriage and motherhood.

I am impressed by the fact that the plaintiff does not assume the posture that she wants to be an alimony drone or seek permanent alimony. Rather she had indicated that she only wants support for herself until she finishes medical school in 5 1/2 years (1 1/2 years more in college and 4 years in medical school) and will try to work when possible.

* * *

Accordingly, * * * the defendant shall pay a total sum of $200 weekly for alimony and child support, so long as she does not remarry and continues to be a full-time student, undertaking a premedical or medical course. (I am taking into consideration plaintiff's agreement to work during her vacation periods when not prohibited by school work.) Completion of her medical school training and the awarding of an M.D. degree shall be deemed a sufficient change of circumstances and I am granting leave to the defendant to apply at such time for an appropriate modification to delete the alimony feature of this award.

NOTES AND QUESTIONS

1.   On appeal, this sensible judgment was reversed:

The alimony of $100 per week awarded below was predicated upon plaintiff's ambition to obtain entrance to medical school and receive an M.D. degree. It is not disputed that the plaintiff has present earning ability, which the court below believed might be at least $10,000 per year. A wife's ability to be self-supporting is relevant when determining the amount of support a husband is to provide. Absent a compelling showing that the wife cannot contribute to her own support, courts have "imputed" or deducted a wife's potential earnings from the amount which would otherwise be found payable as alimony by her ex-husband. *While this Court recognizes plaintiff's goal in medicine, this pursuit was never in the contemplation of the parties during marriage and appears to be of recent origin.* The law requires that the alimony award should be predicated upon the present circumstances of the parties. Although the wife's ambition is most commendable, the court below was in error in including in the alimony award monies for the achievement of that goal.

Morgan v. Morgan, 383 N.Y.S.2d 343 (App. Div. 1976) (emphasis added). Why is it important whether the parties, before they decided to divorce, contemplated that the wife would go to medical school?

2.   Does *Morgan* demonstrate that need should not be the only factor relevant to an alimony award?

3.   In response to the plight of spouses like Mrs. Morgan, many states have amended their support rules to authorize an alimony award based on one spouse's contribution to the career or education of the other. Some states, for example California, now require reimbursement to the marital community "for community contributions to education or training of a party that substantially enhances the earning capacity of the party." CAL. FAM. CODE § 2641. If the supporting spouse is to be reimbursed for funding her husband's education, what costs should be included? Tuition and books only? What about the student-spouse's living expenses?

Other states have made support for the other spouse's education a relevant factor in considering an alimony claim. *See, e.g.,* N.C. GEN. STAT. § 50–16–3(b)(6). Oregon has authorized "compensatory" spousal support when one party makes a "significant" contribution to the other spouse's education. In *In re* Marriage of Harris, 244 P.3d 801 (Or. 2010) the Oregon Supreme Court discusses what constitutes a significant contribution and concludes that the wife made such a contribution. Under the statute, the supporting spouse is entitled to share in some of the educated spouse's post-divorce earnings. In this case the parties met while both were in college. When they married in 1990, the man was going to school full time and the woman was working full time and attending school part time. The man graduated from college in 1992 and entered dental school. When the parties had their first child in 1993, the woman continued to work full time but stopped taking college classes. The woman was the primary caretaker of their child and provided financial support for the family until the husband graduated from dental school in 1996. The man then started working as a dentist, and his income quickly exceeded $350,000 annually. The husband continued to have a successful practice until he filed for divorce in 2006 when the husband was age 37 and the wife was 38. Each party received $720,000 of the marital estate. The husband's annual earning capacity was $400,000, and the wife's estimated annual earning capacity was $30,000–$40,000.

Does Mrs. Harris "need" spousal support more than Mrs.Morgan? Here the parties were married 17 years, while the Morgans were married about 6 years. Should this matter?

The Oregon Supreme Court affirmed an award to Mrs. Harris of $3000 monthly "transitional" support for 4 years, $4000 monthly "maintenance" support for 6 years (decreasing to $2500 monthly for another two years and then to $1000 for 1 year), and "compensatory" monthly support of $2000 for 10 years. That appears to mean that Mrs. Harris will receive total monthly support of $9000 for 4 years, $6000 monthly for another 2 years, $4500 monthly for another 2 years, $3000 for 1 year and $2000 monthly during the tenth year. If spousal support is to be awarded, is it a sensible policy to reduce the amount gradually over time?

4.   The author of a survey concluded that eleven states continue to employ alimony standards, like those contained in UMDA § 308, that permit alimony only when the applicant "is unable to support himself through appropriate employment * * *." In these states, judges "do not have discretion to consider whether a spouse has sacrificed his or her earning capacity for the benefit of the marriage." Mary Frances Lyle & Jeffrey L. Levy, *From Riches to Rags: Does Rehabilitative Alimony Need to Be Rehabilitated?*, 38 FAM. L.Q. 3, 15 (2004).

5.   Assume Mrs. Morgan was working as an executive secretary at divorce, earning $10,000 annually in 1974. Husband is a young lawyer, earning $27,500. Does the wife "need" support? Should the answer to this question be impacted by the parties' decision during marriage that the wife should defer her career plans while the husband completed his education?

MARRIAGE OF HUNTINGTON
California Court of Appeals, 1992.
10 Cal. App. 4th 1513, 14 Cal. Rptr. 2d 1.

KLINE, PRESIDING JUSTICE.

Ann K. Huntington appeals from a judgment of dissolution of marriage. She urges the trial court adopted an erroneous interpretation of Civil Code § 4801 and abused its discretion in awarding her spousal support of $5,000 a month for a period of only six months. * * *

STATEMENT OF THE CASE

On March 27, 1989, respondent filed a petition for legal separation from appellant * * *. The parties had been married on August 24, 1985, and separated three years and seven months later on March 28, 1989.

* * * The trial court ordered spousal support of $5,000 per month for a period of six months, to permanently terminate thereafter, and ordered the parties to bear their own attorney fees and costs. Appellant had been receiving temporary spousal support of $7,500 per month since May 1, 1989, and her attorney had previously received $19,000 from respondent for attorney fees pursuant to prior court order and stipulation.

STATEMENT OF FACTS

Respondent is a wealthy man with a net worth in excess of $15 million. At the time of the marriage, appellant was 28 years old and respondent 47. Appellant had been working as a dental hygienist, earning about $30,000 a year, but stopped working shortly before the marriage when respondent told her it would not be necessary for her to work. The day before the marriage, the parties entered into a premarital agreement providing for their property to remain separate.

The parties' standard of living during the marriage was extremely high. Respondent owns a home in Tiburon valued at two and a half million dollars, an 18.2-acre property in Tahoe worth three million, and nine cars, and the court found he has a controllable annual cash flow of approximately $500,000 from his investments. Appellant testified that she spent about $6,000 a month on clothes alone. Respondent's attorney stipulated that respondent could pay any reasonable amount of spousal support.

Appellant testified that she did not wish to return to work as a dental hygienist because it was a stressful, "dead-end" job with no advancement, she had lost her contacts, she would be "rusty" if she went back, her license had expired and she would have to take a test to revive it, as well as "brush-up" courses. Additionally, according to literature on the subject, dental hygienists "burn-out" after about five years, which was the length of time respondent had been practicing before the marriage. She had prepared a resume and applied for several other jobs (public relations at a winery, part-time writer for the Independent Journal, record company, cellular telephone company, lobbyist firm) but had not been successful. She testified that she did not think she was ready to go to work immediately because she had been through a lot, had not worked in a long time, and wanted to see what her options were and make the right choice before entering something new.

Appellant presented three expert witnesses who testified that she was not emotionally prepared to immediately begin self-supporting employment.

Appellant next contends the trial court erroneously read Civil Code § 4801. This statute authorizes trial courts to order spousal support "for any period of time, as the court may deem just and reasonable, based on the standard of living established during the marriage." In making its award, the trial court is required to consider nine enumerated factors, several of which explicitly refer to the marital standard of living, as well as any others it deems "just and equitable." The trial court is required to "make specific factual findings with respect to the standard of living during the marriage, and, at the request of either party, the court shall make appropriate factual determinations with respect to any other circumstances."

In the present case, the court * * * [found] that appellant had a marketable skill she could make use of with little retraining and was young and healthy, that respondent was very wealthy and had not worked during the marriage, and that the marriage was brief and there were no children.[4] With respect to the question of standard of living, the court made specific reference to respondent's Tiburon home, Tahoe estate and cars, and found the marital lifestyle to be "affluent." The court then addressed the issue of appellant's health and ability to work, reviewing the testimony of each of the experts and concluding that appellant suffered from a personality disorder which was exacerbated by the parties' relationship but which was not adequately debilitating to prevent her from working.

Finally, the court expressed its view that the standard of living factor was meant by the Legislature to reflect the common situation in which couples marry with little and over time jointly acquire assets and enjoy a higher standard of living. In that situation the non-working spouse should not be financially prejudiced by divorce. The "same sociological considerations" do not necessarily apply in a marriage of short duration, the court explained, where neither party worked, one was very wealthy and the standard of living derived from inherited money rather than the efforts of either spouse. * * *

---

[4] The court found appellant had the marketable skill of dental hygienist, for which there was a market within reasonable commuting distance, it would take less than two or three months for appellant to "get up to speed," with no substantial retraining or education required to market her skill, and appellant's period of unemployment had little effect on her current employability and income; issues concerning the supported spouse's contribution to the other spouse's attainment of education or career were irrelevant; respondent had earning capacity, had not worked during the marriage but had assets creating income at a "substantial standard of living" and meeting his needs adequately; respondent had assets approximating $15,000,000 which created an annual available cash flow of approximately $500,000, with fairly small obligations, while appellant "essentially has no assets," owning a vehicle, possibly a condominium in which she did not have much equity, $25,000 or $30,000 saved from the temporary support she had been receiving and something less than $25,000 in assets to be determined when the community property was divided; the marriage lasted three years and seven months; there were no children; respondent's age and health were irrelevant and respondent was of good physical health and in her early to mid-thirties; and tax consequences were "of little meaning" in the case.

Appellant contends that § 4801 does not limit consideration of marital standard of living to situations where the standard of living results from community efforts but requires it to be considered as the starting point in all cases. The trial court's comments, however, make clear that the standard of living *was* considered in determining the spousal support award. The judge simply recognized that the situation of a spouse ending a brief marriage in which the standard of living was determined by the other spouse's separate property assets is different from that of a spouse ending a long-term marriage in which the couple developed a standard of living together. * * * Here, the court properly also considered the duration of the marriage and appellant's ability to become self-supporting in reaching its decision.

NOTES AND QUESTIONS

1.   Did Mrs. Huntington need alimony more than Mrs. Morgan? Or do *Huntington* and *Morgan* provide evidence that

> *need*, the most common criterion for an alimony award under existing law, is employed largely as a conclusory term. Not only do courts use varying definitions of need, but they sometimes grant alimony awards in cases where no need exists under any commonly employed standard * * * [and deny] alimony * * * despite the presence of obvious need.

AM. LAW INSTITUTE, PRINCIPLES OF THE LAW OF FAMILY DISSOLUTION ch. 1 intro., Topic 1, I(b) (2002).

2.   Virtually all alimony statutes cite marital duration as a factor in alimony determination. *See* Robert Kirkman Collins, *The Theory of Marital Residuals: Applying an Income Adjustment Calculus to the Enigma of Alimony*, 24 HARVARD WOMEN'S L.J. 23, 34 (2001). But why should "the situation of a spouse ending a brief marriage in which the standard of living was determined by the other spouse's separate property assets" be treated differently from that "of a spouse ending a long-term marriage in which the couple developed a standard of living together"? What is the *Huntington* court implicitly saying about the alimony entitlement? If "short-term" marriages are different from "long-term" ones, what does "long-term" mean?

In Zinovoy v. Zinovoy, 50 So. 3d 763 (Fla. Dist. Ct. App. 2010) at divorce the husband's monthly income was $38,000, compared to the wife's monthly income of $1200. The parties had been married 16 years, and both were 48 years old. The court of appeals ruled that an award of permanent alimony to the wife of $6370 per month was too low and an abuse of discretion in light of the parties' standard of living during marriage. The wife had asked for $16,000 in monthly alimony. On remand, what should she receive? Is it clear why the wife's claim is accepted in *Zinovoy* but not in *Huntington*?

3.   Professor Garrison found that most alimony decisions made by New York judges could be predicted based on the claimant's income and the

duration of the marriage. For unemployed women married more than ten years, the alimony award rate was 83%; for employed women married less than ten years, it was 23%. Eighty-nine per cent of women earning less than 10% of family income were awarded alimony. *See* Marsha Garrison, *How Do Judges Decide Divorce Cases? An Empirical Analysis of Discretionary Decision Making*, 74 N.C. L. REV. 401, 468–69, tbls. 14–16 (1996). In a related sample of New York cases that were settled during the same time period, only 49% of unemployed women married ten or more years and 58% of women with income representing less than 10% of family income obtained alimony. *Id.* Why would wives who litigate have better alimony prospects than those who settle? One factor may be legal representation. Professor Garrison found that, where both sides in a settled case were represented by counsel, wives obtained alimony in 30% of the cases. No wives received alimony when neither was represented. *See* Marsha Garrison, *Good Intentions Gone Awry: The Impact of New York's Equitable Distribution Law on Divorce Outcomes*, 57 BROOKLYN L. REV. 621, 711, tbl. 48 (1991). (Of course, parties are more likely to be represented by counsel when they have been married longer and have higher incomes).

4.   If marital duration is an important variable, should all "long" marriage cases be treated identically? For example, in the "traditional" marriage, the husband concentrates on working outside the home and the wife assumes the role of primary caretaker of the children, which frequently negatively impacts her lifetime earning capacity. In contrast, spouses can have substantially different earning capacities at divorce for a variety of other reasons. For example, in Michael v. Michael, 791 S.W.2d 772 (Mo. App. 1990) the parties married after both had graduated from college. They did not have children during their marriage. The wife had more career success than the husband, and whenever the wife received a promotion or transfer he moved with her and tried to find some sort of job. Fifteen years later they divorced, when the wife's annual income was over $70,000 and the husband was not working. Here the parties' earning capacities at divorce, after a "longish" marriage, were quite different. Should the husband be awarded spousal support? In *Michael*, the trial court did not award spousal support; the appellate court ruled that this was an abuse of discretion. On remand, what should the trial court do?

The *Huntington* court refers to a "long-term marriage in which the couple developed a standard of living together." What if the parties have a "long" marriage but one of the parties had already developed a successful career before marriage? Should there be a different result?

5.   If "marital duration" is an important factor, what should be included when calculating the marital duration? In a Massachusetts case, the parties first married in 1995 and divorced in 2004. They began to live together in 2007, married in 2012, and the wife filed for divorce in 2013. The Massachusetts Supreme Judicial Court ruled that, to determine the length of marriage (and therefore the duration of the wife's alimony claim), the court correctly included the length of both marriages and the cohabitation. *See* Duff-Kareores v. Kareores, 52 N.E. 3d 115 (Mass. 2016).

B. MARITAL FAULT

PUCHEU V. PUCHEU

Court of Appeal of Louisiana, 2005.
904 So. 2d 69.

GENOVESE, J.

This appeal presents the question of whether mental illness was *issue* sufficiently proven so as to excuse the fault of the wife in the break up of the marriage for purposes of final periodic support. The trial court found *history* that the wife was excused from fault and awarded $2,000.00 per month in final periodic support. For the following reasons, we reverse. - *holding*

FACTS

John Pucheu ("John") and Maxine Guidry Pucheu ("Maxine") were married on December 9, 1988, separated January 9, 2000, and divorced on August 14, 2002. Prior to their marriage, Maxine was employed by the Louisiana Legislature and John was practicing law in Eunice, Louisiana. Upon marrying, Maxine left her job and moved to the Pucheu family home in Eunice. Maxine had no prior children. John had three children from a previous marriage. The couple had no children together, but raised John's three children, who are now adults.

Following a four-day trial on the issues of fault and final periodic support, the trial court found that Maxine's behavior during the marriage constituted fault which led to the dissolution of the marriage. However, the trial court held that Maxine's fault was excused due to her pre-existing mental illness and awarded her final periodic support in the amount of $2,000.00 per month. John appeals. * * *

LAW AND DISCUSSION

Louisiana Civil Code article 111 provides that a court "may award final periodic support to a party free from fault prior to the filing of a proceeding to terminate the marriage."

In the present case, the trial court found that Maxine's behavior during the marriage constituted fault which led to the dissolution of the marriage. * * *

Even though the trial court found that Maxine was at fault in the break up of the marriage, the trial court went on to state that the "behavior which constituted fault in the dissolution of the marriage was involuntarily induced over an extended period of time by her preexisting mental illness and excuses her of the same." * * * In reaching this conclusion, the trial court relied upon Credeur v. Lalonde, 511 So. 2d 65, which states [that * * * "p]articular medical expert testimony is not required for each instance of misconduct at each particular junction of her illness including symptoms which arose to the level of misconduct that constituted fault in the marriage's dissolution when such a reasonable factual basis for their cause exists." * * * Relying on *Credeur*, the trial court reasoned that Maxine did not have to establish by medical evidence that all of her acts constituting fault were caused by her mental illness. This is a * * * misapplication of our holding in *Credeur*.

In *Credeur*, unlike the matter before us, this court was faced with examining only one assertion of fault based on abandonment. The evidentiary issue in *Credeur* arose when a spouse had been diagnosed with a schizophrenic disorder in February of 1984, and did not abandon the matrimonial domicile until August of 1984, some five months later. This court simply stated that the reasons given by the spouse for abandoning the matrimonial domicile were consistent with the diagnosed mental illness disorder, i.e., fear that her husband and daughter were going to do her bodily harm, and that a reasonable fact finder could conclude that there was a causal connection. In contrast, with Maxine, the medical witnesses were not clear concerning which actions were caused by her mental condition and which were not. Dr. Krishna Yalamanchili, Maxine's treating psychiatrist for over twenty years, was unable to state with any degree of medical certainty or probability that Maxine's mental illness was the cause of all of her behavior constituting fault. Thus, we find as a matter of law, the trial court applied the wrong standard to the facts in evidence * * *.

The record in this case reveals that Maxine had underlying emotional problems. However, the factual and medical evidence established long periods between documented medical treatment. Her first hospitalization occurred in 1982, six years before her marriage to John. At this time, Maxine was diagnosed with anxiety disorder and hysterical personality disorder. Despite her illness, she successfully worked at the Louisiana Legislature for eight years and continued to work there until the marriage.

The next hospitalization did not occur until 1996, eight years after the marriage, when she was hospitalized for a personality disorder. Thereafter, she was not hospitalized again until 2001, which was one year after the parties separated for the last time. The diagnosis on this occasion was a major depressive disorder and unspecified personality disorder. The record reveals that Maxine engaged in a variety of behavior. In addition to publicly criticizing her husband and refusing to participate with him in public events, Maxine did not cook, clean house, iron, or maintain any marital sexual relationship. She also exhibited bizarre behavior such as spending most of her time locked in her bedroom with her dog, maintaining the bedroom in such a manner that only the dog felt welcome, starting construction projects in the middle of the night, playing the television intolerably loud so as to alienate everyone in the house, engaging in screaming tantrums, cursing her husband, throwing objects, insisting that he make more money to maintain her required lifestyle, and requiring him to run errands for her during work hours. These were only some examples of her bizarre behavior and activities.

Although there was sufficient proof in the record of mental illness to excuse much of her bizarre and erratic behavior, there was likewise behavior constituting independent fault not proven with any degree of medical certainty to be caused by her specific mental condition. There were periods of remission where the fault inexplicably continued. The mere proof of mental illness does not excuse all fault. In the case at bar, there were numerous incidents and behavior constituting fault which were not proven by a preponderance of the medial evidence to have been caused or excused by the wife's mental illness. A review of the jurisprudence on this issue supports this court's conclusion, that for behavior constituting fault to be excused for purposes of final periodic support, the spouse must establish that each act constituting fault was caused by mental illness. * * *

For the foregoing reasons, we reverse the trial court's judgment excusing Maxine from fault due to her mental illness and awarding her final periodic support. * * *

DECUIR, J., dissenting.

* * * The trial court's conclusions are well supported by the evidence. Maxine's psychiatric history shows a longstanding disorder which directly affected the marriage and ultimately caused its failure. Her disorder was characterized by poor judgment, hysteria, depression, and social and marital stress. The testimony * * * depict Maxine as a very troubled and emotional person. These symptoms culminated in and caused Maxine's behavior and ended her relationship with her husband. Medical evidence directly linking each act of fault with Maxine's diagnosis is unnecessary when the record so clearly depicts a woman whose disorders took over the household.

The majority, however, holds Maxine to an impossible burden. That she, as a mentally ill, depressed and anxious wife, with at times minimal functioning capabilities, could provide psychological evidence regarding each and every act of misbehavior, as described by her husband and over the course of a twelve-year marriage, is preposterous. Tellingly, the majority is unable to describe, and not even once hint at, which behaviors might not be excusable and which are. How then could Maxine? That, of course, is the province of the trial court and the rationale of *Credeur*.

Because I find no manifest error in the conclusion that Maxine met her burden of proving a causal connection between her mental illness and her fault in causing the failure of the marriage, I respectfully dissent from the reversal of the trial court's judgment.

NOTES AND QUESTIONS

1.   Given the evidence in *Pucheu*, was Maxine at fault in causing the dissolution of her marriage? Is fault vs. no-fault a useful way of determining whether Maxine should obtain an alimony award?

2.   The states are about equally divided on whether fault is relevant to an alimony award. *See* Linda D. Elrod & Robert G. Spector, *A Review of the Year in Family Law: Working Toward More Uniformity in Laws Relating to Families*, 44 FAM. L.Q. 469, 510, chart 1 (2011). Reviewing decisions on fault, Professor Peter Swisher concluded that "the current judicial trend in many states * * * [is] to severely limit the * * * effect of fault-based statutory divorce factors except in serious or egregious circumstances." Peter Nash Swisher, *The ALI Principles: A Farewell to Fault*, 8 DUKE J. GENDER L. & POL'Y 213, 227 (2001). Today, only a handful of states follow the *Puecheu* approach and bar an alimony award when the claimant spouse has been found guilty of fault causing the dissolution of the marriage. *See, e.g.*, GA. CODE ANN. § 19–6–1(b) (alimony barred when claimant guilty of adultery or desertion); Romulus v. Romulus, 715 S.E.2d 308 (N.C. App. 2011) (wife's illicit sexual behavior during marriage barred her receipt of post-divorce alimony). A New Jersey court has stated that alimony should be barred if the claimant was guilty of "egregious economic fault." Clark v. Clark, 57 A.3d 1 (N.J. Super. App. Div. 2012).

3.   The German Civil Code explicitly limits the alimony court to consideration of egregious fault:

> A claim for support must be denied, reduced or limited in duration, if the imposition of the obligation—also considering the rights of a child of the obligor and obligee that is in the obligee's custody—would be unconscionable (grossly inequitable) because * * * (2) The obligee is guilty of a crime or of a severe intentional offense against the obligor or against a near relative of the obligor; (3) The obligee has caused his or her own need intentionally or recklessly; (4) The obligee has intentionally or recklessly disregarded significant financial interests of the obligor; (5) For a considerable period of time before the separation, the obligee has grossly violated his or her duty to contribute to the support of the family; (6) The obligee is responsible for obviously serious, clearly unilateral misconduct against the obligor * * *.

GERMAN CIVIL CODE § 1579. What are the pros and cons of the German approach as compared to that outlined in *Pucheu* and the interpretive approach described by Professor Swisher?

4.   Principles of marital dissolution developed under the auspices of the American Law Institute (ALI) eschew any consideration of marital fault:

> The potentially valid functions of a fault principle are better served by the tort and criminal law, and attempting to serve them through a fault rule risks serious distortions in the resolution of the dissolution action. One possible function of a fault rule, punishment

of bad conduct, is generally disavowed even by fault states. It is better left to the criminal law, which is designed to serve it, and in doing so appropriately reaches a much narrower range of marital misconduct * * *. The second possible function, compensation for the nonfinancial losses imposed by the other spouse's battery or emotional abuse, is better left to tort law. With the general demise of interspousal immunity, tort remedies for spousal violence are readily available. Most courts have been more cautious in recognizing interspousal claims for emotional abuse unaccompanied by physical violence, but the grounds for their caution apply equally to consideration of emotional distress claims in a dissolution action * * *.

AM. LAW INSTITUTE, PRINCIPLES OF THE LAW OF FAMILY DISSOLUTION ch. 1 intro., at Topic 2, VI (2002). In evaluating the ALI position, review current law on spousal tort actions (see Chapter 4) and consider this assessment of marital torts:

> [A]lthough appellate opinions may suggest that there are a vast number of tort cases associated with divorce, in practice there are relatively few cases that are actually brought and even fewer where there has actually been a recovery. The reasons for this are not doctrinal but practical. Matrimonial lawyers overwhelmingly indicate that * * * practically all clients show a distaste for the prolonging of the process that a civil case would entail. * * * Second, even when the client is willing to bring a separate tort action there may not be a source of funds to pay the damages. Most homeowners insurance policies no longer cover intentional torts.

Robert G. Spector, *Marital Torts: The Current Legal Landscape*, 33 FAM. L.Q. 745, 762–63 (1999).

5. Should the fault of the obligor be relevant to an alimony award? In Dyer v. Tsapis, 249 S.E.2d 509 (W. Va. 1978), the West Virginia Supreme Court said yes:

> * * * Once all divorces, like all tort actions, were predicated upon a legal wrong; alimony, like tort damages, served both punitive and compensatory purposes. Now, increasingly, divorces are awarded on no-fault grounds and awards of alimony, like contract damages increasingly emphasize restitution to the exclusion of punishment. * * * Reluctantly, and possibly because of the difficulty in determining fault in the context of a complex interpersonal relationship, we have shifted the focus of the divorce inquiry from fault evidence to more dignified and reliable economic evidence. Nonetheless, the more modern approach must be alloyed with the more ancient. * * *
>
> We hold * * * that in a divorce action based upon [one year's voluntary separation], a spouse seeking alimony must show the other spouse guilty of inequitable conduct. Although inequitable conduct

need not be so serious as to fall into one of the standard fault categories it must be a significant wrong * * *. In the case before us, while the husband may or may not have committed adultery, his conduct was found to give rise to a strong suspicion of adultery. Conduct of this sort, which would lead persons in the community reasonably to believe that the husband committed adultery, and, therefore, to hold the wife up to ridicule and contempt, could reasonably be considered inequitable. * * * [A] totally blameless party can never be charged with alimony. When, however, there has been inequitable conduct on the part of the husband and it appears that the wife has been comparatively blameless, the trial court [may] * * * award * * * alimony. * * *

6.   The split among jurisdictions regarding the role of fault in alimony decision making reflects the lack of consensus about alimony's purpose. *If* alimony is compensation for tortious conduct, the payor spouse's wrongdoing should increase the "damage" award. *If* alimony is compensation for breach of the marital contract, the victimized spouse should be able to recover, but not the wrongdoer spouse. *If* alimony represents accrued economic interests in the marriage relationship, fault should be irrelevant. *If* alimony represents a replacement of lost earnings or pay for unpaid services, fault should be irrelevant. *If* divorce terminates spousal support obligations, then there should be no alimony at all, fault or no fault.

7.   Evaluate the following approaches to fault as a factor in alimony decision making:

a.   the approach of the *Pucheu* majority;

b.   the approach of the *Pucheu* dissent;

c.   the approach of the German Civil Code (note 3, *supra*);

d.   the ALI approach (note 4, *supra*);

e.   the *Dyer* approach (note 5, *supra*);

f.   disallowing a showing of fault in alimony determination, but permitting spouses to bring claims for intentional infliction of emotional distress (*see* Chapter 4).

What policy goals underlie each approach? Can you predict which approach will produce the most alimony awards? The least? On balance, is one approach clearly preferable to the others?

C. CONTRACTUAL COMMITMENTS

It was mentioned above in Chapter 5 that many, but not all, states will enforce an alimony waiver contained in a premarital agreement.

If one spouse has signed U.S. immigration sponsorship documents for the other spouse during marriage, the question has arisen whether this should be treated as a commitment to pay spousal support if they divorce.

Some courts have treated them as contractual commitments to pay alimony. *See* Love v. Love, 33 A.3d 1268 (Pa. Super. 2011); Naik v. Naik, 944 A.2d 713 (N.J. Super. App. Div. 2008); Erler v. Erler, 824 F.3d 1173 (9th Cir. 2016). Others have not. *See* Barnett v. Barnett, 238 P.3d 594 (Alaska 2010).

3. THE DURATION AND VALUE OF ALIMONY

A. THE DURATION OF ALIMONY

In many states, there are three types of alimony: (1) transitional or rehabilitative alimony, which is received for a specified period after divorce; (2) reimbursement alimony, to repay a spouse for support provided while the other spouse was educated during marriage; and (3) indefinite-term alimony, which is paid until the recipient remarries or either party dies. There is no clear agreement regarding when transitional support is warranted and when indefinite-term support should be awarded.

OTIS V. OTIS
Supreme Court of Minnesota 1980.
299 N.W.2d 114.

TODD, JUSTICE.

Emmanuel and Georgia Contos Otis' marriage was terminated by divorce. Georgia Otis has appealed from that portion of the decree which terminates her maintenance after four years. We affirm.

The parties were married on June 6, 1954. At the time of the marriage, Mrs. Otis was a skilled executive secretary, earning a substantial income. She left her employment to give birth to the parties' only child and has remained absent from the employment market since that time. Mr. Otis has achieved a high degree of success in the business world and is employed by Control Data Corporation as an executive vice president. At the time of the divorce, Mrs. Otis was 45 and Mr. Otis was 46 years of age.

* * *

At the time of the divorce, Mr. Otis received an annual salary in excess of $120,000, plus bonuses. The trial court found that Mrs. Otis was in good health and had held a highly paid secretarial job in the past. Further, the court found that Mrs. Otis, with some additional training, is capable of earning $12,000 to $18,000 per year.

* * *

In addition to the property settlement * * * Mrs. Otis was awarded as "alimony" the sum of $2,000 per month [for four years]. * * * The only issue presented by this appeal is the correctness of the trial court's order terminating monthly payments to the wife after four years.

* * *

The divorce decree divided the property of the parties[, awarding Mrs. Otis assets worth $225,704.50 and Mr. Otis assets worth $210,620.50. Both parties received a mix of liquid and nonliquid assets.] * * * Mr. Otis was also awarded his substantial interest in his vested pension plan. In addition, he was awarded property in Greece valued at $85,000 which he had inherited.

* * *

The grounds for awarding "maintenance" were established by Minn. Stat. § 518.552 * * *[,] taken in large part from the Uniform Marriage and Divorce Act * * *.

> The basic attitudinal change reflected in the new provision has been summarized as follows:

> * * * Traditionally, spousal support was a permanent award because it was assumed that a wife had neither the ability nor the resources to become self-sustaining. However, with the mounting dissolution rate, the advent of no-fault dissolution, and the growth of the women's liberation movement, the focal point of spousal support determinations has shifted from the sex of the recipient to the individual's ability to become financially independent. This change in focus has given rise to the concept of rehabilitative alimony, also called maintenance, spousal support, limited alimony, or step-down spousal support.

Rehabilitative Spousal Support: In Need of a More Comprehensive Approach to Mitigating Dissolution Trauma, 12 U.S.F. L. REV. 493, 494–95 (1978).

* * *

The Florida Court of Appeals, which has * * * adopted an approach similar to that of the Uniform Act[,] * * * emphasized, in setting aside a 20-year award of alimony, that rehabilitative alimony must be of reasonable duration:

> Rehabilitative alimony is * * * clearly an incentive to assist one in reclaiming employment skills outside the home which have atrophied during the marital relationship. * * * [W]hen a wife has completed her maternal role, and provided she is in good health, she should make every effort to rehabilitate herself within a reasonable time thereafter, and when she has done so, rehabilitative alimony is to be discontinued.

Robinson v. Robinson, 366 So. 2d 1210, 1211–12 (Fla. App. 1979).

* * *

* * * [T]he focus of this court must now be on a determination of the two basic standards established by the new legislation; namely, we must determine if the spouse seeking maintenance—

(a) Lacks sufficient property, including marital property apportioned to him, to provide for his reasonable needs, especially during a period of training or education, and

(b) Is unable to support himself through appropriate employment or is the custodian of a child whose condition or circumstances make it appropriate that the custodian not be required to seek employment outside the home.

* * * Applying these standards to the findings of the trial court * * *, we conclude that the decision of the trial court is not clearly erroneous.

Affirmed.

OTIS, JUSTICE (dissenting) joined by SHERAN, C.J., and WAHL, J.

In this decision, the majority applies a section of the Minnesota session laws which was not effective until after this case was tried and then holds that it dictates that appellant, who has not held a job outside her home for 23 years, may be denied all alimony after only four years have elapsed. In my opinion it is manifestly unjust and inappropriate to deprive a wife of an expectancy on which she had a right to rely after a marriage of 25 years and accordingly I respectfully dissent.

* * *

The parties were married in June 1954. Today, respondent, is a vice-president of Control Data Corporation, earning more than $120,000 per year. Appellant has not been employed since her son was born, at which time she abandoned a promising career as an executive secretary in order to fulfill the expected, traditional role of wife and hostess for a rising and successful business executive. She performed this role so well that in 1977 she was selected to serve as hostess to the board of directors of Control Data Corporation during a week-long meeting in Greece, which was her homeland and that of her husband. When her husband was being considered for his present position, appellant was herself interviewed to determine whether she could fill the role required of her in her husband's business career. A number of years previously she had been anxious to resume a career of her own. Her husband forbade it stating that he was "not going to have any wife of mine pound a typewriter."

There is no evidentiary support for the trial court's finding that her earning capacity is substantial. There is no showing that at her age, now approximately forty-seven, she can be gainfully employed at her prior occupation after a lapse of more than twenty years. * * * Accordingly, I would continue the $2,000 per month payment indefinitely, subject only to a substantial change in circumstances at some later date.

NOTES AND QUESTIONS

1.   Here the parties were married 26 years and raised one child together. They now have very different career prospects, at least in part due to the roles assumed during their marriage.

2.   The husband's monthly salary is $10,000, plus bonuses. The wife's monthly salary, after training, will be $1000–$1500. Does she need support? She is 45 years old and will receive $225,000 in marital assets. Will she "lack sufficient property to provide for her reasonable needs"?

3.   The husband's income after divorce will be much higher than the wife's. Does the fact that they will be "divorced" mean he should not have to share any post-divorce income with her? Or is there some reason that, despite the divorce, he should share some post-divorce income? If he should share some post-divorce income, how much should he share and for how long?

CHAMBERLAIN V. CHAMBERLAIN
Court of Appeals of Minnesota, 2000.
615 N.W.2d 405.

ANDERSON, J.

FACTS

Appellant Paul W. Chamberlain and respondent Mary Lou Chamberlain, both now 50 years old, sought to end their 20-year marriage by a dissolution petition filed January 21, 1998. The parties have two sons, now ages 13 and 19. Both appellant and respondent have enjoyed successful careers. He is an attorney in solo practice, and her master's degree has furthered her career as a second-grade teacher in a suburban school district. They earn about $200,000 and $63,000 per year, respectively. Appellant enjoyed increased, but out-of-the-ordinary, income totaling $335,000 in 1994 and $426,000 in 1996. Respondent has worked as a teacher since 1971, except for a five-year period following the birth of their first son.

To say that the parties experienced an affluent lifestyle is an understatement of the facts. The record contains references to: (1) the parties' Lake Minnetonka home that sold in November 1999 for nearly $1.3 million * * *; (2) numerous vacations, including biannual cruises, annual Hawaiian Christmas trips, and travel to ski destinations such as Vail, Colorado; (3) dining at expensive restaurants several times each week; (4) memberships at athletic and social clubs; (5) expensive designer and custom-made clothing; (6) luxury vehicles; and (7) frequent elective cosmetic surgeries.

* * *

After debt payments, the approximately $1.3 million in marital property was distributed nearly equally. * * * The district court awarded respondent permanent maintenance of $2,400 per month. [Petitioner appeals from that order.] * * *

ANALYSIS

Appellant * * * claims that the district court abused its discretion by awarding appellant permanent maintenance of $2,400 per month. Appellant argues that respondent is not a suitable candidate for permanent maintenance because she has had, throughout the 20-year marriage, her own successful career as a teacher and presently earns the top salary in her profession—more than $63,000 annually. Appellant contends that because respondent does not need rehabilitation to become self-sufficient, and has significant financial resources available to her, she is not in need of maintenance, let alone permanent maintenance. * * *

husband's argument

Spousal maintenance * * * may be granted if the spouse seeking maintenance demonstrates that he or she:

Rule

(a) lacks sufficient property, including marital property apportioned to the spouse, to provide for reasonable needs of the spouse considering the standard of living established during the marriage, especially, but not limited to, a period of training or education, or

(b) is unable to provide adequate self-support, after considering the standard of living established during the marriage and all relevant circumstances, through appropriate employment, or is the custodian of a child whose condition or circumstances make it appropriate that the custodian not be required to seek employment outside the home.

Minn. Stat. § 518.552, subd. 1 (1998).

When determining the amount and duration of maintenance, district courts must consider all relevant factors, including factors that address the financial resources of the spouse seeking maintenance to provide for his or her needs independently, the time necessary to acquire education to find appropriate employment, the age and health of the recipient spouse, the standard of living established during the marriage, the length of the marriage, the contribution and economic sacrifices of a homemaker, and the resources of the spouse from whom maintenance is sought. Minn. Stat. § 518.552, subd. 2(a)–(h) (1998). In the questionable case, the statute directs that the district court order permanent maintenance, leaving the order open for later modification. Maintenance-related findings of fact are not set aside unless clearly erroneous.

The district court found that the parties' standard of living reflected a lifestyle that was beyond their means and reduced or eliminated some of respondent's claimed reasonable expenses, such as elective surgery and dining at high-priced restaurants. * * *Despite these reductions, the district court * * * determined that the facts supported a permanent maintenance award * * * [:]

> [T]he simple fact of the matter is that Respondent needs spousal maintenance in order [to] duplicate a standard of living that already represents a substantial reduction from the standard of living born of deficit spending.

Considering the marital standard of living that would have been within the parties' means, the district court found respondent's and her unemancipated son's reasonable monthly expenses to be $6,627. Respondent's monthly income of $3,046 and the $1,483 child-support award did not cover the reasonable expenses as determined by the district court. The district court found that appellant was able to pay monthly maintenance. Appellant's monthly needs of $6,846 left nearly $6,000 of monthly after-tax income with which to support respondent and their youngest son. The district court awarded respondent permanent monthly maintenance of $2,400.

In order to properly understand the result reached by the district court * * * some historical perspective is helpful. In 1984, the then-existing maintenance statute was functionally read as disfavoring permanent maintenance. * * *

* * * 1985 amendments * * * require[d] a district court, when considering maintenance questions, to consider the parties' marital standard of living * * * [and] stat[ed] that when evaluation of the factors in Minn. Stat. § 518.552, subd. 2, produce uncertainty about the need for permanent maintenance, that uncertainty "shall" be resolved in favor of a permanent award left open for future modification. * * *

* * *

* * * Appellant correctly notes that there are no appellate decisions in Minnesota affirming an award of permanent maintenance with a fact pattern similar to the present controversy. But the analysis does not stop with this observation. The district court correctly focused on the standard of living of the parties, a standard of living arrived at jointly and experienced by the parties for many years, in determining that permanent maintenance was appropriate and made findings that appellant's income was sufficient to support a permanent maintenance award. The district court correctly noted that the legislature could have excluded an affluent

lifestyle as a consideration but chose not to do so. Indeed, a review of the legislative history reveals that the legislature amended the maintenance statute to expand the definition of "reasonable needs," as well as "adequate self support" to include specifically a consideration of the standard of living established during the marriage.

What is at issue in this case, and what is unresolved by the statutory language and the decisions of the appellate courts of Minnesota, is whether *issue* the permanent-maintenance "factors" are equal in terms of the weight to be assigned to each or whether some should be more significant than others. Appellant argues, with more than a little persuasive logic, that the district court judgment here determines, in effect, that standard of living is a "trump card" overruling other factors which in this case would normally not support an award of permanent maintenance. Respondent is in good health, 50 years old, at the top of her teaching career, did not play the role of a traditional homemaker for most of the marriage, needs no further education or rehabilitation, and does not suffer health problems that affect her ability to work. In addition, she received a substantial property award as a result of the dissolution.

But, to adopt appellant's view of the law would essentially eliminate the statutorily required consideration of the marital standard of living from the maintenance analysis. * * * It is our conclusion that, absent further direction from the legislature or the supreme court, the long-standing affluent lifestyle of the parties is an appropriate factor for the district court to consider, and given the court's findings regarding appellant's income and the wide discretion afforded the district court, we affirm the award of permanent maintenance in this case. While a different result is supportable, and we might have reached a different result, on this record we cannot say an award of permanent maintenance is an abuse of discretion. * * * *legislature fixed what happened in Otis*

[The court did remand the case for a reduction in the amount of the award.]

NOTES AND QUESTIONS

1. Why was Mrs. Chamberlain eligible for alimony when Mrs. Morgan was not?

2. Could Mrs. Otis have obtained permanent alimony under *Chamberlain*? Under the Texas statute printed earlier in this chaper? Could Mrs. Chamberlain have obtained permanent alimony under the *Otis* decision? The Texas statute?

3. In *Otis*, the court discusses the concept of "rehabilitative alimony." This reflects the idea that alimony should be for a limited term if it seems reasonable to predict that the recipient can "rehabilitate" his or her career. What does this mean? That the recipient will then be able to earn enough

money to maintain a standard of living approximating the marital standard, or is it sufficient that the recipient will be able to maintain a much more modest standard of living? In *Otis*, the husband at divorce was earning an annual salary of $120,000. The court predicted that, with additional training, the wife's annual income would be $12,000 to $18,000. After a 23-year marriage where the wife raised their child, what amount and duration of support should be awarded?

4.   In *Chamberlain*, the claimant had worked outside the home throughout most of the marriage. Should this impact her alimony claim? If so, how?

5.   In *Otis*, it seems unlikely that the wife will be able to maintain the marital standard of living after divorce, even during the 4-year period she will receive support. In contrast, the court in *Chamberlain* affirms the support award because the court found that she needed the support to maintain the marital standard of living.

6.   In Andrews v. Andrews, 344 S.W.3d 321 (Tenn. App. 2010) the court held that rehabilitative limited-term support (as opposed to permanent support) should be awarded at the end of a 12-year marriage only where the payor spouse demonstrates that the recipient will be able to generate income sufficient to support the standard of living during marriage at the expiration of the alimony term. Is this a sensible rule?

What if the court awards fixed-term support, assuming the recipient can rehabilitate his or her career by the expiration of the term, but this does not happen? Should the recipient be able to successfully petition the court to extend the term?

7.   The shift in Minnesota's alimony law described in *Chamberlain* is not unique. In reaction to decisions like *Otis,* many states, by statute or judicial decision, have now established alimony standards that reject the UMDA approach in the case of a long-married homemaker. This shift implicitly accepts dissenting Justice Otis's claim that when the wife's marital "role * * * was to expend her youth and intelligence and talents in the home and with her children and in family-related activities of which her husband approved," she should not be penalized at divorce. But if the concept of rehabilitative alimony cannot fairly be applied to the Mrs. Otises of the world, does that necessarily imply that it cannot fairly be applied to the Mrs. Chamberlains? Put somewhat differently, does *Chamberlain* foreclose future claims by prospective alimony obligors that alimony should be limited to the period necessary to enable the obligee to "provide adequate self-support"? Is there some standard other than standard of living during marriage that would be a better standard?

8.   In studying divorce decision making in New York, Professor Garrison found that permanent alimony was much more common in marriages of at least twenty years duration; 46% of judicial awards to wives in this group were permanent as compared to 24% in marriages of less than ten years. The likelihood of a permanent award also declined significantly over a ten-year

period when the marriage was less than twenty years, while for marriages over twenty years it did not. *See* Marsha Garrison, *How Do Judges Decide Divorce Cases? An Empirical Analysis of Divorce Decision Making*, 74 N.C. L. REV. 401, 471–72 (1996). *See also* Joan B. Krauskopf, *Rehabilitative Alimony: Uses and Abuses of Limited Duration Alimony*, 21 FAM. L. Q. 573, 579–89 (1988) (concluding, based on appellate opinion survey, that "it is likely that marriages over fifteen years will be considered long-term ones and that time limits on alimony needed at the divorce by the long-term, traditional homemaker will not be justified.").

Garrison also investigated the predictability of alimony permanence and found that, for judicial decisions at the trial level, the most significant factors in predicting whether an alimony award was permanent or fixed-term were marital duration and the political party of the judge who made the decision; Republican judges awarded permanent alimony in 40% of the cases they decided while Democratic judges awarded permanent alimony in only 25%. After appeals were taken into account, the most significant predictive factors were marital duration and the year of decision; later decisions were more likely to produce fixed-term awards. Both before and after appeal, decisions on the length of a fixed-term award were completely unpredictable. Garrison, *supra,* at 486–88, 503.

9.   In Marriage of Brankin, 967 N.E.2d 358 (Ill. App. 2012), the couple was divorcing after 30 years of marriage. They had raised one child together, who was an adult at the time of divorce. The husband, almost age 60, earned $30,000 a month and had just had a heart attack. The wife, age 55, earned $6,333 per month. The wife asked for permanent maintenance in addition to the $600,000 in marital assets she was to receive. The appellate court emphasized the extent to which the divorce court has discretion when ordering maintenance. The court stated the post-divorce equalization of income is neither required or prohibited. The appellate court affirmed the trial court's decision to order $3,000 in monthly permanent maintenance.

10.   In contrast to the *Otis* and *Chamberlain* approaches, some states have adopted rules that base alimony duration on marital duration. For example, the California statute provides that "the goal [of alimony] is for the supported party [to become] self-supporting within a reasonable period of time" and defines "reasonable period of time" to mean one-half the duration of the marriage (except in a marriage of ten or more years). CAL. FAM. CODE § 4320(l). *See also* DEL. CODE ANN. tit. 13, § 1512(d) (alimony award cannot exceed a period equal to one-half the length of the marriage unless the marriage had continued for twenty or more years); 19–A ME. REV. STATS. § 951–A(2)(A)(1) (same duration limit as Delaware for marriages of 10–20 years duration); UTAH CODE ANN. § 30–3–5(8)(h) (limiting alimony period to the number of years of the marriage, absent "extenuating circumstances"). In Massachusetts, if parties divorce and have been married for fewer than 20 years, the maximum alimony duration is a specified fraction of the marital duration; there is no maximum duration for marriages that lasted for 20 years or more. *See* MASS. GEN. LAWS, Chapter 208, § 49. In Biskie v. Biskie, 37 So. 3d 970 (Fla. Dist. Ct.

App. 2010) the court stated that a marriage ending in divorce after 15 years is "in the gray area" where there is no presumption in favor or against permanent alimony.

11. In *Otis* and *Chamberlain*, the spouses raised a child together during marriage. Should the alimony analysis be different if the parties did not raise a child together? For heterosexual couples, should the analysis be different if the higher earner is a man or a woman? Should the analysis be different for gay couples?

12. Is it clear that if a marriage lasted 20 years indefinite-term support is generally justified? Can you imagine types of long-term marriages where the parties' incomes are quite different at divorce and no spousal support seems justified? If support is justified, in a long-term marriage how long should the support last, and what should be grounds for modification? For example, assume the spouses are both 45 when they divorce. Unless the recipient remarries, should the support continue until the first spouse dies? If the obligor's income substantially increases after divorce, should the support amount be increased? What if the payor spouse retires at age 65 and his income is significantly reduced? What if the recipient establishes another stable romantic relationship with a new partner who has a significant income, but does not live with the new partner and does not remarry? What if the obligor spouse establishes a new relationship with a party with substantial needs?

In Texas, if parties have been married 25 years spousal support cannot exceed 7 years unless the recipient is permanently disabled or the primary caretaker of a disabled child. Why do you think no other state has adopted this type of durational limit for support after a long marriage?

13. In terms of fairness and predictability, what are the advantages and disadvantages of: (a) the traditional approach (i.e., all alimony awards are permanent; (b) the UMDA approach used in *Otis*; (c) the *Chamberlain* approach; (d) the Texas approach; (e) the California approach; or (f) the Massachusetts approach?

B. THE VALUE OF ALIMONY

Except for the Texas statute set forth above, alimony statutes seldom specify either a ceiling or a floor for the value of alimony; alimony decisions seldom explain, or justify, the dollar value of an award. The result, in all probability, is a fairly high level of inconsistency. In her study of judicial divorce decision making in New York, Professor Garrison found that, in cases with minor children, adding alimony to the child support award *reduced* the overall predictability of the decision-making process. For cases without minor children, the only factors significantly related to the value of the alimony award were the husband's property (husbands with more valuable assets tended to pay more alimony) and the appellate department in which the case was brought; neither the wife's nor the husband's income was significantly related to alimony value. *See* Garrison, *supra* note 4, at

490–94. A survey in which Ohio divorce judges were asked to make spousal support decisions in several sample cases also revealed wide disparity in the duration and value of awards. For example, in the case of a 25-year marriage between a 54-year-old physician earning $400,000 annually and a college-educated 50-year-old homemaker who had been primary caretaker for the couple's two emancipated children but never worked outside the home, 100% of the 185 responding judges awarded spousal support to the wife—but the awards ranged from a low of $101 per week to a high of $3,400 per week. 28% of the awards were permanent, while 63% were for periods between five and twenty years. *See* Leslie Herndon Spillane, *Spousal Support: The Other Ohio Lottery*, 24 OHIO N.U. L. REV. 282, 296 (1998).

In order to prevent such inconsistency, some jurisdictions have begun to move toward alimony "guidelines" that produce presumptive alimony values based on specific case characteristics. Interestingly, Pennsylvania—which maintains the extremely discretionary take-everything-conceivably-relevant approach to the *determination* of whether alimony should be awarded that you saw in the statute on p. 971 has been in the guideline forefront.

MASCARO V. MASCARO

Supreme Court of Pennsylvania, 2002.
569 Pa. 255, 803 A.2d 1186.

NEWMAN, JUSTICE.

We granted appeal in this matter to determine whether the support guidelines apply to spousal support cases where the parties' combined net income exceeds $15,000 per month ($180,000 per year). Because we hold that they do apply, we reverse the decision of the Superior Court * * *.

FACTS AND PROCEDURAL HISTORY

Joseph Mascaro (Husband) and Rosemary Mascaro (Wife) were married in August of 1978, and separated in October of 1994. They had one child, born on November 14, 1984. On June 4, 1996, Wife filed a Complaint for Support, and on September 25, 1996, a master issued a recommendation that Husband pay Wife $2,500 per week ($130,000 per year) tax free for spousal and child support.[3] Both parties filed exceptions,

---

[3] Pa. R.C.P. 1910.16–4(f)(1) provides:

An order awarding both spousal and child support may be unallocated or state the amount of support allocable to the spouse and the amount allocable to the child. However, the formula provided by these rules assume that an order will be unallocated. Therefore, if the order is to be allocated, the formula set forth in this Rule shall be utilized to determine the amount allocable to the spouse. If allocation of an order utilizing the formula would be inequitable, the court shall make an appropriate allocation. Also, if an order is to be allocated, an adjustment shall be made to the award giving consideration

following which the trial court held a de novo hearing. The trial court determined that Husband had monthly after-tax income of nearly $52,000 ($624,000 per year). The parties agreed that Wife had no earning capacity.

On June 10, 1998, the trial court ordered Husband to pay Wife $19,786 per month ($237,432 per year) in child and spousal support. Husband sought reconsideration [and] * * * the trial court ordered Husband to pay Wife $13,000 per month ($156,000 per year) as tax-free unallocated spousal and child support. The court determined that where monthly income exceeds the limit provided in the support guidelines, both child support and spousal support must be calculated pursuant to the formula set forth in *Melzer v. Witsberger,* 505 Pa. 462, 480 A.2d 991 (1984). On appeal, the Superior Court affirmed the order of the trial court.

DISCUSSION

* * *

The statutory basis for the support guidelines is found in Section 4322 of the Divorce Code, which provides:

> *(a) Statewide guideline.*—Child and spousal support shall be awarded pursuant to a Statewide guideline * * * so that persons similarly situated shall be treated similarly. The guideline shall be based upon the reasonable needs of the child or spouse seeking support and the ability of the obligor to provide support. In determining the reasonable needs of the child or spouse seeking support and the ability of the obligor to provide support, the guideline shall place primary emphasis on the net incomes and earning capacities of the parties, with allowable deviations for unusual needs, extraordinary expenses and other factors, such as the parties' assets, as warrant special attention. * * *

23 Pa.C.S. § 4322. * * *

[T]he guidelines are based upon the Income Shares Model * * *. Because authoritative economic studies demonstrate the average amount of money that intact families with a monthly net income of $15,000 or less spend on their children, such amounts serve as the basic child support schedule set forth in Pa.R.C.P. 1910.16–3.

Pa.R.C.P. 1910.16–4 provides the following method by which to calculate spousal support * * * when the parties have dependent children:

---

to the federal income tax consequences of an allocated order as may be appropriate under the circumstances.

Spousal Support (With Dependent Children)

12. Obligor's Monthly Net Income (line 4)   _____

13. Less Obligor's support, alimony pendente lite or alimony obligations, if any, to children or former spouses who are not part of this action (See Rule 1910.16–2(c)(2))   (_____)

14. Less Obligee's Monthly Net Income (Line 4)   (_____)

15. Difference   _____

16. Less Obligor's Total Child Support Obligation (line 11)   (_____)

17. Difference   _____

18. Multiply by 30%[4]   x .30

19. Amount of Monthly Spousal Support or APL   _____

An award of child or spousal support determined under the support guidelines is a rebuttable presumption, from which the trier of fact may deviate [based on]: * * *

(1) unusual needs and unusual fixed obligations;

(2) other support obligations of the parties;

(3) other income in the household;

(4) ages of the children;

(5) assets of the parties;

(6) medical expenses not covered by insurance;

(7) standard of living of the parties and their children;

(8) in a spousal support or alimony pendente lite case, the period of time during which the parties lived together from the date of marriage to the date of final separation; and

(9) other relevant and appropriate factors, including the best interests of the child or children.

Pa.R.C.P. 1910.16–5. * * *

---

[4] Pa.R.C.P. 1910.16–4(a) Part IV provides that where the obligor does not have a child support obligation, the obligee receives forty percent of the difference between the obligor's net income and the obligee's net income as spousal support or APL. However, where the obligor does have a child support obligation, as in the instant matter, the obligee receives thirty percent of the difference between the obligor's net income and the obligee's net income.

Despite the existence of a framework to employ when determining a spousal support award, the trial court rejected the guidelines, and instead performed a *Melzer* analysis regarding the reasonable needs of Wife and the parties' child. * * * [T]he Superior Court correctly noted, "[a]s to child support, the guidelines recognized that they were not applicable to high income cases because the model does not contain data which would establish the children's reasonable needs." Where we disagree with the Superior Court is in its analysis regarding the application of the spousal support guidelines to high-income cases. The Superior Court stated:

> Our research has not revealed any data in the guidelines model that make the guidelines applicable to spousal support in high income families. Therefore, we conclude that the guidelines are not designed to calculate spousal support in high income families where after tax income exceeds $15,000.00 per month. To conclude otherwise, would result in awards that were not contemplated by the model which underpins the guideline system and one that is not based on an analysis of the reasonable needs of the dependent spouse. In such high income cases, the determination of spousal support, as in high income child support cases, must be based on the factors found in *Melzer*. In the absence of a statement in the guidelines themselves that they are applicable, we conclude they are not.

* * * Clearly, the income shares model relates only to child support. Because the income shares model bears no relation to the spousal support guidelines, it cannot "underpin" the spousal support formula. Therefore, the Superior Court acted unreasonably in refusing to follow the guidelines simply because they do not state that they apply to high-income cases.

Determining spousal support solely on the parties' net incomes and the obligor's other support obligations treats similarly situated persons similarly, which is the goal expressed in Section 4322 of the Divorce Code (Support Guidelines). Allowing for deviations from the presumptive amount of support by permitting the trier of fact to consider the factors set forth in Rule 1910.16–5 prevents the goal of uniformity from leading to an unnecessarily harsh result where findings of fact justify the amount of the deviation. Furthermore, by emphasizing the parties' income instead of their standard of living, the guideline formula obviates the need for inquiry into details of the parties' frugality or extravagance with regard to clothing, entertainment, household expenses, etc. Thus, under the guideline formula, an obligee will not be prejudiced by the fact that during the marriage the obligor required him or her to live below the parties' means. Conversely, an obligor whose spouse spent profligately during the marriage will not be required to fund such a lifestyle unless it can be justified by the parties' income.

* * * [T]he trial court erred when it failed to calculate Wife's spousal support award based on Rule 1910.16–4, with an upward or downward modification pursuant to the factors set forth in Rule 1910.16–5 [and] * * * when it ignored the specific requirements of *Melzer* by failing to calculate the child's reasonable needs separately from those of Wife. Pinpointing the child's needs is crucial not only to determining his or her support, but for determining Wife's support as well, because the spousal support calculation set forth in Rule 1910.16–4 allows the obligor to deduct child support obligations from his or her net income. Accordingly, upon remand the trial court must engage in a thorough *Melzer* analysis * * *.

CONCLUSION

Spousal support in all cases, regardless of income level, is based on the formula in Rule 1910.16–4. Any deviation from this must be made pursuant to Rule 1910.16–5. Prior to determining spousal support, the finder of fact must first calculate the payor's child support obligation. In cases where the combined net income exceeds $15,000 per month ($180,000 per year), the child support obligation must be determined based on the child's reasonable needs, as required by *Melzer*. While the reasonable needs of a child are paramount in a high-income child support matter, the reasonable needs of a spouse are not a proper consideration when calculating spousal support or APL.

Therefore, we reverse the Order of the Superior Court and remand this matter to the trial court for further proceedings consistent with this Opinion.

NOTES AND QUESTIONS

1.   Alimony guidelines like those utilized in *Mascaro* are still rare. A 2004 survey revealed local or statewide alimony guidelines in effect in only eight states. *See* Twila B. Larkin, *Guidelines for Alimony: The New Mexico Experiment*, 38 FAM. L.Q. 29, 31–32 (2004).

2.   Under the guidelines in *Mascaro*, the focus is no longer on how much the claimant needs to maintain the standard of living during marriage. The claimant has a presumptive claim to a percentage of the difference in the parties' post-divorce net incomes. What are the advantages and disadvantages of such an approach? If the claim should be for a percentage of the difference in the spouses' respective net incomes at divorce, is 30% the right figure, or should it be higher or lower? *See also,* J. Thomas Oldham, *Changes in the Economic Consequences of Divorces, 1958–2008,* 42 FAM. L.Q. 419, 443–446 (2008). During the past five years, Illinois, Colorado and New York have adopted spousal support guidelines. *See* J. Thomas Oldham, *Economic Consequences of Divorce in the United States: Recent Developments,* in FAMILY LAW IN BRITAIN AND AMERICA IN THE NEW CENTURY (John Eekelaar Ed. 2016) 55.

1006 SPOUSAL SUPPORT CH. 16

3.   Under *Mascaro*, how much support should have been awarded Mrs. Otis? Mrs. Chamberlain? Assume that Mrs. Otis earns $15,000 per year and that she and Chamberlain both pay 25% of their gross salaries in taxes; assume that Mr. Otis and Mr. Chamberlain pay 35%. Do the awards generated by the Pennsylvania formula seem more or less fair than those devised by the *Otis* and *Chamberlain* trial courts? On remand, the trial court awarded Mrs. Chamberlain $1,975 per month. The award reflected a reduction in her housing allowance to $1,575 based on actual housing costs of $2,227.03 per month. The appellate court affirmed the award. *See* Chamberlain v. Chamberlain, 2002 WL 857783 (Minn. App. 2002) (unpublished).

4.   Why should the alimony value be set at 30% of the difference in spousal net incomes in cases where there are children and 40% where there are not? Do the numbers suggest any theory of alimony? *Cf.* TEX. FAM. CODE § 8.055 (restricting alimony award (but not child support) to the lesser of $5000 per month or 20% of payor's average monthly gross income); LA. CIV. CODE art. 112(C) (alimony award restricted to one-third of the obligor's net income).

5.   If alimony is limited to 40% of the difference in spousal net incomes, the alimony obligor will typically have a higher living standard than will the obligee. This living standard gap is not unique to the Pennsylvania guideline: virtually every divorce researcher to date has reported that, on average, the post-divorce living standard of former wives (and children in their custody) falls, while that of former husbands (and children in their custody) rises. Most researchers report a living standard decline for divorced wives of around 30%. *See* Alicia Brokars Kelly, *Rehabilitating Partnership Marriage as a Theory of Wealth Distribution at Divorce: In Recognition of a Shared Life*, 19 WIS. WOMEN'S L.J. 141, 160 (2004). Despite the fact that virtually all state "factor lists" include the marital standard of living, alimony case law (to the extent it considers the issue at all) rejects the claim that alimony should enable the supported spouse to enjoy a standard of living equivalent to that of the payor spouse:

> Appellee does not contend that the * * * alimony awarded is inadequate to meet her living expenses; instead, she argues that it is inequitable and unreasonable not to allow her to share in the higher standard of living that appellant enjoys as his income increases. R.C. § 3105.18(B) lists standard of living as one of eleven factors a trial court is to consider in determining the amount of alimony. Some of the factors enumerated in R.C. 3105.18(B) are more pertinent than others in the process of reaching an equitable property division, while some are more relevant in ascertaining the need for an amount of sustenance alimony. However, all the statutory factors must be considered. The goal is to reach an equitable result. The method by which the goal is achieved cannot be reduced to a mathematical formula. Therefore, we hold that in making a[n] * * * alimony determination, the court must consider all the factors listed in R.C. § 3105.18(B) and not base its determination upon any one of those factors taken in isolation. * * * [T]he court of appeals erred in its

suggestion that an alimony award must establish an equal standard of living for the parties.

Kaechele v. Kaechele, 518 N.E.2d 1197, 1200 (Ohio 1988). *See also In re Marriage of Reynard*, 801 N.E.2d 591 (Ill. App. 2003) (rejecting wife's argument that trial court should have used alimony award to equalize spouses' income); Stone v. Stone, 488 S.E.2d 15 (W.Va. 1997) (same).

Remember, for example, that Mrs. Otis was awarded $2000 per month when the difference in the parties' annual incomes exceeded $100,000, and that Mrs. Chamberlain (on remand) was awarded $1975 per month when the obligor earned $137,000 more per year that she did.

If equalizing post-divorce spousal living standards is *not* a goal of alimony decision making, are we any closer to discerning the purpose of alimony?

6.   *Calculating the Amount to be Paid:* In Pennsylvania, the calculation of the presumptive amount of spousal support is unaffected by the duration of the marriage. Other guideline models have proposed that marital duration should be an important factor in the calculation. For example, in Maricopa County, if divorcing parties have no minor children, the court first subtracts the gross income of the lower earner from the other spouse's gross income. Then this amount is multiplied by (.015 x years of marriage) to arrive at the presumptive support amount. *See* Ira Mark Ellman, *The Maturing Law of Divorce Finances: Toward Rules and Guidelines,* 33 FAM. L.Q. 801, 812 (1999); Cullum v. Cullum, 160 P.3d 231, 235 (Ariz. 2007). So, in a 10-year marriage the support would be 15% of the difference in income, and after a 20-year marriage the support would be 30% of the difference. If spousal support formulas are to be accepted, does it make sense to incorporate marital duration as an element of the calculation? Canada has promulgated advisory guidelines for spousal support; the formula for couples with no minor children is similar to the Maricopa County formula. *See* Carol Rogerson & Rollie Thompson, *The Canadian Experiment with Spousal Support Guidelines,* 45 FAM. L.Q. 241 (2011).

7.   *Duration of the Award*: Some guidelines incorporate a way to arrive at a presumptive duration. In New Mexico, for marriages that lasted 10–20 years the suggested duration is .3 to .5 the length of the marriage. *See* Oldham, *supra* note 2, 42 FAM. L. Q. at 445–446.

8.   *Deciding When to Award Spousal Support*: Before guidelines can be utilized a standard must be established for how to determine if spousal support should be awarded. Should the court be given discretion to make this initial determination? If not, how could it be clarified when support should be awarded?

4. THE ALIMONY DEBATE: ARE CURRENT STANDARDS FAIR?

RICHARD POSNER, ECONOMIC ANALYSIS OF LAW
136–37 (3d ed. 1986).

Alimony is analytically quite complex. It appears to serve three distinct economic functions:

1.   It is a form of damages for breach of the marital contract. * * *

2.   Alimony is a method of repaying the wife (in the traditional marriage) her share of the marital partnership's assets. * * *

3.   The last and perhaps most important economic function of alimony is to provide the wife with a form of severance pay or unemployment benefits. In the traditional family, where the wife specializes in household production, any skills that she may have had in market production depreciate and eventually her prime employment possibilities—should the present marriage dissolve—narrow down to the prospect of remarrying and forming a new household where she can ply her trade. Although she could always find some kind of work in the market, the skilled household producer forced to work as a waitress or file clerk is like the lawyer who, unable to find a legal job, becomes a process server.

Because the search for a suitable spouse is often protracted, and because age may depreciate a person's ability (especially if a woman) to form a new marriage that will yield her as much real income as the previous marriage did, it makes sense to provide as a standard term in the marriage contract a form of severance pay or unemployment compensation that will maintain the divorced wife at her previous standard of living during the search for a new husband. Consider an analogy to law practice. By agreeing to work for a law firm that specialized exclusively in negotiating oil-tanker mortgages, a lawyer might make it very difficult for himself, in the event he was ever laid off, to find an equally remunerative position (why?). But that is all the more reason why he might demand, as a condition of working for such a firm, that it agree that should it ever lay him off it will continue his salary until he finds equally remunerative work, even if the search is protracted.

An alternative in both the housewife's and the lawyer's case would be a higher wage to compensate for the risk of prolonged unemployment in the event of layoff. But in the case of marriage, the husband may be incapable of making the necessary transfer payments to the wife, especially during the early years of the marriage, when the household may not have substantial liquid assets. Also, to calculate in advance the appropriate compensation for a risk as difficult to quantify as that of divorce would be costly, especially since the relevant probability is really a schedule of probabilities of divorce in each year of the marriage. This of course is a reason for awarding alimony on a period basis even if the rationale is damages.

Just as severance pay is awarded without regard to whether the employer was at fault in laying off the worker—indeed, often without regard to whether the employee quit or was fired—so alimony, viewed as a form of severance pay, is not dependent on notions of fault. But just as an employee might forfeit his entitlement to severance pay by having quit in breach of his employment contract, so alimony should be denied or reduced (and sometimes it is) if the wife was seriously at fault in procuring dissolution of a marriage. Better, any damages she caused the family by walking out on the marriage could be subtracted from her alimony payments if her share of the marital assets was insufficient to cover them.

NOTES AND QUESTIONS

1.   Would the abolition of alimony affect marital roles or the marriage rate? At least one economist has argued that the answer is yes:

> * * * I find that a legal prohibition on alimony reduces the gains from marriage. In states which prohibit alimony, I find both a lower proportion of young women marrying and reduced marital fertility among those who do, even when the variables found to be important in the economic literature on marriage and fertility are held constant. * * * The empirical results in this paper suggest that the alimony system, as administered, acts to compensate wives for their opportunity costs incurred by entering and investing in marriage. This interpretation of the economic function of alimony is directly opposed to the common allegation that alimony is an 'anachronistic' manifestation of the wife's dependency upon her husband. Nevertheless, increasing participation of married women in the labor force and declining marital fertility suggest that the importance of alimony will diminish over time with decreasing levels of household specialization.

Elizabeth Landes, *The Economics of Alimony*, 7 J. LEG. STUD. 35 (1978). Are prospective wives more likely to be deterred from marrying by legal rules that limit alimony claims than are prospective husbands deterred from marrying by legal rules that authorize generous, long-term awards?

2.   While some commentators oppose alimony primarily because of its potential to impose "lifetime peonage" on divorced husbands, it is also possible to make a case against alimony based on its impact on women:

> In the long run, * * * I do not believe that we should encourage future couples entering marriage to make choices that will be economically disabling for women, thereby perpetuating their traditional financial dependence upon men and contributing to their inequality with men at divorce. I do not mean to suggest that these choices are unjustified.

For most couples, they are based on the presence of children in the family. The infant's claim to love and nurturance is a compelling one both on moral and developmental grounds. Throughout history, the choice of the mother as the primary nurturing parent has been the most common response to the infant's claim. * * * But other choices are possible. * * * Women, like men, should be able to lead productive, independent lives outside the family. Female dependency should no longer be the necessary result of motherhood.

I do not propose that the state attempt to implement this view of family life by enacting laws requiring mothers to work or mandating that fathers spend time at home with their children. But * * * since Anglo-American family law has traditionally reflected the social division of function by sex within marriage, it will be necessary to withdraw existing legal supports for that arrangement as a cultural norm. * * *

Herma Hill Kay, *Equality and Difference: A Perspective on No-Fault Divorce and Its Aftermath*, 56 U. Cin. L. Rev. 1, 80, 84–85 (1989). What factual assumptions underlie Professor Kay's view? Judge Posner's? Which assumptions are sound?

Ira M. Ellman, The Theory of Alimony
77 Cal. L. Rev. 1, 17–18, 41–42, 79–80 (1989).

A theory of alimony must explain why spouses should be liable for each other's needs after their marriage has ended. Why should the needy person's former spouse provide support rather than his parents, his children, or society as a whole?

* * *

[Although] the ordinary marriage appears to have many attributes of contract[,] * * * the essential problem with a contract analysis should be clear: The wife expects that the marriage itself will compensate her economic sacrifice, by providing not only personal satisfaction but also a share in her husband's financial success. * * * A formal contract claim would therefore require, as its basis, an allegation that the marriage's termination is due to the husband's breach. * * * Making such a showing would be difficult. * * * Indeed, one might well argue that couples divorce precisely because they discover, as specific issues arise after some years of marriage, that in fact there never was a clear contract, that they do not have the same understanding of their mutual commitment.

* * *

If contract does not work, then what principles can we look to in fashioning alimony rules? The question is fundamental, for by shifting away from contract we necessarily shift away from a conception of alimony as a claim based on promise or commitment, to one grounded in some other policy. What should that policy be? Examination of analogous commercial arrangements may be instructive.

* * *

Marriage is usually intended to be a long-term arrangement. The typical commercial arrangement is not; although it may in fact continue over many years, in most cases there is no agreement legally binding the parties over a long term. In some cases, however, parties make a long-term commitment. One reason they do is relevant here: A contracting party might seek a long-term commitment because the relationship requires that party to make an investment that he cannot otherwise justify. * * * For example, the owner of a building might be willing to modify it for a prospective tenant only if that tenant signs a long-term lease; a supplier to IBM might be willing to invest the capital necessary to produce a part only if it is assured that IBM will not change suppliers the next year.

* * *

The traditional marriage bears many similarities to this arrangement. It is a relationship in which the wife makes many initial investments of value only to her husband, investments a self-interested bargainer would make only in return for a long-term commitment. Her investments may be obvious, such as supporting him through a degree or training program, or they may be more subtle, such as providing him with the emotional support or domestic services that allow him to enhance his earning capacity. Her bearing and raising of children, while of value to him, also provides value to her, but—as with the commercial investors—give her no prospects for a return in the open market commensurate with her investment. The traditional marriage thus involves considerable up-front investment by the wife which, like the idiosyncratic improvements in the building or the purchase of equipment needed for the production of a unique part, has little general market value even though it has value to the one person for whom it was made. Like the owner or part supplier, she risks great loss if her husband stops buying.

* * *

* * * [D]ivorce typically burdens the wife more than her husband for two reasons: She has more difficulty finding a new spouse, and she suffers disproportionate financial loss because of her domestic role. * * * Marriage thus poses unavoidable risks for the wife, risks that are different and greater than those assumed by her husband. * * *

* * *

The function of alimony [should be] * * * to reallocate the postdivorce financial consequences of marriage in order to prevent distorting incentives. * * * This conception of alimony differs fundamentally from prevailing law. It casts alimony as an entitlement earned through marital investment, and as a tool to eliminate distorting financial incentives, and not as a way of relieving need. * * * [It] allows recovery for lost earning capacity when that loss arises from marital investment. * * * [O]nly financially rational sharing behavior can qualify as such marital investment. Lost earning capacity is thus not compensable if it arises from financially irrational behavior, with * * * one major exception [for] losses resulting from the care of children.

* * *

When one spouse cedes a market opportunity in favor of the other spouse's we must provide a remedy. Otherwise, a marital decision made on the assumption that the spouses are a single economic unit will burden the sharing spouse disproportionately when divorce renders them financially separate. In contrast, when one spouse forgoes a market opportunity to accommodate a lifestyle preference, both spouses know that lower income will result. On divorce, the spouse who made the financial sacrifice suffers no additional financial burden as a result, beyond that already incurred during the marriage. Even if the sacrifice was made entirely to accommodate the other spouse's lifestyle desires, the real complaint on divorce is not the economic sacrifice itself, which the spouse would have borne even if the marriage had remained intact. The real complaint is that the marriage did not remain intact despite the economic sacrifice. That complaint, though real, is simply beyond the scope of the alimony remedy, which can never compensate marital partners for the personal loss of marital dissolution.

* * * If we do not impose a limit, we would have to consider every sacrifice one makes for one's mate, and this would extend to nonfinancial losses as well. Suppose an attorney gives up his prospects for a faculty position to accommodate his wife; would she have to compensate him his lost chance at the professor's life if that was what he really wanted, despite the lower income? Allowing compensation for financial losses incurred for nonfinancial reasons is no less troublesome. If she had a change of heart and sought divorce, would the Duchess of Windsor then owe the Duke for his throne?

Marriage necessarily involves much give and take that the law cannot address or equalize upon divorce. This theory assumes that we can sensibly isolate decisions that a couple rationally expects will enhance their aggregate income, and ensure that in making such a decision neither takes a risk of disproportionate loss if divorce then occurs. * * *

The difficulties involved in proving lost earning capacity are significant but not fatal. Even crude approximations of theoretically defensible criteria are probably better than intuitive estimates of what is 'fair' under a system lacking established principles of 'fairness' in the first place. Moreover, the establishment of rules clearly specifying the facts that are relevant in judging alimony claims, and the precise impact of these facts on the amount of the claim may itself motivate studies that increase the amount of relevant data. * * *

J. THOMAS OLDHAM, CHANGES IN THE ECONOMIC CONSEQUENCES OF DIVORCES, 1958–2008

42 FAM. L.Q. 419, 425–27 (Fall 2008).

When a couple has one or more children, the career of at least one parent frequently is affected. The parent who decides to be the primary caregiver in many instances either quits work for a period or takes part-time work in order to be able to fulfill child-care responsibilities. Because of such career choices, the primary caretaker's career is impacted. That parent loses seniority, and skills erode. Only 34% of married women with children younger than age six work full time.

The impact on the primary caretaker's career prospects can be significant. One investigator found that female nonmothers earned 90% of what men earned at age 30; in contrast, mothers earned on average 70% of the male wage. Twenty years ago, another investigator found that a primary caretaker's lifetime earnings were reduced, on average, by $22,000, $43,000, and $64,000 for raising one, two, or three children, respectively. Another study found an average wage penalty of approximately 7% per child for American women.

Some recent trends may be reducing the career impact of motherhood. Recent studies show that more women are working during most of their pregnancy and are returning to work quickly. For example, in the early 1960s, 44% of mothers worked at all while pregnant; forty years later, this percentage had increased to 67%. Forty percent of pregnant mothers worked full time in the 1960s; this percentage increased to 57% in the early 2000s. Of those pregnant mothers who worked during pregnancy in the early 1960s, 13% stopped working during the first trimester, while 35% kept working until within one month or less of the child's birth. Forty years later, 4% of pregnant working mothers quit work during the first trimester, and 80% worked until one month or less of giving birth. As family income increases, however, mothers with children younger than age 18 are less likely to work full time.

The percentage of women receiving paid leave (maternity, sick leave, or vacation time) increased from 37% in the early 1980s to 49% twenty years later. Mothers today are returning to work sooner after giving birth. In the early 1960s, 14% of all mothers were working within six months of giving birth; by 2000 to 2002, 55% of all mothers were working within six months of giving birth, and 64% were working within twelve months. One study has found that when mothers return quickly to the work force after giving birth, the wage penalty of motherhood is reduced.

Another recent study found that current effects of divorce on women are less substantial than they were in the past; they argue that this is the result of the increased labor force participation of married women. Education levels of mothers have significantly increased. In 2000, 25% of all mothers had completed sixteen or more years of school, compared to 9% in 1970.

Two investigators have attempted to compare the lifetime earnings penalty incurred by mothers in various Western countries. They found that the lifetime earning penalty for mothers in the U.S. was significantly lower than that incurred by mothers in Germany or the Netherlands. Nevertheless, they found that in the United States, mothers earn 11% to 19% less during their lifetimes than nonmothers.

JANE RUTHERFORD, DUTY IN DIVORCE: SHARED INCOME AS A PATH TO EQUALITY
58 FORDHAM L. REV. 539, 563–64, 573, 578–83, 592 (1990).

* * * Alimony seems to perpetuate the vicious circle of women assuming more household duties because they earn less and then earning less because they have more household duties. Hence, alimony can be viewed as paternalistic for three reasons. First, it encourages women to be dependent instead of self-sufficient. Second, it leaves women under the control of men because women cannot remarry without losing their alimony. Third, it condones the disparity in earning power between men and women because some of that difference will be made up by alimony. * * *

* * *

A need-based approach [to alimony] has at least three problems. One of the reasons spouses and partners are willing to devote their efforts to such relationships is the belief that they will share in future profits. Although they take the risk that such profits will not materialize, they do not expect to limit their share of actual profits to need. To do so would embrace a more Marxist view: "[f]rom each according to his ability, to each according to his needs!"

Second, limiting one spouse to need while allowing the other one to prosper is inherently unfair; focusing on need leaves spouses in an unequal position because one spouse is limited to the bare essentials while the other enjoys an improved lifestyle.

Finally, there is a stigma associated with need-based alimony. Because only the functionally unemployable are entitled to maintenance on a pure need-based standard, accepting support can lower the spouse's self-esteem.

A need-based standard denigrates the needy spouse either in terms of party expectations or lowered self-esteem. We should be striving instead for a system based on sharing and caring. * * *

In order to avoid the problems of need * * *, some reformers have focused on a contribution standard. * * * The contribution theory has two major problems, however. First, it fails to account for expectations. Second, it overcompensates earners and undercompensates homemakers because economic contributions are easier to measure. * * *

* * * [I]t seems more intellectually honest and fairer simply to admit that spouses expect to share income when they are married. Thus we should adopt some form of income sharing.

Income sharing refers to a system in which the incomes of the former couple would be added and divided by the number of people to be supported. Each member of the family would receive an equal share. Income sharing differs from traditional permanent alimony in at least two respects. First, income sharing does not take the form of a fixed award of a specific dollar amount. Indeed, income sharing is not fixed at any given time. Instead, it recognizes the inevitable changes inherent in the passage of time. Rather than fixing a specific award that can only adapt to changed circumstances by court order, income sharing creates a formula that automatically adjusts to changed circumstances. Such income sharing should continue at least until remarriage. * * *

* * * [T]he theoretical basis for income sharing is quite different from that of alimony. Income sharing is not based on need, pre-divorce standard of living, prior contributions, or fault. Instead, it represents a conscious effort to achieve equality between spouses who have divided their labors during marriage. If spouses have not divided the labor, either because they were not married long enough, or because they did not have children, then income sharing should not apply.

* * *

Income sharing has four distinct advantages. First, it fosters the kind of sharing and caring that should typify families. Second, income sharing offers a way out of the fault conundrum. Third, income sharing empowers the financially disadvantaged who may be economically trapped in destructive relationships. Fourth, it provides a path to equality that automatically adjusts to reflect the actual market situation of the parties over time. * * *

Shared income after divorce fosters caring in two ways. First, it reinforces sharing as the model for family life. Law is not only a mechanism to settle disputes. It also sets normative standards for how we ought to behave. If the family is viewed as a shared enterprise for the common good, our rules about income distribution within the family should reflect sharing principles.

* * *

Income sharing may actually foster a more equal division of labor at home. Currently, the UMDA encourages couples to maximize individual profits. This creates an incentive for the party with greater earning ability to shift homemaking tasks to the party who earns less in order to maximize income.

If men and women earned equal amounts in the job market, there would be a greater incentive to share homemaking burdens to avoid jeopardizing either job. Therefore, income sharing provides divorced men with an incentive to help eradicate gender discrimination in the job market. Similarly, there will be a greater incentive to share the burdens of childcare, as the economic burden will be reduced if each contributes enough childcare to enable the former spouse to earn an equal amount of money. Most of the earning disparity between married men and married women can be accounted for by the difference in their family burdens.

* * * Finally, income sharing can address * * * changing needs without report to repeated court battles over need and changed circumstances. Changed circumstances will be accounted for simply by continuing to share the couple's available income. * * *

* * *

Some might argue that saddling an earner with a non-earning spouse for life is a strict penalty for an improvident marriage. Indeed, the case for income sharing is weakest in childless marriages of young people, who have the time and the opportunity to improve their circumstances, and in cases of those married a short time. Income sharing is a better option in marriages that have lasted for many years because the spouses have relied on each other and therefore restricted their options. This problem can be solved by creating a grace period of three to five years before a childless divorced couple is required to share income.

* * * Income sharing is * * * a legal duty, similar to the fiduciary duties of partnership, which society should impose on spouses at divorce. It is a duty not because spouses have agreed to assume it, but because of the mutuality inherent in the division of labor within a marriage. It is a duty required to encourage sharing and equality.

N<small>OTES AND</small> Q<small>UESTIONS</small>

1.   While alimony based entirely on lost earning capacity is a novel idea, in some states career damage during marriage may be taken into account in determining whether to award alimony. *See* Gerth v. Gerth, 465 N.W.2d 507, 509 (Wis. 1990); M<small>INN.</small> S<small>TAT.</small> § 518.552(2)(e).

2.   Professors Ellman and Rutherford agree that alimony should not be based on need or some notion of marital contract. Each emphasizes marriage partners' expectations of sharing and the desirability, from a public policy perspective, of encouraging sharing behavior in marriage. But their proposals for replacing current alimony law are quite different. Why? Is one analysis more persuasive than the other? What are the pros and cons of each approach to the alimony problem?

In evaluating Ellman's and Rutherford's theories of alimony, consider these questions:

a.   Application of Professor Ellman's theory would produce an award representing the capitalized value of lost earning capacity resulting from a financially rational marital investment. Would Mrs. Morgan, Mrs. Huntington, Mrs. Otis, and Mrs. Chamberlain be eligible for alimony if it were so defined? Should they be?

b.   If, as Professor Ellman suggests, financially irrational decisions should not be compensable, then why should losses arising from child care responsibilities? *See* Robert Kirkman Collins, *The Theory of Marital Residuals: Applying an Income Adjustment Calculus to the Enigma of Alimony*, 24 HARV. WOMEN'S L.J. 23, 64 (2001) (arguing that there is "no cogent reason to privilege sacrifices of a career or other opportunities to be the caregiver for a child or a needy relative over other equally noble sacrifices—the expenditure of premarital or separate capital to fund the family through a crisis, or a child's education. Every such decision is grounded in reliance on the continuance of the marriage to justify the uncommon sacrifice; it is unclear why some such contributions or losses should be singled out for compensation while others are ignored.")

c.   Assuming the desirability of Professor Rutherford's income sharing approach, why should sharing continue until income equalization occurs or the recipient remarries? Professor Singer has proposed that income equalization should continue for one-half the duration of the marriage. *See* Jana Singer, *Divorce Reform and Gender Justice*, 67 N.C.L. REV. 1103 (1989); Jana Singer, *Alimony and Efficiency: The Gendered Costs and Benefits of the Economic Justification for Alimony*, 82 GEO. L. J. 2423 (1994). What are the pros and cons of Rutherford's and Singer's approaches? What assumptions underlie each?

d.   Should an income-sharing approach require equality? Professor Sugarman has proposed a system in which each spouse's interest in the other's earning capacity would be based on marital duration. For example, "one might obtain a 1.5% or 2% interest in the other for every year together, and presumably this interest would survive the remarriage of either party. Such a regime might be subject to minimum vesting rules restricting when the right accrues (such as after three or five years of marriage) and it might possibly be subject to a ceiling (such as 40% or twenty years)." Stephen D. Sugarman, *Dividing Financial Interests at Divorce*, *in* DIVORCE REFORM AT THE CROSSROADS 159–60 (1990). What are the pros and cons of Rutherford's and Sugarman's approaches? What assumptions underlie each?

　　e.　If equal income sharing is desirable, what is the appropriate measure of equality? If Bill, with an income of $2,000 per month, and Ann, with an income of $1,000 per month, divorce and Ann obtains custody of the couple's two minor children, a transfer of $500 per month would be necessary to achieve equal household *incomes*. To achieve equal *living standards*, it would take $1,070. Should income-sharing aim at equal incomes or living standards? (Living standard calculations in this example are based on the "household equivalence scale" contained in the widely-utilized U.S. Bureau of Labor Standards household budgets. To read up on household equivalence scales, see Chapter 17).

　　f.　What post-divorce events should affect an income-sharing award? Should the spouses have an obligation to maximize income? What if the ex-spouse marries someone with substantial needs or has a needy parent? Decides to take a less stressful (and lower-paying) job or stay home to raise children?

Problem 16-5: Reinventing Alimony

The state legislature is considering replacing its current alimony law (identical to the Pennsylvania statute reprinted at p. 971) with standards recently approved by the American Law Institute. *See* AM. LAW INSTITUTE, PRINCIPLES OF THE LAW OF FAMILY DISSOLUTION: ANALYSIS AND RECOMMENDATIONS (2002) (hereinafter "Principles"). Under the Principles, "[a]limony becomes a remedy for unfair loss allocation, rather than for relief of need. * * * The change from need to loss transforms alimony from a plea for help to a claim for an entitlement, allowing—indeed, requiring—more certain rules of adjudication." Ira M. Ellman, *Inventing Family Law*, 32 U.C. DAVIS L. REV. 855, 879–80 (1999).

The Principles specify that spouses in a "long" [to be defined by each state] marriage would annually accrue a percentage-based interest in the other's earning capacity. Post-divorce, the high-earning spouse would pay alimony to the lower-earning spouse in an amount equal to the accrued percentage multiplied by the difference in spousal earnings. *See* Principles § 5.04.

Under the Principles, an alimony claim may also arise from the assumption of child-care responsibilities. *See* Principles § 5.05. To establish such a claim, a spouse must show that he or she assumed the majority of the family's child-care responsibilities for more than a minimum period and has an earning capacity at divorce that is substantially less than that of the other spouse. The amount of the award is based on the "child care durational factor," determined by multiplying the claimant spouse's years of primary child care by a state-established percentage. The higher-earning spouse must pay as alimony that percentage of the earnings difference. So, if the claimant cared for a child for ten years and the relevant state percentage was .015, the claimant would be awarded 15% of the difference between his or her post-divorce earnings and those of the higher-earning spouse.

An award under both §§ 5.04 and 5.05 may be made in the same case. However, the total award may not exceed the state's maximum percentage for an award under § 5.04 alone (say, 40% or 50%). *See* Principles § 5.05. Awards under both §§ 5.04 and 5.05 are modifiable based on a post-divorce change in circumstances. *See* Principles § 5.08.

Awards under both §§ 5.04 and 5.05 are presumed to be for an indefinite period if the marriage meets specified minimum requirements. Under § 5.04, the requirements are marital duration and age; under § 5.05, the requirements are age and child-care duration. Each enacting state is to set the relevant minima. *See* Principles § 5.07. In a case where the requirements for an indefinite award have not been met, payments under § 5.04 extend for a period determined by multiplying the length of marriage by a state-determined percentage; payments under § 5.05 extend for a period determined by multiplying the child-care period by a state-determined percentage.

If an award is unavailable under both §§ 5.04 and 5.05, the Principles suggest that an award should not be made unless: (1) the claimant spouse is unable to recover after divorce the standard of living he or she enjoyed at the time of marriage; and (2) the living-standard loss is due to responsibilities assumed by the claimant during marriage. *See* Principles § 5.13.

Here is an example of how the ALI Principles work. It assumes a child-care durational factor of .015 (§ 5.05), a durational factor of .01 (§ 5.04), and a maximum equal to .4.

> Husband and wife have been married for 18 years, during 15 of which the wife has been the primary caretaker of the couple's children, who are 15 and 11 at the time of divorce. Husband is a plumber earning $5000 monthly; Wife attended a junior college, has worked occasionally as a teacher's aide in a nursery school, and at the time of divorce can find regular work paying $750 monthly.
>
> Under the particular implementation of the ALI Principles that the draft assumes in setting out this example, the applicable guideline would recognize both an award based on marital duration and one based on the child care period. [Considered

separately, the two sections entitle Wife to concurrent awards for 7.5 years of (.225) ($4,250), or $956.25, and for 9 years of (.18) ($4,250), or $765. But the maximum is slightly exceeded in this case, since .225 plus .18 equals .405. Therefore the combined award for the first 7.5 years is not $1,721.25 but rather] * * * $1700 monthly for seven and a half years, with the award based upon the marital duration alone continuing for an additional year and a half at a monthly amount of $765.

Ellman, *supra,* at 881 n. 55 (describing Principles § 5.05, illus. 5–6).

The ALI approach has been criticized on several counts. Professor Penelope Eileen Bryan contends that the Principles' "focus on 'loss' * * * fosters a narrow vision of entitlement":

> The * * * Principles acknowledge only the standard of living an individual loses after a long-term marriage or the individuals's reduced earning capacity due to caretaking responsibilities. The household labor that facilitated the husband's ideal worker status becomes conceptually peripheral, weakening the justification for her entitlement to a share of his post-divorce income. A more comprehensive justification would recognize that spouses (frequently wives) who perform the bulk of marital labor suffer losses *and* make contributions that entitle them to a share of their husbands' post-divorce income. The * * * Principles explicitly reject this contribution justification.

Penelope Eileen Bryan, *Vacant Promises? The ALI Principles of the Law of Family Dissolution and the Post-Divorce Financial Circumstances of Women,* 8 DUKE J. GENDER L. & POL'Y 167, 169–70 (2001). Professor Allen M. Parkman more broadly argues that "[t]he *Principles* do not provide a logical reason why ex-spouses' incomes should be shared just because they were married, even when there is no discernable sacrifice involved":

> * * * Among workers with similar attributes, those willing to work harder and accept jobs with fewer attractive attributes tend to have higher earnings. Consequently, it can be unfair to force a higher paid ex-spouse to subsidize a lower paid exspouse. Secondly, injustices will occur because sacrifices are not considered. Long-duration marriages would result in compensatory payments regardless of whether there were sacrifices during the marriage. A spouse may have left the labor force not so much to emphasize domestic work as to obtain a more leisurely life. This person will receive the same transfers as a spouse who made significant career sacrifices to provide valuable services in the home. * * * Moreover, if a spouse limits a career to provide important services in the home and that loss is recognized at dissolution as the basis for compensatory payments, it will not

disappear even if the person remarries (when the *Principles* would normally terminate compensation.)

Injustices will also occur because the *Principles* assume that the lower-income earning spouse only deserves compensation if that person's income is substantially below that of the other spouse. If the primary caretaker does not have an income that is substantially less than the other spouse, she will receive no compensation for any reduction in her future income due to her working in the home.

Allen M. Parkman, *The ALI Principles and Marital Quality*, 8 DUKE J. GENDER L. & POL'Y 157, 169–70 (2001).

The legislature in your state is certain that it would like to reduce alimony-related litigation and improve the consistency of alimony awards. It is also sure that it wants to achieve results that are fair. But, legislators have freely admitted to you, many are not quite sure what fairness means in this context. You have been asked to advise the legislature on several issues:

1.   What results would the ALI principles produce in the *Morgan, Huntington, Otis* and *Chamberlain* cases? Assume the same percentages as in the example given above.

2.   What policy goals underlie the ALI Principles? Are there other goals the state should aim to achieve that the Principles do not address? If so, what are they?

3.   Would women's groups (NOW, etc.) support or oppose passage of the ALI Principles? What about MUDD ("Men United against Divorce Discrimination")? Advocates of "family values"? The Matrimonial Lawyers Association?

4.   Would adoption of the ALI Principles likely produce an increase or decrease in the rate, duration, and value of alimony awards?

5.   On balance, should the state adopt the ALI Principles? If not, what alimony rules should the state employ?

CHAPTER 17

CHILD SUPPORT

▪ ▪ ▪

1. AN HISTORICAL PERSPECTIVE

WILLIAM BLACKSTONE, COMMENTARIES ON THE LAWS OF ENGLAND, BOOK I
(1765).

The duty of parents to provide for the *maintenance* of their children is a principle of natural law; an obligation, says Puffendorf, laid on them not only by nature herself, but by their own proper act, in bringing them into the world: for they would be in highest manner injurious to their issue, if they only gave the children life, that they might afterwards see them perish. By begetting them therefore they have entered into a voluntary obligation, to endeavour, as far as in them lies, that the life which they have bestowed shall be supported and preserved. And thus the children will have a perfect *right* of receiving maintenance from their parents. * * *

The municipal laws of well-regulated states have taken care to enforce this duty: though providence has done it more effectually than any laws, by implanting in the breast of every parent that * * * insuperable degree of affection, which not even the deformity of person or mind, not even the wickedness, ingratitude, and rebellion of children, can totally suppress or extinguish. * * *

No person is bound to provide a maintenance for his issue, unless where the children are impotent and unable to work, either through infancy, disease, or accident; and then is only obliged to find them with necessaries, the penalty on refusal being no more than 20 s. a month. For the policy of our laws, which are ever watchful to promote industry, did not mean to compel a father to maintain his idle and lazy children in ease and indolence: but thought it unjust to oblige the parent, against his will, to provide them with superfluities, and other indulgences of fortune; imagining they might trust to the impulse of nature, if the children were deserving of such favours.

Blackstone describes the common law approach to child support, which treated parental duty as a *moral,* but not a *legal,* obligation. Under the common law, neither the child nor a parent suing on his behalf could obtain an enforceable support order.

The common law's failure to accord the child an enforceable support right derived, in part, from the legal unity of the family. As you saw in Chapter 4, during Blackstone's day virtually all income and property rights were vested in the male household head: wives had no more entitlement to support than their children; both wives and children had extremely limited inheritance rights; neither wife nor child could individually maintain a lawsuit, even against an individual outside the family.

Parents in Blackstone's day did have a *public* obligation to support their children, imposed under the Elizabethan Poor Laws (43 Eliz. 1, ch. 2, § vi (1601)) and their colonial counterparts. The Poor Laws instituted both a comprehensive public welfare program and a legal duty to reimburse the state for benefits. This reimbursement obligation was not restricted to parents; grandparents were liable for the support of their grandchildren, as were husbands for support of their wives, and adult children for support of their parents. The manner and rate of payment were determined by county Justices of the Peace. Default resulted, as Blackstone notes, in a standard penalty of twenty shillings per month. *Id.* at ch. 2, § vi. *See* JOYCE O. APPLEBY, ECONOMIC THOUGHT AND IDEOLOGY IN SEVENTEENTH-CENTURY ENGLAND 129–57 (1978); Jacobus ten Broek, *California's Dual System of Family Law: Its Origins, Development, and Present Status, Part I,* 16 STAN. L. REV. 258–87 (1964).

The Industrial Revolution brought with it a wave of laws that pierced the legal unity of the family. Statutory divorce laws [Chapter 12], the Married Women's Property Acts [Chapter 4], and the alimony claim [Chapter 16] all came into being during this period; so did the modern child support obligation. A hundred years after Blackstone wrote, American family law recognized a paternal support obligation that was enforceable on behalf of the child rather than the public and which applied whether or not the child was in danger of becoming a public charge.

The new child support obligation reflected some, but not all, of the Poor Law concepts that preceded it. Like the public relief applicant, the child who sought support was required to show dependence and worthiness; children who were emancipated from parental control or who refused to obey reasonable parental commands were no more entitled to parental support than were the able-bodied to public funds. In contrast to the Poor Law approach, however, the relief obtainable under the new child support laws was not limited to subsistence. Instead, just as they did in the alimony context, courts held that the child was entitled to support that reflected, insofar as the father's current means permitted, the family's income and prior standard of living. The value of the support obligation was thus left to the discretion of the presiding judge; even when initially fixed, the award was subject to modification based on changes in the child's or father's circumstances. *See generally* HOMER H. CLARK, JR., THE LAW OF DOMESTIC RELATIONS IN THE UNITED STATES 496–507 (1st ed. 1968).

As *McGuire* [see Chapter 2] shows, courts are reluctant to intervene in disputes involving intact families. So, courts will not normally intervene to resolve financial disputes in intact families. Perhaps this is based on a fairly reasonable assumption that, in disputes relating to expenditures regarding children in the household, parents will resolve such disputes in good faith. Separated parents are treated differently. There is ample empirical evidence confirming that separated parents will not voluntarily provide adequately for children. So, judicial involvement is needed. This principal is reflected in Marriage of Wilson and Bodine, 143 Cal. Rptr. 3d 803 (App. 2012) . In this case, the parties had two children before marriage and the man was ordered to pay child support. The parties then married. The appellate court held that upon marriage the support order was nullified as to support due during marriage.

One exception to the principle discussed in the preceding paragraph involves situations where a child under 18 is incarcerated. In a number of states, parents are charged "child support" for the period their child is incarcerated, regardless of whether the parents have separated or are living together. *See* Kinzi Abou-Sabe, Brenda Breslauer and Ronald Farrow, *Double Punishment: When Your Kid Goes to Jail and You Get a Bill*, NBC News, March 6, 2017.

2. WHO OWES SUPPORT?

A. THE BASIS OF THE SUPPORT OBLIGATION

STRAUB V. B.M.T

Supreme Court of Indiana, 1994.
645 N.E.2d 597.

SHEPARD, CHIEF JUSTICE.

Francine Todd wanted to have a child, but she did not want to be married. She and Edward Straub signed an agreement providing that Edward Straub would not be responsible for supporting any child the two might procreate. B.M.T. was born in the wake of this agreement. When Straub offered this agreement as a defense to a claim for child support, the trial court held it void. When the validity of that agreement was before the Indiana Court of Appeals, it provoked a debate about the public policy surrounding a parent's child support obligation. We conclude that the agreement was void.

I. SUMMARY OF FACTS

The facts most favorable to the judgment reveal that in 1986 Francine Todd and Edward Straub engaged in a romantic relationship and sexual relations. In December of that year, Todd informed Straub of her desire to have a child. Straub was a divorcee with five children from a previous marriage, and he expressed resistance to fathering another child. Todd threatened to end the relationship, however, unless he agreed to impregnate her.

Straub handwrote the following statement and told Todd he would attempt to impregnate her if she signed it.

To whom it may concern

I Francine Todd in sound mind & fore thought have decided not to marry, but would like to have a baby of my own. To support financially & emotionally. I have approached several men who will not be held responsible financially or emotionally, who's [sic] names will be kept secret for life.

Signed <u>Francine E. Todd</u>

Dec. 15, 1986

Todd signed the statement, and the couple thereafter began having unprotected intercourse. Todd became pregnant in March 1987 and gave birth that November. The birth certificate did not list anyone as the father.

On January 7, 1991, Todd filed a petition asking the trial court to declare Straub the father of the child and require him to pay child support and certain medical expenses. The trial court found Straub to be the father of the child and ordered him to pay support in the sum of $130 per week, arrearages of $20 per week and certain medical expenses.

Straub appealed this decision and the Court of Appeals affirmed. * * * Straub raises * * * [the question]: whether parent may contract away his or her rights and obligations to a child and/or the child's right to support through a preconception contract for fertilization. We * * * affirm.

II. SOME AGREEMENTS CONCERNING CHILDREN ARE VOID

Three rudimentary elements must be present before an agreement may be considered a contract: offer, acceptance of the offer and consideration. If these components are present, legal obligation results from the bargaining of the parties as found in their language or by implication from other circumstances, as affected by the rules of law. *See, e.g.,* U.C.C. § 1–201(3).

There are instances, however in which an agreement is not an enforceable contract despite proper formation. Where a properly formed agreement contravenes the public policy of Indiana, for instance, courts have traditionally said it is void and unenforceable. Leading commentators frame the principle somewhat differently, saying that in such circumstances there is no contract, because such an agreement produces no legal obligation upon the part of the promisor. It may well be more exact to say that where an agreement violates public policy, no contract is created.

In any event, certain agreements are prohibited outright by statute and thus void. *See, e.g.*, IND. CODE ANN. § 26–2–5–1 (rendering void provisions which indemnify a promisee against liability for negligence by promisee or his or her independent contractors). There are even court rules outlawing certain agreements. *See, e.g.*, Ind. Professional Conduct Rule 1.5(d)(2) (no contingency fees in criminal cases).

More often, though, the question of whether an agreement is void on public policy grounds is a question of law to be determined from the surrounding circumstances of a given case. Where public policy is not explicit, we look to the overall implications of constitutional and statutory enactments, practices of officials and judicial decisions to disclose the public policy of this State. Where there is not a clear manifestation of public policy we will find an agreement void only if it has a tendency to injure the public, is against the public good or is inconsistent with sound policy and good morals.

Rule

One well-established public policy of this State is protecting the welfare of children. Expressed by all three branches of Indiana government, this policy is of the utmost importance. In keeping with this public policy, Indiana courts have from time to time voided agreements reached by parents. Agreements which yield up a support opportunity for a child have been especially suspect. We have treated custodial parents who receive child support as trustees of the payments for the use and the benefit of the child. Neither parent has the right to contract away these support benefits. The right to the support lies exclusively with the child. Any agreement purporting to contract away these rights is directly contrary to this State's public policy of protecting the welfare of children, as it narrows the basis for support to one parent.

parent cannot contract away support duties

Seeking to avoid the rules that agreements between parents giving up a child's right to support are void, Straub contended during oral argument and in his appellate briefs that he was not a traditional parent but merely a sperm donor for Todd's "artificial insemination." The Indiana legislature has acknowledged the use of artificial insemination, though it has not addressed the support obligation of parents where artificial fertilization leads to the conception of the child. Nonetheless, citizens of this State execute contracts for such fertilization. These contracts have the ability to impact significantly the support responsibility of biological and nonbiological parents. Other jurisdictions have addressed the support

∆ argument

issues surrounding artificial fertilization through the adoption of statutes based on the Uniform Parentage Act ("UPA"), and the Uniform Status of Children of Assisted Conception Act ("USCACA"). The majority of states adopting legislation similar to these acts hold that the donor of semen or ova, provided to a licensed physician for use in the artificial fertilization of a woman, is treated under the law as if he or she were not the natural parent of the child thereby conceived. Otherwise, whether the impregnation occurs through artificial fertilization or intercourse, there *can* be a determination of parentage. *See, e.g., Jhordan C. v. Mary K.* [Chapter 9]. * * *

III. ARE AGREEMENTS LIKE THIS ONE ENFORCEABLE?

While Indiana does not have statutes on assisted conception, common law courts certainly have the ability to fashion and refashion the law of contract, as Judge Conover suggested in his dissenting opinion to the Court of Appeals.[8] Accordingly, we evaluate the Todd agreement within the parameters of common law as influenced by the emerging contract principles surrounding reproductive technology.

This agreement falls on multiple accounts. First, it looks for all the world as a rather traditional attempt to forego this child's right to support from *Straub*, which contravenes public policy. We conclude there is no such thing as "artificial insemination by intercourse" as *Straub* contends. The emerging law on contracts for artificial insemination so suggests.

Second, consideration for this agreement, received by Straub, was sexual intercourse with Todd. Using sexual intercourse as consideration is itself against public policy.

Third, the agreement contains none of the formalities and protections which the legislatures and courts of other jurisdictions have thought necessary to address when enabling childless individuals to bear children.[10] For these reasons, we hold the Todd agreement to be void and unenforceable. * * *

DEBRULER, JUSTICE, dissenting.

I agree with the majority that one cannot contract away the right of a child to financial support from one of her parents. One cannot contract away one's liability for negligence either, but we do permit people to buy

---

[8] Judge Conover explained: "Thus, in my opinion, the contract in question is valid and enforceable because it is conversant with current public policy. Todd had an absolute right to contract with *Straub* as she did, and is absolutely bound by the obligations she incurred under that contract. Quite simply, she bargained away the right to file a paternity action against *Straub* and to publicly name him as the child's father." *Straub*, 626 N.E.2d, at 855–56.

[10] For example, prerequisites such as physician involvement are essential for protecting the health and welfare of the child conceived. *Jhordan C.*, [p. 453] (physician involvement essential to obtain donor's complete medical history which child may later need and creates a formal structure for donation which reduces misunderstandings of the relationship between donor and recipient and donor, recipient and child).

insurance. If an individual's insurance coverage is inadequate then that person must pay. However, we do not void insurance contracts by invoking a public policy of imposing liability for negligence. The proper procedure to make certain that B.M.T. receives adequate support is that suggested by Judge Chezem's opinion in the Court of Appeals. If a person promises to pay the father's share of child support then, if that person is able, he or she should pay.

NOTES AND QUESTIONS

1.   How does the approach advocated by dissenting Judge DeBruler differ from that of the majority? When would Judge DeBruler enforce a child support waiver?

2.   *Straub* reflects the general rule that, because the parental support obligation is owed directly to the child, it is independent of both the parental relationship and any agreement between the parents. *See* G.E.B. v. S.R.W. [Chapter 7]. A waiver of child support in a premarital agreement is thus unenforceable. *See* UPAA § 3 [Chapter 5].

Why is the man obligated to support his biological child in this instance, but has no child support obligation if he donates sperm to a licensed physician who then inseminates the woman?

3.   Fathers who have sought to avoid support obligations based on the mother's "contraceptive fraud" have also been unsuccessful. For example, in *In re* Pamela P., 443 N.Y.S.2d 343 (Fam. Ct. 1981), the trial court found "the evidence [is] entirely clear and convincing that petitioner falsely told respondent she was 'on the pill' and thereby purposely deceived him with regard to contraception." Noting that this was a case of first impression, the court ruled that the father should pay support only to the extent that the mother's means were insufficient to provide the child with a living standard equivalent to the father's. But the New York Court of Appeals disagreed:

> [T]he [support] statute mandates consideration of two factors—the needs of the child for support * * * and the financial ability of the parents to contribute to that support. The statute does not require, nor, we believe, does it permit, consideration of the "fault" or wrongful conduct of one of the parents in causing the child's conception. * * *

The Court was equally unimpressed with the father's constitutional argument:

> The * * * respondent's constitutional entitlement to avoid procreation does not encompass a right to avoid a child support obligation simply because another private person has not fully respected his desires in this regard. However unfairly respondent may have been treated by petitioner's failure to allow him an equal voice in the decision to conceive a child, such a wrong does not rise to the level of a constitutional violation.

In re L. Pamela P. v. Frank S., 449 N.E.2d 713 (N.Y. 1983). Other courts confronted with allegations of contraceptive fraud have agreed with the *L. Pamela P.* court's constitutional analysis; they have accordingly treated allegations of misrepresentation as irrelevant to the support obligation. *See, e.g.,* N.E. v. Hedges, 391 F.3d 832 (6th Cir. 2004).

4. Could an unwilling father maintain a tort action based on the mother's fraud? Courts have uniformly said no. *See, e.g.,* Wallis v. Smith, 22 P.3d 682 (N. M. App. 2001) (dismissing complaint and noting that "[t]o our knowledge, no jurisdiction recognizes contraceptive fraud or breach of promise to practice birth control as a ground for adjusting a natural parent's obligation to pay child support.") *See generally* Anne M. Payne, Annot., *Sexual Partner's Tort Liability to Other Partner for Fraudulent Misrepresentation Regarding Sterility or Use of Birth Control Resulting in Pregnancy,* 2 A.L.R.5th 301 (1992).

5. A number of cases involve situations where a minor impregnates an older woman in situations that constitute statutory rape. Should the minor have to support such a child? Courts have imposed a child support obligation. In *In re* Parentage of J.S., 550 N.E.2d 257 (Ill. App. 1990) the court stated:

> The respondent initially argues that he should not be required to support his child, because he was a 15-year-old minor when the child was conceived. * * * We note that . . . Illinois public policy has never offered blanket protection to reckless minors. * * * We find the public policy mandating parental support of children overrides any policy of protecting a minor from improvident acts.

See also, Hermesmann v. Seyer, 847 P.2d 1273 (Kan. 1993) (involving a boy who was 12 when the girl became pregnant); *In re* Paternity of K. B., 104 P.3d 1132 (Okla. App. 2004) (boy age 15 must pay child support).

If a 12-year-old girl is raped and conceives a child, should she have a child support obligation? If an adult woman is raped and conceives, should she have a child support obligation?

T.F. v. B.L.

Supreme Judicial Court of Massachusetts, 2004.
442 Mass. 522, 813 N.E.2d 1244.

COWIN, J.

The plaintiff, T.F., and the defendant, B.L., are two women who lived together from 1996 to 2000. During this time, the plaintiff became pregnant through artificial insemination, and in July, 2000, after the couple had separated, she gave birth to a child. In January, 2001, the plaintiff filed a complaint in the Probate and Family Court Department. Based on theories of promissory estoppel and breach of an oral contract, she requested that the defendant be ordered to pay child support under the child support guidelines. The judge found that there was an agreement "to create a child," which the defendant had breached * * * [and] reported the matter to the Appeals Court * * * for a determination whether "parenthood by contract is the law of Massachusetts." If this question were answered in the affirmative, she opined, "then [the defendant] is a parent." * * *

We conclude that while the plaintiff has established the existence of an implied agreement, "parenthood by contract" is not the law of Massachusetts and the agreement is unenforceable as against public policy. Therefore, this defendant has no obligation of child support and the Probate and Family Court cannot create such an obligation pursuant to its equity jurisdiction. * * *

The plaintiff and defendant met in 1995, and began living together in the fall of 1996. On May 30, 1999, the couple held a "commitment ceremony." Subsequently, they pooled their money and nominated each other as beneficiaries of their respective life insurance policies and retirement plans. The plaintiff had long wanted to have a child, and communicated her feelings to the defendant on several occasions. * * * The defendant, who had grown up in an abusive household, doubted her own fitness to be a parent. She also had experienced psychological problems in the past, and was undergoing treatment for a recurrence of depression in the spring and summer of 1999. The defendant continued her resistance to having a child until one day in June or July of 1999, when she telephoned the plaintiff at work and told her that she had changed her mind. * * * [After further conversations and medical consultations,] the parties decided to proceed with the plaintiff's artificial insemination.

* * * The parties worked together to select an anonymous [sperm] donor. The couple used joint funds for insemination and prenatal care expenses. The defendant's actions during this period were at least in part an effort to preserve her relationship with the plaintiff, which she believed would have suffered had she attempted to prevent the plaintiff from having a child. The defendant told her sister and a friend that, from the time of the 1999 conversation, she "went along" with having a baby because she got "tired of the arguments" and "didn't want to take [the plaintiff's] dream away."

* * * In December, 1999, the plaintiff became pregnant as the result of the second insemination. The parties' relationship deteriorated in the following months, and the defendant moved out of their apartment in May, 2000. Prior to leaving, the defendant expressed her regrets about being a "separated parent," said she desired to adopt the child, and "promised financial support and promised to talk later about the details since she wanted to just focus on the break-up of the relationship at that time." On July 1, 2000, the plaintiff went into premature labor and gave birth to a boy. * * * The defendant visited the mother and child in the hospital several times, participated in selecting his name, and promised to provide support

and to change her work hours to help raise him. During one of these visits, the defendant gave the plaintiff $800. On July 26, 2000, the defendant sent pictures of herself with the child, via the Internet, to friends accompanied by the message: "I hope you all enjoy the pics of my wonderful, beautiful boy." In October, 2000, the parties argued for over an hour about support for the child, who, as the result of his premature birth, required a great deal of medical attention. * * * The defendant "acknowledged that she was not paying child support because she was angry at [the plaintiff]." Later that month, the defendant sent a letter to the plaintiff, declaring that she desired no further contact with the plaintiff or the child.

* * *

a.   *"Parenthood by contract."* The plaintiff does not contend that there was any express written agreement between the parties, but rather that the defendant's initial statement, in the summer of 1999, that she wished to discuss having a child, followed by her course of conduct, reflect an implied contract to create a child. In the absence of an express agreement, an implied contract may be inferred from (1) the conduct of the parties and (2) the relationship of the parties. An implied contract requires proof that there was a benefit to the defendant, that the plaintiff expected the defendant to pay for that benefit, and that the defendant expected, or a reasonable person should have expected, that he or she would have to pay for that benefit. When the defendant was, or should have been, aware of the plaintiff's expectations in this regard, the defendant's failure to object can create a contract. The defendant's subjective intent is irrelevant when she knows or has reason to know that her objective actions manifest the existence of an agreement.

In this case, the evidence warranted the judge's finding that there was an agreement by the defendant to undertake the responsibilities of a parent in consideration of the plaintiff's conceiving and bearing a child. Although the defendant claims that the plaintiff should not have relied on her passive silence, the judge reasonably concluded that the circumstances and relations of the parties, as stated in her findings, told a different story. The parties cohabited for several years as a couple, pooling all their financial resources. After the 1999 conversation, the plaintiff agreed to conceive and give birth to a child. Following this agreement, the defendant not only did not object, but actively participated in medical decisions and procedures, and in discussions about the child's future and the finances related to the conception and raising of the child. Furthermore, the judge found that the defendant intentionally manifested an outward desire to have a child in order to maintain her relationship with the plaintiff. A finding of an implied contract based on these facts, while not compelled, was certainly permissible.

* * * [T]he question remains whether the court can enforce this contract. Contracts between unmarried cohabitants regarding property, finance, and other matters are normally enforceable. Such contracts may concern the welfare and support of children, provided they do not contravene the best interests of the child. * * * However, when a contract violates or conflicts with public policy, we treat it as void and will not enforce it. This is such a contract.

In *A.Z. v. B.Z.* [Chapter 9], we refused to enforce an agreement that compelled a party "to become a parent against his or her will." In that case, the plaintiff successfully prevented his estranged wife from using his own sperm (which had been frozen and stored by an in vitro fertilization clinic) to create a child. "[F]orced procreation," we concluded, "is not an area amenable to judicial enforcement." The present case is factually distinguishable in that the defendant's contribution to the conception and birth of the child arose from contractual intent rather than from her genetic material. However, important concerns underlying that decision also apply here. We determine public policy by looking "to the expressions of the Legislature and to those of this court." In the *A.Z.* case we noted that, by statute, a contract to enter into a marital relationship is not enforceable. We also discussed earlier cases that had "indicated a reluctance to enforce prior agreements that bind individuals to future family relationships." *Id.*, citing R.R. v. M.H. (agreement by which surrogate mother agreed to give up child at birth was unenforceable unless agreement contained, inter alia, "reasonable" waiting period consistent with waiting period in adoption surrender); Capazzoli v. Holzwasser (contract requiring individual to abandon marriage unenforceable). We concluded that in order to protect the "freedom of personal choice in matters of marriage and family life," *quoting* Moore v. East Cleveland [Chapter 1], "prior agreements to enter into familial relationships (marriage or parenthood) should not be enforced against individuals who subsequently reconsider their decisions."

The principles expressed by this court in *A.Z.* are applicable, and of like force, in the present case. The decision to become, or not to become, a parent is a personal right of "such delicate and intimate character that direct enforcement . . . by any process of the court should never be attempted." *Id.* * * *

In the present case, the appropriate inquiry is whether there was a specific identifiable agreement to support the child contained within the implied contract to create and parent the child, and, if so, whether that agreement is severable from the implied contract. The Probate and Family Court judge suggested that an agreement to become a parent inherently involves four promises: (1) that the "parties will continue to love the child," (2) "support each other," (3) "provide child care," and (4) "provide financial support for the child." Nothing in the record gives substance or meaning to any specific promise to provide child support separate and apart from the implied agreement to create a child; support was, as the judge stated, one of the inherent consequences of parenthood. Furthermore, where a portion of a contract is separably enforceable, that portion would ordinarily confer delineated benefits and obligations on both sides. But here, nothing in the record shows a distinct consideration in return for child support apart from the core, unenforceable promise to coparent. Therefore, any implied promise that the defendant made respecting child support is inextricably linked to her unenforceable promise to coparent the child, and is similarly unenforceable.[10]

b.   *Equity power of the Probate and Family Court.* * * * The duty to support a minor child is statutory. * * * Here, the defendant is not a parent of the child under any statutory provision. She has not become a "de facto" parent by virtue of a long-term relationship with the child. Apart from the unenforceable contractual obligation found by the Probate and Family Court judge, the defendant is legally a stranger to the child. * * *

* * * Equity is not an all-purpose judicial tool by which the "right thing to do" can be fashioned into a legal obligation possessing the legitimacy of legislative enactment. Similarly, the "best interests of the child" is not a free-floating concept that empowers probate judges to impose legal obligations on people who have no legal obligations to begin with. * * * It may be the case that a child is better off with two persons responsible for providing support than with only one such person, and that it will always be in the child's "best interest" to impose a support order on some second person. But that second person may not be imposed on, by way of equity or the "best interests" standard, until and unless the Legislature establishes that he or she is among a class of persons who have a legal obligation to the child. * * *

* * * [W]e conclude that "parenthood by contract" is not the law in Massachusetts. This case is remanded to the Probate and Family Court for further proceedings consistent with this opinion.

---

[10] The dissent's conclusion that "parenthood by contract" is not the law, yet that a separate support obligation may nevertheless be imposed on a nonparent, is conspicuously silent on the possible ramifications of such a conclusion. Given the unprecedented nature of imposing a long-lasting support obligation independent of parenthood, we have no recognized legal principles for determining the defendant's status. For example, although the defendant voluntarily ceased visitation, would she have visitation rights, or some right to resume contact with the child, that she could seek to enforce? While presumably not having a right to custody, would she have any say in some aspects of the child's care, or at least in those aspects that would profoundly affect her own financial obligations (e.g., the decision to send the child to private as opposed to public school)? What if the plaintiff marries and her spouse wants to adopt the child? * * * Given the novel and unprecedented status the defendant would have under the dissent's theory, the Probate and Family Court would be called on to supervise the relationship between the parties and the child for many years to come, and none of them would fully comprehend their rights and obligations until each such right and obligation gave rise to a disagreement and was later defined by way of litigation.

GREANEY, J. (concurring in part and dissenting in part, with whom MARSHALL, C.J., and Ireland, J., join).

* * * The defendant cannot be held to be a parent by contract, but her agreement with the plaintiff includes a promise to support the child that she and the plaintiff agreed to create * * * and to parent together. * * * A person cannot participate, in the way the defendant did, in bringing a child into the world, and then walk away from a support obligation.

* * * The Legislature has * * * expressed, in unmistakable terms, that "dependent children shall be maintained, as completely as possible, from the resources of their parents" and not by the taxpayers, and that support determinations should be made in "the best interests of the child." * * * [T]he Legislature [also] made clear that the parentage of children born as a result of artificial insemination does not depend on biology but may be determined on the basis of consent. * * *

The prerequisites for a successful claim based on a theory of promissory estoppel are met in this case: (1) promises to parent and support a child that (2) the defendant should reasonably have known would cause the plaintiff to proceed with their joint plan for her to become pregnant by means of artificial insemination (3) which the plaintiff did (4) justifiably relying on the defendant's affirmative conduct and promises, leaving the plaintiff in circumstances such that (5) injustice (to the plaintiff and to the child) can be avoided only by enforcement of the promise to support.

In summary: even though we do not recognize parenthood by contract, an agreement between the parties has been proved, which includes a promise of support, and the Probate and Family Court * * * has jurisdiction to hear the case and specifically to enforce that promise. * * * The court's concerns over what rights, if any, the defendant, if ordered to pay child support, might seek in the future with respect to the child address issues that are beyond the scope of this opinion. * * * The same types of concerns have been raised, and dealt with, in other cases presenting novel or difficult family law issues.

NOTES AND QUESTIONS

1. Does *A.Z.* compel the holding in *T.F.*? Does *Straub* compel the holding in *T.F.*? Does *Moore* compel the holding in *T.F.*?

2. A number of courts have imposed a support obligation on a nonparent who, like the *T.F.* defendant, made promises that led the parent to utilize artificial insemination to bear a child. For example, in Buzzanca v. Buzzanca [Chapter 9], a California appellate court relied on the doctrine of equitable estoppel to impose a support obligation upon the husband of an intended mother based on his agreement, before the child's birth, to act as a parent. In *Kristine H. v. Lisa R.* [Chapter 9], the California Supreme Court relied on the

estoppel doctrine in imposing a support obligation on a former same-sex partner who had stipulated to the issuance of a written judgment of parentage and "enjoyed the benefits of that judgment for nearly two years." And in L.S.K. v. H.A.N., 813 A.2d 872 (Pa. Super. 2002), the court imposed a support obligation on a former same-sex partner who had encouraged the mother to utilize artificial insemination to bear both a son and quadruplets during their relationship but had never explicitly promised to help support the children. At the time support was sought, the partner had sought and obtained joint legal custody and visitation rights; the court held that she could not both allege that she had acquired rights in relation to the children and deny any obligation to support them based on the lack of an explicit agreement. Can *Buzzanca*, *Kristine H.*, and *L.S.K.* be distinguished from *T.F.*? How would you expect that the Massachusetts Supreme Judicial Court would rule in these cases? *See generally* Annot., *Child Support Obligations of Former Same-Sex Partners*, 5 A.L.R. 6th 303 (2005).

3.   What outcome should a court reach in a case like *T.F.*: What legal and equitable principles are relevant? What public policies and practical problems should be taken into account? On balance, what decision should a court reach and why?

4.   *Stepparents:* Under the common law, a stepparent relationship created no rights or obligations. Stepchildren were not entitled to support from a stepparent; if the stepparent died intestate, his stepchild took nothing. Most states maintain the common law approach, although some do impose statutory support obligations on stepparents during their marriage to the child's custodial parent. *See, e.g.,* WASH. REV. CODE § 26.16.205; DEL. CODE tit. 13, § 501(b). But a "during marriage" support obligation is terminable at will. Given the tradition of noninterference with spending decisions in an intact family, it is also unenforceable most of the time. Without adoption by the stepparent, courts have imposed support obligations that survive divorce from the child's parent only in cases involving special circumstances. For example, one court ordered a stepparent to pay child support after divorce when he was seeking post-divorce custody of the children. *See* A.S. v. I.S., 42 Fam. L. Rep. (BNA) 1111 (Pa. 2015). Contracts requiring post-divorce support have been enforced. *See, e.g., In re* Marriage of Dawley, 551 P.2d 323 (Cal. 1976). The equitable estoppel doctrine has also been used to impose post-divorce support. *See* Annot., *Stepparent's Postdivorce Duty to Support Stepchild*, 44 A.L.R.4th 521 (1986). Can stepparents be distinguished from a same-sex partner like the *T.F.* defendant?

5.   In Canada, a court may order a divorcing stepparent to pay support when he or she "stands in the place of a parent." Chartier v. Chartier, [1999] 1 S.C.R. 242. This inquiry, according to the Canadian Supreme Court, depends on "the nature of the relationship" and not on "formal expressions of intent":

> The court must determine the nature of the relationship by looking at a number of factors, among which is intention. Intention will not only be expressed formally. The court must also infer intention from

actions, and take into consideration that even expressed intentions may sometimes change. The actual fact of forming a new family is the key factor * * *.The relevant factors * * * include, but are not limited to, whether the child participates in the extended family in the same way as would a biological child; whether the person provides financially for the child * * *; whether the person disciplines the child as a parent; whether the person represents to the child, the family, the world, either explicitly or implicitly, that he or she is responsible as a parent * * *; the nature or existence of the child's relationship with the absent biological parent. * * * Every case must be determined on its own facts.

Id. How does the *in loco parentis* approach differ from the equitable estoppel approach? What are the advantages and disadvantages of each in determining stepparent obligations?

6. *Grandparents:* Some states impose a support responsibility on grandparents for children born to the grandparent's minor children, as long as the parents are minors. *See* MO. STAT. § 201.847; S.C. CODE § 20–7–936. In Lovelace v. Gross, 605 N.E.2d 339 (N.Y. 1992), the New York Court of Appeals rejected a constitutional challenge to a grandparent-support policy applicable to children receiving state public assistance. Is a grandparent support policy consistent with the result in *T.F.*?

J.R. v. L.R.

N.J. Super. Ct., Appellate Division, 2006.
386 N.J. Super. 475, 902 A.2d 261.

COLLESTER, J.A.D.

The focus of this case is fifteen-year-old Jessica, who has been denied love, comfort and support by two fathers: her biological father, who was unknown to her until these proceedings, and the man she called Dad for almost ten years. Following two plenary hearings Judge Daniel M. Waldman directed that each pay $75 per week for Jessica's support. Only S.G., the biological father, has appealed.

J.R. and L.R. were married on November 5, 1988. Two children were born during the marriage: Nicholas, born June 20, 1989, and Jessica, born January 19, 1991. The relationship between their parents was stormy and at times violent. After an argument in April 1990, L.R. went to a bar and met S.G., whom she had known before. Later they engaged in sexual intercourse. When she discovered she was pregnant, L.R. did not tell J.R. about her brief affair. J.R. raised Jessica as his daughter and had no reason to doubt he was her biological father until nine and one-half years later when L.R. said during an argument that S.G. was the father. J.R. called S.G. and told him what L.R. had said. Taken aback by the call, S.G. said he had no idea what L.R. was talking about.

J.R. and L.R. separated. L.R. remained in Florida with the children while J.R. moved to North Carolina. Later that summer Jessica, then nine years old, was on her computer conversing with J.R. on a live, on-line computer service called AOL Instant Messenger when he typed her a message saying she should find her real father and tell Nicholas that his father was dead. L.R. was in the same room with Jessica and told her that J.R. was just angry about the separation. When Jessica continued to press her mother on the subject, L.R. told her there was a possibility that J.R. was not her father.

During this time L.R. abused alcohol and was unable to support her children financially or emotionally. She applied for and received public assistance, and as a result, the Ocean County Board of Social Services, together with L.R., filed a complaint against J.R. for support of the two children. At an appearance before a hearing officer, J.R. raised the issue of paternity of the children and requested they be tested. The hearing officer explained she had no jurisdiction to decide the matter and submitted a recommendation that J.R. pay $193 per week for both children, which was adopted by the judge.

J.R. then filed a separate motion for paternity testing of the children using the docket number of the support action. Even though a paternity complaint had not been filed, an order was signed by the Family Part judge for genetic testing of J.R., Nicholas and Jessica. The results disclosed that J.R. was the biological father of Nicholas but not Jessica. The judge then modified the support order to require that J.R. only pay support for Nicholas.

Five days later J.R. left New Jersey. He has lived outside this state since that time. While he has stayed in contact with Nicholas, his relationship with Jessica completely deteriorated. At Christmas in 2003 he sent her a gift with a note telling her he was sorry, that he loved her and wanted to be her friend. Jessica crumpled up the note. She has not seen or spoken to J.R. since early 2002.

After she received the order eliminating J.R.'s obligation to support Jessica, L.R. called S.G. She told him that the test showed J.R. was not Jessica's father and that she believed S.G. was the biological parent. She asked him to contribute money for her support, but he refused. L.R. then filed a paternity complaint in Monmouth County claiming that S.G. was Jessica's father and demanding he submit to genetic testing and pay support. An order for S.G. to submit to testing was entered by the Monmouth County judge but later was vacated after S.G. made a motion to vacate under *R.* 4:50–1(f) and raised the issue of whether such testing was in Jessica's best interests. *See M.F. v. N.H.,* 252 N.J. Super. 420, 429–30, 599 A.2d 1297 (App. Div. 1991).

Meanwhile, J.R. filed a motion for a reduction in child support, for joint custody of both Jessica and Nicholas and for an order compelling L.R. to produce Jessica's biological father for a support hearing. The motion was consolidated with the paternity action and transferred to Monmouth County where the children lived. Judge Waldman appointed counsel to represent Jessica's interest on the issues of paternity and support. He also appointed Lillian Haber Gordon, L.C.S.W., to interview all parties to the action and submit a report as to whether Jessica's best interests would be served by the genetic testing. Gordon interviewed S.G. who told her that he wanted no relationship with Jessica under any circumstances and believed his other children would be emotionally harmed if they found out about her. Jessica told Gordon that she did not want a relationship with J.R. but did want to know the identity of her natural father, even if he wanted nothing to do with her. Gordon concluded that Jessica deserved to know the identity of her biological father and recommended S.G. be ordered to submit to genetic testing.

Judge Waldman conducted a hearing over two days, during which J.R., L.R., S.G., C.G. (S.G.'s wife), Gordon and Jessica testified.[2] He issued a lengthy written opinion in which he concluded that the evidence and the genetic testing overcame the presumption of N.J.S.A. 9:17–43(a) that J.R. was Jessica's father and that there was an articulable reason to suspect S.G. was her biological parent. He also found that Jessica knew J.R. was not her father and that her relationship with him was "nearly non-existent." He said Jessica wanted to know the identity of her biological father even though she understood that if it was S.G., he probably would reject her. Accordingly, Judge Waldman held that the factors set forth in *M.F. v. N.H., supra,* 252 N.J.Super. at 429–30, 599 A.2d 1297, had been satisfied, and it was in Jessica's best interests to order that S.G. submit to genetic testing.

After the test results indicated a 99.9 percent probability that S.G. was Jessica's biological father, Judge Waldman held a hearing on the support issue. Both S.G. and J.R. testified and supplied proof of their income and expenses. Judge Waldman issued a comprehensive written opinion in which he held that as Jessica's biological father, S.G. was responsible for her support. However, he also found that S.G. was unable to pay the entire amount of her support because of his income and the financial demands of his family, including his other children. Finding that the proper support for Jessica required $150 per week, he directed S.G. to pay $75 per week. He then turned to J.R., whom he found to be Jessica's psychological father and found, based on his income and expenses, that he should pay the remaining amount of Jessica's necessary support of $75 per week.

---

[2]　Sadly, S.G. and C.G. declined to be present for Jessica's testimony, and J.R. left the courtroom shortly after her testimony began.

S.G. argument

Only S.G. has appealed. He does not dispute that he is Jessica's biological father or contend he is unable to pay $75 per week for her support. He argues first that the orders directing that both he and J.R. submit to paternity testing were erroneous under the New Jersey Parentage Act, N.J.S.A. 9:17–38 to –59, as well as contrary to Jessica's best interests since the testing results were destructive to her relationship with J.R., who was the only father she had ever known.

Under the Parentage Act there is a presumption that a child born during marriage is the offspring of the husband. N.J.S.A. 9:17–43(a)(1). Since the Act disfavors a finding of illegitimacy, the presumption may be rebutted only by clear and convincing evidence that another man is the biological father and that "'there is no possible escape' from that conclusion."

S.G.'s argument that the results of the genetic testing which excluded J.R. as Jessica's father should be suppressed as contrary to Jessica's best interests has no merit. Following a conference pursuant to N.J.S.A. 9:17–48 of the Parentage Act, a consent order was entered testing J.R. There is no record of any proceedings, and no appeal was taken. Although there was no finding that the testing of J.R. was in Jessica's best interests, the record is clear that Jessica had been told more than a year earlier by her mother and J.R. that he was not her natural father. In any event, we cannot turn back the clock and ignore the fact that prior to the paternity action against S.G., Jessica was fully aware that the genetic testing confirmed what she already knew and that there was no father/daughter relationship with J.R. to protect.

S.G.'s argument that he should not have been ordered to submit to testing is equally unpersuasive. The order was grounded on N.J.S.A. 9:17–41(g), which provides that,

> [T]he child and other parties in a contested paternity case shall submit to a genetic test upon the request of one of the parties, unless that person has good cause for refusal, if the request is supported by a sworn statement by the requesting party: (1) alleging paternity and setting forth the facts establishing a reasonable possibility of the requisite sexual conduct between the parties. . .

Judge Waldman made detailed factual findings to which we assign special deference. The record supports that there was much more than a reasonable possibility of the requisite sexual contact between L.R. and S.G. and that Jessica's desire to ascertain the identity of her biological father was in accord with her best interests. Accordingly, S.G. was properly ordered to submit to the testing.

S.G. next argues that since J.R. was and is Jessica's psychological parent, he should be solely responsible for her support under the doctrine of equitable estoppel. But it is settled law that the natural parent is the primary source for the support of a child, and the duty cannot be switched to a stepparent absent exceptional circumstances. J.W.P v. W.W., 255 N.J. Super. 1, 3, 604 A.2d 603 (App. Div.1991). That exception arises when a stepfather actively interferes with the child's support from the natural father, and, as a result, he may be equitably estopped from disclaiming that obligation in the future. As we stated in J.W.P. v. W.W., equitable estoppel is "a safety net for the child whose stepfather has affirmatively interfered with his right to be supported by his natural father." This exception is obviously inapplicable here. J.R. never interfered with a relationship between S.G. and Jessica. They have never had a relationship and, sadly, probably never will.

Finally, S.G. contends that it is simply inequitable to require him to be financially responsible for Jessica after so much time passed before L.R. made him aware of Jessica's existence and also because acknowledging and supporting her would harm his wife and other children. But reality cannot be ignored, and the reality is that S.G. has a daughter who is in need of support and is legally entitled to it. As her father, S.G. is responsible for her proper support to the extent that he is financially able, even though there is no relationship between them. Finally, the result is hardly inequitable in light of the fact that Judge Waldman found S.G. could not bear the entire burden of supporting Jessica and directed that J.R., as her psychological father, should equally share in the responsibility The decision is legally correct and equitably just.

Affirmed.

NOTES AND QUESTIONS

1. The appellate court refers to the husband as a stepfather and then concludes that these facts do not justify the imposition of a support obligation on him as a stepparent. But the trial court imposed a child support obligation on the husband. Does this mean that if the husband had appealed, he could have avoided paying child support? Does it make sense to treat the husband as a "stepfather" in this case?

2. The biological father argues unsuccessfully that, because he had not been notified of the child's existence for such a long time, he should not have a child support obligation. In most states, this has not been considered a defense to the imposition of a child support obligation. Perhaps the more interesting issue is whether his lack of notice should impact a court's decision regarding whether to award retroactive support. When the mother has not notified the biological father of the child's existence, some courts have not awarded retroactive support. *See In re* Loomis, 587 N.W.2d 427 (S.D. 1998); *In re* Hilborn, 58 P.3d 905 (Wash. App. 2002); Webb v. Menix, 90 P.3d 989 (N.M. 2004). Other courts have awarded retroactive support, particularly if the father was aware of the child's existence. *See* Bennett v. Peterson, 657 N.W. 2d

(S.D. 2002); *In re* A.B., 368 S.W.3d 850 (Tex. App. 2012); Ellison v. Walter, 834 P.2d 680 (Wyo. 1992); Reitenour v. Montgomery, 807 A.2d 1259 (N.H. 2002). Is this fair? If so, in what amount? In Arkansas, retroactive child support from the date the child was born must be awarded to a mother who is not married to the father. *See* Walden v. Jackson, 506 S.W.3d 904 (Ark. App. 2016).

3.   In Fischer v. Zollino, 35 A.3d 270 (Conn. 2012) the Connecticut Supreme Court held that a man in J.R.'s position could sue the biological father for support provided by J.R. for the child during the period J.R. mistakenly believed he was the biological father.

B. LIMITATIONS ON THE PARENTAL SUPPORT OBLIGATION

1. The Child's Behavior

ROE V. DOE

Court of Appeals of New York, 1971.
29 N.Y.2d 188, 324 N.Y.S.2d 71, 272 N.E.2d 567.

SCILEPPI, JUDGE.

* * * Petitioner is the court-appointed guardian for a 20-year-old student at the University of Louisville who had been fully and generously supported by her father, a prominent New York attorney, until April of 1970. Afforded the opportunity of attending college away from home, and after living in the college dormitory for a time, the daughter, contrary to the father's prior instructions and without his knowledge, took up residence with a female classmate in an off-campus apartment. Upon learning of this deception, the father cut off all further support and instructed her to return to New York.

Ignoring her father's demands, the daughter sold her automobile (an earlier gift from her father) and elected to finish out the school year, living off the proceeds realized upon the sale, some $1,000. During the following summer, the daughter enrolled in summer courses at the university and upon her return to New York chose to reside with the parents of a female classmate on Long Island. The family situation has been tense and somewhat less than stable. The daughter was three years old when her mother died and her father has remarried several times since, most recently in the spring of 1970. Academically, the daughter fared poorly, and was placed on academic probation during her freshman year; though, on a reduced credit work load, she has managed to improve her academic standing over the past year. She has experimented with drugs (LSD and marijuana), apparently without addiction. The girl has been comfortably maintained, and there is no real question about the father's ability to provide. Tuition payments, approximately $1,000 per semester, for the academic year 1970–71, are long past due and petitioner has commenced this support proceeding, alleging that the respondent has refused and neglected to provide fair and reasonable support.

The Family Court entered two separate orders: a temporary order of support (August 21, 1970), requiring the father to remit a tuition payment for the then pending semester and to provide for reasonable medical, dental, eye and psychiatric care; and a final order of support (November 30, 1970), requiring that the father pay $250 per month in support for the period between December 1, 1970 and October 20, 1971, the daughter's twenty-first birthday. Respondent was found to have willfully failed to comply with the temporary order of support and was committed to jail for 30 days, the commitment to be stayed until December 28, 1970 and at that time vacated on condition that he post a cash bond in the sum of $5,750 covering his liability for support. The order of commitment was stayed pending appeal.

On appeal, the Appellate Division modified the temporary order * * * and directed that the father pay only those university and health bills actually rendered prior to November 30, 1970. The final order of November 30, 1970, requiring that the father pay $250 per month in support for the period between December 1, 1970 and October 20, 1971, the daughter's twenty-first birthday, plus tuition payments through the September, 1971 semester, was reversed * * *. As it is our conclusion that where, as in the case at bar, a minor of employable age and in full possession of her faculties, voluntarily and without cause, abandons the parent's home, against the will of the parent and for the purpose of avoiding parental control she forfeits her right to demand support, the order appealed from should be affirmed.

It has always been, and remains a matter of fundamental policy within this State, that a father of a minor child is chargeable with the discipline and support of that child * * * and none would dispute that the obligation cannot be avoided merely became a young enough child is at odds with her parents or has disobeyed their instructions: delinquent behavior of itself, even if unexplained or persistent, does not generally carry with it the termination of the duty of a parent to support.

On the other hand, while the duty to support is a continuing one, the child's right to support and the parent's right to custody and services are reciprocal: the father in return for maintenance and support may establish and impose reasonable regulations for his child. * * * Accordingly, though the question is novel in this State, it has been held, in circumstances such as here, that where by no fault on the parent's part, a child "voluntarily abandons the parent's home for the purpose of seeking its fortune in the world or to avoid parental discipline and restraint [that child] forfeit the claim to support" (C.J.S. Parent and Child § 16). * * * To hold otherwise would be to allow, at least in the case before us, a minor of employable age to deliberately flout the legitimate mandates of her father while requiring that the latter support her in her decision to place herself beyond his effective control.

It is the natural right, as well as the legal duty, of a parent to care for, control and protect his child from potential harm, whatever the source and absent a clear showing of misfeasance, abuse or neglect, courts should not interfere with that delicate responsibility. Here, the daughter, asserting her independence, chose to assume a status inconsistent with that of parental control. The Family Court set about establishing its own standards of decorum, and, having determined that those standards were met, sought to substitute its judgment for that of the father. Needless to say, the intrusion was unwarranted.

We do not have before us the case of a father who casts his helpless daughter upon the world, forcing her to fend for herself; nor has the father been arbitrary in his requests that the daughter heed his demands. The obligations of parenthood, under natural and civil law, require of the child "submission to reasonable restraint, and demands habits of propriety, obedience, and conformity to domestic discipline" * * *. True, a minor, rather than submit to what her father considers to be proper discipline, may be induced to abandon the latter's home; but in so doing, however impatient of parental authority, she cannot enlist the aid of the court in frustrating that authority, reasonably exercised, by requiring that her father accede to her demands and underwrite her chosen lifestyle or as here, run the risk of incarceration.

Nor can we say that the father was unreasonable or capricious in his request that the daughter take up residence in the college dormitory or return to New York. In view of her past derelictions, and, to use the Appellate Division's words, "the temptations that abound outside," * * * we can only conclude that it was reasonable for her father to decide that it was in her own best interests that she do so. And the fact that the father doggedly persisted in his demands despite similar evils which may have lurked within the campus residence, or psychiatric advice that the daughter live off campus, cannot be said to amount to a showing of misconduct, neglect or abuse which would justify the Family Court's action. The father has the right, in the absence of caprice, misconduct or neglect, to require that the daughter conform to his reasonable demands. Should she disagree, and at her age that is surely her prerogative, she may elect not to comply; but in so doing, she subjects herself to her father's lawful wrath. Where, as here, she abandons her home, she forfeits her right to support.

The order appealed from should be affirmed.

NOTES AND QUESTIONS

1.   The *Roe* principle has been widely followed, although there are many decisions refusing to relieve a parent of support obligations toward a younger child despite a child's obstreperous behavior. *See* Annot., *What Voluntary Acts of Child, Other than Marriage or Entry into Military Service, Terminate Parent's Obligation to Support*, 55 A.L.R.5th 557 (1998); *In re* Marriage of Brown, 597 N.E.2d 1297 (Ind. App. 1992) (finding that minor child who lived apart from her parents, had abandoned her father's surname, and refused to visit her father, was not emancipated for purposes of support). Courts have typically been far more willing to relieve parents of support obligations for college-age children than for younger children. What factors likely explain this case-law pattern?

2.   Should the *Roe* principle apply when state officials seek reimbursement for public assistance benefits? In Parker v. Stage, 371 N.E.2d 513 (N.Y. 1977), involving a child who had left home "to live with her paramour and have his child," the New York Court of Appeals said yes:

> It was once the policy of this State to place the financial burden of supporting needy individuals upon designated relatives, rather than the public, in order to reduce the amount of welfare expenditures. * * * In recent years however * * * [t]he laws were amended to relieve individuals of the obligation to support grandchildren, adult children and parents who were unemployed and destitute. Thereafter the burden passed to the public. * * * Of course the fact that the child is eligible for public assistance may as is evident here, permit her to avoid her father's authority and demands however reasonable they may be. But it does not follow that the parent must then finish what has been begun by underwriting the lifestyle which his daughter chose against his reasonable wishes and repeated counsel. * * *

What practical and policy concerns offer arguments against the *Parker* approach? On balance, what approach is best?

3.   A New Jersey case involved a girl, age 18, who moved out of the family home due to a dispute about the boy she was dating, among other things. When she moved out, she was attending a parochial school. She filed suit agaist her parents, asking the court to order them to continue to pay for the costs of her attending school. What should the court do? *See* http://abcnews.go.com/US/rachel-canning-loses-suit-make-parents-pay-high/story?id=22.

4.   Assume a girl living in an intact family is about to graduate from high school in a state where the duty of support continues until age 21. Further assume she is accepted by a public college and a more expensive private university. The parents discussed the situation with the daughter and informed the girl that they wanted her to attend the public university, and will pay for these costs. If the daughter instead chooses to attend the private school and petitions a court to order her parents to pay those costs, what should the court do?

2. Age

In the United States, the age of majority traditionally was 21. Over the past three decades, most states lowered the age of majority to 18. This shift has generated a number of child support issues: Should support continue past 18 if the child has not graduated from high school? Should it continue if the child is disabled or unable to support himself? Should it continue if the child had an expectation of parental support in college? Does *Roe* mean that a minor has a "right" to be supported in college by his parents if he follows their reasonable instructions? Should it make a difference if the age of majority were 21 instead of 18?

NEUDECKER V. NEUDECKER

Supreme Court of Indiana, 1991.
577 N.E.2d 960.

DICKSON, JUSTICE.

The parties' 1975 dissolution decree determined that Wendy Neudecker should have custody of the two children and ordered Rolland Neudecker to pay * * * all costs for the older child to attend college for four years following high school. The Court of Appeals affirmed.

history

* * *

Rolland contends that the Court of Appeals erred in upholding the constitutionality of Ind. Code § 31–1–11.5–12(b)(l). He argues that the statute is unconstitutionally vague, that it impermissibly treats unmarried parents and their children differently from married parents and their children, and that it infringes upon his fundamental child-rearing rights. * * *

Rejecting the claim of unconstitutional vagueness, the Court of Appeals noted the rules of interpretation that favor construing statutes as constitutional if reasonably possible, found that the statute provides sufficient guidelines for a trial court to exercise its discretion, and observed that parents "seeking to dissolve their marriages are aware that the trial court may, in its discretion, order them to pay for their children's education." We approve of the determination of this issue by the Court of Appeals.

We likewise agree with the disposition of Rolland's claim that equal protection rights are violated because a divorced parent can be ordered to pay for his child's education, while a married parent may unilaterally refuse to do so.

It is true that there is no absolute legal duty on the part of parents to provide a college education for their children. However, common experience teaches that one of the major concerns of most families is that qualified children be encouraged to pursue a college education in a manner consistent with individual family values. The statutory authorization in dissolution cases to order either or both parents to pay sums for their child's education expenses constitutes a reasonable implementation of the child support criteria that the court must consider the standard of living the child would have enjoyed had the marriage not been dissolved. This factor is applicable in support modification proceedings, particularly those in which educational expense is an issue.

When an initial support order or its modification is otherwise appropriate, a party seeking to include therein the required payment of college expense must establish by a preponderance of the evidence that such order is reasonable considering the statutory factors * * *. In this regard, the "standard of living the child would have enjoyed had the marriage not been dissolved" means whether and to what extent the parents, if still married, would have contributed to the child's college expenses.

In finding a rational relationship between the child support statutory scheme and the state interest in seeing that children of divorced parents are afforded the same opportunities as children of married parents; the Court of Appeals was correct.

* * *

The expenses of college are not unlike those of orthodontia, music lessons, summer camp, and various other optional undertakings within the discretion of married parents but subject to compulsory payment by inclusion in a child support order in the event of dissolution. The statutes which authorize such orders do not infringe upon fundamental child-rearing rights.

The judgment of the trial court is affirmed.

NOTES AND QUESTIONS

1. *The Age of Majority*: In all states, child support presumptively terminates at the age of majority. In some, the support obligation ends at the earlier of graduation from high school or age 19. *See* CAL. FAM. CODE §§ 3901; DEL. CODE tit. 13 § 501(d). In others, child support ends at age 18 unless the child is still attending high school. *See* TENN. CODE § 34–11–102; TEX. FAM. CODE § 154.001(a). A few states still mandate support to the age of 21. *See, e.g.*, N.Y. DOM. REL. L. § 240.

2. *Emancipation*: Emancipation—marriage, joining the armed forces, or other voluntary acts by which the child establishes independence from parental control—will typically terminate the support obligation, but a number of courts have found that such events are inadequate to terminate support if the child is still in need. *See, e.g., In re* Schoby, 4 P.3d 604 (Kan. 2000) (16-year-old boy's marriage did not terminate father's support obligation when

child was still supported by his mother); Dunson v. Dunson, 769 N.E.2d 1120 (Ind. 2002) (child must be self-supporting); Sakovits v. Sakovits, 429 A.2d 1091 (N.J. Super. 1981) ("regardless of the fact the child may have been formally declared emancipated, the parents *may* in a given case be called upon to contribute to the college education of such child"). Some courts have also reinstated support when an emancipated child loses the capacity for self-support and thus becomes unemancipated. *See, e.g.,* Crimmins v. Crimmins, 745 N.Y.S.2d 686 (Fam. Ct. 2002).

3. *Post-Majority College Support*: Although married parents may not be ordered to support their children during college, most courts that have considered the issue have agreed with the *Neudecker* court that statutes which authorize the divorce court to order a divorced parent to provide college support are constitutional. *See, e.g.,* McLeod v. Starnes, 723 S.E.2d 198 (S.C. 2012); Kohring v. Snodgrass, 999 S.W.2d 228 (Mo. 1999); *In re* Crocker, 22 P.3d 759 (Or. 2001). But the Pennsylvania Supreme Court disagreed:

> Act 62 classifies young adults according to the marital status of their parents, establishing for one group an action to obtain a benefit enforceable by court order that is not available to the other group. The relevant category under consideration is children in need of funds for a post-secondary education. The Act divides these persons, similarly situated with respect to their need for assistance, into groups according to the marital status of their parents, i.e., children of divorced/separated/ never-married parents and children of intact families.
>
> It will not do to argue that this classification is rationally related to the legitimate governmental purpose of obviating difficulties encountered by those in non-intact families who want parental financial assistance for post-secondary education, because such a statement of the governmental purpose assumes the validity of the classification. Recognizing that within the category of young adults in need of financial help to attend college there are some having a parent or parents unwilling to provide such help, the question remains whether the authority of the state may be selectively applied to empower only those from non-intact families to compel such help. We hold that it may not.

Curtis v. Kline, 666 A.2d 265 (Pa. 1995). Is *Curtis* or *Neudecker* better reasoned? Which opinion is more consistent with the Supreme Court's analysis of classifications based on marital status? Oregon has dealt with the problem noted in *Curtis* by making a college support order available in all situations regardless of the marital status of the parents. *See* OR. REV. STAT. tit. 11, §§ 108.110, 107.108. Is this a good solution?

4. In many states, a divorce court cannot order post-majority college support, *See, e.g.,* Cartee v. Cartee, 239 P.3d 707 (Alaska 2010). In 2006, seventeen state child support laws explicitly authorized college-support orders. *See* Laura W. Morgan, *Child Support Guidelines*, 39 FAM. L.Q. 919 chart 3

(2006). Since 2006, Alabma and Indiana have changed their policies and no longer permit a divorce court to order child support for a college student. *See* Leslie Joan Harris, *Child Support for Post-Secondary Education: Empirical and Historical Perspectives,* 29 J. AM. ACAD. MAT. LAW. 299, 317 (2017). *See also,* Monica Hof Wallace, *A Federal Referendum; Extending Child Support for Higher Education,* 58 U. KAN. L. REV. 665 (2010). And even without explicit statutory authorization, some courts have interpreted child support laws as authorizing such support. *See* Childers v. Childers, 575 P.2d 201 (Wash. 1978) (divorce courts had the power to award post-majority support based on the fact that the legislature had amended the support statute to eliminate any reference to the court's power to award support to "minor" children only). In those states that do not permit judges to order support during college, courts may still enforce parental agreements. *See* Bruni v. Bruni, 924 S.W.2d 366 (Tex. 1996). *See generally* Madeline Marzano-Lesnevich & Scott Adam Laterra, *Child Support and College: What is the Correct Result?,* 22 J. AM. ACAD. MATRIM. LAW 335, 339 (2009); National Conference of State Legislatures, *Termination of Support-College Support Beyond the Age of Majority,* http:// www.ncsl.org/research/human-services/termination-of-support-college-support.aspx (last visited December 31, 2016) (providing state-by-state chart of statutes and case law regarding the duty to provide college support).

5. Some child support statutes establish a maximum age for court-ordered college support. *See, e.g.,* OR. REV. STAT. tit. 11, § 107.108 (limiting college support to students younger than 21); CONN.GEN. STAT. § 46b–56c (post-majority college support must terminate when the child turns 23); Allen v. Allen, 54 N.E.3d 344 (Ind. 2016) (divorced parents can't be ordered to pay for graduate or professional school expenses); Kelman v. Kelman, 860 A.2d 292 (Conn. App. 2004) (college support duration cannot exceed four years). Others do not. *See, e.g.,* 750 ILL. COMP. STATS. § 5/513 (referring to the court's power to award support for "college education or professional training" with no age limit). What are the pros and cons of each approach? Note that a parent can extend the support obligation contractually. *See* Flomer v. Farthing, 64 So. 3d 36 (Ala. Civ. App. 2010) (agreement to pay all "reasonable costs of post-secondary education" included graduate school).

6. If support for a child attending college can be imposed, how should the amount of support be calculated? *See,* Jacoby v. Jacoby, 47 A.3d 40 (N.J. App. Div. 2012) (child support guidelines should not be used to determine the amount of college support). Should a parent be required to pay all costs, including living expenses? What if the parent wants the child to attend a state school, but the child prefers a private school? *See* Pharoah v. Lapes, 571 A.2d 1070 (Pa. Super. 1990) (father ordered to pay cost of attending MIT, which the child selected, despite receiving a tuition-free education offer from Georgia Tech). *See also,* Dykes v. Scopetti, 121 A.3d 684 (Vt. 2015); Pamela T. v. Marc B., 930 N.Y.S.2d 857 (Sup. Ct. 2011). In a few cases, an appellate court has affirmed a trial court order establishing that the obligor would not have to pay any more than a certain percentage of the total cost of attending a state university. *See* Jones v. Jones, 958 S.W.2d 607 (Mo. App. 1998); Hinesley-Petry

v. Petry, 894 N.E.2d 277 (Ind. App. 2008). In Iowa, the amount of college support ordered may not exceed one-third of the total cost of attending a state college. *See* IOWA CODE ANN. § 598.21F. In Connecticut, the college support order may not exceed the amount charged by the University of Connecticut for a full-time in-state student. *See* CONN. GEN. STAT. § 46b–56c. Are either of these limits sensible? *Cf.* Tishman v. Bogatin, 942 N.Y.S.2d 516 (App. Div. 2012) (whether to cap the support obligor's obligation at the cost of attending a state school should be determined on a case-by-case basis). Some statutes permit the court to order a parent to pay only certain types of expenses. *See* Barbour v. Barbour, 113 A.3d 77 (Conn. App. 2015) (court cannot order a parent to pay for transportation expenses or incidental expenses). *Cf. In re Marriage of Shipley*, 892 N.W.2d 874 (Iowa App. 2016) (college support order can include room and board, tuition, books, fees, and anticipated personal expenses). If the child can obtain loans, should this reduce the support obligation? Should the court assume the child will work part-time during the school year or during the summer? *See generally* Abraham Kuhl, *Post-Majority Educational Support for Children in the Twenty-first Century,* 21 J. AM. ACAD. MAT. LAW 763 (2008).

7. The *Roe* principle is, of course, applicable to college support. What type of parent-child disagreements, if any, should terminate a college-support obligation? *Cf.* Flomer v. Farthing, 64 So. 3d 36 (Ala. Civ. App. 2010) (holding that the fact that the parent and child are estranged does not extinguish that right of support). *Cf.,* IOWA CODE ANN. § 598.21F(4) (college support should not be awarded if the child has repudiated the parent.

8. Should the college-support obligation terminate if the child fails to maintain good grades? *See* OR. REV. STAT. tit. 11, § 107.108 (requiring child to maintain at least a C average); IOWA CODE § 598.21F(5) (college support generally should terminate at the end of the first calendar year the student attends school if the child fails to maintain a GPA "in the median range or above"). *See also* Marriage of Moore, 702 N.W.2d 517 (Iowa App. 2005) (ending college support obligation in part due to the student's 1.92 GPA). Should it matter if the child has other resources or can obtain a college loan?

9. UIFSA establishes that the initial child support order governs the duration of the obligation. So, if the original order does not include a college support obligation, a court of another state modifying that order cannot award college support. *See* Schneider and Almgren, 268 P.3d 215 (Wash. 2011).

10. *Disabled Children*: There is a split of authority regarding a parent's obligation to support disabled children. In nine states, the support obligation ends when the child reaches the age of majority. The majority rule is that the support obligation can continue beyond the age of majority, but only if the child was disabled at that time. *See* TEX. FAM. CODE § 154.066(a)(4); Loza v. Marin, 198 So. 3d 1017 (Fla. App. 2016) (petition for adult support must be filed when the child is younger than 18). *See generally* Hays v. Alexander, 114 So.3d 704, 710 n. 9 (Miss. 2013) (King, J. dissenting) (citing to many state statutes and cases). A significant number of states have accepted a third view that a parent

can have a support obligation even if the child becomes disabled as an adult. *See generally*, Sande L. Buhai, *Parental Support of Adult Children with Disabilities*, 91 MINN. L. REV. 710 (2006–2007). Why have many states conditioned the continuing support obligation upon the disability arising before the child reaches the age of majority? *See, e.g.*, ARIZ. REV. STAT. § 25–320; DEL. CODE tit. 13 § 501; TEX. FAM. CODE § 154.001 (a).

3. The Obligor's Death

"[E]vidence of complete freedom of testation can be found only twice in history, viz., in Republican Rome and in England * * *." MAX WEBER, LAW IN ECONOMY AND SOCIETY 137 (Max Rheinstein ed. 1954).

WILLIAM BLACKSTONE, COMMENTARIES ON THE LAWS OF ENGLAND, BOOK I

(1765).

Our law has made no provision to prevent the disinheriting of children by will; leaving every man's property in his own disposal, upon a principle of liberty in this, as well as every other, action: though perhaps it had not been amiss, if the parent had been bound to leave them at the least a necessary subsistence. By the custom of London indeed, (which was formerly universal throughout the kingdom) the children of freemen are entitled to one third of their father's effects, to be equally divided among them; of which he cannot deprive them. And, among persons of any rank or fortune, a competence is generally provided for younger children, and the bulk of the estate settled upon the eldest, by the marriage-articles. Heirs also, and children, are favourites of our courts of justice, and cannot be disinherited by any dubious or ambiguous words; there being required the utmost certainty of the testator's intentions to take away the right of an heir.

Except for Louisiana, which follows the civil law approach, all American states maintain the common law approach described by Blackstone: parents are free to disinherit their child at will. The U.S. stance is atypical. In civil law countries, children are entitled to a "legitime" share of the parent's estate; only where the child has done something shocking (i.e., tried to kill the parent, etc.) is the legitime right forfeited. *See* George Pelletier & Michael Sonnenreich, *A Comparative Analysis of Civil Law of Succession*, 11 VILLANOVA L. REV. 323 (1966). The U.K. has now abandoned the common law rule that a decedent may disinherit his children; any needy child, whether a minor or adult, may petition the court for reasonable support from the decedent's estate. PROVISION FOR FAMILY & DEPENDANTS ACT, 1975, c. 63, 1(1)(a)–(e). The laws of New Zealand and Australia are similar. *See* JOHN DEGROOT & BRUCE NICKEL, FAMILY

PROVISION IN AUSTRALIA AND NEW ZEALAND (1993). Indeed, it now appears that, at least in the developed world, parents have the right to disinherit needy children only the United States and parts of Canada.

Despite academic criticism and law reform efforts, most states apply the common law approach to child support as well as inheritance. In these states, the death of the obligor terminates all support obligations. Professor Oldham has theorized that U.S. legislators have failed to respond to repeated criticisms of the common law approach because that approach reflects "American resistance to government control" and the fact that "American parents need a threat of disinheritance because * * * the American parent-child bond generally is weaker than that in other countries." In sum, Oldham sees the approach as based in "the extreme individualism of American culture." J. Thomas Oldham, *What Does the U.S. System Regarding Inheritance Rights of Children Reveal About American Families?*, 33 FAM. L.Q. 265, 272–73 (1999). Can you think of evidence from family law that supports Professor Oldham's claims? That tends to refute it? What other factors might be relevant to lawmakers' reluctance to overturn the traditional, common law approach?

In most U.S. states, a child support obligation ends when the obligor dies, even if the child has not reached the age of majority. A few states have abolished this rule, and consider the continuing child support obligations a claim on the decedent's estate. See TEX. FAM. CODE § 154.015. Which seems a more sensible rule?

C. RECIPROCITY: SHOULD ADULT CHILDREN SUPPORT THEIR PARENTS?

WILLIAM BLACKSTONE, COMMENTARIES ON THE LAWS OF ENGLAND, BOOK I
(1765).

3.   The *duties* of children to their parents arise from a principle of natural justice and retribution. For to those, who gave us existence, we naturally owe subjection and obedience during our minority, and honour and reverence ever after; they, who protected the weakness of our infancy, are entitled to our protection in the infirmity of their age; they who by sustenance and education have enabled their offspring to prosper, ought in return to be supported by that offspring, in case they stand in need of assistance. Upon this principle proceed all the duties of children to their parents, which are enjoined by positive laws. * * *

The law does not hold the tie of nature to be dissolved by any misbehaviour of the parent; and therefore a child is equally justifiable in defending the person, or maintaining the cause or suit, of a bad parent, as a good one; and is equally compellable, if of sufficient ability, to maintain and provide for a wicked and unnatural progenitor as for one who has strewn the greatest tenderness and parental piety.

In days not long past, the family constituted the primary economic safety net. Parents provided for their children when they were unable to provide for themselves and *vice versa*. The more children parents had, the more they paid to their "retirement fund" during their productive years and the greater their "pension" during old age. Today, the federal social security system has largely supplanted children's contributions as a source of support for the elderly. Of course, social security taxes paid by "children" indirectly fund benefits for parents. And many states continue to impose direct support responsibilities on children when parents are indigent.

CANNON V. JURAS
Oregon Court of Appeals, 1973.
15 Or. App. 265, 515 P.2d 428.

FOLEY, JUDGE.

Petitioner appeals from a "Final Order" * * * determining petitioner's liability in the amount of $384 to that agency for public assistance furnished his needy mother. We affirm.

Petitioner claims he is exempt from contribution under ORS § 416.030(2)(c) because he was abandoned or driven from the home as a child. The evidence was that petitioner, when 15 years of age, voluntarily began to work in logging camps. He returned home during his 16th year and found his mother living with a man. Claimant is not sure whether his mother was married to the man at that time or not. The man met petitioner at the door and refused to let him enter. Petitioner's mother was present, did not step forward or make any statement. Petitioner testified:

ATTORNEY: Okay, and what happened?

CLAIMANT: And a * * * well he met me at the door. He said that I wasn't welcome there and I said well I'm not going anywhere I'm not welcome and a * * * before that I'd worked in the shipyards and I'd paid the bills there because my mother said that she didn't get any help from her husband, her first husband. And so I had a little disagreement in the shipyards and I went somewhere else and I worked there and I still helped.

Petitioner further testified that he was allowed to return to obtain his belongings but did not again return to his mother's home until he was out of the Army several years later.

The hearing officer concluded that petitioner had emancipated himself and thus was not abandoned or deserted. We need not decide whether petitioner was emancipated. The only evidence of abandonment or desertion was that his mother did not take a stand when the man told him he was not welcome there at the home where his mother was living. We have previously held that

> * * * expulsion of the child from the home must have been accompanied with a bad purpose or wrongful intent on the part of the mother if petitioner is to be exempt.

Cheatham v. Juras, 11 Or. App. 108, 501 P.2d 988 (1972).

Petitioner presented no evidence to show his mother acted with a bad purpose or wrongful intent. The fact that the mother did not assert herself to overcome the man's refusal to welcome petitioner into the home occupied by herself and the putative stepfather is not a sufficient basis to conclude that she acted with a bad purpose or wrongful intent.

Petitioner's other contentions are without merit. Affirmed.

NOTES AND QUESTIONS

1. What justifies the imposition of support responsibilities in a case like *Cannon*? Should it matter that the child makes contributions to the Social Security system that indirectly fund government payments to the elderly? Should *Roe*-type defenses be available to an adult child from whom filial support is sought? If yes, is *Cannon* an appropriate case for such a defense?

2. Relative responsibility laws have survived a variety of constitutional challenges. *See, e.g.,* Swoap v. Superior Court of Sacramento County, 516 P.2d 840 (Cal. 1973); Americana Healthcare Center v. Randall, 513 N.W.2d 566 (S.D. 1994).

3. In 2001, thirty states had filial responsibility laws. *See* Seymour Moskowitz, *Filial Responsibility Statutes: Legal and Policy Considerations*, 9 J.L. & POL'Y 709 (2001) (listing and categorizing statutes); Katherine C. Pearson, *Filial Support Laws in the Modern Era; Domestic and International Comparison of Enforcement Practices for Laws Requiring Adult Children to Support Indigent Parents*, 20 ELDER L.J. 269 (2013). But the laws on the books are rarely utilized. One survey found eleven states with laws that seemingly "had never been invoked." *See* Katie Wise, Note, *Caring for Our Parents in an Aging World: Sharing Public and Private Responsibility for the Elderly*, 5 NYU J. LEGIS. & PUB. POL'Y 53, 574 (2001–02). Filial responsibility laws appear to be in decline worldwide, and "[m]ost industrialized countries have abolished their family responsibility laws altogether." *Id.* at 591. But these statutes sometimes have been enforced in recent decades. *See* Americana Healthcare Center v. Randall, 513 N.W.2d 566 (S.D. 1994); Prairie Lakes Health Care Sys. v. Wookey, 583 N.W.2d 405 (S.D. 1998) (son is liable for his parents' hospital bills of $70,091); Presbyterian Medical Center v. Budd, 832 A.2d 1066 (Pa. Super. 2003); Health Care & Retirement Corp. of America (HCA) v. Pittas, 46

A.3d 719 (Pa. Super. 2012) (son is liable for $92,943, the amount charged his mother for care at a skilled nursing facility).

4.   One survey of elderly American parents found that only about 10% believed that adult children should provide financial assistance to parents. *See* ALVIN SCHORR, "HONOR THY FATHER AND THY MOTHER . . . ": A SECOND LOOK AT FILIAL RESPONSIBILITY AND FAMILY POLICY 12 (U.S. Dept. of Health & Human Serv., Pub. No. 3–11953 (1980)). But when Singapore enacted a law requiring adult children to support their parents, many parents filed suit. *See* Peter Waldman, *In Singapore, Mother of All Lawsuits Is Often Filed by Mom*, WALL STREET J., Sept. 17, 1996, at A1 col. 4. What facts might explain this seeming difference in parental attitudes?

3.   CALCULATING SUPPORT: HOW MUCH WOULD PARENTS PAY?

A.   FROM DISCRETION TO BRIGHT-LINE RULES

UNIFORM MARRIAGE AND DIVORCE ACT § 309
9A U.L.A. 400 (1987).

In a proceeding for dissolution of marriage, legal separation, maintenance, or child support, the court may order either or both parents owing a duty of support to a child of the marriage to pay an amount reasonable or necessary for his support, without regard to marital misconduct, after considering all relevant factors including:

(1) the financial resources of the child; (2) the financial resources of the custodial parent; (3) the standard of living the child would have enjoyed had the marriage not been dissolved; (4) the physical and emotional condition of the child, and his educational needs; and (5) the financial resources and needs of the noncustodial parent.

The UMDA reflects the traditional, highly discretionary approach to determining the value of child support. Under this approach, the support statute sets out factors relevant to support determination; the court applies those factors and determines the amount of support to be paid.

While in most states the discretionary approach survives intact in alimony and property distribution law, discretion is now much more rigidly cabined in child support determination. The impetus for this shift has come from the federal government. The federal government's entrance into child support law, traditionally left to the states, was motivated by a rising tide of single parenting, children's poverty, and welfare dependence—plus national survey evidence showing that only three-fifths of parents eligible to receive child support had obtained support orders. Only about half of those awarded support received full payment. The average value of child support paid was less than half of what economists estimate as typical child-rearing costs and only 12% of average male earnings for that year. Research at the state level also documented considerable variation in award values, even among families of similar size and socioeconomic characteristics.

Marsha Garrison, *Autonomy or Community? An Evaluation of Two Models of Parental Obligation*, 86 CAL. L. REV. 31 (1998). Researchers also showed that child support eligibility was associated with a wide range of serious risks:

> More than half of children in mother-only households are poverty-stricken; in black and Hispanic mother-only households, more than two-thirds are poor. Children in single-parent households are also more likely to experience poor health, behavioral problems, delinquency, and low educational attainment than are their peers in intact families; as adults they have higher rates of poverty, early childbearing, and divorce. Moreover, although "the poor outcomes associated with growing up in a single-parent household do not result solely from reduced economic status, this factor appears to be the most important of the identifiable causes."

Id. In sum, the recent federal initiatives were motivated by the same concerns that produced the first support laws enacted in Elizabethan England. And, like the Poor Laws, the new rules reflect and reinforce public assistance principles. Thus, just as contemporary welfare law has abandoned individualized assessment of merit and need in favor of standardized eligibility criteria and grants, Congress required the states to replace discretionary child-support laws with standardized, numerical guidelines.

When Congress mandated the development of numerical support guidelines in the mid 1980s, it specified that they:

> 1.   Take into consideration all earnings and income of the absent parent;
>
> 2.   Be based on specific descriptive and numeric criteria and result in a computation of the support obligation; and
>
> 3.   Provide for the children's health care needs, through health insurance or other means.

45 C.F.R. § 302.56. But Congress did not specify a particular formula or model. As a result, each state was left to make its own decisions on the values that would guide the development of child support policy, how those values would be ordered, and how they would be implemented:

* * * Put more concretely, states had to resolve—explicitly or implicitly—these questions: To whom does the income of individual family members belong? Exactly what do parents owe their children and each other? What do they owe the public, that may be forced to pick up the tab for children's needs that parents have failed to meet?

As none of these questions have uncontroversial answers, one would expect spirited debate as well as a range of legislative outcomes. And in the early days of the guidelines movement scholars did offer legislators a variety of policy options.

Garrison, *supra,* at 57–58. Three basic approaches garnered the most attention:

(1) *Continuity of expenditure*: This approach seeks to ensure that the child receives the same proportion of total parental income that he or she would have received if the parents lived together. It relies on estimates of typical child-related outlay in intact families to derive a support percentage (calculated either on the basis of gross or net income), which is then prorated between the parents. Both the "percentage-of-obligor-income" and "income-shares" support models are based on a continuity-of-expenditure goal, but because these models incorporate different assumptions about child-related expense, they typically produce different awards.

(2) *Equal outcomes*: This approach (sometimes referred to as a "share the suffering" approach) seeks to ensure that each household in the separated family has the same living standard. It relies on a "household equivalence scale" to calculate the percentage of total family income needed by each family; the value of child support is the noncustodial parent's "excess" income.

(3) *Poverty prevention*: This approach focuses on ensuring that the child's basic needs, calculated from a minimal needs assessment such as the federal poverty thresholds or foster care reimbursement rates, are met. A needs standard, that does not vary by parental income level, is established and child support calculated on that basis. After the support need is established, it is prorated on the basis of parental income.

While these three approaches garnered the most attention, legislators could also have opted for a utilitarian model or one that aimed at ensuring the child an adequate, rather than minimal, income:

But while the range of policy options was extensive, policy debate was muted and rarely focused either on the underlying choice between individualist and sharing norms within the family or the ordering of community and familial obligation. * * * One reason for this constricted debate was the speed with which the guidelines movement came to fruition: Prior to 1984, when

Congress first required states to adopt advisory support guidelines, only a handful of states and localities utilized guidelines of any description; within a few months of the October 1989 deadline imposed by Congress, all states had adopted guidelines meeting the federal requirement. Perhaps unwittingly, the federal government also set the tone of the debate by commissioning an economic analysis of child-rearing costs; most states fell in line with this numbers-crunching approach. When the deadline passed and the dust settled, no state had adopted an equal-outcomes, utilitarian, or minimum-income approach. Three had adopted guidelines that took poverty prevention as their basic aim. All others adopted guidelines utilizing the continuity-of-expenditure approach. * * * Thus, despite the fact that the guidelines legislation evidenced no central philosophy and required no particular approach, all state guidelines today aim, to some extent, at maintaining continuity of expenditure; in a handful, poverty-prevention is also an articulated goal.

Id. at 59.

At the time guidelines were developed, no one seriously advocated that guidelines should attempt to *maintain* the child's standard of living. Although traditional, discretionary child support standards typically listed "the standard of living the child would have enjoyed had the marriage not been dissolved" (UMDA § 309) as a factor to be considered in determining child support, actual support awards almost invariably fell far short of what would be required to maintain the child's standard of living. One reason for this result is simply that two households cannot live as cheaply as one; thus the federal poverty level for a family of three is approximately 50% less than that of a family of one plus a family of two. *See* U.S. BUREAU OF THE CENSUS, POVERTY THRESHOLDS 2005, http://www.census.gov/hhes/www/poverty/. Divorce or separation therefore ensures that some portion of the divided family will experience a living standard loss. Because mothers typically earn less than fathers and obtain custody of the children 80–90% of the time, very large support transfers would typically be required to maintain the children's predivorce living standard.

To use an extreme example, consider the case of Mr. and Mrs. A, who have six minor children and an annual income of $30,000, all earned by Mr. A. If Mrs. A assumes sole custody of the children post-divorce and continues to earn no income, ensuring that the children suffer no living standard loss would require a transfer of $26,763, or 89% of Mr. A's income, leaving him with only $3237 to meet his own needs![1] A law requiring

---

[1] The support obligation is calculated using the "household equivalence scale" contained in the U.S. Bureau of Labor Standards moderate income budgets. For more on household equivalence scales, *see* Burt Barnow, *Economic Studies of Expenditures on Children and Their Relationship to Child Support Guidelines*, at p. 888.

transfers of this magnitude would produce several practical problems. One is enforcement. Researchers report, not surprisingly, that higher support obligations tend to produce a lower percentage of support paid. Even if Mr. A could somehow be forced to pay up, his incentive to keep earning $30,000 per year would be small; why should he work hard to retain only 10%, or even 25%, of his income? Because high support obligations produce significant payment and work disincentives, it is unfeasible, in a case like that of the A's, to maintain the child's former standard of living.

All guidelines—no matter what their goals and methodology—must deal with these practical concerns. A guideline must preserve work incentives for both parents. It must be enforceable as well as fair.

JANE C. VENOHR & ROBERT G. WILLIAMS, THE IMPLEMENTATION AND PERIODIC REVIEW OF STATE CHILD SUPPORT GUIDELINES
33 FAM. L.Q. 7, 10–18 (1999).

1. *Percentage-of-Obligor-Income*

The Percentage of Obligor Income model is the simplest of the four formulas. It determines the child support order amount by applying a state-determined percentage to obligor income. * * * [The model can be applied to gross or net income.] Most Percentage of Obligor Income states using gross income follow Wisconsin's model, which was one of the earliest formulas implemented. It applies the following percentages to obligor gross income for one, two, and three children:

One child	17 percent
Two children	25 percent
Three children	29 percent

* * *

Generally, Percentage of Obligor Income states using net income apply higher percentages to compensate for the impact of taxes. For example, Minnesota applies the following percentages to obligor net incomes above $1,001 per month for one, two and three children.

One child	25 percent
Two children	30 percent
Three children	35 percent

Minnesota applies lower percentages to obligor net incomes of $1,000 or less. Two other Percentage of Obligor Income states (Arkansas and North Dakota) also apply a varying percentage of net income.

2.   *Income Shares Model*

The Income Shares model * * * [begins with an] estimate of actual child-rearing expenditures in an intact family [which] forms the basic child support obligation. * * * [T]he basic child support obligation is prorated according to each parent's income. Barring adjustments for child care, medical expenses, or other factors, the nonresidential parent's prorated share is the amount of the child support ordered. * * * All but a handful of the Income Shares states * * * adopted the prototype Income Share model * * * [using] estimates of child-rearing expenditures * * * derived from a study * * * by Dr. Thomas Espenshade based on data from the 1972–73 Consumer Expenditure Survey. * * * [M]any of these states subsequently updated their child support schedules for more recent estimates of child-rearing expenditures developed by Dr. David Betson.

* * *

The Income Shares model can be based on net or gross income. * * * [M]ore than half of Income Shares states base the child support calculation on gross income, with the remainder starting from net. The end result of the calculation differs little because the tables used in gross income states take into account the impact of federal and state income taxes, FICA, and the earned income tax credit.

3.   *Melson Formula*

* * * The Melson formula calculates child support in three steps:

Step 1: Provide for Each Parent's Minimal Self Support Needs. After determining net income for each parent, a self-support reserve (also called a "primary support allowance") is subtracted from each parent's income. The purpose of the self-support reserve is to allow each parent enough income to maintain subsistence. Typically, the reserve amount is near the federal poverty level for one person. Current, for example, Delaware sets the self-support reserve at $750 per month.

Step 2: Provide for Children's Primary Support Needs. Each parent's income less the self-support reserve is applied to the child support obligation calculation. First, the primary support needs of the child are considered. Similar to the self-support reserve for the parents, the primary support needs of the child represents the minimum amount required to provide a subsistence living for the child. The current levels are:

One child	$210
Two children	$575
Three children	$815

Actual amounts for child care and children's extraordinary medical expenses are added to the above amounts to obtain the total primary support needs. The total primary support needs of the child are prorated to each parent according to his or her share of the combined income.

Step 3: Determine Standard of Living Allowances (SOLA): To the extent that either parent has income available after covering the self-support reserve and his or her share of the child's primary support needs, an additional percentage (the SOLA) of the remaining income is applied to the child support obligation. The current SOLA amounts for one, two, and three children in Delaware are listed below:

One child	16 percent
Two children	26 percent
Three children	33 percent

A total child support obligation for each parent is determined by adding the amounts in Steps 2 and 3. The residential parent is assumed to spend his or her obligation directly on the child. The nonresidential parent's share is payable as child support.

* * *

4.   *Percentage of Obligor Income Hybrid*

Massachusetts and the District of Columbia implement a hybrid of the Percentage of Obligor Income and Income Shares models. If obligee income is below a specified threshold, a Percentage of Obligor Income model is applied. If obligee income is above the specified threshold, an Income Shares approach is used.

In Massachusetts, obligee gross income net of child care expenses must be greater than [$20,000] before obligee income is considered in the child support calculation. The District of Columbia has set the threshold somewhat lower. * * *

NOTES AND QUESTIONS

1.   *Implementation Trends:* By 2013, 39 states used an income-shares guideline, 9 used the percentage of obligor's income, and 3 used the Melson Formula. *See generally* Jane C. Venohr, *Child Support Guidelines and Guidelines Reviews; State Differences and Common Issues,* 47 FAM. L. Q. 327, 329–30 (2013). For citations to the guidelines in each state, *see generally* LAURA W. MORGAN, CHILD SUPPORT GUIDELINES: INTERPRETATION AND APPLICATION (2010), Table 1–1, at page 1–13.

2.   Income-shares and Melson-type guidelines typically rely on income schedules and worksheets. For example, as set forth below, Table 1 contains an excerpt from an income-shares schedule and Figure 1 shows how the schedule is used to arrive at a child support award.

Table 1. Excerpt of the Oregon Income Shares Schedule.

Combined Adjusted Monthly Gross Income	One Child	Two Children	Three Children	Four Children	Five Children
4000.00	672	932	1,069	1,192	1,113
4050.00	678	940	1,077	1,201	1.321
4100.00	684	947	1,086	1,210	1,332
4150.00	689	955	1,094	1,220	1,342
4200.00	695	962	1,102	1,229	1,352
4250.00	700	970	1,111	1,238	1,362
4300.00	706	978	1,119	1,248	1,372
4350.00	712	985	1,127	1,257	1,382
4400.00	717	993	1,135	1,266	1,393

Figure 1. Example of an Income Shares Guidelines Calculation Using 2003 Median Earnings and the Oregon Income Shares Schedule.

		Mother		Father		Combined
1.	Gross Monthly Income	$1,762		$2,631	=	$4,393
2.	Each Parent's Share	40%	+	60%	=	100%
3.	Expenditures on Children in Intact Family (One child amount from schedule in Table 1)			$ 717		
4.	Each Parent's Share of Obligation (Each parent's Line 2 x Line 3 Combined)	$ 287	+	$ 430	=	$ 717

Reprinted from Jane C. Venohr & Tracy E. Griffith, *Child Support Guidelines: Issues and Reviews*, 43 FAM. CT. REV. 415 (2005).

     3.   *Deviation:* Under federal law, all state guidelines must establish a *presumptive* award. 42 U.S.C. § 667(b)(2) requires that "[t]here shall be a rebuttable presumption * * * that the amount of the award which would result from the application of such guidelines is the correct amount of child support to be awarded. A written finding or specific finding on the record that the application of the guidelines would be unjust or inappropriate in a particular case, as determined under criteria established by the State, shall be sufficient to rebut the presumption in that case." *See also* 45 C.F.R. § 302.56(f). Judges

are thus free to depart from the guideline if they make written findings describing the basis for a deviation. Many state guidelines contain lists of factors that might justify deviation, including: the child's special needs, an obligation to support children from prior relationships, a large amount of debt, unusually high living expenses, a needy family member, or substantial expenses incurred in connection with visiting the child (which could occur if the custodial parent lives a significant distance from the obligor).

The fact that most states utilize an income-shares methodology does not mean that presumptive awards are consistent. Because of variation in the definition of income, the percentages used to calculate support, and "add-ons" to the basic support value, income-shares guidelines produce wildly different results. Thus a review of 1997 guidelines reports, for a sample middle-income case, that the highest presumptive award ($1,054) was in Nebraska, an income-shares state, and that the second lowest ($604) was in Kentucky, another income-shares state. *See* Laura W. Morgan & Mark C. Lino, *A Comparison of Child Support Awards Calculated Under States Child Support Guidelines with Expenditures on Children Calculated by the U.S. Department of Agriculture*, 33 FAM. L.Q. 191, 209 tbl. 4 (1999). A more recent comparison found similar variation in award amounts among states. See Jane C Venohr, *Difference in State Child Support Guidelines Amounts: Guidelines Models, Economic Basis, and Other Issues*, 29 J. AM. ACAD. MAT. LAW. 377 (2017).

Empirical evidence also suggests that judges in some states deviate from the presumptive guideline values frequently. State surveys report deviation in anywhere from 10% to more than 60% of cases. *See* David Arnaudo, *Deviation from State Child Support Guidelines, in* CHILD SUPPORT GUIDELINES: THE NEXT GENERATION 85, 88–94 (Margaret Campbell Haynes ed. 1994) (describing and summarizing research). Most deviation is downward. *Id.* (88% of deviations downward in Kansas survey; 85% in Washington survey; 80% in Colorado survey). What facts might explain the high rate of deviation and its typical direction?

If the child has special needs, a court may well order support above the guideline amounts, unless the obligor is poor. *See* Carver v. Carver, 488 S.W.3d 585 (Ky. 2016).

Sometimes a primary custodian might be willing to agree that the other parent will not have a child support obligation as long as he or she seeks no contact with the child. A court usually will not enforce such a waiver. *See* Perkinson v. Perkinson, 989 N.E.2d 758 (Ind. 2013) (contrary to public policy).

4. *Adjustments:* Most guidelines require adjustment of the basic award.

a. *Child Care:* While the percentage-of-income model does not typically take child-care expenses into account in computing the support obligation, income shares guidelines almost invariably treat work-related, child-care expenses as a mandatory "add-on" to the basic child support obligation. Under this approach, "reasonable" work-related expenses are typically prorated in accordance with the parents' relative proportion of family income; the obligor's portion is added to his basic support obligation. In 2005, 30 states treated child-care expenses as a mandatory add-on; in four additional states, the guideline treated these expenses as a permissive add-on. *See* Linda D. Elrod & Robert G. Spector, *A Review of the Year in Family Law: Same-Sex Marriage Issue Dominates Headlines*, 38 FAM. L.Q. 865 chart 3 (2005). *See also* LAURA W. MORGAN, CHILD SUPPORT GUIDELINES: INTERPRETATION AND APPLICATION § 3.02[b] (2010). Significant issues relating to child care include: (1) whether to factor in the federal tax credit; (2) whether to include child-care expenses related to a job search; (3) whether to limit consideration of such expenses (i.e. define "reasonable" costs); and (4) how to take into account direct expenditures for child care by the noncustodial parent.

b.   *Extraordinary Medical Expenses:* In 2006, all but two state guidelines had special provisions relating to extraordinary medical expenses. Most states mandated adjustment of the basic support order to take account of such expenses, typically by prorating expenses in accordance with parental income. *See* Laura W. Morgan, *Child Support Guidelines*, 39 FAM. L.Q. 919 chart 3 (2006). *See also* Laura Morgan, *supra,* § 3.01[b]. A primary problem in determining whether an adjustment is warranted is determining what level of expense is extraordinary: "A few states describe the type of services; others set a dollar amount. A few define the type of service or illness as well as the amount. Others leave it totally to the decision maker's discretion." Linda Henry Elrod, *Adding to the Basic Support Obligation, in* CHILD SUPPORT GUIDELINES: THE NEXT GENERATION 62, 64 (Margaret Campbell Haynes ed. 1994).

c.   *Health Insurance:* Federal regulations require state guidelines to provide for children's health care needs through health insurance or other means. Based on this mandate, many state guidelines provide a credit to the parent who funds health insurance or otherwise prorate health insurance costs. *See* Laura Morgan, *supra,* § 3.01 [a]. 29 U.S.C. § 1169 also requires group insurance plans to honor a qualified medical child support order (QMCSO) issued by a divorce court.

5.   *Case Processing:* Although administrative proceedings are sometimes used to prepare orders for judicial approval, American child support orders are still typically made by courts. Internationally, the trend is toward administrative case processing due to its lower cost both to government and the parties. Some states have begun to experiment with administrative processing of child support cases. State high courts have disagreed on the constitutionality of administrative proceedings. *Compare* State v. Gocha, 555 N.W.2d 683 (Iowa 1996) (administrative processing constitutional) *with* Seubert v. Seubert, 301 Mont. 382, 13 P.3d 365 (2000) (administrative processing violated state constitution's separation of powers provisions). The success of administrative case processing may depend on the extent of

discretion available and the guideline's complexity. In England, for example, administrative processing using a complicated formula produced a high incidence of miscalculated awards, with resulting public criticism. *See* J. Thomas Oldham, *Lessons from the New English and Australian Child Support Systems,* 29 VAND. J. TRANSNAT'L L. 691 (1996).

6.   *Popularity of the Income Shares Method:* Most states now utilize the income shares approach. Is it clear why this is true? Australia, which had adopted a percentage of obligor income approach, replaced it with an income shares guideline in 2008. The chair of the committee that recommended the change emphasized that, among other things, (i) the income shares approach incorporated the evidence that parents spend a lower percentage of their income on their children as their income increases, and (ii) the income shares approach considers the income of both parents. *See* Patrick Parkinson, *The Future of Child Support,* 33 U. WEST AUST. L. REV. 179 (2006–2007).

7.   *State vs. Federal:* Many experts believe that a federal guideline is needed to ensure uniformity and preclude forum shopping:

> The advantage of a federal formula related to the father's ability to pay may be substantial. It would provide uniformity (with appropriate adjustments for local factors) and consequently fairness throughout the country, and it would assure that absent fathers are not asked to pay too little or too much. The latter possibility is of equally crucial importance as the former. The total impact of a support order that is pegged too high may be productive of more mischief than if no support order were entered at all. If a support obligation to a first family is imposed that would make it difficult or impossible for the father to meet his other obligations, the net result may be two families on welfare instead of one. This would produce a greater ultimate cost to the taxpayer in terms of welfare dollars spent than if the taxpayer undertook to take care of the first family, not to speak of the social cost of the disarray that would be caused by breaking up the father's new family.

Harry D. Krause, Review of Part X, Child Support, 92d Cong., 2d Sess., Soc. Sec. Amend. of 1972, Committee on Finance, U.S. Senate, H.R. 1 (unpublished consultant's paper, at 52–53). Is Professor Krause correct that a federal guideline would ensure that "absent fathers are not asked to pay too little or too much"?

8.   *U.S. Guidelines in International Context:* Child support guidelines are not a uniquely American phenomenon. But the amount of support sought under guidelines varies widely:

> The amount of income sought from absent parents obviously has some relation to the level of public support for single-parent families. In countries with minimal public support programs for such families, like Australia and the United States, the percentage chosen is relatively high. In other countries with more substantial public

support programs for such families, such as Denmark or Sweden, the percentage chosen has been lower. For example, a Danish absent parent with an average income of about $40,000 pays 4% of his gross income as child support for one child. Similarly, in Sweden the average child support order for one child amounts to about 6% of the obligor's gross income. Germany has adopted a level of support somewhere between the levels sought in Australia and those found in Scandinavia. A German obligor is asked to pay between 10–15% of his net income as child support for two children.

Oldham, *supra* note 5, at 711. Is the pattern described by Professor Oldham consistent with filial responsibility trends? If yes, what are the pros and cons of substituting public for private child support obligations? Put somewhat differently, should public and private responsibilities for the elderly and for children be consistent: How does public support for the elderly differ from public child support? Are these differences adequate to justify different levels of public support?

9. In a few states the amount of child support due depends on the age of the child, based on the assumption that older children are more expensive than younger children. Is this a good idea?

10. *Guidelines and Children in College:* The amount of child support due while a child is attending college should not be determined solely based on guidelines. *See* Jacoby v. Jacoby, 47 A.3d 40 (N.J. Super. App. Div. 2012). In Hudson v. Hudson, 719 A.2d 211 (N.J. Super. App. Div. 1998) the court stated that "child support and contribution to college expenses are two discrete yet related obligations imposed on parents." *See also* Madeline Marzano-Lesnevich & Scott Adam Laterra, *Child Support and College: What is the Correct Result?* 22 J. AM. ACAD. MAT. LAW. 335 (2009).

Problem 17-1:

Recalculate the child support obligation for the couple shown in note 2 using: (a) the Delaware Melson formula; (b) the Wisconsin percentage-of-income model; (c) the Minnesota formula. Assume that mother has monthly child-care expenses of $300 per month.

Problem 17-2:

Assume that father will be the custodial parent and that his child care expenses are identical to mother's. Calculate mother's support obligation under: (a) the Delaware Melson formula; (b) the Wisconsin percentage of income model; (c) the Minnesota formula; (d) the income shares guideline shown in note 2.

B. APPLYING THE GUIDELINES: RECURRING CASES

1. Obligor Wealth

McGINLEY V. HERMAN

California Court of Appeals, 1996.
50 Cal. App. 4th 936, 57 Cal. Rptr. 2d 921.

MASTERSON, ASSOCIATE JUSTICE.

financial evidence

Children are entitled to share in the standard of living of both parents. To this end a presumption exists that the amount of a child support award is determined pursuant to uniform guidelines. However, the presumption may be rebutted if one of the parents has an "extraordinarily high income." In this case, after finding that the father had an extraordinarily high income, the court awarded child support in an amount that did not relate to the father's standard of living in any meaningful way. We find this award to constitute an abuse of discretion. Accordingly, on the mother's appeal asserting that the amount of support awarded from the father was inadequate, we reverse and remand for a new support determination.

In February 1994, Lori McGinley filed a complaint to establish that Stan Herman is the father of her child, born out of wedlock in January 1993, and for child support. In an accompanying income and expense declaration, McGinley stated that she had a monthly net disposable income of $400 and expenses of $7,627 per month. She sought support from Herman, who she claimed to be "one of the most successful real estate agents in the entire Los Angeles area," in an unspecified amount to be established under the uniform child support guidelines.

In response, Herman admitted paternity and agreed to pay "reasonable child support based on the 18 month old minor child's reasonable needs." He declared that, as a real estate investor, he recently suffered substantial losses due to the downturn in the real estate market and the Northridge earthquake. His income and expense statement indicated an "average cash flow deficit of $42,532." Herman submitted evidence, including the declaration of a certified public accountant, in support of this figure. Herman's evidence placed his "living expenses" at $31,457 a month. Herman also disputed several of McGinley's claimed expenses.

In reply, McGinley submitted the declaration of a certified public account who, based on an examination of Herman's business records, concluded that Herman's net worth was over $11 million, that his living expenses were $80,390 per month, and that he had $116,256 "cash available for support" each month. Utilizing the latter figure, the accountant calculated Herman's monthly support obligation under the uniform guidelines at $14,617. McGinley requested support in this amount.

The only evidence taken at trial concerned McGinley's lifestyle. McGinley testified that she did not graduate from high school. She is not employed and is studying to get a real estate license. She owns a house that she rents out and lives with her child in a 600 square foot apartment which is next to a busy highway. McGinley described the expenses she incurs for the child's preschool, swim lessons, and baby-sitting. She would like to live somewhere with a backyard in which the child can play.

McGinley argued to the court that, under controlling law, her child was entitled to be supported in a manner that reflected the lifestyle of his father. Herman argued that a monthly award of $1,500, with an additional $500 per month into a blocked account for college expenses, would meet the child's present actual needs, espccially since he is not yet in school or involved in other activities.

In making its ruling, the trial court stated that it would be "nonsensical" to award McGinley the guidelines amount of child support based on a "casual relationship that result[ed] in the birth of a child." The court stated that a support figure of $2,000 "came to mind, because we have a lot of cases like this. And that's usually been the real limits that I've seen." The court further stated that, "without a specific finding as to the exact amount, [Herman] has an extraordinarily high earning capacity and/or real income." The court also found that McGinley has a net disposable income of zero.

Based on these and other findings discussed *infra*, the trial court awarded monthly child support of $1,750, with an additional $400 per month for one-half of McGinley's child care expenses, for a total of $2,150.

* * * We find that the trial court's discretion was not exercised along legal lines. We therefore reverse and remand for a new support determination

This case is governed by the Statewide Uniform Child Support Guidelines * * *. Under these guidelines, the interests of the child are given "top priority." (§ 4053, subd. (e).) "Children should share in the standard of living of both parents. Child support may therefore appropriately improve the standard of living of the custodial household to improve the lives of the children." (§ 4053, subd. (f).) The guidelines set forth a complex formula for determining child support based on the circumstances of the parents and child. The support amount rendered under the guidelines formula "is intended to be presumptively correct in all cases . . . " (§ 4053, subd. (k)). This presumption may, however, be rebutted by evidence of various factors, including that [t]he parent being ordered to pay child support has an extraordinarily high income and the amount determined under the formula would exceed the needs of the children.

Long before these principles were incorporated into statute, it was well established that "[a] child, legitimate or illegitimate, is entitled to be supported in a style and condition consonant with the position in society of its parents." "The father's duty of support for his children does not end with the furnishing of mere necessities if he is able to afford more."

McGinley places great reliance on two more recent cases that have applied these principles, albeit before the uniform child support guidelines were enacted—*In re Marriage of Catalano*, 204 Cal. App. 3d 543, 251 Cal. Rptr. 370 (1988) and *In re Marriage of Hubner*, 205 Cal. App. 3d 660, 252 Cal. Rptr. 428 (1988). In *Catalano,* the mother sought an increase in child support from $475 to $2,000 per month. The trial court increased the amount to $1,110 and both parents appealed. The father was concededly wealthy, owning at least two residences and numerous automobiles, including a Rolls Royce. The mother's lifestyle had been in decline since separation from the father, resulting in the need for her to invade capital.[4] The court observed that "[a] child's 'need' for more than the bare necessities . . . varies with the parents' circumstances. Accordingly, where the supporting parent enjoys a lifestyle that far exceeds that of the custodial parent, child support must to some degree reflect the more opulent lifestyle even though this may, as a practical matter, produce a benefit for the custodial parent." The *Catalano* court found that, under the circumstances presented, "the only tolerable award would be the full $2,000 that [the mother] requested. Anything less would ignore the tremendous disparity between [the child's] lifestyle and that of his father."

In *Hubner*, the mother's net disposable monthly income was $1,000 and the father's was over $43,000. The support guidelines then in effect were discretionary and included a statement of "legislative intent that children share in their parents' standard of living." Pursuant to a schedule developed under these guidelines, the mother asked for child support of not less than $6,000 a month.

The trial court awarded $2,215, finding that " 'the child's standard of living must be based on the reasonable lifestyle of both parents. . . [I]t would be inappropriate for the court to make an order which was a disguised form of support for the [mother] herself as opposed to support directed merely toward the child.' " On appeal, the mother argued that the award was inadequate because it was less than half of the discretionary guideline amount. Without stating what a proper support payment would be, the *Hubner* court held that the support award of $2,215 constituted an abuse of discretion. In explaining its holding the court found that, "at least where the ability of the noncustodial parent to pay a high level of child support is undisputed, and that level is also consistent with the guidelines, the inability of the custodial parent to make a meaningful financial contribution should not significantly affect the level of support ordered."

---

[4]   Evidence was presented in this case that Herman had recently purchased (and sold) a Bentley automobile, and that McGinley was invading capital for living expenses.

It would be difficult to imagine any greater discrepancy between a mother's and father's assessment of the father's earnings than exists here. Scant evidence was presented. Thus, we must assume that the trial court considered Herman's income to be the amount reflected in the declaration of McGinley's accountant—i.e., $116,256 a month, or just under $1.4 million a year.

The only basis that we can glean from the record for an award amount of $2,150 is the trial court's comment that this figure "came to mind, because we have a lot of cases like this. And that's usually been the real limits that I've seen." As we view the law, reliance on what has *"usually been the real limits"* is the antithesis of how a trial court should approach what is, by statutory definition, an *extraordinary* situation. The reason that the presumptive guideline amount of support may be rebutted by extraordinarily high earning is set forth in the second clause of the statute: "the amount determined under the formula would exceed the needs of the children." (§ 4057, subd.(b)(3).) Thus, rather than relying on the usual, the trial court must at least approximate at what point the support amount calculated under the formula would exceed the children's needs, and therefore at what point the income of the party paying support becomes extraordinarily high.

We think it no more than common sense that a parent who rebuts the guidelines support presumption because of an extraordinarily high income not be permitted to pay less support than a parent whose income is not extraordinarily high. Because of the lack of meaningful findings in this case, we have no way of ascertaining the level of income which must have been imputed to Herman in order to yield a figure of $2,150 monthly child support under the guidelines formula. What we can say with certainty is that, if this imputed amount of income were less than the level of income that could properly be considered extraordinarily high, the support award of $2,150 would be prima facie inadequate.

We note that the trial court found that its support award was "consistent with the best interest of the child."

Nonetheless, this conclusionary finding falls far short of providing *reasons* why the level of support that the trial court awarded is consistent with the child's interests as required by § 4056, subd. (a)(3).

As with our conclusion regarding the finding specified in § 4056, subd. (a)(1), we do not hold that the trial court's failure to comply with subd. (a)(3) of the statute is necessarily fatal. However, in this case it would appear that the trial court's assessment of the best interests of the child did not give sufficient consideration to the child's right to share in the standard of living of his extraordinarily high earning father. For example, in *In re Marriage of Hubner, supra,* a support award of $2,215 a month was considered so low as to constitute an abuse of discretion in the case of a father whose annual income was in excess of $500,000. In *Estevez v. Superior Court*, 22 Cal. App. 4th 423, 27 Cal. Rptr. 2d 470, a monthly support package in excess of $14,000 was provided by a father who conceded that his gross income was over $1.4 million a year.

Utilizing *Hubner* as our guidepost, it is clear that the child support award in this case constituted an abuse of discretion. We will not, however, fathom a guess as to the dollar amounts that define the parameters of this discretion. A proper exercise of discretion in this case would require a statement of the reason(s) why a given amount of support awarded would meet the needs of Herman and McGinley's child. It is not enough to simply say that, because the presumption of the guidelines has been rebutted, the "usual" amount of support should be awarded. Moreover, a satisfactory reason for determining that a support award would be adequate requires at least an approximation of Herman's net disposable monthly income and of the point at which that income became extraordinarily high. Without these findings, the support award might be set in an amount lower than that required of an ordinarily high earner, thus according Herman an undue advantage from his ability to rebut the guidelines presumption based on his extraordinarily high earnings. We remand the matter to the trial court to reassess McGinley's support request under the appropriate criteria.

The order under review is reversed and the matter is remanded for a new support determination. McGinley to recover costs on appeal.

NOTES AND QUESTIONS

1.   The *McGinley* court says that "children are entitled to share in the standard of living of both parents" and that the California guideline does not apply to all income when the noncustodial parent's income is "extraordinarily high." Are these two statements consistent? What does it mean in this context that the child, who will be living with the mother, should be able to "share in the standard of living of both parents?" It can't mean that the standards of living in both households will be the same, can it? If it doesn't mean that, what does it mean?

2.   The federal Department of Health and Human Services has specified that:

> The [Family Support] Act clearly requires guidelines to be used as a rebuttable presumption in any judicial or administrative proceeding for the award of child support. Therefore * * * *States may not simply exempt an entire category of cases with incomes above or below a specific dollar level from application of the guidelines.*

56 Fed. Reg. 22343 (May 15, 1991) (emphasis added). Does *McGinley* comply with the federal standard? How?

3.   What factual and policy assumptions underlie a decision that the rich parent owes a smaller percentage of his income in child support? Are those assumptions sound?

4.   The trial court in *McGinley* appeared reluctant to award substantial child support in this situation. Can you guess why?

5.   Assuming that rich parents should pay a smaller percentage of their incomes in child support than other parents, how should a court calculate the obligation?

a.   A 2005 review of the California case law indicates that "[t]hus far, no California case has specified the minimum annual income level that qualifies as extraordinarily high income under the statute. However, a review of all the relevant reported cases appears to establish clearly that an annual income in the range of $1.4 million brings the payor parent squarely within the purview of Section 4057(b)(3). * * * [F]or a payor whose annual income is $1 million, a guideline child support award for one child will be approximately $6,300 per month." Dennis M. Wasser & Bruce E. Cooperman, *Million Dollar Babies: The Family Code Anticipates That in Extraordinarily High-Income Cases Guideline Child Support May Exceed the Needs of the Children*, LOS ANGELES LAWYER 36 (Feb. 2005).

b.   In *McGinley*, the custodial mother alleged that the noncustodial father earned $116,000 per month and asked for "only" $14,617 per month. In the *Estevez* case cited in *McGinley*, monthly support in excess of $14,000 was ordered when the father, actor Emilio Estevez, conceded that his gross income was over $1.4 million a year (or at least $116,000 per month). Can you guess where the *McGinley* plaintiff's $14,000 figure came from? Precedent aside, why is 10% of gross income an appropriate support percentage for a very wealthy obligor? Would it be unreasonable, if the court accepted the evidence that Mr. Herman's monthly living expenses were $80,000, to order monthly child support of $23,000? Would it be unreasonable to order support at less than $14,000?

c.   What expenses are relevant? If the parents had lived together, presumably the court would attempt to determine what amount would be needed to maintain that standard of living after the parties separated. But what should the standard be when the parents have never shared the same household? Should the child support order be fashioned so that the mother could move to a better neighborhood? If so, how much better, and to what type of home? Should the court assume the woman would rent a house or buy a house? Should the order include the cost of private school? A full-time nanny? A new car? Riding lessons? A horse? A stable? In Ciampa v. Ciampa, 415 S.W.3d 97 (Ky. App. 2013) the father was an oral surgeon and the mother was the primary caretaker of their 3 children. The father's annual income was $817,000. In her request for support, the mother asked for funds to pay for a horse, a nutritionist, and a personal trainer, which the court rejected. In S. P. v. F. G., 208 Cal. Rptr. 3d 903 (App. 2016) the father's net worth exceeded $400 million and the parties had never lived together. The trial court awarded $14,840 in monthly child support, not accepting the mother's request for $78,000, and this was affirmed. *See generally* Laura Raatjes, *High-Income Child Support Guidelines: Harmonizing the Need for Limits With the Best Interests of the Child*, 86 CHI.-KENT L. REV. 317 (2011). *Cf. In re* Marriage of Left, 2016 WL 816090 (Cal. App.) (unpublished) (affirming a child support monthly award of $37,500).

d.   The *McGinley* trial court initially awarded $2,215 per month based on a finding that "it would be inappropriate for the court to make an order which was a disguised form of support for the [mother] herself as opposed to support directed merely toward the child." On remand, may the court take benefits conferred on the custodial parent into account? Should such benefits be relevant? How can the court allow the child to "share in the father's standard of living" without providing benefits to the mother?

e.   The trial court noted the "casual relationship" between the parties as another basis for its award. On remand, may the court take the nature of the relationship and its duration into account? Should the parents' relationship affect the support obligation? Can you imagine why the trial court was reluctant to grant substantial support for a child who was the result of a brief intimate relationship?

f.   Assume that you are the trial court judge to whom the *McGinley* case is remanded and that you find the mother's allegations regarding the father's income and expenses are accurate. What child support will you order? How will you justify your decision?

g.   It was mentioned above that one concern in a case like *McGinley* is the child should "share in the standard of living of both parents." What if the wealthy parent lives a frugal lifestyle? Is this a factor that should result in a lower support amount? *See* Schieffer v. Schieffer, 826 N.W.2d 627 (S.D. 2013) (yes).

6.   *Child Support Trusts:* Many state courts and some state legislatures, have authorized the use of child support trusts to secure the child's right to support in cases where the obligor's high earning potential may be short-lived or his income variable. Some states have specific statutes which expressly authorize the family court to impose a trust on property to ensure payment of child support. For example, WIS. STAT. § 767.25(2) provides that "(t)he court may protect and promote the best interests of the minor children by setting aside a portion of the child support which either party is ordered to pay in a separate fund or trust for the support, education and welfare of such children."

7. *Defining Income:* Wealthy obligors often have unusual forms of income such as stock options and expense accounts. State definitions of income and allowable deductions from income vary substantially. When the guideline itself is silent, the court must determine whether the particular benefit should be classified as income and how to value it. Many courts, including California's, have employed their discretion expansively. *See, e.g.,* Cheriton v. Fraser, 111 Cal. Rptr. 2d 755 (App. 2001) (multimillion dollar stock options were includible in income). *See generally* Annot., *Excessiveness or Adequacy of Money Awarded as Child Support*, 27 A.L.R.4th 864, 880–881, § 4 (1984) & 2012 Supp. at 145–153.

Guideline definitions of income and allowable deductions are not necessarily consistent with tax law definitions. Courts have generally held that consistency is not required. *See e.g.,* Turner v. Turner, 586 A.2d 1182 (Del. 1991); *In re* Sullivan, 794 P.2d 687 (Mont. 1990). *Should* tax and child support laws employ consistent definitions of income and expenses? Why?

8. *Imputing Income:* In cases where the obligor has substantial property but low income, courts have sometimes based the support obligation on assets as well as income. *See, e.g.,* County of Kern v. Castle, 89 Cal. Rptr. 2d 874 (App. 1999) (inheritance should have been taken into account in determining support obligation); *In re* Marriage of Dacumos, 90 Cal. Rptr. 2d 159 (App. 1999) (rental income imputed to obligor based on the fair market value of his real property and his net equity in it, despite the fact that those rental properties were actually losing money).

Chapter 20 will discuss whether a support award should be reduced, after the original order is issued, if an obligor's income decreases as a result of some choice by the obligor. A related point is whether a divorced parent's original support obligation should be based on his or her *actual* income, or his or her earning *potential*. For example, in Armbrister v. Armbrister, 2011 WL 5830466 (Tenn. App.), the husband had a law degree and an MBA. Throughout most of the marriage, the husband ran a performing arts camp. At divorce, he testified that he was earning $2750 per month. In Robinson v. Tyson, 461 S.E.2d 397 (S.C. App. 1995) at divorce the father was a lawyer who represented poor people, and he earned $700 per month. In both instances their wives argued they were "underemployed" and their child support obligations should be based on their earning *potential,* not their actual earnings. How should a court rule in these situations? Is the issue whether the parent is pursuing his or her career path in good faith? Or does a divorcing parent have the obligation to maximize his or her earning potential?

9. In Australia, which until recently employed a percentage-of-income type support guideline, obligor income in excess of 250% of the average Australian wage was ignored. In Texas, for an obligor with a monthly income of $7,500 or more, a support order cannot exceed the guideline value for $7,500 unless the child has additional "proven needs." TEX. FAM. CODE § 154.126. And you already learned that, in Pennsylvania, when parents' combined net income exceeds $15,000 per month, child support is calculated based on the *Melzer*

formula, which requires an evaluation of "the reasonable expenses of raising the children involved." *See* Mascaro v. Mascaro (Chapter 16). What awards would the Australian, Texas, and Pennsylvania approaches produce in *McGinley*? What are the pros and cons of the Australian, Texas, and Pennsylvania approaches as compared to that described in *McGinley*?

In Florida (an income shares state), once combined monthly net income of both parents exceeds $10,000, for one child the presumptive amount of child support due is 5% of any excess net income. *See* FLA. STAT. ANN. § 61.30.

Should the child support obligation of a parent earning $12 million per year be greater than that for a parent who earns $1 million? *See* Johnson v. Superior Court, 77 Cal. Rptr. 2d 624 (App. 1998) (arguing that it should be greater).

10. Should guidelines apply when the noncustodial parent earns considerably less than the custodial parent? *See* J. Thomas Oldham, *The Appropriate Child Support Award When the Noncustodial Parent Earns Less Than the Custodial Parent*, 31 HOUS. L. REV. 585 (1994).

2. Obligor Poverty

If a special approach is warranted for a high-income obligor, is one also warranted for the obligor at the other end of the income scale? There is no consensus on the answer to this question. The percentage-of-income model applies at all income levels without variation; low-income obligors are not granted special treatment. By contrast, both the original Income Shares model and the Melson formula provide a "self-support reserve" for a one-person household; if the support obligor's income falls below the reserve value, the guideline support values do not apply. In 2005, twenty-eight states provided low-income obligors with a self-support reserve and eleven others provided some type of guideline adjustment. The value of the self-support reserve ranged from a low of $447 to a high of $1048. *See* Jane C. Venohr & Tracy E. Griffith, *Child Support Guidelines: Issues and Reviews*, 43 FAM. CT. REV. 415, 423 tbl. 3 (2005).

In states where the guideline values do not apply to low-income parents, three basic approaches have been utilized:

> Under one approach, in cases of extremely low income, that is, where income is below the poverty level, the guidelines will presume that an award of $50 per month per child is the appropriate award; as in any other case, the appropriateness of this award can be rebutted downward. When this method is used in a percentage of income state, for example Tennessee or Texas, the $50 is not stated; rather, the support is calculated by means of the percentage formula. * * *

Under the second approach, an absolute mandatory minimum award, usually $20 to $50, must be made. There can be no downward deviation from this absolute minimum award. * * *

Under the third approach, the amount of support is left to the discretion of the judge, without any presumptive amount stated.

Laura Morgan, *Child Support and the Anomalous Cases of the High-Income and Low-Income Parent,* 13 CAN. J. FAM. L. 161 (1996).

Some states also utilize a low-income adjustment formula. For example, in California:

> In all cases in which the net disposable income per month of the obligor is less than one thousand dollars ($1,000), there shall be a rebuttable presumption that the obligor is entitled to a low-income adjustment. The presumption may be rebutted by evidence showing that the application of the low-income adjustment would be unjust and inappropriate in the particular case. In determining whether the presumption is rebutted, the court shall consider the principles provided in Section 4053, and the impact of the contemplated adjustment on the respective net incomes of the obligor and the obligee. The low-income adjustment shall reduce the child support amount otherwise determined under this section by an amount that is no greater than the amount calculated by multiplying the child support amount otherwise determined under this section by a fraction, the numerator of which is 1,000 minus the obligor's net disposable income per month, and the denominator of which is 1,000.

CAL. FAM. CODE § 4055(7).

NOTES AND QUESTIONS

1.   *Support Minima:* Some state courts have held that guidelines prescribing an invariable support minimum conflict with the federal rebuttable-presumption requirement and are thus invalid under the Supremacy Clause. *See In re* Marriage of Gilbert, 945 P.2d 238 (Wash. App. 1997); Rose ex rel. Clancy v. Moody, 629 N.E.2d 378 (N.Y. 1993).

2.   *Public Assistance Exclusions:* 42 U.S.C. § 407(a) states that "none of the moneys paid or payable under [SSI] shall be subject to execution, levy, attachment, garnishment, or other legal process." Some state courts have interpreted section 407(a) to forbid the inclusion of SSI payments when calculating a support obligation. *See, e.g.,* Department of Public Aid ex rel. Lozada v. Rivera, 755 N.E.2d 548 (Ill. App. 2001) (SSI exists not to support the recipient and her dependents but only to provide a subsistence income for the recipient herself). *But see* Whitmore v. Kenney, 626 A.2d 1180 (Pa. Super. 1993). Some state support guidelines also explicitly exclude SSI or other public assistance benefits from support calculation. *See* N. Y. DOM. REL. L. § 240.1–

b(b)(5)(vii). *Should* public assistance benefits be excluded from support calculation: What policy values support and oppose such an exclusion? Could an exclusion withstand an equal protection challenge from an obligor who earned less than an SSI allowance?

3.   Under traditional, discretionary child-support principles, the available evidence suggests that support awards were regressive, with low-income parents typically paying significantly higher proportions of their incomes in child support than high-income parents. *See* LENORE J. WEITZMAN, THE DIVORCE REVOLUTION: THE UNEXPECTED SOCIAL AND ECONOMIC CONSEQUENCES FOR WOMEN AND CHILDREN IN AMERICA 462–69 (1985) (California); Marsha Garrison, *Good Intentions Gone Awry: The Impact of New York's Equitable Distribution Law on Divorce Outcomes*, 57 BROOKLYN L.REV. 621, 718 tbl. 53 (1991) (New York); James B. McLindon, *Separate But Unequal: The Economic Disaster of Divorce for Women and Children*, 21 FAM. L.Q. 351, 371–72 (1987) (Connecticut). Both the Melson and income-shares model produce regressive results *except* for obligors with incomes below the "self-support" reserve, where both produce much lower rates for below-poverty-level obligors. Under the percentage-of-income model, obligors at all income levels presumptively pay the same percentage of income in child support. What are the pros and cons of each approach?

4.   A self-support reserve is inconsistent with the aim of a continuity-of-expenditure approach: poor parents in intact families share income with their children to at least the same extent as do wealthier parents. Some studies have found that parents spend approximately the same percentage of household income on their children at all income levels. Others have found that poor parents spend more on their children than their wealthier counterparts. *See, e.g.*, THOMAS ESPENSHADE, INVESTING IN CHILDREN: NEW ESTIMATES OF PARENTAL EXPENDITURES (1984) (poor parents spent 26% of their income on one child, while parents with significantly higher incomes spent 15.2%). It is for this reason that percentage-of-obligor income guidelines do not authorize deviation from the presumptive support award in the case of low-income parents. *See* IRWIN GARFINKEL, ASSURING CHILD SUPPORT 134 (1992) ("No research suggests that * * * the poor spend a smaller proportion of income on their children than middle-income fathers. Indeed, the evidence suggests either that the proportions are about the same or that the poor actually spend a slightly higher percentage.") Given its inconsistency with tradition, the economic research, and the goal of the continuity of expenditure, why would policymakers adopt a policy that imposes low support obligations on poor support obligors?

5.   We discussed in Chapter 16 that a divorce court can order one spouse to pay the other spousal support in certain situations if the spouse needs the support. In addition, a few courts have held that, if the primary custodian has a substantially higher income than the other parent, the primary custodian can be ordered to pay child support to the other parent, if it would be in the best interest of the child. *See In re* Marriage of Turk, 12 N.E. 3d 40 (Ill. 2014);

Williamson v. Williamson, 748 S.E.2d 679 (Ga. 2013); Grant v. Hager, 868 N.E.2d 801 (Ind. 2007).

6. *The Unemployed Obligor:* Frequently a parent who has a duty to support his or her child does not have a job. Sometimes courts in such a situation calculate a child support obligation by imputing income to the parent at the minimum wage working a 40-hour week. *See* Rallo v. Rallo, 477 S.W.3d 29 (Mo. App. 2015). Is this fair?

7. A regulation recently adopted by the Office of Child Support Enforcement requires state child support guidelines to consider a child support obligor's subsistence needs when determining the amount of child suppor for a low-income obligor. See Jane C. Venohr, *Differences in State Child Support Guidelines Amounts: Guidelines Models, Economic Basis, and Other Issues*, 29 J. AM. ACAD. MAT. LAW. 377, 381 (2017). This eventually should reduce child support awards for poor obligors.

3. Joint and Split Custody: The Problem of "Extra" Visitation

Most guidelines were originally drafted with sole custody, where one parent is the primary caretaker and the other has occasional visitation, in mind. Is a different approach needed when both parents have the child in their care for substantial time periods?

IN RE SEAY
Supreme Court of Iowa, 2008.
746 N.W.2d 833.

APPEL, JUSTICE.

In this case, we must determine the proper method of calculating child support in a case where the district court awards joint physical care, but where the district court order provides that one party has actual physical care for more days a year than the other. We hold that under our rules, child support in all joint physical care cases should be decided using the offset method provided in Iowa Court Rule 9.14.

I. Factual and Procedural Background.

DeAngelo Seay and Andrea Thomas were never married, but had three children. Seay filed a petition to determine custody arrangement, child support, and liability for resulting court costs. The parties agreed that the court should award the parties joint legal custody of the children. The parties disagreed on the issues of physical care, child support, and apportionment of court costs and fees.

The district court order "awarded joint physical care" of the children to Seay and Thomas. The district court order further established a physical care schedule under which the parties alternated "physical care" on weekends and most holidays and vacations. The court provided that Seay would have "physical care" from 6:00 pm on Tuesdays and Thursdays until the beginning of school on Wednesdays and Fridays respectively. Under the schedule, the children would reside with Seay for 158 days and with Thomas for 206 days.

The district court awarded child support pursuant to the Child Support Guidelines Worksheet. Using undisputed income figures provided by the parties, the district court calculated that under the guidelines, Seay's child support obligation for the three children was $331 per month. Pursuant to Iowa Court Rule 9.9, the district court then reduced Seay's child support obligation by 25 percent as a result of extraordinary visitation. As a result, the district court ordered that Seay pay Thomas child support of $248 per month.

Seay appealed. He argued that the district court erred in calculating his child support obligation. According to Seay, the district court erred in not applying Iowa Court Rule 9.14 in calculating child support. Iowa Court Rule 9.14 provides that "[i]n cases of court-ordered joint (equally shared) physical care, child support shall be calculated" using an offset approach. Under the offset approach of the rule, the child support that would be required of each party is calculated as if they were a noncustodial parent. Child support is determined by calculating the difference between these two amounts.

Thomas cross-appealed. She claimed that the district court should have reduced Seay's child support obligation by only 20 percent because Seay's court-ordered visitation was more than 148 days but less than 167 days per year. *See* Iowa Ct. R. 9.9. Thomas also contended that Seay's support obligation should be increased because the court awarded two children to Seay as dependents for tax purposes, and only one to Thomas. She also sought an award of appellate attorneys' fees.

II. Scope of Review.

This case involves the interpretation of court rules regarding the award of child support where joint physical care is awarded.

III. Discussion.

In this case, there is no dispute that the district court ordered joint physical care of the parties' three children and that aspect of the district court's order is not challenged on appeal. The fighting issue in this case is whether Iowa Court Rule 9.14 applies to a case involving joint physical care where the district court establishes a schedule pursuant to which one party has physical care for a somewhat longer period than the other. The district court declined to apply the rule on the grounds that physical care in this case was not "equally shared."

States have taken a variety of approaches to the issue of whether generally applicable child support guidelines should apply in cases where the court awards joint physical care or its equivalent to both parents. Some states have decided that generally applicable child support guidelines should be applied in the first instance, subject to any adjustments that might be justified under all the facts and circumstances. Other states by judicial decision have adopted variants of the offset method in situations involving joint physical care. *See generally* Stephanie Giggetts, *Application of Child-Support Guidelines to Cases of Joint-, Split-, or Similar Shared-Custody Arrangements*, 57 A.L.R.5th 389, 389 (1998).

In Iowa, we have adopted a rule which requires application of the offset method for calculating child support in cases involving joint physical care. Iowa Ct. R. 9.14. The rule reflects the difference between joint physical care and other parental arrangements. Under Iowa Code section 598.1(4) (2007), parties awarded joint physical care have equal responsibility to maintain homes and provide routine care for the child. No party has superior rights or responsibilities with respect to the child. In contrast, the legal rights and responsibilities of a party with only joint legal custody and visitation is more limited. *See* Iowa Code § 598.1(3). As a result, ordinarily a parent with joint physical care directly expends more for the support of a child than a party awarded joint legal custody and visitation. Application of the offset method as a starting point in determining child support recognizes these differences.

On appeal, Thomas argues that Iowa Court Rule 9.14 should not apply under the facts and circumstances presented to the district court. She draws our attention to *In re Marriage of Fox*, 559 N.W.2d 26 (Iowa 1997). In *Fox*, the parties had agreed to what they termed "shared physical care" whereby one child lived with the father one third of the time. *Fox*, 559 N.W.2d at 27. Under the circumstances presented, we ruled that the "shared parenting" arrangement gave the father nothing more than what amounted to liberal visitation and applied the child support guidelines applicable to a noncustodial parent. *Id.* at 29.

We find *Fox* inapposite. In *Fox*, we found that the arrangement of the parties amounted to "liberal visitation." In this case, the district court specifically awarded "joint physical care" to the parties. *Nolte v. Mehrens*, 648 N.W.2d 727, 730 (Minn. App. 2002) (district court description determines nature of custody arrangements). The distinction between "liberal visitation" and "joint physical care" is crucial on the issue of the proper manner in determining child support. Iowa Court Rule 9.14 applies to situations where the parties are awarded "joint physical care."

Thomas stresses that Iowa Court Rule 9.14 contains the parenthetical "equally shared" and argues that, as a result, it does not apply to this case because physical care of the children was not equally divided on a calendar basis. Although the text of Iowa Court Rule 9.14 uses the parenthetical "equally shared," this phrase is a generalized description of the responsibilities and decision-making authority of each party. Under joint physical care, the parties are equally responsible for routine, daily decisions to be made regarding the child or children regardless of residential arrangements at the time. While joint physical care does require equal responsibility on routine, daily decision-making, it does not require that the residential arrangements be determined with mathematical precision. *Hynick,* 727 N.W.2d at 579 ("Joint physical care anticipates that parents will have equal, or roughly equal, residential time with the child."); *Janney v. Janney,* 943 So. 2d 396, 399–400 (La. Ct. App.2 006) (45.3 percent physical custody amounted to shared custody under child support statute).

For the above reasons, we hold that because the district court awarded joint physical care, Iowa Court Rule 9.14 is applicable. As a result, the district court erred in failing to utilize the offset method in calculating Seay's child support.

Our holding, however, does not end the matter. The amount of child support calculated pursuant to the rules is not cast in stone. Instead, under Iowa Court Rule 9.11, the amount of child support for parents awarded joint physical care pursuant to Iowa Court Rule 9.14 is a guideline that is presumptively valid but may be varied if the district court makes written findings that application of the guidelines would be unjust or inappropriate according to established criteria. *See* Iowa Code § 598.21(B)(1)(*c*), (*d*). Upon remand, the district court should determine whether there is any basis for a departure from an award of child support calculated pursuant to the offset method contained in Iowa Court Rule 9.14.

NOTES AND QUESTIONS

1.   As of 2005, 34 states had guidelines providing formulas for calculating child support when parents shared residential time. The amount of shared parenting required to trigger the formula varied widely. For example, the New Jersey formula applied when the child had one or more overnight visit per year; the Kentucky and Louisiana formulae did not apply unless the parents had nearly equal time with the child. *See* Jane C. Venohr & Tracy E. Griffith, *Child Support Guidelines: Issues and Reviews,* 43 FAM. CT. REV. 415, 423 tbl. 3 (2005). Here is an example of a shared-custody formula:

ARIZ. REV. STAT. § 25–320. Adjustment   for   Costs   Associated   with   Parenting Time

> To adjust for the costs of parenting time, first determine the total annual amount of parenting time indicated in a court order or parenting plan or by the expectation or historical practice of the parents. * * * After determining the total number of parenting time days, refer to "Parenting Time Table A" below. The left column of the table sets forth numbers of parenting time days in increasingly higher ranges. Adjacent to each range is an adjustment percentage. The parenting time adjustment is calculated

as follows: locate the total number of parenting time days per year in the left column of "Parenting Time Table A" and select the adjustment percentage from the adjacent column. Multiply the Basic Child Support Obligation * * * by the appropriate adjustment percentage. The number resulting from this multiplication then is subtracted from the proportionate share of the Total Child Support Obligation of the parent who exercises parenting time.

PARENTING TIME TABLE A

Number of Parenting Time Days		Adjustment Percentage
0	3	0
4	20	.012
21	38	.031
39	57	.050
58	72	.068
163	172	.085
173	182	.486

As the number of parenting time days approaches equal time sharing (143 days and above), certain costs usually incurred only in the custodial household are assumed to be substantially or equally shared by both parents. * * * If this assumption is rebutted by proof, for example, that such costs are not substantially or equally shared in each household, only "Parenting Time Table B" must be used to calculate the parenting time adjustment for this range of days. * * *

PARENTING TIME TABLE B

Number of Parenting Time Days		Adjustment Percentage
143	152	.275
153	162	.293
163	172	.312
173	182	.331

Some other states utilize the proportional offset method but first increase the basic child support obligation. *See, e.g.,* COLO. REV. STAT. § 14–10–115 (50% increase). The American Law Institute has recommended a similar, but not identical, approach. Under the ALI model, the decision maker "should calculate each parent's child-support obligation to the other, and require the parent with the larger obligation to pay the difference between the obligations to the parent with the smaller obligation. Each parent's obligation to the other should be established by calculating the amount that each parent would pay

* * * if the other were the sole residential parent; multiplying that amount by 1.5 to take into account the increased cost of dual residence; and multiplying the result by the other parent's proportional share of residential responsibility." AM. LAW INSTITUTE, PRINCIPLES OF FAMILY DISSOLUTION § 3.08(2) (2002).

Assuming that a formula is desirable, what are the respective merits of the Arizona, Colorado, Iowa and ALI approaches?

2.   How should child support be computed when there is "split" custody or divided residency (i.e., where each parent is primary custodian of at least one child)? *See* KY. REV. STAT. § 403.212(6); Lawrence v. Webber, 894 A.2d 480 (Me. 2006); Annot., *Application of Child Support Guidelines to Cases of Joint-, Split-, or Similar Shared-Custody Arrangements*, 57 A.L.R.5th 389 (1998). One common approach is to calculate the respective child support obligations each parent would have under the guidelines for the children not living with them. The parent with the higher support obligation would pay support to the other, after subtracting the lower obligation. See Naveen v. Naveen, 825 N.W.2d 863 (N.D. 2012).

3.   In England, when guidelines were first accepted one component of support awards for children under fourteen represented compensation for the custodial parent's time spent and career damage incurred due to child care responsibilities. *See* J. Thomas Oldham, *Lessons from the New English and Australian Child Support Systems*, 29 VAND. J. TRANSNAT'L L. 691 (1996). Is such compensation appropriate? If yes, how should a compensatory award be calculated in a joint custody case?

4.   In addition to *Seay*, other states have accepted the offset method for determining child support when there is joint physical custody. Some apply only if each parent has the child 50% of the time (*see* Serr v. Serr, 746 N.W.2d 416 (N.D. 2008)) while others apply it even if one parent has the child slightly more than half the time (*see* Rivero v. Rivero, 216 P.3d 213 (Nev. 2009)).

5.   In some states, child support must be reduced if the obligor has substantial visitation. For example, in Florida child support must be lowered from the guideline amount if the obligor has the child more than 20% of the time. *See* FLA. STAT. ANN. § 61.30(11)(b); Seiberlich v. Wolf, 859 So. 2d 570 (Fla. Dist. Ct. App. 2003).

4.   Child Living in Another Place with a Different Cost of Living

Courts have disagreed regarding whether a court should consider, when awarding child support, differences in the cost of living where the parties live.

TERAN V. RITTLEY
Court of Appeals of Michigan, 2015.
882 N.W.2d 181.

PER CURIAM.

SUMMARY OF FACTS AND PROCEEDINGS

In 2006, while defendant was in the military and stationed abroad in Ecuador, he fathered a child with plaintiff. The child was born on November 18, 2006, in Quito, Ecuador. Defendant left Ecuador shortly after the child was born and did not leave plaintiff any contact information.

On September 30, 2010, plaintiff filed the instant paternity action to determine custody, parental responsibility, and child support. The trial court permitted both parties to appear telephonically at scheduled hearings. A stipulated order for paternity testing was entered on April 25, 2011. DNA testing was performed on samples from the parties and the child. The results of the DNA testing were that defendant could not be excluded as the child's father. The probability that defendant was, in fact, the child's father was 99.99%. On August 26, 2011, the parties stipulated to the entry of an order of filiation, and the matter was referred to the Friend of the Court (FOC) for an investigation regarding child support. Using $22,892 for plaintiff's gross income, and $109,774 for defendant's gross income, the FOC recommended setting defendant's child support obligation at $1,211 a month.

In May 2013, the court conducted a two-day trial regarding child support at which both plaintiff and defendant testified via telephone. The main issues were the amount of child support and whether the court should deviate from the child support formula because plaintiff and the child lived in Ecuador. Defendant presented the testimony of Stan Smith, Ph.D. (University of Chicago), whom the trial court recognized as an expert in economics. Dr. Smith testified that he examined the cost of living in Quito, Ecuador, and Washington, D.C., and converted the costs of living in those cities to the cost of living in Detroit, Michigan. According to Dr. Smith, plaintiff's income of $22,900 in Quito equated to $36,914 of purchasing power in Michigan, and defendant's income of $127,000 in Washington, D.C., equated to $89,557 of purchasing power in Michigan. Using this determination of the parties' respective purchasing power in Michigan dollars ($36,914 and $89,557), Dr. Smith calculated that the amount of child support should be $1,021 per month. Dr. Smith further testified that in order to achieve the equivalent of $1,021 purchasing power in Michigan, a person in Ecuador would need only $634.00 (as of January 2012) or $567.00 (as of May 2013).

On September 24, 2013, the trial court issued a written opinion and order setting the amount of child support at $1,211 a month, as the FOC had recommended. The trial court rejected defendant's argument that it would not be a deviation to reduce the formula-recommended child support to an amount consistent with Dr. Smith's testimony regarding the relative purchasing power in the different locales. The trial court also rejected defendant's substantive arguments that a deviation from the child support formula was warranted. The court reviewed caselaw from other jurisdictions, finding the reasoning of a Maryland decision, *Gladis v. Gladisova*, 382 Md. 654, 856 A.2d 703 (2004), the most persuasive. The court also noted that our Supreme Court in *Verbeke v. Verbeke*, 352 Mich. 632, 90 N.W.2d 489 (1958), which was decided before the current statutory scheme of the child support formula, had rejected international variations in the costs of living as reasons for modifying child support.

The trial court first reasoned that defendant's proposal would be administratively unworkable, require expert testimony in many cases, place undue burdens on litigants and the judicial system, and delay entry of support orders. Second, the court reasoned that child support should not depend on the parents' choice of residences, but on the economic ability of the child's parents to provide support. The court also noted that the cost of living corresponding to a specific geographic location had not been made an explicit factor that could justify a deviation from the child support formula. The trial court therefore ruled that it would not consider the variation in the costs of living at different locales as a factor in establishing child support.

DEVIATION FROM THE CHILD SUPPORT FORMULA

DISCUSSION

Defendant asserts that the trial court erred by not deviating from the MCSF-recommended child support on the basis of the costs of living relative to where the child resides and where defendant, the support payer, resides. As an issue of first impression, we hold that the trial court may not, as a general rule, deviate from the MCSF-recommended child support on the basis of any differences between the general costs of living where the parents and the child reside. We also conclude that the trial court did not abuse its discretion by finding that the MCSF-recommended child support was not "unjust or inappropriate" as required by MCL 552.605(2) to support a deviation.

In setting the amount of child support, the Legislature has required that a trial court must generally follow the formula developed by the state Friend of the Court Bureau:

> Except as otherwise provided in this section, the court shall order child support in an amount determined by application of the child support formula developed by the state friend of the court bureau as required in section 19 of the friend of the court act, MCL 552.519. The court may enter an order that deviates from the formula *if the court determines from the facts of the case that*

application of the child support formula would be unjust or inappropriate and sets forth in writing or on the record all of the following:

(a) The child support amount determined by application of the child support formula.

(b) How the child support order deviates from the child support formula.

(c) The value of property or other support awarded instead of the payment of child support, if applicable.

(d) The reasons why application of the child support formula would be unjust or inappropriate in the case. [MCL 552.605(2) (emphasis added).]

As the trial court recognized, other jurisdictions are split on the issue whether differences in costs of living based on geographic location should factor into determining child support. In *Gladis*, 382 Md. at 657, 856 A.2d 703, the father lived in the United States, and the mother and child lived in the Slovak Republic. The trial court concluded that applying the Maryland child support guidelines was "inappropriate when there is a wide disparity in the cost of living," and therefore reduced the amount of the monthly award from $497 to $225. The mother filed a motion to amend that decision, and a different judge ordered the father to pay $497 per month in accordance with the guidelines. Maryland's highest appellate court, the Maryland Court of Appeals, issued a writ of certiorari before any action was taken by the Court of Special Appeals, Maryland's intermediate appellate court.

In *Gladis*, 382 Md. at 665–668, 856 A.2d 703, after recognizing the conflicting views among state courts that have addressed the issue, the Maryland Court of Appeals held "that the better position is to prohibit courts from deviating from the Guidelines based on the standards of living in different areas." The court reasoned that the Maryland legislature did not explicitly make the standards of living in relevant geographic areas part of the child support formula, that the child should enjoy the standard of living that he or she would have enjoyed if the child's parents had stayed together, and that there is nothing wrong with a child support award that would allow a child to enjoy an above-average standard of living that corresponds with the economic circumstances of the child's parent. The court also recognized that permitting the trial court to consider the costs of living on a case-by-case basis would create more frequent deviations from the child support guidelines and would frustrate the purposes of requiring courts to use the guidelines—to ensure that child support awards meet the needs of children, to improve the consistency and equity of awards, and to improve the efficiency of adjudicating child support issues.

In contrast, other jurisdictions have allowed differences in costs of living to be a proper factor in determining whether to deviate from child support guidelines. In *People ex rel. A.K.*, 72 P.3d 402, 404 (Colo. App. 2003), the court found that the trial court erred by not considering whether the difference between living expenses in Colorado and Russia would render applying the guidelines "inequitable, unjust, or inappropriate." Similarly, in *Booth v. Booth, 44 Ohio St.3d 142, 144, 541 N.E.2d 1028 (1989)*, the Supreme Court of Ohio addressed whether the trial court erred by deviating from the child support guidelines because of the "substantial difference" between the parents' costs of living in New York and Ohio. The court found that the trial court did not abuse its discretion in deviating from the guidelines. According to the court, after "a careful review of the facts and circumstances of this cause, we find that the child support order herein was proper in all respects, and was neither unreasonable, arbitrary nor unconscionable."

Like the trial court, we agree that the reasoning of the Maryland Court of Appeals in *Gladis* is persuasive. But, more importantly, principles of statutory construction dictate that we affirm the trial court. This Court has summarized the pertinent principles of statutory construction:

> The primary goal of judicial interpretation of statutes is to ascertain and give effect to the intent of the Legislature. The first criterion in determining intent is the specific language of the statute. The Legislature is presumed to have intended the meaning it plainly expressed. Nothing will be read into a clear statute that is not within the manifest intention of the Legislature as derived from the language of the statute itself. [*Polkton Twp.*, 265 Mich.App. at 101–102, 693 N.W.2d 170 (citations omitted).]

Neither the Legislature, in MCL 552.605(2), nor the Friend of the Court Bureau, which is tasked with developing the MCSF "based upon the needs of the child and the actual resources of each parent," MCL 552.519(3)(a)(*vi*), has specifically included geographic variations in the costs of living as a factor that may justify deviation from the MCSF-recommended child support amount. See 2013 MCSF 1.04(D); *Ewald*, 292 Mich. App. at 715–718, 810 N.W.2d 396. The statute is clear: "*Except as otherwise provided in this section,* the court *shall* order child support in an amount determined by application of the child support formula developed by the state friend of the court bureau as required in section 19 of the friend of the court act, MCL 552.519." MCL 552.605(2) (emphasis added). Nothing in the plain language of the statute or the MCSF manifests an intent to permit geographic variations in the costs of living to justify deviating from the MCSF-recommended child support amount.

Accordingly, because a difference between the cost of living at the payer parent's location and the cost of living at the child's location is not a proper basis for deviating from the child support formula, the trial court's application of the child support formula was not "unjust or inappropriate" under these circumstances, MCL 552.605(2), and therefore, the trial court did not abuse its discretion by establishing child support in the amount recommended by the MCSF. We affirm.

4. EVALUATING CURRENT GUIDELINES

Problem 17-3:

In one evaluation, researchers compared awards generated by state guidelines with the most recent evidence on child-related expenditure in intact families. This is sometimes referred to as a "continuity-of-expenditure" evaluation of child support guidelines. In lower-income families (defined as those with combined parental income of $21,600 or less), no state guidelines produced awards that would permit continuity-of-expenditure. For middle-income families (with combined parental income of at least $46,100), the guidelines of only one state (Nebraska) produced such an award, and for high-income families (those with parental income of $75,000 or more) nine jurisdictions (the District of Columbia, Georgia, Massachusetts, Minnesota, Nebraska, Nevada, New York, Tennessee, and Wisconsin) did. *See* Laura W. Morgan & Mark C. Lino, *A Comparison of Child Support Awards Calculated Under States' Child Support Guidelines with Expenditures on Children Calculated by the U.S. Department of Agriculture*, 33 FAM. L.Q. 191, 215–18 (1999). A more recent review, using different child-rearing expenditure estimates and "a typical case scenario where the residential parent's income reflects female median earnings and the nonresidential parent's income reflects male median earnings and support is being determined for one child" found that 22 states currently had child support guidelines that yielded amounts below the lower bound of the range of estimates of child-rearing expenditures for this case scenario. *See* Venohr & Griffith, *supra*, 43 FAM. CT. REV., at 421–22. The American Law Institute's (ALI) child support proposals take a different approach. The ALI support principles are designed to ensure that "parents share income with a child in order that the child enjoy"

> a) a minimum decent standard of living when the combined income of the parents is sufficient to achieve such result without impoverishing either parent and
>
> b) a standard of living not grossly inferior to that of either parent[.]

PRINCIPLES *supra* at § 3.04 (2002) [hereinafter Principles]. The Principles thus reject the continuity-of-expenditure aim that underlies most current guidelines:

Although the[ ] Principles do to some extent embody the marginal-expenditure notion of justice for the nonresidential parent, this notion of justice arguably overstates the nonresidential parent's claim. The continuity of the marginal-expenditure measure may be understood to be predicated on the view that, insofar as the nonresidential parent is the dominant earner, that parent should be held harmless by divorce, that is, should be no worse off economically after divorce than during marriage. Yet being no worse off suggests, in the alternative, that the nonresidential parent should not be heard to complain so long as that parent does not suffer a decline in standard of living. To the extent that there is no such decline (using household-equivalence measures), there is no persuasive reason the nonresidential parent should not pay more than what he or she would have spent on the children were they living in the same home as the nonresidential parent. * * *

Id. at § 3.04 cmt. f.

Professor Garrison has also noted that the ALI formula, in many cases, produces results more or less equivalent to those that would be achieved using an equal-outcomes approach:

The ALI * * * model deviates from a typical continuity-of-expenditure guideline in two important respects: it provides a self-support reserve for the child's household and it includes a supplement explicitly designed to enhance the likelihood that the supported child will enjoy a both a "minimum decent standard of living" and a living standard "not grossly inferior" to that of the nonresidential parent. The supplement is expressed as an income percentage and added to the base, marginal expenditure percentage. * * * The ALI approach thus starts with a continuity-of-expenditure methodology, but incorporates supplements to "attain the dual objectives of [income] adequacy and avoidance of gross disproportion [of living standards]." In fact, it achieves approximately equal living standards in many cases. * * *

Marsha Garrison, *Child Support: Guidelines and Goals*, 33 FAM. L.Q. 157, 184–85 (1999).

Why did the ALI reject an equal-outcomes approach in favor of a complex methodology that achieves relatively equal outcomes in some cases but not others? And is that rejection appropriate? A draft of the Principles notes that the equal-outcomes approach

is most likely to protect children from poverty and to enable them to enjoy a relatively high standard of living. * * * [But t]he difficulties with an equal living standard system * * * are two fold: first, it gives no weight to the primacy of the earner's claims to his own earnings. It would treat the nonresidential parent's income as unconditionally available to the residential household up to the point at which the nonresidential parent would suffer more than the residential household. Whether or not this treatment is ethically sound, it would seem culturally unacceptable and politically unrealizable. * * * [T]he equal living standards model * * * also would create [a] substantial work disincentive for the residential parent. Every dollar earned by the residential parent would be heavily taxed * * *.

ALI PRINCIPLES OF THE LAW OF FAMILY DISSOLUTION § 3.04 cmt. d(i), § 3.05A cmt. j (Council Draft No. 4 (1997)). Garrison argues that the ALI's rejection of equal outcomes makes little "sense in light of the ALI's own recommendations":

First, the drafters of the ALI recommendations clearly understood that any and all guidelines can be modified to take account of work disincentives; indeed, an important feature of the enhanced model is an "imputed income" provision designed to do just that. * * * [A]n equal outcomes approach—or any support model—can be similarly modified. Second, if equal outcomes are "culturally unacceptable," it would appear that the enhanced model proposed by the ALI should also be unacceptable. * * * [T]he enhanced model benefits [some] * * * nonresidential parent[s, but] the two approaches [often] produce remarkably similar initial awards.

Garrison, *supra*, at 186. And Garrison contends that "[t]he equal outcomes approach holds one clear advantage over the [ALI] model * * *: It is conceptually much simpler. As the ALI reporter herself put it, the [ALI] model's 'basic measure of child support as not as susceptible to easy definition as are [standard continuity of expenditure guidelines and the equal outcomes model]'." She also urges that the equal outcomes model is better equipped to "consistently take account of changes in family composition in a way that treats the needs of both parents equally." *Id.* at 183,186. Garrison nonetheless concludes that "[d]espite these negatives, the * * * [ALI] model marks a vast improvement over first-generation continuity-of-expenditure guidelines. For policymakers who wish to emphasize income adequacy instead of equity, it * * * deserves serious consideration." *Id.* at 188.

Approaching the issue of guidelines from a different perspective, Professor Sanford Braver has argued that the post-divorce living standard gap between children and their nonresidential parents that has been so often reported is, in fact, "vanishingly small." Braver argues that research showing a larger gap results from failure to take account of earned-income and child-care credits that sometimes reduce the custodial parent's federal tax liability. Using his own sample of Arizona cases from the late 1980s, Braver calculated income-to-needs ratios using a computer program designed to capture these tax effects; he found that noncustodial fathers experienced an average gain of only 13% while custodial mothers experienced an average loss of 16%. After again "correcting" the data by assuming that the children's expenses "travel" with them during visitation periods, Braver concluded that the living standard of noncustodial fathers increased, on average, only 2% after divorce while that of custodial mothers decreased 8%. *See* Sanford Braver, *The Gender Gap in Standard of Living After Divorce: Vanishingly Small?*, 33 FAM. L.Q. 111, 123–29 (1999). Braver concludes that "[t]here is reason to think that recent reforms of the child support guidelines has [sic] actually reversed the conventional wisdom: fathers in certain states may now be more impoverished by divorce than mothers. There is also reason to think that this tendency will worsen as longer term effects are assessed." *Id.* at 134.

While the ALI model received a great deal of attention from commentators, it has not been accepted by state legislatures. The continuity-of-expenditure model is still the accepted model for child support guidelines in the United States.

CHAPTER 18

SEPARATION AGREEMENTS

■ ■ ■

1. NEGOTIATING AND DRAFTING
THE AGREEMENT

A. NEGOTIATING A SETTLEMENT

Because litigation is expensive, time-consuming, and sometimes unpredictable, many divorcing couples, either by themselves or through their attorneys, prefer to negotiate a settlement. Experts estimate that no more than 10% of all divorce cases go to trial. Marygold S. Melli, Howard S. Erlanger & Elizabeth Chambliss found that

> * * * [o]ver the last two decades, many studies, * * * have found that the predominant mode of dispute resolution is not litigation, but negotiation. Of the 349 files examined in the first phase of our study, only 32 involved a dispute between the parties that had to be settled by a judge. Several commentators have noted that, given findings such as these, to speak of negotiation as "alternative dispute resolution" is nonsensical. Marc Galanter has argued: "On the contemporary American legal scene the negotiation of disputes is not an alternative to litigation * * * [I]t is not some marginal peripheral aspect of legal disputing in America; it is the central core. * * * Negotiation is not just the typical outcome; it is also the expected mode of dispute resolution in the minds of the parties and their lawyers."

Marygold S. Melli et al., *The Process of Negotiation: An Exploratory Investigation in The Context of No-fault Divorce*, 40 RUTGERS L. REV. 1133, 1142 (1988).

The aim of settlement negotiations is a result acceptable to all parties. This does not mean that the law is unimportant; negotiations take place in the "shadow" of state laws on child custody, visitation, child support, and marital property.

ROBERT MNOOKIN & LEWIS KORNHAUSER, BARGAINING IN THE SHADOW OF THE LAW: THE CASE OF DIVORCE
88 YALE L.J. 950, 986 (1979).*

* * *

Ideally, a bargaining theory would allow us to predict how alternative legal rules would affect negotiations between particular spouses and the deal, if any, they would strike. Such a theory might be combined with knowledge of how the characteristics that determine bargaining behavior are distributed among divorcing couples. Alternative rules and procedures could then be compared by evaluating the patterns of bargains that would result under each. Unfortunately, no existing theory of bargaining allows confident prediction of how different legal rules and procedures would influence outcomes. * * *

What follows is not a complete theory. Instead, we identify five factors that seem to be important influences or determinants of the outcomes of bargain, and then offer some observations on the bargaining process. The factors are (1) the preferences of the divorcing parents; (2) the bargain endowments created by legal rules that indicate the particular allocation a court will impose if the parties fail to reach agreement; (3) the degree of uncertainty concerning the legal outcome if the parties go to court, which is linked to the parties' attitudes toward risk; (4) transaction costs and the parties' respective abilities to bear them; and (5) strategic behavior.

* * *

If one accepts the proposition that the primary function of the legal system should be to facilitate private ordering and dispute resolution, then several important questions come into sharp focus. To what extent does the participation of lawyers facilitate dispute resolution? Are there fairer and less costly procedures in which lawyers would play a lesser role?

Many observers are very critical of the way some lawyers behave in divorce negotiations. Lawyers may make negotiations more adversarial and painful, and thereby make it more difficult and costly for the spouses to reach agreement. Indeed lawyers may be more likely than lay people to adopt negotiating strategies involving threats and the strategic misrepresentation of their clients' true preferences in the hope of reaching a more favorable settlement for the client. Ivan Illich has suggested that a broad range of illnesses are "iatrogenic": induced and created by medical treatment and the health industry. The same charge might be made against the legal profession. The participation of lawyers in the divorce

* REPRINTED BY PERMISSION OF THE YALE LAW JOURNAL COMPANY AND FRED B. ROTHMAN & CO. FROM THE YALE LAW JOURNAL.

process may on balance lead to more disputes and higher costs without improving the fairness of outcomes.

Yet, there are also arguments that lawyers facilitate dispute settlement. Lawyers may make negotiations more rational, minimize the number of disputes, discover outcomes preferable to both parties, increase the opportunities for resolution out of court, and ensure that the outcomes reflect the applicable legal norms. Professor Eisenberg has suggested that a pair of lawyers—each acting for his client—may make the process of negotiation very much like adjudication, in which "rules, precedents, and reasoned elaboration * * * may be expected to determine outcomes." When each disputant is represented, the lawyers "are likely to find themselves allied with each other as well as with the disputants, because of their relative emotional detachment, their interest in resolving the dispute, and, in some cases, their shared professional values. Each * * * therefore tends to take on a Janus-like role, facing the other as an advocate of his principal, and facing his principal as an advocate of that which is reasonable in the other's position."

* * * "Because a lawyer is both a personal advisor and a technical expert, each actor-disputant is likely to accept a settlement his lawyer recommends."

In view of the critical role of lawyers and the disparate functions they may perform, it is startling how little we know about how lawyers actually behave. Obviously, lawyers are not all the same. Their styles and talents differ. Some lawyers are known within the profession as negotiators who strive to find middle ground acceptable to both sides; others are fighters who love the courtroom battle. Research could usefully explore how much specialization there is and, more importantly, the extent to which clients, when they are choosing a lawyer at the time of divorce, have any notion at all of their lawyers' skills or preferences for these various roles. More generally, systematic empirical research might illustrate how often, and in what circumstances, lawyers facilitate dispute settlement at the time of divorce, and how often, and in what circumstances, they hinder it.

––––––––––

At the time Mnookin and Kornhauser wrote, there were few studies of lawyer behavior in divorce cases. More recent research on twenty lawyers and their clients revealed that lawyers typically advise their clients to try to settle rather than litigate. *See* AUSTIN SARAT & WILLIAM L.F. FELSTINER, DIVORCE LAWYERS AND THEIR CLIENTS: POWER AND MEANING IN THE LEGAL PROCESS 56, 108–09, 148 (1995):

> While, at least at the outset, many clients think of the legal process as an arena for a full adversarial contest, most divorce disputes are not resolved in this manner * * * Clients often resist

the pro-settlement message of their lawyers and deploy various tactics of resistance to keep alive the possibility of contested hearings or trials. Thus the selling of settlement is a risky business for lawyers. * * * In their interactions with clients divorce lawyers try to manage that risk in two ways: first, by stressing that the ultimate decision about, and responsibility for, settlement rests with the client; and, second, by describing negotiation as an adversarial process in which lawyers look for an edge and advance their clients' interests even as they seek a consensual outcome.

Lawyers use an array of strategies to try to construct a particular meaning of what is "realistic" and to persuade their clients to adopt a particular definition of what is, in their view, legally possible. Of course, their knowledge of legal rules and process, and the information that they have about specific players, such as other lawyers, judges, and mediators, provide powerful arguments. * * * In addition to their feel for the legal system and for the dramatis personae, lawyers, particularly specialists in family law, benefit from their experiences in prior cases.

* * * Divorce lawyers realize that when the case for settlement is first proposed to them, may clients cannot be convinced at a single stroke to abandon trial as a mode of disposition and embrace negotiations. They must not only be persuaded that settlement is the more prudent course, they must also be emotionally prepared to engage in negotiations with the very party who has upset their life. * * *

See also J. DEWAR & S. PARKER, LAW & THE FAMILY 18–19 (2d ed. 1992) (concluding that U.S. divorce lawyers push disputes towards settlement in part because "lawyers are supreme in the world of settlements whereas in courts they must cede power to the judges.")

The client's attitude toward the divorce will often color both his willingness to enter into settlement negotiations and his attitude toward settlement proposals. For example, Melli, Erlanger & Chambliss compared settlement agreements containing child support awards based on whether the support obligor was "reluctant" to end the marriage, "impatient" to end the marriage, or "accepting" of the divorce. Reluctant obligors agreed to pay an average of 19% of their income in child support, accepting obligors 24%, and impatient obligors 29%. Similarly, reluctant obligees obtained agreements requiring an average of 30% of the obligor's income to be paid in support, while accepting obligees obtained 24%, and impatient obligees received 19%. *See* Melli et al., *supra* p. 1093, at 1133.

What steps can (and should) a lawyer take to counsel a client whose emotional state may make him or her inclined to accept an unreasonable offer, or reject a reasonable offer? Are there any malpractice risks here?

B. DRAFTING THE AGREEMENT

Once an agreement has been made, it must be reduced to clear and unambiguous written form. This sounds simple, but it is easier said than done!

STEWART V. STEWART
Missouri Court of Appeals, 1987.
727 S.W.2d 416.

CRIST, JUDGE.

Respondent (father) filed a motion to cite appellant (mother) for contempt for failing to pay him his equity in the marital residence after their youngest son had reached his majority, as provided by their separate agreement and dissolution decree. Father also asked the trial court for its order to sell the residence to satisfy his claim to the equity. Mother filed an answer asking that father be cited for contempt for failing to pay past child support. The trial court denied both motions for contempt, but ordered the sale of the residence with father to get one-half of the equity of such residence as of the time of sale. We reverse and remand with directions.

The seminal issue is whether father was to get one-half the equity at the time of sale, or whether he was to get one-half the equity at the time of dissolution decree on October 22, 1975. The equity in the real estate has increased in value from approximately $12,000 to at least $38,000.

At the time of the divorce, the parties were joint owners of the marital residence. The terms of the dissolution decree referred to a written separation agreement incorporated therein. A portion of the separation agreement provides:

> Party of the First Part (mother) shall be entitled to the Parties' home located at 119 Flesher in Ellisville, Missouri. At the time the Parties' youngest son, Steven Paul Stewart, shall reach the age of majority or be fully emancipated, it shall become the obligation of the Party of the First Part to pay to the Party of the Second Part (father) a sum of money equal to one-half (1/2) of the current equity in the said real estate less all proper expenses of selling said home, taxes and other fees. It is further agreed that the fair market value of said property as of the signing of this Agreement is Twenty Eight Thousand ($28,000) Dollars.

At no time since the dissolution has there been any conveyance of the marital residence, and title continues in both mother and father. Their youngest son became twenty-one years of age on January 28, 1984. Father testified he thought he was to receive one-half of the equity valued at the time of the sale. Mother testified he was to receive one-half the equity, valued at the time of the dissolution decree. There was little evidence on the question of the intention of the parties at the execution of the separation agreement.

Excepting for the words "less all proper expenses of selling said home, taxes and other fees," there can be little question about the intention of the parties at the time of the execution of their agreement. The parties would not have used the term "current equity" or provided that "the fair market value * * * as of the signing * * * is twenty-eight thousand dollars," unless the equity to be paid to father was to be calculated based upon the value of the home at the time of the dissolution decree.

Mother was to get the marital residence. When their youngest son reached his majority mother had to pay father a sum of money equal to one-half of the equity value at the time of dissolution, which was approximately $12,000. We do not know why the parties chose to add the words "less all proper expenses of selling said home, taxes and other fees," and no reasonable explanation is offered by the parties; but we are not permitted to make an agreement other than that of the parties. In any event, the parties agree that if the property must be sold, each must share the payment of the sale expenses.

The wording of the agreement regarding the proceeds of the marital residence is not ambiguous. The parties are bound by its terms.

The judgment of the trial court that "current equity" was to be measured as of the time mother's obligation to pay had matured rather than the time of the dissolution decree is reversed. The separation agreement shall be interpreted to mean father may receive his "current equity" measured as of the time of the dissolution decree. Mother shall have the right to pay the equity due father in lieu of sale of the marital residence. In all other respects, the judgment of the trial court is affirmed. The trial court is directed to enter an order in accordance with this opinion.

Judgment reversed and remanded.

NOTES AND QUESTIONS

1. *Stewart* involves a provision in an agreement that many types of lawyers must learn to draft. In many different agreements, the parties wish to give one or both parties the right to buy out the other's interest in something in the future. Such agreements need to address numerous issues.

a. *Valuation.* Who will determine the value of the interest, and by what methodology? If the appraiser is to be paid a fee, who will pay the fee?

b. *Offsets.* Once the value of the interest is obtained, is anything to be deducted from the gross value of the interest when determining the net amount the buyer must pay? The agreement in *Stewart* provided that the buyer could deduct "all proper expenses of selling said home, taxes and other fees." Is this clear?

c. *Payment terms.* Does the buyer have to pay the purchase price in cash? If so, within how many days after exercising the option to purchase? If payment over time is permitted, what would be the term and the interest rate? Would the payment obligation be secured?

2. The case of *In re* Garza, 217 B.R. 197 (Bkrtcy. N.D. Tex. 1998) involved an obligation, set forth in the parties' divorce decree, that the husband would promptly pay the wife 50% of the first $50,000.00 received from any settlement or judgment in a lawsuit pending at the time of divorce, and 60% of the second $50,000.00 received. When the husband agreed to a settlement of the lawsuit, the wife contended she should receive a percentage of the gross settlement amount, while the husband argued that legal fees, expenses, and taxes should be deducted before calculating the wife's share. How could this ambiguity have been clarified?

3. If a clause in a separation agreement includes a provision that equity shall be divided "upon sale of the property," is division required when foreclosure occurs? *See* Troy Savings Bank v. Calacone, 617 N.Y.S.2d 995 (App. Div. 1994) (yes).

4. In a settlement negotiation, what role should the client play? Should the lawyer initially let the parties try to reach an acceptable settlement on their own, without the lawyer's participation? When might this be a bad idea?

Problem 18-1:

Redraft the disputed provision in *Stewart* twice to clearly and unambiguously convey both of its possible meanings.

Problem 18-2:

Assume you are representing the divorcing party who will be primary custodian of the parties' minor children. Further assume that in this state the obligor's support obligation ends upon death, and that the obligation may be secured by a life insurance policy on the obligor's life, naming your client as the beneficiary. How would you draft such a provision? *See* Tupper v. Roan, 243 P.3d 50 (Or. 2010). What future potential problems would you address?

2. DURESS, NONDISCLOSURE AND MISREPRESENTATION

HRESKO V. HRESKO

Maryland Court of Appeals, 1990.
83 Md. App. 228, 574 A.2d 24.

ALPERT, JUDGE.

In *Hamilos v. Hamilos*, 297 Md. 99, 465 A.2d 445 (1983), the Court of Appeals held that an enrolled decree will not be vacated even though obtained by use of forged documents, perjured testimony, or any other frauds which are intrinsic to the trial of the case itself. In the present case, this court encounters for the first time the question of whether the fraudulent concealment of assets by one spouse during negotiations leading to a separation and property settlement agreement subsequently incorporated into a divorce decree is intrinsic or extrinsic to the divorce litigation.

During the spring or early summer of 1985, James and Marie Hresko decided to terminate their 24-year marriage. The parties agreed to and signed a separation and property settlement agreement on July 10, 1985. According to terms of the settlement agreement, James (appellant) agreed to pay $400 per month in child support, to pay the total costs of the minor child's college education, and to assume payment of certain family consumer debts. The agreement further provided that Marie (appellee) had the option of buying out appellant's interest in the family home three years from the date of the settlement agreement.

In the summer of 1988, appellee exercised her option to buy out appellant's interest in the family home and on the day of settlement, August 4, 1988, paid appellant $80,000 in cash for his one-half interest. Appellant had assumed that appellee would require a mortgage to purchase his interest in the house and claimed that he was "stunned" when she fulfilled her obligation with cash. He then became convinced that a fraud had been perpetrated against him during the 1985 negotiations that led to the property settlement. This alleged fraud involved the concealment, by appellee, of at least $80,000 in cash at the time of the agreement. As a result of this belief, appellant filed a Motion to Revise Judgment and to Rescind Separation and Property Settlement Agreement, together with a memorandum of law and an affidavit. Appellee responded by filing a motion to dismiss appellant's motion. Judge Cawood held a hearing on appellee's motion on June 7, 1989. After briefly holding the matter sub curia, the judge issued a written opinion on June 13, 1989, granting appellee's motion to dismiss appellant's motion to revise judgment.

In an action to set aside an enrolled judgment or decree, the moving party must initially produce evidence sufficient to show that the judgment in question was the product of fraud, mistake or irregularity. Furthermore, it has long been black letter law in Maryland that the type of fraud which is required to authorize the reopening of an enrolled judgment is extrinsic fraud and not fraud which is intrinsic to the trial itself.

Appellant contends that appellee concealed from him an unknown, but apparently sizable, sum of money at the time the two parties were negotiating the subject separation and property settlement agreement.

Assuming without deciding that appellant has produced facts and circumstances sufficient to establish fraud, we will address whether this alleged fraud is extrinsic or intrinsic to the trial itself. We hold, based on appellant's claims and verified statements, that appellee's alleged concealment of funds is an example of, at most, intrinsic fraud.

Intrinsic fraud is defined as "[t]hat which pertains to issues involved in the original action or where acts constituting fraud were, or could have been, litigated therein." *Black's Law Dictionary* (5th ed. 1979). Extrinsic fraud, on the other had, is "[f]raud which is collateral to the issues tried in the case where the judgment is rendered." *Id.*

Fraud is extrinsic when it actually prevents an adversarial trial. In determining whether or not extrinsic fraud exists, the question is not whether the fraud operated to cause the trier of fact to reach an unjust conclusion, but whether the fraud prevented the actual dispute from being submitted to the fact finder at all. In *Schwartz v. Merchants Mortgage Co.,* 272 Md. 305, 309, 322 A.2d 544 (1974), the Court of Appeals * * * provided examples of what would be considered extrinsic fraud:

> Where the unsuccessful party has been prevented from exhibiting fully his case, by fraud or deception practiced on him by his opponent, as by keeping him away from court, a false promise of a compromise; or where the defendant never had knowledge of the suit, being kept in ignorance by the acts of the plaintiff; or where an attorney fraudulently or without authority assumes to represent a party and connives at his defeat; . . . or where the attorney regularly employed corruptly sells out his client's interest in the other side—these, and similar cases which show that there has never been a real contest in the trial or hearing of the case, are reasons for which a new suit may be sustained to set aside and annul the former judgment or decree, and open the case for a new and a fair hearing.

Schwartz, 272 Md. at 309, 322 A.2d 544.

Appellant contends that appellee's alleged fraudulent representations were extrinsic to the subsequent divorce action because they took place over two years before its inception and served to prevent appellant from taking advantage of his right to an adversarial proceeding. He argues that appellee's concealment is a "fraud or deception practiced upon the unsuccessful party by his opponent as by keeping him away from court or making a false promise of a compromise."

As stated above, the issue of whether appellee's alleged fraudulent concealment of assets during pre-separation agreement negotiations is intrinsic or extrinsic to the divorce litigation is one of first impression in Maryland courts. Upon looking to other jurisdictions for guidance, we find conflict among our sister states.

California courts have uniformly recognized that the failure of one spouse to disclose the existence of community property assets constitutes extrinsic fraud. The principle underlying these cases is that each spouse has an obligation to inform the other spouse of the existence of community property assets. This duty stems in part from the confidential nature of the marital relationship and from the fiduciary relationship that exists between spouses with respect to the control of community property.

In *Daffin v. Daffin*, 567 S.W.2d 672 (Mo. App. 1978), the Missouri Court of Appeals set aside property provisions of a dissolution of marriage decree. There, equity intervened, not because of the deception that affected the substance of the court's judgment (the concealment of assets) but because of the husband's breach of the relationship of confidence between husband and wife.

Other courts have found extrinsic fraud holding, as appellant would have us do, that a spouse's concealment or misrepresentation of assets can be classified as an intentional act by which the one spouse has prevented the other spouse from having a fair submission of the controversy and thus amounts to extrinsic fraud.

Other jurisdictions have reached the opposite result, determining that the fraudulent concealment of assets by one spouse during a property settlement agreement is intrinsic to the divorce litigation. Recently, in *Altman v. Altman*, 150 A.D.2d 304, 542 N.Y.S.2d 7, 9 (1989), the New York Supreme Court, Appellate Division, held that alleged fraud in the negotiations of the separation agreement involves the issue in controversy and is not a deprivation of the opportunity to make a full and fair defense. The court reasoned that the alleged misrepresentations of financial status are in essence no different from any other type of perjury committed in the course of litigation and thus constitute intrinsic fraud.

Similarly, in *Chapman v. Chapman*, 591 S.W.2d 574, 577 (Tex. Civ. App. 1979), the Texas court refused to overturn on the basis of fraud a property settlement agreement incorporated into a divorce decree. The court stated that the fraud alleged at most related to untruths which misled the wife into acquiescence and approval an unjust division of property. Because these misrepresentations bore only on issues in the trial (or which could have been at issue in the trial), they, therefore, amounted to no more than intrinsic fraud.

We are persuaded that these latter cases are the better reasoned ones. Misrepresentations or concealment of assets made in negotiations leading to a voluntary separation and property settlement agreement later incorporated into a divorce decree represent matters intrinsic to the trial itself. In fact, a determination of each party's respective assets, far from being a collateral issue, would seem to be a central issue in a property settlement agreement.

We reject appellant's contention that appellee's misrepresentations are extrinsic to the divorce action because it occurred two years prior to the action and prevented appellant from taking advantage of his right to an adversarial proceeding. The property settlement agreement, which appellant asserts was derived from the fraudulent representations of appellee,[2] was the same agreement that the parties submitted to the court for incorporation into the divorce decree. Appellant had every opportunity to examine these representations through discovery methods or in court. Instead, he chose to file an uncontested answer and permitted the matter to go to judgment.

In *Hamilos, supra*, the Court of Appeals held that an enrolled decree would not be vacated even though obtained by use of perjured testimony. As the trial judge stated in his written opinion and order, "It would be anomalous to give an alleged false statement in a letter (or given orally) greater stature than perjury during the course of the proceedings. If any fraud exists, it is intrinsic to the proceedings, which is not sufficient." We agree.

No "extrinsic fraud" prevented appellant from seeking trial and this court will not, therefore, reopen the decree in the present case. To rule otherwise would be to subject every enrolled divorce decree that includes a property settlement to revision upon discovery of alleged fraud in the inducement of the settlement. Public policy of this state demands an end to litigation once the parties have had an opportunity to present in court a matter for determination, the decision has been rendered, and the litigants afforded every opportunity for review.

Judgment affirmed; costs to be paid by appellant.

---

[2]   We note that the actual settlement agreement made no representations as to the recent assets of either party. Furthermore, Subsection 18.2 of the agreement expressly states that there are no other representations, statements, understandings, promises, either oral or written, which are relied upon by either party.

NOTES AND QUESTIONS

1.   Courts have not reached consensus on how to handle post-divorce disputes regarding assets not disclosed at divorce:

a.   In community property states, spouses remain co-owners of community property after divorce until the property is divided. *See* Henn v. Henn, 605 P.2d 10 (Cal. 1980). In California, if a spouse fraudulently fails to disclose community property in connection with a divorce property settlement, the victimized spouse who later discovers the property is entitled to 100% of its value. *See* Marriage of Rossi, 108 Cal. Rptr. 2d 270 (App. 2001). Is this a good idea? Should a spouse who fails to disclose property be penalized? If so, in what way?

b.   Most common law states divide into the two camps described in *Hresko*. In some states, even if the separation agreement cannot be rescinded when a spouse discovers additional hidden marital assets, the spouse may bring a separate action to divide the discovered property. *See* Gehm v. Gehm, 707 S.W.2d 491 (Mo. App. 1986); Marriage of Hiner, 669 P.2d 135 (Colo. App. 1983) (court expressly retained jurisdiction in the original decree to divide undisclosed assets subsequently discovered). In others, the provisions of the separation agreement remain in effect. Even in those states where a party can sue after divorce to recover omitted assets, the statute of limitations might ban such a claim. *See* Klineline v. Klineline, 481 S.W.3d 551 (Mo. App. 2015).

c.   Some common law states resolve the issue presented in *Hresko* by determining whether the spouses had fiduciary obligations to each other when the agreement was negotiated; a spouse with fiduciary obligations has a duty to disclose all material facts, and the failure to do so constitutes fraud. *See* Marriage of Palacios, 656 N.E.2d 107 (Ill. App. 1995); Etzion v. Etzion, 880 N.Y.S.2d 79 (App. Div. 2009); Greenland v. Greenland, 29 So. 3d 647 (La. App. 2009). Most courts agree that either the separation of the parties or a spouse's retention of a lawyer terminates the couple's fiduciary obligations. *See* Daughtry v. Daughtry, 497 S.E.2d 105 (N.C. App. 1998); Barnes v. Barnes, 340 S.E.2d 803 (Va. 1986). *See also* Terwilliger v. Terwilliger, 64 S.W.3d 816 (Ky. 2002) (holding that, when neither spouse was represented by counsel in negotiating a separation agreement, the parties' fiduciary obligations continued, with the result that one spouse's undervaluation of marital assets was fraud sufficient to permit rescission of the agreement). *See generally* Amanda K. Esquibel, *Fiduciary Duties: The Legal Effect of the Beneficiary's Retention of Counsel on the Fiduciary Relationship*, 33 RUTGERS L.J. 329 (2002).

2.   What policies does the *Hresko* approach further? the *Daffin* and fiduciary-obligation approaches? Which policy, on balance, is best?

3.　　Assuming Maryland has abolished spousal tort immunity, could Mr. Hresko bring an action for fraud?

4.　　Does footnote 2 of the *Hresko* opinion suggest that the husband's lawyer should have added another provision to the settlement agreement? In Hess v. Hess, 580 A.2d 357 (Pa. Super. 1990) the wife obtained compensatory and punitive damages from her former husband where he had concealed assets and the settlement agreement included a warranty that both parties had fully disclosed their assets.

5.　　In Quiring v. Quiring, 944 P.2d 695 (Idaho 1997) the wife promised not to contact the police about the husband's alleged sexual contact with their daughter if he would agree to a disproportionate financial settlement. When the husband agreed to the settlement and later challenged it, should the settlement be rescinded?

3.　WHAT TERMS ARE PERMISSIBLE?

A.　FAIRNESS

Should a court review the substantive fairness of a separation agreement?

UNIFORM MARRIAGE AND DIVORCE ACT　§ 306. [SEPARATION AGREEMENT]

(a)　To promote amicable settlement of disputes between parties to a marriage attendant upon their separation or the dissolution of their marriage, the parties may enter into a written separation agreement containing provisions for disposition of any property owned by either of them, maintenance of either of them, and support, custody, and visitation of their children.

(b)　In a proceeding for dissolution of marriage or for legal separation, the terms of the separation agreement, except those providing for the support, custody, and visitation of children, are binding upon the court unless it finds, after considering the economic circumstances of the parties and any other relevant evidence produced by the parties, on their own motion or on request of the court, that the separation agreement is unconscionable.

(c)　If the court finds the separation agreement unconscionable, it may request the parties to submit a revised separation agreement or may make orders for the disposition of property, maintenance, and support.

(d)　If the court finds that the separation agreement is not unconscionable as to disposition of property or maintenance, and not unsatisfactory as to support:

(1) unless the separation agreement provide to the contrary, its terms shall be set forth in the decree of dissolution or legal separation and the parties shall he ordered to perform them, or

(2) if the separation agreement provides that its terms shall not be set forth in the decree, the decree shall identify the separation agreement and state that the court has found the terms not unconscionable.

(e) Terms of the agreement set forth in the decree are enforceable by all remedies available for enforcement of a judgment, including contempt, and are enforceable as contract terms.

(f) Except for forms concerning the support, custody, or visitation of children, the decree may expressly preclude or limit modification of terms set forth in the decree if the separation agreement so provides.

Otherwise, terms of a separation agreement set forth in the decree are automatically modified by modification of the decree.

Official Comment

An important aspect of the effort to reduce the adversary trappings of marital dissolution is the attempt, made by § 306, to encourage the parties to reach an amicable disposition of the financial and other incidents of their marriage. This section entirely reverses the older view that property settlement agreements are against public policy because they tend to promote divorce. Rather, when a marriage has broken down irretrievably, public policy will be served by allowing the parties to plan their future by agreeing upon a disposition of their property, their maintenance, and the support, custody, and visitation of their children.

Subsection (b) undergirds the freedom allowed the parties by making clear that the terms of the agreement respecting maintenance and property disposition are binding upon the court unless those terms are found to be unconscionable. The standard of unconscionability is used in commercial law, where its meaning includes protection against one-sidedness, oppression, or unfair surprise (see § 2–302, Uniform Commercial Code), and in contract law * * *. It has been used in cases respecting divorce settlements or awards. Hence the act does not introduce a novel standard unknown to the law. In the context of negotiations between spouses as to the financial incidents of their marriage, the standard includes protection against overreaching, concealment of assets, and sharp dealing not consistent with the obligations of marital partners to deal fairly with each other.

In order to determine whether the agreement is unconscionable, the court may look to the economic circumstances of the parties resulting from the agreement, and any other relevant evidence such as the conditions under which the agreement was made, including the knowledge of the other party. If the court finds the agreement not unconscionable, its terms respecting property division and maintenance may not be altered by the court at the hearing.

The terms of the agreement respecting support, custody, and visitation of children are not binding upon the court even if these terms are not unconscionable. The court should perform its duty to provide for the children by careful examination of the agreement as to these terms in light of the standards established by § 309 for support and by Part IV for custody and visitation. * * *

IN RE MARRIAGE OF BISQUE

Colorado Court of Appeals, 2001.
31 P.3d 175.

TAUBMAN, J.

Matthew L. Bisque (husband) appeals the permanent orders dissolving his marriage to Cheryl L. Bisque (wife) and awarding her approximately 91% of the marital property, as provided in an agreement the parties signed and included in a mail-order Mexican divorce kit. We reverse and remand for further proceedings.

During this childless seven-year marriage, both parties were employed. Husband worked for a company owned by his brother, while wife has worked for large, publicly-held companies where she made more money than husband.

On March 23, 1998 wife purchased and received a kit to obtain a mail-order Mexican divorce. Without the benefit of counsel, the parties signed an agreement before a notary public on March 25, 1998, under which wife received the bulk of the marital estate, including the marital home and adjacent lot. * * *

The next day, the parties mailed the completed paperwork for the Mexican divorce, which included special powers of attorney referencing the March 25 agreement. The eventual Mexican decree also referenced the March 25 agreement and indicated that the case was filed March 27 1998, and that a divorce was granted a week later on April 3, 1998.

Approximately two months later, husband filed this Colorado action for dissolution. Wife then requested a declaratory judgment that the marriage had already been dissolved by the Mexican court. Determining that the parties' mail-order Mexican divorce was invalid, the court granted dissolution.

The court also found that the agreement was "extremely" and "grossly" unfair, and that husband signed the agreement because "(h)is will was simply overborne by his aggressive persistent, overbearing spouse." The court noted that wife "seems to be centered on money and very pushy," and was "unusually aggressive and demanding," while husband was "unusually passive and co-dependent." The court found that husband "is less driven by money than is" wife, and that wife was unhappy because husband's "job did not produce the income she thought appropriate."

However, the court concluded that the agreement was a marital agreement, rather than a separation agreement, because it was signed prior to the filing of the Colorado dissolution action. The court further concluded that the agreement is valid because husband signed it voluntarily after fair and reasonable disclosure of the parties' assets. * * *

I. MARITAL OR SEPARATION AGREEMENT?

Husband contends the court erred in concluding that the agreement constituted a marital agreement, rather than separation agreement, solely because it was signed before the filing of the Colorado dissolution of marriage action. More specifically, husband argues that the agreement, which was signed two months before the petition for the Colorado dissolution, but just the day before it was mailed with the Mexican divorce papers, constitutes a separation agreement because it was "attendant upon" the parties' dissolution of marriage. We agree.

A marital agreement is "an agreement either between prospective spouses made in contemplation of marriage or between present spouses, but only if signed by both parties prior to the filing of an action for dissolution of marriage or for legal separation." Section 14–2–302(1), C.R.S.2000. In contrast, a separation agreement promotes "the amicable settlement of disputes between the parties to a marriage attendant upon their separation or the dissolution of their marriage." Section 14–10–112(1), C.R.S.2000.

The two types of agreement are subject to different standards of review. A marital agreement is enforceable unless it was executed involuntarily or there was not a fair and reasonable disclosure of the property or financial obligations involved. In contrast, a separation agreement is enforceable unless it is found to be unconscionable.

The conscionability standard applicable to separation agreements is different "because of the public policy concern for safeguarding the interests of a spouse whose consent to the agreement may have been obtained under more emotionally stressful circumstances, especially if that spouse is unrepresented by counsel." *In re Marriage of Manzo*, 659 P.2d 669, 675 (Colo. 1983). * * *

The clear and unambiguous intent of § 14–10–112(1) is that, if an agreement is executed under circumstances accompanying, connected with, or surrounding a contemplated divorce or separation, it is a separation agreement.

The bright line rule in § 14–2–302(1), describing marital agreements as those made prior to filing for dissolution or legal separation, is equally clear and unambiguous.

The apparent conflict between these statutes may be resolved by requiring the trial court to make a specific factual finding whether an agreement is "connected with" or "attendant upon" a contemplated dissolution of marriage or legal separation.

Accordingly, we hold that when an agreement between present spouses is entered into "attendant upon" separation or dissolution, the agreement must be considered a separation agreement, even if it was signed prior to filing for dissolution or legal separation. In our view, this interpretation furthers the policy of safeguarding the interests of a spouse contemplating and preparing for the emotionally stressful step of dissolution of marriage.

Here, the findings and record indicate that the agreement was signed just two days before filling of the Mexican case. Furthermore, in its bench ruling, the court specifically found that the agreement "was made in anticipation or contemplation of the divorce."

Thus, the court made sufficient findings, based on the record, which support the conclusion that the agreement was clearly "attendant upon" a dissolution. Accordingly, the trial court erred reaching the legal conclusion that the agreement constituted a marital agreement. Instead, it constitutes a separation agreement and is entitled to review under the conscionability standard.

II.   UNCONSCIONABILITY OF SEPARATION AGREEMENT

Husband contends next that the separation agreement must be set aside as unconscionable. Again, we agree.

The trial court made oral findings supporting the determination that husband's emotional state was adversely affected by the circumstances surrounding the execution of the agreement. First, the court found that there is "no question" but that wife was the "impetus for the divorce" and that she "is a very driven woman; insisting, consistently pushing for those things which she desires, and somewhat manipulative in the way that she does it." The court found that "those were the factors in this ultimate dissolution and agreement." This sentiment is mirrored in the written finding that husband's "will was simply overborne by his aggressive, persistent, overbearing spouse."

Furthermore, the court, in both its oral and written findings, made numerous emphatic references to the unfairness of this separation agreement. The court found that "[i]f marital agreements could be set aside in Colorado solely because they divide the marital estate unfairly, this one would be set aside." Thus, the only reason the court declined to set aside the agreement was its legal conclusion that an agreement entered into prior to the parties' filing for dissolution must be considered a marital agreement. However, since we have concluded otherwise, this agreement * * * must be set aside.

On remand, the court shall divide the marital property equitably without reference to the separation agreement.

NOTES AND QUESTIONS

1. Most states use the unconscionability standard described in *Bisque* in determining whether a divorce settlement agreement should be set aside due to unfairness. *See* Wasserman v. Wasserman, 629 N.Y.S.2d 69 (App. Div. 1995); Weber v. Weber, 548 N.W.2d 781 (N.D. 1996). In a few states, a separation agreement is enforceable only if it is fair. *See* TEX. FAM. CODE § 7.006.

2. What percentage award to the husband would the *Bisque* court consider conscionable? Put somewhat differently, why is the agreement in *Bisque* unconscionable? Would the court have found the *Bisque* agreement conscionable if the wife had a significantly lower income than the husband? Would the court have found the agreement conscionable if the wife had been less domineering? *Compare* Galloway v. Galloway, 622 S.E.2d 267 (Va. App. 2005) (upholding agreement giving one spouse 94% of marital assents based on the other spouse's failure to show overreaching or oppressive influence) *with* Shraberg v. Shraberg, 939 S.W.2d 330 (Ky. 1997) (rejecting argument that a one-sided agreement should not be set aside on grounds of unconscionability unless the claimant spouse can show fraud, undue influence or overreaching).

3. What if one spouse says to the other, "Accept the economic terms I have proposed or I will seek custody." Is this duress? If yes, should duress be a ground for rescission of the agreement? *Compare* Marriage of Lawrence, 642 P.2d 1043 (Mont. 1982) ("custody is frequently a bargaining chip, whether we like it or not") *with* Fanning v. Fanning, 828 S.W.2d 135 (Tex. App. 1992) (custody-contest threat is relevant to unconscionability).

4. If one lawyer represented both spouses in connection with the separation agreement, should this affect its enforceability? *Compare* Levine v. Levine, 436 N.E.2d 476 (N.Y. 1982) *with* Marriage of Egedi, 105 Cal. Rptr. 2d 518 (App. 2001) (and *see* chapter 11 *supra*).

5. The ALI has proposed that:

The terms of a separation agreement [relating to property division or spousal support] are unenforceable if they substantially limit or augment [property rights or spousal support rights] otherwise due under law, and enforcement of the terms would substantially impair the economic well-being of a party who has or will have:

(a) primary or dual residential responsibility for a child or

(b)   substantially fewer economic resources than the other party.

ALI PRINCIPLES § 7.09 (2).

How does the ALI standard differ from the UMDA approach? What are the pros and cons of both approaches? On balance, which one is preferable?

6.   Under both the UMDA and ALI PRINCIPLES, agreements regarding children (support, visitation, custody) are unenforceable without court approval. *See* UMDA § 306(b); ALI *Principles* § 7.09(5). *See also* RESTATEMENT (SECOND) OF CONTRACTS § 191 (1981) ("A promise affecting the right of custody of a minor child is unenforceable on grounds of public policy unless the disposition as to custody is consistent with the best interest of the child.") For example, in Kelley v. Kelley, 449 S.E.2d 55 (Va. 1994), the husband agreed that the wife could have the total equity in the marital home in return for the wife's agreement that if he would be freed of any child support obligation. The wife agreed to indemnify him for any child support he ever had to pay. When she later sued for support, he tried to enforce the indemnity agreement; the court ruled the wife couldn't contract away the child's right to support. In Bell v. Bell, 572 So. 2d 841 (Miss. 1990), the husband and wife agreed that neither would relocate with the children without the other's consent. When the husband tried to enforce this agreement the court refused to enforce it and instead determined what would be in the child's best interest.

Is this approach sensible? Custody, support, and visitation are typically basic and integral factors in the negotiation between the parties. Moreover, during the marriage, parents may do *anything* they please with their minor children, barring abuse or neglect. Why should they not be equally autonomous on divorce? Specifically, if the mother agrees to a smaller property settlement than she might otherwise have accepted because the husband agrees to let her have custody of the children (thereby imposing long-run child support and, possibly, alimony obligations upon himself), why should the father be able to relitigate the custody issue when he could not if he had traded alimony for property? If the family home is relinquished to the wife in exchange for generous visitation arrangements or if child support was set deliberately low and alimony deliberately high so as to gain a tax advantage, how can a separation agreement be structured to avoid potential problems?

7.   Because divorce is part of the consideration for a separation agreement, the couple's reconciliation will ordinarily nullify the agreement. *See* Estate of K.J.R., 792 A.2d 561 (N.J. Super. App. Div. 2002). But a court may nonetheless enforce the agreement if it finds that the parties intended the agreement as a *postnuptial contract*. *See* Vaccarello v. Vaccarello, 757 A.2d 909 (Pa. 2000) (enforcing agreement signed during separation as postnuptial agreement despite parties' 12-year reconciliation); *In re* Marriage of Patterson and Kanaga, 255 P.3d 634 (Or. App. 2011).

8.   Should the same rescission standards apply to separation and postnuptial agreements? *See* chapter 5 *supra*. If not, how can the two situations be distinguished? Which should be easier to challenge?

FRANCE V. FRANCE

North Carolina Court of Appeals, 2011.
705 S.E.2d 399.

McGEE, JUDGE.

Plaintiff and Defendant entered into a Contract of Separation, Property Settlement, Child Support, Child Custody and Alimony Agreement (the Agreement) on 17 December 2007. One of the provisions of the Agreement concerned confidentiality. Plaintiff and Defendant agreed that "neither party [would] disclose any financial information relating to the other party or any provision of th[e] Agreement to anyone except" certain professionals, such as their attorneys and financial advisors, unless compelled by law. Plaintiff and Defendant further agreed to keep private certain personal information regarding each other "unless either party is legally compelled to disclose any such information[.]"

[Based on the parties' confidentiality agreement, the parties petitioned the court to close the proceedings and bar the public from witnessing them. The court denied the motion and the parties appealed.]

We must now decide whether Judge Culler was correct in ruling that "there are no compelling countervailing public interests as related to these parties which outweigh the public's right and access to open court proceedings." Our Supreme Court has stated:

> The paramount duty of the trial judge is to supervise and control the course of the trial so as to prevent injustice. Thus, even though court records may generally be public records under N.C.G.S. § 132–1, a trial court may, in the proper circumstances, shield portions of *court proceedings* and records from the public; the power to do so is a necessary power rightfully pertaining to the judiciary as a separate branch of the government, and the General Assembly has "no power" to diminish it in any manner. N.C. Const. art. IV, § 1 [.] This necessary and inherent power of the judiciary should only be exercised, however, when its use is required in the interest of the proper and fair administration of justice or where, for reasons of public policy, the openness ordinarily required of our government will be more harmful than beneficial.

Article I, Section 18 [of the North Carolina Constitution] provides the public access to our courts. Article I, Section 18 of the North Carolina Constitution guarantees a *qualified* constitutional right on the part of the public to attend civil court proceedings. We begin with the presumption that the civil court proceedings and records at issue in this case must be open to the public, including the news media, under Article I, Section 18.

The qualified public right of access to civil court proceedings guaranteed by Article I, Section 18 is not absolute and is subject to reasonable limitations imposed in the interest of the fair administration of justice or for other compelling public purposes. Thus, although the public has a qualified right of access to civil court proceedings and records, the trial court may limit this right when there is a compelling countervailing public interest and closure of the court proceedings or sealing of documents is required to protect such countervailing public interest. In performing this analysis, the trial court must consider alternatives to closure. Unless such an overriding interest exists, the civil court proceedings and records will be open to the public. Where the trial court closes proceedings or seals records and documents, it must make findings of fact which are specific enough to allow appellate review to determine whether the proceedings or records were required to be open to the public by virtue of the constitutional presumption of access.

Beginning with the presumption that the civil court proceedings and records at issue in this case must be open to the public, including the news media, under Article I, Section 18, we find no abuse of the trial court's discretion in ruling that Plaintiff failed to overcome this presumption by demonstrating that the public's right to open proceedings was outweighed by a countervailing public interest. Plaintiff argues that the qualified right to open court proceedings is outweighed by his constitutional right to contract, the right to seek redress for injury, and "the right of privacy in matters related to minor children and . . . personal and financial affairs."

In his argument concerning his right to contract, Plaintiff states that "unless a contract is contrary to public policy or prohibited by statute, the freedom to contract requires that it be enforced." We hold that if the Agreement requires automatic and complete closure of the proceedings in this matter, then the Agreement *is* in violation of public policy—the qualified public right of access to civil court proceedings guaranteed by Article I, Section 18. Were we to adopt Plaintiff's position, any civil proceeding could be closed to the public merely because any party involved executed a contract with a confidentiality clause similar to that contained in the Agreement in this matter. Plaintiff's right to contract is in no way violated; we merely hold that Plaintiff cannot, by contract, circumvent established public policy—the qualified public right of access to civil court proceedings. Plaintiff must show some independent countervailing public policy concern sufficient to outweigh the qualified right of access to civil court proceedings.

Plaintiff's position would also render meaningless provisions of the Public Records Act, N.C. Gen. Stat. § 132–1 (1995). *Virmani,* 350 N.C. at 462–63, 515 S.E.2d at 685 (Transcripts of civil court proceedings are public records under the Public Records Act. "The term 'public records,' as used in N.C.G.S. § 132–1, includes all documents and papers made or received by any agency of North Carolina government in the course of conducting its public proceedings. N.C.G.S. § 132–1(a) (1995). The public's right of access to court records is provided by N.C.G.S. § 7A–109(a), which specifically grants the public the right to inspect court records in criminal and civil proceedings. N.C.G.S. § 7A–109(a) (1995).").

We hold that, in the present case, the trial court was correct to determine whether proceedings should be closed based upon the nature of the evidence to be admitted and the facts of this specific case. Evidence otherwise appropriate for open court may not be sealed merely because an agreement is involved that purports to render the contents of that agreement confidential. Certain kinds of evidence may be such that the public policy factors in favor of confidentiality outweigh the public policy factors supporting free access of the public to public records and proceedings. *See, e.g.,* N.C. Gen. Stat. § 15–166 (2009) ("In the trial of cases for rape or sex offense or attempt to commit rape or attempt to commit a sex offense, the trial judge may, during the taking of the testimony of the [victim], exclude from the courtroom all persons except the officers of the court, the defendant and those engaged in the trial of the case."); N.C. Gen. Stat. § 48–2–203 (2009) ("A judicial hearing in any proceeding pursuant to this Chapter [adoption of a minor child] shall be held in closed court."); N.C. Gen. Stat. § 66–156 (2009) ("In an action under this Article, a court shall protect an alleged trade secret by reasonable steps which may include granting protective orders in connection with discovery proceedings, holding in-camera hearings, sealing the records of the action subject to further court order, and ordering any person who gains access to an alleged trade secret during the litigation not to disclose such alleged trade secret without prior court approval."); *Virmani,* 350 N.C. at 478, 515 S.E.2d at 694 ("The public's interest in access to these court proceedings, records and documents is outweighed by the compelling public interest in protecting the confidentiality of medical peer review records in order to foster effective, frank and uninhibited exchange among medical peer review committee members."); *Knight,* 172 N.C.App. at 495, 616 S.E.2d at 609 ("Whatever the General Assembly's policy considerations, the language employed by the General Assembly shows that it was concerned about protecting the confidentiality of public hospital personnel information, thereby specifically exempting this information from broad public access.").

We hold that Plaintiff's claim that his "constitutional right of privacy, particularly with respect to matters surrounding the parenting of minor children," will be violated is without merit, and Plaintiff fails to show that any such right to privacy outweighs the qualified right of the public to open proceedings. Plaintiff cites no authority in support of his claim that any "compelling interest" exists to close the proceedings in the *present* case for the protection of his children, especially as Plaintiff argues that the entire proceeding should be closed, not just the portions involving information concerning his minor children. While a trial court may close proceedings to protect minors in certain situations, such as where a child is testifying about alleged abuse that child has suffered, or adoption proceedings, N.C.G.S. § 48–2–203, we can find no case supporting the closing of an entire proceeding merely because some evidence relating to a minor child would be admitted. We hold that it is the province of the trial court to determine when a proceeding will be closed to protect a minor child, absent a specific statutory mandate such as in N.C.G.S. § 48–2–203.

In most instances, a proceeding will only be closed during the testimony of the minor child. Plaintiff has presented nothing on appeal demonstrating that the trial court abused its discretion by denying Plaintiff's motion to close the proceeding merely because some evidence concerning his minor children could be admitted. If, during the course of a proceeding, the trial court determines that any part of the proceeding should be closed to protect a minor child, the trial court remains free to make that determination. We hold that the trial court did not abuse its discretion in denying Plaintiff's motion to close the proceeding to the public, which included the media.

B. TERMS ENCOURAGING DIVORCE

RESTATEMENT (SECOND) OF CONTRACTS § 190 (1981)

Comment to § 190.

b.   *Separation agreements.* The policy that limits the parties in modifying the marital relationship does not apply if that relationship has ended. The rule stated in Subsection (1) thus does not apply to a promise that is part of an enforceable separation agreement. To be enforceable, a separation agreement must be made after the parties have separated or when they contemplate immediate separation, so that the marriage has, in effect, already disintegrated. It must also be fair in the circumstances, a matter as to which the court may exercise its continuing discretionary powers. Separation agreements commonly deal with such matters as support and are generally enforceable because the parties could usually accomplish the same result through a judicial separation. They are still subject to the rule stated in Subsection (2) if they tend unreasonably to encourage divorce.

Illustration:

2.   A and B who are married but have decided to separate, make a separation agreement that is fair in the circumstances, in which A promises to pay B a stated sum each month in return for B's promise to relinquish all other claims to support. Although the promises of A and B change an essential incident of the marital relationship, their enforcement is not for that reason precluded on grounds of public policy because they are part of a separation agreement.

c.   *Tending to encourage divorce or separation.* When persons contemplating marriage or married persons seek to determine by agreement their rights in the event of a divorce or separation, the rule stated in Subsection (2) comes into play, along with that stated in Subsection (1). See Illustration 2. Because of the public interest in the marriage relationship * * *, a promise that undermines that relationship by tending unreasonably to encourage divorce or separation is unenforceable. Although the parties are free, if they choose, to terminate their relationship under the law providing for divorce or separation, a commitment that tends unreasonably in this direction will not be enforced. Whether a promise tends unreasonably to encourage divorce or separation in a particular case is a question of fact that depends on all the circumstances, including the state of disintegration of the marriage at the time the promise is made. A promise that merely disposes of property rights in the event of divorce or separation does not of itself tend unreasonably to encourage either.

Illustrations:

3.   A, who is married to B, promises to pay B $50,000 in return for B's promise to obtain a divorce. The promises of A and B tend unreasonably to encourage divorce and are unenforceable on grounds of public policy. The result does not depend on whether or not there are grounds for divorce or on whether or not B has performed.

4.   A, who was married to B but has obtained a divorce that can possibly be set aside for fraud, promises to pay B $50,000 in return for B's promise not to attempt to have the divorce set aside. The promises of both A and B tend unreasonably to encourage divorce and are unenforceable on grounds of public policy. The result does not depend on whether or not B has performed.

5.   A, who has begun divorce proceedings against B, promises B that if divorce is granted, alimony shall be fixed at a stated sum, in return for B's agreement to relinquish all other claims to alimony. A court may decide that in view of the disintegration of the marriage relationship, the promises of A and B do not tend unreasonably to encourage divorce and their enforcement is not precluded on grounds of public policy.

Courts distinguish between provisions of an agreement that facilitate divorce and those that induce it. A separation agreement does not induce divorce because the parties have already separated and the marriage has broken down. Similarly, in Glickman v. Collins, 533 P.2d 204 (Cal. 1975), the prospective second wife of the husband agreed to guarantee the obligations of the husband to the first wife under the separation agreement; in return, the first wife agreed to facilitate the divorce. The court concluded that, because the marriage of the first wife and the husband had already broken down at the time the agreement was signed and grounds for divorce existed, the agreement was enforceable. By contrast, a court may not enforce an agreement that induces a spouse to divorce if the spouses are still cohabiting. *See* Capazzoli v. Holzwasser, 490 N.E.2d 420 (Mass. 1986) (involving a boyfriend's promise of support to induce a wife of another to divorce her husband).

4. ENFORCEMENT AND MODIFICATION OF THE AGREEMENT

A. MERGER OF THE AGREEMENT INTO THE DECREE

After a settlement agreement is signed, the court will normally enter a divorce decree reflecting the terms of the agreement. This presents the technical, but important, question of whether the contract remains in effect once a decree has been entered. If the contract is still in effect, does modification of the divorce decree inferentially modify the contract as well?

MURPHY V. MURPHY
Delaware Family Court, 1983.
467 A.2d 129.

GALLAGHER, JUDGE.

A petition has been filed by petitioner, (father) against respondent (mother) seeking to modify an order entered by this court on June 17, 1982, incorporating into a divorce decree the parties' separation agreement dated October 7, 1981. Under the agreement father is to pay to mother unallocated alimony and child support in the sum of $462 each week. Father now asks that his support obligation be reduced to $250 a week because his income estimations at the time the agreement was entered into were higher than his actual income has turned out to be. Father also suggests that the *Melson* formula, often utilized by this court in determining child support obligations, be utilized by the court if it should produce a lower support figure.

Respondent filed an answer opposing the relief requested by the petition. Although unwilling to relinquish any of her rights under the agreement, mother does admit that father is presently financially unable to meet his obligations under the agreement and indicates a willingness to be satisfied presently with payment of $350 per week support.

Father, in support of his request that the court modify the separation agreement, argues that when the agreement was incorporated into the divorce decree the court gained full power to modify that agreement under 13 Del.C § 1519.

Mother, in response, insists that the agreement retains its contractual nature despite incorporation into the decree. Therefore, according to mother, the court has no power to modify the terms of the agreement.

Under paragraph 7 of the agreement either party may at any time cause the agreement "to be filed of record in any court of competent jurisdiction". By stipulated order dated June 17,1983, the agreement was incorporated into the divorce decree entered herein.

There is a body of well established law defining the powers of, and limitations on, a court in modifying or enforcing a marital agreement. Where the parties have contracted with respect to their rights, privileges and obligations they are bound by their agreement and the court does not have the power either under 18 Del.C. § 1519, or independently, to modify the same. The existence of an agreement treating matters such as child support, custody and visitation will not preclude the court from entering an independent inconsistent order with respect to these matters, the rationale being that since the children were not parties to the agreement neither they nor the court are bound thereby. But even though a court is free to disregard contractual undertakings respecting children it will normally consider those undertakings and, if reasonable, make them the basis for a court order.

But is the situation any different where the divorce or other decree touches upon the agreement itself? Does it matter whether the agreement is merely incorporated into the divorce decree or merged therein?

If the agreement is merely incorporated into the decree it retains, for all intents and purposes, its contractual character, and the decree is limited by the terms of the contract. The purpose of incorporation by reference is to identify and verify the agreement of the parties, provide a basis for *res judicata* and, perhaps, promote enforcement in a foreign forum. But since the court looks exclusively to the agreement for resolution of the parties' post-nuptial rights, privileges and obligations it does not have the power, unless contractually given by the parties, to modify the agreement. In short, incorporation of the agreement into the decree does not empower the court to modify the agreement, pursuant to 13 Del.C. § 1519, as it might alter a judicial disposition because the terms of the order are entirely the product of its contractual genesis. It would also follow that a contempt citation should not issue in the first instance for breach of an agreement incorporated into a decree.

If the court thereafter enters an order inconsistent with any provision of the agreement as regards children such an order does not modify the agreement of the parties. It has been held that in such event suit might then be brought on the contract to recover any monetary differential created by the order.

But if the agreement is merged into the decree the result is entirely different. In that event the rights, privileges and obligations of the parties under the agreement are displaced by the judgment or decree. * * * and the court has full power to modify the agreement (now an order) to the extent that it has jurisdiction to do so. Following merger the contract between the parties no longer exists and in its stead there is a judgment or decree under which the rights, privileges and obligations of the parties are to be defined and enforced thereafter. The contempt citation would alto be available *ab initio.*

Does the fact that the court cannot modify an incorporated separation agreement mean that in every case the court must order the respondent to perform his obligations under the agreement to the letter? The answer is no. The court has the power to award specific performance on such terms and conditions as justice requires even though the performance ordered is not identical with the performance required by the agreement.

I cannot modify the incorporated agreement now before the court to reduce father's support obligation thereunder. I will give mother a judgment for the full amount of support arrears and for counsel fees. I will, nevertheless, order that father pay not less than $325 each week, a lesser sum than the sum specified by the agreement, and so long as he pays the lesser sum ordered by the court he will not be held in contempt for failure to pay the contractual support. Let me emphasize again that the support arrears will continue to accrue and that with respect to those arrears mother can obtain a judgment and execution thereon in the Superior Court.

IT IS SO ORDERED.

NOTES AND QUESTIONS

1. The Delaware Supreme Court has since changed its rule for modifying alimony agreements merged into a decree. *See* Rockwell v. Rockwell, 681 A.2d 1017 (Del. 1996) (such obligations should be treated as contractual and are generally not modifiable). Still, the *Murphy* approach is applied by a number of courts.

The decision whether to merge the settlement agreement into the decree is surprisingly important in a number of states. If the agreement is only incorporated, but not merged, it remains an enforceable contract. In such a case, some courts (like *Murphy*) permit modification of the decree, but not the agreement; so, if the amount due under the decree is reduced and the obligor pays the new amount, the obligor can still be sued on the contract. *See* Mendelson v. Mendelson, 541 A.2d 1331 (Md. App. 1988). Other courts will not modify even the decree unless it expressly states that is intended to have validity independent from the agreement. *See* Riffenburg v. Riffenburg, 585 A.2d 627 (R.I. 1991). Even if the agreement is considered merged into the decree, support provisions are not modifiable if the court finds they are part of an integrated agreement. *See* Keeler v. Keeler, 958 P.2d 599 (Idaho App. 1998).

2. Merger can affect the range of remedies available. A merged agreement can be enforced through a contempt proceeding, while a non-merged agreement can only be enforced through an action for breach of contract. *See* Oedekoven v. Oedekoven, 538 P.2d 1292 (Wyo. 1975). *See also,* Davis v. Davis, 489 S.W.3d 225 (Ky. 2016). Merger thus will be preferable to incorporation for the spouse whose primary concern is child support enforcement. But, if the contractual support obligation exceeds that which a court could impose, incorporation may be preferable. For example, in many states a court may not order post-majority support during college; in some, such an obligation cannot be enforced if the agreement is merged into the decree. *See, e.g.,* Noble v. Fisher, 894 P.2d 118 (Idaho 1995).

3. Some rights can't be divided by court order but can be divided if the parties so agree. Thus, in Hoskins v. Skojec, 696 N.Y.S.2d 303 (App. Div. 1999), the court found that the parties' agreement was incorporated, but not merged into the divorce decree and enforced a provision dividing the husband's veteran's disability benefits, which could not have been divided by court order.

4. Courts have not reached consensus on what to do if the divorce decree does not expressly state whether the parties intend to merge the agreement into the decree. *See* Doris Brogan, *Divorce Settlement Agreements: The Problem of Merger or Incorporation and the Status of the Agreement in Relation to the Decree*, 67 NEB. L. REV. 235 (1988).

5. Under UMDA § 306(d), the parties to a separation agreement are not required to decide whether to merge the agreement into the decree; those terms set forth in the decree may be enforced by judicial enforcement procedures:

> [This] permit[s] the parties, in drawing the separation agreement, to choose whether its terms shall or shall not be set forth in the decree. In the former event, the provisions of subsection (e), making these terms enforceable through the remedies available for the enforcement of a judgment, but retaining also the enforceability of them as contract terms, apply. This represents a reversal of the policy of the original 1970 Act, which required a choice between "merging" the agreement in the judgment and retaining in character as a contract. Strong representations as to the undesirability of such a choice, in the light of foreign doctrines as to the enforceability of judgment, as compared with contract terms, in this area of the law, made by persons and groups whose expertise entitled them to respect, led the Conference, in 1971, to change its former decision.
>
> There still remains a place for agreements the terms of which are not set forth in the decree, if the parties prefer that it retain the status of a private contract, only. In this instance, the remedies for the enforcement of a judgment will not be available, but the court's determination, in the decree, that the terms are not unconscionable, under the ordinary rules of res adjudicata, will prevent a later successful claim of unconscionability. Such an agreement, unless its terms expressly so permit, will not be modifiable as to economic

matters. Other subjects, relating to the children, by subsection (b) do not bind the Court.

Official Comments to § 306.

6.   When a settlement agreement is not merged in the decree, does a material breach of the agreement by one party excuse the nonbreaching party from the performance of his or her obligations under the contract and/or under the decree? *See* Herbert v. Herbert, 754 S.W.2d 141 (Tex. 1988) (holding that nonbreaching party was excused).

B. ENFORCEMENT BY CONTEMPT

OEDEKOVEN V. OEDEKOVEN
Supreme Court of Wyoming, 1975.
538 P.2d 1292.

RAPER, J.

One serious question, as we see it, arises in this appeal: Is contempt the proper path to travel when a property settlement agreement is only *issue* ratified and confirmed by the divorce decree, without incorporating a direction that the parties comply with its terms? There are other significant queries raised by appellant intertwined with that problem which we shall dispose of at the time they are reached. * * *

The rule is plainly stated in 24 Am.Jur.2d (Divorce and Separation) § 921, p. 1049: "Assuming that performance of an act called for by a property settlement may be enforced by a contempt proceeding where the court distinctly orders performance, performance will not be so enforced where the decree is not to be construed as including such an order. Thus, if the decree approves a property settlement but does not order the parties to perform its obligations, the violation of the agreement is not a violation of the decree and is not a contempt of court."

* * *

* * * [M]ere approval of a property settlement agreement is not a command to pay what is due by its terms and so, therefore, there is no order of the court or decree of the court that has been violated. Furthermore, there are hovering in the background constitutional implications that a person may not be imprisoned for debt but we avoid nailing our decision to that reason. The result we then have is when a party to a divorce action, where the court has only approved and ratified the agreement, asserts nonpayment under its conditions, he or she is confined to a claim on contract not enforceable by contempt proceedings. We so hold and consider it fundamental reversible error to hold defendant in contempt with all its overtones of punishment under such circumstances, even in absence of objection. The obligation sought to be enforced is negotiated and

contractual and while arising out of marriage, the remedy must conform to the right asserted—one consistent with contract and not a decree enforceable by attachment of the person.

C. WAIVER OF THE RIGHT TO MODIFY

KARON V. KARON
Supreme Court of Minnesota, 1989.
435 N.W.2d 501.

YETKA, JUSTICE.

This case is before the court on the appeal by the petitioner of a decision of the Hennepin County District Court, affirmed by the court of appeals, which modified an award of maintenance originally made pursuant to a stipulation of the parties in which the parties waived any right to future modification of maintenance. We reverse the trial court and reinstate the original terms of the decree of dissolution.

Frima and Howard Karon executed a stipulation in this dissolution action on June 27, 1981, and the trial court incorporated the terms of the stipulation into its judgment and decree. The decree awarded temporary maintenance to Frima for a 10-year period. The stipulation, as well as the judgment and decree, states that the parties waived any right to maintenance except as provided therein and that the court was divested of jurisdiction to alter the agreement or maintenance.

On February 7, 1986, the referee recommended and the court held, pursuant to Frima's motion, that it had jurisdiction to modify the dissolution decree pursuant to Minn. Stat. § 518.64 (Supp. 1985). On March 11, the court affirmed the referee's recommendation. After a discovery period, the referee recommended and the court ordered that the judgment and decree be modified to increase the amount of maintenance to Frima and made the maintenance award permanent rather than temporary. The court made the increase in maintenance retroactive to October 1, 1986, and an amended judgment and decree was entered on May 14, 1987.

Howard appealed the issue of whether the court had authority to modify the decree while Frima appealed the amount of the modification and the amount of attorney fees awarded. The court of appeals affirmed the trial court. Howard appealed to this court.

Howard F. and Frima M. Karon married on December 21, 1952. Howard commenced a dissolution proceeding in 1979, and the parties executed a stipulation on June 27, 1981. The court entered its judgment and decree on August 28, 1981, incorporating the terms of the stipulation. Both documents provided that Howard would pay Frima $1,200 per month for 6 years and $600 per month for 4 years thereafter. Both documents also stated:

> Except for the aforesaid maintenance, each party waives and is forever barred from receiving any spousal maintenance whatsoever from one another, and this court is divested from having any jurisdiction whatsoever to award temporary or permanent spousal maintenance to either of the parties.

In late 1985, Frima moved the court for a modification of the maintenance award, requesting permanent maintenance of $3,500 month. Howard challenged the court's authority to modify the maintenance provision, arguing that the parties had waived any alteration of maintenance in the stipulation and that the court had divested itself of jurisdiction to alter the decree. A referee held that Minn. Stat. § 518.64 (Supp. 1985) granted it such authority and ordered that it would hear the modification motion on the merits after a discovery period. The district court affirmed this order.

After the completion of discovery, a referee heard the merits of the motion and ruled that a substantial change in circumstances had occurred, warranting a maintenance modification pursuant to § 518.64. The referee determined, however, that Frima had the capacity to earn $1,000 per month and thus increased maintenance to $1,500 per month rather than the $3,500 requested. The referee also made the award permanent because Frima had an uncertain future earning capacity. Finally, the referee awarded Frima $1,000 in attorney fees. The district court affirmed the referee's order.

Howard appealed the jurisdictional decision and the decision on the merits. Frima appealed the decision on the merits and the decision on attorney fees. She claimed that the court had abused its discretion by not awarding the requested amounts.

The court of appeals affirmed the trial court. This court granted Howard's petition for further review which, like the arguments before the court of appeals, presented only jurisdictional issues. Frima never filed a petition for further review.

The parties have confused and compounded numerous issues, but we believe the question before us is whether one of the adult parties to a stipulation in a dissolution matter made in 1981, which was approved by the trial court and which settled all issues, including maintenance, and which further provided that the parties expressly waived any right to maintenance except as provided in the original agreement, may now re-open the issue of maintenance to seek an increase therein. The trial court allowed reconsideration of the maintenance issue and the court of appeals affirmed. We reverse.

Howard argues that the terms of the original judgment and decree denied the court any further jurisdiction over the issue of maintenance. We agree. The language of the judgment and decree purports to divest jurisdiction. Section 518.64, however, states that the court may modify a maintenance award upon petition of a party. The court must decide, therefore, whether the maintenance issue was res judicata or whether the court correctly modified the maintenance award under § 518.64 regardless of the original order's language.

Initially, the legal doctrines at issue need clarification. Howard, in essence, argues that the form of res judicata known as direct estoppel precludes relitigation of the maintenance issue. Direct estoppel is issue preclusion in a second action on the same claim. Restatement (Second) of Judgments § 27 comment b (1982). The seminal issue, therefore, becomes whether the original decree constituted a final judgment in the dissolution on the maintenance issue. If so, it should have had the res judicata effect of preventing the court from hearing the modification motion. Phrased in other words, we must decide whether the district court properly divested itself of jurisdiction over the issue in 1981. We hold that it did.

It is not the parties to the stipulation who have divested the court of ability to relitigate the issue of maintenance. The court had the authority to refuse to accept the terms of the stipulation in part or *in toto*. The trial court stands in place and on behalf of the citizens of the state as a third party to dissolution actions. It has a duty to protect the interests of both parties and all the citizens of the state to ensure that the stipulation is fair and reasonable to all. The court did so here and approved the stipulation and incorporated the terms therein in its decree. Thus, the decree is final absent fraud.

We have recognized that parties may stipulate to waive all maintenance at the time of the initial decree and that the courts are without authority to award it in the future. Likewise, we have held that if maintenance is awarded and the term has expired, the court is equally without authority to award further maintenance.

We see no valid distinction between the two situations outlined above and the one now before us. Counsel for respondent would have us believe that waiver of a statutory right is without precedent. One can quickly see the fallacy of such an argument. In probate law, for example, heirs frequently enter into stipulations to distribute property or to waive statutory allowances. Antenuptial agreements have become quite common in the past several decades. In criminal law, we have held on numerous occasions that a defendant can waive constitutional rights.

Normally, stipulations are carefully drawn compromises which affect property distribution, real and personal, as well as future income. One may, for example, give or take certain items in order to have another reduced or eliminated. Setting aside one portion of the stipulation may totally warp the effects of other portions of the document. It would be difficult to imagine why anyone would agree to temporary maintenance or even maintenance itself for an indefinite period if the agreement could be later nullified. Why not litigate the matter at the time of the original dissolution proceedings? In the interest of judicial economy, parties should be encouraged to compromise their differences and not to litigate them. It is in the litigation of difficult dissolution matters where much of the acrimony and long-term scars are created, leading to still more litigation.

For any of these reasons, we reverse the modification of the original dissolution decree and remand to the trial court with instructions to enforce the terms of that initial dissolution decree.

NOTES AND QUESTIONS

1.   Should a waiver of the right to modify a family law obligation be treated differently from other types of waiver?

2.   Why would a party agree to waive the right to modify? *- security*

3.   The *Karon* dissent expressed concern that the court's decision would prevent the recipient from obtaining increased support even if she became disabled. *See* 435 N.W.2d at 504. Is this an accurate interpretation of the majority decision? If so, did the *Karon* majority reach the wrong result? Can you think of a better approach to limiting modification rights?

4.   Would the *Karon* court have reached the same result if the issue were the custodial parent's right to increase child support? What result under UMDA § 306?

5.   The *Karon* court enforced the modification waiver when the obligor's income increased. *See also* Toni v. Toni, 636 N.W.2d 396 (N.D. 2001) (alimony); Marriage of McInnis, 110 P.3d 639 (Or. App. 2005) (alimony). Courts have also enforced a waiver of the right to modify when the obligor's income has decreased. *See* Honore v. Honore, 439 N.W.2d 827 (Wis. App. 1989) (child support); Josic v. Josic, 397 N.E.2d 204 (Ill. App. 1979) (alimony). One court refused to terminate an alimony obligation when the recipient had married, in light of the provision in the marital settlement agreement providing that the alimony obligation as set forth in the agreement was not modifiable. *See* Vick v. Hicks, 2014 WL 6333965 (Tenn. App. 2014).

6.   Almost all the cases cited above involve alimony, not child support. In *Honore*, the court enforced a no-modification clause regarding child support that extended for three years, when the obligor's income decreased and the obligor petitioned to reduce support. Should the result be the same when the child support recipient is petitioning for an increase in child support due to an increase in the obligor's income? In Matar v. Harake, 270 P.3d 257 (Or. App. 2011) the court enforced the parties' agreement not to modify child support, but stated that such an agreement should not be enforced if it would be

contrary to public policy. In May v. May, 813 N.W.2d 179 (Wis. 2012), while the court enforced an agreement that the child support could not be reduced during a 33-month period, the court stated that an agreement barring child support modification for an indefinite period would "likely violate public policy." In Tomlinson v. Tomlinson, 46 A.3d 112 (Conn. 2012) the court ruled that the husband's child support obligation was modifiable when he was granted primary physical custody of the child, even though the parties' separation agreement characterized his obligation as nonmodifiable.

7.   Courts have enforced other contractual limits relating to modification of support. For example, in Gentry v. Morgan, 83 So. 3d 924 (Fla. Dist. Ct. App. 2012) the parties agreed that the father would pay $2500 in monthly child support and that the child support could not be changed unless the obligor's annual income exceeded $2.5 million or was less than $500,000. The appellate court ruled that, in light of this agreement, the child support should not be increased when the obligor had received a raise, but his income did not exceed $2.5 million.

Problem 18-3:

Harry signed a separation agreement in which he agreed to pay Wendy $250 per month in permanent maintenance. Harry did so because he believed, based on the prevailing pattern of judicial decision making, that Wendy stood a good chance of obtaining permanent maintenance should the case go to trial. Shortly thereafter, the legislature limited maintenance to a period of 121 months. Can Harry obtain modification of the separation agreement based on the change in the law? *See In re* Marriage of Jones, 921 P.2d 839 (Kan. App. 1996).

CHAPTER 19

LEGAL CONSEQUENCES OF CHILD SUPPORT, PROPERTY DIVISION AND ALIMONY DISTINGUISHED: TAXATION AND BANKRUPTCY

■ ■ ■

1. BASIC OVERVIEW

Awards of property, alimony, and child support do not have the same legal consequences:

1.   *Federal Income Tax:* Alimony is deductible from the income of the payor and includable in the income of the recipient; a property settlement or child support is not. A property transfer produces no immediate capital gains consequences; a spouse who receives a property distribution incident to divorce takes the transferor's adjusted basis in the property. A "QDRO" pension distribution produces no tax consequences until pension payments are received.

2.   *Federal Gift and Estate Tax:* Transfers between spouses qualify for an unlimited marital deduction; no gift or estate tax liability is incurred.

3.   *Compromise:* A right to alimony (usually) and property distributions (always) may be compromised, settled or waived; a parental waiver of the child support obligation does not bind the child and thus will not bar a court from reopening the child support issue if the child is in need.

4.   *Modification:* Alimony (unless the separation agreement or divorce decree specifies otherwise) and child support are subject to modification if circumstances change; a property settlement is final and not modifiable.

5.   *Enforcement:* Alimony and child support may be enforced through civil or criminal contempt proceedings; special nonsupport remedies (e.g., wage garnishment, driver's license revocation) are also available. A property settlement normally is enforceable only through regular civil enforcement proceedings.

6.   *Termination of Obligation:* Alimony usually terminates upon the recipient's remarriage (or possibly, cohabitation); child support usually

terminates when the child reaches majority; property settlement obligations are due until paid. Property settlement obligations can sometimes be discharged in bankruptcy, while child support and alimony cannot.

7. *Effect of Payor or Recipient's Death:* Alimony and child support generally terminate upon the death of either the recipient or the payor; property settlement obligations are enforceable by and against an estate.

So far, so good! We are barely into this Chapter and know most of the law as well as many practical considerations. Before we go on to consider some complexities of alimony, property settlements and child support in this chapter and the next, the basic simplicity of *all* these transactions must be kept in mind: One spouse transfers or promises to transfer value (typically money or property) to other spouse. That is all! A pays or promises to pay money to B.

The wild card in this pack is classification of a transaction as alimony, child support or a property distribution. Appearances can be deceiving: alimony and child support may be paid as lump sums; property may be distributed in short-term or long-term installments. These approaches are not unusual. Property settlements are paid in installments for a variety of reasons, including issues of liquidity, marketability, or taxation; the alimony recipient may bargain to obtain a lump-sum payment in order to avoid future problems with later modification or enforcement of the obligation. Worse—and very important—is the fact that what bears one label in one context may bear another in a different context. The label attached—and whether that label "sticks" in different contexts—will produce a range of legal consequences; the payment's enforceability, taxability, modifiability, duration and terminability may all be affected.

"Anyone may so arrange his affairs [Ed. note: and why not marriages and divorces?] that his taxes shall be as low as possible; he is not bound to choose that pattern which will best pay the Treasury; there is not even a patriotic duty to increase one's taxes." Helvering v. Gregory, 69 F.2d 809, 810 (2d Cir. 1934), aff'd 293 U.S. 465 (1935) (Learned Hand, J.).

2. TAXATION

A. DURING THE ONGOING MARRIAGE

Although the U.S. tax system once taxed family members as individuals, since 1948 a married couple has been treated as one tax unit. Since 1986, most income of minor children has been taxed at the rate applicable to their parents.[1]

---

[1] The 1986 Tax Reform Act ended most possibilities for income-splitting with minor children. For children, a very small amount of unearned income is taxed at the child's own rate, with the rest taxed at the custodial parent's marginal rate.

The purpose of this "family tax unit" approach is to avoid "income-splitting" by spouses in order to obtain a lower tax rate. Prior to the 1948 spousal tax unit reform, married couples in community property states could allocate 50% of the income of a high-income spouse to a homemaker spouse in order to reduce the rate at which the income was taxed.[2] Couples in community property states could do this because each spouse held a vested one-half interest in wages earned by either during marriage. *See* Poe v. Seaborn, 282 U.S. 101 (1930). Couples in common law states, who had no legal interest in each other's income, could not. Or so held the Supreme Court in Lucas v. Earl, 281 U.S. 111 (1930). *Earl* caused a sudden brief rush of support for community property; six common law states adopted a community property system between 1939 and 1949. The adoption of the spousal tax unit principle ended this flurry of enthusiasm for community property. *See* Pamela B. Gann, *Abandoning Marital Status as a Factor in Allocating Income Tax Burdens*, 59 TEX. L. REV. 1 (1980); Lawrence Zelenak, *Marriage and the Income Tax*, 67 S. CAL. L. REV. 339 (1994).

Although the 1948 reforms eliminated the income-splitting problem, they created a marriage "penalty" for two-income couples with relatively equal wages and a marriage "bonus" for couples in which one spouse earned the lion's share of the household income. The Congressional Budget Office calculated that in 1996 more than 21 million married couples paid a total of $29 billion in marriage penalties, while 25 million married couples enjoyed a marriage bonus totaling more than $33 billion. *See* Lawrence Zelenek, *Doing Something About Marriage Penalties: A Guide for the Perplexed*, 54 TAX L. REV. 1 (2000).

The marriage penalty was politically unpopular; recent amendments have largely eliminated it except for couples with relatively high incomes. For example, in 2017 single adults are taxed at a rate of 10% on the first $9,325 of income, and married couples on the first $18,650; the 15% marginal tax rate applies to income up to $37,950 for single adults and $75,900 for married couples. *See* http://www.irs.gov/pub/irs-pdf/i1040tt. pdf. The marriage bonus still exists. *See* Deborah A. Widiss, *Changing the Marriage Equation*, 89 WASH. U. LAW. REV. 721, 749 (2012). Of course, these rules could be changed significantly if Congress substantially revises the tax code, as some members of Congress have advocated.

Spouses may file separate tax returns, but because a couple will almost always pay less tax if they file jointly, most married couples do so. If spouses file a joint return, they are each individually liable for all income

---

[2] Assume that the first $25,000 of individual income was taxed at a 20% rate and that additional income at a 40% rate. If one spouse earning $50,000 assigned half of his income to the other, who earned nothing, the couple would pay tax at a rate of 20% on all their income (a total tax of $10,000). If all income would be allocated to the wage earner, he or she would pay tax at a rate of 20% on half his or her income and at a rate of 40% on the other half (for a total tax of $5,000 plus $10,000, or $15,000).

tax liability accrued during their marriage. Even if the deficiency is not revealed until after a divorce has been finalized, both spouses are liable to the Internal Revenue Service. If a spouse qualifies as an "innocent spouse" who had no knowledge of the funds received, he or she is not liable (*see* I.R.C. § 6015); it is fairly difficult to qualify as an innocent spouse, however. *See* Demeter v. Commissioner, 41 Fam. L. Rep. (BNA) 1062 (Tenn. App. 2014) (qualifying as an innocent spouse); U.S. v. Tilford, 810 F.3d 370 (9th Cir. 2016) (a claim of innocent spouse status is not a defense when the government is enforcing a criminal judgement against a spouse); Rose v. Rose, 364 P.3d 1244 (Mont. 2016) (even where wife was found to be an innocent spouse, the tax liability was a joint marital obligation in their divorce); Cheshire v. Commissioner, 282 F.3d 326 (5th Cir. 2002); Lilly Kahng, *Innocent Spouses: A Critique of the New Tax Laws Governing Joint and Several Tax Liability*, 49 VILL. L. REV. 261 (2004). (Of course, one spouse could agree to indemnify the other in a divorce separation agreement for any future tax liability.)

B. AT DIVORCE

1. Timing the Divorce Decree

The Internal Revenue Service (IRS) determines each taxpayer's marital status as of December 31. If a couple marries on December 30, they are treated as if married for the entire year; if they divorce on December 30, they are treated as if divorced for the entire year. If settlement negotiations are winding up toward the end of the year, the lawyer should consider whether the parties will owe less income tax that year if married or divorced. This generally would involve an analysis of whether the couple would qualify for a "marriage bonus" for the calendar year if they were married December 31.

Other concerns can also be relevant. As will be mentioned below, spouses can shield more gain on the sale of a primary residence than a single person can, so this might be a reason to stay married until the house is sold. In contrast, spouses are limited to deducting mortgage interest on $1 million in mortgage debt, while two single adults can each deduct interest on $1 million dollars in mortgage debt. *See Another Reason Not To Get Married, Courtesy of the IRS*, 42 FAM. L. REP. (BNA) 1504 (2016).

2. Property Division (IRC § 1041)

Under the Internal Revenue Code, a taxpayer owes tax only if a "taxable event" occurs. Since 1984, a division of property at divorce is not normally a taxable event. This does not mean that a family lawyer can ignore tax issues in negotiating a property division. A spouse who receives property pursuant to a divorce decree takes the transferor spouse's "basis" (normally the original cost of the property). If and when that property is sold, capital gains tax will be assessed on the extent to which the net sales price exceeds the seller's basis; low basis property is thus, at divorce, worth less, after tax, than is high basis property. The client who plans to sell appreciated property after divorce needs to be told that there will be tax liability at the time of sale.

Pensions divided at divorce also pose potential tax problems. As you will recall from Chapter 15, the value of pension payments are taxed to the recipient if the pension plan is covered by ERISA *and the order requiring the payments is a qualified domestic relations order.* In Hawkins v. Commissioner, 102 T.C 61 (1994), the court determined that a decree awarding a nonemployee spouse $1,000,000 from the employee's pension plan was not a QDRO, so the distribution to the nonemployee was taxed to the employee. Such potential malpractice minefields explain why most family lawyers have divorce decrees involving significant amounts of property reviewed by competent tax counsel.

For sales of a primary residence after May 6, 1997, each divorced spouse may exclude a gain of up to $250,000 as long as the house was the spouse's primary residence for at least two of the last five years and the spouse had not already used such an exclusion within two years. For sales before divorce, spouses filing a joint return may exclude $500,000. So, for divorcing spouses whose house has appreciated more than $250,000 and who plan to sell the house in the near future, in some instances they would pay less tax if they sell it before divorce and file a joint return for that tax year. (Both spouses need not hold record title to qualify for the $500,000 exclusion.) *See* Margot Slade, *Gainful Way to Splitsville*, N.Y. TIMES, March 8, 1998, Business Section, p. 10.

Division of the right to receive future income can also present non-obvious tax problems. For example, in Kochansky v. Commissioner, 92 F.3d 957 (9th Cir. 1996), a lawyer-spouse had a potential right to receive a contingent fee after divorce. In the divorce he agreed to give his spouse one half of any fee he received. He did receive a fee and paid her 50% of it. The court held that, based on the "assignment of income" doctrine, he owed tax on the entire fee, even though he only kept half. (This may not be true in a community property state. *See* P.L.R. 2005 46026, released 11/18/05, 32 Fam. L. Rep. (BNA) 1118.)

If vested nonqualified stock options are transferred from an employee to a non-employee spouse at divorce, no tax is due at that time. At the time of exercise, the recipient must include in his gross income the difference between the market value on the date of exercise and the price paid. Revenue Ruling 2002–22.

If the parties want to divide funds in an IRA, this can be done free of tax, but only if the funds are distributed to the other spouse and then deposited into that spouse's IRA. *See* Cohen v. Commissioner, 2004 WL 2251801 (U.S. Tax Ct.).

3.   Child Support and Alimony (IRC §§ 71 and 215)

Alimony is deductible from the taxable income of the payor and includable in the taxable income of the recipient; since 1976, the alimony deduction has been available even to taxpayers who do not itemize deductions. Although the recent "flattening" of tax rates has reduced the scope and value of the alimony deduction, tax savings are still possible. In 2016, the highest federal tax rate for individuals was about 40%. If an obligor is in the 40% marginal tax bracket and the recipient is in the 15% tax bracket, every $100 in alimony costs the obligor $60 after tax, but is worth $85 to the recipient after tax.

In such a high-low rate situation, there are potential tax advantages to each spouse of substituting a larger amount of alimony for what would otherwise have been paid in child support. There are risks to this strategy, however. The IRS will treat payments to a former spouse as alimony only if those payments meet the requirements of the Internal Revenue Code. To qualify:[3]

(1)   Payments must be in cash or cash equivalent to or for the benefit of a former spouse;

(2)   Payments must be required by a:

   a)   written separation agreement;

   b)   divorce or separate maintenance decree; or

   c)   other support decree such as an order for temporary support.

(3)   If the payments are made after a final decree of divorce or legal separation, the payor and payee cannot live in the same household; the parties have a one-month grace period to establish separate households.

(4)   The payment obligation must end at the payee's death; the payor cannot be required to make substitute payments to the payee's estate or third parties after the payee's death.

(5)   The payments must not be "fixed" to a minor child.

See IRC §§ 71, 215.

---

[3]   Alimony payments required under pre-1985 court orders or agreements incident to divorce or separation are and remain deductible under the *old* rules. Under these rules, payments must be: i) based on the marital or family relationship, ii) paid after the decree, and iii) paid on a "periodic" basis. The payment period must be in excess of 10 years or subject to specific contingencies such as the death of either spouse, the remarriage of the alimony recipient, or a change in the economic status of either spouse. Pre-1985 alimony obligations may be brought under the new rules by specifying in an amendment that the new rules are to apply.

Payments will be treated as "fixed" to a minor child (even if characterized in the decree as alimony) if:

(1) Payments are to be reduced not more than six months before or after the date the child is to attain the age of 18, 21, or the local age of majority, or

(2) Payments are to be reduced on two or more occasions which occur not more than one year before or after a different child of the payor spouse attains a certain age between the ages of 18 and 24, inclusive.

Internal Revenue Service Temp. Reg. § 1.71–1T, Q–18.

So, if an obligation terminates when a child graduates from high school, this is a payment of child support and not alimony for tax purposes. *See* Johnson v. Commissioner, 40 Fam. L. Rep. (BNA) 1287 (Tax Ct. Memo. 2014–67). Payments made while a divorce is pending can constitute alimony. *See* Anderson v. Commissioner, 42 Fam. L. Rep. (BNA) 1227 (Tax. Ct. Memo. 2016–47).

While lump-sum as well as periodic payments may qualify as alimony, alimony "recapture" provisions may apply if the annual value of alimony paid decreases by more than $15,000 during the first three post-separation years. The recapture provisions are intended to bar spouses from characterizing a property settlement as alimony in order to save taxes. The recapture calculation is done once, in the third year after payments begin. The formula requires a comparison of total alimony paid during Year 2 with total alimony paid in Year 3, then a comparison of total alimony paid in Year 1 with the *average* of total alimony paid in Years 2 and 3, as follows:

1. Subtract [the amount paid in Year 3 plus $15,000] from the amount paid in Year 2 to get R1.

2. Average [the amount paid in Year 2 plus the amount paid in Year 3 minus R1]. Add $15,000 to this amount, and subtract all from the amount paid in Year 1 to get R2.

3. Add R1 and R2 to get the amount of alimony subject to recapture.

Thus, if H pays W $60,000 in Year 1, $30,000 in Year 2, and 0 in Year 3, the formula works this way:

1. $30,000 (Yr 2 alimony) – [$0 (Yr 3 alimony) + $15,000 (allowable variation)] = $15,000 = R1

2. $60,000 (Yr 1 alimony) – [($30,000 + $0 – $15,000)/2 + $15,000] = $37,500 = R2

3. $15,000 + $37,500 = $52,500 = Amount recaptured in Year 3.

Or, if W pays H $45,000 in Year 1, $30,000 in Year 2, and $15,000 in Year 3, the formula works this way:

1. $30,000 (Year 2)—$15,000 (allowable yearly variation) = $15,000

2. $15,000 (allowable variation)—$15,000 (Year 3 total) = $0 = R1

3. $45,000 (Year 1 alimony)—[($30,000 + $15,000)/2 + $15,000] = $2,500 = R2

4. $0 + $2,500 = $2,500 = Amount recaptured in Year 3.

Note that the same total sum of money ($90,000) was paid in alimony in both examples. But the amount subject to recapture varied by $50,000 depending on how the payments were structured. Alimony payments thus should be structured to avoid, or at least minimize, recapture.

The recapture provisions apply to *payments*, not obligations. The payor who falls into arrears in Year 2 or Year 3 on his alimony obligations may find that he has lost the tax advantage of the alimony deduction in Year 1 or Year 2 through recapture. Recapture will not apply, however, if: the payments cease due to death of either party or remarriage of the recipient; the payments are made under a temporary support order; or payments are to be made for at least three years in an amount representing a fixed percentage of the income from a business, property, or employment rather than a dollar amount.

4. Medical Expenses, Dependency Exemptions, Child, Child Care and Earned Income Credits

While either parent may claim medical expenses actually paid on behalf of the child (IRC § 213(d)(5)), the Internal Revenue Code generally assigns tax benefits associated with a child to the parent who has primary physical custody. *Only* the custodial parent may claim the child care credit, available to some parents with earned income who pay for child care to enable them to work (IRC § 21(d)(5)); *only* the custodial parent may claim the earned income credit (IRC § 32). The custodial parent is also entitled to the dependency exemption *unless* he or she agrees in writing to relinquish the exemption to the other parent; the waiver may be for one or more years. *See* IRC § 152(3). Tax credits for children and education credits are available only to the parent with the dependency exemption.

There has been a good deal of litigation on the power of a divorce court to order the custodial parent to execute a dependency exemption waiver. Most, but not all, state courts have held that the divorce judge does have authority to mandate such a waiver. *Compare* Eric M. v. Laura M., 790 S.E. 2d 929 (W. Va. 2016); Dodge v. Sturdivant, 335 P.3d 510 (Alaska 2014); Freed v. Freed, 2015 WL 6663274 (Ohio App. 2015); Macias v. Macias, 968 P.2d 814 (N.M. App. 1998), and Serrano v. Serrano, 566 A.2d 413 (Conn. 1989) (majority rule) *with* Hulsey v. Hulsey, 792 S.E.2d 709 (Ga. 2016) (minority rule), *See also* Benson, *The Power of State Courts to Award the Federal Dependency Exemption at Divorce*, 16 U. DAYTON L. REV. 29 (1990). If the divorce court awards the exemption to the non-custodial parent but does not order the custodial parent to execute a waiver, it is probably ineffective. *See* Lystad v. Lystad, 916 S.W.2d 617 (Tex. App. 1996). If the exemption is to be given to the parent who is not the primary custodian, the IRS Form 8332 should be filled out and signed by the parties, and attached to their tax returns. *See* Cappel v. Commissioner, 42 Fam. L. Rep. (BNA) 1479 (Tax. Ct. Memo. 2016–150).

Note that the tax benefit of the dependency exemption can be significantly reduced if the parent's income is sufficiently high. I.R.C. § 151 (d) (3). (In 2009, for a single person the value of the exemption began to be reduced if adjusted gross income exceeded $166,800). So, if one parent has a high income and the other's is much lower, it would make sense to give the exemption to the parent who could derive the greater benefit from it.

Since 1998, in addition to a dependency *exemption*, a tax *credit* for children has been available. The credit amount is $1000 per qualifying child in 2016. The value of this credit may be reduced or eliminated if the parent's income is too high; an unmarried parent begins to lose the full value of the credit in 2016 with an income exceeding $75,000. *See* http://www.irs.gov/pub/irs-pdf/p972.pdf. To be entitled to the tax credit, a parent must be entitled to the dependency exemption. I. R. C. § 24(c)(1)(A). Additional websites with relevant information are:

https://www.irs.gov/pub/irs-drop/rp-16-55.pdf

https://www.irs.gov/uac/ten-facts-about-the-child-tax-credit

http://turbotax.intuit.com/tax-tools/tax-tips/Family/Tax-Exemptions-and-Deductions-for-families/INF12053.html.

Legal fees incident to obtaining taxable alimony or other tax benefits are deductible but, since such fees are now categorized among "miscellaneous" itemized deductions, they are deductible only if itemized deductions exceed 2% of the taxpayer's adjusted gross income.

Some courts have ruled that a divorce court can order divorcing spouses to sign a joint tax return. See Butler v. Simmons-Butler, 863 N.W.2d 677 (Mich. App. 2014).

Problem 19-1:

During their marriage, Jennifer and Brad bought shares of two companies, X Co. and Y Co., with marital funds. They paid $50,000 for the X Co. shares and $75,000 for the Y Co. shares. At divorce, the X Co. shares and the Y Co. shares are each worth $100,000. Which shares would you prefer to get for your client?

3. BANKRUPTCY

A. AFTER DIVORCE

JOHNSON V. JOHNSON

U.S. Bankruptcy Court, M.D., North Carolina, 2008.
397 B.R. 289.

MEMORANDUM OPINION DENYING
CONFIRMATION OF CHAPTER 13 PLAN

THOMAS W. WALDREP, JR., BANKRUPTCY JUDGE.

This matter came before the Court on November 20, 2007 upon the Notice and Proposed Order of Confirmation (the "Plan"), filed by Travis and Amy Johnson (the "Debtors") on October 26, 2007; the Objection to Confirmation or Reclassification of Debt (the "Objection"), filed by Christy C. Snow ("Mrs.Snow") on November 14, 2007; and the Response to Objection to Order Confirming Plan by Christy C. Snow (the "Response"), filed by the Debtors on November 19, 2007. After consideration of the Plan, the Objection, the Response, the evidence presented at the hearing, the arguments of the parties, and the relevant law, the Court will sustain the Objection and deny confirmation of the Plan.

II. FACTS

The male Debtor ("Mr. Johnson") and Mrs. Snow were married on December 7, 2001. One child, Meagan Johnson, was born to the marriage. On November 23, 2005, Mr. Johnson and Mrs. Snow entered into a Separation Agreement (the "Separation Agreement"). The Separation Agreement was drafted by Mr. Johnson's divorce attorney and was revised on at least three occasions prior to entry. Paragraph one releases Mr. Johnson "from any and all obligations for alimony and support" of Mrs. Snow. Paragraphs three and four of the Separation Agreement provide that Mr. Johnson will pay for the support and medical insurance coverage of Meagan Johnson. Paragraph five provides that Mr. Johnson and Mrs. Snow will equally share the costs of a college education for Meagan Johnson. Paragraph nineteen of the Separation Agreement provides that Mr. Johnson and Mrs. Snow will purchase life insurance policies and designate Meagan Johnson as the beneficiary.

Mr. Johnson and Mrs. Snow owned real property located at 121 Cedar Bluff Trail, Dobson, North Carolina (the "Real Property") as tenants by the entirety. Pursuant to paragraph six of the Separation Agreement, Mr. Johnson agreed to convey his undivided, one half interest in the Real Property to Mrs. Snow. Two deeds of trust encumber the Real Property. The first deed of trust is in favor of Piedmont Federal Savings and Loan Association ("Piedmont"), and it secures a debt in the original principal amount of $56,000.00. Mrs. Snow agreed to assume sole responsibility for payment of the debt secured by the Piedmont deed of trust.

The second deed of trust is in favor of Wachovia Bank and Trust Company ("Wachovia"); it secures a line of credit with an outstanding balance, as of the signing of the Separation Agreement, of $22,000.00 (the "Wachovia Debt"). The Wachovia Debt was incurred to purchase personal property items for Mr. Johnson, Mrs. Snow, Meagan Johnson, and their household. During the marriage, Mr. Johnson and Mrs. Snow made payments on the interest portion of the Wachovia Debt. Because Mrs. Snow could not afford to pay both deeds of trust on the Real Property, Mr. Johnson agreed to assume sole responsibility for payment of the Wachovia Debt. Meagan Johnson was accustomed to living in the residence, and both Mr. Johnson and Mrs. Snow wanted her to remain living there. Mr. Johnson was aware that Mrs. Snow intended to remain in the residence with Meagan Johnson after the separation and divorce. At the time that the parties entered into the Separation Agreement, there was roughly $30,000.00 of equity in the Real Property.

On September 18, 2006, a divorce judgment was entered in state court, terminating the marriage of Mr. Johnson and Mrs. Snow and incorporating the Separation Agreement. Mr. Johnson married the female Debtor in November of 2006. Mrs. Snow remarried in the spring of 2007.

Mr. Johnson made payments on the Wachovia Debt from September of 2005 through August of 2007. On August 16, 2007, the Debtors filed jointly for Chapter 13 bankruptcy relief. On October 4, 2007, Mrs. Snow filed a proof of claim totaling $22,283.47, which represents the principal balance of the Wachovia Debt as of the petition date. On October 26, 2007, the Plan was filed; it provides for a plan payment of $505.00 each month for 60 months. The Plan proposes no payments on the Wachovia Debt.

On their Schedule E, the Debtors checked the box stating that there were domestic support obligations owing. Mrs. Snow is listed as an unsecured, nonpriority creditor on Schedule F. Schedule F lists the Wachovia Debt as "domestic support obligations arising from separation agreement and divorce judgment." Wachovia Bank is also listed as an unsecured, nonpriority creditor for the "second deed of trust on property conveyed to former spouse." On Schedule H, Mrs. Snow is listed as a codebtor on the Wachovia Debt.

On November 14, 2007, Mrs. Snow filed the Objection. Mrs. Snow argues that confirmation should be denied and that the balance owed on the Wachovia Debt is a nondischargeable domestic support obligation pursuant to Section 523(a)(5) of the Bankruptcy Code. On November 19, 2007, the Response was filed. The Debtors agree that Mr. Johnson has ongoing obligations pursuant to paragraphs three, four, and five of the Separation Agreement. Further, the Debtors agree that such obligations are priority, nondischargeable obligations pursuant to Sections 507(a)(1) and 523(a)(5) of the Bankruptcy Code. However, the Debtors assert that paragraph six of the Separation Agreement, which addresses the Real Property, provides for a property settlement, not a nondischargeable domestic support obligation ("DSO") pursuant to Section 523(a)(5). Mr. Johnson contends that he did not intend for the assumption of the Wachovia Debt to be for alimony or child support. He admitted that he wanted to provide for Meagan Johnson, and that he was willing to do anything to secure a divorce.

The issue before the Court is whether the portion of the Separation Agreement pertaining to the Wachovia Debt constitutes a nondischargeable DSO or a dischargeable property settlement.

III. DISCUSSION

A.   The Statute

Section 523 of the Bankruptcy Code specifies that certain debts are nondischargeable in a bankruptcy case. The pertinent portions of Section 523, as amended by the Bankruptcy Abuse Prevention and Consumer Protection Act of 2005 ("BAPCPA"), specify:

(a) A discharge under section 727, 1141, 1228(a), 1228(b), or 1328(b) of this title does not discharge an individual debtor from any debt—

. . .

(5) for a domestic support obligation;

. . .

(15) to a spouse, former spouse, or child of the debtor and not of the kind described in paragraph (5) that is incurred by the debtor in the course of a divorce or separation or in connection with a separation agreement, divorce decree or other order of a court of record, or a determination made in accordance with State or territorial law by a government unit; . . .

BAPCPA added the term "domestic support obligation" ("DSO") to the Code. Section 101(14A) provides that a DSO is:

a debt that accrues before, on, or after the date of the order of relief in a case under this title, including interest that accrues on that debt as provided under applicable nonbankruptcy law notwithstanding any other provision of this title, that is—

(A) owed to or recoverable by—

(I)   a spouse, former spouse, or child of the debtor or such child's parent, legal guardian, or responsible relative; or

(ii)   a governmental unit;

(B) in the nature of alimony, maintenance, or support (including assistance provided by a governmental unit) of such spouse, former spouse, or child of the debtor or such child's parent, without regard to whether such debt is expressly so designated;

(C) established or subject to establishment before, on, or after the date of the order for relief in a case under this title, by reason of applicable provisions of—

(I)   a separation agreement, divorce decree, or property settlement agreement;

(ii)   an order of a court of record; or

(iii) a determination made in accordance with applicable nonbankruptcy law by a governmental unit; and

(D) not assigned to a nongovernmental entity, unless that obligation is assigned voluntarily by the spouse, former spouse, child of the debtor, or such child's parent, legal guardian, or responsible relative for the purpose of collecting the debt.

11 U.S.C. § 101(14A) (2005).

Sections 523(a)(5) and (15) operate to provide greater protection for alimony, maintenance, and support obligations owing to a spouse, former spouse, or child of a debtor in bankruptcy. Alan N. Resnick, *2007 Collier Pamphlet Edition Bankruptcy Code* 42–43, 590 (Alan N. Resnick & Henry J. Sommer eds., 2007). "[A] debtor should not use the protection of a bankruptcy filing in order to avoid legitimate marital and child support obligations." *Id.* (quoting 140 Cong. Rec. H 10,769 (October 4, 1994)). These provisions are intended to make "non-dischargeable any debts resulting from an agreement by the debtor to hold the debtor's spouse harmless on joint debts, to the extent that the agreement is in payment of alimony, maintenance, or support of the spouse, as determined under bankruptcy law considerations as to whether a particular agreement to pay money to a spouse is actually alimony or a property settlement." S.Rep. No. 95–989, at 79 (1978), *as reprinted in* 1978 U.S.C.C.A.N. 5787, 5865.

B.   Determination of Domestic Support Obligation

In cases under Chapters 7, 11, and 12 of the Bankruptcy Code, the distinctions between DSOs, governed by Section 523(a)(5), and other types of post-marital obligations, governed by Section 523(a)(15), are immaterial because both types of debts are nondischargeable and must be paid in full. But in Chapter 13 cases, an important distinction is drawn. DSOs may not be discharged in a Chapter 13 plan. 11 U.S.C. § 1328(a)(2); 11 U.S.C.

§ 523(a)(5). However, other post-marital obligations, including property settlements, are dischargeable in Chapter 13. 11 U.S.C. § 1328(a)(2); 11 U.S.C. § 523(a)(15). If an obligation is deemed a DSO, pursuant to Section 523(a)(5), then the obligation is a priority debt, pursuant to Section 507(a)(1)(A), and the Chapter 13 plan must provide for its full payment, pursuant to Section 1322(a)(2). In fact, the discharge will not be granted until the DSO has been paid in full pursuant to Section 1328(a). Therefore, the Court must determine whether Mr. Johnson's obligation to pay the Wachovia Debt is a DSO under Section 523(a)(5).

For the Wachovia Debt to be considered a DSO, the Court must determine that the obligation (1) is owed to or recoverable by Mrs. Snow; (2) is in the nature of alimony, maintenance, or support; (3) was established before the debtor filed for bankruptcy relief by a separation agreement or divorce decree; and (4) has not been assigned other than for collection purposes. 11 U.S.C. § 101(14A)(B).

Payment of the support, maintenance, or alimony need not be paid directly to the spouse or ex-spouse. The Wachovia Debt is owed by Mr. Johnson and Mrs. Snow to Wachovia. The debt would be recoverable from Mrs. Snow or Mr. Johnson if Mr. Johnson did not pay. Due to the language in the Separation Agreement by which Mr. Johnson agreed to hold her harmless, if Mrs. Snow were forced to pay the Wachovia Debt, then Mr. Johnson would be liable to Mrs. Snow. Thus, the Wachovia Debt is owed to or recoverable by Mrs. Snow.

The Wachovia Debt was established pursuant to a Separation Agreement entered on November 23, 2006, which is prior in time to the Debtors' Chapter 13 bankruptcy. The Wachovia Debt has not been assigned to any other entity.

The final prong of the DSO analysis requires the Court to determine whether the payment of the Wachovia Debt is in the nature of alimony, maintenance, or support, which is a fact specific analysis. The complaining spouse has the burden to demonstrate that the obligation at issue is in the nature of alimony, maintenance or support.

Federal bankruptcy law, not state law, determines whether a debt is in the nature of support. The court must not rely only on the label used by the parties or the state court, but must look beyond the label to examine whether the debt actually is in the nature of support or alimony. *Cummings v. Cummings*, 244 F.3d 1263, 1265 (11th Cir.2001); *In re Brody*, 3 F.3d 35, 38 (2d Cir.1993).

DSO is a term derived from the definition of a nondischargeable debt for alimony, maintenance, and support contained in the former Section 523(a)(5); therefore, case law construing the former Section 523(a)(5) is relevant and persuasive.

In the Fourth Circuit, courts first look at the mutual or shared intent of the parties to create a support obligation. The labels attached to certain provisions in a separation agreement are not dispositive of their "nature," but the labels are persuasive evidence of the parties' intent.

Courts in the Fourth Circuit have articulated an "unofficial" test for the intent inquiry, which provides for the court to look at: (1) the actual substance and language of the agreement, (2) the financial situation of the parties at the time of the agreement, (3) the function served by the obligation at the time of the agreement (i.e. daily necessities), and (4) whether there is any evidence of overbearing at the time of the agreement that should cause the court to question the intent of a spouse. Furthermore, because this list is non-exclusive and the inquiry is fact intensive, courts should consider all relevant evidence. Ultimately, courts may look beyond the four corners of a divorce decree or the agreement of the parties to determine the nature of the payments constituting the debts sought to be discharged.

Numerous courts have held that an obligation that is essential to enable a party to maintain basic necessities or to protect a residence constitutes a nondischargeable support obligation. On nearly identical facts to those in this case, the *Gianakas* court held that an obligation to make payments on a second mortgage was in the nature of support and therefore nondischargeable. *Gianakas*, 917 F.2d at 764. The court reasoned that at the time of the divorce the parties intended the ex-spouse to remain in the former marital home with the couple's children. The court looked at the nature of the obligation at the time that it was undertaken, regardless of the parties' current financial situation. The court ruled that the agreement to provide shelter should be construed as an obligation to provide support.

Further, an agreement to indemnify and hold an ex-spouse harmless on a debt is nondischargeable for the same reasons that an obligation to enable a family to maintain shelter is nondischargeable. In *Calhoun*, 715 F.2d, at 1107, the court noted that where hold harmless clauses relate to debts in the nature of alimony or support "[b]ankruptcy courts have uniformly found hold harmless clauses to create nondischargeable obligations." The hold harmless agreement imposes liability upon the assuming spouse for all consequences of failure to pay.

What was the mutual intent of Mrs. Snow and Mr. Johnson at the time of entering into the Separation Agreement? They both knew that Mrs. Snow would be unable to afford to remain living on the Real Property with Meagan Johnson unless Mr. Johnson assumed the Wachovia Debt. Mr. Johnson testified that he was willing to do whatever it took to get out of the marriage. The Court finds that at the time of the Separation Agreement the parties intended Mr. Johnson's payment of the Wachovia Debt to serve as a contribution toward maintenance and support of lodging for Ms. Snow and Meagan Johnson.

The Separation Agreement did not designate the obligation to pay the Wachovia Debt as support. In fact, the Separation Agreement did not label any obligation as support. Nor did it label any obligation as being a part of the property settlement. No provision in the agreement was labeled. But the agreement to pay the Wachovia Debt was essential to protect the former marital residence, and Mr. Johnson agreed to indemnify and hold Ms. Snow harmless on the debt. As discussed above, an obligation that enables one's family to maintain shelter is in the nature of support, and an agreement to indemnify and hold the former spouse harmless on that debt is nondischargeable under Section 523(a)(5).

All of the circumstances taken together, including the intent of the parties, the financial circumstances of the parties at the time of entering into the Separation Agreement, and the function served by Mr. Johnson paying the Wachovia Debt, justify a finding that the obligation of Mr. Johnson to pay the Wachovia Debt is a DSO. The obligation to pay the Wachovia Debt is "in the nature of alimony, maintenance, or support," and therefore constitutes a DSO that must be paid in full under the Debtors' Plan.

IV. CONCLUSION

The obligation of Mr. Johnson to pay the Wachovia Debt constitutes a DSO pursuant to Section 523(a)(5) of the Bankruptcy Code. As such, the debt is nondischargeable and must be paid in full under the Debtors' Plan. Confirmation of the Plan will be denied, and the Objection will be sustained. The Debtors shall be given the opportunity to file a new plan in compliance with this opinion.

NOTES AND QUESTIONS

1. Property division obligations have traditionally been dischargeable in bankruptcy while support obligations were not. *See generally* Sheryl L. Scheible, *Bankruptcy and the Modification of Support: Fresh Start, Head Start, or False Start?*, 69 N. C. L. REV. 577, 578 (1991). 1994 amendments to the Bankruptcy Code made it more difficult to extinguish property division obligations. Under § 523(a)(15), such obligations could not be discharged unless (1) the debtor does not have the ability to pay such debt from income or property of the debtor not reasonably necessary to be expended for the maintenance or support of the debtor or a dependent of the debtor; (2) the debtor does not have enough income or property to pay the debt after paying necessary business expenses if the debtor owns a business; or (3) discharging the debt would "result in a benefit to the debtor that outweighs the detrimental consequences to the obligee." 11 U.S.C.A. § 523(a)(15).

2.   The 2005 amendments to the Bankruptcy Code again changed the rules regarding discharging family law obligations. Under this law, neither a support nor a property award may be discharged under a Chapter 7 liquidation, traditionally the most popular bankruptcy procedure, or a proceeding under Chapter 11. *See* 11 U.S.C. § 523(a)(15). *See In re* Mason, 58 A.3d 1153 (N.H. 2012); Avelino-Catabran v. Catabran, 42 Fam. L. Rep. (BNA) 1392 (N.J. Super. App. Div. 2016) (obligation to pay a child's college expenses not impacted by Chapter 11 bankruptcy). *See also, In re* Hardesty, 553 B.R. 86 (Bankr. E.D. Va. 2016) (indemnity obligation under property settlement agreement is dischargeable). For cases holding other obligations not dischargeable in Chapter 13 because they were domestic support obligations, *see In re* Thomas, 511 B.R. 89 (6th Cir. 2014) (an obligation to pay a second mortgage); Quinn v. Quinn, 528 B.R. 203 (D. Mass. 2015) (same). However, property awards remain dischargeable under Chapter 13. For a Chapter 13 plan to be confirmed, all of the debtor's domestic support obligations must be current, and to obtain discharge at the end of the plan period the debtor must certify that all of his domestic support obligations are current. *See* 11 U.S.C. §§ 1325 (a), 1328(a). *See generally* Daniel A. Austin, *Discharge of Marital Debt Obligations Under the Bankruptcy Abuse Prevention and Consumer Protection Act of 2005*, 51 WAYNE L. REV. 1369 (2005).

3.   For cases holding that a family law obligation was not a domestic support obligation, and therefore dischargeable in chapter 13 bankruptcy, see *In re* Nolan, 2010 WL 3926870 (D. Minn.); *In re* Trentadue, 827 F.3d 743 (7th Cir. 2016) (family law legal fees).

HOWARD V. HOWARD

Supreme Court of Kentucky, 2011.
336 S.W.3d 433.

MINTON, J.

I.   INTRODUCTION.

We accepted discretionary review of this case primarily to resolve whether a trial court could properly enforce, through its contempt powers, an obligation under a divorce decree to make payments to a creditor on a marital debt even after the former husband, who had been ordered to make the payments, received a post-decree Chapter 7 bankruptcy discharge, and the former wife failed to institute an adversary proceeding in bankruptcy court. We conclude that the trial court could properly enforce the former husband's divorce obligation through contempt proceedings. Following recent amendments to the federal bankruptcy code, this obligation is excepted from discharge in bankruptcy with no requirement for an adversary proceeding in bankruptcy court.

II. FACTS.

The decree dissolving the marriage of Roy Shane Howard and Sondra Howard provided for joint custody of their minor child with Sondra serving as the primary residential custodian and Shane paying her child support. The amount of child support was not derived from Shane's actual earnings at the time of the divorce decree but, from his recent history of earnings as a federal prison guard. The decree stated that Shane "is voluntarily under employed since he voluntarily quit his job and gave no testimony which would justify him quitting his employment."

Shane claimed in pre-decree papers that he and Sondra agreed that he should quit his job at the federal prison because Sondra also worked there as a guard, and their marital split created an awkward working environment. Sondra denied making such an agreement and alleged that Shane's continued employment at the federal prison would not pose a problem because they worked different shifts. Shane also claimed in his papers that he unsuccessfully tried to regain employment as a federal prison guard.

In addition to ordering Shane to pay child support, the trial court divided the parties' marital property and determined which marital debts each party was to pay. Relevant to the issues raised before us, the decree stated that the trial court found, as a matter of fact, that "[t]he parties have agreed" that Shane would be liable for certain debts incurred by the parties, including a National City loan on the parties' Dodge Durango, which was repossessed by the time of the decree.

Some fifteen months after entry of the decree, Shane filed a motion in the trial court to reduce his child support obligation because of an alleged material change in circumstances. With his motion, Shane filed a supporting affidavit in which he claimed health problems, inability to find correctional work or similarly lucrative positions, and filing for bankruptcy. He requested that his child support obligation be reduced retroactive to the date he filed his motion.

The trial court conducted a hearing on this motion and also heard motions brought by Sondra. Sondra sought payment of her attorney's fees and sought to have Shane held in contempt for failure to pay the debt on the repossessed Durango, for which she had been subjected to collection efforts by the creditor. Both parties testified about their current income levels, insurance, and childcare expenses. Shane testified to filing bankruptcy shortly after entry of the decree, to receiving a discharge in bankruptcy, and to not having a deficiency judgment entered against him following the repossession of the Dodge Durango.

The parties acknowledged at the hearing that Sondra received notice of Shane's filing for bankruptcy and that she did nothing to challenge the discharge of his debts. They also acknowledged that Shane received a

Chapter 7 discharge and that the creditor then sought collection from Sondra, rather than Shane, on the repossessed Durango.[1] But Shane admitted that he was responsible for paying the debt on the Durango under the divorce decree and even seemed willing to admit that this was a nondischargeable marital debt before his attorney lodged an objection to characterizing this debt as nondischargeable.

The trial court found Shane to be in contempt for failure to pay the debt on the repossessed Durango. Shane appealed all of these rulings to the Court of Appeals, which affirmed on all issues. And we affirm, addressing each issue in turn.

III. ANALYSIS.

B.　No Reversible Error in Contempt Finding.

Shane argues that the trial court erred in holding him in contempt for failing to comply with a divorce decree provision requiring him to make payments on the loan for the Dodge Durango vehicle because of his bankruptcy discharge. Apparently, Shane and Sondra jointly obtained the loan on the Dodge Durango before the decree, the vehicle was repossessed before the decree, and the decree stated that Shane would be responsible for payments on the Durango loan in accordance with the parties' agreement. But Shane did not explicitly agree to hold Sondra harmless for the debt on the repossessed Durango.

After the decree, Shane failed to make these payments and filed for bankruptcy under Chapter 7. Sondra received notice of his bankruptcy filing, but she did not file an adversary proceeding challenging Shane's discharge of the Durango debt. After Shane received a bankruptcy discharge, the creditor pursued collection from Sondra, who testified to experiencing credit problems as a result. She filed a motion with the trial court to hold Shane in contempt for failing to make payments on the Durango loan. The trial court held Shane in contempt, although it did not impose a sanction for Shane's contempt of court.

The Court of Appeals affirmed the contempt finding, concluding that Shane's obligation was not discharged under 11 United States Code (U.S.C.) § 523(a)(15). The Court of Appeals noted that this statute had been amended, effective in 2005, to provide that a discharge under Chapter 7(11 U.S.C. § 727) does not discharge the debtor from any debt "to a spouse, former spouse or child" for something other than a "domestic support obligation" (*i.e.,* child support or maintenance)[14] that "is incurred by the

---

[1]　There seems to be no dispute that Shane filed for Chapter 7 bankruptcy, that Sondra received notice of his filing for bankruptcy, and that Shane received a discharge in bankruptcy. But the parties have not shown us, nor have we located upon our own review of the record, any written documentation concerning the bankruptcy proceeding.

[14]　11 U.S.C. § 523(a)(15) provides for an exception to discharge of a debt "not of the kind described in paragraph (5)" meeting the other elements of 11 U.S.C. § 523(a)(15). 11 U.S.C.

debtor in the course of a divorce or separation or in connection with a separation agreement, divorce decree or other order of a court of record, or a determination made in accordance with State or territorial law by a governmental unit."

As the Court of Appeals states, obviously Shane had an obligation to pay the Durango debt under the divorce decree. But the tricky question is whether this was a debt to his former spouse that would not be subject to discharge under the post-BAPCPA version of 11 U.S.C. § 523(a)(15). Obviously, Shane was not required to make a direct payment to Sondra under the relevant divorce decree provision, which simply stated that he was responsible for making payments to the creditor.

1.   *State Courts Have Jurisdiction to Construe Discharge and Determine if Particular Debt is Within Discharge.*

Before we address the merits on this issue, we must first address whether Kentucky state courts have jurisdiction to determine the dischargeability of a debt. As we recently stated, "[w]hile . . . state courts lack jurisdiction to modify or to grant relief from a bankruptcy court's discharge injunction, they retain, with a few exceptions not pertinent here, concurrent jurisdiction under 28 U.S.C. § 1334(b) to construe the discharge and determine whether a particular debt is or is not within the discharge." We also note recent federal authority that: "Aside from determinations of dischargeability under 11 U.S.C. § 523(a)(2), (4), or (6) [not implicated in present case], state courts have concurrent jurisdiction to determine the dischargeability of a debt." So Kentucky state courts have jurisdiction to determine whether Shane's obligation to make payments on the bank loan on the repossessed Durango was discharged in his Chapter 7 bankruptcy.

2.   *Under Prior Law, Necessity for Adversary Proceeding to Determine Exception from Discharge for Non-Support Divorce Debt under 11 U.S.C. § 523(a)(15).*

Shane contends that he was discharged of any obligation to pay the Durango deficiency debt because he received a Chapter 7 bankruptcy discharge, citing the 2004 Kentucky Court of Appeals case of *Holbrook v. Holbrook.*[18] In *Holbrook,* the Court of Appeals held that an ex-spouse who received notice of the debtor's bankruptcy filing was unable to recover arrearages on the debtor's obligation under the divorce decree to distribute a portion of pension benefits to her because she failed to file a complaint in bankruptcy court to determine that the pension arrearage debt, which was not claimed to be child support or maintenance, should be excepted from discharge under 11 U.S.C. § 523(a)(15). But, as Sondra noted, federal bankruptcy statutes have been significantly amended since *Holbrook* by

---

§ 523(a)(5) refers to a "domestic support obligation" as another exception to discharge. A "domestic support obligation" generally refers to child support or maintenance. 11 U.S.C. § 101(14A)(B).

    [18]   151 S.W.3d 825 (Ky.App.2004).

the BAPCPA in such a way that *Holbrook*'s holding requiring the filing of a complaint in bankruptcy court to obtain a determination of exception to discharge under 11 U.S.C. § 523(a)(15) does not apply to cases where filing for Chapter 7 bankruptcy occurred following the effective date of the BAPCPA amendments (mid-October 2005).

Before the enactment of BAPCPA in 2005, 11 U.S.C. § 523(a) provided that a Chapter 7 discharge did not discharge a debtor from: "any debt . . . (5) to a spouse, former spouse, or child of the debtor" for child support or maintenance under a separation agreement or divorce decree. Also excepted from discharge under Chapter 7 was "any debt . . . (15) not of a kind described in paragraph 5 [*i.e.*, not for child support or maintenance] that is incurred by the debtor in the course of a divorce or separation or in connection with a separation agreement, divorce decree or other order of a court of record" unless the debtor was not reasonably able to pay the debt and the benefits of discharge to the debtor outweighed the detriment to the spouse, ex-spouse, or child. Although debts for child support or maintenance were simply not discharged in Chapter 7, at that time, 11 U.S.C. § 523(c)(1) stated that the debtor "shall be discharged" from other divorce-related debts under 11 U.S.C. § 523(a)(15) "unless, on request of the creditor to whom such debt is owed, and after notice and a hearing, the court determines such debt to be excepted from discharge" under 11 U.S.C. § 523(a)(15).

In other words, under pre-BAPCPA bankruptcy laws, an ex-spouse was required to take action in a former spouse's Chapter 7 bankruptcy case, or a non-support divorce debt would be discharged if the debtor received a Chapter 7 discharge. So as to pre-BAPCPA cases, *Holbrook* dictates that an ex-spouse, who receives notice of the debtor's Chapter 7 bankruptcy filing but who fails to file an adversary complaint in the bankruptcy court to obtain a determination that a non-support divorce debt is excepted from discharge, cannot obtain enforcement of that debt in state court once the bankruptcy court has granted a Chapter 7 discharge to the debtor.

3.   *Post-BAPCPA, Debt Incurred in Divorce Excepted From Discharge Without Necessity for Adversary Proceeding in Bankruptcy Court.*

Following the BAPCPA amendments, 11 U.S.C. § 523(a)(5) recognized an exception to discharge for debts "for a domestic support obligation" without explicitly requiring that such debts be to a spouse, former spouse, or child. On the other hand, 11 U.S.C. § 523(a)(15) was amended to add language requiring that other divorce-related debts be "to a spouse, former spouse or child of the debtor" to be excepted from discharge. 11 U.S.C. § 523(a)(15) was also amended to delete the former language that allowed for discharge if the debtor was not reasonably able to pay the debt and the benefits to the debtor outweighed the detriment to the other person(s) affected.

Not only was 11 U.S.C. § 523(a)(15) amended to require that the debt be to a present or former spouse or a child and to no longer permit discharge upon consideration of the debtor's ability to pay and balancing of the benefits and burdens on both sides, but 11 U.S.C. § 523(c)(1) was also significantly amended. Contrary to the pre-BAPCPA requirement that divorce debts other than those for child support or maintenance would be discharged unless the present or former spouse or child filed a complaint for an exception to discharge under 11 U.S.C. § 523(a)(15), the post-BAPCPA version of 11 U.S.C. § 523(c)(1) no longer includes debts under subsection (a)(15) among its list of debts that will be discharged unless the creditor takes action to obtain a determination that the debt is excepted from discharge. So a non-support divorce debt (one that is not for child support or maintenance) *to a present or former spouse or a child* is excepted from discharge, and there is no requirement that the present or former spouse or child take part in the bankruptcy action for the debt to be excepted from discharge.

4.   The Obligation to Pay Debt on Repossessed Durango Under the Divorce Decree is a Nondischarged Debt to Sondra Even Without Hold Harmless Clause.

But the question here is whether Shane's obligation under the divorce decree to pay the bank loan on the repossessed Durango is a debt to his former spouse, Sondra. If the obligation to make payments on the bank loan on the repossessed Durango meets the requirements of 11 U.S.C. § 523(a)(15) as a debt to Sondra under the divorce decree, then Sondra is correct that she was not required to file anything in bankruptcy court in order later to obtain enforcement of Shane's obligation to her under the divorce decree in state court.[29] We conclude that the obligation does meet the requirements of 11 U.S.C. § 523(a)(15) and that Sondra was not required to file anything in bankruptcy court regarding Shane's Chapter 7 filing in order to preserve her right to enforcement in state court of Shane's obligation to her under the divorce decree.

Shane argues that because he was ordered to make payments to the bank, rather than directly to Sondra, that he did not owe any debt to her. Meanwhile, Sondra contends that the divorce decree established an obligation to her for him to make payments to the bank so it really is a debt to her.

Actually, in the divorce decree provision incorporating the parties' agreement that Shane would make the payments on the bank loan on the

---

[29] *See Fast v. Fast*, 766 N.W.2d 47, 49 (Minn.Ct.App.2009), *citing, e.g., In re Dumontier*, 389 B.R. 890, 896 (Bankr. D. Mont. 2008); *In re Douglas*, 369 B.R. 462, 464 (Bankr.E.D.Ark.2007); *In re Schweitzer*, 370 B.R. 145, 150–51 (Bankr.S.D.Ohio 2007) ("Spouses are no longer required to participate in the bankruptcy proceedings to preserve their rights to enforce such marital obligations. Federal courts have consistently interpreted the 2005 amendments as written.").

repossessed Durango, "two distinct obligations" are at issue.[30] Naturally, there is an underlying marital debt on the bank loan on the repossessed Durango. But the divorce decree also establishes a separate obligation to Sondra that Shane make payments on this loan as part of the division of marital property and debts even though there is no hold harmless provision.

* * *

While the creditor presumably accepted Shane's obligation to it under the car loan had been discharged in bankruptcy, Shane's obligation to Sondra under the divorce decree to make the payments to the creditor was excepted from discharge under 11 U.S.C. § 523(a)(15) because this constitutes a debt to a former spouse under a divorce decree. *Debt* is defined in 11 U.S.C. § 101(12) (2007) as "liability on a claim." And a *claim* is basically defined as a "right to payment" or a "right to an equitable remedy for breach of performance if such breach gives rise to a right to payment" under 11 U.S.C. § 101(5) (2007). So, despite the language specifying a debt to a present or former spouse, the broad definition of debt has been interpreted to encompass divorce decree-imposed obligations to a former spouse to make payments on a loan from a third party.[34] So the trial court could properly enforce Shane's obligation *to Sondra* under the divorce decree even if Shane's obligation *to the bank* on the repossessed Durango had been discharged.[35]

While the debtor's obligation on an underlying debt to a third-party creditor may be discharged because that underlying debt was not *to a spouse or former spouse or child,* the weight of authority holds that a separate, otherwise enforceable, obligation to one's present or former spouse under a separation agreement or a divorce decree to make payments on third-party debt is not dischargeable in Chapter 7 bankruptcy following the BAPCPA amendments.[36] Our holding today is premised on the broad

---

[30] *See McDonald,* 882 S.W.2d at 136. ("There are two distinct obligations involved in an agreement to assume former joint marital debts—the underlying debt owed to the mutual creditor and the obligation owed directly to the former spouse to hold the spouse harmless on the underlying debt.").

[34] *See Cheatham v. Cheatham (In re Cheatham),* Bankruptcy No. 08–63664, Adversary No. 09–6034, 2009 WL 2827951 at *5 (Bankr.N.D.Ohio Sept. 2, 2009) ("the mere fact that Defendant's debt is *payable* to First National Bank of Orrville still does not mean that the debt is not 'to' Plaintiff within the meaning of the Bankruptcy Code. Under the Code, the term 'debt' means liability on a 'claim.' 11 U.S.C. § 101(12). A 'claim' in turn, can mean either a right to payment or a right to an equitable remedy for breach of performance if such breach gives rise to a right to payment. 11 U.S.C. § 101(5)."). *See also Wodark v. Wodark (In re Wodark),* 425 B.R. 834, 837–38 (B.A.P. 10th Cir.2010) ("What matters in a § 523(a)(15) case is (1) the nature of the debt[ ] and (2) whether the debt was incurred in the course of a divorce or separation. The fact that the underlying obligation was payable to [third-party bank] does not mean that [debtor] did not incur a separate obligation to [spouse] that is, in itself, a nondischargeable debt.") (footnotes omitted).

[35] Because the bank is not a party to this appeal, we need not reach the question of whether any obligation Shane owed to the bank was discharged in bankruptcy.

[36] *See In re Williams,* 398 B.R. 464, 469 (Bankr. N.D. Ohio 2008) ("Nowhere in § 523(a)(15) is it provided that a marital debt cannot be 'incurred' [in the course of a divorce or separation] for

definition of debt encompassed within the bankruptcy statutes. This holding is especially clear in cases where the debtor-spouse has not only been ordered to, or agreed to, pay the debt, but has also been ordered to, or agreed to, hold the other spouse harmless or indemnify the other spouse.[37]

When one spouse's obligation to make payments on third-party debt under a separation agreement or divorce decree is not accompanied by a hold harmless or indemnification clause, the law is perhaps somewhat less settled.[38] But some courts have still recognized that even in the absence of an indemnification or hold harmless provision, the debtor spouse's divorce-related obligation to make payments on third party debt is not dischargeable.[39]

While the issue of whether the absence of a hold harmless provision would preclude an exception to discharge for a divorce-related obligation to make payments on a non-support debt to a third party has apparently not been squarely addressed by the Sixth Circuit Court of Appeals since the 2005 BAPCPA amendments, pre-BAPCPA Sixth Circuit precedent rejected the view that absence of a hold harmless provision would necessarily result in the dischargeability of a divorce-related obligation to pay a debt to a third party. Rather, the Sixth Circuit held that the bankruptcy court must look to applicable non-bankruptcy law (*i.e.*, state law governing enforceability of obligations to pay such debt under a divorce decree). And we are aware of no authority that would prevent a Kentucky state court from enforcing with contempt sanctions such an obligation to pay a third-party debt under a divorce decree in the absence of an indemnification or hold harmless clause. In fact, a trial court's power to enforce provisions of a divorce decree through its contempt powers is clearly established under Kentucky law.

In view of the broad definition of debt under federal bankruptcy law and a Kentucky trial court's authority to use its contempt powers to enforce obligations under divorce decrees, we conclude that Shane's obligation to Sondra under the divorce decree for him to make payments on the bank loan debt on the repossessed Durango was not discharged in Chapter 7 bankruptcy. While perhaps the trial court's ordering Shane to make payments *to the bank* may be problematic because any direct obligation he

---

purposes of the statute simply because the underlying debt is owed to a third party."). *See also Fast*, 766 N.W.2d 47.

[37] *See In re Schweitzer*, 370 B.R. at 150–54; *Fast*, 766 N.W.2d 47.

[38] *See In re Johnson*, 2007 WL 3129951 at *4 (Bankr.N.D.Ohio October 23, 2007) ("Courts are divided on the issue of whether debts owing to third parties and not subject to indemnification or hold harmless language fall within the ambit of § 523(a)(15)."); *In re Wodark*, 425 B.R. at 838 ("Nothing in § 532(a)(15) addresses the presence or absence of indemnification provisions."). *See also id.* at 837 (noting that prior to BAPCPA amendments, "courts were divided on the matter of whether debts delegated to divorcing/separating spouses in separation agreements or divorce decrees without express hold harmless or indemnification provisions were excepted from discharge under § 523(a)(15).").

[39] *See In re Johnson*, 2007 WL 3129951 at *6; *In re Wodark*, 425 B.R. at 839–40.

owed *to the bank* was apparently discharged in bankruptcy and the bank was not a party to these proceedings, the trial court clearly retained the authority to enforce Shane's obligations to Sondra under the divorce decree. And, in any case, given the fact that the contempt finding was not accompanied by a fine or jail time sanction, his injury in being found in contempt appears negligible.

IV. CONCLUSION.

For the foregoing reasons, we affirm the decision of the Court of Appeals.

B. DURING THE DIVORCE

WHITE V. WHITE
Court of Appeals, Sixth Circuit, 1988.
851 F.2d 170.

WELLFORD, CIRCUIT JUDGE.

The debtor-appellant challenges in this appeal the bankruptcy court's decision to lift an automatic stay to allow divorce proceedings brought by his wife to proceed in state court. The debtor claims an abuse of discretion because lifting the stay divested the bankruptcy court of its alleged exclusive jurisdiction in favor of a state tribunal. We disagree.

Patricia White, appellee, instituted divorce proceedings against her husband, John, on February 7, 1985, in Ashtabula County, Ohio. The divorce court ordered him to make temporary alimony payments of $800 weekly. When her husband made no payments under this order, Mrs. White moved for the appointment of a receiver for Mr. White's property.

John Paul White countered by instituting Chapter 11 bankruptcy proceedings in the bankruptcy court. For a time he remained in control of the bankruptcy estate, principally his oil and gas business, but later a bankruptcy trustee was appointed to manage the financial affairs of the bankruptcy estate. Debtor still operates the business. The effect of Mr. White's bankruptcy petition was to halt the divorce proceedings because of the automatic stay provisions of 11 U.S.C. § 362.

Mrs. White thereafter moved to lift the stay in order to allow the divorce action to proceed. She seeks permission for the state court to make an appropriate division of the marital estate which, of course, also constitutes the husband's bankruptcy estate. Mrs. White maintains that the state court's previous assumption of jurisdiction over the marital property took precedence over the bankruptcy court, citing *In re Washington*, 623 F.2d 1169 (6th Cir. 1980), *cert. denied sub nom. Wasserman v. Washington*, 449 U.S. 1101 (1981). The bankruptcy court granted her motion and lifted the stay so that divorce proceedings, including an apportionment of the marital estate, could be accomplished. In lifting the stay, the court noted that the state court had prior *in rem* jurisdiction. While specifying that it was not allowing the state court to appoint a receiver, the bankruptcy court stated the case could be disposed of in an orderly fashion by first allowing the state court to determine, under state law, how the property should be appropriately divided between the husband and wife.

On appeal, the district court upheld this action despite debtor's challenges to its jurisdictional propriety. The district court decided that the bankruptcy court order at issue did not improperly give up bankruptcy jurisdiction to the divorce court. Further, it noted that if the state court were to overstep its role, the problem could be rectified by actions under 11 U.S.C. § 105(a). Appeal to this court followed.

Appellant argues that the jurisdiction granted the bankruptcy court in 28 U.S.C. § 1334(d) is exclusive and may not be given up in favor of a state court proceeding for any reason. He also claims that *In re Washington, supra,* is no longer valid in light of 1984 amendments to the Bankruptcy Code.

We do not believe *In re Washington* controls the outcome of this case. That decision reversed a bankruptcy court's determination that it could assert jurisdiction over a debtor's property even when a state divorce court already had *in rem* jurisdiction over it. Our decision to award superior jurisdiction to the state court was based on "traditional notions of comity, which require that, as between state and federal courts, jurisdiction must be yielded to the court that first acquires jurisdiction over the property." 623 F.2d at 1172. We traced this holding to a broader doctrine which advocates granting exclusive jurisdiction to the first court asserting *in rem* jurisdiction, when both courts base jurisdiction on control of the same property. *See, e.g., Princess Lida of Thurn and Taxis v. Thompson,* 305 U.S. 456, 466 (1939).

Despite the federalism interests served by such a rule, we agree with debtor's argument that the 1978 and 1984 changes to the Bankruptcy Code were primarily aimed at getting away from the kind of *in rem* jurisdiction set out in *Princess Lida* and *In re Washington.* The jurisdiction granted in 28 U.S.C. § 1334(d) indicates a conscious effort by Congress to grant the bankruptcy court special jurisdiction and to preclude the type of jurisdictional disputes evidenced in those cases.

This interpretation has been followed by other courts presented with similar circumstances. *In re Modern Boats, Inc.,* 775 F.2d 619 (5th Cir. 1985) presented the situation in which an admiralty court had obtained *in rem* jurisdiction over the debtor's ship before bankruptcy was declared. Despite this previously-claimed jurisdiction, the bankruptcy court took control of the vessel. The court in *Modern Boats* declared this action to be appropriate because once a bankruptcy petition was filed, the admiralty court was stripped of jurisdiction and it became the exclusive province of the bankruptcy court. *Id.* at 620. The same result was reached in another case where, prior to bankruptcy, the admiralty court had sold a ship and only approval of the sale remained. *See In re Louisiana Ship Management, Inc.*, 761 F.2d 1025 (5th Cir. 1985). The outcome in these decisions is premised upon the changes Congress made in bankruptcy court jurisdiction, and we believe we must also follow the intent reflected in the amended language of § 1334(d). The rule in *In re Washington* should therefore no longer apply to give the state court jurisdiction over property simply because it may have been the first court to exercise control over the property.

Whether the bankruptcy court may suspend its jurisdiction, however, is a different question. Lifting the automatic stay as provided in 11 U.S.C. § 362(d) in this case will permit the state court to exercise limited jurisdiction in the kind of matter that is traditionally exclusively reserved for state divorce courts. Bankruptcy courts in other cases have not declined to lift the stay to allow divorce proceedings to conclude. *See In re Johnson*, 51 B.R. 439 (Bankr. E.D. Pa. 1985), and *Schulze v. Schulze*, 15 B.R. 106 (Bankr. S.D. Ohio 1981). The Bankruptcy Code does not define a debtor's interest in property; the answer to that question must be made after reference to state law. 4 L. King, *Collier on Bankruptcy* § 541.07 p. 541–29 (15th ed. 1983); *cf. Selby v. Ford Motor Co.*, 590 F.2d 642 (6th Cir. 1979) (court looked to Michigan treatment of property rights in deciding bankrupt's interest in trust funds). With regard to the present pending state court divorce proceedings, the bankruptcy court has acted to permit the state court with expertise in such matters to decide questions that are an inherent part of the divorce process.

While the bankruptcy court under § 105(a) may enforce the Code for the benefit of the parties before it, and may seek a just result in light of the interests of creditors and others concerned with the bankruptcy process, we are not sure that it can review or reject the state court's action in allocation of the marital estate once the stay is lifted. This, therefore, represents some abrogation of the bankruptcy court's authority, at least as far as its ability to determine the rights in marital property. Nevertheless, we are persuaded that:

> It is appropriate for bankruptcy courts to avoid invasions into family law matters 'out of consideration of court economy, judicial restraint, and deference to our state court brethren and their established expertise in such matters.'

In re MacDonald, 755 F.2d 715, 717 (9th Cir. 1985) (quoting *In re Graham*, 14 B.R. 246, 248 (Bankr. W.D. Ky. 1981)). *See also Schulze, supra. Schulze* considered the position of the nondebtor spouse and concluded his or her status would be seriously compromised if the bankruptcy proceedings continued while the divorce proceedings were stayed. This was deemed to be "cause" sufficient to lift the stay within the guidelines of § 362(d)(1). 15 B.R. at 108–09. The language of § 362(d) has not been changed by the 1984 amendments to the Code and we believe the bankruptcy court properly deferred to the divorce court's greater expertise on the question of what property belongs to whom.

The 1984 amendments to the Bankruptcy Code have not rendered it a self-contained mechanism to operate entirely without reference to state law. We therefore find no abuse of discretion in the bankruptcy court's decision to defer to the traditional and expert judgment of the divorce court of the State of Ohio for the sole purpose of deciding interests in the marital estate of the debtor husband and wife. The debtor's argument simply proves too much in urging that a bankruptcy court may never give up its jurisdiction for any reason, even for a limited purpose. The provisions for lifting the stay found in § 362(d) should be deemed to apply in these circumstances for the limited purpose of allowing the state court to exercise its exclusive domestic relations authority, including decisions concerning fair allocation of the marital estate.

We find no error, therefore, in the reasoning of Judge Bodoh that, "[U]ntil the court of Common Pleas for Ashtabula County, Ohio, makes a specific determination of the property rights as between the Debtor and his spouse, what is property of the Debtor's estate in this cause is unclear, and the reorganization of Debtor's business cannot proceed in an orderly fashion." The bankruptcy judge proceeded to lift the stay so that the state court might "determine the substantive rights of the parties under applicable, non-bankruptcy domestic relations law and to allow the parties to reach, or the state court to impose, a property settlement based on the state court's inquiry into the need for support and other factors under state law." At the same time, the bankruptcy court indicated its "exclusive jurisdiction over property of the Debtor * * * when the state court defines what is the property of the Debtor. * * * "

As noted above, the district court believed any problems encountered in handing partial resolution of the matter to the divorce courts could be remedied by resort to 11 U.S.C. § 105. We agree that this is an adequate safeguard, and we also suggest that the courts below urge the trustee to appear in the divorce action. By setting out his position as representative of the debtor's creditors, the trustee could make the state court aware that other parties' interests will be affected by the property division, thus possibly facilitating a fairer settlement for all parties concerned.

We affirm the decision to lift the stay under the circumstances here because we are concerned that the Bankruptcy Code could otherwise be abused as a weapon in a marital dispute. We believe the decision to lift the stay in this case was a proper exercise of discretion, but we do not wish to establish a per se rule in every bankruptcy case involving a domestic relations situation that the bankruptcy stay must be lifted. For example, there might be times when the bankruptcy court suspects collusion between the spouses to stage a divorce to avoid payment of the just claims of creditors, and granting a stay in that situation would obviously not serve the ends of bankruptcy or divorce jurisprudence. We simply hold that whether or not to lift the automatic stay in that type of bankruptcy proceeding lies within the reasonable discretion of the bankruptcy court or the district court as the case may be.

We therefore AFFIRM the challenged action in this case.

NOTES AND QUESTIONS

1.   *Howard* considers a situation where a spouse obtains a bankruptcy discharge *after* the divorce, If a spouse obtains a bankruptcy discharge after the dicorce petition was filed but *before* the divorce decree is entered, that could impact the court's ability to order each spouse to pay marital debts. *See* Horvath v. Horvath, 2010 WL. 338209 (Ohio App.).

A Summary. The family lawyer must carefully and precisely assess the tax consequences of a proposed settlement. The tax rules present opportunities for benefits to both parties—but also present a minefield of potential mistakes. For example, in Hoover v. Commissioner, 23 Fam. L. Rep. (BNA) 1104 (6th Cir. 1996), the divorce decree labelled payments as alimony, but failed to specify that the obligation would terminate upon the recipient's death. Because it was not clear under Ohio law that alimony automatically terminated if the recipient died, the obligor could not deduct any of the payments. This is not something you want to happen to one of your clients. Think! Read carefully! And get the advice of competent tax counsel.

Other bodies of law, such as bankruptcy, must also be considered. What may look and be treated like an installment property transfer or a mere contractual obligation may, under the bankruptcy laws, be considered in the "nature of" alimony or child support and thus not held to be dischargeable.

Finally, practical concerns must be assessed. If a divorcing woman is thinking of early remarriage, or if her ex-husband is near death, she may be much better off with a small, but final and indefeasible, property settlement than with generous alimony which would terminate on either party's death or her remarriage; where there is an antagonistic and bitter ex-husband, an alimony judgment, with its threat of jail for contempt, may be preferable to a larger installment property settlement; a large, installment-type property settlement from a man in a high-risk (of bankruptcy) business may be worth a lot less than a much more modest (but not dischargeable) alimony obligation.

CHAPTER 20

MODIFICATION AND ENFORCEMENT
OF SUPPORT AWARDS

■ ■ ■

1. MODIFICATION: SOME GENERAL THEMES

Child and indefinite (*i.e.*, permanent) spousal support awards are modifiable; property division and lump-sum alimony awards orders are not. *See* Pittman v. Pittman, 419 So. 2d 1376 (Ala. 1982); Marriage of Dundas, 823 N.E.2d 239 (Ill. App. 2005). Courts have disagreed on whether rehabilitative spousal support granted for a fixed term may be extended if the recipient does not become economically independent within the prescribed time. *Compare* Self v. Self, 861 S.W.2d 360 (Tenn. 1993) *with* Bentz v. Bentz, 435 N.W.2d 293 (Wis. App. 1988).

The traditional basis for modification of a support order is a "substantial (or material) and unforeseeable change in the circumstances of one of the parties." J. Thomas Oldham, *Cohabitation by an Alimony Recipient Revisited*, 20 J. FAM. L. 615 (1982). This is a relatively vague standard; the materials in this chapter describe how courts have interpreted it.

A central problem in modification policy is attaining the right balance between stability and flexibility. Support orders can often remain in effect for a long while. The child who is age 2 at divorce will be entitled to support until age 18 (or 21, depending on state law); the spouse who obtains permanent alimony will be entitled to support until remarriage or the death of either party. Because of their duration, support orders must be flexible; a support order based on the obligor's high income will quickly become unconscionable if he loses his job. But judicial economy and the parties' need for reasonably certain income entitlements also demand stability; we do not want divorced couples to continually relitigate the amount of support owed.

The "substantial change in circumstances" test is an attempt to balance the goals of stability and flexibility. The Uniform Marriage and Divorce Act comes down more firmly on the side of stability, requiring that, to warrant modification, a change in circumstances must be "so substantial and continuing as to be unconscionable." UMDA § 316. In recent years, child support policy has come down more firmly on the side of flexibility.

When child support orders are initially entered, many parents are young and have relatively low incomes. As time goes by, inflation typically diminishes the value of the initial award, while the noncustodial parent's income typically increases. *See* Elizabeth Phillips & Irwin Garfinkel, *Income Growth Among Nonresident Fathers: Evidence from Wisconsin*, 30 DEMOGRAPHY 227 (1993). In response to this pattern, alimony and child support modification principles have begun to diverge. The federal government now requires review of support orders for children receiving federal public assistance benefits every three years for possible modification; it does not require review of alimony orders. 42 U.S.C. § 666(a)(9)(C). The requirement that child support orders must be periodically reviewed (and modified if appropriate) is made more burdensome by the rule applicable in most states that the amount of child support cannot be adjusted automatically based on the parties' incomes at that time; some court action is needed to modify the order. *See In re* Kahle, 138 P.3d 1129 (Wash. App. 2006).

Some states have gone further in the direction of flexibility than the federal government requires. *See* J. Thomas Oldham, *Abating the Feminization of Poverty: Changing the Rules Governing Post-Decree Modification of Child Support Obligations*, 1994 B.Y.U. L. REV. 841. Wisconsin, for example, now permits (but does not require) courts to order child support expressed as a fraction of the obligor's income instead of a dollar value. (Because Wisconsin calculates child support from gross income, the calculation is relatively simple.) This approach has shown some success when the support obligor has stable employment, but has worked less well when the obligor is self-employed. *See* Oldham, *supra*. Minnesota has adopted a system to adjust child support orders for inflation. Every two years, each support obligor receives notice of an increase in the support obligation equal to the annual percentage increase in the cost of living index. The increase is presumptive and will not be imposed if the obligor can show that the cost of living increase exceeds his or her wage increase during the relevant period. While the Minnesota approach is simpler to administer than the Wisconsin model, it fails to capture any real increase in the obligor's earnings. Other states have retained the substantial change in circumstances standard, coupled with a presumption that a substantial change in circumstances has occurred if a new support award, based on the current guidelines and the parents' current incomes, deviates from the initial award by more than a specified percentage. *See* TEX. FAM. CODE § 156.401 (a) (2). Specified percentages adopted by states thus far range from ten to thirty percent.

The materials below explore how courts have construed the substantial change in circumstances principle and the rule that spousal support ends at "remarriage."

2. MODIFICATION BASED ON A SHIFT IN INCOME

A. THE OBLIGOR'S INCOME

MARRIAGE OF MEEGAN

California Court of Appeals, 1992.
11 Cal. App. 4th 156, 13 Cal. Rptr. 2d 799.

MOORE, ASSOCIATE JUSTICE.

In a marital dissolution judgment, a husband is ordered to pay monthly spousal support and does so for some years. Thereafter, however, he voluntarily resigns his high-paying job and enters a monastery to pursue a life of religious observance and prayer. In this case of first impression, we must decide whether it was an abuse of discretion for the trial court to grant the husband's request to reduce the spousal support award to zero.

After more than 23 years of marriage, Elizabeth and Patrick Meegan were divorced on May 17, 1988. At the time of the dissolution, Patrick's net disposable income was $4,700 per month. Although the financial records submitted to the court were incomplete, the evidence indicated Elizabeth, who was a nurse, had a monthly net disposable income of $1,900. Patrick was ordered to pay $739 per month spousal support.

In early 1991, Patrick decided to pursue a life of religious observance and prayer. He resigned his job as a sales executive, joined an order of the Catholic church, and entered the Holy Trinity Monastery in St. David, Arizona. He supported himself from his savings and, though he was no longer employed, continued to contribute $875 per month toward his two adult daughters' college educations and expenses. Patrick agreed to pay his 25-year-old daughter $300 per month, and his 19-year-old daughter $425 per month plus $150 a month for her car insurance, until they graduated and found employment.

On March 22, Patrick, then in his mid-50s, filed an order to show cause for modification seeking to terminate his obligation to pay spousal support, stating: "I am no longer employed and I cannot continue my former vocation due to its stress which has caused me depression, and my conscience and desire to become a Catholic priest dictate I follow a path of good works and services. In preparation to become a priest, I plan to work at 'Holy Trinity Monestary' [sic] for a year of voluntary community work. During the next few years I do not anticipate I will be earning income. I plan to support myself from my separate property from my divorce. I cannot afford to pay spousal support during the time I have no income."

Patrick estimated it would take four and a half to five years to become a permanent member of the religious order, prior to which time he could be asked to leave. He conceded the church might not permit him to become a priest because he had been married previously and would have to obtain an annulment before he could make his vows. At the time of the hearing, he had not started the annulment process. He was not obligated to pay money to the church for his residence at the monastery, and the church supplied his food and drink.

Patrick had $4,873 in checking accounts, $16,379 in a savings account, and stock worth $73,000. He received $4,700 from his pension plan when he resigned his job. In the year prior to the order to show cause (OSC) hearing, Patrick gave $4,000 to the church. Elizabeth testified her income was $28,000 per year at the time of the dissolution and that she had $70,000 in assets, including equity in her home. Patrick contended Elizabeth's income increased 30 percent between the time of the dissolution and the time of the OSC.

The court entered an order reducing the spousal support to zero, ruling: "The judgment of dissolution of marriage * * * is modified. Spousal support is reduced to zero * * *, with the court reserving jurisdiction over it. In the event [Patrick] obtains employment the spousal support order made in [the] judgment of dissolution of marriage is reinstated upon [Patrick's] receipt of a first paycheck, until a court of competent jurisdiction can evaluate the then existing financial situation in order to make a new order. * * *"

The court determined Patrick was acting in good faith and did not resign his job to avoid his spousal support obligations. The court also found that Elizabeth had a capacity "to be financially independent without a substantial reduction in her standard of living," and emphasized its decision would have been different if Elizabeth was "unemployable and faced with an impoverished situation as [compared] to being employable and faced with a minimal reduction in standard of living." The court found support should be reduced to zero based upon Patrick's "being no longer income-producing and his rights to a free [ ] alienation of his existing property." The court also stated that Patrick had "the ability to pay until he has no further money. That's patently obvious from the facts presented. The question [is] should the court take from him all capital as a response to this relief presuming that there was a division of community property with some rule of reason as to that division * * * some four years ago. The question now is: do I have jurisdiction to take from [Patrick] all that he has, and the answer is no, I do not have that jurisdiction and I will not do that."[1]

---

[1] The trial court considered numerous hypotheticals and emphasized the importance of this case to the bench and bar. For example, the judge considered a scenario where a wealthy stockbroker from Newport Beach divorces his wife and moves to Utah to rent canoes for $25,000 a year leaving the wife and family destitute. He also considered the possibility of a trial attorney making $250,000 a year deciding to become a judge and earn $80,000 a year. The judge noted that

Elizabeth contends the trial court abused its discretion by reducing the spousal support to zero and by denying her request to create a lien in her favor on monies and other property owned by Patrick to secure payment to her of any future spousal support payments ordered made by Patrick.

Spousal support is not a mandatory requirement in dissolution proceedings. (*See* Civ. Code, § 4801.) "Spousal support must be determined according to the needs of both parties and their respective abilities to meet these needs. In this regard, a trial court has broad discretion and an abuse thereof only occurs when it can be said that no judge reasonably could have made the same order."

Similarly, modification of a spousal support order is a matter for the sound exercise of the court's discretion, based upon a showing of a material change of circumstances since the last spousal support order.

In re Marriage of Sinks, 204 Cal. App. 3d 586, 251 Cal. Rptr. 379, affirmed the trial court's decision refusing to reduce spousal support. However, the court based its conclusion on the fact that the husband retired from his job in "an attempt to shirk his support obligation." (*Id.* at p. 594, 251 Cal. Rptr. 379.) Because the trial court found the husband's retirement "was improperly motivated," the Court of Appeal did not address the question of first impression raised here. As Elizabeth concedes, the trial court here found Patrick was "well motivated."

Here, the trial court found that Patrick did not quit his job to avoid his spousal support obligation and was acting in good faith. Credibility is a matter within the trial court's discretion. The court believed Patrick's testimony that he could not continue his former employment due to stress and depression, and due to the fact that his "conscience and desire to become a Catholic priest dictate [he] follow a path of good works and services in preparation to becoming a priest." The evidence was uncontroverted that he did, in fact, take residence at the monastery, that he was no longer employed, and that he was earning no income. Patrick estimated it would take four and a half to five years for him to become a permanent member of the religious order, at which time he would be required to take a vow of poverty. Deferring to the trial court's findings on these credibility issues, as we must, we conclude there was no abuse of discretion in reducing Elizabeth's spousal support to zero.

Elizabeth also asks us to find that spousal support should be based on Patrick's ability to earn, rather than on his actual earnings. In light of the trial court's determinations, we may not do so. "It has long been the rule the court can consider the payor's earning capacity when determining . . . spousal support. However, this rule has been applied only where the parent has demonstrated a willful intention to avoid fulfilling financial obligations

---

courts have concluded that there are "no rules we could come up with, no pattern . . . Every case would be analyzed on an individual basis."

through deliberate misconduct." *In re Marriage of Regnery*, 214 Cal. App. 3d 1367, 1371, 263 Cal. Rptr. 243 (1989). No such facts exist here.

The judgment is affirmed.

HARVEY V. ROBINSON

Supreme Court of Maine, 1995.
665 A.2d 215.

LIPEZ, J.

Cheryl Robinson appeals from a judgment entered in the Superior Court affirming the judgment of the District Court substantially reducing the amount of her former husband's child support payments. Robinson argues that the District Court erred when it approved a reduced level of child support that did not reflect her former husband's current full-time earning capacity. We agree, and accordingly we vacate the judgment.

I.

In a 1988 divorce judgment the District Court determined that Robinson and Harvey's two children, Karen (born 1980) and Sara (born 1981), would reside principally with Robinson and that Harvey would pay to Robinson as child support $345 bi-weekly. In 1991, Harvey made $26,000 as a civilian employee of the National Guard and another $3,500 for weekend Guard service. He had a total income of approximately $35,500 because of additional work with an ambulance service.

In 1992, having completed 20 years of service with the National Guard, Harvey anticipated that he might face involuntary retirement. Rather than waiting to see if this involuntary retirement occurred, Harvey retired from the Guard voluntarily to pursue his long deferred dream of going to college and medical school. He is currently a full-time undergraduate student.

As a result of this decision, Harvey now has a gross income of approximately $13,840. This amount reflects the income from part-time work he is able to do while in school and some educational grant money.

After Harvey left his full-time job with the Guard, he stopped making child support payments. In July 1992 he moved to reduce his support obligation. In November 1992 he cashed in his retirement pension to obtain funds to pay a child support arrearage of $3,400. In December, however, he again stopped making child support payments.

In May 1993, the District Court heard Harvey's motion to reduce his support obligation. Harvey had just completed his first year of undergraduate schooling and was behind approximately $3,800 in his child support payments. Robinson testified that Harvey's failure to make these payments had prevented her from purchasing winter boots and coats for her daughters and had forced them to forego gymnastics, an activity in which they had participated for five or six years. At that time Robinson was employed full-time as a medical secretary earning $21,000 annually. Seven years remained before Harvey would complete medical school, at approximately the same time his younger daughter would no longer be a minor.

Despite Robinson's urging, the court used Harvey's current gross income as a full-time student to calculate the appropriate child support obligation, instead of his earning capacity before beginning college.[1] The court found that Harvey's decision to leave his full-time employment was made in good faith, and, therefore, using $13,840 as Harvey's gross income and $21,000 as Robinson's gross income, established a support payment for Harvey of $60 per week. The court found, however, that it was equitable in this instance, particularly because Harvey had recently purchased a new automobile, to deviate upward from this amount. The court also stated that it was considering the effects on the children of the reduced support payments. Accordingly, it ordered Harvey to pay $80 per week, increasing to $86 per week in December 1993 when his younger daughter reached twelve years of age. Robinson unsuccessfully argued that based on Harvey's earning capacity, his gross income should be $36,000 and his weekly child support payment pursuant to the work sheet should be $213, increasing to $236 in December 1993. The Superior Court affirmed the order and Robinson's appeal followed.

II.

We review for abuse of discretion the court's decision to base a child support award on Harvey's current income as a part-time employee rather than his current earning capacity as a full-time employee, and we "will overturn the trial court's decision only if it results in a plain and unmistakable injustice, so apparent that it is instantly visible without argument." In *Rich v. Narofsky*, 624 A.2d 937, 939 (Me. 1993), the mother sought to amend the divorce judgment to modify her support obligation after leaving her full-time job to enroll in college. Although she was capable of working part-time while pursuing her studies and full-time during summers, she saw no need to do so. The trial court designated the father as the primary caretaker and relieved the mother of any child support obligations. We held that the District Court abused its discretion by eliminating the mother's obligations "without some consideration of her part-time and summer earning capacity."

---

[1]   The statutory child support guidelines include the following provision on the earning capacity of a party:

> Gross income may include the difference between the amount a party is earning and that party's earning capacity when the party voluntarily becomes or remains unemployed or under employed, if sufficient evidence is introduced concerning the party's current earning capacity. 19 M.R.S.A. § 311(5)(D) (Supp. 1994).

Although Harvey, unlike the mother in *Rich*, is working as many hours as his educational commitments permit, his decision to change his career and pursue a full-time educational program has imposed needless hardships on his children. Harvey's priorities have the same effect on his children as the unwillingness of the mother in *Rich* to use her part-time and summer earning capacity to help support her children.

As justification for its order, the trial court noted that Harvey's decision to pursue a college degree was made in good faith. That is undoubtedly true. There is no suggestion in the record that Harvey opted for school in an effort to avoid his obligation to his children. Harvey's good faith, however, does not ameliorate the dramatic effect on the children of his decision to give up full-time work. That good faith consideration must be balanced by an evaluation of the effect that Harvey's under employment decision has on the interests of his children. By its nature, an order for child support serves the interests of the child by compelling parents to meet their financial responsibilities to their children. *See* 19 M.R.S.A. § 306 (Supp. 1994).

Although the court acknowledged the effects on the children of reduced child support payments, the court approved that reduction because it accepted Harvey's decision to forego full-time employment in favor of full-time education. The court does not explain how this accommodation to Harvey's preferences serves the interests of the children in any way. Harvey's decision cannot be justified as one that will serve the interests of his children eventually despite their current deprivations. Harvey will complete medical school when his youngest child becomes an adult and he no longer has a legal obligation to support either of his children. This case is markedly different than *Rowland v. Kingman*, 629 A.2d 613 (Me. 1993) (cert. denied 114 S. Ct. 884 (1994)), in which we approved a decrease in the amount of child support to be paid by the mother based on our recognition that she had closed her medical practice in Maine in anticipation of her move to Oregon with her children. Her decline in income would only be temporary: "There is evidence in the record that because of the time required to rebuild her practice, Rowland would not be able to immediately achieve her previous level of income." *Id.* at 617. In this case, Harvey has no medical practice to rebuild. His practice is years away, when the children are adults.[3]

---

[3]   The age of Harvey's children and the length of his educational program also distinguish this case from *Rich v. Narofsky*, 624 A.2d 937 (Me. 1993). In *Rich,* the two children were 8 and 5 at the time the trial court made its decision. The mother anticipated an educational program of five years. Rich argued on appeal that her enhanced education credentials would permit her to increase her financial support for her children. Harvey's children were 13 and 11 at the time the court made its decision. He had seven years to go in his educational program. He acknowledged that his children would be adults when he finished medical school. He does not argue that his enhanced education credentials will permit him to increase his financial support for his children.

In a tacit acknowledgment that the interests of the children matter, Harvey argues that an interests analysis that focuses on money is too narrow:

> This [focus on money] fails completely to consider that children may actually suffer through watching parents stay in bad jobs; the children may suffer if maintaining a certain job keeps the parent from spending time with his/her children; and the children may indeed suffer if they are taught at an early age that having children absolutely bars a parent from continuing his/her education. Certainly more than just money must be considered when ascertaining the best interests of children.

Even if there is some abstract merit in this argument, there is not a testimonial word in the record that supports it.

As further justification for its order, the court noted that Harvey delayed his secondary education so that he could work and earn income while Robinson attended school. Harvey cannot reduce his child support obligations by arguing that it is now his turn to go to college. Robinson pursued her education at a time when the family was intact and her educational endeavors would eventually benefit the family and herself. Harvey's educational endeavors benefit only himself and deprive the children. He has permitted his preferences to override the interests of his children.

Although we recognize the difficult issues posed for the trial court by these cases, the dilemma here was not insoluble. Harvey could work full time and go to school part time. In that way, he could fulfill his support obligation to his children while pursuing his educational interests. If medical school were unattainable through a part time education, he might have to make necessary adjustments to fulfill his parental obligation. The decision to relieve Harvey of that obligation of adequate support "results in a plain or unmistakable injustice, so apparent that it is instantly visible without argument." *Tardif*, 617 A.2d at 1033. This case must be remanded for reconsideration of the child support determination based on Harvey's current earning capacity as a full-time employee.

Judgment vacated.

DANA, J., with whom ROBERTS, J. joins, dissenting.

I respectfully dissent. When determining a party's gross income for purposes of computing child support payments, the trial court "may include the difference between the amount a party is earning and that party's earning capacity when the party voluntarily becomes or remains unemployed or underemployed, if sufficient evidence is introduced concerning a party's current earning capacity." 19 M.R.S.A. § 311(5)(D) (Supp. 1994). Consideration of earning capacity as opposed to present income is not mandatory and we should not disturb a court's decision whether to consider earning capacity absent an abuse of discretion. Moreover, we accord "unusual deference" to a court's findings in an order modifying the amount of child support and "will overturn the trial court's decision of such a question only if it results in a plain and unmistakable injustice, so apparent that it is instantly visible without argument." *Tardif v. Cutchin*, 617 A.2d 1032, 1033 (Me. 1992).

Unlike determinations of parental rights and responsibilities, determinations of child support payments are not based solely on the standard of the "best interests of the child." *Compare* 19 M.R.S.A. §§ 311–320 (Supp. 1994) *with* 19 M.R.S.A. § 752(5) (Supp. 1994). Following dissolution of marriage, the custodial parent and children cannot be allowed to freeze the other parent in his employment or otherwise preclude him from seeking economic improvement for himself and his family. So long as his employment, educational or investment decisions are undertaken in good faith and not deliberately designed to avoid responsibility for those dependent on him, he should be permitted to attempt to enhance his economic fortunes without penalty.

The trial court carefully considered the motivations behind Harvey's decision to leave his full-time job in order to pursue a college education while maintaining three part-time jobs. The court reached a conclusion that the decision was one based on good faith and not one motivated by a desire to avoid child support payments. There is substantial evidence to support this finding. Moreover, there is no indication that the court did not consider the best interests of the children when it adjusted Harvey's monthly payments to an amount significantly greater than that suggested by the child support payment guidelines.

I find the trial court's action to be within its considerable discretion, and I would affirm the judgment.

NOTES AND QUESTIONS

1.   While the court grants downward modification in *Meegan*, an alimony case, and denies it in *Harvey*, a child support case, don't assume that modification outcomes will invariably follow this pattern. Courts often refuse to permit downward modification of an alimony award when the obligor voluntarily reduces his income. *See, e.g.,* Vriesenga v. Vriesenga, 931 So. 2d 213 (Fla. Dist. Ct. App. 2006); Barbarine v. Barbarine, 925 S.W.2d 831 (Ky. App. 1996). Should the standard for downward modification be the same for purposes of child support and spousal support? If the standard should be different, in what way should it be different?

Should it be relevant in *Harvey* that the husband delayed obtaining his college education during marriage to support the family while the wife completed her education?

For an example of a situation similar to *Meegan* involving a motion to reduce child support, which was not granted, *see* Andrews v. Andrews, 719 S.E.2d 128 (N.C. App. 2011).

2.   The availability of modification based on a voluntary reduction in income varies substantially from one state to the next. Some courts look primarily at the voluntariness of income reduction, refusing modification whenever the change was in the obligor's control. *See, e.g.,* Shaughnessy v. Shaughnessy, 793 P.2d 1116 (Ariz. App. 1990); Aguiar v. Aguiar, 127 P.3d 234 (Idaho App. 2005). Some refuse modification whenever there is a negative impact on the payee spouse or child. *See, e.g.,* Moseley v. Moseley, 216 So. 2d 852 (La. App. 1968). Many take a multifactor approach. *See, e.g.,* Deegan v. Deegan, 603 A.2d 542 (N.J. Super. App. Div. 1992); *In re* Marriage of Smith, 396 N.E.2d 859 (Ill. App. 1979). All look to the obligor's intentions; if the obligor quits a job for the sole purpose of harming the custodial parent and child, no court would permit modification. *See* Hutto v. Kneipp, 627 So. 2d 802 (La. App. 1993). What are the pros and cons of these various approaches? Which, on balance, seems preferable? *See generally* Lewis Becker, *Spousal and Child Support and the "Voluntary Reduction of Income" Doctrine,* 29 CONN. L. REV. 647 (1997).

3.   Is it possible to harmonize the results in *Meegan* and *Harvey*? If so, on what basis?

4.   What, if any, recourse would Mrs. Meegan and Ms. Robinson have had if they had remained married and opposed their husbands' career changes?

5.   The *Meegan* court holds that the obligor should not have to exhaust all available resources before the support obligation is suspended. Why? Is this approach fair?

6.   Which of these income reductions justify downward modification of support obligations? (Assume in each case that neither the obligee's income nor needs have substantially changed.)

a.   A successful dentist, who has long wanted to be a lawyer, plans to attend law school and seeks downward modification of his child support obligation while attending school. His former wife's income has not increased. *See* McKenna v. Steen, 422 So. 2d 615 (La. App. 1982).

b.   A support obligor is fired from his job for cause (but not because he was trying to reduce his support obligation) and cannot find a comparable job elsewhere. *See* Busche v. Busche, 272 P.3d 748 (Utah App. 2012); Klahold v. Kroh, 649 A.2d 701 (Pa. Super. 1994); Lambert v. Lambert, 617 N.W.2d 645 (Neb. App. 2000).

c.   A support obligor is involuntarily laid off and finds employment at a considerably lower salary in a different town. After moving, he is recalled to his former job, but declines the opportunity to return. *See* McKinney v. McKinney, 813 S.W.2d 828 (Ky. App. 1991).

d.   The support obligor has committed a crime and has been incarcerated. *See* Herring v. Herring, 24 A.3d 574 (Vt. 2011); Clark v. Clark, 902 N.E.2d 813 (Ind. 2009); Thomasson v. Johnson, 903 P.2d 254 (N.M. App. 1995); Franzen v. Borders, 521 N.W.2d 626 (Minn. App. 1994).

e.   The obligor commits a felony, loses his job, and cannot find comparable work. *See* Bendinelli v. Bendinelli, 2011 WL 7163124 (Ark. App.); Hayes v. Hayes, 949 So. 2d 150 (Ala. App. 2006).

f.   The obligor has remarried. His new spouse is offered, and takes, a new job in a distant city at a substantially higher salary; the obligor moves with his new spouse and cannot find employment at a comparable salary.

g.   The obligor has an extremely stressful job and "burns out." He takes a less stressful but less remunerative position.

h.   Before marriage, husband and wife agree that husband will maintain his current stressful employment as an investment banker for ten years and then pursue his long-term career aim of becoming a minister. Husband and wife divorce after six years of marriage; in year ten, husband quits his job and goes to divinity school.

i.   The support obligor wishes to retire. *See* Suarez v. Sanchez, 43 So. 3d 118 (Fla. Dist. Ct. App. 2010); Marriage of Reynolds, 74 Cal. Rptr. 2d 636 (App. 1998).

j.   The obligor was in the military, voluntarily did not reenlist, and could not find work paying the same salary. *See* Dill v. Dill, 908 So. 2d 198 (Miss. App. 2005).

k.   The obligor decides to retire, thereby reducing his or her income. *See* Hemmingsen v. Hemmingsen, 767 N.W.2d 711 (Minn. App. 2009). Should it matter whether it is the "customary" retirement age?

l.   The primary custodian relocates to another location with the parties' child. Assume the support obligor moves to that location and cannot find a comparable job. *See* DuBois v. DuBois, 956 S.W.2d 607 (Tex. App. 1997).

7.   Assume the custodial parent chooses not to work outside the home. Is this underemployment? *See* Stanton v. Abbey, 874 S.W.2d 493 (Mo. App. 1994). Should the answer depend upon the age of the child? Would the answer be different if the custodial parent was working outside the home for a period but then quits the job to care for a child she conceived with a new partner?

8.   Spousal support orders are generally modifiable if an unforeseen event causes a continuing, material change in circumstances for a party.

a.   One recurring fact pattern involves a recipient spouse who has not become self-sufficient by the time rehabilitative support was to end. In Schmitz v. Schmitz, 586 N.W.2d 490 (N.D. 1998), the court held that increases in the ex-husband's earnings after divorce were not unforeseen and could not be the basis for an increase in support. But the ex-wife's failure to become financially independent as quickly as she and the court had hoped was an unforeseen change in circumstances that warranted an extension of the period of support.

b.   Assume at the time of divorce the support obligor has been diagnosed with multiple sclerosis. If the obligor's health continues to deteriorate and at some point can no longer work, should this be a ground for spousal support modification? *See* Garvey v. Garvey, 138 So. 3d 115 (Fla. Dist. Ct. App. 2014) (yes).

9.   *Increased Obligor Income:* A child support modification petition may also be based on an increase in the obligor's income. Although most courts generally would increase the amount of child support payable if it found either that the obligor's income had substantially increased or had increased more than the percentage specified in the applicable state statute, a few courts have held that in such instances support should be increased only if it is established that he child's needs have increased. *See* Thomas v. Thomas, 518 S.E.2d 513 (N.C. 1999); Snipes v. Snipes, 454 S.E.2d 864 (N.C. App. 1995) (invalidating a provision that the support obligation would be adjusted annually based on the consumer price index).

In the introduction of the chapter it was mentioned that some states have enacted a rebuttable presumption that, if applying the guidelines to the parties' current circumstances would change the support amount by more than a specified percent, that constitutes a substantial change in circumstances which warrants modification. *See* Dudgeon v. Dudgeon, 318 S.W.3d 106 (Ky. App. 2010) (15% change).

If the obligor had a very high income when the original child support order was entered, the question arises whether a later substantial additional increase in income warrants an increase. For example, in Smith v. Freeman, 814 A.2d 65 (Md. App. 2002), the obligor earned $1.2 million annually when he agreed to pay $4200 in monthly support. If a few years later the obligor's annual income is $3.2 million and the child's situation is no different, what should happen if the primary custodian petitions for an increase? If the obligor is a professional athlete (presumably with a short period of high income), should this be relevant? *See* Boone v. Holmes, 2015 WL 3562658 (Ohio App.) (discussing numerous cases).

10. Although a recipient generally should be able to obtain an increase in child support if the obligor's income substantially increases, and an obligor should be able to obtain a reduction in his or her child support obligation if he or she is laid off from work, in each case the party desiring modification needs to navigate the child support system to modify the order. The recipient in many instances, can get assistance to increase the award from the state child support office, while in most states the child support office will not help the obligor reduce the award when his or her income is significantly reduced. So, a child support order may remain unchanged even though the parties' circumstances

have substantially changed for the worse after the order was calculated. For obligors who are no longer receiving any income, if the order is not changed this can quickly result in a substantial amount of unpaid child support, which can dramatically impact the obligor for much of his or her future. *See* Daniel L. Hatcher, *Forgotten Fathers,* 93 B.U. L. REV. 897 (2013).

11. *Visitation Changes:* A change in visitation can result in a modification of child support. For example, if the original child support amount was decreased from the guideline presumptive level due to the amount of time the obligor intended to spend with the child, the amount due can be increased if the obligor's level of contact is lower than what was envisioned. *See* Buhler v. Buhler, 83 So. 3d 790 (Fla. Dist. Ct. App. 2011). Similarly, the court can deviate from the guidelines and order more child support if the obligor is not visiting the child, thereby increasing the expenses of the primary custodian. *See In re* Selley, 359 P.3d 891 (Wash. App. 2015). A substantial change in the amount of time the child spends with each parent can be grounds for a child support modification. *See In re* Handley, 385 P.3d 1148 (Or. App. 2016).

B. THE RECIPIENT'S INCOME

CARTER V. CARTER
Supreme Court of Utah, 1978.
584 P.2d 904.

CROCKETT, JUSTICE.

In this proceeding, plaintiff, Norman G. Carter, sought to have his obligation of paying $350 per month alimony to his former wife, defendant, Pauline Carter, terminated. Upon a plenary hearing and due consideration of the appropriate factors, the trial court granted his petition only to the extent of reducing the alimony to $100 per month. Plaintiff appeals.

* * * The parties had been married in 1945 and thus, at the time of the divorce in 1976, the marriage had endured for 31 years. They had reared a family of four children, all of whom were of age and independent. At that time, their principal assets were a home worth about $80,000, a mountain cabin worth about $10,000, and household furniture, equipment and other adjunctive assets of the usual character, including an automobile for each.

The plaintiff had worked for * * * U.S. Steel in Orem for almost 30 years and his yearly salary was about $18,000 and he also had a Veteran's pension of $300 per month. Defendant Pauline was unemployed, though she was qualified to follow her former vocation as a school teacher. The decree made an equitable distribution of the property (about which no complaint is made in this proceeding) and awarded the defendant alimony of $275 per month while she lived in the family home and until it was sold, and thereafter $350 per month.

Ten months later, the plaintiff filed the instant petition to have the $350 per month alimony eliminated. His counsel stated to the court that they made no contention that plaintiff's income or economic status had diminished since the divorce was granted, but that the ground relied on for termination of alimony was that the defendant Pauline had become employed as a school teacher at a monthly salary of $636.27, and that because of that, together with other fixed income of about $150 per month, she has adequate income for her support and that therefore alimony should be eliminated entirely.

It is not difficult to appreciate that the plaintiff desires to be relieved entirely from the payment of alimony. Neither are we insensitive to the fact that there is some merit to his argument that alimony is primarily to provide support for the recipient. But in adjudicating his petition, it is necessary and proper for the court to consider not only his point of view, but all of the factors bearing on the total problem. This includes the effect its determination will have on each of the parties at present, and also in the future; and, moreover, how its ruling will harmonize with the underlying policy of the law and thus affect society generally.

One of the important factors is that it should be the policy of the law to encourage one receiving alimony to seek employment. This purpose would not be served if a wife who manifests sufficient initiative and industry to get a job is penalized by having her alimony cut off entirely. In that connection it is also noteworthy that in this case the defendant is 58 years old; and even though she has present employment with a fairly good salary, there is the likelihood that it may not last very long and she would be left without that income and likewise without alimony.

Another matter of significance is that where parties have been married for many years and reared their family, it is natural to assume that the wife has been occupied mainly with taking care of the home and the family, and thus in comparative isolation from the competitive world, while the husband has been out in it earning a living. He therefore has the advantage of the training, experience and seniority which normally gives him the greater earning potential. Nonetheless, whatever degree of financial success and standard of living they have attained should properly be regarded as a result of their joint efforts. Consistent with this view and in accord with the determination made by the trial court in this matter, it would seem to be manifestly unfair to eliminate the alimony entirely and in effect turn the wife out to fend for herself.

Correlated to the above is the fact that upon consideration of all of the circumstances, the trial court did grant the plaintiff substantial relief by reducing his obligation to pay alimony from $350 to $100 per month.

NOTES AND QUESTIONS

1.   What is the probable basis of the trial court's determination that the husband's maintenance obligation should be reduced from $350 to $100, based on his wife's additional monthly income of $636? Given that her income was still substantially lower than her husband's, why didn't the court maintain the husband's obligation?

2.   The court notes that it does not want to apply a rule that would deter alimony recipients from finding work. Is the court's approach effective?

3.   In those states whose guidelines consider the income of the custodial parent, a significant reduction in income of the custodial parent could warrant a child support increase. Of course, if the reduction is voluntary, not all states would consider it. *See* Stanton v. Abbey, 874 S.W.2d 493 (Mo. App. 1994) (custodial parent quit her job after remarriage).

4.   The parties might attempt to specify in the decree when spousal support will end. For example, in *In re* C.P.Y., 364 S.W.3d 411 (Tex. App. 2012) the decree provided that the support would continue until the recipient "returned to work on a full-time basis." When the recipient became employed by a law firm as a contract attorney, the obligor filed a petition asking the court to confirm that his support obligation had terminated. The recipient contended that the support obligation should not terminate, because she was rarely asked to work 40 or more hours per week, so she was not working "full time." What would be a fair result? Can you think of a more precise standard the parties could have established for when the support would stop? What if the claimant qualifies for a Social Security longevity benefit but has chosen not to begin receipt of the benefits? *See* McKernan v. McKernan, 135 A.3d 1116 (Pa. Super. 2016). Should that be considered a ground for reducing the spousal support?

Problem 20-1:

You are a family court judge. When the original child support order was calculated two years ago, the obligor was earning $6,300,000 annually. The original order was for weekly support payments of $760. The primary custodian has filed a petition to modify support because the obligor's annual income now is more than $9 million. Should the order be modified? Davis v. Knafel, 837 N.E.2d 585 (Ind. App. 2005). If so, by how much?

Problem 20-2:

At divorce the husband, a medical doctor who earns more than $200,000 annually, is ordered to pay $2500 monthly child support and $2500 monthly spousal maintenance. He then develops a cocaine addiction and has his medical license suspended, which reduces his monthly income to $1238. He files a motion to terminate his spousal support obligation. You are the clerk for the family court judge; she asks you to review the motion and make a recommendation. What would you recommend? *See In re* Luty, 263 P.3d 1067 (Or. App. 2011) (appellate court ruled that the husband's spousal support obligation should be terminated).

3. MODIFICATION BASED ON NEW RELATIONSHIPS

A. COHABITATION BY THE ALIMONY RECIPIENT

If an alimony recipient remarries, in most states the alimony terminates. *See generally* Cynthia Starnes, *Alimony, Intuition, and the Remarriage-Termination Rule*, 81 IND. L. J. 971 (2006). In light of this rule, courts and legislatures have had to specify what should occur if the recipient cohabits.

TAAKE V. TAAKE
Supreme Court of Wisconsin, 1975.
70 Wis. 2d 115, 233 N.W.2d 449.

BEILFUSS, JUSTICE.

On October 31, 1966, the plaintiff-respondent, E. Robert Taake, was granted an absolute divorce from the defendant-appellant, Barbara A. Taake, upon the ground of cruel and inhuman treatment. From the findings of fact and judgment on file and a part of the record on appeal, it appears the parties had been married about twelve years. They had three minor children—two of their own and an adopted child. The plaintiff-husband was and still is a physician and surgeon; the defendant-wife was a housewife. The parties resided in Beaver Dam. Pursuant to stipulation of the parties, the court awarded the custody of the children to the wife and required a support money payment of $550 per month by the plaintiff-husband. As a division of estate, the wife was awarded the home of the parties, the household goods, her personal effects and an automobile. In addition, she was awarded alimony in the amount of $200 per month.

On February 6, 1968, based upon a stipulation of the parties, the judgment was amended to provide that the husband have custody of the children, and the provision for support money payments was deleted.

Shortly thereafter the defendant sold the house in Beaver Dam and moved to an apartment complex in Sun Prairie. She lived there for about a year and then moved to an apartment in Madison, where she lived until December, 1971. She worked intermittently as a personnel worker.

During the year 1971 the defendant, Mrs. Taake, met Lyle Fink. Fink was divorced from his wife and was employed as a maintenance painter for the Madison school system. Fink was negotiating for the purchase of a home on School Road in Madison. For a period of four to five weeks prior to actual occupancy of the School Road home, Fink lived with Mrs. Taake in her Madison apartment.

In December of 1971 both Mr. Fink and Mrs. Taake moved into his newly purchased home on School Road and both were still living there at the time of the hearing in this matter in May of 1973. The arrangements were that she was to pay him $25 per month rent and pay for a part of the groceries, and do at least a part of the housework. She had a separate bedroom. Mrs. Taake has been unemployed a part of the time due to alleged emotional problems. Fink suffered an injury while at work, has received some workmen's compensation benefits but is unemployed.

Mrs. Taake admits having occasional sexual relations with Fink and failing to correct persons when they refer to her as Mrs. Fink, although she has not affirmatively identified herself as Fink's wife. Her name does appear as Barbara Fink in a city directory.

Fink testified he considered Mrs. Taake to be his wife but later changed his testimony to the effect that they were very, very good friends. Mrs. Taake and Mr. Fink have not married at any time.

In September of 1972 the respondent, Robert Taake, ceased making the monthly $200 alimony payments and in May of 1973 petitioned the court for an order amending the judgment to terminate alimony.

As stated, the order amending the judgment expunged the alimony arrearages, terminated alimony and barred future alimony.

In a memorandum decision the trial court found that Mrs. Taake and Lyle Fink had a *de facto* marriage relationship and that Mrs. Taake had and was engaging in misconduct of such a nature so as to require a termination of her former husband's obligation to pay her alimony.

The trial court concluded that Mrs. Taake should not be permitted to enjoy both the benefits of her *de facto* marriage relationship with Lyle Fink and the benefit of alimony from her former husband; and that to permit a divorced woman to do so might dissuade her from remarriage. The trial court also concluded that Mrs. Taake's legal misconduct was the kind of misconduct which this court has heretofore recognized as warranting a change or elimination of alimony.

* * *

We acknowledge that a divorced wife owes no duty of sexual fidelity to her former husband. However, her cohabitation with another man can be acknowledged as a change of circumstances affecting her former husband's responsibility to provide alimony for her support. The manner and extent of the cohabitation and circumstances should be considered in determining whether alimony payments are to be changed.

In this case there are several changed circumstances that can be considered. Mrs. Taake was given a substantial division of estate, including the home and household furniture of the parties for the obvious reason that it was going to be used as the home for the minor children. Further, because she was awarded the children, her opportunity for supporting herself was limited. She stipulated that the custody be transferred to the husband and sold the house. These were material changes in the circumstances that the court considered when the original award of alimony was made. Her cohabitation with Lyle Fink was not an occasional indiscretion but continuous cohabitation with arrangements for joint support.

We believe this change of circumstances was sufficient to permit the trial court to expunge the delinquencies in alimony payments and to amend the judgment to delete the provision for alimony. We conclude the trial court did not abuse its discretion in these respects and those parts of the order must be affirmed.

The order also barred any future alimony. This we think goes too far. If, at a subsequent hearing, it appears that Mrs. Taake is not married, is not cohabiting in the manner set forth above, and other circumstances warrant a resumption of alimony in some degree, the court should not be powerless to act. That part of the order barring future alimony must be reversed.

HEFFERNAN, JUSTICE (dissenting).

In Wisconsin it is the rule that, upon divorce, a husband has a continuing obligation to support his former wife in the manner to which she was accustomed. * * *

There may well be good reasons to conclude that, in this day of equal rights, in cases where both parties have the capacity to be self-supporting, the entire concept of alimony should be re-examined. Suffice it to say that alimony serves the public interest where, as here, it is necessary for the maintenance of one party to the divorce and without which the dependent former spouse would become a public charge. It is in the public interest that alimony usually be paid, for without such post-divorce provision for support, there is a substantial likelihood that a divorced spouse would become a public charge.

Bearing in mind this overriding purpose of alimony, what are the facts of this case? Dr. Taake, a Beaver Dam physician, whose ability to pay his divorced wife, the mother of his children, the sum of $200 per month for her support is unquestioned, petitioned the court to be relieved of his legal obligation solely because of his former wife's alleged misconduct.

There was no proof that Dr. Taake could not pay the amount previously decreed, nor was there any proof that Barbara Taake's financial circumstances had changed so that the alimony payments were not necessary for her maintenance.

Rather, the facts indisputably show that, at the time of the hearing, she was ill, was unable to work, and was unable to pay her rent.

The situation of Fink and Barbara Taake is more to be deplored in our society than to be blamed. He is unemployed and is not able to contribute substantially to Barbara's support. In fact, she has been paying him rent. The relationship was one that arose out of mutual economic necessity—a necessity that the record shows continues in respect to Barbara Taake. * * *

It was admitted that Fink and Barbara had intercourse on several occasions, that they lived in the same house, that Barbara on no occasion held herself out as the wife of Fink, but on occasion had failed to correct persons who addressed her as Mrs. Fink. There was evidence that her mail was received under the name of Barbara Taake, not Barbara Fink. No neighbors were called as witnesses to testify that they believed that Fink and Barbara Taake were apparently living in a marital, rather than in an illicit, relationship.

On the basis of this evidence, however, the trial judge concluded that a *de facto* marriage existed between Fink and Barbara Taake. Under the statutory law of Wisconsin, only a remarriage bars alimony as a matter of law.

* * *

Clearly, the relationship between Barbara Taake and Lyle Fink was not a marriage sanctioned by the law of this state. This state specifically outlaws *de facto* or common law marriages. The law, for obvious public-policy reasons, does not clothe a legally unsanctioned male-female cohabitative relationship with any of the legal protections of a marriage. No legal relationship ever arose between Barbara and Fink except that of landlord and tenant. The trial judge's characterization of the relationship as a *de facto* marriage is without significance except as a shibboleth on which to predicate a desired result. In states where a common law marriage is recognized, it is indeed true that a common law marriage would, if proved, terminate the obligation to pay alimony just as a *de jure* marriage would. The reason for that is, of course, that in a common law marriage there is the manifestation that the relationship is permanent and that each party to it assumes the reciprocal obligations of marriage, including the obligation of support and fidelity. * * *

The relationship that the trial judge considered in this case was, however, only a temporary expedient. A true common law marriage requires the common law husband to support the wife, and the need for alimony for a divorced wife would be supplanted by the obligation of the common law husband to support. In such circumstances the divorced husband ought to be relieved of his obligation. In the instant case no obligation was assumed by Fink to support Barbara Taake. The facts that might be pertinent in the event of a common law remarriage do not appear in this case.

The trial judge abused his discretion when he gave the same legal effect to the relationship between the parties as he would have to a legally recognized marriage.

NOTES AND QUESTIONS

1.   State rules dealing with the effect of cohabitation on alimony vary. *See, e.g.,* CAL. FAM. CODE § 4323 (cohabitation creates a "rebuttable presumption, affecting the burden of proof, of decreased need for support"); N.Y. DOM. REL. L. § 248 (court may modify support payment upon proof that "wife is habitually living with another man and holding herself out as his wife, although not married to such man"); Brister v. Brister, 594 P.2d 1167 (N.M. 1979) (support from a "paramour," living with the ex-wife, may be considered as evidence of changed financial circumstances in determining whether her alimony should be reduced; "[t]he focal point in each case is the recipient's need for support."); 750 ILL. COMP. STAT. § 5/510 (support is to be terminated if the recipient is cohabiting with another on a "resident, continuing conjugal basis."). Strickland v. Stickland, 650 S.E.2d 465 (S.C. 2007) (terminate alimony if the recipient resides with another person in a romantic relationship for ninety or more consecutive days); Campbell v. Campbell, 41 So. 3d 775 (Ala. App. 2009) (terminate alimony if the recipient is cohabiting with a member of the opposite sex in a relationship of some permanency).

2.   Evaluate the following fact patterns under the laws of California, New York, Illinois, South Carolina, and New Mexico. In cases b, c, and d, assume that the alimony recipient is employed at a low-wage job and earns the same salary as she did when awarded alimony:

a.   The *Taake* case.

b.   Mrs. Morrison, a recipient of indefinite-term alimony ($1500 per month), now has a sexual relationship with Mr. Adams, who has moved into her home and pays her $800 for "room and board." Mrs. Morrison continues to use the name Morrison; neighbors do not believe that she and Mr. Adams are married. Mr. Adams's annual income is $54,000. *See* Morrison v. Morrison, 910 P.2d 1176 (Or. App. 1996).

c.   Mrs. Sappington, a recipient of indefinite-term alimony ($750 per month), has for the past two years allowed Mr. Adams to share her home. According to Mrs. Sappington, she charges Adams $120 per month for rent; they share the utilities bills and grocery payments. Mrs. Sappington and Mr. Adams both state that they do not have a sexual relationship and that they have never slept in the same bed. They do, however, typically share meals. Sometimes they go out together. Mr. Adams's annual income is $30,000. Mrs. Sappington continues to use the name Sappington; neighbors do not believe that she and Mr. Adams are married. *See In re* Marriage of Sappington, 478 N.E.2d 376 (Ill. 1985). *See also,* Atkinson v. Atkinson, 157 So. 3d 473 (Fla. Dist. Ct. App. 2015).

d.   Mrs. Schroeder, a recipient of indefinite-term alimony, has a sexual relationship with Mr. Adams, and for the past year has allowed him to live in her home. She pays all the household expenses and grocery bills. Mr. Adams pays no rent or utilities; he does pay for occasional entertainment and dining out. He has also done occasional repair work on the house, allows her the use of his car, and gave her a $4200 diamond ring that formerly belonged to his mother. Mr. Adams is currently unemployed and has no income. Mrs. Schroeder sometimes uses the name Mrs. Adams, particularly when she and Mr. Adams have travelled together. The neighbors do not believe that she and Mr. Adams are married. *See In re* Marriage of Schroeder, 238 Cal. Rptr. 12 (App. 1987).

e.   Mrs. Chopin is awarded alimony for 8 years beginning in 2006. She began a romantic relationship with another man in 2007. They became engaged to be married in January 2008 but ended their relationship in December 2008. During 2007 and 2008, each party had separate residences, although the man sometimes stayed overnight in Mrs. Chopin's home and they vacationed together. *See* Chopin v. Chopin, 232 P.3d 99 (Ariz. App. 2010).

f.   Ms. McKinney agrees to pay Mr. Pedery permanent alimony. Mr. Pedery subsequently established a romantic relationship with another woman. She typically stayed in Mr. Pedery's home from Wednesday afternoon until Monday morning. From Monday morning until Wednesday afternoon, she went to a nearby city to work as a nanny for her grandchildren and stayed there overnight. *See* McKinney v. Pedery, 776 S.E.2d 566 (S.C. 2015). Cf. *In re* Marriage of Knoll, 381 P.3d 490 (Kan. App. 2016); Rehm v. Rehm, 409 S.E.2d 723 (N.C. 1991).

3.   In a few states remarriage of the support recipient is a ground for modifying spousal support. See Scott v. Scott, 368 P.3d 133 n.17 (Utah App. 2016). In most states, support automatically terminates if the recipient remarries. *See* Keller v. O'Brien, 652 N.E.2d 589 (Mass. 1995); Oman v. Oman, 702 N.W.2d 11 (S.D. 2005); Miller v. Miller, 892 A.2d 175 (Vt. 2005). *See generally* Cynthia Starnes, *Alimony, Intuition, and the Remarriage-Termination Rule,* 81 IND. L.J. 971 (2006); Principles of the Law of Family Disolution § 5.09 comment a (2002); Cynthia Lee Starnes, *I'll Be Watching You: Alimony and the Cohabitation Rule,* 50 FAM. L. Q. 261 (2016). This rule can be changed by contract. *See* Simpson v. Simpson, 352 S.W.3d 362 (Mo. 2011) In Herbst v. Herbst, 153 So. 3d 290 (Fla. Dist. Ct. App. 2014) the court held that the alimony obligation was not terminated by the remarriage of the recipient where the decree stated that the payments were nonmodifiable, and would cease only upon the death of the recipient).

But consider Grove v. Grove, 571 P.2d 477 (Or. 1977):

We turn now to the question upon which we requested argument: whether spousal support awards should routinely provide that the support payments will terminate upon the remarriage of the supported spouse. We hold that they should not. * * * Although this court has expressed the opinion that it was against public policy to permit a woman to look for her support to two different men, that policy has never been held in this state to operate automatically without regard to the particular circumstances. The cases announcing the position that it does not were decided at a time when the husband was considered to have an absolute unilateral obligation to support his wife. We would not now hold otherwise, when legal duties of spousal support are mutual. Public policy does not require that a woman whose first marriage has been dissolved be free to remarry only if her new husband is able to support her. If remarriage by the supported spouse is not, as a matter of law, grounds for automatic termination of spousal support, we cannot approve the general practice of inserting provisions to that effect in support decrees as a matter of routine. Unless there is reason, at the time the decree is entered, to predict a remarriage which will substantially change the circumstances relevant to the support award, the question of the effect of remarriage upon a support decree should await the event and proper application for modification of the decree. * * *

Which approach is preferable? Why?

4.   If "remarriage" automatically terminates alimony, does the marriage have to be legally valid? *See* Montini v. Lenhardt, 713 N.W.2d 193 (Wis. App. 2006) (no, applying the concept of estoppel). *Cf. In re* Marriage of Left, 2016 WL 816090 (Cal. App.) (a "commitment ceremony" alone is not grounds for terminating support).

5.   In *Taake,* the court characterizes the recipient's relationship as a *"de facto* remarriage," based on the recipient sometimes using her partner's surname and their sporadic sexual relationship. Other courts have considered it important whether the recipient has established a *de facto* remarriage, but have engaged in a more detailed inquiry as to whether, for example, the parties pooled their finances, or have named each other as beneficiaries under wills or life insurance policies. *See* C.K. v. B.K., 325 S.W.3d 431 (Mo. App. 2010); Overton v. Overton, 34 So. 3d 759 (Fla. Dist. Ct. App. 2010). In these cases, the courts found no *de facto* remarriages. In most states, alimony is terminated upon a showing that the recipient is living with another and having a sexual relationship; no *de facto* remarriage need be shown. In contrast, when asked to define what should establish "cohabitation" that would justify a termination of alimony, one judge stated:

> cohabitation is comprised of several distinct elements; (1) living with (2) an unrelated adult (3) with an expectation of permanence (4) in an intimate relationship (5) without being married. In my view, the extent to which a couple intermingles its finances is pertinent to whether . . . the parties intended a long-term commitment.

Graev v. Graev, 898 N.E.2d 909 (N.Y. 2008) (Graffeo J., dissenting).

6. Should the issue in these cases be (i) whether the parties are living together in a romantic relationship of some permanence, (ii) whether the recipient is receiving financial support from his or her partner, (iii) whether the parties have established a *de facto* remarriage, or (iv) whether the parties have established a stable romantic relationship of some significant duration regardless of whether they live together?

7. If support terminates upon remarriage, without the need for any additional showing of changed circumstances, can a different policy be justified for cohabitation? If yes, should long-term cohabitation be treated like remarriage?

8. In those states where only the financial effects of cohabitation by the alimony recipient are relevant, should cohabitation and an increase in the recipient's salary be treated identically?

9. Should the financial effects (either positive or negative) of cohabitation or remarriage by the alimony obligor be taken into account as a ground for alimony modification? In Gammell v. Gammell, 153 Cal. Rptr. 169 (App. 1979), the court held that it should be:

> The California courts have held that, while a husband's remarriage does not alone justify reduction of support payments to his former wife, the remarriage with its additional burdens is a factor to be considered. Since a remarriage with its additional burdens is a factor to be considered in modifying support payments, it appears fair and equitable that a remarriage with its additional benefits also ought to be considered. Furthermore, spousal support is determined according to the needs of both parties and the respective ability of the parties to meet those needs. Although the second wife's income in this case is her separate property, as a pragmatic matter this income directly or indirectly reduces the needs of the husband and it directly or indirectly affects the husband's ability to meet the needs of his former wife.

Post-*Gammell*, the California legislature adopted a rule that any income of the obligor's new spouse or cohabitant should be ignored when computing spousal support. *See* CAL. FAM. CODE § 4323. Why might the California legislature have disagreed with the *Gammell* court?

10. If a recipient has a long-term romantic relationship with another, but they maintain separate households, how should this impact a spousal support obligation? *Compare* Rehm v. Rehm, 409 S.E.2d 723 (N.C. App. 1991) *with* McKinney v. Pedery, 776 S.E.2d 566 (S.C. 2015).

11. In a few states, only heterosexual cohabitation by an alimony recipient justifies termination or modification of support. *See* J.L.M. v. S.A.K., 18 So. 3d 384 (Ala. App. 2008). In most states, it appears gay and heterosexual cohabitation is treated the same. *See* Luttrell v. Cucco, 784 S.E.2d 707 (Va. 2016).

12. In Jones v. Jones, 2016 WL 4123920 (Del.), the Delaware Supreme Court held that the divorce court could award alimony in the divorce to a wife

who had cohabited with another after separating from her husband, when the cohabitation relationship had ended before the alimony hearing in the divorce.

13. Spouses may define the terms under which the alimony obligation will cease in a separation agreement. This approach holds the potential for curing any imprecision in state statutory standards, but realizing that potential is not easy. In O'Connor Brothers Abalone Co. v. Brando, 114 Cal. Rptr. 773 (App. 1974), for example, the court was required to interpret this clause in Marlon and Movita Brando's separation agreement:

> (a)   Defendant agrees to pay or cause to be paid to Plaintiff, the amount of $1,400.00 per month commencing on the first day of the calendar month next succeeding the month in which this Agreement is executed and continuing for a period of one-hundred fifty-six (156) months, or *until she remarries or dies, whichever occurs sooner. For the purposes of this Agreement, 'remarriage' shall include, without limitation, Plaintiff's appearing to* <u>maintain a marital relationship</u> *with* <u>any person,</u> *or any ceremonial marriage entered into by Plaintiff even though the same may later be annulled or otherwise terminated or rendered invalid.* (Emphasis added.)

[Movita argued] that the phrase 'appearing to maintain a marital relationship' means a holding out by Movita that she was in fact married or conduct on her part that would imply a marriage in fact. According to this version, a meretricious relationship, no matter how intimate and enduring, would not terminate the obligation for support payments so long as it was made clear to the world that Movita and her paramour were not married. This interpretation would place a premium on the persistence with which Movita publicized the illicit nature of the relationship.

* * * Marlon contend[ed] that the Agreement was designed to prevent Movita from maintaining a relationship with a male companion as a result of which the latter appeared to enjoy the usual rewards of marriage without assuming the obligations which flow from a ceremony of marriage. According to Marlon the Agreement means a "marital type" relationship and such interpretation is necessary to avoid what he sought to avoid, i.e., the possibility that Movita's male companion, in sharing Movita's shelter, bed and board, would also benefit from the support payments which Marlon was providing. * * *

The final Agreement evolved from two previously written drafts. The first draft simply used the phrase "until she remarries" without further definition. To this Marlon objected. The second draft defined remarriage as "cohabitation by plaintiff with any person." To this Movita objected. Mr. Garey testified that Movita's attorney indicated that the objection to "cohabitation" was based on a fear that the word might apply to so-called "one night stands."

* * *

Clearly the purpose of the Agreement was not to circumscribe Movita's sexual activity per se as she was free to engage in sexual intercourse with other men. The Agreement sought to embrace actual ceremonial marriages on the one hand and on the other, relationships which were not marriages but which had the attributes of marriage such as companionship of substantial duration, the sharing of habitation, eating together and sexual intimacy. The characterization of such a relationship as "marital" does not depend on whether third persons are led to believe the existence of a ceremonial marriage. In fact, public belief that Movita and Ford were actually married would be less demeaning to Marlon than their conduct of "living" together while disavowing an actual marriage.

What is important here from the standpoint of the objectives of the Agreement is that such a relationship creates the strong probability that the male partner will derive benefit from the support payments. And that, in fact, is what occurred here. O'Connor contends in its brief that there was no common financial or economic relationship between Ford and Movita and that this detracts from the "marital" character of the relationship. Interestingly enough, however, in respondent's support of this argument it is admitted that Movita paid for the upkeep of her cars which Ford drove. She paid for the groceries which Ford charged, and she paid for the department store purchases which Ford charged. It appears without contradiction that Movita paid for the maintenance of the house in which they lived.

We interpret the phrase "appearing to maintain a marital relationship" as including the appearance of "living together" under circumstances such as existed here, whether or not there is the appearance of marriage in fact. This appears to us to be the only possible reasonable interpretation of the Agreement.

How could the agreement have been drafted to embody Marlon's point of view? Movita's?

14. Evaluate J. Thomas Oldham, *The Effect of Unmarried Cohabitation by a Former Spouse Upon His or Her Right to Continue to Receive Alimony*, 17 J. FAM. LAW 249, 267–68 (1978–79):

It is submitted that the optimum approach to unmarried cohabitation by an ex-spouse receiving alimony would be the two-step analysis outlined below. First, a court should consider whether the cohabitants either (i) have lived together for a sufficient length of time and the cohabitant's income is at such a level that it would be equitable, considering the surrounding circumstances, to require the cohabitant to support the ex-spouse, or (ii) whether the alimony recipient has established a de facto remarriage. In connection with the former determination, the length of the marriage, the alimony payor's income, and any other equitable factors should be considered. In connection with the latter determination, all relevant factors, such as the length of the cohabitation and the manner in which the couple conducts their financial affairs, should be considered; the presumption set forth above could be utilized. If it is found that a de facto remarriage occurred, spousal support should be terminated. If it is decided that it would be fair to require the cohabitant to support the ex-spouse, alimony should be suspended for the duration of cohabitation. If it is determined that it would not be fair to require the cohabitant to support the ex-spouse, and that a de facto remarriage has not occurred, the court should consider whether the cohabitation reduces the support needs of the ex-spouse and reduce or suspend the alimony obligation, as appropriate, if it finds such a reduced need.

15. Cohabitation by a child support recipient can also cause litigation. For example, in Bacardi v. Bacardi, 727 So. 2d 1137 (Fla. Dist. Ct. App. 1999) the father—who had agreed to pay $16,900 per month in child support as part of the divorce settlement—sued for "an accounting of child support payments" after he learned that the children's mother had bought her boyfriend a car and was paying his travel expenses. The trial court granted his motion and ordered the mother "to report all expenditures * * * made for the children" during the preceding five months.

Is the *Bacardi* approach sound? What expenditures can be fairly attributable to the children? How much of the mortgage payment, the utility bills, and the food budget, for example, were "made for the children"? Assuming that the children's expenses can be calculated and that they equal or exceed the support order, would relief to the support obligor be precluded? If the children's calculable expenses are less than the support order, would relief to the support obligor be ensured? (The appellate court held that Dad had not presented evidence adequate to justify such a "monumental intrusion into [the mother's] financial records.")

A number of states give courts discretion to order some form of financial accounting from child support recipients. *See* Laura Morgan, *A Custodial Parent's (Non) Duty To Account for Child Support,* 12 DIV. LITIG. 57 (April 2000). Is this a good idea?

Problem 20-3:

You are counsel to the New York State Legislature's Family Law Committee, which is considering a change in its law dealing with the effect of cohabitation on alimony. The Committee has concluded that the current standard is unworkable in an era of widespread cohabitation. Its goal is a statutory standard that "reflects current economic and social realities, treats like situations in a like manner, and resists attempts at evasion and fraud." Draft a statute for the Committee's consideration. Make sure your statute specifies when, if at all, alimony is to be:

(a)   cut off fully and permanently;

(b)   cut off only to the extent the ex-spouse's financial circumstances have actually changed and only for the duration of the changed circumstances.

Problem 20-4:

In a divorce, the husband agreed to pay the wife alimony until the wife remarried or either party died. The decree stated the obligation was otherwise non-modifiable. Seven years later, the husband petitioned the court to terminate his support obligation because his former wife had attempted to hire someone to kill him. What should the court do? Richardson v. Richardson, 218 S.W.3d 426 (Mo. 2007).

B. REMARRIAGE OF EITHER PARENT

IN RE MARRIAGE OF NIMMO

Supreme Court of Colorado, 1995.
891 P.2d 1002.

ERICKSON, J.

We granted certiorari to review *In re Marriage of Seanor*, 876 P.2d 44 (Colo. App. 1993). The court of appeals concluded the trial court properly denied Nick Nimmo's motion to compel discovery of Margaret E. Nimmo's (now Margaret E. Seanor) (Ms. Seanor's) present spouse's income for purposes of § 14–10–115(7)(a)(I)(A), 6B C.R.S. (1987 & 1994 Supp.).[2] We affirm in part, reverse in part, and return this case to the court of appeals for remand for further proceedings consistent with this opinion.

I

A decree of dissolution of marriage was entered on May 4, 1989. In that decree, the trial court approved and incorporated the parties' separation agreement. Among other things, the agreement granted Ms. Seanor primary physical custody and Nimmo sole legal custody of the parties' two children. The agreement provided that Nimmo would pay maintenance to Ms. Seanor until June 1991. After June 1991, Nimmo would pay child support in accordance with § 14–10–115, 6B C.R.S. (1987 & 1994 Supp.).

---

[2]   For calculating child support, § 14–10–115(7)(A)(I)(A) provides:

"Gross income" includes income from any source and includes, but is not limited to, income from salaries, wages, including tips calculated pursuant to the federal internal revenue service percentage of gross wages, commissions, bonuses, dividends, severance pay, pensions, interest, trust income, annuities, capital gains, social security benefits, workers' compensation benefits, unemployment insurance benefits, disability insurance benefits, gifts, prizes, and alimony or maintenance received. Gross income does not include child support payments received. § 14–10–115(7)(a)(I)(A), 6B C.R.S.

In October 1991, Ms. Seanor filed a motion to increase child support payments. In preparation for the hearing, Nimmo submitted interrogatories in November 1991. The interrogatories sought information from Ms. Seanor regarding her income since June 1, 1991. Nimmo's definition of "income" included "all funds available for * * * [Ms. Seanor's] use, including gifts." Nimmo wanted a list of "all gifts, including without limitation, jewelry, clothes, entertainment, travel, and restaurant meals provided to * * * [Ms. Seanor] or to the children" by Ms. Seanor's present spouse (Mr. Seanor). Nimmo also requested a list of "all amounts paid by Mr. Seanor either directly to * * * [Ms. Seanor] or to third parties from which * * * [Ms. Seanor] received a benefit. * * * " The interrogatories also sought copies of checking account registers, bank statements, and credit card records.

When Ms. Seanor failed to provide answers to the interrogatories, Nimmo filed a motion to compel discovery. The trial court denied the motion on the grounds that the income and contributions of Mr. Seanor were immaterial to the determination of Nimmo's child support obligation. Also, because Mr. and Ms. Seanor shared checking and savings accounts, granting the motion would constitute an invasion of Mr. Seanor's privacy.

In its order of October 14, 1992, the trial court granted Ms. Seanor's motion to increase Nimmo's child support payments. The trial court found Ms. Seanor had no income. Nimmo was ordered to pay, based on his income, $1,341 per month as child support plus $4,906 in back payments. Nimmo appealed.

The court of appeals found Nimmo's definition of income to be "significantly broader than the definition of income set forth in the child support guidelines." The court of appeals emphasized the common law rule that the income of third parties is not considered when determining income for child support purposes. The court of appeals concluded the child support guidelines did not change the common law rule and held that "the trial court did not abuse its discretion in denying the motion to compel."

II

C.R.C.P. 26(b)(1) allows parties to "obtain discovery regarding any matter, not privileged, which is relevant to the subject matter involved in the pending action. * * * " Child support obligations are determined by establishing the "combined gross income," which "means the combined monthly adjusted gross incomes of both parents." § 14–10–115(10)(a)(II), 6B C.R.S. (1987 & 1994 Supp.) " 'Adjusted gross income' means gross income less preexisting child support obligations and less alimony or maintenance actually paid by a parent." *Id*. Using the statutory schedule, child support amounts are extrapolated based on the combined gross income and the number of children due support. *See* § 14–10–115(10)(b), 6B C.R.S. (1987 & 1994 Supp.). Each parent's obligation is determined by dividing the combined gross income "in proportion to their adjusted gross incomes." § 14–10–115(10)(a)(I), 6B C.R.S. (1987).

The statutory definition of " 'gross income' includes income from any source and includes, but is not limited to, income from salaries, wages, * * * commissions, bonuses, dividends, severance pay, pensions, interest, trust income, annuities, capital gains, social security benefits, workers' compensation benefits, unemployment insurance benefits, disability insurance benefits, gifts, prizes, and alimony or maintenance received." § 14–10–115(7)(a)(I)(A). For purposes of calculating "gross income," the plain language of the statute "includes all payments from a financial resource, whatever the source thereof." *In re Marriage of Armstrong*, 831 P.2d 501, 503 (Colo. App. 1992).

We are aware that various sources of income under the statute are treated differently for tax purposes. However, the statute makes no distinction between sources of income based on the federal or state tax codes. Also, because sources of income are "not limited to" the enumerated items of § 14–10–115(7)(a)(I)(A), domestic relations courts would be required to undergo a complex tax analysis to determine income under the guidelines. Such a tortured analysis thwarts the goals of the guidelines and explains why tax definitions are irrelevant to an interpretation of § 14–10–115.

The court of appeals properly noted that the factors considered in determining child support at common law did not include the financial resources of third-parties. *See also In re Marriage of Conradson*, 43 Colo. App. 432, 604 P.2d 701 (1979) (holding that the financial resources of an aunt with whom the child was living were not to be considered in making a support award); *Garrow v. Garrow*, 152 Colo. 480, 382 P.2d 809 (1963) (concluding that the contributions of third parties were immaterial to a determination of father's duty of support). The opinion also correctly stated that "by the adoption of the child support guidelines, the General Assembly did not intend to change the common law rule set forth" in *Conradson* and *Garrow*. Based on these principles, the court of appeals concluded the income of Mr. Seanor was not relevant to the determination of child support.

The court of appeals came to the correct conclusion concerning the discovery of Mr. Seanor's income. However, the focus of the court's opinion failed to adequately address the plain language of the child support guidelines. The source of money available to Ms. Seanor is not the relevant factor. Instead, under the guidelines the existence of that money is the relevant inquiry. The guidelines require an examination of the existence of parental income. The source of that income is irrelevant to a determination of child support.

Income may come "from any source," and the definition of "gross income" expressly includes "gifts." § 14–10–115(7)(a)(I)(A). However, the income "could come from relatives, friends, investments, trusts, or the lottery." Because "gifts" are included in calculating income for child support, we must determine whether Nimmo may discover Ms. Seanor's income as defined in § 14–10–115(7)(a)(I)(A). Concluding that Mr. Seanor's income is not relevant does not resolve Nimmo's motion to compel.

III

Colorado's child support guidelines are based on the Income Shares Model. * * * The guidelines were enacted to prevent a drastic decrease in the standard of living of children and custodial parents resulting from divorce. By ensuring child support obligations are proportionate to both parents' combined income, the guidelines attempt to rectify this dramatic decrease in lifestyle. The guidelines were not enacted to prevent an increase in a child's standard of living by denying a child the fruits of one parent's good fortune after a divorce. The standard of living of a child if the parents maintained their marriage is only one factor for the court to consider, which does not lock the child into a single standard of living until emancipation.

IV

We are persuaded by the rule announced in *Barnier v. Wells*, 476 N.W.2d 795 (Minn. Ct. App. 1991). In *Barnier*, the court stated "if a gift is regularly received from a dependable source, it may properly be used to determine the amount of a child support obligation." *Id.* at 797. The court found that the father received $833 per month from his father and periodic payments of $5,000 from his grandmother.

The court of appeals found *Barnier* to be inapplicable "since husband did not establish either that * * * [Ms. Seanor] received monetary payments or, if so, that such payments were regularly received. * * *" However, by not allowing Nimmo to discover Ms. Seanor's income "from any source," the court denied Nimmo the ability to "establish * * * monetary payments" and "that such payments were regularly received."

Information sought through discovery "need not be admissible at the * * * [hearing] if the information sought appears reasonably calculated to lead to the discovery of admissible evidence." C.R.C.P. 26(b)(1). Although Mr. Seanor's income is not discoverable, Nimmo must be able to discover Ms. Seanor's income to properly meet the motion to increase his child support payments. Attempts to discover Ms. Seanor's income "from any source" are "reasonably calculated to lead to the discovery of admissible evidence." Nimmo must be able to obtain information regarding gifts received by Ms. Seanor, so he can attempt to establish that they are "regularly received from a dependable source." *See Barnier*, 476 N.W.2d at

797. Without proper discovery Nimmo cannot establish the *Barnier* requirements.

Pursuant to § 14–10–115(7)(a)(I)(A) Nimmo may not discover the source of Ms. Seanor's income. However, Nimmo may discover the existence of Ms. Seanor's income, "whatever the source thereof." When attempting to establish gift income, a party is subject to the same requirements of proof he or she would face trying to show any other type of income. In a hearing to determine child support, a party must establish with reasonable certainty that the amounts are regularly received from a dependable source. Claims that are too speculative may not be used to determine child support. However, receipt of periodic checks, as in *Barnier*, may be more easily established.

This analysis supports the discovery request for all amounts paid by Mr. Seanor directly to Ms. Seanor. However, it does not extend to amounts paid by Mr. Seanor to third parties for cable television, mortgage payments, car and home repairs, insurance or utilities. The amounts Mr. Seanor may pay to provide himself and his family with certain necessities should not be considered as income to Ms. Seanor. Mr. Seanor is not making a gift of income to Ms. Seanor by paying these expenses. He is satisfying the household's obligations. The fact Ms. Seanor may receive some benefit does not convert the payment into income. It appears this discovery request for the household expenses is an indirect attempt to determine Mr. Seanor's income, which, as previously noted, is irrelevant.

Discovery of the receipt of isolated and irregular tokens would also not be permissible. Mementos or keepsakes do not qualify as "gifts" for purposes of the child support guidelines. These occasional presents fall outside the statute. They are not relevant to a determination of child support because they are not regularly received from a dependable source. Also, the speculative nature of these items, combined with their irrelevance, prevents their discovery.

Accordingly, we affirm the court of appeals decision to not permit the discovery of Mr. Seanor's income and reverse the court of appeals denial of Mr. Nimmo's motion to compel discovery of Ms. Seanor's income. We return this case to the court of appeals for remand to the district court for further proceedings consistent with this opinion.

JUSTICE MULLARKEY concurring in part and dissenting in part.

* * * Because I would affirm the court of appeals' decision, I respectfully dissent from the partial reversal.

The majority in this case holds that "the source of money available to Ms. Seanor is not the relevant factor," and, in order to determine Ms. Seanor's income, the majority allows discovery of all amounts Mr. Seanor has paid directly to her. It excludes direct payments made by Mr. Seanor to third parties for household expenses. Because I do not believe that such family expenses, whether paid by Ms. Seanor with cash provided to her by Mr. Seanor or paid by Mr. Seanor directly to third parties, are "income" under the Uniform Dissolution of Marriage Act (UDMA), I would hold that none of the information requested in the interrogatories is discoverable.

* * *

In the motion to compel answers to interrogatories, Mr. Nimmo requests [various items paid by Mr. Seanor].

I interpret this motion to request discovery of all the ordinary and necessary household expenses paid by Mr. Seanor for his household which includes Ms. Seanor and Mr. Nimmo's children. In my view, this information is not relevant and therefore not discoverable because: (1) such expenses are not income to Ms. Seanor for purposes of the child support guidelines; (2) the stepparent, Mr. Seanor, has no obligation to support Mr. Nimmo's children; and (3) this discovery request is an impermissible attempt to circumvent the trial court's refusal to impute income to Ms. Seanor because the court found that Ms. Seanor was not intentionally unemployed or underemployed.

In conclusion, I would rule that none of the information requested by Mr. Nimmo is relevant to determining Ms. Seanor's income because the enumerated expenses normally arise from a marital relationship. As such, they cannot be construed as income and are not discoverable. I would also hold that a gift does not have to be regularly received from a dependable source under the UDMA.

NOTES AND QUESTIONS

1.   In most states, a stepparent does not have a duty to support a child of his spouse. *See* Chapter 17. Is *Nimmo* consistent with this rule?

2.   In light of *Nimmo*, what advice would you give a Colorado child support recipient planning to remarry someone with a substantial income? (*See also* Murray v. Super, 26 N.E.3d 1116 (Mass. App. 2015) (new husband of child support recipient made regular weekly payments to her)).

3.   If the income of the new spouse would be considered in an action to modify support, how might that rule impact the remarriage behavior of parents paying or receiving child support?

4.   There is no consensus among the states on whether a new spouse's income may be taken into account in determining the child support obligation. Some states permit consideration of the income of a new spouse. *See* Rodgers v. Rodgers, 887 P.2d 269 (Nev. 1994); Hutchinson v. Hutchinson, 619 N.E.2d 466 (Ohio App. 1993). Some permit the income of a new spouse to be taken into account if the support obligor seeks downward modification of a support award based on his obligations to subsequent children. *See* Bock v. Bock, 506 N.W.2d

321 (Minn. App. 1993); Johnson v. Johnson, 468 N.W.2d 648 (S.D. 1991). But most do not permit consideration of a new spouse's income except in unusual circumstances. *See* Blumenshine v. Hall, 765 S.E.2d 647 (Ga. App. 2014); Murray v. Super, 26 N.E.3d 1116 (Mass. App. 2015); Miller v. Miller, 491 N.W.2d 104 (Wis. App. 1992). Although the case law is less plentiful, states that forbid consideration of a new spouse's income should logically forbid consideration of a new spouse's needs. *See* TEX. FAM. CODE § 154.069. *Cf.* Linge v. Meyerink, 806 N.W.2d 245 (S.D. 2011) (reducing the father's child support obligation by $300 due to his current wife's medical expenses).

5.   In Moore v. Moore, 763 N.W.2d 536 (S.D. 2009) the court ruled that, in connection with an alimony claimant's petition to increase the alimony, the income of the obligor's new spouse should not be considered.

C. SUBSEQUENT CHILDREN

MILLER V. TASHIE
Supreme Court of Georgia, 1995.
265 Ga. 147, 454 S.E.2d 498.

BENHAM, PRESIDING JUSTICE.

When the parties were divorced, appellee-mother was awarded custody of the one minor child of the parties and appellant-father was ordered to pay a total of $6,400.00 per year in child support. Since that time, these changes have occurred: both parties have remarried; appellant has fathered two more children and has undertaken custody of his child from a marriage preceding his marriage to appellee; and appellant's gross annual income has increased by $7,738.00. Based on those changes, appellant sought a downward modification of his support obligation to the child of his marriage to appellee. The trial court dismissed appellant's petition, holding, in essence, that the increase in appellant's gross income was an absolute bar to modification and that appellant's additional support obligations were not factors which could be considered in determining whether there had been a change in his financial status. Concluding that both those rulings are too broad, we reverse.

1.   With regard to the trial court's holding that an increase in the petitioning parent's income is an absolute bar to modification, we note first the general rule that "either parent may seek modification of support based on a change in either of their financial circumstances . . . " *Allen v. Georgia Dep't of Human Resources*, 262 Ga. 521, 524 (423 S.E.2d 383) (1992). Nothing in either the statute or the case law limits the right to seek modification to an obligor parent whose income has decreased. OCGA § 19–6–19 "allows revision if the petitioning former spouse shows a change in the income and financial status of either former spouse or in the needs of the child or children." Appellee's reliance on *Wright v. Wright*, 246 Ga. 81 (268 S.E.2d 666) (1980), is misplaced: that case holds only that the trial

court did not abuse its discretion in increasing the support obligation of a parent whose income had increased, notwithstanding that the obligor-parent's expenses had increased. There was no holding there that an increase in income would bar a petition for modification or even that such an increase would absolutely preclude a trial court's conclusion that the financial status of the obligor parent had changed in such a way as to warrant reconsideration of the amount of the support obligation. We hold, therefore, that dismissal of the petition on the ground that an increase in appellant's income barred the petition was error.

2.   The trial court held that appellant's increased responsibility for the support of children other than the one involved in this case did not constitute a change in his financial status. Appellant and appellee have focused on the issue of whether the factors listed in OCGA § 19–6–15(c)(6) as authorizing variation from guideline amounts require that the trial court take into account obligations to support other children. We look instead to the plain language of OCGA § 19–6–19(a):

> The judgment of a court providing permanent alimony for the support of a child or children . . . shall be subject to revision upon petition filed by either former spouse showing a change in the income and financial status of either former spouse or in the needs of the child or children.

The statute requires only a showing of "a change in the income and financial status" of either parent. "In determining a change of the financial condition of a parent, the court should consider every relevant fact. * * *" *Decker v. Decker*, 256 Ga. 513 (350 S.E.2d 434) (1986).

The proper scope of the trial court's consideration in this case was whether there had been, as alleged by appellant, such a change in the financial status of each parent as would support a reconsideration of the level of appellant's obligation to provide financial support for the parties' child. Focusing solely on the fact that appellant's gross income has increased since the initial child support award was error.

Judgment reversed. All the Justices concur.

NOTES AND QUESTIONS

1.   Traditionally, courts refused to modify a child support obligation based on the support obligor's acquisition of subsequent children; the theory is that the obligor knew his obligations to the first family before the later children were born or adopted. Some courts continue to apply this approach, at least to intact second families. *See, e.g.,* Brown v. Brown, 503 N.W.2d 280 (Wis. App. 1993); Fantanzo v. Decker, 614 N.Y.S.2d 671 (Fam. Ct. 1994). But an increasing number of recent decisions take the needs of a second family into account. *See, e.g.,* Martinez v. Martinez, 660 A.2d 13 (N.J. Super. Ch. Div. 1995). As in *Miller,* courts in many states may now deviate from the

presumptive award under state guidelines based on the needs of a second family. *See* Czaplewski v. Czaplewski, 483 N.W.2d 751 (Neb. 1992); Ainsworth v. Ainsworth, 574 A.2d 772 (Vt. 1990); Burch v. Burch, 916 P.2d 443 (Wash. App. 1996). *See generally* Comment, 20 WM. MITCHELL L.REV. 967 (1994).

2.   If you were the trial judge, what decision would you make in *Miller* on remand? In Bock v. Bock, 506 N.W.2d 321 (Minn. App. 1993), the trial court was directed to equalize, to the extent possible, support to both families. Is this a desirable approach? If yes, how should equalization be accomplished?

3.   In Texas (a percentage of obligor income state), the percentage of income owed by a support obligor is reduced based on the number of his other children:

TEX. FAM. CODE § 154.129

MULTIPLE FAMILY ADJUSTED GUIDELINES
% OF NET RESOURCES

Number of children before the court

		1	*2*	*3*	*4*	*5*	*6*	*7*
Number of other children for whom the obligor has a duty to support	0	20.00	25.00	30.00	35.00	40.00	40.00	40.00
	1	17.50	22.50	27.38	32.20	37.33	37.71	38.00
	2	16.00	20.63	25.20	30.33	35.43	36.00	36.44
	3	14.75	19.00	24.00	29.00	34.00	34.67	35.20
	4	13.60	18.33	23.14	28.00	32.89	33.60	34.18
	5	13.33	17.86	22.50	27.22	32.00	32.73	33.33
	6	13.14	17.50	22.00	26.60	31.27	32.00	32.62
	7	13.00	17.22	21.60	26.09	30.67	31.38	32.00

What are the pros and cons of this approach?

4.   In *Miller*, the court distinguished between "natural" (and presumably adopted) children and stepchildren; it held that the former might justify deviation from the guidelines, but not the latter. Researchers have found that stepparents do in fact contribute to the support of stepchildren, even in states where they have no legal support duty. *See* David Chambers, *Stepparents, Biologic Parents, and the Law's Perceptions of 'Family' after Divorce, in* DIVORCE REFORM AT THE CROSSROADS 102, 105 (Stephen D. Sugarman & Herma H. Kay, eds., 1990). Given this fact, would it make sense to permit modification of the support obligation if the "natural" parent of the stepchildren is not providing support? In Marriage of Zacapu, 368 P.3d 242

(Wash. App. 2016) the court affirmed the trial court's decision to deviate downward from the guidelines in its child support determination due to the obligor's six stepchildren.

4. ENFORCEMENT OF SUPPORT OBLIGATIONS

[The parental support obligation] is so well secured by the strength of natural affection that it seldom [needs] to be enforced by human laws.

Chancellor Kent

Although Chancellor Kent's assertion may well be correct for intact families, it certainly is not correct for non-intact families. This section outlines the enforcement procedures now available to obtain payment from delinquent support obligors.

A. INCARCERATION

AMERICAN LAW INSTITUTE, MODEL PENAL CODE AND COMMENTARIES
454–58 (1980).

§ 230.5 Persistent Non-support

A person commits a misdemeanor if he persistently fails to provide support which he can provide and which he knows he is legally obliged to provide to a spouse, child or other dependent.

Comment

1. *Antecedent Legislation.* Section 230.5 applies to persistent nonsupport of a spouse, child, or other dependent. Failure to support a spouse or child did not constitute a crime at common law. However, the law of all American jurisdictions at the time the Model Code provision was drafted contained criminal penalties addressed to desertion or nonsupport of minor children, and all but three punished desertion or nonsupport of one's wife. * * *

* * *

Imprisonment authorized by legislation in effect when the Model Code was drafted varied from three months to as much as 20 years. Most states had maxima of one year or less. However, the primary objective of the non-support law appeared to be to coerce the accused to support his family, rather than to impose exemplary punishment. Frequently, provision was made for releasing from custody for non-support a defendant who gave assurance of complying with his support obligation. Thus a criminal prosecution for non-support could result in a judicial order that differed from the ordinary civil support order only in the availability of a previously determined sentence of imprisonment that could be invoked if the defendant failed to comply. Used in this way, criminal non-support statutes parallel the usual enforcement mechanisms of a civil order backed by the summary power of the court to punish for contempt.

COMMONWEALTH V. POULIOT

Supreme Judicial Court of Massachusetts, 1935.
292 Mass. 229, 198 N.E. 256.

RUGG, C.J.

Manifestly, it is not slavery or involuntary servitude as thus authoritatively defined to sentence this defendant if he fails to perform his duty to support his family. The obligation of a husband and father to maintain his family, if in any way able to do so, is one of the primary responsibilities established by human nature and by civilized society. The statute enforces this duty by appropriate sanctions. A reasonable opportunity is afforded to the defendant by the city to provide for the support of his wife and children. The statutes require that support at the public expense be provided for the poor and indigent residing or found in the several towns. * * * In a period of depression like the present, it is reasonable to require one in the position of the defendant to work under the conditions shown in the case at bar in order to meet his obligation to his family. If occasion arises, the officers of the city can be compelled to perform their functions with respect to the defendant in a lawful way and without oppression.

CHILD SUPPORT RECOVERY ACT OF 1992

18 U.S.C.A. § 228 (West. 2000).

§ 228. Failure to pay legal child support obligations

(a) **Offense.**—Any person who—

(1) willfully fails to pay a support obligation with respect to a child who resides in another State, if such obligation has remained unpaid for a period longer than 1 year, or is greater than $5,000;

(2) travels in interstate or foreign commerce with the intent to evade a support obligation, if such obligation has remained unpaid for a period longer than 1 year, or is greater than $5,000; or

(3) willfully fails to pay a support obligation with respect to a child who resides in another State, if such obligation has remained unpaid for a period longer than 2 years, or is greater than $10,000; shall be punished as provided in subsection (c).

(b) **Presumption.**—The existence of a support obligation that was in effect for the time period charged in the indictment or information creates a rebuttable presumption that the obligor has the ability to pay the support obligation for that time period.

(c) Punishment.—The punishment for an offense under this section is—

(1) in the case of a first offense under subsection (a)(1), a fine under this title, imprisonment for not more than 6 months, or both; and

(2) in the case of an offense under paragraph (2) or (3) of subsection (a), a fine under this title, imprisonment for not more than 2 years, or both.

(d) Mandatory Restitution.—Upon a conviction under this section, the court shall order restitution under § 3663A in an amount equal to the total unpaid support obligation as it exists at the time of sentencing.

* * *

(f) Definitions.—As used in this section—

* * *

(3) the term "support obligation" means any amount determined under a court order or an order of an administrative process pursuant to the law of a State or of an Indian tribe to be due from a person for the support and maintenance of a child or of a child and the parent with whom the child is living.

NOTES AND QUESTIONS

1.   Federal appeals courts have uniformly rejected arguments that Congress has violated the Tenth Amendment or exceeded its power under the Commerce Clause in enacting the CSRA. *See* U.S. v. Klinzing, 315 F.3d 803 (7th Cir. 2003) (discussing numerous cases); U.S. v. Faasse, 265 F.3d 475 (6th Cir. 2001).

2.   Although researchers have found that the threat of jail is an effective tool in enforcing child support orders (*see* DAVID CHAMBERS, MAKING FATHERS PAY (1979)), most judges are reluctant to put a support obligor in jail. What factors might explain this reluctance?

3.   In U.S. v. Hill, 257 F.3d 1116 (9th Cir. 2001), a wife helped her husband relocate from the United States to Mexico to avoid a child support obligation. He had been indicted pursuant to 18 U.S.C. § 228. The Ninth Circuit held that she could be prosecuted for harboring a fugitive.

B. CONTEMPT

Civil and criminal contempt proceedings are possible in connection with family law matters. Criminal contempt is intended as punishment. In contrast, civil contempt is coercive, in the sense that the defendant may free himself by complying with the court's order. So, if the defendant would be sentenced to a jail term, but could free himself at any time by paying a certain amount of child support arrearage, this would be an example of civil contempt.

Under federal law, a defendant in a criminal contempt case is entitled to the protections given all criminal defendants; those protections do not extend to civil contempt. *See* Hicks v. Feiock, 485 U.S. 624 (1988). In criminal contempt actions, any fines would be paid to the court; in civil matters, the complainant is entitled to any fine imposed. In Turner v. Rogers (2011), the court held that, in a petition for civil contempt brought by a child support recipient who was not represented by a lawyer, the Due Process Clause did not require appointment of counsel for the defendant child support obligor.

Some states impose more stringent requirements in civil contempt proceedings than those mandated under *Feiock* and *Turner*. Michigan, for example, guarantees the right to a jury trial in a civil contempt proceeding. *See* Mead v. Batchlor, 460 N.W.2d 493 (Mich. 1990). Some states provide counsel for indigent defendants when a jail sentence is possible. *See In re* Marriage of Stariha, 509 N.E.2d 1117 (Ind. App. 1987).

Sometimes the question has arisen whether there are any limits on a court's ability to incarcerate for civil contempt. For example, in Chadwick v. Janecka, 302 F.3d 107 (3d Cir. 2002), a divorce court ordered one spouse to transfer to the other $2.5 million from an escrow account. The spouse refused and the divorce court entered an order that he should, be incarcerated for civil contempt until he agreed to transfer the funds. Seven years later, he applied to the federal district court for release. The district court held that, because of the length of the confinement, the contempt order had lost its coercive effect and that confinement was no longer constitutional. The appellate court reversed, noting that the spouse still had the present ability to comply with the court order.

Inability to pay is a defense in a contempt proceeding to collect child support. *See In re* Smith, 354 S.W.3d 431 (Tex. App. 2011). Courts narrowly construe this defense; a claim that support payments can't be made because of mortgage payments for a new home or car payments for a luxury car will not succeed.

Statutes setting forth the maximum penalty for contempt can be misleading, as each violation of the court's order can constitute a separate act of contempt. The support obligor who fails to pay on more than one occasion thus may face multiple charges of contempt. *See* Johnson v. Iowa District Court for Mahaska Cnty., 385 N.W.2d 562 (Iowa 1986). As *Chadwick* shows, civil contempt can be used to enforce the divorce property division. *See* Ingle v. Ingle, 2013 Ark. App. 660 (2013).

C. INCREASING FEDERAL INVOLVEMENT AND ITS IMPACT ON SUPPORT ENFORCEMENT

In 1975, hoping to significantly reduce the cost of the Aid to Families with Dependent Children (AFDC) program, Congress enacted sweeping legislation to strengthen enforcement of child support obligations across the nation (P.L. 93–647). Since that time, although state authority and state laws remain the primary vehicles for paternity establishment and child support collection, the federal government has been an active stimulator, overseer, and financier of state collection systems.

Under the 1975 legislation, each state enforcement agency—now commonly known as a "IV-D Agency" as a reflection of the section of statute discussing such state agencies—was required to meet standards imposed by the federal Office of Child Support Enforcement (OCSE) as a condition of receiving federal AFDC reimbursement. Under the legislation, state agencies were required, *inter alia*, to: collect data; use the social security numbers of all AFDC applicants as identification; notify the state child support enforcement agency whenever benefits are granted to deserted children; and open its records to support enforcement officials. Public assistance applicants were required to assign their right to uncollected child support to the state and to agree to cooperate in locating the absent parent, establish paternity, obtain a support judgment if none is outstanding, and secure payments. In case of an applicant's unjustified failure to cooperate, AFDC benefits were to be withheld from the applicant. (Since 1996, states have been given discretion to define both "cooperation," and "good cause" for noncooperation, and to determine the penalty for noncooperation (as long as it is not less than 25% of the family's grant).)

The 1975 legislation also required the states to maintain a "parent locator service" equipped to search state and local records for information regarding the whereabouts of absent parents. Using this service, enforcement authorities may call upon the sophisticated, computerized federal parent locator service based in Washington with access to Social Security, Internal Revenue, and other federal information sources. Once the absent (or alleged) parent is located, the state must, if necessary and possible, establish paternity, obtain a support judgment, and enforce the obligation through either in-state or interstate proceedings. All states must cooperate fully with their sister states; access to the federal courts is a last resort. If other efforts have failed, a state may request that OCSE certify to the Internal Revenue Service any outstanding judgments for collection. Past due support is also collectible from state and federal income tax refunds. After collection, the state must disburse child support payments, keeping detailed records and reporting to OCSE. To encourage local participation in child support enforcement, a portion of the proceeds is turned over to the collecting unit of local government.

While the 1975 legislation was aimed at reducing public assistance costs, legislators recognized that preventing the need for public assistance was as important as collecting support for the population already receiving benefits. IV-D services were thus made available to all parents who pay a reasonable fee; by 1994, eight million non-AFDC clients used IV-D services. OFFICE OF CHILD SUPPORT ENFORCEMENT, NINETEENTH ANNUAL REPORT TO CONGRESS (1994).

The Child Support Enforcement Amendments of 1984 (CSEA), P.L. 98–378, 98 Stat. 1205 (1984), required the states to add new enforcement weapons to their arsenal. The law required states to make wage withholding immediate in most new or modified orders using the IV-D system beginning in October 1990 and in most new orders issued after January 1, 1994. It also required the imposition of liens against the property of defaulting support obligors, expedited hearings—judicial or administrative—in support cases, and statutes of limitation permitting the establishment of paternity up to 18 years after the child's birth. The CSEA also allowed credit companies to be informed of unpaid child support in excess of $1,000 and established mechanisms for the deduction of unpaid support from federal and state income tax refunds. Additional requirements enacted as part of the Family Support Act of 1988, P.L. 100–485m, 102 Stat. 234 (1988), included automatic wage withholding for all support orders issued in public assistance cases after 1993 and compelled genetic testing in contested paternity cases; the federal government also promised to pay 90% of the cost of those genetic tests.

The Personal Responsibility and Work Opportunity Reconciliation Act of 1996 (PRWORA), Pub. L. No. 98–378, 98 Stat. 1205 (1996), further extended federal support enforcement requirements. PRWORA mandated a number of innovations in paternity establishment. States were required to provide that a signed voluntary admission of paternity is binding unless challenged within a sixty-day period or in certain other limited circumstances. They were also required to simplify and streamline the process of paternity establishment. The key piece in these new simplified procedures is "up-front" genetic testing without the necessity of filing a paternity action. These procedures complement 1993 legislation that required states to have procedures which establish either a rebuttable or conclusive presumption of paternity based upon genetic test results showing a threshold probability of paternity.

PRWORA also set up additional informational resources for the Parent Locator Services; the Act established a national Directory of New Hires and required that state agencies have access to state and local government records (including vital statistics, tax and revenue records, motor vehicle records, and occupational and professional licenses) as well as certain private records, including customer records of public utilities and cable television companies.

Finally, PRWORA mandated certain "expedited procedures" for handling routine cases. These expedited procedures must permit the state child support agency to undertake routine enforcement procedures (for example, the imposition of a lien on a defaulting obligor's assets) "without the necessity of obtaining an order from any other judicial or administrative tribunal." PRWORA § 325. Other expedited case processing mechanisms were also required. *See generally* Paul Legler, *The Coming Revolution in Child Support Policy: Implications of the 1996 Welfare Act*, 30 FAM. L.Q. 519 (1996). Updated information on federal child support initiatives is available on the Office of Child Support Enforcement Home Page [http://www.acf.dhhs.gov/ACFPrograms/CSE/].

PRWORA also provides funds for work programs for unemployed fathers (§ 365) and authorizes state IV-D programs to improve the obligor's access to children (§ 469B).

NOTES AND QUESTIONS

1.   *Wage Garnishment:* Automatic wage withholding in IV-D cases is now required by federal law unless the support obligor can show "good cause." *See* 42 U.S.C.A. § 666 (b). Withholding can be a very useful tool for the custodial parent as long as the obligor is a stable employee or has another reliable source of income. *See* Irwin Garfinkel & Marieka Klawitter, *The Effect of Routine Income Withholding on Child Support Collections*, 9 J. POLICY ANALYSIS & MGMT. 155, 168 (1990) (finding some improvement in collections). The Office of Child Support Enforcement found that about 65% of state IV-D agencies' support collections in 2002 were obtained via income withholding. See U.S. Dept. of Health and Human Services, *Child Support Enforcement Report for FY 2002* (2003). If the employee is self-employed or changes jobs frequently, the remedy is less effective. If the obligor moves to other states or countries, more problems can be encountered.

2.   *License Suspension:* Another weapon in the child support enforcement arsenal is license suspension, also mandated by PRWORA. *See* 42 U.S.C.A. § 666 (a) (16). Under state suspension rules, delinquency for a specified period may cause the obligor to lose any of various state licenses; licenses commonly covered include driver's licenses and professional licenses, such as those required to practice law or medicine. *See* S.D. CODE §§ 32–12–116, 25–7A–56. Results to date suggest that these programs are very effective enforcement tools. *See* Michael Holmes, *Millions Culled in Child Support*, HOUSTON CHRONICLE, Sept. 10, 1996, page 20A, col. 2; Margaret Graham Teba, *When Dad Won't Pay*, 86 A.B.A.J., (Sept. 2000) at 54, 56 (reporting that Maryland reported significantly improved collections in 1999 when such a system was established).

State license suspension system systems have withstood constitutional challenges. *See* Farley v. Santa Clara County, 2011 WL 4802813 (N.D. Cal. 2011); Alaska Dept. of Rev. v. Beans, 965 P.2d 725 (Alaska 1998); Tolces v. Trask, 90 Cal. Rptr. 2d 294 (App. 1999). The Washington Supreme Court also upheld the constitutionality of its driver's license suspension scheme; three justices dissented, however, arguing that there was no rational relationship between road safety (the perceived purpose of driver's licenses) and child support payment. *See* Amunrud v. Board of Appeals, 143 P.3d 571 (Wash. 2006).

If a state uses license suspension as a remedy for child-support nonpayment, should it also use license suspension as a remedy for nonpayment of other judgments? Should a custodial parent who doesn't comply with a visitation order have his or her licenses suspended?

In Texas, if an obligor has made no child support payments for at least six months when their automobile registration needs to be renewed, the new registration cannot be obtained until the obligor contacts the Texas Attorney General and agrees to a payment plan. *See* Mara Flanagan Friesen, *Child Support Debt Affects Vehicle Registration Renewal,* Vol. 39 (No. 3) Child Support Report, Office of Child Support Enforcement (March/April 2017) at page 6.

3.   *Passport Revocation:* Under 42 U.S.C. § 652 (k), a person who owes over $2,500 in past-due support may have his passport revoked. In Weinstein v. Albright, 261 F.3d 127 (2d Cir. 2001), the court held that this law violated neither the Due Process nor the Equal Protection clauses of the U.S. Constitution. *See also* Eunique v. Powell, 281 F.3d 940 (9th Cir. 2002).

4.   *Other "Creative" Sanctions:* In State v. Oakley, 629 N.W.2d 200 (Wis. 2001), the court upheld an order placing the male support obligor on probation for 5 years; during that period he could not have more children unless he demonstrated he was supporting his existing children and could support another child. Is this a useful approach?

A number of states have promulgated "most wanted" posters publicizing egregious cases of nonpayment of child support. Another idea is to "boot" (immobilize) the car owned by obligors who owe past-due support. *See* Drew A. Swank, *Das Boot! A National Survey of Booting Programs' Impact on Child Support Compliance,* 4 J.L. & FAM. STUD. 265 (2002).

5.   *Liens for Child Support Arrearages:* Federal law requires each state to provide a procedure for the creation of a lien on the obligor's property for support arrearages. *See* 42 U.S.C. § 666 (a)(4).

6.   *Paternity Establishment Increases:* Under PRWORA, an unmarried father may not be listed on a child's birth certificate unless he has signed a paternity acknowledgment or has been found to be the father by a court or administrative tribunal. *See* 42 U.S.C.A. § 666 (a) (5). This and other changes in paternity-establishment procedures mandated by PRWORA have resulted in a substantial increase in paternity establishment, largely due to substantial increases in voluntary paternity acknowledgment. One study found that between 1992 and 2000, the number of children for whom paternity was established annually increased from 500,000 to 1,500,000. *See* PAUL LEGLER, LOW-INCOME FATHERS AND CHILD SUPPORT: STARTING OFF ON THE RIGHT

TRACK 6 (Annie E. Casey Foundation 2003). *See also* Virginia Ellis, *Fathers' Legal Ties That Bind*, L.A. TIMES, Mar. 8, 1998, at A1 (finding that, after the effective date of PRWORA, there was a 600% increase in the number of fathers signing paternity declarations in 1997).

7. *New Administrative Support Procedures:* Administrative support procedures are becoming increasingly common; in Holmberg v. Holmberg, 588 N.W.2d 720 (Minn. 1999), the Minnesota court held the administrative system in that state was an unconstitutional transfer of power from the judicial to the executive branch.

8. *Incorporation or Merger?* You learned in Chapter 18 that procedures available for the enforcement of a divorce settlement might depend on whether the divorce settlement was incorporated or merged into the divorce decree. Thus, in states in which a court cannot order a support obligor to pay for his child's college expenses, an agreement by the obligor to pay those expenses may not be enforceable if the agreement was merged in the divorce decree. *See* Noble v. Fisher, 894 P.2d 118 (Idaho 1995) (finding that agreement was merged and that post-majority support obligation could not be enforced as a contract).

9. *Who May Sue To Enforce:* In Burt v. Burt, 841 So. 2d 108 (Miss. 2001), the court affirmed the trial court's order letting the child sue to collect child support arrearages that accrued after the custodial parent died. In Waterbury v. Waterbury, 388 P.3d 532 (Wyo. 2017) the husband had been ordered to pay certain college expenses for his daughters. The court held that the judgment for any deficiency should be awarded to the mother, not the daughters.

10. *Informal Settlements of Arrearages:* Spouses sometimes informally settle a claim for child support arrearages for less than the full amount due. Subject to a possible claim for estoppel or laches (discussed below), such a settlement made without judicial approval would not be considered binding. *See* Williams v. Patton, 821 S.W.2d 141 (Tex. 1991). Furthermore, federal law now bars retroactive modification of child support arrearages. *See* 42 U.S.C.A § 666(a)(9)(c).

11. *Garnishing Social Security Benefits:* A number of states permit the collection of child support arrearages long after the child reaches the age of majority. In such instances, it could be important that 65% of social security benefits can be attached to pay child support obligations. *See* 42 U.S.C. § 666(b)(1).

12. *Increases in the Amount of Child Support Collected:* The creation of various new child support enforcement procedures has had an effect upon collections. For example, one study estimated that aggregate child support collections increased from $8 billion in 1992 to $18 billion in 2000. *See* Paul Legler, *supra* n. 6, at 6.

13. *The Limits of Child Support Enforcement:* There are some obligors who can afford to pay child support but choose not to. *See* Robert Pear, *U.S. Agents Arrest Dozens of Fathers in Support Cases,* N.Y. TIMES, Aug. 19, 2002 at A1 (describing obligors who were not paying support, including a

professional football player and a psychiatrist). However, most arrearages are owed by poor obligors. A national study found that 42% of delinquent obligors had no earnings and an additional 28% had annual earnings of less than $10,000. *See* U.S. DEPT. OF HEALTH & HUMAN SERVICES, OFFICE OF CHILD SUPPORT ENFORCEMENT, UNDERSTANDING CHILD SUPPORT DEBT: A GUIDE TO EXPLORING CHILD SUPPORT DEBT IN YOUR STATE 4–6 (Pub. No. DCL–04–28, 2004). Only 4% was owed by obligors with annual income above $40,000. *Id. See generally* Ann Cammett, *Deadbeats, Deadbrokes, and Prisoners,* 18 GEO. J. ON POVERTY L. & POLICY 127 (2011).

Some commentators contend that governmental efforts to improve paternity establishment and support-payment rates among poor fathers have substantially harmed poor families. *See* Jane C. Murphy, *Legal Images of Fatherhood: Welfare Reform, Child Support Enforcement, and Fatherless Children,* 81 NOTRE DAME L. REV. 325 (2005); Laurie S. Kohn, *Engaging Men as Fathers: The Courts, the Law, and Father-Absence in Low-Income Families,* 35 CARDOZO L. Rev. 511 (2013). Others argue that current policies are ineffective. *See* ELAINE SORENSEN & HELEN OLIVER, POLICY REFORMS ARE NEEDED TO INCREASE CHILD SUPPORT FROM POOR FATHERS (Urban Institute 2002).

Is it realistic to expect significant improvement in support payment by poor fathers? If yes, what enforcement policies should government adopt? If no, what policy changes should government make?

14. Given the recent focus on enforcing child support obligations, it might be surprising to learn that of those custodial parents who were owed child support in 2013, only 45.6% received the full amount due, 28.6% received partial payment, and 25.9%, received nothing. *See* Timothy Grall, U.S. Bureau of the Census, Current Population Reports, *Custodial Mothers and Fathers and Their Child Support 2013,* at 9 *(2016).*

D. STATUTES OF LIMITATION

Statutes of limitation apply to family law obligations. Divorce property division obligations must be enforced fairly quickly. For example, in Texas such obligations need to be enforced within two years of the divorce. *See* TEX. FAM. CODE § 9.003. In Nevada, the statute of limitations is six years. *See* Davidson v. Davidson, 382 P.3d 880 (Nev. 2016).

Some states have enacted longer statutes of limitations to enforce child support arrearages. For example, the statute of limitations in Washington to collect child support arrearages is 10 years after the child turns 18, while the Indiana limit is 20 years. *See* Bell v. Heflin, 383 P.3d 1031 (Wash. 2016); Wilson v. Steward, 937 N.E.2d 826 (Ind. App. 2010) (20-year limit applies to judgements). *See also* Overton v. Overton, 2011 WL 398040 (Tex. App.) (permitting enforcement of child support order rendered in 1970).

5. DEFENSES TO THE OBLIGATION TO PAY SUPPORT

A. LACK OF ACCESS

In some states the duty to pay support is conditioned on a right to access (i.e., visitation). *See, e.g.,* OHIO REV. CODE ANN. § 3109.05; R. I. GEN. LAWS § 15–5–16; F.S.P. v. A.H.R., 844 N.Y.S.2d 644 (Fam. Ct. 2007). A few others authorize courts to consider interference with visitation a ground for support modification. *See* OR. REV. STAT. ANN. § 107.431. In most states, however, visitation and support are treated as independent obligations; visitation denial does not affect the support obligation (or vice versa). *See* Moffat v. Moffat, 612 P.2d 967 (Cal. 1980). *See generally* HOMER CLARK, THE LAW OF DOMESTIC RELATIONS IN THE UNITED STATES 682 (2d ed. 1988); Dee Phelps, *Child Support v. Rights to Visitation*, 16 STETSON L. REV. 139 (1986). Under the majority view, an obligor who is being denied visitation should seek enforcement by contempt; the child should not suffer a loss of support due to the actions of the custodial parent.

Some courts have distinguished between frustration of visitation rights and active concealment of the location of the child. In the latter case, some "majority view" states will not permit an action for support arrearages accruing during the period of concealment. *See* Damico v. Damico, 872 P.2d 126 (Cal. 1994) (emphasizing that the child had been concealed until the child became an adult and the obligor made reasonably diligent efforts to try to locate the child); *In re* Marriage of Boswell, 171 Cal. Rptr. 3d 100 (App. 2014) (concealment for 15 years); Hoffman v. Foley, 541 So. 2d 145 (Fla. Dist. Ct. App. 1989); Williams v. Williams, 781 P.2d 1170 (N.M. App. 1989).

Courts generally rule a child support order is enforceable regardless whether the obligor has any contact with the child. *See* Burt v. Burt, 841 So. 2d 108 (Miss. 2001); Thrasher v. Wilburn, 574 So. 2d 839 (Ala. Civ. App. 1990). In extreme situations involving older children, courts have terminated the support obligation due to the child's hostile behavior. *See* Roberts v. Brown, 805 So. 2d 649 (Miss. App. 2002); Marriage of Baker, 485 N.W.2d 860 (Iowa App. 1992); McKay v. McKay, 644 N.E.2d 164 (Ind. App. 1994).

B. ESTOPPEL

Sometimes parents will make an agreement that the obligor will not have to pay support if visitation rights are waived. If a custodial parent then later attempts to collect past due support payments, courts must determine whether he or she is estopped. A few courts have held that the custodial parent is estopped in this situation (*see* Brown v. Brown, 399 So. 2d 1083 (Fla. Dist. Ct. App. 1981); Dubroc v. Dubroc, 388 So. 2d 377 (La.

1980)), particularly if the obligor has changed his position in reliance on the agreement (*see* Lewis v. Lewis, 185 S.W.3d 621 (Ark. App. 2004); Marriage of Shorten, 967 P.2d 797 (Mont. 1998)). Some courts have barred collection of past due support based on such an agreement, but permitted the custodial parent to retract his or her consent with respect to future payments (*see* Malekos v. Chloe Ann Yin, 655 P.2d 728 (Alaska 1982); Chitwood v. Chitwood, 211 S.W.3d 547 (Ark. App. 2005)). Most courts, however, do not apply estoppel in this situation. *See* Office of the Attorney General of Texas v. Scholer, 403 S.W.3d 859 (Tex. 2013); Hailey v. Holden, 457 So. 2d 947 (Miss. 1984); Starzinger v. Starzinger, 727 P.2d 168 (Or. App. 1986); Peebles v. Disher, 310 S.E.2d 823 (S.C. App. 1983).

In Ramsey v. Ramsey, 861 S.W.2d 313 (Ark. App. 1993), the mother had been named the primary custodian and the father was ordered to pay child support. The child later chose to live with a sibling and not the mother. The father stopped paying child support to the mother; he gave the support to the child. The mother later sued to collect support not paid during this period. The court held that the suit was barred based on principles of equitable estoppel.

In a South Carolina case, the parties divorced in 1988 and the court awarded the wife $1200 in indefinite-duration alimony, and this award was increased to $1400 monthly in 1990. Despite this order, the husband paid the wife $300 per month for 7 years and then made no more payments. The wife took no action until late 2004, when a lawyer retained by the wife contacted the husband regarding the past-due alimony. The court held that, based on the wife's inaction, her claim for past-due alimony was based on equitable estoppel. *See* Strickland v. Strickland, 650 S.E.2d 465 (S.C. 2007).

C. LACHES

Some courts have permitted a laches defense if the custodial parent has delayed seeking enforcement of past-due support payments, particularly if the obligor has been prejudiced by the delay. Laches is sometimes found if the parties had agreed that the obligor would no longer attempt to visit the children if the other parent would not require the payment of child support. *See* Wing v. Wing, 464 So. 2d 1342 (Fla. Dist. Ct. App. 1985); Marriage of Copeman, 108 Cal. Rptr. 2d 801 (App. 2001); Marriage of Fogarty, 93 Cal. Rptr. 2d 653 (App. 2000); Tepper v. Hoch, 536 S.E.2d 654 (N.C. App. 2000). *See also* State v. Base, 126 P.3d 79 (Wash. App. 2006) (applying laches to an action for retroactive support filed on behalf of the state). In most situations, however, it appears that courts will not find prejudice. *See* Myers v. Myers, 768 N.E.2d 1201 (Ohio App. 2002); Gardiner v. Gardiner, 705 So. 2d 1018 (Fla. Dist. Ct. App. 1998); Marriage of Cutler, 79 Cal. App. 4th 460, 94 Cal. Rptr. 2d 156 (2000); Hammond v. Hammond, 14 P.3d 199 (Wyo. 2000). And some courts do not permit a laches defense in a child support obligation proceeding even if prejudice can be shown. *See* Wornkey v. Wornkey, 749 P.2d 1045 (Kan. App. 1988); Pickett v. Pickett, 470 N.E.2d 751 (Ind. App. 1984). *See generally* Annotation, 5 A.L.R.4th 1015 (1981).

A few courts have held that laches is not a defense to the obligation to pay the principal amount of a child support arrearage but can be a defense to accrued interest. *See In re* Johnson, 380 P.3d 150 (Colo. 2016); Brochu v. McLead, 148 A.3d 1220 (Me. 2016). Other courts have held that laches is not a defense to an action to collect a child support arrearage. *See In re* Boswell, 171 Cal. Rptr. 3d 100 (App. 2014); Lombardi v. Lombardi, 862 N.E.2d 436 (Mass. App. 2007).

Federal legislation now bars retroactive modification of child support. 42 U.S.C. § 666(a)(9)(C). How will this development affect the ability of the obligor to argue that concealment, laches or estoppel should be a defense to an action for arrearages?

A number of states have relaxed or abolished statutes of limitation regarding child support arrearages. An example of this trend can be seen in an Illinois case where an obligor did not pay child support when ordered to, during a period from 1966–82. In 2004, the custodial parent sued to collect $375,000 in arrearages and interest. The obligor unsuccessfully argued that the claim was barred by the statute of limitations. *See In re* Saputo, 845 N.E.2d 901 (Ill. App. 2006).

D. PARENTAL ALIENATION OR ESTRANGEMENT

In New York, a support obligation may be suspended if the court finds that the recipient has intentionally alienated the children from the obligor. *See* Usack v. Usack, 793 N.Y.S.2d 223 (App. Div. 2005). In addition, a support obligation can be suspended if, through no fault of the obligor, the child refuses all contact with the obligor. *See* Labanowski v. Labanowski, 857 N.Y.S.2d 737 (App. Div. 2008); Coull v. Rottman, 15 N.Y.S.3d 834 (App. Div. 2015). In Wuebelling v. Clark, 502 S.W.3d 676 (Mo. App. 2016) the appellate court affirmed the trial court's order abating the father's child support obligation during the period where the mother created a toxic atmosphere and interfered with the father's visitation.

E. INFORMAL CUSTODY CHANGES

In Rosen v. Rosen, 63 N.E.3d 394 (Mass. App. 2016) the parties' children were living with the mother at the time of divorce. After that, the children eventually chose to live with the father, but no formal action was taken to modify the father's child support obligation. When the wife tried to enforce the order, the appellate court affirmed the trial court's order giving the father an "equitable credit" against arrearages for the period the children were living with him. *See also*, Jackson v. Jackson, 124 Cal. Rptr. 101 (App. 1975).

F. ATTEMPTED RECONCILIATION

In Helgestad v. Vargas, 180 Cal. Rptr. 3d 318 (App. 2014), the father had been ordered to pay child support while he was living separately from his children. He then attempted to reconcile with the mother. The family lived together for 9 months before they once again separated. No action was taken to modify or suspend the child support order. About 9 months after he moved out, he asked the court to calculate the amount of his child support arrearages. The court of appeals held that the father should receive a child support credit for the support due while he was living with his children.

INDEX

References are to Pages